The Value of a Dollar

1860 - 2004

The Value of a Dollar

Prices and Incomes in the United States

1860 - 2004

By Scott Derks

Grey House Publishing

MILLERTON, NY 12546

PUBLISHER:	Leslie Mackenzie
EDITORIAL DIRECTOR:	Laura Mars-Proietti
AUTHOR:	Scott Derks
CONTRIBUTORS:	Elizabeth Derks, Tony Smith
COPYEDITOR:	Elaine Alibrandi
COMPOSITION & DESIGN:	Atlis Graphics
MARKETING DIRECTOR:	Jessica Moody

A Universal Reference Book
Grey House Publishing, Inc.
185 Millerton Road
Millerton, NY 12546
518.789.8700
FAX 518.789.0545
www.greyhouse.com
e-mail: books @greyhouse.com

Publisher's Cataloging-In-Publication Data
(Prepared by The Donohue Group, Inc.)

The Value of a Dollar : Prices and Incomes in the United States, 1860-2004 / by Scott Derks. — 3rd ed.—

 660pp. ; 3.048cm.
 ISBN: 1-592-37074-8

1. Prices—United States—History. 2. Wages—United States—History. 3. Purchasing power—United States—History. 4. Cost and standard of living—United States—History. I. Derks, Scott.

HB235.U6 V35 2004
338.5/2/0973

For Ellen, Elizabeth, Marshall, Lucia, and Hal

ACKNOWLEDGMENTS

The author wishes to acknowledge and thank first of all Tony Smith, whose energy, insight and knowledge made the new Trends section possible. Thanks also go to Greg Flowers, chief researcher, whose work extended over two years; Edna Horning, who played a vital role in updating the 2000 section; Linda Kelly, whose skills have blessed five books; and children Elizabeth and Marshall Derks, whose work has appeared in several books. Thanks also to the librarians across the nation who have made suggestions and comments through the years.

Introduction

Welcome to the third edition of *The Value of a Dollar, 1860-2004*. This edition, although similar to previous editions in many ways, has several new features. In fact, one new feature, **Pricing Trends**, can be used to track a report in a recent *New York Times (9/9/04)* article by Virginia Postrel* on spending trends. According to Postrel, as incomes go up, Americans spend more on intangibles and less on goods. New economic value comes increasingly from experiences, not goods, she reports.

Value of a Dollar's **Pricing Trends** not only compares the cost of everyday products and Postrel's intangibles over a specified number of years, but also shows how those prices compare to today's dollar. Using both bar charts and numeric tables, you'll see that a first class postage stamp was actually more expensive in 1900 (.41) than in 2000 (.33), and that the salary that the President of the United States receives is worth considerably less today than in earlier years. You can also compare cost and value of hotel stays and tickets to sporting events which, based on the article referenced above, Americans are spending a larger percentage of their income on.

In addition to **Pricing Trends**, there are other exciting changes to this edition of *Value of a Dollar*. You'll notice a new and consistent design. We have added hundreds of photos throughout the book to give more meaning to all the numbers and tabular data. And you'll find hundreds of new items in both the *Selected Income* and *Selected Prices* sections from 1860 to 2004. In fact, this edition is bigger than the last edition by more than 200 pages. This third edition now has an Index, to make searching for specific topics easier.

This book is still about practical economy: what things have cost and how much money people have had to buy them. *The Value of a Dollar* records the actual prices of thousands of items that consumers purchased from the Civil War to the present, along with facts about investment options and income opportunities. Most consumers do not make personal economic decisions based on models, indexes and trends. Their buying choices are typically based on weighed options: the need to pay a large electricity bill versus a desire to buy a new dress; the enjoyment of eating in expensive restaurants measured against the pleasure of owning a nice automobile; buying four-for-a-dollar summer corn versus a happy-hour draft beer. It may be valuable to keep in mind, however, Postrel's report that American consumer spending trends change with their income.

Pricing is an inexact science. In any given year the same item—a raincoat, for example—might be sold at widely varying prices in the same store, based on the season, the availability, the retailer's need for cash or the consumer's demand. Within the same city the price of an item may vary based on the cost of inventory, overhead, competitive pressures, demographics of the retailer's customer base, a holiday sales promotion, cash flow or simply the whim of the owner. Many statistical studies accurately trace wholesale prices; few attempt to define the value of a dollar to the consumer at the point of purchase. The sources of prices reported in this book are the same as those available to the consumer at the time: trade cards in the 1880s, newspapers, magazines, catalogues, direct-mail letters and posters. In all, more than 500 sources were used.

Section One

The first section of this book is divided into six chapters, all of which follow a standard format, except the first, which covers the era from the Civil War to 1899, when the groundwork was being laid for a national consumer economy. Because less information is available for that period, less is reported than in other chapters. For most of this first 40-year span, government statistical gathering was in its infancy; few newspapers and fewer magazines carried specific product advertising, and advertisements for jobs were few. Trade cards, newspapers, magazines and some government reports served as the primary resources for this period.

Subsequent chapters cover the periods 1900–1919; 1920–1939; 1940–1959; 1960–1979; and 1980–2004. Each chapter begins with a background essay describing the major social and economic forces of the period. The price and income reports are grouped in five-year subchapters. Each subchapter includes the following elements:

Historical Snapshot — A chronology of key economic and historical events from each year.

Consumer Expenditures — A report on per-capita consumer prices of the day nationwide to serve as a benchmark for specific wage and price information. This information, based on reports compiled by the U.S. Bureau of Economic Analysis, is available annually from 1929 to present. Before 1929 it was compiled only for certain years — 1909,1914 and at two-year intervals beginning in 1919. Totals given are for the items listed only. Such costs as federal, state and local taxes are not included.

Investments — A selection of investment returns compiled from Federal Reserve reports, including a diversified portfolio of common stocks, monitored annually with splits and dividends noted. Dividends were not reported in a standardized fashion until 1927, and thus annual dividends have not been indicated here before that date.

Selected Income — A section of jobs listed in the want ads of major newspapers and reported in the language of the ad. The selected income represents the types of jobs available and the wages offered across the country. This section allows a view of the job market unavailable in average-wage tables. Until fairly recently, for example, many ads specified the sex, age and race acceptable to the employer. Care was taken in the collection process to include newly created jobs, such as advertising copywriters in the 1920s and female factory workers during World War II.

Income, Standard Jobs — A selection of national average wages paid for representative jobs traced annually and based primarily on reports compiled by the Bureau of Economic Analysis. Though job opportunities and wages varied from region to region, this section provides a general guide to the wage-earning capacity of the average American.

Food Basket — A regional report of food pricing compiled from reports by the Bureau of Labor Statistics. The prices or ordinary food items from four sections of the country are traced throughout the twentieth century. Items listed in the food basket are changed over the 90-year period to reflect changing food fashions and government statistical gathering techniques; lard, for example, is reported in the century but not later, and quantities reported are adjusted to correspond with the custom of the marketplace.

Selected Prices — A selection of priced items selected from advertisements of the period. Advertising has one purpose: to sell products — sometimes through fashion or need, but often through price. The prices advertised in magazines, newspapers, sales catalogues, posters and direct-mail letters were used to create the bulk of selected prices. A description of each object helps indicate whether the advertised price was discounted; whether the object was the top of the line or a bargain-basement sale item. The source of the advertisement provides geographic clues to offerings and pricings. Dates of the advertisement in which the price was offered are provided in the sources column.

Standard Prices — A selection of representative items tracked annually, allowing the user to trace price fluctuations. This section demonstrates the range of forces that can affect the price a retailer places on an object. During a twenty-year period new brands appear and disappear; technology drives the price radically up or down; consumer demand requires different styles or fashions; competitive pressures require a company to make an item available in several styles or variations. In some cases, as during World War II, circumstances will cause an item to be unavailable for sale. An effort was made in the gathering of this information to trace products over long periods of time, but it was often necessary to change the description of the "base" item. For example, a push lawn mower used from 1900 to 1919 bears little resemblance to a gasoline-powered, 3.5 horsepower mower used as the standard from 1960 to 1980.

Miscellany — A selection of anecdotal price and income reports from publications of the period concludes each subchapter. Sources are reported at the back of the book.

Section Two

Pricing Trends is divided into seven categories, from *Around the House* to *Travel & Entertainment*. Here is where you'll discover how the cost of things changed over the years, and how that cost relates to the value of money over the years. This section profiles 92 items and services, such as *The New York Sunday Times* to a ticket to a baseball World Series Game. And the data is presented in two ways – bar charts allow you to make quick analyses, and numeric tables give you the specifics, down to the penny.

In addition to a new Index, *The Value of a Dollar* includes several Source documents and a Bibliography for those wishing to do further research.

Audience

As with previous editions, this book has been prepared for people curious about social history: students studying the topics that require knowledge about everyday life in America; teachers who seek information to enliven classroom discussions while broadening their students' understanding of the quality of American life; writers who need access to the basic facts of American commerce; business historians seeking data to establish a framework of wage and price information during a specific period; reporters seeking to enhance a story with economic details. *The Value of a Dollar* is for both the user who simply wants to know what life was like during the time of his or her great-grandparents and the serious historical researcher. Now, with the new **Pricing Trends**, this edition of *The Value of a Dollar* is even more useful and more interesting than ever before.

*Virginia Postrel is the author of "The Substance of Style: How the Rise of Aesthetic Value Is Remaking Commerce, Culture and Consciousness," *recently published in paperback by Perennial.*

Contents

1980-2004: From Recession to the Era of Possibilities

1980-1984

1985-1989

1990-1994

1995-1999

2000-2004

1900-2000: Trends

Around the House

Fashion

The Value of a Dollar, 1860-2003

Composite Consumer Price Index; 1860=1

Year	Amount	Year	Amount	Year	Amount	Year	Amount
1860	$1.00	1896	$1.01	1932	$1.64	1968	$4.18
1861	$1.06	1897	$1.00	1933	$1.56	1969	$4.40
1862	$1.21	1898	$1.00	1934	$1.61	1970	$4.66
1863	$1.51	1899	$1.00	1935	$1.64	1971	$4.86
1864	$1.89	1900	$1.01	1936	$1.67	1972	$5.02
1865	$1.96	1901	$1.02	1937	$1.73	1973	$5.33
1866	$1.91	1902	$1.03	1938	$1.69	1974	$5.92
1867	$1.78	1903	$1.06	1939	$1.67	1975	$6.46
1868	$1.71	1904	$1.07	1940	$1.68	1976	$6.83
1869	$1.64	1905	$1.06	1941	$1.76	1977	$7.27
1870	$1.57	1906	$1.08	1942	$1.96	1978	$7.82
1871	$1.47	1907	$1.13	1943	$2.08	1979	$8.71
1872	$1.47	1908	$1.11	1944	$2.11	1980	$9.89
1873	$1.44	1909	$1.09	1945	$2.16	1981	$10.91
1874	$1.37	1910	$1.14	1946	$2.34	1982	$11.58
1875	$1.32	1911	$1.14	1947	$2.68	1983	$11.95
1876	$1.29	1912	$1.17	1948	$2.89	1984	$12.47
1877	$1.26	1913	$1.19	1949	$2.86	1985	$12.91
1878	$1.20	1914	$1.20	1950	$2.89	1986	$13.15
1879	$1.20	1915	$1.21	1951	$3.12	1987	$13.63
1880	$1.23	1916	$1.31	1952	$3.18	1988	$14.19
1881	$1.23	1917	$1.54	1953	$3.20	1989	$14.88
1882	$1.23	1918	$1.81	1954	$3.23	1990	$15.68
1883	$1.21	1919	$2.08	1955	$3.22	1991	$16.34
1884	$1.18	1920	$2.40	1956	$3.26	1992	$16.83
1885	$1.16	1921	$2.15	1957	$3.37	1993	$17.34
1886	$1.13	1922	$2.02	1958	$3.47	1994	$17.78
1887	$1.14	1923	$2.05	1959	$3.49	1995	$18.29
1888	$1.14	1924	$2.05	1960	$3.55	1996	$18.82
1889	$1.11	1925	$2.10	1961	$3.59	1997	$19.26
1890	$1.09	1926	$2.12	1962	$3.62	1998	$19.56
1891	$1.09	1927	$2.09	1963	$3.67	1999	$19.99
1892	$1.09	1928	$2.05	1964	$3.72	2000	$20.66
1893	$1.08	1929	$2.05	1965	$3.78	2001	$21.25
1894	$1.03	1930	$2.00	1966	$3.89	2002	$21.59
1895	$1.01	1931	$1.82	1967	$4.01	2003	$22.07

1860–1899

The Age of Endeavor

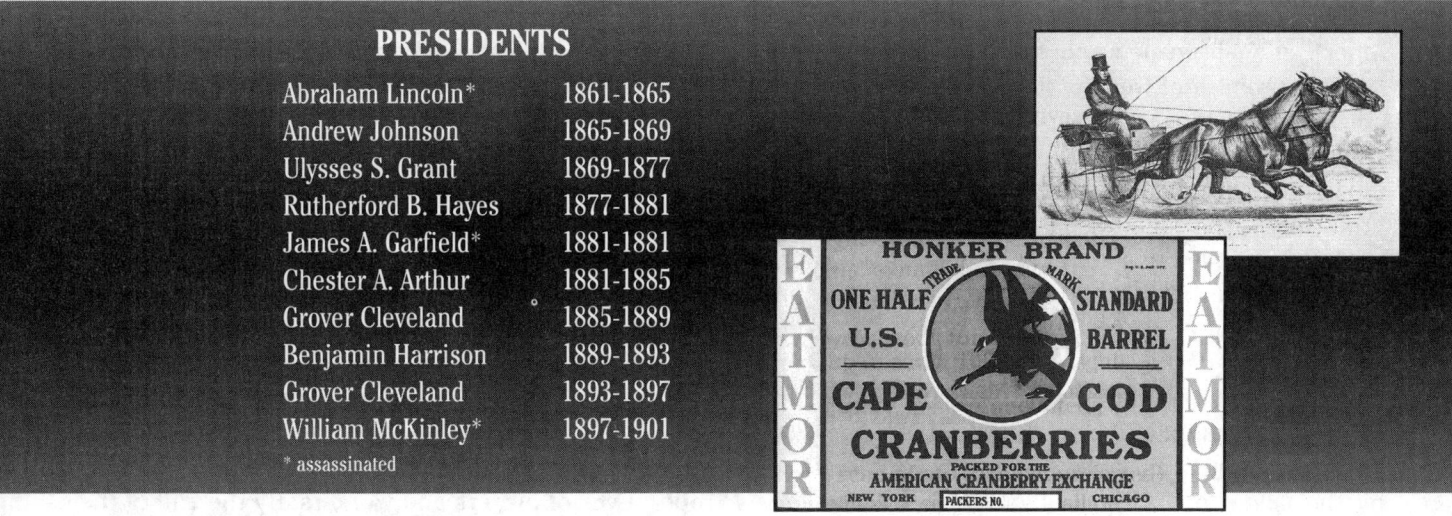

Historians disagree about whether the Civil War was a revolutionary stimulus to the American economy, a violent interruption of industrial development, or something in between. It is clear that after the war business and industry came to dominate American life. The combination of advances in technology, increases in manufacturing capacity, the development of a national system of railroads to transport goods, and the accumulation of capital that allowed the industrial barons of the age to build financial empires established the United States as a world economic power and transformed Americans into the world's most avid consumers. By 1900 the population and the per-capita income of the U.S. were double that of the United Kingdom.

Railroads were the nation's pioneer big business. They delivered raw materials to manufacturing centers, finished goods to market, food from the farm to the city, and people to centers of commercial opportunity. From 1865 to 1900 track mileage nationwide increased from 35,000 to 192,556, a clear indication of the industrial boom railroads stimulated. During the same time the total labor force more than doubled; the amount of capital invested in manufacturing increased tenfold; and the gross national product tripled.

The energy required to drive the industrial boom was enormous. Between 1860 and 1900, the total horse-power generated to meet the needs of the economy increased 500 percent, with railroads and factories accounting for 76 percent of the total by 1900. They had to be fueled. By 1890, 25 percent of the world output of coal was mined in the United States. Annual production of crude petroleum went from 500,000 barrels in 1860 to 63.6 million in 1900. With the introduction of electricity in the 1870s a powerful energy source was made available that had relatively little effect in the nineteenth century but profoundly affected consumers and the products they purchased beginning in the early years of the twentieth century.

Innovation was a significant element in the Age of Endeavor. Not only were goods manufactured on a scale unimaginable before the Civil War, but entrepreneurs created new products and invented ways to produce them. Between 1860 and 1869, 77,355 patents were issued; in the last decade of the century, the number had risen to 234,749. The Pullman sleeping car and the Westinghouse air brake expanded the uses of trains. Barbed wire, the wind-powered electrical generator, the hay baler, and the twine binder revolutionized farm life; the telephone, typewriter, cash register, and adding machine contributed mightily to the development of commerce.

Despite the financial promise of the Age of Endeavor, the economy was unstable, due partly to

1

irresponsible speculation but more generally to the stubborn adherence of the federal government to a gold standard as the basis of value for currency. Prices went into a steady decline after the Civil War, reaching bottom with the Panic of 1893, and only then beginning a long-term recovery. Congress reacted with increasingly restrictive tariffs to protect American businessmen from foreign competition.

The promise of wealth offered by investment opportunities gave rise to irresponsible speculation that had national repercussions. In September 1873 the failure of the banking house of Jay Cooke & Co., the most prominent in the country, due to overextension in railroad securities led to a series of failures among banks and brokerage houses and related bankruptcies of businesses that relied on them for capital. The result was a five-year decline in the economy despite the continued expansion of industry and increases in equipment purchases. After a brief recovery the depression resumed, reaching its nadir in 1893 with a crisis caused by the failure of Baring Brothers, a British banking house, and the resulting sale of American securities held abroad. The drain of gold caused American reserves to fall to dangerously low levels. Investors panicked; Congress reacted with gold-price supports.

The last half of the nineteenth century was a period of expansion for the United States. Population went from 31.5 million in 1860 to 76 million in 1900, of whom about 13 million were immigrants. Twelve states were added to the Union, bringing the total to forty-five. Alaska, Hawaii, the Philippines, and Puerto Rico were either purchased or annexed. To encourage the economic development of the West, the Homestead Act of 1862 offered any American citizen 160 acres of government land free if the homesteader lived on it for five years; after six months' residence a homesteader could purchase the land from the government for $1.25 per acre. The result was a 700 percent (3.5 million persons) growth in population in the West between 1860 and 1900. At the beginning of the period the South was the most populated region of the United States, with over 35 percent of the total population, followed by the North, with 34 percent; at the end of the period the North Central region had grown to nearly 35 percent, followed by the South, with 32 percent.

The social changes imposed by the capitalistic fervor of the Age of Endeavor prompted energetic reform movements. Labor unions protested against the abuse of workers. Wages were low, sixty-hour workweeks were common, and working conditions in factories were often deplorable. Between 1880 and 1900 unions organized twenty-three thousand strikes, sometimes violent, involving 6.5 million workers. National attention was focused on labor unrest by such highly publicized clashes as the Haymarket Massacre of 1886 in Chicago (7 killed, 70 wounded), the Homestead Massacre of 1892 in Homestead, Pennsylvania (7 killed), and the Pullman Strike of 1894 which paralyzed railroads throughout the Midwest (with 3,400 special deputies sworn in to keep trains running). First the National Labor Union in the 1860s and early 1870s then the 700,000-member Knights of Labor in the 1870s and 1880s led the labor-reform movement with platforms that called for an eight-hour workday, child-labor regulation, and cooperatives of owners and workers. By the end of the century the newly formed American Federation of Labor had gained supremacy as the chief labor advocate in America. By 1904, eighteen years after it was founded, the AF of L claimed 1.676 million of 2.07 million total union members.

Agricultural reform was advocated by the Granger Movement, which attracted 850,000 farmers seeking cooperative marketing, higher prices for agricultural products, and relief from high railroad freight rates. With support from merchants the Grangers were successful in sponsoring legislation regulating railroad rates and in gaining popular support for their opposition to monopolies.

The most-visible social-reform movements were those organized by women suffragists, who fought for women's right to vote, and the temperance crusaders, who sought the prohibition of alcohol. Both issues were hotly debated during the period, and the groundwork was laid for constitutional amendments addressing the reformers' concerns: the 18th Amendment (1919) prohibited the manufacture, sale, or transportation of intoxicating beverages; and the 19th Amendment (1920) extended to women the right to vote.

HISTORICAL SNAPSHOT 1860-1899

1860

- Abraham Lincoln elected president with 40 percent of the popular vote
- U.S. cotton exports equal $192 million of the nation's export total of $334 million
- John D. Rockefeller enters the oil business
- Elizabeth Cady Stanton urges women's suffrage in an address to a joint session of the New York State Legislature
- Oneida Community grosses $100,000 from the sale of the Newhouse animal trap
- First Pony Express Riders deliver mail from St. Joseph, MO, to Sacramento, CA, in ten days; Rates range from $2 to $10 per ounce, depending on distance
- Palmolive Soap created using a new soap-milling machine demonstrated at the St. Louis Exposition
- New York's Tiffany & Co. sells a pearl necklace for $1 million
- Checkered Game of Life board game is introduced by Springfield, MA, lithographer Milton Bradley
- U.S. population reaches 31.4 million, double its 1840 level

1861

- Ten Southern states secede from the Union
- Civil War begins when Fort Sumter, in Charleston Harbor, SC, is fired upon
- New York's Bellevue Hospital Medical College is established
- Louis Pasteur refutes the idea of spontaneous generation and advances germ theory
- Congress levies first U.S. income tax; law taxes incomes in excess of $800 at the rate of 3 percent
- U.S. banks suspend payments in gold
- MIT, University of Colorado, University of Washington founded
- I. M. Singer sells more sewing machines abroad than in America, has profits of $200,000
- John Wanamaker opens a Philadelphia menswear shop, becomes pioneer of fixed-price sales

- Elisha G. Otis patents a steam-powered elevator
- The McCormick reaper sells for $150, up from $100 in 1849
- Baltimore canner Isaac Solomon reduces the average processing time for canned goods from 6 hours to 30 minutes using calcium chloride

1862

- Homestead Act provides 160 acres, free to settlers of western land
- Western Union's telegraph forces Pony Express into bankruptcy
- John Hancock Life Insurance Company founded
- Land Grant Act funds land grant college for the education of farmers
- Beer taxed at $1 per barrel to finance war effort

1863

- President Abraham Lincoln's Emancipation Proclamation takes effect, frees nearly 4 million slaves
- Government guarantees Central Pacific and Union Pacific Railroads $16,000 for every mile of track laid, $48,000 per mile through mountains
- Boston College founded
- Travelers Insurance Company created to insure accidents
- Bay Sugar Refining Company starts in San Francisco

1864

- Ulysses S. Grant given command of Union Army
- Inflation devalues Confederate currency to $4.60 per $100
- The University of Kansas and University of Denver formed
- George M. Pullman and Ben Feld patent railway sleeping car
- U.S. wheat prices reach $4 per bushel
- European immigrants pour into U.S. for Homestead Act free land and factory jobs left vacant due to the war

1865

- Civil War ends and President Lincoln assassinated; War claims a total of 360,222 Union men, 258,000 Confederate

- Union Pacific Railroad construction reaches Kansas City
- Inflation reduces value of Confederate money to $1.76 per $100
- Linus Yale patents Yale Lock
- W. R. Grace & Co. formed to engage in South American trade

1866

- Prices begin rapid rise following war
- Tin can with a key opener is patented
- Breyer's Ice Cream founded
- Jack Daniel's Tennessee Sour Mash Whiskey introduced
- Nebraska admitted to Union

1867

- French engineer George Leclanche invents first practical dry-cell battery
- Pacific Mail Steamship Company begins service from San Francisco to Hong Kong
- University of Illinois and University of West Virginia founded
- More than half of all U.S. working people employed on farms

1868

- House of Representatives votes to impeach President Andrew Johnson
- Navajo chiefs forced to sign treaty establishing 3.5-million-acre reservation
- Metropolitan Life Insurance Company founded under reorganization of National Travelers Insurance Company
- Rand McNally & Co. founded
- U.S. wheat prices fall to 67 cents per bushel
- Tabasco sauce introduced by Edmund McIlhenny

1869

- Union Pacific Railroad and Central Pacific reduce New York to San Francisco travel time from three weeks to eight days
- Wall Street suffers first "Black Friday," ruining many small investors

- Stanley Rule and Level Co. buys patent rights to first metal plane
- Purdue University founded in Lafayette, IN
- First U.S. plow with a moldboard entirely of chilled steel patented
- Armour & Co. adds beef to its line of pork products

1870

- New York's F. A. O. Schwartz toy shop opens on Broadway
- First through railway cars from the Pacific Coast reach New York City
- Steamships account for 16 percent of world shipping
- Smith Brothers Cough Drops are patented by William "Trade" and Andrew "Mark," whose bearded faces serve as trademark
- Women enter University of Michigan for first time since it was founded in 1817
- Texas Christian University founded in Fort Worth
- U.S. corn crop reaches 1 million bushels for the first time

1871

- 1836 Colt redesigned to extend its effective range
- First shipload of bananas lands at Boston, 14 days out of Kingston, Jamaica
- University of Arkansas founded at Fayetteville
- Barnum's Circus opens in Brooklyn, NY; grosses $400,000 in first season
- C. A. Pillsbury & Co. founded by Minneapolis miller Charles Alfred Pillsbury
- U.S. population reaches 39 million, surpassing France, Italy, and Great Britain

1872

- U. S. Grant reelected despite charges of corruption
- Susan B. Anthony arrested for attempting to vote in presidential election
- Commercial production of celluloid begins under a patent obtained by John Wesley Hyatt
- Vanderbilt University founded in Nashville, TN, with a grant from Commodore Vanderbilt
- Congress enacts first consumer protection law, making it illegal to use the mail fraudulently

- Montgomery Ward Co. founded in Chicago, aimed at members of the Grange

1873

- Congress makes gold the sole U.S. monetary standard
- U.S. silver yield reaches $36 million, up from $157,000 in 1860
- Greenback party organized, claiming a shortage of money to be the cause of hard times
- U.S. suffers second "Black Friday"; stocks fall; 5,000 business firms fail
- San Francisco's cable streetcar goes into service
- Henri Nestle's Infant Milk Food introduced in U.S.
- Barbed wire exhibited at the DeKalb, IL, county fair

1874

- R. H. Macy & Co. displays doll collection in the world's first Christmas window
- Remington typewriter introduced by F. Remington & Sons Fire Arms Co., costing $125 each
- Levi Strauss blue jeans add rivets and sell for $13.50 per dozen
- Margarine is introduced in U.S.
- Women's Christian Temperance Union founded at Cleveland
- New pressure-cooking technique improves canning process

1875

- Prudential Insurance Co. is founded in Newark, NJ
- George F. Green patents electric dental drill
- Vaseline petroleum jelly introduced by Chesebrough Manufacturing Co.
- U.S. cigarette production reaches 50 million
- Chinese orchard man in Oregon develops Bing cherry
- New York Condensed Milk Co. begins selling canned milk

1876

- First Fred Harvey restaurant opens in the Santa Fe Railroad depot at Topeka, KS
- Heinz Tomato Ketchup introduced
- Bananas introduced as foil-wrapped novelty at the Philadelphia fair costing 10¢ each
- W. Atlee Burpee & Co. founded to sell livestock by mail

- New York's Central Park completed
- BVD underwear introduced by New York's Bradley, Voorhees, and Day
- McCall's magazine begins publication under the name The Queen
- Eli Lilly Company founded

1877

- Granola introduced by James Harvey Kellogg
- First low-rent housing project opens in Brooklyn, NY. Businessman Alfred Tredway White charges tenants $14 per month
- Singer Manufacturing company cuts price of sewing machines in half as depression of 1873 continues
- Washington Post begins publication, charging 3¢ per copy
- Bessemer steelmaking process cuts barbed wire prices from 18¢ per pound to 8¢ per pound
- First telephone exchange organized at Lowell, MS

1878

- Chase and Sanborn packs first roasted coffee in sealed can
- Edison Electric Light Co. founded
- 10,500 businesses fail as depression of 1873 continues
- Bland-Allison Act makes the silver dollar legal tender
- Mennen's Sure Corn Killer introduced by Newark, NJ, pharmacist Gerhard Mennen
- 287.42-carat Tiffany diamond discovered in South Africa's Kimberly Mine
- Hutchinson Bottle Stopper invented to seal in carbonation of effervescent drinks

1879

- Thomas Edison demonstrates first practical incandescent light bulb
- Cleveland and San Francisco install arc-lamp streetlights
- Standardization of pharmaceutical drugs pioneered by Parke Davis & Company
- McCormick's reaper sells for $1,500, up from $150 in 1861
- Photography revolutionized by Speed Dry Plate
- Scott Paper Company founded in Chester, PA

- Lambert Pharmaceutical Company founded in St. Louis
- Women given right to practice law before the Supreme Court

1880

- 539,000 Singer sewing machines sold, up from 250,000 in 1875
- U.S. has 100 millionaires
- New England's ice crop fails because of warm weather; ice prices soar
- A&P grocery stores operate 95 stores from Boston to Milwaukee
- Plush Del Monte Hotel in Monterey, CA, opens
- Halftone photographic illustrations appear in newspapers for the first time
- Midwest farmers burn corn for fuel; prices too low to warrant shipping

1881

- President James Garfield assassinated
- Supreme Court rules 1862 federal income tax law unconstitutional
- Diamond Match Co. created
- Southern Pacific Railway links New Orleans with San Francisco
- Marquette University founded in Milwaukee
- Barnum & Bailey's Circus formed through merger of two companies
- Marshall, Field & Co. created by reorganization
- Chicago meatpacker Gustavus F. Swift perfects refrigerator car to take Chicago-dressed meat to East Coast

1882

- An internal combustion engine powered by gasoline is invented by German engineer Gottlieb Saimler
- Electric cable cars are installed in Chicago; they travel 20 blocks, averaging less than 2 miles per hour
- Only 2 percent of New York homes have water connections
- Andrew Jergens Company founded to produce soaps, cosmetics, and lotions
- Canadian Club whiskey introduced by Hiram Walker distillery
- Van Camp Packing Company Incorporated produces 6 million cans of pork and beans for shipment to Europe and U.S. markets

1883

- Brooklyn Bridge opens

- *Ladies' Home Journal* begins publication; Cyrus H. K. Curtis is publisher
- Thomas Edison invents the radio tube
- First malted milk produced in Racine, WI
- First successful pea-podder machine installed in Owasco, NY, replacing 600 cannery workers

1884

- Linotype typesetting machine patented by Ottmar Mergenthaler, revolutionizing newspaper composing rooms
- More than 80 percent of the petroleum from U.S. oil wells is marketed by John D. Rockefeller's Standard Oil Trust
- National Cash Register Company (NCR) founded
- Waterman pen invented by New York insurance agent Lewis Edson Waterman
- Montgomery Ward catalogue offers 10,000 items

1885

- Westinghouse Electric & Manufacturing Co. founded
- Evaporated milk produced commercially for first time
- Maryland oyster catch reaches 15 million bushels
- Johnson & Johnson Company founded
- Corn crop tops 2 billion bushels per year for first time
- *Good Housekeeping* magazine begins publication
- Parker Brothers founded to market board games

1886

- A record 610,000 workers strike nationwide seeking 8-hour day, better working conditions
- Capture of Geronimo ends last major Indian war
- Commercial aluminum production pioneered
- Johnson's Wax introduced at Racine, WI
- A decade of intermittent drought begins on Great Plains; nearly 60 percent of range livestock dies
- Coca-Cola sold for first time, at Jacob's Pharmacy in Atlanta
- Hires' Root Beer introduced in bottles

- Statue of Liberty dedicated

1887

- Quaker Mill Company registers the first trademark for a breakfast cereal—a man in Quaker garb
- First ready-to-use surgical dressings introduced by Johnson & Johnson
- Railroads ordered by Congress to keep rates fair and reasonable
- Thomas Edison invents first motor-driven phonograph
- Telephone listings surpass 200,000
- Wheat prices fall to 67¢ per bushel
- Log Cabin Syrup introduced by St. Paul, MN, grocer
- White Rock Mineral Springs Company established in Wisconsin
- Ball-Mason jars introduced
- Ice-making machines supercede blocks of ice at Western Cold Storage Company in Chicago

1888

- Alternating-current electric motor developed
- Anti-Chinese riots erupt in Seattle
- Burroughs adding machine patented
- *National Geographic* begins publication
- First typewriter stencil introduced
- Parker Pen Company started in Janesville, WI
- Immigration from Britain peaks
- Tobacco merchant Washington B. Duke produces 744 million cigarettes
- Ponce de Leon Hotel opened at St. Augustine, FL

1889

- Oklahoma Territory lands formerly reserved for Indians opened to white settlers
- Safety bicycle introduced; more than 1 million will be sold in the following four years
- Electric lights installed in White House
- *Wall Street Journal* begins publication
- I. M. Singer Company introduces first electric sewing machine
- Aunt Jemima pancake flour invented at St. Joseph, MO
- Calumet baking powder created in Chicago

1890

- Congress increases import duty to record highs
- First commercial dry-cell battery introduced
- 3 percent of Americans age 18 to 21 attend college
- *Literary Digest* begins publication
- Population of Los Angeles reaches 50,000, up 40,000 in ten years
- Two-thirds of nation's 62.9 million people live in rural areas
- First aluminum saucepan produced

1891

- Restrictive antiblack "Jim Crow" laws enacted across South
- First full-service advertising agency established in New York City
- First electric oven for commercial sale introduced at St. Paul, MN
- Thousands of Kansas farmers bankrupted by tight money conditions
- $3 million Tampa Bay Hotel completed in Florida
- American Express Traveler's Cheque copyrighted
- Ceresota flour introduced by Northwestern Consolidated Milling Company

1892

- Steelworkers strike Carnegie-Phipps mill at Homestead, PA; violence erupts
- Improved carburetor invented
- General Electric Company created through merger
- $1 Ingersoll pocket watch introduced
- Chicago's first elevated railways go into operation to begin the Loop
- First U.S. motorcar produced at Springfield, MA, by the Duryea brothers
- Hamilton Watch Company founded
- Country has 4,000 millionaires
- First successful gasoline tractor produced by Waterloo, IA, farmer

1893

- Philadelphia and Reading Railroad goes into receivership
- Recession continues; Chicago's Pullman Palace Car Company reduces wages by one-fourth
- First Ford motorcar road tested
- Wrigley's Spearming and Juicy Fruit chewing gum introduced by William Wrigley Jr.
- Name Sears, Roebuck & Company used for first time
- Cream of Wheat introduced by Diamond Mill of Grand Forks, ND
- New York's 13-story Waldorf Hotel opens

1894

- Income tax imposed on annual incomes of $4,000 or more
- Strikes cripple railroads; federal government intervenes
- 750,000 workers strike during year
- Oil discovered at Corsicana, TX
- Hershey Bar introduced
- Wheat prices down to 49¢ per bushel
- Winchester M1894 lever-action rifle introduced

1895

- Pneumatic tires put on motorcars for first time
- Underwood Typewriter Company founded
- Treasury gold reserves fall to $41 million as depression continues
- *Collier's Weekly* and *Field and Stream* magazines begin publication
- $4.1 million Biltmore House, world's largest private home, completed at Asheville, NC
- Pocket Kodak camera introduced by Eastman Kodak

1896

- Utah admitted to Union
- Bicycle industry reports sales of $60 million; average bike sells for $100
- S&H Green Stamps issued for first time

- Michelob beer introduced
- Cracker Jack and Tootsie Roll candies introduced
- Klondike gold rush begins
- Radioactivity discovered in uranium

1897

- Bituminous coal miners stage 12-week walkout
- Continental Casualty Company founded
- Dow Chemical Company incorporated
- Winton Motor Carriage Company organized
- Mail Pouch tobacco introduced
- Wheat prices rise to $1.09 per bushel
- Jell-O introduced by Pearl B. Wait
- Boston's H. P. Hill uses glass bottles to distribute milk

1898

- First shots of Spanish-American War fired
- Louisiana "grandfather clause" restricts most blacks from voting
- Union Carbide Company is founded
- Motorcar production reaches 1,000 per year
- Goodyear Tire and Rubber Company founded
- *New York Times* drops price from 3¢ to 1¢ daily; circulation triples
- Pepsi-Cola introduced by New Bern, NC, pharmacist Caleb D. "Doc" Bradham
- Uneeda Biscuits created

1899

- J. P. Stevens & Company founded in New York
- Trolly replaces horsecars in Boston
- Automobile production surpasses 2,500
- Wesson Oil developed
- United Mine Workers of America founded
- First concrete grain elevator erected near Minneapolis
- Boll weevil begins spreading across cotton-growing southern states

SELECTED INCOME 1860-1899

Job	Source	Description	Pay
Actor	Philip B. Kunhardt, Philip B. Kunhardt III, and Peter W. Kunhardt, *P.T. Barnum, America's Greatest Showman* (1995)	Three-year contract of Commodore George Washington Morrison Nutt with P. T. Barnum Circus, beginning in 1862	$30,000
Circus Owner	Kunhardt, *P.T. Barnum, America's Greatest Showman* (1995)	Annual income of P. T. Barnum in 1879	$87,850
Composer	Edwin S. Grosvenor and Morgan Wesson, *Alexander Graham Bell* (1997)	Payment to Richard Wagner to compose the patriotic *Centennial March* for the International Centennial Exhibition in 1876, staged in Philadelphia to celebrate the signing of the Declaration of Independence	$5,000
Golfer	Vincent Tompkins, ed., *American Eras: Development of the Industrial United States, 1878-1899* (1997)	Purse to Horace Rawlins in 1895 for winning first U.S. Open	$150 and Gold Medal worth $50
Photographer	James D. Horan, *Mathew Brady: Historian with a Camera* (1965)	Payment to Mathew Brady by Congress in 1875 to purchase his collection of historical and war photographs; the famous photographer was in bankruptcy and forced to sell his life's work (valued at more than $150,000)	$25,000
Photography Retouching	*San Francisco Examiner* (1895)	Ladies, training provided	$10/wk
Political Cartoonist	J. Chal Vinson, *Thomas Nast, Political Cartoonist* (1967)	Annual salary of Thomas Nast at *Harper's Weekly* in 1871; Nast turned down a $50,000 bribe to leave publication from William Marcy "Boss" Tweed	$5,000
Teacher	Robert A. Margo, *Race and Schooling in the South* (1990)	Average annual income of black teachers in Alabama in 1890	$255
Teacher	Margo, *Race and Schooling in the South* (1990)	Average annual income of white teachers in Alabama in 1890	$215

INVESTMENTS 1870-1899

Investment	1870	1871	1872	1873	1874
Basic Yield, Common Stocks, Total		5.26	5.70	6.54	6.89
Index of Common Stocks (1941–1943=10)		4.69	5.03	4.80	4.57

Investment	1875	1876	1877	1878	1879
Basic Yield, Common Stocks, Total	6.51	7.02	5.78	5.12	4.70
Index of Common Stocks (1941–1943=10)	4.45	4.06	3.14	3.38	4.12

Investment	1880	1881	1882	1883	1884
Basic Yield, Common Stocks, Total	4.78	4.84	5.18	5.69	6.31
Index of Common Stocks (1941–1943=10)	5.21	6.25	5.90	5.63	4.74

Investment	1885	1886	1887	1888	1889
Basic Yield, Common Stocks, Total	5.09	3.85	4.24	4.18	3.88
Index of Common Stocks (1941–1943=10)	4.60	5.36	5.53	5.20	5.32

Investment	1890	1891	1892	1893	1894
Short-term Interest Rates, 4–6 Months, Prime Commercial Paper	6.91	6.48	5.40	7.64	5.22
Basic Yield, Common Stocks, Total	4.01	4.28	4.16	5.03	4.62
Index of Common Stocks (1941–1943=10)	5.27	5.03	5.55	4.78	4.39

Investment	1895	1896	1897	1898	1899
Short-term Interest Rates, 4–6 Months, Prime Commercial Paper	5.80	7.02	4.72	5.34	5.50
Basic Yield, Common Stocks, Total	3.97	4.15	3.90	3.72	3.21
Index of Common Stocks (1941–1943=10)	4.53	4.23	4.45	5.05	6.29

STANDARD JOBS 1860-1864

Job Type	1860	1861	1862	1863	1864
Bricklayers (Massachusetts)	$1.53/day	$1.81/day	$1.79/day	$2.05/day	$2.31/day
Avg hrs/wk	60	61	60	60	60
Carpenters and Joiners (Connecticut)	$1.65/day	$1.50/day	$1.48/day	$1.86/day	$2.05/day
Avg hrs/wk	61	60	60	60	60
Engineers, Stationary (New York)	$1.63/day	$1.82/day	$1.77/day	$1.69/day	$2.04/day
	68	68	70	67	73
Farm Labor (New York)	$0.88/day	$0.88/day	$1/day	$1.13	$1.50/day
	66	66	66	66	66
Firemen (Massachusetts)	$1.33/day	$1.38/day	$1.41/day	$1.48/day	$1.25/day
	70	66	66	66	72
Glassblowers, Bottles (New Jersey)	$2.59/day	$2.44/day	$2.95/day	$2.95/day	$2.95/day
	NR	NR	NR	NR	NR
Hod Carriers (Massachusetts)	$1/day	$1.08/day	$1.18/day	$1.19/day	$1.43/day
	56	61	63	63	63
Marble Cutters (New York)	$2.04/day	$1.62/day	$1.58/day	$1.95/day	$2.52/day
	60	60	60	60	60
Painters (New York)	$1.97/day	$1.93/day	$1.98/day	$2.21/day	$2.93/day
	60	60	60	60	60
Plasterers (Pennsylvania)	$1.69/day	$1.66/day	$1.67/day	$1.92/day	$1.93/day
	60	60	60	60	60
Plumbers (New York)	$1.88/day	$1.88/day	$1.93/day	$2.50/day	$3.50/day
	60	60	60	60	60
Stonemasons (New York)	$2.50/day	$2.50/day	$2.05/day	$1.98/day	$2.35/day
	60	60	60	60	60

STANDARD JOBS 1865-1869

Job Type	1865	1866	1867	1868	1869
Bricklayers (Massachusetts)	$2.59/day	$2.95/day	$3.17/day	$3.76/day	$3.44/day
Avg hrs/wk	60	60	60	60	60
Carpenters and Joiners (Connecticut)	$2.25/day	$2.63/day	$3.03/day	$3.05/day	$2.98/day
Avg hrs/wk	60	61	60	60	60
Engineers, Stationary (New York)	$2.34/day	$2.43/day	$2.63/day	$2.66/day	$2.66/day
	70	70	70	70	69
Farm Labor (New York)	$1.50/day	$1.50/day	$1.50/day	$1.50/day	$1.75/day
	66	66	66	66	66
Firemen (Massachusetts)	$1.51/day	$1.58/day	$1.67/day	$1.64/day	$1.67/day
	66	66	66	66	66
Glassblowers, Bottles (New Jersey)	$3.95/day	$3.95/day	$5.14/day	$5.19/day	$5.19/day
	NR	NR	NR	NR	NR
Hod Carriers (Massachusetts)	$1.55/day	$1.74/day	$1.59/day	$2/day	$1.93/day
	60	60	60	60	60
Marble Cutters (New York)	$2.91/day	$2.94/day	$3.39/day	$3.46/day	$3.69/day
	60	60	60	60	60

Job Type	1865	1866	1867	1868	1869
Painters (New York)	$2.82/day 60	$3.35/day 60	$3.86/day 60	$3.43/day 60	$4.29/day 60
Plasterers (Pennsylvania)	$2.29/day 60	$2.60/day 60	$3.70/day 60	$3.67/day 60	$3.67/day 60
Plumbers (New York)	$3.5/day 60	$3.50/day 60	$3.85/day 60	$3.85/day 60	$3.85/day 60
Stonemasons (New York)	$2.40/day 60	$2.73/day 60	$2.72/day 60	$2.72/day 60	$2.72/day 60

STANDARD JOBS 1870-1874

Job Type	1870	1871	1872	1873	1874
Bricklayers (Massachusetts) Avg hrs/wk	$3.97/day 60	$4.07/day 60	$3.86/day 60	$3.88/day 60	$3.50/day 60
Carpenters and Joiners (Connecticut) Avg hrs/wk	$2.77/day 60	$2.79/day 60	$2.73/day 60	$3.04/day 60	$2.89/day 60
Engineers, Stationary (New York)	$2.97/day 66	$2.86/day 70	$2.62/day 65	$2.70/day 64	$2.94/day 67
Farm Labor (New York)	$1.50/day 66	$1.50/day 66	$1.50/day 66	$1.50/day 66	$1.25/day 66
Firemen (Massachusetts)	$1.73/day 66	$1.86/day 63	$1.61/day 66	$1.67/day 66	$1.72/day 66
Glassblowers, Bottles (New Jersey)	$5.19/day NR	$5.17/day NR	$5.19/day NR	$5.19/day NR	$4.96/day NR
Hod Carriers (Massachusetts)	$2.12/day 60	$2.09/day 60	$1.98/day 60	$2.03/day 60	$1.95/day 60
Marble Cutters (New York)	$3.19/day 60	$3.22/day 60	$3.27/day 60	$3.25/day 60	$3.19/day 60
Painters (New York)	$3.15/day 60	$3.16/day 60	$3.12/day 60	$3.13/day 60	$3.02/day 60
Plasterers (Pennsylvania)	$2.86/day 60	$2.88/day 60	$2.86/day 60	$2.92/day 60	$2.86/day 60
Plumbers (New York)	$3.37/day 57	$3.36/day 57	$3.22/day 57	$3.18/day 57	$3.11/day 57
Stonemasons (New York)	$3.41/day 60	$3.42/day 60	$3.38/day 60	$3.36/day 60	$2.95/day 60

STANDARD JOBS 1875-1879

Job Type	1875	1876	1877	1878	1879
Bricklayers (Massachusetts)	$3.48/day	$3.45/day	$2.96/day	$2.90/day	$2.71
Avg hrs/wk	60	60	60	60	60
Carpenters and Joiners (Connecticut)	NR	NR	NR	NR	NR
Avg hrs/wk					
Engineers, Stationary (New York)	$3.21/day	$3.09/day	$3.10/day	$3.04/day	$2.55/day
	71	70	70	70	72
Farm Labor (New York)	$1.25/day	$1.25/day	$1/day	$0.88/day	$0.88/day
	66	63	63	63	63
Firemen (Massachusetts)	$1.60/day	$1.57/day	$1.51/day	$1.49/day	$1.39/day
	60	60	60	60	60
Glassblowers, Bottles (New Jersey)	$4.64/day	$4.36/day	$3.68/day	$3.68/day	$3.68/day
	NR	NR	NR	NR	NR
Hod Carriers (Massachusetts)	$1.91/day	$1.84/day	$1.79/day	$1.83/day	$1.82/day
	60	60	60	60	60
Marble Cutters (New York)	$3.10/day	$2.93/day	$2.77/day	$2.47/day	$2.38/day
	60	60	60	60	60
Painters (New York)	$3.08/day	$3.02/day	$2.59/day	$2.61/day	$2.84/day
	60	60	60	60	60
Plasterers (Pennsylvania)	$2.88/day	$2.31/day	$1.94/day	$1.94/day	$1.58/day
	60	60	60	60	60
Plumbers (New York)	$3.16/day	$3.13/day	$3.16/day	$3.13/day	$3.12/day
	57	57	57	54	54
Stonemasons (New York)	$3.01/day	$2.52/day	$2.12/day	$2.11/day	$2.47/day
	60	60	60	60	60

STANDARD JOBS 1880-1884

Job Type	1880	1881	1882	1883	1884
Bricklayers (Massachusetts)	$2.68/day	$2.83/day	$3.18/day	$3.23/day	$3.20/day
Avg hrs/wk	60	60	60	60	60
Carpenters and Joiners (Connecticut)	$2.15/day	$2.33/day	2.49/day	$2.57/day	$2.53/day
Avg hrs/wk	61	60	61	60	60
Engineers, Stationary (New York)	$2.48/day	$2.29/day	$2.29/day	$2.24/day	$2.28/day
	65	65	62	64	64
Farm Labor (New York)	$1.25/day	$1.25/day	$1.50/day	$1.25/day	$1.25/day
	63	63	63	63	63
Firemen (Massachusetts)	$1.37/day	$1.42/day	$1.39/day	$1.50/day	$1.48/day
	60	60	60	60	60
Glassblowers, Bottles (New Jersey)	NR	NR	NR	$4.23/day	$4.08/day
				51	51
Hod Carriers (Massachusetts)	$1.82/day	$1.62/day	$1.71/day	$1.94/day	$1.72/day
	60	60	60	60	60
Marble Cutters (New York)	$2.40/day	$2.57/day	$2.05/day	$2.69/day	$2.85/day
	60	60	60	60	60
Painters (New York)	$2.94/day	$2.76/day	$2.86/day	$3.25/day	$3.26/day
	60	58	58	58	58
Plasterers (Pennsylvania)	$1.81/day	$1.97/day	$2.39/day	$2.98/day	$3.25/day
	60	60	60	59	59
Plumbers (New York)	$3.37/day	$3.43/day	$3.50/day	$3.50/day	$3.50/day
	54	54	54	58	60
Stonemasons (New York)	$2.58/day	$2.92/day	$3.22/day	$3.31/day	$3.26/day
	60	60	60	60	60

STANDARD JOBS 1885-1889

Job Type	1885	1886	1887	1888	1889
Bricklayers (Massachusetts)	$3.37/day	$3.50/day	$2.94/day	$3.30/day	$3.46/day
Avg hrs/wk	60	59	58	56	56
Carpenters and Joiners (Connecticut)	$2.32/day	$2.46/day	$2.24/day	$2.56/day	NR
Avg hrs/wk	61	58	55	54	56
Engineers, Stationary (New York)	$2.32/day	$2.34/day	$2.12/day	$2.45/day	$2/day
	64	61	64	63	65
Farm Labor (New York)	$1.38/day	$1.38/day	$1.38/day	$1.40/day	$1.50/day
	63	63	63	63	63
Firemen (Massachusetts)	$1.54/day	$1.63/day	$1.53/day	$1.43/day	NR
	60	57	59	60	
Glassblowers, Bottles (New Jersey)	$4.14/day	$4.22/day	NR	$4.95/day	$4.05/day
	52	54		52	54
Hod Carriers (Massachusetts)	$1.66/day	$1.69/day	$1.67/day	$1.73/day	$1.69/day
	60	60	56	58	58
Marble Cutters (New York)	$2.82/day	$2.94/day	$2.98/day	$3.01/day	$2.89/day
	60	60	60	54	54
Painters (New York)	$2.96/day	$3.18/day	$2.93/day	$2.59/day	$3.40/day
	60	54	54	57	55
Plasterers (Pennsylvania)	$3.50/day	$2.85/day	$3/day	$3.50/day	$3.50/day
	54	52	54	54	54
Plumbers (New York)	$3.17/day	$3.28/day	$3.52/day	$3.37/day	$3.59/day
	56	54	52	54	48
Stonemasons (New York)	$3.05/day	$2.75/day	$3.35/day	$3.37/day	$3.32/day
	56	54	56	55	57

STANDARD JOBS 1890-1894

Job Type	1890	1891	1892	1893	1894
Bricklayers (Massachusetts)	$3.55/day	$3.51/day	$3.68/day	$3.75/day	$3.65/day
Avg hrs/wk	55	56	54	54	52
Carpenters and Joiners (Connecticut)	NR	NR	$2.63/day	$2.53/day	$2.26/day
Avg hrs/wk	60	56	56	60	60
Engineers, Stationary (New York)	$2.26/day	$2.26/day	$2.72/day	$2.26/day	$2/day
	63	63	63	63	60
Farm Labor (New York)	$1.49/day	$1.37/day	NR	$1.17/day	$1.25/day
	63	63	66	60	
Glassblowers, Bottles (New Jersey)	$3.80	$5.15	$5.15	NR	NR
	51	NR	NR		
Hod Carriers (Massachusetts)	$1.80/day	$1.77/day	$2.24/day	$2.22/day	$2.19/day
	57	58	54	54	52
Marble Cutters (NewYork)	$3.21/day	$3.27/day	$3.38/day	$2.51/day	$2.77/day
	54	50	49	53	54
Painters (New York)	$2.16/day	$2.09/day	$3.43/day	$2.93/day	$2.61/day
	55	51	51	50	54
Plasterers (Pennsylvania)	$3.50/day	$3.20/day	$3.20/day	$2.17/day	NR
	54	48	48	57	
Plumbers (New York)	$2.94/day	$2.87/day	$3.58/day	$3.53/day	$3.72/day
	48	48	48	49	48
Stonemasons (New York)	$3.39/day	$3.18/day	$3.90/day	$3/07/day	$3.95/day
	50	49	49	51	48

 # STANDARD JOBS 1895-1899

Job Type	1895	1896	1897	1898	1899
Bricklayers (Massachusetts)	$3.34/day	$3.87/day	$3.45/day	$3.41/day	$3.60/day
Avg hrs/wk	48	50	48	48	48
Carpenters and Joiners (Connecticut	2.27/day	$2.04/day	$2.33/day	NR	NR
Avg hrs/wk	62	60	58		
Engineers, Stationary (New York)	$2.52/day	$2.67/day	$3/day	$3.17/day	$2.63/day
	59	63	70	60	56
Glassblowers, Bottles (New Jersey)	NR	NR	NR	$3.97/day	NR
				54	
Hod Carriers (Massachusetts)	$2/day	$2.15/day	$2/day	$1.97/day	$2.10/day
	48	49	48	48	48
Marble Cutters (New York)	$2.80/day	$2.83/day	$3.94/day	$4.22/day	NR
	54	54	48	48	
Painters (New York)	$2.32/day	$2.96/day	$2.45/day	$2.47/day	$2.57/day
	56	51	49	50	52
Plasterers (Pennsylvania)	NR	$3.19/day	NR	NR	$3.20/day
			49		48
Plumbers (New York)	$3.74/day	$3.49/day	$3.73/day	$3.74/day	$3.92/day
	48	49	48	48	50
Stonemasons (New York)	$3.94/day	$3.92/day	$3.38/day	$3.67/day	$3.06/day
	48	49	48	48	48

SELECTED PRICES 1860-1899

Item	Source	Description	Price
Advertising			
Advertising Budget	Cecil Munsey, *The Illustrated Guide to the Collectibles of Coca-Cola* (1972)	*Coca-Cola;* amount spent for advertising in 1886	$73.96
Advertising Rate	*The Plantation* (1872)	Full page	$20.00
Advertising Rate	*Demorest's Illustrated Monthly* (1873)	Per line solid agate space	$0.75
Apparel, Children's			
Hat	*Advertising Trade Card* (1892)	Boy's school hat	$0.25
Knee Pants	*The Delineator* (1896)	Boy's; we take remnants of fine woolens, give them to our merchant tailoring department, and make them into boy's knee pants	$0.50/$0.75/$1.00
Parasol	*New York Times* (1877)	Sun umbrellas	$0.50
School Outfit	*Ladies' Home Journal* (1893)	Our combination suit; extra pair pants and hat to match; for boys 4 to 14 years	$5.00
Shoes	*Advertising Trade Card* (1875)	Button boats; $10,000 worth of boots and shoes better than ever	$0.60
Snap Waist	*Ladies' Home Journal* (1893)	*Cupid;* no more buttons to sew on; no buttonholes, no buckles	$1.00
Suit	*Advertising Trade Card* (1885)	*Nobby*	$2.00
Suit	*Chicago Daily Tribune* (1882)	Jerome suits; 4 to 11 years old	$3.00
Suit	*Ladies' Home Journal* (1893)	Boy's combination; consisting of double-breasted coat, two pairs of knee pants, and a nice hat—all made to match	$5.00
Suits	*Advertising Trade Card* (1892)	Cooperative clothing, come and be convinced; we are the people that quote the lowest prices	
Apparel, Men's			
Clothing	*R. H. Macy & Co. Advertising Flyer* (1881)	Silk walking costumes; in solid colors	$16.84
Collar	*New York Times* (1895)	*Keep's;* best four-ply linen	$0.15
Collar	*Harper's Weekly* (1865)	*American Steel;* snow-white; linen-finished; illusion-stitched	$1.25
Collars and Cuffs	*The Ledger Monthly* (1899)	*Linene;* stylish, convenient, economical, made of fine cloth; the turn-down collars are reversible and give double service; ten collars or five pairs of cuffs	$0.25

Item	Source	Description	Price
Cuff Holder	*Demorest's Family Magazine* (1890)	Invisible; just out; impossible to get out of order	$1.00/2 dozen
Cuffs	*The Youth's Companion* (1898)	*Linene;* reversible; look well, feel well, wear well; made of fine cloth; when soiled, reverse, wear again, then discard	$0.25/5 pairs
Gloves	*Spirit Of The Times* (1877)	Kid and dogskin, embroidered backs, all shades	$1.50
Golf Cap	*New York Times* (1895)	*Keep's;* correct styles	$1.00
Half Hose	*Spirit Of The Times* (1877)	Elegant; in cotton worsted and merino	$0.40
Hat	*Spirit Of The Times* (1877)	*Sola;* made of waterproof duck, dead grass color, and in same style as east India hats; absolute guarantee against sunstroke	$3.00
Hat	*New York Times* (1895)	Fall styles; silk derbies	$6.00
Necktie	*Demorest's Illustrated Monthly* (1873)	Designed to supersede all other methods for fastening the bow to a turn-down collar	$0.10
Necktie	*Demorest's Illustrated Monthly* (1873)	*Demorest's;* black bows in rich red silk	$0.50
Neckware	*Spirit Of The Times* (1877)	Ties, bows, and scarves	$0.25
Pants	*New York Times* (1877)	English trousers; many specialties to order	$9.00
Pants	*Advertising Trade Card* (1885)	Good cassimere pants	$2.00
Shirt	*Spirit Of The Times* (1877)	*Wamsutta;* muslin	$1.00
Shirt	*San Francisco Examiner* (1895)	Standard shirts; a shirt that will fit, look and wear like finest custom-made	$1.50
Shirt Bosoms	*New York Times* (1863)	*Kinzey's gent's;* various styles	$0.28-$0.50
Shirts	*The New Orleans Picayune* (1875)	Stylish shirts	$1.50
Shirts	*New York Times* (1895)	*Keep's;* made to order	$9.00/6
Shoes	*Advertising Trade Card* (1875)	Working; $10,000 worth of boots and shoes better than ever	$0.98
Shoes	*The State* (Columbia, SC) (1891)	*Hanan's;* handmade	$3.00
Shoes	*Advertising Trade Card* (1892)	Man's good working shoes	$1.00

Item	Source	Description	Price
Shooting Coat	*Spirit Of The Times* (1877)	W. H. Holabird; complete waterproof duck coat	$6.00
Suit	*Advertising Trade Card* (1875)	Fine imported Scotch suits	$10.00
Suit	*Advertising Trade Card* (1875)	Durable working suits	$4.00
Suit	*Advertising Trade Card* (1875)	Fine all-wool suits	$8.00
Suit	*Advertising Trade Card* (1875)	Fine English cassimere suits	$12.00
Suit	*Chicago Daily Tribune* (1882)	*Putnam Apparel House;* men's single-breast frock suit; made with Scotch cassimere	$12.50
Suit	*New York Times* (1877)	Cheviot; black and blue	$20.00
Suit	*New York Times* (1877)	*Regents;* striped cassimere	$22.00
Suit	*Advertising Trade Card* (1885)	Black cheviot	$7.50
Suit	*The Delineator* (1896)	All-wool suit equal to any clothier's $12 garments	$5.95
Suspenders	*The Yorkville Enquirer* (Yorkville, SC) (1892)	$0.05 will buy a regular $0.15 suspender	$0.05
Top coat	*New York Times* (1895)	English design	$10.00

Apparel, Women's

Item	Source	Description	Price
Bicycle Costume	*The Delineator* (1896)		$7.50
Bicycle Skirt	*The Youth's Companion* (1898)	Tailor-made; our new designs in bicycle skirts are recognized everywhere as the most practical skirts for wheeling that have yet been produced	$2.50
Bust Form	*The Delineator* (1896)	*The New Hygeia;* as light as a feather, tastefully covered so that the forms can be removed and the covering washed	$0.50
Cape	*Harper's Weekly* (1875)	Young & Conant; gossamer, waterproof; the best storm garment ever worn; 56" long	$8.25
Corset	*Demorest's Monthly Magazine* (1881)	*Hercules;* supporting; woven, spoon steel, cannot stretch, break or lose its shape, avoids all pressure on the chest	$3.00
Corset	*Demorest's Family Magazine* (1890)	*Madame Foy's;* skirt supporting; graceful form, health and comfort	$1.40
Corset	*The Delineator* (1896)	F. P.; create handsome forms	$1.00
Corset	*The Delineator* (1896)	*The Henderson Flexo Girdle;* every inch of it fits	$1.25
Corset	*The Delineator* (1896)	*W. B. Cyclist Athletic;* perfect freedom combined with the shape and gracefulness of W. B. corsets	$1.00

Item	Source	Description	Price
Corset	*The Spartan* (Spartanburg, SC) (1898)	*Featherbone;* every one guaranteed	$0.18
Corset	*The Youth's Companion* (1898)	*Warner's* '98 models; the quality is the finest thing to consider in corsets; all figures suited at these prices	$1.00
Dress Shield	*Demorest's Family Magazine* (1890)	*Canfield Seamless;* the only reliable dress shield in the world	$0.25
Dress Shield	*The Delineator* (1896)	OMO: better than rubber, absolutely odorless; impervious to perspiration	$0.25
Glove Hook	*Harper's Weekly* (1887)	*H. H. Tammen;* moss agate	4/$0.05
Gloves	*Advertising Trade Card* (1875)	Perfumed kid gloves; pure elastic; any shade or color Two-button gloves Four-button gloves	 $1.00 $1.50
Gloves	*The Delineator* (1896)	*Kayser Patent Finger-Tipped;* the tips wear as long as the gloves	$0.50
Hat	*New York Times* (1877)	Trimmed	$2.50
Parasols	*Chicago Daily Tribune* (1882)	*Pardridges'* Semiannual Reduction Sale; satin parasols, regular $5.00; now	$3.90
Scarf	*New York Times* (1877)	Spanish and Brusells net; 2 1/2 yards long	$0.75
Shoes	*Advertising Trade Card* (1875)	*Lace;* $10,000 worth of boots and shoes better than ever	$0.63
Shoes	*The State* (Columbia, SC) (1891)	*Ziegler's;* button; 100 pairs available	9/$0.05
Shoes	*Advertising Trade Card* (1892)	*Dongola;* button shoes	$1.50
Skirt	*The Delineator* (1896)	*Brilliantine*	$1.75
Skirt	*The Delineator* (1896)	*Lustre;* wool; the best and lightest all year round skirt, regardless of price; five gored, 3 1/3 yards wide	$2.50
Skirt	*The Delineator* (1896)	Skirt made of heavily figured brilliantine, full flare and ripple back	$2.49
Sleeve Buttons	*Harper's Weekly* (1865)	Ivory and pearl; top quality	$3.00/pair
Suit	*Advertising Trade Card* (1885)	All-wool evening suit	$6.00
Turban	*Ladies' Home Journal* (1893)	Neatly made of cloth and velvet and trimmed in all colors and combinations to match any suit	$0.98
Undergarments	*Ladies' Home Journal* (1893)	Ladies' cotton and wool combination suits, natural color; send bust measurements	$2.00 to $3.00
Waist	*The Delineator* (1896)	*Chicago;* size 6-D; gives such comfort . . . allows perfect freedom of motion and perfect development of the body	$1.00
Waist	*The Delineator* (1896)	Fine silk dress waists, brocade or plain surah; sizes 32 to 42	

Item	Source	Description	Price
Appliances			
Burner and Chimney	*Harper's Weekly* (1887)	*Royal Argand;* large, white, steady light without a flicker	$1.25
Oil Heater	*Ladies' Home Journal* (1893)	*Barler's Ideal;* costs less than $0.01 an hour to heat a room 16' square; no coal; no ashes; no odor	
Baby Products			
Diaper	*Demorest's Family Magazine* (1890)	*The Canfield;* the only article of its kind that affords perfect protection without harmful results	6/$0.05
Shoes	*Advertising Trade Card* (1875)	$10,000 worth of boots and shoes better than ever	$0.15
Soap	*Advertising Trade Card* (1870)	*B. T. Babbitt's;* only the purest vegetable oils used; a certain preventative of chafing, itching, etc.	$2.50
Business Equipment & Supplies			
Business Cards	*Demorest's Monthly Magazine* (1881)	*Chromo;* in sets of one dozen assorted styles	$0.05
Harness	*Chicago Daily Tribune* (1882)	Double buggy harness	$25.00
Insurance Rates	*The New Orleans Picayune* (1875)	Life insurance, per $1,000, cost per year Age 40 Age 50	$21.02 433.17
Printing Press	*Harper's Weekly* (1865)	*Taylor;* double cylinder, five roller, table distribution, bed 38 x 51"	$3,500
Printing Press	*Demorest's Family Magazine* (1890)	Self-inker; printing press with script type outfit	$5.00
Rubber Stamp	*Demorest's Family Magazine* (1890)	With name on, ink pad, pencil & pen; one ring and agent's outfit	$0.10
Typewriter	*Harper's Weekly* (1887)	*Hall;* guaranteed to do better work, and a greater variety, than any other typewriter in the world	$40.00
Typewriter	*The Delineator* (1896)	Anderson's shorthand is taking the place of stenography because it is quickly learned	$25.00
Collectibles			
Engravings	*Harper's Weekly* (1887)	President and Mrs. Cleveland; far superior to lithographs; each portrait 7" x 11"	$0.50
Figures	*The Century Magazine* (1884)	Rogers Group; *The Peddler At The Fair;* these groups are packed without charge to go to any part of the world	$15.00
Photographs	*Ingalls' Home Magazine* (1889)	President and Mrs. Harrison; two cabinet photos	$0.15
Prints	*Spirit Of The Times* (1877)	*Currier & Ives;* pictures of the great trotters; all in action, showing just their gait and style; size 13 1/2" x 17 3/4"	$0.20
Stamps	*The Youth's Companion* (1898)	Shanghai, China; 100 rare stamps	$0.10

Item	Source	Description	Price
Education			
Dance Lessons	*San Francisco Examiner* (1895)	Waltz guaranteed in private; 3 months' tuition	$10.00
Fees	*Southern Christian Advocate* (1897)	*Clemson College;* board, washing, fuel, lights for session; 40 weeks	$59.00
Piano Lessons	*New York Times* (1863)	Twenty-four lessons on the piano, at pupils' residences	$8.00
School	*San Francisco Examiner* (1895)	*Miss Bolte's home school;* board; English, French, German, Music, Dancing	$30.00/month
Tuition	*New York Times* (1868)	*Rockland Female Institute;* for board and English tuition, Nyack on the Hudson	$360/year
Tuition	*New York Times* (1868)	*West Branch Board School;* for boys 10 to 16 years of age, Jersey shore, Lycoming County, Penn.	$225/year
Tuition	*The Plantation* (1872)	*Rome Female College;* for the illustration of scientific facts and principles; extra charges will be made for music, French, oil painting and drawing	$125
Tuition	*Spirit Of The Times* (1877)	Special training for teachers; renowned music school and school of elocution, oratory, modern languages, drawing and painting Classes of three pupils Private	 $10.00/quarter $30.00/quarter
Tuition	*The State* (Columbia, SC) (1896)	*Columbia Female College;* curricula on university plan; students entering every department according to preparation, none held back	$200/year
Tuition	*The Delineator* (1896)	*University of the City of New York Law School;* Two-year Post-graduate	 $200 $125
Entertainment			
Aquarium Ticket	*New York Times* (1877)	*The Great American Aquarium;* marvelous triple-tailed Japanese fishes, beautiful vari-colored fish, for which $2,000 was offered and refused Children Adult	 $0.25 $0.50
Concert	*The New Orleans Picayune* (1875)	Grand Concert featuring Miss Corinne Bouligny Per ticket	 $1.00
Concert Ticket	*San Francisco Daily Examiner* (1875)	Grand Concert of Music; Madame Z. Dennis, late of the Italian Opera, Paris and lately from the French Opera, New Orleans, will make her first appearance	$1.00
Concert Ticket	*Spirit Of The Times* (1877)	*Gilmore's Concert Garden;* Gilmore's Great Military Band and other eminent artists Per seat Box seating four	 $0.50 $3.00
Exhibition Tickets	*San Francisco Daily Examiner* (1875)	Industrial Exhibition, single season tickets	$3.00
Exhibition Ticket	*New York Times* (1877)	*Academy of Design Painting Exhibition;* the fifty-second Grand Annual Exhibition, 23rd St. and 4th Avenue	$0.25
Exhibition Ticket	*Spirit Of The Times* (1877)	*Russian Horse Trotter Exhibition at Fleetwood Park;* a display of all horses as shown at fairs in Russia, with all styles of horse clothing and trappings used there	$1.00

Item	Source	Description	Price
Game Ticket	*Spirit Of The Times* (1877)	*Tammy Hall Grand Billiards Match;* for the champion gold medal valued at $600 between Wm. Sexton (champion) and Cyearillic Dion; ladies accompanied by gentlemen free	
		General admission	$0.50
		Reserved seats	$1.00
Horse Racing	*Chicago Daily Tribune* (1882)	*Six Great Contests of Speed;* The Cup Day and Chicago Stakes	
		Admission	$0.50
Lecture Ticket	*New York Times* (1863)	*"How To End The War";* lecture by Col. O. T. Beard	$0.25
Museum Ticket	*New York Times* (1863)	*Banvard's Hall of Art;* four Grand Panoramas on the same night	
		Children	$0.15
		Adults	$0.25
Museum Ticket	*New York Times* (1863)	*Barnum's American Museum;* featuring the smallest pair of human beings ever seen	
		Children under 10	$0.15
		Adults	$0.25
Museum Ticket	*Harper's Weekly* (1865)	*Barnum's New American Museum;* nothing to offend the most fastidious, but everything to gratify healthy curiosity and refined taste; two performances daily	
		Children	$0.15
		Adults	$0.30
Museum Ticket	*New York Times* (1877)	*P. T. Barnum at Gilmore Gardens;* the very last opportunity to witness the most tremendous amusement combination of modern times	$0.25/$0.50/$0.75
Opera Ticket	*San Francisco Daily Examiner* (1875)	Grand English Opera, MaGuire's New Theatre; *Marriage of Figaro;* reserved seats	$1/$1.50/$2
Orchestra Ticket	*New York Times* (1895)	Symphony Orchestra, Walter Damrosch, conductor	$0.25/$0.50/$1
Show Ticket	*Spirit Of The Times* (1894)	*Buffalo Bill's Wild West Show;* Ambrose Park, South Brooklyn; twice daily, rain or shine; 20,000 covered seats	
		Children	$0.25
		Adults	$0.50
Skating Ticket	*New York Times* (1863)	*Fifth Avenue Skating Pond;* single ticket	
		Ladies'	$2.50
		Gentlemen's	$5.00
Race Ticket	*Spirit Of The Times* (1894)	*Chicago Race-Track At Harlem;* six races each day	$0.75
Theater Ticket	*New York Times* (1868)	*Wood's Museum and Metropolitan Theatre;* Miss Susan Galton will appear in two of Offenbach's comic operettas, introducing the songs of "Home Sweet Home" and "Lo! Hear the Gentle Lark"	
		Children under 10	$0.25
		Adults	$0.50
Theater Ticket	*New York Times* (1877)	*Mark Twain American Drama at Park Theatre;* farewell engagement of John T. Raymond in his creation of Col. Mulberry Sellers	$0.50 to $1.50
Theater Ticket	*New York Times* (1895)	*Comic Elephants,* by George Lockhart	$0.40

Entertainment, Home

Item	Source	Description	Price
Card Game	*The Youth's Companion* (1898)	*Dominola;* home card game; fun for young and old	$0.20

Item	Source	Description	Price
Magic Lantern Attachment	*The Ledger Monthly* (1899)	Makes pictures 6' high, plus 36 views	$1.00
Music Box	*Spirit Of The Times* (1877)	*Distin;* everything in the musical line	$2.50
Music Box	*The Delineator* (1896)	*The Capital;* self-playing; plays any number of tunes; standard and popular airs 44 teeth in comb, 8 tunes 162 teeth in comb, 12 tunes	 $15.00 $75.00
Music Boxes	*Harper's New Monthly Magazine* (1866)	Playing from one to 36 different tunes	$5.50 to $6.00
Recording	*Demorest's Illustrated Monthly* (1873)	*Elocutionist's Annual*	$0.25
Song Sheet	*Spirit Of The Times* (1877)	*"Life's Wheat is Full of Tares, My Boy,"* by H. P. Danks; a motto song of uncommon sense and excellence	 $0.30
Stereoscopic Pictures	*New York Times* (1863)	*Leggat Brothers;* magnificent colored pictures	$1.50/dozen

Farm Equipment & Supplies

Item	Source	Description	Price
Boarding Fee	*Spirit Of The Times* (1877)	Horses; for winter at farm in Stamford, Conn.	$8.00/month
Condition Powder for Chickens	*The Youth's Companion* (1898)	*Sheridan's;* to get more eggs there is no better plan than that of daily mixing the food given to poultry	$0.25
Corn Seed	*The Plantation* (1872)	*Dent;* very early and prolific and succeeds well in our (southern) climate	$1.00
Cotton Seeds	*R. H. Macy & Co. Advertising Flyer* (1881)	*Duncan's Mammoth Prolific;* yields 6590 lbs. seed cotton per acre; for 100 seeds	$0.10
Fertilizer	*The Plantation* (1872)	*Dickson;* ground raw bone	$40/ton
Harness Soap	*Spirit Of The Times* (1877)	*Colgate's;* try it and you will use no other	3/$0.05/cake
Hog	*The Plantation* (1872)	*Berkshire;* one boar, over twelve months old, large and handsome	$40/pair
Hoof Ointment	*Spirit Of The Times* (1877)	*Knickerbocker;* for horses; cures quarter cracks, corns, brittle hoofs, and all diseases arising from dryness of the hoof	$1.00/jar
Horse Medicine	*Spirit Of The Times* (1877)	*Wilder's Constitution Powders for Horses;* a public blessing to horses and cattle; cures all diseases common to horses, gives vitality, purifies the blood, and gives new lease of life	$0.50/box
Horse Muzzle	*Spirit Of The Times* (1877)	*Gedney's;* wire; invaluable for biters and cribbers	$6.00
Horse Muzzle	*Spirit Of The Times* (1894)	*Gillespies' Patent;* it prevents bolting and waste of food, it corrects digestion	$2.50
Insecticide	*Spirit Of The Times* (1894)	*Tough on Flies;* protect your horses and cattle from any annoyance for flies, gnats, and insects of any kind	$1.00/quart

Item	Source	Description	Price
Oat Seeds	*Spirit Of The Times* (1877)	A distinct and hardy winter crop; free from rust; makes good fall pasture	$1.00/bushel
Oats	*The Plantation* (1872)	*Red Rust Proof;* 500 bushels available	$2.00
Raisin Grape Vines	*Demorest's Monthly Magazine* (1881)	Best varieties by mail	3/$0.05
Stud Fee	*Spirit Of The Times* (1877)	Trotter *Alamo;* the only son of Almont, the great sire of trotters; mares not proving in foal can return next season free of charge	$50.00

Financial Products & Services

Item	Source	Description	Price
Gold Investments	*The Delineator* (1896)	Ladies and gentlemen investing $100 per month for ten months in our 5 percent bonds receive $1,000 in gold as a premium; no risk, loss impossible	$100
Money Order	*Advertising Trade Card* (1893)	*United States Express;* cheapest, safest, and most convenient; $5 to $50	
		Not over $5	$0.05
		$5–$9.99	$0.08
		$10.00–$19.99	$0.10
		$20–$29.99	$0.12
Money Order		$30–$39.99	$0.15
		$40–$50	$0.20
Safety Deposit	*The State Box Rental* (1891)	Loan and Exchange Bank (Columbia, SC)	$4 to $12/year

Food Products

Item	Source	Description	Price
Baking Powder	*Advertising Trade Card* (1870)	*Kenton;* it has few equals and no superior	$0.20
Baking Powder	*Ladies' Home Journal* (1893)	Cleveland's; food raised with Cleveland's baking powder has no bitter taste, but is sweet and keeps sweet and fresh; a quarter-pound can	$0.15
BonBons	*The Delineator* (1896)	*Lowney's Chocolate;* name on every piece	$0.60
Candy	*Demorest's Family Magazine* (1890)	One box candy, 100 colored pictures, 1 pack new cards	$0.06
Candy	*Ladies' Home Journal* (1893)	*Plows';* that's what your Chicago friends bought when you were visiting the World's Fair; tin boxes $0.10 extra	$0.80/pound
Chocolate	*San Francisco Examiner* (1895)	Venard's Eagle chocolate	$0.20/pound
Chocolate Icing	*Ladies' Home Journal* (1893)	*Lang's Readymade;* making chocolate cake easily and successfully; sample can, enough for a three-layer cake	$0.20
Codfish	*The Delineator* (1896)	*Beardsley's;* shredded; clean-wholesome-sweet, requires no boiling or soaking	$0.10/package
Coffee	*New York Times* (1863)	Gillies' Old Plantation; to all lovers of fine flavored coffee	$0.25/pound
Coffee	*New York Times* (1863)	*Rubia Mills Government;* put up in tin-foil pound papers, 48 in a box	$0.07/pound
Coffee	*The Spartan* (Spartanburg, SC) (1898)	*Chapman's Grocer's;* 11 pounds, parched	$1.00

Item	Source	Description	Price
Corned and Roast Beef	*The State* (Columbia, SC) (1896)	Key cans	$0.10/pound
Crackers	*The Youth's Companion* (1898)	*Baby Educator;* a hard, nutritious cracker, the shape of a ring; six in a box	$0.20
Cream Cheese	*The State* (Columbia, SC) (1896)	Extra fine	$0.15/pound
Extract of Beef	*Ladies' Home Journal* (1893)	*Liebig Company's;* one can will make excellent stock; it is possible to make a quart of good stock at a cost of about $0.10 for the meat flavor	$0.10
Flour	*The State* (Columbia, SC) (1896)	*Perfection* Half-barrel Barrel	$2.50 $4.75
Food Supplement	*Demorest's Family Magazine* (1894)	*Ridge's Food for Children;* supplement medicine that brings back strength; the most reliable food on the market for rearing of children	3/$0.05
Gelatin	*Demorest's Family Magazine* (1890)	*Chalmer's;* superior to the imported and much cheaper; two-ounce packets	$1.40/dozen
Gelatin	*The Youth's Companion* (1898)	*Knox's;* sparkling; no acids, no odor, no taste; pink gelatin for fancy desserts with every package; two-quart package	$0.15
Instantaneous Chocolate	*Demorest's Family Magazine* (1890)	No trouble, no boiling, the greatest invention of the age; one-pound tin can	$0.75
Lactated Baby Food	*Ladies' Home Journal* (1893)	When four months old we gave him lactated food and since then he has grown strong and healthy	$0.25
Lactated Food	*Advertising Trade Card* (1888)	*Wills Richardson;* 150 meals per can; it makes them healthy, happy, hearty	$1.00
Lactated Food	*Advertising Trade Card* (1890)	It makes them healthy, happy; hearty; that's why they love it; for 150 meals	$1.00
Molasses	*The State* (Columbia, SC) (1896)	Cheap; straight New Orleans molasses, dark colored, but good; by the barrel only	$0.10/gallon
Pineapple Cheese	*The State* (Columbia, SC) (1896)	Picnic; of best quality	$0.40
Pork & Beans	*The Youth's Companion* (1898)	*Van Camp's;* a day's fuel, a day's worry and care, are done away with in ten minutes; where economy tastes good	$0.06
Powdered Chocolate	*Demorest's Family Magazine* (1890)	*Wilbur's Cocoa-Theta;* the finest powdered chocolate for family use	$0.10
Rice	*The State* (Columbia, SC) (1896)	Fancy white rice in 240-pound sacks	$0.04/pound
Sarsaparilla	*The Yorkville Enquirer* (Yorkville, SC) (1892)	*Ayeare's;* superior to all other preparations claiming to be blood-purifiers; cures catarrh	$1.00

Item	Source	Description	Price
Seeds	*Demorest's Family Magazine* (1890)	Ten varieties best and new and popular annuals	$0.25
Smoked Herring	*The State* (Columbia, SC) (1896)	$0.15/box	
Soup	*Ladies' Home Journal* (1893)	*White Label* per case, 2 dozen pint cans Per case, 2 dozen quart cans	$2.00 $3.00
Sugar	*The State* (Columbia, SC) (1896)	Best granulated and refined in 100-pound sack	$0.04/pound
Tea	*Demorest's Family Magazine* (1890)	*Sirocco;* direct from our own gardens in India and Ceylon; per tin	$0.60/$0.80/$1.00
Tea	*The New Orleans Picayune* (1875)	*J. W. Platt's Imperial Green Tea;* Per size	$0.50 $0.75 $0.90 $1.10
Tea	*The Yorkville Enquirer* (Yorkville, SC) (1892)	Best First-class breakfast tea	6/$0.05
Tea	*The Youth's Companion* (1898)	*Salada Ceylon;* sold only in lead packets	$0.50/pound

Furniture

Item	Source	Description	Price
Bed	*San Francisco Daily Examiner* (1875)	Folding bed	$15.00
Bedroom Set	*San Francisco Daily Examiner* (1875)	4 pieces; antique	$11.00
Chair	*San Francisco Daily Examiner* (1875)	New solid oak high-back chairs	$1.00
Safe	*Demorest's Illustrated Monthly* (1873)	*Marvin's;* boudoir; every woman should have one in her dressing room to protect jewelry; highly ornamental	$100

Garden Equipment & Supplies

Item	Source	Description	Price
Chrysanthemums	*The Delineator* (1896)	3 beautiful chrysanthemums	$0.10
Dwarf French Cannas	*The Delineator* (1896)	At prices as low as geraniums; one fine healthy plant	$0.15
Florida Palms	*The Delineator* (1896)	Palms are considered the rich man's plant because so high priced in the north	$0.20
Grapevines	*Demorest's Family Magazine* (1890)	3 sample vines; 100 varieties	$0.15
Pesticide	*The State* (Columbia, SC) (1896)	*Anti-Skeet;* kills mosquitoes; six wafers in a box	$0.10

Item	Source	Description	Price
Plant Sprinkler	*Ladies' Home Journal* (1893)	*Tyearian;* just like rain	$0.75
Roses	*The Delineator* (1896)	Six lovely roses: Snowflake, Maurice Rouvier, Star of Gold, Mde. Sai Carnot, Mlle F. Kruger, Mde. Scwaller	$0.25
Roses	*The Delineator* (1896)	*Everblooming;* six strong one-year plants	$0.25
Sweet Pea Seeds	*The Delineator* (1896)	Ten full packets	$0.10
Tomato Seeds	*Demorest's Family Magazine* (1890)	*Lorillard;* the most solid and delicious variety grown; a packet	$0.15
Vegetable Seeds	*The Modern Priscilla* (1893) In Silver	*Finch's;* packet each of Finch's tree tomato, Mansfield tomato, evergreen cucumber, surehead cabbage, perfection lettuce $0.25 in stamps	$0.30
Vegetable Seeds	*The Youth's Companion* (1898)	Vaughan's; radish 100; beauty lettuce 100; blackest beet 50; early cabbage 100; white onion 100; gem melon 100; cucumber 50; beefsteak tomato 50; giant pumpkin 30; mixed herbs 125; for 20 packets	$0.20

Hotel Rates

Item	Source	Description	Price
Hotel Room	*Spirit Of The Times* (1877)	Cincinnati, Ohio; on the European plan	$1.00/day
Hotel Room	*Spirit Of The Times* (1877)	New York, New York; European plan, prices reduced	$1.00/day
Hotel Room	*Spirit Of The Times* (1877)	Augusta, Georgia; conveniently located, newly fitted up in first-class order; board reduced; special arrangement to theatrical troops	$2.00/day
Hotel Room	*The State* (Columbia, SC) (1891)	Columbia, South Carolina; largest hotel in the city, newly remodeled and refurnished	$2 to $2.50/day
Room	*San Francisco Daily Examiner* (1875)	*Lyon;* for two gentlemen; bedroom and parlor; highly furnished	$20 per month

Household Products

Item	Source	Description	Price
Atomizer and Sprinkler	*Ingalls' Home Magazine* (1889)	Spray appears like fog; best clothes sprinkler in the world	$0.50
Broom Holder	*Demorest's Family Magazine* (1890)	Holds a broom either end up; keeps a wet broom from rotting	$0.15
Cake Tins	*The Delineator* (1896)	*Perfection;* delicate cake removed without breaking; two round layered tins	3/$0.05
Cake Turner	*The Delineator*	Revolving; you press the handle, it turns the cake	$0.20
Carpet	*The State* (Columbia, SC) (1896)	1/$0.09/yard	
China	*New York Times* (1868)	*Washington Hadley's White French;* dinner set, 130 pieces	$30.00
Cloth	*Chicago Daily Tribune* (1882)	Silk and wool plaid cloth; worth $0.60 per yard	$0.25

Item	Source	Description	Price
Cloth	*Chicago Daily Tribune* (1882)	44-inch all wool nun's veiling in navy blue, myeartle and bronze green, embroidered with silk flowers; worth $2.25 per yard Special yard price	$0.50
Cloth	*The New Orleans Picayune* (1875) (1896)	White linen; per yard	$0.30
Cookie and Biscuit Cutter	*Ladies' Home Journal* (1893)	Dough will not stick to it; saves hours of work; wonderful rotary wire	$0.15
Detergent	*Advertising Trade Card* (1885)	*Boraxine;* saves toil and drudgery; large package	$0.10
Detergent Dye	*The Youth's Companion* (1898)	*Maypole Soap;* home dyeing a pleasure at last; washes and dyes in one operation; all colors	$0.15
Dinner and Tea Set	*The Delineator* (1896)	English decorated dinner and tea set; packed and delivered	$7.00
Dinner Knives	*Demorest's Monthly Magazine* (1881)	Silver plated; orders boxed and placed on car or steamer, free of charge	$3.00/dozen
Dinner Set	*Demorest's Monthly Magazine* (1881)	English porcelain; 100 pieces white china	$14.00
Dishes	*Demorest's Monthly Magazine* (1881)	Dinner set; French china; 149 pieces fine white china	$30.00
Disinfectant	*Demorest's Monthly Magazine* (1881)	*Milson's Patent Ozone;* nature's great disinfectant; includes generator and diffuser which will purify the atmosphere of dwellings; small size	$8.00
Doilies	*The Ledger Monthly* (1899)	Linen; nine handsome butter doilies stamped on fine white linen	$0.10
Dye	*Demorest's Family Magazine* (1890)	Fancy dyeing at home, fast colors, 50 popular shades for cotton, wool and silk Per package Per dozen	 $0.10 $0.80
Fork	*American Silver Flatware* (1890)	*Graft & Niemann Earl Patent;* for children; the child will naturally place its finger in the shield, which prevents finger slipping and proper control of the fork; sterling; child's size	$2.00
Fruit, Wine, and Jelly Press	*Advertising Trade Card* (1880)	Enterprise; not intended for making cider	$3.00
Glass Cutter and Putty Knife	*Harper's Weekly* (1875)	*Lovejoy's;* will cut glass better than a diamond	$0.50
Linoleum	*The State* (Columbia, SC) (1896)	*A-quality;* laid	$0.80/yard
Nutmeg Grater	*Ingalls' Home Magazine* (1889)	Lady agents wanted in every town to sell this useful article	$0.25
Paint	*Sales Flier* (1892)	Enamel; for decorating tables, chairs, wicker ware, picture frames, baskets, earthenware, metal, glass, etc.	$0.25
Pesticide	*The Ledger Monthly* (1899)	*Stearns Electric Paste;* don't feed roaches and bedbugs on the exterminating powders, which don't even make the bugs sick	$0.25

Item	Source	Description	Price
Polish	The Delineator (1896)	Lemonoide; the perfect polish, makes your piano or organ conspicuous for its beauty	$0.50
Raisin and Grape Seeder	Advertising Trade Card (1880)	Enterprise; removes every seed without waste Family size Hotel size	$1.00 $2.50
Rubber Roofing	Harper's Weekly (1887)	For house, barn and all out buildings	$2.00/100 square feet
Shingles	The Yorkville Enquirer (Yorkville, SC) (1892)	North Carolina Heart of Pine; standard 4" size	$2.50/thousand
Shingles	The Spartan (Spartanburg, SC) (1892)	G. O. Fike Lumber Co.; we'll sell the best $2 shingles on this market	$2.00
Shower Bath Ring	The Delineator (1896)	Kelly; prevents wetting the head and floor; nickel-plated rings and 6' of hot waterproof hose	$2.00
Silver Polish	Demorest's Family Magazine (1890)	Electro-Silicon; silver polish imparts to precious metals the highest degree of brilliancy, without the least detriment; price in stamps for a full-sized bottle	$0.15
Soap	Advertising Trade Card (1881)	Enoch Morgan's Sun Sapolio Cleanser; no one article known that will do so many kinds of work about the house	$0.10
Soap	Advertising Trade Card (1885)	Boque's; $100 reward for a bar of Boque's Soap that will not do all that is claimed for it; cakes	$0.25/3
Soap	Advertising Trade Card (1885)	Enoch Morgan's Sun Sapolio; a cake of Sapolio, a bowl of water and a brush, cloth or sponge, will make housecleaning an easy and quick job	$0.10
Stain	Sales Flier (1892)	Ebony black; can be used on woodwork, furniture, etc., to produce an exact imitation of ebony	$0.25
Stove-Polishing Mitten	The Delineator (1896)	Polishes the stove better and quicker than a brush	$0.25
Table Covers	Ingalls' Home Magazine (1889)	Felt; two yards square, stamped with pansies on the corners	$2.50
Tidies	Ingalls' Home Magazine (1889)	Fringed linen; size 15" x 20" including fringe	$0.04
Toilet Set	Ingalls' Home Magazine (1889)	Set of 7 pieces stamped on fine Momie cloth, designs of fuchsias, daisies, and roses	$0.60
Vase	The Century Magazine (1884)	West's; terraline; ready without further preparation to receive Winsor & Newtons, Schoenfelds, or other oil colors without firing or baking	$2.00
Wallpaper	The Modern Priscilla (1893)	Alfred Peats; handsome gold parlor paper with wide borders and ceilings to match	$0.15/roll
Wallpaper	The Delineator (1896)	Over 2 million rolls carried in stock	$0.10/roll
Wallpaper	The Youth's Companion (1898)	Alfred Peats 1898 Prize; new floral, silk, chintz, delft, denim stripe effects for parlors and bedrooms	$0.03 to $0.10/roll
Window Shades	The State (Columbia, SC) (1891)	Per window	3/$0.03

Item	Source	Description	Price
Window Shades	*The State* (Columbia, SC) (1896)	Per window	2/$0.02

Insurance Rates

Fire Insurance	*Insurance Policy* (1899)	$500 fire coverage two wood frame houses in Columbia, South Carolina	$4.75/year
Insurance Policy	*The Yorkville Enquirer* (Yorkville, SC) (1892)	No salaried officers to support, no capitalist to enrich, no loss—no expense; on $1,000 per annual	$1.50

Jewelry

Cuff Buttons	*Ingalls' Home Magazine* (1889)	Oxidized silver jewelry	$0.25/pr
Glove Hook	*Ingalls' Home Magazine* (1889)	Oxidized silver jewelry	$0.10
Pocket Watch	*Harper's Weekly* (1865)	Imperial officer; our whole stock of imported watches being of rich and novel designs, are now offered at reduced prices	$10.00
Pocket Watch	*Spirit Of The Times* (1877)	J. Bride & Co.; the greatest imitation gold watch in the market for trading purposes; genuine American movement	$12.00
Scarf Pins	*New York Times* (1863)	For gentlemen	$1/$2/$3
Scarf Pins	*Ingalls' Home Magazine* (1889)	Oxidized silver jewelry	$0.15
Watch	*Demorest's Illustrated Monthly* (1873)	Ladies'	$29.00
Watch	*The Modern Priscilla* (1893)	*Hill;* lady's chatlette; genuine coin; silver case; 14K gold-plated bow and swivel	$5.00

Meals

Dinner	*American Silver Flatware* (1868)	Santa Fe route; menu includes: puree of tomato; whitefish stuffed, Spanish sauce; shoulder of mutton, sauce soubise; roast beef; loin of pork, shrimp salad au mayonnaise; ox tongue; rice pudding; apple pie, edam and Roquefort cheese	$0.75
Dinner	*Spirit Of The Times* (1894)	*Martin Restaurant;* the best table d'hôtel dinner in New York	$1.25

Medical Products & Services

Artificial Leg	*Harper's Weekly* (1865)	*Weston's;* metallic; lightest, cheapest, most durable, and most natural ever invented	$75.00
Consultation Fee	*New York Times* (1863)	For diseases of the pelvic area; for rupture, piles, varicocele, and fistula, radically cured with the knife or ligature	$5.00
Dental Fees	*Advertising Trade Card* (1880)	Vitalized or gas	$0.25
Dental Fees	*Advertising Trade Card* (1880)	Teeth extracted free when plates are ordered	$5.00

Item	Source	Description	Price
Dental Fees	*Advertising Trade Card* (1880)	Extracting	$0.25
Dental Fees	*Advertising Trade Card* (1880)	Silver Fillings Gold Fillings	$0.50 $1.00
Dental Fees	*Queen City Dentists* (1883)	Teeth extracted free when plates are ordered; gold filling	$1.00
Medical Care	*San Francisco Examiner* (1895)	*The Copeland Institute;* relief from the tortures of chronic diseases; medicines included	$5.00/month
Nonprescription Drug	*New York Times* (1863)	*Dr. Sterling's Ambrosia;* a stimulating oil extract of roots, barks and herbs; it will cure diseases of the scalp and itching of the head; box contains two bottles	$1.00
Nonprescription Drug	*Harper's Weekly* (1865)	*Dr. R. Goodale's Catarrh Remedy;* treatment cures the most hopeless cases	$1.00
Nonprescription Drug	*New York Times* (1868)	*Dr. Hunter's Botanic Cordial;* restores vigor of youth in one week; per bottle	$5.00
Nonprescription Drug	*New York Times* (1868)	*Portuguese Female Monthly Pills;* in all cases of stoppage or irregularity	$5.00/box
Nonprescription Drug	*Harper's Weekly* (1875)	*Dr. Van Holm Perfezione;* strengthens, enlarges, and develops all parts of the body	$1.00
Nonprescription Drug	*Spirit Of The Times* (1877)	*Dr. Melvin Capsicum Porous Plaster;* the greatest medical discovery since the creation of man, or since the commencement of the Christian era	$0.25
Nonprescription Drug	*Spirit Of The Times* (1877)	*Dr. Van Holm Nervous Debility Pills;* strengthens, enlarges, and develops all parts of the body	$1.00
Nonprescription Drug	*Advertising Trade Card* (1880)	*Horsfords Acid Phosphate;* for mental and physical exhaustion; it makes a delicious drink with water and sugar only	$0.50
Nonprescription Drug	*Advertising Trade Card* (1880)	*Little Hop Pills;* headache is positively cured	$0.25
Nonprescription Drug	*Harper's Weekly* (1887)	*Ayer's Cherry Pectoral;* it saved my life	$1.00
Nonprescription Drug	*Ingalls' Home Magazine* (1889)	Tobacco cure; in one week it will remove all desire for smoking and chewing	$0.50
Nonprescription Drug	Adelaide Hechtlinger, *The Great Patent Medicine Era* (1970)	*Ford's Female Regulator;* effective and reliable medicine in all cases of female complaints, such as amenorrhea, sysmenorrhea, suppressed or irregular menses [cost in 1890]	$0.50
Nonprescription Drug	Hechtlinger, *The Great Patent Medicine Era* (1970)	*Juno Drops;* any woman can bring the blush of health to her cheeks, a perfect plumpness to her figure [cost in 1890]	$1.00
Nonprescription Drug	Hechtlinger, *The Great Patent Medicine Era* (1970)	*Con-Formagen Ointment;* sprinkled on loose or ill-fitting plate makes it conform to mouth and securely fastens it there [cost in 1890]	$0.10
Nonprescription Drug	Hechtlinger, *The Great Patent Medicine Era* (1970)	*Dr. Rose's Obesity Powders;* fat folks, they reduce the weight in a comparatively short time [cost in 1890]	$0.58

Item	Source	Description	Price
Nonprescription Drug	Hechtlinger, *The Great Patent Medicine Era* (1970)	*Dr. Williams Pink Pills for Pale People;* miraculous cure [cost in 1890]	$0.50
Nonprescription Drug	*The Modern Priscilla* (1893)	Root, Bark and Blossom; two months' supply; remedy stomach, liver, kidney, and blood	$1.00
Nonprescription Drug	*New York Times* (1895)	*Rikers Expectorant;* a certain cure for a cough, cold, croup, pneumonia, or any disease of throat or lungs	$0.60
Nonprescription Drug	*The Delineator* (1896)	*Scott's Emulsion of Cod Liver Oil;* it produces force with the whip; to all druggists	$0.50
Nonprescription Drug	*The Delineator* (1896)	*Dr. Edison Obesity Pills;* get thin and well; two months' treatment	$6.00
Nonprescription Drug	*Southern Christian Advocate* (1897)	*Perry Davis Pain Killer;* for cramps, colic, colds	$0.25
Nonprescription Drug	*The Spartan* (Spartanburg, SC) (1898)	*Electric Bitters;* three physicians had given me up; fortunately a friend advised trying electric bitters	$0.50
Nonprescription Drug	*The Youth's Companion* (1898)	*Hyomei Bronchitis or Incipient Consumption Cure;* it is nature's own remedy, given through the air you breathe Extra inhalant	$1.00 $0.50
Nonprescription Drug	*The Youth's Companion* (1898)	*Arid Air Spiral Spring;* new hospital method, direct cure for coughs, colds, catarrh, asthma; a year without refilling	$0.25
Nonprescription Drug	*The Spartan* (Spartanburg, SC) (1898)	*Bucklen's Arivica Salve;* the best salve in the world for cuts, bruises, sores, ulcers, salt rheum fever sores, tetter, chapped hands, chilblains, corns, and all skin eruptions, and positively cures piles or no pay required	$0.25
Nonprescription Drug	*The Spartan* (Spartanburg, SC) (1898)	*Castoria Medicine;* for infants and children; promotes digestion, cheerfulness and rest; contains neither opium, morphine or mineral; not narcotic; 35 doses per bottle	3$0.05
Nonpresciption Drug	*The Youth's Companion* (1898)	*Morgan's Cod Liver Oil and Horehound Drops;* cure your cough; free from taste and odor	$0.05
Nonprescription Drug	*The Spartan* (Spartanburg, SC) (1898)	*Mother's Friend Liniment;* good for only one purpose, to relieve motherhood of danger and pain	$1.00
Nonprescription Drug	*The Ledger Monthly* (1899)	*Dr. Campbell's Arsenic Complexion Wafers;* pimples and freckles are things of the past	$0.10
Nonprescription Drug	*The Ledger Monthly* (1899)	*Ayer's Cherry Pectoral;* when a cough medicine is good, it's worth ten times its price	$1.00
Nonprescription Drug	*The Ledger Monthly* (1899)	*Mentholette Cure;* the true Japanese headache cure instantly relieves and cures headache and other pains by simply rubbing	$0.10

Motorized Vehicle, Supplies, & Services

Automobile	*Sears, Roebuck* (1899)	*The Winton Motor Carriage;* a road locomotive; it does not take an engineer to run it	$1,000
Automobile	*Scientific American* (1899)	*The Winton Motor Carriage;* variable speed up to 18 miles per hour and under perfect control; no agents	$1,000

Musical Instruments

Autoharp	*The Delineator* (1896)	Easy to play, easy to buy; the autoharp is a musical instrument in its full range of styles	$7.50

Item	Source	Description	Price
Organ	*Demorest's Illustrated Monthly* (1873)	*Mason and Hamlin;* one to twenty stops	$55 to $500
Organ	*Demorest's Monthly Magazine* (1881)	*Mason & Hamilton Baby;* especially adapted to children	$22.00
Piano	*New York Times* (1863)	Seven-octave; French action, rosewood; cost including stool and cover	$300
Piano	*Demorest's Illustrated Monthly* (1873)	*U.S.;* first-class 7 octave piano	$290
Piano	*Demorest's Family Magazine* (1890)	*University;* sold direct to families; no middleman	$180
Piano	*San Francisco Examiner* (1895)	Used *Steinway* upright; must have cash	$200
Violin	*Spirit Of The Times* (1877)	With bow, case, and instruction book	$5.00
Xylophone	*Spirit Of The Times* (1877)	Wood and straw instruments as used in orchestras	$4.50

Other

Item	Source	Description	Price
Bow Knot Alphabet	*The Modern Priscilla* (1893)	2 3/4" high, perforated on linen bond paper	$0.10
Buggy Carriage	*Spirit Of The Times* (1877)	*Baker & Son;* top side-bar and end-spring road wagon; equal in style, finish, and durability to any made	$135
Carriage	*Demorest's Family Magazine* (1890)	Adjustable top, nickel-plated rod, springs, axles, and braces; wire or wooden wheels same price; delivered free east of the Mississippi	$12.35
Carriage	*The Delineator* (1896)	With iron axles, steel wheels and parasol top	$3.75 to $31.00
Decalcomania	*Demorest's Illustrated Monthly* (1873)	Chromos, vases, picture frames, passe-partouts, Swiss carved goods, wax flower materials, boxes of assorted wax with tools. For learners.	$5.00
Draft Exemption Fee	*New York Times* (1863)	Civil War; to be arranged by the Secretary of War	$300
Entry Fee	*Spirit Of The Times* (1877)	One-mile swimming race; a suitable prize will be given	$1.00
Fire Engine	*New York Times* (1863)	Steam; for Engine Company No. 10, New York City	$4,000
Fountain Pen	*The Yorkville Enquirer* (Yorkville, SC) (1892)	*Rapid Writer;* no. 2 gold mounted	$3.00
Fountain Pen	*Ladies' Home Journal* (1893)	*The Pittsburg;* largest and best pen for the price; solid-gold ink feed, long and short nibs	$3.50
Fountain Pen	*The State* (Columbia, SC) (1896)	*Waterman's;* J. W. Gibbes Stationery Company, Columbia, South Carolina	$4.00
Fountain Pen	*The Ledger Monthly* (1899)	*R. W. Whitney;* 14K pen for bookkeepers, correspondents and stenographers	$1.50

Item	Source	Description	Price
Gas Sunlight Apparatus	*Demorest's Illustrated Monthly* (1873)	A flood of light; consists of a hemispherical cup of flint glass	$2.00
Glass Cards	*Harper's Weekly* (1875)	*F. K. Smith & Co.;* red, blue, white, clear and transparent; beautifully printed in gold	$0.50/dozen
Japanese Fan	*New York Times* (1877)		$0.02
Lottery Ticket	*Spirit Of The Times* (1877)	Louisiana State Lottery Co.; capital prize $30,000; 100,000 tickets	$2.00
Magic Inkstand	*Harper's Weekly* (1875)	Ten quarts of fine ink; no refilling fluid	$2.00
Microscope	*New York Times* (1863)	*Craig;* sent with 6 beautiful mounted objects	$3.00
Money Belt	*Harper's Weekly* (1865)	*Howard's;* for soldier; sweat-proof; top quality	$3.00
Pen	*Harper's Weekly* (1865)	*Morton's;* gold; all first quality, in silver-mounted desk-holders; no. 5	$6.25
Photograph Pin	*The Ledger Monthly* (1899)	Your Face On A Button; send photo (cabinet preferred) and receive post-paid, pin-back celluloid medallion with your photo on same	$0.10
Reward	*New York Times* (1863)	Small dog, part terrier breed; hair long and a yellow tan color; nose and eyes brown	$10.00
Silver Engraving	*American Silver Flatware* (1886)	*Benjamin Allen & Co.;* Old English style	$0.10/liter
Silver Engraving	*American Silver Flatware* (1886)	*Benjamin Allen & Co.;* script style on dessert or tablespoons	$0.38/liter
Squirrel Skins	*New York Times* (1868)	500; reported as part of a theft from Solomon Bloomenstock store in New York City	$400
Statuary	*Harper's Weekly* (1875)	*John Rogers';* the tap on the window	$15.00
Ventriloquist Instructions	*Harper's Weekly* (1865)	*M. A. Jagger's;* full instructions by which any person can master the art of ventriloquism in a few hours	$1.00
Weather House	*Harper's Weekly* (1875)	*Lovejoy's;* metallic; indicates the change in the weather, and are pretty mantel ornaments	$2.00
Writing Paper	*Ladies' Home Journal* (1893)	*Metcalf;* linen; the finest made for polite correspondence; for 3 quires (72 sheets) and envelopes to match up	$0.75

Personal Care Products

Item	Source	Description	Price
Blush	*Demorest's Family Magazine* (1890)	*Extract Of Turkish Rose Leaves;* indelible tint, for the lips and face, soft as the blush of the rose	$1.00
Cologne	*Spirit Of The Times* (1877)	*Mitchell's Memorial;* the most exquisite perfume of the century; small bottle	$0.25
Cologne	*Advertising Trade Card* (1880)	*Austen's Forest Flower;* the most fashionable perfume of the day	$0.25/$0.50/$1.00
Cologne	*Advertising Trade Card* (1883)	*Austen's Forest Flower;* the most fashionable perfume of the day	$0.25/$0.50/$1.00

Item	Source	Description	Price
Cologne	*Advertising Trade Card* (1888)	*Hoyt's German;* fragrant and lasting Trial size Medium size Large size	$0.25 $0.50 $1.00
Combing Sacque	*The Delineator* (1896)	Of excellent quality of flannelette in pretty pink and blue stripes	$0.98
Dandruff Cure	*The Ledger Monthly* (1899)	*Coke;* if you want to keep your hair, get rid of your dandruff	$1.00
Face Bleach	*The Delineator* (1896)	*Madame Rupert's;* removes tan, pimples, eczema, moth and all diseases the skin is heir to	$2.00
Face Lotion	*The Modern Priscilla* (1893)	*Dr. Hebra's Voila Cream;* removes freckles, pimples, liver-moles, blackheads, sunburn and tan	$0.50
Face Powder	*The Delineator* (1896)	*Lablanche;* the purest and most perfect face powder that science and skill can produce	$0.50
Facial Cloth	*Ingalls' Home Magazine* (1889)	*Koriza;* removes pimples, blackheads, wrinkles and crows feet	$0.30
Hair Curler	*Harper's Weekly* (1865)	*Brazilian;* warranted to curl the most straight and stubborn hair into wavy ringlets	$1.00
Hair Curler	*Ingalls' Home Magazine* (1889)	Nickel-plated with enameled handles; can be used with absolute safety, as the source of heat is under perfect control	$0.50
Hair Remover	*Demorest's Family Magazine* (1890)	*Kosmeo Depilatory;* no blemish so terrible to a pretty woman as superfluous hair upon the face	$1.00
Hair Remover	*The Delineator* (1896)	*Modene;* hair on the face, neck, arms or any part of the person quickly dissolved or removed	$1.00
Hair Restorer	Hechtlinger, *The Great Patent Medicine Era* (1970)	*Princess Tonie* [cost in 1890]	$0.57
Hair Treatment	*Harper's Weekly* (1865)	*Boswell & Warner Colorific;* don't dye the hair; one application, no wash, no trouble; large bottle	$1.00
Hair Wave	*Demorest's Monthly Magazine* (1881)	*Thompson;* natural curly hair; indispensable to all ladies whose front hair is thin or will not remain in crimps	$6 to $12
Lotion	*Demorest's Family Magazine* (1890)	*Planta Beatrice;* a sanitary preparation for the complexion	$1.25
Lotion	*The Modern Priscilla* (1893)	*Hawley's Corn Salve;* cure guaranteed	$0.25
Lotion	*The Delineator* (1896)	*Wrinkleine;* guaranteed to permanently remove wrinkles, flesh worms, etc.	$1.00
Nail Trimmer	*The Ledger Monthly* (1899)	Closes compactly and can be carried in vest pocket or purse	$0.25
Perfume	*Ladies' Home Journal* (1893)	*Seely's Easter Lily;* delicate, fragrant, lasting; one-oz bottle	$0.50
Perfume	*The Delineator* (1896)	*Forest Fringe Violet;* just like a bunch of the freshly gathered flowers of the woods	$1.00
Powder	*The Delineator* (1896)	*Gossamer;* faces fair are made fairer with a touch of Tetlow's Gossamer Powder	$0.25
Sachet Powders	*Ingalls' Home Magazine* (1889)	*Ingalls;* odors include new mown hay, white rose, heliotrope, jockey club, violet, rose, geranium	$0.15/package

Item	Source	Description	Price
Shaving Soap	*Advertising Trade Card* (1880)	*Williams;* oldest and most famous shaving soap in the world; for six cakes (one pound)	$0.40
Shaving Soap	*Advertising Trade Card* (1884)	*Williams;* 6 round cakes equal one pound; oldest and most famous shaving soap in the world	$0.40
Shaving-Soap Stick	*Harper's Weekly* (1887)	*Williams;* each stick in a turned-wood case	$0.25
Skin Cleaner	*The Delineator* (1896)	*Campbell's Safe Complexion Wafers;* removes pimples, freckles, moth, blackheads, redness, oiliness and all other beauty marring defects	$1.00
Skin Mask	*Demorest's Family Magazine* (1890)	Beautify	$2.00
Soap	*New York Times* (1868)	*Phalon's;* for the toilet, bath and nursery	$0.25
Soap	*Demorest's Family Magazine* (1894)	*Wrisley's Cucumber Complexion Toilet Soap;* combines the healthful cleansing of pure sweet soap with the grateful emollient quantities of cucumber juice	1/$0.02
Soap	*The Delineator* (1896)	*Sweet Home;* a chautangua reclining chair or a chautangua desk with a combination box	$0.10
Soap	*The Delineator* (1896)	*Charmant Turkish Wonder Bar;* this is no patent medicine but a soap that has been used in Turkey for hundreds of years; for salve and soap	$1.00
Soap	*The Delineator* (1896)	*Copco Bath Soap;* soap-wise folks say it's a decade in advance of soap making progress	$0.05
Tooth Cleaner	*Demorest's Family Magazine* (1890)	*Rubiform For The Teeth;* deliciously flavored; a perfect liquid dentifrice	$0.25
Tooth Cleaner	*The Youth's Companion* (1898)	*Dr. Sheffield's Creme Dentifrice;* cream in collapsible tubes; it removes from the teeth all stains and whatever would cause decay	$0.25
Tooth Soap	*The Delineator* (1896)	*Arnica;* others imitate; none equals	$0.25
Tooth Soap	*The Delineator* (1896)	*Wright's Myearrh;* without the taste of soap; large china box	$0.25
Whisker and Mustache Grower	*Harper's Weekly* (1865)	*Graham's;* my ointment will force them to grow heavily in six weeks (upon the smoothest face)	$1.00
Wig	*Demorest's Family Magazine* (1890)	Parted bang; made of natural curly hair, guaranteed becoming to ladies who wear their hair parted	$6.00

Publications

Item	Source	Description	Price
Book	*New York Times* (1863)	*Army and Navy Pocket Dictionary;* in flexible leather, marbled edges	$0.75
Book	*Harper's Weekly* (1865)	*Portrait Gallery of the War;* civil, military, and naval; edited by Frank More; full gilt	$7.50
Book	*Harper's Weekly* (1865)	*Speke's Africa;* journal of the discovery of the source of the Nile; by Captain John Hanning Speke; cloth	$4.00
Book	*Harper's New Monthly Magazine* (1866)	*Medical Common Sense;* 400 pages; 100 illustrated	$1.50
Book	*Harper's New Monthly Magazine* (1866)	*New Physiognomy; or Signs of Character;* as manifested through temperament and external forms, and especially in the Human Face Divine	$5.00
Book	*Harper's Weekly* (1875)	*The Ugly Girl Papers: Or Hints for the Toilet*	$1.00

Item	Source	Description	Price
Book	*Spirit Of The Times* (1877)	*Scott's Fishing in American Waters;* has an interesting addition to it, such as coast and inland fishing of the South; has numerous new engravings	$3.50
Book	*Demorest's Monthly Magazine* (1881)	*Vick's Floral Guide;* elegant book of 100 pages, one colored flower plate, and 600 illustrations; in English or German	$0.10
Book	*The Century Magazine* (1884)	*Illustrations of Artistic Homes* (Fuller, Wheeler & Prescott); contains 76 full-page illustrations of Queen Anne and Colonial villas and cottages	$3.50
Book	*Harper's Weekly* (1887)	*Harper's Pictorial History of the Rebellion;* containing 1,000 of its famous war pictures; in full Turkey Morocco, gilt edges	$35.00
Book	*Ladies' Home Journal* (1893)	Portrait scrapbooks; scrapbooks made from newspaper pictures are the latest fad For 30 For 70 For 400	 $0.10 $0.20 $1.00
Magazine	*Harper's Weekly* (1865)	*Demorest's Monthly Magazine;* the model parlor magazine of America	$3/year
Magazine	*Harper's Weekly* (1865)	*Harper's Weekly*	$0.10/week
Magazine	*Harper's New Monthly Magazine* (1866)	*American Educational Monthly;* no educator can afford to be without it	$1.50/year
Magazine	*Harper's Weekly* (1887)	*Ridley's Fashion Magazine;* quarterly	$0.15/quarter
Magazine	*Ingalls' Home Magazine* (1889)	*Ingalls' Home Magazine;* monthly	$0.15/month
Magazine	*Demorest's Family Magazine* (1891)	*The Great Divide;* premium: 20 gemstones cut free from the successful monthly of the wild and wooly west	$1.00/year
Magazine	*Demorest's Family Magazine* (1891)	*Demorest's Family Magazine;* monthly	$0.20
Magazine	*Ladies' Home Journal* (1893)	*Ladies' Home Journal* Single issue Per year	 $0.10 $1.00
Magazine	*The Modern Priscilla* (1893)	*The Modern Priscilla;* monthly	$0.50
Magazine	*The Ledger Monthly* (1899)	*The Ledger Monthly;* single copy	$0.05
Newspaper	*New York Times* (1863)	*New York Times;* daily	$0.03/day
Newspaper	*Wall Street Journal* (1890)	Annual subscription	$5.00
Newspaper	*The Weekly Bulletin* (1885)	*The Weekly Bulletin*	$1.00
Pamphlet	*The Delineator* (1896)	*Recitations and How to Recite*	$0.25
Prohibition Fliers	*Demorest's Family Magazine* (1890)	Logical and convenient tracts for circulation in your neighborhood Per 100 Per 1,000	 $0.05

Item	Source	Description	Price
Real Estate			
Building	*New York Times* (1863)	For sale; four-story; high-stoop basement and under-cellar brownstone house with all modern improvements; near 4th Avenue on 23rd St	$21,000
Business Opportunity	*San Francisco Examiner* (1895)	Saloon; one block off Market Street; daily receipts $20 and over	$650
House	*New York Times* (1863)	For sale; Harlem; two-story and half-frame cottage; 125th Street, near 5th Ave., with gas and water and 2 1/2 lots of ground	$7,800
House	*New York Times* (1863)	For rent; Brooklyn; two-story; Franklin Ave and Myeartle; with basement and subcellar	$250/year
House	*New York Times* (1863)	For sale; Brooklyn; three-story brick; has marble mantels, gas fixtures, near the Hamilton Ferry	$3,500
House	*New York Times* (1863)	For rent; Brooklyn; three-story; 2nd St. and Williamsburg; with front and back basement near the Ferry	$300/year
House	*New York Times* (1868)	For sale; same block Dr. Cuyler's Church, near Green Ave.; three-story brick and brownstone; basement	$7,000
House	*New York Times* (1868)	For rent; unfurnished, the first-class house; no. 31 Washington Square, four story, low stoop	$2,600/year
House	*New York Times* (1877)	For rent; four-story English; basement; brick; 232 West 43rd St., all improvements	$1,100/year
House	*New York Times* (1877)	For rent; furnished nine rooms, fine view and grounds, well of purest water; 300 fruit trees; one hour from city	$70/month
House	*The Yorkville Enquirer* (York, SC) (1892)	New; six rooms; broad hall, closet, pantry; good well of water on the back porch; one acre, enclosed	$825
House for Sale	*San Francisco Examiner* (1895)	Four-room cottage in Berkeview; lot 50' X 100'; near station	$1,800
Land	*San Francisco Daily Examiner* (1875)	10 acres level land in Alameda County; 1 1/2 acres fruit trees; running water in creek	$1,800
Land Rental	*The New Orleans Picayune* (1875)	618 acres in Red River County, Texas, improved; 200 acres in a good fence and under cultivation Rent per acre	$3.00
Retail Business	*San Francisco Daily Examiner* (1875)	Half interest in oldest and best news book and stationery store in Portland, Oregon; doing $20,000 a year in business	$3,500
Room	*The New Orleans Picayune* (1875)	Furnished room with board; good table, Magazine Street Per month	$25.00
Sewing Equipment & Supplies			
Cloth	*New York Times* (1863)	*Kinzey's;* sewing cotton; two spools	$0.01
Cloth	*New York Times* (1863)	*Kinzey's;* ladies' fine grass linen; the Eighth Ave. cheap store	$0.25/yard
Cloth	*New York Times* (1877)	Imported black dress silks	$0.80/yard
Cloth	*New York Times* (1877)	Examine our American black silks	$1.30/yard
Cloth	*New York Times* (1877)	Imported stripe silks	$0.60/yard
Cloth	*The State* (Columbia, SC) (1891)	*Sea Island Dress Goods;* yd wide	$0.05

Item	Source	Description	Price
Cloth	*Ladies' Home Journal* (1893)	Evening silks; pongees and silks of a crepe character, two designs in each, all light colorings	$0.50
Cloth	*The Modern Priscilla* (1893)	Waste embroidery silk; 1 oz of silk; assorted colors (equal to 100 skeins) in every box	$0.40
Cloth	*The Delineator* (1896)	Shirting percales	1/$0.03/yard
Cloth	*The Delineator* (1896)	Silk stripe challis; exclusive designs	7/$0.09/yard
Cloth	*The Ledger Monthly* (1899)	Silk remnants for crazy work; from 100 to 120 pieces, carefully trimmed	$0.25
Cross-Stitch Book	*The Modern Priscilla* (1893)	*Priscilla;* contains over 100 patterns	$0.50
Embroidery Frame	*Ingalls' Home Magazine* (1899)	*Priscilla;* 9" without holder, of polished wood	3/$0.05
Embroidery Silk	*Ingalls' Home Magazine* (1889)	For overlaid embroidery; 10 yd skein	$0.03
Oil Colors	*Ingalls' Home Magazine* (1889)	*M. Fuchs & Co.;* German; finest made; tube	$0.05
Pattern	*Demorest's Monthly Magazine* (1881)	Chelsea jacket for child, ornamented with the favorite Capuchin hood, a turned-down collar, and reverse on the double-breasted fronts; sizes for 12 to 16 years	$0.20
Pattern	*The Delineator* (1896)	Combination and decoration for a lady's Louis XIV; 13 sizes, 28" to 48" bust measure	$0.40
Pattern	*The Delineator* (1896)	*Bosquets;* double-breasted ripple basque, with gored sleeves in four sections	$0.30
Pattern	*The Delineator* (1896)	Pattern for lady's basque waist with waist decoration; in thirteen sizes for ladies from 28" to 46" bust measure	$0.30
Quilting Squares	*Demorest's Family Magazine* (1890)	60 beautiful silk and satins, enough to cover 500 square inches	$0.20
Sewing Machine	*Harper's Weekly* (1865)	*Family Gem;* the embodiment of practical utility and extreme simplicity	$5.00
Sewing Machine	*The Delineator* (1896)	*Singer;* buy the improved Singer sewing machine with a complete set of attachments	$9.00
Sewing Machine	*Southern Christian Advocate* (1897)	The best and lightest running machine	$19.50
Sewing-Machine Attachments	*Demorest's Illustrated Monthly* (1873)	*Palmer's;* combination; the perfection of making and arranging every style of dress trimming with as much ease and simplicity as running up an ordinary seam	$3.00
Sewing Needle	*The Delineator* (1896)	Sewing made easy; for each paper	$0.05
Sewing Needles	*The Ledger Monthly* (1899)	Self-threading; can't bend 'em pins; package of four	$0.25
Skirt Binding	*The Delineator* (1896)	*Manhattan Mohair;* yard dyed, seam shrunk and fast color; for five-yd piece	$0.20
Stamping Paint	*Ingalls' Home Magazine* (1889)	*Ingalls;* for stamping felt, velvet, plush, and park goods; large tube	$0.25

Item	Source	Description	Price
Tassels	*Ingalls' Home Magazine* (1889)	*Ingalls;* Chenille; all colors	$0.06
Thread	*Demorest's Family Magazine* (1890)	Twilled lace; for crocheting, makes beautiful lace; per spool, 500 yards	$0.10
Tinsel Cord	*Ingalls' Home Magazine* (1889)	Imported; furnished in light and dark gold, three shades of silver, pink, iridescent, copper	$0.10
Tissue Papers	*Ingalls' Home Magazine* (1889)	*Dennison's;* for flower decoration; beginner's outfit contains 12 half-sheets assorted tissues, wire tubing for stems and leaves, culots, sprays and a book of instructions	3/$0.05
Tracing Wheel	*Demorest's Illustrated Monthly* (1873)	Ladies pentagraph; used for tracing pattern	$0.25
Turkish Rug Patterns	*Ingalls' Home Magazine* (1889)	1/2 yard x 1 yard shows vine of morning glories running around the rug for a border, and a small cluster of flowers in center	$0.40
Work Books	*Ingalls' Home Magazin* (1889)	Fancy; darned lace patterns	$0.15
Yarn	*New York Times* (1863)	*Kinzey's;* French floss; best; spool	$0.02
Yarn	*Ingalls' Home Magazine* (1889)	*Madonna;* crochet cotton; for tidies, lambrequins 25-gram ball	$0.15
Watercolor	*Ingalls' Home and Gilding Magazine* (1889)	Perfection; box contains six pans and assorted colors	4/$0.03
Whisk Broom Holder	*Ingalls' Home Magazine* (1889)	Linen; made and bound with designs stamped on them to be worked	$0.20

Sports Equipment

Item	Source	Description	Price
Bait	*Spirit Of The Times* (1877)	Artificial; a bait that excels all others for taking black bass	$0.75
Baseball	*Spirit Of The Times* (1877)	*Peck & Snyder Treble Match-Ball;* buy our popular brands of baseballs; popular professional ball, red or white; each ball is wrapped in tinfoil and boxed; by mail	$1.50
Baseball Mask	*Spirit Of The Times* (1877)	*Peck & Snyder;* catcher's; in case the swift ball misses the catcher's ready grasp and strikes the face, the blow is harmless	$3.00
Bicycle	*New York Times* (1895)	*Waverly Scorcher;* 21 pounds	$85.00
Bicycle	*San Francisco Examiner* (1895)	*Waverly*	$85.00
Bicycle	*The Delineator* (1896)	*Windsor American Beauties;* for 1896 . . . bicycling should be pure happiness	$85.00
Bicycle	*The Delineator* (1896)	*Columbia;* standard of the world; before buying a bicycle said to be just as good as Columbia, it is well to compare the prices at which the machines sell second hand	$100
Bicycle	*The Delineator* (1896)	*Gladiator Cycles;* perfect machines, strong, light, speedy	$85.00

Item	Source	Description	Price
Bicycle	*The Youth's Companion* (1898)	*Acme;* same grade as agents sell for $75; eight elegant models	$34.50
Bicycle	*Popular Mechanics Picture History of American Transportation* (1952)	*Columbia;* combine the best results of 22 years experience [cost in 1899]	$75.00
Bicycle	*Scientific American* (1899)	*Ideal;* fit every member old and young	$20.00
Bicycle Lamp	*The Youth's Companion* (1898)	*Klondike;* fine 2 1/2" magnifying lens; colored side lights; perfect ventilation; throws a big light	$2.00
Bicycle Seat	*The Delineator* (1896)	*The Hunt Ladies' Saddle;* especially designed to meet the peculiar requirements of lady cyclists	$5.00
Boxing Gloves	*Spirit Of The Times* (1877)	Pecks and Snyders; net price per set, includes two pairs	$2.50 to $6.00
Fishing Rod	*Spirit Of The Times* (1877)	*Conroy, Bisset & Malleson;* salmon; six-strip, two tips	$50.00
Fly Rod	*Spirit Of The Times* (1877)	*Conroy, Bissett & Malleson;* split bamboo; six-strip hexagonal rods, two tips	$25.00
Pistol	*Spirit Of The Times* (1877)	*W&C Scott & Sons;* .45 caliber; celebrated double-action revolvers; central fire	$20.00
Pocket Gymnasium	*Spirit Of The Times* (1877)	*Goodyear No. 6;* for gentlemen of moderate strength, used standing, sitting, or reclining	$1.50
Rifle	*Spirit Of The Times* (1877)	*The Remington;* sporting rifle No. 1 model; 30"	$30.00
Skates	*Harper's Weekly* (1875)	*Peck & Snyder's American Club;* the only perfect self-fastening skate that adjusts without heel-plates, shapes or key; fully polished	$7.00

Telephone Equipment & Services

Item	Source	Description	Price
Telephone Charges	*New York Times* (1895)	600 local messages, two-party line	$75.00
		Direct line	$90.00
		1,000 messages, two-party line	$105
		Direct line	$120
		1,500 messages, two-party line	$135
		Direct line	$150

Tobacco Products

Item	Source	Description	Price
Cigar	*The Weekly Bulletin* (1885)	Best nickel cigar in town	$0.05
Cigarette	*Spirit Of The Times* (1877)	*L'Amerique;* only best French cigarette paper used; sample pack	$0.15
Pipes	Hechtlinger, *The Great Patent Medicine Era* (1970)	*Cobb;* assorted styles [cost in 1890]	3/$0.03/dozen

Item	Source	Description	Price
Toys			
Game	*Harper's Weekly* (1875)	*Punch and Judy;* jolliest game in the whole world	$1.00
Paper Dolls	*Ingalls' Home Magazine* (1889)	Set contains three paper dolls, 2 girls, 1 boy, and an elegant wardrobe of 30 pieces	$0.15
Travel & Transportation			
Boat Fare	*Advertising Trade Card* (1885)	Delightful ocean trip to the Point of Pines leaving Foster's Wharf; round trip	$0.40
Boat Fare	*New York Times* (1895)	New York to Boston	$2.00
Boat Fare	*New York Times* (1895)	New York to Southampton	$60.00
Coach Fare	*Spirit Of The Times* (1877)	Leaves Brunswick, New York, at 4:30 p.m. and the Getty House, Yonkers, 8 a.m. daily (Box seats $0.50 extra each way)	$1.50
Railroad Fare	Edward L. Throm, ed., *Popular Mechanics Picture History of American Transportation* (1952)	New York Elevated Railway [cost in 1876] Rush hour Regular hours	 $0.05 $0.10
Railroad Fare	*New York Times* (1895)	107 miles from New York on the banks of the Delaware River; round trip	$1.00
Railroad Fare	*The Spartan* (Spartanburg, SC) (1898)	Western Carolina Railroad; Spartanburg, South Carolina, to Augusta, Georgia, round trip for Merry Maker's Week	$4.70
Railroad Freight Charge	Throm, ed., *Popular Mechanics Picture History of American Transportation* (1952)	Charge for barrel of oil from Macksburgh, Ohio, to Marietta, Ohio [cost in 1885] Standard Oil Company All Other Companies	 $0.10 3/$0.05
Steamship	*The New Orleans Picayune* (1875)	New Orleans to Key West Cabin Steerage	 $40.00 $20.00
Steamship Fare	*New York Times* (1863)	New York to Liverpool, payable in gold or its equivalent in U.S. currency Second Cabin Chief Cabin	 $80.00 $132.50
Steamship Fare	*New York Times* (1863)	New York to Nassau	$45.00
Steamship Fare	*New York Times* (1868)	New York to Liverpool, one-way, first-class iron steamship; cabin in gold Steerage First class	 $30.00 $80.00
Steamship Fare	*New York Times* (1868)	*State Line;* New York to Glasgow, Liverpool, Belfast and Londonderry Second cabin First cabin	 $45.00 $65 to $70
Steamship Fare	*New York Times* (1877)	*Cunard Line;* New York to Liverpool and Queenstown	$80 to $130

Item	Source	Description	Price
Steamship Fare	*Spirit Of The Times* (1877)	General TransAtlantic Company; New York to Havre, calling at Plymouth (G.B.); price of passage in gold (including wine)	
		Steerage	$26.00
		Third Cabin	$35.00
		Second Cabin	$65.00
		First Cabin	$100
Steamship Fare	*New York Times* (1895)	*Cooks Tours Nile Steamers;* New York to Egypt	$675 to $1225
Train	*Chicago Daily Tribune* (1882)	July 4th Excursion to South Park, Chicago; under the auspices of the Women's Christian Temperance Union; good on all suburban trains of the Illinois Central Railroad Roundtrip	$0.25

MISCELLANY 1860-1899

The Barber

A negro came to Green Bay, Wisconsin, to keep a barber's shop. Soon after he opened a Western speculator presented himself to be shaved. His charge was asked: the barber said 25 cents. The customer named several cities he had been shaved at, and all for less money. The negro straightened himself up, and said: "Do you suppose I am going to leave society in the East and come here among you backwoodsmen to shave men for ten cents?"

Harper's New Monthly Magazine, October 1866

Harper's Hand-book for Travellers in Europe and the East

Being a guide through France, Belgium, Holland, Germany, Austria, Italy, Sicily, Egypt, Syria, Turkey, Greece, Switzerland, Russia, Denmark, Sweden, Spain, and Great Britain and Ireland. By W. Pembroke Fetridge. Fifth Year. Large 12mo, Leather, Pocket-Book form. $7.50

Harper's New Monthly Magazine, October 1866

Anesthetics in the Military

The surgeon-general has recommended Congress to pay Dr. G. Morton $200,000 for the use of anesthetics in the army and navy. Dr. Morton personally appeared before the Committee of Ways and Means this morning to urge its adoption.

New York Times, March 3, 1863

Concerning Dickens's 1869 American Tour

Queuing for tickets to hear Dickens had begun the night before the box office opened; an hour before opening time the queue was already half a mile long; all tickets were sold out in a hectic eleven hours and fourteen thousand dollars were taken in for the first reading in Boston. (Promoter George) Dolby sold tickets at two dollars each. Scalpers were re-selling them at anything up to twenty-six dollars.

Charles Dickens, An Authentic Account of His Life and Times, by Martin Fido, 1968

Rental prices in Washington, D. C. in 1865

The Washington city to which (photographer Mathew) Brady returned after the war was a dirty, brawling, lusty city, one step removed from the frontier. In the summer of 1865 living quarters were impossible to find and too expensive. A house which rented for three hundred dollars a season before the war now brought twelve hundred to its owner.

Mathew Brady, Historian with A Camera, by James D. Horan, 1955

Thomas Nast, Political Cartoonist

Early the next year (1862) he accepted a job at $50 a week from his former employer, Frank Leslie. After a short time, Leslie, perhaps because of financial stress, cut Nast to $30 a week and let him go a month later. After (U. S.) Grant's nomination (1868), however, the journal (Harper's) offered Nast a regular fee of $150 per double page cartoon, five times more than his rate in 1862.

Thomas Nast, Political Cartoonist, by Chal Vinson, 1967

Publications and the Civil War

To unite the North, to make the mystical concept of Union a rallying point, Abraham Lincoln encouraged communications in every way. By then, there were 3,000 U.S. publications. Suddenly the Civil War increased circulation substantially. People depended on day-to-day reports from the battlefields. The Union increased mail subsidies and land grants to railroads. It started the Pony Express and then completed the transcontinental telegraph and pushed for a transcontinental railway. The Lincoln Administration established the three-cent postage delivery of a one-ounce letter anywhere in the Union. It initiated free, city-wide postal delivery and collection in 49 cities of 20,000 or more population. It gave newspapers especially low postage rates—half a cent to mail a newspaper, and postage could be billed. Many times papers never paid. Railroad car post offers were now on all important railroads. Registered letters and money orders began.

Sears and Wards: The First Hundred Years Are the Toughest, by Cecil C. Hoge, Sr., 1988

MISCELLANY 1860-1899

Montgomery Ward Catalog

In the fall (1874), Montgomery Ward issued a 100-page catalog measuring 3 1/2" X 7". It listed several hundred articles with prices. Sales for Ward passed $100,000 in 1874 . . . In 1878, Montgomery Ward passed $400,000 in sales. For the next few years, the biggest Ward item in dollar sales was the sewing machine. Ward sold sewing machines much cheaper—as low as $26 for a machine which otherwise sold for $50.

Sears and Wards: The First Hundred Years Are the Toughest,
by Cecil C. Hoge, Sr., 1988

The One-Price System

In 1878, a successful (Philadelphia) merchant named John Wanamaker had opened what he called a "New Kind of Store," which incorporated something called the one-price system. Instead of negotiating a price with each customer, the merchant marked the price plainly and customers paid the posted price. Wanamaker was not the first merchant to adopt the one-price system—Lord and Taylor in New York used it as early as 1835—but he was the first to adopt it on such a large scale.

Belk, A Century of Retail Leadership,
by Howard E. Covington, Jr., 1988

The Centennial Exposition of 1876

The immense buildings that housed the Centennial Exposition of 1876 were mostly taken down when it was over. Highly permanent, however, was another huge structure that also much impressed visitors to Philadelphia that memorable and influential summer—the towered and towering bulk of the new City Hall nearing completion in the square of the middle of town, where seventy years earlier Oliver Evans' wheeled steam monster had been demonstrated. Even in those days of low prices the building cost some $10,000,000. It covers ground enough for almost six football fields and, counting in the 20-foot figure of William Penn on the central tower, rises 450 feet above street level.

The Americans: A Social History of the United States
1587–1914, by J. C. Furnas, 1969

Chinese Labor

In 1870 a New England shoe manufacturer named Calvin T. Sampson fired his unioned workers and imported 75 Chinese laborers from the Pacific coast. The Chinese signed a contract to work for three years at $26 a month, and settled down in North Adams, Massachusetts, where they attended the Methodist Sunday school, saved their money, and reduced Mr. Sampson's costs $840 a week. A writer in *Scribner's* magazine hastened to praise this experiment, saying, "If for no other purpose than the breaking up of . . . labor combinations and 'Trade Unions . . . the advent of Chinese labor should be hailed with warm welcome by all who have the true interests of . . . the laboring classes at heart.'"

The American Past, by Roger Butterfield, 1947

Drug Store for Sale

A Bona-Fide Bargain. A retail drug business in Brooklyn, established 20 years in its present location. Price $4000. F. E. Tower, 482 B. 2nd St., Brooklyn.

Harper's Weekly, January 2, 1875

Method of Cleaning Plaster

The Prussian Government has lately a prize of about $750 for the discovery of a new method of cleaning plaster casts, statues, etc., and one of $2,500 for the invention of a new material possessing the properties of plaster, but which shall not deteriorate by repeated washings.

Harper's Weekly, September 25, 1875

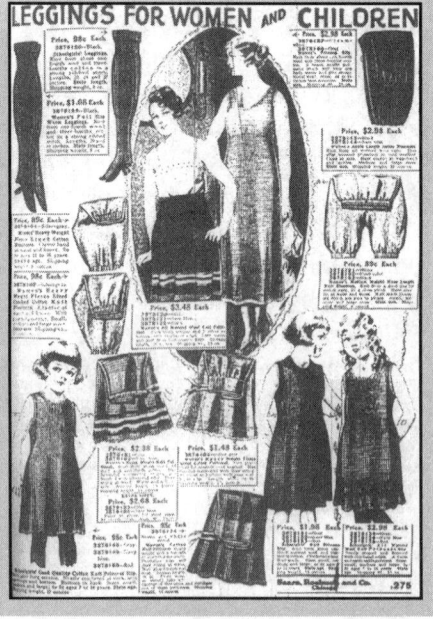

1900-1919

The Progressive Era and World War II

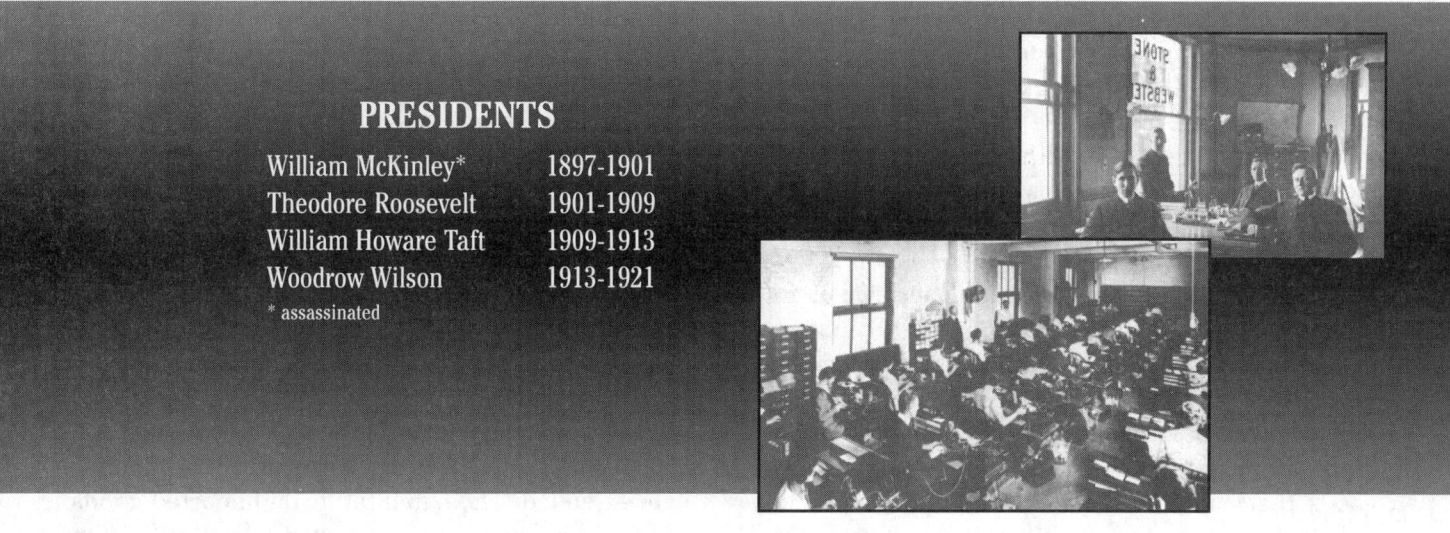

PRESIDENTS

William McKinley*	1897-1901
Theodore Roosevelt	1901-1909
William Howare Taft	1909-1913
Woodrow Wilson	1913-1921

* assassinated

Social and economic historians divide the first twenty years of the twentieth century into two periods: The Progressive Era (1900–1914), during which Americans confronted the social unrest of early industrialism; and the time of World War I (1914–1918) during which the nation assumed fully the responsibilities of world citizenship and experienced the effects of a centrally managed wartime economy. Despite economic downturns in 1903 and 1907, the beginning of the century was a time of prosperity and stability for the newly emerging middle class; unimaginable profits for the industrial barons; and unrelieved misery for the lower class of workers who toiled, often under unsafe and unhealthy conditions, for a pittance in wages.

"Reform" is the word most often associated with the Progressive Era. The nation had changed too quickly, demographically and economically, to suit the newly prosperous middle class, who sought to maintain their comfortable positions in society while expressing concern about the lack of values in this new age. Big business had been largely responsible for the transformations industrialism brought to American life, and business was an easy target for the misgivings people had about the commercial world. Examples of children, women, and immigrants exploited mercilessly in the cause of commercial enter-

prise—if not simple greed—were common, and people wanted controls on the excesses of unscrupulous businessmen. The labor movement defended the interests of workers, but its greatest impact came after World War I. Women sought the vote and with it a voice in the business of the nation, but they were not successful until 1920. There was popular sentiment against the monopolistic trusts that threatened to engulf American business, but although antitrust legislation was enacted, most Americans felt the business men had their way.

Nationalism had taken on a new meaning in America by 1900. Railway expansion in the middle of the nineteenth century had made it possible to move goods quickly and efficiently throughout the country. As a result, commerce, which had been based largely on local production of goods for local consumption, expanded enormously. Ambitious merchants seized the opportunity to expand their businesses by appealing to broader markets. In 1900 there were 58 chain stores (businesses with more than one retail outlet) in the country; by 1920 the total had risen to 808. The number of clothing chains alone rose from 7 to 125 during the period.

The increase in productivity and consumerism radically changed the character of American life. Manufacturing plants drew people from the country into cities. Between 1900 and 1920 urban population increased by 80 percent compared to just over 12 percent for rural population. During the same time the non-farm workforce went from 783,000 people to 2.2 million. Unlike farmers, these workers drew a regular paycheck and spent it. Government statistics show that disposable income rose from $20 billion to $71.5 billion in the first two decades of this century, during the same time that cars were first available to transport people from home to store. Perhaps the most telling statistic about the change in American life-styles during this period is that in 1900 only 4,192 automobiles were registered; in 1920 there were 1.9 million.

Moreover, the electrical-energy-generating capacity of the country increased tenfold over the first two decades of the century, with dramatic effects. This new energy supplied the power to operate the plants that provided the expanding workforce with jobs and money. Just as important, it expanded the universe of goods that could be manufactured and sold in the enlarged marketplace. Radios, electric lights, telephones, and powered vacuum cleaners were possible for the first time and quickly established themselves as essential household items. Stimulated by the possibilities of an energized world, inventors were more active than ever before. In 1916, the last year of the period before wartime economic controls went into effect, 43,892 patents were issued, 75 percent more than in 1900.

World War I had a dramatic impact on the American economy. When the war broke out in Europe, American exports were required to support the Allied war effort. America's intervention in 1917 required that two million men be drafted, opening up jobs in home-front industries and requiring production at higher levels than ever before to support the war effort. To finance the war, the federal government issued more money, borrowed from citizens in the form of war bonds, and used the newly enacted income-tax legislation to raise funds (businesses with over $1 million in income were taxed at 77 percent); to control inflation, the government imposed strict price controls, forming the most closely controlled federal economy in American history.

The war forced Americans to confront one more important transformation. The United States had become a full participant in the world economy, and as a result the perimeters of American commerce were extended. The hated tariffs on imported goods were reduced, and exports reached an all-time high in 1919 and 1920, further stimulating American industry. The United States earned the respect of the world during the war; in the postwar years American business capitalized on this attitude.

By 1920 urban Americans had begun to define themselves—for their neighbors and for the world—in terms of what they consumed. It was a turning point in the social and economic history of the nation.

HISTORICAL SNAPSHOT
1900-1904

1900

- President William McKinley campaigns for reelection, emphasizing prosperity by using the "Full Dinner Pail" as his symbol
- Average life expectancy at birth is 47 years
- 13,824 motorcars are on the road
- Franklin, Peerless, and Stearns motorcars are introduced
- Hamburger introduced by Louis Lassen in New Haven, Connecticut
- Firestone Tire and Rubber Company founded on patent for attaching tires to rims
- 30,000 trolley cars operate on 15,000 miles of track
- Excavation begins on New York subway system
- U.S. railroads charge an average 75¢ per ton-mile, down from $1.22 in 1883
- First modern submarine, *Holland,* is purchased by navy
- Cripple Creek goldfield in Colorado yields $20 million
- Brownie box camera introduced by Eastman Kodak Company with a sales price of $1.00
- Uneeda Biscuits achieves sales of more than 10 million packages per month

1901

- President William McKinley assassinated; Theodore Roosevelt assumes presidency
- United States Steel Company created by J. P. Morgan
- Monsanto Chemical Company funded with a capitalization of $5,000

- New York City streetcars and elevators convert to electric power
- Andrew Carnegie gives the New York Public Library $5.2 million to open its first branches
- Jergen's Lotion for chapped hands introduced
- King C. Gillette and William Nickerson start American Safety Razor Company with $5,000; becomes the Gillette Safety Razor Company the following year
- Japanese-American chemist Satroi Kato of Chicago introduces the first soluble "instant" coffee at the Pan-American Exhibition

1902

- John Mitchell leads 5-month strike of 147,000 anthracite coal workers
- Price of coal in New York goes from $5 to $30 per ton
- Membership in the AF of L reaches the million mark
- Rayon is patented by U.S. chemist A. D. Little
- Carnegie Institute of Washington established with a $10 million gift
- Russian-American Morris Michtom and his wife introduce the teddy bear with movable arms, legs, and head
- Philip Morris Corporation, Ltd., is incorporated in New York
- Charles Lewis Tiffany, founder of Tiffany and Co., dies leaving estate of $35 million
- The first Automat restaurant is opened by Horn & Hardart Baking Company in Philadelphia

1903

- Wright Brothers make first sustained manned flights in a controlled gasoline-powered aircraft
- Twenty-four hp Chadwick motorcar introduced; capable of 60 mph; $4,000
- Massachusetts creates first automobile license plate
- Bottle-blowing machine cuts cost of electric light bulb
- Harley-Davidson motorcycle introduced
- An automatic machine to cut off a salmon's head and tail, and clean it is devised by A. K. Smith
- Sanka Coffee introduced by German coffee-importer Ludwig Roselius

1904

- Marie Curie discovers two new radioactive elements, radium and polonium
- Post Toasties introduced by the Postum Company
- Joseph Campbell Preserve Company introduces Campbell's Pork and Beans
- St. Louis fair spawns iced tea and the ice-cream cone
- *Ladies' Home Journal* publishes exposé of the U.S. patent-medicine business
- Montgomery Ward distributes free catalogues, mailing 3 million books; Sears, Roebuck distributes a million copies of its spring catalogue
- Pope-Toledo motorcar introduced at $650
- E. F. Hutton and Company is founded by Edward Francis Hutton

SELECTED INCOME 1900-1904

Job	Source	Description	Pay
Assistant	*Milwaukee Journal* (1904)	Boy; steady advancement and good chance to learn trade if industrious; no boy who thinks he is 'it' because he swears and smokes cigarettes need apply.	$3.50/wk
Baseball Players	*American Chronicle* (1999)	Each winner's share of the 1903 Baseball World Series	$1,316
Business Representative	*New York Times* (1903)	Wanted—Trustworthy persons in each state to manage business of wealthy corporation; salary in cash each Thursday direct from headquarters; expense money advanced	$18/wk
Businessman	Vincent Tompkins, ed. *American Decades: 1900-1909* (1996)	Annual salary of Charles M. Schwab as first president of U.S. Steel in 1903	$2 million
Carpenter	*San Francisco Examiner* (1913)	House carpenter, work on ranch	$3.25/day
Casual Labor	*New York Times* (1903)	Boys, we will give you a perfect timepiece for working for us a few hours. H. W. Wright Co., Baltimore, Md.	Watch
Circular Distributors	*Distributors National Union,* Cincinnati, OH (1902)	Pay advanced; no canvassing	$5/1,000
Clerk	*Chicago Tribune* (1902)	Bookkeeper and Stenographer	$20/wk
Collection Agent	*Chicago Tribune* (1904)	Man—To travel and collect; salary, all expenses, and commission; position will net $4,000 a year; $100 cash security required. Abbott Co.	$100/mo
Collection Agent	*Chicago Tribune* (1902)	German speaking; middle aged or men who cannot work hard	$2/day for 3 days; rest of week commission
Cook	*New York Times* (1900)	Wanted—To remain in the city all summer, a competent, young cook who is also a good laundress and who has first-class city references, wages	$25/mo
Cook	*Chicago Tribune* (1900)	Situation wanted—Competent cook	$50/mo
Cook	*San Francisco Examiner* (1913)	A man cook for hotel, country town	$50/mo
Dressmaker	*New York Times* (1901)	First-class fitter and trimmer; work by day; all latest fancy waists; remodeling	$2.50/day
Editor	Justin Kaplan, *Lincoln Steffens* (1974)	Annual salary of Lincoln Steffens as managing Editor of McClure's magazine in 1901	$5,000
Electric Linemen	*New York Tribune* (1902)	Daily pay for nine hours' work as an electric lineman with Pittsburgh and Allegheny Company	$2.50
Letter Carrier	*New York Tribune* (1902)	Yearly pay of America's 75,000 letter carriers is determined by length of service	
		First year	$600
		2nd year	$800
		3rd year	$1000
		Thereafter	$1200
Light Labor	*Chicago Tribune* (1900)	Situation wanted—Light, by refined young man, 19 years old; some outside work attached	$7/wk

Job	Source	Description	Pay
Mine Engineers	*New York Tribune* (1902)	Daily pay of Hoisting Engineers for Amalgamated Copper Company	$4
Nurse	*Chicago Tribune* (1904)	Situated Wanted—by a thoroughly competent nurse to care for an infant and day; wages.	$8/wk
Painter/Wallpaperer	*York (SC) Times* (1901)	Good work done cheap; rooms painted, papered	$1.25/day $1.75/day
Railroad Worker	*Milwaukee Journal* (1904)	Strong Young Men—For firemen and brakemen, Wisconsin and other railroads. Name position preferred. Send stamp for particulars. Railway Association. Firemen, engineers and brakemen conductors	$65/mo $125/mo $60/mo $105/mo
Sales	*Chicago Tribune* (1900)	We want a few active hustlers in city to sell our new patent reflectors for Welsbach lights; evening 6 to 9 p.m.; exclusive territory	$1.50-$3/night
Sales	*Chicago Tribune* (1900)	Agents—introducing our "super-asbestos" wicks; just out; beats electricity; address Fireproof Safety Wick Works.	$3–$5/day
Sales	*Chicago Tribune* (1902)	No experience needed; our circulars teach you the business and our patented goods do the rest; if you are making less than $300 per month write to us	$25/day
Sales	*Milwaukee Journal* (1904)	Wanted—Female Help "Lady"—For census work and distributing sample magazines; steady employment (home work)	$15/wk
Sales	*Milwaukee Journal* (1904)	General Agents—; every business man buys a new best pocket invention $3. Big holiday business.	$20-$50/wk
Stenographer	*Milwaukee Journal* (1904)	At once—An experienced male stenographer; Smith Premier operator; must also be a bookkeeper. A good position for the right party.	$50/mo
Vaudeville Actor	*American Chronicle* (1999)	Weekly wages of Vaudeville star Lillian Russell in 1902	$3,500
Vaudeville Actor	*American Chronicle* (1999)	Weekly pay of Eva Tanquay at Hammerstein's Victoria Theater	$3,500

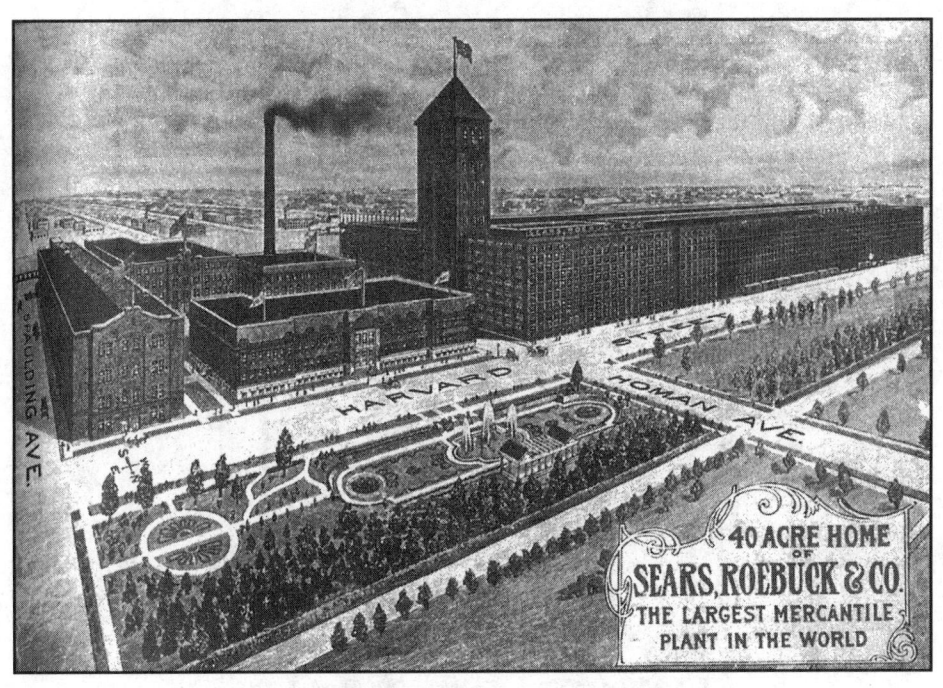

INVESTMENTS 1900-1904

Investment	1900	1901	1902	1903	1904
Basic Yield, One-year Corporate Bonds	3.97	3.25	3.30	3.45	3.60
Short-term Interest Rates, 4–6 Months, Prime Commercial Paper	5.71	5.40	5.81	6.16	5.14
Basic Yield, Common Stocks, Total	4.50	3.85	3.71	4.65	4.18
Index of Common Stocks (1941−1943=10)	6.15	7.84	8.42	7.21	7.05
COMMON STOCKS, CLOSING PRICE AND YIELD, FIRST BUSINESS DAY OF YEAR					
Allis Chalmers (Inc. 5/7/01)				82 ⅛	50
AT & T (5/15/00 first date of issue)		93	96	163	126
American Tobacco (Inc. 10/19/04)					
Anaconda (Inc. 6/18/1895)	40 ½	48 ⅝	30 ⅝	99	76
B & O (Chartered 1827)	58 ¾	85 ⅞	108 ⅛	101	78 ½
Bethlehem Steel (Inc. 12/10/04)					
Corn Products				30 ½	17 ½
General Electric (Inc. 4/15/1892) (66 2/3% stock dividend, 6/25/02)			282	183	170 ½
Intl Harvester (Inc. 8/12/02)					
National Biscuit (Inc. 2/3/1898)	90 ¼	41 ¾	43 ¼	45 ⅛	36
US Steel (Inc. 2/25/01)			43	36 ⅞	11 ¾
Western Union (Inc. 4/1/1851 as NY & Mississippi Valley Printing Telegraph Co.; name changed to Western Union in 1856)	84 ¾	83	92 ½	88 ¾	86

STANDARD JOBS 1900-1904

Job Type	1900	1901	1902	1903	1904
Average of All Industries, excl. farm labor	$490/yr	$508/yr	$519/yr	$543/yr	$540/yr
Average of All Industries, incl. farm labor	$438/yr	$454/yr	$467/yr	$489/yr	$490/yr
Bituminous Coal Mining	20¢/hr	23¢/hr	24¢/hr	27¢/hr	27¢/hr
Avg hrs/wk	52.60	52.40	52.30	52.20	51.60
Building Trades, Union Workers	37¢/hr	39¢/hr	41¢/hr	44¢/hr	44¢/hr
Avg hrs/wk	48.30	47.50	46.70	46.30	46.10
Clerical Workers in Mfg. & Steam RR	$1011/yr	$1009/yr	$1025/yr	$1037/yr	$1056/yr
Domestics	$240/yr	$243/yr	$264/yr	$270/yr	$277/yr
Farm Labor	$247/yr	$255/yr	$264/yr	$277/yr	$290/yr
Federal Civilian	$940/yr	$974/yr	$967/yr	$1009/yr	$971/yr
Federal Employees, Executive Depts.	$1033/yr	$1047/yr	$1061/yr	$1067/yr	$1066/yr
Finance, Insurance, & Real Estate	$1040/yr	$1037/yr	$1051/yr	$1078/yr	$1099/yr
Gas & Electricity Workers	$620/yr	$615/yr	NA	NA	$556/yr
Lower-Skilled Labor	$459/yr	$471/yr	$481/yr	$501/yr	$512/yr
Manufacturing, Payroll	15¢/hr	15¢/hr	16¢/hr	17¢/hr	16¢/hr
Avg hrs/wk	62.10	61.90	61.50	61.20	61.10
Manufacturing, Union Workers	34¢/hr	35¢/hr	36¢/hr	37¢/hr	37¢/hr
Avg hrs/wk	53.00	52.40	51.80	51.40	51.10
Medical/Health Services Workers	$256/yr	$258/yr	$267/yr	$275/yr	$283/yr
Ministers	$731/yr	$730/yr	$737/yr	$761/yr	$759/yr
Nonprofit Org. Workers	$652/yr	$651/yr	$657/yr	$679/yr	$677/yr
Postal Employees	37¢/hr	38¢/hr	37¢/hr	37¢/hr	37¢/hr
Avg hrs/wk	48.00	48.00	48.00	48.00	48.00
Public School Teachers	$328/yr	$337/yr	$346/yr	$358/yr	$377/yr
and Local Govt. Workers	$590/yr	$605/yr	$612/yr	$621/yr	$640/yr
State and Local Govt. Workers	$590/yr	$605/yr	$612/yr	$621/yr	$640/yr
Steam Railroads, Wage Earners	$548/yr	$549/yr	$562/yr	$593/yr	$600/yr
Street Railway Workers	$604/yr	$601/yr	$576/yr	$582/yr	$610/yr
Telegraph Ind. Workers	NA	NA	$544/yr	$573/yr	$601/yr
Telephone Ind. Workers	NA	NA	$408/yr	$397/yr	$392/yr
Wholesale and Retail Trade Workers	$508/yr	$510/yr	$521/yr	$537/yr	$551/yr

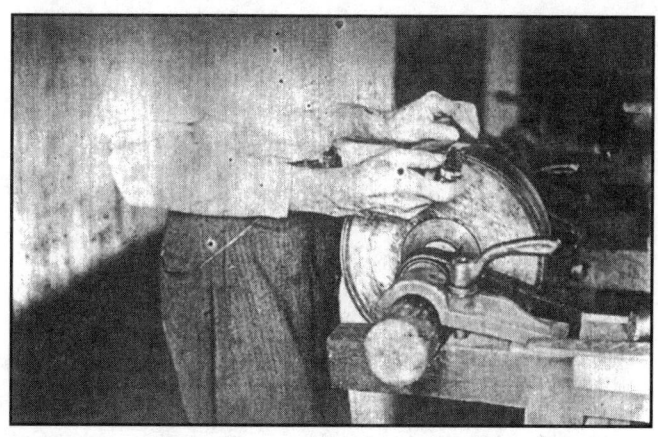

FOOD BASKET 1900-1904

Commodity	Year	New York	Atlanta	Chicago	Denver	Los Angeles
Apples, Evaporated, per pound	1900	10¢	10¢	7.67¢	NR	9.67¢
	1901	10¢	10¢	8.67¢	NR	9.33¢
	1902	10¢	10¢	10.71¢	NR	9.83¢
	1903	10¢	10¢	12.50¢	NR	9.67¢
	1904	12¢	10¢	10¢	10¢	10¢
Beans, Dry, per quart	1900	10¢	10¢	8.75¢	NR	5.63¢
	1901	10¢	15¢	8.67¢	NR	5.63¢
	1902	10¢	15¢	8.50¢	NR	7.03¢
	1903	10¢	10¢	10¢	NR	7.50¢
	1904	10¢	10¢	10¢	9.38¢	7.50¢
Beef, Fresh, Roasts, per pound	1900	18¢	18¢	13¢	15.67¢	17¢
	1901	18¢	18¢	13¢	16.67¢	17.67¢
	1902	20.67¢	20¢	14.42¢	21.79¢	18¢
	1903	20¢	17.71¢	14.42¢	21.17¢	18¢
	1904	14.83¢	12.50¢	9.92¢	12.50¢	15¢
Beef, Salt (Corned), per pound	1900	6¢	NR	7.25¢	NR	8.33¢
	1901	6.33¢	NR	7.25¢	NR	8.33¢
	1902	8.83¢	NR	7.75¢	NR	8.33¢
	1903	6.17¢	NR	8¢	NR	8.33¢
	1904	8¢	12.50¢	6.33¢	6.42¢	10¢
Beef, Steaks (Round), per pound	1900	16¢	13.63¢	12¢	12.50¢	10¢
	1901	16.33¢	15¢	12.67¢	14.17¢	10¢
	1902	16.33¢	15¢	13.25¢	14.58¢	11.88¢
	1903	18¢	15¢	12.50¢	11.33¢	12.50¢
	1904	16¢	12.50¢	10.50¢	10¢	12.50¢
Bread, Wheat, per loaf	1900	5¢	5¢	5¢	5¢	5¢
	1901	5¢	5¢	5¢	5¢	5¢
	1902	5¢	5¢	5¢	5¢	5¢
	1903	5¢	5¢	5¢	5¢	5¢
	1904	5¢	5¢	5¢	5¢	5¢
Butter, per pound	1900	26.67¢	28.75¢	22.67¢	27.92¢	25.48¢
	1901	24.67¢	26.25¢	24.58¢	29.17¢	25.24¢
	1902	27.67¢	30.42¢	24¢	31.25	28.81¢
	1903	29.33¢	30.83¢	26.58¢	30.83¢	30.48¢
	1904	26.25¢	27.92¢	25.58¢	25.42¢	26.25¢
Cheese, per pound	1900	14.17¢	17.58¢	17.33¢	20¢	18¢
	1901	14¢	17.25¢	17¢	20¢	19.33¢
	1902	17¢	18¢	17.33¢	20¢	20¢
	1903	19.17¢	18.33¢	16.58¢	20¢	20¢
	1904	16.17¢	15.42¢	16.92¢	20¢	20¢
Chickens, per pound	1900	12.50¢	14¢	10.75¢	NR	NR
	1901	12.17¢	15.25¢	10.92¢	NR	NR
	1902	12.75¢	15.33¢	13.25¢	NR	NR
	1903	12.75¢	16.83¢	16.33¢	NR	NR
	1904	18¢	16.04¢	15.42¢	13¢	23.75¢
Coffee, per pound	1900	15.75¢	12.67¢	13.33¢	12.50¢	25¢
	1901	16¢	13¢	13.67¢	12.50¢	25¢
	1902	16¢	11.33¢	13.33¢	12.50¢	25¢
	1903	15¢	11.08¢	15.42¢	12.38¢	25¢
Cornmeal, per pound	1900	3¢	1.67¢	1.75¢	2¢	2¢
	1901	3¢	2.08¢	2.25¢	2¢	2¢
	1902	3¢	2.08¢	2.50¢	2¢	2.75¢
	1903	3¢	1.77¢	2.50¢	2¢	3¢
	1904	2.95¢	2¢	2.50¢	2.50¢	3¢

Commodity	Year	New York	Atlanta	Chicago	Denver	Los Angeles
Eggs, per dozen	1900	22.83¢	18¢	18.25¢	19.92¢	26.67¢
	1901	22.50¢	19¢	19.17¢	25.21¢	26.25¢
	1902	26.17¢	21¢	22.58¢	25.42¢	29.83¢
	1903	28¢	21.21¢	22.75¢	28¢	29.79¢
	1904	29.17¢	22.13¢	23.92	28.33¢	28.33
Fish, Fresh, per pound	1900	12¢	12.50¢	11.71¢	NR	10¢
	1901	12¢	12.50¢	11.71¢	NR	10¢
	1902	12¢	12.50¢	11.71¢	NR	10¢
	1903	11.83¢	10¢	11.71¢	NR	9.50¢
	1904	11.50¢	10.83¢	9.25¢	14¢	10¢
Fish, Salt, per pound	1900	9.75¢	14.33¢	6.46¢	NR	NR
	1901	9.33¢	15¢	7.71¢	NR	NR
	1902	9¢	14.92¢	6.17¢	NR	NR
	1903	9¢	15¢	9.17¢	NR	NR
	1904	11¢	12.42¢	10¢	14.81¢	8.33¢
Flour, Wheat, per pound	1900	2.31¢	2.78¢	2.30¢	1.65¢	2.50¢
	1901	2.28¢	3.05¢	2.30¢	1.85¢	2.50¢
	1902	2.61¢	3.05¢	2.30¢	1.90¢	2.50¢
	1903	2.82¢	3.11¢	2.43¢	2.18¢	2.79¢
—per one-eighth barrel bag	1904	81.67¢	84.58¢	74.58¢	61.67¢	73.33¢
Lard, per pound	1900	8.33¢	9.13¢	10¢	10.67¢	NR
	1901	10.21¢	11.08¢	10¢	12.42¢	NR
	1902	12.67¢	12.38¢	11.08¢	14.29¢	NR
	1903	11.33¢	10.46¢	10.67¢	15¢	NR
	1904	11.29¢	9.38¢	10.42¢	10¢	12.50¢
Milk, Fresh, per quart	1900	5¢	8¢	6¢	6.25¢	10¢
	1901	5¢	8¢	6¢	6.25¢	10¢
	1902	4.75¢	8¢	6¢	6.25¢	10¢
	1903	5¢	8¢	6¢	6.62¢	10¢
	1904	6¢	8¢	7¢	6.25¢	9.33¢
Molasses, per gallon	1900	50¢	50¢	60¢	65¢	70¢
	1901	50¢	50¢	60¢	65¢	70¢
	1902	50¢	50¢	60¢	65¢	70¢
	1903	57.50¢	50¢	60¢	65¢	70¢
	1904	53.75¢	50¢	50¢	50¢	50¢
Mutton and Lamb, Leg, per pound	1900	9.75¢	20¢	8¢	15¢	15¢
	1901	10.17¢	20¢	8¢	15¢	15¢
	1902	12.75¢	20¢	8¢	15¢	16.42¢
	1903	12.75¢	17.71¢	10.67¢	11.13¢	18.50¢
	1904	12.42¢	15¢	10.83¢	12.50¢	12.50¢
Pork, Fresh, per pound	1900	14.75¢	NR	9.25¢	12.50¢	15¢
	1901	15¢	NR	9.92¢	14.17¢	15¢
	1902	17.33¢	NR	11.67¢	16.04¢	16.58¢
	1903	18.67¢	NR	10.08¢	13.75¢	17.50¢
	1904	13.38¢	12.50¢	10.25¢	11¢	15¢
Pork, Salt, Bacon, per pound	1900	16.75¢	11¢	12.25¢	13.17¢	13.25¢
	1901	17.58¢	11.17¢	13.75¢	13.71¢	13.75¢
	1902	19¢	12¢	14.58¢	16.42¢	15.50¢
	1903	18¢	17.08¢	15.92¢	17.25¢	17.75¢
	1904	16.33¢	12.96¢	14.50¢	20¢	18¢
Pork, Salt, Dry or Pickled, per pound	1900	13.33¢	NR	8¢	NR	NR
	1901	14¢	NR	10¢	NR	NR
	1902	15¢	NR	12¢	NR	NR
	1903	14¢	NR	12¢	NR	NR
	1904	12.71¢	10¢	11.33¢	11.38¢	12.50¢
Pork, Salt, Ham, per pound	1900	14.08¢	15¢	11¢	13.54¢	14.83¢
	1901	15.08¢	15¢	12.50¢	13.71¢	15.21¢
	1902	14.42¢	15¢	12.50¢	15.96¢	16.08¢
	1903	15.75¢	14.33¢	12.50¢	15.50¢	15.50¢
	1904	20¢	20¢	16.33¢	20¢	20¢

Commodity	Year	New York	Atlanta	Chicago	Denver	Los Angeles
Potatoes, Irish, per bushel	1900	61.33¢	$1.2083	38.64¢	71.25¢	85.75¢
	1901	83.58¢	99.17¢	68.18¢	93¢	94¢
	1902	94.58¢	$1.0250	82.73¢	95.75¢	94.25¢
	1903	99.58¢	90.42¢	71.67¢	93¢	$1.0125
—per peck	1904	30.67¢	19.58¢	18¢	23.81¢	24.69¢
Prunes, per pound	1900	10¢	NR	7.67¢	NR	8.75¢
	1901	10¢	NR	7.33¢	NR	8.33¢
	1902	8¢	NR	7.75¢	NR	8.33¢
	1903	10¢	NR	7.50¢	NR	6¢
	1904	7.83¢	8.33¢	8.50¢	8¢	5¢
Rice, per pound	1900	7¢	7¢	5¢	8.33¢	7¢
	1901	7¢	7¢	5.83¢	8.33¢	7¢
	1902	7¢	7¢	6¢	8.33¢	6.50¢
	1903	7¢	7¢	5¢	8.33¢	6.79¢
	1904	7.58¢	7.50¢	9¢	8.33¢	8¢
Sugar, per pound	1900	5.75¢	5.90¢	5.79¢	5.85¢	NR
	1901	5.92¢	6.04¢	5.71¢	5.74¢	NR
	1902	6¢	5.38¢	5.54¢	5.36¢	NR
	1903	6¢	5.38¢	5¢	5.45¢	NR
	1904	5.58¢	5.67¢	5.33¢	6.25¢	6.35¢
Tea, per pound	1900	50¢	60¢	47.50¢	60¢	50¢
	1901	50¢	61.67¢	50¢	60¢	50¢
	1902	50¢	60¢	50¢	60¢	50¢
	1903	50¢	50¢	50¢	60¢	50¢
	1904	50¢	50¢	50¢	35¢	50¢
Veal, per pound	1900	12.08¢	NR	10.25¢	NR	NR
	1901	12.25¢	NR	12¢	NR	NR
	1902	14¢	NR	12.13¢	NR	NR
	1903	12.75¢	NR	12¢	NR	NR
	1904	20.50¢	15¢	16.33¢	13.96¢	20¢
Vinegar, per gallon	1900	28¢	NR	20¢	NR	40¢
	1901	28¢	NR	20¢	NR	42.50¢
	1902	28¢	NR	20¢	NR	50¢
	1903	32¢	NR	20¢	NR	50¢
	1904	20¢	20¢	20¢	30¢	50¢

SELECTED PRICES 1900-1904

Item	Source	Description	Price
Alcohol			
Whiskey	*The New Orleans Picayune* (1903)	White Line Whiskey Gallon Quart	$3.50 $1.00
Whiskey	*Atlanta Constitution* (1904)	*Golden Grain;* a whiskey that will make good with all who know good whiskey	$1.00/quart
Wine	*Atlanta Constitution* (1904)	Zinfandel; 12 quarts	$5.00/case
Apparel, Children's			
Hat	*The New Orleans Picayune* (1903)	Children's lawn or straw hats, trimmed worth $0.98; Special	$0.49
Hosiery	*Ladies' Home Journal* (1904)	Black Cat; serviceable five-thread hose for boys; fine mercerized hose for girls	$0.35/pair
Overcoat	*Yorkville Enquirer* (Yorkville, SC) (1900)	Boy's, 6 to 12 years; best quality	$2.50
Play Suit	*Ladies' Home Journal* (1904)	Little Tudor; a complete top-to-toe garment	$0.50
Silk Bonnet	*Southern Christian Advocate* (1902)	60 Children's silk bonnets; reg $1	$0.50
Suit	*New York Times* (1901)	Three-piece; a camera free with every suit; reg $5	$2.98
Underwear	*The State* (Columbia, SC) (1903)	Jersey ribbed, fleeced, lined vests and pants	$0.15
Apparel, Men's			
Hat	*New York Times* (1901)	Alpines and derbies	$3.49
Heel Cushions	*Ladies' Home Journal* (1904)	*Gilbert's;* make yourself taller; worn inside the shoe; 1/2"	$0.25
Overcoat	*New York Times* (1901)	Spring weight	$6.50
Shirt	*New York Times* (1901)	Madras, open back and front, two detached cuffs	$0.94
Shirt	*Sears, Roebuck* (1902)	French percale; fast colors, yoke back, pearl buttons	$0.40
Shoes	*New York Times* (1901)	*W. L. Douglas;* My large business permits me to buy the high-grade leathers used in $5 shoes	$3.50
Shoes	*Greenville News* (Greenville, SC) (1902)	Satin calf	$0.93
Suit	*The State* (Columbia, SC) (1903)	*Fitzmaurice;* sack business suit; worn by most business men of your acquaintance	$8.50
Suspenders	*Harper's Monthly Magazine* (1903)	President suspenders make walking easy; the "give and take" principle; metal trimmings cannot rust.	$0.50 to $1.00

Item	Source	Description	Price
Apparel, Women's			
Belt	*The State* (Columbia, SC) (1903)	Silk and elastic; large oxidized buckle, something very swell	$0.50
Corset	*New York Tribune* (1902)	*James McCreery and Company corsets;* straight front, long hip, batiste Value Sale price	 $2.25 $1.45
Corset	*Sears, Roebuck* (1902)	Special four-hook short corset for medium frame	$0.50
Crash Skirts	*Atlanta Constitution* (1904)	Linen; black and colors; $1.25 value	$0.69
Dress	*New York Times* (1901)	Spring; percale	$4.88
Handkerchiefs	*New York Times* (1901)	Hemstitched; 1" and 2" hems	$3.00/dozen
Hat	*Sears, Roebuck* (1902)	Jaunty large black turban, with a very richly designed straw braid	$2.25
Hose	*New York Times* (1901)	*Lisle* thread and fine cotton; regularly $0.50	$0.29
Lawn Dress	*New York Times* (1901)	Satin-striped, figured	$10.41
Opera Bag	*The State* (Columbia, SC) (1903)	Positively the newest things	$1.50 to $3.50
Parasol	*Sears, Roebuck* (1900)	Pure white China silk	$1.25
Shoes	*Greenville News* (Greenville, SC) (1902)	*Dongola* shoes	$0.89
Shoes	*Ladies' Home Journal* (1904)	*La France;* the Oxford is the smartest shoe of the season	$3.00
Shoe Inserts	*Harper's Monthly Magazine* (1903)	*Astra* soles keep your feet dry, clean, and healthy—cool in summer and warm in winter. Worn all the year round, they absorb perspiration entirely, prevent catarrh and rheumatism, and save shoes and stockings	$0.25 for 10 pairs
Suit	*New York Times* (1901)	Shirt-waist suit, comfortable successor to the ill-fitting wrapper and house dress	$2.25 to $4.50
Summer Suit	*Ladies' Home Journal* (1904)	Tailored suits Mohair and brilliantine suits Traveling dresses	$8 to $50 $8 to $40 $8 to $30
Undervest	*The State* (Columbia, SC) (1903)	Fleece lined	$0.39
Appliances			
Home Heater	*Sears, Roebuck* (1902)	*Acme Seroco;* hot-blast, air-tight sheet-steel heater for hard or soft coal; 16" diameter	$9.55
Linen Washer and Press	*Harper's Monthly Magazine* (1903)	Washer and heated steel roll mangle; produces crisp, clean linen that can be had in a few minutes; the ideal laundry apparatus for the home	$150 for both
Radiator	*Sears, Roebuck* (1902)	*Acme;* direct steam or water; latest thing in radiator design and construction	$9.45
Range	*Sears, Roebuck* (1902)	*Acme Regal;* 20" x 21" x 14"; steel range is highly nickel plated throughout	$20.55
Range	*Sears, Roebuck* (1902)	Steel; 8" lids; over 17" x 21" x 12"; 475 lbs; terms: $8 cash, $3/mo, no interest	$22.90

Item	Source	Description	Price
Refrigerator	*Sears, Roebuck* (1902)	*Acme Seroco;* ice receptacle holds 125 lbs of ice, and a 100 lb piece will go in easily without any chipping	$27.50
Refrigerator	*Ladies' Home Journal* (1904)	Leonard Cleanable; lined with genuine porcelain enamel fired on sheet steel; 35" x 22" x 46"; beware of imitations made with white paint	$27.50
Stove	*The Housewife* (1903)	*Acme Wonder* cook stove; extra fine finish	$4.85
Washer	*Sears, Roebuck* (1902)	*Fulton American #1;* machine made of white pine, painted and grained as ash color; will wash five shirts clean without the use of a washboard	$4.44
Washing Machine	*The Housewife* (1903)	Wonder washing machine; the equal of washing machines that sell for two or three times the price	$1.95
Water Closet	*Sears, Roebuck* (1902)	Siphon jet water closet; tank copper lined	$19.75

Baby Products

Item	Source	Description	Price
Baby Powder	*Sears, Roebuck* (1902)	*Talcum;* nicely perfumed and put up handsomely; decorated metal boxes with sprinkler tops	$0.08/box
Baby Spoon and Food Pusher	*Ladies' Home Journal* (1904)		$1.00
Baby Tender	*Ladies' Home Journal* (1904)	*E-Z-Go;* teaches baby to walk	$2.75
Hygienic Absorbent Pads	*Ladies' Home Journal* (1904)	Keep the baby dry and clean; shield wt. 4 oz	$1.50 each
Hygienic Dip Pins	*Ladies' Home Journal* (1904)	*Boston;* if you buy 3, 1 will be sent free	$0.10 each
Infant's Long Dress	*Ladies' Home Journal* (1904)	*Nainsook,* yoke of fine beading and featherstitching	$1.35
Nipple	*Ladies' Home Journal* (1904)	*Clingfast;* pure gum right size; outlasts three ordinary nipples	$0.50/dozen
Pants for babies	*Ladies' Home Journal* (1904)	*Stork;* made to cover the diaper; absolutely waterproof	$0.05
Rattle Pacifier	*Sears, Roebuck* (1902)	Best rattle, teething ring, and plaything ever invented for the babies	$0.09
Rubber Teething Ring	*Ladies' Home Journal* (1904)	*Bailey's;* expands the gums, keeping them soft; comforts and amuses the child	$0.10

Buggy Carriages & Supplies

Item	Source	Description	Price
Buggy	*Sears, Roebuck* (1900)	Jump seat; the body is made of good material; 25" x 54"	$59.75
Buggy	*Sears, Roebuck* (1902)	*Acme* Royal Top	$54.90
Buggy Whip	*Sears, Roebuck* (1900)	Black star finish, waterproof cover; 6"	$0.69
Buggy Whip	Edward L. Throm, ed., *Popular Mechanics Picture History of American Transportation* (1952)	Twisted; hickory handle covered with sheepskin [cost in 1900]	$0.25
Driving Wagon	*Ladies' Home Journal* (1904)	Open trap style; bike gear and 7/8" Kelly rubber tires	$83.00
Driving Wagon	*Ladies' Home Journal* (1904)	With basket seat	$57.50

Business Equipment & Supplies

Item	Source	Description	Price
Telephone Rates	*New York Tribune* (1902)	Manhattan rates for business service, New York Telephone Company Per month	$5.00

57

Item	Source	Description	Price
Wireless Machine	*Ladies' Home Journal* (1904)	*Lambert;* it is a dwarf in size but a giant in its work; complete	$25.00
Collectibles			
Book	*New York Tribune* (1902)	First edition of "The Loving Ballad" by William Makepeace Thackeray	$42.50
Painting	*New York Tribune* (1902)	*The Holy Family* by Peter Paul Rubens sold in auction	$50,000
Painting	*New York Tribune* (1902)	*Harvesting the Poppies* by Jules Breton sold in auction	$35,000
Painting	*New York Tribune* (1902)	*Arabs Crossing a Stream* by A. Schreyer sold in action	$11,000
Painting	*American* Chronicle (1999)	Anton Mauve's *Sheep Coming Out of the Forest;* sold at auction	$40,200
Proof Sheet	*New York Tribune* (1902)	Original proof sheet of "Charge of the Light Brigade" with margin correction by poet	$440
Education			
Boarding School	*Harper's Monthly Magazine* (1903)	*Dr. Holbrook's School for Boys;* full term begins September 24, 1903; Ossining-on-Hudson, New York	$700
Boarding School	*Harper's Monthly Magazine* (1903)	*Fort Edward Collegiate Institute for Girls;* location unsurpassed; college preparatory; choice of six courses of study; departments also in Music, Art, Elocution, Physical Culture; Fort Edward, New York. Yearly rate	$300 to $400
Boarding School	*Harper's Monthly Magazine* (1903)	*Lawrence Academy;* endowed, limited school for boys over ten; founded 1793. Fits for all colleges, scientific and technical schools; Groton, Massachusetts	$500
Boarding School	*Southern Christian Advocate* (1902)	*Wofford College Fitting School;* Spartanburg, South Carolina; board, fuel, lights and all fees	$110
Boarding School	*The Salem Academy Magazine* (1903)	*The Bingham School;* Mebane, North Carolina; U. S. Army officer detailed; Bible, physical culture, and penmanship emphasized	$125/half-term
Business School	*Harper's Monthly Magazine* (1903)	*Eastman,* "The Best Business School in America;" One hundred dollars pay entire expense of tuition, books, stationery, board, room rent, fuel and lights during three months; Poughkeepsie, New York	$100
Dance Lessons	*New York Times* (1901)	Waltz, two-step polka, waltz quadrille; five private four-class lessons	$5.00
Seminary	*Harper's Monthly Magazine* (1903)	*Ashland Seminary;* certificate admits to Wellesley and other colleges. A delightful church school in the heart of the beautiful Blue Grass region. In the Diocese of Lexington, Kentucky; yearly charge	$250
Entertainment			
Broadway Play	*New York Tribune* (1902)	*Sleeping Beauty and the Beast;* matinee	$50.00 to $1.50
Circus	*New York Tribune* (1902)	*Great 4-Paw and Sells Brothers Enormous Shows United;* at Madison Square Garden, featuring Diavalo's Loop the Loop	$0.25 to $2.00
Orchestral Concert	*New York Tribune* (1902)	*Wetzler Orchestral Concert;* featuring soloist Paderewski Seats	$1 to $2
Vaudeville	*New York Tribune* (1902)	Big Vaudeville Comedy; 25 star acts Seats Reserved Box	$0.25 and $0.50 $0.75 $1.00

Item	Source	Description	Price
Show Ticket	*Sears, Roebuck* (1901)	*Buffalo Bill's Wild West and Rough Riders Show,* Madison Square Garden Gallery	$0.25
		Second balcony	$0.50
		First balcony	$0.75
		Arena	$1.00
		First-tier boxes	$9.00
		Arena boxes	$12.00
Theater Ticket	*Atlanta Constitution* (1904)	Eagle Minstrels; Singers, dancers, comedians patriotic first part; funny mock initiation	$0.25/$0.50/$0.75

Entertainment, Home

Item	Source	Description	Price
Board Game	*Sears, Roebuck* (1902)	*Ouija;* the most interesting and mystifying production of the age	$1.00
Bone Dice	*Sears, Roebuck* (1902)	Square corners, No. 6, 1/2"	$0.09/dozen
Camera	*Sears, Roebuck* (1902)	*Delmar* folding camera	$3.75
Playing Cards	*Sears, Roebuck* (1902)	*Dougherty Climax;* enameled, round-cornered, linen cards	$0.24/package
Talking Machine	*Sears, Roebuck* (1900)	*Graphophone;* not a toy but a high-grade and complete graphophone	$5.00
Talking Machine	*Sears, Roebuck* (1902)	*Graphophone Grand*	$25.00

Farm Equipment & Supplies

Item	Source	Description	Price
Dehorning Clippers	*Sears, Roebuck* (1900)	*Keystone;* the latest improved and most powerful instrument for dehorning cattle	$12.00
Pony Plow	*Sears, Roebuck* (1902)	All-steel, wood beam, one-horse plow, 8" cut	$2.39

Financial Products and Services

Item	Source	Description	Price
U.S. Money Orders	*Advertising Trade Card* (1900)	$5–$1,000	$0.08
		$2,000–$3,000	$0.12
		$3,000–$4,000	$0.15
		$4,000–$5,000	$0.20

Food Products

Item	Source	Description	Price
Breakfast Cereal	*Ladies' Home Journal* (1904)	*Ralston;* over a million people know Ralston is the best	$0.15/package
Butter	*Atlanta Constitution* (1904)	*Elgin;* best of this famous brand; delivered on ice	$0.28/pound
Coffee	*Sears, Roebuck* (1902)	Ten-pound tin, special grade	$2.10
Coffee	*Greenville News* (Greenville, SC) (1903)		13¢/pound
Coffee	*Ladies' Home Journal* (1904)	*Pomja;* a selected blend of the highest grades of coffee	$0.30/pound
Coffee	*The Ladies' Home Journal* (1904)	*Pomja* coffee; sold in sealed one-pound packages	$0.30
Corn Syrup	*Ladies' Home Journal* (1904)	*Karo;* the great spread for daily bread in air-tight, friction-top tins	$0.10/$0.25/$0.50
Cream Puffs	*The Salem Academy and Cupcakes Magazine* (1903)		$0.20/dozen
Dessert Jelly	*The Ladies' Home Journal* (1904)	*Bro-Man-Gel-On;* the one perfect dessert jelly One package	$0.13

Item	Source	Description	Price
Flour	*Greenville News* (Greenville, SC) (1903)	Virginia flour; ground from selected winter wheat	$4.75/bushel
Gelatin	*Ladies' Home Journal* (1904)	*Bro-Man-Gel-On;* the one perfect dessert jello	13¢/package
Jam	*Atlanta Constitution* (1904)	*A&P;* One-pint jar	$0.16/jar
Marshmallows	*Sears, Roebuck* (1902)	Five-pound box	$0.67
Milk Cocoa	*Ladies' Home Journal* (1904)	*Croft's Swiss;* nothing in it but pure pasteurized milk, the finest cocoa beans, and sugar; makes 40 cups	$0.15
Pork Sausage	*Greenville News* (Greenville, SC) (1902)	$0.10/pound	
Prunes	*Greenville News* (Greenville, SC) (1903)	Large jar	$0.10
Soda Crackers	*Sears, Roebuck* (1902)	Twenty-pound box	$0.99
Sweet Pickled Peaches	*Greenville News* (Greenville, SC) (1903)	Large jars	$0.47
Tea	*Atlanta Constitution* (1904)	*Ceylonia Iced;* highest grade	$0.70/pound
Tea	*The Ladies' Home Journal* (1904)	*Ceylon* tea; a delight to all connoisseurs Per package	$0.70
Vanilla Wafers	*The Salem Academy* and *Macaroons Magazine* (1903)		$0.10/dozen
Water	*The New Orleans Picayune* (1903)	*Sparkling Abita;* the perfect table water Per dozen pints	$1.75

Furniture

Item	Source	Description	Price
Banquet Lamp	*Sears, Roebuck* (1902) 25" high	*Cerise;* globe and bowl are of one dark red shade with the velvet finish, making a very soft light at night; $5.90	
Bed	*New York Times* (1901)	White enamelled brass, heavy posts	$2.98
Bed	*Sears, Roebuck* (1902)	Brass trimmed iron; baked white-enamel finish, 1/2 brass-top rail on both head and foot	$4.75
Bed	*Atlanta Constitution* (1904)	Sanitary folding; metal, worth $10	$5.00
Bedroom Suite	*Sears, Roebuck* (1900)	With Cheval dresser; made of hardwood	$21.00
Bedroom Suite	*Sears, Roebuck* (1902)	Full-size bed, dresser, 18" x 34" commode, oak	$16.95
Bookcase	*Ladies' Home Journal* (1904)	Sectioned; can be added to as your library grows; 49" high, art glass doors, quarter-sawed oak or mahogany finish	$18.25
Carpet	*Sears, Roebuck* (1902)	Heavy weight; ingrain; all-wool super ingrain carpet in one of the richest dark red backgrounds and newest bright floral designs shown this season	$0.58/yard
Dining Room Suite	*The New Orleans Picayune* (1903)	*The Union Furniture Company;* suite includes one sideboard, one extension table, six cane seat chairs; in solid golden oak	$23.00

Item	Source	Description	Price
Furniture	*New York Times* (1901)	Parlor suits: 3-piece suite, sofa, arm and wall chair; inlaid frames, carved legs, satin damask cover	$90 to $135
Home Desk	*Ladies' Home Journal* (1904)	28" x 40", tambour front; dust proof; quarter-sawed oak; golden finish	$27.00
Lantern	*Sears, Roebuck* (1902)	*Dietz;* a strongly guarded crystal tubular lantern with a glass front instead of tin	$0.68
Mantel	*Harper's Monthly Magazine* (1903)	The newest and most artistic fireplace mantels are made of ornamental brick in Colonial, Elizabethan, Renaissance, Empire, and other styles; any capable brickmason can set them up with our plans	$12.00 and up
Mattress	*Sears, Roebuck* (1902)	You are in luck to sleep on a climax mattress	$10.00
Parlor Suite	*Sears, Roebuck* (1902)	Three-piece; divan, arm chair, and parlor chair; birch construction, mahogany finish; price depending on fabric selection	$9.95-$11.95
Rocking Chair	*Sears, Roebuck* (1900)	High back, richly carved	$2.85
Rolltop Desk	*Sears, Roebuck* (1902)	All oak; 48" long, 30" wide, 46" high; 5 drawers	$11.95

Garden Equipment & Supplies

Item	Source	Description	Price
Fertilizer	*New York Tribune* (1902)	*Bowker's* bone and wood ash fertilizer; 100-pound bag One ton	$2.00 $25.00
Flower Bulb	*Greenville News* (Greenville, SC) (1902)	Calladium	$0.15
Garden Hose	*Greenville News* (Greenville, SC) (1903)	½" ¾"	$0.10/foot $0.125/foot
Lawn Dressing	*New York Tribune* (1902)	*Bowker's* lawn and garden dressing; anyone can apply, sufficient for one-quarter acre 100 pounds	$3.00
Pruning Shears	*Sears, Roebuck and Co. Catalogue* (1902)	*Henry Pattern* pruning shears; high-grade steel blades	$0.27

Hotel Rates

Item	Source	Description	Price
Hotel Room	*New York Tribune* (1902)	*Hotel Stratford;* ocean front, Atlantic City, New Jersey, European plan Per day	$2.50 to $3.00
Hotel Room	*New York Tribune* (1902)	*The Rittenhouse;* Atlantic City, New Jersey, strictly high-class, refined hotel, cuisine and service unsurpassed Spring rates per day Saturday to Monday	$12 to $17 $4.00
Hotel Room	*New York Tribune* (1902)	*Hotel Windsor;* the most reasonably priced first-class hotel in the world, 140 rooms, American plan Per day, per person	$2.50
Hotel Room	*The New Orleans Picayune* (1903)	*Hotel Denechaud;* New Orleans; per day American plan European plan	$2 and up $1 and up
Hotel Room	*The Salem Academy Magazine* (1903)	*Hotel Jones;* all modern conveniences provided, electrical lights and bells	$2.00/day

Household Products

Item	Source	Description	Price
Alarm Clock	*Sears, Roebuck* (1902)	Oxidized, no battery necessary; 2 lb	$2.50

Item	Source	Description	Price
Asphalt Coating	*Ladies' Home Journal* (1904)	*Elliott's Durable;* will add at least ten years to the life of a new or old leaky shingle, tin, or felt roof	$0.75/gallon
Blanket	*Yorkville Enquirer* (Yorkville, SC) (1900)	In grey and white	$0.50
Carpet	*Ladies' Home Journal* (1904)	Can be selected at your own fireside from our catalogue; Sultan cottage carpets All-wool extra super ingrains	$0.25/yard $0.59/yard
Carpet Sweeper	*Ladies' Home Journal* (1904)	*Bissell;* it is little short of pathetic to see a woman in this age sweeping with a corn broom	$2.00 to $4.00
Carpet Sweeper	*Sears, Roebuck* (1902)	Acme; does not wear out a carpet like a broom does	$1.65
China	*Sears, Roebuck* (1902)	*Waverly;* 100-piece, semi-porcelain dinner set, service for 12; decorated in green, blue, or brown	$5.98
Cleanser	*Sears, Roebuck* (1902)	*Cleanit Liquid;* the best compound in the world for removing paint or grease stains, 4-oz bottle	$0.15/bottle
Curtains	*The State* (Columbia, SC) (1903)	Very handsome patterns	$3.50/pair
Curtains	*New York Tribune* (1902)	*Lord and Taylor* ruffled muslin curtains; Per pair	$1.00 $2.00 $3.00
Fleece Blanket	*Ladies' Home Journal* (1904)	*The Suffolk Sanitary;* beautiful to see, healthful to use, light to handle; full-size pair	$1.00
Floor Mop	*Atlanta Constitution* (1904)	Regular 1$0.09 kind	$0.10
Fountain Brush	*Ladies' Home Journal* (1904)	*The Knickerbocker;* for your bath; 595 little streams and rubber tips bathe and massage at once	$3.50
Glassware	*Sears, Roebuck* (1902)	40-piece outfit; imitation cut glass, includes 6 glass tumblers, 6 goblets, 12 berry saucers"	$1.75
Grille Fencing	*Ladies' Home Journal* (1904)	48" long with pole Decorative and inexpensive 60" long $5.75	$5.00
Kitchen Cabinet	*Ladies' Home Journal* (1904)	*Hoosier;* storeroom, pantry, kitchen table in one	$14.00
Lead Paint	*The State* (Columbia, SC) (1903)	*Masury's Railroad;* it will stay white	$07¼ cents/pound
Light Bulb	*Harper's Monthly Magazine* (1903)	*Block light;* a wonderful, new white light of intense brilliancy produced by the perfect combination of air and any kind of gas—city gas, natural gas and gasoline gas; complete block light	$1.50
Milk Can	*Sears, Roebuck* (1902)	*Wisconsin Pattern;* is in use all over the United States as a wagon can for hauling milk or cream to creameries; 10 gallons	$1.60
Nail Hammer	*Sears, Roebuck* (1902)	*Sears & Roebuck;* 1 ½", 1 lb claw hammer	$0.53
Paint	*Sears, Roebuck* (1902)	Ready mix	$0.98/gallon
Pesticide	*Sears, Roebuck* (1900)	*Strangle Food;* the surest and quickest death to bugs	$0.25/can
Pillow	*The New Orleans Picayune* (1903)	Large size feather pillows covered with best feather ticking	$0.49
Pineapple Knife and Shredder	*Ladies' Home Journal* (1904)	Seams and eyes quickly and easily removed	$0.25

Item	Source	Description	Price
Porch Shades	*Ladies Home Journal* (1904)	*Vudor;* shut out the sun and at the same time let in the air, making the porch a cool, cozy, and comfortable room on warm summer days	$2.00
Prepared Wax	*Ladies' Home Journal* (1904)	*Johnson;* the hardwood floor authorities 1 lb can 8 lb can	$0.60 $2.00
Rubber Gloves	*Ladies' Home Journal* (1904)	*Non-Pa-Reil;* preserve the beauty of the hands	$1.00/pair
Saw	*Sears, Roebuck* (1902)	*Henry Disston & Sons;* 22" panel saw, 12 points	$1.13
Sawed Wood	*The State* (Columbia, SC) (1903)	Palmetto Ice Company	$3.25/cord
Sheet	*The State* (Columbia, SC) (1903)	Bleached; 81" x 90"	$0.98
Silver Tea Strainer	*Ladies' Home Journal* (1904)	Made of solid white metal quadruple silver-plated, ebonized handle four inches long	$0.35
Silverware Set	*Sears, Roebuck* (1902)	26 pieces	$4.95
Sponge	*Ladies' Home Journal* (1904)	*Kleanwell;* for perfect hands, the only thoroughly hygienic and sanitary sponge in existence; Toilet size Bath size	$0.50 $0.75 to $1.00
Tool Chest	*Sears, Roebuck* (1902)	Made of selected chestnut hardwood moldings; sliding tray; 28" x 15" x 14"	$5.40
Wallpaper	*Sears, Roebuck* (1902)	All-purpose for home; dark gray background with beautiful festoons of daisies; includes 9" border; double roll	$0.09
Washcloth	*Ladies' Home Journal* (1904)	*Aercel;* made by an entirely new process; it cleans itself	$0.05

Jewelry

Item	Source	Description	Price
Badge or Class Pin	*Ladies' Home Journal* (1904)	Be loyal to your college, school, class, society, or club Silver plate Sterling silver	$1.00/dozen $2.50
Pocket Flask	*Sears, Roebuck* (1902)	Pocket drinking flask; glass-covered with leather	$0.80
Pocket Watch	*Sears, Roebuck* (1902)	17-jewel, 20-year guarantee a gold-filled case	$11.00
Watch	*Greenville News* (Greenville, SC) (1903)	Nickel, 21 extra-fine red-ruby jewels	$100

Meals

Item	Source	Description	Price
Lunch	*American Silver Flatware* (1901)	*New York Central Railroad;* menu includes: Baked chicken pie; boiled ox tongue with spinach; roast ribs of beef, new golden wax beans, stewed tomatoes, lettuce salad, potato salad, bread and butter, custard pudding	$1.00

Medical Products & Services

Item	Source	Description	Price
Alcohol Cure	*Sears, Roebuck* (1902)	It creates an appetite for food instead of liquor	$0.42
Glasses	*New York Times* (1901)	*Keene's Optical;* free exam with purchase of glasses, Regular Gold-spring eyeglasses	$1.00 $2.50
Glasses	*Sears, Roebuck* (1902)	Gold-filled spectacles	$1.90
Homeopathic Remedies	*Sears, Roebuck* (1902)	Twelve bottles of homeopathic remedies, medicine case, and instruction sheet free	$1.50

Item	Source	Description	Price
Nonprescription Drug	*Sears, Roebuck* (1900)	*Pasteur's Death of Microbes;* will prevent lagrippe, catarrh, consumption, malaria, blood poison, and rheumatism	$0.80/half-gallon
Nonprescription Drug	*Sears, Roebuck* (1900)	*Wonderful Little Liver Pills;* constipation, that most hideous and deadly demon of sickness, is an easy enough thing to cure	$0.12/bottle
Nonprescription Drug	*Sears, Roebuck* (1902)	*Dr. Rose's French Arsenic Complexion Wafers;* for even the coarsest and most repulsive skin and complexion	$0.35/50 wafers
Nonprescription Drug	*Sears, Roebuck* (1902)	*Electric Liniment;* for rheumatism, sprains, wounds, bruises, lame back, contracted muscles	$0.25
Nonprescription Drug	*Greenville News* (Greenville, SC) (1903)	*Castoria;* remedy for constipation, sour stomach, convulsion, and loss of sleep	$0.35/35 doses
Nonprescription Drug	*Greenville News* (Greenville, SC) (1903)	*Wine of Gardui;* 1,500,000 afflicted women have been cured of female diseases	$1.00/bottle
Nonprescription Drug	*Atlanta Constitution* (1904)	*Botanic Blood Balm;* cures eczema, all skin and blood diseases, cold sores	$1.00/bottle
Painkiller	*Sears, Roebuck* (1902)	At the first sign of a cramp, relief comes at once	$0.25
Teeth	*The New Orleans Picayune* (1903)	*National Dental Parlors;* the Celebrated English Teeth, mounted on Sampson Red Rubber Set of teeth Porcelain crowns Gold fillings	 $3.00 $3.00 $0.75
Tobacco Cure	*Sears, Roebuck* (1902)	Can be chewed the same as tobacco	$0.40
Truss	*Sears, Roebuck* (1900)	Double scrotal; we recommend it in very severe cases	$10.00
Truss	*Sears, Roebuck* (1902)	*Lea's;* fitted with improved safety clutch fastenings; elastic; complete with the celebrated water pad; adult size, single adult size, double	 $0.98 $1.75
Witch Hazel Extract	*Sears, Roebuck* (1902)	Useful for sore throat, hemorrhage, wounds, sprains, bruises, sore eyes, stiff joints, burns; ½-pt bottle	$0.12

Motorized Vehicles, Supplies, & Services

Item	Source	Description	Price
Automobile	Joseph J. Schroeder Jr., *The Wonderful World of Automobiles* (1971)	*Hoffman Motor Car;* 8 hp; equal to any $2,500 automobile made [cost in 1902]	$800
Automobile	Schroeder, *The Wonderful World of Automobiles* (1971)	*Rochester Carriage;* new steam model [cost in 1902]	$600
Automobile	*Columbus State Automobile Club* (1902)	*The Santo-Dumont;* in appearance, power, and general results fully the equal of any $6,000 French car on the market	$1,500
Automobile	Schroeder, *The Wonderful World of Automobiles* (1971)	*The Century Tourist;* 7 hp gasoline car; a light touring car at a reasonable price [cost in 1903]	$750
Automobile	Schroeder, *The Wonderful World of Automobiles* (1971)	*The Flint Roadster;* the touring car for two [cost in 1903]	$850

Item	Source	Description	Price
Automobile	Schroeder, *The Wonderful World of Automobiles* (1971)	*Graham Roadster;* complete with lamps and mud guards; wheel steering, if preferred, same price; electric or gasoline [cost in 1903]	$850
Automobile	Schroeder, *The Wonderful World of Automobiles* (1971)	*Jones-Corbin Gasoline Car;* Runabout, 8 hp, 750 lbs Tonneau 9 hp, 1,000 lbs [cost in 1903]	$1,000 $1,500
Automobile	Schroeder, *The Wonderful World of Automobiles* (1971)	*Autocar;* two-passenger; 10 hp; chainless drive; ball-bearing transmission [cost in 1904]	$1,900
Automobile	Schroeder, *The Wonderful World of Automobiles* (1971)	*The Convert;* the ideal light car for town or country [cost in 1904]	$750
Automobile	Schroeder, *The Wonderful World of Automobiles* (1971)	*Crestmobile Model D;* 8 hp to about 1000 lbs weight of vehicle; shaft drive (no chains); slightest possible vibration; [cost in 1904] two-person four-person	 $800 $900
Automobile	*Ladies' Home Journal* (1971)	*Oldsmobile;* quality is apparent in every line Standard runabout Touring runabout Light tonneau	 $650 $750 $950
Automobile	Schroeder, *The Wonderful World of Automobiles* (1971)	*Packard Voiture Grey World;* broke all American records, running a mile in 46 2/5 seconds and a kilometer in .29⅗ seconds [cost in 1904]	$3,000
Automobile	Schroeder, *The Wonderful World of Automobiles* (1971)	*The Santos-Dumont;* high-grade two-cylinder tonneau; fully the equal of any $6,000 French car on the market [cost in 1904]	$1,500
Automobile	*Sears, Roebuck* (1903)	*The Yale Touring Car;* simplicity reduced to a science; starts and stops in a second	$1,750
Motor Bicycle	*Advertising Trade Card* (1902)	*Thomas;* the motor does the work; no hills—no head winds, always coasting—any speed—any distance	$200

Musical Instruments

Item	Source	Description	Price
Autoharp	*Sears, Roebuck* (1902)	23 strings, 5 bars; produces five chords	$2.95
Cornet	*The Housewife* (1903)	*Marceau B Flat cornet;* short model	$6.45
Piano	*New York Times* (1901)	*Waters;* upright; cash price Installments: $10 down and $7/mo	$225 $250
Piano	*Sears, Roebuck* (1902)	Home favorite piano-organ upright; A-grade	$59.45
Violin	*Sears, Roebuck* (1902)	Stradivarius model Genuine Lowendall violin	$2.45 $19.95

Other

Item	Source	Description	Price
Baseball Calendar	*New York Times* (1901)	Part I: July–December 1901	$0.30
Crematory Services	*American* Chronicle (1999)	Adult charges, receptacles free	$30.00
Fine	*New York Tribune* (1902)	Cost of a speeding ticket for automobile dealer Frank Homan of Amsterdam Ave., New York City	$10.00

Item	Source	Description	Price
Fireworks	*Atlanta Constitution* (1904)	Roman candle; 15-ball style	$0.06
Ink	*Sears, Roebuck* (1902)	*Dann's Black;* glass bottle	$0.04/2 ounces
Kid Gloves, Cleaned	*Ladies' Home Journal* (1904)	Scientifically cleaned; ordinary length	$0.10/pair
Palm Reading	*The State* (Columbia, SC) (1903)	Prof. Edwin Chase, psychic; there is no more profitable and interesting way to spend a half-hour; Private reading	$2.00
Pencils	*Sears, Roebuck* (1900)	*Dixon's American Graphite;* round, plain, cedar, 7" long, extra quality	$0.05/dozen
Steam-Cleaning	*The State* (Columbia, SC) (1903)	Blankets	$0.50/pair
Steam-Cleaning	*The State* (Columbia, SC) (1903)	Lace Curtains	$0.35 to $1/pair
Tombstone	*Sears, Roebuck* (1900)	Royal blue Vermont marble; unheard-of value; height 3' 8"	$29.00
Tombstone	*Sears, Roebuck* (1902)	Royal blue marble marker made of unfading Vermont marble; 24" high, 18" wide; 206 lbs	$7.65
Wedding Invitation	*Ladies' Home Journal* (1904)	Worded as you wish, elegant royal vellum stock; 100 cards, double set of envelopes	$2.25

Personal Care Products

Item	Source	Description	Price
Barber's Razor	*Sears, Roebuck* (1900)	Extra hollow ground, 1/2"blade	$1.50
Bust Developer	*Sears, Roebuck* (1902)	*Princess;* combined with the use of the bust cream or food, forms a full, firm, well-developed bust in a few days' use, per bottle	$1.50/bottle
Comb	*Ladies' Home Journal* (1904)	Utility pompadour; throw away your unhealthy hair rat and use the adjustable comb	$0.25
Cream Paste	*Sears, Roebuck* (1902)	*Dan's;* embodies the latest results of advanced chemical research in Department of Adhesives	$0.04/1 ounce tube
Electric Belt	*Sears, Roebuck* (1902)	*Heidelberg;* primary; the 20-gauge current is just the right strength for the pains of the back, loins, and groin	$4.00
Family Soap	*Sears, Roebuck* (1902)	100-bar box	$2.95
Fountain Comb	*Ladies' Home Journal* (1904)	Scalp-Sprayer; applies any liquid to scalp or hair, no waste, merely press the bulb	$1.00
Hair Bleach	*Sears, Roebuck* (1902)	*Blondine;* the famous hair bleach; small trial-size bottle / Large bottle	$0.42 / $0.70
Hair Rolls	*Ladies' Home Journal* (1904)	Cool and sanitary, can't injure the hair, braided-wire, 8" / 12"	$0.10 / $0.15
Human Hair Wig	*Ladies' Home Journal* (1904)	Natural curly pompadour	$2.50
Liniment	*The New Orleans Picayune* (1903)	*Sloan's Liniment;* a genuine remedy / Per bottle	$0.25
Patent Leather Polish	*Ladies' Home Journal* (1904)	*Superb;* best of all polishes for all patent-leather and shiny shoes	$0.10/box
Petroleum Jelly	*Sears, Roebuck* (1902)	Another name for pure vaseline or cosmoline	$0.04/jar
Sanitary Protector	*Sears, Roebuck* (1902)	*The Venus;* no woman who values comfort, cleanliness, and health should be without it	$0.47

Item	Source	Description	Price
Skin Cream	*Harper's Monthly Magazine* (1903)	*Hydrozone;* cures eczema, salt rheum, pimples, ring-worm, itch, ivy poison, acne or other skin troubles Trial size	$0.25
Shoe Dressing	*Ladies' Home Journal* (1904)	*Whittemore's Gilt-Edge Oil;* imparts a beautiful lustre to all black shoes	$0.25/bottle
Soap	*Ladies' Home Journal* (1904)	*Palmolive;* the refinement of soap for gentlefolk	$0.05/bar
Toilet Powder	*The Housewife* (1903)	*Mennen's Borated Talcum Toilet Powder;* a positive relief for prickly heat, chafing and sunburn Per can	$0.25
Toothbrush	*Sears, Roebuck* (1902)	Good four-row tooth brush, good bristles	$0.04
Toothbrush	*Sears, Roebuck* (1902)	The highest grade of fine imported French tooth brushes	$0.25
Trimmer Shears	*Sears, Roebuck* (1902)	8" straight trimmer, Japanned handles, steel-laid blade	3/$0.06

Publications

Item	Source	Description	Price
Book	*New York Tribune* (1902)	*My Early Travels and Adventures in America and Asia* by Henry M. Stanley, two volumes Regularly Sale	$3.00 $0.75
Book	*Harper's Monthly Magazine* (1903)	*A History of the American People* by Woodrow Wilson in five volumes; a new, epoch-making, work—the only complete narrative history of the great Republic in existence today	$25.00
Catalogue	*Sears, Roebuck* (1900)	*Sears, Roebuck & Co. Catalogue*	$0.15/year
Catalogue	*Sears, Roebuck* (1902)	*Sears, Roebuck & Co. Catalogue*	$0.50/year
Cook Book	*The Ladies' Home Journal* (1904)	From Grandmother's time until now; every improvement, as well as famous recipes of Grandma's day. Marion Harland's *New Complete Cook Book*	$2.00
Magazine	*Ladies' Home Journal* (1904)	*Popular Mechanics;* Per copy Per year Year's subscription and easy electrical experiments	$0.10 $1.00 $1.50
Newspaper	*The Daily Picayune* (New Orleans, LA) (1900)	*The Daily Picayune*	$0.10
Newspaper	*Yorkville Enquirer* (Yorkville, SC) (1900)	*Yorkville Enquirer;* twice weekly	$0.05
Newspaper	*New York Tribune* (1902)	*New York Tribune* Sunday Daily 12 Months	$0.05 $0.03 $10.00
Periodical	*The Philistine*	*The Philistine;* a periodical of protests Monthly	$1.00

Real Estate

Item	Source	Description	Price
Apartment Building	*New York Times* (1901)	For sale; 20-family, cold-water tenement; five-story; rents over $2,900/year	$3,000
House Plans	*The Ladies' Home Journal* (1904)	Large book of 125 plans giving views, plans, description and estimate to build	$0.25
House	*New York Times* (1901)	Country homes in the Palisades	$800
House	*New York Times* (1901)	Prospect Park South; 10–14 room houses, tiled vestibules and two baths	$10,000 + up

Item	Source	Description	Price
House	*New York Times* (1901)	South Midwood, Flatbush Avenue, Brooklyn; 35 minutes from New York City	$7,000 to $12,000
House	*Greenville News* (Greenville, SC) (1903)	Seven-room house, West Washington St., 90'x 200'	$2,800
House	*Ladies' Home Journal* (1904)	California; seashore cottage of Swiss design contains eight rooms and bath	$2,200
House	*Ladies' Home Journal* (1904)	California; shingle bungalow of five rooms; building cost	$1,200
House	*Ladies' Home Journal* (1904)	California; most attractive and spacious cottage of four rooms and bathroom	$1,100
House	*Ladies' Home Journal* (1904)	California; teacher's bungalow and artist's studio	$2,000
Room	*New York Tribune* (1902)	Room with bath; private halls, elegant suite, elevator, hall boy service; Apply at 30 West 128th Street, New York City Per month	$50.00
Room	*New York Tribune* (1902)	Modern, high-class, absolutely fireproof apartment 1109 Madison Avenue Per year	$1,600

Sewing Equipment & Supplies

Item	Source	Description	Price
Broadcloth	*The State* (Columbia, SC) (1903)	52" wide in all colors	$1.00/yard
Cloth	*Sears, Roebuck* (1900)	Fancy percale; both dress and shirting styles in figures, scrolls, and fancy stripes	$0.10/yard
Cloth	*New York Times* (1901)	French batiste all-wool fabrics; reg $0.50	$0.38
Cloth	*Southern Christian Advocate* (1902)	500 yards flannelettes; reg $0.15	$0.10
Cloth	*Sears, Roebuck* (1902)	Broadcloth in all-fashion colors	$1.00/yard
Cloth	*The State* (Columbia, SC) (1903)	Granite stripe madras; new weaves for winter waists	$0.25 to $0.35/yard
Pants Cuffs	*Sears, Roebuck* (1900)	Highwater; enables the wearer to quickly transform regular trousers into bicycle, golf, or riding breeches	$0.25/pair
Pattern	*Ladies' Home Journal* (1904)	Baby wardrobe; 35 patterns for baby's long clothes	$0.25
Sewing Machine	*Sears, Roebuck* (1902)	*Minnesota;* automatic drop desk cabinet	$23.20
Sewing Needle Case	*Sears, Roebuck* (1902)	Contains four papers of needles, also other needles and pins	$0.02
Thimble	*Sears, Roebuck* (1902)	Solid silver Solid 14-karat gold	$0.15 $3.75

Sports Equipment

Item	Source	Description	Price
Bicycle	*New York Times* (1901)	*Viking;* special offer	$15.50
Bicycle	*Sears, Roebuck* (1902)	Lady's	$8.95
Bicycle Tire	*New York Times* (1901)	*H. Rausch*	$2.65
Book	*Harper's Monthly Magazine* (1903)	*Practical Golf* by Walter J. Travis, Former Amateur Golf Champion of the United States; profusely illustrated from photographs	$2.00

Item	Source	Description	Price
Carver	*Sears, Roebuck* (1902)	Fancy blade stag-handle carver; 8" knife and fork	$1.62/pair
Field Glasses	*Sears, Roebuck* (1902)	Highest grade genuine Jena	$12.95
Jackknife	*Sears, Roebuck* (1902)	Stag handle, brass lining, finished inside and out	$0.47
League Baseball	*Sears, Roebuck* (1900)	*S. R. & Co.;* made entirely by hand, by old, experienced workmen only	$0.90
Police Revolver	*Sears, Roebuck* (1900)	*Colt;* side-ejecting revolver; 32-caliber, nickle plated	$12.50
Shotgun	*Sears, Roebuck* (1902)		$27.75
Shotgun	*Harper's Monthly Magazine* (1903)	*Iver Johnson* top snap	$7.00

Telephone Equipment & Services

Telegraph	Susan J. Douglas, *Inventing American Broadcasting* (1987)	Charge to steamship companies to report the arrival of ships at Nantucket [cost in 1901]	$5.00/vessel
Telephone Charges	Douglas, *Telephone: The First Hundred Years* (1987)	Residential rates (Cleveland) for 1901	$48.00/year
Telephone Charges	Douglas, *Telephone: The First Hundred Years* (1987)	Business Rates (Asheville, North Carolina) for 1903	$40.00

Tobacco Products

Cigar	*The New Orleans Picayune* (1903)	*Tulane College* cigar; the leading five-cent cigar; Union Labor; Not in the Trust	$0.05
Cigar	*Advertising Trade Card* (1901)		$0.05
Pipe	*Sears, Roebuck* (1902)	*Applewood;* wood pipe with silver derrule and rubber stem, 2 1/2" long	$0.04
Pipe	*Sears, Roebuck* (1902)	*Yale Student;* heavy briar pipe with bent Chinese amber bit, heavy Bull-Bitch shape	3/$0.09

Travel & Transportation

Cruise	*New York Tribune* (1902)	European Tour, 103-day trip to include Gibraltar, Morocco, Spain, Italy, Austria, Switzerland, Germany, the Rhine, Belgium, France, England	$240 to $975
Ship Fare	*New York Tribune* (1902)	Dominion Line; fast twin screw service Boston to Queenstown to Liverpool	
		Saloon	$50.00
		Second saloon	$40.00
Ship Fare	*New York Tribune* (1902)	Mediterranean, service from New York to Gibraltar, Naples, Genoa	
		Saloon	$75.00 and up
		Second saloon	$50.00
Taxi Fare	*New York Tribune* (1902)	Carriage ride from White Star pier in New York City to any point in the city south of 59th Street	
		One person	$2.00
		Two or three persons	$3.00
		Four persons	$4.00

MISCELLANY 1900-1904

Jack Zelig, (1882–1912): Gang Leader and Murderer

A handsome, brutish killer, Big Jack's services were always available for hire to any bidder, high or low. There is no record of the gang leader ever turning down any job of violence. A Zelig henchman once gave the police Big Jack's price list:

Slash of cheek with knife	$1–10
Shot in leg	1–25
Shot in arm	5–25
Throwing a bomb	5–50
Murder	10–100

The Encyclopedia of American Crime

Liquor Licenses

In 1900, licensed retail liquor saloons annually paid $500 for a license in Chicago, but were charged $1,100 in Philadelphia. In Boston, innkeepers paid $2000, common victualers, $1,100, while common victualers, second, and third calls, $500. In Bridgeport, Conn., the amount of the license ran $450—reduced to $250 for the sale of beer only. San Francisco had one of the nation's lowest license fees at $84 a year.

Bulletin of the Department of Labor, September 1901

Nickelodeon

The Sears Roebuck catalog of 1902 offered prospective operators the Edison Projection Kinetoscope (with either an electric arc lamp or a calcium burner) for $105 and a wide selection of titles, some 20 minutes in length. THE FIVE CENT THEATER IS HERE TO STAY . . . almost any vacant store room can be made into a five-cent theater.

Sears and Wards, The First Hundred Years Are the Toughest

Automobile Production, 1903

Complete statistics from 85 per cent of the automobile manufacturers in the United States to September 3 indicate that the actual sales for the year 1903 will be 11,000 cars, valued at $12,000,000. This is double the business of 1902, to which must be added to the foreign importation of 200 cars, valued at $800,000. The importation of foreign cars is about the same as last year. Trade in foreign-made cars is probably at its maximum and will slowly decline, as the American manufacturers are rapidly supplying the demand.

Scientific American, January 1904

Twenty-five Flower Beds for Little Money

The prices of the various tender plants, as begonias, geraniums, cannas and coleus, will run at the rate of $5 to $8 a hundred; dahlias, $8 to $10; roses about $10; and hardy plants as day lilies, phloxes and ferns about $10 a hundred. In fewer numbers the prices may be a trifle higher.

Ladies' Home Journal, May 1904

Diamond in the Rough

There has been exhibited in London a diamond which is the second largest gem of its description in the world. It weighs 336 ½ carats. It is of a yellowish color and worth about $10,000. If the color had been better, the stone would have been worth a fabulous amount. It was recently extracted from the Ottos Kopje diamond mines at Kimberly.

Scientific American, January 1904

MISCELLANY 1900-1904

Union Dispute

Racine, Wis.—This morning twenty tin shops of Racine went out on strike. The minimum wage scale in the past has been 22 ½ cents an hour, nine hours a day. Their demand is for a minimum scale of 25 cents an hour, nine hours a day. The bosses refused to give the increase in part, claiming that some of the men were worth more than others and refusing to pay it to this class of mechanics. The maximum scale is satisfactory and ranges from 25 cents to 35 cents an hour.

Milwaukee Journal (1901)

The Chorus Girl of To-Day

There are now employed in New York in musical plays between 1,200 and 1,500 women who appear in the chorus; the salaries range anywhere from $15 to $30 a week. Taking a mean average of $20 a week for the chorus girl, it will be seen that no less than $24,000 is paid out every week in chorus girl salaries alone. In a season of thirty weeks the expenditures in salaries for chorus girls would amount to no less than $720,000.

New York Times (1903)

Barbers Wanted

Wanted—men to learn barber trade; can nearly earn expenses before finishing; position waiting graduates; $18 weekly; a few weeks completes course.

Atlanta Constitution (1904)

Men's Salaries Compared to Women's

A chart showing the weekly wages in 2,846 Minnesota business establishments in 1890, showed that 13.79 percent of the male workers earned less than $8 per week compared to 81.33 percent of the female workers at that wage. The highest percentage of male employees received from $9 to $15 per week.

Seventh Biennial Report of the Bureau of Labor of the State of Minnesota, 1899–1900

HISTORICAL SNAPSHOT
1905-1909

1905

- The newly formed Industrial Workers of the World (IWW) attacks AF of L for accepting capitalist system
- A New York law limiting hours of work in the baking industry to 60 per week is ruled unconstitutional by the Supreme Court
- U.S. auto production reaches 15,000 cars/yr, up from 2,500 in 1899
- William Randolph Hearst acquires *Cosmopolitan* magazine for $400,000
- Royal Typewriter Company founded by New York financier Thomas Fortune Ryan

1906

- Excavation of the Panama Canal begins
- Armstrong Linoleum introduced
- Sales of Jell-O reach nearly $1 million
- A-1 Sauce introduced in the United States by Hartford's G. F. Heublein & Bros.
- Planters Nut and Chocolate Company created
- Oklahoma admitted to the Union

- C. W. Post creates Post Toasties cornflakes
- Upton Sinclair's *The Jungle* exposes conditions in U.S. meat-packing industry
- Samuel Hopkins Adams's *The Great American Fraud* exposes the fraudulent claims of many patent medicines

1907

- Economic crises abound with the collapse of the New York Stock Market and runs on banks
- Sears, Roebuck distributes 3 million copies of spring catalogue
- Cadillac is advertised at $800, a Ford Model K at $2,800, horses for $150 to $300
- Wireless telegraphy service links U.S. to Ireland
- Movie projectionist Donald H. Bell founds Bell and Howell Co., pioneers in motion picture photography and projection
- The first canned tuna fish is packed in California

1908

- U.S. banks close as economic depression deepens

- Model-T Ford introduced; flivver costs $850.50
- A C Spark Plug Co. founded by Buick Motor Car president W. C. Durant
- Two subway tunnels open to traffic in New York City
- President Theodore Roosevelt calls White House conference on conservation

1909

- 20,000 members of Ladies' Waist Maker's Union stage three-month strike, win most demands
- Westinghouse Electric is placed in receivership
- General Motors acquires Cadillac from Henry H. Leland for $4.5 million
- $17 million Queensboro bridge opens in New York City
- John D. Rockefeller gives $350 million for worldwide medical research
- Copyright Act of 1909, significantly extending the rights of authorship, approved by Congress and becomes law

SELECTED INCOME 1905-1909

Job	Source	Description	Pay
Actress	*American Chronicle* (1999)	Salary of Lillian Russell for 33-week engagement at Proctor's 23rd Street Theater in New York	$100,000
Actress	Vincent Tomkins, ed., *American Decades: 1900-1909* (1996)	Earnings of Sarah Bernhardt from "The Divine Sarah" tour in 1906	$1 million
Actuary	*New York Times* (1907)	Western insurance concern	$1,000– $12,000/yr
Bookkeeper and Clerk	*New York Times* (1907)	Manufacturing concern	$780/yr
Boxer	Tomkins, ed., *American Decades: 1900-1909* (1996)	Purse of Jack Johnson for winning Heavyweight Boxing Championship in 1908	$5,000
Boxer	*American Chronicle* (1999)	Purse for heavyweight championship fight between Tommy Burns and Jack Johnson in Sydney, Australia in 1908	$30,000
Cook	*New York Tribune* (1908)	Available through Miss FitzGerald Employment Bureau	$35/month
Cook	*New York Tribune* (1908)	Swedish preferred, capable of soups, entrees, desserts; good managers	$30/month
Department Manager	*Chicago Tribune* (1905)	Familiar with farm implements	$2,000/yr
Domestic	*San Francisco Examiner* (1907)	Chambermaid, Lake Tahoe, fares paid both ways	$25/mo
Draftsman	*Chicago Tribune* (1905)	Electrical experience	$75–$125/mo
Electrical Worker	*Chicago Tribune* (1905)	Machine shop	$4/day
Governess	*New York Tribune* (1908)	Nursery governess	$40/month
Navy Serviceman	*Chicago Tribune* (1905)	Includes board, lodging, medical, $60 uniform free	$16–$70/mo
Newspaper Worker	*Chicago Tribune* (1905)	$50/mo	
Nobel Prize	*American Chronicle* (1999)	Theodore Roosevelt's cash award for winning The Nobel Peace Prize recognizing his efforts to mediate the end of the Russo-Japanese War	$40,000
Nurse	*New York Tribune* (1908)	For six-year-old girl	$25/month
Professional Football Player	*American Chronicle* (1999)	Per game pay of Willie Heston to play professional football	$600
Salesman	*Chicago Tribune* (1905)	Man to travel, new line of goods, Chicago	$80/mo
Singer	*New York Times* (1907)	Bass and tenor	$300–$500/yr
Stenographer	*Chicago Tribune* (1905)		$15/mo
Vaudeville Performer	*American Chronicle* (1999)	Weekly pay of Vaudeville headliner Buffalo Bill Cody	$3,000

Job	Source	Description	Pay
Waitress	*San Francisco Examiner* (1907)	First class city hotel, room in or out	$30 or $35/mo

CONSUMER EXPENDITURES 1909

(Per Capita)

Expenditure Type	1909	Expenditure Type	1909
Clothing	$30.00	Health Insurance	NR
Food	$81.43	Personal Business	$9.61
Auto Purchases	$1.85	Personal Care	$2.88
Auto Parts	0.59	Tobacco	$6.33
Gas & Oil	$1.36	Local Transport	$5.12
Housing	$61.48	Intercity Transport	$2.97
Furniture	$3.25	Recreation	$9.49
Utilities	$4.00	Religion/Welfare Activities	$9.05
Telephone & Telegraph	$.91	Private Education & Research	$4.59
Physicians	$3.24	Per Capita Consumption	$318.42
Dentists	$.91		

INVESTMENTS 1905-1909

Investment	1905	1906	1907	1908	1909
Yield, One-year Corporate Bonds	3.50	4.75	4.87	5.10	4.03
Term Interest rates, 4–6 Months, Prime Commercial Paper	5.18	6.25	6.66	5.00	4.67
Basic Yield, Common Stocks, Total	3.53	3.96	5.38	4.93	4.31
Index of Common Stocks (1941−1943=10)	8.99	9.64	7.84	7.78	9.71

COMMON STOCKS, CLOSING PRICE AND YIELD, FIRST BUSINESS DAY OF YEAR

	1905	1906	1907	1908	1909
Allis Chalmers pfd	21 ⅜	22 ¼	16 ⅞	5 ½	15 ½
AT & T	145	138	135	99 ½	127 ½
American Tobacco pfd	145	106	96 ½	72 ¾	93 ½
Anaconda	109	289	290	29 ¼	50 ½
B&O	104 ⅞	113 ⅛	119 ½	82 ½	110
Bethlehem Steel		33 ½	18 ⅛	9 ½	24
Corn Products	21 ¼	18 ⅝	22	10 ⅞	17 ⅛
General Electric	187	177	160	112 ½	157
IBM					
International 1 Harvester					65
(Recapitalization: for 2 shares of common stock exchanged for 1 share of common and one share of preferred, 1/8/07)					
National Biscuit	57 ¼	118 ½	77	67	98 ½
U.S. Steel	29 ⅞	43	48 ¼	26 ¾	53 ⅜
Western Union	92 ½	93 ⅜	83 ½	55	69 ½
(1 1/4% stock dividend, 1/15/08)					
(1 1/4% stock dividend, 4/15/08)					

STANDARD JOBS 1905-1909

Job Type	1905	1906	1907	1908	1909
Average of all Industries, excl. farm labor	$559/yr	$571/yr	$593/yr	$564/yr	$594/yr
Average of all Industries, incl. farm labor	$510/yr	$523/yr	$542/yr	$519/yr	$544/yr
Bituminous Coal Mining	30¢/hr	29¢/hr	29¢/hr	29¢/hr	28¢/hr
Avg hrs/wk	51.60	51.60	51.60	51.60	51.60
Building Trades, Union workers	48¢/hr	50¢/hr	51¢/hr	51¢/hr	45¢/hr
Avg hrs/wk	45.90	45.70	45.60	45.60	46.10
Clerical Workers in Mfg. & Steam RR	$1076/yr	$1074/yr	$1091/yr	$1111/yr	$1136/yr
Domestics	$278/yr	$286/yr	$316/yr	$580/yr	$420/yr
Farm Labor	$302/yr	$315/yr	$319/yr	$324/yr	$328/yr
Federal Employees, Executive Depts.	$1072/yr	$1085/yr	$1094/yr	$1102/yr	$1106/yr
Finance, Insurance, & Real Estate	$1115/yr	$1146/yr	$1180/yr	$1218/yr	$1263/yr
Gas & Electricity Workers	$543/yr	$581/yr	$623/yr	$595/yr	$618/yr
Lower-Skilled Labor	$484/yr	$495/yr	$442/yr	$496/yr	$443/yr
Manufacturing, Payroll	18¢/hr	19¢/hr	18¢/hr	18¢/hr	15¢/hr
Avg hrs/wk	60.70	60.60	60.30	60.20	60.10
Manufacturing, Union Workers	38¢/hr	39¢/hr	40¢/hr	39¢/hr	39¢/hr
Avg hrs/wk	51.10	51	50.80	50.40	50.30
Medical/Health Services Workers	$292/yr	$296/yr	$306/yr	$313/yr	$326/yr
Ministers	$773/yr	$759/yr	$831/yr	$833/yr	$831/yr
Nonprofit Org. Workers	$689/yr	$677/yr	$741/yr	$743/yr	$741/yr
Postal Employees	37¢/hr	38¢/hr	40¢/hr	41¢/hr	38¢/hr
Avg hrs/wk	48.00	48.00	48.00	48.00	48.00
Public School Teachers	$392/yr	$409/yr	$431/yr	$455/yr	$476/yr
State and Local Govt. Workers	$646/yr	$664/yr	$694/yr	$695/yr	$696/yr
Steam Railroads, Wage Earners	$589/yr	$607/yr	$661/yr	$667/yr	$644/yr
Street Railway Workers	$646/yr	$662/yr	$658/yr	$650/yr	$671/yr
Telegraph Ind. Workers	$592/yr	$581/yr	$635/yr	$639/yr	$622/yr
Telephone Ind. Workers	$401/yr	$412/yr	$412/yr	$420/yr	$430/yr
Wholesale and Retail Trade Workers	$393/yr	$580/yr	$593/yr	$609/yr	$561/yr

FOOD BASKET 1905-1909

Commodity	Year	New York	Atlanta	Chicago	Denver	Los Angeles
Apples, Evaporated, per pound	1905	12¢	10¢	12¢	12¢	10¢
	1906	12¢	12¢	13¢	12¢	13¢
	1907	NR	NR	NR	NR	NR
	1908	NR	NR	NR	NR	NR
	1909	NR	NR	NR	NR	NR
Beans, Dry, per quart	1905	10¢	9.44¢	9.33¢	9.38¢	7.50¢
	1906	10.13¢	9.44¢	9.33¢	9.38¢	7.50¢
	1907	NR	NR	NR	NR	NR
	1908	NR	NR	NR	NR	NR
	1909	NR	NR	NR	NR	NR
Beef, Fresh, Roasts, per pound	1905	13.71¢	13.67¢	10.03¢	11¢	12.80¢
	1906	13.02¢	13.98¢	10.29¢	11.14¢	13.35¢
	1907	NR	NR	NR	NR	NR
	1908	NR	NR	NR	NR	NR
	1909	NR	NR	NR	NR	NR
Beef, Steaks (Round), per pound	1905	17.23¢	13.64¢	10.80¢	11.67¢	12.50¢
	1906	17.93¢	13.33¢	10.77¢	11.94¢	12.50¢
	1907	18.13¢	13.75¢	14.25¢	15.20¢	12.50¢
	1908	18.40¢	15¢	14.85¢	15.83¢	12.50¢
	1909	19.20¢	17.50¢	15.93¢	16.55¢	13.19¢
Beef, Salt (Corned), per pound	1905	7.50¢	12.50¢	8.81¢	6.33¢	9¢
	1906	7.72¢	12.50¢	7.31¢	6.33¢	9¢
	1907	NR	NR	NR	NR	NR
	1908	NR	NR	NR	NR	NR
	1909	NR	NR	NR	NR	NR
Bread, Wheat, per loaf	1905	5¢	5¢	5¢	5¢	5¢
	1906	5¢	5¢	5¢	5¢	5¢
	1907	NR	NR	NR	NR	NR
	1908	NR	NR	NR	NR	NR
	1909	NR	NR	NR	NR	NR
Butter, per pound	1905	27.97¢	29.47¢	23.08¢	26.54¢	30.14¢
	1906	29.86¢	29.67¢	23.67¢	26.63¢	33.03¢
	1907	33.14¢	32.75¢	32.04¢	30.28¢	37.64¢
	1908	33.42¢	31.81¢	31.42¢	32.69¢	36.67¢
	1909	35.19¢	37.05¢	32.43¢	34.03¢	37.78¢
Cheese, per pound	1905	17.23¢	16.62¢	17.13¢	18.44¢	20¢
	1906	18.50¢	18.54¢	18.37¢	18.44¢	20¢
	1907	NR	NR	NR	NR	NR
	1908	NR	NR	NR	NR	NR
	1909	NR	NR	NR	NR	NR
Chickens, per pound	1905	16.71¢	16.56¢	15.03¢	15.46¢	23.32¢
	1906	17.35¢	16.97¢	14.78¢	15.49¢	24.5¢
	1907	17.83¢	18.67¢	14.39¢	15.31¢	20¢
	1908	18.36¢	22¢	15.29¢	16.22¢	20¢
	1909	19.02¢	20.83¢	16.22¢	18.03¢	22.33¢
Coffee, per pound	1905	18.33¢	25¢	16.80¢	21.67¢	25¢
	1906	19.41¢	25¢	17¢	22.43¢	25¢
	1907	NR	NR	NR	NR	NR
	1908	NR	NR	NR	NR	NR
	1909	NR	NR	NR	NR	NR
Cornmeal, per pound	1905	3.42¢	1.95¢	2.38¢	2.25¢	2.75¢
	1906	3.09¢	2.06¢	2.38¢	2.25¢	2.75¢
	1907	3.17¢	1.96¢	2.57¢	2.56¢	2.97¢
	1908	3.25¢	2.22¢	2.62¢	2.56¢	3.14¢
	1909	3.33¢	2.62¢	2.94¢	2.56¢	3.03¢

Commodity	Year	New York	Atlanta	Chicago	Denver	Los Angeles
Eggs, per dozen	1905	31.93¢	22.69¢	23.32¢	25.69¢	30.69¢
	1906	32.85¢	24.88¢	23.86¢	24.86¢	32.78¢
	1907	32.40¢	23.79¢	26.63¢	27.92¢	32.33¢
	1908	33.38¢	25.65¢	27.62¢	27.64¢	31.95¢
	1909	35.17¢	27.92¢	29.11¢	29.17¢	33.61¢
Fish, Fresh, per pound	1905	12.09¢	11.22¢	10.40¢	14.67¢	10¢
	1906	12.28¢	11.83¢	11.75¢	15¢	10¢
	1907	NR	NR	NR	NR	NR
	1908	NR	NR	NR	NR	NR
	1909	NR	NR	NR	NR	NR
Fish, Salt, per pound	1905	13.24¢	13.96¢	13.13¢	13.87¢	8.33¢
	1906	14.14¢	13.16¢	13.25¢	13.87¢	8.33¢
	1907	NR	NR	NR	NR	NR
	1908	NR	NR	NR	NR	NR
	1909	NR	NR	NR	NR	NR
Flour, Wheat, per one-eighth Barrel Bag	1905	82.84¢	82.22¢	75.93¢	63.47¢	75¢
	1906	78.96¢	81.81¢	63.94¢	49.93¢	75¢
	1907	81.92¢	77.17¢	74¢	$1.18	$1.31
	1908	84.25¢	79.84¢	78.93¢	$1.34	$1.36
	1909	75¢	87.75¢	84.99¢	$1.54	$1.51
Lard, per pound	1905	12¢	10¢	10.88¢	12.50¢	12.50¢
	1906	12.88¢	12.08¢	11.42¢	12.50¢	13.75¢
	1907	14.83¢	12.50¢	12.42¢	15¢	15¢
	1908	14.33¢	12.33¢	12.17¢	15¢	15¢
	1909	15¢	15¢	13.50¢	15¢	15¢
Milk, Fresh, per quart	1905	6¢	8.33¢	7¢	6.25¢	8.25¢
	1906	6¢	8.33¢	7¢	6.40¢	8.50¢
	1907	8.17¢	8.33¢	7¢	7.14¢	9.50¢
	1908	8.17¢	8.33¢	7.17¢	7.14¢	9¢
	1909	8.17¢	8.33¢	7.17¢	7.54¢	9¢
Molasses, per gallon	1905	60¢	50¢	61.67¢	75¢	60¢
	1906	60¢	50¢	65¢	75¢	60¢
	1907	NR	NR	NR	NR	NR
	1908	NR	NR	NR	NR	NR
	1909	NR	NR	NR	NR	NR
Mutton and Lamb, per pound	1905	13.17¢	15.33¢	12¢	15¢	12.50¢
	1906	13.83¢	17.54¢	12.58¢	15¢	13.54¢
	1907	16.67¢	20¢	15¢	15¢	15¢
	1908	16.67¢	20¢	15.33¢	15.17¢	15¢
	1909	16.67¢	17.54¢	16.33¢	15.42¢	15¢
Pork, Fresh, per pound	1905	16.92¢	15¢	11.75¢	12.50¢	15.17¢
	1906	18.17¢	15¢	12.46¢	12.50¢	17¢
	1907	17.33¢	16.67¢	14.67¢	13.75¢	17.50¢
	1908	16.67¢	19.58¢	15¢	13.75¢	17.50¢
	1909	17¢	20.83¢	15.67¢	16.83¢	20.83¢
Pork, Salt, Bacon, per pound	1905	17.25¢	12.88¢	15.17¢	20¢	20¢
	1906	21¢	15.67¢	17.67¢	20¢	20¢
Pork, Bacon, Sliced, per pound	1907	20¢	20¢	23¢	20¢	25¢
	1908	20¢	20.83¢	26¢	20¢	26.67¢
	1909	20¢	25¢	28¢	20¢	30¢
Pork, Salt, Dry or Pickled, per pound	1905	14¢	10¢	12.58¢	12. ¢	12.50¢
	1906	14.67¢	12.29¢	12.67¢	12¢	13.54¢
Ham, Smoked, Sliced, per pound	1907	23.33¢	20¢	19.67¢	25¢	30¢
	1908	24.33¢	20.83¢	23¢	31.67¢	30¢
	1909	25¢	25¢	23.33¢	30¢	30¢
Pork, Salt, Ham, per pound	1905	15.67¢	19.50¢	13.67¢	25¢	25¢
	1906	16.58¢	20¢	15.17¢	25¢	25¢
	1907	NR	NR	NR	NR	NR
	1908	NR	NR	NR	NR	NR
	1909	NR	NR	NR	NR	NR

Commodity	Year	New York	Atlanta	Chicago	Denver	Los Angeles
Potatoes, Irish, per peck	1905	32.56¢	22.58¢	16.92¢	15.50¢	22.25¢
	1906	33.33¢	25¢	15.67¢	20.38¢	24.56¢
	1907	NR	29.83¢	21¢	$1.54 (per 100 lbs)	$1.95 (per 100 lbs)
	1908	NR	25.83¢	25.17¢	$1.58 (per 100 lbs)	$1.60 (per 100 lbs)
	1909	NR	28.33¢	24¢	$1.58 (per 100 lbs)	$1.79 (per 100 lbs)
Prunes, per pound	1905	10¢	10¢	8¢	10.63¢	5.25¢
	1906	12¢	10¢	9¢	12.50¢	6.81¢
	1907	NR	NR	NR	NR	NR
	1908	NR	NR	NR	NR	NR
	1909	NR	NR	NR	NR	NR
Rice, per pound	1905	8.67¢	7.33¢	9¢	9.25¢	8.33¢
	1906	10¢	9¢	9.42¢	9.25¢	8.33¢
	1907	NR	NR	NR	NR	NR
	1908	NR	NR	NR	NR	NR
	1909	NR	NR	NR	NR	NR
Sugar, per pound	1905	5.43¢	5.71¢	5.71¢	6.49¢	5.93¢
	1906	5.14¢	5.50¢	5¢	5.85¢	5.49¢
	1907	5.43¢	5.61¢	5.42¢	5.92¢	5.88¢
	1908	5.43¢	5.88¢	5.42¢	6.13¢	6.49¢
	1909	5.43¢	5.72¢	5.50¢	5.83¢	6.25¢
Tea, per pound	1905	50¢	50¢	50¢	60¢	50¢
	1906	50¢	50¢	50¢	60¢	50¢
	1907	NR	NR	NR	NR	NR
	1908	NR	NR	NR	NR	NR
	1909	NR	NR	NR	NR	NR
Veal, per pound	1905	22.75¢	15.42¢	16.83¢	20¢	20¢
	1906	25¢	16.46¢	16.83¢	20¢	22.92¢
	1907	NR	NR	NR	NR	NR
	1908	NR	NR	NR	NR	NR
	1909	NR	NR	NR	NR	NR
Vinegar, per gallon	1905	25¢	30¢	20¢	40¢	50¢
	1906	25¢	30¢	20¢	40¢	50¢
	1907	NR	NR	NR	NR	NR
	1908	NR	NR	NR	NR	NR
	1909	NR	NR	NR	NR	NR

SELECTED PRICES 1905-1909

Item	Source	Description	Price
Alcohol			
Ale	*Chicago Tribune* (1905)	*Ye Olde Inn*	$1.50/dozen
Beer	*Atlanta Constitution* (1905)	*Bohemian;* the absolute purity and healthfulness of A. B. C. Beer makes it the safest and best for home use	$1.50/12 pints
Corn Whiskey	*The State* (Columbia, SC) (1905)	*Amulet;* five years old, copper distilled	$2.65/gallon
Whiskey	*The State* (Columbia, SC) (1905)	*Cockade Rye;* 5 years old, smooth and mellow	$3.15/gallon
Whiskey	*The State* (Columbia, SC) (1909)	*Clark's Pure Rye;* 100 Proof	$5.00/gallon
Whiskey	*Atlanta Constitution* (1905)	*H. O. Wise Pure Rye;* Double copper distilled and aged	$3.50/gallon
Apparel, Children's			
Hosiery	*Ladies' Home Journal* (1905)	*Black Cat;* for boys & girls; the highest quality of yarn, the fastest of dyes	$0.25/pair
Knit Waist	*Sears, Roebuck and Co. Catalogue* (1908)	*E. Z. Waist;* thoroughly reinforced over the shoulders and down the back with tubular bands. For boys or girls	$0.19
Shoes	*New York Times* (1905)	Boy's	$1.75
Suit	*San Francisco Examiner* (1908)	*Ruf Wear* for boys; Ruf Wear pertains to the strength of the cloth	$5.00
Underwear	*New York Tribune* (1908)	*Porosknit underwear;* coolest for summer wear Shirts Union suit	$0.25 $0.50
Apparel, Men's			
Collar	*Century Magazine* (1909)	*Arrow* collars; most of the successful styles appear first in *Arrow* collars Olympic 2 3/8-inch-high Carlton 2 1/8-inch-high	$0.15 each
Coat	*New York Times* (1907)	Australian opossum fur automobile coats, long model venetian yoke; regularly $50	$37.50
Coat	*New York Times* (1907)	Raccoon fur automobile coat	$47.50
Cuffs	*Century Magazine* (1909)	*Arrow* cuffs	$0.25/pair
Gloves	*New York Times* (1907)	*Perrin;* regularly $2	$1.30
Handkerchief	*Chicago Tribune* (1905)	White linen hemstitched handkerchiefs; 1/4" to 1/2" hem	$0.50
Hat	*Chicago Tribune* (1905)	Bishop's hat	$3.00
Hat	*New York Times* (1907)	Derby (clear nutria)	$2.75

Item	Source	Description	Price
Hat	*New York Times* (1909)	Deluxe hats	$6.00
Overcoat	*New York Times* (1905)	Spring weight	$15 to $35
Pajamas	*Chicago Tribune* (1907)	Serviceable quality of cheviot, military collars	$1.15
Pajamas	*Sears, Roebuck* (1908)	Military cut; coat and trousers	$0.96
Shirt	*New York Times* (1905)	From the most celebrated looms in Scotland	$4.00
Shirt	*The State* (Columbia, SC) (1905)	*The Emery;* put on a great front	$1.00
Shirt	*New York Times* (1907)	Men's negligee shirt, coat model with cuffs attached	$0.98
Shirt	*New York Times* (1907)	Fine cottons; special designs	$5.50
Shirt	*Century Magazine* (1909)	*Cluett;* dress	$1.50 and up
Shoes	*Atlanta Constitution* (1905)	French tan blucher Oxfords for men; were $5	$3.50
Shoes	*Van Norden Magazine* (1907)	They keep the feet healthy, prevent their getting damp and cold	$4.00
Shoes	*New York Times* (1909)	*Boyden's Famous;* any size, style; per pair regularly $6–$7	$4.75
Socks	*New York Times* (1907)	*Lisle* half-hose for men, lisle thread/instep silk, hand embroidered	$1.00/3 pairs
Suit	*San Francisco Examiner* (1908)	*Cholly Knickerbocker;* 30 styles, 100 colors; the foxiest clothes ever made	$12.50
Suit and Overcoat	*San Francisco Examiner* (1908)	Suits and overcoats	$15 to $45
Suspenders	*Van Norden Magazine* (1907)	*Bull Dog*	$0.50/pair
Tie	*New York Times* (1907)	Odds and ends sale	$0.27
Trousers	*New York Times* (1907)	Odds and ends sale	$1.35
Work Shirts	*Sears, Roebuck* (1908)	Chambray; lightweight cotton, fine finish	$0.46

Apparel, Women's

Item	Source	Description	Price
Clothing	*Chicago Tribune* (1905)	Tailor-made suits for women	$35.00
Coat	*Chicago Tribune* (1907)	Women's fine coats for fall and winter; broadcloth	$40.00
Coat	*New York Tribune* (1908)	Stern Brothers fur-lined coats; long moiré pony coat	$125
Coin Purses	*San Francisco Examiner* (1908)		$0.25
Corset	*Ladies' Home Journal* (1905)	*W. B.;* stitched fan front to restrain and flatten abdomen	$1.50
Corset	*Ladies' Home Journal* (1905)	*W. B.;* has the new high bust effect	$1.00

Item	Source	Description	Price
Corset	Sears, Roebuck (1908)	Are you too stout? Will do what an abdominal corset cannot; size 20–30 size 31–36 size 37–40	$2.25 $2.50 $2.75
Embroidery Waists	Chicago Tribune (1905)	Full blouse front with dainty tucks, form yoke effect	$4.50
Gloves	Chicago Tribune (1905)	Trefousse; kid gloves; regularly $1.75, sale price	$1.35
Hat	San Francisco Examiner (1908)	Pretty hats for Easter with ribbon	$6.50
Hat	Sears, Roebuck and Co. Catalogue (1908)	A large flaring mushroom style with long drooping back, rich in trimmings	$2.38
Kimono	San Francisco Examiner (1907)	Long lawn kimonos	$0.59
Petticoat	San Francisco Examiner (1907)	Heather bloom petticoats	$1.39
Petticoat	The Taylor-Trotwood Magazine (1908)	A guaranteed quality Simon's Regatta taffeta silk	$4.95
Shoes	Ladies' Home Journal (1905)	American Lady; with the character of the woman	$3.00
Shoes	Van Norden Magazine (1907)	They keep the feet healthy, prevent their getting damp and cold	$3.00
Shoes	Sears, Roebuck (1908)	Made of Conora coltskin, a foot-fitting low shoe	$1.39
Skirt	San Francisco Examiner (1907)	Alpaca walking skirt	$2.95
Stockings	New York Times (1909)	Pure French silk stockings	$4.50/pair
Stockings	Ladies' Home Journal (1905)		$0.25
Suit	New York Tribune (1908)	Saks and Company tailored suits of fine broadcloths or cheviots; new hipless models, satin lined Regularly $35, special	$19.50
Suits	San Francisco Examiner (1907)	Charming new Pony and Eton suits	$14.95

Appliances

Item	Source	Description	Price
Coffee Pot	Century Magazine (1909)	The Marion Harland coffee pot; full nickel-plated copper cover and silver-plated strainer 2-cup size (1 pint) 4-cup size (1 quart) 8-cup size (2 quarts) 12-cup size (3 quarts)	$1.25 $1.60 $1.90 $2.20
Iron Stove	The State (Columbia, SC) (1908)	Black	$19.50
Refrigerator	The State (Columbia, SC) (1908)	Big Line Hall; saves every drop of melted ice as drinking water; You can buy $20 worth of furniture for $2 cash and $0.50 per week	$16.50 and up
Steel Range	Sears, Roebuck (1908)	Massive blue steel, six-hole range	$29.27

Item	Source	Description	Price
Washing Machine	Sears, Roebuck (1908)	Ball-bearing washing machine	$6.38
Water Heater	Ladies' Home Journal (1906)	Heat your home with hot water; average price	$198

Baby Products

Item	Source	Description	Price
Baby Carriage	Sears, Roebuck (1908)	Finest grade of imported round reeds entirely woven by hand	$16.95
Baby Carriage	Sears, Roebuck (1908)	16" steel wheels with 3/8" rubber	$4.25
Baby Walker	Sears, Roebuck and Co. Catalogue (1908)	Combination walker, table and swing on a hardwood frame	$1.80
Cloaks	Sears, Roebuck and Co. Catalogue (1908)	Infants' long cloaks in cashmere, Bedford cord and silk Cashmere Cashmere with silk trim	$1.95 $3.29
Gown	Sears, Roebuck and Co. Catalogue (1908)	Beautiful Jap silk set; yoke is trimmed with three rows of lace. The underskirt is made of Jap silk Slip and shirt set	$4.25
Ring	Sears, Roebuck and Co. Catalogue (1908)	Baby ring, 1 ruby doublet, 2 enamel pearls, size 0 to 4	$0.65

Business Equipment & Supplies

Item	Source	Description	Price
Adding Machine	Forestry and Irrigation (1905)	The Locke Adder; famous calculating machine	$5 to $10
Bowling Alley	New York Tribune (1908)	American Box Ball Company can put you in the popular bowling game; Alleys pay $25 to $65 each per week Investment	$150 per lane
Carbon Paper	Van Norden Magazine (1907)	Whitfield; No Smudge, No Blur; 8" x 13"	$0.50/25sheets
Player Piano	American Chronicle (1999)	Wurlitzer; 65-note, coin-operated player piano	$700
Pushpins	Ladies' Home Journal (1905)	Moore; Here's a Pin, Push it In; made of steel and polished glass	$0.10/half-dozen
Typewriter	New York Tribune (1908)	Typewriter Exchange, bargains Remingtons Hammonds Franklins	$15.00 $10.00 $10.00
Typewriter Rental	New York Times (1907)		$2.00/month

Collectibles

Item	Source	Description	Price
Book	New York Times (1907)	First edition of Endymion (1818) by John Keats	$91.00
Glasses	American Collector (1942)	Rare set of eight early green wine glasses, broken pontles, The Loft, West Chester, Pennsylvania [In 1909]	$48.00
Letter	New York Times (1907)	By King Ferdinand and Queen Isabella signed 5 May 1495; earliest document mentioning American Indians	$85.00
Painting	American Chronicle (1999)	Thomas Gainsborough's Portrait of John Revett; sold at auction [In 1907]	$40.00

Education

Item	Source	Description	Price
Home Language Lessons	Century Magazine (1909)	Learn Spanish, French, Italian, German; taught as if actually in the presence of the teacher	$5/language

Item	Source	Description	Price
Language Classes	*Century Magazine* (1909)	Learn to speak fluently in Spanish, French, Italian or German. Pupils taught as if actually in the presence of the teacher. Ten-week course, per language	$5.00
Preparatory School	*The Taylor-Trotwood Magazine* (1908)	*Bethel Military Academy;* fifty miles from Washington. Prepares for business, universities and government academies. Warrenton, Virginia	$275
Seminary for Young Women	*Century Magazine* (1909)	*Martha Washington Seminary;* two-year course for high school graduates Per year	$500
Tuition	*American Chronicle* (1999)	*University of Michigan;* cost per semester in 1909	$40.00

Entertainment

Item	Source	Description	Price
Concert	*New York Tribune* (1908)	Violin soloist John Spargur; Broadway Theater; all seats reserved Tickets	$0.50 $0.75 $1.00
Horse Race	*The State* (Columbia, SC) (1909)	Spring; 300 Horses from Big circuit	$0.50
Opera Ticket	*New York Times* (1905)	*Die Meistersinger*	$1/$1.50/$2/$3
Snake Fight	*New York Times* (1907)	Mr. Rattlesnake v. Mr. Kingsnake	$2.00
Theater	*New York Tribune* (1908)	Klaw and Erlanger's Musical Comedy *Little Nemo;* Wednesday matinee	$1.50
Theater Ticket	*Chicago Tribune* (1905)	Klaw & Erlanger Co. Production	$0.75/$1/$1.50
Theater Ticket	*San Francisco Examiner* (1907)	Novelty Theatre presents Sidewalks of New York	$0.25/$0.50
Theater Ticket	*The State* (Columbia, SC) (1908)	*What Women Will Do*—Friday Night; *Dr. Jekyll and Mr. Hyde*—Saturday Night	$0.15/$0.25/$0.35
Ticket	*New York Times* (1909)	The greatest girl show ever seen in New York City; table seats	$1.00
Wrestling	*The State* (Columbia, SC) (1908)	Wrestling Dan McLeod v. Charles Conkle; Gallery Balcony Orchestra Stage seats	$0.25 $0.50 $0.75 $1.00

Entertainment, Home

Item	Source	Description	Price
Camera	*Century Magazine* (1909)	*Speed Kodak;* fitted with the Kodak Focal Plane Shutter having a range of automatic exposure from slow instantaneous to 1-1000 of a second	$50
Camera	*Sears, Roebuck* (1908)	*Conley Long Focus;* includes Conley Safety Shutter, 4" x 5"	$13.90
Camera	*Sears, Roebuck* (1908)	Improved compact; 4" x 5" size, rack and pinion focus movement	$6.95
Camera	*New York Times* (1909)	*Kodak;* N. 4A Speed; 4 1/4" x 6 1/2" (without lens)	$50.00
Card Game	*Ladies' Home Journal* (1905)	A decided novelty for your friends Gilt edged	$0.50 $0.75

Item	Source	Description	Price
Game	Sears, Roebuck and Co. Catalogue (1908)	Parchesi; the popular home game	$0.65
Magic Lantern	Sears, Roebuck (1908)	Includes 12 colored slides with four pictures on each slide	$4.98 to $6.98
Playing Cards	Century Magazine (1909)	Bicycle	$0.25
Playing Cards	Century Magazine (1909)	Congress; gold edges; 90 picture backs	$0.50
Records	Century Magazine (1909)	New Victor Records—"Fairest of the Fair," March, Sousa's Band; "Flanagan's New Year's Call," Steve Porter; "The Little Red Drum," Whitney Brothers Quartet—10"	$0.60 each
		"Pamplona Waltz," Victor Dance Orchestra; "When I Get Back Again to Bonnie Scotland," Harry Lauder; "The Flag He Loved So Well," Nat M. Wills—12"	$1 each
Records	Sears, Roebuck (1908)	Wax-cylinder; standard size; your own selection of subjects	$0.18
Records	Century Magazine (1909)	Phonograph; in a class by themselves—above price competition; 10" 12"	$0.60 $1.00
Stereoscopic Views	Sears, Roebuck (1908)	St. Louis World's Fair, 100 views	$0.85
Stereoscopic Views	Sears, Roebuck (1908)	The siege of Port Arthur; 100 views of the Japanese-Russian War	$0.85
Stereoscopic Views	Sears, Roebuck (1908)	50 views of the great plant of Sears, Roebuck & Co.	$0.35
Stereoscopic Viewer	Sears, Roebuck (1908)	Standard Special Aluminum	$0.28 $0.49
Talking Machine	Chicago Tribune (1907)	Wurlitzer	$29.50
Talking Machine	Sears, Roebuck (1908)	Oxford; cylinder talking machine	$14.95
Talking Machine	Century Magazine (1909)	The actual living, breathing voices of the world's greatest opera singers in all their power, sweetness, and purity	$10.00

Farm Equipment & Supplies

Item	Source	Description	Price
Bit	Sears, Roebuck and Co. Catalogue (1902)	Dexter driving bit; large, heavy cheeks; large, heavy tapered mouthpiece	$0.50
Cabbage Plants	The State (Columbia, SC) (1905)		$1.50/thousand
Chicks	New York Times (1907)	Barred Rocks, White Leghorns	$0.15/each
Cream Separator	Sears, Roebuck and Co. Catalogue (1908)	Improved economy cream separator, outskimmed all others. Capacity 250 to 300 pounds per hour, suitable for dairy of two to eight cows	$26.30
Engine	The Housewife (1903)	Best gasoline engine made complete with tank, tools and fittings. For pumping water 1-Horsepower 2-Horsepower 3-Horsepower	$69.00 $95.00 $112.25
Harness	Sears, Roebuck and Co. Catalogue (1902)	Iowa single harness; for 900- to 1200-pound horse; weight, boxed, 23 pounds	$8.95

Item	Source	Description	Price
Horse Harness	*Sears, Roebuck and Co. Catalogue* (1908)	*Hercules Farm Harness;* double and stitched trace, 6 feet long, with clip cockeye riveted on. 1 1/2 inch traces	$20.99
Incubator	*Wood's Special Poultry Supply Catalog* T. W. Wood and Sons Richmond, VA (1909)	*Cyphers' Standard* fireproofed incubator, 144-egg size	$22.00
Incubator	*The Ladies' Home Journal* (1911)	125-egg incubator and brooder	$10.00 for both
Insecticide	*The Ladies' Home Journal* (1910)	*Daisy Fly Killer*—attracts and kills flies. Made of metal; cannot spill or tip over Per box	$0.20
Medicine for Chickens	*Wood's Special Poultry Supply Catalog* T. W. Wood and Sons Richmond, VA (1908)	*Sterling Cholera Cure* is one of the best possible remedies for cholera. Cholera is the most deadly disease affecting poultry	$0.50
Sheep Shears	*Sears, Roebuck and Co. Catalogue* (1908)	Imported English double bow sheep shears, made in Sheffield, England 6 1/2 inch 7 inch	$1.04 $1.24
Shoe	*Sears, Roebuck and Co. Catalogue* (1908)	Plow shoe; made from Milwaukee oil grain leather	$1.35
Separator	*The Housewife* (1903)	Cream separator; most economical and most thorough hand cream separator	$48.75
Saddle	*Sears, Roebuck and Co. Catalogue* (1902) $0.20	Cheyenne Cowboy saddle; made of oiled russet skirting leather on a 15-inch Hidalgo steel fork rawhide covered tree	$19.90
Walking Plow	*Sears, Roebuck* (1908)	They score perfectly	$8.62

Food Products

Item	Source	Description	Price
Baking Powder	*New York Times* (1905)		$0.38/pound
Baking Powder	*The State* (Columbia, SC) (1905)	*Good Luck;* positively pure and has unsurpassed leavening qualities	$0.10/pound
Bananas	*Chicago Tribune* (1905)		$0.50 to $1.25/bunch
Beets	*Chicago Tribune* (1905)		$2 to $3.50/bushel
Beverages	*The Taylor-Trotwood Magazine* (1908)	Teas and coffees, the supplying of Catholic Institutions, clergymen and large consumers a specialty. By the pound Finest teas Finest coffees	$0.19 $0.27 $0.12 $0.13 $0.18
Catsup	*New York Times* (1905)		$0.20/pint

Item	Source	Description	Price
Cereal	*Ladies' Home Journal* (1905)	*Egg-o-See;* the whole grain of the very best white wheat; a large package	$0.10
Chocolate	*New York Tribune* (1908)	*Taylor-made Sorority Chocolates;* a new sensation One pound box	$0.60
Chocolate Bonbons	*Ladies' Home Journal* (1905)	*Caillers*	$1.35/pound
Clam Chowder	*Ladies' Home Journal* (1905)	*Scarboro Beach;* appetizing, nutritious, and absolutely pure	$0.10/can
Cracker	*The State* (Columbia, SC) (1908)	*Uneeda Biscuit;* the world's best soda cracker; in dust-tight moisture proof packages	$0.05
Dressed Chicken	*Chicago Tribune* (1905)		$0.12/pound
Eggs	*The State* (Columbia, SC) (1909)	One-day old; they will cost you more than eggs from two weeks to two months	$0.30/dozen
Flour	*San Francisco Examiner* (1908)		$5.40 to $6/barrel
Flour	*The State* (Columbia, SC) (1908)	*Silver Leaf*	$2.65/98-pound sack
Flour	*The State* (Columbia, SC) (1909)	*Piedmont*	$0.90/24 pounds
Gelatin	*Ladies' Home Journal* (1905)	*Jell-O;* six flavors	$0.10/package
Grape Juice	*Ladies' Home Journal* (1905)	*Welch's;* the food value of a grape	$3.00/dozen
Ham	*The State* (Columbia, SC) (1909)	*Swifts Premium*	$0.16/pound
Ice Cream	*Ladies' Home Journal* (1905)	*Jell-O;* four kinds	$0.25/2 packages
Mackerel in Tomato Sauce	*Sears, Roebuck* (1908)		$0.71/5 tins
Oranges	*Chicago Tribune* (1905)		$1.50 to $3.75/box
Peanuts	*Sears, Roebuck* (1908)	*Garlandis;* Salted peanuts, 1/2 lb can	$0.21
Potatoes	*San Francisco Examiner* (1908)		$0.40 to $0.85/sack
Potatoes	*The State* (Columbia, SC) (1908)	New York Table	$2.50/sack
Prunes	*The State* (Columbia, SC) (1908)	California; most wholesome food of this season; 25 lb box	$0.10/pound
Sardines	*New York Times* (1905)	Contains 14 fish per can	$0.35/half-can
Soft Drinks	*The State* (Columbia, SC) (1908)	*Bludwine;* King of soft drinks	$0.05/each; $1.90/ 6 dozen
Strawberries	*San Francisco Examiner* (1908)		$0.15/basket

Item	Source	Description	Price
Sugar	*The State* (Columbia, SC) (1909)	Granulated	$1/20 pounds
Sugar Wafers	*Century Magazine* (1909)	*Nabisco;* no other dessert confection has ever so satisfied that wholesome desire for a delicate sweet	$0.10 to $0.25/tin
Tea	*Ladies' Home Journal* (1905)	*Matsuri Tea Co., Importers;* express prepaid	$1.00/pound
Tea	*New York Times* (1905)		$0.50/pound
Toffee	*Ladies' Home Journal* (1905)	*Mackintosh's;* the great international candy	$1.60/4 pounds
Wafer	*Century Magazine* (1909)	*Nabisco Sugar Wafers;* no other dessert confection has ever so satisfied that wholesome desire for a delicate sweet Small tin Large tin	 $0.10 $0.25

Furniture

Item	Source	Description	Price
Bed	*Sears, Roebuck* (1908)	Massive high-grade continuous post brass bed	$28.85
Bed	*Sears, Roebuck* (1908)	Iron bed has corner posts made of drawn steel tubing, finished with white enamel only	$1.89
Chair	*Chicago Tribune* (1905)	Spanish leather-bag cushion rocker	$9.75
Chair	*Sears, Roebuck* (1908)	Golden oak, upholstered seat and back, fabric-covered leather	$4.45
Chair	*The State* (Columbia, SC) (1908)	Back porch rocker; Reed-seat and three-slat back	$2.35
Chair	*Sears, Roebuck and Co. Catalogue* (1908)	Adjustable reclining swing chair, made of oak, figured velour cushion	$6.25
Clock	*Ladies' Home Journal* (1905)	Grandfather; 79" high, regularly $55 Mahogany	$30.00 $34.00
Clock	*Sears, Roebuck* (1908)	Mantel; case imitates black Italian marble and Mexican onyx	$5.05
Clock	*Sears, Roebuck* (1908)	Empress design veneered with highly figured quarter-sawed oak; 78" long x 30" wide	$12.15
Desk	*New York Tribune* (1908)	60-inch Sanitary Rolltop Desk	$37.50
Dining Table	*New York Times* (1907)	Golden oak, round, pedestal base	$11.25
Hall Mirror and Hall Seat	*San Francisco Examiner* (1908)	Hall mirrors Hall seats	$3.00 $10.00
Rug	*Chicago Tribune* (1905)	Oriental; 9.5' x 13.7', regularly $315	$235

Garden Equipment & Supplies

Item	Source	Description	Price
Flower Bupounds	*Childs' Fall Catalogue of Bupounds and Plants that Bloom* John Lewis Childs Floral Park, NY (1908)	*Hyacinthus belgicus;* it resembles the Grape Hyacinth more than any other; pure white, shell pink, blue	$0.20 for 3 of each

Item	Source	Description	Price
Flower Bupounds	*Childs' Fall Catalogue of Bupounds and Plants that Bloom John Lewis Childs Floral Park, NY* (1908)	*Darwin tulips;* produce only solid self colors and bloom early in May	$0.50 per dozen
Lawn Mower	*The State* (Columbia, SC) (1909)	*Panama;* self-sharpening; 14" cut 16" cut	$6.50 $7.50
Roses	*Ladies' Home Journal* (1905)	Blooming size plants	$1/24 plants
Seeds	*Ladies' Home Journal* (1905)	Giant sweet peas	$0.10/5 packages
Tree Protectors	*Forestry and Irrigation* (1905)	Do not wait until rabbits and mice ruin your trees	$0.75/100

Hotel Rates

Item	Source	Description	Price
Hotel Room	*Century Magazine* (1909)	*The Jefferson Hotel;* the most magnificent hotel in the South. Rooms single and en suite, with and without bath. Richmond, Virginia	$1.50 per day
Hotel Room	*Atlanta Constitution* (1905)	*Hotel Earlington;* rooms with detached bar	$1.00/day
Hotel Room	*Chicago Tribune* (1905)	*Hotel Johnson;* 336 Dearborn, furnished with bath and gas	$2.00/week
Hotel Room	*Chicago Tribune* (1905)	*The Plaza;* the world's most luxurious hotel With bath With parlor, bedroom, and bath	$2.50/day $4 to $6/day $12 to $20/day
Hotel Room	*Van Norden Magazine* (1907)	*Lenox Hotel;* our rapid electric carriages Exclusively for patrons	$1.50/day
Hotel Room	*New York Times* (1909)	*Jefferson Hotel,* Richmond, Virginia; most magnificent hotel in the South	$1.50/day

Household Goods

Item	Source	Description	Price
Blanket	*New York Times* (1905)		$3.25
Blanket	*Ladies' Home Journal* (1905)	*Suffolk Sanitary Fleece;* superior to woolen blankets	$1.50/pair
Bowl	*Ladies' Home Journal* (1906)	Cut-glass fruit or berry bowl; 7" bowl	$3.00
Bread Maker	*Ladies' Home Journal* (1905)	*Universal;* mixes and kneads bread thoroughly in three minutes; four-loaf capacity, large family size	$3.25
Carriage Bag	*New York Times* (1905)	*Walrus;* vienna covered frame 6", 7", 8" and 9" in tan, brown, and black; value $4	$1.95
Cleaner	*Ladies' Home Journal* (1906)	*Old Dutch;* a natural product, cleanest and cheapest agent that ever blessed the housewife; large cans with sifting top	$0.10
Coffee Pot	*Century Magazine* (1909)	*Marion Harland;* full nickel-plated copper cover and silver-plated strainer; One pint size Three quarts	$1.25 $2.20
Curtains	*Ladies' Home Journal* (1905)	Lace; Point De Luxe, Motifany, Queen Anne made on real babbinet	$2.00/pair
Draperies	*Chicago Tribune* (1905)	Cotton; artistically hand-painted cretonnes	$0.13/yd

Item	Source	Description	Price
House Paint	*Sears, Roebuck* (1908)	*Ready* mixed paint ($9.10 for two-story wood frame house)	$0.98/gallon
Liquid Glaze	*Ladies' Home Journal* (1905)	*Varno;* revives all varnished surfaces	$0.30/5-ounce can
Matches	*Sears, Roebuck* (1908)	Red Brand	$0.58/12,000
Mattress	*Ladies' Home Journal* (1905)	*Ostermoor;* 6' 3" long, 3' 6" wide; pure, elastic hand-laid, sheeted mattress not dangerous animal fibre, 4' 6" wide	$11.70 $15.00
Pesticide	*Ladies' Home Journal* (1905)	*Rough on Rats;* Why feed rats? Rough on Rats kills them	$0.15
Plumbing	*Century Magazine* (1909)	*Mott's;* Imperial solid porcelain	$85 to $300
Silver Polish	*Century Magazine* (1909)	*Electro;* silicon; does not scratch or wear	$0.15/jar
Soap	*Ladies' Home Journal* (1905)	*Palmolive;* more than ordinary soap	$0.10
Stove Polish	*Ladies' Home Journal* (1905)	*Black Satin in Can;* the perfect stove polish	$0.25/can
Suitcase	*Atlanta Constitution* (1905)	$4 leather suitcase	$3.00
Tablecloth	*New York Times* (1905)	Irish Satin Damask; 2 yds x 3 yds	$3.00
Tableware	*Sears, Roebuck* (1908)	28 pieces, solid Alaska metal, 6 dinner forks, dinner knives, full-size tablespoons and teaspoons, 1 butter knife, sugar shell and salt and pepper	$4.66
Tooth Cleanser	*Ladies' Home Journal* (1906)	*Rubifoam;* for a well-kept mouth	$0.25/tube
Towels	*New York Times* (1905)	250 dozen spoke, hemstitched, huckaback	$3.00/dozen
Trunk	*Sears, Roebuck* (1908)	32" x 21" x 23 1/2"	$6.88
Varnish	*Sears, Roebuck* (1908)	Fine carriage varnishes $1.60/ 1/2 gal	4/$0.05/ pint
Water Softener	*The State* (Columbia, SC) (1909)	*Lavadura;* it softens the water and makes easy work of washing the clothes	$0.05 to $0.10/pack

Insurance Rates

Item	Source	Description	Price
Fire Insurance	*Insurance Policy* (1908)	$500 fire coverage for two-story wood frame building in Columbia, SC	$4.50
Life Insurance	*Century Magazine* (1909)	Whole life plan (at age 30 equals $50 monthly for 20 years)	$167.35

Jewelry

Item	Source	Description	Price
Bracelet	*Sears, Roebuck and Co. Catalogue* (1908)	Oval tubing, gold filled, bright polish, patent pull-out spring bracelet	$3.82
Cuff Links	*The State* (Columbia, SC) (1908)	Solid gold cuff; several patterns to select from; regularly $3	$2.00
Watch	*Sears, Roebuck* (1908)	Pocket watch; 7-jewel, nickel plate, size 16	$2.76
Watch	*Sears, Roebuck* (1908)	*Elgin;* pocket watch; 15-jewel; size 16	$8.15
Watch	*Sears, Roebuck* (1908)	Pocket watch; 21-jewel, solid 14K gold, size 16	$32.50

Item	Source	Description	Price
Watch	*Century Magazine* (1909)	*Howard;* pocket watch; 17-jewel, gold filled 23-jewel, 14K solid gold	$36.00 $150

Meals

Dinner	*Atlanta Constitution* (1905)	*Hotel Earlington,* New York City; table d'hote	$0.75

Medical Products & Services

Dentist	*Atlanta Constitution* (1905)	Dr. E. G. Griffin's Gold Crowns and Bridge Work; work at lowest cash prices	$4.00
Dentist	*San Francisco Examiner* (1908)	Fillings Teeth re-enameled Gold plate	$1.00 $2.00 $5 to $8
Glasses	*Sears, Roebuck* (1908)	Man's, cable bow, gold-filled spectacles	$1.98
Nonprescription Drug	*New York Times* (1905)	*Caster Oil Tablets*	$0.10/box
Nonprescription Drug	*The State* (Columbia, SC) (1905)	*Dr. Bell's Pine-Tar-Honey;* will always prevent a cold if taken on coming in out of the wet	$0.25/bottle
Nonprescription Drug	*Sears, Roebuck* (1906)	*Blackberry Balsam;* a pleasant, safe, speedy, and l effectua remedy for dysentery, diarrhea, looseness, cholera morbus	$0.20/bottle
Nonprescription Drug	*Sears, Roebuck* (1906)	*Carolene;* cures while you sleep; a remedy for whooping cough, asthma, catarrh, diphtheria, croup, colds, cough, etc.	$0.89
Nonprescription Drug	*Sears, Roebuck* (1906)	*Castoria;* the best-known remedy for all stomach and bowel complaints of infants and children; regular price $0.35	$0.26/bottle
Nonprescription Drug	*Sears, Roebuck* (1906)	Eye Remedy; a safe and positive cure for eye troubles	$0.40
Nonprescription Drug	*Sears, Roebuck* 1906)	*Red Clover Compound;* the great cure for worn out, tired, and exhausted conditions of the system	$0.68
Nonprescription Drug	*Sears, Roebuck* (1906)	*Reliable Worm Syrup;* no other disease is so fatal to children as worms	$0.18/bottle
Sanitarium	*San Francisco Examiner* (1908)	*Dr. Juilly's;* confinement with ten days' care	$30 to $60

Motorized Vehicles, Services, & Supplies

Automobile	*Century Magazine* (1909)	The "30" Locomobile shaft drive touring car	$3,500
Automobile	*Sears, Roebuck* (1905)	*Franklin Light Tonneau;* 4-cylinder air-cooled motor	$1,650
Automobile	*Sears, Roebuck* (1905)	*White Steam Car;* the ideal closed automobile	$3,200
Automobile	*Cycle and Automobile Trade Journal* (1905)	*Zent High-grade Car;* the simplest car on earth; has ample power, the 3-cylinder engine developing full 18 hp and over; price for the present	$1,350
Automobile	*New York Times* (1907)	*Elmore Three;* 3 cylinder, valveless, two-cycle engine	$1,750
Automobile	*New York Times* (1907)	*Waltham Orient;* Two-passenger Runabout, 4 hp	$400
Automobile	*New York Times* (1908)	*Oldsmobile Palace Touring Car;* Four cylinders	$2,750

Item	Source	Description	Price
Automobile	*New York Times* (1909)	*Rambler Model 44;* 34 hp, seven passengers	$2,250
Automobile Seat	*Sears, Roebuck* (1908)	Two-seat surrey with extension top	$77.45
Boat Steering Gears	*Cycle and Automobile Trade Journal* (1905)	*Edson;* the side steering quadrant will come as a valued aid to the man who wishes to steer his own boat and to run the engine as well	$8.00
Carburetor	*Cycle and Automobile Trade Journal* (1905)	*Schebler;* the heart of the automobile; cost saved through reduced gasoline bills in a few weeks	$18.00
Jack	*Cycle and Automobile Trade Journal* (1905)	*Kenosha;* durable handsomely finished and carefully made in our own factory; everything for the man with the car	$4.00
Marine Motor	*Cycle and Automobile Trade Journal* (1905)	*Clifton;* 1-cylinder; one of the improvements is the use of the jump spark system of ignition	$600
Marine Motor	*Cycle and Automobile Trade Journal* (1905)	*Lawrence;* 2-cycle 12 hp; weighs 600 pounds, runs 450 r.p.m.	$850
Motor Oil	*Cycle and Automobile Trade Journal* (1905)	*Ideal;* for automobile and marine engines; pure hydrocarbon high fire test, low cold test; no gum, no carbon	$0.60/gallon
Motorboat	*Cycle and Automobile Trade Journal* (1905)	18-ft. launch, driven by DuBrie's 2 hp motor, regular speed 8 miles per hour, gasoline consumption about two gallons in 10 hours running; seats 8	$175
Motorcycle	*Popular Mechanics Picture History of American Travel* (1909)	*Curtis;* 7 hp double cylinder	$275
Road Wagon	*Sears, Roebuck* (1908)	*Blue Ribbon Runabouts*	$32.15 to $34.15

Musical Instruments

Item	Source	Description	Price
Piano	*New York Times* (1905)	*Kimbrall;* New Used	$450 $200
Piano	*New York Times* (1905)	*Weber;* New Used	$625 $440
Piano	*Sears, Roebuck* (1908)	Special concert grand piano	$195
Piano	*Century Magazine* (1909)	*Steinway;* miniature grand ebonized case	$800
Violin	*Sears, Roebuck* (1908)	*Pisani;* Stradivarius model	$45.00
Violin	*New York Times* (1909)	Student Regular	$15.00 $100

Other

Item	Source	Description	Price
College Poster	*Forestry and Irrigation* (1905)	In the colors of the college they represent (14" x 22")	$25.00
Fountain Pen	*Forestry and Irrigation* (1905)	Pocket companion; regularly $3, reduced	$1.00

Item	Source	Description	Price
Photographs	*The State* (Columbia, SC) (1908)	Fine cabinet photos in folders	$3.00/dozen
Photography	*American Chronicle* (1999)	Financier J. P. Morgan's pledge to support a photo collection of North American Indians in 1907	$75,000
Postcards	*New York Times* (1909)	Set of 12, showing 90 hp Locomobile winning 1908 International Race for Vanderbilt Cup	$0.10/set
Stationery	*Ladies' Home Journal* (1905)	*Autocrat;* for social correspondence; special combination cabinet, containing correspondence cards, writing papers and exclusive deep flap envelopes	$0.50
Whiskey Flask	*The State* (Columbia, SC) (1908)	Sterling silver; regularly $12	$9.00

Personal Care Products

Item	Source	Description	Price
Cold Cream	*Century Magazine* (1909)	*Daggett and Ramsdell's Perfect Cold Cream;* a beauty clean-up in cold weather when pores are contracted and inactive Jar Tube	 $0.35 $0.10
Cold Cream	*Century Magazine* (1909)	The skin needs emollient cleansing $0.35/jar	$0.10/tube
Combination Case	*Ladies' Home Journal* (1905)	*Larkin*	$10.00
Digestive Aid	*Sears, Roebuck* (1908)	*Essence of Pepsin;* for treatment of indigestion, sour stomach, dyspepsia, bad breath	$0.43/8 ounces
Face Powder	*Ladies' Home Journal* (1905)	*LaBlache;* flesh, white, pink, cream	$0.50/box
Face Whitener	*Sears, Roebuck* (1908) (1906)	*White Lily;* great face, neck, and arm whitener; the ladies' favorite toilet preparation prevents decay	4/$0.05 $0.25
Razor	*Van Norden Magazine* (1907)	*Razac Ready;* complete outfit, genuine leather case	$3.50
Safety Razor	*Century Magazine* (1909)	*Gillette;* no stropping, no honing; standard set	$5.00
Skin Cream	*Century Magazine* (1909)	*Strong's Arnica Jelly;* ideal for sunburn, keeps the skin soft and smooth Tube	 $0.25
Soap	*Century Magazine* (1909)	*Fairy;* the floating oval cake	$0.50
Sunburn Remedy	*Century Magazine* (1909)	*Arnica Jelly;* ideal for sunburn, keeps the skin soft and smooth	$0.25/tube
Talcum Powder	*Century Magazine* (1909)	*Mennen's Borated;* baby's best brief, relieves and prevents chapped hands and chafing; a non-refillable box	$0.25
Toothpaste	*Ladies' Home Journal* (1906)	*Dentacura;* cleans the teeth, destroys bacteria, prevents decay	$0.25
Tooth Soap	*Century Magazine* (1909)	*Arnica;* sweetens the breath, hardens the gums, whitens the teeth; metal package at all druggists	$0.25

Publications

Item	Source	Description	Price
Book	*Century Magazine* (1909)	*The World I Live In* by Helen Keller, an autobiographical record	$1.20
Book	*Century Magazine* (1909)	*The Trail of the Lonesome Pine;* by John Fox Jr., illustrated	$1.50

Item	Source	Description	Price
Magazine	*Century Magazine* (1909)	*St. Nicholas Magazine;* St. Nicholas is not only a joy to the children for whom it is primarily intended, but has also an unfading attraction for the older folk 12 Issues, One-year subscription	$3.00
Magazine	*Century Magazine* (1909)	*The American Magazine*; January issue contains a new story by David Grayson One-year subscription	$1.00
Magazine	*Forestry and Irrigation* (1905)	*Scientific American;* anyone sending a sketch and a description may quickly ascertain our opinion on whether an invention is probably patentable	$3.00/year
Magazine	*Van Norden Magazine* (1907)	*The Financial Forum*	$1.00/year
Magazine	*Century Magazine* (1909)	*St. Nicholas Magazine*; monthly for children	$3.00/year
Newspaper	*New York Times* (1905)	*New York Times*, daily issue	$0.01

Real Estate

Item	Source	Description	Price
Apartment	*New York Tribune* (1908)	*Hoffman Arms Apartments* from 5 to 20 rooms with kitchen or restaurant service; 59th St. and Madison Ave. Rent per year	$1,200 to $4,000
Apartment	*San Francisco Examiner* (1908)	For rent; furnished apartments, gas ranges, sinks, closets	$17.50/month
Apartment Building	*New York Times* (1907)	For sale; Central Park view apartment house, Central Park West and Eighty-sixth Street, New York City; 100' x 150' plot, 12-story building, 47 apartments	$1,200,000
Farm	*Atlanta Constitution* (1905)	124 acres 16 miles from Atlanta, 1 mile from R. R., heavily timbered, enough timber to pay for place twice	$20.00/acre
House	*New York Tribune* (1908)	Three-story brick dwelling in Flushing, New York; 8 acres, 17 rooms, two bathrooms, large kitchen and laundry in basement	$75,000
House	*Atlanta Constitution* (1905)	10-room home near Peachtree	$4,500
House	*Ladies' Home Journal* (1905)	Three-room house (Carpentry and hardware $675, masonry $125, plumbing $125, painting $75)	$1,000
House	*The State* (Columbia, SC) (1905)	One eight-room dwelling on East Gervais Street, delightful neighborhood	$5,500
House	*Atlanta Constitution* (1905)	For rent; 7-rooms; equipped with furnace heat, gas and electric lights and all conveniences	$35.00/month
House	*Atlanta Constitution* (1905)	Lee Street Cottage; $200 cash, balance $15 per month	$1,500
House	*The State* (Columbia, SC) (1908)	For rent; 7 rooms	$19.00/month
House	*The State* (Columbia, SC) (1908)	For rent; 7-room house, bath both floors, Columbia, SC	$35/month
House	*Sears, Roebuck* (1908)	Plows, all materials for two-story, six-room house	$725
Land	*Chicago Tribune* (1905)	Kansas Wheat	$6 to $12/acre
Land	*Chicago Tribune* (1905)	Colorado and Nebraska ranch land (payment one-tenth in cash)	$1.75 to $4/acre
Lot	*Atlanta Constitution* (1905)	50 x 250 lot; This is the place to save your money and we can make you $100 profit on each lot by spring	$250

Item	Source	Description	Price
Lot	*Chicago Tribune* (1905)	24 x 110, old cottage thrown in	$1,800
Lot	*New York Times* (1909)	120 lots in the choicest section of Bogota Estates, Bogota, New Jersey	$250 to $300
Office	*New York Times* (1907)	For rent; Times Square Building; 18 yards x 24 yards, 4th floor, best lighted in New York City, elevators run all night	$1,400/year
Room	*New York Times* (1907)	For rent; eastside New York City, furnished with board, running water, steam heat	$8.00
Room	*New York Times* (1907)	For rent; furnished room, 124th St, 68th East, heated, running water, hall room	$2.00
Warehouse and Factory	*Chicago Tribune* (1905)	244 yds x 130 yds with two-story brick warehouse and factory less than one mile from city hall	$40,000

Sewing Equipment & Supplies

Item	Source	Description	Price
Cloth	*New York Times* (1907)	Stirling black taffeta silks 26" wide	$1.10/yard
Cloth	*San Francisco Examiner* (1907)	Japanese wash silk in the latest patterns and colorings	$0.39/yard
Sewing Machine	*Sears, Roebuck and Co. Catalogue* (1908)	*Belmont* five-drawer drop head, oak cabinet sewing machine	$9.85
Sewing Machine	*Sears, Roebuck* (1908)	5-drawer, drop head with oak cabinet	$9.85
Sewing Machine	*Sears, Roebuck* (1908)	7-drawer, drop leaf and box cover with oak cabinet	$13.85

Sports Equipment

Item	Source	Description	Price
Baseball Glove	*Sears, Roebuck* (1908)	Made of horsehide, correctly padded	$1.90
Basketball Goal	*Sears, Roebuck and Co. Catalogue* (1908)	Regulation style made of iron frame with cotton netting, weight per pair, 12 pounds	$2.74
Bicycle	*Sears, Roebuck* (1908)	Man's Roadster model	$14.95
Bicycle Pump	*Sears, Roebuck* (1908)	Compound action, hose connection will fit all valves	$0.09
Field Glasses	*Sears, Roebuck* (1908)	Highest grade genuine Jena special field glass	$12.95
Fishing Rod	*Sears, Roebuck* (1908)	Two-jointed, 5 1/2" with double cork grip	$1.29
Fishing Tackle	*Sears, Roebuck and Co. Catalogue* (1908)	Complete bait casting outfit suitable for bait casting or trolling	$5.98
Pistol	*Sears, Roebuck* (1908)	Automatic self-cocking revolver	$3.75
Shot Gun	*Sears, Roebuck* (1908)	Double-barrel, breech loading	$11.95
Supporter	*Sears, Roebuck and Co. Catalogue* (1908)	Admiral elastic supporters; the most sanitary, most practical jockey strap on the market	$0.44

Telephone Equipment & Services

Item	Source	Description	Price
Telephone	*Sears, Roebuck* (1908)	Five-magnet, 1600 ohm, compact, briding telephone; more power than is required in actual practice	$9.95

Item	Source	Description	Price
Telephone Service	John Brooks, *Telephone The First Hundred Years* (1976)	Annual rates (Pittsburgh) for 1906 Residential Business	 $100 $125
Telegraph Charges	Susan J. Douglas, *Inventing American Broadcasting* (1987)	Rates for 1907	$0.05 to $0.25/word

Tobacco Products

Item	Source	Description	Price
Cigar	*New York Times* (1905)		$0.05
Cigarettes	*Century Magazine* (1909)	*Nestor Cigarettes;* if you must have the very best, smoke *Nestor's* and ignore the rest Nestor Green Label Imported Royal Nestor	 $0.25 $0.40 $0.15
Cigarettes	*Century Magazine* (1909)	*Nestor Cigarettes;* if you must have the very best and ignore the rest, pack of 10, Blue Label Green Label Imported	 $0.15/pack $0.25/pack $0.40/pack
Cigarettes	*New York Times* (1907)		$0.15/ten
Cigarettes	*The State* (Columbia, SC) (1908)	*Piedmont;* famous for the quality of fine old tobacco; packaged in tin foil	$0.05/ten
Cigars	*Sears, Roebuck* (1908)	*Perfectos;* box of 50	$1.20/box

Toys

Item	Source	Description	Price
Doll	*Sears, Roebuck and Co. Catalogue* (1908)	Full jointed papier maché doll; natural appearance and beautifully proportioned 19" 24" 30"	 $1.19 $2.88 $4.89
Teddy Bears	*Sears, Roebuck and Co. Catalogue* (1908)	Teddy bears; the best plaything ever invested, not a fad or campaign article 10" high 12" high 14" high 16" high	 $0.75 $1.19 $1.75 $2.38
Wondergraph	*Sears, Roebuck and Co. Catalogue* (1908)	*Wondergraph;* makes, as if by magic, beautiful designs no artist can draw; a child can operate	$0.95

Travel & Transportation

Item	Source	Description	Price
Boat	*New York Tribune* (1908)	Hudson River Night Lines; between New York and Albany	$2.65 $1.50
Cruise	*New York Times* (1909)	To the Orient; 80 Days	$300
Cruise	*New York Times* (1909)	South America; stopping at all the important cities en route to the Straits of Magellan; duration, 81 days	$350
Cruise	*New York Times* (1909)	World; thirty tours to Europe	$250
Railroad Ticket	*Atlanta Constitution* (1905)	Weekend railroad tickets, Atlanta to Atlantic Beach (Florida) and return	$8.85
Railroad Ticket	*Chicago Tribune* (1905)	Chicago to San Francisco; The best of everything	$33.00

Item	Source	Description	Price
Railroad Ticket	*New York Times* (1905)		$1.44/mile
Railroad Ticket	*New York Times* (1905)	New York to Washington	$12 to $14.50
Railroad Ticket	*New York Times* (1905)	New York to New Orleans for Mardi Gras (Pullman Berth/all meals); round trip	$75.00
Railroad Ticket	*New York Times* (1905)	New York to Pinehurst (Golf Championship) (Pullman Berth/all meals/3 days board at Hotel Carolina)	$35.00
Railroad Ticket	*Forestry and Irrigation* (1905)	St. Paul, Minnesota, to Billings, Montana	$20.00
Railroad Ticket	*Forestry and Irrigation* (1905)	St. Paul, Minnesota, to northern Pacific coastal points	$25.00
Railroad Ticket	*San Francisco Examiner* (1907)	Rock Island Railroad Transportation; *San Francisco* to New Orleans; round trip	$67.50
Railroad Ticket	*San Francisco Examiner* (1907)	Rock Island Railroad Transportation; San Francisco to New York	$108.50
Railroad Ticket	*New York Times* (1907)	New York to Atlantic City, lenten outings; round trip, two days' board	$10 to $12
Railroad Ticket	*The State* (Columbia, SC) (1908)		$0.03/mile
Railroad Ticket	*The State* (Columbia, SC) (1908)	St. Louis to Portland	$35.50
Steamship	*New York Tribune* (1908)	Steamship *Yale;* fare between New York and Boston	$2.65
Steamship Fare	*New York Times* (1909)	Delightful afternoon excursion from New York to West Point; round trip	$1.00
Train	*Forestry and Irrigation* (1905)	Northern Pacific Railway; train trip to northern Pacific Coast points. From St. Paul, stopovers at will west of Billings, Montana	$25.00
Train	*New York Tribune* (1908)	Special train to Savannah Automobile Races, under direction of Twentieth Century Automobile Club, price includes sleeping accommodations and meals during trip, plus grandstand seats for both racing days	$65.00

MISCELLANY 1905-1909

Auction Results

Several rarities were included in a three day book sale which ended at the Merwin-Clayton rooms, in Eastern Twentieth Street yesterday. A first edition of "England's Parnassus," by Robert Allot, the earliest poetical anthology of English literature, fetched $120. A first edition of Thomas Bancroft's "Two Books of Epigrammes" sold for $125.

A letter of Ferdinand and Isabella of Spain, Madrid, May 5, 1495, sold for $85. The first edition of John Gay's "Fables" brought $80. The Grolier Club's "Rubaiyat of Omar Khayyam," fetched $148. First editions of "Endymion" and "Lamia" by John Keats, sold respectively for $91 and $101. The letter of Ferdinand and Isabella is said to be the earliest original document extant in America mentioning the American Indians.

New York Times, March 1, 1905

Convenient Schedules via Western and Atlantic Railroad

From Atlanta to the following points and return at the rates named:

Lookout Mountain, Tenn. $4.10
Dalton, Ga. $3.00
Monteagle, Tenn. $6.55

Atlanta Constitution, July 1905

Steam Rate War Ended

The Allen and Donaldson Steamship Lines, after a month of rate cutting, came to terms today with regard to second and third class trans-atlantic passenger tickets. The second class rate was restored to $35, and the third class to $25.

Atlanta Constitution, August 1, 1905

Wanted to Chop Their Salaries

Somewhat of a stir was created in the House yesterday when the general appropriations bill was under discussion by an amendment offered by Mr. Knight of Berrian, proposing to reduce the salaries of the members of the railroad commission from $2,500 to $1,000 each.

Mr. Knight said $1,000 was all the railroad commissioners were worth, considering the service they rendered the state.

Atlanta Constitution, August 1, 1905

Player Sold to Atlanta

Jackson fans did not relish the parting with their star pitcher, Arthur Raymond, and some harsh things were said of the management for selling him to Atlanta.

The Jackson News said of Raymond: "The regret over Raymond's departure was not one-sided. The big fellow was all broken up over the transaction, notwithstanding the fact that it gives him a salary of $200 per month with a mighty good chance of being in the American or National League next season."

Atlanta Constitution, August 1, 1905

Expansion or Inflation

The National Bank Loans for the country increased $395,000,000 during 1906, this increase being almost entirely outside of New York City. A conservative banker from Dakota stated recently that his deposits had decreased because he could not bring himself to compete with his neighbors. Eighteen months ago, farms about his town were selling at $5 to $10 per acre. Now they are held at $125. He loaned only on the old valuation, while others willing to advance more secured the business.

Van Norden Magazine, April 1907

Investor Buys $1,250,000 Apartment House on Central Park West

John H. Berry has sold the Monticello Realty Company to David H. Taylor for investment, the Central Park View apartment house, at the southwest corner at Central Park West and Eighty-sixth Street, a twelve-story structure containing forty-seven apartments, on a plot 100 by 150. The price is reported to have been $1,250,000.

New York Times, March 1, 1907

$439,370 for Paintings

There was a large crowd at Christie's to-day to witness the dispersal of Sir Cuthbert Quilter's famous collection of paintings. Turner's "Venus and Adonis" brought only $20,000. This was far below anticipations, but was considerably above the price paid for the same canvas in 1885, when it sold for $9,250. In 1830 it brought only $215. Ramney's "Portrait of Mrs. Jordan" for which Quilter had refused $80,000, brought only $24,000.

New York Times, July 25, 1909

HISTORICAL SNAPSHOT
1910-1914

1910

- Western Union abolishes the 40¢ to 50¢ charge for placing telegraph messages by telephone
- *Women's Wear Daily* begins publication in New York
- U. S. cigarette sales reach 8.6 billion cigarettes, with 62 percent controlled by the American Tobacco Trust
- Florida orange shipments rebound to 1894 level
- 70 percent of bread is baked at home, down from 80 percent in 1890
- Flexner Report shows most North American medical schools are inferior to those in Europe

1911

- California women gain suffrage by constitutional amendment
- F. W. Woolworth Co. is incorporated
- Electric self-starter for motorcar perfected and immediately adopted by Cadillac
- Chevrolet Motor Co. founded by race car driver Louis Chevrolet

- First Indianapolis 500-mile race is won by a Marmon Wasp averaging 75 miles per hour
- Carnegie Corporation of New York created through $125 million gift from Andrew Carnegie to encourage education
- Direct telephone link opens between New York and Denver
- New York's Ellis Island has a record one-day influx of 11,745 immigrants

1912

- Congress extends the 8-hour day to all federal employees
- Ford produces more than 22 percent of all U. S. motorcars
- L. L. Bean, Inc., is founded by merchant Leon Leonwood Bean
- SS *Titanic* sinks during maiden voyage
- Oreo biscuits introduced by National Biscuit Company to compete with "biscuit bon bons"
- Merger of U. S. film producers creates Universal Pictures Corp.
- A&P begins rapid expansion based on economy stores that operate on cash and carry basis

1913

- Brillo Manufacturing Corp. founded
- Camel cigarettes introduced by R. J. Reynolds, creating the first modern blended cigarette
- 60-story Woolworth building opens in New York
- Congress strengthens the Pure Food and Drug Law of 1906
- Peppermint Life Savers introduced as a summer seller when chocolate sales are reduced

1914

- World War I begins in Europe
- Henry Ford offers workers a minimum wage of $5 a day
- Panama Canal opens to traffic, linking Atlantic and Pacific across 50 miles of land
- Cleveland installs red and green lights to control traffic
- Gulf Oil distributes the first U. S. automobile maps
- Consumers eat 5 pounds of butter for every pound of margarine
- Mary Phelps Jacob patents elastic brassiere, destined to replace corset

SELECTED INCOME 1910-1914

Job	Source	Description	Pay
Accountant	*New York Times* (1911)	Bookkeeper; books opened, audited, system installed; firm not employing bookkeepers	$2.50/wk
Actress	*American Chronicle* (1999)	Mary Pickford's annual salary, following the release of the movie Tess of the Storm Country in 1914	$104,000
Address Collection	*Atlanta Constitution* (1914)	Men/Women, to collect all kinds of names and addresses; no canvassing	$25/week
Autoworker	*Atlanta Constitution* (1913)	Colored men taught to build automobiles	$100–$500/mo
Barber	*The New Orleans Picayune* (1912)	Good barber for Saturday and Sunday; wage guaranteed	$4
Ballroom Dancers	Tomkins, ed., *American Decades: 1910-1919* (1996)	Nightly fee for Vernon and Irene Castle in 1913	$1,000
Baseball Player	Tomkins, ed., *American Decades: 1910-1919* (1996)	Annual salary and bonus of Washington Senator pitcher Walter Johnson in 1914	$26,000
Baseball Player	Tomkins, ed., *American Decades: 1910-1919* (1996)	Average salary of a professional baseball player in 1910	$3,000
Baseball Player	Tomkins, ed., *American Decades: 1910-1919* (1996)	Annual salary of Detroit Tigers' Ty Cobb in 1910	$9,000
Bookkepper	*San Francisco Examiner* (1913)	Complete charge of office and finance	$125/mo
Bookkeeper	*New York Times* (1914)	Situation Wanted: Practical accountant 14 years' experience modern methods, systematizer, seeks responsible position	$25/wk
Broadway Productions	George Cohan: *Prince of the American Theater* (1943)	Annual income of George Cohen for Broadway productions	$1.5 million
Businessman	*American Chronicle* (1999)	Annual salary of business executive William Gillette in 1912	$300,000
Carpenter	*San Francisco Examiner* (1913)	House carpenter, work on ranch	$3.25/day
Clerk	*New York Times* (1912)	Bright office boy about 16; one living within walking distance of Madison Square preferred	$5/wk
Cook	*San Francisco Examiner* (1913)	A man cook for hotel, country town	$50/mo
Delivery Man	*Atlanta Constitution* (1913)	Colored hustler in each locality; just spare time; experience unnecessary	$100/mo
Detective	*Atlanta Constitution* (1913)	Be a detective; travel over the world	$150–$300/mo

Job	Source	Description	Pay
Evangelist	Lyle W. Dorsett, *Bill Sunday and the Redemption of Urban American* (1991)	Annual income of former professional baseball player turned evangelist Billy Sunday in 1914	$200,000
Hotel Manager	*The New Orleans Picayune* (1912)	Total compensation of an assistant manager of The Hotel Plaza in New York, including payment from steamship lines and liquor distributors	$8,400
Hotel Worker	*San Francisco Examiner* (1913)	Janitor, new hotel plus room	$40/mo
Machine Miner	*San Francisco Examiner* (1913)		$90/mo
Physician	*Atlanta Constitution* (1914)	For lumber company and good outside practice	$125/mo
Railway Mail Clerks	*Chicago Tribune* (1914)	Men 18–35	$75/mo
Raise Mushrooms	*Atlanta Constitution* (1913)	Anybody can earn $20 weekly; raising mushrooms, entire year, in cellars, sheds, boxes, etc.; markets waiting	$20/wk
Sales	*New York Times* (1912)	Young man, let us show you how to make $30 weekly; pleasant outdoor work; no experience necessary	$30/wk
Sales	*Chicago Tribune* (1914)	$18 monthly and expenses to travel, distribute samples and take orders or appoint agents, permanent; Jap-American Co.	$18/mo
Secretary	*Chicago Tribune* (1911)	Situation wanted: stenographer or secretary; well educated and competent; good correspondence; mechanical and sales experience; A-1 references	$90/mo
Situation Wanted	*New York Times* (1911)	Need an assistant? Am nineteen years old and want to connect with firm where attention to business will be rewarded. Want a chance to prove I am worth twelve dollars per week. Shall I call?	$12/wk
Stenographer	*Chicago Tribune* (1910)	At least one year's experience; starting salary according to ability	$10–$12/wk
Stenographer	*New York Times* (1910)	Young man, Christian, neat, careful, accurate, steady, familiar with detail work; not afraid of hard work	$12/wk
Teacher	Margo, *Race and Schooling in the South* (1990)	Average annual income of black teachers in Alabama	$311
Teacher	Margo, *Race and Schooling in the South* (1990)	Average annual income of white teachers in Alabama	$790
Typist	*New York Times* (1911)	Young woman typist for copy work only; must be expert on Remington machine	$12/wk
World Series Earnings	*The New Orleans Picayune* (1912)	Amount paid in 1911 to each member of the Philadelphia Baseball Team for winning the World Series	$3,654.59

CONSUMER EXPENDITURES 1914

(Per Capita)

Expenditure Type	1914	Expenditure Type	1914
Clothing	$29.52	Health Insurance	NR
Food	$90.34	Personal Business	$9.86
Auto Purchases	$4.21	Personal Care	$3.08
Auto Parts	$1.09	Tobacco	$7.39
Gas & Oil	$2.35	Local Transport	$6.13
Housing	$62.78	Intercity Transport	$3.32
Furniture	$3.47	Recreation	$10.06
Utilities	$4.64	Religion/Welfare Activities	$8.44
Telephone & Telegraph	$1.13	Private Education & Research	$4.97
Physicians	$2.99	Per Capita Consumption	$336.95
Dentists	$0.95		

INVESTMENTS 1910-1914

Investment	1910	1911	1912	1913	1914
Basic Yield, One-year Corporate Bonds	4.25	4.09	4.04	4.74	4.64
Short-term Interest Rates, 4–6 Months, Prime Commercial Paper	5.72	4.75	5.41	6.20	5.47
Basic Yield, Common Stocks, Total	4.84	4.92	4.85	5.37	5.01
Index of Common Stocks (1941−1943=10)	9.35	9.24	9.53	8.51	8.08

COMMON STOCKS, CLOSING PRICE AND YIELD, FIRST BUSINESS DAY OF YEAR

	1910	1911	1912	1913	1914
Allis Chalmers	14 3/4	7 1/2	1 3/8	2	8 3/4
(Foreclosure 4/26/13)					
(assets acquired by Allis Chalmers Corp.)					
(1 share common exchanged for .35 share of common and 1 share preferred)					
AT&T	140 5/8	140	137 7/8	139 1/4	117 1/2
American Tobacco pfd	94 1/2	93 1/4	103	103	102
Anaconda	32 3/4	38 1/8	38 1/8	41 1/2	34 1/4
B&O	117 5/8	105 1/8	103 1/4	105 3/4	92 3/4
Bethlehem Steel	33 1/2	29	31 7/8	39 1/4	29 3/4
Corn Products	22 7/8	14 1/4	10 1/2	14 3/4	9 3/8
General Electric (30% stock dividend, 12/31/12)	159	151 1/4	153	185 1/2	139
General Motors					37 3/8
(Inc. 9/16/08; 150% stock dividend, 11/15/09)					37 3/8
IBM					
Intl Harvester	117	109 1/2	109	112	101
National Biscuit	115	117	140	127	120
US Steel	89 1/8	72 1/8	69	68 7/8	58 3/8
Western Union	76 5/8	72 1/2	78 1/2	74 5/8	59 3/4

STANDARD JOBS 1910-1914

Job Type	1910	1911	1912	1913	1914
Average of All Industries, excl. farm labor	$630/yr	$629/yr	$646/yr	$675/yr	$682/yr
Average of All Industries, incl. farm labor	$574/yr	$575/yr	$592/yr	$621/yr	$627/yr
Bituminous Coal Mining	30¢/hr	31¢/hr	32¢/hr	32¢/hr	32¢/hr
Avg hrs/wk	51.60	51.60	51.60	51.60	51.60
Building Trades, Union Workers	52¢/hr	53¢/hr	54¢/hr	56¢/hr	57¢/hr
Avg hrs/wk	45.20	45	45	44.90	44.70
Clerical Workers in Mfg. & Steam RR	$1156/yr	$1213/yr	$1209/yr	$1236/yr	$1257/yr
Domestics	$337/yr	$343/yr	$350/yr	$357/yr	$355/yr
Farm Labor	$336/yr	$338/yr	$348/yr	$360/yr	$351/yr
Federal Civilian	$1096/yr	$1133/yr	$1140/yr	$1169/yr	$1197/yr
Federal Employees, Executive Depts.	$1108/yr	$1116/yr	$1128/yr	$1136/yr	$1140/yr
Finance, Insurance & Real Estate	$1301/yr	$1355/yr	$1338/yr	$1349/yr	$1368/yr
Gas & Electricity Workers	$622/yr	$648/yr	$641/yr	$661/yr	$651/yr
Lower-Skilled Labor	$506/yr	$496/yr	$521/yr	$536/yr	$492/yr
Manufacturing, Payroll	19¢/hr	19¢/hr	20¢/hr	21¢/hr	21¢/hr
Avg hrs/wk	59.80	59.60	59.30	58.80	58.30
Manufacturing, Union Workers	40¢/hr	41¢/hr	42¢/hr	43¢/hr	44¢/hr
Avg hrs/wk	50.10	49.80	49.50	49.20	48.80
Medical/Health Services Workers	$338/yr	$352/yr	$352/yr	$357/yr	$366/yr
Ministers	$856/yr	$802/yr	$879/yr	$899/yr	$938/yr
Nonprofit Org. Workers	$715/yr	$763/yr	$784/yr	$802/yr	$837/yr
Postal Employees	42¢/hr	43¢/hr	44¢/hr	45¢/hr	46¢/hr
Avg hrs/wk	48.00	48.00	48.00	48.00	48.00
Public School Teachers	$492/yr	$509/yr	$529/yr	$547/yr	$564/yr
State and Local Govt. Workers	$699/yr	$712/yr	$724/yr	$779/yr	$788/yr
Steam Railroads, Wage Earners	$677/yr	$705/yr	$721/yr	$760/yr	$795/yr
Street Railway Workers	$681/yr	$685/yr	$674/yr	$704/yr	$737/yr
Telegraph Ind. Workers	$649/yr	$670/yr	$669/yr	$717/yr	$742/yr
Telephone Ind. Workers	$417/yr	$419/yr	$438/yr	$438/yr	$476/yr
Wholesale and Retail Trade Workers	$630/yr	$666/yr	$666/yr	$685/yr	$706/yr

FOOD BASKET 1910-1914

Commodity	Year	New York	Atlanta	Chicago	Denver	Los Angeles
Beef, Rib Roasts, per pound	1910	19.33¢	20¢	17.50¢	18.33¢	20¢
	1911	19.83¢	20¢	19.33¢	18.96¢	20¢
	1912	NR	NR	NR	NR	NR
	1913	NR	NR	NR	NR	NR
	1914	NR	NR	NR	NR	NR
Beef Steaks, (Round), per pound	1910	20¢	20¢	20¢	15.83¢	15¢
	1911	20¢	20¢	16.33¢	20¢	20¢
	1912	25¢	20¢	22¢	25¢	20¢
	1913	25¢	21.10¢	20.20¢	20.90¢	20.80¢
	1914	26.30¢	22.20¢	22.40¢	21.70¢	21.20¢
Bread, Wheat, per loaf	1910	NR	NR	NR	NR	NR
	1911	NR	NR	NR	NR	NR
	1912	5¢	5¢	5¢	5¢	10¢
	1913	6.10¢	5.90¢	6.10¢	5.40¢	6.10¢
	1914	6.20¢	5.90¢	6.10¢	5.50¢	6.20¢
Butter, per pound	1910	39¢	38.33¢	36¢	36.67¢	40¢
	1911	35.17¢	37.50¢	32.17¢	33.75¢	36.25¢
	1912	43¢	37.50¢	40¢	40¢	45¢
	1913	38.20¢	39.90¢	36.20¢	37.30¢	39.60¢
	1914	36.20¢	37.40¢	33.30¢	34¢	35.80¢
Cheese, per pound	1910	NR	NR	NR	NR	NR
	1911	NR	NR	NR	NR	NR
	1912	NR	NR	NR	NR	NR
	1913	19.70¢	25¢	25.20¢	26.10¢	19.50¢
	1914	19.90¢	25¢	25.20¢	26.10¢	20¢
Chickens, per pound	1910	18.67¢	21.67¢	19.83¢	21.33¢	25¢
	1911	19.58¢	22.92¢	17.50¢	17.96¢	25¢
	1912	20¢	20¢	17¢	20¢	20¢
	1913	21.40¢	20.20¢	19.30¢	20.30¢	26.60¢
	1914	21.80¢	21.40¢	19.60¢	20.50¢	27.10¢
Coffee, per pound	1910	NR	NR	NR	NR	NR
	1911	NR	NR	NR	NR	NR
	1912	NR	NR	NR	NR	NR
	1913	27.40¢	32¢	30.50¢	29.40¢	36.30¢
	1914	26.30¢	32.80¢	30¢	29.40¢	36.30¢
Cornmeal, per pound	1910	3¢	2.78¢	3¢	2.75¢	3¢
	1911	3¢	2.68	3¢	2.58¢	2.67¢
	1912	3¢	2.50¢	3¢	2.78¢	3.50¢
	1913	3.40¢	2.50¢	2.90¢	2.50¢	3.33¢
	1914	3.50¢	2.80¢	2.80¢	2.60¢	3.60¢
Eggs, per dozen	1910	36.33¢	31.67¢	30.17¢	28.33¢	30.69¢
	1911	34.92¢	26.88¢	27.25¢	32.08¢	33.75¢
	1912	35¢	40¢	26¢	30¢	45¢
	1913	40.30¢	29.20¢	29.20¢	32¢	38.33¢
	1914	41.30¢	31.10¢	29.80¢	32¢	39.20¢
Flour, Wheat, per one-eighth-barrel bag	1910	90¢	90¢	77.50¢	71.50¢	91.67¢
	1911	90¢	90¢	81.67¢	65.84¢	85¢
	1912	84¢	90¢	70¢	65¢	85¢
	1913	3.20¢	3.60¢	2.80¢	2.60¢	3.50¢ (per lb)
	1914	3.40¢	3.50¢	3.10¢	2.70¢	3.70¢ (per lb)
Ham, Smoked, Sliced, per pound	1910	26¢	27.83¢	24¢	33.33¢	35¢
	1911	25.33¢	28.75¢	24¢	33.75¢	35¢
	1912	28¢	30¢	30¢	25¢	35¢
	1913	29¢	29.80¢	31.80¢	30.20¢	35.30¢
	1914	30.20¢	30.30¢	32.60¢	30.60¢	35.60¢

Commodity	Year	New York	Atlanta	Chicago	Denver	Los Angeles
Lard, per pound	1910	16.67¢	16.25¢	16.17¢	17.50¢	18¢
	1911	14.33¢	13.75¢	12.50¢	13.96¢	18¢
	1912	16¢	15¢	15¢	16¢	18¢
	1913	16.10¢	15.40¢	14.90¢	16.20¢	18¢
	1914	15.70¢	15.60¢	15.10¢	15.90¢	17.50¢
Milk, Fresh, per quart	1910	8.50¢	9.44¢	8¢	8.33¢	9¢
	1911	9¢	10¢	8¢	8.33¢	9.92¢
	1912	9¢	10¢	8¢	8.33¢	10¢
	1913	9¢	10.20¢	8¢	8.40¢	10¢
	1914	9¢	10.30¢	8¢	8.40¢	10¢
Mutton and Lamb, per pound	1910	17.67¢	19.79¢	17.67¢	16.83¢	16¢
	1911	16¢	20¢	17.42¢	16¢	16¢
	1912	16.50¢	20¢	18¢	15¢	17¢
	1913	16.50¢	20.10¢	19.80¢	16.40¢	18.80¢
	1914	16.50¢	20.20¢	19.80¢	17.10¢	19.10¢
Pork, Bacon, Sliced, per pound	1910	25.50¢	27.83¢	28¢	33.33¢	34.17¢
	1911	23.83¢	28.75¢	28¢	33.75¢	34.17¢
	1912	24¢	30¢	28¢	30¢	35¢
	1913	25.10¢	31.70¢	31.60¢	28.30¢	33.70¢
	1914	25.80¢	31¢	31.70¢	28.80¢	34.10¢
Pork Chops, per pound	1910	19.33¢	21.67¢	17.33¢	17.50¢	20¢
	1911	17.83¢	19.79¢	15.25¢	16.88¢	20¢
	1912	20¢	20¢	16¢	17.50¢	25¢
	1913	21.50¢	23.10¢	19¢	19.50¢	25.10¢
	1914	22.90¢	23.50¢	19.80¢	20.80¢	26¢
Potatoes, Irish, per pound	1910	NR	NR	NR	NR	NR
	1911	NR	NR	NR	NR	NR
	1912	40¢ (per peck)	27.50¢ (per peck)	20¢ (per 15 lbs)	$1.25 (per 100 lbs)	$1.25 (per 100 lbs)
	1913	2.50¢	2.20¢	1.60¢	1.40¢	1.50¢
	1914	2.63¢	2.40¢	1.70¢	1.70¢	1.80¢
Rice, per pound	1910	NR	NR	NR	NR	NR
	1911	NR	NR	NR	NR	NR
	1912	NR	NR	NR	NR	NR
	1913	8¢	8.60¢	8.90¢	8.60¢	7.70¢
	1914	8.30¢	8.60¢	9¢	8.60¢	8¢
Sugar, per pound	1910	5.43¢	5.83¢	5.71¢	6.13¢	6.53¢
	1911	5.91¢	6.44¢	6.50¢	6.54¢	6.28¢
	1912	5.43¢	5.88¢	5.50¢	6¢	5.88¢
	1913	4.90¢	5.70¢	5.10¢	5.50¢	5.40¢
	1914	5.30¢	6.10¢	5.60¢	5.70¢	5.90¢
Tea, per pound	1910	NR	NR	NR	NR	NR
	1911	NR	NR	NR	NR	NR
	1912	NR	NR	NR	NR	NR
	1913	43.30¢	60¢	54¢	52.80¢	54.50¢
	1914	43.33¢	60¢	54.30¢	52.80¢	54.50¢

SELECTED PRICES 1910-1914

Item	Source	Description	Price
Alcohol			
Whiskey	*The New Orleans Daily Picayune* (1912)	*Hayner Bottled-in-Bond Whiskey;* per quart	$0.80
Whiskey	*New Orleans Daily Picayune* (1910)	*Duffy's Pure Malt;* it corrects the defective digestion of the food, increases the appetite, strengthens the heart	$1.00/bottle
Apparel, Children's			
Army Uniform	*Sears, Roebuck* (1912)	Boy's; the regular army play suit of olive-colored khaki drill	$1.50
Baby Wear	*New York Times* (1910)	*Abraham and Straus;* lawn dress	$0.98
Dress	*Sears, Roebuck* (1913)	Girl's shepherd check; cut in one-piece sailor style with sailor collar	$1.65
Fabric	*The Ladies' Home Journal* (1911)	All wool dress serge. Dressmakers' width for family use Per yard	$0.75
Hat	*Sears, Roebuck* (1910)	Washable; the entire brim of this hat is of fluted mall, with full double ruffle on edge	$0.44
Hose	*The Ladies' Home Journal* (1911)	*Black Cat Hosiery*—a beautiful, fine mercerized hose Girls, per pair	$0.35
Hose Support	*Ladies' Home Journal* (1911)	*Wilson;* children can't stand restraining clothing; that's why their garters are important for comfort	$0.25
Infant's Pants	*Ladies' Home Journal* (1911)	*OMO;* a dainty, comfortable garment that will keep baby's clothes dry and clean	$0.25
Knee Pants	*John M. Smyth Company* (1911)	Boys; these pants are actually worth 75¢—$1.25 per pair	$0.45
Knitted Legging Drawers	*Sears, Roebuck* (1913)	Drawstring at waist	$0.19
Long Cambric Slip	*Sears, Roebuck* (1913)	Infant's; trimmed with lace edge on neck and sleeves	$0.09
Night Gown	*The New Orleans Daily Picayune* (1912)	Soft, fleecy flannelette nightgown	$0.22
Overall Suit	*Sears, Roebuck* (1912)	*Rip-Proof;* neat gray-stripe denim	$1.40
Overcoat	*Sears, Roebuck* (1912)	*Ucanttear;* of strong wool and cotton fabric	$1.75
Stockings	*Sears, Roebuck* (1913)	Girl's tearproof; elastic ribbed black cotton stockings	$0.19
Sweater	*The New Orleans Daily Picayune* (1912)	All-wool sweaters, sizes 20 to 34	$0.50
Apparel, Men's			
Automobile Duster	*John M. Smyth Company* (1911)	Man's fancy; made from fancy herring-bone striped natural linen	$1.95
Boots	*The New Orleans Daily Picayune* (1912)	*Dull Calf Blucher boots;* heavy, double sole; splendid shoes for businessmen	$2.45

Item	Source	Description	Price
Coat	*John M. Smyth Company* (1911)	*Alpaca;* the ideal hot weather coat	$1.95
Coat	*John M. Smyth Company* (1911)	English slip-on motor coat; made from fine imported English Roseberry cloth	$10.98
Coat	*John M. Smyth Company* (1911)	*Storm King Mackintosh;* single-breasted with fly front wide black velvet collars, fancy woven plaid lining	$3.98
Coat	*John M. Smyth Company* (1911)	Ministerial coat; made from black Drap D'Ete cloth	$5.00
Coat	*John M. Smyth Company* (1911)	*Presto Model Cravenette Raincoat;* fine black broadcloth	$16.50
Coat	*Sears, Roebuck* (1912)	Sheepskin-lined corduroy; with sheepskin collars	$4.95
Coat	*Sears, Roebuck* (1912)	Waterproof brown duck; made from 8-ounce duck with heavy fancy blanket lining and oiled slicker cloth	$2.10
Coat	*Sears, Roebuck* (1913)	Sweater coat; in popular zig-zag style	$2.48
Collars	*Sears, Roebuck* (1913)	Low style, lots of tie space	$0.59/6
Hat	*Sears, Roebuck* (1913)	*Cornwell;* Lennox Jr. style black or nutria tan	$2.00
Overcoat	*New York Times* (1910)	*Hart, Schaffner and Marx;* large size 40–52	$12.50
Overcoat	*John M. Smyth Company* (1911)	Grey vicuna cloth; full silk lined	$18.00
Pajamas	*Sears, Roebuck* (1913)	Quality madras trimmed with frog fasteners and large pearl buttons	$1.45
Scarf	*Sears, Roebuck* (1913)	Shetland wool motor scarf; veil in medium size mesh with face-knitted border; size about 20 x 54	$1.05
Suit	*John M. Smyth Company* (1911)	*Glory B;* satin-lined blue serge; the most wonderful suit of the century	$7.98
Suit	*John M. Smyth Company* (1911)	*Smyth Made Model 86;* three piece, fancy, olive, striped, worsted; a tasteful, elegant, and dressy pattern	$7.98
Suit	*John M. Smyth Company* (1911)	Young man's biplane model; navy blue serge three piece	$7.98
Support Hose	*Sears, Roebuck* (1913)	Elastic; exceptionally good value at $0.25 a pair	$0.12/pair
Trousers	*John M. Smyth Company* (1911)	*Smyth Made Model K;* novelty smoke-gray fancy striped worsted trousers	$3.00
Trousers	*John M. Smyth Company*(1911)	*U.S.A. Khaki;* more popular this season than ever before	$0.98
Trousers	*John M. Smyth Company* (1911)	College style, peg top; made from extra-fine all-wool fancy cassimere	$3.50
Umbrella	*Sears, Roebuck* (1913)	Genuine paragon steel frames with mixed silk taffeta cover cover and selected boxwood handle	$2.25
Undershirt	*Sears, Roebuck* (1913)	Winter fleeced; extra heavy flat-knit cotton	$0.44

Item	Source	Description	Price
Vest	John M. Smyth Company (1911)	Men's fancy vest; every man should have one or two fancyvests in his wardrobe	$1.48
Work Shirt	Sears, Roebuck (1913)	Khaki tan; double-yoke shoulders	$0.45

Apparel, Women's

Item	Source	Description	Price
Blouse	Sears, Roebuck (1913)	Sweater blouse; has high fitting turndown collar	$1.19
Coat	Sears, Roebuck (1913)	Furlike; black boucle cloth coat (imitation Persian lamb)	$13.95
Coat	Sears, Roebuck (1913)	Misses winter weight; heavy gray cloth coat, double texture plaid trimmed	$8.95
Corset	Sears, Roebuck (1910)	Long hip style; our Frances model gives the straight slender effect which is so much desired	$1.38
Corset	Ladies' Home Journal (1911)	W. B. Nuform; for average or full figures; low bust and low under arms	$2.00
Corset	Ladies' Home Journal (1911)	W. B. Reduso; for average large figures; medium high bust, long over hips and abdomen	$3.00
Corset	The Ladies' Home Journal (1911)	Nuform, Style 101—for average figures. Medium high bust, long over hips and back	$1.50
Dress	New Orleans Daily Picayune (1910)	Silk; Pongees, in natural color and light summery shades	$10.95
Dress	Sears, Roebuck (1913)	Misses lace-trimmed mohair; looks worth fully twice the price we ask	$5.15
Furs	The New Orleans Daily Picayune (1912)	Exclusive Shop; Eastern mink set, regularly $300; on sale	$270
Gloves	Sears, Roebuck (1910)	Gauntlet	$0.06
Gloves	Ladies' Home Journal (1911)	Fownes; silk; it's a Fownes—that's all you need to know about a glove	$0.50
Gloves	The State (Columbia, SC) (1911)	Open at wrist 2-clasp, elegant quality pure silk, 16-button length	$0.69
Gloves	Sears, Roebuck (1913)	Lined fabric; imported black cashmerette gloves	$0.23
Hair Net	Ladies' Home Journal (1911)	Con-tour; very convenient and stylish; a favorite with fashionable ladies everywhere	$0.15
Handkerchief	Sears, Roebuck (1910)	White Swiss embroidered scalloped handkerchiefs	$0.14
Hat	New York Times (1910)	Poke bonnet; made of fancy black braid, trimmed with cluster of royal and pink roses, and silver-lace foliage	$27.89
Hat	Sears, Roebuck (1913)	Dressy; a charming poke style turban	$3.15
Hat Pins	New Orleans Daily Picayune (1910)	Rhinestone; a splendid selection of attractive styles	$0.50
Hose	Ladies' Home Journal (1911)	Gordon Dollar Silk; pure thread silk, heavy lisle soles, heel and toe, extra garter hem protection	$1.00
Muff	Sears, Roebuck (1912)	Opossum fur; made in large well-padded semi-barrel style	$8.25
Nightgown	Sears, Roebuck (1913)	Misses; very fine quality nainsook Empire style	$0.99

Item	Source	Description	Price
Ostrich Plume	*The New Orleans Daily Picayune* (1912)	Bull Head four-tie willow ostrich plume, black only	$18.00
Petticoat	*New York Times* (1910)	Satin	$7.75
Petticoat	*New Orleans Daily Picayune* (1910)	White; nainsook tops, lawn flounces	$1.69
Petticoat	*Ladies' Home Journal* (1911)	*Klosfit;* made so that it fits the figure as a silk glove fits the hand	$1.00
Petticoat	*Sears, Roebuck* (1913)	Made of splendid cotton fabric, closely woven	$1.48
Purse	*Sears, Roebuck* (1913)	Silk velvet; ninety-nine steel studs, silver English frame 8"x7"	$1.65
Shoes	*The New Orleans Daily Picayune* (1912)	Maison Blanche Queen Quality shoes; no matter the occasion, whether walking, street or dress wear, you'll find a style suited to your needs	$3.50 to $5.00
Shoes	*New Orleans Daily Picayune* (1910)	*Queen Quality;* fifty new styles	$3.50
Shoes	*Ladies' Home Journal* (1911)	*Red Cross;* the Red Cross shoe never needs breaking in; You can put it on in the store and wear it home; Oxford style	$3.50
Skirt	*The Ladies' Home Journal* (1911)	The *National Maternity Skirt* makes possible outdoor exercise, fresh air, sunshine and health for the prospective mother.	$5.98 to $10.00
Skirt	*Ladies' Home Journal* (1911)	*National Maternity;* it does away with the stay-at-home, the gloom and depression of the maternity period	$5.98
Skirt	*Sears, Roebuck* (1913)	Panama style; made in popular straight hanging style with full length front panel	$2.89
Suit	*New York Times* 1910)	*O'Neill Adams Spring Suit;* an exceedingly smart suit of French serge, with the full-length of coat	$29.75
Supporter	*The Ladies' Home Journal* (1911)	Princess Chic supporter produces ideal figure lines State waist measure	$0.50 to $1.00
Union Suit	*Sears, Roebuck* (1913)	Winter weight; elastic-ribbed fleece-lined union suit	$0.48

Appliances

Item	Source	Description	Price
Vacuum Cleaner	*Ladies' Home Journal* (1911)	*Eureka;* no other indoor dry method of cleaning than suction can make your home really clean	$35.00
Vacuum Cleaner	*Sears, Roebuck* (1912)	*Eckhardt;* makes clean houses cleaner	$46.75

Baby Products

Item	Source	Description	Price
Baby Walker	*The Ladies' Home Journal* (1911)	*E-Z-GO Baby Tender.* Teaches baby to walk in the easy way. Does a large part of a nurse's children's work Express, prepaid	$2.75
Bottle	*The Ladies' World* 1910	*Hygeia* nursing bottle, only bottle with a breast; germs of disease have no hiding place 8-ounce bottle and nipple 12-ounce bottle and nipple	$0.38 $0.50
Diaper Cover	*Sears, Roebuck* (1913)	Of white cambric, coated with a specially prepared composition making it waterproof	$0.35
Nipples	*Sears, Roebuck* (1912)	Best black rubber nipples to fit over neck of nursing bottle	$0.10/3
Portable Folding Bathtub	*Sears, Roebuck* (1913)	Tub when open is 36 long, 22 high and 16 wide	$4.98

Item	Source	Description	Price
Wrapper	*The New Orleans Daily Picayune* (1912)	Infant's fleece-lined knit wrapper	$0.17

Business Equipment & Supplies

Item	Source	Description	Price
Express Mail Flat Rate	*The New Orleans Daily Picayune* (1912)	Express charge for any package, up to 11 pounds, in United States	$0.27
Typewriter Rentals	*New York Times* (1910)	$100 machines; rental allowed to apply if purchased	$3/mo
Wagon	*The New Orleans Picayune* (1912)	Top delivery wagon	$97.00

Collectibles

Item	Source	Description	Price
Painting	*American Chronicle* (1999)	Claude Monet's *Fishing Boats;* sold at auction in 1910	$240
Painting	*American Chronicle* (1999)	Rembrandt's *Portrait of Admiral Campbell;* sold at auction in 1910	$4,400
Spade	*The New Orleans Daily Picayune* (1912)	Shovel used by Jane Addams to open The Priscilla Inn, a hotel home for self-supporting women in 1912; spade sold in auction	$900

Education

Item	Source	Description	Price
Tuition	*American Decades* (1911)	Harvard University	$150/year
Tuition	*American Decades* (1911)	Colgate University	$60.00/year
Tuition	*The Magazine of Wall Street* (1913)	*Raymond Riordon School* (Highland, New York); high school, college preparatory, special courses and department for younger boys	$800

Entertainment

Item	Source	Description	Price
Aviation Exhibition	*New York Tribune* (1911)	International Aviation Meet; thirty world-famous men and women aviators demonstrate speed, duration and altitude Admission Seats at starting line Auto space	$0.50 $1.00 $5.00
Baseball Game	*The New Orleans Picayune* (1912)	Greenwall Theatre; World Series baseball games played on stage by electrical scoreboard; also Monster Burlesque Show Night prices and Ball Game matinees	$0.10 to $0.50
Concert Ticket	*New York Times* (1910)	*Carnegie Hall;* Sembrich Frank LaForge at piano	$2.50
Festival Ticket	*New Orleans Daily Picayune* (1910)	*Grand May Festival and Picnic at Southern Park;* given by the Gardners' Mutual Protective Association; admission to grounds	$0.25 to $1.00
Musical	*The New Orleans Picayune* (1912)	*The Balkan Princess;* includes a special orchestra Nights	$0.25 to $1.50
Musical Comedy	*The New Orleans Daily Picayune* (1912)	*Louisiana Lou* by the La Salle Opera-House Company at Tulane Nights and Saturday matinee, per seat	From $0.25 to $1.50
Play	*The New Orleans Daily Picayune* (1912)	*The Confession;* from a successful run at the Broadway Bijou Theatre, New York Nights, seats	From $0.15 to $0.75
Theater Ticket	*New Orleans Daily Picayune* (1910)	*American Music Hall;* summer season popular vaudeville; this week Albert Wild, Hilman & Roberts, George Smedley and other features; all seats	$0.10

Item	Source	Description	Price
Theater Ticket	*New York Times* (1910)	*Metropolis;* Harry Bryant's Burlesque Co.	$0.35
Theater Ticket	*New York Times* (1910)	New Amsterdam Theatre; *Madame X;* supreme drama of tears and thrills, best seats	$1.50
Theater Ticket	*New York Times* (1910)	*The New Theatre; The School for Scandal,* Sheridan's delightful comedy	$0.50
Theater Ticket	*San Francisco Examiner* (1913)	Henry W. Savage's play, *The Merry Widow,* all-star revival	$0.50 to $2.00
Theater Ticket	*San Francisco Examiner* (1913)	Thomas A. Edison's Talking Moving Pictures, exclusively at The Orpheum	$0.10 to $1.00

Entertainment, Home

Item	Source	Description	Price
Card Game	*Sears, Roebuck* (1912)	*Old Maid;* too well known to need description	$0.19
Crayons	*Sears, Roebuck* (1913)	*Paragon Drawing;* twenty-eight colors	$0.04
Dominoes	*Sears, Roebuck* (1912)	*Black Cat;* high-grade black composition double six dominoes	$0.33
Game	*Sears, Roebuck* (1912)	*Jolly Coon Race;* a new and very comical game for two or three people; metal figures of darkies with moveable arms, racing along three poles	$0.89
Record	*The Magazine of Wall Street* (1913)	*Columbia Double Disc Phonograph;* fits your machine	$0.65
Statue	*Sears, Roebuck* (1912)	Musical negroes; darkies playing accordion and flute	$0.98
Talking Machine	*Sears, Roebuck* (1912)	*J. F. Oxford;* flower-shaped metal horn, 18" in diameter	$14.95

Farm Equipment & Supplies

Item	Source	Description	Price
Egg Incubator and Brooder	*Ladies' Home Journal* (1911)	Hot water, copper tanks, double walls, double glass doors, freight paid east of Rockies; 125 egg capacity	$10.00
Milk Bucket	*Sears, Roebuck* (1910)	Tin; flaring open-top pail; 4 1/2 quart capacity	$0.08

Financial Products & Services

Item	Source	Description	Price
Interest Rate	*The New Orleans Picayune* (1912)	Interstate Bank interest payment on savings accounts	4%

Food Products

Item	Source	Description	Price
Candy	*Sears, Roebuck* (1912)	Peanut Butter Kisses; Preferred by many to the usual taffy; 2 1/2 pound box	$0.46
Cereal	*The Ladies' World* 1910	Gigantic kernels of wheat or rice, puffed to eight times natural size. Made so porous and crisp that they melt in the mouth Puffed wheat Puffed rice	 $0.10 $0.15 (except in extreme West)
Cereal	*The Ladies' Home Journal* (1911)	*Quaker Oats Puffed Rice.* They taste like bubbled nuts	$0.15 (except in far West)
Chocolate	*The Ladies' World* 1910	*Baker's Caracas Sweet Chocolate,* a delightful combination of the highest grade cocoa, pure sugar and vanilla, one package	$0.10

Item	Source	Description	Price
Cracker	*New York Times* (1910)	*Uneeda Biscuit;* made today and packaged snugly in their protecting package	$0.05
Marshmallows	*Sears, Roebuck* (1912)	200 finest soft delicious marshmallows in a box	$0.42
Seasoning	*New Orleans Daily Picayune* (1910)	*Genuine Creole;* there is no trouble; nothing to learn; regular-size bottle	$0.25
Soup	*The Ladies' Home Journal* (1911)	*Campbell's Soup*—a perfect dinner course; 21 kinds	$0.10
Soup	*Ladies' Home Journal* (1911)	Tomato; the way to his heart	$0.10
Wafers	*Overland Monthly* (1910)	*Nabisco Sugar Wafers;* always in good form Two sizes	$0.10 and $0.25

Furniture

Item	Source	Description	Price
Bed	*San Francisco Examiner* (1913)	High-class sleigh bed in mahogany or circassian walnut	$39.50
Chair	*New Orleans Daily Picayune* (1910)	Porch rocker; double cane seat and back, with wide arms and seat	$2.25
Chair	*Ladies' Home Journal* (1911)	*Come-Packt Morris;* in quartered white oak—save half or more buying direct from our factory	$8.75
Chair	*Sears, Roebuck* (1912)	Bowback wooden kitchen chair; made of especially selected northern hardwood	$0.78
Chair	*Sears, Roebuck* (1912)	Morris rocker; solid comfort every minute	$5.35
Furniture Package	*New Orleans Daily Picayune* (1910)	4-Room outfit consisting of full bedroom suite, dining suite, parlor suite and kitchen outfit	$147.50
Kitchen Cabinet	*Sears, Roebuck* (1912)	*Wilson Oak;* cupboard and kitchen table in a single piece of furniture	$23.85
Lamp	*Sears, Roebuck* (1912)	*Art Glass;* electric portable; wired complete with chain pull socket	$7.50
Mirror	*New Orleans Daily Picayune* (1910)	*Chiffonier;* mirror 14 x 22 , double shaped top 20 x 36; full-quartered oak with golden finish, serpentine front	$14.90
Table	*Sears, Roebuck* (1912)	Parlor; made of seasoned quarter sawed oak	$2.85
Tea Wagon	*The Magazine of Wall Street* (1913)	*Willow;* painted to match chintz	$16.50
Turkish Bath Cabinet	*New York Times* (1910)	The best means in the world for breaking up colds or grippe	$4.50 to $18

Garden Equipment & Supplies

Item	Source	Description	Price
Manure Spreader	*Sears, Roebuck* (1912)	*David Bradley;* when not needed to spread, lift off box and you have a splendid farm truck with wheel truck	$69.50
Potato Planter	*Sears, Roebuck* (1912)	*Schofield;* all iron and steel except pole	$19.85

Hotel Rates

Item	Source	Description	Price
Hotel Room	*The Magazine of Wall Street* (1913)	*Hotel Puritan;* Boston; a public house for those who demand the best single rooms	$2.00/day

Item	Source	Description	Price
Room	*The New Orleans Daily Picayune* (1912)	*Hotel Victoria;* fronting on Fifth Avenue and Broadway, New York City; all rooms have hot and cold running water	
		Rooms	$1.50
		Rooms with bath	$2.00 and up
Room	*Overland Monthly* (1910)	*Hotel Normandie,* San Francisco, California; fine air, elevation, location	
		American plan, per day	$3.00 and up
		European plan, per day	$1.50 and up
Room	*Overland Monthly* (1910)	*Hotel St. Francis,* San Francisco, California	
		European plan, per day	$2.00 and up
Room	*Overland Monthly* (1910)	*Hotel Windsor,* 308-310 West 58th Street, New York; 100 feet from Broadway; 100 suites, each with bath	
		Per day	$2.50 to $10.00

Household Products

Item	Source	Description	Price
Ammonia	*Sears, Roebuck* (1912)	*Violet;* for the toilet and bath	$0.17
Bedspread	*Sears, Roebuck* (1910)	Pure white, hemmed, crochet, bedspread; 68 x 79	$0.68
Blanket	*Sears, Roebuck* (1912)	All-wool; splendid wearing qualities and rich appearance	$3.98
Cake Turner	*Sears, Roebuck* (1913)	Steel; length about 12	$0.02
China	*New York Tribune* (1911)	White and gold monogrammed china; 100-piece dinner set with coin gold border	$52.50
Cistern	*The New Orleans Daily Picayune*	*Cypress cistern,* in good order	$6.50
Cleanser	*The Ladies' Home Journal* (1911)	Scour pots and pans with *Old Dutch Cleanser* Large sifter can	$0.10
Cleanser	*Ladies' Home Journal* (1911)	*Old Dutch;* cuts the grease and burn from tinware, agateware, aluminum ware, graniteware, etc.	$0.10
Couch Covers	*Sears, Roebuck* (1912)	Tapestry; in rich oriental design 2 7/8 yrds long by 56 wide	$1.75
Desk	*Sears, Roebuck* (1912)	*Simplex;* single desk; one of our most stable and durable patterns	$1.75
Finish	*Ladies' Home Journal* (1911)	*Johnson's Under-Lac;* a thin, elastic spirit finish far superior to varnish or shellac	$0.70/quart
Flashlight	*Sears, Roebuck* (1912)	*Ever Ready;* the most efficient flashlight of its size ever made with Merchlor battery	$0.98
Floor Wax	*Sears, Roebuck* (1912)	*Seroco;* dirt and dust will not stick to floors waxed with Seroco floor wax	$0.22/pound can
Hammer	*Sears, Roebuck* (1912)	*Fulton Special;* solid tool steel, full nickel plated; 13 oz.	$0.66
Inlaid Linoleum	*Sears, Roebuck* (1912)	Fine quality domestic inlaid linoleum	$2.35/yard
Lamp Burner	*Sears, Roebuck* (1913)	Brass; by including these items with other goods you usually get them without paying any more freight	$0.04
Lavatory	*Sears, Roebuck* (1912)	Porcelain-enameled one-piece square with nickel-plated model waste and wall hanger	$8.40
Paint	*Sears, Roebuck* (1910)	For entire house; this cottage measures 18' wide x 32' long and 12' high; for body 4 gallons, for trimming 1 gallon	$4.90/gallon
Picture Hooks	*Sears, Roebuck* (1910)		$0.04/dozen
Pot Holder	*Sears, Roebuck* (1913)	Iron; asbestos filled	$0.02

Item	Source	Description	Price
Potato Baker	*Ladies' Home Journal* (1911)	*Handi-Kwick;* saves burning your arms and hands, bakes six at a time	$0.10
Rug	*New York Times* (1910)	*Joseph Wild Prairie;* a superior weave of tough grass; carried in plain green or brown; 4' x 7'	$9.50
Shovel	*Sears, Roebuck* (1910)	*Invincible D Handle;* plain back, solid steel	$0.48
Silverware	*The State* (Columbia, SC) (1911)	*1847 Rogers Brothers;* knives and forks warranted 16-dwt pure silver on every dozen (6 knives and 6 forks)	$3.93/dozen
Soap	*Ladies' Home Journal* (1911)	*Grandma;* borax powdered; Grandma is not a washing powder but a powdered soap	$0.05
Soap	*Sears, Roebuck* (1912)	*Lifebuoy;* removes the dirt you see while destroying the germs which you cannot see	$0.51/12 cakes
Suitcase	*Sears, Roebuck* (1913)	Lightweight cane made over strong wood frame	$4.95
Toilet Paper	*Sears, Roebuck* (1912)	*Jewel;* about 1,000 sheets to roll	$0.27/6 rolls
Trunk	*Sears, Roebuck* (1913)	*Gibraltar;* guaranteed to last a lifetime of ordinary service; 38 x 22 x 24	$16.95
Umbrella	*New York Times* (1910)	*Abraham and Straus;* woman's style	$2.74
Wallpaper	*Sears, Roebuck* (1912)	*The Eugenia;* red and pink roses in a frame of gilt Border Ceiling	$0.02/double roll $0.15/double roll
Wall Paper	*New York Tribune* (1911)	Fine foreign wallpapers; values $1 to $4; sold in room lots Now	$0.25 a piece
Wood Stain	*The Magazine of Wall Street* (1913)	*Devoe* wood stain; ready for use after dissolving in water	$0.50/can

Insurance Rates

Item	Source	Description	Price
Fire Insurance	Insurance Policy (1911)	Rate 2.51; $250 coverage fire damage on brick and frame one-story building in Columbia, SC	$6.27/year

Jewelry

Item	Source	Description	Price
Diamond Ring	*New Orleans Daily Picayune* (1910)	Man's solitaire; pure blue-white stone; perfect in cut	$100
Diamonds	*The New Orleans Picayune* (1912)	*Weinfurter's;* blue tinged, finest white diamonds; weight 7/8 and 1/16 carat stone	$185
Watch	*The New Orleans Picayune* (1912)	Waltham gold pocket watch; seventeen jewel	$10.50

Medical Products & Services

Item	Source	Description	Price
Dental Crowns	*The New Orleans Daily Picayune* (1912)	*Union Dental Company;* highest quality and workmanship Per tooth	$4.00
False Teeth	*The New Orleans Daily Picayune* (1912)	*Union Dental Company;* a good set of teeth on a rubber base, guaranteed to wear well Per set	$5.00
Laxative	*The New Orleans Daily Picayune* (1912)	*Castoria;* for infants and children; a vegetable preparation for stimulating the food and regulating the stomach and bowels 35 doses per bottle	$0.35

Item	Source	Description	Price
Liquor Cure	*The State* (Columbia, SC) (1911)	From the third day after I started treatment I can honestly say I have had no desire for a drink of whiskey or beer; includes board, lodging, and necessary attention	$35/mo
Nonprescription Drug	*Sears, Roebuck* (1912)	Elixir pepsin compound; pleasant to take and largely sold for indigestion and stomach complaints	$0.49/16-ounce bottle
Teething Powders	*The Ladies' World* (1910)	*Dr. StedMen's Teething Powders,* absolutely free from morphia or any other alkaloid or constituent of opium opium; One packet	$0.25

Motorized Vehicles, Services, & Supplies

Item	Source	Description	Price
Automobile	Throm, ed., *Popular Mechanics Picture History of American Transportation* (1952)	*Black Crow;* biggest, handsomest, greatest value cars ever offered for these prices, 25–30hp	$1,000
Automobile	Joseph J. Schroeder Jr., *The Wonderful World of Automobiles* (1971)	*Franklin 1910;* only one percent of the roads in this country is macadam; the rest are ordinary dirt roads; do you want an automobile that is comfortable only on macadam roads or on all roads?; 4-cylinder, 28 hp, five-passenger touring car	$2,800
Automobile	Schroeder, *The Wonderful World of Automobiles* (1971)	*Glide Special;* 7-passenger, 45 hp touring car [cost in 1910]	$2,500
Automobile	*New York Times* (1910)	*Marmon Thirty-two;* 5-passenger touring car, shaft drive, double system ignition; the positive car	$2,700
Automobile	*New York Times* (1910)	*Mora;* there is no other power plant like it	$1,050
Automobile	*New York Times* (1910)	*Paige-Detroit;* a low-priced, high-powered roadster that at once satisfies the power crank, the speed fiend, and the endurance runner	$800
Automobile	Schroeder, *The Wonderful World of Automobiles* (1971)	*Rambler;* featuring the offset crank-shaft, straight-line drive, spare wheel and new expanding clutch [cost in 1910]	$1,800
Automobile	Schroeder, *The Wonderful World of Automobiles* (1971)	*Sears Motor Car;* so simple that anyone can operate; Model H, 14 hp, air-cooled motor [cost in 1910]	$395
Automobile	Schroeder, *The Wonderful World of Automobiles* (1971)	*American Underslung Traveler Special;* six passengers, the last word in grace and beauty [cost in 1912]	$4,500
Automobile	Schroeder, *The Wonderful World of Automobiles* (1971)	*Elmore Torpedo;* five-passenger light torpedo with top and windshield [cost in 1912]	$1,350
Automobile	Schroeder, *The Wonderful World of Automobiles* (1971)	*Overland 610-T;* five-passenger 45 hp touring car; the shifting levers are in the center of the car [cost in 1912]	$1,500
Automobile	Schroeder, *The Wonderful World of Automobiles* (1971)	*Garford Six;* electrically started; all lights are electric; the horn is electric, 60 hp, five-passenger touring car [cost in 1913]	$2,750

Item	Source	Description	Price
Automobile	Schroeder, *The Wonderful World of Automobiles* (1971)	*Jackson;* no hill too steep no sand too deep, 50 hp, 4 cylinder motor, five-passenger [cost in 1913]	$1,800
Automobile	Schroeder, *The Wonderful World of Automobiles* (1971)	*Maxwell Mercury;* an ideal car for touring [cost in 1913]	$1,150
Automobile	Schroeder, *The Wonderful World of Automobiles* (1971)	*Oakland Greyhound;* four-, five-, and seven-passenger touring cars [cost in 1913]	$2,550
Machine Oil	*Sears, Roebuck* (1913)	Best grade of mineral oil for light machinery	$0.06/3-ounce bottle
Transmission Grease	*Sears, Roebuck* (1912)	We cannot use the manufacturer's name for the reason that we are selling it at a greatly reduced price	$0.80/5-pound pail
Used Automobile	*The New Orleans Daily Picayune* (1912)	*Stoddard-Dayton touring car;* five-passenger; fully equipped	$600
Windshield	Schroeder, *The Wonderful World of Automobiles* (1971)	*Mezger Automatic;* up or down with one hand without slackening speed [cost in 1910]	$25.00

Musical Instruments

Item	Source	Description	Price
Piano	*The New Orleans Daily Picayune* (1912)	Steinway baby grand piano	$2,000 and up
Piano-Organ	*Sears, Roebuck* (1912)	*Beckwith Queen;* leads all others in quality, finish, design, and tone	$68.00
Violin	*Sears, Roebuck* (1912)	*Stradivarius Model;* violin outfits of this grade are generally sold for $35	$19.95

Other

Item	Source	Description	Price
Film Developer	*The Ladies' World* (1910)	Hayden film tank, the best, simplest and most improved film tank on the market Film printing frame Convertible plate tank 5 x 7	$0.75 $1.75
Home Plans	Ladies' Home *Journal* (1911)	*MacLagan's;* suburban; 200 building plans of bungalows, suburban and country homes, actually erected costing from $400 up to $10,000; plans and specifications	$5 and up
Mask	*Sears, Roebuck* (1912)	Santa Claus; fancy waxed-cloth mask with heavy eyebrows	$0.09
Plumes	*Ladies' Home Journal* (1911)	French; carefully selected raw material from the male bird; full 15	$1.90
Prize, Billiards Match	*New Orleans Daily Picayune* (1910)	Championship; Harry P. Cline, of Philadelphia, the present title holder at 18.2 balk line billiards, has agreed to meet Willie Hoppe for the world's championship; prize includes championship emblem	$1,000
Wrapping Paper	*Sears, Roebuck* (1912)	Christmas Bells; Red tissue paper; beautiful for Christmas decoration	$0.09/pkg of 2

Personal Care Products

Item	Source	Description	Price
Cluster Puffs	Ladies' Home *Journal* (1911)	*Recamier;* just send us a lock of your hair and we will send you this lovely set of Recamier Cluster Puffs	$2.85

Item	Source	Description	Price
Face Powder	*The Ladies' Home Journal* (1910)	*Lablache face powder* keeps complexions smooth and velvety Per box	$0.50
Hair Aid	*The Ladies' World* (1910)	Parker's Hair Balsam cleanses and beautifies the hair. Promotes a luxuriant growth; cures scalp diseases and hair falling Small bottle Large bottle	 $0.50 $1.00
Hair Barrette	*Sears, Roebuck* (1913)	Silvered filigree; 42 rhinestones	$0.49
Soap Dispenser	*New York Times* (1910)	*The Soapator;* supplies soap in the most delightful form, includes soapator and box of assorted soaps	$5.00
Toothpaste	*New York Times* (1910)	*Sanitol;* a perfect dentifrice—you can get it in either powder or paste form	$0.25
Toothpaste	*New Orleans Daily Picayune* (1910)	*Sanitol;* your general health will be better	$0.25
Tooth Soap	*Sears, Roebuck* (1912)	*Albi-Denta;* for hardening gums and preserving the teeth	$0.10/3 ounce
Toupee	*Sears, Roebuck* (1913)	Man's; made on the finest quality silk gauze foundation	$21.65

Publications

The *Daily Picayune*	*The New Orleans Daily Picayune* (1912)	Published seven days a week One-year subscription	$12.00
Magazine	*Overland Monthly* (1910)	*The Jewish Times;* weekly	$3.00
Magazine	*Ladies' Home Journal* (1911)	*Ladies' Home Journal;* biweekly	$0.10
Magazine	*The Magazine of Wall Street* (1913)	*Broadmoor Bungalow;* elevation half tone reproductions of photographs of California bungalows	$0.50
Magazine	*The Magazine of Wall Street* (1913)	*Collier's;* weekly	$0.05
Magazine	*The Magazine of Wall Street* (1913)	*Illustrated World Magazine;* monthly	$0.05

Real Estate

Apartment	*New York Times* (1910)	West End Ave 712 Apartment A (96th St. subway); Light, heat, hot water; cleanliness	$5.00/week
Apartment	*New York Times* (1910)	2 and 3 rooms, just completed, overlooking Morningside and Central Parks; vacuum cleaning system	$40 to $55/month
Apartment Building	*New York Times* (1910)	Eight-, nine-, ten-room (3 bath) suites; at 36 Gramercy Park-East	$8,900
House	*The Ladies' Home Journal* (1911)	*Aladdin Readi-Cut Houses.* All the materials for a complete house	$557
House	*New York Times* (1910)	Artistic houses	$4,750
House	*New Orleans Daily Picayune* (1910)	Double, two-story house, New Orleans; 6 rooms each side; driveways, stable, etc.; 938-940 Felicity	$5,100

Item	Source	Description	Price
House	*New York Times* (1910)	New Jersey; 7 rooms, bath, cellar, furnace, gas and electricity, hardwood trim; train and trolly; 15 minutes to city	$5,400
Land	*New Orleans Daily Picayune* (1910)	Three lots between Freret and Robertson *Street*s New Orleans	$6,000
Land	*The New Orleans Daily Picayune* (1912)	Texas timberland, walnut, oak, pine, ebony; within 100 miles of gulf port Per acre	$2.00 to $5.00
Land	*The New Orleans Daily Picayune* (1912)	Choice lots in the heart of Mandeville, Louisiana; six blocks from beach and railroad depot Per lot	$30.00
Land	*New York Times* (1910)	Long Island plot; 100 x 145 feet, overlooking Manhasset Bay; water privileges; improvements; eight minutes to either water or station	$3,000
Lots and Commercial Business	*The New Orleans Picayune* (1912)	Sale of The New Orleans Home for Incurables to Transmississippi Terminal Company, two lots	$12,625
Plantation	*New Orleans Daily Picayune* (1910)	Killoden Plantation Monroe, Lousiana; the plantation contains 3,006 acres of land	$45,675
Room	*New York Times* (1910)	18th St., 26 West; newly furnished, heated	$2.00/week
Room	*New York Times* (1910)	80th St. West, furnished; exceptionally beautiful, exclusive, private residence; three minutes subway L	$10/week
Room	*New York Times* (1910)	28th, 16 East Bachelors; single, double rooms, swimming pool, showers	$6 to $8/week
Room	*The New Orleans Daily Picayune* (1912)	Furnished front room for rent in a private home; includes housekeeping Per month	$7.00
Vineyard	*Overland Monthly* (1910)	28 acres of land, 16 acres in hay, 10 in vines; seven miles from San Jose, California	$5,500

Sewing Equipment & Supplies

Item	Source	Description	Price
Buttons	*The Ladies' Home Journal* (1911)	Buy buttons by the name *Chalmers Pearls* and you buy utmost value Card of 12	$0.05
Buttons	*Ladies' Home Journal* (1911)	*Chalmers;* pearl; you can always match the same style again; 12 buttons per card	5¢/card
Buttons	*Sears, Roebuck* (1913)	Mother of Pearl; choice of three styles	$0.10/dozen
Cloth	*Sears, Roebuck* (1910)	*Zephyr;* dress gingham; new 1910 styling	$0.09/yard
Cloth	*New York Times* (1910)	Crepe Charmeuse; 44wide; usually $5/yard	$2.25/yard
Cloth	*New York Times* (1910)	Imported dress satin; 35 wide, usually $3.50/yard	$1.78/yard
Cloth	*The State* (Columbia, SC) (1911)	Black taffeta; the wanted quality and weight for summer wear; a regular value, 36 wide	$0.67/yard
Cloth	*The State* (Columbia, SC) (1911)	Marquisette and voile; 40 wide and the cheapest yard in the lot is worth regular price of $0.25/yard	$0.15/yard
Cloth	*Ladies' Home Journal* (1911)	Irish linette; a beautiful sheer fabric will make up into a dress that will attract on account of the simplicity and daintiness of the designs	$0.19/yard

Item	Source	Description	Price
Cloth	*The State* (Columbia, SC) (1911)	Old English poplin; pure snowy white; the finest mercerized in the yarn material for dresses, coat suits, and separate skirts	$0.25/yard
Cloth	*Sears, Roebuck* (1913)	Dress and shirting percale; a very satisfactory cloth at a low price; full yard wide	$0.08/yard
Cloth	*Sears, Roebuck* (1913)	Mohair brilliantine; made in this country; very hard twisted thread	$0.36/yard
Cloth	*Sears, Roebuck* (1913)	Persian silk; neat and attractive in appearance; 19" wide	$1.00/yard
Cloth	*Sears, Roebuck* (1913)	Scotch table damask; every fiber guaranteed pure flax; 66 wide	$0.66/yard
Suiting Cloth	*Sears, Roebuck* (1913)	A heavy all pure-wool serge, soft and smoothly finished 56" wide	$3.00/yard

Sports Equipment

Item	Source	Description	Price
Baseball	*Sears, Roebuck* (1913)	$0.10 value	$0.06
Bicycle	*Sears, Roebuck* (1910)	*Napoleon;* For quality and value our Napoleon is second only to our Peerless.	$15.95
Bicycle	*Ladies' Home Journal* (1911)	*Mead 1911;* with coaster-brakes and puncture-proof tires	$10 to $27

Telephone Equipment & Services

Item	Source	Description	Price
Telephone	*Sears, Roebuck* (1912)	*Briding Five Magnet;* Southwestern style price, with two dry batteries	$10.20

Tobacco Products

Item	Source	Description	Price
Cigarettes	*New York Times* (1910)	*Turkey Red;* success has many roads	$0.10/pack

Toys

Item	Source	Description	Price
Aeroplane	*Sears, Roebuck* (1912)	Splendid copy made of flexible wire and silk	$0.98
Climbing Monkey	*Sears, Roebuck* (1912)	Distinctly a boy's toy; mechanical monkey which moves at will up and down heavy cord	$0.21
Doll	*Sears, Roebuck* (1912)	*Schoenhut;* performing unbreakable art dolls; extra-good quality cloth body with papier mache forearms; height including hat 18	$0.98
Floor Train	*Sears, Roebuck* (1912)	Large 15 1/2 engine and tender, and three 13 1/2 red, white and blue Pullman cars	$1.37
Water Pistol	*Sears, Roebuck* (1912)	Made of metal, nickel finished with hollow rubber handle.	$0.21
Wool Sheep Animal	*Sears, Roebuck* (1912)	Natural bleat, mounted on metal wheels. 13 1/2 x 15	$1.85

Travel & Transportation

Item	Source	Description	Price
Airplane Fare	*Airports of Columbia Photograph* (1910)	*Stark Airplane Flight;* sightseeing flight over Columbia, South Carolina	$5.00
Bus Fare	Throm, ed., *Popular Mechanics Picture History of American Transportation* (1952)	Hibbing to Alice, Minnesota [cost in 1914]	$0.15

Item	Source	Description	Price
Ocean Liner Fare	*New York Times* (1910)	New York to Rotterdam; Russian American Line on promenade deck	$50.00
Ocean Liner Fare	*New York Times* (1910)	New York to Glasgow; Anchor Line; Glasgow via Londonderry, first cabin	$67.50 to $72.50
Steamship Fare	*The New Orleans Daily Picayune* (1912)	Steamer *New Camelia;* excursions on Tchefuncta River	$0.75
Steamship Ticket	*San Francisco Examiner* (1913)	San Francisco to Los Angeles; round trip	$12.00
Train Fare	*The New Orleans Daily Picayune* (1912)	Roundtrip train ride from New Orleans, Louisiana, to Dallas, Texas; featured attraction, The Dallas Fair	$18.30
Train Fare	*Overland Monthly* (1910)	San Francisco to natural hot sulphur and iron baths in Lake County, California Round trip	$7.00

MISCELLANY 1910-1914

Autograph Auction

An article discussing a recent Rare Autographs Auction at Anderson's in New York City reported, "the autograph receipt for 1,600 ducats of gold by Michelangelo, in part payment for his work on the tomb of Pope Julius II, brought $170. It was dated Rome, June 7, 1513. A Frederick County land survey in George Washington's handwriting, Oct. 22, 1750, went for $74. A civil war letter of W. S. Grant, City Point, Va., March 12, 1865 to Secretary of War Stanton went for $32. Two early Abraham Lincoln legal documents, dated 1844 and 1853, sold respectively, for $37 and $29."

New York Times, March 2, 1910

Public Roads: Mileage and Expenditures

In 1911 the population per mile of road in the United States equalled 41 people, the total estimated expenditures nationwide was $142,144,191 and the expenditure per mile of public road was $64.63.

Statistical Abstract, 1911, U. S. Department of Labor, 1923

The Story of Cotton

Pickers usually carry a sack strapped over their shoulders as they walk or crawl along the rows. The cotton is picked from the stalk by hand and dropped into his sack. Hand labor is expensive and the cost of picking ranges from forty cents to one dollar a hundred pounds.

New Orleans Daily Picayune, May 15, 1910

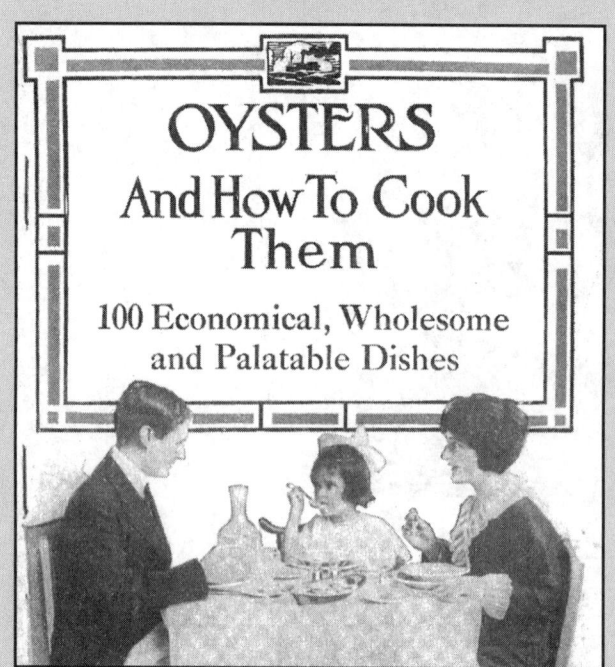

OYSTERS
And How To Cook Them
100 Economical, Wholesome and Palatable Dishes

Oyster Legislation

I believe the time has come, said he, when the dredging of our natural oyster reefs must cease, and that the canneries and packers should be given facilities for producing their oysters on state lands. For instance I believe the State of Louisiana should say to Mr. Packer that after 1913 or 1914, or whatever time may be agreed upon, that they must not dredge on natural reefs of this state. However, lease to these packers liberal allotments of hard bottoms, on which they can plant oysters and produce them. The state should furnish the seed oysters.

Give the packers a sufficiently long term lease that it would pay them to enter into the contract: say twenty to twenty-five years: certainly not longer than twenty-five years. The state would furnish police protection and charge them an acreage rental. It should be sufficient to reimburse the state but should not be excessive. Offhand, I should say $1 per acre for the first ten years: $2 per acre for the next ten years, and $5 per acre per year for the last five years.

In that way the state would be recouping its wasted oyster bottoms, and they would be returning a steady income every year during the time.

New Orleans Daily Picayune, May 15, 1910

Yale Worth $24,000,000; Property Value Thus Figured, Exclusive of University Equipment

New Haven, Conn. Dec. 10—The total resources of Yale University, not including equipment, art, book and other collections, has been figured at $24,000,000. Recently the trustee of the Sheffield Scientific School made an appraisal of that property basing their figures on the assessments of the New Haven tax office, and placed the total at $3,000,000. The same method has been applied to the whole university.

The larger items in the total of $24,000,000 are the bi-centennial buildings, the campus land, and dormitories. Investment funds make up about half the total.

New York Times, December 11, 1910

MISCELLANY 1910-1914

Predicts 16-Cent Copper; Adolph Lewisohn Expects an Increased Demand Soon

Adolph Lewisohn, President of the Miami Copper Company and a Director in other mining and smelting companies, predicted yesterday that copper would soon be selling at 10 cents.

"The copper market," he said, "is in excellent condition. Stocks of the metal everywhere have been greatly reduced and are now very moderate. The advance has been gradual on actual demand. At present the price is firm at 15 cents a pound, and only limited quantities are to be had at that figure. I am of the opinion that when the strike situation in England has clarified, demand for the metal in the country will materially increase. I believe copper will further advance and within a reasonable time reach 16 cents a pound. While it is true that most of the large producers are making good profits at present prices, yet it must be taken into consideration that good copper mines are very scarce. The mill of the Miami Copper Company has about been completed, and the company is producing at the rate of approximately 3,000,000 pounds of copper a month. I am extremely optimistic in regard to the future of this property and of the metal market."

New York Times, March 22, 1912

EDWARD H. COY
Yale

THOMAS L. SHEVLIN
Yale

WALTER W. HEFFELFINGER
Yale

The Minnesota Rate Cases and What They Mean

One of the gravest and most important results of the (rate) reductions under discussion was their effect upon long distance rates. St. Paul lies near the eastern boundary of Minnesota, and practically all freight shipped from States south and east of Minnesota and destined for towns within that State passes through St. Paul. The former through rate from Chicago to Wadena (a small town in the western part of Minnesota) was $1.09 per 100 pounds. But by shipping such freight from Chicago to St. Paul, and then reshipping it from St. Paul to Wadena at the lower interstate rate imposed by Minnesota Commission, the total rate from Chicago to Wadena amounts to less than $1.01 per 100 pounds.

The Magazine of Wall Street, June 1913

HISTORICAL SNAPSHOT
1915-1919

1915

♦ British steamer *Lusitania* sunk by Germans, killing 1,198, including 128 Americans

♦ U.S. Pullman-car porters paid $27.50 per month, prompting U.S. Commission on Industrial Relations to ask if wages are too high

♦ IWW organizer Joe Hill executed by firing squad

♦ Emory University founded in Atlanta with support of Coca-Cola family money

♦ Kraft processed cheese introduced by Chicago-based J. L. Kraft and Bros.

♦ Pyrex glass developed by Corning Glass researchers

1916

♦ Workman's Compensation Act protects 500,000 federal employees from disability losses

♦ Kellogg's All-Bran introduced by the Battle Creek Toasted Corn Flakes Co.

♦ Supreme Court upholds constitutionality of federal income tax

♦ Hetty Green, the "witch of Wall Street," dies leaving an estate of more than $100 million

♦ Stanford University psychologist Lewis Madison Terman introduces the term *intelligence quotient* (IQ)

♦ Lucky Strike cigarettes introduced by American Tobacco, outsells Sweet Corporal and Pall Mall

♦ Converse basketball shoes and U.S. Keds introduced

1917

♦ U.S. declares war on Germany

♦ Charlie Chaplin, Mary Pickford, and Douglas Fairbanks help sell $18.7 billion in Liberty Bonds to support war effort, despite low 3.5% interest rate

♦ Anchor Oil and Gas Company, founded in 1903, is reincorporated as Phillips Petroleum Company, as oil prices double because of war

♦ First air-conditioned theater installed in Empire theatre in Montgomery, AL

♦ Del Monte begins national advertising of canned fruits and vegetables

♦ Clarence Birdseye pursues commercial exploitation of freezing foods

1918

♦ Amalgamated Clothing Workers Union stages first of 534 strikes over six years protesting open shops, sweat shops, and piecework pay

♦ First U.S. airmail stamps issued costing 24 cents as service begins between New York and Washington, DC

♦ The world's first granulated laundry soap, Rinso, is introduced by Lever Brothers

♦ Charles Strite patents the first automatic pop-up toaster

♦ U.S. corn belt acreage sells for two to three times 1915 price

1919

♦ Treaty of Versailles assigns Germany sole responsibility for causing the Great War

♦ Boston police strike against pay scales of 21 to 23 cents per hour for 83- to 98-hour weeks

♦ Nineteenth Amendment, granting women suffrage, is adopted

♦ Cost of living in New York City up 79 percent from 1914

♦ Dial telephone introduced in Norfolk, VA

♦ Grand Canyon National Park established

♦ Wheat prices soar to $3.50 per bushel as famine sweeps Europe

♦ U.S. ice cream sales reach 150 million gallons, up from 30 million in 1909

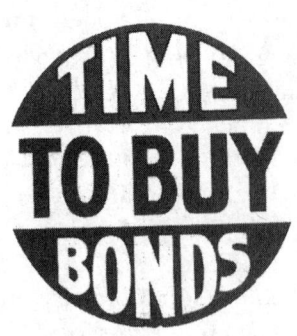

SELECTED INCOME 1915-1919

Job	Source	Description	Pay
Actor	Catherine Legrand and Robyn Karney, *Chronicle of the Cinema* (1995)	Payment for three movies to Mary Pickford in 1918	$900,000
Actor	Scott Eyman, *Mary Pickford America's Sweetheart* (1990)	Annual income of Mary Pickford in 1917	$560,00
Actor	Catherine Legrand and Robyn Karney, *Chronicle of the Cinema* (1995)	Weekly income of Douglas Fairbanks in 1917	$10,000
Actor, Director	*American Chronicle* (1999)	Movie star Charles Chaplin's annual salary with Mutual starting in 1916	$675,000
Actor/Producer	*Time* (1916)	Weekly income of Charlie Chaplin in 1916	$10,000
Actress	*American Chronicle* (1999)	Annual pay of movie star Mary Pickford in 1918	$1 million
Barber	*New York Times* (1918)	No Sunday work	$14–20/wk
Baseball Player	Vincent Tomkins, ed., *American Decades: 1910-1919* (1996)	Annual salary of Detroit Tigers' Ty Cobb in 1915	$20,000
Baseball Player	Harvey Frommer, *Shoeless Joe and Ragtime Baseball* (1992)	Annual salary of Chicago White Sox player Joe Jackson in 1919	$6,000
Bookkeeper	*New York Times* (1918)	Assistant, American; in office of large manufacturing concern	$18/wk
Boy Wanted	*New York Times* (1916)	15–16 years old; in advertising business; references required; unusual opportunity for advancement	$5/wk
Boy Wanted	*New York Times* (1918)	Bright boy wanted in large woolen house; splendid chance for advancement	$7/wk
Cabinetmaker	*The Chicago Daily Tribune* (1917)	Washington Employment Agency Per week	$18–$20
Driver	*Chicago Tribune* (1915)	Man to drive laundry wagon	$18/wk
Electrical Draftsman	*The Chicago Daily Tribune* (1917)	Must be familiar with isolated plants, installation layouts and interior light and power Per month	$150
Elevator Operator	*New York Times* (1918)	Elderly man desired; steady and easy position	$5/wk
Errand Boy	*New York Times* (1918)	New York office of large textile concern desires boy 16 or 17 to run errands	$5/wk
Football Player	Tomkins, ed., *American Decades: 1910-1919* (1996)	Payment per game to Jim Thorpe, former Olympic Champion and professional football player with Canton, Ohio, Bulldogs in 1915	$250

Job	Source	Description	Pay
Foreign Stenographer	*New York Times* (1918)	We are having numerous calls for stenographers in Spanish and English; also French and English; only those experienced in taking dictation in two languages can be used	$20–30/wk
Illustrator	*MastroNet Auction Catalog* (2004)	Fee paid painter Leslie Thrasher to create a "Chew Beech Nut Tobacco" advertisement by P. Lorillard & Co. [In 1918]	$1,500
Movie Actor	*Seventy Years of the Cinema* (1969)	Silent movie actor Charlie Chaplin signed with Mutual for a record salary, annual [1916]	$650,000
Office Worker	*New York Times* (1918)	Boy for office work in wholesale jewelry house	$8/wk
Packers	*Chicago Tribune* (1918)	Boys over 16 years of age to act as packer boys on rotary presses	$12/wk
Racehorse	Vincent Tompkins, ed., *American Decades: 1910-1919* (1996)	One year winnings of Triple Crown winner Sir Barton in 1919	$88,250
Situation Wanted—Accountant	*New York Times* (1916)	Experienced; all lines; books opened, closed, disentangled, audited, systems installed	$2.50/wk
Situation Wanted—Accountant	*Chicago Tribune* (1918)	Just mustered out; accountant or assistant credit manager; experienced; best references; future must be assured	$125–150/mo
Situation Wanted—Bookkeeper	*New York Times* (1916)	Fourteen years' experience	$20/wk
Situation Wanted—Bookkeeper	*Chicago Tribune* (1918)	Married; 33	$20/wk
Situation Wanted—Office Worker	*Chicago Tribune* (1918)	Experienced young man, age 19	$16/wk
Situation Wanted—Secretary	*Chicago Tribune* (1918)	Young lady, exceptional ability, stenographer, secretary; 6 years' experience	$26/wk
Solicitor	*Chicago Tribune* (1915)	Two magazine men preferred; to call on regular customers; new proposition; permanent employment	$18/wk
Spy	Tomkins, ed., *American Decades: 1910-1919*	Payment to Dr. Heinrich Albert by Germany to sabotage American munitions plants in 1915	$28 million
Stenographer	*Chicago Tribune* (1915)	Excellent appearance, high class, with good personality, Protestant, 16–22; for private office; must be capable; this is a first-class position for a HIGH CLASS GIRL ONLY	$8/wk
Truckers	*The Chicago Daily Tribune* (1917)	Washington Employment Agency Per week	$70 - $80
Typists	*New York Times* (1918)		$15/wk
Wagon Boy	*The Chicago Daily Tribune* (1917)	Must be over 16 years of age Per week	$8

CONSUMER EXPENDITURES 1919

(Per Capita)

Expenditure Type	1919	Expenditure Type	1919
Clothing	$55.52	Health Insurance	NR
Food	$177.53	Personal Business	$19.83
Auto Purchases	$12.44	Personal Care	$5.88
Auto Parts	$5.54	Tobacco	$13.67
Gas & Oil	$11.73	Local Transport	$7.78
Housing	$76.98	Intercity Transport	$5.43
Furniture	$6.97	Recreation	$20.64
Utilities	$6.76	Religion/Welfare Activities	$13.92
Telephone & Telegraph	$1.93	Private Education & Research	$7.19
Physicians	$6.87	Per Capita Consumption	$579.57
Dentists	$2.65		

INVESTMENTS 1915-1919

Investment	1915	1916	1917	1918	1919
Basic Yield, One-Year Corporate Bonds	4.47	3.48	4.05	5.48	5.58
Short-term Interest Rates, 4–6 Months, Prime Commercial Paper	4.01	3.84	5.07	6.02	5.37
Basic Yield, Common Stocks, Total	4.98	5.62	7.82	7.24	5.75
Index of Common Stocks (1941−1943=10)	8.31	9.47	8.50	7.54	8.78

COMMON STOCKS, CLOSING PRICE AND YIELD, FIRST BUSINESS DAY OF YEAR

	1915	1916	1917	1918	1919
Allis Chalmers	6 1/2	31	27 3/8	19 1/2	32
AT & T	116 1/4	127 1/8	123 3/8	106 3/8	100 1/2
American Tobacco	217 1/2	208 1/2	108 1/2	142 1/8	196
Anaconda	25	90 1/4	83 1/4	62 3/8	60 3/4
B&O	68 1/4	95 3/8	84 1/2	52 3/8	49 5/8
Bethlehem Steel	46 5/8	458	510	79 1/2	61
(Dividend 2 shares of Common B @ $120.75, 2/17/17)					
Corn Products	8	20 3/8	23 1/4	31 3/4	48 3/8
General Electric	139	174 1/2	168 1/4	134 5/8	151 3/4
(2% stock dividend, 12/7/17)					
(2% stock dividend, 6/8/17; 2% stock dividend, 12/7/17)					
General Motors	81	495	138 1/4	115	132 1/2
IBM					
Intl Harvester	73	75	121	59	113
(Merged with Intl Harvester of New Jersey 9/19/18; for each share of IH New Jersey, 1 1/2 share of new common; for each share of IH Corp, 2/3 share of new common)					
National Biscuit	118 1/4	124			105
US Steel	49 3/8	88 1/2	109 5/8	95 7/8	95 1/4
Western Union	57 5/8	88 1/2	95 3/4	86 3/4	86 1/2

STANDARD JOBS 1915-1919

Job Type	1915	1916	1917	1918	1919
Average of All Industries, excl. farm labor	$687/yr	$765/yr	$887/yr	$1115/yr	$1272/yr
Average of All Industries, inc. farm labor	$633/yr	$708/yr	$830/yr	$1047/yr	$1201/yr
Bituminous Coal Mining	38¢/hr	48¢/hr	60¢/hr	70¢/hr	34¢/hr
Avg hrs/wk	51.60	49.80	48.70	48.40	51.60
Building Trades, Union Workers	59¢/hr	62¢/hr	68¢/hr	78¢/hr	57¢/hr
Avg hrs/wk	47.50	44.40	44.10	44	44.80
Clerical Workers in Mfg. & Steam RR	$1327/yr	$1427/yr	$1552/yr	$1765/yr	$1999/yr
Domestics	$342/yr	$357/yr	$389/yr	$432/yr	$538/yr
Farm Labor	$355/yr	$388/yr	$481/yr	$604/yr	$706/yr
Federal Civilian	$940/yr	$974/yr	$967/yr	$1009/yr	$971/yr
Federal Employees, Executive Depts.	$1152/yr	$1211/yr	$1295/yr	$1380/yr	$1520/yr
Finance, Insurance, & Real Estate	$1040/yr	$1037/yr	$1051/yr	$1078/yr	$1099/yr
Gas & Electricity Workers	$620/yr	$615/yr	NR	NR	$556/yr
Lower-Skilled Labor	$905/yr	$925/yr	$964/yr	$984/yr	$991/yr
Manufacturing, Union Workers	34¢/hr	35¢/hr	36¢/hr	37¢/hr	37¢/hr
Avg hrs/wk	53.00	52.40	51.80	51.40	51.10
Manufacturing, Payroll	15¢/hr	16¢/hr	17¢/hr	16¢/hr	15¢/hr
Avg hrs/wk	61.90	61.50	61.20	61.10	62.10
Medical/Health Services Workers	$381/yr	$407/yr	$451/yr	$520/yr	$606/yr
Ministers	$730/yr	$731/yr	$737/yr	$761/yr	$759/yr
Nonprofit Org. Workers	$652/yr	$651/yr	$657/yr	$679/yr	$677/yr
Postal Employees	38¢/hr	37¢/hr	37¢/hr	37¢/hr	38¢/hr
Avg hrs/wk	48.00	48.00	48.00	48.00	48.00
Public School Teachers	$328/yr	$337/yr	$346/yr	$358/yr	$377/yr
State and Local Govt. Workers	$590/yr	$605/yr	$612/yr	$621/yr	$640/yr
Steam Railroads, Wage Earners	$548/yr	$549/yr	$563/yr	$593/yr	$600/yr
Street Railway Workers	$604/yr	$601/yr	$576/yr	$582/yr	$610/yr
Telegraph Ind. Workers	NR	NR	$544/yr	$573/yr	$601/yr
Telephone Ind. Workers	NR	NR	$408/yr	$397/yr	$392/yr
Wholesale and Retail Trade Workers	$510/yr	$521/yr	$537/yr	$551/yr	$508/yr

FOOD BASKET 1915-1919

Commodity	Year	New York	Atlanta	Chicago	Denver	Los Angeles
Beans, Navy, per pound	1915	8.4¢	9.70¢	7.50¢	7.90¢	7.20¢
	1916	10.90¢	11.20¢	10.90¢	10.10¢	10¢
	1917	17.60¢	17.50¢	18.10¢	17.40¢	14.80¢
	1918	17.60¢	18.60¢	17.20¢	16.60¢	17¢
	1919	12.90¢	14.90¢	12¢	13.20¢	25.30¢
Beef, Rib Roasts, per pound	1915	22.20¢	18.30¢	21.30¢	18.30¢	19¢
	1916	23.20¢	19¢	21.90¢	18.80¢	20¢
	1917	27.40¢	22.90¢	22.30¢	22.30¢	22.10¢
	1918	35.30¢	28.30¢	29.70¢	27.50¢	27.70¢
	1919	39.10¢	30.20¢	31.40¢	29.10¢	28.70¢
Beef, Steaks (Round), per pound	1915	26¢	20.40¢	22.10¢	21.20¢	20.10¢
	1916	27.40¢	20.90¢	22.60¢	21.20¢	21¢
	1917	32.60¢	26.20¢	25.80¢	26.20¢	23.10¢
	1918	42.30¢	34.10¢	32.30¢	38.80¢	29.70¢
	1919	45.70¢	36.50¢	34.30¢	34.50¢	30.50¢
Bread, Wheat, per loaf	1915	6.10¢	6.80¢	5.90¢	5.60¢	6.30¢
	1916	6.20¢	7.20¢	6.10¢	6.20¢	6.30¢
	1917	8.30¢	9.50¢	8.50¢	8.50¢	7.30¢
	1918	NR	10¢	NR	NR	NR
	1919	NR	10¢	NR	NR	NR
Butter, per pound	1915	35.80¢	37.90¢	33.60¢	34.10¢	33.10¢
	1916	39.50¢	40.80¢	37.60¢	37.50¢	37.30¢
	1917	48.80¢	50.60¢	46.40¢	45.80¢	45.90¢
	1918	57.80¢	60.20¢	54.50¢	54.50¢	56.90¢
	1919	68.60¢	70.90¢	63.90¢	65.30¢	67.50¢
Cheese, per pound	1915	23.10¢	23.50¢	23.20¢	24.60¢	24.10¢
	1916	24.60¢	26.20¢	26.10¢	26.20¢	25.10¢
	1917	32.90¢	33.60¢	34.20¢	34.30¢	32¢
	1918	34.90¢	36.80¢	37.30¢	36.70¢	35.90¢
	1919	42.70¢	41.80¢	42.90¢	43.80¢	44.40¢
Chickens, per pound	1915	21.60¢	19.10¢	19¢	19.70¢	25.60¢
	1916	24.50¢	20.50¢	22.30¢	21.50¢	26.70¢
	1917	29.30¢	26.30¢	26.80¢	26.40¢	29.10¢
	1918	39.40¢	35.60¢	33.90¢	34.40¢	39.20¢
	1919	41¢	38¢	36.60¢	37.30¢	46.30¢
Coffee, per pound	1915	28.70¢	29.30¢	30¢	20.60¢	32.70¢
	1916	27.20¢	28.20¢	30¢	29.50¢	32.20¢
	1917	26.40¢	29.20¢	28.90¢	29.90¢	30.70¢
	1918	27.70¢	29.70¢	28.60¢	30.40¢	30.60¢
	1919	39.90¢	43.30¢	39.70¢	44¢	42.10¢
Cornmeal, per pound	1915	3.50¢	2.70¢	3.10¢	2.80¢	3.60¢
	1916	4.10¢	2.70¢	3.30¢	2.70¢	3.90¢
	1917	6.70¢	4.80¢	5.70¢	4.90¢	6.20¢
	1918	7.90¢	5.60¢	6.80¢	6¢	7.60¢
	1919	7¢	5.70¢	6.10¢	5.80¢	7.20¢
Eggs, per dozen	1915	39¢	28.50¢	30.70¢	32.20¢	36.30¢
	1916	42.70¢	33.10¢	33.40¢	36¢	38.90¢
	1917	55.10¢	43.60¢	44.70¢	45.50¢	45.40¢
	1918	64.20¢	52.70¢	52¢	53.70¢	58.30¢
	1919	70.80¢	57.20¢	58.10¢	59.80¢	62.60¢

Commodity	Year	New York	Atlanta	Chicago	Denver	Los Angeles
Flour, Wheat, per pound	1915	4.20¢	4.10¢	3.80¢	3.40¢	4.30¢
	1916	4.50¢	4.40¢	4¢	3.60¢	4.40¢
	1917	7.30¢	6.80¢	6.50¢	5.80¢	6.60¢
	1918	7.20¢	7¢	6.40¢	5.70¢	6.80¢
	1919	7.50¢	7.30¢	7¢	6.20¢	7.30¢
Ham, Smoked, Sliced, per pound	1915	28.70¢	28.80¢	32.80¢	29.90¢	34.10¢
	1916	31.50¢	31.60¢	34¢	32¢	36¢
	1917	42¢	39.10¢	40¢	42.10¢	46.30¢
	1918	50.20¢	55.40¢	54.70¢	55.40¢	59.90¢
	1919	51.30¢	59.50¢	58.10¢	58.30¢	63.80¢
Lard, per pound	1915	15.20¢	15¢	14.50¢	15.20¢	17¢
	1916	17.40¢	17.90¢	16.80¢	17.70¢	18¢
	1917	27.50¢	27.50¢	26.20¢	28.60¢	27.10¢
	1918	33.20¢	34.20¢	32.20¢	34¢	33.80¢
	1919	36.90¢	37.60¢	35.30¢	38¢	36.10¢
Milk, Fresh, per quart	1915	9¢	10.40¢	8¢	8.40¢	8.50¢
	1916	9.20¢	11.20¢	8.40¢	8.40¢	8.30¢
	1917	11.90¢	14.30¢	10.30¢	10¢	10.40¢
	1918	14.50¢	19.10¢	12.50¢	11.80¢	13.80¢
	1919	16.10¢	21.30¢	14.20¢	12.70¢	14.30¢
Mutton and Lamb, Leg, per pound	1915	18.40¢	17.80¢	21¢	21.10¢	18.40¢
	1916	19.90¢	23.60¢	22.40¢	19.40¢	20.80¢
	1917	26¢	29.50¢	28.20¢	27.40¢	26.70¢
	1918	31.40¢	36.90¢	33.80¢	32.60¢	32.50¢
	1919	31.80¢	38.50¢	35.40¢	31.60¢	32.40¢
Pork Chops, per pound	1915	21¢	21.50¢	19¢	18.50¢	24.10¢
	1916	23.70¢	23.30¢	21.10¢	20.60¢	25.10¢
	1917	32.70¢	31.90¢	29.40¢	31.30¢	32.90¢
	1918	40.40¢	39.10¢	35.40¢	37.60¢	42¢
	1919	44.40¢	40.30¢	38.30¢	41.10¢	46.20¢
Pork, Bacon, Sliced, per pound	1915	25.10¢	29.30¢	30.50¢	26.90¢	33.50¢
	1916	26.40¢	30.70¢	31.80¢	30.30¢	34.60¢
	1917	39.40¢	41.60¢	42.20¢	43.50¢	46.10¢
	1918	50.20¢	55.40¢	54.70¢	55.40¢	59.90¢
	1919	63.80¢	59.50¢	58.10¢	58.30¢	63.80¢
Potatoes, Irish, per peck	1915	1.90¢	1.90¢	1.30¢	1.60¢	1.80¢
	1916	3.30¢	3.20¢	2.50¢	2.50¢	2.60¢
	1917	5.10¢	5¢	4.20¢	4.20¢	3.80¢
	1918	3.80¢	4.10¢	2.70¢	2.70¢	2.60¢
	1919	4.40¢	5¢	3.50¢	3.50¢	3.80¢
Prunes, Dried, per pound	1915	14.50¢	13.60¢	13.80¢	13.70¢	11.30¢
	1916	13.70¢	13.10¢	13.10¢	13.30¢	11.40¢
	1917	15.70¢	16.50¢	15.40¢	16.30¢	14.80¢
	1918	18.30¢	18¢	17.20¢	17.50¢	17¢
	1919	28¢	21.80¢	25.80¢	24.60¢	25.30¢
Rice, per pound	1915	9.20¢	8.50¢	9.50¢	9¢	9.60¢
	1916	9.20¢	7.90¢	9.40¢	9.20¢	9.40¢
	1917	10.30¢	9.60¢	10.10¢	10.60¢	9.80¢
	1918	12.80¢	13.20¢	12.80¢	13.40¢	12.90¢
	1919	14.80¢	14.90¢	14.70¢	15.30¢	14.80¢
Sugar, per pound	1915	5.90¢	6.80¢	6.20¢	7¢	6.50¢
	1916	7.50¢	8.60¢	7.40¢	8¢	7.70¢
	1917	8.80¢	10¢	8.60¢	8.90¢	8.40¢
	1918	9.40¢	9.90¢	9.20¢	9.90¢	9.30¢
	1919	10.40¢	12.50¢	11.40¢	11.60¢	11¢

Commodity	Year	New York	Atlanta	Chicago	Denver	Los Angeles
Tea, per pound	1915	45.20¢	61.50¢	51.20¢	52.10¢	53.10¢
	1916	44.50¢	61.70¢	52.10¢	50¢	55.10¢
	1917	50¢	73.30¢	55.90¢	55¢	55.70¢
	1918	54¢	85.20¢	59.10¢	60.70¢	63.30¢
	1919	55.70¢	88.40¢	63.50¢	69.10¢	69.10¢

1869-1919
50TH ANNIVERSARY—FIFTY YEARS OF PROGRESS

HEINZ
Spaghetti
Ready cooked ready to serve

FIRST the Spaghetti is made in the spotless home of the 57 Varieties.

It is Heinz Spaghetti.

Then it is cooked in the Heinz kitchens.

The original recipe was Italian but Heinz famous tomato sauce takes the place of the ordinary kind and with it is combined a special cheese of peculiar merit.

The result can only be expressed by the word "Perfection."

Keep the pantry shelves supplied with it, for experience has proved that, once tried, it becomes a permanent addition to the family menu.

It is delicious, nutritive and economical.

Some of the **57** Varieties

Vinegars   Baked Beans
Tomato Ketchup   Mince Meat

SELECTED PRICES 1915-1919

Item	Source	Description	Price
Alcohol			
Gin	*New York Times* (1919)	*Imperial* Gin	$2.15/fifth
Rum	*New York Times* (1919)	*Bacardi Rum*	$3.20/fifth
Whiskey	*New York Times* (1919)	*Old Bridgeport Whiskey;* 6 years old	$3.10/fifth
Apparel, Children's			
Baby Shoes	*Powell & Campbell Catalogue* (1915)	*Lyons & Co.;* patent-leather vamp, white-kid top, soft sole	$0.50/each
Dress	*Sears, Roebuck* (1917)	Babies' long white dress; yoke of lace insertions, satin ribbon	$1.33
Gloves	*Chicago Daily Tribune* (1917)	Children's Scotch knit wool gloves, seamless fingers	$0.75
Hood	*Sears, Roebuck* (1917)	Pretty hand-crocheted silk hood	$0.78
Overcoat	*Sears, Roebuck* (1917)	Winter weight; made very large and cut full in every way	$5.48
Shoes	*The Asheville (NC) Times* (1919)	Children's white Oxfords, English toe	$1.45
Skirt	*Sears, Roebuck* (1917)	Girl's; made of all-wool double-twisted wrap serge	$4.38
Suit	*Sears, Roebuck* (1917)	*Knickerbocker;* boys; rich olive-brown cassimere	$6.75
Suit	*Chicago Tribune* (1919)	Boy's suits of excellent quality chambray	$2.95
Apparel, Men's			
Boots	*Powell & Campbell Catalogue* (1915)	Tan elk; oak sole	$21.00
Coat	*Sears, Roebuck* (1917)	80 percent camel hair and 20 percent wool	$4.85
Gloves	*Sears, Roebuck* (1917)	14-ounce canvas gloves, knitted wrists	$1.50/dozen
Hat	*Sears, Roebuck* (1917)	Alpine style; the crown is 5 1/2" high; raw edge brim 2 1/2" wide	$2.25
Hat	*Chicago Tribune* (1919)	*Newmark;* Easter style; considering style and quality, the lowest prices in town	$5.00
Heel	*Powell & Campbell Catalogue* (1915)	*Foster;* orthopedic; rubber; especially beneficial to people troubled with flat foot; men's whole heel	$0.75/pair
Nightshirt	*Sears, Roebuck* (1917)	Collarless; finished 60" long with full-size bell-shape body	$1.15
Overcoat	*Sears, Roebuck* (1917)	Chesterfield style; four-button fly front	$9.00

Item	Source	Description	Price
Overcoat	*Chicago Tribune* (1919)		$30
Pants	*Sears, Roebuck* (1917)	*Rip Proof;* inexpensive herringbone-weave brown striped cheviot Rip-Proof work pants	$1.50
Shirt	*Sears, Roebuck* (1917)	Medium weight wool; mixed sacking flannel shirt	$1.49
Shoes	*The Asheville (NC) Times* (1919)	Men's Oxfords in English high toe, button and lace black and tan	$4.95
Suit	*Sears, Roebuck* (1917)	Stylish; good quality pure-wool worsted	$16.50
Suit	*Chicago Tribune* (1919)	*Joseph Sobel;* tailored; made-to-order spring suits, extra pants free	$33.00
Union Suit	*Today's Housewife* (1917)	*Chalmer's Underwear;* as easy to wear as your skin	$1.25
Work Shirt	*Sears, Roebuck* (1917)	Coat style; heavy-weight chambray	$0.75

Apparel, Women's

Item	Source	Description	Price
Bloomers	*Altman's Spring Catalogue* (1919)	Of pink or white batists, elastic band at waist and knee	$0.90
Blouse	*Sears, Roebuck* (1917)	*George;* Crepe daintily adorned with fine white silk embroidery	$5.50
Corset	*Sears, Roebuck* (1917)	Low bust with elastic webbing; designed for exclusive dancing and outdoor wear	$1.59
Corset Cover	*Altman's Spring Catalogue* (1919)	Nainsook; cap sleeves, trimmed with Valenciennes lace; size 36 to 44 in bust	$1.50
Dress	*Sears, Roebuck* (1917)	*Homestead* house dress made of good quality washable gingham	$ 1.59
Dress	*Sears, Roebuck* (1917)	Junior; about one-third wool, shepherd check	$6.25
Dress	*Sears, Roebuck* (1917)	Nobby velveteen corduroy; heart shaped pockets on the skirt	$5.48
Dress	*Sears, Roebuck* (1917)	For stout woman; half-wool serge; a pretty embroidered dress, especially designed for women of full figure	$8.98
Fur Coat	*Sears, Roebuck* (1917)	Full-length muskrat; natural blue-black Jersey Muskrat coat, with deep square cape effect, collar, cuffs, pocket pieces and button of high-grade	$115
Gloves	*Sears, Roebuck* (1917)	Chamois; wash them like you wash your hands	$1.19
Hose	*Sears, Roebuck* (1917)	Seamless artificial silk; reinforced with cotton at the top	$0.35
Mesh Bag	*Chicago Tribune* (1919)	Silverplated; in pouch shape, and with plain polished mountings	$7.50
Raincoat	*Sears, Roebuck* (1917)	The outer fabric is a fine twill-wool mixed cashmere	$10.98
Shoes	*Cohan and Harris Theatre Program* (1917)	*Hood Leisure Shoes;* add a touch of distinction to any frock	$3.00 to $4.00
Shoes	*Sears, Roebuck* (1917)	*Sears, Roebuck;* patent-leather button, black brocade cloth top, cuban louis heel	$3.85
Shoes	*Chicago Tribune* (1919)	*Victory Pumps;* patent leather or dull kid, slender louis heel.	$5.85

Item	Source	Description	Price
Slippers	*Powell & Campbell Catalogue* (1915)	*P&C;* in patent, mat kid, black satin, black satin	$2.25
Suit	*Sears, Roebuck* (1917)	Fall; made of good wearing quality velveteen; lined throughout	$29.75
Underwear	*Altman's Spring Catalogue*) (1919)	Nainsook; Valenciennes lace edge	$1.25
Union Suit	*Sears, Roebuck* (1917)	Nursing; elastic-ribbed wool	$2.68

Appliances

Item	Source	Description	Price
Electric Radiator	*Sears, Roebuck* (1917)	*Majestic;* fine for that cold bathroom, bedroom, small office	$5.75
Indoor Toilet	*Hearth and Home* (1917)	*Kawnear Cabinet;* no more outside back yard inconveniences; no chambers to empty; no sewer or cesspool	$0.01/week /person
Radiator	*The World's Work* (1917)	*American Radiator Company;* ideal boiler and 350 sq. ft. of 38" American radiator will heat a cottage	$1.95
Vacuum Cleaner	*Sears, Roebuck* (1917)	Electric; if your house is lighted by electricity from a central station, you can operate one of the above cleaners	$24.50

Baby Products

Item	Source	Description	Price
Blanket	*Sears, Roebuck* (1917)	The most popular baby blankets on the market	$0.75
Safety Pin	*Today's Housewife* (1917)	*Clinton;* send $0.10 for a big $0.10 worth of pins and a dainty pin tray as well	$0.10
Swing	*Today's Housewife* (1917)	*Rock-A-Bye;* baby amuses himself away from dirt, out of drafts; he can't fall out and the swing can't break or wear out	$1.00

Business Equipment & Supplies

Item	Source	Description	Price
Telephone Call	*American Chronicle* (1999)	Three-minute long-distance charges between New York and San Francisco in 1915	$20.70
Typewriter	*The World's Work* (1917)	*Corona;* the personal writing machine; makes you independent of your office	$50.00
Typewriter	*Sears, Roebuck* (1917)	*Standard Visible;* writes faster, cleaner, plainer and easier than pen or pencil	$46.50
Typewriter	*The World's Work* (1917)	*Underwood;* guaranteed for five years; includes two color ribbons, back spacer, tabulator, everything complete	$43.85

Collectibles

Item	Source	Description	Price
Bust	*Sears, Roebuck* (1917)	Bronze-plated metal bust of President Wilson; stands 2 1/2" high	$0.10
Painting	*American Chronicle* (1999)	Sandro Botticelli's *Madonna and Child;* sold at auction in 1915	$20,000

Education

Item	Source	Description	Price
Tuition	*The Craftsman* (1915)	*The Raymond Riordon School;* Highland, New York; high school, college preparatory, special courses; not merely a recitation hall but a preparation for life's work	$800/year
Tuition	*The World's Work* (1917)	*Cascadilla School for Boys;* a fitting school for Cornell	$675/year
Tuition	*The World's Work* (1917)	*Loomis School for Boys;* Windsor, Connecticut; practical training for boys intending to enter business or farming on graduation	$400/year

Item	Source	Description	Price
Tuition	*American Magazine* (1917)	*Wilbraham Academy;* Wilbraham, Massachusetts; fits for life and college work	$600/year

Entertainment

Item	Source	Description	Price
Annual Ball Ticket	*The Playhouse Playbill,* New York City (1916)	The Second Annual Ball of the Allied Arts of the Theatre in behalf of the Actors' Fund of America; Hotel Astor, March 30, 1916, 10 p.m.	$5.00 each
Dance Lessons	*Cohan and Harris Theatre Program* (1917)	Dancing Carnival, 200 instructors, 50,000 square feet of floor space Private lessons, per half hour	$0.50
Exposition	*Chicago Daily Tribune* (1917)	Home Furnishing Exposition; everything for the home Adults Children	$0.50 $0.25
Lecture	*Chicago Daily Tribune* (1917)	Captain R. Hugh Knyvett presents "The Real Thing," War lectures Seats	$0.75 $1.00 $1.50
Movie	*The Asheville (NC) Times* (1919)	Mary Pickford in *Rags* Children Adults Including war tax	$0.10 $0.15
Musical	*The Asheville (NC) Times* (1919)	*Flo-Flo;* classy, snappy, catchy, girly musical entertainment	$0.25 $0.75 $1.00 $2.00
Opera	*Chicago Daily Tribune* (1917)	*Aida;* by the Boston English Opera Company; Strand Theatre, Chicago Nights	$0.50 $0.75 $1.00
Theater Tickets	*Cohan and Harris Theatre Program* (1917)	Cohan and Harris Theatre Evening Orchestra, including war tax Saturday Evening Orchestra, including war tax First Balcony, including war tax	$2.20 $2.75 $0.55 to $2.20

Entertainment, Home

Item	Source	Description	Price
Camera	*Sears, Roebuck* (1917)	*Kodac Kewpie Kameras;* the Kewpie always gets the picture; for 2 1/2" x 4 1/2" picture	$2.80
Camera	*Sears, Roebuck* (1917)	*Conley Model C;* roll film model; beautifully made in every detail	$16.40
Card Game	*Sears, Roebuck* (1917)	*Rook;* one of the most popular games on the market	$0.42
Game	*Sears, Roebuck* (1917)	*Major League Baseball;* plays all the National League teams with over 240 players	$2.45
Novelty	*Sears, Roebuck* (1917)	Boxing darkies; these little fellows thump each other merrily and heartily as the music plays; rides on needle arm	$1.06
Phonograph	*Sears, Roebuck* (1917)	*Silvertone;* plays every disc record made	$6.95
Phonograph	*The World's Work* (1917)	*Starr;* Jacobean style; for the chosen few of music lovers	$250
Phonograph	*Chicago Tribune* (1919)	*Stark Grafonola;* including Grafonola type D-2 and 14 selections	$65.95
Phonograph Record	*The Craftsman* (1915)	*Columbia;* double disc	$0.65

Item	Source	Description	Price
Phonograph Record	*Chicago Tribune* (1919)	*Columbia;* Ponselle's first *Butterfly* record; a record that justifies the critics' acclaim of Ponselle as the world's greatest dramatic soprano	$1.50

Financial Products & Services

Travelers' Checks	*The World's Work* (1917)	*K. N. & K.;* safer than currency to carry; experienced travelers use them	$0.50

Food Products

Candy	*Sears, Roebuck* (1917)	*Pep-O-Mint Life Savers;* a dainty confection	$0.05/rl
Cereal	*The Youth's Companion* (1919)	*Quaker Oats;* the best way to cut down your food cost is to breakfast on Quaker Oats	
		Regular size	$0.12 to $0.13
		Large size	$0.30 to $0.32
Chewing Gum	*Sears, Roebuck* (1917)	*Wrigley's Doublemint;* 25 packages to each box	$0.73/box
Latest prices of Ohio market	Toledo (Ohio) *Weekly Blade* (1917)	Lard, per pound	$0.24
		Corn, shelled, per bushel	$1.75
		Spring wheat, per bbl	$15.50
		Purina whole wheat, per bbl	$15.00
Milk	*Chicago Daily Tribune* (1917)	Bowman Dairy Company perfectly pasteurized milk Quart bottle	$0.12
Macaroni	*Today's Housewife* (1917)	*Skinner's;* made from the highest-grade Durum wheat; cooks in 12 minutes	$0.25
Peanut Sandwich	*The Playhouse Playbill,* New York City (1916)	*National Biscuit Company,* Peanut Sandwich—a generous spread of peanut butter between a slightly salted biscuit. Per box	$0.10
Puffed Rice	*American Magazine* (1917)	No other process makes whole-grain so easy to digest	$0.15/box
Puffed Wheat	*Today's Housewife* (1917)	Puffed grains are all nutrition	$0.15/box
Radium Water	*Cohan and Harris Theatre Program* (1917)	*Muidar Radium Water;* Every glass of water contains radium Case of 50, 24-ounce bottles	$25.00

Furniture

Bed and Mattress	*The Gentlewoman* (1919)	*Spiegel, May, Stern Co.;* Sturdy Steel Bed; Colonial design, standard full size, springs and Restwell mattress	$19.95
Bed	*Hearth and Home* (1917)	Feather; full weight 40 lbs	$8.95
Bookcase	*The World's Work* (1917)	*Lundstrom Universal;* solid oak with disappearing glass doors	$8.00
Buffet	*Sears, Roebuck* (1917) quarter sawn oak	Colonial design; large double-door cupboard, seasoned hardwood, imitation of $14.95	
Chair	*The Craftsman* (1915)	Reclining; with adjustable back and spring cushion; with sheepskin cushions	$37.00
Chair	*Sears, Roebuck* (1917)	Morris rocker; artificial black leather upholstery	$7.45
Chair	*Sears, Roebuck* (1917)	Washingtonian-style box-seat dining cushions; the distinctive feature of this fine chair is the extra-high curved back	$4.95
Chair	*Sears, Roebuck* (1917)	Turkish rocker; artificial black leather	$12.55
Chiffonier	*Sears, Roebuck* (1917)	Six drawers with quarter-sawed veneer serpentine front	$11.60

Item	Source	Description	Price
Hall Furniture Rack	Sears, Roebuck (1917)	French bevel plate mirror	$9.85
Settee	The Craftsman (1915)	7' long, seat 34" deep and 16" high, back 36" high; spring seat cushion of soft leather	$96.50
Table	The Craftsman (1915)	Craftsman; fumed oak table is suitable for library or living room	$19.00
TeachCart	Chicago Daily Tribune (1917)	John A. Colby and Sons English TeachCart; finished in old English walnut or brown mahogany	$27.00
Tea Wagon	The Craftsman (1915)	Willow; new designs in Willow	$16.50

Garden Equipment & Supplies

Item	Source	Description	Price
Seed	The World's Work (1917)	Burpee's Sweet Pea; 40-50 seeds; packets of Cherub, King White, Margaret Allee, Rosabelle, and Wedgewood	$0.25

Hotel Rates

Item	Source	Description	Price
Hotel Room	The World's Work (1917)	Hotel Butler; Seattle, Washington; large airy rooms, care without peer	$1.00/day

Household Products

Item	Source	Description	Price
Canvas Shoe Cleaner	Powell & Campbell Catalogue (1915)	Eagle Brand Nova; the perfect white cleaner	$0.25/package
Clock	Sears, Roebuck (1917)	Hanging wall regulator clock; eight-day clock; 35" high, 12" dial	$5.22
Clock	Sears, Roebuck (1917)	National Call 8-day; alarm; an eight-day run on one winding	$2.00
Ice Cream Freezer	Today's Housewife (1917)	Auto vacuum; today's method of making ice cream is automatic, accurate and economical; there's no crank to turn—no labor	$3.00
Kitchen Cabinet	Sears, Roebuck (1917)	Wilson; roll-curtain front cabinet	$19.85
Linoleum and Floor Oil	Sears, Roebuck (1917)	Seroco; cloth finish; puts a coating on linoleum and drys hard	$0.48/quart
Oil	Hearth and Home (1917)	Kibler's All 'Round; the oil with a thousand uses	$0.25/bottle
Oil	Today's Housewife (1917)	3-In-One; a little 3-in-One oil on a damp cloth will restore the lustre and cause surface scratches to vanish	$0.25
Polish	Today's Housewife (1917)	O-Cedar; it cleans as it polishes	$0.25
Polish	Sears, Roebuck (1917)	Whittmore's Albo; cleans and whitens canvas, duck, NuBuck, and suede shoes	$0.08
Rug	Chicago Tribune (1919)	Royal Wilton; 6' x 9'	$43.50
Sheet	Sears, Roebuck (1917)	White cotton; extra-quality regular length; 54" x 8"	$1.07
Soap	The Asheville (NC) Times (1919)	Grandma's Powdered Soap; just a teaspoon replaces the chipping, slicing and rubbing Per box	$0.05
Tablespoon	Sears, Roebuck (1917)	Salem; silver plate; Broadfield pattern; set of six	$4.40/set
Tapestry	Sears, Roebuck (1917)	Tallulla; worsted; 9' x 12'	$16.85
Toilet Paper	Sears, Roebuck (1917)	Sterling; large roll	$0.07

Item	Source	Description	Price
Trunk	*Sears, Roebuck* (1917)	Round cornered Vulcanized fiber; made of three-ply veneer lumber	$18.75
Vacuum Food Jar	*Sears, Roebuck* (1917)	For salads, stews, hot vegetables; quart size	$3.90
Washing Powder	*Today's Housewife* (1917)	*Fairbank's Gold Dust;* to clean pots, pans, refrigerator, and bathroom fixtures; purifies while it cleans	$0.05

Insurance Rates

Health Insurance	*The World's Work* (1917)	*Aetna;* get $25 a week up to 52 weeks while you are ill	$60.00/year

Jewelry

Watch	*Sears, Roebuck* (1917)	Woman's bracelet watch; 10-year gold filled case; fitted with a 7-jewel imported movement	$7.00

Meals

Dinner	*Cohan and Harris Theatre Program* (1917)	Murray's, 42nd Street, just west of Broadway Old Dominion Beefsteak Dinner	$1.50
Hot Dog	*American Chronicle* (1999)	Nathan's hotdogs at Coney Island	$0.05 each
Lunch	*Cohan and Harris Theatre Program* (1917)	Murray's Exceptional Luncheon, for tired shoppers and theatergoers	$0.70

Medical Products & Services

Cough Drops	*The Playhouse Playbill,* New York City (1916)	*Smith Brothers Cough Drops*—after the show, be sure to bundle up good and take a few S.B. Cough Drops Per box	$0.05
Laxative	*Chicago Daily Tribune* (1917)	*Nujol* for constipation Pint bottle	$0.69
Laxative	*Chicago Daily Tribune* (1917)	*Phillips Milk of Magnesia*	$0.33
Lozenges	*The Youth's Companion* (1919)	*Brown's Bronchial Troches;* quick relief from sore throat, coughing, hoarseness, tickling in the throat, loss of voice Four sizes	$0.15 $0.35 $0.75 $1.25
Nonprescription Drug	*The World's Work* (1917)	*Absorbine Jr.;* real help for tired feet	$1.00
Nonprescription Drug	*Today's Housewife* (1917)	*Blue-Jay Corn Medicine;* immediate relief—then the corn comes out in 48 hours	$0.15
Nonprescription Drug	*The World's Work* (1917)	*Brown's Bronchial Troches;* for that hacking cough; speedy, effective, harmless	$0.25
Nonprescription Drug	*The World's Work* (1917)	*Forhan's Pyorrhea Preparation;* at the first sign of inflamed or receding gums	$0.50
Nonprescription Drug	*The World's Work* (1917)	*Luden's Menthol Candy Cough Drops;* throat irritations won't disturb your sleep; in yellow box	$0.05

Motorized Vehicles, Services, & Supplies

Automobile	*The Playhouse Playbill,* New York City (1916)	Hudson—the super-six motor has made Hudson cars supreme; the motor is 80% more efficient than other like-size motors The Cabriolet at Detroit	$1,675

Item	Source	Description	Price
Automobile	*Cohan and Harris Theatre Program* (1917)	Standard "8", The Magneto Equipped Eight; built by steel masters famous for their railroad rolling stock	$2,450
Automobile	*The Craftsman* (1915)	*King Motor Car;* eight-cylinder, 40–45 hp; too successful to change this year	$1,350
Automobile	Joseph J. Schroeder Jr. *The Wonderful World of Automobiles* (1971)	*Chandler Six;* leads in service, style, and price [cost in 1916]	$1,295
Automobile	Schroeder, *The Wonderful World of Automobiles* (1971)	*Jackson Wolverine Eight;* eight-cylinder car, goes from a walking pace to sixty miles per hour [cost in 1916]	$1,295
Automobile	Schroeder, *The Wonderful World of Automobiles* (1971)	*Maxwell Touring Car;* completely equipped, including electric starter and lights [cost in 1916]	$915
Automobile	Schroeder, *The Wonderful World of Automobiles* (1971)	*Saxon Six;* in the salesrooms of over 2,000 Saxon dealers throughout the country you will find Saxon Sixes [cost in 1916]	$815
Automobile	Schroeder, *The Wonderful World of Automobiles* (1971)	*Allen;* 37 hp, full-floating rear axle, large, easy-acting brakes [cost in 1917]	$795
Automobile	Schroeder, *The Wonderful World of Automobiles* (1971)	*Briscoe 4-24;* the car with the half-million-dollar motor [cost in 1917]	$625
Automobile	*The World's Work* (1917)	*Chandler Six;* seven-passenger touring car	$1,395
Automobile	*The World's Work* (1917)	*Chandler Six;* four-passenger convertible coupe	$1,995
Automobile	*The World's Work* (1917)	*Franklin;* runabout; 2,160 pounds	$1,900
Automobile	*The World's Work* (1917)	*Marion-Handley The Six Pre-Eminent Six-60;* 7-passenger touring, 125" wheel base	$1,575
Automobile	*The World's Work* (1917)	*Paige Statford Six-51;* 7-passenger car; the most beautiful car in America	$1,495
Automobile	Schroeder, *The Wonderful World of Automobiles* (1971)	*Studebaker Convertible Sedan;* door window lowers into frame, others slide into individual compartments under rear seat [cost in 1917]	$1,700
Automobile	Schroeder, *The Wonderful World of Automobiles* (1971)	*Willys-Knight Touring Sedan;* rear glass lowers, other between rear seat upholstery and tonneau casing [cost in 1917]	$1,950
Carbon Remover	*American Magazine* (1917)	*Johnson;* the engine laxative	$1.00

Musical Instruments

Clarinet	*Sears, Roebuck* (1917)	*LaFayette;* 15 keys, 2 rings, in the key of A, B flat, or E flat	$18.45
Player Piano	*Sears, Roebuck* (1917)	*Beckwith;* the versatility of this instrument makes it one of the most desirable of all instruments for home use	$397

Item	Source	Description	Price
Other			
Cup	*Sears, Roebuck* (1917)	Collapsible; aluminum; just the thing for school children	$0.05
Friction Tape	*Sears, Roebuck* (1917)	Insulating; for electric wires or bicycles	$0.02
Glue	*Hearth and Home* (1917)	*Lepage's;* stronger than nails	$0.10
Home Building Materials	*Today's Housewife* (1917)	*Montgomery Ward Ready Cut;* all lumber, lath, shingles, doors, windows, frames, hardware, pipe, gutter and painting materials for this pretty, roomy bungalow	$548
House Barometer	*The World's Work* (1917)	*Tycos;* make your own weather forecasts	$10
Ink	*Today's Housewife* (1917)	*Payson's Indelible;* ready for use with a common pen	$0.25
Interest Rate	*American Chronicle* (1999)	Interest paid on $2 billion in War Savings Certificates and Liberty Loans to support World War I	3%
Mousetrap	*Sears, Roebuck* (1917)	Easy to set, a sure killer	$0.02
Printing Press	*American Magazine* (1917)	*Multigraph Senior;* produces real printing and form-typewriting rapidly, economically, privately in your own establishment; deluxe model	$765
Telephone Call	*Milwaukee Journal* (1916)	Three-minute call from New York to San Francisco	$20.70
Telephone Call	*Milwaukee Journal* (1916)	Three-minute call from New York to Chicago	$14.45
Personal Care Products			
Comb	*Chicago Daily Tribune* (1917)	Ladies' French ivory combs	$0.69
Comb	*Sears, Roebuck* (1917)	4 1/2" ornamental; set with tiny colored beads	$0.43
Comb	*Hearth and Home* (1917)	*Prof. Long's Magnette;* they remove dandruff, stop falling hair; relieve headaches	$0.02
Cream	*Today's Housewife* (1917)	*Ingram's Milkweed;* there is beauty in every jar	$0.50
Deodorant Cream	*Today's Housewife* (1917)	*Mum;* takes all the odor out of perspiration	$0.25
Eye Treatment	*Today's Housewife* (1917)	*Lash-Brow-ine;* nourishes the eyebrows and lashes	$0.25
Face Powder	*Today's Housewife* (1917)	*Nadine;* soft and velvety, adheres until washed off; popular tints: flesh, pink, brunette, white	$0.50
Hair Color	*Hearth and Home* (1917)	*Duby's;* darken your gray hair; package makes one pint	$0.25/package
Hair Curlers	*Today's Housewife* (1917)	*West Electric;* wave or curl your hair; every curler electrified—imparting strength to the hair	$0.25
Hair Pins	*Today's Housewife* (1917)	*Hump;* you'll need only one-third as many HUMP Hair pins to get better results; 5 sizes	$0.05
Powder	*Today's Housewife* (1917)	*Air Float Talc;* assorted odors: rose, wisteria, corylopsis, lilac, violet	$0.10
Powder	*Today's Housewife* (1917)	*Delatone;* removes hair or fuzz from face, neck or arm	$1/ounce jar
Powder	*Today's Housewife* (1917)	*Hinds Talcum;* a pure borated talc, powdered to an indescribable fineness	$0.25

Item	Source	Description	Price
Razor Blades	*Chicago Daily* Tribune (1917)	*Ever-Ready* razor blades Package of 10	$0.33
Shampoo	*Chicago Daily Tribune* (1917)	*Hay's Coconut Oil Shampoo*	$0.33
Shampoo	*Today's Housewife* (1917)	*Canthrox;* natural beauty and fluffiness of the hair is brought out to its best advantage; 15 exhilarating shampoos	$0.50
Soap	*Chicago Tribune* (1919)	*Kirk's Jap Rose;* opposite Marshall Fields	$0.07

Publications

Item	Source	Description	Price
Book	*The World's Work* (1917)	*Sea Warfare;* Kipling master war correspondent	$1.25
Magazine	*Leslie's* (1919)	*Film Fun;* puts you on speaking terms with your favorite star Per copy Per year	 $0.15 $1.50
Magazine	*The World's Work* (1917)	*The World's Work;* monthly	$0.25
Magazine	*The World's Work* (1917)	*Vanity Fair;* monthly	$0.25
Newspaper	*Wall Street Journal* (1916)	Annual subscription	$12.00
Newspaper	*The Youth's Companion* (1919)	*The Youth's Companion;* The Best of American Life in fiction, fact and comment; published weekly Per year	 $2.00

Real Estate

Item	Source	Description	Price
Apartment	*Chicago Daily Tribune* (1917)	Seven-room apartment, three baths, overlooking Lake Michigan Per month	 $175
Apartment	*Chicago Daily Tribune* (1917)	Near elevated station; four-room flat, stove heat Per month	 $12.00
Apartment Building	*Chicago Tribune* (1919)	Highgrade 3-apartment building, Chicago; 1/2 block from lake in Rogers Park	$26,000
Boiler Shop	*Chicago Daily Tribune*	One story brick boiler shop; Halsted Street, Chicago	$20,000
Farm	Toledo (Ohio) *Weekly Blade* (1917)	160-acre farm with 15 acres of corn, 7 of wheat, 3 acres of potatoes, comfortable residence with telephone	$4,500
Farm Land	Toledo (Ohio) *Weekly Blade* (1917) (1917)	Low terms for small or large tracts in Michigan's fruit and clover belt Per acre	 $15.00 to $25.00
Fruit Farm	*Chicago Daily Tribune* (1917)	Fennville, Michigan 22-acre farm, 500 fruit trees	$6,000
House	*The Asheville (NC) Times* (1919)	Nice house, five rooms with sleeping porch, good neighborhood	$4,200
Land	*The Asheville (NC) Times* (1919)	Six lots in Norwood Park, frontage 250 feet; suitable for handsome residence	$6,500
Land	*Chicago Tribune* (1919)	180 acres, northern Wisconsin; dairy, grain, and stock farm, near town, lake, and river	$9,000

Item	Source	Description	Price
Lot	*Chicago Daily Tribune* (1917)	Vacant corner lot fronting lake and Sheridan Road	$40,000
Room	*Chicago Tribune* (1919)	*The Gibsonia;* Chicago, Illinois; single room; to rent, beautiful large room, separate beds	$4.00/week

Sewing Equipment & Supplies

Item	Source	Description	Price
Cloth	*Sears, Roebuck* (1917)	Mixed wool fabric; possess the much desired softness	$0.32/yard
Dress Pattern	*Hearth and Home* (1917)	*Hearth and Home;* this dress has a broad box plait at the center front and the dress fastens under this	$0.10
Sewing Needles	*Sears, Roebuck* (1917)	For sewing machines of any make	$0.15/dozen

Sports Equipment

Item	Source	Description	Price
Baseball Glove	*Sears, Roebuck* (1917)	*J. C. Higgins Professional;* pliable horsehide throughout	$3.00
Golf Bag	*Chicago Tribune* (1919)	5", canvas, leather trim, white or tan; regularly $5	$3.45
Oil	*The Youth's Companion* (1919)	3-in-One Oil; the right oil for guns 3 sizes, East of Rocky Mountain states	$0.15 $0.25 $0.50
Shotgun	*Sears, Roebuck* (1917)	*Remington Repeating;* six-shot takedown model made in 12-gauge only	$32.70

Telephone Equipment & Services

Item	Source	Description	Price
Telephone	*Sears, Roebuck* (1917)	*Briding;* five-magnet compact briding telephone with 1,000 ohm ringer; price with two dry batteries	$11.25

Tobacco Products

Item	Source	Description	Price
Cigarettes	*The Playhouse Playbill,* New York City (1916)	*Murad,* The Turkish Cigarette	$0.15
Cigarettes	*Cohan and Harris Theatre Program* (1917)	*Egyptian Deities;* The utmost in cigarettes Plain end or cork tip, per box	$0.25
Cigars	*Chicago Tribune* (1919)	*Cyro;* the original idea of putting $0.15 worth of smoke in a $0.10 cigar	$0.10
Cigars	*Sears, Roebuck* (1917)	*Berriman's Handmade Havana;* made at Tampa, Florida; can of 25 cigars	$1.27/can
Cigars	*Sears, Roebuck* (1917)	*Sardou;* the sweet domestic cigar; box of 50	$2.47/box
Cigarettes	*Chicago Tribune* (1919)	*Camel;* expertly blended choice Turkish and choice domestic tobaccos	$0.18/pack
Tobacco	*Chicago Tribune* (1919)	*Falk's Serene Mixture;* the great pipe smoke	$0.15/package

Toys

Item	Source	Description	Price
Hobby Horse	*Sears, Roebuck* (1917)	He longs to conquer the fiery steed when placed on a rocking horse like this	$2.98
Wooden Blocks	*Sears, Roebuck* (1917)	Consists of twenty painted square blocks on which are Mother Goose nursery rhymes	$0.79

Item	Source	Description	Price
Travel & Transportation			
Steamship Fare	*The World's Work* (1917)	From New York to Australia on Sydney Short Line via Honolulu and Samoa aboard splendid 10,000 ton, twin-screw American steamer	$337.50
Streetcar Fare	Edward L. Throm, ed. *Popular Mechanics Picture History of American Transportation* (1952)	Horse and mule; Bleecker Street, New York [cost in 1917]	$0.30
Trolley Fare	*American Chronicle* (1999)	Cost of a cross-town trolley ride in Boston in 1917	$0.05

MISCELLANY 1915-1919

What Price Doctors

Between 1917 and 1923, the eighteen general hospitals reporting to the United Hospital Fund increased their receipts for ward service from $1.46 to $2.67 per day. The average ward rates now charged in the majority of cases are between $3 and $4.

New York Times, May 4, 1919

Liquor and Prohibition

This is the time to acquire your wines and liquors. Prices are advancing daily and will continue to advance whether Prohibition becomes effective July 1, 1919, or January 20, 1920. Henry Hollander 149–151 West 36th Street New York City.

Imperial Gin	$2.15
Doul Gin	$2.30
Gordon Gin	$2.45
Cocktail Rum	$2.75
Bacardi Rum	$3.20
Allash Kummel	$2.60
Old Bridgeport Whiskey	$3.10
Green Creme De Menthe	$3.00

Chicago Tribune, April 19, 1919

MARS adds 17,000 Millionaires to American List

Recent estimates made public at Washington were that not fewer than 17,000 men and women in the United States had graduated into the millionaire class in the last two years. It is estimated that not fewer than 7,000 of their number, and possibly 10,000, are residents of New York.

Chicago Tribune, April 19, 1919

Gas Rates and Politics

As part of his campaign platform for City Council, Charles A. Brady of Columbia, S.C., called for another gas and electric power company, for we need competition, as our rates are too high as compared with other cities.

For 1916, he listed electric current for residence use of 7¢ per KWH in Jacksonville, Fla., 10¢ per KWH for Greenville, S. C., and 7¢ per KWH in New Orleans, La.

Gas prices for residence use were $1.15 per 1000 cu. ft. in Jacksonville, Fla.; $1.35 per 1000 cu. ft. in Greenville, S. C. and $1.10 per 1000 cu. ft. in New Orleans. The rates he was protesting in Columbia, S. C. were 12¢ per KWH and $1.35 per 1000 cu. ft. of gas.

Campaign Flier

Interview with Football Player Red Grange

1. I started working summers on the ice truck when I was a kid and I kept it up for years, even after I became a professional football player (in 1925). I'd start at six in the morning, and many a day I'd work until seven or eight at night, six days a week. We got five dollars a day until the union came in, and they upped our salary to $37.50 a week.

2. When I joined the (Chicago) Bears (football team) in 1929, except for my salary the entire payroll—all the coaches and players and even the trainer—was about three thousand dollars a game. I remember some of the early games at Wrigley Field in Chicago; our trainer would wait until they had sold a dozen tickets, then he'd take the ticket money across the street to a drugstore and buy the tape for our ankles. So help me, that's true.

Robert S. Gallagher, American Heritage Magazine,
December 1974

MISCELLANY 1915-1919

Rapid Dish Washer

At first view, the Rapid Electric Dish Washer appears to be only a beautiful kitchen table with silvery top and spacious lower compartment. Upon lifting the lid, which extends across a portion of the top, one sees a most interesting interior, consisting of removable racks for dishes, so made that there are spaces for all kinds of china and utensils.

All one has to do in order to operate this machine is scrape the dishes, place them in their proper compartments, pour in eight quarts of boiling water, in which a good washing powder has been mixed, close the lid tight, turn on the current—and go about one's other duties. The price is $40.

The World's Work, February 1917

The Price of Fixing

Before 1919 the fixing of baseball games for betting purposes was by no means unheard of. But in that year it went too far: the 'unthinkable' happened; a World Series was fixed by eight star players for the Chicago White Sox. Testimony showed that most of the players had gotten $5,000 for their parts in the fix, while Chicago first baseman Charles Arnold 'Chick' Gandil had kept $35,000 for himself.

The Encyclopedia of American Crime

1920-1939

Return to "Normalcy," the Great Depression, and Recovery

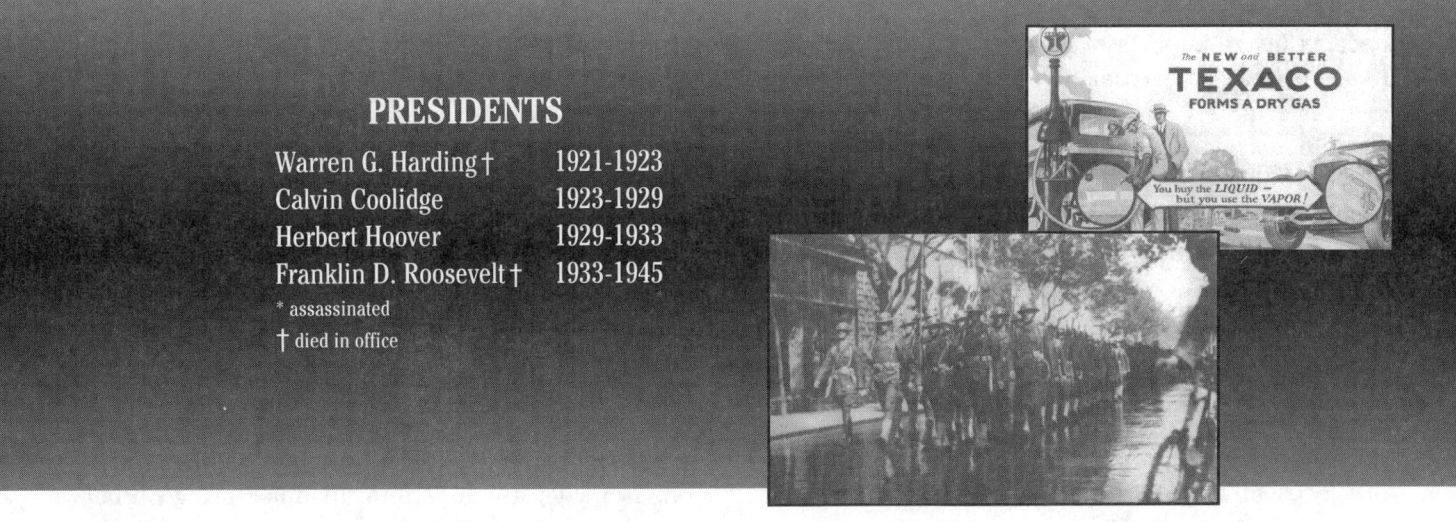

PRESIDENTS

Warren G. Harding†	1921-1923
Calvin Coolidge	1923-1929
Herbert Hoover	1929-1933
Franklin D. Roosevelt†	1933-1945

* assassinated

† died in office

The second twenty years of the twentieth century are divided into two major periods by historians: the Return to Normalcy (1920-1929), following the First World War, a decade of expansion and speculation, and the Great Depression and Recovery (1930-1939), which threw millions out of work and dramatically changed the role of the federal government.

The attitude of many Americans during the first half of the era is expressed in President Calvin Coolidge's famous statement, "the chief business of the American people is business"; the role of the federal government remained small and federal expenditures actually declined following the war effort. Harry Donaldson's song "How Ya Gonna Keep 'Em Down on the Farm After They've Seen Paree?" described another basic shift in American society after the war. The 1920 census reported that more than 50 percent of the population—54 million people—lived in urban areas. The move to the cities was the result of changed expectations after the war and the migration of millions of southern Blacks to the industrialized urban North.

The dream of normalcy lasted through most of a fitful decade, during which the United States became more than a land of big cities, big money, and big factories filled with machines. Following the war years, women who had worked men's jobs during the wartime mobilization usually remained in the work force, although at lower wages. Average family earnings increased slightly during the first half of the period while prices and hours worked both declined. The forty-eight-hour work week became standard, providing greater leisure time. At least 40 million persons went to the movies every week. Expanding use of electricity, appliances, and automobiles was the consequence of rapidly changing lifestyles. Automobile production rose from 1.5 million in 1921 to 4.8 million in 1929 while the prices declined dramatically. By 1929 one American in five owned an automobile, ushering in weekend trips, tourist cabins, road-sign advertising, and gas stations. Within the home the availability of electricity brought an array of timesaving appliances. Radio brought the world to small-town America; the automobile and expanding railroad service took small-town America to the world.

Despite a growing middle class, the share of disposable income going to the top 5 percent of the population moved from approximately one-quarter to nearly one-third of the total. Fifty percent of the people, by one estimate, lived in poverty. By 1929 the average factory worker made less than $1,500 annually. Coal and textile workers, southern farmers, unorganized labor, the elderly, single women, and most blacks were excluded from the economic giddiness of the period. Union membership declined throughout the 1920s, canceling the gains of the war years, despite a rapidly expanding work force. Labor strikes also declined during the period from a peak of 4,450 in 1917 to 732 in 1927.

American exports more than doubled during the decade; heavy imports of European goods were virtually halted, a reversal of the progressive movement's flirtation with free trade. Immigration laws were increasingly restrictive during the 1920s. The 1924 National Origins Act limited immigration from each country to a percent of its proportional population of resident aliens based on the census of 1890. It cut immigration to a trickle.

In 1929 America appeared to be in an era of unending prosperity. U.S. goods and services reached an all-time high. Industrial production rose 50 percent during the decade as the concept of mass production was refined and broadly applied. The sale of electrical appliances, radios, refrigerators, and other durable goods skyrocketed. Consumers were able to purchase newly produced goods through the extended use of credit. Debt accumulated faster than wealth. By 1930 personal debt had increased to one-third of personal wealth.

The next decade, following the nightmare on Wall Street in October 1929, was marked by economic paralysis: bank failures, railway insolvency, high unemployment, closed factories, and sharply reduced foreign trade. By 1932 one in four Americans was jobless. One of every four farms was sold for taxes. Five thousand banks closed their doors. Durable goods production did not regain the 1929 peak until 1940. Prosperity had disappeared.

Despite continued assurances to the contrary from government and business leaders, the crash of 1929 was not simply a correction of inflated values. Farm income was cut in half. Members of the middle class lost their savings, their houses, their jobs, and their hope. President Hoover, the great humanitarian of 1928, became regarded as the dupe. The stage was set for change and the New Deal as presented by Franklin D. Roosevelt.

Roosevelt's first series of social experiments was characterized by Relief, Recovery, and Reform. This program carried two key objectives: to raise prices by restricting output while controlling competition, and to inflate the dollar. Believing that the expansion of the United States economy was finished, the Roosevelt administration paid attention to better distribution and planned production. The Civilian Conservation Corps (CCC), for example, put 250,000 jobless young men to work in the forests at $1 a day. By 1935 government deficit spending spurred economic change. By 1937 total manufacturing output exceeded that of 1929; prices and wages rose briskly. Inflation fears forced curtailed spending and restrictions on bank lending, driving the Depression into a serious dip in the late 1930s.

During the second half of the 1930s social security began, and estate and gift taxes were increased, as were the income taxes of large corporations. Organized labor, which hit a low point in 1933, gained expanded rights to organize and rapidly began to use its new-found muscle. Despite progress, 10 million workers were still unemployed in 1938, and farm prices lagged far behind manufacturing progress. Full recovery would not occur until the United States mobilized for World War II.

HISTORICAL SNAPSHOT
1920-1924

1920

- Chanel No. 5 perfume introduced
- Youngs Rubber Company is founded to make Trojan brand condoms
- Flour consumption falls to 179 pounds per capita from 224 pounds in 1900, as meat, fish, and vegetable consumption rises
- Baby Ruth candy introduced by Curtiss Candy Company, priced at 5 cents
- Coca-Cola sales exceed $4 million
- World sugar price drops from 30 cents per pound to 8 cents
- The Volstead Act, enforcing national prohibition of alcohol, goes into effect
- Soybean harvest reaches 1 million bushels

1921

- Drano drain cleaner introduced
- Wise Potato Chips introduced by Berwick, PA, grocer Earl V. Wise
- Mounds candy bars introduced by the Peter Paul Manufacturing Company
- Molasses prices drop to 2 cents per gallon, down from 20 cents
- Wholesale butter prices fall to 29 cents per pound, down from its wartime high of 76 cents

- Salt iodized with potassium iodide
- Cigarette consumption reaches 43 billion cigarettes
- Arrow shirt introduced to meet demand for collar-attached shirts

1922

- New York's Delmonico's Restaurant closes
- Thom McAn shoe store introduces mass-produced shoes sold through chain store for $3.99 per pair
- California becomes year-round source of oranges
- Most farmers in deep depression
- First commercially prepared baby food marketed
- Camden, NJ canning company, founded in 1869, changes name to Campbell's Soup Company
- Mah-jongg craze sweeps nation, game sets outsell radio

1923

- Popsicle patented under name Epsicle
- Butterfinger candy bar created and marketed by dropping parachuted bars from airplane
- Commercially canned tomato juice marketed by Libby McNeill & Libby
- First practical electric shaver patented by Schick

- A. C. Nielsen Company founded
- Chicago Radio Laboratory, founded in 1918, is incorporated as Zenith Radio Corporation
- 10 automakers account for 90 percent of sales; 108 companies producing cars
- Hertz Drive Ur Self System founded; creates world's first auto rental concern

1924

- Thirty percent of bread baked at home, down from 70 percent in 1910
- First effective chemical pesticides introduced
- *American Mercury* begins publication
- Radio set ownership reaches 3 million
- James Buchanan "Buck" Duke donates $47 million to Trinity College at Durham, NC, which changes its name to Duke
- Ford produces 2 million Model T motorcars; price of touring car falls to $290
- Dean Witter and Company founded
- Maxwell Motor Corporation (run by Walter Chrysler), Ford, and General Motors produce approximately 80 percent of U. S. cars

SELECTED INCOME 1920-1924

Job	Source	Description	Pay
Actor	Legrand and Karney, *Chronicle of the Cinema* (1995)	Weekly income of Rudolph Valentino after the release of the silent movie *The Sheik* in 1921	$1,250
Bookkeeper	*San Francisco Examiner* (1921)		$115/wk
Classical Concert Pianist (1922)	*Guinness Book of World Records* (1981)	Single year earnings of classical pianist Ignace Jan Paderewski	$500,000
Clearing House Clerk	*San Francisco Examiner* (1921)	Bank	$70/wk
Clerk	*Chicago Tribune* (1920)	Young man; bright; willing; experienced at figures	$22/wk to start
Clerk	*Chicago Tribune* (1920)	Young men 16 and 21; junior clerical position; excellent chance to learn profession while you earn a salary	$14-16/wk
Clerk	*Chicago Tribune* (1922)	Good at figures, reliable, and willing to work some evenings; office experience helpful but not necessary	$35/wk
House Messenger	*Chicago Tribune* (1920)	A boy who wants to start as a house messenger and junior stock clerk, where he can develop and earn a good salary, will find a splendid opportunity now	$17/wk
Industrialist	*American Chronicle* (1999)	Billionaire manufacturer Henry Ford's daily income in 1922	$264,000
Mechanical Draftsman	*Chicago Tribune* (1920)	Experienced, preferably with railway experience	$225/mo
Miscellaneous	*Chicago Tribune* (1920)	Boys and young men mechanically inclined; no experience required; steady employment	$15–25/wk
Office Boy	*Chicago Tribune* (1920)	Where is there an office boy with some AMBITION, who wants a good position in an advertising office?	$12/wk
Porcelain	*Chicago Tribune* (1920)	Man—young to learn porcelain work	$15/wk
Sales	*Chicago Tribune* (1920)	No experience necessary; we train you and assist you to make big money	$80–300/wk
Sales	*Chicago Tribune* (1920)	Ambitious and energetic young man 20 years old; married; College education; 5 years successful record in sales promotion	$65/wk
Sales	*Chicago Tribune* (1922)	Men; have openings for some live young men on special house-to-house work satisfied with $32 to start; selling experience not necessary	$32/wk
Sales	*Chicago Tribune* (1922)	Work with manager on renewals, 20 popular magazine clubs	$40/wk
Sales	*Chicago Tribune* (1922)	Jewish of good personality to represent the largest Jewish publishing house in the world; our work makes an appeal to all classes of Jews and we can offer you exclusive territory and leads	$100–$125/wk
Secretary	*Chicago Tribune* (1920)	Situation wanted: steno and dictaphone operator; 10 years' experience	$30–35/wk

Job	Source	Description	Pay
Sewer	*Picture Play* Magazine (1923)	Decorate pillow tops at home; experience unnecessary; particulars for stamp; tapestry Paint Co., 110 LaGrange, Indiana	$6–18/dozen
Steno-Clerk	*San Francisco Examiner* (1921)	Small Office	$75/wk
Stenographer	*Chicago Tribune* (1920)	The editor and executive of a Catholic publishing house desires to secure the services of a competent stenographer with secretarial experience, preferring one who writes and speaks French	$30/wk to start
Stenographer	*Chicago Tribune* (1920)	Who can do some ledger posting; excellent opportunity for right party	$18/wk
Stenographer	*New York Times* (1923)	Openings for capable refined young women; steno; law	$25–30/wk
Stenographer	*Chicago Tribune* (1924)	Situation Wanted: Steno-Corr; Small office; Loop; efficiency and common sense	$30/wk
Switchboard Operator	*Chicago Tribune* (1920)	Experienced, capable, and competent; small board; some office work. Jewish preferred	$23–25/wk
Telephone Operator	*New York Times* (1923)	Hours 6 a.m. to 2:10 p.m. and from 4–6 p.m. Busy board	$20/wk
Ticket Press	*Chicago Tribune* (1920)	Boys over 16; extra pay for good work	$14/wk
Typist	*Chicago Tribune* (1920)	Good permanent position with chance to advance; dictaphone experience preferred but not necessary	$20/wk to start

CONSUMER EXPENDITURES 1921, 1923

(Per Capita)

Expenditure Type	1921	1923	Expenditure Type	1921	1923
Clothing	$56.45	$64.52	Housing	$89.20	$94.80
Food	$128.14		Furniture	$6.36	$8.78
Auto Purchases	$10.66	$20.45	Utilities	$7.63	$8.97
Auto Parts	$3.46	$4.97	Telephone & Telegraph	$2.35	$2.71
Gas & Oil	$11.57	$12.38	Physicians	$4.79	$7.15
Dentists	$1.71	$2.72	Intercity Transport	$5.16	$5.22
Health Insurance	NR	NR	Recreation	$19.05	$23.44
Personal Business	$17.95	$22.17	Religion/Welfare Activities	$12.57	$11.57
Personal Care	$5.55	$7.79	Private Education & Research	$6.87	$7.26

INVESTMENTS 1920-1924

Investment	1920	1921	1922	1923	1924
Basic Yield, One-year Corporate Bonds	6.11	6.94	5.31	5.01	5.02
Short-term interest Rates, 4–6 Months, Prime Commercial Paper	7.50	6.62	4.52	5.07	3.98
Basic Yield, Common Stocks, Total	6.13	6.49	5.80	5.94	5.87
Index of Common Stocks (1941–1943=10)	7.98	6.86	8.41	8.57	9.05

COMMON STOCKS, CLOSING PRICE AND YIELD, FIRST BUSINESS DAY OF YEAR

	1920	1921	1922	1923	1924
Allis Chalmers	53 3/8	30 7/8	38	46 7/8	44 1/4
AT&T	97 3/8	96	114 7/8	123 1/2	125 1/4
American Tobacco (75% stock dividend in Common B, 7/15/20)	270	114	129 1/2	155	148 1/2
Anaconda	65	35 1/2	49	49 7/8	38
B&O	33 1/4	36	34	42 3/4	58 3/4
Bethlehem Steel A	93	53	52 5/8	61 3/4	53 5/8
Corn Products	86 3/4	67	93	128 5/8	157
General Electric (2% stock dividend, 6/7/19; 2% stock dividend, 12/6/19) (2% stock dividend, 6/10/20; stock dividend, 12/8/20) (2% stock dividend, 6/8/21; 2% stock dividend, 12/8/21) (5% stock dividend in special stock, 9/7/22) (5% stock dividend in special stock, 9/5/23)	172	122 1/4	137	182	194
General Motors (10 shares for 1 split, 3/1/20; 2 1/2% stock dividend, 7/5/20; 2 1/2% stock dividend, 10/5/20)	338	14 3/8	9 1/2	14 7/8	14 7/8
Intl Harvester (12 1/2% stock dividend, 9/15/20) (2% stock dividend, 1/25/21; 2% stock dividend, 7/25/21) (2% stock dividend, 1/25/22; 2% stock dividend, 7/25/22) (2% stock dividend, 1/25/23)	130	95 3/8	79 1/48	88	79
National Biscuit (4 shares for 1 split, 12/30/22; 75% stock dividend, 12/30/22)	121		123	38 1/2	41 1/4
US Steel	107 7/8	81 1/2	82 1/2	107 1/4	98 7/8
Western Union	88	84	90 5/8	112 1/2	107

STANDARD JOBS 1920-1924

Job Type	1920	1921	1922	1923	1924
Average of All Industries, excl. farm labor	$1489/yr	$1349/yr	$1305/yr	$1393/yr	$1402/yr
Average of All Industries, inc. farm labor	$1407/yr	$1233/yr	$1201/yr	$1299/yr	$1303/yr
Bituminous Coal Mining	85¢/hr	83¢/hr	86¢/hr	81¢/hr	78¢/hr
Avg hrs/wk	48.20	48.40	48.40	48.50	48.20
Building Trades, Union Workers	$1.08/hr	$1.01/hr	$1.11/hr	$1.19/hr	$1.05/hr
Avg hrs/wk	43.80	43.80	43.90	43.80	43.80
Clerical Workers in Mfg. & Steam RR	$2160/yr	$2134/yr	$2067/yr	$2126/yr	$2196/yr
Domestics	$655/yr	$649/yr	$649/yr	$711/yr	$732/yr
Farm Labor	$810/yr	$522/yr	$508/yr	$572/yr	$574/yr
Federal Civilian	$1707/yr	$1683/yr	$1694/yr	$1704/yr	$1747/yr
Federal Employees, Executive Depts.	$1648/yr	$1593/yr	$1625/yr	$1658/yr	$1708/yr
Finance, Insurance, & Real Estate	$1758/yr	$1860/yr	$1932/yr	$1896/yr	$1944/yr
Gas & Electricity Workers	$1432/yr	$1364/yr	$1343/yr	$1339/yr	$1417/yr
Lower-Skilled Labor	$1207/yr	$780/yr	$807/yr	$984/yr	$1128/yr
Manufacturing, Payroll	47¢/hr	44¢/hr	49¢/hr	50¢/hr	56¢/hr
Avg hrs/wk	52.70	53.40	53	52.10	53.50
Manufacturing, Union Workers	88¢/hr	92¢/hr	87¢/hr	91¢/hr	97¢/hr
Avg hrs/wk	45.70	46.10	46.20	46.30	46.10
Medical/Health Services Workers	$752/yr	$983/yr	$912/yr	$845/yr	$845/yr
Ministers	$1556/yr	$1428/yr	$1622/yr	$1620/yr	$1678/yr
Nonprofit Org. Workers	$1286/yr	$1392/yr	$1446/yr	$1454/yr	$1507/yr
Postal Employees	76¢/hr	75¢/hr	76¢/hr	78¢/hr	74¢/hr
Avg hrs/wk	47.40	47.40	47.20	47.20	48.00
Public School Teachers	$970/yr	$1109/yr	$1206/yr	$1239/yr	$1269/yr
State and Local Govt. Workers	$1164/yr	$1296/yr	$1316/yr	$1336/yr	$1346/yr
Steam Railroads, Wage Earners	$1817/yr	$1632/yr	$1591/yr	$1585/yr	$1570/yr
Street Railway Workers	$1608/yr	$1539/yr	$1436/yr	$1493/yr	$1544/yr
Telegraph Ind. Workers	$1159/yr	$1145/yr	$1110/yr	$1133/yr	$1150/yr
Telephone Ind. Workers	$980/yr	$1038/yr	$1064/yr	$1069/yr	$1104/yr
Wholesale and Retail Trade Workers	$1270/yr	$1260/yr	$1261/yr	$1272/yr	$1314/yr

FOOD BASKET 1920-1924

(NR-Not Reported)

Commodity	Year	New York	Atlanta	Chicago	Denver	Los Angeles
Beans, Navy, per pound	1920	12¢	13.50¢	11.60¢	12.70¢	9.90¢
	1921	8.90¢	10¢	7.90¢	9.10¢	8¢
	1922	10¢	11.10¢	9.80¢	10.10¢	9.10¢
	1923	11.60¢	12.80¢	11.10¢	12.10¢	9.80¢
	1924	10.80¢	12.30¢	9.90¢	11¢	9.50¢
Beef, Rib Roasts, per pound	1920	40.50¢	30.70¢	33.50¢	28.40¢	30¢
	1921	36.40¢	27.40¢	30.20¢	23.60¢	29.30¢
	1922	35.30¢	26.70¢	28.80¢	22.90¢	28.30¢
	1923	36.30¢	26.90¢	30.20¢	22.40¢	28.10¢
	1924	36.90¢	26.60¢	31.60¢	22.20¢	28.80¢
Beef, Steaks (Round), per pound	1920	47.30¢	36.70¢	34.70¢	34.20¢	32.40¢
	1921	41.30¢	32.80¢	31¢	27.20¢	29.90¢
	1922	39.60¢	31.20¢	29.10¢	25.80¢	28.20¢
	1923	40.80¢	30.90¢	31.50¢	26.40¢	27.60¢
	1924	40.40¢	31.80¢	32.10¢	26.50¢	29.10¢
Bread, per loaf	1920	11.70¢	12.20¢	11.60¢	11.80¢	10.10¢
	1921	10.30¢	11.10¢	10.30¢	10.30¢	9.30¢
	1922	9.50¢	9.90¢	9.70¢	8.30¢	9¢
	1923	9.60¢	9.10¢	9.70¢	8¢	9¢
	1924	9.50¢	9.10¢	9.80¢	7.80¢	8.80¢
Butter, per pound	1920	70.50¢	73.30¢	63.40¢	64.80¢	68.90¢
	1921	52.40¢	54.10¢	48.90¢	47¢	52.40¢
	1922	48.00¢	49.10¢	45.20¢	42.60¢	51.80¢
	1923	55.50¢	56.40¢	53.50¢	51.10¢	57.50¢
	1924	52.20¢	53.80¢	49.80¢	47.30¢	52.50¢
Cheese, per pound	1920	42.10¢	40.20¢	42.20¢	43.90¢	43.90¢
	1921	35.40¢	32.70¢	37¢	36.10¢	38.20¢
	1922	33.30¢	32.40¢	35¢	35.10¢	36.10¢
	1923	37.90¢	35.80¢	40.20¢	38.60¢	37.40¢
	1924	37.10¢	33.30¢	39.20¢	37.40¢	38.20¢
Chickens, per pound	1920	43.50¢	39.50¢	41.60¢	40.80¢	49¢
	1921	42.10¢	33.80¢	36.70¢	35.60¢	44.80¢
	1922	37.40¢	31.30¢	33.70¢	30.70¢	41.30¢
	1923	36.10¢	31.30¢	32.80¢	29.20¢	39.70¢
	1924	37.60¢	31.80¢	34¢	29.40¢	40.20¢
Coffee, per pound	1920	43.10¢	50.30¢	39.70¢	48¢	44.80¢
	1921	32.40¢	34.60¢	33.60¢	36.40¢	37.90¢
	1922	33.50¢	35.90¢	34.50¢	35.50¢	38¢
	1923	34.80¢	37.10¢	38¢	36.60¢	39.50¢
	1924	40.80¢	42.40¢	43.90¢	42¢	47.80¢
Cornmeal, per pound	1920	7.90¢	5.50¢	6.80¢	5.80¢	7.50¢
	1921	6.50¢	3.40¢	6.10¢	3.50¢	5.20¢
	1922	5.40¢	2.90¢	5.20¢	3.10¢	4.30¢
	1923	5.40¢	3.60¢	5.30¢	3.30¢	4.40¢
	1924	5.80¢	4¢	5.60¢	3.60¢	4.70¢
Eggs, per dozen	1920	78¢	69¢	71.20¢	63.40¢	64.50¢
	1921	1.80¢	44.60¢	48.90¢	47.20¢	50.20¢
	1922	53.70¢	38.30¢	42.70¢	40.70¢	44.80¢
	1923	57.10¢	41.40¢	46¢	42.10¢	46.50¢
	1924	57.80¢	43.70¢	47.80¢	43.60¢	46.40¢

Commodity	Year	New York	Atlanta	Chicago	Denver	Los Angeles
Flour, Wheat, per pound	1920	8.70¢	8¢	7.60¢	6.70¢	7.80¢
	1921	5.90¢	6.20¢	5.20¢	4.30¢	5.80¢
	1922	5.20¢	5.50¢	4.60¢	3.90¢	4.90¢
	1923	4.80¢	5.30¢	4.10¢	3.80¢	4.70¢
	1924	5.10¢	5.60¢	4.40¢	3.90¢	4.70¢
Lard, per pound	1920	29.90¢	30.30¢	27.80¢	32.20¢	32¢
	1921	19.10¢	18.90¢	17.30¢	19.80¢	19.20¢
	1922	17.10¢	17.90¢	16.30¢	18.80¢	18.70¢
	1923	18.20¢	18.20¢	17.20¢	19.10¢	19.60¢
	1924	19.60¢	18.90¢	19.10¢	19¢	20.30¢
Milk, Fresh, per quart	1920	16.70¢	25¢	15¢	12.90¢	17¢
	1921	15.1¢	19.10¢	13.40¢	11.40¢	12.10¢
	1922	14.60¢	16.40¢	12¢	10¢	14.20¢
	1923	14.80¢	16.70¢	13.50¢	11.80¢	15¢
	1924	13.80¢	17.60¢	14¢	11.70¢	15.70¢
Mutton and Lamb, Leg, per pound	1920	34.40¢	41.70¢	38.70¢	34.10¢	35.50¢
	1921	32.90¢	34.30¢	33.40¢	31¢	31.40¢
	1922	35.30¢	36.60¢	36¢	34.30¢	32.50¢
	1923	35.80¢	35.50¢	35.60¢	35¢	33.30¢
	1924	36.30¢	35.20¢	36.50¢	34.80¢	33.80¢
Pork chops, per pound	1920	44.10¢	40.50¢	38.10¢	40.40¢	48.90¢
	1921	38.10¢	33.50¢	32.10¢	32.90¢	41.30¢
	1922	35.70¢	31.80¢	30.30¢	30.90	38.60¢
	1923	33¢	28.50¢	27.30¢	28.60¢	36.90¢
	1924	33¢	29.10¢	28.40¢	29¢	37.80¢
Pork, Bacon, Sliced, per pound	1920	49.19¢	54.30¢	56.40¢	55.20¢	62.80¢
	1921	40.80¢	43.60¢	50.20¢	46.40¢	54.20¢
	1922	38.20¢	38.60¢	45.90¢	43.40¢	51.50¢
	1923	37.90¢	35.80¢	44.30¢	42.70¢	49.80¢
	1924	36.60¢	34.90¢	42.20¢	41¢	47.70¢
Pork, Ham, Sliced, per pound	1920	59.90¢	55.80¢	56¢	60.10¢	65.80¢
	1921	53.40¢	48.50¢	50.60¢	53.80¢	60.80¢
	1922	54.60¢	47.60¢	49.40¢	53.60¢	61.20¢
	1923	45.70¢	47.80¢	49.70¢	49.70¢	58¢
	1924	49.90¢	45.20¢	47.30¢	48¢	58.40¢
Potatoes, Irish, per pound	1920	6.60¢	7.70¢	6.60¢	6.40¢	6.35¢
	1921	3.70¢	4¢	2.90¢	2.80¢	3.20¢
	1922	3.40¢	3.90¢	2.70¢	2.50¢	2.90¢
	1923	3.70¢	4¢	2.60¢	2.40¢	3.20¢
	1924	3.40¢	3.60¢	2.60¢	2.70¢	3.50¢
Prunes, Dried, per pound	1920	27¢	27.80¢	28.60¢	30.10¢	27.40¢
	1921	19.30¢	20.70¢	20.60¢	20.30¢	18.10¢
	1922	33.50¢	21.10¢	20.70¢	20.80¢	19.40¢
	1923	17.30¢	19.80¢	19.90¢	20.30¢	18.90¢
	1924	16.10¢	18.10¢	18.80¢	18.40¢	16.90¢
Rice, per pound	1920	16.90¢	16.70¢	16.80¢	17.60¢	16.90¢
	1921	9.20¢	8.40¢	9.40¢	9.40¢	9.90¢
	1922	9.10¢	9.10¢	9.80¢	9.70¢	9.70¢
	1923	9.40¢	8.60¢	10.10¢	9.60¢	9.80¢
	1924	9.80¢	9.50¢	10.60¢	10¢	10.40¢
Sugar, per pound	1920	18.20¢	19.90¢	19.60¢	14.70¢	18¢
	1921	7.20¢	8.30¢	7.50¢	8.60¢	8¢
	1922	6.60¢	7.70¢	6.60¢	8¢	7.40¢
	1923	9.40¢	10.60¢	9.40¢	10.80¢	10.30¢
	1924	8.40¢	9.70¢	8.80¢	9.80¢	9.10¢

Commodity	Year	New York	Atlanta	Chicago	Denver	Los Angeles
Tea, per pound	1920	57.40¢	92.30¢	70.20¢	72.70¢	73.40¢
	1921	52.50¢	90.90¢	65.70¢	71.40¢	69¢
	1922	49.10¢	88.10¢	64¢	69.60¢	70.20¢
	1923	55.40¢	92.90¢	71.30¢	67.70¢	69.80¢
	1924	60.30	93.50¢	73¢	68.20¢	70.70¢

SELECTED PRICES 1920-1924

Item	Source	Description	Price
Advertising			
Advertising Budget	Roland Marchand, *Advertising the American Dream* (1985)	Crane Company (plumbing supplies) budget for 1921	$79,000/year
Advertising Budget	Marchand, *Advertising the American Dream* (1985)	*Maxwell House coffee;* for magazine advertisements in 1921	$19,955/year
Appliances			
Carpet Sweeper	*The Literary Digest* (1924)	*Bissell Sweeper,* get ten years' of quick, thorough, easy sweeping	$5.00
Electric Cooker	*Kalamazoo Stove Co.* (1923)	*Kalamazoo;* automatic; like an electric range—cooks, bakes, roasts, fries, boils and toasts; just turn the switch and let the electricity heat the food	$28.85
Electric Percolator	*Kalamazoo Stove Co.* (1923)	Coffee tastes better when percolated; 9 cup size	$7.15
Fountain Percolator	*Kalamazoo Stove Co.* (1923)	*Kalamazoo;* six-cup size, aluminum, comes with spreader and valve	$3.87
Gas Grill	*National Geographic Magazine* (1924)	*American Kampkook;* plan to take kitchen convenience with you on your vacation; deluxe model	$15.00
Heating Unit	*Kalamazoo Stove Co.* (1923)	*Vulcan Utility;* with warm and cold air through one big register; it has long been one of our most popular styles	$84.65
Iron	*Kalamazoo Stove Co.* (1923)	*Kalamazoo Comfort;* gasoline; the comfort is ready for use half a minute after lighting	$4.45
Laundry Stove	*Kalamazoo Stove Co.* (1923)	*Kalamazoo;* you can cook and heat irons at the same time—thereby saving fuel	$8.85
Oil Heater	*Kalamazoo Stove Co.* (1923)	*Kalamazoo;* take the chill out of cold rooms; light and convenient	$4.95
Range	*Kalamazoo Stove Co.* (1923)	*Kalamazoo Emperor;* Blue-enamel brass with nickel; improved high closet with smoke pipe behind the clear white-enameled splasher back	
		Cash price	$72.25
		Credit price	$79.25
Range	*Kalamazoo Stove Co.* (1923)	*Kalamazoo Prince;* porcelain blue enamel; burns all fuels, regularly furnished with duplex grates for burning soft coal, wood, or coke	
		Cash price	$84.95
		Credit price	$93.45
Refrigerator	*Kalamazoo Stove Co.* (1923)	*Kalamazoo North Star;* white, enamel-lined; a dandy little food saver at a little price	$27.95
Refrigerator	*Kalamazoo Stove Co.* (1923)	All steel; for lifetime service, ice capacity 100 pounds	$56.95
Table Stove	*The World's Work* (1923)	*Armstrong;* cooks three things at once, makes waffles too	$12.50
Vacuum Cleaner	*Kalamazoo Stove Co.* (1923)	*Kalamazoo;* put pleasure into your house work; safe for your rugs	$33.95
Waffle Iron	*The World's Work* (1923)	*Armstrong;* electrical dealers in your town will be glad to show you	$4.00
Washer	*Kalamazoo Stove Co.* (1923)	*Kalamazoo;* an electric washer founded upon a washing principle that has been tried and proven in the largest steam laundries—with the revolving wooden cylinder; capacity, six sheets or equal amount of other clothes	$112.50

Item	Source	Description	Price
Wood Heater	*Kalamazoo Stove Co.* (1923)	*Kalamazoo Star;* truly a dandy little air-tight parlor heater; made to burn wood only	$17.80

Apparel, Children's

Item	Source	Description	Price
Baseball Outfit	*Sears, Roebuck* (1924)	Boy's; quality gray cotton flannel with maroon stripes	$1.79
Bathing Suit	*B. Altman & Co.* (1923)	One-piece; wool jersey in white and navy blue, white-and-rose, or white and copenhagen	$2.95
Camping and Hiking Suit	*B. Altman & Co.* (1923)	Girl's; khaki-colored twill, includes coat, knickers and wrap-around skirt	$14.50
Dress	*B. Altman & Co.* (1923)	Girls; middy; cotton twill, lacing in front, patch pocket	$1.55
Children's Shoes	*The Youth's Companion* (1920)	*Selz Liberty Bell Shoes;* save your children from the foot miseries most adults know	$5.00 and up
Dress	*B. Altman & Co.* (1923)	Baby's; hand-made; long; of nainsook, hand tucks, and hand-hemstitching formed yoke	$2.95
Frock	*B. Altman & Co.* (1923)	Girl's; cotton voile, belted with smocking	$3.85
Nightrobe	*B. Altman & Co.* (1923)	Baby's; of cotton stockinette, drawstring at bottom, one year	$0.95
Romper	*B. Altman & Co.* (1923)	Boy's; of chambray in cadet blue on tan	$1.35
Sailor Suit	*B. Altman & Co.* (1923)	Boy's; French blouse; unbleached jean with black trimming	$3.25
Shoes	*B. Altman & Co.* (1923)	Lace; of dark tan calfskin, sizes 7 to 11	$4.50
Shoes	*B. Altman & Co.* (1923)	*Keds;* boy's; of heavy white or brown duck; Goodyear glove band	$0.75
Skirt	*B. Altman & Co.* (1923)	Baby's; long; of nainsook, ruffle of embroidery	$0.85
Suit	*Chicago Tribune* (1920)	*Starr Best;* boy's wash; of plain blue denim trimmed with lighter blue	$2.95
Suit	*B. Altman & Co.* (1923)	Boy's; regulation middy; elaborately trimmed with embroidery and taping; yoke, black silk tie	$2.95

Apparel, Men's

Item	Source	Description	Price
Bathing Suit	*B. Altman & Co.* (1923)	Of worsted; in black or navy blue	$5.00
Collars	*Sears, Roebuck* (1920)	Vanderbilt style; soft; points 2 1/4"; back 1 1/2"; package of six	$1.25/package
Handkerchiefs	*B. Altman & Co.* (1923)	Plain; white lawn, shirred, hemstitched	$1.80/dozen
Hose	*B. Altman & Co.* (1923)	Ribbed wool; half hose; for tennis in white	$1.50/pair
Hose	*B. Altman & Co.* (1923)	*Lisle;* half hose; black, white, cordovan, gray, navy, blue, tan	$0.75/pair
Riding Breeches	*B. Altman & Co.* (1923)	Tan linen crash, with full reinforcement of the material	$12.00
Shirt	*Chicago Tribune* (1922)	*Manhattan;* white Oxford; you're going to like this shirt a lot	$2.75
Shirt	*B. Altman & Co.* (1923)	Polo; white Oxford, with collar attached	$2.50
Shoes	*Chicago Tribune* (1920)	*Henry L. Lytton & Sons Palm Beach Oxford;* made in custom or medium broad toes with solid leather soles	$7.00
Shoes	*B. Altman & Co.* (1923)	Brogue Oxford; of tan or black Norwegian grain leather	$8.50/pair

Item	Source	Description	Price
Slippers	B. Altman & Co. (1923)	Of brown or black leather	$3.65
Suit	Chicago Tribune (1920)	Hart Schaffner & Marx; silk lined; made to sell at $75, $80, $85	$50.00
Suit	Chicago Tribune (1922)	Gold and Sports; four-piece suits in imported and domestic tweeds	$45.00
Tie	Sears, Roebuck (1924)	Fancy knit; of fiber silk	$0.39
Undershirt	B. Altman & Co. (1923)	White cotton, gauze-weight, sleeveless	$0.75
Underwear	Collier's (1924)	B.V.D. knee-length drawers; tailored with balance and grace Each	$0.85
Union Suit	B. Altman & Co. (1923)	White plaid, madras, sleeveless, knee length; webbing at back	$1.15
Union Suit	National Geographic Magazine (1924)	BVD; there is only one BVD underwear	$1.50
Work Shoe	Kalamazoo Stove Co. (1923)	A sturdy genuine brown all-leather, dairy-proof shoe that gives you dependable and long wear	$3.45

Apparel, Women's

Item	Source	Description	Price
Apron	Sears, Roebuck (1920)	Waterproof; made of cotton material coated with high-grade composition rubber	$0.98
Bathing Suit	B. Altman & Co. (1923)	Black sports stain, trimmed with colored stitching	$8.50
Bloomers	B. Altman & Co. (1923)	Tailored silk model in pink, black or orchid	$3.95
Bloomers	B. Altman & Co. (1923)	Mercerized cotton; white or pink	$1.10
Blouse	Sears, Roebuck (1920)	Silk crepe de chine; a very special value in a stylish and well-made garment; narrow pin tucks down front panel	$4.95
Blouse	San Francisco Examiner (1921)	Forsythe blouse; favorites for tailored and sports wear	$2.95
Boudoir Cap	B. Altman & Co. (1923)	Cream net, the crown trimmed with ruffles of Valenciennes lace	$2.95
Boudoir Sacque	B. Altman & Co. (1923)	Valenciennes; a slipover model of Georgette crepe	$6.95
Brassiere	Sears, Roebuck (1920)	In camisole style	$0.79
Cap	B. Altman & Co. (1923)	Maid's cap; fluted white organdie, black ribbon	$0.45
Cape	Chicago Tribune (1922)	The Resale Shop; made of genuine American mink	$55.00
Coat	B. Altman & Co. (1923)	Tailored wool; double breasted, trimmed with leather-covered buttons	$12.75
Corselet and Brassiere Combination	B. Altman & Co. (1923)	Pink batiste; very long, with deep elastic gores of hips and back	$3.00
Corset	B. Altman & Co. (1923)	Fasso; silk; pink figured batiste, daintily trimmed top and bottom with fine net ribbon and silk flowers	$20.50
Dress	New York Times (1923)	Lehman; cotton; over 300 voiles, crepes, dotted swisses, linens, and chintzes dramatically reduced	$14.00
Dress	B. Altman & Co. (1923)	Flowered Georgette crepe; for afternoon wear with wide flowering sleeves that reveal a bit of the arm	$49.50

Item	Source	Description	Price
Fan	B. Altman & Co. (1923)	Uncurled ostrich feathers mounted on three amber-colored sticks, in coral, jade, turquoise blue, or American beauty	$7.75
Frock	B. Altman & Co. (1923)	Checked gingham smartly trimmed with novelty edging of white organdie	$5.75
Frock	B. Altman & Co. (1923)	The chiffon falling in soft panels on each side, and dipping below the skirt give something of an Oriental touch for evening wear	$39.50
Frock	B. Altman & Co. (1923)	Cotton voile; the skirt is made with a plaited apron front, irregular in outline, and with panels at the back, which are plaited and these are all trimmed with ribbon	$13.25
Frock	B. Altman & Co. (1923)	Black silk braid of interesting design on this frock of navy-blue wool twill	$29.75
Gloves	B. Altman & Co. (1923)	*Marvex;* suede and kidskin; eight-button length	$5.50
Gown	New York Times (1923)	Lingerie; the workmanship is exquisite with lace	$88.00
Handbag	B. Altman & Co. (1923)	Striped moire silk; silk lined throughout; inside compartment and mirror	$4.90
Hat	Chicago Tribune (1920)	*Silk Sport;* fashioned in this season's smartest styles	$13.75
Hat	B. Altman & Co. (1923)	Straw and tafetta; with a slightly rolled brim all around	$10.50
Hose	B. Altman & Co. (1923)	Cotton; semi-fashioned, black, white, or African brown	$0.35
Hose	B. Altman & Co. (1923)	Silk; gossamer weight in black, white, and the fashionable colors	$3.95
Hose	Chicago Tribune (1920)	*O'Connor & Goldberg;* pure silk; with semi-fashioned seam	$1.59
Nightrobe	B. Altman & Co. (1923)	Nainsook trimmed with medallions of embroidery and Valenciennes lace	$1.95
Outercoat	B. Altman & Co. (1923)	Coat of bandella cloth, an all-wool material, closing with ornamental clasp at the left side	$75.00
Overblouse	B. Altman & Co. (1923)	Crepe de chine of heavy quality with contrasting embroidery of individual design	$18.50
Nightrobe	B. Altman & Co. (1923)	Nainsook trimmed with medallions of embroidery and Valenciennes lace	$1.95
Pajamas	B. Altman & Co. (1923)	Silk; washable; pointed effect at lower edge	$7.95
Panel Collar	B. Altman & Co. (1923)	Detachable; cream embroidered net	$3.50
Pantalet	B. Altman & Co. (1923)	Cotton gauge; low neck and sleeveless	$0.55
Parasol Umbrella	Sears, Roebuck (1920)	Rain or shine; eight-rib paragon steel frame	$5.95
Petticoat	B. Altman & Co. (1923)	Radium silk; trimmed with lace insertion and lace edge	$6.85
Robe	B. Altman & Co. (1923)	*Eiderdown;* in blue, with collar, cuffs and pockets in blue-and-white checked material	$6.75
Sandals	New York Times (1923)	*Novelty;* strap with military, Cuban, and Louis XVI heels	$9.95
Shoes	B. Altman & Co. (1923)	Sports Oxford; tie; of white buckskin with patent-leather apron, rubber soles and heels	$11.50
Skirt	San Francisco Examiner (1921)	Wool sports skirts; plaids and stripes	$14.95

Item	Source	Description	Price
Slip	B. Altman & Co. (1923)	Plaited meteor trimmed with wide Valenciennes lace	$9.75
Slippers	B. Altman & Co. (1923)	Of patent leather	$7.50
Suit	Sears, Roebuck (1920)	Tailored; all-wool double-twisted warp serge	$27.95
Suit	B. Altman & Co. (1923)	Tweed; comprising coat, suit, and knickers—making a serviceable and smart three-piece suit for sports	$36.50
Suit	B. Altman & Co. (1923)	Three-piece; both the cape and one-piece dress being of black canton crepe richly embroidered in black	$90.00
Sweater	New York Times (1923)	R. H. Macy & Co.; sleeveless; coatee model of mohair and fiber, with novel collar	$10.74
Undergarment	B. Altman & Co. (1923)	Combination of Nainsook, knickbocker drawers, drop seat	$1.45
Union Suit	Sears, Roebuck (1920)	Elastic-ribbed cotton, double-body, heavyweight	$1.65
Vest	B. Altman & Co. (1923)	Silk chemise; machine scalloped and embroidered, in pink, peach color, or orchid, length 21" and 23"	$3.95
Work Boot	Sears, Roebuck (1920)	Cromax; leather sole; guaranteed to wear six months	$3.98

Baby Products

Item	Source	Description	Price
Baby's High Chair	B. Altman & Co. (1923)	Of white-enameled reed	$7.00
Crib	B. Altman & Co. (1923)	White-enameled metal, drop sides, 28" x 52"	$17.50
Portable Bathtub	B. Altman & Co. (1923)	Rubber, with faucet at the bottom made on a wooden folding frame in natural color	$5.75
Wardrobe	B. Altman & Co. (1923)	Baby's; white-enameled wicker, with folding drawers	$24.50

Business Equipment & Supplies

Item	Source	Description	Price
Steel Pens	The Youth's Companion (1920)	Spencerian Steel Pens; the standard for over half a century Ten different pens	$0.10
Typewriter	The National Geographic Magazine (1924)	Remington De Luxe Portable typewriter in ivory tone finish with brown leather carrying case	$75.00
Typewriter	Typewriter Flier (1921)	Underwood; reconstructed; each worn part replaced with a new part	$31.50
Typewriter	The Mentor (1923)	Underwood; portable; typed words are winged words	$50.00
Typewriter	National Geographic Magazine (1924)	Remington; portable; an ideal gift for graduates	$60.00
Typewriter Ribbon	Typewriter Flier Magazine (1924)	Condo Typocraft; medium-black inking; each ribbon foil wrapped in tin box	$3/dozen

Education

Item	Source	Description	Price
College Tuition	The Progressive Farmer (1924)	Clemson College, S. C., for students seeking classes in agriculture Per session	$40.00
Dance Lessons	San Francisco Examiner (1921)	Ladies taught by gentlemen; per couple	$1.00

Item	Source	Description	Price
Entertainment			
Swimming Lessons	*New York Times* (1923)	*Madison Square Garden Gymnasium;* largest swimming pool in United States	$5/6 lessons
Theater Ticket	*Chicago Tribune* (1920)	*Colonial Theatre Musical Review;* Raymond Hitchcock in his all-new musical review *Hitchy Koo 1919;* matinees	$2.00
Theater Ticket	*New York Times* (1923)	*Globe Plays;* fifth annual production of George White's *Scandals;* best seats	$2.50
Entertainment, Home			
Camera	*Collier's* (1924)	*Autographic Kodak Camera;* you'll get good pictures from the first	$6.50 and up
Camera	*The Mentor* (1923)	*Kodak No. 1;* autographic; exposures as fast as 1/200 of a second	$50.00
Game	*Sears, Roebuck* (1923)	Mah-jongg; the royal game of China that is sweeping the country like wildfire; ivory pyrain tiles, mahogany box with five compartments	$22.95
Poker Set	*B. Altman & Co.* (1923)	In small leather case, with 100 chips, two packs of playing cards and book of rules	$6.25
Radio	*New York Times* (1923)	*Crosley 50;* Oh, boy! There's London! Last night I had Honolulu and the night before that Puerto Rico	$14.50
Records	*The National Geographic Magazine* (1924)	Victor Records featuring The Philadelphia Orchestra; *Carmen*—Prelude to Act I and *March of the Caucasian,* double-faced	$1.50
Talking Machine	*The National Geographic Magazine* (1924)	*Victrola No. 405;* walnut case, electric	$290
Table Covers	*The World's Work* (1923)	For Mah-jongg; well made of green, heavy felt, to exactly fit any 30" card table top	$5.00
Talking Machine	*The World's Work* (1923)	*Victrola;* Victor Talking Machine Co., Camden, New Jersey; place your order now while all the 21 instrument styles are available	$25 and up
Talking Machine	*National Geographic Magazine* (1924)	*Victrola;* mahogany, oak or walnut cabinet	$125
Farm Equipment & Supplies			
Hen	*Rhode Island Red Journal* (1923)	S.C. Red; first and color hen at National Red meet at Kansas City, Missouri, 1919	$25.00
Insecticide	*Rhode Island Red Journal* (1923)	*Licecil;* kill the lice the best and sure way	$1.00/bottle
Insect Poison	*The Progressive Farmer* (1924)	*So-Bos-So;* guaranteed to rid your cows of flies and gnats Per 15-gallon drum	$15.00
Medicine for Chickens	*Rhode Island Red Journal* (1923)	*Sunny Life White;* Diarrhea tablets; recommended by thousands of the world's foremost poultry raisers	$0.75/100 tablets
Portable Power Plant	*The Progressive Farmer* (1924)	*Homelite* portable electric light and power plant; power for pumping, grinding, shelling corn, drilling, boring and milking; will run on gasoline, kerosene, fuel oil; Model D-11	$250
Pullet	*Rhode Island Red Journal* (1923)	S.C. Red; sired by a 296-egg cock, out of 247- and 218-egg hens	$5.00
Separator	*Kalamazoo Stove Co.* (1923)	*Kalamazoo;* a cream separator often means as much as $20 extra from every cow; 600 lb capacity	$69.95

Item	Source	Description	Price
Food Products			
Biscuits	*National Geographic Magazine* (1924)	*Huntley & Palmers;* the sweetmeats of kings; special package	$1
Champagne	*New York Times* (1923)	*R. H. Macy's Mount Zircon Ginger Champagne;* bottles by the Moon Tide Spring in Mount Zircon	$0.19
Chocolate	*World's Work* (1923)	*Wilbur Buds;* exquisite morsels of vanilla chocolate, wrapped in pure tin foil	$1.00/1 pound
Chocolate Bars	*Sears, Roebuck* (1922)	*Hershey's;* 24 sweet milk bars	$0.98
Coffee	*New York Times* (1923)	*Macy's Vienna Brand;* a rich and delicious blend of South American Coffees	$0.34/lb
Condensed Soup	*National Geographic Magazine* (1924)	*Campbell's;* look for the red and white label; 21 kinds	$0.12/can
Curry Powder	*New York Times* (1923)	*R. H. Macy Madras;* our own importation from India	$0.29/half-lb
Eggs	*Rhode Island Red Journal* (1923)	S.C. Red; eggs from special color matching for the Southern trade fall hatching	$5.00/15
French Peas	*New York Times* (1923)	*Marceau Brand;* regular size tins; extra fine	$0.37
Gum	*Sears, Roebuck* (1922)	*Wrigley Juicy Fruit*	$0.39/10 pkgs
Instant Coffee	*National Geographic Magazine* (1924)	*G. Washington's;* even the best roasted coffee can be spoiled in the making; why risk failure?	$0.10
Olives	*New York Times* (1923)	*La Forge Stuffed Spanish Queen;* stuffed with red peppers	$0.29
Salmon	*New York Times* (1923)	*Lily White;* Columbia River fine quality: No. 1 flat can	$0.44
Tenderloin Steak	*San Francisco Examiner* (1921)	From "A" No. 1 prime steer beef	$0.55/pound
Furniture			
Bookcase	*Chicago Tribune* (1922)	Sectional; sections are 9" x 11" and 13"	$4.80
Chest	*Kalamazoo Stove Co.* (1923)	Beautiful colonial design; finished in natural cedar and trimmed with satin-polished copper; size: 36" x 16" x 16"	$12.55
Davenette	*Kalamazoo Stove Co.* (1923)	*Kalamazoo;* two pieces of furniture in one—combining davenette and full sized bed	$46.50
Dresser	*Chicago Tribune* (1920)	Walnut; Louis XVI style; 46" wide, carefully constructed, and has a mirror of generous proportions	$98.00
Furniture Set	*Kalamazoo Stove Co.* (1923)	*Arts and Crafts Oak Mission;* seven-piece set includes arm chair, reception chair, arm rocker, rocker, tabourette, bookends, and table	$28.50
Kitchen Cabinet	*Kalamazoo Stove Co.* (1923)	Oak; modern kitchen efficiency in your home is practically impossible unless you have a convenient place for everything; has a white porcelain top	$32.50
Metal Bed	*Kalamazoo Stove Co.* (1923)	Continuous post; 2" posts, includes bed, mattress and spring	$26.95
Garden Equipment & Supplies			
Birdhouse	*The National Geographic Magazine* (1924)	*Dodson's Queen Anne Martin House;* 48 rooms; white with green trim; pine with copper roof; 36 x 26 x 37 inches	$60.00
Daffodils	*National Geographic Magazine* (1924)	*Elliott Nursery;* 60-bulb collection	$4.00

Item	Source	Description	Price
Lawnmower	*The Literary Digest* (1924)	*Montamower,* no gears, no long blades, trims and cuts at the same time	$18.00
Lawn Mower	*New York Times* (1923)	*James McCreery & Co. New England Mower;* ball bearing with three 14-inch steel blades	$9.95
Lawn Mower	*National Geographic Magazine* (1924)	*Montague Montamower;* the new easy way to cut lawns	$18.00

Hotel Rates

Item	Source	Description	Price
Hotel Room	*Chicago Tribune* (1920)	*Hotel Wychmere;* 150 clean comfortable outside rooms, at exceptionally attractive rates; electric lights, steam heat, running water	$1-$1.50/day
Hotel Room	*New York Times* (1923)	*Hotel Monticello New York;* 35–37 West 6th Street, between Broadway and Central Park with shower and bath	$3.00/day
Hotel Room	*The Journal of the American Dental Association* (1924)	*Waldorf Dallas;* with bath, two persons	$4 to $6/day
Room	*The National Geographic Magazine* (1924)	*Jasper Park Lodge,* in Canadian Rockies, American plan	$6.00 per day

Household Goods

Item	Source	Description	Price
Alarm Clock	*Sears, Roebuck* (1921)	*National;* 8-day alarm	$2.50
Barn Paint	*Kalamazoo Stove Co.* (1923)	*Kalamazoo;* real insurance against rot and decay	$1.54/gallon
Bath Tub	*Kalamazoo Stove Co.* (1923)	*Handee Modern;* Handee bath tub includes a stove and water heater combination that gives you real city comfort; Outfit complete	$29.95
Blanket	*B. Altman & Co.* (1923)	All-wool; white, blue, or pink borders; 60" x 84"	$14.50/pair
Bonbon Box	*B. Altman & Co.* (1923)	Engraved glass, sterling silver deposit; with cover	$4.00
Borax	*New York Times* (1923)	*Red Star Brand;* guaranteed absolutely pure	$0.49/5 pounds
Cookware	*Kalamazoo Stove Co.* (1923)	25-piece aluminum service; includes 5-piece combination cooker and steamer, 2 quart welded spout percolator with spreader, new round toaster, 5 quart tea kettle, 1 quart lipped sauce pan, 2 quart lipped sauce pan, cake turner, soup ladle, 2 bottom cake pans	$10.95
Fence	*Kalamazoo Stove Co.* (1923)	*Perfection;* open hearth; basic steel, heavily galvanized; a real improvement in farm fencing; 47" high	$0.62/rod
Floor Covering	*Chicago Tribune* (1920)	*Texoleum;* adapted to use in all parts of the house— on stains, in the halls, upstairs and down	$0.66/sq yd
Floor Paint	*Kalamazoo Stove Co.* (1920)	*Kalamazoo;* dress up your old floors; colors include yellow, maroon, light gray, buff, oak, and dark gray	$1.95/gallon
Food Jar	*B. Altman & Co.* (1923)	*Thermalware;* keeps food or liquids hot or cold; capacity one gallon	$10.00
Hat Box	*B. Altman & Co.* (1923)	Circular-shaped of enameled duck; cretonne-lined; leather handle	$5.00
House Paint	*Kalamazoo Stove Co.* (1923)	*Kalamazoo;* save the surface and you save all	$2.15/gallon
Lamp	*Kalamazoo Stove Co.* (1923)	*Nulite Match-Lite;* is 20 times as powerful as the old style cool oil lamp, but operates without a wick or grease, lamp black or smell that is so distasteful; burns 14 hours on one filling of three pints of common motor gasoline	$7.35
Meat Platter	*B. Altman & Co.* (1923)	Silver plate; well and tree design; 17"	$10.50

Item	Source	Description	Price
Roaster	Kalamazoo Stove Co. (1923)	Aluminum; a roaster that has every modern improvement; with rack	$4.82
Salt and Pepper Set	B. Altman & Co. (1923)	Sterling silver; six shakers in case	$4.00/case
Suitcase	B. Altman & Co. (1923)	Black enameled duck, cretonne-lined, leather corners and handles; 24" x 15" x 9"	$6.00
Tablecloth	B. Altman & Co. (1923)	Fine quality durable satin damask; 72" x 108"	$17.25
Toilet	Kalamazoo Stove Co. (1923)	Simply place the sanitary closet in any out of the way place —a closet, under the stairs or wherever a private corner can be found; it is absolutely sanitary and odorless	$6.95
Toilet Cleaner	National Geographic Magazine (1924)	Sani-Flush; cleans the toilet bowl better than any other means	$0.25
Traveling Bag	B. Altman & Co. (1923)	Tan cowhide, leather-lined, size 16"	$10.50
Vacuum Bottle	B. Altman & Co. (1923)	Green enamel; aluminum top; capacity one quart	$2.25

Insurance Rates

Item	Source	Description	Price
Fire Insurance	Insurance Policy (1920)	Charleston Insurance And Trust Co.; $750 fire coverage on one-story frame house	$11.10/year
Fire Insurance	Insurance Policy (1921)	Charleston Insurance & Trust Co.; (rate $0.68 per $100); $500 fire insurance on brick building in Columbia, South Carolina	$3.40/year
Fire Insurance	Insurance Policy (1922)	New Jersey Insurance Co.; $2,000 fire insurance; two story, wood frame building	$22.40/year
Life Insurance	Chicago Tribune (1920)	Merchant's Reserve Life Insurance; pure life insurance; annual premium per $1,000, whole life, age 35	$16.40/year

Jewelry

Item	Source	Description	Price
Blue Diamond	National Geographic Magazine (1924)	Black Starr & Frost; the largest blue diamond ever discovered; 1 9/32" by 1 5/32"	$3 million
Cigarette Case	Sears, Roebuck (1920)	Sterling silver; engraved ornamentation with shield; gold plated inside	$11.72
Cuff Buttons	The World's Work (1923)	The Baer & Wilde Co. Kum-A-Part Kuff; the button for soft cuffs that clicks open, snaps shut	$25/pair
Cuff Links	The World's Work (1923)	J.F. Sturdy's Sons & Co. Sta-Lokt; the perfected separable cuff link	$1.50 to $7.50/pair
Lapel Button	Reunion Pamphlet, 81st Division Wildcats (1920)	Wildcat Insignia Co.; 81st division Wildcat reunion; screw buttons to be worn on coat lapels; a very neat insignia sterling silver / 10-k gold	$1.00 / $4.50
Necklace	The World's Work (1923)	The Henshel Co.; bluebird pearl; the rare depth and iridescence of the most expensive natural pearls; platinum safety clasp with brilliant diamond; 24" long	$85.00
Pendant Earrings	B. Altman & Co. (1923)	Imitation pearls in the shower design; French backs	$4/pair
Pin	B. Altman & Co. (1923)	Rhinestone bar; set in sterling silver	$2.25
Pocket Watch	Spiegel Catalog (1920)	Illinois railroad nickel or gold filled; 18 size; swing-ring case; 21-jewel; genuine Bunn special movement	$43.50
Pocket Watch	Spiegel Catalog (1920)	Illinois railroad nickel; twenty-year double strats; gold-filled open face; popular 16 size; fitted with Bunn movement; 23-jewel	$63.50

Item	Source	Description	Price
Ring	*Reunion Pamphlet, 81st Division Wildcats* (1920)	*Wildcat Insignia Co.;* 81st division Wildcat reunion; the center of the seal is a relief form of the wildcat; sterling silver 10-k gold	$3.50 $12.50
Ring	*Chicago Tribune* (1920)	*Lewy Brothers Co.;* sincere, personal service; black pearl	$3,500
Strap Watch	*The World's Work* (1923)	*Hamilton Watch Co.;* all Hamiltons have true beauty of design	$38 to $42
Wristwatch	*Chicago Tribune* (1920)	*Lebolt & Co.;* woman's; 15-jewel movement; gold filled case, hand engraved	$22.00
Wristwatch	*B. Altman & Co.* (1923)	Woman's; sterling silver; 15 jewels; Swiss movement mounted on black ribbon	$20.00

Meals

Lunch	*San Francisco Examiner* (1921)	Luncheon: Fruit or combination salad; boiled chicken or boiled steak; mashed potatoes, steamed potatoes, string beans, choice of pudding	$1.00

Medical Products & Services

Electric Heating Oven	*The Journal of the American Dental Association* (1924)	*Buffdentco;* for wax elimination and general heating purposes in the dental laboratory	$55.00
Laboratory Work Bench	*The Journal of the American Dental Association* (1924)	*Alcasco;* designed for the present day restricted working space	$47.50
Medicine	*The Youth's Companion* (1920)	New-Skin—Keeps Little Hurts from Getting Big; it forms a covering that keeps out germs	$0.15 to $0.30
Nonprescription Drug	*Sears, Roebuck* (1921)	Aromatic castor oil; to make it more palatable; 8-oz bottle	$0.69
Nonprescription Drug	*The World's Work* (1923)	*Eno's Fruit Salt Derivative Compound;* just a teaspoonful of ENO's in a glass of water will clear your blood stream and give you a new and happier aspect	$0.75/can
Nonprescription Drug	*Sears, Roebuck* (1924)	*Milk of Magnesia Laxative;* well-known mild laxative and stomach anti-acid corrective; $0.50 size	$0.39
Regulating Dental Appliances	*The Journal of the American Dental Association* (1924)	*Jackson's;* improvement in orthodontic methods enables us to turn out mechanically correctly constructed appliances; gold plated	$7.00
Smock	*The Journal of the American Dental Association* (1924)	*Angelica Jacket Co.;* of finely woven white bleached twill with indestructible knotted tape buttons	$2.00

Motorized Vehicles, Services, & Supplies

Automobile	*The Literary Digest* (1924)	*Willys-Knight coupe-sedan,* powered by same type engine used in Daimler, Panhard, Mercedes, Minerva	$1,450
Automobile	Joseph J. Schroeder Jr. *The Wonderful World of Automobiles* (1971)	*Hendley Knight;* standard 7-passenger touring car; an ever-increasing appeal to the business man [cost in 1922]	$2,450
Automobile	Schroeder, *The Wonderful World of Automobiles* (1971)	*Kline Car;* Kline lowers manufacturing costs by utilizing its own shops [cost in 1922] Coupe Sedan	 $3,050 $3,090
Automobile	Schroeder, *The Wonderful World of Automobiles* (1971)	*Case;* Sedan; exceptional performance is an outstanding feature of this car [cost in 1922]	$2,790

Item	Source	Description	Price
Automobile	*The World's Work* (1923)	*1924 Haynes 60 DeLuxe Sedan;* improved six cylinder Haynes-built motor—created from the Haynes motor which had established a wonderful eight-year record for dependability	$1,895
Automobile	Schroeder, *The Wonderful World of Automobiles* (1971)	*Durant Four;* 5-passenger touring car; the new motor is a revelation in power and flexibility [cost in 1924]	$890
Automobile	Schroeder, *The Wonderful World of Automobiles* (1971)	*Buick Standard Six;* open model; 5-passenger touring car [cost in 1924]	$1,175
Automobile	Schroeder, *The Wonderful World of Automobiles* (1971)	*Willys-Overland;* the champion economy car [cost in 1924]	$695
Automobile	*National Geographic Magazine* (1924)	*Chrysler Six Phaeton*	$1,395
Automobile	*National Geographic Magazine* (1924)	*Chandler;* touring car; change speeds without clashing; the traffic transmission is acknowledged to be the most important automotive improvement of the decade	$1,485
Automotive Accessories	*Collier's* (1924)	Oldsmobile Six accessories available at any Oldsmobile dealer:	
		Front bumper	$15.00
		Road spot light	$5.00
		Rear view mirror	$1.75
		Trunk rails, set of four	$6.80
		Windshield wings, pair	$17.00
Heat Indicator	*Collier's* (1924)	*Safe-T-Stat* engine heat indicator; accurate and visible at all times on the dashboard of your car	$10.00
Ignition System	*The Progressive Farmer* (1924)	*Bosch Type 600* ignition system for Fords; insures quick, easy starts	$12.75
Motor Oil	*Collier's* (1924)	*Mobiloil* from Vacuum Oil Company; the new sealed one-quart can is ideal while touring	$0.35

Musical Instruments

Piano	*World's Work* (1923)	*Steinway & Sons;* the instrument of the immortals;	
		Upright	$875
		Grand	$1,425
Piano	*New York Times* (1923)	*Mathushek Grand Opera;* size only 36"	$635

Other

Adoption	*The American Legion Weekly* (1920)	Cost to adopt a French orphan	$75.00
Dolly Washer	*Kalamazoo Stove Co.* (1923)	Hand powered; it is so constructed that even a child can run it	$15.60
Exercise Program	*Picture Play Magazine* (1923)	*Luthy's Daily Five Minute Basic Physical Exercise;* to keep one agile, healthy and young	$5.00
Exploration	*The National Geographic Magazine* (1924)	Cost to National Geographic Society for series of expeditions into Peru to investigate the traces of the Inca race	$50,000
Fountain Pen	*Picture Play Magazine* (1923)	*Waterman Ideal;* self-filling type, mottled with gold-filled level and clip	$7.50

Item	Source	Description	Price
Grid Batteries	*National Geographic Magazine* (1924)	*Philco Diamon;* for low-voltage peanut tubes; east of the Mississippi	$8.00
Incense	*Picture Play Magazine* (1923)	*Temple of Allah;* this rare, choice incense is even used as a cachet by fastidious women; it sweetens the air and keeps away flies and other pests; deluxe set with large metal burner and incense	$1.00
Mail Order House	*National Geographic Magazine* (1924)	*Aladdin;* 7 room; price includes all lumber cut to fit; highest grade interior woodwork, siding, flooring, windows, doors, glass, paints, hardware, nails, lath, roofing, with complete instructions and drawings	$975
Mechanical Pencil	*National Geographic Magazine* (1924)	*Wahl Eversharp;* the superior writing companion; economy model	$3.00
Pen	*National Geographic Magazine* (1924)	*Parker Duofold Duette;* handsomer than gold—mightier than the sword	$7.00
Photographs	*Picture Play Magazine* (1923)	*Homer S. Howry Co.;* movie stars original photos; over 250 stars including Mary Pickford, Doug Fairbanks, Debe Daniels, Betty Compson, Priscilla Dyan; size 8" x 10"	$0.50
Stationery	*The World's Work* (1923)	*Hampshire Paper Co. Old Hampshire;* the stationery of a gentleman; 24 sheets and envelopes of royal club size	$1.50/box

Personal Care Products

Item	Source	Description	Price
Bath Salts	*B. Altman & Co.* (1923)	*Alsam Bouquet*	$1.50/jar
Brush	*B. Altman & Co.* (1923)	*Ideal Hair;* waterproof	$1.65
Dental Cream	*The Mentor* (1923)	*Colgate Ribbon;* cannot roll off the brush	$0.25
Dental Cream	*National Geographic Magazine* (1924)	*Colgate's;* cleans teeth the right way; large tube	$0.25
Dressing Case	*B. Altman & Co.* (1923)	Man's; of black walrus-grain leather; contains comb, ebony-back military brush, ebonized soap box, toothbrush holder, metal shaving-brush holder, metal shaving-soap tube, and space for razor	$5.00
Eyelash Treatment	*Picture Play Magazine* (1923)	*Maybelline;* makes every face more beautiful	$0.75
Face Cream	*Picture Play Magazine* (1923)	*Hinds Honey and Almond Cream;* an excellent base for face powder, comes in four tints	$0.15
Face Powder	*Picture Play Magazine* (1923)	*Lablache;* protect your complexion; use only a safe powder	$0.50
Hair Comb	*B. Altman & Co.* (1923)	Spanish; crystal-colored celluloid, sapphire studded	$5.25
Hair Remover	*Picture Play Magazine* (1923)	*Neet;* removes hair harmlessly	$0.50
Insect Repellent	*The Progressive Farmer* (1924)	*Black Flag;* kills mosquitoes; just burn a little powder in your bedroom; the smoke is deadly to mosquitoes Powder, per bottle	$0.15 $0.40 $0.75
Liniment	*The Literary Digest* (1924)	*Absorbine Jr.,* the antiseptic liniment Per bottle	$1.25

Item	Source	Description	Price
Lipstick	*Picture Play Magazine* (1923)	*Jasmynette;* the latest Parisian novelty; 18kt gold-plated container with mirror	$1.00
Mouthwash	*Sears, Roebuck* (1924)	*Listerine;* $1 size	$0.79
Mouthwash	*National Geographic Magazine* (1924)	*Forhan's For the Gums;* check Pyorrhea with Forhan's large size	$0.60
Paste Polish	*Sears, Roebuck* (1924)	*Shinola;* produces a lustrous polish	$0.08
Perfume & Toilet Water	*Picture Play Magazine* (1923)	*Rieger's Flower Drops;* Flower Drops is the most exquisite perfume ever produced; made without alcohol; souvenir box of five 25-cent bottles	$1/5 bottles
Permanent Wave Hairstyle	*New York Times* (1923)	*Permanent Waving Beauty Salon;* Lane Bryant; using the most approved of method—which is absolutely safe and results in a wave that retains its beauty for months; whole head wave (regularly $25)	$15
Shaving Brush	*B. Altman & Co.* (1923)	The brush in this box has been sterilized	$1.25
Shaving Stick	*B. Altman & Co.* (1923)	*Colgate;* handy-grip shaving stick	$0.35
Soap	*Sears, Roebuck* (1923)	*Pear's Unscented;* three cakes	$0.24
Soap	*Sears, Roebuck* (1921)	*Lifebuoy;* well-known toilet and bath soap	$0.29/3
Straight Razor	*Sears, Roebuck* (1922)	*Silverking;* blade of English steel	$2.90
Tooth Brush	*The Literary Digest* (1924)	*Dr. West's Tooth Brush,* where health hangs in the balance Adult size Youth size Children's size	 $0.50 $0.35 $0.25
Tooth Brush	*The Journal of the American Dental Association* (1924)	*Pepsodent Co.;* decorator; the new era tooth brush, home style	$0.50
Water Softener	*Picture Play Magazine* (1923)	*Bathasweet;* adorable skin; let softened water help you achieve it and keep it; large size	$1.00

Publications

Item	Source	Description	Price
Book	*Collier's* (1924)	"Love, Marriage and Other Perils" by Uncle Henry; 28 stories from *Collier's*	$1.00
Book	*The Literary Digest* (1924)	*Practical Radio;* know all there is to be known about radio; its amazing development, how radio messages pass through our bodies, how radio outfits are made; 427 pages	$1.75
Book	*The World's Work* (1923)	*The Rover* by Joseph Conrad; finest novel in three years; 377 copies deluxe autographed	$2.00 $25.00
Book	*Picture Play Magazine* (1923)	*The Long, Long Trail,* by George Owen Baxter; a western story	$1.75
Magazine	*Collier's* (1924)	*Colliers, The National Weekly* Per issue	 $0.05
Magazine	*The Progressive Farmer* (1924)	One-year subscription to *The Progressive Farmer*	$1.00
Magazine	*The World's Work* (1923)	*Life;* weekly	$5.00/year

Item	Source	Description	Price
Magazine	*The World's Work* (1923)	*The World's Work;* Doubleday, Page & Co.; monthly	$0.35
Magazine	*The World's Work* (1923)	*The Freeman;* a liberal education for educated liberals	$6.50/year

Real Estate

Apartment	*San Francisco Examiner* (1921)	Sacramento at Franklin; 5-room apartment; very attractive new building; rooms finished in ivory; plenty of steam heat	$70/month
Apartment	*San Francisco Examiner* (1921)	A clean, quiet place; 2-room apartment for adults; hot water	$25/month
Grocery Store	*New York Times* (1923)	In best business section of New Rochelle; includes two Dodge delivery cars	$6,000
Hotel	*American Chronicle* (1999)	Cost to construct the 1,200-room Shelton Hotel in New York City in 1923	$8 million
House	*Chicago Tribune* (1920)	For rent; 6-room summer cottage; Fox Lake, Illinois; 100' lake frontage (for season July–Sept.)	$350
House	*New York Times* (1923)	Furnished; New York City; West 50s—23 fine rooms, 6 baths, straight lease	$3,000
Store	*Chicago Tribune* (1920)	For rent; large; with living rooms, steam heat, hot water	$55/month

Sewing Equipment & Supplies

Bodkin Set	*B. Altman & Co.* (1923)	Sterling silver; 4 pieces, in case	$1.90
Sewing Thread	*Sears, Roebuck* (1924)	*Barbour's;* linen; 100 yds to the spool	$0.09

Sports Equipment

Baseball Glove	*Sears, Roebuck* (1922)	Professional Wagner model; made of high quality, tan color, oil treated horsehide	$4.20
Boat	*New York Times* (1923)	*Cabrilla;* motor yacht; a delightful cruising boat; waterline 110'; beam 12' 6"	$20,000
Canoe	*The National Geographic Magazine* (1924)	*Old Town Canoe,* remarkably steady and easy to handle	$64.00
Field Glasses	*The Literary Digest* (1924)	German Army officers' field glasses; finest achromatic day and night lenses; 40mm Slightly used	$9.85
Golf Bag	*B. Altman & Co.* (1923)	Tan or white canvas, with 4 steel stays; hooded top and lock; 5" rawhide bottom	$6.50
Handball Gloves	*Sears, Roebuck* (1924)	*Draper-Maynard Co.;* brown napa leather, stitched front and well padded	$3.50/pair
Tennis Racquet	*B. Altman & Co.* (1923)	Fine quality frame, reinforced at shoulders; strung with best English gut	$10.50

Tobacco Products

Ashtrays	*B. Altman & Co.* (1923)	Nickel-plated, lined with red, blue, green or yellow glass, set of four	$2.75
Cigarettes	*Collier's* (1924)	*Reedsdale Cigarettes;* liked by many smokers of sophisticated taste Per package of 20	$0.20
Cigarettes	*The American Legion Weekly* (1920)	*Camel Cigarettes;* an expert blend of Turkish and domestic tobaccos Per package of 20	$0.20
Cigarettes	*The World's Work* (1923)	*Pall Mall;* try them tonight for your luxury hour—that easy-chair hour when every man feels entitled to life's best per 20 west of the Rockies	$0.30 $0.35

Item	Source	Description	Price
Cigars	*The World's Work* (1923)	*Robert Burns Panatela;* give a brand that is known for Christmas box of 50	$0.10/each 44.75
Pipe	*B. Altman & Co.* (1923)	Genuine briar; straight stem, mouthpiece of hard rubber	$1.00

Travel & Transportation

Item	Source	Description	Price
Airline Ticket	Edward L. Throm, ed. *Popular Mechanics Picture History of American Transportation* (1952)	Los Angeles to San Francisco; one way [cost in 1922]	$50.00
Beach Camping	*The American Legion Weekly* (1920)	*Camp Franklin D'Olier,* the vacation center operated by The Atlantic City Legionnaire Post; spend a week under canvas near the beach; breakfast and light lunch available Per week	$15.00
Cruise	*The World's Work* (1923)	*Frank C. Clark;* around the world in four months on specially chartered Cunarder "Laconia"	$1,000
Cruise	*National Geographic Magazine* (1924)	A joyful week of cruising on four great lakes; meals and berth included	$74.50
Cruise	*National Geographic Magazine* (1924)	*Coates Tours;* world cruises; 30 days of delightful travel	$425
European Tour	*The National Geographic Magazine* (1924)	*American Express Travel;* Mediterranean tour to Naples with comprehensive European itinerary	$1,370
Hawaii Tour	*The National Geographic Magazine* (1924)	Hawaii in the summer; dark-skinned imps dive for your dimes; travel from Seattle or Los Angeles, includes hotel, sightseeing including visit to Volcano Kilaueachin Hawaii National Park, 3 to 4 weeks	$300 to $400
Motor Tour	*The National Geographic Magazine* (1924)	Yosemite National Park tour covering 240 miles round trip from Merced, California	$35.00
Railroad Ticket	*Chicago Tribune* (1920)	Santa Fe railroad from Chicago direct to *San Francisco* for National Democratic Convention; round trip from Chicago	$89
Steamship Ticket	*San Francisco Examiner* (1921)	San Francisco to Seattle; round trip; every Tuesday	$75.00
Steamship Ticket	*San Francisco Examiner* (1921)	*Pacific Steamline;* Los Angeles to Alaska; first class; includes berth and meals	$18.00
Steamship Ticket	*New York Times* (1923)	*Colonial Line;* New York to Boston	$5.19
Train Ticket	*The National Geographic Magazine* (1924)	Northern Pacific Railway roundtrip trip from Chicago to Yellowstone Park	$56.50
Train Ticket	*National Geographic Magazine* (1924)	*Pacific Northwest Railroad;* the route will take you to the very gates of five of the nation's greatest scenic attractions: Glacier Park, Yellowstone Park, Crater Lake National Park, Rainier National Park, the Alaskan Tour	$86.00

MISCELLANY 1920-1924

$11,000 Booze Raid In Loop Traps 3 at Bar; Labor Trouble at Still Fills U.S. Cells

Whiskey valued at $11,000 was seized in a saloon at 201 North State Street and the two proprietors and a bartender were arrested yesterday by federal prohibition agents. The men are Edward Stevens and Charles McDermott, owners, and M. J. O'Rourke, the bartender. Bonds were set by Commissioner Lewis F. Mason, at $2,500 for the proprietors and $2,000 for the bartender.

Chicago Tribune, April 17, 1920

Gas Rates Up; It Now Costs $1.15 Per Thousand

Chicago's gas rate was increased from 85¢ to $1.15 a thousand cubic feet by an order of the state public utilities commission yesterday. The commission also fixed a minimum charge of 60¢ a month.

Chicago Tribune, June 16, 1920

L Men Accept Raise; Company to Ask 10¢ Fare

As a result of the 15¢ wage increase awarded the street car workers on Monday and the acceptance last night of an equal boost in pay by 2,000 elevated employees, Chicago straphangers are asked to pay an 8¢ street car fare and a 10¢ fare on the overhead lines after July 1.

Chicago Tribune, June 17, 1920

Cement Makers Cut Prices for State Highways

Cement manufacturers today expressed their willingness to do their bit toward maximum highway construction in Illinois in 1922 when they offered to supply 4,000,000 barrels of cement to the state at prices ranging from $1.20 to $1.40 a barrel.

The lowest bid, offering 600,000 barrels at $1.20 a barrel, was made by the Marquette Portland Cement Company, a reduction of 25¢ a barrel from the bids made Jan. 8, which were rejected.

Chicago Tribune, March 6, 1922

Retirement Bonuses

A hundred dollars for each of the fifty years' service was the reward to Rudolph Zimmerman and Louis Moses, who recently completed a half century in the employ of the drug and laboratory firm of Eimer & Amend. At a dinner celebrating the occasion last week each of the veterans, who began as errand boys and are now heads of important departments, received $5,000.

New York Times, June 17, 1923

Americans Pay Lures German Housegirls

Relief appears to be at hand for women who have been wrestling with the servant girl problem. Europe is beginning to send a new and better supply of domestic workers, evidence of this fact having been furnished a few days ago when the Royal Mail liner Orca brought thirty expert servant girls who had embarked at Hamburg and were readily permitted to pass the portals of Ellis Island. They had been earning the equivalent of less than $2 a week in Germany, and when told that many American housewives would gladly pay $10 weekly, their surprise was unbounded.

New York Time, June 17, 1923

MISCELLANY 1920-1924

Senator David A. Reed of Pennsylvania Urges Cut in Tax on Earned Income

The present system of taxing the earned income is a discrimination in favor of the person whose income is unearned. The man who works for a living can be taxed 58 percent, whereas the man who invests all his capital enjoys exemptions behind which he can take refuge and that man can "get by" with a tax of only 12 1/2 percent.

New York Times, June 17, 1923

Letter to the Editor

When these productions are shown for the first time at big theatres, at prices as high as $1.50 or $2.00, the claim is often made in the advertising that they will not be shown in the same city at a lower price within a year. But often within a month, they are shown at the regular movie houses for thirty cents.

Picture Play Magazine, October 1923

Dental Practices For Sale

Indiana Practice for Sale—Light competition. Averaging $6,000 a year cash practice. Many advances to this deal. Salaried Appointment transferable. Practice to go perhaps $10,000 a year with full time. Moderate Investment.

For Sale—Dental practice in Chicago suburb doing $12,000 cash a year.

The Journal of the American Dental Association, September 1924

Valentines

A beautiful assortment from ½¢ to 25¢ each. Just the kind you may want. Palmetto Drug Co.

Union Progress, Union, SC, February 6, 1924

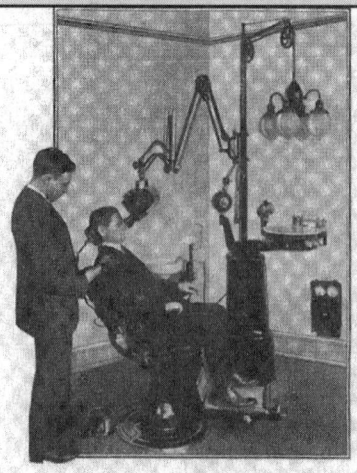

HISTORICAL SNAPSHOT 1925-1929

1925

- Refrigerator sales reach 75,000, up from 10,000 in 1920
- Florida land prices collapse as investors discover that many lots they bought are underwater; Ponzi scheme gains notoriety
- $10 million Boca Raton Hotel in Florida completed
- Aunt Jemima Mills acquired by Quaker Oats Company for $4 million
- Al Capone takes control of Chicago bootlegging
- Chesterfield cigarettes marketed to women for first time
- Simmons Beautyrest mattress introduced
- President Coolidge opposes cancellation of French and British war debt

1926

- Book-of-the-Month Club founded
- Machine-made ice production exceeds 56 million pounds; up from 1.5 million in 1894
- First ham in a can introduced by Hormel
- Philadelphia's Warwick Hotel opens

- First blue jeans with slide fasteners introduced by H. D. Lee company
- Synthetic rubber pioneered by B. F. Goodrich Rubber Company chemist Waldo Lonsbury Sermon

1927

- 20 million cars on roads, up from 13,824 in 1900
- First compulsory automobile insurance law passed in Massachusetts
- Transatlantic telephone service between London and New York begins; call cost $75 for three minutes
- Wonder Bread introduced

1928

- Broccoli marketed in United States
- Rice Krispies introduced by W. K. Kellogg
- Peanut butter cracker sandwich packets sold under the name NAB by National Biscuit Company for 5 cents each
- U.S. per capita consumption of crude oil reaches 7.62 barrels
- Florida's 143-mile Tamiami Trail links Miami to Fort Myers through Everglades at a cost of $48,000 per mile

- Presidential candidate Herbert Hoover calls for "a chicken in every pot and two cars in every garage"

1929

- J. C. Penney goes public
- 513 Americans have incomes of more than $1 million
- Income tax rate is 1.5 percent on first $7,500 of net income
- Auto production exceeds 5 million
- Commercial airlines carry 180,000 passengers, up from 37,000 in 1927
- Delta Air Service, formerly a crop-dusting business, inaugurates passenger service and secures air-mail contracts
- 20 million telephones in use, double 1918 figures
- Average price of refrigerator falls to $292 from $600 in 1920
- Seven-Up introduced under name Lithiated Lemon
- Coca-Cola has gross sales of $39 million
- Stock market crashes, $30 billion capital disappears.

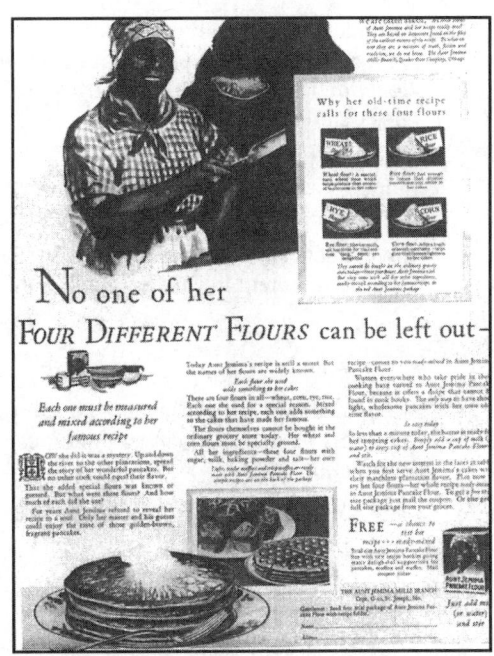

SELECTED INCOME 1925-1929

Job	Source	Description	Pay
Actor	Legrand and Karney, *Chronicle of the Cinema* (1995)	Al Jolson's earnings for *The Jazz Singer* (1927), the first motion picture to utilize spoken dialogue	$75,000
Actor	Legrand and Karney, *Chronicle of the Cinema* (1995)	Weekly income of Gloria Swanson when she moved to United Artist to produce her own films in 1926	$20,000
Actor	Legrand and Karney, *Chronicle of the Cinema* (1995)	Weekly income of Greta Garbo after the release of *Flesh and the Devil* in 1927	$5,000
Aviator	Joyce Milton, *Loss of Eden: A Biography of Charles and Anne Morrow Lindbergh* (1993)	Earnings of Charles Lindbergh following his historic transatlantic flight, including $25,000 for the Orteig Prize as the first pilot to fly from New York to Paris, and from the Guggenheim Fund honorarium for his U.S. tour following the flight in 1927	$50,000 $500,000
Barber	*Washington Post* (1928)	Short hours; weekly pay	$30–$35 weekly
Barber	*Washington Post* (1928)	First class; must speak good English; weekly pay	$30 per week + commission
Barber	*Washington Post* (1926)	Italian preferred, hours 9:00 a.m. to 7:30 p.m.	$30.00/week
Bookkeeper	*New York Times* (1929)	Experienced; wanted by manufacturing concern to take care of small set of books and do some typing; good appearance required; five-day wk all year	$20.00/week
Carpenter	*Chicago Tribune* (1929)	Situation Wanted: Own tools	$0.60/hr
Chemist	*Popular Science Monthly* (1927)	Annual pay	$4,000
Doorman	*New York Times* (1928)	Prominent automobile company requires services of a courteous, willing, and obliging white man; location Columbus Circle district; steady position with possibilities; uniform furnished	$27.50/week to start
Engineer	*New York Times* (1928)	Junior mechanical engineer at automobile plant close to New York, college-trained preferred	$27/month
Entrepeneur	James Grant, Bernard Baruch, *The Adventures of a Wall Street Legend* (1983)	Investment profits in 1926 of Bernard Baruch from a 1909 investment in Gulf Sulphur Company	$8 million
Gangster (1927)	*Guinness Book of World Records* (1981)	Reported income of Chicago gangster Al Capone, whose enterprises included illegal liquor, gambling, vice and protection racket	$105 million
Inspector	*Popular Science Monthly* (1927)	Weekly pay of Illinois Corn Inspector	$20.00
Loan Clerk	*New York Times* (1928)	Bank, know securities	$2,400/yr

Job	Source	Description	Pay
Miscellaneous	*Chicago Tribune* (1927)	I want 3 men now employed to do some special work for me three evenings a wk.	$30/wk
Pushcart Peddler	*The Youth's Companion* (1925)	Seller of every commodity from fish to umbrellas, occupation of 7,800 people in New York City. Weekly sales	$75 to $126
Plasterer	*Popular Science Monthly* (1927)	Day rate of Union certified plasterer for eight hours	$13.00
Radio Engineer	*New York Times* (1928)	Radio production managers	$10–100/wk
Record Producer	Mary A. Bufwack and Robert K. Oerman, *Finding Her Voice, The Saga of Women in Country Music* (1993)	Income in 1925 of Ralph Peer, country record producer and talent scout	$16,000
Sales	*Washington Post* (1926)	Catholic; if you have sold books, magazines, pictures or insurance and are a hustler, we can offer you a position	$40/wk
Salesman	*Washington Post* (1928)	Salesman with selling experience; exceptional opportunity; small orders bring large commission	$32.50 order brings $6 in advance and bonus
Salesman	*Washington Post* (1928)	Experienced specialty salesman for large manufacturing firm	$400–$1200 per month
Shipping Room	*Chicago Tribune* (1925)	Young with shipping room experience; ambitious and energetic; must be able to fill orders and pack shipments	$20/wk to start
Stenographer	*Washington Post* (1928)	Office clerk; part-time work, 25 hours Per week Per hour	$15 $.75
Stenographer	*Chicago Tribune* (1925)	Young man for stenographic position in executive office; large corporation	$125/month
Stenographer	*New York Times* (1926)	Stenographer and typist with knowledge of bookkeeping; 18–19 years of age; in customs broker's office; good opportunity for advancement; give previous experience and state religion	$18/wk to begin
Textile Worker	*Time* (1928)	Average wages of workers in New Bedford, Mass. Mills Per week	$19
Well Digger	*The Farm Journal* (1927)	Average weekly gross income of well digger L. E. Haffner of Donnellson, Iowa using a Lisle Manufacturing machine	$180.00

CONSUMER EXPENDITURES 1925, 1927, 1929

(Per Capita)

Expenditure Type	1925	1927	1929
Clothing	$62.04	$63.92	$63.24
Food	$160.59	$153.89	$160.14
Auto Purchases	$20.82	$16.76	$21.35
Auto Parts	$6.96	$7.09	$4.92
Gas & Oil	$15.70	$13.39	$14.78
Housing	$98.89	$95.09	$96.08
Furniture	$9.49	$9.43	$9.85
Utilities	$9.82	$10.33	$24.64
Telephone & Telegraph	$5.88	$6.33	$4.93
Physicians	$7.68	$7.79	$8.21
Dentists	$3.26	$3.24	$4.11
Health Insurance	NR	NR	82¢
Personal Business	$27.33	$31.67	$32.85
Personal Care	$7.79	$8.75	$9.03
Tobacco	$13.13	$13.58	$13.96
Local Transport	$9.13	$9.45	$9.03
Intercity Transport	$4.95	$4.77	$4.11
Recreation	$24.52	$26.39	$35.31
Religion/Welfare Activities	$11.31	$12.16	$9.85
Private Education & Research	$7.72	$8.46	$5.75
Per Capita Consumption	$619.45	$626.45	$634.82

INVESTMENTS 1925-1929

Investment	1925	1926	1927	1928	1929
Basic Yield, One-Year Corporate Bonds	3.85	4.40	4.30	4.05	5.27
Short-Term Interest Rates, 4–6 Months, Prime Commercial Paper	4.02	4.34	4.11	4.85	5.85
Basic Yield, Common Stocks, Total	5.19	5.32	4.77	3.98	3.48
Index of Common Stocks (1941–1943=10)	11.15	12.59	15.34	19.95	26.02

COMMON STOCKS, CLOSING PRICE AND DIVIDEND, FIRST BUSINESS DAY OF YEAR

(Parenthetical number is annual dividend in dollars)

	1925	1926	1927	1928	1929
Allis Chalmers	73 1/2	93 (6)	39 1/8 (7)	117 7/8 (3)	190
AT&T	132 3/8	142 3/4 (9)	149 7/8 (9)	179 3/8 (9)	195 (9)
American Tobacco (2 for 1 split, 11/28/42)	86 3/8	115 3/8 (8)	121 3/4 (8)	175 3/4 (8)	177 (8)
Anaconda	47 1/4	49 7/8 (3)	47 3/4 (3)	58 3/4 (3)	118 1/2 (6)
B&O	30 3/8	94 1/8 (5)	107 1/2 (6)	117 1/2 (4)	123 (6)
Bethlehem Steel	51	48 1/4 (-)	46 1/2 (-)	58 1/8 (-)	88 (-)
Corn Products	41 1/8	42 1/8 (2)	47 3/4 (2)	64 7/8 (2)	91 1/8 (2)
General Electric (5% stock dividend in special stock, 9/4/24) (share for share distribution of Electric Bond and Share Securities Corp @ 67 1/2, 1/15/25) (5% dividend in special stock, 9/3/25) (4 shares for 1 split, 5/26/26) (10% stock dividend in special, 6/7/26)	315	326 1/2 (8)	83 3/4 (3)	137 1/2 (4)	125 1/4 (4)
General Motors (1 share for 4 reverse split, 9/19/24) (50% stock dividend, 8/21/26) (2 shares for 1 split, 9/16/27)	65 7/8	118 (6)	150 5/8 (7)	137 3/4 (5)	209 (5)
International Business Machines (20% stock dividend, 12/1/25) (3 shares for 1 split, 2/16/26) (5% stock dividend, 12/28/28)	118 3/4	147 1/2 (8)	54 (3)	119 1/2 (5)	154 1/4 (5)
National Biscuit	73 1/4	77 3/4 (3)	97 (4)	173 1/8 (6)	195 1/2 (6)
US Steel (40% stock dividend, 6/1/27)	120 1/4	136 4/8 (5)	155 (7)	151 3/4 (7)	162 3/4 (7)
Western Union	116 1/4	135 5/8 (3)	146 1/2 (8)	177 (8)	182 7/8 (8)

STANDARD JOBS 1925-1929

Job Type	1925	1926	1927	1928	1929
Average of all Industries, excl. Farm Labor	$1434/yr	$1473/yr	$1487/yr	$1490/yr	$1534/yr
Average of all Industries incl. Farm Labor	$1434/yr	$1473/yr	$1380/yr	$1384/yr	$1425/yr
Bituminous Coal Mining	72¢/hr	$1446/yr	$1342/yr	$1293/yr	72¢/hr
Avg hrs/wk	48.40	NR	NR	NR	48.50
Building Trades, Union Workers	$1.31/hr	$1708/yr	$1719/yr	$1674/yr	$1.23/hr
Avg hrs/wk	43.80	NR	NR	NR	43.90
Clerical Workers in Mfg. & Steam RR	$2239/yr	$2310/yr	NR	NR	NR
Domestics	$741/yr	$748/yr	$756/yr	$725/yr	$731/yr
Farm Labor	$382/yr	$386/yr	$387/yr	$385/yr	$378/yr
Federal Civilian	$1762/yr	$1888/yr	$1907/yr	$1916/yr	$1916/yr
Federal Employees, Executive Depts.	$1776/yr	$1809/yr	NR	NR	NR
Finance, Insurance, & Real Estate	$1997/yr	$2008/yr	$2019/yr	$2043/yr	$2062/y
Gas & Electricity Workers	$1552/yr	$1571/yr	$1558/yr	$1591/yr	$1589/yr
Lower-Skilled Labor	$1095/yr	NR	NR	NR	$1065/yr
Manufacturing, Payroll	49¢/hr	$1502/yr	$1534/yr	$1543/yr	49¢/hr
Avg hrs/wk	52.20				52.20
Manufacturing, Union Workers	99¢/hr	$1.01/hr	NR	NR	NR
Avg hrs/wk	45.90	45.90	NR	NR	NR
Medical/Health Services Workers	$916/yr	$857/yr	$931/yr	$930/yr	$925/yr
Ministers	$1826/yr	$1769/yr	NR	NR	NR
Nonprofit Org. Workers	$1578/yr	$1607/yr	$1647/yr	$1675/yr	$1712/yr
Postal Employees	87¢/hr				84¢/hr
Avg hrs/wk	47.20	NR	NR	NR	47.20
Public School Teachers	$1299/yr	$1342/yr	$1393/yr	$1433/yr	$1445/yr
State and Local Govt. Workers	$1377/yr	$1422/yr	$1488/yr	$1500/yr	$1549/yr
Steam Railroads, Wage Earners	$1597/yr	$1613/yr	$1687/yr	$1720/yr	$1749/yr
Street Railway Workers	$1565/yr	$1566/yr	$1549/yr	$1553/yr	$1598/yr
Telegraph Ind. Workers	$1161/yr	$1215/yr	NR	NR	NR
Telephone Ind. Workers	$1108/yr	$1117/yr	NR	NR	NR
Wholesale and Retail Trade Workers	$1416/yr	$1480/yr	$1573/yr	$1594/yr	1359/yr

FOOD BASKET 1925-1929

Commodity	Year	New York	Atlanta	Chicago	Denver	Los Angeles
Beans, Navy, per pound	1925	11.20¢	12.30¢	9.90¢	10.90¢	10.30¢
	1926	10.40¢	10.60¢	9.40¢	10¢	9.30¢
	1927	10.10¢	10.40¢	9.60¢	9.90¢	9.50¢
	1928	12.37¢	12.78¢	11.91¢	11.50¢	11.60¢
	1929	14.80¢	16¢	13.60¢	12.90¢	13.40¢
Beef, Rib Roasts, per pound	1925	38.80¢	28.50¢	33.60¢	22.60¢	28.60¢
	1926	38.80¢	31.60¢	34.90¢	24.10¢	29.40¢
	1927	40.40¢	32.60¢	35.60¢	25.10¢	30¢
	1928	44¢	35.10¢	39.70¢	30.20¢	33.80¢
	1929	43.60¢	36.60¢	40.40¢	31.10¢	35.40¢
Beef, Steaks (Round), per pound	1925	43.10¢	33.90¢	34.20¢	27.60¢	29.70¢
	1926	43.50¢	36.10¢	35.90¢	30¢	30¢
	1927	45.20¢	38¢	37.20¢	31.30¢	31.10¢
	1928	49.40¢	41.70¢	43¢	36.70¢	35.50¢
	1929	50.90¢	44.60¢	45.70¢	38.10¢	38.40¢
Bread, per loaf	1925	9.60¢	10.30¢	9.90¢	8.30¢	9.30¢
	1926	9.60¢	10.60¢	9.80¢	8.30¢	8.60¢
	1927	9.70¢	10.80¢	9.90¢	8¢	8.50¢
	1928	8.80¢	10.80¢	9.70¢	8¢	8.80¢
	1929	8.60¢	10.50¢	9.80¢	7.60¢	8.60¢
Butter, per pound	1925	55.30¢	57.20¢	52.20¢	50.20¢	57.20¢
	1926	53.90¢	56.30¢	51¢	47.60¢	53¢
	1927	57.20¢	57¢	54.70¢	50.30¢	54.20¢
	1928	57.10¢	57.80¢	54.80¢	51.60¢	55.30¢
	1929	55.60¢	57.50¢	52.90¢	49.90¢	54.70¢
Cheese, per pound	1925	37.40¢	35.20¢	40.80¢	39¢	38.40¢
	1926	38.20¢	35.10¢	41.50¢	37.70¢	39.30¢
	1927	39¢	36.90¢	42.30¢	38¢	38.30¢
	1928	38.50¢	36.50¢	43.40¢	39.80¢	38.50¢
	1929	40.80¢	36.30¢	42¢	38.80¢	38.40¢
Chickens, per pound	1925	38.70¢	32.80¢	36.50¢	29.80¢	42¢
	1926	41.20¢	37.40¢	39.20¢	32.50¢	44.40¢
	1927	39.20¢	35.80¢	37.40¢	30.70¢	42.80¢
	1928	39.50¢	35.50¢	38.90¢	31.10¢	44¢
	1929	41.80¢	37.10¢	41.40¢	32.80¢	38.70¢
Coffee, per pound	1925	47.40¢	50.80¢	52¢	51.90¢	53.20¢
	1926	47.70¢	51.40¢	51.40¢	51.70¢	54.20¢
	1927	45.40¢	49.70¢	48.20¢	49.40¢	51.60¢
	1928	46.10¢	49.70¢	48¢	49.80¢	53.50¢
	1929	44.70¢	51.20¢	47.10¢	49.60¢	53.40¢
Cornmeal, per pound	1925	6.60¢	4.60¢	6.50¢	4.40¢	5.70¢
	1926	6.40¢	4.10¢	6.20¢	4.20¢	5.30¢
	1927	6.50¢	6.70¢	4.40¢	5.40¢	6.50¢
	1928	6.60¢	4.20¢	6.90¢	4.50¢	5.80¢
	1929	6.70¢	4.40¢	6.60¢	4.60¢	5.70¢
Eggs, per dozen	1925	62.90¢	47.20¢	51.50¢	47.50¢	50.50¢
	1926	59.60¢	45.90¢	49.10¢	44.40¢	46.30¢
	1927	57.30¢	43¢	46.20¢	41.10¢	41.60¢
	1928	57.40¢	44¢	48¢	41.40¢	43.70¢
	1929	59.40¢	46.80¢	50.50¢	42.80¢	47.50¢

Commodity	Year	New York	Atlanta	Chicago	Denver	Los Angeles
Flour, Wheat, per pound	1925	6.20¢	6.90¢	5.60¢	5.20¢	5.90¢
	1926	6¢	6.90¢	5.60¢	4.90¢	5.60¢
	1927	5.50¢	6.50¢	5.10¢	4.30¢	5.30¢
	1928	5.20¢	6.60¢	4.80¢	4.30¢	5.20¢
	1929	5¢	6.40¢	4.60¢	3.90¢	4.80¢
Lard, per pound	1925	23.70¢	23.20¢	22.90¢	24.30¢	24.10¢
	1926	22.40¢	21.70¢	21.60¢	22.70¢	23.70¢
	1927	20.20¢	19.10¢	19.30¢	19.60¢	20.20¢
	1928	19.50¢	18.10¢	18.80¢	18.60¢	20¢
	1929	19.30¢	18¢	18.50¢	18.50¢	19.70¢
Milk, Fresh, per quart	1925	14.80¢	17.20¢	14¢	11.40¢	15¢
	1926	15¢	19.40¢	14¢	12¢	15¢
	1927	15.30¢	18.10¢	14¢	12¢	15¢
	1928	15.60¢	17.10¢	14¢	12¢	15¢
	1929	16¢	16.60¢	14¢	12¢	15¢
Mutton and Lamb, Leg, per pound	1925	36.90¢	37¢	38.10¢	35.60¢	37¢
	1926	37.40¢	38.10¢	39.60¢	36.50¢	36.90¢
	1927	37.40¢	40.40¢	39.10¢	36.60¢	36.70¢
	1928	38.40¢	40.40¢	39.40¢	36.70¢	37.70¢
	1929	38.90¢	41.30¢	40.50¢	37¢	38.70¢
Pork Chops, per pound	1925	39.70¢	34.80¢	34.60¢	34.40¢	44.30¢
	1926	42.50¢	37.60¢	38¢	37.30¢	45.70¢
	1927	42.50¢	35.60¢	35.70¢	33.70¢	43.50¢
	1928	38.80¢	34¢	34¢	32.90¢	41.10¢
	1929	39¢	35.20¢	37.20¢	35.30¢	43.50¢
Pork, Bacon, Sliced, per pound	1925	46.69¢	44.50¢	49.80¢	48.40¢	54.90¢
	1926	51.30¢	48.20¢	54.20¢	51.30¢	59.30¢
	1927	48.70¢	45.20¢	51.10¢	47.40¢	55.30¢
	1928	45.90¢	42.40¢	47.90¢	43.20¢	50.90¢
	1929	45.30¢	40.80¢	48.20¢	41.60¢	50.20¢
Ham, Sliced, per pound	1925	57.70¢	53.40¢	52.70¢	54.90¢	63.90¢
	1926	62.10¢	57.80¢	56.60¢	58¢	69.20¢
	1927	62.10¢	56.60¢	55.70¢	54.60¢	68.40¢
	1928	57.20¢	53.10¢	53.50¢	52.90¢	67.10¢
	1929	58.20¢	56.10¢	54.80¢	54.70¢	68.30¢
Potatoes, Irish, per pound	1925	3.80¢	4.60¢	3.50¢	3.40¢	4.35¢
	1926	5.30¢	6¢	4.80¢	4.20¢	4.70¢
	1927	4¢	5¢	3.70¢	3.60¢	4¢
	1928	3.10¢	3.90¢	2.70¢	2.10¢	2.70¢
	1929	3.60¢	4¢	3.20¢	2.80¢	3.30¢
Prunes, Dried, per pound	1925	16¢	17.50¢	18.40¢	18.80¢	16¢
	1926	15.60¢	18.30¢	18.50¢	18.20¢	16.40¢
	1927	13.50¢	16.70¢	17.40¢	15.60¢	14.10¢
	1928	12.90¢	14.70¢	15.30¢	14.60¢	12.60¢
	1929	14.50¢	16.50¢	17.20¢	16.80¢	15.20¢
Rice, per pound	1925	10.50¢	10.70¢	11.50¢	11.20¢	11.20¢
	1926	10.70¢	11.50¢	11.80¢	11.30¢	11.20¢
	1927	9.90¢	10.10¢	11.20¢	9.90¢	10.20¢
	1928	9.90¢	9.10¢	10.50¢	9.10¢	10.10¢
	1929	9.60¢	9.50¢	10.50¢	8.90¢	9.70¢
Sugar, per pound	1925	6.40¢	7.70¢	6.90¢	7.80¢	6.90¢
	1926	6.10¢	7.30¢	6.60¢	7.40¢	6.70¢
	1927	6.50¢	7.70¢	7.10¢	7.80¢	7¢
	1928	6.30¢	7.60¢	6.90¢	7.50¢	6.80¢
	1929	5.90¢	7.10¢	6.40¢	7.20¢	6.20¢

Commodity	Year	New York	Atlanta	Chicago	Denver	Los Angeles
Tea, per pound	1925	63.80¢	99.10¢	74¢	67.70¢	76¢
	1926	65¢	$1.0480	73.10¢	68.40¢	75.30¢
	1927	66.40¢	$1.0440	72.80¢	68.90¢	74.50¢
	1928	67.80¢	$1.60	69.30¢	69.80¢	74.70¢
	1929	67.60¢	$1.04	70¢	69.40¢	73.80¢

SELECTED PRICES 1925-1929

Item	Source	Description	Price
Advertising			
Advertisement	Roland Marchand, *Advertising the American Dream* (1985)	Full page, four-color in *Saturday Evening Post* [cost in 1926]	$11,000/pg
Advertising Budget	Marchand, *Advertising the American Dream* (1985)	Crane Company (plumbing supplies) [cost in 1925]	$436,000/yr
Advertising Budget	Marchand, *Advertising the American Dream* (1985)	For Maxwell House coffee [cost in 1927]	$509,000/yr
Testimonial Fee	Marchand, *Advertising the American Dream* (1985)	Price paid to a football player for a testimonial for Lucky Strike cigarettes [cost in 1926]	$4,000
Apparel, Children's			
Baby Outfits	*Sears, Roebuck* (1927)	44 pieces including white lawn dress, nainsook dress, white flannelette Gertrude undershirt, booties, bibs, diapers, talcum powder	$9.48
Coat	*Sears, Roebuck* (1927)	Smartly hand-smocked for girls; lovely model adapted in fine quality, silky lustrous all-wool broadcloth; styled on fetching lines	$10.50
Football Pants	*Lorick & Lowrance Hardware* (1928)	Made of good quality 8-oz olive drab duck; Notre Dame-style leg	$7
Hockey Cap	*Sears, Roebuck* (1927)	Knit in double thickness all-wool worsted in fancy pineapple stitch	$0.47
Play Suit	*Sears, Roebuck* (1927)	Boy's; he'll have lots of fun with this khaki drill coat with bright red trimmings; khaki drill pants and headdress	$1.89
Romper	*Sears, Roebuck* (1927)	Boy's; sturdy play suits	$0.59
Shoes	*The Youth's Companion* (1925)	*Keds* athletic shoes. Complete line of canvas rubber-soled shoes	$1.25 to $4.50
Suit	*Store Calendar* (1925)	Two-pants knicker suit and overcoat, sizes 6–18	$10.50
Apparel, Men's			
Chauffeur's Outfit	*Vogue* (1925)	*Brill Brothers;* suit, overcoat, and cap to match	$78
Hat	*Sears, Roebuck* (1927)	A smart and rakish broad-brim fancy-band hat; made of a good-quality fur felt	$3.45
Hose Supporter	*John Martin* (1927)	Velvet grip	$0.12
Hunting Coat	*Lorick & Lowrance Hardware* (1928)	*Red Head;* medium-weight forest-brown regimental duck	$3.50
Overcoat	*Sears, Roebuck* (1927)	Storm proof; heavy all-wool sheep-lined ulter, has a large shawl-style collar of Australian opossum fur	$29.95
Shirt	*Time* (1928)	Custom shirt maker	$3

Item	Source	Description	Price
Sombrero	Sears, Roebuck (1927)	Man's good quality wool felt sombrero work hat; the crown is about 4 3/4" high	$1.98
Suit	Sears, Roebuck (1927)	Fancy weaves for fall—pure all-wool worsted	$21.50
Suit and Overcoat	Store Calendar (1925)	Two pants, suit and overcoat; the extra pair doubles the wear	$10.50

Apparel, Women's

Item	Source	Description	Price
Brassiere Corset	Vogue (1925)	Royal Worcester Bon Ton; makes you appear slim, supple, and tailored in this smooth-fitting, one-piece garment	$3.50
Coat	Sears, Roebuck (1927)	Opossum fur; collegiate style; called the tomboy model, having been especially made for hard strenuous service and cut on loose, comfortable lines	$129
Coat	Sears, Roebuck (1927)	All-wool suede velour; true reproduction of French model; satin de chine lining, mandel-fur trimming	$27.50
Corset	Sears, Roebuck (1927)	It confines the bust and hip and diaphragm, is light, yet is strong and flexible	$1.69
Frock	Vogue (1925)	Bromely Shepard; one-piece dress of red jersey with black and red braid	$25
Galoshes	Sears, Roebuck (1927)	Silk and wool snap-on	$2.48
Handbag	Sears, Roebuck (1927)	Back strap; newest shape and leathers	$2.98
Handbag	Sears, Roebuck (1927)	Newest French-tailored; of soft extra-quality smooth calf leather; has three large pockets; coin purse	$4.95
Hose	Delineator (1928)	Allen-A Hosiery; pure silk the entire length of the hose Per pair	$1.50 to $3.00
Maternity Corset	Vogue (1925)	Lane Bryant; the best corset in the world	$6.95
Nursing Brassiere	Sears, Roebuck (1927)	Fastens with hooks and eyes at each side of panel in front without the least inconvenience	$0.85
Shoes	Vogue (1925)	Shoecraft; snakeskin and kid model	$22.50
Short Corset	Sears, Roebuck (1927)	Berthe May; for expectant mothers; very comfortable, no boning over hips	$2.48

Appliances

Item	Source	Description	Price
Coffee Pot	Modern Priscilla (1929)	Universal; the percolator that has brought perfect coffee to millions Empire pattern, 4 to 14 cups Continental pattern, electric, 2 to 6 cups	$4.50 to $6.00 $9.00 to $10.00
Corn Popper	Sears, Roebuck (1927)	Enjoy fresh-popped corn, right on your living room table; will make popcorn a daily habit	$1.75
Desk Fan	Lorick & Lowrance Hardware (1928)	Hunter; electric; alternating current, three speeds, 12" blades	$30
Heating Stove	Lorick & Lowrance Hardware (1928)	Enterprise Burnside; for coal; 363 pounds	$51
Hot Water Heater	Delineator (1928)	American Radiator Company Hotcoil gas water heater; perfect heating at lowest fuel price 20 gallon	$55.00 plus installation
Iron	Sears, Roebuck (1927)	The Aristocrat; the ultimate in beautiful design, ease of work, and perfect ironing convenience, full weight, 6 1/2 lbs	$4.95

Item	Source	Description	Price
Iron	*The Farm Journal* (1927)	*Coleman,* self-heating iron; asbestos-lined lid keeps handle cool while iron gets hot	$5.00
Juice Extractor	*Modern Priscilla* (1929)	*Sunkist Junior Orange and Lemon Juice Extractor;* electrically powered; extracts all the juice	$14.95
Omelet Pan	*Modern Priscilla* (1929)	Omelet pan; made from the super-metal Hyb-Lum; is light as aluminum but stronger	$6.75
Range	*The Literary Digest* (1928)	*Campbell Automatic Electric Fireless Cooker;* an electric range with new quick-ring heating elements which actually cook as fast as gas	$25.50
Range	*Lorick & Lowrance Hardware* (1928)	*Supreme Enterprise;* cast with duplex grate for coal or wood	$78
Table Stove	*Sears, Roebuck* (1927)	Heavy cast stoves for kitchenette use; for 110-volt current only	$5.25
Toaster	*Antique Week* (1926)	*Toastermaster Automatic;* pop-up toaster	$12.50
Toaster	*Lorick & Lowrance Hardware* (1928)	*Universal;* electric; has bread-pack drop that never fails to work	$4.95
Vacuum Cleaner	*Delineator* (1928)	*Hoover* vacuum; cleaning that tires you not at all; positive agitation	
		Model 700	$75.00
		Model 543	$59.50
Vacuum Cleaner	*Sears, Roebuck* (1927)	*Greater Energex;* attachments complete and with airizer device for 110-volt city current only	$33.90
Waffle Iron	*Lorick & Lowrance Hardware* (1928)	*Universal;* electric; pure aluminum; 7 1/2" grids that require no greasing	$9.75

Baby Products

Baby Bottle Kit	*Time* (1928)	Sterilizer and carrier; pack it with ice—carry anywhere	$5

Business Equipment & Supplies

Amplifier	*Popular Science Monthly* (1927)	*Thordarson Power Compact* is the only power supply foundation unit available to the home constructor; transform your radio set	
		Power Compact R-171	$15.00
Bonds	*The Youth's Companion* (1925)	*Smith Bonds;* sold in denominations of $100, $500 and $1,000 with maturities from 2 years to 15 years	7%
Counter	*Popular Science Monthly* (1927)	*Veeder Set-Back Rotary Ratchet Counter;* for presses and metal-stamping machines with reciprocating movement	$11.50
Drill Press	*Popular Science Monthly* (1927)	*Knapp Drill Press,* drills wood, iron, copper, brass, aluminum, lead, slate, bakelite	$4.50
		Denver West	$4.75
Lathe	*Popular Science Monthly* (1927)	*Junior South Bend Lathe;* practical for handling the finest work in the machine shop, manufacturing plant or tool room	$175
Trucks	*Time* (1928)	White trucks earn the most profit	
		Light delivery, 1 1/2-ton chassis	$2,125
		Heavy duty, 3-ton chassis	$4,650

Collectibles

Autograph	*The Youth's Companion* (1925)	Signature of Button Gwinnett, one of the 56 signers of The Declaration of Independence, representing Georgia	$14,000
Gun	*Antique Gun and Military Catalog* (1925)	*Kentucky Flintlock Smooth Bore;* with heavy octagonal barrel, 36", 9/16" bore	$50

Item	Source	Description	Price
Gun	*Antique Gun and Military Catalog* (1925)	*Smooth Bore Flint-lock Musket;* 3/4" bore; good, cleaned condition; perhaps made about 1840	$14
Gun	*Antique Gun and Military Catalog* (1925)	Revolving double-barrel flintlock, one hammer with two flash pans, one attached to each barrel	$120
Pistol	*Antique Gun and Military Catalog* (1925)	Pepper-box revolving barrel, 6-shot, top hammer, engraved frame	$12
Rifle	*Antique Gun and Military Catalog* (1925)	*Flintlock 1766;* 21" octagonal barrel, engraved "fowler" on barrel "1766"	$25

Education

Item	Source	Description	Price
Camp for Girls	*Delineator* (1928)	*Camp Sequoya* for girls in Allegheny Mountains; water sports, tennis, hockey Bristol, Virginia 8-week term	$225
Cornell University	*Popular Science Monthly* (1927)	Total annual cost of Cornell, including tuition and living expenses	$1,400
Prep School	*Delineator* (1928)	*Dean Academy;* young men and young women find a home-like atmosphere Per year	$500 to $600
School for Boys	*Delineator* (1928)	*Curtis,* a school for 30 young boys, home-life, strong, clean influence, Brookfield, Connecticut	$1,200
School for Boys	*Delineator* (1928)	*Dakotah School for Boys;* a home school in the country for boys under 15; Dakota, Illinois Rates	$600 to $650
School for Boys	*Delineator* (1928)	*Gettysburg Academy;* a school for 100 boys, new gymnasium and swimming pool, Gettysburg, Pennsylvania Per year	$475 to $575

Entertainment

Item	Source	Description	Price
Boxing Match	*Guinness Book of World Records* (1981)	Ring-side ticket price for Tunney vs. Dempsey heavy weight title fight in 1926	$27.50
Concert Ticket	*Washington Post* (1926)	London String Quartette; Washington Auditorium	$1–$2

Entertainment, Home

Item	Source	Description	Price
Butterfly Shades	*Modern Priscilla* (1929)	All materials and directions for making exquisite butterfly shade	$5.00
Camera	*Time* (1928)	*Graflex;* Graflex is the only camera which shows the action in the finder exactly as on the negative; Series B, 3 1/4" x 4 1/2"; speed up to 1/1000 second	$80
Camera	*Time* (1928)	*Graflex;* the camera that shows the action in the finder exactly as on the negative Series B, speed up to 1/1000 second	$80.00
Microscope	*Popular Science Monthly* (1927)	*Wollensak Optical* 250 power microscope	$16.50
Radio	*Sears, Roebuck* (1927)	*Model XVIII;* six tube; receiver only	$39.95
Radio	*Sears, Roebuck* (1927)	*Model XX;* six-tube receiver with all accessories; includes two large detector-amplifiers, storage battery, tubes, two large-duty 45-volt "B" batteries; one 100 ampere-hour storage battery, aerial; weight 205 lbs.	$99.95

Item	Source	Description	Price
Radio	*Literary Digest* (1928)	*Atwater Kent Model 30:* powerful one-dial, six-tube receiver	$65
Radio	*Literary Digest* (1928)	*Atwater Kent Model 33;* one dial, six tube receiver with solid mahogany cabinet; effective when distance getting is essential	$75
Radio	*Time* (1928)	*Gembox;* 6-tube electric radio	$65
Radio	*Time* (1928)	*Showbox;* 8-tube AC electric radio	$80

Farm Equipment & Supplies

Item	Source	Description	Price
Dog Medicine	*The Farm Journal* (1927)	*Glover's* Mange Medicine	$0.65
		Glover's Imperial Medicated Soap	$0.30
		Glover's Distemper Medicine	$1.25
Fence	*The Farm Journal* (1927)	Kokomo ornamental wire fence, costs less than wood Per foot	$0.06
Horse Treatment	*The Farm Journal* (1927)	*Absorbine* reduces thickened, swollen tissues, curbs filled tendons, soreness from bruises or strains Per box	$2.50
Lamb	*The Farm Journal* (1927)	Average of 29 ewes sold by Caldwell County, Missouri farmer	$16.69
Medicine for Chickens	*Carolina Gazette* (1925)	Absolutely rids chickens of sorehead	$0.35
Plow	*Lorick & Lowrance Hardware* (1928)	*Oliver;* one-horse; right-hand capacity, 4" deep by 7" wide	$8.25
Poultry Medicine	*The Farm Journal* (1927)	*Walko White Diarrheach Remedy;* reduces chicken loss Per package	$0.50
Spark Plug	*The Farm Journal* (1927)	*Champion X* spark plugs; exclusively for Ford cars, trucks and Fordson tractors Set of four	$2.40
Udder Balm	*The Farm Journal* (1927)	Bag Balm, for dairy cattle udder and teats; will heal between milkings 10-ounce package	$0.60

Food Products

Item	Source	Description	Price
Milk Chocolate	*Sears, Roebuck* (1926)	*Hershey's;* box of 24 $0.05 bars	$0.97/box
Strained Vegetables	*Modern Priscilla* (1929)	*Gerber's;* vegetables for baby; fresh to the cooker; per can	
		Strained vegetable soup	$0.25
		Strained carrots	$0.15
		Strained peas	$0.15

Household Products

Item	Source	Description	Price
Blanket	*Modern Priscilla* (1929)	Nashua part wool blanket in color sets Per pair, 72" x 84"	$4.95
Cleaner	*Modern Priscilla* (1929)	*Sani-Flush* cleans closet bowls without scoring Per can	$0.25
Cleaning Fluid	*Modern Priscilla* (1929)	*Energine;* removes spots quickly, dries instantly and leaves no odor Handy sized can	$0.35
Hammer	*Popular Science Monthly* (1927)	*Plumb Ball Pein* hammer; a safe hammer for car or work bench	$1.30
Pots	*Delineator* (1928)	Mirror aluminum pots; cook the new way with vapo-seal lids 10-quart size	$6.50 (more in far West) and South

Item	Source	Description	Price
Soap	*Modern Priscilla* (1929)	*Super Suds;* beads of soap make clothes whiter, dishes brighter Big box size	$0.10
Tarnish Tissues	*Modern Priscilla* (1929)	*Dexstar Staybrite Tissues;* silverware will not show the slightest tarnish when wrapped in tissues Sample, including 48 sheets (size 20 x 30 inches)	$1.00
Water Softner	*Delineator* (1928)	*Mel'o, a Real Water Softner;* a teaspoon in the dishpan is enough Full-sized can	$0.10

Garden Equipment & Supplies

Item	Source	Description	Price
Ax	*Lorick & Lowrance Hardware* (1928)	*Kelly Falls City;* single bit; handled, 4 pounds	$1.20
Ax	*Lorick & Lowrance Hardware* (1928)	*Box Scout;* official ax of Boy Scouts of America; 1 1/4 lbs, with Canvas Sheath	$1.65
Plant	*The Literary Digest* (1928)	New water fern; thrives in a vase of water	$0.50
Saw	*Carolina Gazette* (1925)	*Graves;* one-man saw; one man can do the work of two with this saw	$10
Saw	*Lorick & Lowrance Hardware* (1928)	*Handy Hand;* skew-back 24" saw	$2.35
Wheelbarrow	*Lorick & Lowrance Hardware* (1928)	General purpose; weight 43 lbs	$6.25

Household Products

Item	Source	Description	Price
Alarm Clock	*Lorick & Lowrance Hardware* (1928)	*Westclox Big Ben;* mellow toned; rings on back gong	$3.25
Bathroom Fixtures	Marchand, *Advertising the American Dream* (1985)	Meeting the modern demand for color in bathroom fixtures; includes sink, toilet, and tub [cost in 1929]	$157.45
Bathroom Outfit	*Sears, Roebuck* (1927)	*Fairview;* bathtub, lavatory and closet, with lavatory supply and waste pipes to wall	$64.75
Battery	*Lorick & Lowrance Hardware* (1928)	*Ray-O-Vac;* dry-cell A; 1 1/2 volts; diameter 2 1/2"; height 6"	$0.50
Blanket	*Sears, Roebuck* (1927)	Cotton plaid; these best staple cotton blankets are one-fifth lower than they were a year ago; 64" x 76"; weight per pair, 2 1/2 lbs	$1.72
Ceiling Fan	*Lorick & Lowrance Hardware* (1928)	*Hunter;* electric; 52" sweep, four basswood blades, three speeds	$52
Chisels	*Lorick & Lowrance Hardware* (1928)	Cabinet; six different sizes in a box	$10.20/bx
Clothes Pins	*Lorick & Lowrance Hardware* (1928)	One-piece standard pattern; hardwood	$3.50/5 gross case
Comforter	*Vogue* (1925)	*Carlin;* with lamb's wool filling; in Japanese silks	$21
Condiment Set	*Sears, Roebuck* (1927)	Made of Japanese lusterware decorated with cherry blossoms; set consists of one tray, one mustard jar, and one salt and pepper shaker	$0.85

Item	Source	Description	Price
Corn Cake Pans	*Lorick & Lowrance Hardware* (1928)	14 1/4" x 7 5/8" pan; makes 11	$0.85
Egg Beater	*Lorick & Lowrance Hardware* (1928)	*Blue Whirl;* no splash, even when whipping cream or mixing salad dressing	$1
Fireplace Grate	*Lorick & Lowrance Hardware* (1928)	*Cahill;* three-piece frame, 10" opening, 39 lbs., oxidized copper	$10
Fuse Plug	*Lorick & Lowrance Hardware* (1928)	*Universal;* made to fit all Universal electric hollow ware	$1.20
Grist Mill	*Lorick & Lowrance Hardware* (1928)	*Black Hawk;* will grind corn, wheat, rye, rice, or other small grain, beans, peas, spices, etc.	$4
Hacksaw	*Lorick & Lowrance Hardware* (1928)	*Miller Falls;* pistol grip, 10" blade	$2
Ice Cream Disher	*Lorick & Lowrance Hardware* (1928)	*Gilchrist;* automatic; pressing the thumb piece rotates the scraper	$2
Ironing Table	*Lorick & Lowrance Hardware* (1928)	*Daisy;* adjustable to four different heights	$2.35
Knives	*Lorick & Lowrance Hardware* (1928)	*Universal Resistain;* set of six steel paring knives	$0.45
Lantern	*Lorick & Lowrance Hardware* (1928)	*Dietz Monarch;* 13 1/2" height; fount capacity 18 hours	$12.50
Lavatory	*Lorick & Lowrance Hardware* (1928)	*Kohler Columbia;* enameled lavatory 20" x 24"	$50.70
Luggage	*Time* (1928)	Five bags combined in one at practically the price of one	$26.95
Mousetrap	*Lorick & Lowrance Hardware* (1928)	*Victor;* sheet-metal bait trigger	$1.80
Nail Hammer	*Lorick & Lowrance Hardware* (1928)	*Plumb;* adze eye, bell face; 1 lb	$1.75
Paint	*Lorick & Lowrance Hardware* (1928)	*Johnston's Dulle Kote;* for interior use; cleans easily with soap and water	$2.75
Pocketknife	*Lorick & Lowrance Hardware* (1928)	*Remington;* pearl handle; three blades	$3.50
Rule	*Lorick & Lowrance Hardware* (1928)	*Lufkin Folding Aluminum Rule;* 6' length, 6" folds	$2.10
Scale	*Vogue* (1925)	*Detecto;* watches your weight	$15
Soap	*Sears, Roebuck* (1927)	Toilet soap	$0.83
Soap	*Sears, Roebuck* (1927)	Bar toilet soap	$0.57
Spray Painting Machine	*Time* (1928)	Portable; will cut your maintenance painting costs in half	$115

Item	Source	Description	Price
Toilet	*Lorick & Lowrance Hardware* (1928)	*Kohler;* dorking; vitreous china wash-down closet combination	$35.05
Tool Chest	*Lorick & Lowrance Hardware* (1928)	*Stanley;* includes 12 tools	$15
Turpentine Measure	*Lorick & Lowrance Hardware* (1928)	Capacity 8 qt	$2
Vase	*Sears, Roebuck* (1927)	Imported; made of Japanese tokannabe pottery in antique design; height about 10"	$1.25
Waterproofer	*Sears, Roebuck* (1927)	Will make canvas waterproof and mildew proof; white	$1.25
Wood Varnish	*Lorick & Lowrance Hardware* (1928)	*Luxeberry;* for interior trim	$1.45

Insurance Rates

Item	Source	Description	Price
Accident and Sickness	*The Literary Digest Insurance* (1928)	No medical examination, men and women 16–70 years	accepted$10/yr
Fire Insurance	*Insurance Policy* (1926)	$500 fire coverage on two-story wood-frame building	$9/yr

Jewelry

Item	Source	Description	Price
Pocket Watch	*Illinois Watch Catalogue* (1928)	Man's size 12; 21 jewels engraved empire 14k; extremely thin for the business or professional man	$240
Watch	*The Farm Journal* (1927)	*Ingersolls* have earned a reputation for dependability Wrist watch Waterbury pocket watch	$3.50 $8.00
Watch	*Washington Post* (1926)	*Gruen* watch; 15 jewels; 14k gold; 25-year guarantee	$35
Wristwatch	*Sears, Roebuck* (1927)	Man's; 14-carat solid white gold; hand engraved bezel and sides; curved back to fit wrist; 15-jewel movement	$38.50

Meals

Item	Source	Description	Price
Dinner	*Washington Post* (1926)	The Rendezvous Restaurant; George Washington Birthday Dinner; home-cooked food at moderate prices	$1

Medical Products & Services

Item	Source	Description	Price
Dust Mask	*The Farm Journal* (1927)	*Dr. Willson's Dust and Spray Mask,* for all dusty farm and factory work	$2.25
Nonprescription Drug	*Carolina Gazette* (1925)	*6006 Blood Tablets;* safer than 606	$2
Nonprescription Drug	*Time* (1928)	*Gastrogen;* tablets; quick digestive relief and brings no hiccup or gas	$0.20
Nonprescription Drug	*The Literary Digest* (1928)	*Squibb's Milk of Magnesia;* promotes proper alimentation	$0.25
Sanatorium Care	*Report of the Board of Trustees, Brotherhood of Railroad Trainmen* (1928)	Average cost of 15 tuberculosis sanatoriums per year as paid by Brotherhood of Railroad Trainmen	$2,092.30/yr
Sanatorium Care	*Report of the Board of Trustees, Brotherhood of Railroad Trainmen* (1928)	*Thompson Sanatorium;* Kenneiller, Texas	$5/day
Sanatorium Care	*Report of the Board of Trustees, Brotherhood of Railroad Trainmen* (1928)	*Thomas Davis Clinic;* Tucson, Arizona	$4/day

Item	Source	Description	Price
Motorized Vehicles, Services, & Supplies			
Airplane	*Popular Science Monthly* (1927)	Cost of private flying aircraft, single engine	$2,000 and up
Airplane	*Popular Science Monthly* (1927)	Cost of Charles Lindbergh's Ryan Monoplane	$18,000
Auto Camp Fee	*The Farm Journal* (1927)	Connecticut Auto Camp charge per night	$0.50
Automobile	Joseph J. Schroeder Jr., *The Wonderful World of Automobiles* (1971)	*Hudson Coach;* 6-cylinder; world's greatest buy [cost in 1925]	$1,250
Automobile	Schroeder, *The Wonderful World of Automobiles* (1971)	*Star Coupster;* the ideal business car [cost in 1925]	$625
Automobile	Schroeder, *The Wonderful World of Automobiles* (1971)	*Willys-Knight Coupe-Sedan;* you have longed for a car you could keep and enjoy for years [cost in 1925]	$1,495
Automobile	Schroeder, *The Wonderful World of Automobiles* (1971)	*Chrysler '70 Roadster;* changed in no way except lower prices [cost in 1926]	$1,525
Automobile	*Time* (1928)	*Lincoln;* seven-passenger sport touring, restful touring comfort even across a continent	$4,600–$7,300
Automobile	*Time* (1928)	*Plymouth;* 4-cylinder roadster, coupe	$670
Automobile	Schroeder, *The Wonderful World of Automobiles* (1971)	*Chrysler Imperial 80;* town sedan, 112 hp [cost in 1928]	$2,995
Automobile	Schroeder, *The Wonderful World of Automobiles* (1971)	*Dodge Brothers Senior Six;* swift response and impressive reserves of quiet power [cost in 1928]	$1,575
Automobile	*The Literary Digest* (1928)	*Packard Custom Eight;* lower prices make it possible for many additional thousands to step up to the possession of America's finest and most modern car 2-Passenger Convertible Coupe 4-Passenger Coupe 7-Passenger Limousine	$4,150 $4,450 $4,550
Automobile	*Washington Post* (1926)	*Peerless Sedan* demonstrator; 5-passenger; 6-cylinder; new car guarantee	$2,100
Automobile, Used	*Washington Post* (1926)	1924 Chevrolet, perfect condition; 4 new tires; wheel lock	$125
Delivery Truck	*Time* (1928)	*White;* delivers the most money-earning miles	$1,545
Motorbike	*Sears, Roebuck* (1927)	High-grade motor bike at fully one-third less than it would cost anywhere else	$25.75
Motorcycle	*Popular Science Monthly* (1927)	*Harley-Davidson Motorcycle;* The single that travels 80 miles per gallon	$235
Radiator Repair	*The Farm Journal* (1927)	*X Liquid* repairs leaky radiators, harmless to metal, rubber and leather For Fords, Stars and Chevrolets	$0.75

Item	Source	Description	Price
Tire Chains	*The Literary Digest* (1928)	*Woodworth Easyon;* don't let your wife drive without them	$0.35
Truck Tire	*Sears, Roebuck* (1927)	*Cushion;* size 30" x 3 1/2"; complete with rim which has four lugs to fit Fords and Chevrolet; ready for mounting	$16.45

Musical Instruments

Harmonica	*John Martin* (1926)	*Hohner;* Anyone can play the Hohner harmonica	$0.50

Other

Christmas Cards	*Modern Priscilla* (1929)	Charming Christmas cards with envelopes for hand coloring	25 per package $1.00
Dog Collar Padlock	*Lorick & Lowrance Hardware* (1928)	*Eagle;* assortment	$4.20
Dog Medicine	*The Literary Digest* (1928)	*Glover's Imperial Dog Medicines;* dogs need these aids to health	$0.65
Funeral Expenses	*Report of the Board of Trustees, Brotherhood of Railroad Trainmen* (1928)	*D. L. Case*	$935
Grave Marker	*Confederate Veteran Magazine* (1928)	"Lest We Forget" markers for Confederate graves; approved by the UDC	$1.50
Lumber	*John Martin* (1926)	*Bildmor Blox;* well-cut building lumber accurately cut on the system of "multiple units" so that inter-locking construction is possible	$3.50
Silver Plate Knives	*Delineator* (1928)	Community deluxe stainless knives; blades as sharp as a Turk's scimitar Paul Revere design, per half dozen	$9.00

Personal Care Products

Cream	*Delineator* (1928)	*Helena Rubinstein's Valaze Pasteurized Face Cream;* cleans the skin immaculately	$1.00
Cream	*Delineator* (1928)	*Ingram's Milkweed Cream;* for cleansing face twice a day Jar Theatrical size	$0.50 $1.75
Curling Iron Heater	*Sears, Roebuck* (1927)	Heats your iron the safe, clean electric way; strong aluminum tube which keeps the iron warm for some time after the current is turned off	$2.55
Dental Cream	*Sears, Roebuck* (1927)		$0.75
Dental Cream	*Sears, Roebuck* (1927)	*Ribbon;* add 7¢ postage	$0.43
Dental Cream	*The Literary Digest* (1928)	*Squibb's;* make your teeth and gums safe at the danger line	$0.40
Eye Care	*Modern Priscilla* (1929)	*Murine* for your eyes; every woman longs for clear, bright eyes Month's supply	$0.60
False Teeth Holder	*The Literary Digest* (1928)	*Klutch;* forms a comfort cushion; holds the plate so snug it can't rock	$0.50
Hair Dryer	*Lorick & Lowrance Hardware* (1928)	*Polar Cub;* electric; for drying hair, shoes, delicate fabrics, motor-driven blower type	$4.95

193

Item	Source	Description	Price
Hair Treatment	*Sears, Roebuck* (1927)	*Water Waver for Hair;* beautiful deep graceful water waves assured; set of 6	$2.45/set
Hairpins	*Sears, Roebuck* (1927)	*Celluloid;* brown-shell or yellow-amber color; 24 pins per box	$0.23/bx
Lipstick	*Vogue* (1925)	*Tangee;* be beautiful with Tangee	$1
Mouthwash	*Sears, Roebuck* (1927)		$0.79
Razor	*The Farm Journal* (1927)	*Durham-Duplex Razor*—the blades men swear by, not at Set includes razor and two $0.50 packages of blades	$1.50
Razor Blade	*Lorick & Lowrance Hardware* (1928)	*Gillette;* double edge; half packet 5 blades	$0.50
Safety Razor	*Lorick & Lowrance Hardware* (1928)	*Enders;* knurled razor handle made of dualumin	$1
Safety Razor	*Lorick & Lowrance Hardware* (1928)	*Gillette New Standard;* genuine-leather-covered case, purple velvet and satin lined	$5
Shaving Lotion	*Sears, Roebuck* (1927)	*Talc for Men*	$0.19
Shaving Soap	*Sears, Roebuck* (1927)	*Colgate's Barber's Bar;* 1 lb equals 8 cakes	$0.49/lb
Suntan Lotion	*Delineator* (1928)	*Helena Rubinstein's Valaze Suntan Lotion*	$2.50
Tissue	*Lorick & Lowrance Hardware* (1928)	*Scott;* the soft, smooth tissue with purity, whiteness and quick absorbency; 50 roll case	$6.50/case
Tissue	Roland Marchand, *Advertising the American Dream* (1985)	*Scott;* now doctors ask you: is your bathroom paper safe? [cost in 1928]	$0.25
Toilet Tissue	*Delineator* (1928)	*A. P. W. Satin Tissue;* soft, absorbent, pure; scientifically safe One year's supply, 10,000 sheets in rolls One year's supply, 9,000 sheets flat	 $2.00 $2.45
Toothpaste	*The Literary Digest* (1928)	*Listerine;* the best paste that scientific knowledge could achieve	$0.25
Toothbrush	*Sears, Roebuck* (1927)	A popular type brush highly recommended by dentists	$0.25
Toothbrush	*The Literary Digest* (1928)	*Prophylactic;* reaches every tooth every time you brush	$0.50

Publications

Item	Source	Description	Price
Article	Marchand, *Advertising the American Dream* (1985)	"Truth is Stranger than Fiction" (1929)	$0.25
Book	*Washington Post* (1926)	Abraham Lincoln, *The Prairie Years* by Carl Sandburg; two-volume set	$10
Book	*Confederate Veteran Magazine* (1928)	*Echoes From Dixie, The Best Collection of the Real Old Songs of the South*	$1
Book	*John Martin* (1927)	*Winnie The Pooh;* amusing as only Christopher Robin's 'Bear of the Little Brain' could make it	$2
Magazine	*The Youth's Companion* (1925)	*The Youth's Companion,* published weekly, one-year subscription	$2.50

Item	Source	Description	Price
Magazine	*The Farm Journal* (1927)	The Farm Journal—inserts no humbug advertising, published monthly	
		One year	$0.25
		Four years	$1.00
Magazine	*Modern Priscilla* (1929)	*Modern Priscilla Monthly*	
		Per year	$2.00
Newspaper	*Wall Street Journal* (1928)	Annual subscription	$15

Real Estate

Item	Source	Description	Price
House	*The Farm Journal* (1927)	Gordon-Van Tine home; 5 rooms, bath, sun porch; all materials precut and shipped by rail for your construction	$1,932
House	*Carolina Gazette* (1925)	For rent; Bluffton, South Carolina; tent house with four spring cots, mattresses, and pillows	$10/wk
Land	*Popular Science Monthly* (1927)	10 acres near White River in Ozarks	$100 ($5.00 per month)

Sewing Equipment & Supplies

Item	Source	Description	Price
Cloth	*Sears, Roebuck* (1927)	All-wool flannel shirting; a fine quality twilled flannel in a small check; medium weight; width about 54"	$1.59/yd
Cloth	*Sears, Roebuck* (1927)	Half-wool shirting flannel; makes excellent children's play suits because it is washable; width about 27"	$0.39/yd
Dye	*Modern Priscilla* (1929)	*Diamond Dyes;* give richer colors to faded or out-of-date dresses	
		Blue package for silk and wool only	$0.15
		White package for every kind of fabric	$0.15
Sewing Machine	*Sears, Roebuck* (1927)	Six-drawer, drop-head ball-bearing sewing machine, plain oak woodwork	$33.95
Sewing Machine	*Modern Priscilla* (1929)	*Priscilla Electric Consolette Sewing Machine;* 15 monthly payments of $5	$79.00
Thread	*Modern Priscilla* (1929)	Boil fast mercerized thread; smooth enough to slip without friction through the filmiest chiffons	
		100-yard spool	$0.05

Sports Equipment

Item	Source	Description	Price
Baseball	*Sears, Roebuck* (1927)	*Wilson Official League;* selected horsehide cover sewed with best linen thread	$1.39
Baseball Bat	*Lorick & Lowrance Hardware* (1928)	*Louisville Slugger;* Ty Cobb style	$2
Baseball Glove	*Sears, Roebuck* (1927)	Youth model first baseman's mitt; good quality, soft and pliable horsehide leather	$1.75
Baseball Glove	*Sears, Roebuck* (1927)	*G. C. Alexander;* professional league model; diverted seams prevent ripping	$3.39
Baseball Glove	*Lorick & Lowrance Hardware* (1928)	*Rawlings Junior;* cross-lace fielder's glove; Willow horsehide, full glovolium oiled	$3
Baseball Mask	*Sears, Roebuck* (1927)	Catcher's; electrically welded dull-black-enameled steel-wire frame	$1.89
Basketball	*Lorick & Lowrance Hardware* (1928)	Made in four sections from tanned pebble grain cowhide	$18
Bicycle	*Lorick & Lowrance Hardware* (1928)	*Williams;* steel; wood-lined rims	$41
Boxing Gloves	*Lorick & Lowrance Hardware* (1928)	*U.S. Army Special;* weight 10 oz	$3.65

Item	Source	Description	Price
Fishing Line	*Lorick & Lowrance Hardware* (1928)	*Mayo;* twisted; made of Irish linen	$5.60
Fishing Plug	*Sears, Roebuck* (1927)	*South Bend Wiz-Oreno;* practically weedless, single hook, swiveling spinner, hankle fly and pork-rind snap	$0.87
Fishing Reel	*Sears, Roebuck* (1927)	*Shakespeare Criterion Level;* winding; 100-yd capacity; full quadruple-multiplying correct-level winding	$4.37
Fishing Reel	*Lorick & Lowrance Hardware* (1928)	*Shakespeare Criterion Level;* winding; capacity 100 yds	$5
Football	*Sears, Roebuck* (1927)	*Glenn F. Thistlewaite;* official; stemless bladder, ready-laced and ready to be inflated	$6.85
Football	*Lorick & Lowrance Hardware* (1928)	*Rawlings Official Intercollegiate;* pebble-grain leather	$12
Football Helmet	*Lorick & Lowrance Hardware* (1928)	Black strap leather; white felt padding	$5.50
Football Pants	*Sears, Roebuck* (1927)	*Red Grange;* boys; made of good quality duck-felt pad at top, reinforced with tape; autographed photograph of Red Grange furnished with each pair of pants	$3.89
Golf Ball	*Time* (1928)	*Dunlop;* Have you ever heard anyone ask for a better ball than a Dunlop? Each	$1.00
Golf Ball	*Time* (1928)	*Practo;* Practo makes perfect; this knitted golf ball will not travel far and it can't break anything	$0.25
Golf Ball	*Lorick & Lowrance Hardware* (1928)	*U. S. Royal;* recessed marking	$1
Golf Club	*Lorick & Lowrance Hardware* (1928)	*Macgregor Master;* driver	$15
Golf Clubs	*Lorick & Lowrance Hardware* (1928)	*Macgregor Duralite Uni-Set;* irons; set of eight	$78
Golf Tee	*Time* (1928)	Be sure you get the original and genuine	$0.25
Golf Tee	*Time* (1928)	*The Reddy Tee* 18 for	$0.25
Gun	*Lorick & Lowrance Hardware* (1928)	*L. C. Smith Field Grade;* double-barrel shotgun; made entirely of steel	$40
Gun	*Sears, Roebuck* (1927)	*Winchester Model 94;* solid-frame repeating rifle; the well known lever action style, noted for its simple mechanism, accuracy, and reliability	$31.98
Knife	*Lorick & Lowrance Hardware* (1928)	*Official Boy Scouts of America;* stag handle, four blades	$1.80
Rifle	*The Farm Journal* (1927)	*J. Stevens Arms Company;* manufactured over 10 million arms; single shot, .22 long rifle	$8.00
Rifle	*Antique Gun and Military Catalog* (1925)	*German Breech-loading Target Rifle:* heavy octagonal barrel, fine muzzle front sight, sliding-leaf peep sight	$16
Scooter	*Sears, Roebuck* (1927)	DeLuxe all-steel roller-bearing scooter	$3.98
Shotgun	*Sears, Roebuck* (1927)	Single barrel; matted top rib, trap-style automatic ejector, 12 gauge	$12.35

Item	Source	Description	Price
Shotgun	Sears, Roebuck (1927)	Single barrel; barrel is drilled from solid bar of special gun barrel steel, 12 gauge, 20" barrel	$8.95
Shotgun Shells	Lorick & Lowrance Hardware (1928)	Remington New Club; loaded with blank powder; 12 gauge; case of 100	$37/case
Tennis Racket	Lorick & Lowrance Hardware (1928)	Narragansett; 3-piece; full-beveled laminated frame, 60 line	$15
Tent	Sears, Roebuck (1927)	Army duck waterproofed umbrella style; new popular empire green color, size 9 3/4' x 10 1/2"	$37.85

Telephone Equipment & Services

Long Distance Charges	John Brooks, Telephone: The First Hundred Years (1987)	New York to London [rate for 1927]	$45

Tobacco Products

Pipe Tobacco	Popular Science Monthly (1927)	Old Briar tobacco is bringing smokers back to the pipe Per box	$0.50 $1.00 $2.00

Toys

Board Game	Sears, Roebuck (1927)	Ouija; apparently answers questions concerning your past, present and future, equipped with Fauld's new patented transparent indicator	$0.98
Board Game	Sears, Roebuck (1927)	Special Auto Race; no more exciting game; each kiddie has his own metal racer; two or four can play	$0.39
Cash Register	John Martin (1927)	Ask your dealer for Uncle Sam's registering and adding savings banks	$3
Construction Set	John Martin (1927)	Lincoln Logs; the all-American toy 53 Logs 234 Logs	$1 $4
Construction Set	Sears, Roebuck (1927)	Tinker Toy Wonder Builder; will build operating models; an ideal wood construction toy for the younger child	$0.63
Crayons	John Martin (1926)	Rubens Crayola; 24 bright permanent colors	$0.30
Doll	John Martin (1926)	Amberg Newborn Baskit Babe; get the guaranteed Amberg Newborn Babe	$1
Doll	Sears, Roebuck (1927)	The New Happy Baby; smiling-faced, dimpled baby doll, sure to bring Sunshine and Happiness to your little daughter; 23", 4 1/2 lbs	$6.48
Doll	John Martin (1927)	Chase Stockinet; most prized and loved by the little folks	$3.50
Doll Carriage	Lorick & Lowrance Hardware (1928)	Machine-woven flat fibre body, weight 17 lbs	$3.50
Dollhouse Furniture	John Martin (1927)	Four-poster bedroom; 14 pieces	$14.25
Doll Embroidery Outfits	John Martin (1927)	These attractive outfits for "Dolly" will interest your child in sewing and embroidery	$1
Erector Set	John Martin (1926)	Super erector No. 7 builds 533 models	$10
Erector Set With Motor	Sears, Roebuck (1927)	235 parts, builds 500 models; a very popular size which will make anybody happy	$4.47

Item	Source	Description	Price
Horseshoes	*Sears, Roebuck* (1927)	*Pitch-Em;* indoor; if in doubt as to how to entertain your friends some evening, just bring out your horseshoe game	$0.89
Juvenile Chevrolet Automobile	*Lorick & Lowrance Hardware* (1928)	Adjustable peddles, 35" long, weight 36 pounds	$11.25
Kitchen Cabinet	*John Martin* (1927)	Just like mother's; 39" high	$11
Motor Driven Toy	*John Martin* (1926)	*Kingsbury;* motor truck 25" long; spring motor, wound crank-fashion from the front	$15
Pedal Car	*Sears, Roebuck* (1927)	Made from heavy-gauge automobile steel; every boy can now haul ice, groceries, wood, anything, and drive it himself	$14.98
Scooter	*Lorick & Lowrance Hardware* (1928)	*American;* steel footboard, 15" long, weight 46 lbs	$2.40
Sewing Machine	*John Martin* (1926)	A real sewing machine for your very own	$5
Stencils	*John Martin* (1927)	*Junior Art-Kraft;* draw and paint artistic pictures, decorate with stencils	$1.50
Toymaker	*John Martin* (1926)	Builds boys as well as toys; boys and girls are now making boats, aeroplanes, radio sets, and many other dandy toys	$2
Train Set	*Popular Science Monthly* (1927)	*Lionel Electric Trains;* real enough for a man to enjoy, simple enough for a boy to operate Sets	$5.75 to $300
Tricycle	*Sears, Roebuck* (1927)	*High Class Fall Tubular Kidobike;* tubular-steel-frame velocipede for youngsters 2 to 4	$3.89
Trucks	*The Youth's Companion* (1925)	*Structo Toys*—for any kid who likes to play with real working toys Giant steam shovel Dump truck Grab bucket Racing auto	$2.50 $1.20 $1.35 $1.75
Wagon	*Sears, Roebuck* (1927)	*Faultless;* special play wagon for little tots; hardwood bottom, heavy sheet-metal sides	$1

Travel & Transportation

Item	Source	Description	Price
Cruise	*The Literary Digest* (1928)	Mediterranean luxury; 71 days of delightful diversion on the *Rotterdam*	$955
Cruise	*The Literary Digest* (1928)	New York to Havana; an entrancing trip of fascinating interest to a gay and scintillating foreign capital; 10 to 17 days	$85
Cruise	*The Literary Digest* (1928)	31 days of tropical contrast; New York to Trinidad	$300
Railroad Ticket	*The Farm Journal* (1927)	Low summer roundtrip fares from Chicago to California	$90.30
Steamship	*Delineator* (1928)	*Floating University;* The World Its Campus, 8 months, 26 countries All expenses	$2,500 to $4,150
Tour	*The Literary Digest* (1928)	*Collegiate;* Europe; visit five countries, all expenses	$38

MISCELLANY 1925-1929

Random Prices

Cost of the modes nine-room rented house at 21 Massasoit Avenue, Northampton, Mass. rented by President Calvin Coolidge on election day, November, 1928: $32.50 a month.

Wages paid the Marx Brothers for filming a movie version of *The Cocoanuts* for Paramount: $100,000.

The Year of the Great Crash, 1929, by William K. Klingaman
(New York: Harper and Row)

What Price Doctors

Excluding the fees of attending physicians and surgeons, actual records selected at random show that a private case of myocardial insufficiency requiring a hospital stay of fifty-five days cost $1,166, approximately half of the expense being for private nursing care and most of the remainder for room and board. A case of appendicitis cost $450; of mastoiditis over $750; of sinus infection $360.

Harpers, 1927

Prices and Wages

In April, 1928, New Bedford, Mass. wages for mill workers manufacturing high quality cloth was cut from $19 to $17 a week.

During an undercover prohibition police raid on Helen Morgan's summer home, outside New York City, a policeman and his wife paid $15 per pint for brandy.

Time, August 13, 1928

Men and Women

In 1928 the Detroit Survey of advertising wages showed that although 50 percent of the men were then receiving salaries of over $5,000 a year, no woman was being paid more than $3,500.

Advertising the American Dream, by Roland Marchand
(University of California Press)

Coolidge Raises Pay

President Coolidge approved a schedule of pay increases between $60 and $400 per annum for some 5,400 employees of the Navy Department in offices outside Washington—employees overlooked by the Welch Act.

Time, August 13, 1928

Sears Says We Pay the Postage

Sears, Roebuck and Co. announces with the issuance of this catalog the greatest single step forward in Mail Order merchandising since the establishment of the Parcel Post.

Every article in this catalog which can be conveniently sent by parcel post will be shipped to you postage prepaid.

Sears and Roebuck Catalogue, Spring 1929

Beef Steer Prices

Beef steers attained a strong position at the highest price level of the year during last week. Buyers ran short and scrambled for finished weighty cattle after midweek. New highs were established, prime 1,570 lb beefs for fancy eastern trade at $13.50 being 25¢ above the previous top this year and highest for heavy cattle since the fall of 1925.

Chicago Tribune, March 17, 1927

One Cent A Day Brings $100 A Month

Kansas City, Mo.—Accident insurance at a cost of one cent a day is being featured in a policy issued by the National Protective Insurance Association. The benefits are $1,200 to $1,800 at death. The premium is only $3.65 a year or exactly one cent a day.

Chicago Tribune, March 17, 1927

Borah Turns Back $2,500 Increase In His Pay as Senator

Washington, D.C.—Senator Borah of Idaho has been turning back into the treasury $2,500 of his annual salary since Congress, two years ago, increased the pay of senators and representatives from $7,500 to $10,000. And he says he intends to do so until the completion of his present term in 1931.

Chicago Tribune, March 17, 1927

MISCELLANY 1925-1929

Cost of Medical Service

A study of the cost of medical service was made by the Bureau of Labor Statistics from information secured in the first week of April 1928, from its personnel of 117 persons, other than the commissioner, assistant commissioner, and agents in the field. One hundred and fourteen satisfactory schedules were secured.

The term cost of medical service as used in this study, covers all direct expenditures for health purposes, including the care of the teeth and eyes, medicines, hospital and nursing charges, surgical appliances, etc. as well as the services of physicians and surgeons.

The principal points developed from the study are as follows: the average annual expenditures per employee for medical services were $98.92 for the salary group earning less than $2,000 per year; $146.13 for the salary group $2,000 to $3,000; and $190.63 for the salary group $3,000 and over. The average medical costs represented 6.2 percent of salary in the lower salary group; 6.3 percent in the middle group; and 5.5 percent in the upper group.

Handbook of Labor Statistics, 1929

HISTORICAL SNAPSHOT
1930-1934

1930

- Unemployment passes 4 million
- University of Pennsylvania professor creates beginnings of Gross National Product Index
- More than 1,352 banks close
- First analog computer is placed in operation by Vannevar Bush
- U.S. has one passenger car per 5.5 persons
- Gasoline consumption rises to nearly 16 billion gallons
- Radio set sales increase to 13.5 million
- Advertisers spend $60 million on radio commercials
- *Fortune Magazine* launched by Henry R. Luce; cost $1 per issue

1931

- Car sales collapse; 1,000,000 auto workers laid off
- Ford halts production of Model A
- 2,294 banks close
- Unemployment reaches 8 million
- Alka-Seltzer introduced by Miles Laboratories
- Chicago gangster Al Capone convicted of evading $231,000 in federal income taxes
- Clairol Hair products introduced by U.S. chemists
- New York's Waldorf-Astoria Hotel opens

- Safeway Stores reach their peak of 3,527 stores
- Birds Eye Frosted Foods sold nationally for first time

1932

- Average weekly wage falls to $17; breadlines form
- Wall Street's Dow Jones Industrials Average drops to 41.22
- AF of L urges that work be spread through a 30-hour week
- Patent application for a parking meter is made by *Oklahoma City News* editor Carl C. Magee
- Beech Aircraft Corporation founded at Wichita, KS
- *Family Circle* magazine begins publication
- Zippo lighter introduced
- Farm prices fall to 40 percent of 1929 levels
- Campbell's tomato juice introduced

1933

- City of Detroit defaults on $400 million debt
- Average earnings for a physician are $3,382; $8,663 for a congressman; $1,227 for a public school teacher
- U.S. abandons the gold standard
- National bank holiday proclaimed March 5

- Gasoline sells for 18¢ a gallon
- General Motors assumes leadership in motorcar sales, followed by Chrysler, then Ford
- IBM enters the typewriter business
- *Esquire* magazine is launched
- Agricultural Adjustment Act approved by Congress
- Ritz Crackers introduced by National Biscuit Company
- A&P stores control 11 percent of grocery stores sales

1934

- United Airlines is created when United Aircraft and Transportation Company, a holding company, is divided into three parts
- Price of gold stabilized by Department of Treasury at $35
- Greyhound cuts business fares in half to $8 between New York and Chicago
- Seagram's 7 Crown blended whiskey introduced
- Soybean acreage increases to 1 million
- Drought reduces corn crop by nearly 1 billion bushels
- Securities and Exchange Commission is created
- 4.7 million families are on relief
- Los Angeles Farmers Market opens; booths cost 50¢ a day
- Royal Crown Cola is introduced

SELECTED INCOME 1930-1934

Job	Source	Description	Pay
Accountant	*New York Times* (1932)	Certified, diversified experience; public, private position	$45/wk
Actor	*The Scribner Encyclopedia of American Lives,* 1987	Weekly salary of movie star Pat O'Brien, lead in Flying High in 1931	$1,750
Actor	Catherine Legrand and Robyn Karney, *Chronicle of the Cinema* (1995)	Weekly income of Johnny Weissmuller to play Tarzan the Ape Man in 1932	$250
Baseball Player Basketball Player	*Sports Illustrated* Victor Bondi, ed., *American Decades: 1930–1939* (1995)	Annual salary of New York Yankees' Babe Ruth in 1930 Monthly earnings of Babe Didrikson while touring with a mixed gender professional basketball team in 1934	$80,000 $1,500
Cook	*Chicago Tribune* (1931)	White, expd. woman. No Sunday work	$15/wk
Cook	*San Francisco Examiner* (1932)	Housework, care for infant; good home	$15/mo
Domestic	*New York Herald Tribune* (1930)	Want white, Protestant girl, with good disposition for cooking and downstairs work in the country. Must be willing to share large corner bedroom and bath with other maid	$75/mo
Domestic	*San Francisco Examiner* (1932)	Spanish-American lady for light housework	$10/mo
Dressmaker	*New Orleans Times-Picayune* (1930)	German; coats, suits, dresses; at home or out	$5/wk
Driver	*New Orleans Times-Picayune* (1931)	Route of 60 families; reliable hustler can start earning and increase rapidly	$35/wk
Government Jobs	*The State* (Columbia, SC) (1930)	Government jobs; men, women; 18 and up; common education usually sufficient; sample coaching; full particulars free	$1,260–$3,400/yr
Miscellaneous	*Chicago Tribune* (1931)	Girls over 21; three permanent positions.	$22.50/wk to start
Miscellaneous	*Chicago Tribune* (1933)	A man, permanent position; old established company only energetic men with best references need apply.	$50/wk
Musicians	Mary A. Bufwack and Robert K. Oerman, *Finding Her Voice, The Saga of Women in Country Music* (1993)	Nightly payment for The Vagabonds' appearance on *The Grand Old Opry* in 1933	$75
Office Assistant	*New York Times* (1934)	Young man, quick and accurate at figures; state age, education, experience if any; references	$15/wk

Job	Source	Description	Pay
Painter	*San Francisco Examiner* (1932)	Painting, exterior-interior; ceiling	$2.50/day
Phone Solicitor	*Chicago Tribune* (1931)		$22/wk
Refrigeration Salesman	*New York Times* (1932)	One of the world's largest manufacturers selling nationally known electric refrigerator; leads, promotion; only those willing to work with experienced manager	$30–$50/wk
Routemen	*New York Times* (1933)	With cars, established good routes	$40/wk
Sales	*New York Times* (1933)	Girls (2) inexperienced; attractive personality; cosmetics department, advancement	$15/wk
Sales	*The State* (Columbia, SC) (1930)	Permanent connection with weekly guarantee handling desirable fast-selling specialty; men earning $150 weekly	$40/wk
Sales	*New Orleans Times-Picayune* (1931)	Our business is radio selling and business is good	$30–$50/wk
Sales	*New Orleans Times-Picayune* (1934)	Nationally known concern selling products through wholesale grocery jobbers wants junior salesman. Must own Ford or Chevrolet coach that can be operated cheap.	$100 per month
U.S. President	*Sports Illustrated* (1996)	Annual salary of President Herbert Hoover in 1930	$75,000

CONSUMER EXPENDITURES 1930-1934

(Per Capita)

Expenditure Type	1930	1931	1932	1933	1934
Clothing	$54.39	$45.91	$32.01	$29.44	$36.37
Food	$145.31	$118.41	$91.24	$92.29	$90.13
Auto Usage	$38.15	$30.61	$24.01	$24.66	$29.15
New Auto Purchase	$12.99	$8.86	$4.80	$6.36	$7.91
Auto Parts	$4.06	$3.22	$2.40	$2.39	$2.37
Gas & Oil	$13.80	$12.08	$12.00	$11.93	$12.65
Housing	$90.92	$84.58	$73.63	$64.44	$61.67
Furniture	$7.30	$6.44	$4	$3.98	$3.95
Utilities	$25.16	$22.55	$20.81	$20.69	$21.35
Telephone & Telegraph	$4.87	$4.83	$4.00	$3.18	$3.16
Physicians	$7.30	$6.44	$5.60	$4.77	$5.53
Dentists	$4.06	$3.22	$2.40	$2.39	$2.37
Health Insurance	81¢	81¢	80¢	79¢	79¢
Personal Business	$28.41	$25.78	$21.61	$21.48	$21.35
Personal Care	$8.12	$8.05	$6.40	$5.57	$6.32
Tobacco	$12.18	$12.08	$10.40	$9.55	$11.07
Local Transport	$8.93	$7.25	$6.40	$5.57	$6.32
Intercity Transport	$3.25	$2.42	$2.40	$1.59	$2.37
Recreation	$32.41	$26.58	$19.21	$17.50	$18.97
Religion/Welfare Activities	$5.68	$5.64	$4.80	$3.98	$7.12
Private Education & Research	$5.68	$5.64	$4.80	$3.98	$3.95
Per Capita Consumption	$567.74	$487.73	$388.96	$364.39	$406.37

INVESTMENTS 1930-1934

Investment	1930	1931	1932	1933	1934
Basic Yield, One-Year Corporate Bonds	4.40	3.05	3.99	2.60	2.62
Short-Term Interest Rates, 4–6 Months, Prime Commercial Paper	3.59	2.64	2.73	1.73	1.02
Basic Yield, Common Stocks, Total	4.26	5.58	6.69	4.05	3.92
Index of Common Stocks (1941–1943=10)	21.03	13.66	6.93	8.96	9.84

COMMON STOCKS, CLOSING PRICE AND YIELD, FIRST BUSINESS DAY OF YEAR

(Parenthetical number is annual dividend in dollars)

	1930	1931	1932	1933	1934
Allis Chalmers	49 1/2	34 7/8	11	6 3/8	17 1/4
(4 for 1 split, 9/20/29)	(3)	(3)	(1)	(/)	(/)
AT&T	220	181	112 1/4	103	108 1/2
	(5)	(9)	(9)	(9)	(9)
American Tobacco	201	106	67	55 3/8	67
(2 for 1 split, 9/4/30)	(8)	(5)	(5)	(5)	(5)
Anaconda	72 3/8	32	16 3/8	7 3/8	14 1/8
	(7)	(2 1/2)	(/)	(/)	(/)
B&O	116 3/4	71 7/8	14 7/8	8 7/8	23 3/8
	(7)	(4)	(/)	(/)	(/)
Bethlehem Steel	93 1/4	52 7/8	18 1/2	14 1/2	36 3/8
	(6)	(6)	(4 1/2)	(/)	(/)
Corn Products	89 3/4	80 1/2	38 7/8	53 1/2	75
	(3)	(3)	(3)	(3)	(3)
General Electric	242 1/4	45 3/8	23 1/4	14 7/8	19 1/2
(4 shares for 1 split, 1/24/30)	(1.60)	(1.60)	(1.60)	(.40)	(.40)
General Motors	40 1/2	37 3/8	20 3/4	13 1/8	35
(2 1/2 shares for 1 split, 1/7/29)	(3)	(3)	(3)	(1)	(1)
International Business Machines	164 1/4	152	100	89	142
(5% stock dividend, 1/10/30)	(6)	(6)	(6)	(6)	(6)
(5% stock dividend, 1/11/32)					
(5% stock dividend, 1/11/32)					
Intl Harvester	79	50 3/8	24	20 3/4	39 3/8
	(2)	(2 1/2)	(2 1/2)	(1.20)	(.60)
National Biscuit	177	79	38 3/4	38 3/8	46 1/8
(2 1/2 shares for 1 split, 11/15/22)	(6)	(2.80)	(2.80)	(2.80)	(2.80)
US Steel	167 1/4	142	37 1/8	27 1/8	47 3/4
	(7)	(7)	(4)	(/)	(/)
Western Union	194	134 1/2	33 5/8	26 1/2	53 3/4
	(8)	(8)	(6)	(/)	(/)

STANDARD JOBS 1930-1934

Job Type	1930	1931	1932	1933	1934
Average of all Industries, excl. farm labor	$1494/yr	$1406/yr	$1244/yr	$1136/yr	$1146/yr
Average of all Industries, inc. farm labor	$1388/yr	$1298/yr	$1141/yr	$1045/yr	$1066/yr
Bituminous Coal Mining	$909/yr	$723/yr	$748/yr	$900/yr	$1119/yr
Building Trades	$1233/yr	$907/yr	$869/yr	$942/yr	$1526/yr
Domestics	$676/yr	$584/yr	$497/yr	$460/yr	$473/yr
Farm Labor	$444/yr	$355/yr	$279/yr	$259/yr	$286/yr
Federal Civilian	$1768/yr	$1895/yr	$1824/yr	$1673/yr	$1717/yr
Federal Employees, Executive Depts.	$1492/yr	$1549/yr	$1504/yr	$1213/yr	$1178/yr
Federal Military	$1182/yr	$1164/yr	$1070/yr	$1070/yr	$1191/yr
Finance, Insurance, & Real Estate	$1973/yr	$1858/yr	$1652/yr	$1555/yr	$1601/yr
Gas & Electricity Workers	$1603/yr	$1600/yr	$1542/yr	$1453/yr	$1510/yr
Manufacturing, Durable Goods	$1391/yr	$1127/yr	$1087/yr	$1171/yr	$1556/yr
Manufacturing, Nondurable Goods	$1425/yr	$1352/yr	$1166/yr	$1086/yr	$1139/yr
Medical/Health Services Workers	$933/yr	$919/yr	$865/yr	$810/yr	$801/yr
Miscellaneous Manufacturing	$1466/yr	$1230/yr	$1166/yr	$1195/yr	$1535/yr
Motion Picture Services	$2179/yr	$2175/yr	$1950/yr	$1891/yr	$1844/yr
Nonprofit Org. Workers	$1698/yr	$1653/yr	$1545/yr	$1442/yr	$1440/yr
Passenger Transportation Workers, Local and Highway	$1587/yr	$1500/yr	$1328/yr	$1219/yr	$1310/yr
Personal Services	$1200/yr	$1136/yr	$996/yr	$889/yr	$905/yr
Public School Teachers	$1455/yr	$1463/yr	$1399/yr	$1300/yr	$1265/yr
Radio Broadcasting & Television Workers	$2624/yr	$2732/yr	$2740/yr	$2510/yr	$2198/yr
Railroads	$1717/yr	$1661/yr	$1461/yr	$1439/yr	$1505/yr
State and Local Govt. Workers	$1517/yr	$1497/yr	$1427/yr	$1333/yr	$1289/yr
Telephone & Telegraph Workers	$1410/yr	$1436/yr	$1335/yr	$1245/yr	$1338/yr
Wholesale and Retail Trade Workers	$1569/yr	$1495/yr	$1315/yr	$1183/yr	$1228/yr

FOOD BASKET 1930-1934

(NR=Not Reported)

Commodity	Year	New York	Atlanta	Chicago	Denver	Los Angeles
Beans, Navy, per pound	1930	13.60¢	13.10¢	11.90¢	10.30¢	11.70¢
	1931	10.10¢	8.60¢	7.90¢	7.30¢	7.80¢
	1932	5.70¢	6.10¢	5¢	5.10¢	5.60¢
	1933	5.80¢	6.30¢	4.90¢	5.50¢	5.80¢
	1934	7.50¢	7¢	6¢	6.40¢	6.70¢
Beef, Rib Roasts, per pound	1930	40.50¢	32.40¢	38.20¢	29.10¢	32.90¢
	1931	35.10¢	28.40¢	32.70¢	25.20¢	26.90¢
	1932	30.20¢	24.10¢	26.30¢	20.80¢	22.70¢
	1933	25.20¢	21.30¢	22.30¢	18¢	21.60¢
	1934	27.10¢	21.60¢	23.50¢	18¢	20.90¢
Beef, Steaks, (Round), per pound	1930	47.50¢	42.20¢	43.10¢	34.70¢	35.90¢
	1931	40.10¢	37.30¢	35.10¢	28.50¢	28.30¢
	1932	35.80¢	32.50¢	28.10¢	23.40¢	24.80¢
	1933	29.40¢	27.50¢	23.60¢	21.60¢	24.40¢
	1934	31.90¢	28.40¢	25.40¢	23.90¢	24.70¢
Bread, White, per loaf	1930	8.60¢	9.70¢	9.30¢	7.50¢	8.60¢
	1931	7.70¢	7.90¢	8.70¢	6.50¢	7.50¢
	1932	7.40¢	6.80¢	7.50¢	5.90¢	6.70¢
	1933	7.80¢	7.40¢	6.50¢	6.40¢	7.70¢
	1934	8.90¢	8.90¢	7.40¢	7.60¢	7.80¢
Butter, per pound	1930	46.10¢	50.30¢	44¢	41.50¢	44.90¢
	1931	35.90¢	40¢	34¢	33.20¢	36.10¢
	1932	28.30¢	30¢	26.90¢	25.60¢	28.40¢
	1933	28.90¢	28.70¢	27.50¢	26.20¢	27.30¢
	1934	32.50¢	31.40¢	31¢	30.60¢	31.50¢
Cheese, per pound	1930	38¢	31.50¢	39.60¢	36.70¢	35.30¢
	1931	32.20¢	24.80¢	31¢	28.70¢	28.10¢
	1932	28.60¢	21¢	26.10¢	24.50¢	24.50¢
	1933	26.90¢	20.50¢	25.50¢	24.40¢	23.80¢
	1934	27.40¢	21.10¢	26.50¢	24.20¢	23.60¢
Chickens, per pound	1930	37.30¢	34.20¢	31.50¢	29¢	41.10¢
	1931	32.50¢	28.90¢	32.70¢	26.10¢	35.10¢
	1932	26.50¢	21.80¢	26.10¢	18¢	28.80¢
	1933	22.60¢	18.20¢	21.70¢	18¢	26.30¢
	1934	27.60¢	23.10¢	25.80¢	19.70¢	27.90¢
Coffee, per pound	1930	36.50¢	39.50¢	40.20¢	43.40¢	44.20¢
	1931	31.10¢	34.50¢	33.80¢	40.30¢	37.80¢
	1932	28.70¢	29.10¢	31¢	32.50¢	33.20¢
	1933	25.90¢	25.30¢	27.50¢	32.50¢	30.20¢
	1934	26.90¢	26¢	27¢	31.20¢	30.90¢
Cornmeal, per pound	1930	6.50¢	4¢	6.80¢	4.60¢	5.60¢
	1931	5.90¢	3¢	5.60¢	4.20¢	4.80¢
	1932	5.30¢	2.10¢	5.30¢	4.10¢	4.10¢
	1933	5.10¢	2.30¢	4.90¢	3.80¢	3.50¢
	1934	5.80¢	2.80¢	5.40¢	4.50¢	4.40¢
Eggs, per dozen	1930	51.60¢	39.50¢	41.40¢	35¢	38.80¢
	1931	41.70¢	30¢	33¢	26.60¢	32.80¢
	1932	36.90¢	24.70¢	27.60¢	24.10¢	28.10¢
	1933	35¢	23.60¢	26.40¢	25¢	28¢
	1934	38¢	28.20¢	30.30¢	29¢	30.10¢

Commodity	Year	New York	Atlanta	Chicago	Denver	Los Angeles
Flour, Wheat, per pound	1930	4.40¢	5.50¢	4.10¢	3.60¢	4.40¢
	1931	3.50¢	4.10¢	3.30¢	2.70¢	3.30¢
	1932	3.40¢	3.60¢	2.80¢	2.40¢	2.90¢
	1933	4¢	4.40¢	3.70¢	3.20¢	3.60¢
	1934	5.30¢	4.40¢	4.70¢	4¢	4.50¢
Lard, per pound	1930	17.70¢	16.50¢	17.30¢	16.40¢	17.30¢
	1931	14.10¢	12.70¢	13¢	13.10¢	13.70¢
	1932	9.80¢	8.40¢	8.90¢	8.90¢	9.40¢
	1933	9.90¢	9.10¢	9.10¢	8.60¢	9.50¢
	1934	12.20¢	11.90¢	11.30¢	11.70¢	11.90¢
Milk, Fresh, per quart	1930	15.70¢	16.20¢	14¢	11.40¢	14.50¢
	1931	14.70¢	14.70¢	13¢	10.30¢	12.60¢
	1932	11.90¢	13.30¢	11.20¢	10.10¢	10.60¢
	1933	11.20¢	12.40¢	9.90¢	10¢	10.70¢
	1934	12.40¢	12.20¢	9.50¢	10.10¢	10.80¢
Mutton and Lamb, Leg, per pound	1930	33.90¢	36.50¢	34.90¢	32.10¢	32.30¢
	1931	28.90¢	29.80¢	30.40¢	27¢	25.30¢
	1932	23.20¢	22.70¢	24.20¢	20.80¢	21.30¢
	1933	21.40¢	21.60¢	21.80¢	19.60¢	21.40¢
	1934	25.20¢	23.10¢	24.80¢	22.40¢	24¢
Pork, Bacon, Sliced, per pound	1930	45¢	38.50¢	46.50¢	40.40¢	40.20¢
	1931	39.10¢	31.50¢	40.40¢	35.10¢	38.20¢
	1932	27.40¢	20.50¢	27.20¢	24.10¢	27.90¢
	1933	24.80¢	21.30¢	25¢	21.80¢	21.70¢
	1934	31.40¢	27.20¢	30.40¢	29¢	32.50¢
Pork Chops, per pound	1930	39¢	33.50¢	35.60¢	34.30¢	40.90¢
	1931	32.10¢	27.70¢	29.60¢	28¢	32.70¢
	1932	24.10¢	21.20¢	21.30¢	18.70¢	24.30¢
	1933	21.70¢	19.70¢	19.90¢	17.90¢	25.40¢
	1934	26.60¢	24.60¢	25.40¢	23.80¢	30.20¢
Pork, Ham, Sliced, per pound	1930	55.30¢	51.80¢	55.40¢	52.50¢	65¢
	1931	48.30¢	44.30¢	48.20¢	45¢	53.10¢
	1932	39.10¢	33.20¢	36.10¢	35.10¢	41.40¢
	1933	35.10¢	30.40¢	30.70¢	31.90¢	38.10¢
	1934	39¢	36.20¢	36.60¢	37.40¢	46.40
Potatoes, Irish, per pound	1930	3.80¢	4.40¢	3.70¢	3.40¢	3.65¢
	1931	2.60¢	3.10¢	2.40¢	2.20¢	2.30¢
	1932	2¢	2.30¢	1.80¢	1.80¢	1.90¢
	1933	2.60¢	2.70¢	2.30¢	2.20¢	2.20¢
	1934	2.70¢	2.70¢	2.50¢	2.30¢	2.20¢
Prunes, Dried, per pound	1930	14.90¢	16.90¢	17.10¢	17.30¢	14.80¢
	1931	10.70¢	11.80¢	12.70¢	13.30¢	10.40¢
	1932	8.40¢	9.70¢	10.60¢	10.80¢	8.70¢
	1933	8.80¢	9.40¢	10.90¢	10.90¢	8.60¢
	1934	10.90¢	11.50¢	12.90¢	12.80¢	10.40¢
Rice, per pound	1930	9.10¢	8.50¢	10.10¢	8.90¢	9.20¢
	1931	8¢	7.60¢	8.20¢	7.70¢	7.70¢
	1932	6.50¢	6¢	7.10¢	6.40¢	6.60¢
	1933	6¢	5.70¢	6.50¢	6.20¢	6.10¢
	1934	5.80¢	7.70¢	8.10¢	8.40¢	8.10¢
Sugar, per pound	1930	5.50¢	6.50¢	6.20¢	6.70¢	5.80¢
	1931	5.20¢	6¢	5.70¢	6.20¢	5.40¢
	1932	4.80¢	5.20¢	5.20¢	5.70¢	4.90¢
	1933	5¢	5.60¢	5.40¢	6¢	5¢
	1934	5.30¢	5.80¢	5.70¢	6.10¢	5.10¢

Commodity	Year	New York	Atlanta	Chicago	Denver	Los Angeles
Tea, per pound	1930	66.40¢	96.70¢	72.90¢	71.60¢	73.50¢
	1931	64¢	93.40¢	70.10¢	73.70¢	74.70¢
	1932	57.20¢	80.60¢	66.60¢	71.50¢	73.80¢
	1933	55.80¢	70.10¢	65.90¢	68¢	74¢
	1934	64.20¢	70.90¢	74.30¢	72.60¢	79.50¢

SELECTED PRICES 1930-1934

Item	Source	Description	Price
Advertising			
Advertisement	Roland Marchand, *Advertising The American Dream* (1985)	*Ladies' Home Journal* [cost in 1933]	$12,500/full pg
Advertisement	Marchand, *Advertising The American Dream* (1985)	Weekly advertising cost for *Comic Weekly* and other nationally syndicated Sunday comic supplements [cost in 1933]	$16,000–$17,000/pg
Apparel, Children's			
Baby Skirt	*Montgomery Ward & Co.* (1932)	*Amoskeag Gertrude;* flannelette; skirt long, infant's size only	$0.21
Frock	*Montgomery Ward & Co.* (1932)	*Sunnymorn;* bolero effect youthfully styled	$0.77
Galoshes	*Montgomery Ward & Co.* (1932)	All rubber; three snap fasteners; light-colored lining; reduced from $1.19	$0.98
Gym Suit	*Sears, Roebuck* (1932)	Girl's one-piece; we formerly got $1.89 for this type garment	$1
Knickers	*Montgomery Ward & Co.* (1932)	Boy's; made in golf style, fully lined, and strongly sewn throughout	$0.77
Overalls	*Pee Dee Advocate* Bennettsville, SC (1934)	All sizes at Belk's Department Store	$0.30
Rubber Pants	*Montgomery Ward & Co.* (1932)	Gum; washable; ruffled side ventilation	$0.22/3 pr
Shoes	*Montgomery Ward & Co.* (1932)	Little girl's; patent or calf-grain; extra-good quality; long wearing leather soles	$1.39
Shoes	*Sears, Roebuck* (1932)	*Airway Lightfoot;* fastest shoe on the playground	$0.75
Slip	*Montgomery Ward & Co.* (1932)	*Rayon;* ages 4 to 14 years; ruffled flounce slip with built-up shoulder	$0.39
Sweater	*Sears, Roebuck* (1932)	Girl's; worsted-wool shaker; good quality	$2.19
Vest	*Montgomery Ward & Co.* (1932)	10 percent wool; rayon; striped; pin-back style	$0.35
Apparel, Men's			
Boots	*Montgomery Ward & Co.* (1932)	*Wonderwear* combination rubber soles; double tanned	$1.59
Boots	*Montgomery Ward & Co.* (1932)	All black rubber; absolutely waterproof; great for farm wear	$1.77

Item	Source	Description	Price
Coats	*Curry Brothers Oil Company Catalogue* (1931)	*Fish Brand;* reflex waterproof coats; 44" long	$56/dz
Gloves	*Montgomery Ward & Co.* (1932)	Standard-wear work gloves; the harder the work the better you will like them	$0.79
Handkerchief	*Sears, Roebuck* (1932)	Cotton bandana; neat designs	$0.58/dz
Hat	*Collier's* (1934)	*Dunlap;* America's smartest hats	$5
Hose Supporter	*Sears, Roebuck* (1932)	*Buster Brown;* with non-elastic top	$0.24
Overalls	*Montgomery Ward & Co.* (1932)	Mill shrunk, pure Indigo dyed	$0.85
Shirt	*Montgomery Ward & Co.* (1932)	*Yukon Permana;* Shrunk suede cloth; whatever size you buy stays that size because it's fully guaranteed full shrunk, coat style, with two large button-through pockets	$1
Shirts	*Pee Dee Advocate* Bennettsville, SC (1934)	Heavy covert shirts	$0.65
Shoes	*Montgomery Ward & Co.* (1932)	Plain-toe Oxford tie shoe; black calf-grain leather	$2.48
Shoes	*Sears, Roebuck* (1932)	*Green Grip;* nowhere do we know of stronger, more rugged leather or finer workmanship	$3.98
Suit	*Sears, Roebuck* (1932)	Tailored wool; $10 to $30 lower than for equal quality offered elsewhere	$16.50
Suit	*Montgomery Ward & Co.* (1932)	*Stillson Yale Model;* features all-wool worsted cheviots in a two-button notch lapel coat	$10.88
Sweater	*Montgomery Ward & Co.* (1932)	Men's; all-wool worsted; fits snugly and keeps its shape	$1.88
Trousers	*Montgomery Ward & Co.* (1932)	*Cheviot;* All-wool dress; a new high-rise trouser that will stick with style leaders	$2.89

Apparel, Women's

Item	Source	Description	Price
Bag	*Montgomery Ward & Co.* (1932)	Woman's; a new smart steerhide bag of the quality that has been sold everywhere at $2.95	$1.77
Bloomers	*Sears, Roebuck* (1932)	Nainsook; famous for long hard wear	$0.23
Bloomers	*Montgomery Ward & Co.* (1932)	Run-resistant rayon; stout size; flesh, peach; reinforced crotch	$0.55
Coat	*Sears, Roebuck* (1932)	Wool, fur-lined; full length	$13.74
Corselet	*Montgomery Ward & Co.* (1932)	Fine brocade belted; rayon and cotton tricot Jersey top, knitted elastic panels	$1.88
Corset	*San Francisco Examiner* (1932)	Some innerbelt models for heavier women	$1.00
Dress	*Sears, Roebuck* (1932)	Silk; flat crepe; the savings will thrill you	$2.98

Item	Source	Description	Price
Frock	Montgomery Ward & Co. (1932)	Fruit of the Loom; youthful cotton print; flattering neck line set off with piping and two-tone bow	$1
Girdle	Montgomery Ward & Co. (1932)	Durolastic; for average height figures; 12" length	$1.74
Gloves	San Francisco Examiner (1932)	4-button and fancy kidskins	$1.45
Gloves	Sears, Roebuck (1932)	Imported glacé lambskin; usually called kid gloves	$1.95
Handbag	Sears, Roebuck (1932)	Back-strap style; calf leather; inverted frame pouch	$1.79
Hat	Sears, Roebuck (1932)	Peanut straw body; with the new lifted left-side brim line	$0.95
Hosiery	Montgomery Ward & Co. (1932)	Golden Crest; pure silk top to toe; medium service weight	$0.89
Mesh Bag	Sears, Roebuck (1932)	Lined dresden; predomination colors: green and white; size 4" x 5 3/4"	$2.95
Shoes	Pee Dee Advocate Bennettsville, SC (1934)	Suede shoes, regular $2.95—on sale	$1.95
Shoes	Montgomery Ward & Co. (1932)	Anita style, smooth calf-grain tip and back	$2.67
Shoes	Sears, Roebuck (1932)	Goodyear Welt; low heels with rubber top lifts patent leather	$2.48
Slip	Montgomery Ward & Co. (1932)	All-silk crepe de chine; nobody ever dreamed of a slip like this; others ask $1.79	$1
Sweater	Montgomery Ward & Co. (1932)	All-wool elastic rib knit; a sweater like this is not only practical, but economical	$2.25

Appliances

Item	Source	Description	Price
Batteries	Pee Dee Advocate Bennettsville, SC (1934)	Radio batteries recharged Auto batteries recharged	$0.45 $0.75
Cook Stove	Montgomery Ward & Co. (1932)	Juniper Windsor; heavy all-cast-iron cook stove	$21.50
Electric Heater	Montgomery Ward & Co. (1932)	Guaranteed element; in copper bowl, green enamel frame	$1
Electric Washer	Montgomery Ward & Co. (1932)	Big value combination! Electric ironer with deluxe porcelain or copper tub	$79.85
Iron	Montgomery Ward & Co. (1932)	Electric; don't bother to repair your old iron now—it actually costs less to buy a better one	$1
Iron	Montgomery Ward & Co. (1932)	Gasoline; costs 1/2¢ an hour to operate; burns 3 1/2 hours with one filling	$3.98
Mixer	Dallas Hospitality Magazine (1932)	Sunbeam Mix-Master; mix batters, mash potatoes, beat eggs, extract juice from oranges, etc., make mayonnaise, malted milk	$21

Item	Source	Description	Price
Range	*Montgomery Ward & Co.* (1932)	*Windsor Seminole;* kerosene; 5-burner	$28.95
Toaster	*Montgomery Ward & Co.* (1932)	Electric; it automatically turns the toast when doors are lowered	$1
Vacuum Cleaner	*Montgomery Ward & Co.* (1932)	*Majestic;* beating, sweeping, suction; motor-driven brush	$28.95
Vacuum Cleaner	*Dallas Hospitality Magazine* (1932)	*Premier Duplex;* easy one-hand operation and great ability to pick up threads, etc.	$49.50
Waffle Iron	*Dallas Hospitality Magazine* (1932)	*Westinghouse Crisp-Grid;* it bakes waffles for a houseful of guests at a cost of a couple of cents	$7.95
Washing Machine	*Montgomery Ward & Co.* (1932)	*Wardway DeLuxe Gyrator;* greatest washer value in America; twice winner of the whiteness tests	$57.95

Baby Products

Item	Source	Description	Price
Baby Powder	*Montgomery Ward & Co.* (1932)	*Johnson & Johnson;* two $0.25 cans; a real savings	$0.29
Blanket	*Sears, Roebuck* (1932)	*Pepperell;* a woven cotton-twill fabric with a soft downy-fleeced finish	$0.31
Dusting Powder	*Sears, Roebuck* (1932)	*My Baby's;* a cooling, soothing, healing powder	$0.39
Nipple	*Sears, Roebuck* (1932)	*Faultless Wonder;* pure-gum nipple	$0.34
Walker	*Sears, Roebuck* (1932)	Ball bearing walker; non-tipping, with adjustable seat straps	$2.29

Business Equipment & Supplies

Item	Source	Description	Price
Typewriter	*Sears, Roebuck* (1932)	*L. C. Smith;* the world's only ball-bearing typewriter	$45
Typewriter	*Montgomery Ward & Co.* (1932)	*Underwood;* portable; four full key rows, 84 characters; paper space up to 9 1/2" wide	$49.50
Typewriter	*Popular Mechanics* (1933)	*International Typewriter Exchange Underwood No. 5;* includes standard 4-row keyboard, backspacer, automatic ribbon reverse, shift-lock key, 2-color ribbon	$39.90
Typewriter	*Popular Mechanics* (1933)	*Underwood;* positively the greatest bargain ever offered; Regular $100 model	$39
Typewriter Ribbons	*Pee Dee Advocate* Bennettsville, SC (1934)	The best silk ribbons	$0.75

Entertainment

Item	Source	Description	Price
Concert Ticket	*The Raleigh (NC) Times* (1931)	Ken Hackley's Oklahoma Cowboys Famous Radio Artists, 4 shows daily Matinee Night	 $0.10 to $0.30 $0.10 to $0.40
Movie Ticket	*Pee Dee Advocate* Bennettsville, SC (1934)	*Footlight Parade* starring James Cagney and Ruby Keeler Adults Children Balcony for Colored	 $0.25 $0.10 $0.10

Item	Source	Description	Price
Entertainment, Home			
Camera	*Collier's* (1934)	*Kodak Six-20;* with F 6.3 lens, pictures 2 1/2" 4 1/2"	$20
Cards	*New York Times Magazine* (1931)	*Currier & Ives;* there are 18 subjects, and each subject comes in two sizes 3" x 4" 5" x 6"	$0.10 $0.15
Microphone	*Popular Mechanics* (1933)	*Master Mike;* with mike ring; reproduces your own voice through your radio; a million dollars worth of fun	$1
Model Airplane	*Popular Mechanics* (1933)	*Cleveland Model and Supply Co. Inc. Boeing 247;* hailed as a masterpiece in model flying aircraft; nearly 5' span, weight 16 oz	$6.50
Moving Picture Camera and Projector	*Popular Mechanics* (1933)	Get professional moving pictures; uses 50' roll of 16mm film	$13.75
Phonograph Records	*Montgomery Ward & Co.* (1932)	*Paramount Hill Country Melodies;* full 10" size; double-face song *When the Moon Comes Over the Mountain;* lot of five	$0.29
Radio	*Montgomery Ward & Co.* (1932)	*Airline 7-tube Super Heterodyne;* thrilling new power and almost unbelievable realism of tone	$39.85
Radio	*Popular Mechanics* (1933)	*Midwest Radio Corp. Super Deluxe;* 16-tube all wave; world's greatest radio value with new deluxe auditorium-type speaker	$49.50
Radio	*Collier's* (1934)	*Philco 16x All Wave;* no longer is the Atlantic or the Pacific a barrier to your search for radio entertainment	$175
Radio	*Collier's* (1934)	*Philco 8413;* a wonderful little radio in an attractive two-tone cabinet	$20
Radio	*Rock Hill Herald* (Rock Hill, SC) (1933)	*Philco;* make your home the center of the world	$18.75–$295
Shortwave Receiver	*Popular Mechanics* (1933)	*Powertown-Wallace Try-Mo Radio;* price with blueprints and 1 coil	$14.70
Victrola	*The Raleigh (NC) Times* (1931)	Used portable Victrola with records Contact Raleigh Loan Office	$3.90
Farming Equipment & Supplies			
Barbed Wire	*Montgomery Ward & Co.* (1932)	Galvanized; 80-rod spool, 53 lbs	$1.43
Barbed Wire	*Sears, Roebuck* (1932)	4-point galvanized cattle wire	$2.28
Cod Liver Oil	*Montgomery Ward & Co.* (1932)	For healthier poultry and livestock	$1.79/gal
Frogs	*Popular Mechanics* (1933)	Breeders lay 10,000 eggs; unlimited market; book, *Fortune in Frogs*	$1–$3/dz
Hog Troughs	*Montgomery Ward & Co.* (1932)	20-gauge steel, welded and soldered; lots of six	$0.48
Home Hatcher	*Montgomery Ward & Co.* (1932)	*Ward's;* continuous electric entirely eliminates the variation of temperature in the egg chamber	$39.95
Mules and Horses	*Rock Hill Herald* (Rock Hill, SC) (1933)	*W. L. Abernathy,* Fort Lawn, South Carolina; the kind to make a cheap crop	$35/$63/$75

Item	Source	Description	Price
Food Products			
Apples	*New York Times Magazine* (1931)	*Jonathan* apples	$3.25/bx
Candy Bar	*Sears, Roebuck* (1932)	*Hershey's Almond;* 25 $0.05 almond bars	$1
Figs	*San Francisco Examiner* (1932)	California Syrup Figs	$0.35
Fruit	*Rock Hill Herald* (Rock Hill, SC) (1933)	*Gator Fruit Store,* Rock Hill, South Carolina; oranges grapefruit bananas	$0.30–$0.40/peck $0.05/2 $0.19/4 lbs
Ice Cream	*The Raleigh (NC) Times* (1931)	Get your favorite flavor at these special prices from White Dairy Products Company One Pint White's Ice Cream Two Pints White's Ice Cream	$0.25 $0.35
Marshmallows	*Sears, Roebuck* (1932)	*Kraft;* fresh, soft, fluffy vanilla-flavored marshmallows; box of 200	$0.65/bx
Marshmallows	*Montgomery Ward & Co.* (1932)	Creamy; wholesome and nutritious; box of 200	$0.46/bx
Salt Mackerel Fillets	*Collier's* (1934)	18 extra-large mackerel fillets by mail	$3
Vanilla Extract	*Sears, Roebuck* (1932)	*Montclair;* equal of any nationally advertised brand	$0.42
Furniture			
Bathroom	*Montgomery Ward & Co.* (1932)	*Deerfield;* 3-piece outfit includes bathtub, closet and outfit, Combination and lavatory	$61.45
Bed	*Montgomery Ward & Co.* (1932)	All steel; continuous seamless 2" main posts; includes bed, coil spring, and mattress	$14.35
Bathroom Suite	*Montgomery Ward & Co.* (1932)	3-piece; panel bed, chest, and 36" dresser	$32.75
Cedar Chest	*Montgomery Ward & Co.* (1932)	Solid 3/4", genuine Tennessee red cedar, 40" x 17" x 18 3/4" walnut finish	$12.95
Chair	*Montgomery Ward & Co.* (1932)	Solid oak; positively the first time at this price	$1
Chair	*Montgomery Ward & Co.* (1932)	Nursery; enameled; comfy seat opening, swing over tray	$1
Chair	*Montgomery Ward & Co.* (1932)	Bow-back style; golden oak; made of select hardwood; well-braced, heavy seat	$1
Chifforobe	*Sears, Roebuck* (1932)	Of good-quality seasoned hardwood	$18.95
Clock	*Montgomery Ward & Co.* (1932)	*Gilbert;* mahogany-finished case with burled panels; strikes hours and half hours on cathedral gong	$5.95
Davenport	*Montgomery Ward & Co.* (1932)	*Jacquard;* velour two-tone; serpentine front; never-sag steel under construction	$19.95

Item	Source	Description	Price
Mattress	Montgomery Ward & Co. (1932)	Full 50-pound all felted cotton mattress; 54"	$4.65
Radio Bench	Montgomery Ward & Co. (1932)	Rich tapestry upholstering	$1
Rug	Montgomery Ward & Co. (1932)	Seamless velvet; floral designs on a tan taupe ground; blue border; 9' by 12'	$14.95
Stool	Sears, Roebuck (1932)	All metal; eight cross braces; green	$0.97

Fuel

Item	Source	Description	Price
Coal	Pee Dee Advocate Bennettsville, SC (1934)	Free burning, grate and stove coal Per ton Per half ton	$7.50 $4.00

Garden Equipment & Supplies

Item	Source	Description	Price
Evergreen Shrubbery	Rock Hill Herald (Rock Hill, SC) (1933)	Belk Department Store; a great variety of large healthy evergreens—broad leaf and conifers	$0.50–$1
Flowers	New York Times Magazine (1931)	Fargo; 20 double early tulips	$1.10
Lawn Mower	Montgomery Ward & Co. (1932)	Lakeside; five years ago this same quality mower sold for twice as much; self-adjusting, ball-bearing, quiet and easy running; 9" wheels; 14" blade	$5.49
Plants	The Raleigh (NC) Times (1931)	Live ferns from Job P. Wyatt and Sons Company	$0.10 each
Shovels	Curry Brothers Oil Company Catalogue (1931)	Ames 3-Star; contractor's or digging blade; 9 1/2" x 12 1/4"; handle length 26 1/2"	$25/dz

Household Products

Item	Source	Description	Price
Blanket	Montgomery Ward & Co. (1932)	Fleecy down staple cotton; plain; extra large size; 72" x 84"	$1.25
Blankets	Sears, Roebuck (1932)	Falcon; all virgin wool	$7.35/pr
Blankets	Montgomery Ward & Co. (1932)	All wool; double; extra heavy 6 1/2 lbs; size 70" x 80"	$4.48/pr
Borax	Sears, Roebuck (1932)	Muleteam; a wonderful and natural water softener for laundry work	$0.27/2 bxs
Bottle Opener and Resealer	New York Times Magazine (1931)	Spear-Cap; opens and reseals your milk bottle; made of frosted aluminum with nickel-silver spear	$0.10
Brace and Bit Set	Sears, Roebuck (1932)	Fulton; Brace, 7 auger bits, and screwdriver set	$2.80
Coffee Pot	Rock Hill Herald (Rock Hill, SC) (1933)		$0.50
Cookery Parchment	New York Times Magazine (1931)	Patapar; banishes cooking odors, improves flavors, saves food values	$0.10
Dinner Plates	Butler Brothers Sales Flier (1934)	Butler Brother; imported; plain white semi-porcelain	$0.84/dz

Item	Source	Description	Price
Fire Pails	*Curry Brothers Oil Company Catalogue* (1931)	Round bottom; made of steel, galvanized outside and inside and painted red outside; 10 1/2" x 10 1/2"	$8.55/dz
Flatware	*Sears, Roebuck* (1932)	*Rogers Bros.;* silver plate; 26-piece set	$28.45
Flatware	*Montgomery Ward & Co.* (1932)	*Rogers;* nickel-silver; made to withstand the constant handling of everyday service	$2.79
Grinder	*Popular Mechanics* (1933)	*Chicago Wheel & Mfg. Co. Handee;* just plug in and start grinding—electronically	$10
Hammer	*Curry Brothers Oil Company Catalogue* (1931)	*Stanley Atha Plain Face Adze Eye;* 13 1/2" length overall	$1.50/ea
Hammer	*Montgomery Ward & Co.* (1932)	Ball-peen; size 2/0—12 oz drop forged tempered head	$0.19
Ice Box	*San Francisco Examiner* (1932)	Ideal for the average family	$18.75
Lathe	*Popular Mechanics* (1933)	*Southbend;* back-geared, screw cutting precision lathes, 11" x 4'	$340
Leather Treatment	*Curry Brothers Oil Company Catalogue* (1931)	*Viscol Dressing;* softens and preserves shoes, harnesses, belts, and everything else made of leather; 1/4 pint cans	$2.23/dz
Light Bulbs	*Montgomery Ward & Co.* (1932)	40-watt bulb, package of eight	$1/pkg
Motor Grinder	*Popular Mechanics* (1933)	Powerful; operates on AC or DC, sturdy, durable, and Buffer quality built	$4.95
Oil	*Curry Brothers Oil Company Catalogue* (1931)	*3-In-One;* a blend of animal, mineral and vegetable oils, scientifically compounded 3 oz can 8 oz bottle	 $0.30 $0.60
Oriental Rug	*San Francisco Examiner* (1932)	Approximate size 9 x 12; the designs are exact copies of priceless Persian pieces	$119.00
Percolator	*Montgomery Ward & Co.* (1932)	9-cup; with guaranteed element and cord set; others ask $1.50	$1
Percolators	*Rock Hill Herald* (Rock Hill, SC) (1933)		$0.25–$0.30
Photography Light Bulb	*Collier's* (1934)	*General Electric Mazda;* photoflood; makes pictures easy to snap indoors	$0.35/ea
Pins	*Sears, Roebuck* (1932)	*Stewart's;* duplex safety pins; box of 6 dozen	$0.39/box
Rule	*Montgomery Ward & Co.* (1932)	*Lakeside;* flexible; length 6', graduated in 16ths; Swedish steel, tempered	$1.59
Salad Bowls	*Butler Brothers Sales Flier* (1934)	*Butler Brothers;* imported; embossed edge; 9 1/2" wide	$1.28/dz
Saw	*Montgomery Ward & Co.* (1932)	*Lakeside Champion Tooth;* one-man and supplementary handles; 3 1/2' length	$1.48
Screwdriver	*Curry Brothers Oil Company Catalogue* (1931)	*Tobrin;* machinists; 9 1/2" overall	$10/dz

Item	Source	Description	Price
Screwdriver	Montgomery Ward & Co. (1932)	Spiral Ratchet; works right or left, spiral or ratchet; two size bits	$1
Sheets	Montgomery Ward & Co. (1932)	Longwear; bleached; size before hemming 81" x 90"	$0.65/ea
Towels	Montgomery Ward & Co. (1932)	Cannon; fast-color borders	$1/12
Towels	Montgomery Ward & Co. (1932)	Cannon; only a few weeks ago, the identical quality sold for $0.85/6	$0.65/6
Towels	Sears, Roebuck (1932)	Cotton husk; beautiful border on an equally beautiful towel	$0.90/6
Varnish	Montgomery Ward & Co. (1932)	Diamond W; color; stains and varnishes in one brush stroke	$0.42/qt
Wood Filler	Popular Mechanics (1933)	Plastic Wood; this canned wood makes home repairs easy	$0.25/tube
Wrenches	Curry Brothers Oil Company Catalogue (1931)	Starrett; ratchet; for engineers, machinists, and motor mechanics; complete set	$15

Jewelry

Item	Source	Description	Price
Pocket Watch	Illinois Watch Catalogue (1930)	Man's 23-jewel railroad watch; 60 hour, 6 position, motor barrel 14K filled 14K solid	$90 $150
Pocket Watch	Montgomery Ward & Co. (1934)	Hamilton Railroad; the watch of railroad accuracy; 14K white-gold filled	$65
Pocket Watch	Montgomery Ward & Co. (1934)	Ingersoll Buck Rogers; Buck Rogers and Wilma are shown in action; the hands are shaped like cosmic rays	$0.75
Pocket Watch	Montgomery Ward & Co. (1934)	Ingersoll Mickey Mouse; "I keep time for 1 1/2 million happy children"; in a gift box	$1.50
Watch	Delineator (1928)	Elgin, the Madame Jenny; chic and styleful	$35.00
Wristwatch	Saturday Evening Post (1930)	Lady Elgin; the lowest price ever offered on such an Elgin watch	$25
Wristwatch	Montgomery Ward & Co. (1932)	Man's reliable 6-jewel Swiss movement	$5.98
Wristwatch	Sears, Roebuck (1932)	Elgin; Man's 15-Jewel; 14-karat solid white gold case	$33.25
Wristwatch	Montgomery Ward & Co. (1934)	Ingersoll Mickey Mouse; the demand is so heavy that there is often a scarcity	$2.95

Meals

Item	Source	Description	Price
Dinner	The Raleigh (NC) Times (1931)	Special Sunday Luncheon and Dinner at California Fruit Store Luncheon Dinner	$0.50 $0.75
Meal	Rock Hill Herald (Rock Hill, SC) (1932)	Southern Hotel and Dining Room; the best meal 35 cents can buy	$0.35

Item	Source	Description	Price
Sunday Dinner	*The Raleigh (NC) Times* (1931)	*Wilson's Coffee Shop* open Sundays, specialty juicy western steaks and chops	$0.45

Medical Products & Services

Item	Source	Description	Price
Camphor	*San Francisco Examiner* (1932)	Spirits of Camphor; 2 oz.	$0.13
Laxative	*Montgomery Ward & Co.* (1932)	*Milk of Magnesia;* mild laxative, antacid, and mouthwash	$0.46/2 btls
Mineral Oil	*Montgomery Ward & Co.* (1932)	Russian; colorless, odorless, pleasant to take	$0.83/qt
Soda	*San Francisco Examiner* (1932)	*Fleet's Phospho-soda*	$0.39
Thermometer	*Montgomery Ward & Co.* (1932)	Fever thermometer; tested according to U.S. Bureau of Standards; one-minute style	$0.79
Truss	*Montgomery Ward & Co.* (1932)	*Boston;* electric; for ordinary size ruptures; with leather-covered soft factis pads	$1.59

Motorized Vehicles, Services, & Supplies

Item	Source	Description	Price
Automobile	*Collier's* (1934)	*Reo Motor Car Co.;* why shackle yourself to a gearshift lever; the Reo self-shifter does it automatically	$795
Automobiles	*The Raleigh (NC) Times* (1931)	Low-priced specials: Used 1929 Olds Sedan Used 1927 Dodge, 4-door	 $275 $150
Automobile Cover	*Sears, Roebuck* (1932)	*Society Brand;* slip-on; no fasteners required	$1.45
Car Cleaner	*Sears, Roebuck* (1932)	*Simoniz Kleener;* it makes old cars look new; 12 oz. can	$0.44/can
Highway Flare Torches	*Curry Brothers Oil Company Catalogue* (1931)	Made of steel; will burn kerosene or light fuel oil	$24/dz
Jack	*Montgomery Ward & Co.* (1932)	Super-lift hydraulic; capacity 3,080 lbs; lifting range 7 1/2" to 15"	$3.29
Liquid Solder	*Collier's* (1934)	*Warner;* pour a can into the radiator; it finds all leaks and repairs them permanently	$0.50/can
Motor Oil	*Sears, Roebuck* (1932)	*Corona;* for all passenger cars and light trucks	$0.49/gal
Radio	*Collier's* (1934)	*Philco Auto;* featuring a full-size dynamic speaker, four-point tone control, more powerful	$55
Spark Plug	*Sears, Roebuck* (1932)	*Champion;* for Ford Model T	$0.55
Spark Plug	*Popular Mechanics* (1933)	*A. C. Spark Plug Co.;* always the quality spark plug offered at the lowest price in Canada	 $0.60 $0.75
Tire	*Sears, Roebuck* (1932)	*AllState;* 6-ply balloon; 31 x 6.50-19 fits Buick, 1930, 1931; Graham Paige 1928, 1929, 1930	$1.54
Tire and Tube	*Popular Mechanics* (1933)	*Goodyear Firestone Goodrich;* balloon tire; 30 x 5.25-20 size and rim Tire Tube	 $2.95 $1.15

Item	Source	Description	Price
Tire and Tube	*Popular Mechanics* (1933)	*Goodyear Firestone Goodrich;* cord tire; 32 x 4 Tire Tube	 $2.95 $0.85
Tire	*Montgomery Ward & Co.* (1932)	*Chevrolet;* 29 x 4.40-21; 4–ply balloons; order in pairs	$4.65/ea
Tire	*Montgomery Ward & Co.* (1932)	*Studebaker;* 31 x 6.50-19; 6–ply balloons; order in pairs	$11.92/ea
Wax	*Popular Mechanics* (1933)	*Johnson's Wax;* try this amazing new method on your car; enough for 4 or 5 waxings; adds $50–$200 to trade-in values	$0.35/can

Musical Instruments

Item	Source	Description	Price
Trombone	*The Raleigh (NC) Times* (1931)	Used sliding trombone, perfect Contact Raleigh Loan Office	$12.50

Other

Item	Source	Description	Price
Cooking Fuel	*Montgomery Ward & Co.* (1932)	*Sterno Canned Heat;* a clean dependable fuel that meets every light cooking need; normally $0.10 per can	$0.29/4 cans
Engine	*Popular Mechanics* (1933)	*Briggs-Stratton;* 1/2 horsepower, new	$27.50
Memory Course	*Popular Mechanics* (1933)	*Bott 15-Minute;* how to remember names, faces, numbers, etc.	$1
Microscope Outfit	*Popular Mechanics* (1933)	*J. W. Winn Manufacturing Co. Winnerset;* complete set contains 100x Wallensak precision-built microscope, dissecting scissors, blade and needle, professional slides, bottle of balsam, specimen jar, tweezers, pipette, book of lens paper, glass rod	$6
Motor	*Popular Mechanics* (1933)	*Dumore-Racine Universal;* with pulley, cord, and plug; operates on AC or DC, 110 volts	$1.95
Radio Tube	*Montgomery Ward & Co.* (1932)	*Trail Blazer;* four-prong tube for AC sets; replaces any tube with number ending in 25	$0.42/ea
Signs	*Curry Brothers Oil Company Catalogue* (1931)	*Line-O-Graph;* highway traffic and safety zone marks; operated by one man; eliminates hand painting	$150
Storage Battery	*Montgomery Ward & Co.* (1932)	*Riverside;* sturdy, leak-proof composition case with bail handle	$5.19
Valentines	*Montgomery Ward & Co.* (1932)	Cunning and colorful hearts with just the right verse; 16 cards	$0.25

Personal Care Products

Item	Source	Description	Price
Cold Cream	*Montgomery Ward & Co.* (1932)	*Tre-Jur;* cleans the pores and leaves the skin smooth and glowing; 1 lb jar	$0.49
Comb	*Sears, Roebuck* (1932)	Lightweight dressing; especially suitable for ladies with medium length hair	$0.33
Hair Clipper	*Sears, Roebuck* (1932)	*Brown and Sharpe;* the choice of professional barbers	$3.87
Hair Color Treatment	*Montgomery Ward & Co.* (1932)	*Mary T. Goldman;* slate color	$1.29/btl
Hair Cut	*Rock Hill Herald* (Rock Hill, SC) (1933)	*Sanitary Barber Shop,* Rock Hill, South Carolina; why not have the best at this reduced price	$0.20

Item	Source	Description	Price
Hair Lotion	*Montgomery Ward & Co.* (1932)	*Bay Rum;* buy one bottle at Ward's usual low price, $0.36, and get another free	$0.36/2 btls
Hair Tonic	*Montgomery Ward & Co.* (1932)	*Lucky Tiger;* with a free comb	$0.79
Hand Cream	*Montgomery Ward & Co.* (1932)	*Pacquin's;* delightful for chapped hands or face	$0.74
Lotion	*Collier's* (1934)	*Zemo For Skin Irritation;* itching stops the moment Zemo touches the tender and inflamed skin; to clear away rashes, pimples, eczema, ringworm and restore skin	$0.35/$0.60/$1
Powder	*San Francisco Examiner* (1932)	LaBlache face powder	$0.33
Sanitary Napkin	*Sears, Roebuck* (1932)	*Kotex;* the ideal comfort napkin	$0.85/dz
Sanitary Pads	*Montgomery Ward & Co.* (1932)	*Modess;* famous Johnson & Johnson Red Cross quality	$1/5 bxs
Shampoo	*Montgomery Ward & Co.* (1932)	Coconut oil; the favorite of many thousands of our customers; three 50¢ bottles	$0.49
Shave Cream	*Collier's* (1934)	*Colgate Rapid;* dewaterproof your whiskers and make shaving easier; large size tube	$0.25
Soap	*Montgomery Ward & Co.* (1932)	*Woodbury Castile;* made from pure imported Spanish olive oil; bars	$0.57/4

Publications

Item	Source	Description	Price
Book	*Popular Mechanics* (1933)	*Popular Chemistry Experiment Book;* for junior chemists, adopted by the New York Public Library	$0.50
Magazine	*Popular Mechanics* (1933)	*Popular Mechanics* magazine; monthly	$0.25
Newspaper	*The Raleigh (NC) Times* (1931)	One-year subscription to *The Raleigh Times*, published every evening except Sunday By carrier By mail	 $7.50 $6.00

Real Estate

Item	Source	Description	Price
Apartment	*San Francisco Examiner* (1932)	Furnished; 45th Avenue; sunny four rooms; two beds	$25/mo
Room	*The Raleigh (NC) Times* (1931)	Heated room with board, 102 New Bern Avenue Per week	 $7.00

Sewing Equipment & Supplies

Item	Source	Description	Price
Cloth	*Montgomery Ward & Co.* (1932)	Cotton outing flannel; soft, warmly fleeced on both sides; we've slashed the price and then thrown in 2 extra yards	$1/12 yds
Cloth	*Montgomery Ward & Co.* (1932)	Silk and cotton crepe; here are the prints that will be worn this spring and summer	$0.35/yd
Cloth	*Montgomery Ward & Co.* (1932)	*Gold Stripe;* stifel rawhide; copper-riveted western style	$0.95/yd
Knitting Yarn	*Sears, Roebuck* (1932)	*Golden Crown;* a 4-fold yarn mixture of pure wool and rayon	$0.17

Item	Source	Description	Price
Sewing Machine	*Montgomery Ward & Co.* (1932)	*Brunswick;* prices haven't been this low since 1923; golden oak, 5 drawers	$19.95

Sports Equipment

Item	Source	Description	Price
Baseball	*Sears, Roebuck* (1932)	*J. C. Higgins;* official outseam playground and diamond ball	$0.95
Binoculars	*Sears, Roebuck* (1932)	*Dr. Wobler's;* for sportsmen, marine, or mountain use	$33.48
Boat	*Popular Mechanics* (1933)	*Hammond Lumber Co. Wilson Fold-Flat;* wooden; fold in one minute; carry on running board; 10'; weight 80 lbs; price FOB Los Angeles; slightly higher New York or Chicago	$39
Canoe	*Collier's* (1934)	*Old Town Canoe Co.;* a graceful sweep of cedar, tight planked, strong ribbed, covered with water-tight canvas	$68
Fish Hooks	*Sears, Roebuck* (1932)	Eyed; assorted sizes and patterns	$0.23/100
Fishing Line	*Sears, Roebuck* (1932)	*King Fisher Black Wonder;* silk; extra hard braided	$1.35
Golf Ball	*Sears, Roebuck* (1932)	*Aristo;* built to improve the game	$0.59
Knife	*Sears, Roebuck* (1932)	*Official Boy Scout;* full size 3 5/8", bone stag handle	$1.23
Shotgun	*Sears, Roebuck* (1932)	*Fox Sterlingworth;* double barrel; fitted with Jostam antiflinch recoil pad	$36.98
Tent	*Sears, Roebuck* (1932)	Boy's camp tent; 5' x 7' with 2' side walls and 4' 8" height at center	$4.95

Telephone Equipment & Services

Item	Source	Description	Price
Long Distance Rates	John Brooks, *Telephone: The First Hundred Years* (1987)	*Bell Telephone;* New York to London [cost in 1930]	$30/3 min

Tobacco Products

Item	Source	Description	Price
Cigarettes	*Collier's* (1934)	*Kool Mild Menthol;* a new champion in throat comfort	$0.15/pk
Pipe	*Popular Mechanics* (1933)	*Drinkless Kaywoodie Presidential Model;* by actual measurement 51% purer smoke, 51% better taste from your tobacco	$3.50
Pony Clamps	*Popular Mechanics* (1933)	*Jorgensen Pony;* fittings go on ordinary 3/4" pipe to make clamps of any length	$3
Smoking Tobacco	*Popular Mechanics* (1933)	*Brown & Williamson Tobacco Corp. Sir Walter Raleigh;* for pipe and cigarettes	$0.15/tin

Toys

Item	Source	Description	Price
Bicycle	*Sears, Roebuck* (1932)	*Peerless Junior;* strongly built for safety	$17.50
Croquet Set	*Sears, Roebuck* (1932)	Deluxe; others ask as much as $7.50 for this set	$3.98
Junior Caster Outfit	*Rapaport Catalogue* (1934)	Make your own metal toys; U.S. soldier outfit, baseball player outfit	$2.25
Wagon	*Sears, Roebuck* (1932)	*Chummy Coaster;* child's full size body, 14 3/4" x 33 3/4" of 20 gauge auto steel	$3.69

Travel & Transportation

Item	Source	Description	Price
Bus Excursion	*The Raleigh (NC) Times* (1931)	Weekend bus trips, roundtrip from Raleigh, North Carolina to Wilmington, North Carolina	$3.90
		Charleston, South Carolina	$7.20
		Richmond, Virginia	$4.30
		Washington, D.C.	$7.00

MISCELLANY 1930-1934

Old Money Wanted

Will pay fifty dollars for nickel of 1913 with Liberty head (no buffalo). We pay cash premiums for all rare coins. Send 4¢ for large coin folder.

Popular Mechanics, October 1933

To the Stockholders of Woodside Cotton Mills Company

Your Board of Directors, at a meeting held this day, decided that in view of the depressed condition of the cotton textile business throughout the country and its effect on the earnings of this company during the past six months, it is important that all the resources of the company be conserved to the fullest at this time, and that it would be unwise to declare and pay any dividends on the common and preferred stocks this July.

Letter from Woodside Cotton Mills Company,
Greenville, S.C., June 26, 1930

Why I Change To Marlboro Contest

I smoked 15-cent cigarettes until I realized that only a few cents are left to buy tobacco—considering the 6 percent per package U.S. tax and tremendous advertising expenditures.

I smoke Marlboros because they are better—better not because of a more clever catchword or slogan—but better because that extra nickel buys better tobacco. Irwin Shaffer, New York.

New York Times Magazine, October 25, 1931

F. Scott Fitzgerald's Income

F. Scott Fitzgerald's income in 1931 was $37,599. His income statement included nine magazine stories, for which he was paid $4,000 each—minus a 10 percent commission. Royalties from his books that year included $12.90 for *This Side of Paradise* and $17.90 for *The Great Gatsby.* 1931 was Fitzgerald's best year of earnings before he went permanently to Hollywood in 1937.

The Romantic Egoists: Pictorial
Autobiography from the Scrapbooks
and Albums of Scott and Zelda Fitzgerald

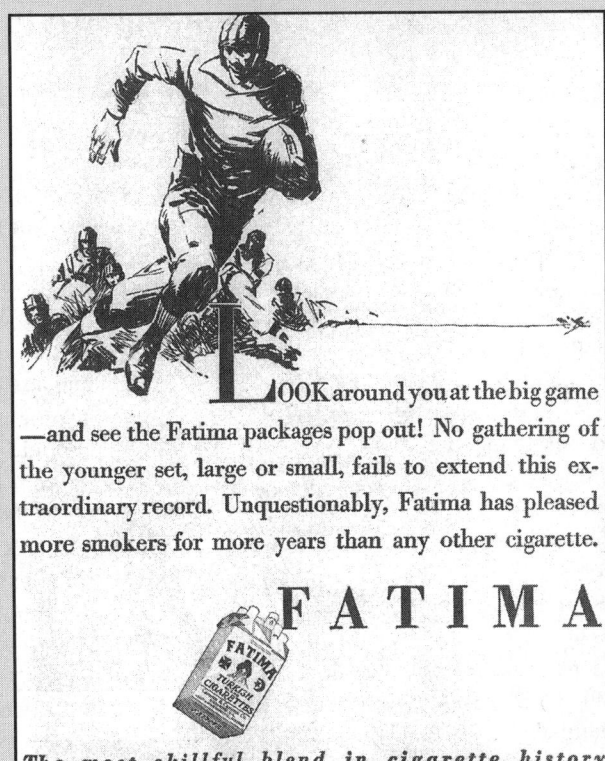

LOOK around you at the big game —and see the Fatima packages pop out! No gathering of the younger set, large or small, fails to extend this extraordinary record. Unquestionably, Fatima has pleased more smokers for more years than any other cigarette.

FATIMA

The most skillful blend in cigarette history

LIGGETT & MYERS TOBACCO CO.

Mention of Harper's Magazine is the best introduction to our advertisers

Joseph Aiello

Joseph Aiello and his brothers, Dominick, Antonio, and Andrew, were enemies of Al Capone in the struggle for control of organized crime in Chicago. Aiello tried to have Capone killed in somewhat novel ways, e.g., attempting to bribe a restaurant chef $10,000 to put prussic acid in Capone's soup and, on another occasion, offering a reward of $50,000 for Big Al's head. These efforts called for extraordinary vengeance on Capone's part and he ordered his enemy killed "real good." On October 23, 1930 Aiello was gunned down on North Kolmar Avenue, struck by 59 bullets, weighing altogether well over a pound.

The Encyclopedia of American Crime, June 1934

HISTORICAL SNAPSHOT
1935-1939

1935
- Social Security Act passed by Congress
- Emergency Relief Appropriation Act authorizes $5 billion to create jobs
- Fort Knox becomes repository for U.S. gold bullion
- Kodachrome color film introduced by Eastman Kodak Company
- One-tenth of 1 percent of U.S. corporations earn 50 percent of all corporate income
- Sulfa-drug chemotherapy introduced
- Nylon developed by E. I. Du Pont Corp.
- General Telephone Corporation created
- Beer in cans introduced
- 240 million cases of canned goods shipped
- One-third of farmers receive U.S. Treasury allotment checks for not growing food or crops

1936
- 38 percent of families have incomes of less than $1,000 a year
- Population reaches 127 million
- Ford's V-8 engine unveiled

- *Life* magazine begins publication
- New York's Triborough Bridge opens; charges 25¢ toll
- Mercedes-Benz creates first diesel-fuel passenger car

1937
- United Automobile Workers recognized by General Motors as sole bargaining agent for employees
- Principle of minimum wage for women upheld by Supreme Court
- Packard Motor Car Company sells a record 109,000 cars
- General Motors introduces automatic transmission
- Icemen continue to make regular deliveries to more than 50 percent of middle-class households
- Spam introduced by George A. Hormel & Co.
- *Popular Photography* magazine begins publication

1938
- Congress's wage-and-hour law limits work week to 44 hours
- Recovery stumbles, Wall Street's Dow Jones Industrials Average falls to 98.95

- Eastern Airlines created
- Owens-Corning Fiberglass Corporation is incorporated to produce products utilizing newly developed fiberglass
- First high-definition color television demonstrated
- Ballpoint pen patented
- Consumption of beef and dairy produce increases by 3 percent
- First Xerox image produced
- First nylon stockings go on sale

1939
- World War II begins in Europe
- New York's La Guardia Airport opens
- Only 3 percent of Americans qualify to pay income tax
- 42,500 taxpayers declare incomes of more than $25,000
- 5-minute Cream of Wheat introduced
- First food stamp program instituted in Rochester, NY
- 25 percent of American workers are farmers
- Pesticide DDT introduced for crops
- 13,500 motels and tourist courts in business

SELECTED INCOME 1935-1939

Job	Source	Description	Pay
Accountant	*Atlanta Constitution* (1937)	For large local concern, age 25 to 30. Must know general accounting, and be familiar with tax work.	$150/wk
Actor	Lee O. Miller, *The Great Cowboy Stars of Movies and Television*	Income in 1938 of William Boyd, better known as Hopalong Cassidy, for eight films	$100,000
Advertising Executive	*Time* (1939)	Annual compensation of Eddie Bernays, promoter of products for Proctor & Gamble	$25,000
Banker	*New York Herald* (1935)	Senior Accountant, factoring or finance experience	$2,600/yr
Bookkeepers	*New York Times* (1936)	Complete charge or assistants	$8–$25/wk
Comic Strip Artist	*Literary Digest* (1936)	Income in 1936 of Bud Fisher for his comic strip *Mutt and Jeff*	$93,600
Cook	*Atlanta Constitution* (1935)	Colored cooks, maids for North Side jobs	$6–$10/wk
Dentist	*New York Times* (1938)	Dentist seeks position, experienced contractor and extractor, careful operator, expert inlays, personality	$40/mo
Draftsman	*Chicago Tribune* (1936)	Sheet metal experience	$125/mo
Driver	*Atlanta Constitution* (1935)	Local tea and coffee route	$60/wk
Engineer	*New York Herald* (1935)	Aircraft designers	$40–$55/wk
Nurse	*New York Times* (1936)	Situation wanted. English; American graduate (24); to care for invalid lady; will travel; New York references	$90/mo
Photographer	*New York Times* (1938)	Commercial still life; bring samples, complete charge	$25/wk
Railway Postal Clerk	*Mechanics Illustrated* (1938)	First year pay; requires travel; clerks on long runs work three days on then three days off	$1,900
Receptionist	*New York Times* (1938)	Attractive college graduate, well poised, good personality	$15/wk
Route Driver	*Atlanta Constitution* (1936)	Automobile offered as bonus for covering local coffee route	$45/wk
Sales	*Atlanta Constitution* (1935)	Ladies wanted immediately to demonstrate actual samples of snag-proofed hosiery to friends	$22/wk206
Sales	*New York Herald* (1935)	Marine Oil Sales Supervisor, under 40, out-of-town	$4,000/yr
Sales	*Chicago Tribune* (1936)	Married man over 35 yrs to call on new and old customers for 75-year-old house furnishings concern. Must have good references. Car furnished and satisfied with commission	$25–$30/wk
Sales	*Chicago Tribune* (1936)	Auto parts	$1,800/yr
Stenographer	*Atlanta Constitution* (1939)	Large North Georgia manufacturer has position available as Assistant Secretary to President	$109/wk
Stenographer-Bookkeeper	*New York Times* (1936)	Intelligent	$12/wk

Job	Source	Description	Pay
Teacher	*Atlanta Constitution* (1939)	Degree men, teach mathematics and coaching	$95/wk
Teacher	*Atlanta Constitution* (1939)	Degree women, grades 2 to 7	$70–$90/wk
Writer	Catherine and Legrand and Robyn Karney, *Chronicle of the Cinema* (1995)	Payment by Metro-Goldwyn-Mayer in 1936 to Margaret Mitchell for movie rights to her book Gone With The Wind	$50,000

CONSUMER EXPENDITURES 1935-1939

(Per Capita)

Expenditure Type	1935	1936	1937	1938	1939
Clothing	$39.26	$42.13	$42.65	$42.32	$45.03
Auto Usage	$33.76	$39.01	$41.87	$34.62	$39.69
New Auto Purchase	$11.78	$14.82	$15.51	$9.23	$12.21
Auto Parts	$3.14	$3.12	$3.10	$3.08	$3.82
Gas & Oil	$13.35	$14.82	$16.28	$16.16	$16.79
Housing	$62.03	$63.97	$68.24	$70.79	$71.74
Furniture	$5.49	$6.24	$6.98	$6.16	$6.87
Utilities	$21.98	$23.40	$23.26	$23.08	$23.66
Telephone & Telegraph	$3.93	$3.90	$3.88	$3.85	$4.58
Physicians	$5.49	$5.43	$6.16	$6.92	$6.87
Dentists	$2.36	$2.34	$3.10	$3.08	$3.05
Health Insurance	79¢	78¢	78¢	77¢	$1.53
Personal Business	$22.77	$24.18	$25.59	$23.85	$24.42
Personal Care	$6.28	$7.02	$7.75	$7.69	$7.63
Tobacco	$10.99	$11.70	$13.18	$13.08	$13.74
Local Transport	$6.28	$6.24	$6.98	$6.16	$6.87
Intercity Transport	$2.36	$2.34	$3.10	$2.31	$3.05
Recreation	$20.41	$23.40	$26.36	$24.62	$26.71
Religion/Welfare Activities	$7.07	$7.02	$6.98	$7.69	$7.63
Private Education & Research	$3.93	$3.90	$4.65	$4.62	$4.58
Per Capita Consumption	$438.12	$483.69	$517.21	$493.19	$511.34

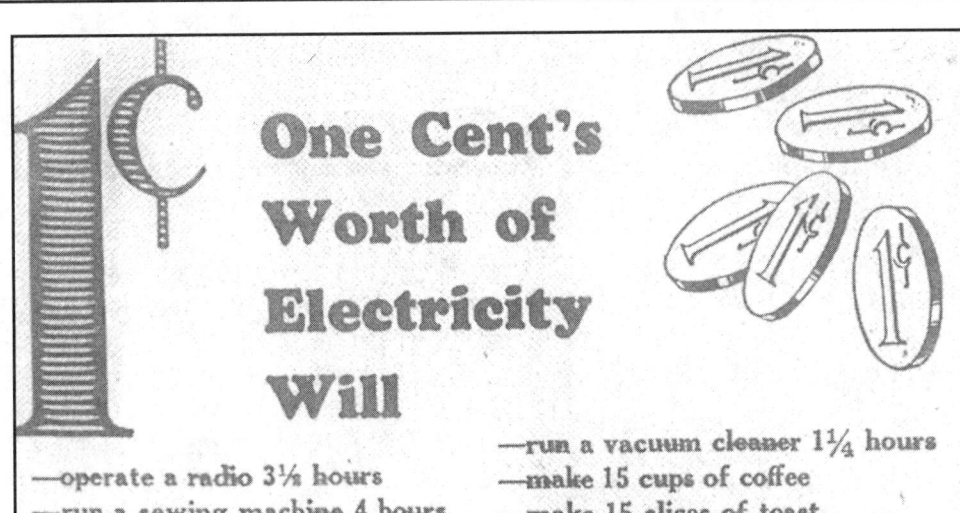

INVESTMENTS 1935-1939

Investment	1935	1936	1937	1938	1939
Basic Yield, One-Year Corporate Bonds	1.05	.61	.69	.85	.57
Short-Term Interest Rates, 4–6 Months, Prime Commercial Paper	.75	.75	.94	.81	.59
Basic Yield, Common Stocks, Total (Moody's)	4.01	3.50	4.63	4.30	4.14
Index of Common Stocks (1941–1943=10)	10.60	15.47	15.41	11.49	12.06

COMMON STOCKS, CLOSING PRICE AND YIELD, FIRST BUSINESS DAY OF YEAR

(Parenthetical number is annual dividend in dollars)

	1935	1936	1937	1938	1939
Allis Chalmers	17 1/8	36 1/2	77 3/4	46 1/2	47 3/8
			(1 1/2)	(3.50)	(1.50)
AT&T	105 3/8	158 3/4	185	144 3/4	150
	(9)	(9)	(9)	(9)	(9)
American Tobacco	82 3/4	97 3/8	95	60 3/4	86
	(5)	(5)	(5)	(5)	(5)
Anaconda	11 3/4	29 1/2	53 3/8	29	35 1/4
			(1)	(1.75)	(.50)
B&O	13 7/8	16 1/2	21 1/8	9	8 3/8
Bethlehem Steel	32 1/4	52 1/2	74 7/8	58	79 7/8
			(1 1/2)	(5)	
Corn Products	63 3/4	69 1/2	67	59 1/4	66 1/2
	(3)	(3)	(3)	(3)	(3)
General Electric	22 1/8	38	53 3/4	40 3/4	43 1/2
	(.60)	(.70)	(1)	(2.20)	(.90)
General Motors	34 1/8	55 3/4	62 1/8	29 1/8	50 3/8
	(1)	(2)	(3 1/4)	(3.75)	(1.50)
International Business Machines	152	176 1/2			184 1/4
(2% stock dividend, 1/10/35)	(5)	(6)			(6)
(3% stock dividend, 2/10/36)					
(5% stock dividend, 4/1/37)					
(5% stock dividend, 4/1/38)					
(5% stock dividend, 4/1/39)					
Intl Harvester	43 5/8	61 1/2	105 3/8	61 1/8	59
	(.60)	(1.20)	(2 1/2)	(4)	(1.92 1/2)
National Biscuit	29	33 5/8	31 7/8	18 1/8	25 3/8
	(2)	(1.60)	(1.60)	(1.60)	(1.60)
U.S. Steel	38 1/4	49 3/8	76 1/4	53	
Western Union	33 7/8	74 1/4	77 1/2	24 5/8	
		(2)	(2 3/4)	(2.25)	

STANDARD JOBS 1935-1939

Job Type	1935	1936	1937	1938	1939
Average of all Industries, excl. farm labor	$1195/yr	$1226/yr	$1341/yr	$1303/yr	$1346/yr
Average of all Industries, incl. farm labor	$1115/yr	$1146/yr	$1259/yr	$1221/yr	$1266/yr
Bituminous Coal Mining	$957/yr	$1103/yr	$1170/yr	$1050/yr	$1197/yr
Building Trades	$1027/yr	$1178/yr	$1278/yr	$1193/yr	$1268/yr
Domestics	$485/yr	$506/yr	$558/yr	$527/yr	$544/yr
Farm Labor	$324/yr	$351/yr	$407/yr	$420/yr	$436/yr
Federal Civilian	$1759/yr	$1896/yr	$1797/yr	$1832/yr	$1843/yr
Federal Employees, Executive Depts.	$1183/yr	$1112/yr	$1188/yr	$1149/yr	$1137/yr
Federal Military	$1154/yr	$1152/yr	$1132/yr	$1120/yr	$1134/yr
Finance, Insurance, & Real Estate	$1632/yr	$1713/yr	$1788/yr	$1731/yr	$1729/yr
Gas & Electricity Workers	$1589/yr	$1615/yr	$1705/yr	$1749/yr	$1766/yr
Manufacturing, Durable Goods	$1264/yr	$1376/yr	$1491/yr	$1365/yr	$1479/yr
Manufacturing, Nondurable Goods	$1178/yr	$1210/yr	$1267/yr	$1241/yr	$1263/yr
Medical/Health Services Workers	$829/yr	$851/yr	$876/yr	$899/yr	$908/yr
Miscellaneous Manufacturing	$1244/yr	$1298/yr	$1359/yr	$1274/yr	$1337/yr
Motion Picture Services	$1892/yr	$1896/yr	$1972/yr	$1942/yr	$1971/yr
Nonprofit Org. Workers	$1435/yr	$1465/yr	$1497/yr	$1529/yr	$1546/yr
Passenger Transportation Workers, Local and Highway	$1361/yr	$1433/yr	$1505/yr	$1529/yr	$1569/yr
Personal Services	$915/yr	$940/yr	$978/yr	$992/yr	$1034/yr
Public School Teachers	$1293/yr	$1329/yr	$1367/yr	$1406/yr	$1403/yr
Radio Broadcasting & Television Workers	$2089/yr	$2223/yr	$2361/yr	$2497/yr	$2427/yr
Railroads	$1645/yr	$1724/yr	$1774/yr	$1849/yr	$1877/yr
State and Local Govt. Workers	$1361/yr	$1433/yr	$1505/yr	$1529/yr	$1569/yr
Telephone & Telegraph Workers	$1378/yr	$1420/yr	$1481/yr	$1580/yr	$1600/yr
Wholesale and Retail Trade Workers	$1279/yr	$1295/yr	$1352/yr	$1352/yr	$1360/yr

FOOD BASKET 1935-1939

(NR=Not Reported)

Commodity	Year	New York	Atlanta	Chicago	Denver	Los Angeles
Apples, Fresh, per pound	1935	6.50¢	5.50¢	6.50¢	5.90¢	6.20¢
	1936	6.40¢	5.80¢	6.50¢	6.10¢	6.10¢
	1937	NR	NR	NR	NR	NR
	1938	NR	NR	NR	NR	NR
	1939	NR	NR	NR	NR	NR
Beans, Navy, per pound	1935	8.30¢	7.10¢	6¢	6.98¢	7.40¢
	1936	8.90¢	7¢	6.50¢	6.70¢	8¢
	1937	NR	NR	NR	NR	NR
	1938	NR	NR	NR	NR	NR
	1939	NR	NR	NR	NR	NR
Beef, Rib Roasts, per pound	1935	34.10¢	29.20¢	32.20¢	24.20¢	27.60¢
	1936	31.80¢	29.50¢	31.60¢	24.70¢	27.40¢
	1937	NR	NR	NR	NR	NR
	1938	NR	NR	NR	NR	NR
	1939	NR	NR	NR	NR	NR
Beef, Steaks (Round), per pound	1935	39.20¢	36.20¢	34.70¢	31¢	31.30¢
	1936	36.80¢	35.70¢	33.50¢	30.90¢	31.40¢
	1937	NR	NR	NR	NR	NR
	1938	NR	NR	NR	NR	NR
	1939	NR	NR	NR	NR	NR
Bread, White, per loaf	1935	5.60¢	5.60¢	5.20¢	4.10¢	4.50¢
	1936	5.20¢	5.10¢	4.80¢	3.80¢	4.30¢
	1937	NR	NR	NR	NR	NR
	1938	NR	NR	NR	NR	NR
	1939	NR	NR	NR	NR	NR
Butter, per pound	1935	37.10¢	37.50¢	35.60¢	35.40¢	36.50¢
	1936	40.50¢	40¢	39.20¢	38.80¢	39.10¢
	1937	NR	NR	NR	NR	NR
	1938	NR	NR	NR	NR	NR
	1939	NR	NR	NR	NR	NR
Cheese, per pound	1935	28.90¢	24.20¢	28.60¢	27.40¢	27.10¢
	1936	30.50¢	24.50¢	30.40¢	28.50¢	27.70¢
	1937	NR	NR	NR	NR	NR
	1938	NR	NR	NR	NR	NR
	1939	NR	NR	NR	NR	NR
Chickens, per pound	1935	31.80¢	25.10¢	30.30¢	26.50¢	33¢
	1936	33.50¢	26.10¢	32¢	28.90¢	35¢
	1937	NR	NR	NR	NR	NR
	1938	NR	NR	NR	NR	NR
	1939	NR	NR	NR	NR	NR
Coffee, per pound	1935	26¢	24.30¢	26.20¢	30.90¢	28.70¢
	1936	24.50¢	22.90¢	24.70¢	31.80¢	27.30¢
	1937	NR	NR	NR	NR	NR
	1938	NR	NR	NR	NR	NR
	1939	NR	NR	NR	NR	NR
Cornmeal, per pound	1935	6.30¢	3¢	6.10¢	5.40¢	5.10¢
	1936	6.50¢	3¢	6.10¢	5.20¢	4.90¢
	1937	NR	NR	NR	NR	NR
	1938	NR	NR	NR	NR	NR
	1939	NR	NR	NR	NR	NR

Commodity	Year	New York	Atlanta	Chicago	Denver	Los Angeles
Eggs, per dozen	1935	44.20¢	34.60¢	35.60¢	37.10¢	35¢
	1936	43.80¢	34.10¢	36.20¢	35.90¢	32¢
	1937	NR	NR	NR	NR	NR
	1938	NR	NR	NR	NR	NR
	1939	NR	NR	NR	NR	NR
Flour, Wheat, per pound	1935	5.60¢	5.10¢	5.20¢	4.10¢	4¢
	1936	5.20¢	5.10¢	4.80¢	3.80¢	4.30¢
	1937	NR	NR	NR	NR	NR
	1938	NR	NR	NR	NR	NR
	1939	NR	NR	NR	NR	NR
Lard, per pound	1935	19.90¢	19.50¢	19.50¢	20.80¢	22¢
	1936	17.90¢	16¢	17¢	17.40¢	16.30¢
	1937	NR	NR	NR	NR	NR
	1938	NR	NR	NR	NR	NR
	1939	NR	NR	NR	NR	NR
Milk, Fresh, per quart	1935	13¢	14¢	10.70¢	10.80¢	11.20¢
	1936	13.10¢	14.40¢	11.40¢	10.80¢	10.90¢
	1937	NR	NR	NR	NR	NR
	1938	NR	NR	NR	NR	NR
	1939	NR	NR	NR	NR	NR
Molasses, per gallon	1935	15.70¢	14.70¢	14.40¢	12.60¢	14.10¢
	1936	14.70¢	14.90¢	14.40¢	12.10¢	13.40¢
	1937	NR	NR	NR	NR	NR
	1938	NR	NR	NR	NR	NR
	1939	NR	NR	NR	NR	NR
Mutton and Lamb, Leg, per pound	1935	27.80¢	26¢	28.30¢	24.60¢	26.20¢
	1936	29.10¢	28.20¢	29.70¢	26.20¢	27.60¢
	1937	NR	NR	NR	NR	NR
	1938	NR	NR	NR	NR	NR
	1939	NR	NR	NR	NR	NR
Pork Chops, per pound	1935	36¢	33.20¢	36¢	33.40¢	40.10¢
	1936	34.90¢	32.50¢	34.10¢	32.20¢	39.10¢
	1937	NR	NR	NR	NR	NR
	1938	NR	NR	NR	NR	NR
	1939	NR	NR	NR	NR	NR
Pork, Bacon, Sliced, per pound	1935	42.40¢	38.90¢	43¢	40.40¢	44.60¢
	1936	42.10¢	38.90¢	42.80¢	41.20¢	43.20¢
	1937	NR	NR	NR	NR	NR
	1938	NR	NR	NR	NR	NR
	1939	NR	NR	NR	NR	NR
Pork, Salt, Dry or Pickled, per pound	1935	31.90¢	26.30¢	31¢	26.80¢	29.70¢
	1936	31.20¢	24.20¢	30.10¢	26¢	28.70¢
	1937	NR	NR	NR	NR	NR
	1938	NR	NR	NR	NR	NR
	1939	NR	NR	NR	NR	NR
Pork, Ham, Sliced, per pound	1935	47.30¢	46.80¢	46.40¢	47.80¢	60.40¢
	1936	48.40¢	49.40¢	50.50¢	51.50¢	63.30¢
	1937	NR	NR	NR	NR	NR
	1938	NR	NR	NR	NR	NR
	1939	NR	NR	NR	NR	NR
Pork, Salt, Ham, per pound	1935	31.90¢	26.30¢	31¢	26.80¢	29.70¢
	1936	31.20¢	24.20¢	30.10¢	26¢	28.70¢
	1937	NR	NR	NR	NR	NR
	1938	NR	NR	NR	NR	NR
	1939	NR	NR	NR	NR	NR
Potatoes, Irish, per pound	1935	2.10¢	2.20¢	2.20¢	2.10¢	2.30¢
	1936	3.50¢	3.60¢	3.30¢	3.10¢	3.50¢
	1937	NR	NR	NR	NR	NR
	1938	NR	NR	NR	NR	NR
	1939	NR	NR	NR	NR	NR

Commodity	Year	New York	Atlanta	Chicago	Denver	Los Angeles
Prunes, Dried, per pound	1935	10.80¢	10.80¢	12.30¢	11.90¢	9.80¢
	1936	9.70¢	9.90¢	11.10¢	10.20¢	8.90¢
	1937	NR	NR	NR	NR	NR
	1938	NR	NR	NR	NR	NR
	1939	NR	NR	NR	NR	NR
Rice, per pound	1935	8.80¢	7.90¢	8.50¢	8.40¢	8.80¢
	1936	8.90¢	8.40¢	9.10¢	8.90¢	9.40¢
	1937	NR	NR	NR	NR	NR
	1938	NR	NR	NR	NR	NR
	1939	NR	NR	NR	NR	NR
Sugar, per pound	1935	5.40¢	5.90¢	5.80¢	6¢	5.20¢
	1936	5.40¢	5.70¢	5.80¢	6.10¢	5.10¢
	1937	NR	NR	NR	NR	NR
	1938	NR	NR	NR	NR	NR
	1939	NR	NR	NR	NR	NR
Tea, per pound	1935	64.60¢	76.50¢	81.10¢	78.50¢	74.90¢
	1936	66.10¢	76.90¢	83.20¢	83.10¢	77.40¢
	1937	NR	NR	NR	NR	NR
	1938	NR	NR	NR	NR	NR
	1939	NR	NR	NR	NR	NR
Veal, per pound	1935	44.20¢	36.80¢	36.80¢	34.20¢	41¢
	1936	46.80¢	39.10¢	39¢	35.80¢	42.60¢
	1937	NR	NR	NR	NR	NR
	1938	NR	NR	NR	NR	NR
	1939	NR	NR	NR	NR	NR

SELECTED PRICES 1935-1939

Item	Source	Description	Price
Appliances			
Coffee Mill	*Time* (1939)	*Kitchen Aid Electric Coffee Mill* for the home	$9.75
Fan	*Goodyear Spring and Summer Catalog* (1937)	*Samson Safe-Flex Home Fan;* 30% more breeze and even baby's fingers are safe	$2.90
Fan	*Sears, Roebuck* (1939)	*Cold Wave;* oscillating; guaranteed five years if oiled twice each season	$5.50
Kitchen Range	*Sears, Roebuck* (1939)	Easy cleaning; lustrous surfaces everywhere	$76.95
Refrigerator	*Sears, Roebuck* (1939)	*Cold Spot;* kerosene; costs only $0.04 to $0.07 per day to operate	$169.50
Refrigerator	*Sears, Roebuck* (1939)	*Polar Air;* air-conditioned ice; modern in style and efficiency—a $40 value	$22.98
Stove	*Sears, Roebuck* (1938)	Cast iron; big pull-out hearth for quick firing or easy emptying of ashes	$29.85
Toaster	*Sears, Roebuck* (1938)	*Heatmaster;* record-smashing value	$1.85
Vacuum Cleaner	*Sears, Roebuck* (1938)	*Kenmore DeLuxe;* triple-action cleaning; beating sweeping suction	$31.45
Washing Machine	*Sears, Roebuck* (1939)	*Challenger;* gasoline; does a big day's wash for less than a dime	$39.95
Apparel, Children's			
Slacks	*Sears, Roebuck* (1939)	Boy's; Sanforized-shrunk, heavy weight, washable, deep tone, cotton twill	$0.98
Suit	*Sears, Roebuck* (1939)	Boy's; double-breasted; 1-knicker suit, 40% wool, balance rayon, cotton	$4.98
Apparel, Men's			
Hat	*Collier's* (1938)	*Stetson;* stag brown; he doesn't see how he could afford to wear anything else	$5 to $10
Shoes	*Collier's* (1938)	*Florsheim Brookfield Style;* we lowered the price and raised the value	$8.75
Shoes	*Collier's* (1938)	*Bostonian;* they're walk fitted	$7.50 to $11
Shorts	*Sears, Roebuck* (1938)	Cotton broadcloth; they won't shrink out of fit or rip	$0.22
Sleeping Robe	*Hunting and Life* (1936)	*Woods Arctic Down;* your Woods robe keeps all warmth in, all cold out; large size	$62.50
Socks	*Sears, Roebuck* (1939)	All wool; for work	$0.28
Suit	*Sears, Roebuck* (1939)	Cassimere; herringbone with an overplaid, in a strong all-wool fabric	$13.95
Tie	*Sears, Roebuck* (1939)	Fine rayon	$0.23
Apparel, Women's			
Charmode	*Sears, Roebuck* (1939)	All-in-one; fits as though it were made for you alone	$2.89

Item	Source	Description	Price
Corset	*Sears, Roebuck* (1939)	Maternity; perfectly designed for correct support before childbirth	$2.98
Dress	*Sears, Roebuck* (1939)	Maternity; spun rayon	$2.98
Frock	*Sears, Roebuck* (1938)	*Eileen Drury;* all-rayon French-type drape	$1.98
Girdle	*Sears, Roebuck* (1939)	Soft-textured 2-way stretch dura-latex	$0.79
Hose	*Time* (1939)	*Davencrepes by Humming Bird;* America's high-style hosiery; every inch is guarded by invisible extra silk Per pair	$1.15
Shoes	*Time* (1939)	*Matrix Originals,* your footprint in leather; oh so comfortable Per pair	$10.00
Slip	*Sears, Roebuck* (1938)	Silk crepe; with shadowproof panels	$1.55
Stockings	*Sears, Roebuck* (1939)	Silk; the same quality that's around $0.29 in most other stores	$0.21

Baby Products

Carriage	*Sears, Roebuck* (1936)	Loom-woven baby seat; back and half of sides lined with cotton	$12.98
Crib	*Sears, Roebuck* (1938)	All steel; new Humpty-Dumpty decoration, sides 20" high	$9.15
Hair Treatment	*Sears, Roebuck* (1938)	*Nestle's;* encourages the natural curliness of the hair	$0.83

Business Equipment & Supplies

Typewriter	*Sears, Roebuck* (1939)	*Corona Standard;* terms, $5 down, $5/mth	$54.50

Collectibles

Arrowheads	*Hunting and Fishing* (1936)	100 good ancient arrowheads	$3.00

Entertainment

Broadway Play	*Time* (1939)	Actress Tallulah Bankhead in *The Little Foxes* Nightly seating	$0.55 to $3.30

Entertainment, Home

Camera	*Hunting and Fishing* (1936)	*Moviematic;* the camera that has made movie shooting everyone's sport	$5.95
Camera	*Country Life* (1939)	*Kodak Bantam;* with Kodak Anastigmat Special lens, 1/200-second shutter; plunger-type body shutter release	$22.50
Movie Camera	*Time* (1939)	*Bell and Howell,* Filmo 8; makes both color and black-and-white movies; use Filmo indoors or out	$49.50
Radio	*Hunting and Fishing* (1936)	*Tingtone Pocket;* operates without tubes or batteries	$2.90
Radio	*Sears, Roebuck* (1936)	A full-size personal radio in the latest styles; 5-tube	$16.50
Radio	*Goodyear Spring and Summer Catalog* (1937)	*Goodyear Wings Deluxe-8;* home radio	$38.95
Radio	*Sears, Roebuck* (1938)	*A.C. Electric Tuning Radio;* press button, instantly hear the program—no waiting at all	$49.50

Item	Source	Description	Price
Farm Equipment and Supplies			
Field Tiller	*Sears, Roebuck* (1938)	*David Bradley;* 2-speed transmission	$94.50
Milker	*Sears, Roebuck* (1939)	*Prima;* milking action is similar to the sucking action of a calf	$42.50
Pitchfork	*Sears, Roebuck* (1939)	*Hercules;* heavy, fully polished; 11 tines	$1.35
Financial Products & Services			
Traveler's Checks	*Country Life* (1939)	*American Express Travel;* funds that know no frontiers	$0.75/$100
Food Products			
Fish	*Atlanta Constitution* (1935)	Fancy speckled trout	$0.19/pound
Fish	*Atlanta Constitution* (1935)	Roe Shad	$0.23/pound
Hamburger	*Atlanta Constitution* (1935)	$0.12/half lb	
Olive Oil	*Sears, Roebuck* (1936)	*Gaillard;* unexcelled for baby's first bath; 1/2 pint	$0.39
Sausage	*Atlanta Constitution* (1935)	Country sausage	$0.20/pound
Shrimp	*Atlanta Constitution* (1935)	Cooked, peeled shrimp	$0.23/half pound
Furniture			
Bathroom Cabinet	*Morgan Millwork Co.* (1936)	*Miami Metal;* 16" x 24"; 3 coats of high-grade baked enamel	$14.00
Bed	*Country Life* (1939)	Louis XIV with Simmons Beautyrest box spring and mattress; custom-made oversize mattress, 6' 4 1/2" long, 6' wide	$345
Bed	*Sears, Roebuck* (1939)	*Lifetime Steel;* complete outfit of bed, mattress, and coil spring	$16.50
Bedroom Set	*Atlanta Constitution* (1935)	12-piece bedroom group; bed, vanity, chest, bench, mattress, 2 pillows, rug, shades, boudoir chair, Simmons coil spring	$89.00
China Cabinet	*Morgan Millwork Co.* (1936)	*Morgan;* designed especially for use in the smaller homes and in apartments; Extra width 2' 9"; height 7'; pine	$32.50
Kitchen Unit	*Morgan Millwork Co.* (1936)	3' 8" wide; 1' 10" deep; six wood drawers, two pan and lid racks, one pair of flush doors	$30.38
Mantel	*Morgan Millwork Co.* (1936)	*Morgan Colonial;* with 5' 11" long shelf, 6 1/2" wide; fancy Greek design	$31.88
Mirror	*Warren's Paint & Varnish Prod.* (1937)	Frameless Venetian; polished v-cut mitered lines are ground on the face side, as well as floral design at the top, peach on blue	$37.72
Sofa and Chair	*Sears, Roebuck* (1939)	Swedish modern; today's most talked of style	$66.85
Table	*Sears, Roebuck* (1936)	Gateleg; with the popular circular leaves opens to 45" x 36"; select hardwoods	$8.69
Table	*Country Life* (1939)	*Hammacher Schlemmer;* rattan serving; easy to carry; firm standing	$10.50
Table	*Country Life* (1939)	*Hammacher Schlemmer;* wrought-iron dining table with glass top	$56.00

Item	Source	Description	Price
Garden Equipment and Supplies			
Ax	*Sears, Roebuck* (1939)	*Merit;* forged-steel head	$0.98
Garden Tractor	*Sears, Roebuck* (1936)	*Handiman;* 4 hp motor	$242
Garden Tractor	*Sears, Roebuck* (1938)	*Handiman;* 2-speed transmission	$299.50
Hotel Rates			
Hotel Room	*Time* (1939)	*Commodore;* New York's best located hotel; 2,000 large outside rooms, all with private baths From	$4.00
Hotel Room	*Time* (1939)	*Hotel Taft* in New York at Radio City; 2,000 rooms with bath and radio From	$2.50 per day
Hotel Room	*Country Life* (1939)	*Copley Plaza Luxury;* Boston, Massachusetts; without pretension and extravagance	$4/night
Room Rates	*Time* (1939)	*Ambassador Hotel;* large, luxurious rooms in New York Single from Double from Suite from	$6.00 $8.00 $12.00
Room Rates	*Time* (1939)	*Traymore on The Boardwalk,* Atlantic City; cruise ashore European plan With meals	$5.00 $8.00
Room Rates	*Time* (1939)	*Mayfair of St. Louis;* location, comfort, fine food Single Double	$3.50 or less $5.00 or less
Household Products			
Broiler Pan	*Sears, Roebuck* (1936)	Oval aluminum	$0.75
Crock	*Sullivan Hardware Co., Inc.* (1936)	12-gallon stone crock	$1.68
Dinnerware	*Sears, Roebuck* (1939)	Semi-porcelain; service for six, includes 32 pieces	$4.98
Disinfectant	*Sears, Roebuck* (1938)	*Lysol;* Used in the care of the famous Dionne Quintuplets since their birth. Large size	$0.83
Flashlight	*Goodyear Spring and Summer Catalog* (1937	*Zephyrlites Flashlight;* 3-cell, 10 1/16" length, 500' beam; Tiffany of flashlights $1.39	
Flashlight	*Sears, Roebuck* (1939)	*Challenge;* long-range piercing finger of light that reaches 750'	$0.55
Flatware	*Sears, Roebuck* (1939)	*Community Plate;* service for 6	$29.75
Furniture Varnish	*Sears, Roebuck* (1936)	*Seroco;* long-wearing clear, hard gloss	$0.77/quart
Glasses	*Sears, Roebuck* (1939)	Cocktail glasses; 7-piece set, includes 6 glasses and shaker	$0.79
Grill	*Goodyear Spring and Summer Catalog* (1937)	Picnic grill; burns charcoal; folds into small compact carrying carton	$1.95
House Paint	*Warren's Paint & Varnish Prod.* (1937)	*Protex;* a rich linseed oil paint, unexcelled in hiding qualities	$4.08/gal

Item	Source	Description	Price
Kitchen Cabinet	*Sears, Roebuck* (1938)	*Hamper;* heavy spot-welded steel in a smart octagon style	$9.98
Lawn Mower	*Country Life* (1939)	*Stearns;* power; no longer a luxury, 10 models, 6-wheel drive and 4-roll drive	$69.50 to $260
Light Bulbs	*Collier's* (1938)	*Edison Mazda General Electric;* eyestrain season is here; homework and dark winter evenings call for light conditioning 100 watt bulb 150 watt bulb	$0.15 $0.20
Paint	*Warren's Paint & Varnish Prod.* (1937)	*Southern Colonial Aluminum;* highly recommended for interior work, and for work on radiators, pipes, machinery, etc	$4.25/gallon
Paintbrush	*Warren's Paint & Varnish Prod.* (1937)	For flat wall paint; 4" width, 2 3/4" length	$0.90
Patching Plaster	*Warren's Paint & Varnish Prod.* (1937)	*Old Newark;* has been on the American market for 118 years; 5 lb package	$0.10
Pressure Cooker	*Sears, Roebuck* (1939)	*Kook-Kwick* 1/3 the time, 1/3 the fuel, 8-quart size	$7.45
Rug	*Sears, Roebuck* (1939)	*Velflor;* the economy rug; 9' x 12'	$8.75
Towels	*Sears, Roebuck* (1936)	*Morninglow;* bath towel; 20" x 40" triple-stripe border	$0.79/4
Wall Clock	*Sears, Roebuck* (1939)	*Ingraham Regulator;* non-striking, for offices, churches, schools, and halls	$6.98
Waterhose	*Sullivan Hardware Co., Inc.* (1936)	25' green 5/8" hose	$3.00
Window Cleaner	*Goodyear Spring and Summer Catalog* (1937)	*Windex;* cleans and polishes auto glass without water	$0.39
Wood Filler	*Collier's* (1938)	*Plastic Wood;* this canned wood makes all home repairs easy	$0.35/can
Wood Lathe	*Sears, Roebuck* (1936)	*Companion;* 44" bed, 4-speed	$11.95

Jewelry

Item	Source	Description	Price
Watch	*Time* (1939)	*Longines President Lincoln* watch for men; 14 carat gold, 17 jewels, pink gold dial	$100
Watch	*Time* (1939)	*Longines Ella Wilcox* watch for women; yellow gold filled, 17 jewels	$47.50

Medical Products & Services

Item	Source	Description	Price
Camphor	*Sears, Roebuck* (1938)	U.S.P. quality in cake form; 1 oz cake	$0.29
Laxative	*Sears, Roebuck* (1939)	*Ex-Lax;* chocolated; 18 tablets	$0.19
Nonprescription Drug	*Hunting and Fishing* (1936)	*Dr. Van Vleck's Absorption Treatment;* for the treatment of piles	$1.00

Item	Source	Description	Price
Motorized Vehicles, Services, and Supplies			
Antifreeze	*Collier's* (1938)	*DuPont Zerone;* get improved engine performance due to better heat dissipation	$1/gallon
		west of the Rockies	$1.20/gallon
Automobile	*Time* (1939)	*Plymouth* stands out; 82-horsepower, L-head engine; price includes front and rear bumpers, bumper guards,	
		spare wheel, tire and tube, foot control for headlight beam, ashtray in front and rear, sun visor, safety glass and big trunk space	
		Coupes start at	$645
		Sedans start at	$685
Automobile	*Time* (1939)	*Hudson;* more room for passenger and luggage; safe stopping with Double-Safe Hydraulics; protection when a tire blows	
		Delivered in Detroit	$695
Battery	*Goodyear Spring and Summer Catalog* (1937)	*Goodyear Double Eagle;* a 24-month or 24,000 mile super-feature battery	$16.95
Compass	*Hunting and Fishing* (1936)	*Hull;* this new airplane-type compass constantly tells your direction of travel	$1.95
Fender Guide	*Goodyear Spring and Summer Catalog* (1937)	Illuminated; necessary on the new cars with high hoods and low curved-peak fenders	$1.19
Polish	*Goodyear Spring and Summer Catalog* (1937)	*Duco No. 7 Auto Polish;* just rub it on, let it dry, then wipe it off	$0.59/pint
Radio	*Goodyear Spring and Summer Catalog* (1937)	*Wings Challenger;* auto radio; the gem of the low-price field; 6 tubes	$17.95
Scooter	*Time* (1939)	*Moto-Skoot;* can be ridden standing up; enclosed engine	$109
Seat Covers	*Goodyear Spring and Summer Catalog* (1937)	*Cool Wave;* cool in summer, warm in winter	
		Coupe	$2.79
		Sedan	$5.85
Spark Plug	*Goodyear Spring and Summer Catalog* (1937)	*Goodyear Spark Plug;* they are built to high standards throughout	$0.60
Tire	*Goodyear Spring and Summer Catalog* (1937)	*Goodyear Double Eagle;* the finest tire the world has ever seen	$18.75
Tire	*Goodyear Spring and Summer Catalog* (1937)	*Goodyear All Weather;* for 1936 Ford	$15.55
Tire Plug	*Goodyear Spring and Summer Catalog* (1937)	*Goodyear Rubber;* can add thousands of miles to tire life	$0.10
Musical Instruments			
Guitar	*Sears, Roebuck* (1936)	*Lone Ranger;* with he-man figures of radio's most-beloved characters	$4.45
Guitar	*Sears, Roebuck* (1938)	*Supertone Gene Autry;* large concert size	$8.45

Item	Source	Description	Price
Other			
Birdbath	*Country Life* (1939)	*Lombard & Co.;* imported English sandstone	$50.00
Charcoal Briquettes	*Goodyear Spring and Summer Catalog* (1937)	5 lb bag	$0.25
Dog Food	*Hunting and Fishing* (1936)	*Miller's Kibbles;* nearly 1/2 pound beef in every pound	$1/8 pounds
Dogs	*Hunting and Fishing* (1936)	Pair of rabbit hounds; 2 1/2 years old, medium size, long ears, good voices, fast, true, steady drivers; 10 day trial	$20.00
Dogs	*Country Life* (1939)	*Giralda Farms;* English Cocker Spaniel pups sired by Blackmoor Beacon out of imported bitches	$50
Door and Frame	*Morgan Millwork Co.* (1936)	*Morgan Colonial Style Exterior;* door, No. 1 pine, heavy 1 3/4" solid panels, flush on outside with beaded edges	$25.00
Entry Fee	*Hunting and Fishing* (1936)	*National Skeet Championship;* 20-gauge championship at 100 targets (includes targets)	$7.00
Film Enlargement Service	*Hunting and Fishing* (1936)	*Diamond Photo Service;* Kodak film enlarged to 8" x 10", negative returned	$0.29
Fountain Pen	*Collier's* (1938)	*Esterbrook Re-New-Point;* the common sense fountain pen complete fountain pen duracrome renew-point	$1.00 $0.25
House Kit	*Hunting and Fishing* (1936)	*Aladdin's Build It Yourself House;* price includes all lumber, readi-cut, millwork, windows, doors, interior woodwork, hardware, roofing, glass, nails, paints, varnish and stains; we pay freight	$493
Laundry Cleaning	*City Directory* (Greenville, SC) (1937)	*Ideal Laundry;* why wash at home? 15 lbs; ideal damp wash	$0.49
Pedestal Lavatory	*Sears, Roebuck* (1936)	*Mayflower;* it will give your bathroom distinctiveness	$15.00
Shoe Polish	*Sears, Roebuck* (1936)	*Bixby's Jet Oil;* for all-black smooth leather shoes; 13 oz	$0.14
Sunlamp	*Sears, Roebuck* (1939)	*Carbon Arc;* make that flattering tan a year round asset	$6.75
Windows	*Morgan Millwork Co.* (1936)	*Andersen Casement;* twin frame, glazed	$10.03
Personal Care Products			
Bath Salts	*Country Life* (1939)	*Elizabeth Arden Pebble;* make your bath fragrant and restful	$2.50/$6.50
Dental Cream	*Sears, Roebuck* (1939)	*Colgate Ribbon;* an old favorite; 7 oz	$0.33
Dental Cream	*Sears, Roebuck* (1939)	*Milk of Magnesia;* large-size tubes	$0.08
Hair Tonic	*Sears, Roebuck* (1938	*Wildroot*	$0.47
Itch Relief	*Hunting and Fishing* (1936)	*Absorbine Jr.;* wonderful relief for just about every kind of trouble that befalls the camper	$1.25/bottle
Lotion	*Sears, Roebuck* (1936)	*Jergens;* famous for softening dry, harsh, chapped skin; 13 1/2 oz	$0.69
Mouthwash	*Sears, Roebuck* (1939)	*Listerine;* large size, 14 oz	$0.59

Item	Source	Description	Price
Razor Blade	*Hunting and Fishing* (1936)	*Double Keen;* the blades they are talking about at the club	$1.00
Soap	*Sears, Roebuck* (1938)	*Woodbury's;* facial soap; unquestioned purity; 3 cakes	$0.25
Toothbrush	*Collier's* (1938)	*Johnson & Johnson Tek;* using one Tek toothbrush in the morning and one at night, allows the bristles to dry, clean better, and last longer	$0.51/2
Toothpaste	*Collier's* (1938)	*Listerine;* supercharged with luster-foam (C14 H27 O5 Na) regular tube double size tube	$0.25 $0.40

Publications

Item	Source	Description	Price
Book	*Sears, Roebuck* (1936)	*Ripley's Believe It or Not;* over 350 illustrations	$0.85
Book	*Hunting and Fishing* (1936)	*Sportsman's Encyclopedia,* by William Bruette; 150 illustrations	$1.00
Book	*Sears, Roebuck* (1939)	*Same Sex Life,* by H. W. Long, M.D.; helpful to married couples or those about to marry	$1.85

Real Estate

Item	Source	Description	Price
House	*Country Life* (1939)	Old brick home for sale; 27 miles south of Washington, 9 rooms, 3 baths, basement, steam heat, electricity, hand carved woodwork, 143 acres	$18,000
Land	*Country Life* (1939)	Dairy estate property for sale; 90 miles from New York City; big income, milk retails; illness, sacrifice	$125,000
Land	*Country Life* (1939)	New Hampshire lake shore farm; 400 foot frontage, 150 acres; trout brook; farm house; 2 barns; includes beautiful building site overlooking lake and Mount Monadnock	$15,000

Sewing Equipment & Supplies

Item	Source	Description	Price
Paper Pattern	*Sears, Roebuck* for Dress	Each pattern may be made up in two or more styles (1936)	$0.15
Sewing Machine	*Sears, Roebuck* (1938)	*Franklin Foot Power;* first with all-level sewing surface	$31.95
Yarn	*Sears, Roebuck* (1936)	*Golden Crown Saxony;* threefold territorial wools	$0.23

Sports Equipment

Item	Source	Description	Price
Bait	*Hunting and Fishing* (1936)	Night Crawlers	$1/quart
Basketball	*Sears, Roebuck* (1938)	*J. C. Higgins;* regular pebbled-top-grain cowhide	$3.59
Bicycle	*Goodyear Spring and Summer Catalog* (1937)	*Goodyear;* deluxe boy's bicycle; nothing has been left undone to make it the sort of bike wanted by anyone who appreciates the best there is	$43.95
Bicycle Tires	*Goodyear Spring and Summer Catalog* (1937)	*Goodyear;* balloon bicycle tires; 26" x 2.125"; made of highest quality live rubber	$1.90
Camp Cottage	*Country Life* (1939)	*Hodgson;* simply fit the ready-made sections together and draw them tight with special Hodgson bolts	$200
Camper's Ax	*Sears, Roebuck* (1939)217	*Craftsman;* don't miss this $1.70 value	$1.00
Decoys	*Hunting and Fishing* (1936)	*C. A. Frakes;* canvas; light, durable, lasting, lifelike	$2.95/dozen

Item	Source	Description	Price
Fishing Outfit	*Sears, Roebuck* (1939)	22-piece starter kit for children	$0.98
Fishing Reel	*Hunting and Fishing* (1936)	*Pfluger Capitol;* all special features of former model retained	$8.25
Gun Bluer	*Hunting and Fishing* (1936)	New method; makes old guns like new	$1.00
Gun Case	*Hunting and Fishing* (1936)	*Nichols Lambskin;* custom-made	$3.00
Motor Yacht	*Country Life* (1939)	*Elco 53;* brings you luxurious yachting at a surprising low cost	$26,300
Pocketknife	*Sears, Roebuck* (1939)	*Sta-Sharp;* 3-Blade perfect for stock men, ranchers, craftsmen; 3 1/4" long	$0.95
Pocket Telescope	*Hunting and Fishing* (1936)	*Robie-Sawyer;* brings distant objects 6 times nearer	$1.00
Rifle	*Sears, Roebuck* (1936)	*Savage Model;* .22 caliber	$19.85
Rifle	*Hunting and Fishing* (1936)	*Winchester 94 Carbine;* .30-.30 caliber	$26.50
Saddle	*Sears, Roebuck* (1938)	*Peerless;* a good saddle for all around use	$27.95
Shotgun	*Hunting and Fishing* (1936)	*Iver Johnson;* double barrel; the greatest double gun value on the market	$30.00
Skittle Set	*Country Life* (1939)	*Abercrombie and Fitch Penguin;* for beach or lawn, six penguins, two balls	$10.00
Sunglasses	*Goodyear Spring and Summer Catalog* (1937)	Deluxe shell sport sun goggles optical finish adjustable temples	$1.98
Table Tennis Set	*Sears, Roebuck* (1939)	4-paddle	$2.95
Target Pistol	*Hunting and Fishing* (1936)	.22 automatic; a target pistol built by gun experts	$20.00
Velocipede	*Goodyear Spring and Summer Catalog* (1937)	Pneumatic tire; the riding velocipede for young America	$13.45

Telephone Equipment & Services

Item	Source	Description	Price
Telephone Rates	*Time* (1939)	*Bell System Overseas;* a three-minute, weekday call between New York and Puerto Rico	$11.25

Tobacco Products

Item	Source	Description	Price
Cigar	*Time* (1939)	Webster custom-made cigars; each Golden Wedding	$0.10
		Perfecto Chico	$0.10
		Queens, 2 for	$0.25
		Fancy Tales	$0.15
Pipe	*Sears, Roebuck* (1939)	*Chesterfield;* known for its sweet smoking qualities; 5" size	$0.39
Pipe Filters	*Collier's* (1938)	*Frank Medico Absorbent;* finest briar money can buy	$1.00
Smoking Tobacco	*Hunting and Fishing* (1936)	*Union Leader;* a dime's no longer small change; it's mighty important money when it buys that big red tin of Union Leader tobacco	$0.10
Smoking Tobacco	*Hunting and Fishing* (1936)	*Sir Walter Raleigh;* switch to the brand of grand aroma	$0.15/can

Item	Source	Description	Price
Toys			
Wagon	*Goodyear Spring and Summer Catalog* (1937)	*Playboy DeLuxe Model Wagon;* all-steel safety body; 41" long, 19" wide	$15.45
Travel & Transportation			
Airline Fare	*Collier's* (1938)	*American Airlines;* let America's flagships-serving 57 major cities-give you extra days for living; costs are often less than first class ground travel; Los Angeles to New York	$149.95
Airline Fare	*Collier's* (1938)	*American Airlines;* New York to Chicago	$44.95
Cruise	*Time* (1939)	*Red Star Line;* one-class travel to Europe; enjoy the run-of-the-ship	$100.50 and up
Cruise	*Time* (1939)	*Norwegian American Line;* from New York to Oslofjord; membership limited to 425	$485 and up

MISCELLANY 1935-1939

Publicity for Salaries

The House Ways and Means Committee has made public every corporate salary of $15,000 or more. In all, 18,000 persons have discovered that their salaries are open to public inspection. Many of them have been printed in the newspapers, and the general feeling of the goldfish is dismay and anger.

Yet it should be recognized that there is a difference between opening up a man's whole income and revealing his salary for the information of the stockholders of his corporation. A corporate officer is only the servant of his stockholder. They are his employers. An employer should know what he is paying his employees. It is not anybody else's business. Neither taxpayers, insurance solicitors, creditors, nor neighbors have any right to the information.

Business Week, January 18, 1936

Down Goes Liquor; 50% Tariff Cut on Imported Liquor and Gin Starts a Wide Series of Price Reductions

Seagram led the parade. Its "V.O." bonded whisky was cut (in New York) from $2.59 a pt. to $2.09; its Five Crown (blend) went from $1.42 a pt. to $1.19.

Hiram Walker retorted with a cut of its Canadian Club (bonded) from $2.49 a pt. to $2.08; its cheaper blends were reduced to $1.19 a pt.

Business Week, February 1, 1936

Bootleg Wiring; Electrical Industry Makes Drive for More and Better Wiring and Against Unlicensed Work

Ten years ago 2% of the building cost was considered a fair allowance for the wiring of a new home. Recent surveys by *Electrical Contracting* show that 1 1/4% is now a fair average and thousands of six-room houses are being wired today for less than $50.

If 1% of the existing homes were rewired each year to the electrical industry's standard of modern adequacy, it would double the volume of the contracting business.

Business Week, February 1, 1936

Only 9,000,000 Now Idle, Commerce Experts Find

Commerce Department experts reported today that unofficial check-ups indicate there are now fewer than 9,000,000 unemployed.

They said that the number of those out of work has been falling off steadily this year and "was slightly less than 9,000,000 at the end of September."

This compared with their estimates of 11,000,000 for January and 9,550,000 in August.

New York Times, November 11, 1936

Socialists Have Surplus; Report to House Shows Campaign Outlay $2,287 Less Than Gifts

The Socialist Party wound up its Presidential campaign with money in the bank.

A post-election report to the Clerk of the House listed expenditures of $20,937, or $2,287 less than contributions.

Major parties are expected to show deficits of $500,000 or more.

New York Times, November 11, 1936

Are There a Million Aliens on Relief?

There may be as many as one million aliens of illegal entry on our relief rolls, supported by taxpayers, according to Arthur Krock, of *The New York Times.* Mr. Krock offers this as another explanation of the administration's curious hesitation to take a census of the unemployed.

He suggests that Congress may be about to be asked virtually to suspend the naturalization laws, that this army of aliens of illegal entry may quickly be made citizens in as good standing as any other.

Saturday Evening Post, January 23, 1937

The Effects of the Gift Tax

Also a Treasury official has testified that a single gift tax of $18,802,978 was paid in 1934, which means that one individual gave another as much as $45,000,000. Just before the tax went into effect, and to avoid its provisions, two taxpayers transferred upward of $150,000,000, according to Treasury information.

Gift-tax rates are three-fourths the estate-tax rates for a given amount and for the same bracket. Thus a rich man saves in two ways by making gifts. He is taxed at a lower rate on the amount given away and he takes the top off his fortune; thereby making another big saving on what is left. If he confines his gifts to $5,000 apiece and to a number of different donees through successive years, he can distribute his whole fortune without incurring any estate-tax obligations.

Saturday Evening Post, February 27, 1937

MISCELLANY 1935-1939

Clothing Brand Cuts Prices First Time In 15 Years

That department stores are experiencing slowness in the sale of men's clothing was indicated yesterday when one large store cut the price of its leading brand for the first time in fifteen years.

The revision was announced in a mailing to charge account customers only, inviting them to a private sale. The amount of the reduction was approximately 15 percent. The sale will be conducted for three days, starting today.

New York Times, October 21, 1937

Radio Would Print News In the Home

G. C. Hamilton, manager of the McClatchy newspapers, announced that an application had been filed with the Federal Communications Commission for a permit to start this form of "radio newspaper" in Sacramento and Fresno. The "radio newspaper" will be two columns wide.

The system is understood to be a modifica- tion of stylus radio receiving, which has been in development for many years.

The company intends to broadcast from midnight until 6 a.m., supplementing the regular schedules.

Because the radio facsimile recorder for home use is not yet manufactured in mass quantity, it is planned to acquire 100 of the devices and install them in the homes of fifty Sacramento residents and in the homes of as many Fresno residents to determine the value of the service.

New York Times, October 21, 1937

Farm Group Also Sees President and Proposes 60-Cent Aid for Producers

President Roosevelt, Secretary Wallace and Secretary Morgenthau prepared today to go ahead with loans to corn producers in advance of the special session of Congress. A loan of about 46 cents a bushel will probably be approved.

New York Times, October 21, 1937

Deepest Hole in the World

And K.C.L. A-2 (in San Joaquin Valley) excels by 1,878 feet the next deepest *producer,* Union Oil Co.'s Rio Bravo discovery well, located about fourteen miles away. Plugged back to 13,180 feet, K.C.L. A-2 is currently producing 450 barrels (or about $520

worth) of crude a day, the allowable permitted under California's proration agreements; and it has produced as much as 3,600 barrels during a twenty-four-hour test, through a one-inch flow bean or choke.

Even beaned down to the present low output, K.C.L. A-2 is expected to pay out—i.e., return the investment—in about three years. Provided, of course, that K.C.L. A-2's type of crude maintains anything like the current price of $1.15 a barrel.

Fortune, July 1938

Akron Disturbed; City Is Startled as Goodrich Plans Big Factory Elsewhere, with Cheaper Labor

A year ago the United Rubber Workers union at the B. F. Goodrich Co.'s Akron plants overwhelmingly voted down a wage cut proposed by the company to its competitive position.

Goodrich, first rubber factory west of the Alleghenies, warned that the city might lose 5,000 jobs if the slash, averaging 12.3% were not accepted. Average hourly earnings for all its Akron workers then were $1.046, while hourly wage rates in all tire and tube plants outside the city averaged but 84¢, Bureau of Labor Statistics showed.

Goodrich, with U.S. Rubber as its main rival, specializes more than other Akron firms in mechanical rubber goods production, where it contended high wages handicapped it more than in the tire and tube end of the business. Outside Akron 59.7¢ was the average hourly wage in 150 mechanical goods plants.

Business Week, May 6, 1939

Wage-Hour Law on Farm

Not yet satisfied by the House Labor Committee's amendments to the wage-hour law, the farm organizations will try to patch the bill on the floor. The farmer's choler will not block passage, however, for they will take the best they can get rather than let harvest time roll 'round with the law unchanged as it now affects farm hands.

The farm organizations claim that, in liberalizing the hours provisions of the law by allowing a 60-hour week for "first process" workers the House Committee slipped a lot more of the laborers under the wage provisions of the law.

Farmers are afraid, of course, that increased costs will be passed back to them and not ahead to the consumers.

Business Week, May 6, 1939

1940-1959

World War II, Recovery, and the Cold War

PRESIDENTS

Franklin D. Roosevelt †   1933-1945
Harry S. Truman   1945-1953
Dwight D. Eisenhower   1953-1961
† died in office

The twenty-year period from 1940 to 1959 includes the turbulent World War II years, when Americans were consumed by the national war effort and recovery, and the contrasting 1950s, when, after resolution of the Korean War, the U.S. was focused on recovery and increasing the prosperity of the middle class. During the first period the economy was radically disrupted as the work force, national wealth, and social demographics were realigned. The 1950s brought the flight to the suburbs, the baby boom, and the creation of truly national products and distribution systems. Even inflation and the minor recessions of 1949 and 1957 caused little anxiety.

While the United States struggled with depression in the 1930s, Germany, Italy, and Japan were preparing for war. Slow at first to mobilize, America responded forcefully. Business worked in partnership with government; strikes were reduced. By 1944 the U.S. was producing twice the total war output of the Axis powers combined. Unemployment all but disappeared. By 1943 the wartime demand for production workers pushed average wage-earner income ahead of that of salaried employees. From 1940 to 1945 the gross national product more than doubled, from $100 billion to $211 billion, despite rationing and the unavailability of many consumer goods such as cars, gasoline, and washing machines. By 1945 government expenditures reached $98 billion—$90 billion over the 1936 New Deal peak of $8 billion. Interest rates were low, and the upward pressure on prices remained high, yet from 1943 to the end of the war the cost of living rose less than 1.5 percent. Following the war, as controls were removed, inflation peaked in 1948; union demands for higher wages accelerated. Between 1945 and 1952 confident Americans, and their growing families, increased consumer-credit by 800 percent.

During the war key New Deal labor concessions were retained, including a 40-hour week and time and a half for overtime. Manufacturing demands increased, the labor pool shrank, and wages and union membership rose. As war industry redistributed the population and the demand for labor, the Pacific Coast gained wealth and power, while the South was able to supply its people much-needed war jobs and provide blacks opportunities in fields previously closed to them. Women entered the work force in unprecedented numbers, reaching 18 million. The net cash income of the American farmer soared 400 percent.

The war years' high employment was followed by the longest sustained period of peacetime prosperity in history. A decade of full employment and pent-up desire produced demands for consumer goods. Businesses of all sizes prospered. Veterans, using the

245

GI Bill of Rights, attended colleges in record numbers. Inflation was the most pressing economic problem, fueled by the Korean War and the Cold War expenditures for defense.

The glamour industries—chemicals, electrical appliances, and electronics—grew at astonishing rates, while the disposable per-capita income more than doubled. The average wage earner benefited more from the industrial system than at any time in national history. The 40-hour workweek became standard in manufacturing. In offices many workers were becoming accustomed to a 35-hour week. During the 1950s an average of seven million new cars and trucks were sold annually. By 1952 two-thirds of all families owned a television set; home freezers and high-fidelity stereo phonographs were considered necessities. Specialized markets developed to meet the consumer needs of such groups as backpackers, amateur photographers, and pet lovers. The adolescent market came of age: shopping malls, supermarkets, and credit cards assumed key roles in the American lifestyle.

By 1960 at least half of all existing dwellings had been built since World War II. Because of Federal Housing Administration and Veterans' Housing Administration programs, a majority of Americans owned their own homes for the first time in the twentieth century. In response to the need for interstate highways, the federal government encouraged the movement from city to suburb. The plan to develop 41,000 miles of highway facilitated the distribution of goods nationally, making national advertising more economical and the concept of a national economy a reality.

Government took on a new role. Following the Korean War, spending remained higher than the 1950 post-World War II low of $45 billion. By 1957 federal spending topped $82 billion—more than half for defense. Big government no longer implied socialism. When Health Education and Welfare secretary Oveta Culp Hobby opposed the free distribution of the polio vaccine as backdoor socialism, the public outcry forced her resignation.

Change was rampant and uneven. By 1950, 25 percent of American wives worked outside the home; by 1960 the number had risen to 40 percent. Scientific innovations and overproduction forced out the small farmer in favor of agribusiness. Up to one-third of the population lived below the government's poverty level, largely overlooked in the midst of prosperity. The Supreme Court's *Brown v. Board of Education* decision to end the "separate but equal" doctrine produced opposition and future opportunities but little immediate equality.

HISTORICAL SNAPSHOT 1940-1944

1940

- France, Belgium, the Netherlands, Luxembourg, Denmark, Norway, and Romania fall to Germans
- President Roosevelt's $8.4 billion budget includes $1.8 billion for defense
- 14.6 percent of work force out of work
- First Social Security checks issued
- Gross National Product is $99 billion
- Arroyo Seco Parkway, first Los Angeles freeway, dedicated
- Chevrolet coupe sells for $659
- Goodyear Dow Corporation formed
- U.S. Blue Cross Insurance programs include 6 million subscribers
- Annual U.S. red-meat consumption reaches 142 pounds per capita
- 33 percent of all farms wired for electric power
- Ford introduces Lincoln Continental

1941

- President's $17.5 billion budget includes nearly $11 billion for defense
- Inflation increases general price level by 10 percent
- U.S. auto production reaches 3.3 million
- Quality Inns founded to franchise motel operations

- Daniel Gerber Fremont Canning Company sells a million cans of baby food weekly
- Cheerios introduced by General Mills
- U.S. food prices up by 61 percent over prewar prices
- Pearl Harbor attacked; U.S. enters war
- Germany declares war on U.S.

1942

- Office of Price Administration formed to control prices
- Tire rationing plan commences; gas rationing begins
- Paine, Webber, Jackson, & Curtis created
- Zinc-coated pennies issued by U.S. Mint
- Florida passes California as leading U.S. producer of oranges
- Kellogg introduces Raisin Bran
- Sunbeam bread introduced
- Maxwell House instant coffee has beginnings in soluble coffee for military's K rations
- Dannon yogurt introduced
- U.S. automobile production halted until 1945

1943

- President Roosevelt's $109 billion budget earmarks $100 billion for war effort
- Congress approves income-tax withholding from paychecks

- Rent controls imposed nationwide
- American Broadcasting Company (ABC) created by Lifesavers millionaire Edward Noble
- Zenith Radio Corporation introduces $40 hearing aid
- Americans rationed three pairs of shoes per year
- Meat rationing set at 28 ounces per week; meat production rises 50 percent
- Sale of sliced bread banned
- Russell Marker pioneers oral contraceptive, Syntex, S.A.

1944

- 176,000 Allied troops land at Normandy beaches; war continues
- President Roosevelt reelected to fourth term
- First automatic, general-purpose digital computer completed at Harvard
- Federal Highway Act establishes interstate highway system
- War costing U.S. $250 million per day
- GI Bill of Rights enacted to finance college educations for veterans; 4 percent home loans available with no down payment
- U.S. soybean production rises as new uses are found for bean
- Chiquita brand banana introduced
- U.S. grocers test self-service meat markets
- Gasoline averages 21 cents per gallon

SELECTED INCOME 1940-1944

Job	Source	Description	Pay
Actress	*Screen Guide* (1941)	Per picture payment to child movie star Carolyn Lee, featured in movie "Virginia"	$10,000
Actor	*Screen Guide* (1941)	Weekly pay of movie actor Henry Fonda	$1,500
Actor	Miller, *The Great Cowboy Stars of Movies and Television* (1979)	Annual income of Gene Autry, King of the Cowboys, in 1941	$600,000
Alderman	*The World Almanac* (1943)	Salary of Chicago Mayor Edward Kelly	$16,200
Army Nurse	*The World Almanac* (1943)	Annual base pay	$1,080
Barber	*Chicago Tribune* (1943)	Steady; good hair cutter; 70% straight; guarantee	$50/wk
Bar Maid	*New Orleans Times Picayune* (1941)	Colored girl; experienced bar maid and waitress; room and board included	$5 per week
Bartender	*New Orleans Times Picayune* (1943)	Night work; meals	$25 week
Baseball Player	Victor Bondi, ed., *American Decades: 1940–1949* (1995)	Earnings of New York Yankee Joe DiMaggio in 1941	$35,000
Bell Boys	*Chicago Tribune* (1941)		$75–$90/mo
Body Man	*Chicago Tribune* (1941)	Experienced to take over growing body shop	$35/wk
Bookkeeper	*New York Times* (1940)	Full charge; 50–55 year; Scot preferred; good health; non-drinker; able to type; permanent; send details: experience, personal photo (nonreturnable), own handwriting	$20/wk
Bookkeeper	*Greenville Piedmont* (Greenville, SC) (1943)	Male	$2600/yr
Bookkeeper/Office Manager	*New York Times* (1943)	Able to prepare weekly payrolls; 300 men for building subcontractor; keep complete double-entry records	$50/wk
Buffer	*New York Times* (1944)	Plastic	$1 plus/hr
Buyer	*New York Times* (1944)	Assistant trimming buyer, dresses	$50/wk
Cabinet Member	*The World Almanac* (1942)	Annual salary of Department of Justice Solicitor General Charles Fahy	$10,000
Carpenters	*New Orleans Times Picayune* (1941)	Residential construction; steady work; state experience	$.80 per hour
Chambermaids	*New York Times* (1944)		$21.25/wk
Clerk (Payroll)	*New York Times* (1943)	40–50 years; experienced	$28/wk
Compositer	*New York Times* (1944)	A-1 man; 48 hrs	$65/wk

Job	Source	Description	Pay
Cook	*New York Times* (1944)	Girls for griddle	$30/wk to start
Cook/Gardener	*New York Times* (1942)	Couple; young cook-houseworker; gardener-houseman; drives	$175/mo
Counter Girl	*New York Times* (1944)	For soda fountain, experienced; 5 1/2 day wk	$35/wk
Dance Instructor	*New York Times* (1944)	Men to teach dancing; no experience	$35–$40/mo
Delivery Man	*The State* (Columbia, SC) (1943)	Colored boy or man	$15/wk
Electrician	*Chicago Tribune* (1943)	Young man 25 to 35 to train for responsible job in electrical industry; must be high-school graduate; night shift; 48-hr wk. Salary during 2-wk training $44.20	$50.83/wk
Elevator Operator	*New York Times* (1944)	Days, Union hrs	$125/mo
Elevator Relief Man	*New York Times* (1944)	18 or over	$122.50/mo
Engineer	*New York Times* (1940)	Wire machinery	$90/mo
Engineer-Draftsman	*Chicago Tribune* (1943)	Long program; 60 hr wk, out of town, all expenses; plant layout; mechanical structural; top men only; confidential	$2.00–$2.50/hr
Factory Girl	*Chicago Tribune* (1941)	Polish or Italian, no experience	$14/wk
Factory War Work	*New York Times* (1943)	Girl, no experience necessary, steady	$25/wk to start
Factory Worker	*Chicago Tribune* (1943)	All trades; men for shops and factories	$40–$50/wk
Factory Workers	*New Orleans Times Picayune* (1943)	Alert white girls; active elderly women; experience unnecessary; light factory work; 8 hours; half pay for over 40 hours	$2.40 per day
File Clerk	*New York Times* (1943)	Young, personable, thoroughly experienced to organize and maintain files; attractive position, Radio City	$30–35/wk
File Clerk	*New York Times* (1944)	Clerk and typist; 5 days; congenial office	$27/wk to start
Food Handler	*Chicago Tribune* (1943)	You can make more in factory, but this is permanent and living conditions ideal	$50/mo
Hospital Chef	*Chicago Tribune* (1941)	Room and board included	$85/mo
Housekeeper	*New York Times* (1942)	Girl, colored; 5 mornings; references	$6.50/wk
Housekeeper	*New York Times* (1942)	Irish; good cook; excellent references	$80–85/mo
Investigator	*New York Times* (1940)	Beginner with car; 24–28; sales exp; Queens res; H. S. Grad	$140/mo
Judge	*The World Almanac* (1943)	Annual salary of New York City Court Judge Joseph Keller	$17,000
Leather-Goods Workers	*New York Times* (1944)	Experienced; desk pads and sets; 52-hr wk	$65/wk
Leather Sander	*New York Times* (1944)	Man, inexperienced, for leather sanding	$39/wk
Library Clerk	*Chicago Tribune* (1943)	Young girl for clerical duties in business library; no experience necessary; 5-day wk, 37 1/2 hrs	$25/wk
Machinist	*New York Times* (1944)	First-class; 10 years' experience; 47 1/2 hrs, 5-day wk	$75/wk
Maid	*Chicago Tribune* (1943)	Temporary; colored; 8 hrs	$3/day

Job	Source	Description	Pay
Maid-Cleaner	*Chicago Tribune* (1943)	No experience necessary, for north side unfurnished apt. bldg.	$70/mo
Maid-Cook	*Chicago Tribune* (1941)	White; light laundry; gentle family; references; private room	$15/wk
Metallurgist	*New York Times* (1940)	Inorganic analysis	$25–$30/wk
Miscellaneous	*New York Times* (1944)	Boys, 17 yrs old; production department of publishers' reps; experience unnec.	$120/mo
Mother's Helper	*New York Times* (1943)	Schoolgirl mother's helper through vacation	$100/mo
Movie Producer	Catherine Legrand and Robyn Karney, *Chronicle of the Cinema* (1995)	Salary of Orson Wells to produce, direct, write and appear in the movie *Citizen Kane* in 1940	$100,000
Movie Star	*Screen Guide* (1941)	Weekly pay of actress Judy Garland, star of *The Wizard of Oz*	$2,500
Musicians	Bufwack and Oerman, *Finding Her Voice, The Saga of Women in Country Music* (1993)	Nightly income of *The Texas Playboys* for Saturday night concerts on Pacific Ocean Piers in Los Angeles in 1943	$20,000
Navy Commander	*The World Almanac* (1943)	1942 annual base pay if less than 30 years of service	$3,500
Nurse	*New York Times* (1944)	Reg. charge; small nursing home	$150/mo
Nurse Trainee	*Chicago Tribune* (1943)	Girl who would like to work in doctor's office, room, board	$60/mo
Nursemaid	*New York Times* (1942)	Trained young adult lady; child; days; sleep out	$30/wk
Order Clerk	*New York Times* (1943)	Spanish-English order clerk for long-established firm, representing Latin-American and other foreign publications; pleasant	$120/mo
Order Fillers	*New York Times* (1944)	Girls as order fillers; 5 days 40 hrs	$21/wk
Page Girl	*New York Times* (1944)	Page Girls and messengers	$20–$25/wk
Painter	Steven Naifeh and Gregory White Smith, *Jackson Pollock: An American Saga* (1989)	Monthly income of Jackson Pollock from promoter Pegg Guggenheim's *Art of This Century* gallery in 1943	$150
Pantry Girl	*Chicago Tribune* (1943)	Experienced to work in loop restaurant	$25/wk and meals
Parking	*New Orleans Times Picayune* (1943)	Young men; 16 or over	$16 week
Pressman	*New Orleans Times Picayune* (1943)	Regular jobs; no extra work; 48 hours	$54.60
Pressers	*New Orleans Times Picayune* (1943)	Women; experienced in wool, linen, silk; steady work assured	$3 per day
Racehorse	Bondi, ed., *American Decades: 1940–1949* (1995)	Earnings for *Pensive* in 1944 *Preakness*	$60,075

Job	Source	Description	Pay
Receptionist	*Chicago Tribune* (1943)	Doctor's office	$65/mo
Record Clerk	*Chicago Tribune* (1943)	40-hr wk; no experience necessary if willing to learn; must be neat penman and be able to use typewriter some	$20/wk
Sales	*Chicago Tribune* (1943)	Every home, every store, tavern, business needs 1 or more of this item. You don't have to be a fancy talker	$25/wk
Sales	*Chicago Tribune* (1943)	Follow-up post cards mailed to old accounts; wearing apparel advance comm	$50–$75/wk
Salesman	*New Orleans Times Picayune* (1943)	Real estate salesman; must own car	$250–$500 per month
Stenographer	*New York Times* (1943)	English-Spanish steno	Up to $45/wk
Teachers	*The State* (Columbia, SC) (1943)	One teacher for 9th and 10th-grade industrial arts and a class in carpentry; college graduate preferred but not necessary	$175/mo
Telephone Solicitor	*New York Times* (1942)	Young man wanted, under 30, with some college education for soliciting of advertising for established publication.	$23.50/wk
Toolroom Foreman	*Chicago Tribune* (1941)		$4,000/yr
Tracers and Letterers	*New York Times* (1940)	Bring samples	$1,200/yr
Truck Driver	*Chicago Tribune* (1943)		$42.50/wk
20-Pin Boys	*Chicago Tribune* (1943)	16 years or over. $0.08 a line.	Up to $10/day
Union President	*The Scribner Encyclopedia of American Lives, 1987*	Annual salary of James Petrillo, president of the American Federation of Musicians in 1941	$46,000
U. S. President	*The World Almanac* (1943)	Annual salary of U. S. President Franklin Delano Roosevelt	$75,000
U. S. Vice President	*The World Almanac* (1943)	Annual salary of U. S. Vice President Henry Wallace	$15,000
Waitress	*New Orleans Times Picayune* (1943)	Experienced; active; intelligent; first class	$.30/hr. plus tips $35–$50 week
Waitress	*New York Times* (1940)	Neat arm service; small tips	$3.50/day
Writer	Bondi, ed., *American Decades: 1940–1949* (1995)	Payment to writer Edna Ferber for movie rights to her unpublished novel "Saratoga Trunk" in 1941	$175,000

CONSUMER EXPENDITURES 1940-1944

(Per Capita)

Expenditure Type	1940	1941	1942	1943	1944
Clothing	$46.93	$53.22	$63.03	$76.79	$83.82
Food	$152.13	$174.66	$210.59	$242.79	$265.18
Auto Usage	$45.41	$53.97	$26.69	$21.21	$21.68
New Auto Purchase	$15.89	$19.49	$74¢	73¢	72¢
Auto Parts	$3.78	$5.25	$2.22	$2.93	$2.89
Gas & Oil	$17.41	$19.49	$19.28	$9.51	$10.12
Housing	$73.42	$77.96	$83.05	$86.29	$88.87
Furniture	$8.33	$9.74	$9.64	$8.78	$9.39
Utilities	$25.73	$26.99	$28.92	$29.98	$30.35
Telephone & Telegraph	$4.54	$5.25	$5.93	$7.31	$7.95
Physicians	$6.81	$7.49	$7.42	$8.04	$9.39
Dentists	$3.03	$3.75	$3.71	$3.66	$4.34
Health Insurance	$1.50	$1.49	$1.48	$2.19	$2.17
Personal Business	$24.22	$25.49	$25.21	$27.06	$28.18
Personal Care	$7.57	$8.99	$10.38	$11.70	$13.01
Tobacco	$14.38	$15.74	$17.05	$19.01	$18.71
Local Transport	$6.81	$7.49	$7.42	$8.04	$12.02
Intercity Transport	$3.03	$2.99	$5.19	$7.31	$7.95
Recreation	$28.76	$31.48	$34.85	$39.49	$39.02
Religion/Welfare Activities	$8.33	$8.25	$9.64	$10.97	$12.28
Private Education & Research	$5.29	$5.25	$5.93	$7.31	$7.23
Per-Capita Consumption	$537.38	$605.69	$656.98	$727.66	$781.81

INVESTMENTS 1940-1944

Investment	1940	1941	1942	1943	1944
Basic Yield, One-Year Corporate Bonds	.41	.41	.81	1.17	1.08
Short-Term Interest Rates, 4–6 Months, Prime Commercial Paper	.56	.53	.66	.69	.73
Basic Yield, Common Stocks, Total	5.31	6.25	6.67	4.89	4.81
Index of Common Stocks (1941–1943=10)	11.02	9.82	8.67	11.50	12.47

COMMON STOCKS, CLOSING PRICE AND YIELD, FIRST BUSINESS DAY OF YEAR

(Parenthetical number is annual dividends in dollars)

	1940	1941	1942	1943	1944
Allis Chalmers	41	36 3/4	30 3/8	26 3/4	38 1/4
	(1.25)	(1.50)	(1.50)	(1)	(1.25)
AT&T	171 7/8	168 3/8	132 1/4	128 1/4	156 1/8
	(9)	(9)	(9)	(9)	(9)
American Tobacco	86 3/4	70 3/4	47 1/2	42 1/8	57 1/2
	(5)	(5)	(4.50)	(3.25)	(3.25)
Anaconda	30 3/4	27 1/8	28 1/8	24 3/8	25
	(1.25)	(2)	(2.50)	(2.50)	(2.50)
B&O	6 1/4	3 1/2	3 1/2	3 3/8	5 1/2
	(/)	(/)	(/)	(/)	(/)
Bethlehem Steel	82	89	66 1/4	56 3/8	56 1/2
	(1.50)	(5)	(6)	(6)	(6)
Corn Products	64 3/4	44 3/8	55 1/4	55 7/8	55 1/2
	(3)	(3)	(3)	(2.80)	(2.60)
General Electric	40 3/4	34 1/4	28 1/4	30 3/4	37
	(1.40)	(1.85)	(1.75)	(1.40)	(1.40)
General Motors	34 7/8	48 1/4	32	44 1/2	52 1/8
	(1.60)	(3.75)	(3.75)	(2)	(2)
International Business Machines	196	160 1/2			173
(5% stock dividend, 4/1/40)	(6)	(6)			(6)
(5% stock dividend, 1/30/41)					
(5% stock dividend, 1/28/42)					
(5% stock dividend, 1/28/43)					
(5% stock dividend, 1/28/44)					
Intl Harvester	62 1/4	50 1/8	47 3/4	59 1/2	73
	(1.60)	(2.40)	(3.10)	(2.50)	(2.50)
National Biscuit	23 3/4	17 3/4	15 3/4	15 3/4	21 1/4
	(1.40)	(1.60)	(1.60)	(1.30)	(1.20)
US Steel		70 3/8		47 7/8	50 1/4
		(3)		(4)	(4)
Western Union		20 1/8		27 1/8	42 1/8
		(1)		(2)	(2)

STANDARD JOBS 1940-1944

Job Type	1940	1941	1942	1943	1944
Average of All Industries, excl. farm labor	$1392/yr	$1561/yr	$1858/yr	$2181/yr	$2360/yr
Average of All Industries, incl. farm labor	$1315/yr	$1492/yr	$1778/yr	$2107/yr	$2292/yr
Bituminous Coal Mining	$1235/yr	$1500/yr	$1715/yr	$2115/yr	$2535/yr
Building Trades	$1330/yr	$1635/yr	$2191/yr	$2503/yr	$2602/yr
Domestics	$554/yr	$601/yr	$706/yr	$919/yr	$1140/yr
Farm Labor	$463/yr	$567/yr	$769/yr	$1002/yr	$1189/yr
Federal Civilian	$1894/yr	$1970/yr	$2265/yr	$2628/yr	$2677/yr
Federal Employees, Executive Depts.	$1125/yr	$1239/yr	$1632/yr	$1792/yr	$1929/yr
Federal Military	$1025/yr	$1113/yr	$1485/yr	$1565/yr	$1763/yr
Finance, Insurance, & Real Estate	$1725/yr	$1777/yr	$1885/yr	$2041/yr	$2191/yr
Gas & Electricity Workers	$1795/yr	$1870/yr	$2040/yr	$2284/yr	$2467/yr
Manufacturing, Durable Goods	$1568/yr	$1840/yr	$2292/yr	$2619/yr	$2774/yr
Manufacturing, Nondurable Goods	$1299/yr	$1440/yr	$1654/yr	$1895/yr	$2081/yr
Medical / Health Services Workers	$927/yr	$955/yr	$1036/yr	$1127/yr	$1262/yr
Miscellaneous Manufacturing	$2320/yr	$1380/yr	$1540/yr	$1882/yr	$2176/yr
Motion Picture Services	$1948/yr	$2016/yr	$2124/yr	$2250/yr	$2379/yr
Nonprofit Org. Workers	$1408/yr	$1379/yr	$1482/yr	$1679/yr	$1795/yr
Passenger Transportation Workers,	$1559/yr	$1664/yr	$1990/yr	$2280/yr	$2458/yr
Local and Highway Personal Services	$1062/yr	$1095/yr	$1199/yr	$1386/yr	$1575/yr
Public School Teachers	$1435/yr	$1462/yr	$1512/yr	$1608/yr	$1730/yr
Radio Broadcasting & Television Workers	$2554/yr	$2581/yr	$2667/yr	$2929/yr	$3333/yr
Railroads	$1906/yr	$2030/yr	$2303/yr	$2585/yr	$2714/yr
State and Local Govt. Workers	$1497/yr	$1522/yr	$1574/yr	$1687/yr	$1797/yr
Telephone & Telegraph Workers	$1610/yr	$1633/yr	$1715/yr	$1878/yr	$2035/yr
Wholesale and Retail Trade Workers	$1382/yr	$1478/yr	$1608/yr	$1781/yr	$1946/yr

FOOD BASKET 1940-1944

Commodity	Year	New York	Atlanta	Chicago	Denver	Los Angeles
Apples, Fresh, per pound	1940	NR	NR	NR	NR	NR
	1941	5.90¢	5.40¢	5.80¢	5.90¢	7¢
	1942	7.10¢	6.30¢	7.40¢	8.10¢	7.50¢
	1943	10.10¢	10.50¢	11.90¢	12.60¢	10.70¢
	1944	11.10¢	11¢	11.80¢	12.40¢	11.40¢
Beans, Navy, per pound	1940	NR	NR	NR	NR	NR
	1941	9.90¢	6.90¢	9.90¢	6.40¢	8.60¢
	1942	10.70¢	8.80¢	9¢	7.90¢	10.60¢
	1943	11.30¢	9.60¢	9.90¢	9.50¢	11.10¢
	1944	11.90¢	10.10¢	10.40¢	10.30¢	11.90¢
Beef, Rib Roasts, per pound	1940	NR	NR	NR	NR	NR
	1941	32¢	29.50¢	32¢	27.20¢	34.40¢
	1942	34.20¢	34.10¢	34.50¢	33.60¢	37.60¢
	1943	36¢	33.50¢	34.60¢	34.10¢	36.70¢
	1944	33.60¢	31.70¢	33.30¢	32.40¢	33.90¢
Beef, Steaks (Round), per pound	1940	NR	NR	NR	NR	NR
	1941	41.20¢	35.80¢	38.10¢	34.80¢	38.40¢
	1942	45.40¢	40.70¢	40.90¢	39.80¢	43.30¢
	1943	45.70¢	41.60¢	41.40¢	40.20¢	42.30¢
	1944	42.80¢	40.20¢	39.90¢	39¢	41.60¢
Bread, White, per pound	1940	NR	NR	NR	NR	NR
	1941	9.20¢	9.20¢	7.10	7.30¢	7¢
	1942	9.60¢	10¢	7.30¢	7.90¢	7.90¢
	1943	9.60¢	9.80¢	7.60¢	8.60¢	8.10¢
	1944	9.40¢	9.80¢	7.70¢	8.40¢	8.30¢
Butter, per pound	1940	NR	NR	NR	NR	NR
	1941	41.90¢	41.70¢	40.50¢	41¢	42.30¢
	1942	48.10¢	47.90¢	46.20¢	49.10¢	48.70¢
	1943	53.10¢	52.40¢	52.10¢	52.60¢	54.10¢
	1944	50.10¢	49.80¢	49.90¢	50.60¢	51.30¢
Cheese, per pound	1940	NR	NR	NR	NR	NR
	1941	32¢	26.90¢	31.10¢	32.30¢	28.80¢
	1942	36.40¢	31.60¢	34.90¢	37.70¢	35.70¢
	1943	37.70¢	35.60¢	36.50¢	40.70¢	38.30¢
	1944	35.20¢	34.50¢	36.30¢	40.80¢	36.80¢
Chickens, per pound	1940	NR	NR	NR	NR	NR
	1941	34.30¢	27.10¢	32.20¢	29.40¢	34.10¢
	1942	40.10¢	32.40¢	39.90¢	37.40¢	41.30¢
	1943	45.20¢	41¢	44.20¢	40.90¢	47.50¢
	1944	45.40¢	40.70¢	45.30¢	40.60¢	44.30¢
Coffee, per pound	1940	NR	NR	NR	NR	NR
	1941	24.20¢	20.30¢	24.50¢	28.10¢	23¢
	1942	29.20¢	25.40¢	29.20¢	31.60¢	28.10¢
	1943	30.30¢	28.60¢	30.40¢	34.60¢	29.50¢
	1944	30.30¢	31.20¢	30.80¢	34.40¢	29.70¢
Cornmeal, per pound	1940	NR	NR	NR	NR	NR
	1941	6.40¢	2.60¢	5.90¢	4.50¢	4.80¢
	1942	6.70¢	3.40¢	6.50¢	5.90¢	6.40¢
	1943	6.50¢	4.80¢	6.10¢	5.90¢	6.40¢
	1944	6.80¢	5.50¢	6.40¢	6.30¢	8.40¢
Eggs, per dozen	1940	NR	NR	NR	NR	NR
	1941	45.30¢	36¢	38.90¢	33.90¢	39¢
	1942	54.60¢	43.70¢	46.50¢	44.40¢	47.20¢
	1943	60.80¢	53.70¢	57.20¢	54.50¢	57.70¢
	1944	58.50¢	50.80¢	54.60¢	53.10¢	56.10¢

Commodity	Year	New York	Atlanta	Chicago	Denver	Los Angeles
Flour, Wheat, per pound	1940	NR	NR	NR	NR	NR
	1941	5.16¢	5.01¢	4.51¢	4.18¢	4.22¢
	1942	5.74¢	5.90¢	5.28¢	4.72¢	4.96¢
	1943	6.19¢	6.86¢	5.78¢	5.30¢	6.04¢
	1944	6.47¢	7.11¢	6.18¢	5.53¢	6.60¢
Lard, per pound	1940	NR	NR	NR	NR	NR
	1941	13.70¢	12.10¢	12.90¢	12.90¢	13.60¢
	1942	18.10¢	16.20¢	17.30¢	17.70¢	18.40¢
	1943	19.40¢	18.80¢	19.40¢	19¢	20.20¢
	1944	18.50¢	18.70¢	19.30¢	19.20¢	20¢
Milk, Fresh, per quart	1940	NR	NR	NR	NR	NR
	1941	15.70¢	15.20¢	14.50¢	12¢	12.80¢
	1942	16.90¢	16.20¢	16.60¢	13.20¢	14.70¢
	1943	17.40¢	17¢	17.50¢	13.60¢	14.50¢
	1944	17¢	17¢	15.50¢	13.70¢	14.50¢
Molasses, per 18-oz can	1940	NR	NR	NR	NR	NR
	1941	14.40¢	13.80¢	14.20¢	11.60¢	11.20¢
	1942	15.70¢	14.90¢	15.80¢	13.30¢	12.90¢
	1943	16.30¢	14.60¢	16.10¢	15.50¢	15.90¢
	1944	16.20¢	14.90¢	16.40¢	15.50¢	16.50¢
Mutton and Lamb, Leg, per pound	1940	NR	NR	NR	NR	NR
	1941	29.10¢	29.90¢	30.10¢	28.20¢	30.40¢
	1942	34.90¢	34¢	34.50¢	35.10¢	36.20¢
	1943	40.70¢	37.40¢	38.10¢	38¢	39.50¢
	1944	39.90¢	38¢	38.70¢	37¢	39.90¢
Pork, Bacon, Sliced, per pound	1940	NR	NR	NR	NR	NR
	1941	34.40¢	34.40¢	36.90¢	36.20¢	37.80¢
	1942	41.40¢	38.80¢	40.90¢	42.80¢	43.50¢
	1943	43.20¢	38.80¢	40.90¢	42.80¢	43.50¢
	1944	40.20¢	40.80¢	41.30¢	43¢	42.60¢
Pork, Chops, per pound	1940	NR	NR	NR	NR	NR
	1941	34.90¢	32.10¢	35.10¢	31.70¢	39.50¢
	1942	41.50¢	37.50¢	41.60¢	41¢	48.20¢
	1943	49.20¢	39.10¢	39.70¢	40.20¢	48.20¢
	1944	38¢	37.80¢	36.80¢	38¢	38.60¢
Pork, Ham, Sliced, per pound	1940	NR	NR	NR	NR	NR
	1941	50.10¢	47.90¢	50.70¢	51¢	62.10¢
	1942	58.20¢	56.10¢	58.60¢	61.50¢	67.60¢
	1943	54.90¢	54.60¢	55¢	56.20¢	60.50¢
	1944	48.30¢	50¢	50.80¢	51¢	53.40¢
Pork, Salt, per pound	1940	NR	NR	NR	NR	NR
	1941	27.30¢	17.90¢	21.50¢	19.20¢	21.10¢
	1942	30.70¢	22.30¢	25.50¢	24.80¢	24.90¢
	1943	26.20¢	23.20¢	23.80¢	23.70¢	26¢
	1944	24.10¢	22.50¢	22.20¢	22.20¢	23.10¢
Potatoes, Irish, per 15 pounds	1940	NR	NR	NR	NR	NR
	1941	37.30¢	37.90¢	39.90¢	32.20¢	36.70¢
	1942	50.80¢	54.20¢	56.80¢	51.80¢	62.60¢
	1943	68.30¢	69.60¢	70.80¢	59.30¢	68.40¢
	1944	68.10¢	70.90¢	74¢	64.30¢	70.30¢
Prunes, Dried, per pound	1940	NR	NR	NR	NR	NR
	1941	10.20¢	8.30¢	10.80¢	10¢	8.30¢
	1942	13.30¢	11.80¢	14.50¢	14.10¢	13.50¢
	1943	13.30¢	11.80¢	14.50¢	16.10¢	16.70¢
	1944	16.70¢	15.80¢	18.50¢	16.80¢	16¢
Rice, per pound	1940	NR	NR	NR	NR	NR
	1941	8.70¢	9.10¢	8.30¢	8.20¢	9.40¢
	1942	12¢	12.80¢	12.80¢	11.10¢	12.80¢
	1943	12.70¢	12.80¢	12.90¢	12.30¢	13.40¢
	1944	13.40¢	12.40¢	12.90¢	12¢	13.50¢

Commodity	Year	New York	Atlanta	Chicago	Denver	Los Angeles
Sugar, per pound	1940	NR	NR	NR	NR	NR
	1941	5.54¢	5.46¢	5.83¢	6.43¢	5.52¢
	1942	6.60¢	6.40¢	6.90¢	7.90¢	6.70¢
	1943	6.60¢	6.50¢	6.90¢	7.90¢	6.80¢
	1944	6.50¢	6.40¢	7¢	7.40¢	6.80¢
Tea, per pound	1940	NR	NR	NR	NR	NR
	1941	75.60¢	75.60¢	81.60¢	90.80¢	77.60¢
	1942	90¢	91.20¢	95.20¢	$1.0040	89.60¢
	1943	89.20¢	96.40¢	92.40¢	$1.0080	94.40¢
	1944	91.20¢	98.80¢	99.60¢	$1.0720	$1.00
Veal, per pound	1940	NR	NR	NR	NR	NR
	1941	52.80¢	45.90¢	46.40¢	42.30¢	52.30¢
	1942	58.90¢	51.80¢	50.40¢	48.20¢	59.10¢
	1943	52.40¢	46.80¢	47.10¢	44.70¢	53.10¢
	1944	45¢	43.70¢	43.10¢	42.30¢	46.30¢

SELECTED PRICES 1940-1944

Item	Source	Description	Price
Alcohol			
Blended Whiskey	*I. Ginsberg Inc. Price List* (1940)	*Seagram's*	$2.70/fifth
Blended Whiskey	*I. Ginsberg Inc. Price List* (1940)	*Seagram's V.O.*	$3.75/fifth
Bourbon	*I. Ginsberg Inc. Price List* (1940)	*Seagram's Five Year*	$3.80/fifth
Cordial	*I. Ginsberg Inc. Price List* (1940)	*Silk Hat*	$1.15/pint
Corn Whiskey	*I. Ginsberg Inc. Price List* (1940)	*Mountain*	$2/quart
Gin	*I. Ginsberg Inc. Price List* (1940)	*Crescent Denby Club*	$1.60/quart
Gin	*I. Ginsberg Inc. Price List* (1940)	*Seagram's King Arthur*	$1.70/fifth
Whiskey	*I. Ginsberg Inc. Price List* (1940)	*Carstairs Blended*	$2.95/fifth
Whiskey	*I. Ginsberg Inc. Price List* (1940)	*Kessler's Private Blend*	$2/fifth
Whiskey	*I. Ginsberg Inc. Price List* (1940)	*Owings Mills Red Moon Corn*	$1.57/quart
Whiskey	*I. Ginsberg Inc. Price List* (1940)	*Seagram's Ancient Bottle Straight Rye*	$3.80/fifth
Whiskey	*I. Ginsberg Inc. Price List* (1940)	*Seagram's Five Crown Blended*	$2.25/fifth
Whiskey	*New York Times* (1940)	*York House Scotch;* outsells the next best selling famous-label Scotch in Macy's Best Cellar by 8 to 1	$2.79/fifth
Apparel, Children's			
Pants	*Sears, Roebuck* (1941)	Sanforized cool tropicals	$1.19
Pants	*Life Magazine* (1942)	*Kleinert's Softex Pad Pants;* refill pads, completely disposable, are the modern solution to the old-fashioned diaper problem	$0.60
Shoes	*Sears, Roebuck* (1941)	*Classic Saddle;* we don't need to tell you about saddle oxfords	$1.69
Slacks	*Sears, Roebuck* (1941)	Leisure coat and slacks; the style hit of the season	$3.98

Item	Source	Description	Price
Apparel, Men's			
Hats	*Chicago Tribune* (1943)	*Dobbs, Stetson and Lee*	$5 to $20
Raincoat	*Life Magazine* (1942)	*Rainfair The Grafton;* for business men; a fine-quality piedmont gabardine	$11.50
Shirt	*Chicago Tribune* (1943)	*Arrow White;* magic for any man's appearance- with a variety of collar styles	$2.75
Shoes	*Liberty* (1944)	*Air-o-Magic* shoes for men; hand-moulded innersoles	$6.00 to $7.50
Shoes	*Life Magazine* (1942)	*Winthrop;* action free shoes with a military-type strap oxford, full-leather lined	$9.50
Shoes	*Life Magazine* (1942)	*Roblee;* kodiak brown; harness stitched; overlay blucher; double sole	$6.00
Shoes	*Consumer Reports* (1943)	*Thom McAnn*	$4.20
Shoes	*Consumer Reports* (1943)	*Towncraft*	$4.79
Sports Jacket	*New York Times* (1940)	*Bloomingdale's;* large selection of wool tweeds and shetlands in shades of blue, grey, brown, and green	$15.00
Suit	*Chicago Tribune* (1941)	*Gulfstream's;* famous gabardine and tropical weaves	$7.95
Tie	*The Saturday Evening Post* (1941)	*Arrow;* as outstanding as Arrow shirts	$1.00
Tie	*Majestic Theatre Program* (1942)	*Arrow;* smart, neat patterns and stripes plus rich fabrics; then, they make the perfect knots	$1/$1.50/$2
Apparel, Women's			
Brassiere	*Majestic Theatre Program* (1942)	*Model Brassieres;* bias cup; be sure your bra really fits— buy your personal cup depth	$1.00
Brassiere	*Life Magazine* (1942)	*Carole;* wears, gives the beauty and style of a $1 brassiere	$0.59
Brassiere	*Majestic Theatre Program* (1942)	*Bali;* in tea rose, white, black nylon	$1.50 to $5.00
Coats	*Chicago Tribune* (1943)	Tweeds, shetlands, herringbones, fleece, twills, gabardines	$20.00
Dress	*New York Times* (1940)	*Knight in Armor;* our gilt-girdled rayon jersey	$22.75
Dress	*Chicago Tribune* (1941)	Vacation sensation; every one of our entire stock of frocks in that famous carefree fabric	$4.45
Dress	*Chicago Tribune* (1941)	*Russeks Prints;* rayon jerseys, rayon crepes; formerly $29.95–$69.95	$21.00
Dress	*Chicago Tribune* (1943)	*Carson, Pirie Scott & Co.;* a simple tailored dress . . . but not so plain as to be uninteresting and dignified without being mature	$7.95
Fur Coat	*New York Times* (1943)	Muskrat; beautiful in its own right, an impressive imitator . . . hardy, reliable, flattering	$245
Fur Coat	*New York Times* (1943)	*John Wanamaker;* silvery, radiant beaver . . . a subtle flatterer and a congenial companion to casual and formal costumes alike	$595
Fur Coat	*Chicago Tribune* (1943)	Persian lamb; from stock or made to measure	$259

Item	Source	Description	Price
Gloves	*Life Magazine* (1942)	*Kayser;* double-wearing leatherette glove, double-woven cotton at a single-woven price	$2.50
Handbag	*Chicago Tribune* (1943)	*Edgewood;* bold banner stripe	$5.00
Handkerchief	*Chicago Tribune* (1943)	Lace; delicately feminine are these petite wisps of linen and cotton; finely edged in lace to carry your Easter wishes	$0.25
Hostess Pajamas	*New York Times* (1943)	*Henri Bendel;* cool, flattering, at ease . . . just right for summer teas and supper; gay flower print; of silk and rayon; white background	$45.00
Jerkin	*Sears, Roebuck* (1941)	Gay candy stripes perk up any costume	$0.89
Purse	*Liberty* (1944)	*The Shopper;* the pocket-size purse for the woman with her hands full; Includes federal tax	$3.60
Shoes	*Majestic Theatre Program* (1942)	*Anoxnia Deluxe;* women's footwear forerunners for the spring mode; it is never too early to refresh your style	$5.98
Shoes	*Life* (1942)	*Enna Jetticks Shoes, Inc.;* Mae Style	$6.00
Shoes	*Life* (1942)	*Enna Jetticks Shoes, Inc. Phyllis Style;* for mother	$6.00
Shoes	*Chicago Tribune* (1943)	*Red Cross;* the Cupid Bow pump; beauty in gabardine	$6.95
Shoes	*Chicago Tribune* (1943)	Black gabardine tie with embroidered eyelets and a tip of patent; a beautiful shoe	$10.95
Slacks Suit	*Chicago Tribune* (1941)	*Rothley;* with new longer-fitted jackets	$6.95
Slacks	*Sears, Roebuck* (1941)	Wool; styles combine classic perfection with new brands of fashion	$2.98
Slips	*Majestic Theatre Program* (1942)	*Miss Swank Exclusive;* straight-plus-bias ends riding and twisting	$2.25 to $7.00
Sports Coat	*Sears, Roebuck* (1941)	We've put gores or pleats and new trims in every one; cut them beautifully, lined them with rich rayon twill	$7.98
Stockings	*The State* (Columbia, SC) (1940)	*Saxon-Cullum No-Mend Silk;* with silk prices up, this sale is more important to you than ever	$0.98
Suit	*Chicago Tribune* (1941)	Our loveliest of all chambray suits for town and country!	$17.95
Suit	*Chicago Tribune* (1943)	*Rothmoor;* of fine all-wool fabrics	$39.95
Washfrocks	*Sears, Roebuck* (1941)	A famous label with a matchless guarantee; $1 value	$0.79

Appliances

Item	Source	Description	Price
Alarm Clock	*Better Homes and Gardens* (1940)	*Westclox Country Club;* electric; for any room in the house; luminous dial; ivory finish	$3.45
Coffee Percolator	*Liberty* (1944)	Vaculator gives you an insurance policy; make the world's finest cup of coffee	$2.95
Deep Freezer	*Better Homes and Gardens* (1940)	*Motor Products Corporation;* electric; allows right at home the large quantity, frozen-food storage some families enjoy in lock systems	$225
Heater	*Better Homes and Gardens* (1940)	*Arvin Electric;* fan-forced; circulating; standard Model 101; 10" high, green enamel finish	$6.95

Item	Source	Description	Price
Home Incinerator	*Better Homes and Gardens* (1940)	*The Majestic Co.;* just connect to your furnace flue—costs nothing to operate	$29.95
Iron	*Better Homes and Gardens* (1940)	*Knapp-Monarch Co. Steam King;* fully automatic, irons with steam and can be used for dry cleaning	$12.95
Mixer	*Better Homes and Gardens* (1940)	*Kitchen-Aid;* superior food mixing; with juicer	$29.95
Mixer	*Better Homes and Gardens* (1940)	*Sunbeam MixMaster;* lighter, higher cakes due to even-mixing and greater aeration; complete with juicer West of Denver	$23.75 $24.50
Oil Burner	*Better Homes and Gardens* (1940)	*General Electric;* can be installed in as short a time as one day; clean, quiet, odorless, full automatic, easy on oil	$268
Range	*Better Homes and Gardens* (1940)	*Frigidaire;* at last I can afford an electric range; super sized twin-unit oven, speed-heat cooking units, high-speed broiler	$100
Washing Machine	*Better Homes and Gardens* (1940)	*Maytag;* available in white or gray finish, with or without water discharge pump	$59.95

Baby Products

Item	Source	Description	Price
Flannelettes	*Sears, Roebuck* (1941)	Sanforized shrunk; medium-heavyweight embroidered	$0.29
Gown	*Sears, Roebuck* (1941)	*Roly Poly;* combed cotton gown, commended by *Parents Magazine*	$0.47
Training Pants	*Sears, Roebuck* (1941)	The quickest easiest way to teach good habits	$0.13

Business Equipment & Supplies

Item	Source	Description	Price
Fountain Pen	*Liberty* (1944)	*Sheaffer's Lifetime Triumph* model pen; 14 karat gold sheath point	$15.00
Typewriter	*Sears, Roebuck* (1941)	Office machine efficiency, portable convenience	$64.50
Typewriter	*Sears, Roebuck* (1941)	*Underwood New Deluxe;* model list price $39.50	$29.75

Collectibles

Item	Source	Description	Price
Furniture	*American Collector* (1942)	Bow front mahogany Hepplewhite chest of drawers, original with exception of brasses; The Loft, West Chester, Pennsylvania	$125

Education

Item	Source	Description	Price
Fee	*New York Times* (1940)	Business school; shorthand, beginners, review, typing, stenotypists, reporting	$1/week

Entertainment

Item	Source	Description	Price
Concert Ticket	*New York Times* (1943)	Benny Goodman and his orchestra; Hotel Astor; Friday and Saturday	$1.25
Concert Ticket	*New York Times* (1944)	Philadelphia Orchestra; Ormandy conducting	$1.20 to $4.20
Movie Ticket	*New York Times* (1940)	*Gone With The Wind;* air conditioned; Little Carnegie	$1.10
Movie Ticket	*New York Times* (1940)	*The Doctor Takes A Wife;* Loretta Young, Ray Milland; plus big stage show; Roxy	$0.25

Item	Source	Description	Price
Movie Ticket	*Chicago Tribune* (1941)	*Wagons Roll At Night;* Humphrey Bogart; State-Lake Before 6:30 After 6:30	 $0.25 $0.40
Movie Ticket	*Chicago Tribune* (1941)	Two features; *That Hamilton Woman* and *The Great American Broadcast;* Oriental; Days Evenings	 $0.25 $0.40
Movie Ticket	*New York Times* (1942)	*My Gal Sal;* Rita Hayworth, Victor Mature, Carole Landis; 10:30 a.m. to 5:00 p.m.; Albee	$0.30
Opera Ticket	*New York Times* (1944)	*La Bohéme;* NY City Center Opera Co.	$0.75 to $2.00
Play Ticket	*Majestic Theatre* (1942)	*Lily of the Valley;* Windsor Theatre Matinees Evenings	 $0.55 to $1.65 $0.55 to $2.20
Play Ticket	*New York Times* (1942)	*Porgy & Bess;* by DuBose Heyward; one of the finest things in the American theater; Majestic	$2.75
Play Ticket	*New York Times* (1944)	*The Streets Are Guarded;* by Laurence Stallings; Henry Miller's	$1.20–$3.60
Theater Ticket	*New York Times* (1944)	*Carmen Jones;* the lowest-price major musical on Broadway	$3.00

Entertainment, Home

Item	Source	Description	Price
Board Game	*Liberty* (1944)	*Quija* board; a spine-tingling, electrifying game	$2.00
Camera	*Sears, Roebuck* (1941)	*Eastman Brownie;* compact, easy to operate	$2.56
Home Movie	*Life Magazine* (1942)	*Castle Films; African Pygmy Thrills;* Africa's tiny pygmies, menaced always by vicious man-eating crocodiles; own this astounding movie now 8mm 16mm	 $5.50 $8.75
Record	*Majestic Theatre Program* (1942)	*Decca;* the glorious Gershwin *Porgy and Bess;* four 12" records	$4.72
Recording Combination	*Better Homes and Gardens* (1940)	*Glamor-tone;* all in one 18" cabinet are radio, phonograph, and home-recording device	$34.50
Recording Disks	*Better Homes and Gardens* (1940)	*Crosley Glameton;* 8" size in cartons of 5	$1.50/carton

Farm Equipment & Supplies

Item	Source	Description	Price
Chicks	*The State* (Columbia, SC) (1940)	Day old; popular breed, post paid in South Carolina; cash with orders	$7.50/100
Seed	*The State* (Columbia, SC) (1940)	*Coker's Abruzzi;* rye seed, 84 percent germination, 100 percent pure	$1.00/bu
Separator	*Sears, Roebuck* (1941)	America's No. 1 separator; finest precision built into the world's most beautifully designed sanitary cream separator; 400 pounds per hour	$58.50
Tractor Tires	*Sears, Roebuck* (1941)	*Allstate;* makes farming easier; cut costs on every job	$35.15

Food Products

Item	Source	Description	Price
Artificial Sweetener	*New York Times* (1940)	*Macy's Saccharin Tablets;* 1/4 gr 1000s	$0.54

Item	Source	Description	Price
Candy	*Liberty* (1944)	*Licorice Sweeties;* gay, candy-coated, licorice-flavored for sweet eating Per box	$0.05
Chocolates	*The Saturday Evening Post* (1941)	*Miss Saylor's;* a tempting lure for lovely ladies; 1 lb tin	$1.00
Chocolates	*The Saturday Evening Post* (1941)	*Whitman's Sampler;* America's outstanding box of fine candy; 5 lb	$5.00
Coffee	*Chicago Tribune* (1943)	*Webb;* ration stamp	$0.33/pound
Drink	*Life* (1942)	*Nesbitt's California Orange Fountain;* favorite for years now in bottles	$0.05
Flour	*Chicago Tribune* (1943)	*Pillsbury;* for pastry, biscuits; not rationed; 24 1/2 lb bag	$1.09
Peanut Butter	*Chicago Tribune* (1943)	*Armours;* 24-oz jar; not rationed	$0.41
Soda Pop	*Better Homes and Gardens* (1940)	*Coca-Cola;* six-pack; delicious and refreshing; plus deposit	$0.25

Furniture

Item	Source	Description	Price
Bedroom Suite	*Chicago Tribune* (1943)	4-piece Early American bedroom suite	$49.50
Bunk Bed	*Sears, Roebuck* (1941)	Two beds for the price of one	$10.98
Chair	*Brochure Furniture by Tomlinson* (1940)	*The Riddle Fan Chair;* width 32", depth 28", height 46"	$85.00
Chest	*Brochure Furniture by Tomlinson* (1940)	*Randolph Tall;* 36" wide; will find a multitude of uses in the apartment or average home	$175
Dresser Base	*Sears, Roebuck* (1941)	An $11.50 value; four spacious drawers give plenty of room for clothing	$6.48
Lamp	*Better Homes and Gardens* (1940)	*General Electric Mazda* 40, 50, 60 Watt 75, 100 Watt	$0.13 $0.15
Mattress	*Better Homes and Gardens* (1940)	*Simmons Beautyrest;* based on our 10-year guarantee, the price comes down to about a penny a night	$39.50
Radio/Phonograph Cabinet	*Better Homes and Gardens* (1940)	*Stewart Warner Concert Grand Sheraton Model 8D9;* for homes where good taste rules	$185
Table	*Brochure Furniture by Tomlinson* (1940)	*Southall;* drop leaf; serves perfectly as a sofa table; top 45" x 26"–68"	$75.00

Garden Equipment & Supplies

Item	Source	Description	Price
Bulbs	*Sears, Roebuck* (1941)	Gladiola; pride of the garden; 10 bulbs	$0.23
Lawn Mower	*Sears, Roebuck* (1941)	We know it sounds unbelievable, but it's TRUE; 18"	$57.50
Pruner	*House and Garden* (1942)	*Seymour Smith & Son, Inc. Snap-cut;* garden scissors, 8"; chrome finish	$2.00
Rose	*Better Homes and Gardens* (1942)	*Jackson & Perkins Dr. Nicolas;* climbing; rose-pink blooms are 5" to 6" across	$1.50

Item	Source	Description	Price
Rose	*House and Garden* (1942)	*Wayside Gardens Heart's Desire Red Rose*	$1.50
Seeds	*House and Garden* (1942)	*Stumpp & Walter Co.;* multiflora hybrid begonia	$0.35/pkg
Seeds	*House and Garden* (1942)	*W. Atlee Burpee Co.;* marigold garden; twelve distinct kinds	$1/12 pkgs

Hotel Rates

Item	Source	Description	Price
Hotel Room	*New York Times* (1940)	*Berkeley-Carteret;* all inclusive weekend rate; Saturday afternoon and Sunday, room with bath, 3 lavish meals	$5.50
Hotel Room	*New York Times* (1940)	*Kathmere Inn and Beach Club;* private beach, pier; Old Greenwich, Conn.; swimming, tennis, delightful, restricted	$14/week
Hotel Room	*Chicago Tribune* (1941)	*McAlpin;* if business beckons you to New York, stay at the McAlpin; single	$3/day
Hotel Room	*New York Times* (1942)	*Hotel Chesterfield;* room with private bath and radio	$2.50/day
Hotel Room	*Majestic Theatre Program* (1942)	*Chelsea, Atlantic City;* dine royally in our beautiful diningroom overlooking the ocean; with meals and bath	$6.50/day
Hotel Room	*New York Times* (1943)	*Hotel Chesterfield;* here's value; room with private bath and radio; at Radio City in Times Square; double	$3.50–$6/day
Hotel Room	*New York Times* (1943)	*The Senator;* Atlantic City; enjoy these famous Senator values; a comfortable room and bath, sun decks, sea water baths, delicious food, just off boardwalk; two to a room	$4/day
Hotel Room	*New York Times* (1943)	*Calderwood;* guest ranch, Ramapo Mountains; northern New Jersey; fine horse, excellent food	$35/week

Household Products

Item	Source	Description	Price
Blanket	*The Saturday Evening Post* (1941)	Lighter, warmer for beauty sleep; 6' x 7 1/2'	$5.95
Casserole	*Better Homes and Gardens* (1940)	*Pyrex;* double duty; cover serves as an extra pie plate; 1 qt size	$0.50
Cheese Slicer	*Better Homes and Gardens* (1940)	*J. C. Brown Hostess;* wire; this sturdy slicer with taut cutting wire is a swifty; at your 5¢ and 10¢	$0.10
Cookware	*Better Homes and Gardens* (1940)	*Wearever Aluminum;* 5-piece matched set is planned to fit the usual oven	$6.40
Cookware	*Sears, Roebuck* (1941)	The kitchen quintuplet 5-purpose cooker	$5.19
Dinnerware	*Sears, Roebuck* (1941)	*Calais;* 32-piece set	$4.98
Draperies	James Bones Wright Jr., *Interiors* (1943)	Glazed chintz	$4/yard
Ice-Cube Tray	*Cheatham-Greenville Hardware Co., Inc.* (1943)		$1.50
Laundry Tub	*Chicago Tribune* (1943)	2-part concrete construction, less fittings	$9.85

Item	Source	Description	Price
Linseed Oil	*Cheatham-Greenville Hardware Co., Inc.* (1943)		$2.50/gal
Paint	*Cheatham-Greenville Hardware Co., Inc.* (1943)	*Dulux;* eggshell enamel	$2/quart
Paint	*Cheatham-Greenville Hardware Co., Inc.* (1943)	Light stone porch and floor paint	$4.50/gallon
Paint	*Chicago Tribune* (1943)	*DuPont;* for interiors and exteriors	$2.45/gallon
Paint	*Chicago Tribune* (1943)	*Ultra Luminal;* has the magic-like synthetic resin base	$2.85/gallon
Pressure Cooker	*Better Homes and Gardens* (1940)	*Presto;* just a twist of the lid horizontally seals the cooker; 3-qt size	$10.50
Salad Set	*Chicago Tribune* (1941)	Sterling silver; for summer buffets and little suppers	$4.75
Stoker	*Better Homes and Gardens* (1940)	Iron; fireman; gives abundant automatic low cost heat; complete with controls	$179.50
Tea Kettle	*Sears, Roebuck* (1941)	Our finest copper teakettle	$3.49
Toast and Jam Set	*Better Homes and Gardens* (1940)	*Toastmaster;* deluxe; includes fully automatic toaster; the handiest of trays, a toast plate and jars for jam or marmalade in colorful Franciscan ware	$17.95
Varnish	*Cheatham-Greenville Hardware Co., Inc.* (1943)	*Tufcote*	$1.43/quart
Wallpaper	*James Bones Wright Jr., Interiors* (1943)	Dining Room	$1.50/roll
Wax	*Cheatham-Greenville Hardware Co., Inc.* (1943)	*Johnson Paste Wax;* 1/4 pound can	$1.90
Weekend Case	*New York Times* (1940)	Grey or brown-striped canvas	$4.98

Jewelry

Item	Source	Description	Price
Engagement Ring	*Liberty* (1944)	5-diamond engagement ring, inspired by Lynn Gardner, Columbia Recording star	$265
Cultured Pearls	*New York Times* (1940)	*Gimbell's;* 46 single-strand necklaces, usually $6.95	$1.98
Watch	*Liberty* (1944)	*Gruen Veri-thin Constance* watch for women; 15 jewel movement	$33.75
Watch	*Chicago Tribune* (1943)	*Benrus;* your choice ladies or gents 15 jewel watch	$24.75
Wedding Ring	*Chicago Tribune* (1943)	Five fine-quality diamonds are set in this neatly engraved 18-k solid white or 14-k solid natural gold	$9.75

Meals

Item	Source	Description	Price
Dinner	*Chicago Tribune* (1941)	*Tracy's Restaurant;* a fresh shrimp cocktail, some relish, then a tender, juicy filet mignon, parsley, new potatoes, and fresh string beans; a farm style salad of fresh cucumbers and sour cream; delicious fresh cherry pie; some hot biscuits and a decanter of coffee	$0.95

Item	Source	Description	Price
Dinner	*New York Times* (1942)	*Taft Grill;* Vincent Lopez and his orchestra; no cover charge	$1.25

Medical Products & Services

Item	Source	Description	Price
Aspirin	*New York Times* (1943)	*St. Joseph;* be sure to insist on genuine St. Joseph aspirin every time; you can't buy aspirin that can do more for you, so why pay more; world's largest seller	$0.35/100
Foot Treatment	*Life* (1942)	*The Mennen Co. Quinsana;* 2-way treatment for athlete's feet	$0.50
Laxative	*Liberty* (1944)	*Inner Clean Herbal Laxative;* helps promote a natural-like movement	$0.30 $0.50 $1.00
Nasal Jelly	*Liberty* (1944)	SNJ for the relief of nose and throat infections Family package, 4 tubes and applicators	$3.00
Nonprescription Drug	*New York Times* (1940)	*Macy's Milk of Magnesia;* 1/2 gallon	$0.61
Nonprescription Drug	*New York Times* (1940)	*Macy's Granular Effervescent Salts;* 1 lb	$0.54
Nonprescription Drug	*Sears, Roebuck* (1941)	*Alka Seltzer;* 8 tablets	$0.24
Nonprescription Drug	*Sears, Roebuck* (1941)	*Listerine;* antiseptic; a favorite in American households for many years	$0.27
Nonprescription Drug	*Sears, Roebuck* (1941)	*Vasoline Camphor Ice;* tube	$0.10
Nonprescription Drug	*Sears, Roebuck* (1941)	*Squibb Spirit of Ammonia;* 1-oz bottle	$0.23
Vitamins	*Life* (1942)	*Vims Vitamin;* contains A, B1, B2, C, D, and P-P; 24 tablets	$1.69

Motorized Vehicles, Supplies, & Services

Item	Source	Description	Price
Automobile	Richard M. Langworth and Graham Robson, *Complete Book of Collectible Cars* (1985)	*American Bantam Convertible Coupe* [cost in 1940]	$399–$565
Automobile	Langworth and Robson, *Complete Book of Collectible Cars* (1985)	*Cadillac Series 60 Special;* 4-door sedan [cost in 1940]	$2,090–$3,820
Automobile	Langworth and Robson, *Complete Book of Collectible Cars* (1985)	*Ford V8 De Luxe V8/85 Convertible Coupe* [cost in 1940]	$600–$947
Automobile	Langworth and Robson *Complete Book of* Collectible Cars (1985)	*Lincoln Continental Club Coupe* [cost in 1940]	$2,783–$2,916
Automobile	Langworth and Robson, *Complete Book of* Collectible Cars (1985)	*Buick Series Century Sport Coupe* [cost in 1941]	$1,128–$1,620

Item	Source	Description	Price
Automobile	Langworth and Robson, *Complete Book of Collectible Cars* (1985)	*Chrysler Windsor Town and Country;* 9-passenger wagon [cost in 1941]	$1,412–$1,685
Automobile	Langworth and Robson, *Complete Book of Collectible Cars* (1985)	*Dodge Custom Convertible* [cost in 1941]	$1,162–$1,245
Automobile	Langworth and Robson, *Complete Book of Collectible Cars* (1985)	*Nash Ambassador Six;* 4-door trunkback sedan [cost in 1941]	$925–$1,130
Automobile	Langworth and Robson, *Complete Book of Collectible Cars* (1985)	*Packard One Ten Convertible Coupe* [cost in 1941]	$1,104–$1,375
Automobile	Langworth and Robson, *Complete Book of Collectible Cars* (1985)	*Chevrolet Fleetline Aerosedan* [cost in 1942]	$880
Automobile	Langworth and Robson, *Complete Book of Collectible Cars* (1985)	*DeSoto Deluxe;* featuring air-foil hidden headlamps [cost in 1942]	$1,010–$1,455
Automobile	Langworth and Robson, *Complete Book of Collectible Cars* (1985)	*Oldsmobile Custom 98 Convertible* [cost in 1942]	$1,079–$1,450
Automobile	Langworth and Robson, *Complete Book of Collectible Cars* (1985)	*Packard Clipper 180;* 4-door sedan [cost in 1942]	$2,099–$2,196
Automobile	Langworth and Robson, *Complete Book of Collectible Cars* (1985)	*Pontiac Steamliner Chieftan;* wood-body wagon [cost in 1942]	$1,030–$1,340
Service	*Authorized Buick Service, Eugene B. Smith, Inc.* (1941)	*Eugene B. Smith Buick Service Saver Plan;* 6 chassis lubrications, 1 front wheel lubrication	$4.25

Other

Item	Source	Description	Price
Billfold	*Life* (1942)	*Amity Leather Products Co.;* special navy model in dress-block cowhide embossed with official coat of arms	$2.50
Cemetery Plots	*New York Times* (1942)	Four-grave family plot; in beautiful Jewish Memorial Park	$100
Garage Door	*Chicago Tribune* (1943)	Overhead; stock worn 8' x 7'	$7.98

Item	Source	Description	Price
Globe	*Chicago Tribune* (1943)	*Marshall Fields & Co.;* follow this global war on a 10" globe	$2.95
Glue	*Better Homes and Gardens* (1940)	*Casco;* save the cost of a new kitchen table; make it stick with Casco	$0.25/tube
Greeting Card	*The Antique Trader Weekly* (1941)	*Gibson Valentine;* with a cellophane-covered candy heart glued into the printed one	$0.10
Greeting Card	*The Antique Trader Weekly* (1943)	*Norcross Valentine;* with a red diagonal ribbon and bow, alongside one printed rose, set off by a plastic dew drop	$1.00
Haircut	*New York Times* (1940)	For boys; summer holidays just ahead for your son . . . this is the time for him to get a shampoo and haircut in our barber shop; here he'll find barbers, expert at his favorite haircut for camp—side part, crew cut or pompadour	$0.50
Haircut	*New York Times* (1942)	Beautifully yours; 1942 windswept; the hair cut that's sweeping the country; fresh looking and so easy to keep it that way; a flick of the comb after a swim and it's set again	$2.00
Moth Spray	*Chicago Tribune* (1943)	*Enoz;* the ideal product to use on rugs, draperies, things you leave in the open air	$1.29/quart
Mural Kit	*Life* (1942)	150' mural on 3 sides of a barn; by Frank Engebretson in South Wayne, Wisconsin	$165 including paint
Open-Air Sunbathing	*New York Times* (1942)	*Grand Central Palace;* also supervised exercise, iced-alcohol massage, 7 courts for squash and handball, steam-salt baths; luncheon served daily; trial visit	$2.00
Paper Trim	*Better Homes and Gardens* (1940)	*Royledge Shelving Paper;* many a model house owes its kitchen charm to Royledge shelving	$0.05/9 feet
Parking	*Majestic Theatre Program* (1942)	*Corvan Garage Theatre;* parking; 122 and 124 West 54th Street	$0.50/day
Shoe Polish	*Sears, Roebuck* (1941)	*Shinola*	$0.09
Soles	*Sears, Roebuck* (1941)	Rubber; stick-on; three pairs	$0.42
Stain Remover	*House and Garden* (1942)	*Consolidated Chemical Works Dog-Tex;* removes dog stains, saves rugs, ends odors	$1.25/pt
Tattoo	*Life* (1942)	Snake design on arm	$0.25
Upholstering	*Chicago Tribune* (1941)	Summer bargain sale; sofa or chair	$10.50
Wallpaper Hanger	*Jesse W. Miller Paper Hanging* (1943)		$0.65/rl

Personal Care Products

Bandages	*The Saturday Evening Post* (1941)	*Johnson & Johnson Adhesive;* use a ready-made sterilized Band-Aid instead of fussing around with awkward, homemade bandages; 36 per box	$0.19
Complexion Powder	*Life* (1942)	*Yardley;* mist-blown, graciously scented with Bond Street; ten radiant shades	$1.00
Denture Adhesive	*Better Homes and Gardens* (1940)	*Polident;* she's not ashamed of her false teeth smile	$0.30

Item	Source	Description	Price
Deodorant	*Chicago Tribune* (1941)	*Dresshield;* an easy-to-apply liquid to check and deodorize underarm perspiration; 2 oz bottle	$0.60
Deodorant Powder	*New York Times* (1940)	*Macy's;* 8 oz	$0.39
Hair Oil	*New York Times* (1940)	*Macy's Perfumed Liquid Petroleum for the Hair;* 6 oz	$0.44
Lip Balm	*Life* (1942)	*Fleet's;* guard lips from weather	$0.25
Lipstick	*Majestic Theatre Program* (1942)	*Chanel;* for impeccable grooming—the fashion correct shades of Chanel lipstick	$1.50
Lipstick	*Consumer Reports* (1942)	*Lentheric Bal Masque Brune Satine*	$1.50
Lipstick	*Consumer Reports* (1942)	*Almay Dark*	$1.10
Lipstick	*Consumer Reports* (1942)	*L'Adonna Light*	$0.50
Lipstick	*Consumer Reports* (1942)	*Elizabeth Post Heavenly Pink*	$0.10
Lipstick	*Life* (1942)	*Yardley, Bond Street;* keeps your lips soft and inviting; in eight shades	$1.00
Makeover	*Majestic Theatre Program* (1942)	*Helena Rubinstein;* complete mid-winter makeover including herbal shampoo, a flattering new coiffure, *posture* exercise, body massage, new make-up	$10.00
Mouthwash	*New York Times* (1940)	*Macy's ZCA's;* 1/2 gallon	$0.71
Perfume Stick	*Life* (1942)	*RIC;* not a liquid; takes perfume off the dressing table and puts it in your purse	$1.00
Razor Blades	*New York Times* (1940)	*Macy's Single Edge;* 50	$0.74
Razor Blades	*Life* (1942)	*Berkeley;* double edge; why pay more, made of fine watch-spring steel; 18 blades to a box	$0.25
Rouge	*Majestic Theatre Program* (1942)	*Coty Air-Spun;* miraculous in the way it clings; buffed by torrents of air	$0.50
Shampoo	*Liberty* (1944)	*Fitch's Saponified Cocoanut Oil Shampoo;* no dull film remains 6-ounce bottle	$0.50
Shaver	*The Saturday Evening Post* (1941)	*Schick Electric;* new 2-M hollow ground head	$9.95
Skin Lotion	*New York Times* (1940)	*Macy's*	$0.94/pint
Sun Oil	*New York Times* (1940)	*Macy's;* scented; 8 oz	$0.89
Toothbrush	*Life* (1942)	*Dr. West's Miracle-Tuft;* includes Exton brand bristling, surgically sterile glass packaging, a full year of effective service	$0.50
Tooth Powder	*New York Times* (1940)	*Macy's;* 1 lb	$0.44
Witch Hazel	*New York Times* (1940)	*Macy's*	$0.82/gallon

Publications

Magazine	*Better Homes and Gardens* (1940)	*Better Homes and Gardens;* monthly	$0.10

Item	Source	Description	Price
Magazine	*Life* (1942)	*Time; weekly* Per issue Per year	$0.10 $4.50

Real Estate

Item	Source	Description	Price
Apartment	*New York Times* (1940)	For rent; 3 rooms, modern, attractive, refrigeration	$35/month
Apartment	*New York Times* (1940)	For rent; 3 rooms, dinette	$75/month
Apartment	*New York Times* (1940)	For rent; off Central Park; 5 rooms; refrigeration, combination sink, tub, shower; references required	$47/month
Chicken Farm	*Chicago Tribune* (1941)	5 1/2 acres; cash	$200
Farm Suburban Estate	*Chicago Tribune* (1941)	House, 2 acres, beautiful hilltop estate, paved road, interior needs modernization	$2,975
Garden Farm	*Chicago Tribune* (1941)	Black garden soil, on newly paved road; nearly 2 acres, electricity; $100 cash, $8 month	$545
House	*New York Times* (1940)	Garden duplex; 5 rooms 2 baths, fireplace; atmosphere	$1,900
House	*New York Times* (1943)	*Baldwin;* 6-room cottage, extra large, spacious rooms, stall shower and tub; steam-oil; 2-car garage; bus at corner	$6,950
House	*New York Times* (1943)	Owner leaving city offers center hall colonial, short walk to station, bus line or shopping; 3 large bedrooms, tile bath and stall shower, fireplace, modern kitchen… complete insulation	$9,000
House	*New York Times* (1943)	Great Neck; price reduced; entirely redecorated; 4 bedrooms, 2 baths; maid's room, bath; sunroom, recreation room with bar; double garage	$16,000
House	*New York Times* (1943)	Exceptionally well-built brick house, painted white, situatedon 3 high acres, water view; walking distance of beach and bus; gardens, fruit trees, lovely grounds	$29,500
House	*Chicago Tribune* (1943)	32 minutes to loop; double garage and hen house, good condition	$1,000
House	*Chicago Tribune* (1943)	Frame home, sleeping porch, furnace heat, low taxes	$7,000
House	*Chicago Tribune* (1943)	Cozy 5-room house on large landscaped lot, garage, fruit trees, flowers	$3,800

Sewing Equipment & Supplies

Item	Source	Description	Price
Cloth	*Sears, Roebuck* (1941)	Monk's cloth; sunfast; plaid; 36" goods	$0.32/yard

Sports Equipment

Item	Source	Description	Price
Golf Clubs	*New York Times* (1942)	*Walter Hagen Power Groove;* set of 5 irons	$12.95
Golf Shoes	*New York Times* (1941)	*Johnny Farrell;* with removable spikes, made on plateau last with selected leather uppers and solid, double-leather outersoles; complete with shoe-horn wrench	$4.99
Head Covers	*New York Times* (1942)	*Poplin Golf Club;* contrasting colors; heavily padded poplin; leather numbers	$1.59/3
Reel	*Sears, Roebuck* (1941)	Top performance; equal quality; the same that costs 1.00/3 more elsewhere; nonbacklash x-port	$3.79
Shotgun	*Sullivan Hardware Co.* (1940)	*Remington 20/26 Model III;* automatic	$39.30

Item	Source	Description	Price
Tobacco Products			
Pipe	*Liberty* (1944)	*Sterling Hall by Briarcraft;* preferred for smoking quality	$3.50
Travel & Transportation			
Airplane Tickets	*New York Times* (1940)	21 flagships daily; only 75 minutes to Boston; go and return any time	
		One way	$11.95
		Round trip	$21.50
Railroad Ticket	*New York Times* (1940)	*New York Central System;* New York-Chicago; the Pacemaker famous deluxe coach train; round trip	$27.25
Railroad Ticket	*New York Times* (1942)	*Montrealer;* round-trip fares to Montreal; summer excursion; upper berth, 60-day return limit	$28.80

1865   1942

A style as American as the red, white and blue feather in the band—with emphasis on quality and accent on wear. This is another Stetson original, made by the exclusive Stetson Vita-Felt process, shown in the new "Freedom Blue" color.

The STETSON *Eagle* $7.50

MISCELLANY 1940-1944

Smith Girls

The job market opens wide for college graduates as war reduces manpower.

The employment boom that is sweeping oldsters, youngsters and mothers of families into jobs left vacant as men go off to war, last spring invaded the nation's colleges, precipitated many a young girl graduate into a juicy job for which she once would have had to labor long and hard.

At Smith College, whereas $1,200 a year was considered a good starting salary in 1941, this year's candidates averaged $1,600 with the promise of speedy raises after a brief training period.

Anita Livingston Willis of Great Neck, Long Island: She is now employed by Macy's in New York, is going through a nine-month training period. Her starting salary is $30 a week.

Marian Frances Carpenter of Brooklyn, N. Y.: Upon graduation, the Office of Price Administration in Washington put in a bid for her services and she went to work there a fortnight after leaving college. She is in the Research Section of Copper, Aluminum and Ferro-Alloys, starting at a yearly salary of $2,000 with a raise to $2,600 promised soon.

Suzanne Cook Vroom of Worcester, Mass.: The job which she took in July (was) with the Liberty Mutual Insurance Co. in Boston. Having first enrolled in a training class for claims adjusters at a yearly salary of $1,300 plus a bonus of about $150, she is now working in the field, investigating accidents.

Life, September 28, 1942

Colored

Come where better jobs are better pay. Largest Colored Dept. to serve you—low fees. Loop Agency 28 E. Jackson 7th Floor.

Chicago Tribune, April 17, 1943

Cigarette, Liquor Taxes in 2 Days Yield $1,834,386

The state treasury netted $1,834,386 from Illinois's new cigarette and liquor taxes in the first two days the new levies were in effect. Finance Director George B. McKibbin reported today.

McKibbin said the cigarette tax, 2 cents on each package of 20, accounted for $676,790 of revenue and the doubled liquor taxes yielded $1,157,596. The figures covered tax stamps sold by the finance department up to July 3, the taxes having become operative July 1.

Stamps sold during the first two days were largely to cover current stocks of liquors and cigarettes on the shelves of retailers and wholesalers. In the future the stocks will reach retailers prestamped by distributors and manufacturers.

Chicago Tribune, July 8, 1941

Hold Furniture Price Hikes to 5%, U.S. Rules

A ceiling of 5 per cent on price boosts was imposed on the furniture industry yesterday by governmental price fixers. The limit was announced as thousands in the industry gathered in Chicago for the summer home furnishings market, which will be held for two weeks at the American Furniture Mart and the Merchandise Mart.

The price stabilizing order by the Office of Price Administration and Civilian Supply was described as a temporary measure in response to the requests of furniture makers for permission to increase wholesale prices. The markups were made necessary by increasing material and labor costs, manufacturers said.

Chicago Tribune, July 8, 1941

MISCELLANY 1940-1944

Farm Land Prices Reported Going Up; OWI Warns Against Repetition of Boom In War of 1917-1918 and Subsequent Collapse

The Office of War Information, comparing current price trends of farm lands with those of the last war, warned today against a general rise of values and a subsequent "disastrous" deflation.

Although values were not at the "boom stage which led to the catastrophe of 1921," the OWI said, farm real estate values on March 3, 1943, were noticeably higher than a year earlier.

On that date, the index of the average per acre values (1912-14 being equal to 100) stood at 99 for the country as a whole, as compared with 91 in March 1942, 85 in 1941, and a low of 73 in 1933.

"The low point reached in 1933 was the final aftermath of an inflationary process set in motion during the last war, a process that reached a climax immediately afterward in 1919 and 1920," the OWI stated.

Swollen land values in those two years came about through the demand for farm land that was paying heavy wartime dividends based on excessive prices received for farm products.

In 1943, for the first time in twenty years, the annual average of farm prices reached parity with other prices, the OWI said.

Since the outbreak of war, it continued, the average of farm prices had risen more than 90 per cent and farm income by about 80 per cent, while the average of prices paid by farmers, including interest and taxes, had increased about 25 per cent.

The Bureau of Agricultural Economics found that as of March 1, 1943, increases in value over those of the previous year were 20 to 24 per cent in thirteen states, 15 to 19 per cent in sixteen states, 10 to 14 percent in eleven states and less than 10 per cent in six states.

New York Times, July 12, 1943

HISTORICAL SNAPSHOT
1945-1949

1945

- President Franklin Delano Roosevelt dies in office; Harry Truman becomes president
- World War II ends
- Penicillin introduced commercially
- Beechcraft Bonanza two-engine private plane introduced
- U.S. Gross National Product is $211 billion, double the GNP of 1928
- Ballpoint pens, costing $12.50 each, go on sale
- Weed killer 2,4-D patented
- Rationing of all items except sugar ends; shortages continue
- Frozen orange juice pioneered
- Tupperware Corporation formed

1946

- Strikes idle 4.6 million workers with a loss of 116 million man-days, worst stoppage since 1919
- Dow Jones Industrials average peaks at post-1929 high of 212.50
- Wage and price controls end on all areas except rents, sugar, and rice
- U.S. college enrollments reach all-time high of more than 2 million
- Ektachrome color film introduced by Kodak Company
- Tide introduced; by 1949 one in four wash detergent consumers will use it
- Timex watches introduced at $6.95 and up

- Hunt Foods establishes "price at time of shipment" contracts with customers
- U.S. birthrate soars to 3.4 million, up from 2.9 million in previous year

1947

- Taft-Hartley Act restricts organized labor
- New York transit fare doubles to ten cents, the first increase since 1904
- B. F. Goodrich Company introduces first tubeless tire
- Ajax cleanser is introduced by Colgate-Palmolive-Peet Company
- U.S. frozen orange juice concentrate sales reach 7 million cans, up from 4.8 in 1946
- Reddi-Whip whipped cream in a can introduced
- Seagram's 7 Crown becomes the world's largest selling brand of whiskey
- Raytheon Company introduces first commercial microwave oven

1948

- Transistor developed by Bell Telephone Laboratories, permitting miniaturization of electronic devices such as computers, radios, and television

- 360,000 soft-coal workers strike demanding $100 per month in retirement benefits at age 62
- Congress passes Anti-Inflationary Act as cost of living rises
- One million homes have television sets
- Nikon camera introduced to compete with Leica
- Dial Soap introduced as first deodorant soap
- Corn production is now 75 percent hybrid
- Gerber Products Company sells 2 million cans and jars of baby food weekly
- The first McDonald's restaurant is opened in San Bernadino, CA

1949

- 500,000 steel workers strike, gain pension demands
- U.S. auto production reaches 5.1 million
- The president's salary is raised to $100,000 per year
- Silly Putty introduced at $1 per ounce
- Sara Lee Cheese Cake introduced
- Minimum wage raised from 40 cents to 70 cents per hour
- CBS introduces long-playing vinyl phonograph record

SELECTED INCOME 1945-1949

Job	Source	Description	Pay
Bakery Salesgirls	*Chicago Tribune* (1949)	Experienced; steady; uniforms furnished	$7/day
Baseball Commissioner	Victor Bondi, ed., *American Decades: 1940-1949* (1995)	Annual salary of Albert "Happy" Chandler in 1945	$50,000
Baseball Player	Bondi, ed., *American Decades: 1940-1949* (1995)	Annual salary of New York Yankee outfielder Joe Dimaggio in 1947	$90,000
Baseball Player	Bondi, ed., *American Decades: 1940-1949* (1995)	Salaries for Professional All-American Girls' Baseball League players in 1948	$40–$100/wk
Baseball Player	Bondi, ed., *American Decades: 1940-1949* (1995)	Annual salary of Boston Red Sox player Ted Williams in 1949	$125,000
Baseball Player	Arnold Rampersad, *Jackie Robinson, A Biography* (1997)	Earnings of Brooklyn Dodgers Jackie Robinson in 1949	$17,500
Boxer	Bondi, ed., *American Decades: 1940-1949*	Joe Louis's earnings for heavyweight boxing championship fight with Billy Conn in 1946	$625,916
Cook	Greenville SC) Piedmont (1945)	Resort; colored woman	$125/mo
Cook	*Atlanta Constitution* (1947)	Good cook and general houseworker; prefer sleeping in; no Thursdays, no Sundays	$20/wk
Counterman	*Chicago Tribune* (1949)		$45/wk
Dictaphone Operator	*Atlanta Constitution* (1947)		$150–175/mo
Director of Home Economics	*Chicago Tribune* (1949)	National food manufacturing company; degree	$7,500/yr
Factory and Warehouse	*Chicago Tribune* (1949)	No experience necessary; choice of shifts	To $1.21/hr
Food Checker	*Chicago Tribune* (1946)	5 days, 9–4; meals included	$25/wk
Football Player	Bondi, ed., *American Decades: 1940-1949* (1995)	Average per player winnings for New York Giants and Chicago Bears Football Championship Game in 1946	$2,000
Golfer	Bondi, ed., *American Decades: 1940-1949*	Annual winnings of Byron Nelson in 1945	$66,000
Hallicrafters	*Chicago Tribune* (1946)	Builders of high-frequency radios: wirers, solderers, assemblers, stenographers, typists, inspectors, sheet metal workers, layout	$0.80–$1.05/hr

Job	Source	Description	Pay
Investigators	*Atlanta Constitution* (1947)	Part-time	$4/day
Junior Cost Man	Greenville (SC) Piedmont (1945)		$175/mo
Machinist	*Chicago Tribune* (1949)	50 hr min; set up and operate; top notch only	$1.25/hr
Maid	*Chicago Tribune* (1946)	White; to do cooking and general housework; must be compatible with family; own room and bath; person with emperament not wanted; must have references	$40/wk
Metal Finisher	*PM* (1977)	Starting hourly wage in General Motors automotive plant in 1947	$1.19
Secretary	*Chicago Tribune* (1949)	For three salesman	$216/mo
Service Station Attendant	*Atlanta Constitution* (1947)	Experienced; Apply ready to work	$40/wk
Shipping Clerk	*Greenville (SC) Piedmont* (1945)		$175/mo
Shoemaker	*Greenville (SC) Piedmont* (1945)	Good working conditions; West Palm Beach, Florida	$60–70/wk
Stenographer	*Greenville (SC) Piedmont* (1945)		$175/mo
Typist	*Greenville (SC) Piedmont* (1945)		$100/mo

CONSUMER EXPENDITURES 1945-1949

(Per Capita)

Expenditure Type	1945	1946	1947	1948	1949
Clothing	$93.62	$106.79	$108.24	$114.57	$107.25
Food	$290.15	$334.54	$363.57	$369.64	$351.90
Auto Usage	$29.30	$67.19	$90.19	$105.71	$126.69
New Auto Purchase	NR	$14.15	$27.75	$34.09	$51.61
Auto Parts	$5.00	$9.90	$9.71	$8.87	$8.04
Gas & Oil	$12.86	$24.05	$27.75	$32.74	$35.53
Housing	$91.48	$100.43	$111.01	$122.08	$131.38
Furniture	$10.72	$15.56	$17.35	$19.09	$18.09
Utilities	$32.16	$35.36	$40.24	$45.01	$43.57
Telephone & Telegraph	$8.58	$9.19	$9.71	$10.91	$11.39
Physicians	$10.01	$12.73	$14.57	$16.37	$16.76
Dentists	$4.29	$5.66	$5.55	$5.46	$6.03
Health Insurance	$2.86	$2.83	$5.55	$5.46	$5.36
Personal Business	$29.30	$33.29	$36.08	$38.87	$39.55
Personal Care	$14.29	$14.85	$15.26	$15.69	$15.42
Tobacco	$20.72	$24.05	$25.67	$27.28	$27.48
Local Transport	$12.15	$13.44	$13.18	$13.64	$13.41
Intercity Transport	$7.86	$7.07	$6.94	$6.82	$6.03
Recreation	$43.59	$60.12	$63.83	$66.15	$67.03
Religion/Welfare Activities	$12.86	$14.85	$14.57	$15.69	$15.42
Private Education & Research	$7.15	$7.78	$9.71	$10.23	$11.39
Per Capita Consumption	$854.73	$1017.76	$1123.32	$1192.79	$1119.51

INVESTMENTS 1945-1949

Investment	1945	1946	1947	1948	1949
Basic Yield, One-year Corporate Bonds	1.02	.86	1.05	1.60	1.60
Short-term Interest Rates, 4–6 Months, Prime Commercial Paper	.75	.81	1.03	1.44	1.49
Basic Yield, Common Stocks, Total	1.02	.86	1.05	1.60	1.60
Index of Common Stocks (1941–1943=10)	102	104.8	103.8	100.8	102.7

COMMON STOCKS, CLOSING PRICE AND DIVIDEND, FIRST BUSINESS DAY OF YEAR

(Parenthetical number is annual dividend in dollars)

	1945	1946	1947	1948	1949
Allis Chalmers	38 1/2	53 3/4	36 7/8	39 1/2	36
	(1.65)	(1.75)	(1.60)	(1.60)	(1.60)
AT&T	163 1/4	190 1/4	171 1/8	152	149 7/8
	(9)	(9)	(9)	(9)	(9)
American Tobacco	65	89 1/4	81	68 1/2	61 1/4
	(3.25)	(3.25)	(3.25)	(3.50)	(3.75)
Anaconda	30	44	39 7/8	34 1/8	33 3/8
	(2.50)	(2.50)	(2.50)	(3)	(3.50)
B&O	12 1/4	25 3/8	21 3/4	13 1/8	10
	(/)	(/)	(/)	(/)	(/)
Bethlehem Steel	65 7/8	95 5/8	91 3/4	103 3/8	31 5/8
	(6)	(6)	(6)	(6)	(2.40)
Corn Products	58 1/2	67 1/4	73 3/4	64	57 3/4
	(2.60)	(2.60)	(2.70)	(3.15)	(3.60)
General Electric	39 3/8	35 1/2	35 7/8	38 7/8	42 3/8
	(1.40)	(1.60)	(1.60)	(1.60)	(1.80)
General Motors	63 7/8	75	54	58	57 3/4
	(3)	(3)	(3.25)	(3)	(4.50)
International Business Machines	185	247 7/8	NR	240	154 1/4
(5% stock dividend, 1/29/45)	(6)	(6)		(6)	(4)
(5 shares for 4 split, 1/26/46)					
(1 3/4 shares for 1 split, 2/6/48)					
(5% stock dividend, 1/28/49)					
Intl Harvester	80	94 3/4	71 3/4	89 1/4	25 1/2
	(3)	(3)	(3)	(5)	(1.35)
National Biscuit	23 7/8	32 1/2	28	30 1/2	30 1/2
	(1.20)	(1.20)	(1.20)	(2)	(2)
US Steel	60 1/2	81	71 5/8	77 5/8	69 1/4
	(7)	(4)	(7)	(5.00)	(5.00)
Western Union	45 3/8	51 3/8	19 1/4	20 1/2	15 1/8
	(2)	(2)	(/)	(/)	(1.00)

STANDARD JOBS 1945-1949

Job Type	1945	1946	1947	1948	1949
Average of All Industries, excl. farm labor	$2424/yr	$2529/yr	$2657/yr	$2999/yr	$3075/yr
Average of All Industries, inc. farm labor	$2364/yr	$2473/yr	$2602/yr	$2933/yr	$3000/yr
Bituminous Coal Mining	$2629/yr	$2724/yr	$3212/yr	$3388/yr	$2922/yr
Building Trades	$2600/yr	$2537/yr	$2829/yr	$3125/yr	$3229/yr
Domestics	$1312/yr	$1411/yr	$1463/yr	$1500/yr	$1498/yr
Farm Labor	$1307/yr	$1394/yr	$1479/yr	$1541/yr	$1501/yr
Federal Civilian	$2646/yr	$2904/yr	$3180/yr	$3256/yr	$3481/yr
Federal Employees, Executive Depts.	$2057/yr	$2490/yr	$2843/yr	$2949/yr	$2995/yr
Federal Military	$1931/yr	$2279/yr	$2556/yr	$2676/yr	$2599/yr
Finance, Insurance, & Real Estate	$2347/yr	$2570/yr	$2740/yr	$2954/yr	$3034/yr
Gas & Electricity Workers	$2596/yr	$2697/yr	$2994/yr	$3223/yr	$3383/yr
Manufacturing, Durable Goods	$2732/yr	$2615/yr	$2883/yr	$3163/yr	$3240/yr
Manufacturing, Nondurable Goods	$2211/yr	$2404/yr	$2683/yr	$2892/yr	$2961/yr
Medical/Health Services Workers	$1401/yr	$1605/yr	$1821/yr	$1918/yr	$1995/yr
Miscellaneous Manufacturing	$2401/yr	$2442/yr	$2657/yr	$2808/yr	$2856/yr
Motion Picture Services	$2567/yr	$2978/yr	$3031/yr	$2964/yr	$3028/yr
Nonprofit Org. Workers	$1876/yr	$2070/yr	$2172/yr	$2334/yr	$2465/yr
Passenger Transportation Workers, Local and Highway	$2596/yr	$2886/yr	$3020/yr	$3101/yr	$3164/yr
Personal Services	$1725/yr	$1881/yr	$2011/yr	$2120/yr	$2189/yr
Public School Teachers	$1822/yr	$2025/yr	$2261/yr	$2538/yr	$2671/yr
Radio Broadcasting & Television Workers	$3515/yr	$3972/yr	$4073/yr	$4234/yr	$4380/yr
Railroads	$2711/yr	$3055/yr	$3216/yr	$3611/yr	$3706/yr
State and Local Govt. Workers	$1938/yr	$2093/yr	$2300/yr	$2593/yr	$2670/yr
Telephone & Telegraph Workers	$2246/yr	$2413/yr	$2583/yr	$2776/yr	$2920/yr
Wholesale and Retail Trade Workers	$2114/yr	$2378/yr	$2632/yr	$2832/yr	$2899/yr

FOOD BASKET 1945-1949

(NR = Not Reported)

Commodity	Year	New York	Atlanta	Chicago	Denver	Los Angeles
Apples, Fresh, per pound	1945	12.60¢	11.80¢	13.70¢	13.30¢	12.80
	1946	13.70¢	13.10¢	13.20¢	14.20¢	14.20¢
	1947	13.10¢	12.90¢	13.20¢	13.50¢	13.50¢
	1948	12.90¢	12.50¢	12¢	12.80¢	13.20¢
	1949	13.60¢	13.20¢	13.20¢	14.20¢	13.80¢
Beans, Navy, per pound	1945	12.90¢	10.40¢	11.60¢	10.50¢	12.50¢
	1946	14.60¢	NR	13.70¢	12.70¢	17.20¢
	1947	22.40¢	20.10¢	20.20¢	18.10¢	25¢
	1948	23.40¢	20.30¢	20¢	19.50¢	24.60¢
	1949	18.50¢	15¢	16.30¢	16¢	18¢
Beef, Rib Roasts, per pound	1945	32.80¢	31.50¢	32.60¢	32.80¢	33.30¢
	1946	NR	41.20¢	44.20¢	41.10¢	45¢
	1947	67.30¢	61.30¢	62.60¢	61.20¢	63.30¢
	1948	76.70¢	73¢	74.30¢	71.40¢	76.20¢
	1949	69.50¢	66.50¢	68.60¢	63.70¢	74.70¢
Beef, Steaks (Round), per pound	1945	41.90¢	39.70¢	39.10¢	39.10¢	41.20¢
	1946	54.70¢	51¢	50.80¢	48.60¢	52.40¢
	1947	80.90¢	76.20¢	73.70¢	71.30¢	70.90
	1948	96.20¢	89.20¢	88.70¢	84.80¢	85.40¢
	1949	88.80¢	84.30¢	83.50¢	75.70¢	82¢
Bread, White, per pound	1945	9.40¢	9.70¢	7.70¢	8.60¢	8.50¢
	1946	11.20¢	10.90¢	9.70¢	10.10¢	10.40¢
	1947	13.80¢	13¢	12¢	12.10¢	13¢
	1948	14.90¢	13.90¢	12¢	13.10¢	14.40¢
	1949	14.90¢	13.80¢	13¢	13.30¢	14.40¢
Butter, per pound	1945	50.80¢	50.50¢	50.90¢	51.10¢	52.10¢
	1946	72.60¢	72¢	70¢	71¢	72.80¢
	1947	81.30¢	85.50¢	79.30¢	80.10¢	82.90¢
	1948	88.40¢	92.30¢	84.30¢	85.90¢	89.90¢
	1949	73.40¢	78¢	70.30¢	73.70¢	72.70¢
Cheese, per pound	1945	33.40¢	33.60¢	36.10¢	40.70¢	36.10¢
	1946	NR	48.50¢	47.90¢	NR	70¢
	1947	64¢	55.40¢	57.10¢	57.10¢	65.70¢
	1948	70.80¢	62.30¢	64.40¢	NR	70¢
	1949	NR	NR	NR	NR	NR
Chickens, per pound	1945	46.90¢	40.70¢	47.20¢	41.30¢	47.90¢
	1946	53.20¢	54.10¢	50.60¢	49.60¢	54.10¢
	1947	55¢	58¢	52.50¢	NR	NR
	1948	61¢	62.30¢	58.30¢	51.10¢	63.30¢
	1949	NR	NR	NR	NR	NR
Coffee, per pound	1945	30.80¢	31.10¢	31.20¢	34.80¢	29.70¢
	1946	35.40¢	35.70¢	33.30¢	37.80¢	35.50¢
	1947	47.30¢	47.70¢	44.90¢	49.30¢	47.40¢
	1948	51.50¢	52.70¢	49.70¢	54.90¢	53¢
	1949	55.30¢	53.70¢	52.90¢	58.30¢	58¢
Cornmeal, per pound	1945	7.10¢	5.70¢	6.60¢	6.80¢	8.60¢
	1946	7.70¢	6.60¢	7.40¢	7.80¢	9.40¢
	1947	10.20¢	7.80¢	10.40¢	10.60¢	11.30¢
	1948	12¢	7.60¢	12¢	11.80¢	12.40¢
	1949	11¢	6.70¢	10.70¢	10.20¢	10.80¢
Eggs, per dozen	1945	59.50¢	56.60¢	58.10¢	58.80¢	59.90¢
	1946	62.90¢	56.10¢	57.10¢	57.90¢	62.40¢
	1947	76.20¢	65.70¢	66.30¢	66.60¢	75.50¢
	1948	79.80¢	66¢	67.40¢	68.50¢	75.60¢
	1949	77¢	65.40¢	66.50¢	68¢	71.20¢

Commodity	Year	New York	Atlanta	Chicago	Denver	Los Angeles
Flour, Wheat, per pound	1945	6.61¢	6.86¢	6.18¢	5.55¢	6.69¢
	1946	7.40¢	7.46¢	6.66¢	6.38¢	7.38¢
	1947	9.56¢	10.40¢	9.44¢	8.94¢	9.82¢
	1948	9.70¢	10.60¢	9.42¢	8.50¢	10.30¢
	1949	9.44¢	10.22¢	9.26¢	8.18¢	9.84¢
Lard, per pound	1945	18.30¢	18.70¢	19¢	19.10¢	19.80¢
	1946	NR	26¢	25.20¢	25.90¢	27.90¢
	1947	32.60¢	31.60¢	30.50¢	30.70¢	33.50¢
	1948	30.90¢	28.80¢	28.40¢	29.40¢	31.90¢
	1949	20.40¢	18.40¢	18.30¢	18.80¢	21¢
Milk, Fresh, per quart	1945	17.20¢	17¢	17.50¢	13.60¢	14.50¢
	1946	19.50¢	18.80¢	18.60¢	15.50¢	16.20¢
	1947	21.20¢	22¢	20.10¢	18.20¢	18.30¢
	1948	24.20¢	22.30¢	22.20¢	19.60¢	20¢
	1949	23.30¢	22¢	20.60¢	20.40¢	19.90¢
Molasses, per 18 oz. Can	1945	16.40¢	14.60¢	16.60¢	14¢	15.80¢
	1946	21.20¢	19.50¢	20.80¢	19.30¢	20.30¢
	1947	15.70¢	14.90¢	15.80¢	13.30¢	12.90¢
	1948	NR	NR	NR	NR	NR
	1949	NR	NR	NR	NR	NR
Mutton and Lamb, Leg, per pound	1945	40.30¢	37.60¢	38.20¢	37.80¢	40.50¢
	1946	49.50¢	48.10¢	47.30¢	45.50¢	49.60¢
	1947	62.50¢	72.50¢	63.10¢	62.20¢	65.60¢
	1948	70.50¢	80.20¢	69.20¢	69.30¢	70.70¢
	1949	69.80¢	83¢	72.80¢	71.50¢	71.20¢
Pork, Chops, per pound	1945	37.40¢	37.80¢	36.50¢	38¢	38.60¢
	1946	49.90¢	47.90¢	47.20¢	48.10¢	52.80¢
	1947	72.80¢	69.10¢	71.20¢	70.80¢	81¢
	1948	79¢	70.70¢	77.80¢	72.70¢	87.20¢
	1949	76.60¢	67.50¢	75¢	69.50¢	82.40¢
Pork, Bacon, Sliced, per pound	1945	41¢	40.80¢	40.90¢	43¢	42.60¢
	1946	53.60¢	53.20¢	51.50¢	54.90¢	57.10¢
	1947	80.20¢	76.90¢	76.50¢	81.60¢	82.80¢
	1948	80.10¢	77.70¢	76.60¢	80¢	81.60¢
	1949	69.60¢	66.90¢	66.90¢	68.40¢	70.30¢
Pork, Ham, Sliced, and Whole, per pound	1945	47.30¢	50¢	49.70¢	50.80¢	53.50¢
	1946	NR	NR	NR	64.20¢	NR
	1947	68.80¢	67.10¢	64.70¢	64.70¢	71.90¢
	1948	70.40¢	66.80¢	65¢	63.40¢	70.10¢
	1949	65.10¢	62.30¢	61.10¢	58.40¢	64.60¢
Pork, Salt, per pound	1945	23.70¢	22.40¢	22.40¢	22.50¢	23.40¢
	1946	NR	33.10¢	33.20¢	33¢	NR
	1947	NR	45.50¢	47.50¢	46¢	51¢
	1948	NR	42.40¢	48.20¢	45.20¢	50.20¢
	1949	NR	35.20¢	40.20¢	34.60¢	39.50¢
Potatoes, Irish, per 15 pounds	1945	71.60¢	70.90¢	78.20¢	64.30¢	70.30¢
	1946	72.50¢	70.80¢	75¢	63.30¢	77.10¢
	1947	76.60¢	75.80¢	84.50¢	71.50¢	77.40¢
	1948	80.40¢	84.20¢	$1.00	81.90¢	90.20¢
	1949	82.30¢	86.50¢	93.50¢	77¢	81.20¢
Prunes, Dried, per pound	1945	16.90¢	16.20¢	18.60¢	17.90¢	18.50¢
	1946	19.50¢	18.50¢	19.20¢	NR	19.40¢
	1947	NR	25.10¢	NR	NR	NR
	1948	21.50¢	22.20¢	21.50¢	NR	19.80¢
	1949	23.90¢	24.60¢	23.60¢	NR	20.80¢
Rice, per pound	1945	13.60¢	12¢	13¢	12¢	13.40¢
	1946	14.50¢	12.50¢	13.10¢	NR	14.10¢
	1947	18.90¢	16.40¢	17.60¢	NR	18.90¢
	1948	21.30¢	20.60¢	20.40¢	21.60¢	22.20¢
	1949	18.30¢	17.80¢	18.50¢	18.20¢	20.30¢

Commodity	Year	New York	Atlanta	Chicago	Denver	Los Angeles
Sugar, per pound	1945	6.50¢	6.50¢	7¢	7.30¢	6.70¢
	1946	7.84¢	7.50¢	7.90¢	8¢	7.60¢
	1947	9.60¢	9.60¢	9.90¢	10.10¢	9.50¢
	1948	9.30¢	9¢	9.50¢	9.80¢	9.20¢
	1949	9.30¢	9.10¢	9.70¢	10¢	9.40¢
Tea, per pound	1945	94.40¢	98.80¢	98¢	$1.07	$1.00
	1946	93.60¢	$1.01	93.60¢	$1.08	$1.04
	1947	NR	NR	NR	NR	NR
	1948	NR	NR	NR	NR	NR
	1949	NR	NR	NR	NR	NR
Veal, per pound	1945	44.10¢	42.30¢	42.30¢	44.20¢	46.60¢
	1946	60.10¢	52.30¢	52.20¢	49.60¢	57¢
	1947	90¢	76.10¢	77.40¢	70.60¢	78.40¢
	1948	$1.074	91.40¢	94.10¢	83.50¢	97.70¢
	1949	$1.091	92.30¢	96.70¢	84.90¢	97.80¢

SELECTED PRICES 1945-1949

Item	Source	Description	Price
Alcohol			
Gin	*Chicago Tribune* (1946)	*Dixie Belle*	$3.12/fifth
Liqueur	*Chicago Tribune* (1946)	*Southern Host;* fine 100-proof liqueur	$4.98/fifth
Rye	*Chicago Tribune* (1946)	*Mount Vernon*	$3.61/fifth
Whiskey	*Chicago Tribune* (1949)	*Old Sunny Brook;* the whiskey that's cheerful as its name	$3.98/fifth
Apparel, Children's			
Cowboy Boots	*Sears, Roebuck* (1946)	Double-tan cowhide	$6.98
Dress	*Sears, Roebuck* (1946)	*Honeysuckle;* for the kindergarten crowd; all have 3" hems, tie sashes	$1.80
Playsuit	*Sears, Roebuck* (1949)	Checked all-in-one in washable cotton percale	$1.49
Shorts	*Sears, Roebuck* (1949)	Clam-digger shorts in Sanforized cotton poplin	$1.39
Socks	*Sears, Roebuck* (1949)	*Boyville;* gaily striped rib-top crew socks	$0.35
Sunsuit	*Sears, Roebuck* (1949)	Cool, summer sun clothes	$0.89
Apparel, Men's			
Boxer Shorts	*Sears, Roebuck* (1946)	Good quality; regular style with grippers or boxer model	$0.65
Hat	*New York Times* (1946)	Pre-shaped Lee	$10.00
Hat	*Chicago Tribune* (1949)	*Homburg Distinction by Stetson*	$12.50
Neckwear	*New York Times* (1946)	All silk crepe; colorful geometric, floral and all-over patterns	$3.50
Pants	*Sears, Roebuck* (1949)	Stockman-style pants	$4.59
Shirt	*Saturday Evening Post* (1948)	*Lion of Troy;* dress; bold collar; wide and handsome with stitching a full 1/2" from the edge	$5.50
Shirt	*Life* (1949)	*TruVal;* TruVal is able to give you more value per dollar than any other shirt on earth	$2.95
Shirt	*Sears, Roebuck* (1949)	Washable; Sanforized cotton broadcloth; sport-type collar	$2.59
Shoes	*Sears, Roebuck* (1949)	Gold-bond tractor tread	$7.35
Shoes	*New York Times* (1946)	The Freeman shoe; durable soles; strain relieving cradle heels	$10.95
Shorts	*Chicago Tribune* (1949)	*Goldblatts;* 100% nylon; boxer style	$1.94
Socks	*Saturday Evening Post* (1948)	*Sarfert;* now in the new light California weight for spring and summer wear; slack length	$1.50
Suit	*Chicago Tribune* (1946)	*Illinois Clothing Manufacturing;* the largest selection in Chicago	$27.00

Item	Source	Description	Price
Suits	*New York Times* (1948)	Imported and domestic fabrics; many patterns, colours and textures; single and double-breasted	$85.00 to $125
Suspenders	*New York Times* (1946)	Elastic; in stripes or solids	$2.50
Sweaters	*New York Times* (1948)	Washable; virgin wool; pullover	$5.98
Tie	*Fortune* (1949)	*Hickey-Freeman;* silk; knitted; in styles that are not too wide or heavy	$3.50
Topcoat	*New York Times* (1946)	California weight; 2/3 camel hair; 1/3 Australia wool	$110
Underwear	*Life* (1949)	*KOPS Bros. Inc.;* a pantie-girdle with the detachable miracle crotch that custom-fits	$5.95
Apparel, Women's			
Belt	*Woman's Home Companion* (1949)	*Calderon;* leather	$4.00
Blouse	*Greenville News* (Greenville, SC) (1949)	*Ivey's Jane Holly;* of luscious soft crepe	$4.95
Blousette	*Sears, Roebuck* (1946)	*Kerrybrooke;* Sears brings you that new style sensation; covers you completely, can be worn without a jacket	$2.69
Chemise	*Frederick's of Hollywood* (1947)	*Frederick's Gay Paree;* shorter, barer, sexier than a slip	$5.98
Dress	*Greenville News* (Greenville, SC) (1949)	*Ruth Rowland;* half size; all the bright colors and black; 14 1/2 to 20 1/2	$22.95
Girdle	*Woman's Home Companion* (1948)	*Bestform;* no finer fit at any price	$7.50
Girdle	*Life* (1949)	*Bestform;* to minimize your waist-line, featuring swing-back elastic band for a flat midriff	$6.95
Gloves	*Sears, Roebuck* (1946)	4-button-length slip-ons for all occasion wear; fine imported skins	$4.50
Gloves	*Life* (1949)	*Kayser Afternoon;* dressmaker detailed, sueded double-woven cotton	$2.10
Gloves	*Woman's Home Companion* (1949)	*Andre's David;* elbow length doeskin	$18.00
Handkerchiefs	*Greenville Piedmont* (Greenville, SC) (1945)	*Ivey's;* initialed; sheer handkerchiefs of fine batiste in time for Mother's Day	$0.59
Mink Coat	*Chicago Tribune* (1946)	Wild; over 50 masterpieces on display, all made in our factory and priced at savings to 35%	$1,650
Nightgown	*Woman's Home Companion* (1949)	*Jonely;* Sanforized simtex flanlet	$5.00
Panties	*Frederick's of Hollywood* (1947)	*Frederick's Bare Illusion;* to wear under your prettiest things when you want to feel extra alluring and just a little naughty, too	$1.98
Panty Girdle	*Life* (1949)	*Jantzen Foundations;* empire tops to make the ribs flat as a pancake	$8.95
Purse	*Sears, Roebuck* (1946)	*Kerrybrooke;* practical plastics; lightweight, easily kept fresh, every new type: embossed, plastic cord	$4.69
Purse	*Woman's Home Companion* (1949)	*Ronay;* smooth calf satchel with brass handles	$11.00

Item	Source	Description	Price
Rainwear	*Life Magazine* (1949)	*The Alligator Co.;* waterproof fabrics in a variety of styles	$10.75
Scarf	*Woman's Home Companion* (1949)	*Strauss & Mueller;* satin with mink	$3.50
Shoes	*Greenville News* (Greenville, SC) (1949)	*Ivey's Softies by Deb;* in black and brown suede with tooled trim	$8.95
Slip	*Woman's Home Companion* (1948)	*Mary Barron;* nylon satin trimmed at top and hem with Alencon type lace	$6.00
Slip	*Greenville News* (Greenville, SC) (1949)	*Miss Swank;* crepe in white and pink tailored and lace trimmed	$3.95
Stockings	*Chicago Tribune* (1949)	*Boulevard by Belle Sharmeer;* a new deep, deep brown nylon shade	$1.95

Appliances

Item	Source	Description	Price
Carpet Sweeper	*New York Times* (1948)	Electric; can be guided over floors; under furniture; into corners; rubber bumpers	$19.95
Coffee Robot	*New York Times* (1948)	*Farberware;* automatically boils water; stirs brew; keeps coffee for hours without change of flavor	$26.95
Dampness Guard	*EveryWomen's Magazine* (1945)	Dri-Air chemical absorbs dampness in basements, game rooms, store room; kills musty odors	$5.50
Electric Floor Polisher	*Woman's Home Companion* (1948)	*Johnson's;* bring out the beauty of the home	$44.50
Electric Knife Sharpener	*New York Times* (1948)	Keeps knives as keen-edged as the day they were bought	$11.95
Hairdryer	*New York Times* (1948)	*Handy-Hanna Electric Hairdryer;* can be held or placed on table stand	$9.95
Humidifier	*Better Homes and Gardens* (1948)	*Fresh'nd-Aire;* guard your family's health; protect your possessions	$59.50
Roaster	*Woman's Home Companion* (1949)	*Westinghouse;* automatic electric roaster; cooks whole meal for eight people	$40.00
Television	*New York Times* (1948)	*Philco* eye-level television consolette; can sit in favorite chair and watch	$349.50
Washer	*Greenville News* (Greenville, SC) 1949)	*Kenmore A;* deluxe model at a standard model price, $5 down, $7 a month	$119.95

Baby Products

Item	Source	Description	Price
Baby Swing	*Sears, Roebuck* (1946)	Steel-frame baby swing	$1.85
Car Seat	*Sears, Roebuck* (1946)	Handy baby seat for auto; you can drive undisturbed without worrying about baby	$1.98
Crib Exerciser	*Sears, Roebuck* (1949)	*Novel;* gym crib exerciser amuses baby by the hour, strengthens young muscles	$1.89
Nursers	*Better Homes and Gardens* (1948)	*Evenflo;* breathes as it feeds; includes nipple, bottle, cap	$0.25
Playpen	*Sears, Roebuck* (1946)	Sturdy indoor or outdoor playpen; easy to fold	$11.98
Play Table and High Chair	*Sears, Roebuck* (1946)	Thousands of mothers have found it an indispensable aid in caring for their babies	$7.83

Item	Source	Description	Price
Rattling Toy Set	*Sears, Roebuck* (1949)	Ideal for bath time; for play in crib or pen; 4-piece	$0.98
Shoes	*Sears, Roebuck* (1946)	*Biltwell;* start baby right with supple-leather Biltwell shoes	$1.79

Business Equipment & Supplies

Item	Source	Description	Price
Adding Machine	*Fortune* (1949)	*Revolutionary Plus;* economical little key-drive machine to handle the addition	$120
Chrome Furniture	*New York Times* (1946)	Chrome furniture for your showroom and reception room; sales and display room; lobbies, etc.; settee; no sag spring seat; durable leatherette; all colors	$45.00
Display Table	*New York Times* (1946)	All steel; shelf can be raised or lowered; work table, packing table or counter; 6 feet long	$54.50
Steel Trailers	*New York Times* (1946)	Heavy duty; one piece; 4,000-pound capacity	$68.50

Collectibles

Item	Source	Description	Price
Baskets	*Antiques* (1945)	*Worcester;* circa 1770; a pair of exquisite blue and white china baskets, complete with pierced covers	$225
Book	*Parke-Bernet Galleries* (1946)	1592 printing of *Pierece Penilefse His Supplication to the Diuell,* by Thomas Nash; first edition, one of three known perfect copies	$2,100
Book	*Parke-Bernet Galleries* (1946)	1616 printing of *The Rape of Lucrece,* by William Shakespeare; one of five known copies; sixth edition and the first to bear Shakespeare's name	$3,700
Book	*Parke-Bernet Galleries* (1946)	1653 printing of *The Compleat Angler or the Contemplative Man's Recreation,* by Isaak Walton; being a discourse of fish and fishing, not unworthy of the perusal of most anglers	$400
Book	*Parke-Bernet Galleries* (1946)	1608 printing of the second quarto of *King Lear,* by William Shakespeare	$4,400
Bookcase Desk	*Antiques* (1945)	Chippendale mahogany; kneehole; height 6' 6 1/2", circa 1760 unusual feetwork top and mullions	$565
Buttons	*Antiques* (1945)	*Francis Bannerman Son;* British military; Royal Marines light infantry	$0.25
China	*Antiques* (1945)	*Olde Lamps Haviland;* scattered roses, 100 pieces, 12-piece setting	$250
Clock	*Antiques* (1948)	English grandfather clock; Emanuel Hopperton, Leeds; mahogany case, brass works, inlay carving	$375
Commode	*Antiques* (1945)	Antique; French inlaid; breakfront; 18th century with two drawers, brass ormolu mounts	$325
Coverlet	*Antiques* (1948)	Antique; woven; 82" x 80"; has "North Lima Ohio 1852" in all corners	$60.00
Desk	*Antiques* (1945)	American; small size; walnut; circa 1750 fine serpentine step-up inlaid interior	$975
Figurine	*Antiques* (1948)	*Meissen;* porcelain parrot in brilliant green 11" high plumage perched on rocky base; period 1790	$250
Mirror	*Antiques* (1945)	*The Stuyvestant Shop, Trenton, NJ;* American hand carved; circa 1918; carved from one block of brown mahogany 19 3/4" x 29"	$185
Pin	*Antiques* (1945)	*Old-Mine Diamond;* spray; Louis-Philippe period	$1,850
Sideboard	*Antiques* (1945)	Circa 1810 mahogany sideboard with five inlays 62" wide, 46" high	$595

Entertainment

Item	Source	Description	Price
Airplane Flight	*Airports of Columbia Photograph* (1946)	*Dixie Aviation;* passenger flight over Columbia, South Carolina	$1.50/person

Item	Source	Description	Price
Movie Ticket	*Chicago Tribune* (1946)	*Obsession;* Basil Rathbone, Eugene Leontovich evenings	$1.20–$3.00
Movie Ticket	*Chicago Tribune* (1949)	*Hamlet;* Academy Award winner; Laurence Olivier; evenings and all day Sunday, all seats	$1.00
Tour	*Fortune* (1949)	*Jungle Garden;* Avery Island, Louisiana; 200-acre jungle garden with its 1,700 varieties of iris, 30,000 zaleas, flame-colored daisies from Africa	$0.25

Entertainment, Home

Item	Source	Description	Price
Board Game	*Sears, Roebuck* (1946)	*Ouija;* mystifying oracle	$1.59
Camera	*Atlanta Constitution* (1947)	*Falcon Magni Vue*	$9.95
Changer	*Chicago Tribune* (1949)	*Wurlizter RCA Victor 45;* this changer brings into your home the amazing 45-rpm system, the new wonder of the world of music	$12.95
Chinese Checkers	*Sears, Roebuck* (1946)	Young and old will like to play this ever popular game	
Clock Radio	*Life* (1949)	*General Electric Model 65;* wakes you to music–gently without shock; stunning ivory plastic	$36.95
Playing Cards	*Greenville News* (Greenville, SC) (1949)	Canasta; double deck with rules	$1.59
Radio	*Sears, Roebuck* (1946)	*Silvertone Commentator;* self-contained loop aerial, automatic control maintains uniform volume; walnut color plastic case	$11.75
Radio	*Saturday Evening Post* (1948)	*Hallicrafters Model S-28;* four bands bring you thrilling, land, sea, air communications from all parts of the world; perfect for den, library, or office	$47.50
Radio Phonograph	*Saturday Evening Post* (1948)	*Spartan FM;* includes handsome modern design cabinet	$199.95
Radio Phonograph	*Chicago Tribune* (1949)	*Packard-Bell Portable;* home recorder	$99.95
Record	*Music Educators Journal* (1947)	*Carl Fischer;* J. M. Coopersmith's Handel's Messiah; an uncut presentation by the Oratorio Society of New York; vocal score	$1.25
Record Player	*Chicago Tribune* (1949)	*RCA Victor;* this compact attachment plugs into your radio and acts silently with trigger-action speed	$12.95
Television	*Chicago Tribune* (1949)	*General Electric;* see all the action clearly on this 12-channel with big 61-square-inch screen	$189.95
Television	*Chicago Tribune* (1949)	*Emerson AM-FM,* auto-phono; 10"; formerly $495	$295

Farm Equipment & Supplies

Item	Source	Description	Price
Chicks	*Greenville Piedmont* (Greenville, SC) (1945)	Pay postman on delivery; top quality Pullorum tested, any sex, any breed	$4.95/100
Traps	*New York Times* (1948)	Rats or weasels; 5 x 5 x 18 squirrels or rabbits; 7 × 7 × 24	$1.75 $3.95

Food Products

Item	Source	Description	Price
Baby Food	*Chicago Tribune* (1949)	*Clapp's;* strained	$0.59
Bacon	*Asheville Citizens Times* (Asheville, NC) (1948)	Available at Purity Market, Asheville, North Carolina	$0.59/pound

Item	Source	Description	Price
Boiled Ham	*Asheville Citizens Times* (Asheville, NC) (1948)	Available at Purity Market, Asheville, North Carolina	$0.49/hf pound
Cereal	*Chicago Tribune* (1949)	*American Family Flakes;* large package	$0.27
Cereal	*Chicago Tribune* (1949)	*Nabisco Honey Grahams;* large package	$0.27
Hot Sauce	*Woman's Home Companion* (1948)	*Frank's;* it perks up your taste buds; 3 full oz	$0.10
Ice Cream	*Greenville News* (Greenville, SC) (1949)	*Sealtest Butterscotch Eclairs;* an out-of-this-world dessert treat; box of 4	$0.59
Pears	*Fortune* (1949)	*Royal Riviera;* the business man's favorite gift for customers, associates, employees; gift box of 10 to 14 pears	$2.95
Shrimp	*Fortune* (1949)		$16/case
Soda Pop	*Greenville Piedmont* (Greenville, SC) (1945)	*Pepsi-Cola;* tops for quality	$0.05
T-Bone Steak	*Asheville Citizens Times* (Asheville, NC) (1948)	Available at Purity Market, Asheville, North Carolina	$0.59/pound

Furniture

Item	Source	Description	Price
Bedroom Suite	*Sears, Roebuck* (1949)	Genuine-walnut veneer, bed, chest, dresser	$89.95
Box Springs	*Sears, Roebuck* (1946)	*Harmony House;* box springs for better sleep, more comfort	$21.98
Cabinet	*Better Homes and Gardens* (1948)	*Fed-Oir;* by day a couch, at night you slide the bed out	$170
Cupboard	*Richmond Times Dispatch* (1949)	*Craftique Hepplewhite;* copied to the last detail out of the same age-old solid mahogany	$179.50
Dinette Set	*Sears, Roebuck* (1949)	5-pc. modern dinette set; 4-legged table, 4 chairs; shining limed oak and chrome	$89.95
Glider	*Richmond Times Dispatch* (1949)	*Troy;* 2-cushion; make your garden your outdoor living room	$59.50
Hassock	*Sears, Roebuck* (1946)	Beauty plus utility best describes this carefully tailored hassock; covered with our finest heavy moleskin-type artificial leather	$7.65
Lamp	*Richmond Times Dispatch* (1949)	Solid brass; 16" opaque drum shade in maroon or green 28" tall	$12.95
Lamp Table	*Better Homes and Gardens* (1948)	*Ruper Lee;* solid cherry; has authentic rose and oak leaf hand-carved pulls; height 25"; top 18" x 14"	$23.45
Mirror	*Better Homes and Gardens* (1948)	Full length; one of the greatest conveniences the well groomed woman can have	$14.90
Record Cabinet	*Sears, Roebuck* (1946)	Protect your records in these beautiful cabinets	$13.50
Sofa Bed	*Greenville News* (Greenville, SC) (1949)	Duran-plastic; makes into a comfortable bed for two in a jiffy	$79.88

Item	Source	Description	Price
Steel Cabinet Ensembles	*Sears, Roebuck* (1949)	Homart 3-piece ensemble of matching base units in two sizes	$179.50
Table	*The American Home* (1948)	*Samson;* folding; famous for strength, for comfort, for wear	$12.95

Garden Equipment & Supplies

Item	Source	Description	Price
Bird Food	*Better Homes and Gardens* (1948)	*Banquest;* wild bird; 50 lbs; feed the wild birds this winter	$9.00
Broad Hatchet	*Sears, Roebuck* (1946)	*Craftsman;* for heavy and rough cutting	$1.69
Flowering Pink	*Richmond Times Dogwood Dispatch* (1949)	Virginia's state flower; 18" to 24" size	$2.85
Greenhouse	*The American Home* (1948)	*Orlyt;* comes in sections for easy assembly; size 10' x 11'	$264
Half Hatchet	*Sears, Roebuck* (1946)	*Craftsman;* has the feel and easy swing that only perfect balance can give	$1.45
Hydrangea	*Greenville News* (Greenville, SC) (1949)	*The Flower Shop;* Italy, Texas; get your beautiful hydrangeas, blooming size, 2-foot plants	$1.00
Lawn Mower	*Richmond Times Dispatch* (1949)	*Eclipse Packhound;* power-driven wheels, power driven reel, power-driven sharpener, positive action; 21" cut	$127.50
Lilies	*Better Homes and Gardens* (1948)	*Burpee Orange Trump;* as many as 8 large blooms to a cluster; package of 3 bulbs	$2.75/pkg
Marigolds	*The American Home* (1948)	*Burpee;* glorious large double blooms up to 4" across; normally $0.75	$0.10/pkg
Roses	*Woman's Home Companion* (1948)	*Armstrong Nurseries Nocturne;* all-American award winner, 1948; deep red; package of 3	$5.25
Roses	*Chicago Tribune* (1949)	Two dozen long red roses in vase	$5.00
Rose Bushes	*Sears, Roebuck* (1946)	Sturdy, easy-to-grow everblooming roses	$1.15
Sprinkler	*Saturday Evening Post* (1948)	*Sunbeam Rain King;* automatic; a turn on the red control dial on top sets this sensational Rain King for any desired circle 5 to 50 feet in diameter West of Denver	$6.95 $7.25
Tuberous Begonias	*The American Home* (1948)	Your choice of nine lovely colors; package of four	$0.50/pkg

Hotel Rates

Item	Source	Description	Price
Hotel Room	*New York Times* (1946)	*The Dorset,* Miami Beach; double room	$12.00 and up
Hotel Room	*New York Times* (1946)	*Croydon Arms,* Miami Beach	$16.00
Hotel Room	*Richmond Times Dispatch* (1949)	*Hotel Richmond;* overlooking Capitol Square; 300 rooms	$3.75/day

Household Goods

Item	Source	Description	Price
Alarm Clock	*Life* (1949)	Gleaming ivory baked enamel case; one key winds both time and alarm	$4.50
Auto Vents	*Better Homes and Gardens* (1948)	*Maid-O-Mist;* for comfort, humidify; put low cost auto-vents on your steam radiators	$5.00

Item	Source	Description	Price
Bedspread	*Greenville News* (Greenville, SC) (1949)	*Baby Chenille;* full or twin sizes, 8 colors; every spread in this special group is worth five precious dollars	$3.99
China	*Greenville News* (Greenville, SC) (1949)	*Wedgwood Woodstock;* Bone china; 20-piece starter set	$75.60
Clog Remover	*Woman's Home Companion* (1948)	*Drano;* opens clogged drains—keeps them running free	$0.25
Coffee Maker	*Woman's Home Companion* (1949)	Automatic; electric; shifts to low heat when coffee is done	$29.00
Dormitory Trunk	*Sears, Roebuck* (1949)	*J. C. Higgins;* 33" x 18 1/2" x 20 1/2"	$20.34
Electric Broom	*Woman's Home Companion* (1948)	*Regina Electrikbroom;* the new revolutionary vacuum cleaner	$44.95
Electric Liquidizer	*Woman's Home Companion* (1949)	Prepares drinks, salad dressing, soups, children's foods	$35.00
Electric Painter	*Saturday Evening Post* (1948)	*Lowell Thoro-spray;* the modern answer to home decorating	$34.95
Faucet	*Better Homes and Gardens* (1948)	*Faucet Queen;* a flick of the finger and you have spray or stream	$0.39
Flatware	*Woman's Home Companion* (1948)	*Gorham;* sterling; to love and to cherish; per place setting	$23.00
Flatware	*Greenville News* (Greenville, SC) (1949)	*Gorham Chantilly;* sterling silver; prices are for 6 piece place settings	$25.50
Food Chopper	*Sears, Roebuck* (1946)	New double action, new streamlined design, new chopping efficiency	$2.98
Glasses	*Better Homes and Gardens* (1948)	*Libby;* decorated with a band of white satin-etched leaves; set includes four 12-oz water tumblers; four 6-oz juice glasses; and four 6-oz sherbets	$4.00
Goblets	*Woman's Home Companion* (1949)	*Tudor;* fine handblown lead cut crystal	$30/dozen
Hammer	*Sears, Roebuck* (1946)	*Craftsman;* for the man who wants only the best; 16 oz	$1.39
Humidifier	*Better Homes and Gardens* (1948)	*Magi-tray;* for storing foods which do not require refrigeration; 10" x 6" x 4 1/2"	$2.50
Lamp Bulb	*Life* (1949)	*General Electric;* 60-watt bulbs; there's a right-size lamp to fill the bill	$0.12
Mattress	*Life* (1949)	*Craftmaster's Gold Label;* hundreds of famous inner-springs buried in soft cotton; 15-year guarantee	$54.50
Mattress and Box Springs	*Woman's Home Companion* (1948)	*Serta Perfect Sleeper;* you sleep on it, not in it	$49.50
Mirror	*Sears, Roebuck* (1946)	*Harmony House;* full-length; hang a full-length mirror on your bedroom, hall or closet door; see yourself as others see you—tip to toe	$5.31
Mothproofer	*Woman's Home Companion* (1948)	*Larvex;* penetrates each tiny woolen fibre and makes the cloth itself mothproof for a whole year	$1.19/quart

Item	Source	Description	Price
Open End Wrenches	*Sears, Roebuck* (1946)	*Craftsman;* set of 6	$2.85
Paint	*Greenville Piedmont* (Greenville, SC) (1945)	*Kem-Tone;* the modern miracle wall finish; paste form	$2.98
Paint	*Richmond Times Dispatch* (1949)	*Glidden Spred-Luster Indoor;* for walls that are truly beautiful choose the original resin-emulsion enamel	$4.98/gallon
Plate	*Antiques* (1945)	*Royal Worcester;* 9" plates; light blue and gold in paisley design	$75/dozen
Platter	*Antiques* (1945)	*Staffordshire Amethyst;* 12" x 14 1/2"; Ridgway Oriental pattern	$15.00
Pressing Cloth	*Woman's Home Companion* (1948)	*Weaver Pres-Kloth;* for a perfect steam press; safe for any fabric	$0.89
Rug Cleaner	*Greenville Piedmont* (Greenville, SC) (1945)	*Tavern;* will clean spots or entire rug	$0.59
Shelving Paper	*Woman's Home Companion* (1948)	*Royledge;* put colorful highlights in your kitchen	$0.08/9 feet
Tablecloth	*Sears, Roebuck* (1946)	*Tablevogue* by Rosmary; 54" x 54"	$1.69
Toaster	*C. O. Allen Company* (1947)		$15.05
Travel Clock	*Saturday Evening Post* (1948)	*Sentinel Wayfarer;* a smart chromium-plated watch with black-enamel numeral dial snuggly fitted into a stand-up metal frame that folds flat	$4.95
Vacuum Cleaner	*Chicago Tribune* (1949)	*General Electric Tidy;* maid-of-all-work for floor and above-the-floor cleaning	$39.95
Waffle Iron	*Woman's Home Companion* (1948)	*Handyhot Twin;* electrical products since 1903	$12.95
Wardrobe Trunk	*Sears, Roebuck* (1949)	*J. C. Higgins;* 3-ply wood veneer body	$56.70
Water Heater	*The National Police Gazette* (1948)	*Presto;* electric; enjoy the luxury of steaming hot water, anytime, anywhere, simply plug heater's cord in socket and presto you have the hot water you want	$4.98

Jewelry

Item	Source	Description	Price
Cuff Links	*Fortune* (1949)	*Jaccard;* matching; initialed; 14K natural gold masterfully engraved	$47.50
Pendant	*Woman's Home Companion* (1949)	*Eisenberg;* rhinestone; on velvet band	$7.50
Watch	*Life* (1949)	*Lord Elgin DeLuxe;* men's; the DuraPower mainspring eliminates 99% of watch repairs due to steel mainspring failures	$47.50
Watch	*Greenville News* (Greenville, SC) (1949)	*Elgin DeLuxe;* 17 jewels adjusted; DuraPower mainspring	$55
Wristwatch	*Woman's Home Companion* (1948)	*Harvel;* beautiful 17-jewel, precision-built, gold-filled watches	$47.50
Zircon	*The National Police Gazette* (1948)	1st quality, pure white; 3 zircons; approximate total weight 2 kts	$6.40

Item	Source	Description	Price
Meals			
Dinner	*Chicago Tribune* (1946)	*The Corner House;* open all nite, air conditioned	$0.95
Lunch	*Chicago Tribune* (1946)	*Heidelberg*	$0.55
Lunch	*Atlanta Constitution* (1947)	*J. J. Newberry;* smothered pork chop, candied yams, buttered green peas, hot rolls and muffins and butter	$0.50
Meal	*Chicago Tribune* (1949)	*Hillmans;* broiled jumbo whitefish, with lemon slice; parsley buttered potatoes	$0.50
Medical Products & Services			
Antacid	*Better Homes and Gardens* (1948)	*Alka-Seltzer;* quick relief for discomfort of colds	$0.30
Antacid	*Chicago Tribune* (1949)	*Tums;* must you avoid favorite foods because of acid stomach?	$0.10
Corn Remover	*Chicago Tribune* (1946)	*Walgreens Freezone;* for corns	$0.16
Mineral Oil	*Chicago Tribune* (1946)	*Walgreens*	$0.05/pint
Skin Whitener Ointment	*Greenville Piedmont* (Greenville, SC) (1945)	*Dr. Fred Palmer's;* loosens blackheads for easy removal	$0.25
Vitamins	*Sears, Roebuck* (1946)	B-Complex capsules; costs only 1 1/3¢ a day; 100-day supply	$1.39
Yeast Tablets	*Sears, Roebuck* (1946)	*Brewer's;* 100 tablets	$0.27
Motorized Vehicles, Services, & Supplies			
Automobile	Richard M. Langworth and Graham Robson, *Complete Book of Collectible Cars* (1985)	*DeSoto Custom Suburban;* 8-passenger sedan [cost in 1946]	$2,093–$2,631
Automobile	Langworth and Robson, *Complete Book of Collectible Cars* (1985)	*Mercury Sportsman Convertible* [cost in 1946]	$2,209
Automobile	Langworth and Robson, *Complete Book of Collectible Cars* (1985)	*Chevrolet Fleetmaster;* 4-door sedan [cost in 1947]	$1,212–$2,013
Automobile	Langworth and Robson, *Complete Book of Collectible Cars* (1985)	*Nash Ambassador Custom Cariolet* [cost in 1948]	$2,345
Automobile	Langworth and Robson, *Complete Book of Collectible Cars* (1985)	*Oldsmobile Futuramic 98 Convertible* [cost in 1948]	$2,078–$2,624
Automobile	Langworth and Robson, *Complete Book of Collectible Cars* (1985)	*Buick Roadmaster Riviera;* two-door hard top [cost in 1949]	$3,203

Item	Source	Description	Price
Automobile	Langworth and Robson, *Complete Book of Collectible Cars* (1985)	*Dodge Wayfarer Roadster* [cost in 1949]	$1,727
Automobile	Langworth and Robson, *Complete Book of Collectible Cars* (1985)	*Packard Super 8 DeLuxe Club Sedan* [cost in 1949]	$2,894–$2,919
Automobile	*Fortune* Magazine (1949)	*Jaguar Sedan;* the finest car of its class in the world	$4,600
Cycle Goggles	*Sears, Roebuck* (1949)	Motorcycle goggles	$3.49
Seat Covers	*Sears, Roebuck* (1946)	*Allstate;* of rich-looking, serviceable fiber, smartly finished with artificial leather	$3.33
Solvent	*Liberty* (1945)	Casite sludge solvent for easy starting Pint can	$0.65

Musical Instruments

Item	Source	Description	Price
Bugle	*Sears, Roebuck* (1946)	*Cadet Bugle;* is pitched to the same key as regular army bugle and can be played in any bugle corps	$0.69
Harmonica	*Sears, Roebuck* (1946)	*Silvertone;* American designed and made	$1.79
Organ	*Greenville News* (Greenville, SC) (1949)	*Hammond;* serving over 18,000 churches today	$1,300
Piano Rolls	*Sears, Roebuck* (1946)	*QRS;* favorite selections. choose from 79 popular, patriotic, sacred songs	$0.95/2
Song Flute	*Sears, Roebuck* (1946)	Ideal for children to learn on; grand for servicemen	$0.94
Trumpet	*Chicago Tribune* (1946)	Postwar-model trumpets; complete with case	$135
Valve Oil	*Music Educators Journal* (1947)	*Speedex;* your instrument will play better and last longer	$0.25

Other

Item	Source	Description	Price
Audubon Kit	*Woman's Home Companion* (1949)	*Lucey's Workshop;* bird modeling; including roughed-out block for six birds	$2.95
Buttons	*Antiques* (1945)	Civil War; eagle buttons with letters A-D-I-C	$0.10
Dry Cleaning	*Greenville News* (Greenville, SC) (1949)	Men's suits, dresses, men's felt hats; cash and carry	$0.50
Dye	*Woman's Home Companion* (1948)	*Rit;* puts the whole rainbow of colors at your fingertips	$0.25
Flying Lessons	*Airports of Columbia Photograph* (1946)	*Dixie Aviation Aeronca Champion;* America's No. 1 low-cost airplane, easy to fly, easy to buy	$2.00
Hairstyling	*Greenville Piedmont* (Greenville, SC) (1945)	*Ideal Beauty Shop;* creme oil permanents; were $8	$6.50
Heat Sealer	*Better Homes and Gardens* (1948)	*Dobeckmun;* for cellophane bags; seals woolens so moths can't reach them; keeps corsages fresh for days	$7.95

Item	Source	Description	Price
Loom	*Sears, Roebuck* (1949)	*Hearthside;* folding floor-model loom	$99.50
Pen	*Greenville News* (Greenville, SC) (1949)	*Waterman;* ball point; finest quality; regularly $3.50	$0.99
Pen	*Life* (1949)	*Parker 51;* 14 precision advances give true newness; writes dry with wet ink	$13.50
Pen Set	*Fortune* (1949)	*Parker Aero-Metric 51;* set in midnight blue; gold filled caps	$29.75
Pesticide	*The American Home* (1948)	*Mouse Seeds;* kills mice	$0.25
Picture	*The National Police Gazette* (1948)	Full color; heavyweight boxing champions; handsome lithograph suitable for framing for hotels, restaurants club rooms, barber shops, bars, gymnasiums and dens; size 22" x 21"	$1.00
Pictures	*The National Police Gazette* (1948)	Women wrestlers; just what the sport fan wants; 8" x 10"; ready for framing	$4.00/6
Rug Frame	*Sears, Roebuck* (1949	For waffle-weave rugs, frame and stand	$5.19
Stationery	*Chicago Tribune* (1946)	Letters; random; 40 sheets, envelopes	$0.13
Sunglasses	*Sears, Roebuck* (1949)	Our best men's aviation style	$6.95
Tool Pack	*Woman's Home Companion* (1949)	*Clement Cook Top;* quality light tools for women	$10.00

Personal Care Products

Item	Source	Description	Price
Aftershave	*Woman's Home Companion* (1949)	*Mennen Skin Bracer*	$0.98
Denture Adhesive	*Sears, Roebuck* (1949)	*Denturfit;* a resilient dental plastic liner for greater comfort and security; 8-oz jar	$0.79
Deodorant	*Woman's Home Companion* (1948)	*Arrid;* don't be half safe	$0.39
Deodorant	*Life* (1949)	*Dryad;* men shy away from a girl who offends with unromantic perspiration odor	$0.10/$0.29/$0.59
Face Cream	*Life* (1949)	*Jergens;* acts as a deep cleaner, a softener, a dry skin cream, and a powder base	$0.20–$1.39/jar
Hair Rinse	*Woman's Home Companion* (1948)	*Marchand's;* there's a blending shade created especially for you; 6 rinses	$0.25
Hair Styling	*Greenville News* (Greenville, SC) (1949)	*White's Machine;* permanent; machineless or cold wave	$5.00
Hand Cream	*Greenville News* (Greenville, SC) (1949)	*Mitchum Esoterica;* new kind of hand cream for fading those brown spots that make your hands look old	$1.50
Home Permanent Kit	*Sears, Roebuck* (1946)	*Toni;* complete kit; everything you need for a beautiful permanent wave	$1.40
Home Permanent Kit	*Life* (1949)	*Richard Hudnut;* problem hair requires the kindest, safest, gentlest type of home permanent	$2.75
Home Permanent Kit	*Life* (1949)	*Toni;* the secret of lovelier hair is yours with a Toni home permanent; includes plastic curlers	$2.00
Lotion	*Better Homes and Gardens* (1948)	*Jergens Lotion;* finer than ever; more protective, too; large size	$1.00

Item	Source	Description	Price
Manicure Set	*Fortune* (1949)	*Clauss;* handsome, smooth, genuine tan-cowhide case with zipper closing	$15.00
Nail Nippers	*Saturday Evening Post* (1948)	*LaCross;* scientifically curved jaws for close, accurate work	$2.50
Night Cream	*Greenville News* (Greenville, SC) (1949)	*Noxema;* millions of women use it as a night cream and as a foundation cream; big $0.85 jar	$0.59
Razor	*Life* (1949)	*Gillette Super-Speed;* instant blade changing, real shaving comfort, double-edge economy; 10 blades	$1.00
Razor Blades	*Saturday Evening Post* (1948)	*Marlin;* double-edge; once over and a clean shave; pkg of 12	$0.28
Shampoo	*Chicago Tribune* (1949)	*Walgreens Beauty Brew Beer;* $0.89 regularly	$0.89/2
Shave Cream	*Woman's Home Companion* (1949)	*Woodbury Lather;* shave-cream kit; includes lotion, shampoo, and talc	$1.10
Shaving Lotion	*Saturday Evening Post* (1948)	*Williams Aqua Velva;* after-shave preparation	$0.50
Soap	*Woman's Home Companion* (1948)	*Yardley English Lavender;* you're enchanting when you're wearing the gay-hearted fragrance	$0.40
Soap	*Chicago Tribune* (1949)	*Walgreen Woodbury's;* regular-size cakes; limit four cakes	$0.23
Tissues	*Life* (1949)	*Tender-Touch;* a finer facial tissue that's actually washed in pure, soft water to give it that soft tender touch; box of 300	$0.27
Toothbrush	*Sears, Roebuck* (1949)	Made of heavy-gauge DuPont nylon bristles	$0.59

Publications

Item	Source	Description	Price
Book	*The National Police Gazette* (1948)	*The Babe Ruth Story;* as told to Bob Considine; this important book by two of the greatest names in baseball	$1
Book	*Better Homes and Gardens* (1948)	*Inside USA,* by John Gunther; Book of the Month Club selection	$3.50
Book	*Sears, Roebuck* (1949)	*Bible;* young folks text Bible; leather	$4.71
Magazine	*Sears, Roebuck* (1946)	*Popular Mechanics*	$3/year
Magazine	*Sears, Roebuck* (1946)	*Jack and Jill;* ten-month subscription	$1.98
Magazine	*Sears, Roebuck* (1946)	*Flower Grower*	$4/2years
Magazine	*Life* (1949)	*Life;* weekly	$0.20

Real Estate

Item	Source	Description	Price
Apartment Building	*Chicago Tribune* (1949)	For sale; six flats; two story; four rooms, bath, stove, heat; $5,000 cash	$9,750
Apartments	*Chicago Tribune* (1949)	For sale; two apartments; brick; 5-6 rooms; no leases; separate furnaces	$9,500
Grocery-Deli	*Chicago Tribune* (1946)	Can add liquor and meats; doing $750 week; cash	$6,500

Item	Source	Description	Price
House	*Greenville Piedmont* (Greenville, SC) (1945)	Attractive, practically new 5-room house in Augusta Rd. section; $1,500 down, balance like rent	$5,700
Tavern	*Chicago Tribune* (1949)	For sale; doing good business; 44' bar; ideal for man and wife; includes inventory	$7,000

Sewing Equipment & Supplies

Item	Source	Description	Price
Cloth	*Atlanta Constitution* (1947)	*Avondale Cotton Chambrays;* for playclothes, bedroom ensembles	$0.49/yard
Sewing Machine	*Greenville News* (Greenville, SC) (1949)	*Singer Portable;* rebuilt electric machines	$42.50
Toy Sewing Machine	*New York Times* (1948)	Stitches so she can make all her own doll clothes; carrying case	$3.98

Sports Equipment

Item	Source	Description	Price
Barbell	*The National Police Gazette* (1948)	*Independent Iron Works;* buy direct from factory	$8.95
Belts	*New York Times* (1948)	Ranger belt	$1.95
Boots	*New York Times* (1948)	Cowboy style	$7.95
Reel	*Saturday Evening Post* (1948)	*Ocean City No. 999;* open face; level wind; quadruple; multiplying 100 yds	$9.95
Saddles	*New York Times* (1948)	Especially made for jumping	$160
Saddles	*New York Times* (1948)	Trooper saddle for English-style riders	$25.00
Sleigh Bells	*New York Times* (1948)		$6.50

Tobacco Products

Item	Source	Description	Price
Ashtray	*New York Times* (1948)	Sports ashtray; gamebirds, cowboy or fox hunt scenes; rimmed with heavy sterling silver	$8.50
Cigarette Holder	*New York Times* (1948)	Sterling silver	$7.50
Cigarette Holder	*Saturday Evening Post* (1948)	*Medico Filtered;* cuts down nicotine; includes box of ten filters	$2.00
Cigarettes	*Chicago Tribune* (1946)	All standard brands; per carton	$1.34
Cigarette Server	*New York Times* (1948)	It appears to be a lamp; shade pushes down; cigarettes emerge to serve guests	$5.00
Lighter	*Saturday Evening Post* (1948)	*Zippo;* your favorite design engraved on a Zippo lighter; brush finish	$3.25
Pipe Lighter	*New York Times* (1948)	Designed for lighting pipes; when tilted acts like small Bunsen burner; shooting flame into pipe bowl	$5.00
Pocket Lighter	*New York Times* (1948)	Outer jacket of 14 karat gold	$160
Table Lighter	*New York Times* (1948)	Gold plated	$15.00

Toys

Item	Source	Description	Price
Balls	*Atlanta Constitution* (1947)	Inflated rubber balls; brightly colored	$0.05/3

Item	Source	Description	Price
Doll	*Atlanta Constitution* (1947)	*Sunbabe;* drinking and wetting rubber dolls; complete in box with diaper and bottle	$1.98
Holster Set	*Sears, Roebuck* (1946)	Low-priced Lone Ranger holster set	$1.15
Model Kit	*Sears, Roebuck* (1946)	4 extra-large model kits	$0.89
Model Kit	*Sears, Roebuck* (1946)	6 small hobby model kits	$0.54
Racer	*Atlanta Constitution* (1947)	Hours of fun from this metal racer, in many colors, key attached; 5" long	$0.39
Scooter	*Atlanta Constitution* (1947)	With red and white-rubber tires	$1.59
Telescope	*Sears, Roebuck* (1946)	6-power telescope with precision-ground lenses	$1.00
Tricycle	*Atlanta Constitution* (1947)	Heavy metal with rubber tires; large size painted ivory and blue; originally $15.98	$5.98
Wagon	*Atlanta Constitution* (1947)	Red steel body; medium	$3.29
Walkie-Talkie	*Sears, Roebuck* (1946)	Brand new; adds more excitement to your games	$1.47
Whistling Rubber Dog	*Sears, Roebuck* (1949)		$0.63
Travel & Transportation			
Airplane Flight	*New York Times* (1948)	LaGuardia one-stop direct to Los Angeles	$99.00
Airplane Flight	*New York Times* (1948)	LaGuardia one-stop direct to Miami	$50.00
Airplane Flight	*New York Times* (1948)	Fly to California overnight	$88.00
Airplane Flight	*New York Times* (1946)	Fly to Miami and back; 21 passengers; complimentary meals aboard	$165
Airline Ticket	*Chicago Tribune* (1949)	*Skycoach;* California from Chicago	$75.00
Railroad Ticket	*Chicago Tribune* (1946)	*Columbian;* Chicago to Washington; round trip	$25.30

MISCELLANY 1945-1949

Bing Signs for New Program $30,000 A Week

Hollywood, Cal. Aug. 15 (AP)—Bing Crosby will return to the radio in October on a weekly program that will be broadcast to 600 stations in the United States, South America, Australia, and Europe.

Everett Crosby, the singer's brother, completed negotiations tonight with James H. Carmine, vice president of Philco Corporation, which will sponsor the programs over the American Broadcasting Company network.

Everett said the salary was the highest ever offered for such a program. Although he declined to specify the amount, other sources indicated Crosby's weekly stipend will be about $30,000, which would be about $2,500 higher than the previous high, paid to Jack Benny.

Chicago Tribune, August 16, 1946

10¢ Buses Open Service to Auto Lots; Fare Hit Some Parkers Balk; Expected 5¢ Trip

Shuttle buses painted in distinctive gray and red to distinguish them from the Chicago Motor Coach company's thru city buses started service yesterday between the automobile parking areas in Grant Park and the Loop.

Patronage was light, as had been expected by traffic experts because the service was new and the weather was favorable to pedestrians. As more motorists become aware of the new, free parking facilities at Soldiers' Field and the shuttle bus service, traffic men said, business will pick up.

Chicago Tribune, August 16, 1946

Estimate Cost to Consumers at $150 Million; Increases Ranging from 3 to 12 Pct.

Washington, D.C. August 25 (AP) Price increases estimated by OPA officials to cost the public "well over 150 million dollars a year" were granted today on such articles as radios, stoves, washing machines, vacuum cleaners, toasters, and irons.

The OPA said the increases were required by the new price controls law which specifies that wholesalers' and retailers' profits must not be cut below their margins on last March 31. Items affected are those on which dealers had been required to absorb part of price increases granted earlier to manufacturers. The OPA said it expects today's increases to be the last on consumers' goods, except for refrigerators, on which the price boost will be announced soon.

The price agency itself announced only that the raises ranged from 3 to 12 per cent. The 150 million dollar estimate was given by an official who would not be quoted by name, in response to a reporter's query on total cost.

Chicago Tribune, August 16, 1946

HISTORICAL SNAPSHOT
1950-1954

1950

- Korean War begins
- Congress increases personal and corporate income taxes and corporation taxes
- Federal Reserve estimates that 4 in 10 families are worth at least $5,000, 1 in 10 have assets of at least $25,000
- Gross National Product reaches $284 billion
- Auto registrations show one car for every 3.7 Americans
- Blue Cross programs cover 3.7 million Americans
- Railroads seized by federal troops to avert a strike
- 5 million homes have television sets; 45 million have radios
- Orlon fiber is introduced by E.I. duPont de Nemours
- Otis Elevator installs first passenger elevator with self-opening doors
- More than 75 percent of U.S. farms electrified
- Average farmer produces enough food for 15.5 people
- Coca-Cola's share of U.S. cola market is 69 percent; Pepsi-Cola's share is 15 percent

1951

- President Truman requests a $10 billion war fund
- First power-producing nuclear fission reactor by Atomic Energy Commission

- $71.6 billion budget submitted to Congress
- Wages and salaries frozen
- Margin profit ceilings placed on 200,000 consumer items
- Income-tax receipts reach $56.1 million
- Univac computer introduced
- CBS broadcasts color television programs, although the FCC later approves the RCA color system as the industry standard
- U.S. telephone call rates go from 5¢ to 10¢
- Denver grocery chain begins offering S&H Green Stamps

1952

- General Dwight David Eisenhower elected president
- 600,000 CIO steelworkers stage 53day strike
- Nation's railroads returned to private control
- 17 million homes have television sets
- Four of five shirts sold in America are white
- Nearly half of U.S. farms have tractors
- First Holiday Inn opens near Memphis

1953

- New York subway fares rise 5¢ to 15¢

- Per capita state taxes average $68.04
- Unemployment hits record lows
- *TV Guide* and *Playboy* begin publication
- New York's Seeman Brothers introduce first instant ice tea

1954

- Sony introduces first pocket-size transistor radio
- Supreme Court declares racial segregation in public schools illegal
- First nuclear-powered submarine, Nautilus, launched
- Gasoline averages 29¢ per gallon
- Texas Instruments introduces first practical silicon transistor
- Taxpayers with incomes of more than $100,000 pay more than $67,000 in taxes
- Sales of Viceroy cigarettes leap as smokers shift to filter-tipped cigarettes
- Open-heart surgery is introduced by Minneapolis physician C. Walton Lillehe
- RCA introduces first color television set
- $13 million, 900-room Fontainebleau Hotel opens at Miami Beach
- Swanson & Sons introduces frozen TV dinners
- Births remain above 4 million per year

SELECTED INCOME 1950-1954

Job	Source	Description	Pay
Actor	Legrand and Karney *Chronicle of the Cinema* (1995)	Annual salary of Clark Gable in 1954	$500,000
Actor	Warren G. Harris, Lucy and Desi: *The Legendary Love Story* (1991)	Contract of Lucy and Desi Arnez for ninety-eight episodes of *"I Love Lucy"* during 1954–1955 season	$4 million
Ad Agency Gal Friday	*New York Times* (1952)	Sten. and ad agency	$85/wk
Attorney	*Chicago Tribune* (1953)	General counsel for independent company; must be well-grounded and experienced corporation lawyer with real-estate experience	$12,000/year
Automechanics	*Chicago Tribune* (1953)	Experienced only	$2/hr
Baseball Player	Rampersad, Jackie Robinson, *A Biography* (1997)	Annual salary of Jackie Robinson in 1951	$39,750
Baseball Radio Announcer	Richard Layman, ed., *American Decades: 1950-1959* (1994)	Annual salary of Red Barber in 1954	$50,000
Biologist	*Chicago Tribune* (1951)	Master's Degree in biology required to be assistant to head of physiology and endocrinology research. Some experience other than academic preferred	$70/wk
Bookkeeper	*New York Times* (1952)	Accounts payable, dress manufacturing experience; 9–5:30, 5 days	$60/wk
Cabinetmakers	*Chicago Tribune* (1953)		$2/hr and up
Comedian	Layman, ed., *American Decades: 1950-1959* (1994)	Annual contract of Milton Berle with NBC in 1951	$200,000
Comedian	Layman, ed., *American Decades: 1950-1959* (1994)	Two-year contract of Jackie Gleason with CBS for weekly show The Honeymooners in 1954	$11 million
Corporate Controller	*New York Times* (1954)	Experience in retail not essential	$25,000
Director of Sales	*New York Times* (1956)	Age 40–55; engineering or physics degree; government contract experience	$25,000
Director of Field Engineering	*New York Times* (1956)	Age 35–55; engineering degree	$19,000
Engineer	*New York Times* (1956)	Senior levels; benefits	$14,000
Executive Accountant	*Chicago Tribune* (1953)	Complete corporation experience for full-charge assignment; manual and machine postings	$10,000/yr
Finance Executive	*New York Times* (1954)	Head of Purchased Paper Department	$10,000

Job	Source	Description	Pay
Hairstylist	*San Francisco Examiner* (1950)	Male; with manager's licence; refs	$75/wk and commission
Mechanical Draftsman	*New York Times* (1956)	Senior level	$167 per week
Millwright Foreman	*Chicago Tribune* (1951)	Experienced in maintenance of machine moving and installing all types of equipment, maintenance of brick work, sheet metal; supervise 15–20 workers	$4,500–$5,000
Physicists	*Chicago Tribune* (1951)		$8,000/yr
Pianist (1954)	*Guinness Book of World Records* (1981)	Single night earnings of Liberace for concert at Madison Square Garden	$138,000
Product Designer	*New York Times* (1956)	Designing new cameras; camera equipment; must be creative	$8,000
Route Man	*Chicago Tribune* (1954)	Towel supply; perm.; 5 day wk; under 35	$82/wk
Salesman	*Chicago Tribune* (1953)	Hats, shoes, slacks, stead; must be A-1 top man in town; able to start at once	$100–$150/wk
Sales Manager	*New York Times* (1956)	Graduate of accounting; retail experience; must know machine accounting methods	$10,000
Secretary	*Chicago Tribune* (1953)	Situation wanted; top notch; 35; personable appearance	$325/mo
Shipping Clerk Assistant	*Chicago Tribune* (1953)	Good opportunity for reliable man	$1.25/hr
Singer	Bufwack and Oerman, *Finding Her Voice, The Saga of Women in Country Music* (1993)	Dorothy Shay's nightly fee for concerts in 1951	$5,000
Singer	Layman, ed., *American Decades: 1950-1959* (1994)	Annual income of Elvis Presley in 1952	$10 million
Social Worker	*Atlanta Constitution* (1953)	Must have sch. soc. wk. training; exc. conditions; give full inf., educ. and exp. in first letter	$225/mo
Stenographer	*Atlanta Constitution* (1953)	One-girl office; 5-day week; national concern	$175/mo
Television Host	Layman, ed., *American Decades: 1950-1959* (1994)	Annual contract of Ed Sullivan for TV show Toast of the Town in 1951	$125,000

CONSUMER EXPENDITURES 1950-1954

(Per Capita)

Expenditure Type	1950	1951	1952	1953	1954
Clothing	$105.48	$113.42	$116.87	$117.19	$116.39
Food	$354.68	$393.42	$408.39	$409.86	$411.35
Auto Usage	$148.99	$143.24	$142.08	$164.19	$160.72
New Auto Purchase	$67.90	$55.74	$50.97	$69.56	$66.51
Auto Parts	$9.89	$9.72	$10.19	$9.40	$8.01
Gas & Oil	$36.26	$39.54	$43.32	$46.38	$48.03
Housing	$143.06	$157.49	$172.02	$187.38	$198.90
Furniture	$20.44	$20.74	$22.29	$23.19	$23.40
Utilities	$48.13	$51.20	$52.88	$54.52	$57.88
Telephone & Telegraph	$12.53	$14.26	$15.29	$16.92	$17.24
Physicians	$17.14	$17.49	$19.11	$20.68	$22.78
Dentists	$6.59	$6.48	$7.00	$7.52	$8.62
Health Insurance	$5.93	$5.83	$7.00	$8.15	$8.62
Personal Business	$42.85	$46.02	$47.15	$50.76	$54.19
Personal Care	$15.82	$17.49	$18.48	$19.43	$20.94
Tobacco	$28.35	$29.17	$31.22	$31.96	$30.17
Local Transport	$12.53	$12.96	$12.74	$12.53	$11.70
Intercity Transport	$5.93	$6.48	$7	$6.89	$6.16
Recreation	$73.18	$75.83	$78.37	$81.47	$83.13
Religion/Welfare Activities	$15.82	$16.85	$19.11	$19.43	$20.94
Private Education & Research	$11.87	$12.31	$13.38	$13.79	$14.16
Per Capita Consumption	$1266.45	$1348.79	$1395.95	$1457.71	$1476.68

new '55 **DODGE** flashes ahead in style!

It's flair-fashioned... and alive with beauty

 # INVESTMENTS 1950-1954

Investment	1950	1951	1952	1953	1954
Basic Yield, One-Year Corporate Bonds	1.42	2.05	2.73	2.62	2.40
Short-term Interest Rates, 4–6 Months, Prime Commercial Paper	1.45	2.16	2.33	2.52	1.58
Basic Yield, Common Stocks, Total	6.27	6.12	5.50	5.49	4.78
Index of Common Stocks (1941-1943=10)	18.40	22.34	24.50	24.73	29.69

COMMON STOCKS, CLOSING PRICE AND YIELD, FIRST BUSINESS DAY OF YEAR

(Parenthetical number is annual dividend in dollars)

	1950	1951	1952	1953	1954
Allis Chalmers	32 5/8	45	50 3/4	59	46 3/4
	(2)	(3.25)	(3.50)	(4)	(4)
AT&T	146 1/4	151 1/2	155 3/8	160 1/4	156 1/2
	(9)	(9)	(9)	(9)	(9)
American Tobacco	74 1/2	66 1/4	62 3/8	65 7/8	62 1/2
	(4)	(4)	(4)	(4)	(3)
Anaconda	28 1/2	40 5/8	50 3/8	43 7/8 30	5/8
	(2.50)	(3)	(3.50)	(3.50)	(3)
B&O	10	20 1/2	19 1/8	28	19 1/2
	(/)	(/)	(/)	(.75)	(1)
Bethlehem Steel	31 5/8	50 1/4	51 5/8	56 1/4	51 1/8
	(2.40)	(4.10)	(4)	(4)	(4)
Corn Products	72 7/8	70	70 1/2	70 1/8	73
	(3.60)	(3.60)	(3.60)	(3.60)	(3.60)
General Electric	42 3/8	50 3/8	NR	72 1/2	88 1/4
	(2.50)	(3.40)		(3.00)	(4)
General Motors (2 shares for 1 split, 10/3/50)	70 3/4	7 1/4	31 3/8	68 1/2	60
	(8)	(2.50)	(4)	(4)	(4)
International Business Machines (5% stock dividend 1/23/50) (5% stock dividend 1/26/51 (5% stock dividend 1/28/52) (5% stock dividend 1/29/53) (2 1/2% stock dividend 1/28/54) (5 share for 4 split, 5/10/54)	213	206	207	234	247
	(4)	(4)	(4)	(4)	(4)
Intl Harvester	27 3/8	32 5/8	28 1/8	32 5/8	28 1/2
	(1.80)	(2)	(2)	(2)	(2)
National Biscuit	39	33	30	35 1/4	36 1/2
	(7)	(2)	(2)	(2)	(2)
US Steel (3 shares for 1 split, 6/2/49)	26 3/8	43	40 1/4	43 1/2	39 7/8
	(1)	(3.45)	(3)	(3)	(3)
Western Union	41 3/8 (3)	40 5.8 (/)	42 3/4 (2.75)	40 (3.00)	41 5/8 (3)

STANDARD JOBS 1950-1954

Job Type	1950	1951	1952	1953	1954
Average of All Industries, excl. farm labor	$3255/yr	$3526/yr	$3732/yr	$3927/yr	$4033/yr
Average of All Industries, inc. farm labor	$3180/yr	$3452/yr	$3660/yr	$3852/yr	$3953/yr
Bituminous Coal Mining	$3245/yr	$3762/yr	$3718/yr	$4061/yr	$3959/yr
Building Trades	$3377/yr	$3774/yr	$4086/yr	$4354/yr	$4484/yr
Domestics	$1502/yr	$1588/yr	$1707/yr	$1805/yr	$1832/yr
Farm Labor	$1454/yr	$1568/yr	$1594/yr	$1464/yr	$1498/yr
Federal Civilian	$3632/yr	$3924/yr	$4202/yr	$4411/yr	$4507/yr
Federal Employees, Executive Depts.	$3220/yr	$3189/yr	$3326/yr	$3410/yr	$3485/yr
Federal Military	$2897/yr	$2788/yr	$2891/yr	$2927/yr	$2997/yr
Finance, Insurance, & Real Estate	$3217/yr	$3356/yr	$3503/yr	$3663/yr	$3828/yr
Gas & Electricity Workers	$3571/yr	$3851/yr	$4125/yr	$4404/yr	$4579/yr
Manufacturing, Durable Goods	$3483/yr	$3862/yr	$4126/yr	$4383/yr	$4452/yr
Manufacturing, Nondurable Goods	$3154/yr	$3386/yr	$3587/yr	$3784/yr	$3923/yr
Medical/Health Services Workers	$2067/yr	$2143/yr	$2262/yr	$2365/yr	$2417/yr
Miscellaneous Manufacturing	$3020/yr	$3240/yr	$3404/yr	$3560/yr	$3640/yr
Motion Picture Services	$3089/yr	$3269/yr	$3485/yr	$3626/yr	$3929/yr
Nonprofit Org. Workers	$2578/yr	$2720/yr	$2898/yr	$3041/yr	$3179/yr
Passenger Transportation Workers, Local and Highway	$3288/yr	$3489/yr	$3645/yr	$3809/yr	$3914/yr
Personal Services	$2254/yr	$2355/yr	$2462/yr	$2573/yr	$2682/yr
Public School Teachers	$2794/yr	$2998/yr	$3169/yr	$3314/yr	$3510/yr
Radio Broadcasting &Television Workers	$4698/yr	$5017/yr	$5417/yr	$5734/yr	$5957/yr
Railroads	$3778/yr	$4163/yr	$4338/yr	$4418/yr	$4544/yr
State and Local Govt. Workers	$2758/yr	$2758/yr	$2950/yr	$3140/yr	$3281/yr
Telephone & Telegraph Workers	$3059/yr	$3253/yr	$3492/yr	$3720/yr	$3914/yr
Wholesale and Retail Trade Workers	$3034/yr	$3171/yr	$3284/yr	$3446/yr	$3558/yr

FOOD BASKET 1950-1954

(NR = Not Reported)

Commodity	Year	New York	Atlanta	Chicago	Denver	Los Angeles
Apples, Fresh, per pound	1950	12.80¢	12.80¢	13.80¢	12.90¢	11.80¢
	1951	10.90¢	12.50¢	12¢	12.10¢	11.80¢
	1952	NR	NR	16.40¢	16.60¢	15.80¢
	1953	16.30¢	16.10¢	16.50	NR	15.90¢
	1954	14.90¢	16.10¢	16.30¢	NR	16.60¢
Beans, Navy, per pound	1950	17.10¢	14.90¢	14.80¢	16¢	15.40¢
	1951	17¢	15.30¢	15.70¢	19.10¢	17.90¢
	1952	16.90¢	15.60¢	15.70¢	16.70¢	16¢
	1953	17.60¢	16.40¢	16.60¢	17.30¢	24.60¢
	1954	18¢	16.90¢	17.50¢	NR	17.90¢
Beef, Rib Roasts, per pound	1950	75.30¢	75.70¢	74.10¢	72.10¢	80.70¢
	1951	87¢	84.10¢	82.90¢	82¢	88¢
	1952	87¢	NR	83.10¢	81.10¢	89.60¢
	1953	71¢	74¢	66.20¢	NR	79¢
	1954	70.10¢	77.70¢	66.70¢	NR	79.20¢
Beef, Steaks (Round), per pound	1950	98.70¢	95.60¢	88.90¢	86.40¢	88.60¢
	1951	$1.15	$1.11	$1.04	$1.01	$1.06
	1952	$1.17	$1.12	$1.04	$1.00	$1.11
	1953	98.40¢	90.70¢	82.40¢	NR	90.50¢
	1954	97.40¢	92¢	81.80¢	NR	89.40¢
Bread, White, per pound	1950	15.30¢	14.40¢	13.20¢	13.90¢	14.70¢
	1951	16.80¢	15.90¢	14.50¢	15.30¢	15.90¢
	1952	17.30¢	15.90¢	15.20¢	15.30¢	16.40¢
	1953	17.90¢	16.20¢	15.20¢	NR	17.30¢
	1954	18.30¢	17.10¢	16.10¢	NR	18.50¢
Butter, per pound	1950	74.20¢	78¢	70.50¢	72.30¢	72.20¢
	1951	82.60¢	86.40¢	80.20¢	81.30¢	81.30¢
	1952	85.30¢	90.30¢	83¢	86.90¢	86.30¢
	1953	80.20¢	84.30¢	77.20¢	NR	80.70¢
	1954	73.70¢	77.60¢	71.60¢	NR	72¢
Cheese, per pound	1950	55¢	54.10¢	50.90¢	46.70¢	48.60¢
	1951	61.30¢	61.20¢	59.10¢	55.55¢	57.40
	1952	62.20¢	NR	60.50¢	58.90¢	61.10¢
	1953	62.70¢	NR	59.60¢	NR	60.80¢
	1954	59.40¢	NR	58¢	NR	57.80¢
Chickens, per pound	1950	44.30¢	54.20¢	47.50¢	65.80¢	58.40¢
	1951	46.50¢	56.90¢	49.90¢	67.70¢	58.90¢
	1952	47.10¢	56.20¢	48.70¢	68.30¢	60.20¢
	1953	45.50¢	54.30¢	46.60¢	NR	57.70¢
	1954	42¢	47.30¢	NR	NR	NR
Coffee, per pound	1950	79.60¢	77¢	77.40¢	82.90¢	81.10¢
	1951	86.70¢	83.50¢	84¢	92.50¢	90.30¢
	1952	86.90¢	83.10¢	83.70¢	92.20¢	90.30¢
	1953	89.90¢	86.30¢	86.80¢	NR	89.70¢
	1954	$1.13	$1.10	$1.11	NR	$1.07
Cornmeal, per pound	1950	10.60¢	6.40¢	10.40¢	9.90¢	10.60¢
	1951	11.10¢	7.10¢	11.10¢	10.80¢	11.20¢
	1952	11.90¢	7.80¢	12.10¢	17.50¢	18.20¢
	1953	12.10¢	8¢	12.20¢	NR	12.70¢
	1954	12.10¢	7.10¢	12.40¢	NR	12.60¢

Commodity	Year	New York	Atlanta	Chicago	Denver	Los Angeles
Eggs, per dozen	1950	67.10¢	57.20¢	56.70¢	59.50¢	61.90¢
	1951	79.40¢	71.10¢	70.80¢	74.10¢	74.40¢
	1952	71.80¢	63.40¢	64.10¢	68.50¢	67¢
	1953	78.20¢	70¢	69.50¢	NR	69.40¢
	1954	67.20¢	58¢	57.20¢	NR	55.80¢
Flour, Wheat, per pound	1950	9.68¢	10.44¢	9.46¢	9.10¢	9.88¢
	1951	10.28¢	11.06¢	10.04¢	9.86¢	10.38¢
	1952	10.26¢	11¢	10¢	10.06¢	10.74¢
	1953	10.40¢	10.62¢	10¢	NR	10.72¢
	1954	10.64¢	10.76¢	10.40¢	NR	10.88¢
Lard, per pound	1950	20.20¢	19¢	18.30¢	18.70¢	20.60¢
	1951	25¢	24.30¢	23.80¢	24.20¢	25.50¢
	1952	19.20¢	18.20¢	17.60¢	18.10¢	20.70¢
	1953	19.60¢	19.60¢	18.20¢	NR	21.70¢
	1954	25.80¢	25.40¢	24.80¢	NR	27.80¢
Milk, Fresh, per quart	1950	21.90¢	21.90¢	20.90¢	20.60¢	19¢
	1951	25¢	25¢	23.60¢	22.60¢	20.70¢
	1952	25.40¢	25.20¢	25.30¢	23.60¢	22.60¢
	1953	25.90¢	25.80¢	25¢	NR	22.90¢
	1954	26.30¢	25.80¢	24.90¢	NR	21.70¢
Mutton and Lamb, Leg, per pound	1950	72¢	79¢	72.80¢	71.90¢	74¢
	1951	81.40¢	86.80¢	80.90¢	79.80¢	84.10¢
	1952	80¢	84.80¢	79.20¢	81¢	81.80¢
	1953	69.50¢	77.90¢	67.90¢	NR	73.20¢
	1954	68.30¢	76¢	67.80¢	NR	70.30¢
Pork, Bacon, Sliced, per pound	1950	68.20¢	64.70¢	63.20¢	64.10¢	68.30¢
	1951	72.10¢	53.20¢	65.50¢	66.20¢	71.20¢
	1952	68.40¢	64.30¢	63.50¢	65.20¢	67.40¢
	1953	83¢	82.20¢	80.80¢	NR	81¢
	1954	88.50¢	82.20¢	80.80¢	NR	85.40¢
Pork, Chops, per pound	1950	76.20¢	68¢	75.30¢	69.90¢	82.60¢
	1951	81.40¢	86.80¢	80.90¢	79.80¢	84.10¢
	1952	80¢	84.80¢	79.20¢	81¢	81.80¢
	1953	69.50¢	77.90¢	67.90¢	NR	73.20¢
	1954	68.30¢	76¢	67.80¢	NR	70.30¢
Pork, Ham, Whole, per pound	1950	64¢	60.90¢	59.60¢	56.60¢	62.50¢
	1951	67.90¢	64.50¢	64¢	61.60¢	67.10¢
	1952	65.80¢	64.40¢	62.60¢	61¢	65.50¢
	1953	71.60¢	69.20¢	67.70¢	NR	71.10¢
	1954	71.80¢	69¢	68¢	NR	70.80¢
Pork, Salt, per pound	1950	43¢	34.70¢	39.20¢	34.60¢	38.70¢
	1951	44.80¢	38.50¢	43.50¢	37.50¢	44¢
	1952	43.60¢	34.50¢	40.30¢	36.40¢	41.10¢
	1953	NR	NR	NR	NR	NR
	1954	NR	NR	NR	NR	NR
Potatoes, Irish, per 15 pounds	1950	65.70¢	73.60¢	83.70¢	67.60¢	72.70¢
	1951	71.20¢	76.40¢	92¢	73.90¢	83.90¢
	1952	$1.05	$1.20	$1.23	$1.04	$1.15
	1953	71.60¢	83.40¢	97.20¢	NR	93.30¢
	1954	69.70¢	73.10¢	91.70¢	NR	$1.00
Prunes, Dried, per pound	1950	24.80¢	NR	25.20¢	24.80¢	22¢
	1951	27.40¢	NR	28.40¢	28.30¢	24.60¢
	1952	NR	NR	NR	NR	NR
	1953	28¢	29.80¢	29.20¢	NR	26.60¢
	1954	29.70¢	31.30¢	31.20¢	NR	27.80¢

Commodity	Year	New York	Atlanta	Chicago	Denver	Los Angeles
Rice, per pound	1950	17.40¢	16¢	16.20¢	16.10¢	17.20¢
	1951	18.60¢	16.80¢	16.70¢	17.40¢	18¢
	1952	18.70¢	17.40¢	17.10¢	17.50¢	18.20¢
	1953	20.30¢	19¢	18.30¢	NR	19.70¢
	1954	19.90¢	18.60¢	17.70¢	NR	20.50¢
Sugar, per pound	1950	9.36¢	9.40¢	9.82¢	10.30¢	9.66¢
	1951	9.74¢	9.84¢	10.22¢	10.70¢	10.06¢
	1952	9.80¢	9.94¢	10.38¢	10.94¢	10.46¢
	1953	9.94¢	9.98¢	10.64¢	NR	10.54¢
	1954	10¢	9.92¢	NR	10.58¢	10.34¢
Tea, per pound	1950	NR	NR	NR	NR	NR
	1951	NR	NR	NR	NR	NR
	1952	NR	NR	NR	NR	NR
	1953	$1.24	$1.29	$1.30	NR	$1.40
	1954	$1.31	$1.37	$1.37	NR	$1.44
Veal, per pound	1950	$1.20	$1.01	$1.00	97.30¢	$1.08
	1951	$1.39	$1.18	$1.14	$1.12	$1.27
	1952	$1.41	$1.17	$1.15	$1.06	$1.28
	1953	$1.29	$1.01	$1.05	NR	$1.12
	1954	$1.23	98.40¢	$1.05	NR	$1.09

SELECTED PRICES 1950-1954

Item	Source	Description	Price
Alcohol			
Blended Whiskey	*New York Times* (1952)	*Old Homestead;* 4/5 quart	$3.19
Bourbon	*New York Times* (1952)	Old Taylor Bonded	$7.35
Bourbon Whiskey	*New York Times* (1952)	*Virginia Lee;* 4/5 quart	$3.69
Canadian Whiskey	*New York Times* (1952)	*Seagram's V.O.*	$6.10
Cognac	*New York Times* (1952)	*Courvoisier V.S.O.P.*	$3.68
Grain Gin	*New York Times* (1952)	*Fifth Avenue Gin;* 4/5 quart	$2.88
Rye	*New York Times* (1952)	*B.P.R. Bonded*	$4.49
Scotch Whiskey	*New York Times* (1952)	*White Abbey;* 4/5 quart	$4.59
Apparel, Children's			
Baseball Suit	*Good Housekeeping* (1950)	*Yankiboy;* Little Leaguers make big hits with these dashingly styled, sturdily made outfits; cotton-flannel shirt and pants, red trim; matching cap	$2.49
Buffalo Bill Costume	*Belk's Christmas Catalog* (1951)	Black-twill pants with chaps, 2-tone flannelette shirt	$2.98
Longies	*Sears, Roebuck* (1952)	Handsome Glen plaid-suspender longies of durable cotton	$1.44
Shirt	*Life* (1950)	*McMullen;* man-tailored shirts get fancy; featuring French cuffs, pique trim, tucked flowed bosom	$10.95–$15.95
Shirt	*Sears, Roebuck* (1952)	Movie star print; has Dale Evans, Roy Rogers, and Trigger on front; old favorites and gay new styles	$0.84
Shoes	*Sears, Roebuck* (1952)	*Jeepers;* Roy Rogers and Trigger imprinted in bright colors to delight every boy, girl	$3.39
Suit	*Good Housekeeping* (1950)	*Botany Eton;* suit for boys; blends the superior quality of Botany Brand 100% virgin worsted with the superb men's wear tailoring of master clothes	$21.00
Apparel, Men's			
Belt	*New York Times* (1952)	Leather	$10.00
Head Warmer	*Woman's Home Companion* (1950)	*Picard;* expert skiers started wearing knitted face-caps last year—now they're your newest perkiest cap for ear-chilling days	$5.00
Jacket	*New York Times* (1952)	Sports jacket, denim striped	$16.50
Jacket	*New York Times* (1952)	Lounging jacket, navy blue silk	$35.00
Pajamas	*New York Times* (1952)	Nylon in gold with navy piping	$14.95
Scarf	*New York Times* (1952)	Silk; in plaids and solids	$10.00

Item	Source	Description	Price
Shirt	*New York Times* (1952)	Clan plaid sports shirt; washable	$16.50
Shirt	*New York Times* (1952)	Oxford cloth button down	$3.95
Shirt	*New York Times* (1952)	Sports shirts; flannels, gabardines or rayon	$3.98
Shirt	*Life* (1950)	*Shirtcraft Airman Model Z;* no buttons on America's newest, smartest business shirt, it zips closed	$3.95
Shirt	*Chicago Tribune* (1951)	Broadcloth; madras	$1.88
Shoes	*Sears, Roebuck* (1952)	Shockless cushion insole; it's smart to be comfortable	$8.98
Shoes	*Sears, Roebuck* (1952)	*Jeepers;* our best quality; pro-type styling	$4.98
Shoes	*New York Times* (1952)	Handsewn moccasins	$13.95
Sweater	*New York Times* (1952)	Sleeveless striped cardigan of imported Alpaca	$23.00
Undershirt	*Life* (1950)	*Arrow;* made by the makers of Arrow shirts	$0.85

Apparel, Women's

Item	Source	Description	Price
Brassiere	*Woman's Day* (1950)	*Flexess;* strapless; of satin, elastic and nylon marquisette	$2.00
Brassiere	*Good Housekeeping* (1950)	Embroidered nylon marquisette cups with rayon satin frame and back	$3.00
Brassiere	*Woman's Home Companion* (1950)	*Maidenform Allo-ette;* 2" band in white satin	$2.00
Brassiere	*Chicago Tribune* (1951)	The Magic Insets gently support from below to give lasting uplift, youthful beauty	$3.00
Brassiere	*Today's Health Magazine* (1952)	*Anne Alt;* maternity and nursing; firm, reliable support to enlarging breasts B&C Cups D Cups	 $2.75 $3.00
Brassiere	*Sears, Roebuck* (1952)	Rayon satin or cotton; was $1.19	$0.98
Dress	*McCall's* (1950)	*Clifford;* diagonally tucked bodice; blouse stops at waistline	$23.00
Dress	*McCall's* (1950)	*Margi Spring Lilac;* with yoke and cuffs of ribbed tucks, tucks below the belt are released to make a full skirt	$40.00
Dress	*McCall's* (1950)	*Hi-Dee;* of Irish linen; sleeveless	$30.00
Dress	*Sears, Roebuck* (1952)	Waffle pique; such gay, young new prints	$3.98
Dress	*Ebony* (1954)	One-piece cotton dress has scoop neck and princess-cut wallpaper waist below empire bust	$15.00
Exercise Suit	*Chicago Tribune* (1951)	*Aqua Sheen Slim-Rite;* coverall; plastic exercise suit	$3.98
Fur	*Chicago Tribune* (1951)	Capes, scarfs, stoles, jackets, coats	$175
Girdle	*Woman's Day* (1950)	*Charvin;* white nylon girdle, sleek as a slither and twice as cute	$6.95
Girdle	*Woman's Day* (1950)	Boned front; with side zipper available in tearose, nylon or satin	$12.50

Item	Source	Description	Price
Girdle	Woman's Home Companion (1950)	Bestform; has nylon-taffeta front, sides, and back and boned-nylon diaphragm	$5.95
Girdle	Chicago Tribune (1951)	The Magic Inset eliminates annoying bones, yet it can't roll over, wrinkle, or bind	$5.95
Golf Suit	Good Housekeeping (1950)	Pro-golfer two-piece woman's outfit; smartly fashioned in sanforized fine-combed cotton	$12.00
Gown	Ebony (1954)	Luxite Red Spice; add spicy variety to your lingerie wardrobe; gay, brilliant, beautiful red for a saucy glimpse of color under a dark hem	$5.95
Robe	Woman's Home Companion (1950)	Evelyn Pearson; in pastel or dark rayon crepe, contrast piping	$13.00
Robe	Woman's Home Companion (1950)	In frost white, harvest rose, tawny gold	$9.95
Shoes	Good Housekeeping (1950)	Wohl Natural Poise; beautifully fashioned; blessedly comfortable and they fit precisely—thanks to the exclusive scientific dimensional equalizer	$8.95
Shoes	Good Housekeeping (1950)	Desco Revelations; rest your arches, look divine	$7.95
Shoes	Today's Health Magazine (1952)	Aerotized Walkmaster; the airway design; you'll be delighted with the slipper-like comfort	$8.95
Slip	Woman's Day (1950)	Seamprufe Marybell; daintily adorned with lace and pin tucking; in fine sanforized wamsutta cotton	$4.00
Slippers	Ebony (1954)	Honeybugs; Robert Haynes, co-starring in Return to Paradise, says "My favorite slippers."	$4.99
Suit	Good Housekeeping (1950)	Side-split skirt for walking ease; sheen gabardine	$70.00

Appliances

Item	Source	Description	Price
Electric Range	McCall's (1950)	Deep Freeze; you can buy them with confidence	$159.95
Gas Range	Chicago Tribune (1951)	Imperial; full size; 36"	$99.00
Gas Range	Chicago Tribune (1951)	Marshall DeLuxe; the best cook in the world is helpless with a bulky, inefficient stove	$159
Home Freezer	McCall's (1950)	Deep Freeze DeLuxe Model; 12.3 cubic feet holds more than 430 lbs of assorted frozen foods	$399.95
Refrigerator	McCall's (1950)	Admiral Dual-Temp; no defrosting—no dish covers needed—no bouncing favors	$189.95
Refrigerator	Chicago Tribune (1951)	Frigidaire; has extra-large frozen food super freezer	$199.75
Steam Radiator	The American Home (1954)	Burnham Portable; steam heat	$60–$108
Washing Machine	Woman's Day (1950)	Bendix Home Appliances; tried and true agitator washing; does 8 pounds of wash at a time	$189.95
Washing Machine	Woman's Day (1950)	Speed Queen; guarantee yourself the most for your money in home laundry service	$99.95–$139.95
Washing Machine	McCall's (1950)	Thor Automagic Spinner-Washer; from suds to spin-dry in a single porcelain tub	$199.50
Washing Machine	Consumer Reports (1950)	Maytag Nonautomatic	$184.95
Washing Machine	Chicago Tribune (1951)	Speed Queen; for easier family washings	$99.95

Item	Source	Description	Price
Baby Products			
Baby Lotion	*McCall's* (1950)	*Johnson's;* hospital-proved the most effective preparation	$0.49/$0.98
Baby Nipple	*Today's Health Magazine* (1952)	*Evenflo;* America's most popular nurser; includes nipple, bottle, cap	$0.25
Baby Oil	*Good Housekeeping* (1950)	*Playtex;* prevent diaper rash with Playtex	$0.79
Crib	*Sears, Roebuck* (1952)	*Honeysuckle;* full-size chest crib; keep baby's pads, shirts, sheets at your finger tips, right where you need them	$49.95
Crib Mattress	*Today's Health Magazine* (1952)	*Bunny Bear;* America's only crib mattress with the unique bonded guarantee	$10.95
Pants	*Woman's Home Companion* (1950)	*Kleinert's;* waterproofed without rubber; three pairs	$3.00
Pants	*McCall's* (1950)	*Playtex;* in pink, white, or blue	$0.69
Pants	*Good Housekeeping* (1950)	*Playtex;* ventilated; it clings gently, gives waterproof fit without cutting off circulation	$0.79
Server	*Good Housekeeping* (1950)	Safety server for babies; prevent tragic highchair accidents; lighten mother's burdens	$15.95
Shoes	*Today's Health Magazine* (1952)	*Moran Wee-Walker;* perfect fit, fine durable leathers	$1.19
Training Pants	*Chicago Tribune* (1951)	White cotton knit; quality	$0.15
Business Equipment & Supplies			
Adding Machine Tape	*Sears, Roebuck* (1952)	Fits all models	$1.79
Carbon Paper	*Sears, Roebuck* (1952)	*Tower Black;* for typewriter copies	$1.19
Paper Punch	*Sears, Roebuck* (1952)	1/4" diameter holes as close as 1/8" from paper edge	$0.89
Stapler	*Life* (1950)	*Bostitch B8R;* pound it, squeeze it, strike it; fastens it better and faster with wire	$2.60
Stapler	*Sears, Roebuck* (1952)	*Arrow;* use as stapler, plier, or tacker	$2.34
Staples	*Sears, Roebuck* (1952)	*Arrow;* fits all standard staplers; box of 5,000	$0.82
Collectibles			
Book	*Rare Books and Manuscripts; Lathrop C. Harper, Inc.* (1953)	*Miguel De Cervantes;* El Ingenioso Hidalgo Don Quichote de la Mancha; Excessively rare second issue of the first edition	$3,500
Book	*Rare Books and Manuscripts; Lathrop C. Harper, Inc.* (1953)	*De Cometis;* First edition of the first printed book on the comets, 1472	$1,250
Coins	*New York Times* (1954)	1953 New Zealand Proof Coin Set; 10 pieces; crown to half-penny in mock leather case; commemorates royal visit of Queen Elizabeth to New Zealand	$14.87

Item	Source	Description	Price
Stamps	*New York Times* (1954)	Triangle stamps from Egypt 100 different 150 different	$1.50 $3.50

Education

Course	*McCall's* (1950)	*DuBarry Success Course For Women;* includes twenty beauty, make-up and hair preparations	$28.50
Course	*Good Housekeeping* (1950)	*DuBarry Success Course;* course, with introductory supply of three DuBarry Beauty Preparations	$12.95
Dance Lessons	*New York Times* (1954)	150 dance courses; 2 hr. lessons	$1.00

Entertainment

Play Ticket	*Chicago Tribune* (1951)	*Point of No Return;* Henry Fonda; a new comedy by Paul Osborn; evenings	$1.80–$5
Sporting Event Ticket	*Chicago Tribune* (1951)	Polo; fast, dangerous action; double-header games General admission Reserved seats	 $1.00 $2.00
Theater Ticket	*Chicago Tribune* (1951)	*Phil Silvers; Top Banana;* 300 good seats	$2.75
Wrestling Ticket	*Chicago Tribune* (1951)	Wrestling; Vern Gagne, NWA Jr. heavyweight champ	$1.30/$2.60/$3.90

Entertainment, Home

Board Game	*Woman's Home Companion* (1950)	*Old MacDonald's Farm;* the fun way to be a farmer—corner the market—trade and unload surplus stocks	$2.00
Board Game	*Woman's Home Companion* (1950)	*Parker Brothers Monopoly;* popular edition, always bound in pebbled green	$4.00
Board Game	*Woman's Home Companion* (1950)	*Parker Brothers Sorry;* an immensely popular board game, unlike any other	$2.50
Board Game	*The American Home* (1954)	*Parker Brothers Monopoly;* the most fascinating game in the world	$3/$4/$10
Camera	*Ebony* (1954)	*Argus;* world's most popular 35 mm camera; perfect for color slides, black and white pictures, action shots	$66.50
Projector	*Ebony* (1954)	*Argus Automatic;* 300-watt projector shows, changes, stores your color slides automatically	$66.50
Record	*Life* (1950)	*Columbia Records; Kiss Me Kate;* up to 50 minutes of music on one record; Alfred Drake, Patricia Morison, and original Broadway cast complete on one record	$4.85
Television	*Chicago Tribune* (1951)	*Scott;* 16"; watch a wonderful world of entertainment—sports, drama, comedy, news and musical events	$299
Television	*The American Home* (1954)	*Crosley;* 17"; fits into a small space	$140
Television	*Ebony* (1954)	*Sylvania;* more picture clarity, more cabinet beauty, more genuine economies, more eye comfort, too	$169.95

Food Products

Cake Mix	*Chicago Tribune* (1951)	*Betty Crocker;* white, devil's food, yellow; your choice; 20 oz	$0.35
Candy Bars	*Chicago Tribune* (1951)	*Mounds, Mars, Almond Joy, Jersey;* limit 4	$0.13/2
Chili Con Carne	*Chicago Tribune* (1951)	With beans; with $0.10 newspaper coupon	$0.25

Item	Source	Description	Price
Chili Sauce	*Saturday Evening Post* (1951)	*Bennett's;* last time you tasted chili sauce like this you spooned it out of a Mason jar back home; 8 oz	$0.25
Coffee	*Chicago Tribune* (1951)	*Holleb;* 1 lb	$0.83
Margarine	*Chicago Tribune* (1951)	*Delrich;* 2 lb	$0.57
Peanut Butter	*Chicago Tribune* (1951)	*Hollob's Supreme;* 12 oz	$0.33
Shortening	*Chicago Tribune* (1951)	*Crisco;* 1 lb	$0.31
Smokie Links	*Chicago Tribune* (1951)	*Oscar Mayer;* deliciously different	$0.59
Wieners	*Chicago Tribune* (1951)	*Oscar Mayer*	$0.49/pound

Furniture

Item	Source	Description	Price
Card Table and Chairs	*The American Home* (1954)	*Cosco Fashionfold;* give the smartest set in town	$49.75
Gun Rack	*The American Home* (1954)	*Nimrod;* 6-gun rack with steel guard	$17.95
Hide-A-Bed	*The American Home* (1954)	*T-Cushion;* with Beautyrest seat cushions, in gold Trigger metallic tweed Apartment size Full size	 $239.50 $249.50
Hope Chest	*Life* (1950)	*Lane;* a Lane chest is the real love-gift; genuine American walnut with tray	$47.95
Rug	*Woman's Day* (1950)	Glamour-rug; handsome, soft-wood-surface 9' x 12"	$29.95
Table and Chairs	*Good Housekeeping* (1950)	*Daystrom;* the tables with the wonder top; set	$74.50

Garden Equipment & Supplies

Item	Source	Description	Price
Garden Hose	*Chicago Tribune* (1951)	*Goodyear Glide;* 50"	$5.95
Lawn Mower	*Chicago Tribune* (1951)	*Davos;* with safety Flex-A-Matic clutch; easy to handle	$88
Trees	*Sears, Roebuck* (1952)	2 Silver Juniper, 4 Pfitzer	$18.95

Hotel Rates

Item	Source	Description	Price
Room Rate	*New York Times* (1954)	*The Versailles;* air conditioned; double occupancy; 2 meals a day included; 7 course dinner	$12.00
Room Rate	*New York Times* (1954)	*The Empress;* European plan available for meals; double occupancy	$14.00
Room Rate	*New York Times* (1954)	*The Broadmoor;* double occupancy	$5.00

Household Products

Item	Source	Description	Price
Automatic Toaster	*Woman's Home Companion* (1950)	*General Mills;* it's double automatic so toast is always timed to perfection	$22.95
Automatic Toaster	*The American Home* (1954)	*General Electric;* extra-high toast lift, 6-position control for any shade of toast	$21.95
Automatic Coffee Maker	*The American Home* (1954)	*General Electric;* makes as few as two cups—as many as 9 —perfectly	$29.50

Item	Source	Description	Price
Blanket	*Chicago Tribune* (1951)	100% wool; $9.95 value	$5.55
Blanket	*The American Home* (1954)	*Kenwood Astra-Ken;* all wool; inspired colorings, borrowed from famous paintings	$50.00
Blanket	*The American Home* (1954)	*Fieldcrest;* a fleecy blend of rayon, wool, and cotton, bordered in stripes	$9.95
Blanket	*The American Home* (1954)	*North Star Flora Nocturne;* strewn with roses, hand-screened and washable	$22.95
Blender	*Today's Health Magazine* (1952)	*Waring Products Model PB-5;* a new kind of food preparation is now at your fingertips	$44.50
Clock	*Life* (1950)	*Telechron;* with the Synchro-sealed motor; keeps time to 1/60th of a second	$3.98
Coffee Maker	*McCall's* (1950)	*Landers, Frary & Clark Universal Coffematic;* America's most popular coffeemaker with the flavor-selector	$24.95
Cooker	*Woman's Home Companion* (1950)	*Universal Cooka-matic;* bakes, grills, toasts, or fries	$29.95
Curtain	*Woman's Day* (1950)	*Duralace;* in patterns to harmonize with every decorative style	$6.00
Defroster	*Woman's Day* (1950)	*Paragon De-Frost-It;* electric; automatic defrosting on your present refrigerator	$9.95
Double Boiler	*Woman's Day* (1950)	*Corning Glass Works Pyrex;* the glass can't change the taste or color of any food; so sturdy—2 1/2 times as strong as ordinary glass	$3.45
Double Snack Toaster	*Woman's Day* (1950)	*Federal;* you can serve tempting, toasted, sealed sandwiches with half the work and half the time	$1.69
Drainboard	*Good Housekeeping* (1950)	*Artwire Drain-A-Tray;* chinalike—super strong plastic	$3.49
Dye	*Woman's Day* (1950)	*Putnam;* you get bright colors the first time you try	$0.15
Electric Cook	*Woman's Day* (1950)	*Arvin Electric Houseware;* America's most versatile cooking appliance—it grills, toasts, fries, bakes waffles	$24.95
Electric Curling Iron	*Sears, Roebuck* (1952)	*Kenmore;* bright finish; wood handle	$1.79
Electric Tool Kit	*The American Home* (1954)	*Black and Decker;* includes 1/4" drill and 14 most useful accessories in tool chest	$29.95
Enamel Wallcovering	*Sears, Roebuck* (1952)	The quality is built right in; 1' 4 1/2" wide	$0.53
Finger Guards	*Saturday Evening Post* (1951)	*Industrial Gloves;* saves fingers, lowers your hand protection cost	$0.10
Flatware	*Woman's Home Companion* (1950)	*Gorham King Edward;* sterling; America's leading silversmiths since 1831; six-piece place setting	$35.00
Flatware	*McCall's* (1950)	*Gorham Chantilly;* place setting, six pieces	$26.00
Floor Cleaner	*McCall's* (1950)	*Bruce;* dry-cleans as it waxes	$0.68/qt
Floor Cleaner	*Woman's Home Companion* (1950)	*Bruce;* easier than any self-polish; far better for your floors	$0.79/qt
Floor Covering	*Woman's Day* (1950)	*Sandura;* new vinyl plastic-coated floor; roll 48" wide 9' long	$2.95
Floor Wax	*Woman's Day* (1950)	*Aerowax;* no rubbing; stop paying fancy prices for floor wax	$0.55/qt

Item	Source	Description	Price
Goblets	*Sears, Roebuck* (1952)	*Harmony House Lace Bouquet;* pattern delicately feminine in design and shape; set of four	$3.35
Gravy Ladle	*Woman's Home Companion* (1950)	*International;* sterling; queen's lace pattern	$10.50
Hair Dryer	*Sears, Roebuck* (1952)	*Ann Barton;* home hair dryer gives you all the convenience of professional shop equipment but right in your own home	$21.50
Ice Cream Freezer	*Woman's Home Companion* (1950)	Homemade ice cream in minutes; 4-qt model	$24.95
Ice Cream Freezer	*The American Home* (1954)	*Silex Freeze-O-Tray;* make delicious ice cream in your own refrigerator	$18.95
Iron	*Woman's Home Companion* (1950)	*General Mills Tru-Heat;* famous for its tapered heel that irons backward as easily as forward	$12.95
Iron	*McCall's* (1950)	*Proctor Champion;* full even heat and over-size soleplate for easier, faster ironing	$9.95
Kitchen Clock	*Woman's Day* (1950)	*General Electric;* things run smoother all day long when you have this accurate, dependable General Electric pantry clock in your kitchen	$3.95
Mattress	*McCall's* (1950)	*Serta Perfect Sleeper;* new improved Serta-foam latex cushioning matching box spring	$49.50
Measure	*Good Housekeeping* (1950)	*Pyrex;* 1-pt size	$0.59
Mixer	*McCall's* (1950)	*General Electric;* to give you faster, more-thorough mixing	$34.95
Mixette	*Woman's Day* (1950)	*Hamilton Beach Portable;* one hand operation, 3-speeds under the thumb West of Denver	$17.75 $18.75
Mop	*Good Housekeeping* (1950)	*Dufold Sponge Mop;* does 9 jobs, keeps hands lovely	$5.95
Paint	*Life* (1950)	*Glidden Spread Satin;* new wonder paint makes winter painting practical; no offensive odor; paint with windows closed	$4.49
Pan	*Good Housekeeping* (1950)	*Pyrex;* loaf pan 9 1/8" size	$0.69
Polisher & Scrubber	*The American Home* (1954)	*Regina Twin-Brush;* does your scrubbing, waxing, polishing	$64.50
Portable Mixer	*The American Home* (1954)	*General Electric;* it actually weighs less than three lbs	$19.50
Sander-Polisher	*Saturday Evening Post* (1951)	*Black & Decker;* 1000 ways to speed home and farm jobs	$32.95
Sheet	*The American Home* (1954)	*Dan River;* percale; bordered with tic-tac-toe pattern	$10.50
Towel	*McCall's* (1950)	*Cannon;* buttercup yellow	$1.19
Vaporizer	*Life* (1950)	*Electric Steam Radiator;* the first and only 3to 24-hour vaporizer that doubles as a room humidifier	$5.95
Weatherstrip	*The American Home* (1954)	*Mortell;* eliminate unhealthy fuel wasting drafts	$1.25/rl
Wood Cream	*Woman's Day* (1950)	*Gold Sea;* gives you lovelier lustre, leaves no oily film	$0.59/pt

Item	Source	Description	Price
Jewelry			
Brooch	*New York Times* (1952)	*Tiffany's* brooch of diamonds and rubies; divides into two clips	$5200
Diamond	*Saturday Evening Post* (1951)	*De Beers Consolidated Mines;* 1 ct	$550–$1165
Ring	*New York Times* (1952)	*Tiffany's* twin stone diamond ring	$2750
Watch	*New York Times* (1952)	*Golden mesh band;* costume buckle; 17 jewel surrounded by filigree and pretend pearls	$45.00
Watch	*Ebony* (1954)	*Gruen;* when you give the revolutionary self-winding Gruen autowind, you are giving the finest gift of all time	$125
Medical Products & Services			
Antacid	*Saturday Evening Post* (1951)	*Tums;* eat like candy, tums for the tummy	$0.10
Aspirin	*Saturday Evening Post* (1951)	100 5-grain tablets; no faster-acting aspirin made	$0.54
Aspirin	*Today's Health* (1952)	*Bayer;* children's size; three ways best for your child; 30 tablets per package	$0.30/pkg
Cough Drops	*Life* (1950)	*Luden's Menthol;* contains more menthol than any other cough drops	$0.05
Glycerine Tablets	*Life* (1950)	*Pine Brothers;* quick throat relief	$0.10
Laxative	*Life* (1950)	*Nature's Remedy NR Tablets;* man's best laxative, 10 herbs in tiny tablet	$0.25
Liniment	*Life* (1950)	*Absorbine Jr.;* the favorite stand-by liniment of many professional athletes for over fifty years	$1.25
Liniment	*Good Housekeeping* (1950)	*Absorbine Jr.;* relieve torturing rheumatic or neuralgic pain; long-lasting bottle	$1.25
Lip Balm	*Life* (1950)	*Chapstick;* keep lips fit	$0.25
Lip Balm	*Saturday Evening Post* (1951)	*Stag;* soothes chapped lips	$0.39
Nail Treatment	*Today's Health* (1952)	*Thumb Nail Biting Medicine;* discourage prolonged and persistent nail biting	$1.20
Nonprescription Drug	*Good Housekeeping* (1950)	*Tabcin;* miserable with cold symptoms?	$0.75
Tincture of Iodine	*Saturday Evening Post* (1951)	First-aid help, with applicator	$0.29
Motorized Vehicles, Supplies, & Services			
Automobile	*New York Times* (1952)	*Dodge '52 Coronet*	$1895
Automobile	*New York Times* (1952)	*Pontiac '52 Club Coupe*	$2195
Automobile	*New York Times* (1952)	*Buick '51 Riviera*	$1995
Automobile	*New York Times* (1952)	*Buick '48;* convertible Roadmaster	$950
Automobile	Richard M. Langworth and Graham Robson, *Complete Book of Collectible Cars* (1985)	*Ford Custom Victoria;* 2-door hardtop	$1925

Item	Source	Description	Price
Automobile	Langworth and Robson, *Complete Book of Collectible Cars* (1985)	*Buick Skylark;* convertible	$5000
Automobile	Langworth and Robson, *Complete Book of Collectible Cars* (1985)	*Cadillac Series 62 Eldorado*	$4,738–$6,286
Automobile	Langworth and Robson, *Complete Book of Collectible Cars* (1985)	*Chevrolet Corvette Roadster*	$2,799–$3,513
Automobile	Langworth and Robson, *Complete Book of Collectible Cars* (1985)	*Nash Rambler;* convertible	$1,550–$2,150
Gasoline Additive	*Saturday Evening Post* (1951)	*Heet;* no more hard starting; prevents frozen gas lines	$0.65

Musical Instruments

Chord Organ	*Chicago Tribune* (1951)	*Hammond;* Love music? Then the new Hammond Chord organ is for you, even without musical training	$975
Piano	*McCall's* (1950)	*Lester Spinet;* dollar for dollar your best piano buy	$595

Other

Dog Food	*Woman's Day* (1950)	Cooked and ready to use; a nourishing food for dogs	$0.10
Gift Kit	*Woman's Home Companion* (1950)	*Palmolive;* Christmas gift kit; with talc, after-shave lotion, and a choice of brushless or latherless shave cream	$1.05
Patent Settlement	*Guinness Book of World Records* (1981)	Settlement paid by Ford Motor Company to the Ferguson Tractor Company in 1952 for a patent-infringement claim filed in 1948.	$9.25 million
Pesticide	*The American Home* (1954)	*Reardon Laboratories Mouse Seed;* kills mice	$0.25
Stationery	*Saturday Evening Post* (1951)	For after-Christmas thank-yous; box of 24 sheets and 24 matching envelopes	$0.49
Wallet	*Sears, Roebuck* (1952)	*Kerrybrooke;* fine-quality leather, smart styling	$3.50

Personal Care Products

Christmas Set	*Woman's Home Companion* (1950)	*Old Spice;* includes aftershave and shaving cream	$1.65
Comb	*Life* (1950)	*Ace;* hard rubber; a type for every purpose	$0.29–$0.39
Cotton Swabs	*Good Housekeeping* (1950)	*Q-Tips;* the largest-selling sterilized swabs; large package	$0.98
Cream	*Good Housekeeping* (1950)	*Sofskin;* new cream softens 3 kinds of dry skin; big jar	$0.25
Cream	*Good Housekeeping* (1950)	*Ponds;* dry skin cream; by day, use lightly under make-up; large jar	$0.89

Item	Source	Description	Price
Cream	*Life* (1950)	*Helena Rubinstein Estrogenic Hormone Cream and Oil Cream;* for hands, face and oil for neck and throat	$3.50
Cream	*McCall's* (1950)	*Jergen's;* doctors' tests show that 8 out of 10 complexions beautifully improved when women used this Vitone-enriched cream	$1.39
Cuticle Scissors	*Sears, Roebuck* (1952)	*Lyric;* fine shaft and rings for holding	$2.00
Deodorant	*McCall's* (1950)	*Stoppette Spray;* 2 1/4 ounces; a quick squeeze checks annoying perspiration, stops odor	$1.25
Deodorant	*McCall's* (1950)	*Odo-Ro-No Cream;* the deodorant without a doubt	$0.25/$0.50
Deodorant	*Today's Health* (1952)	*Heed;* an amazing new underarm deodorant in a lovely cool-green squeezable bottle	$0.59
Electric Shaver	*Life* (1950)	*Schick Colonel;* must outshave blade razors or your money back	$17.50
Hair Color Rinse	*Today's Health* (1952)	*Noreen;* temporary but completely effective	$0.15/$0.30/$0.60
Hair Coloring	*Sears, Roebuck* (1952)	*Ann Barton Glow;* lasting hair color	$1.79
Hair Coloring	*Sears, Roebuck* (1952)	*Clairol;* for easy home use	$0.95
Hair Pomade	*Ebony* (1954)	More hair beauty, more for your money	$0.25
Hair Treatment	*Ebony* (1954)	*Nulox;* 4 oz jar super pre-applied shampoo, 2 oz jar scalp cream; 9 to 12 complete greaseless hair treatment	$2.48
Home Facial	*Woman's Home Companion* (1950)	*Noxema;* look lovelier in 10 days or your money back; big jar	$0.59
Home Permanent Kit	*Life* (1950)	*Rave;* has the Dial-A-Wave to give you the one right wave for your hair	$2.00
Home Permanent Kit	*Life* (1950)	*Richard Hudnut;* scientific tests show creme waving lotion leaves hair springier and stronger	$2.75
Home Permanent Kit	*Chicago Tribune* (1951)	*Stevens Cold Wave;* you ask for it again and again	$15.00
Lipstick	*McCall's* (1950)	*Barbara Gould;* with exclusive greater stay-on formula	$1.00
Nail Kit	*Woman's Home Companion* (1950)	*LaCross Mariner;* with nail file, nail clip, heavy-duty nail scissors and tweezers; in compact leather case	$5.00
Razor	*Saturday Evening Post* (1951)	*Gillette Super-Speed Razor;* improved 10-blade dispenser in styrene travel case	$1.00
Razor Blades	*Saturday Evening Post* (1951)	*Gillette;* 10 blades; sharpest edges ever honed	$0.49
Shampoo	*Good Housekeeping* (1950)	*Shulton;* perfumed with famous Old Spice; 5 3/4 oz bottle	$0.85
Shaver	*Life* (1950)	*Durham-Enders Razor Cord;* the only genuine one-piece razor; nothing to twist or unscrew; package includes five blades	$0.49
Shaving Cream	*Saturday Evening Post* (1951)	*Stag;* brushless; set up whiskers for quick, close, no-sting, no-nick shaving; jumbo tube	$0.49
Toothbrush	*Saturday Evening Post* (1951)	Five styles, long-wearing hyzon bristles	$0.49
Toothbrush	*Today's Health Magazine* (1952)	*Dr. West Miracle-Tuft;* the Exton bristles of this remarkable brush actually repel water	$0.60

Item	Source	Description	Price
Publications			
Magazine	*Woman's Day* (1950)	*Woman's Day*; monthly	$0.05
Magazine	*Life* (1950)	*Life*; weekly	$0.20
Magazine	*McCall's* (1950)	*McCall's*	$0.25
Magazine	*Saturday Evening Post* (1951)	*Saturday Evening Post*; weekly	$0.15
Pamphlets on Communicable Diseases	*Today's Health* (1952)	American Medical Association's topics: common cold, scarlet fever, measles, whooping cough, infantile paralysis	$0.15
Real Estate			
Gas Station and Grocery	*Chicago Tribune* (1951)	Must sell immediately on account of illness	$18,250
House	*Chicago Tribune* (1951)	For sale; ranch bungalow; three bedroom brick	$13,800
House	*Chicago Tribune* (1951)	For sale; nine-room home in excellent condition; 3 1/2 baths, 2 car garage, 2 heated porches; a nice buy	$40,000
House	*Chicago Tribune* (1951)	For sale; 6-bedroom tri-level	$24,750
House	*Chicago Tribune* (1951)	7-room home, 4 bedrooms, 3 baths	$22,500
House Plans	*The American Home* (1954)	*American Home;* traditional stone and wood; one-level plan has three bedrooms, two baths in separate wing	$5.00
Sewing Equipment and Supplies			
Buckle Frame	*Woman's Day* (1950)		$0.14
Fabric	*Woman's Day* (1950)		$3.06
Pattern	*Woman's Day* (1950)		$0.25
Pinking Shears	*Woman's Day* (1950)	*Griffon;* pinks heavier materials, as it cuts for ravel-proof zig-zag edge	$3.95
Slide Fastener	*Woman's Day* (1950)		$0.35
Sports Equipment			
Basketball	*Belk's Christmas Catalog* (1951)	*Collette GC;* official size; valve bladder; inflating needle	$2.98
Fishing Rod & Reel	*New York Times* (1952)	*Weak* fish outfit; split bamboo rod; locking reel seat; 150-yd. size; saltwater reel	$6.99
Fishing Rod & Reel	*New York Times* (1952)	Deep sea outfit; solid glass rod; 3 chromium guides; locking reel seat; 250-yd. free spool; star drag reel	$16.99
Reel	*New York Times* (1952)	*Pflueger "Templar" Reel*	$21.99
Shotgun	*Belk's Christmas Catalog* (1951)	*Louis Max;* double barrel; safety catch; break action loud but safe	$1.98
Sleeping Bag	*Chicago Tribune* (1951)	Vacation special; real U.S. Army	$4.88

Item	Source	Description	Price
Tobacco Products			
Lighter Fluid	*Life* (1950)	*Zippo;* instant lighting, smokeless flame	$0.25
Pipe	*New York Times* (1952)	*Engineer's Desk Pipe;* won't spill ashes	$1.49
Pipe Tobacco	*Saturday Evening Post* (1951)	*Edgeworth;* make your pipe dreams come true; longer lasting; cooler smoking	$0.15
Toys			
Burp Gun	*Belk's Christmas Catalog* (1951)	*Mattel;* realistically designed even to the trigger; fires 1–50 shots at a touch; plenty of smoke pours from the barrel, lots of noise	$2.98
Cash Register	*Belk's Christmas Catalog* (1951)	*Kampkap;* push the key, correct amount $0.01 to $1 plus No Sale pops up in window; aluminum and red finish	$2.49
Doll	*Belk's Christmas Catalog* (1951)	*Madame Alexander Cissy;* the debutante doll with molded figure, shapely feet that wear high-heeled shoes	$19.95
Doll	*Belk's Christmas Catalog* (1951)	*Betty Bows;* rubber body, vinyl head, locked-in plastic eyes with long lashes	$2.98
Doll	*Belk's Christmas Catalog* (1951)	*Tiny Tears;* American character; with molded hair; wears cotton rompers; layette includes lace-trimmed dress, bonnet, panties, booties; 13 1/2"	$7.95
Doll	*Belk's Christmas Catalog* (1951)	*Goldberger;* in party dress; sleeping eyes; rooted hair that can be fixed; cries when squeezed	$3.98
Double Holster Set	*Belk's Christmas Catalog* (1951)	*Carnell;* 50-shot cap pistol; split-grain cowhide	$2.98
Electric Football	*Belk's Christmas Catalog* (1951)	*Tudor;* real football right at the living room table; size 25" x 15 1/4"	$6.95
Farm Set	*Belk's Christmas Catalog* (1951)	*Auburn Rubber;* jumbo; unbreakable vinyl; silo, barn, team, and wagon, tractor, farmer and wife, plus whole yard full of farm friends	$2.98
Heavy Duty Crane	*Belk's Christmas Catalog* (1951)	Nothing to wind, just push; hand-wind boom, lift, removable crane, thick tires	$0.88
Service Station	*Belk's Christmas Catalog* (1951)	*Marx Service Station;* modern as tomorrow; overhead sliding door, cars, garagemen	$3.98
Shooting Gallery	*Belk's Christmas Catalog* (1951)	*Marx;* self-feeding automatic pistol fires steel balls; test of skill	$2.98
Skates	*Sears, Roebuck* (1952)	*J. C. Higgins;* rollerskates are fun galore for boys and girls of all ages	$2.45
Steel Refrigerator	*Belk's Christmas Catalog* (1951)	*Wolverine;* revolving shelf, separate freezer, play food, ice cubes; 17" high	$1.98
Tinkertoy	*Belk's Christmas Catalog* (1951)	Now in color; child learns while selecting parts by color; 149 pieces	$1.98
Tool Set	*Belk's Christmas Catalog* (1951)	*Skil-Craft Handy Andy;* steel chest holds saw, pliers, hammer, chisel, coping saw, mallet, screw driver, try-square, ruler, pencil, sandpaper, manual	$2.98

Item	Source	Description	Price
Vacuum Cleaner	*The American Home* (1954)	*Hoover;* A kid-size Hoover that runs and hums	$14.95
Velocipede	*Belk's Christmas Catalog* (1951)	*Murray Ohio;* strong well-balanced tubular steel frame; 10" ball-bearing front wheel, 1 3/4" tires give speedy ride	$8.95
Washing Machine	*Belk's Christmas Catalog* (1951)	Wind spring, turn switch, it works; rubber drain pipe; just like mother's; fun	$0.88
Travel & Transportation			
Airplane Flights	*New York Times* (1952)	New York to Cologne; round trip	$474.50
		New York to Munich; round trip	$516
		New York to Glasgow; one way	$251
		New York to Glasgow; round trip	$382
Airplane Flights	*New York Times* (1952)	New York to California; save 10% on return	
		One way	$88.00
		Return	$72.00

MISCELLANY 1950-1954

Shirts for Men

Arrow Shirts for men, sold by Cluett, Peabody and Co., Inc. listed five prices for their line of shirts: $3.65, $3.95, $4.50, $5.50, and $7.50.

Life, January 23, 1950

Family Food Cost Down; Annual Market Basket Drops $100 From Post-War Peak

The Agriculture Department said today the annual cost of the family food market basket had dropped almost $100 from its postwar peak. The retail cost of the market basket in January was put at $615, a drop of $7 from the December cost. The post-war peak cost was $713 in July 1948.

New York Times, March 24, 1950

The Lost Women of Social Security

Social Security is a bargain insurance. If the pension your taxes have earned should be the smallest possible—$10 a month—it is property worth about $1,500 at current private annuity rates. The average pension is worth $3,900—no trifling gift to the U.S. Treasury on the day you marry.

The instant dream boy slips that gold band on your third finger he becomes your only social security. The personal contributions you have made cease to be worth a nickel. Well, maybe a nickel.

McCall's, April 1950

Aspirin to Stores In War Shut Off; Bayer Head Angered as Price Is Cut to as Low as 4¢ for 100-Tablet Bottle

Hundred-tablet bottles of Bayer aspirin sold for 4¢ yesterday at Abraham & Straus in Brooklyn. Macy's, Gimbels, and other department stores engaged in the price war offered two bottles for 9¢.

The cost to the stores of the aspirin is believed to be in the neighborhood of 43¢. The hundred-tablet bottle carries a fair trade fixed price of 59¢.

A bitter attack on the stores offering its aspirin at rock-bottom prices is made today by the Bayer Company division of Sterling Drug, Inc., the manufacturers. In full-page advertisements in several leading newspapers, the company notifies the shopping public that it has discontinued sales of Bayer aspirin to price-cutting stores.

New York Times, June 15, 1951

New Model Announced by Willys-Overland Motors

The first conventional-type passenger car line to be built by Willys-Overland Motors since 1942 was announced yesterday by the company. Designated the Aero Willys, the new models will go on display tomorrow in dealer showrooms throughout the country.

New York City delivered prices, exclusive of sales tax, were listed as $1,834 for the Aero Lark, de luxe two-door sedan; $2,083 for the Aero Wing, super de luxe, two-door sedan, and $2,168 for the Aero Ace, custom two-door sedan. Overdrive is optional at extra cost of $86.

New York Times, January 17, 1952

Training Station Salesmen—Key to Shock Absorber Sales

By the end of 1952 there will be 112,000,000 direct action shock absorbers on the road. Since 1907 some 100 types of shock absorbers have been developed, of which only four types have attained general use. Some of these were not only expensive, but were difficult to install. For example the knee-action type cost from $50 to $75, and installation was a major shop job.

Turning to the question of dealer profit (Houdaille shock absorber representative C. A.) Humphrey pointed out that a Houdaille standard carton, containing a pair of shock absorbers with all needed rubber bushings and fittings, costs the dealer $6.55. The dealer can sell a pair of shocks costing him $6.55 for $12.30, plus an installation charge of $1 per shock, for a total sale of $14.30, leaving a gross profit of $7.75.

National Petroleum News, September 3, 1952

MISCELLANY 1950-1954

Resident Offices Report on Trade: Demand for Ready-to-Wear Found Steady with Lingerie, and Sports Lines Active

A number of buyers were in the wholesale markets here last week but the rush has tapered off, according to McGreevey, Werring & Howell Company, resident buying office. Activity in the ready-to-wear field has been steady, lingerie continued active and sportswear and separates are expected to be very popular for spring.

Reorders were received on all types of suits, with better-priced lines stressing beaded and jewel trims. Reorders began to appear for unlined rayon suits. Full-length spring coats received some attention. January cotton promotions on junior dress lines were successful and stores were filling in on the $8.75 to $14.75 price range on summer merchandise.

New York Times, February 1, 1953

HISTORICAL SNAPSHOT
1955-1959

1955

- Racial segregation on interstate buses and trains ordered to end
- Federal minimum wage rises from 75 cents to $1 per hour
- President Eisenhower submits a 10-year $101 billion highway construction program to Congress
- AF of L and CIO merge
- Merger creates second largest bank, Chase Manhattan Bank
- Whirlpool Corporation merges with Seeger Refrigerator Company and begins producing refrigerators, airconditioners, and cooking ranges
- *National Review* and *Village Voice* begin publication
- Crest introduced by Procter and Gamble with stannous fluoride
- Special K breakfast food introduced by Kellogg Company
- Suburban shopping centers now number 1,800

1956

- Congress authorizes 42,500 miles of interstate highways costing $33.5 billion
- First Midas Muffler Shop opens in Macon, GA
- Dow Jones Industrials Average peaks at 521.05

- Salem Cigarettes introduced, become leading mentholated brand in 18 months
- Welch's Grape Juice has sales of $40 million
- Merger creates Beech-Nut Life Savers, Inc.
- Jack Daniel's whiskey acquired by Brown-Forman

1957

- Sputnik I launched by Soviet Union is world's first man-made earth satellite
- Painkiller Darvon introduced by Eli Lilly
- University of Wisconsin study shows that 20 percent of Americans live in poverty
- New York's last trolley car retired
- Frisbee introduced by Wham-O Manufacturing
- Per capita margarine consumption exceeds butter for first time
- Record 4.3 million babies born

1958

- Ford Motor Company introduces Edsel
- Cost of 100,000 computerized multiplication computations falls from $1.26 in 1952 to 26 cents
- First U.S. Earth Satellite launched

- Unemployment reaches postwar high
- Upper 1 percent of Americans enjoy 9 percent of nation's total disposable income
- 64 percent of households have incomes above $4,000 per year
- Gasoline costs 30.4 cents per gallon
- BankAmericard credit card introduced
- First-class postal rates climb to 4 cents per ounce
- U.S. television sets reach 41 million
- Sweet'n Low sugarless sweetener introduced
- Pizza Hut chain begins in Kansas City

1959

- Alaska and Hawaii admitted to the Union
- Japanese automakers produce 79,000 cars
- Volkswagen sales in U.S. top 120,000
- Average U.S. automobile wholesales at $1,880
- Supermarkets comprise 11 percent of food stores, but control 69 percent of sales
- 200,000 retailers offer trading stamps
- New York's Four Seasons restaurant opens

SELECTED INCOME 1955-1959

Job	Source	Description	Pay
Actor	Jeffrey Robinson, Bardot, *An Intimate Portrait* (1994)	Salary of Brigitte Bardot for her role in *Et Dieu A Crée la Femme* (And God Created Woman) in 1957	$11,400
Actor	Legrand and Karney, *Chronicle of the Cinema* (1995)	Per-film fee of Marilyn Monroe, not including a percent of profits, in 1955	$100,000
Baseball Player	Bob Rains, St. Louis Cardinals, *The 100th Anniversary History* (1992)	Annual salary of St. Louis Cardinal Stan Musial in 1958	$100,000
Bookkeeping Machine Operator	*Chicago Tribune* (1955)	Typing experience; 5 day wk; insurance	$75/wk starting
Busboys	*Chicago Tribune* (1957)	Meals and uniforms; short hrs; evenings	$1/hr
Cartoonist	Richard Layman, ed., *American Decades: 1950-1959* (1994)	Annual income of Charles Schultz, the creator of *Peanuts,* in 1958	$90,000
Chemical Trainees	*Chicago Tribune* (1957)	Lab technicians will advance as quickly as they can with expanding company; high school chemistry or better starts you; learn and progress	$350–400/mo
Dry Cleaning and Laundry Man	*Chicago Tribune* (1959)	23 to 35, married with sales ability and willingness to work and progress in a very lively organization; salary/commission	$5000–$6000/yr
Engineer	*San Francisco Examiner* (1959)	Jr. Civil, Jr. Elec., Jr. Mech; apply by 11/19/59	$500–600/mo
Golfer	Layman, ed., *American Decades: 1950-1959* (1994)	Average total purse in an official Professional Golf Association event in 1955	$21,722
Housekeeper	*Charlotte Observer* (1956)	Live in; take care three children; white, age 28–45, room and board; maid on duty for housework	$25–35/wk
Insurance Salesman	*San Francisco Examiner* (1959)	National concern has estab. routes avail.; no experience necessary—we train you	$100/wk
Janitor-Assistant	*Chicago Tribune* (1959)	Mechanical electrical experience; state experience in letter	$350/mo
Manager	*Chicago Tribune* (1957)	Bar-restaurant; night work	$7,500/yr
Office Worker	*Chicago Tribune* (1957)	Men age 21–35; h.s. graduate; for responsible positions in truck billing office; salary plus generous shift bonus	$2.15/hr
Private Secretary	*Chicago Tribune* (1959)	Insurance and investment experience; IBM; age 29	$100/wk
Route Salesman	*Chicago Tribune* (1955)	Interesting positions for right men; married preferred	$85/wk and up

Job	Source	Description	Pay
Salesman	*New Orleans Times-Picayune* (1956)	Settled married man, 25–35, with high school education, to represent one of the leading companies in its field; most of our salesmen average over $400 per month; this is a wonderful opportunityfor man who is willing to apply himself and work hard to get ahead	$60/wk and commission
Switchmen	*Chicago Tribune* (1957)		$18.15/day
Telephone Sales	*Chicago Tribune* (1957)	Men to handle incoming telephone orders 6 evenings a wk, including Friday, Saturday, and Sunday; 37 1/2 hr wk; ideal for intelligent neat appearing man in fifties who has good telephone voice	$1.65/hr

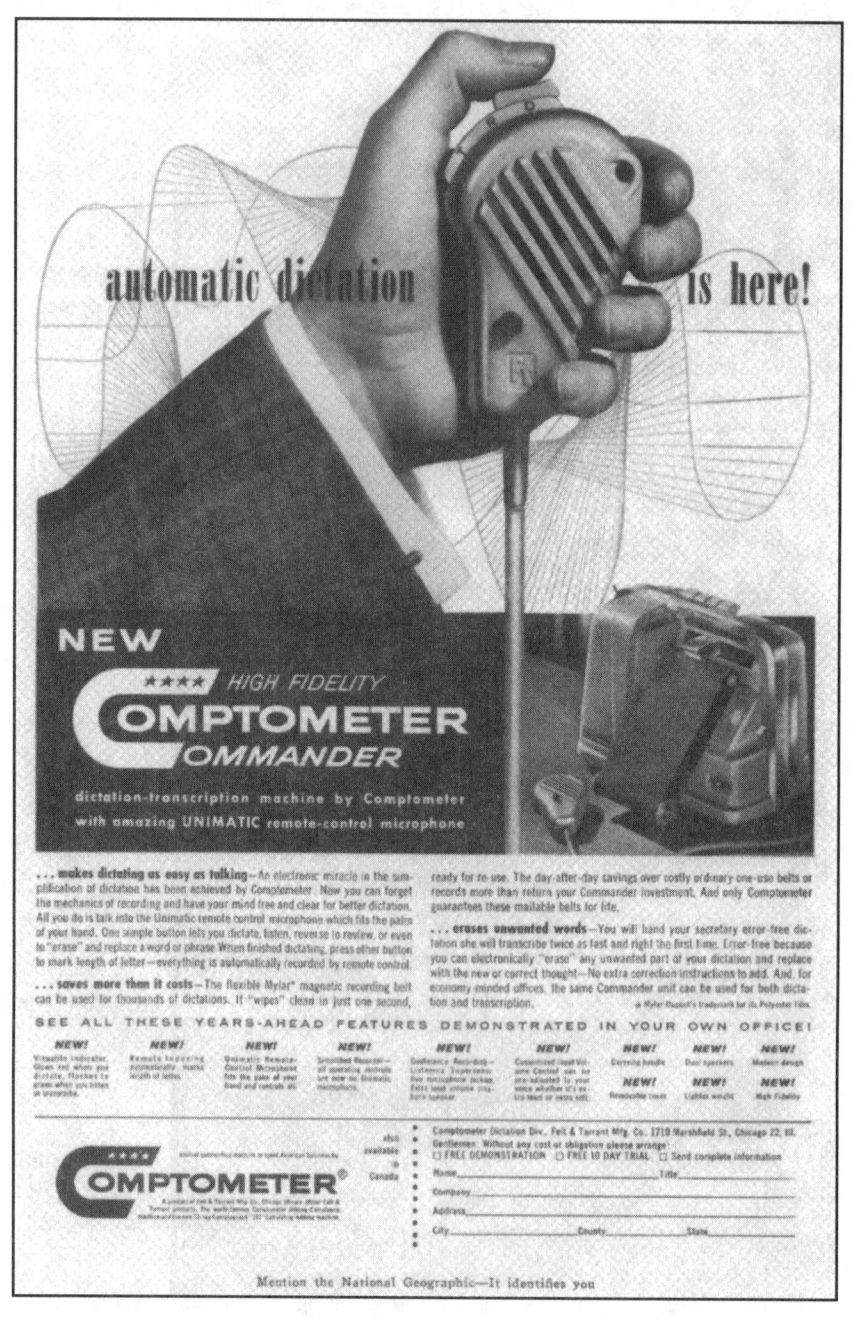

CONSUMER EXPENDITURES 1955-1959

(Per Capita)

Expenditure Type	1955	1956	1957	1958	1959
Clothing	$118.59	$121.86	$120.28	$118.87	$123.71
Food	$414.46	$424.44	$437.89	$447.34	$453.24
Auto Usage	$193.01	$184.88	$196.76	$183.76	$210.88
New Auto Purchase	$83.49	$68.96	$73.57	$55.70	$74.23
Auto Parts	$9.68	$10.11	$11.68	$10.91	$13.49
Gas & Oil	$52.03	$55.88	$59.55	$60.87	$63.54
Housing	$208.14	$218.17	$229.46	$241.18	$253.05
Furniture	$26.62	$27.34	$26.27	$29.29	$26.99
Utilities	$61.72	$64.79	$67.73	$70.63	$72.54
Telephone & Telegraph	$18.76	$19.62	$21.02	$22.39	$23.60
Physicians	$22.99	$24.97	$26.86	$29.29	$30.93
Dentists	$9.08	$10.11	$10.51	$10.91	$11.25
Health Insurance	$8.47	$8.32	$9.34	$8.61	$9.56
Personal Business	$58.69	$63.01	$66.56	$70.06	$74.79
Personal Care	$22.39	$24.37	$26.86	$28.14	$29.24
Tobacco	$30.86	$31.51	$33.28	$34.45	$37.11
Local Transport	$11.49	$11.89	$11.68	$10.91	$11.25
Intercity Transport	$6.66	$6.54	$7.01	$6.32	$6.75
Recreation	$87.73	$91.55	$92.25	$93.03	$98.41
Religion/Welfare Activities	$21.18	$23.18	$23.94	$25.27	$28.12
Private Education & Research	$15.13	$16.64	$18.09	$19.54	$20.24
Per Capita Consumption	$1560.43	$1608.59	$1665.75	$1691.73	$1778.67

INVESTMENTS 1955-1959

Investments	1955	1956	1957	1958	1959
Basic Yield, One-year Corporate Bonds	NR	2.70	3.50	NR	NR
Short-term Interest Rates, 4–6 Months, Prime Commercial Paper	2.18	3.31	3.81	2.46	3.97
Basic Yield, Common Stocks, Total	4.06	4.07	4.33	4.05	3.31
Index of Common Stocks (1941-1943=10)	40.49	42.62	44.38	46.24	57.38

COMMON STOCKS, CLOSING PRICE AND YIELD, FIRST BUSINESS DAY OF YEAR

(Parenthetical number is annual dividend in dollars)

	1955	1956	1957	1958	1959
Allis Chalmers	73 3/4	67	34 3/8	24 5/8	29 5/8
	(4)	(4)	(2)	(2)	(1.25)
AT&T	175 1/4	180	171 1/2	170	225 1/2
	(9)	(9)	(9)	(9)	(9)
American Tobacco	66 1/2	82	73 1/2	77 1/2	96 1/8
	(3.40)	(3.40)	(4)	(4)	(4)
Anaconda	52	70 5/8	71 1/8	41 3/8	60 1/2
	(3)	(4.25)	(5)	(3.75)	(/)
B&O	33 7/8	47 5/8	46 3/8	24 3/4	46 3/8
	(1)	(2)	(2)	(1)	(1.50)
Bethlehem Steel	112 1/4	162 3/4	195 3/8	37 1/8	52 5/8
(4 for 1 split, 1/18/57)	(5.75)	(7.25)	(8.50)	(2.40)	(2.40)
Corn Products	84 1/2	27 7/8	29 1/4	34 1/4	54 1/2
	(3.60)	(1.40)	(1.50)	(1.60)	(2)
General Electric	48 1/4	56 3/4	59 5/8	60 7/8	78 3/4
(3 shares for 1 split, 5/5/54)	(.40)	(.50)	(2)	(2)	(2)
General Motors	103 1/8	45 1/4	43 1/8	34 3/8	50 1/8
(3 shares for 1 split, 9/30/55)	(5)	(1)	(2)	(2)	(2)
International Business Machines	360	404	530	302	529
(2 1/2% stock dividend, 1/27/56)	(4)	(4)	(4)	(2.40)	(2.60)
(5 shares for 4 split, 5/14/56)					
(2 shares for 1 split, 5/12/57)					
(2 1/2% stock dividend, 1/28/59)					
(1 1/2 shares for 1 split, 5/18/59)					
Intl Harvester	37 7/8	36 1/4	38	28 1/8	41 3/8
	(2)	(3)	(2)	(2)	(2)
National Biscuit	43 3/8	38 3/4	35	42 1/8	49 7/8
	(2)	(2)	(2)	(2)	(2)
US Steel	75	56 5/8	71	52 1/2	96 1/4
(2 shares for 1 split, 6/2/55)	(3)	(1.43)	(2.60)	(3)	(3)
Western Union	75	21 1/4	19 1/2	15 1/4	31 7/8
(4 shares for 1 split, 5/23/55)	(3)	(.25)	(1)	(.30)	(1.20)

STANDARD JOBS 1955-1959

Job Type	1955	1956	1957	1958	1959
Average of All Industries, excl. farm labor	$4224/yr	$4445/yr	$4657/yr	$4818/yr	$5069/yr
Average of All Industries, inc. farm labor	$4128/yr	$4342/yr	$4546/yr	$4707/yr	$4965/yr
Bituminous Coal Mining	$4470/yr	$4858/yr	$5086/yr	$4809/yr	$5274/yr
Building Trades	$4607/yr	$4914/yr	$5120/yr	$5305/yr	$5498/yr
Domestics	$1874/yr	$1962/yr	$2050/yr	$2131/yr	$2190/yr
Farm Labor	$1498/yr	$1578/yr	$1657/yr	$1690/yr	$1742/yr
Federal Civilian	$4801/yr	$5025/yr	$5203/yr	$5781/yr	$5852/yr
Federal Employees, Executive Depts.	$3774/yr	$3983/yr	$4073/yr	$4462/yr	$4589/yr
Federal Military	$3237/yr	$3402/yr	$3439/yr	$3697/yr	$3824/yr
Finance, Insurance, & Real Estate	$4005/yr	$4168/yr	$4314/yr	$4523/yr	$4791/yr
Gas & Electricity Workers	$4757/yr	$5000/yr	$5247/yr	$5543/yr	$5815/yr
Manufacturing, Durable Goods	$4737/yr	$4993/yr	$5207/yr	$5478/yr	$5763/yr
Manufacturing, Nondurable Goods	$4134/yr	$4387/yr	$4540/yr	$4725/yr	$4950/yr
Medical/Health Services Workers	$2488/yr	$2532/yr	$2612/yr	$2751/yr	$2881/yr
Miscellaneous Manufacturing	$3789/yr	$4015/yr	$4195/yr	$4408/yr	$4528/yr
Motion Picture Services	$4330/yr	$4587/yr	$4745/yr	$4940/yr	$5315/yr
Nonprofit Org. Workers	$3291/yr	$3395/yr	$3533/yr	$3672/yr	$3815/yr
Passenger Transportation Workers, Local and Highway	$4142/yr	$4306/yr	$4449/yr	$4571/yr	$4789/yr
Personal Services	$2766/yr	$2872/yr	$2999/yr	$3140/yr	$3248/yr
Public School Teachers	$3608/yr	$3827/yr	$4085/yr	$4343/yr	$4522/yr
Radio Broadcasting & Television Workers	$6250/yr	$6613/yr	$6756/yr	$7051/yr	$7210/yr
Railroads	$4701/yr	$5085/yr	$5416/yr	$5836/yr	$6099/yr
State and Local Govt. Workers	$3447/yr	$3564/yr	$3747/yr	$3958/yr	$4152/yr
Telephone & Telegraph Workers	$4153/yr	$4298/yr	$4471/yr	$4707/yr	$5091/yr
Wholesale and Retail Trade Workers	$4616/yr	$4883/yr	$5119/yr	$5294/yr	$5558/yr

FOOD BASKET 1955-1959

Commodity	Year	New York	Atlanta	Chicago	Denver	Los Angeles
Apples, Fresh, per pound	1955	14¢	15.90¢	16.40¢	NR	15.80¢
	1956	15.70¢	16.20¢	NR	NR	15.60
	1957	16¢	17.80¢	18.70¢	NR	17.80¢
	1958	15.80¢	15.50¢	16.40¢	NR	15.20¢
	1959	14.30¢	15.50¢	15.80¢	NR	16.50¢
Beans, Dried, per pound	1955	18.70¢	16.20¢	18.40¢	NR	19.30¢
	1956	16.90¢	15.20¢	17.40¢	NR	16.30¢
	1957	16.80¢	15.10¢	17.60¢	NR	15.70¢
	1958	18¢	18¢	18.50¢	NR	17.70¢
	1959	17.40¢	16.90¢	17.50¢	NR	17.40¢
Beef, Rib Roasts, per pound	1955	70.20¢	75.60¢	69.10¢	NR	80¢
	1956	68.60¢	76.80¢	68¢	NR	80.30¢
	1957	71.20¢	80.90¢	70.30¢	NR	86.30¢
	1958	78.20¢	87.10¢	78.10¢	NR	94.10¢
	1959	77.40¢	87.80¢	80.10¢	NR	95.90¢
Beef, Steaks (Round), per pound	1955	96.50¢	92.10¢	79.70¢	NR	87.20¢
	1956	94.70¢	89¢	76.50¢	NR	86.90¢
	1957	$1.004	92.4¢	79.50¢	NR	93.40¢
	1958	$1.118	$1.018	89.10¢	NR	98.90¢
	1959	$1.165	$1.085	91.20¢	NR	$1.045
Bread, White, per pound	1955	19.1¢	17.5¢	16.70¢	NR	19.30¢
	1956	18.8¢	17.4¢	17¢	NR	19.70¢
	1957	19.6¢	18.5¢	17.10¢	NR	20.80¢
	1958	20.5¢	19.3¢	17.10¢	NR	22.90¢
	1959	21.5¢	19.3¢	18.40¢	NR	22.90¢
Butter, per pound	1955	72.2¢	75¢	70.30¢	NR	70.30¢
	1956	72.5¢	76.3¢	72¢	NR	71.60¢
	1957	74.1¢	78.8¢	73.70¢	NR	73.70¢
	1958	74.2¢	79.4¢	73.20¢	NR	76¢
	1959	75.3¢	80.7¢	74.50¢	NR	78.40¢
Cheese, per pound	1955	59.4¢	NR	58¢	NR	57.60¢
	1956	58.4¢	NR	58¢	NR	56.90¢
	1957	59¢	NR	58.60¢	NR	57¢
	1958	59.7¢	NR	59.30¢	NR	58¢
	1959	59.8¢	65.4¢	59.90¢	NR	57.80¢
Chickens, per pound	1955	45.4¢	50.1¢	55.40¢	NR	65.80¢
	1956	41.9¢	41.4¢	40.30¢	NR	40.10¢
	1957	NR	42.3¢	43.10¢	NR	57.40¢
	1958	NR	43¢	42.70¢	NR	54.80¢
	1959	41.5¢	39.8¢	38.70¢	NR	48.30¢
Coffee, per pound	1955	94.5¢	90.7¢	93¢	NR	92.50¢
	1956	$1.061	$1.039	$1.043	NR	99.60¢
	1957	$1.038	$1.023	$1.008	NR	99.40¢
	1958	92.3¢	93.2¢	89.30¢	NR	88.70¢
	1959	77.6¢	78.7¢	76.40¢	NR	79.50¢
Cornmeal, per pound	1955	12.5¢	7.2¢	12.40¢	NR	12.30¢
	1956	11.9¢	7.1¢	12.40¢	NR	12.80¢
	1957	12.2¢	7.3¢	12.60¢	NR	12.90¢
	1958	12.3¢	7.6¢	12.90¢	NR	13.40¢
	1959	12.20¢	7.20¢	12.90¢	NR	13.80¢

Commodity	Year	New York	Atlanta	Chicago	Denver	Los Angeles
Eggs, per dozen	1955	69.60¢	61¢	59.60¢	NR	57.50¢
	1956	67.60¢	60.70¢	59.90¢	NR	56.50¢
	1957	64.40¢	58.30¢	55.20¢	NR	55¢
	1958	67.60¢	61.80¢	58¢	NR	57.60¢
	1959	60.30¢	52.60¢	49.70¢	NR	NR
Flour, Wheat, per pound	1955	10.60¢	10.04¢	10.28¢	NR	11.14¢
	1956	10.28¢	10.94¢	10.14¢	NR	11.14¢
	1957	10.44¢	11.22¢	10.30¢	NR	12.10¢
	1958	10.70¢	11.48¢	10.32¢	NR	12.66¢
	1959	10.66¢	11.14¢	10.16¢	NR	12.68¢
Lard, per pound	1955	21.90¢	20.10¢	19.80¢	NR	19.80¢
	1956	20.40¢	19.30¢	19¢	NR	21.50¢
	1957	21.90¢	21.80¢	22¢	NR	25¢
	1958	22¢	21.60¢	21.70¢	NR	25¢
	1959	19.40¢	18.40¢	19.30¢	NR	23¢
Milk, Fresh, per quart	1955	26.40¢	25.50¢	26.20¢	NR	21.50¢
	1956	26.50¢	26.50¢	27.80¢	NR	21.70¢
	1957	28.50¢	26.70¢	27.90¢	NR	22.80¢
	1958	30.20¢	27.10¢	25.80¢	NR	23.90¢
	1959	31¢	26.40¢	26.60¢	NR	24.50¢
Mutton and Lamb, Leg, per pound	1955	63.90¢	74.40¢	65.20¢	NR	67.90¢
	1956	64.40¢	76¢	66.60¢	NR	69.50¢
	1957	66.50¢	75.10¢	68.10¢	NR	71.60¢
	1958	73.40¢	82.60¢	73.20¢	NR	77.20¢
	1959	71.10¢	80.70¢	70.90¢	NR	75.20¢
Pork, Bacon, Sliced, per pound	1955	71.10¢	65.90¢	64.40¢	NR	70¢
	1956	61¢	58.70¢	55.50¢	NR	62.40¢
	1957	75.90¢	74¢	71¢	NR	77.90¢
	1958	84.10¢	78.40¢	76.90¢	NR	83.20¢
	1959	72.70¢	66¢	63.90¢	NR	70.10¢
Pork, Chops, per pound	1955	80.80¢	73.10¢	80.90¢	NR	89.90¢
	1956	78.10¢	70.10¢	79.60¢	NR	89.90¢
	1957	87.80¢	76.90¢	85.20¢	NR	98.60¢
	1958	93.80¢	81.50¢	89.80¢	NR	$1.02
	1959	87.80¢	78.50¢	82.50¢	NR	98.40¢
Pork, Ham, Whole, per pound	1955	62.10¢	59.80¢	58.40¢	NR	61.30¢
	1956	60.10¢	58.10¢	58.90¢	NR	60.70¢
	1957	62.80¢	60.80¢	61.40¢	NR	65.60¢
	1958	84.10¢	65.60¢	65.90¢	NR	66.70¢
	1959	64.20¢	60.20¢	60.20¢	NR	61.70¢
Potatoes, Irish, per 10 pounds	1955	51¢	52.10¢	65.80¢	NR	70¢
	1956	59.70¢	65.70¢	78¢	NR	85¢
	1957	50.30¢	55.80¢	63.90¢	NR	70.70¢
	1958	53.80¢	60.60¢	63.90¢	NR	77.80¢
	1959	56.70¢	60.40¢	71.70¢	NR	89.90¢
Prunes, Dried, per pound	1955	32.10¢	34.70¢	34.10¢	NR	31.50¢
	1956	33.50¢	36¢	35.20¢	NR	33.60¢
	1957	32.10¢	33.40¢	33.70¢	NR	30.60¢
	1958	32.50¢	34.70¢	33.40¢	NR	31.80¢
	1959	38¢	40.50¢	39.20¢	NR	38¢
Rice, per pound	1955	19.70¢	19¢	16¢	NR	21.30¢
	1956	19¢	17.60¢	15¢	NR	20.80¢
	1957	19¢	17.90¢	15.50¢	NR	20.80¢
	1958	19.40¢	19.30¢	16.50¢	NR	21.70¢
	1959	19.40¢	19.50¢	NR	NR	22¢

Commodity	Year	New York	Atlanta	Chicago	Denver	Los Angeles
Sugar, per pound	1955	9.94¢	9.80¢	10.50¢	NR	10.32¢
	1956	10.06¢	10.10¢	10.82¢	NR	10.48¢
	1957	10.62¢	10.70¢	11.04¢	NR	10.96¢
	1958	10.92¢	11.16¢	11.02¢	NR	11.30¢
	1959	11.02¢	11.36¢	11.30¢	NR	11.64¢
Tea, Bags, per package of 48 per pound	1955	$1.54	$1.544	$1.592	NR	$1.66
	1956	66.30¢	71.40¢	69¢	NR	74.40¢
	1957	66.30¢	69.30¢	70.80¢	NR	75.30¢
	1958	68.10¢	73.80¢	71.40¢	NR	75.30¢
	1959	69.30¢	73.20¢	71.40¢	NR	75.60¢
Veal, per pound	1955	$1.24	95.60¢	$1.03	NR	$1.07
	1956	$1.26	98.60¢	$1.02	NR	$1.09
	1957	$1.33	$1.04	$1.08	NR	$1.17
	1958	$1.50	$1.20	$1.17	NR	$1.30
	1959	$1.61	$1.31	$1.23	NR	$1.39

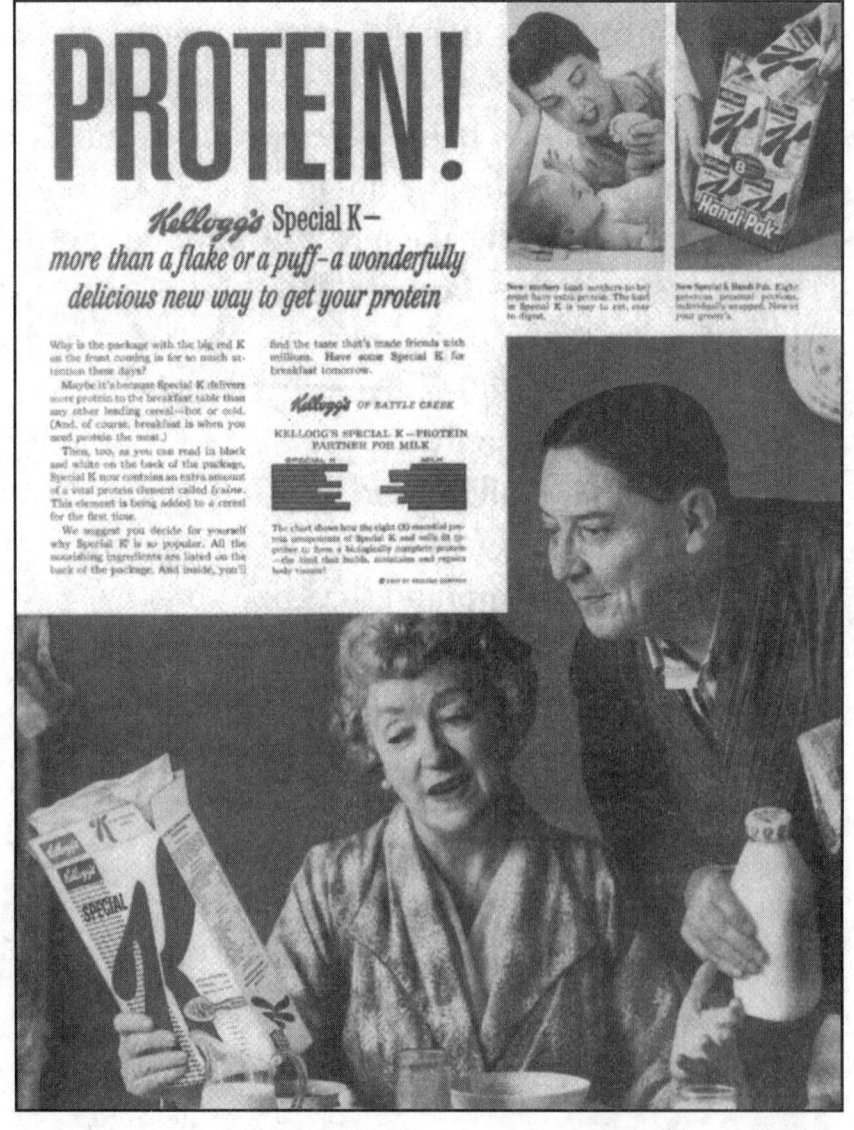

SELECTED PRICES 1955-1959

Item	Source	Description	Price
Alcohol			
Bourbon	*Ben Arnold Co. Price List* (1955)	*Country Fair;* bottled in bond; straight bourbon	$4.88/fifth
Gin	*Ben Arnold Co. Price List* (1955)	*Gordon's*	$4.47/fifth
Scotch	*Ben Arnold Co. Price List* (1955)	*Haig & Haig Pinch;* 100% blended scotch	$7.68/fifth
Scotch	*Ben Arnold Co. Price List* (1955)	*Chivas Regal;* 12 years old	$8.06/fifth
Vermouth	*Ben Arnold Co. Price List* (1955)	*Martini & Rossi;* 16-oz bottle	$1.54
Vodka	*Ben Arnold Co. Price List* (1955)	*Smirnoff*	$5.23/fifth
Whiskey	*Ben Arnold Co. Price List* (1955)	*Seagram's*	$4.89/fifth
Whiskey	*Ben Arnold Co. Price List* (1955)	*Seagram's V.O.*	$6.43/fifth
Whiskey	*Chicago Tribune* (1955)	*Sunny Brook;* Kentucky blend; cheerful as its name	$4.30/fifth
Apparel, Children's			
Camp Shorts	*Sears, Roebuck* (1958)	May be worn with or without attachable suspenders	$1.94
Dress Shirt	*Sears, Roebuck* (1958)	Cotton; with cufflinks, bow tie; grown-up styling for little gentlemen	$1.74
Jeans	*Sears, Roebuck* (1958)	Economy price; 10-oz vat dyed; blue denim	$1.64
Necktie	*Sears, Roebuck* (1958)	Redi-tied; junior size with slip knot and gripper fastener	$0.94
Raincoat	*Sears, Roebuck* (1958)	*Ballerina;* collar converts to cozy hood; elastic-hug waist, roomy raglan sleeves	$5.74
Shirt	*Good Housekeeping* (1955)	*Tam O'Shanter Beau Brummel;* with matching bow tie, poplin boxer longies, and shirt; 3-piece set	$4.98
Shoes	*Life* (1959)	*Buster Brown;* the shoes you were so proud of when you were little are the same shoes that thrill youngsters most today	$5.99–$7.99
Shoes	*Life* (1959)	*Brown's Pedwin;* young ideas in shoes	$9.95
Sweatshirt	*Boy's Life* (1955)	Official Boy Scout; top-quality cotton yarn, fleece-lined for extra warmth	$1.95
Undershirt	*Sears, Roebuck* (1958)	Lighter weight; sleeveless vest; rib knit of white combed cotton; package of three	$1.11/pkg

Item	Source	Description	Price
Uniform	*Boy's Life* (1955)	Boy Scout; summer; includes field cap, v-neck shirt, shorts, web belt, stockings, handkerchief, and slide	$8.97

Apparel, Men's

Item	Source	Description	Price
Coat	*Life* (1959)	*The Alligator Company;* America's most wanted gabardine	$42.75
Golf Jacket	*Life* (1959)	*Dow Finsterwald;* swing in comfort and style; lightweight fabric of 65% dacron, 35% cotton	$11.95
Hosiery	*Life* (1959)	*Kayser-Roth Supp-Hose;* the fashionably sheer way to ease tired legs	$4.95
Shirt	*Sears, Roebuck* (1958)	*Hercules Snap-Front Model;* SNAP—it's open; SNAP—it's closed	$2.34
Shirt	*Life* (1959)	*Jayson;* ready to wear	$5.00
Shirt	*Life* (1959)	*Arrow;* machine-washable, Sanforized fabric	$5.00
Shoes	*Good Housekeeping* (1955)	*Arch Walker Corrective Step;* the arch oxford that cradles your foot	$5.99–$8.99
Shoes	*Chicago Tribune* (1957)	*Johnston Murphy;* the newest concept in smart styling; low, trim lines with slipperflex construction	$32.95
Shoes	*Life* (1959)	*Endicott Johnson Johnsonian Guide Step;* fit the feet in action	$10.95–$14.95
Shoes	*Life* (1959)	*Florsheim Perfecto;* a sensationally new shade	$19.95
Shoes	*Life* (1959)	*Rablee;* executive-styled wingtip style; the shoe with the open-collar feeling	$17.95
Slacks	*Life* (1959)	*Lancer;* safeguarded with scotchgard, repels all stains	$7.88–$12.88
Socks	*Chicago Tribune* (1957)	*Baskin Touch n'Tingle;* unbelievably soft; dacron and cotton	$1.00
Socks	*Sears, Roebuck* (1958)	Double the wear of ordinary cotton socks; in lots of six pairs	$0.37/pr
Socks	*Life* (1959)	*Esquire;* governor style	$1.00
Stockings	*Life* (1959)	*Burlington Hosiery;* support; the fashionable answer to leg fatigue	$4.95
Suit	*Life* (1959)	*Botany 500;* suits and topcoats made for each other	$59.50
Suit	*Life* (1959)	*Brookfield;* 2 Pants, all wool	$55.00
Suit	*Life* (1959)	*Brookfield;* high-priced luxury; these suits look every bit of $65	$39.95
Sweater	*Life* (1959)	*Robert Bruce Magna Cross;* boatneck pullover for men	$8.98
Topcoat	*Life* (1959)	*Botany 500;* suits and topcoats made for each other	$59.50
T-shirt	*Life* (1959)	*Munsingwear;* America's finest T-shirt; crew neck	$1.50

Apparel, Women's

Item	Source	Description	Price
Brassiere	*Good Housekeeping* (1955)	*Warner's Merry Widow;* at the nicest stores here and in Canada	$5.95
Brassiere	*Good Housekeeping* (1955)	*Playtex;* made of elastic and nylon	$3.95

Item	Source	Description	Price
Brassiere	*Life* (1959)	*Maiden Form Star Flower;* white cotton broadcloth, A, B, and C cups	$2.50
Brassiere	*Life* (1959)	*Perma-Lift;* in miracle washeen; the lift that never lets you down	$3.50
Coat	*Life* (1959)	Gold brocade wrap-around coat	$125
Girdle	*Good Housekeeping* (1955)	*Warner's LeGant;* with lend elastic	$13.50
Girdle	*Good Housekeeping* (1955)	*Playtex;* made of wonderful new split-resistant fabricon	$4.95
Gloves	*Life* (1959)	*Pioneer Liquidproof Work Gloves;* nimble fingers; tissue-thin bluettes, knit-cotton lined	$1.49
Hosiery	*Sears, Roebuck* (1958)	*Roy;* purple stretchy garter tops, in white for nurses	$0.97
Nylons	*Good Housekeeping* (1955)	*Kotex Miracle Brand;* stretch; you'll find these full-fashioned nylons a sheer delight	$1.00
Shirt	*Sears, Roebuck* (1958)	Needs little or no ironing	$2.37
Shoes	*Sears, Roebuck* (1958)	*Kerrybroke;* soft leather drape eased through bold vamp buckle	$3.77
Shoes	*Life* (1959)	*Brown AirStep Americana Tulane;* if activity is your kind of living	$13.95
Shoes	*Life* (1959)	*Brown Paddock;* the shoe with the beautiful fit	$12.95
Stockings	*Good Housekeeping* (1955)	*Cannon;* wear longer, too, just like Cannon towels and sheets	$0.99–$1.65
Suit	*Chicago Tribune* (1957)	*Stevens;* our gay crisp suit gives you a smart casual air	$17.95

Business Equipment & Supplies

Item	Source	Description	Price
Boardmaster	*New York Times* (1956)	Graphic pictures of operations at a glance; type or write on cards; snaps in grooves	$49.50 with cards
Lighting	*New York Times* (1956)	Fluorescent and slimline fixtures	$7.60
Photostats	*New York Times* (1956)	Photostats	$0.20 ea.
Shelving	*New York Times* (1956)	Steel Shelving; 24 x 42 x 75	$12.25
Typewriter	*Sears, Roebuck* (1958)	*Smith-Corona;* here's the first electric typewriter in portable size	$209.35
Typewriter	*Life* (1959)	*Smith Corona;* makes all manual portables old-fashioned	$164.50

Collectibles

Item	Source	Description	Price
Bowfront Bureau	*Antiques* (1956)	*Israel Sack;* circa 1780–1800, hepplewhite mahogany, small bowfront bureau with retrained inlay, original signature of maker, H. K. Dorsey	$675
Clock	*Antiques* (1956)	Antique grandfather clock; 6'9" mahogany clock with moon phases	$345
Desk	*Antiques* (1956)	Slant top; circa 1775 Chippendale walnut desk, bold ogee bracket feet	$500
Punch Bowl	*Antiques* (1956)	*Plummer Famille Rose;* circa 1790 presented by King George III, diameter 14 1/4"	$950

Item	Source	Description	Price
Rug	*Antiques* (1956)	*Charles W. Jacobsen Oriental;* 14' x 11.4' tabriz from Iran	$690
Settee	*Antiques* (1956)	*Windsor;* circa 1785; 55 1/2" long; very bold cross stretchers	$375
Soup Tureen	*Antiques* (1956)	*Faience;* 18th century tureen in the form of a setting hen on a shaped plateau; size 13" x 15 1/2"	$350
Stand	*Antiques* (1956)	Converts to desk; mahogany and poplar	$265

Education

Item	Source	Description	Price
Dance Lessons	*New York Times* (1956)	*Fred Astair Dance Club*	$25.00

Entertainment

Item	Source	Description	Price
Ballet	*New York Times* (1956)	*The Royal Danish Ballet*	$7.50
Musical	*New York Times* (1956)	*Shangri-La*	$7.50
Musical	*New York Times* (1956)	*Show Boat*	$1.10
Play	*New York Times* (1956)	*Uncle Vanya*	$3.85

Entertainment, Home

Item	Source	Description	Price
Camera	*Life* (1959)	*Kodak Pony II;* 33 mm color; picture as brilliant as autumn	$29.50
Camera	*Life* (1959)	*Graflex Century 35;* combination viewfinder-range finder permits framing	$49.50
Camera	*Life* (1959)	*Argus Match-Matic C-3;* the color-slide camera you can master in less than a minute	$64.95
Loudspeakers	*Consumer Reports* (1958)	*Acoustic Research AR-2;* high-fidelity; 13 1/2" x 24" x 11"; unfinished birch cabinet	$89/pr
Loudspeakers	*Consumer Reports* (1958)	*KLH;* high fidelity	$209
Movie Projector	*Life* (1959)	*Argus M-500;* shows full 400-ft (half-hour-long) reels	$89.95
Organ	*Life* (1959)	*Magnus 500 Electric Cord Organ;* no lessons, beautiful music the same day	$129.95
Pocket Radio	*Consumer Reports* (1957)	*Zenith Royall 500;* seven-transistor	$75.00
Pocket Radio	*Consumer Reports* (1957)	*Emerson 888;* transistor; price varies by color	$44–$48
Record	*Life* (1959)	*RCA Victor;* Puccini, *La Boheme;* two-record set	$9.98
Refrigerator	*Life* (1959)	*Western Auto Wizard;* 80-lb freezer, roll-out shelf	$259
Stereo	*Life* (1959)	*Webcor;* panoramic sound; three stereo speakers; powerful 8-watt amplifier	$37.95–$399.95
Stereo	*Life* (1959)	*Columbia Stereo I;* the new sound of pleasure	$129.95
Television	*Life* (1959)	*Zenith Lafayette Cabinet Model;* includes space command remote control—built right in	$550

Item	Source	Description	Price
Food Products			
Baby Food	*Chicago Tribune* (1955)	*Gerber's;* strained meat for babies; four 3 1/2 oz glasses	$0.87
Candy	*Boy's Life* (1955)	*Tootsie Roll;* the ideal energy candy to take with you on those long hikes	$0.05
Chocolate Covered Cherries	*Chicago Tribune* (1955)	*Brach's;* 13-oz box	$0.55
Chop Suey Sauce	*Chicago Tribune* (1955)	*Fuji;* two 3-oz bottles	$0.19
Creamer	*Good Housekeeping* (1955)	*Instant Pream;* 100% dairy product	$0.25
Drink Mix	*Boy's Life* (1955)	*Miracle Aid;* makes cold drinks instantly; 6 tempting fruit flavors; 3/4 oz pkg, makes 1/2 gallon	$0.05
Fruit Cocktail	*Chicago Tribune* (1955)	*None-such;* in heavy syrup; four 16-oz tins	$0.93
Macaroni	*Chicago Tribune* (1955)	*Red Cross;* elbow cut; three 7-oz packages	$0.27
Milk	*Cost of Living in Alaska* (1958)		$0.60/quart
Orange Juice	*Cost of Living in Alaska* (1958)		$0.40/glass
Pork and Beans	*Chicago Tribune* (1955)	*Van Camps;* in tomato sauce; two 15-oz tins	$0.25
Soft Drink	*Boy's Life* (1955)	*Lucky Pop Fizz Tablets;* box of 150 drinks; drop one carbonated flavor pill in an 8-oz glass, in seconds a really refreshing soft drink	$1.00
Furniture			
Bedroom Set	*New York Times* (1956)	Hand rubbed walnut; brass inlays; 72"; 9-drawer triple dresser; double chest; night tables; headboard	$645
Bed Frame	*Life* (1959)	*Harvard Frames;* with plastic protecto-caps; can't tear bedding	$12.95
Chair	*New York Times* (1956)	*The Oslochair;* 2 reversible innerspring cushions	$39.95
Chandelier	*Antiques* Magazine (1956)	*Paul Crystal Bohemian;* made of the finest crystal in the world; height 23", width 33"; has 12 arms	$425
Lamp	*Good Housekeeping* (1955)	*Johnny One-Light;* with Velon shade; firestone Velon literally lightens your *life*	$11.95
Sofa	*New York Times* (1956)	*Foamland;* caned arm sofa; zippered covers	$99.50
Sofabed	*New York Times* (1956)	Foam rubber sofabed	$69.95
Step Stool	*Good Housekeeping* (1955)	*Cosco Model 4–M;* chromium or black legs with red, yellow, green, charcoal, pink, or chartreuse upholstery	$12.95
Table	*New York Times* (1956)	Rectangular	$39.00
Table	*New York Times* (1956)	Free form	$59.00
Table	*New York Times* (1956)	Butterfly	$59.00

Item	Source	Description	Price
Garden Equipment & Supplies			
Lawn Sprinkler	*Good Housekeeping* (1955)	*Tuff-Lite;* underlawn sprinkling system; waters 1000 sq. ft	$16.95
Lawn Sprinkler	*Consumer Reports* (1958)	*Allenco Parkside;* rotating model	$6.50
Lawn Sprinkler	*Consumer Reports* (1958)	*Sunbeam Rain King Automatic K-2A*	$9.95
Hotel Rates			
Hotel Room	*Asheville Citizen Times* (Asheville, NC) (1957)	*Mount-Vue Motel*	$4/night
Hotel Room	*Complete Guide to New England* (1958)	*Barnum Hotel;* modern city hotel; 200 rooms, coffee shop, dining room	$4.75/night
Hotel Room	*Complete Guide to New England* (1958)	*Hotel Statler;* Hartford, Connecticut; ultra-modern; all air conditioned with radio and TV Single Double	$7/night $12/night
Hotel Room	*Complete Guide to New England* (1958)	*General Putnam Inn;* Norwalk, Connecticut; small country inn, developed for colonial house; European plan	$4/night
Hotel Room	*Complete Guide to New England* (1958)	*Tremont Motor Court;* New Haven, Connecticut; big, new, modern; 51 air-conditioned units, TV, telephone	$9.50/night
Hotel Room	*Complete Guide to New England* (1958)	*Harbor View Hotel;* Bar Harbour, Maine; near waterfront and next to park; dining room and cocktail lounge; single, in season	$6/night
Hotel Room	*Complete Guide to New England* (1958)	*Bangor House;* Bangor, Maine: commercial-type city hotel, 123 rooms, edge of business district; single	$3.75/night
Hotel Room	*Complete Guide to New England* (1958)	*Green Shutters Inn and Cottages;* Boothbay Harbor, Maine; cottage resort, dining room features New England dishes and seafood; modified American plan; double	$12/night
Hotel Room	*Complete Guide to New England* (1958)	*Hotel Eagle;* Brunswick, Maine; celebrated resort estate, 2 notable dining rooms, Maine specialties, beach and golf course adjacent; per person summer rates	$12/night
Hotel Room	*Complete Guide to New England* (1958)	*Ritz-Carlton Hotel;* Boston, Massachusetts; fashionable, luxurious, and quiet city hotel; main dining room; single	$9/night
Hotel Room	*Complete Guide to New England* (1958)	*Hotel Vendome;* Boston, Massachusetts; transient and residential; 225 rooms; Moulin Rouge supper club and French room restaurant	$5/night
Hotel Room	*Complete Guide to New England* (1958)	*Buzzards Bay Lodge;* Buzzards Bay, Massachusetts; shore setting; 31 modern units, all double or suites, some with TV, many with kitchenette; private beach and dock	$8/night
Hotel Room	*Complete Guide to New England* (1958)	*Commander Hotel;* Cambridge, Massachusetts; across common from Harvard University; all rooms with TV, color TV in apartments; dining room features French cooking Single Double	$6/night $10/night

Item	Source	Description	Price
Household Products			
Blanket	*Good Housekeeping* (1955)	*Chatham Double;* warmer than blankets that cost almost twice as much; the addition of fabulous Orlon to Purrey's patented weave	$10.95
Can Opener	*Good Housekeeping* (1955)	*Rival Can-O-Mat;* most beautiful can opener made; with magnet	$6.98
Cleaner	*Good Housekeeping* (1955)	*Glamorene Wool Rug Cleaner;* made to dry-clean rugs the easy, quick, modern way; 1/2 gallon; cleans two 9' x 12' rugs	$2.29
Coffee Maker	*Consumer Reports* (1958)	Percolator	$16.88
Coffee Maker	*Consumer Reports* (1958)	*Cory;* vacuum type	$39.95
Cooker	*Good Housekeeping* (1955)	*Presto 700;* cooks three times faster	$12.95
Deodorizer	*Chicago Tribune* (1955)	*Colgate;* aerosol	$0.69
Dishes	*Good Housekeeping* (1955)	*International Molded Plastics Brookpark;* plastic non-chipping, non-breaking, modern design; 26-piece starter set, service for four	$14.95
Fry Skillet	*Good Housekeeping* (1955)	*Dominion;* electric-automatic; masters every cooking job better and easier	$15.95
Grill	*Good Housekeeping* (1955)	*Capri Roto-Broil 400;* big 8-way rotisserie barbeque	$79.95
Hearth	*Life* (1959)	*Kos-mark;* ready-made; suitable for burning anything from logs to love letters	$250
Heater	*Life* (1959)	*Arvin Model 5912;* portable; electric; economized in every way	$12.95
Iron	*Life* (1959)	*Western Auto Wizard;* steam dry; fully automatic, fingertip fabric selector	$9.88
Ironing Board Cover	*Life* (1959)	*Magla;* silicone; add zip to your ironing	$1.49
Ironing Table	*Good Housekeeping* (1955)	*Cream City Met-L-Top;* the world's most comfortable ironing table	$13.95
Kitchen Machine	*Good Housekeeping* (1955)	*Rival Kitcheneer;* all-in-one grinder, chopper, slicer, shredder, grater, with interchangeable base	$12.98
Kitchen Towels	*Good Housekeeping* (1955)	*Startex;* so many, many beautiful styles to choose from that you're sure to find just the right patterns for your home	$0.29–$0.49
Mattress	*Life* (1959)	*Serta Perfect Sleeper;* king size at no extra cost	$79.50
Mattress	*Life* (1959)	*Simmons Beautyrest;* the best costs the least	$79.50
Mop	*Good Housekeeping* (1955)	Twice the sponge surface; 5-year written guarantee	$4.98
Paint	*Good Housekeeping* (1955)	*Sherwin-Williams Kem-tone;* paint today, sleep tight tonight; interior paint	$5.59/gallon
Paneling	*Life* (1959)	*Sammara Weldwood;* the only thing expensive is its looks; 12' x 8' wall, 70 panels	$47.00
Photoflash Lamps	*Boy's Life* (1955)	*General Electric M2;* no fuss, no fretting, and they are sure-fire, even on weakened batteries	$0.10
Pillows	*Sears, Roebuck* (1958)	Goose down; extra large, extra soft, and extra comfortable	$14.97

Item	Source	Description	Price
Vacuum Cleaner	*Good Housekeeping* (1955)	*Eureka Super Roto-Matic;* with zip-clip swivel-top and new 4-wheel roto-dolly	$69.95
Vacuum Cleaner	*Good Housekeeping* (1955)	*Electrolux;* world's lightest-weight heavy duty cleaner	$69.75

Insurance Rates

Item	Source	Description	Price
Fire Insurance	*St. Paul Fire and Marine Insurance Co.* (1957)	$14,000 coverage on single-family dwelling	$57.40/year

Jewelry

Item	Source	Description	Price
Chain	*Life* (1959)	Swank sterling silver; initial on golden tones	$2.50
Watch	*Boy's Life* (1955)	*Timex Boy Scout;* American-made wrist watches with top-quality features	$9.95
Watch	*Life* (1959)	*Bulova Royal Clipper;* slim waterproof watches; 17 jewels, self winding	$59.50

Meals

Item	Source	Description	Price
Hamburger	*Associated Press* (1957)	*Burger King Whopper*	$0.37

Medical Products & Services

Item	Source	Description	Price
Cough Syrup	*Life* (1959)	*Troutman's;* friend of the family when coughs come	$0.49
Lotion	*Boy's Life* (1955)	*Clearasil;* starves pimples	$0.59–$0.98
Salve	*Life* (1959)	*Blistex;* best for cold sores, chapped lips, fever blisters	$0.39

Motorized Vehicles, Supplies, & Services

Item	Source	Description	Price
Automobile	Longworth and Robson, *Complete Book of Collectible Cars* (1985)	*Buick Century;* 2-door hardtop	$2,490–$3,420
Automobile	Longworth and Robson, *Complete Book of Collectible Cars* (1985)	*Chrysler New Yorker DeLuxe Newport;* 2-door hardtop [cost in 1955]	$3,652–$4,243
Automobile	Longworth and Robson, *Complete Book of Collectible Cars* (1985)	*Ford Fairlane;* 4-door town sedan [cost in 1955]	$1,914–$2,272
Automobile	Longworth and Robson, *Complete Book of Collectible Cars* (1985)	*Chrysler Imperial Newport;* 2-door hardtop [cost in 1955]	$3,752–$4,072

Item	Source	Description	Price
Automobile	Longworth and Robson, *Complete Book of Collectible Cars* (1985)	*Lincoln Capri Custom;* 2-door hardtop [cost in 1955]	$3,752–$4,072
Automobile	Longworth and Robson, *Complete Book of Collectible Cars* (1985)	*DeSoto Fireflite;* 2-door hardtop [cost in 1956]	$2,727–$3,615
Automobile	Longworth and Robson, *Complete Book of Collectible Cars* (1985)	*Dodge D-500 Royall;* convertible [cost in 1956]	$2,632
Automobile	Longworth and Robson, *Complete Book of Collectible Cars* (1985)	*Packard Caribbean;* 2-door hardtop [cost in 1956]	$5,495–$5,995
Automobile	Longworth and Robson, *Complete Book of Collectible Cars* (1985)	*Plymouth Fury;* 2-door hardtop [cost in 1956]	$2,866
Automobile	Longworth and Robson, *Complete Book of Collectible Cars* (1985)	*Pontiac Bonneville* [cost in 1957]	$5,782
Automobile	Longworth and Robson, *Complete Book of Collectible Cars* (1985)	*Rambler Rebel;* 4-door hardtop [cost in 1957]	$2,786
Automobile	Longworth and Robson, *Complete Book of Collectible Cars* (1985)	*Ford Thunderbird;* 2-door hardtop [cost in 1958]	$3,631–$4,222
Automobile	*Life* (1959)	*Simca DeLuxe;* imported from Paris by Chrysler	$1,698
Automobile	*Life* (1959)	*Buick Opel Caravan Wagon;* German made American style	$2,292.60
Automobile	Longworth and Robson, *Complete Book of Collectible Cars* (1985)	*Cadillac Eldorado Brougham;* 4-door hardtop [cost in 1959]	$13,075
Automobile	Longworth and Robson, *Complete Book of Collectible Cars* (1985)	*Chevrolet Corvette;* convertible [cost in 1959]	$3,631–$3,934

Item	Source	Description	Price
Musical Instruments			
Accordion	*Chicago Tribune* (1957)	*Renelli;* 120-bass accordion with 41 treble keys, 2 treble and 4 bass reeds, 2 treble switches; choice of 3 colors, straps and case included; regularly $295	$189
Cornet	*Chicago Tribune* (1957)	*Lyon Healy;* big tone, easy response, gold-lacquered finish; regularly $112.50	$99.50
Guitar	*Chicago Tribune* (1957)	*Washburn;* Spanish flat-top model with clear-grained spruce top; regularly $35	$27.50
Other			
Air Freshener	*Good Housekeeping* (1955)	*Dazy Spray;* costs less than expensive wicks or throw-away bombs	$0.49
Candygram	*Life* (1959)	*Western Union Candygram;* they'll eat your words	$2.95/pound
Cat Food	*Chicago Tribune* (1955)	*Puss N'Boots;* three 8-oz cans	$0.39
Crystal Prisms	*Antiques* (1956)	Plan colonial; 7" overall	$0.89
Dye	*Good Housekeeping* (1955)	*Rit;* try Rit in your washing machine and amaze yourself	$0.25
Microscope	*Boy's Life* (1955)	*Hy-power;* 100-200-300; 3-turret power	$8.95
Pen	*Life* (1959)	*Listo;* writes on cellophane and everything else	$0.27
Scale	*Good Housekeeping* (1955)	*Health-O-Meter Model 117;* the scale with a lift West of Denver	$8.95 $9.45
Sun and Heat Lamp	*Sears, Roebuck* (1958)	Lets you enjoy the magic of sun-bathing indoors	$72.93
Personal Care Products			
Acne Cream	*Good Housekeeping* (1955)	When acne strikes heartache and loneliness often follow	$0.59
Bandage	*Life* (1959)	*Johnson & Johnson Band-Aid;* plastic strips; extra large	$0.69
Dental Cream	*Life* (1959)	*Colgate-Palmolive;* world's largest selling toothpaste	$0.31/$0.53/ $0.69/$0.83
Deodorant	*Life* (1959)	*Tussy;* guard your charms	$1.00
Eyeliner	*Life* (1959)	*Max Factor Hi-Fi;* smearproof, waterproof, long lasting, never flakes	$1.50
Eyelash Curler	*Good Housekeeping* (1955)	*Maybelline;* naturally, it's the best gold tone	$1.00
Face Powder	*Sears, Roebuck* (1958)	Smooth long-lasting veil	$1.38
Facial Treatment	*Sears, Roebuck* (1958)	*Royal Treatment;* look born beautiful; now, famous royal jelly of the Queen Bee can be yours	$5.50
Home Barber Set	*Sears, Roebuck* (1958)	*Craftsman*	$14.95

Item	Source	Description	Price
Home Permanent	*Good Housekeeping* (1955)	*Proctor & Gamble Lilt Party Curl;* the only ammonia-free children's home permanent	$1.50
Lipstick	*Good Housekeeping* (1955)	*Cashmere Bouquet Rhythm-In-Red;* stays crimson-bright on your lips	$0.49
Lotion	*Good Housekeeping* (1955)	*Jergens;* positively stops detergent hands	$1.00
Lotion	*Life* (1959)	*Shulton Desert Flower;* contains the very heart of lanolin	$2.00
Makeup	*Good Housekeeping* (1955)	*Tangee;* the miracle makeup; actually lets your skin breathe	$0.39/$0.69
Makeup	*Good Housekeeping* (1955)	*Revlon Love-Pat;* it's pressed powder plus foundation; with Lanolite	$1.35
Makeup	*Life* (1959)	*House of Westmore Tru-glo;* liquid; America's most glamorous women applaud Tru-glo	$0.39
Mouthwash	*Life* (1959)	*Vi-Jon Antiseptic Mouthwash;* for colds, sore throats, bad breath; 16-oz family size bottle	$0.74
Perfume	*Life* (1959)	*Dorothy Gray Volate;* incredibly feminine	$5.00
Razor Blades	*Life* (1959)	*Pal Injector;* 20 blades	$0.79
Shampoo	*Good Housekeeping* (1955)	*Woodbury;* for beautiful hair-dos right after shampooing	$0.59
Shaver	*Life* (1959)	*Lady Norelco;* rotary blades no hand setting	$24.95
Shaving Cream	*Life* (1959)	*Shulton Old Spice;* softens beard better than ordinary push-button lathers; regular or mentholated	$1.00

Publications

Item	Source	Description	Price
Book	*Boy's Life* (1955)	Bruce Catton, *Banners at Shenandoah,* Doubleday; Civil War action novel	$3.00
Magazine	*Boy's Life* (1955)	*Boy's Life;* for all boys; monthly	$0.25
Magazine	*Antiques* (1956)	*Antiques;* monthly	$0.75
Magazine	*Life* (1959)	*Life;* weekly	$0.25

Real Estate

Item	Source	Description	Price
Bungalow	*Chicago Tribune* (1955)	For sale; two-bedroom expandable bungalow, extra kitchen	$14,500
House	*Chicago Tribune* (1955)	For sale; 4 bedrooms, 1/2 acre lot	$34,000
House	*Chicago Tribune* (1955)	For sale; bi-level home; only one left	$17,950
House	*Chicago Tribune* (1955)	For sale; four-bedroom frame, living room, dining room, combination, gas heat, single garage	$19,500
House	*Chicago Tribune* (1955)	For sale; three-bedroom, brick ranch; gas radiant heat, vinyl tile, attic fan, 2-car garage, side drive	$18,300

Item	Source	Description	Price
Studio Home	*Chicago Tribune* (1955)	For sale; terms or contract to qualified couple; garden privileges; large first-floor work or storage area	$5,500

Sewing Equipment & Supplies

Sewing Machine	*Life* (1959)	*Singer;* young budget portable model built to meet the sewing needs of young families	$119.50

Sports Equipment

Bait Casting Line	*Boy's Life* (1955)	*Cortland Cam-O-Flag;* braided from nylon test 20 lbs; 50 yds	$1.30
Baseball Glove	*Boy's Life* (1955)	*Rawlings Little League Stan Musial*	$9.95
Baseball Shoes	*Boy's Life* (1955)	*Rawlings;* designed for action, molded rubber soles and cleats	$4.95
Bicycle	*Life* (1959)	*Western Auto Western Flyer;* 26"; features bold Jet-Swept cantilever frame	$64.95
Bicycle Light	*Boy's Life* (1955)	*Delta Electric Rocket Ray;* you'll think you're ready for a flight into space	$2.40
Crow Call	*Boy's Life* (1955)	*Philips S. Olt V-16 Junior Model*	$1.50
Knife Set	*Boy's Life* (1955)	*X-Acto-Inc. No. 82;* includes 10 blades, two knives	$4.20
Lantern	*Boy's Life* (1955)	*Berkshire Designs Campers;* burns with the brightness of a 100-watt bulb for 7 hours	$7.95
License Plate	*Boy's Life* (1955)	*Better Values;* for bicycles; personalized with name or nickname up to 8 letters	$1.00
Outboard Motor	*Boy's Life* (1955)	*Evinrude;* big twin aquasonic, standard model	$430
Outboard Motor	*Boy's Life* (1955)	*Johnson Motors Sea-horse 25;* 25 HP; for the lift of your life	$430
Race Car Kit	*Boy's Life* (1955)	*Pinewood Derby;* contains 8 pre-sawed blocks of clear pine, plus axle supports, wheels, decals and instructions	$2.75
Rifle	*Boy's Life* (1955)	*Harrington & Richardson Pioneer;* .22 cal. bolt action single shot rifle model 750	$17.95
Rifle	*Boy's Life* (1955)	*Remington Model 514;* popular-priced; shoots all 3-sizes of .22s	$15.40
Spinning Tackle	*Boy's Life* (1955)	*Airex Larchmont;* a light weight reel with a precision quadrand brake	$25.00
Stationary Bike	*Sears, Roebuck* (1958)	Home riding exercise	$71.50

Tobacco Products

Cigars	*Life* (1959)	*Trend;* mild little cigars blended with fine Havana; you need not inhale to enjoy them; humidor pack of 20 cigars	$0.35
Lighter	*Life* (1959)	*Zippo;* highly polished durable chrome finish	$4.75

Toys

Doll	*Good Housekeeping* (1955)	*Gerber Baby Doll;* a-cuddle, sleep sweetly; with 6 Gerber food labels	$2.00
Remote Control Robot	*New York Times* (1956)	Electric motor; eyes flash; arms swing back and forth; walks forward or backwards; all metal	$2.78

Item	Source	Description	Price
Toy	*Life* (1959)	*Revell Dr. Seuss Zoo;* we're nutty and new; set of three	$3.98
Truck	*Life* (1959)	*Buddy-L;* Texaco tank truck; lay away for Christmas	$3.50
Travel & Transportation			
Airfare	*Good Housekeeping* (1955)	*TWA;* from New York to London; TWA discount fares; special discounts for couples	
		Round Trip	$482
		Ladies Accompanying Husbands	$282
Airfare	*Chicago Tribune* (1955)	*TWA;* three non-stops to Los Angeles; fly the finest, fly TWA	$76.00
Railroad Fare	*Life* (1959)	Santa Fe Chicago to San Francisco	$63.12
Railroad Fare	*Life* (1959)	*Santa Fe Railroad;* an entire family of four can ride to California and back from Chicago for less than it costs to drive your own car	$212.15

MISCELLANY 1955-1959

Zsa Zsa Gabor

Just discovered why Zsa Zsa Gabor and her daughter, Porfirio Rubirosa, the Herbert Marshalls, Nina Foch, Cy Howard and Gloria Grahame, and Lauritz Melchior are having such a fine time in New York. When one of the richest men in America invited them to his home in Allensville, PA, for his annual New Year's party in honor of his wife, he not only paid all their expenses but gave them an extra check to boot. It was Melchior's third year, but Zsa Zsa claims she got the biggest bonus—$5,000—for being the prettiest guest.

Hollywood entertaining was never like this.

Chicago Tribune, January 8, 1955

Installment Credit Up $15 Million in February

Consumer installment credit outstanding rose $15,000,000 in February, the Federal Reserve Board reported yesterday.

February's rise to a total of $27,784,000,000 compared with an increase of $72,000,000 in February, 1955.

The modest size of the latest increase disguised a much larger rise above the 1955 month's level in new installment credit extended. The $2,769,000,000 in new credit was $45,000,000 above the January total and $353,000,000 above that of February, 1955. Repayments rose even more sharply to $2,754,000,000.

New York Times, April 3, 1956

Action Explained In Six Languages; New Gallery Will Be Opened to the Public Tomorrow—Companies to Exhibit

Information about the operations of the American Stock Exchange is now available in English, French, German, Italian, Spanish and Yiddish. A new gallery, which will be opened to the securities industry today and to the public on Wednesday, is equipped with telephone instructions through which visitors may hear a tape-recorded nine-minute narrative.

New York Times, April 3, 1956

Chain Store Sales Show 15.6% Gain, Best In Six Years

Chain store sales in April registered the sharpest increase over volume of a year earlier since March, 1951, according to a survey completed yesterday by The New York Times.

The gain for forty-four companies was 15.6 per cent, as against 19 per cent in March, 1951. The strong showing was attributed by company executives to the increase in Easter volume. With the holiday three weeks later this year than in 1956, the bulk of the seasonal trade came in April. Last year it came in March.

New York Times, May 14, 1957

1960-1979

The Vietnam War and the Global Economy

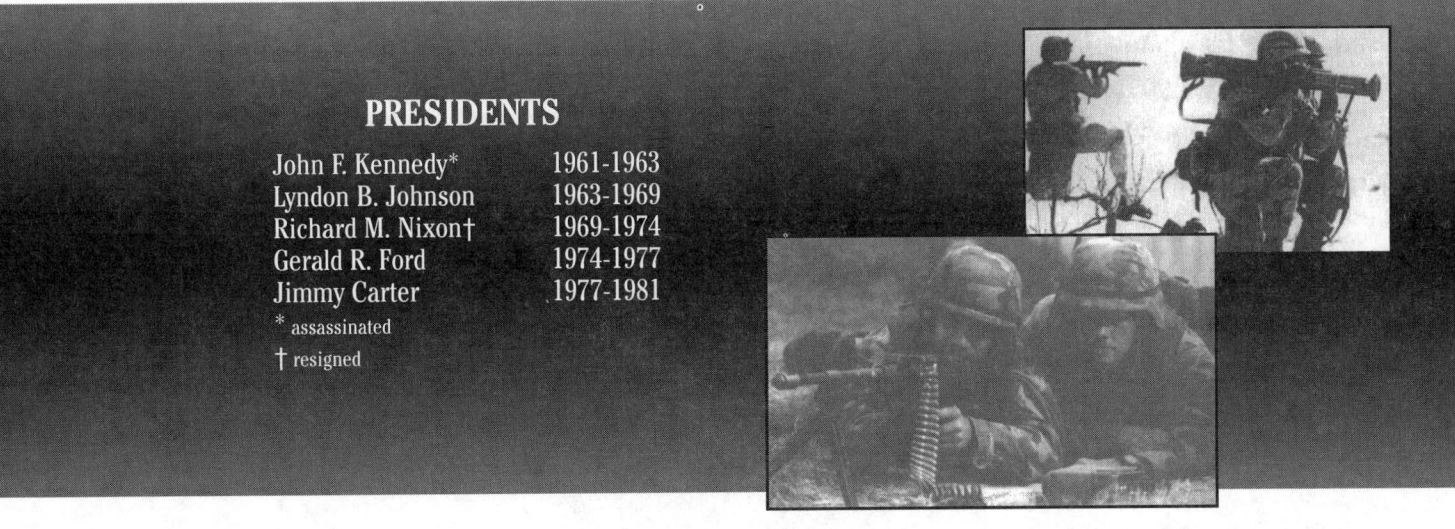

PRESIDENTS

John F. Kennedy*	1961-1963
Lyndon B. Johnson	1963-1969
Richard M. Nixon†	1969-1974
Gerald R. Ford	1974-1977
Jimmy Carter	1977-1981

* assassinated

† resigned

The 1960s and 1970s were full of hope, revolutionary innovation, and disruptive economic change. The role of government grew and transformed American society. World economics and the Vietnam War altered America's view of its invincibility; inflation played a critical role in prices, wages, and politics; the cold war ended as the Soviet Union and lesser communist regimes behind the iron curtain collapsed.

From 1960 to 1964 the economy expanded. Gross national product and total federal spending increased by nearly 25 percent. Inflation was held in check. The power of the United States internationally was immense. Congress gave the young president John F. Kennedy the defense and space-related programs he wanted, but few welfare programs. In the years that followed the erection of the Berlin Wall, the Cuban Missile Crisis, and the initial American involvement in the Vietnam War, all of which occurred during the presidency of John F. Kennedy, Americans were forced to think globally—and not always positively. Economic stability during the period was threatened by inflation. From an annual average of less than 2 percent between 1950 and 1965, the inflation rate soared to almost 9.5 percent in the second half of the 1970s. The rate was frighteningly volatile, ranging from 6 percent to almost 14 percent. Banks found it

difficult to attract deposits as investors sought better rates of return by shifting their money to other markets. For savings and loan institutions the funds shift was a disaster leading to thousands of closures.

In 1963 a presidential commission on women responded to the complex of issues related to women's equality. The National Organization for Women and such feminist statements as Betty Friedan's *The Feminine Mystique* forced women's issues, which are grounded in economics, to the forefront of national attention. By 1980 the twocareer family became the norm. Forty-two percent of all American workers were female, and more than half of all married women and 90 percent of female college graduates worked outside the home. Yet, their median wage was 60 percent of that for men.

In 1973 the economic power of foreign oil became alarming. In just two months' time world oil prices shot up from less than $6 to almost $23 a barrel. Shortfalls and long lines at gas stations resulted. The price at the pump doubled. The second oil shock, in 1978, carried oil prices past $34 a barrel and gas at the pump over $1 a gallon. This situation produced an awareness of U.S. vulnerability and widespread inflation. With roughly 6 percent of the world's people, the U.S. consumed one-third of world petroleum.

Attempts to control inflation by tightening the money supply through higher interest rates and frozen prices and wages created a combination of rising living costs and recession known as stagflation. In 1979 the consumer price index rose 13.3 percent. The following year interest rates and inflation each hit 18 percent.

The Cold War became hotter during conflicts over Cuba and Berlin in the early 1960s. Fears over the international spread of Communism led to America's intervention in a foreign conflict that would become a defining event of the decade: Vietnam. Military involvement in this small Asian country grew from advisory status to full-scale war. Vietnam became a national obsession, producing inflation and discontent. In spring 1970 students on 448 college campuses either staged campus strikes or closed down their institutions. The war was the longest in American history; the total cost was $118 billion, 56,000 dead and 300,000 wounded, and the loss of American prestige abroad. The collapse of communism at the end of the 1980s brought an end to the old world order and set the stage for a realignment of power in which America was still regarded as the strongest nation in the world, but the definition of power was expressed increasingly in economic rather than military terms.

The struggle to bring economic equality to blacks during the period produced massive government spending for school integration, especially in the 1960s. By 1963 the peaceful phase of the civil rights movement ended; street violence, assassinations, and bombings marked the period. In 1967, forty-one cities experienced major disturbances, but by 1972 nearly half of Southern black children sat in integrated classrooms, and about a third all of black families had risen economically into the ranks of the middle class.

HISTORICAL SNAPSHOT
1960-1964

1960

- Organization of Petroleum Exporting Companies (OPEC) meets for first time
- Coal supplies 45 percent of power needs
- Sprite introduced by Coca-Cola Company
- Laser perfected
- Gross national product is $503 billion
- More than 25 million taxpayers declare incomes of $5,000 or more; 5.23 million claim $10,000 or more
- Corporate mergers total 844
- Auto registrations show one passenger car for every three Americans
- Television plays a key role in the Nixon-Kennedy presidential election
- Paperback book sales reach 300 million annually
- 10 percent of work force is on the farm
- Beef consumption reaches 99 pounds a year per capita
- Enovid 10 contraceptive, known widely as the Pill, sells for 55 cents each, costing $11 per month

1961

- DNA genetic code broken
- New York's First National Bank offers fixed-term certificate of deposit
- IBM Selectric typewriter introduced

- Merger creates Harper & Row
- Cigarette makers spend $115 million on television advertising
- R. J. Reynolds acquires Pacific Hawaiian Products Company to diversify
- Canned pet foods are among the three top-selling categories in grocery stores

1962

- Cuban missile crisis pits United States against Soviet Union
- President Kennedy reduces tariff duties to stimulate foreign trade
- Electronic Data Systems founded by H. Ross Perot
- 90 percent of households have at least one television set
- American Broadcasting Company (ABC) begins color telecast for 3.5 hours per week
- *Silent Spring* by U. S. biologist Rachel Carson published
- Diet-Rite Cola introduced as first sugar-free soft drink
- Tab-opening aluminum drink cans introduced

1963

- President Kennedy assassinated; Lyndon Johnson becomes President
- Congress enacts equal-pay-for-equal-work legislation for women
- Jersey Central Power and Light installs first commercial nuclear reactor

- Two-thirds of the world's automobiles are in United States
- Valium introduced by Roche Laboratories
- U.S. factory workers average more than $100 weekly for first time
- Federal budget reaches nearly $100 billion
- First-class postal rates increase to 5 cents per ounce
- Weight Watchers founded in Queens, NY
- Average per capita meat consumption reaches 170.6 pounds; chicken consumption is 37.8 pounds

1964

- Congress approves Tonkin Gulf resolution in North Vietnam
- Civil Rights bill approved
- Soviet coup strips Nikita Khrushev of power
- 24th Amendment, making poll taxes unconstitutional, goes into effect
- Studebaker-Packard Corporation makes seat belts standard equipment
- Ford introduces Mustang
- Gasoline prices are 30.3 cents per gallon
- Zip codes adopted by U.S. Post Office
- Sales through vending machines total $3.5 billion

SELECTED INCOME 1960-1964

Job	Source	Description	Pay
Account Executive	*Chicago Tribune* (1964)	High-caliber man; successful organization servicing established accounts assures you of excellent commission; direct sales experience required	$15,000–$18,000/yr
Accountant	*New York Times* (1961)	Prefer sr.'s or semi's with CPA experience or experience as auditor, controller or F/C bookkeeper; 35–65 years old	$116–$160/wk
Actor	Legrand and Karney *Chronicle of the Cinema* (1995)	Warren Beatty's salary for his role in *Splendor in the Grass* in 1961	$200,000
Actor	Miller, *The Great Cowboy Stars of Movies and Television* (1979)	Clint Eastwood's salary for his role in the movie *A Fistful of Dollars* in 1964	$15,000
Actor	Robinson, *Bardot, An Intimate Portrait* (1994)	Brigitte Bardot's salary for *Contempt* in 1963	$530,300
Administrative Assistant	*New York Times* (1961)	Male; administrative office of industry-wide pension, welfare & vacation plans; college graduate preferred; must be able to coordinate, handle detail & possess writing ability; liberal FREE benefits	$125/wk to start
Advertising Trainees	*Chicago Tribune* (1962)	You will get your feet wet as the department contact man	$500/mo
Agency Director	*Chicago Tribune* (1964)	Life insurance	$17,000/yr
Airlines Trainees	*Chicago Tribune* (1964)	No experience needed; free travel privileges	$385/mo
Assembler	*Chicago Tribune* (1962)		$1.52–$3.60/hr
Assistant Civil Engineer	*San Bernardino (California) Evening Telegram* (1963)	Person desired is college graduate with two years responsible experience in municipal engineering Per month	$708 to $848
Boiler Engineer	*New York Times* (1961)	New York, New Jersey, Florida	$7,000/yr
Broker	*Chicago Tribune* (1962)	Famous brokerage firm needs 3 young men over 20 to learn stock trading; some college helpful; your ability to learn will assure you this spot	$400/mo
Businessman	Harry Hunt III, *Texas Rich: The Hunt Dynasty From The Early Oil Days Through The Silver Crash* (1981)	Gross income of Nelson Bunker Hunt from Sarir oil field, Libya, in 1961	$6 billion
Cartoonist	*National Public Radio Interview* (2004)	Sid Couchy's pay per cartoon page to pencil Richey Rich comic books in 1961	$15
Collection Assistant	*Chicago Tribune* (1964)		$625/mo

Job	Source	Description	Pay
Computer Sales Trainee	*Chicago Tribune* (1964)	Opportunity of a lifetime; fastest growing industry in America; this company will train college men for permanent positions that will earn $25,000–$30,000 annually within four years	$9,000–$11,000/yr
Cook	*Chicago Tribune* (1962)	Chef-sous; chef-sauciers; bakers; institutional cooks	$100–$250/wk
Customer-Service Technicians	*Chicago Tribune* (1964)	General chemical know-how, plus careful training by the employer will make you a top-notch customer-relations representative	$8,000–$9,500/yr
Delivery Man	*San Bernardino (California) Evening Telegram* (1963)	Family man, neat appearing and friendly, to take over local and delivery route Per week to start	$120
Director Public Relations	*Chicago Tribune* (1962)	Industrial background; work with president in all financial areas	$18,000/yr
Editor	*Minneapolis Morning Tribune* (1964)	Editor Trainee to edit monthly house organ and weekly sales magazine Per month	$475
Electrician	*Minneapolis Morning Tribune* (1964)	Alaska Lumber & Pulp Co.; job requires 5 years industrial equipment experience; pulp and mill experience preferred. Rate per hour	$4.10
Executive Assistant	*Chicago Tribune* (1964)	Busy executive will train right young man to assist him; degree not essential	$115/wk
Export Sales	*Chicago Tribune* (1962)	You will get in on this corporation's plans to expand its foreign sales staff! They will hire you and train you in the home office until you are familiar with the operation	$90–$100/wk
Factory Girls	*New York Times* (1961)	No experience; day/night	$65/wk
Factory Men	*New York Times* (1961)	Foundry type operation; 2 yrs recent metal-working experience	$1.56/hr to start
Guard	*New York Times* (1961)	Train as guard; 20 years and over; no experience	$75–$85/wk, plus lunch
Housekeeper	*San Bernardino (California) Evening Telegram* (1963)	Must have driver's license; work from 12:30 to 5:30 pm Per month	$100
Industrial Sales Manager	*New York Times* (1964)	Shipyard or heavy industrial experience leading company, Philadelphia area	$12,000 to $16,000
Machinist	*New York Times* (1961)	Helpers Machinists	$1.75 $3.25
Model Trainees	*New York Times* (1961)	Size 12; coats	$55/wk
Musicians	*Life* (1964)	Payment to the Beatles for their landmark appearance on *The Ed Sullivan Show* in 1964	$4,000
Organic Research Chemist	*Minneapolis Morning Tribune* (1964)	For Minneapolis area, per year	$12,000
Pages (Girl-Woman)	*New York Times* (1961)	Company pays fee; 16 years; housewives ok	$55–$70/wk
Patrolman	*San Bernardino (California) Evening Telegram* (1963)	San Bernardino policeman; high school degree, minimum height 5' 9"; minimum weight 155 lbs. Per month	$529 to $639
Programmer Trainees	*New York Times* (1961)	College graduate; math-statistics, research work; top publisher; no skills	$80–$100/wk

Job	Source	Description	Pay
Public Information	*Chicago Tribune* (1964)	Stable work background; no experience; under 50; 37 1/2 -hour week	$400/mo
Public Opinion Interviewing	*New York Times* (1961)	Part-time; reliable men living in Manhattan needed for evening interviewing in Manhattan	$1.75/hr
Recording Studio	*New York Times* (1961)	College graduate; work in classical music area	$70/wk
Route Runner	*Chicago Tribune* (1962)	Capable of handling part of our north-side vacation routes with help of supervisor. Permanent position with good chance for advancement.	$140/wk plus commission
Sales	*Minneapolis Morning Tribune* (1964)	Pharmaceutical sales in St. Cloud, Fargo and St. Paul; pay includes car Yearly salary	$6,000
Sales	*Chicago Tribune* (1962)	Tired of looking week after week at the same old paycheck? Has your secret dream been to find a leading organization that would give you a chance as a salesman?	$180/wk minimum
Sales Assistant	*Chicago Tribune* (1964)	To vice president; electrical or mechanical education; will train to apply company products to OEM equipment	$11,000–$13,500
Social Security	*San Bernardino (California) Evening Telegram* (1963)	Average Social Security payment at age 65; per month	$127
Tool and Dye Maker	*Chicago Tribune* (1964)	Job shop experience necessary; top pay; best working conditions	$110/wk
Trainee	*Chicago Tribune* (1962)	General factory; experienced; semiskilled	$60–$120/wk
Typist	*New York Times* (1964)	For publishing company Per week	$80
U.S. President	*Look Magazine* (1961)	Annual salary of President John F. Kennedy in 1961	$100,000
Vets	*Chicago Tribune* (1964)	Many Loop positions now open; any armed forces clerical, medical, or technical background qualifies; excellent futures	$375–$450/mo

CONSUMER EXPENDITURES 1960-1964

(Per Capita)

Expenditure Type	1960	1961	1962	1963	1964
Clothing	$123.98	$125.21	$129.73	$131.58	$141.23
Food	$457.74	$462.19	$466.93	$472.94	$492.99
Auto Usage	$218.63	$207.41	$229.44	$245.72	$256.39
New Auto Purchase	$77.49	$65.87	$79.26	$90.89	$93.57
Auto Parts	$13.84	$14.15	$15.01	$15.85	$16.68
Gas & Oil	$66.42	$65.33	$67.55	$68.69	$70.87
Housing	$266.78	$278.73	$293.24	$306.49	$319.98
Furniture	$26.01	$26.13	$27.34	$29.06	$31.79
Utilities	$74.72	$76.21	$79.34	$82.96	$85.47
Telephone & Telegraph	$24.91	$26.13	$27.34	$29.06	$31.27
Physicians	$32.10	$32.12	$34.85	$36.46	$42.73
Dentists	$11.07	$11.43	$12.33	$12.15	$14.07
Health Insurance	$9.96	$10.89	$11.79	$11.63	$12.51
Personal Business	$79.70	$65.87	$79.26	$90.36	$95.89
Personal Care	$30.99	$33.21	$38.59	$39.63	$39.09
Tobacco	$38.19	$38.65	$38.59	$39.63	$39.61
Local Transport	$11.07	$10.89	$10.72	$10.57	$10.42
Intercity Transport	$7.19	$7.62	$8.04	$7.93	$8.86
Recreation	$101.84	$103.98	$110.43	$117.84	$127.16
Religion/Welfare Activities	$29.34	$29.94	$31.09	$32.33	$37.00
Private Education & Research	$21.59	$22.32	$24.12	$25.36	$27.09
Per Capita Consumption	$1830.39	$1856.92	$1943.21	$2016.99	$2133.00

INVESTMENTS 1960-1964

Investment	1960	1961	1962	1963	1964
Basic Yield, One-year Corporate Bonds	NR	NR	NR		
Short-term Interest Rates, 4–6 Months, Prime Commercial Paper	3.85	4.50	4.50		
Basic Yield, Common Stocks, Total	3.60	3.07	3.37		
Index of Common Stocks (1941–1943=10)	55.85	66.27	62.38		

COMMON STOCKS, CLOSING PRICE AND YIELD, FIRST BUSINESS DAY OF YEAR

(Parenthetical number is annual dividend in dollars)

	1960	1961	1962	1963	1964
Allis Chalmers	35 3/4	25	21 7/8	15 3/8	16 5/8
(2 for 1 split, 6/15/56)	(1)	(1.50)	(1.25)	(.75)	(.50)
AT&T	80 3/8	103 1/2	133 5/8	115	139 1/2
(3 for 1 split, 4/24/59)	(3.30)	(3.30)	(3.60)	(3.60)	(3.60)
American Tobacco	107	65 1/4	100 1/4	29 1/4	28 1/
(2 for 1 split, 4/7/60)	(4)		(2.30)	(1.50)	(1.50)
(2 for 1 split, 4/5/62)					
Anaconda	64 7/8	44 1/8	49 1/21/2	41	48
	(2.50)	(2.50)	(2.50)	(2.50)	(2.50)
Bethlehem Steel	56 3/8	41	43	29	32 1/2
	(2.40)	(2.40)	(2.40)	(1.50)	(1.50)
B&O	41 1/4	28 5/8	22 3/8	29 1/8	
(Merged with Chesapeake & Ohio)	(1.50)	(.60)	(/)	(/)	
(B&O shares voluntarily exchanged for 1 share Chessie Systems plus $1.69/share. Shares not exchanged by 5/7/74 were canceled and exchanged for 1 share Chessie Systems)					
Corn Products	56 1/2	78 3/4	56 3/4	49 3/4	60 1/2
	(2)	(2.40)	(1.30)	(1.40)	(1.50)
General Electric	96 5/8	72 1/4	74 3/4	76 3/8	86 3/4
	(2)	(2)	(2)	(2)	(2.20)
General Motors	54 1/2	41 1/2	56 3/8	58 1/4	80 1/4
	(2)	(2)	(2)	(2)	(4)
International Business Machines	437	582 1/2	572	384 3/4	517
(1 1/2 shares for 1 split, 5/16/61)	(2.40)	(3)	(2.40)	(3)	(5)
(5 shares for 4 split, 5/15/64)					
Intl Harvester	49	43 1/4	52 1/8	49 7/8	58 5/8
	(2.40)	(2.40)	(2.40)	(2.40)	(2.40)
National Biscuit	55 1/2	72 1/2	85	43 1/2	57
(2 shares for 1 split, 5/11/62)	(2.40)	(2.80)	(2.80)	(1.50)	(1.60)
US Steel	101 3/8	76 1/8	77 1/8	43 3/4	54 7/8
	(3)	(3)	(3)	(2.75)	(2)
Western Union	50 1/8	40	39 3/4	27	32 3/8
	(1.40)	(1.40)	(1.40)	(1.40)	(1.40)

STANDARD JOBS 1960-1964

Job Type	1960	1961	1962	1963	1964
Average of All Industries, excl. farm labor	$5260/yr	NR	NR	NR	NR
Average of All Industries, incl. farm labor	$4816/yr	$4961/yr	$5155/yr	$5343/yr	$5609/yr
Bituminous Coal Mining	$5367/yr	$5357/yr	$5507/yr	$5786/yr	$6162/yr
Building Trades	$5750/yr	$5938/yr	$6174/yr	$6364/yr	$6709/yr
Domestics	$2336/yr	$2356/yr	$2364/yr	$2418/yr	$2471/yr
Farm Labor	$1848/yr	$1929/yr	$2044/yr	$2166/yr	$2413/yr
Federal Civilian	$6073/yr	$6451/yr	$6643/yr	$6995/yr	$7518/yr
Federal Employees, Executive Depts.	$4721/yr	$4812/yr	$4861/yr	$5137/yr	$5503/yr
Federal Military	$3872/yr	$3813/yr	$3807/yr	$3997/yr	$4284/yr
Finance, Insurance, & Real Estate	$4910/yr	$5203/yr	$5353/yr	$5522/yr	$5797/yr
Gas, Electricity, Sanitation Workers	$6150/yr	$6390/yr	$6655/yr	$6941/yr	$7303/yr
Manufacturing, Durable Goods	$5894/yr	$6048/yr	$6291/yr	$6512/yr	$6842/yr
Manufacturing, Nondurable Goods	$5081/yr	$5250/yr	$5416/yr	$5570/yr	$5836/yr
Medical/Health Services Workers	$3414/yr	$3636/yr	$3831/yr	$4051/yr	$4277/yr
Miscellaneous Manufacturing	$4648/yr	$4753/yr	$4883/yr	$5039/yr	$5301/yr
Motion Picture Services	$5444/yr	$5871/yr	$6008/yr	$6168/yr	$6603/yr
Nonprofit Org. Workers	$3584/yr	$3684/yr	$3787/yr	$3896/yr	$4000/yr
Passenger Transportation Workers, Local and Highway	$4877/yr	$4966/yr	$5081/yr	$5202/yr	$5409/yr
Personal Services	$3665/yr	$3810/yr	$3968/yr	$4063/yr	$4267/yr
Public School Teachers	$4762/yr	$4991/yr	$5291/yr	$5446/yr	$5653/yr
Radio Broadcasting & Television Workers	$7429/yr	$7384/yr	$7713/yr	$8011/yr	$8435/yr
Railroads	$6241/yr	$6440/yr	$6651/yr	$6823/yr	$7105/yr
State and Local Govt. Workers	$4527/yr	$4721/yr	$4987/yr	$5159/yr	$5342/yr
Telephone & Telegraph Workers	$5532/yr	$5793/yr	$6078/yr	$6335/yr	$6687/yr
Wholesale and Retail Trade Workers	$5756/yr	$5932/yr	$6172/yr	$6419/yr	$6703/yr

FOOD BASKET 1960-1964

(NR = Not Reported)

Commodity	Year	New York	Atlanta	Chicago	Denver	Los Angeles
Apples, Fresh, per pound	1960	16.30¢	17.50¢	18.40¢	NR	18.50¢
	1961	17.70¢	18.10¢	19.10¢	NR	19.80¢
	1962	16.80¢	18.60¢	18.10¢	NR	20.40¢
	1963	18.20¢	17.90¢	19.20¢	NR	19.90¢
	1964	19¢	NR	17.60¢	NR	18.60¢
Beans, Dried, per pound	1960	16.20¢	16.60¢	17.50¢	NR	17.40¢
	1961	15.90¢	17.10¢	16.80¢	NR	17.90¢
	1962	16.60¢	16.30¢	17.10¢	NR	19.80¢
	1963	17.20¢	16.90¢	18.30¢	NR	18.90¢
	1964	16.60¢	NR	17¢	NR	18.70¢
Beef, Rib Roasts, per pound	1960	75.50¢	87.80¢	81¢	NR	95.90¢
	1961	73.50¢	86.20¢	81.50¢	NR	94.60¢
	1962	78¢	89.20¢	86.20¢	NR	97¢
	1963	77¢	89¢	88¢	NR	$1.00
	1964	78.20¢	NR	85.60¢	NR	96.70¢
Beef, Steaks (Round), per pound	1960	$1.16	$1.09	89.60¢	NR	$1.00
	1961	$1.14	$1.08	89.20¢	NR	$1.00
	1962	$1.19	$1.10	94.80¢	NR	$1.00
	1963	$1.18	$1.08	91.20¢	NR	98.40¢
	1964	$1.18	NR	88.50¢	NR	94.40¢
Bread, White, per pound	1960	22.80¢	19.40¢	18.90¢	NR	23.40¢
	1961	23.80¢	19.40¢	19¢	NR	24.80¢
	1962	23.90¢	19.30¢	19.80¢	NR	28¢
	1963	25¢	19.40¢	19.50¢	NR	28.60¢
	1964	24.10¢	NR	18.90¢	NR	28.70¢
Butter, per pound	1960	73.80¢	80.50¢	74.60¢	NR	79.40¢
	1961	75.30¢	82.20¢	76.40¢	NR	79.60¢
	1962	74.10¢	81.50¢	74.90¢	NR	76.80¢
	1963	73.90¢	80.40¢	75.80¢	NR	75.50¢
	1964	73.50¢	NR	76.50¢	NR	75.90¢
Cheese, per pound	1960	67¢	67.60¢	66.80¢	NR	72.20¢
	1961	70.20¢	71¢	71.20¢	NR	77¢
	1962	70¢	69.40¢	71¢	NR	77.60¢
	1963	70.40¢	70.60¢	71.60¢	NR	77.60¢
	1964	71¢	NR	72.80¢	NR	78.20¢
Chickens, per pound	1960	43¢	40.90¢	39.20¢	NR	48.60¢
	1961	38.60¢	35.60¢	35.30¢	NR	43.50¢
	1962	41.70¢	37.30¢	38.20¢	NR	43.60¢
	1963	41.50¢	NR	38.10¢	NR	43.50¢
	1964	40.10¢	NR	36.80¢	NR	41.10¢
Coffee, per pound	1960	75¢	78.60¢	74.60¢	NR	77.20¢
	1961	74.60¢	77.30¢	73.90¢	NR	70.60¢
	1962	72.20¢	75.10¢	73.70¢	NR	63.60¢
	1963	69.50¢	72.80¢	72.10¢	NR	64.70¢
	1964	81.10¢	NR	82.30¢	NR	79.50¢
Cornmeal, per pound	1960	12.20¢	7.20¢	12.90¢	NR	14¢
	1961	12.80¢	7.50¢	13¢	NR	14.60¢
	1962	13.30¢	7.70¢	13.60¢	NR	16.20¢
	1963	14.10¢	7.80¢	13.80¢	NR	16.90¢
	1964	NR	NR	NR	NR	NR

Commodity	Year	New York	Atlanta	Chicago	Denver	Los Angeles
Eggs, per dozen	1960	63.40¢	56.80¢	55.10¢	NR	55.90¢
	1961	63.30¢	56¢	56¢	NR	55.10¢
	1962	60.80¢	52.30¢	52.60¢	NR	51¢
	1963	60.90¢	53.60¢	53.20¢	NR	50.70¢
	1964	58.30¢	NR	51.80¢	NR	50.90¢
Flour, Wheat, per pound	1960	10.58¢	11.13¢	10.40¢	NR	13.04¢
	1961	10.62¢	11.36¢	10.68¢	NR	13.04¢
	1962	10.88¢	11.74¢	10.50¢	NR	12.22¢
	1963	11.14¢	11.92¢	10.52¢	NR	11.90¢
	1964	11.26¢	NR	10.84¢	NR	11.70¢
Lard, per pound	1960	19.10¢	17.70¢	18¢	NR	21.50¢
	1961	20.70¢	19.40¢	19.50¢	NR	23.40¢
	1962	20.10¢	18.50¢	19.10¢	NR	23.60¢
	1963	19.70¢	17.80¢	19.30¢	NR	23¢
	1964	NR	NR	NR	NR	NR
Milk, Fresh, per quart	1960	31.80¢	27¢	28.10¢	NR	NR
	1961	31.50¢	27.20¢	28.70¢	NR	25.80¢
	1962	31.20¢	27.20¢	29.30¢	NR	22.80¢
	1963	27¢	26.90¢	29.50¢	NR	23.40¢
	1964	30.50¢	NR	28.95¢	NR	26.95¢
Mutton and Lamb, Leg, per pound	1960	70¢	76.50¢	70.10¢	NR	74.80¢
	1961	65.10¢	73.40¢	66.40¢	NR	72.20¢
	1962	66.70¢	76.60¢	70.20¢	NR	72.50¢
	1963	67.20¢	77.10¢	69.80¢	NR	73.40¢
	1964	$1.33	NR	$1.36	NR	$1.44
Pork, Chops, per pound	1960	89.60¢	78.60¢	86¢	NR	98.10¢
	1961	90.20¢	81.40¢	87.30¢	NR	$1.00
	1962	92.80¢	84.10¢	87.80¢	NR	$1.01
	1963	92.20¢	79.70¢	85.10¢	NR	$1.00
	1964	$1.33	NR	$1.36	NR	$1.44
Pork, Bacon, Sliced, per pound	1960	68.50¢	65.60¢	64.20¢	NR	67.90¢
	1961	73.20¢	70.80¢	68.80¢	NR	72.70¢
	1962	74.40¢	69.60¢	67.70¢	NR	71.10¢
	1963	73.40¢	68.60¢	65.90¢	Denver	67.40¢
	1964	70.30¢	NR	66¢	NR	66.30¢
Pork, Ham, Whole, per pound	1960	62.70¢	59.10¢	58.40¢	NR	59.20¢
	1961	63.60¢	60.50¢	59.30¢	NR	59.70¢
	1962	66.20¢	61.20¢	60.60¢	NR	59.20¢
	1963	65¢	59.50¢	58.50¢	NR	58¢
	1964	63¢	NR	58.40¢	NR	57.30¢
Potatoes, Irish, per 10 pounds	1960	67.30¢	65.30¢	78.30¢	NR	$1.04
	1961	54.90¢	57.70¢	71.50¢	NR	81¢
	1962	57¢	60.70¢	75¢	NR	83¢
	1963	60.30¢	64.30¢	77.60¢	NR	86.90¢
	1964	75.30¢	NR	86.70¢	NR	99.80¢
Prunes, Dried, per pound	1960	37.90¢	39.80¢	39.40¢	NR	37.80¢
	1961	39.20¢	42.50¢	41¢	NR	41.10¢
	1962	38.20¢	40.90¢	40.10¢	NR	39.70¢
	1963	32.70¢	39.20¢	39.60¢	NR	38.70¢
	1964	NR	NR	NR	NR	NR
Rice, per pound	1960	18.70¢	20.70¢	18.70¢	NR	22.10¢
	1961	19.10¢	21.30¢	19¢	NR	22.30¢
	1962	19.90¢	22.70¢	19.30¢	NR	22.50¢
	1963	20.20¢	23.10¢	19.20¢	NR	22.70¢
	1964	19.80¢	NR	19¢	NR	22.30¢

Commodity	Year	New York	Atlanta	Chicago	Denver	Los Angeles
Sugar, per pound	1960	11.06¢	11.40¢	11.30¢	NR	12.18¢
	1961	11.40¢	11.52¢	11.50¢	NR	11.62¢
	1962	11.38¢	11.52¢	11.58¢	NR	10.88¢
	1963	13.76¢	13.88¢	12.86¢	NR	12.50¢
	1964	13.14¢	NR	12.58¢	NR	12¢
Tea bags, per pound or package of 48	1960	69.60¢	74.40¢	69.60¢	NR	75.90¢
	1961	70.20¢	75¢	72.30¢	NR	75.60¢
	1962	70.50¢	74.40¢	72.90¢	NR	75¢
	1963	91.60¢	95.10¢	90.40¢	NR	95¢
	1964	59.60¢	NR	66¢	NR	67¢
Veal, per pound	1960	$1.59	$1.31	$1.22	NR	$1.42
	1961	$1.60	$1.31	$1.24	NR	$1.42
	1962	$1.67	$1.35	$1.28	NR	$1.47
	1963	$1.72	$1.34	$1.30	NR	$1.52
	1964	$1.71	NR	$1.30	NR	$1.47

SELECTED PRICES 1960-1964

Item	Source	Description	Price
Alcohol			
Scotch	*New York Times* (1964)	*Clan MacGregor Rare Scotch;* 4/5 quart	$4.79
Whiskey	*New York Times* (1964)	*Canadian Club Whiskey;* full quart	$7.85
Apparel, Children's			
Blouse	*Ivey's of Charlotte, NC* (1963)	*Liberty;* print cotton; Bermuda collar, roll sleeves; cranberry or loden	$4.00
Blouse	*Ivey's of Charlotte, NC* (1963)	*Smarteens;* print cotton blouse; red and blue on beige	$3.00
Boy Scout Uniform	*Boy's Life* (1962)	Complete uniform including field cap, shirt trousers, web belt, cotton socks, one-color neckerchief, braided slide, metal slide	$10.75
Brassiere	*Ivey's of Charlotte, NC* (1963)	*Teenform Pretty Please Gro-Cup;* helanca nylon stretch lace cups	$1.75
Briefs	*Ivey's of Charlotte, NC* (1963)	*Atkinson;* cotton knit for boys; fit smoothly with just the right amount of snugness	$2/3pr
Coat	*Ivey's of Charlotte, NC* (1963)	*N.Y. Mackintosh;* winter coat for girls; with DuPont Orlon acrylic pile liner with full sleeves	$18.00
Coat	*Ivey's of Charlotte, NC* (1963)	*Atkinson;* muted plaid; all-weather coat with an iridescent gleam	$23.00
Cullotte	*Ivey's of Charlotte, NC* (1963)	*College Teens;* wool flannel, in grey or camel	$8.00
Dress	*Ivey's of Charlotte, NC* (1963)	*Little Star;* plaid cotton dress; deep tones keep fresh through hardest play; black watch or red plaids	$5.00
Duster	*Ivey's of Charlotte, NC* (1963)	*Pettirobe;* printed quilted cotton; a self-ruffle circles the collar cuffs	$8.00
Hat and Bag	*Sears, Roebuck* (1964)	Cotton velveteen	$4.57
Jumper	*Ivey's of Charlotte, NC* (1963)	*Maybro;* madras-inspired wool jumper; fashion-noted with a bateau neckline, self-belt	$11.00
Overalls	*Ivey's of Charlotte, NC* (1963)	*Kid-Bits;* completely washable, long-wearing corduroy	$3.00
Pajamas	*Sears, Roebuck* (1964)	Boys; here's the whole TV gang: Deputy Dog, Terry Bears, Pepiko Mouse	$1.99
Parka	*Ivey's of Charlotte, NC* (1963)	*Walter Jerome of Tidykins;* for girls; reversible quilted nylon, filled with ultra-warm Kodel polyester	$23.00
Shirt	*Ivey's of Charlotte, NC* (1963)	*Atkinson;* combed cotton; for teens; tasteful good looks, just wash-n-wear	$3.00

Item	Source	Description	Price
Shirt	*Ivey's of Charlotte, NC* (1963)	*Atkinson;* short sleeves; cotton knit; wonderfully washable, always handsome with its trimmed fashion collar	$3.00
Shirt	*Sears, Roebuck* (1964)	*Ban-Lon;* knit	$2.97
Shoes	*Boy's Life* (1962)	*Buster Brown Cub Scout Shoe;* sizes 1 to 6; can take it over the roughest trails	$9.99
Shoes	*Ivey's of Charlotte, NC* (1963)	*Jumping Jack The Sabot;* black patent or velvet 8 1/2 to 12 12 1/2 to 14 Big teens	$6.98 $7.98 $8.98
Shoes	*Ivey's of Charlotte, NC* (1963)	*Jumping Jack Loafers;* for girls; in new cordo brown	$7.98
Shoes	*Sears, Roebuck* (1964)	Classic saddle	$3.97
Shoes	*Life* (1964)	*Caumet;* V-toe shoe for teens	$9.99
Ski Hood	*Ivey's of Charlotte, NC* (1963)	*Maybro;* for teens; nylon shell, zipper front, drawstring hood and waist; elastic cuffs	$6.00
Slacks	*Ivey's of Charlotte, NC* (1963)	*Danskin;* stretch nylon; will stay in place, won't ride up; wash easy	$5.00
Slacks	*Ivey's of Charlotte, NC* (1963)	*Atkinson;* combed cotton for teens; Ivy model; wash-n-wear Slims Huskies	$4.00 $5.00
Slicker	*Ivey's of Charlotte, NC* (1963)	*Spatz;* waterproof; fashioned just like a sou'wester with metal-snap fasteners and a protective matching helmet	$4.00
Slip	*Ivey's of Charlotte, NC* (1963)	*Alice Aiken;* blouse slip; DuPont dacron polyester-cotton; delicate lace trim	$4.00
Snowsuit	*Sears, Roebuck* (1964)	*Convert-A-Babe;* a bunting at 6 months; a bootee suit at 12 months; an outdoor suit to 24 months	$9.80
Sweater	*Ivey's of Charlotte, NC* (1963)	*Jacquard;* v-neck cardigan for boys; of DuPont orlon acrylic; charcoal, red	$5.00
Sweater	*Ivey's of Charlotte, NC* (1963)	Scandinavian-type ski sweater for teens; features a colorful snowflake pattern	$7.00

Apparel, Men's

Item	Source	Description	Price
Coat	*Time* (1962)	Forget wrinkles this fall; dacron is here	$90.00
Coat	*Sears, Roebuck* (1964)	Pile lining adds even more warmth	$19.70
Garters	*Sears, Roebuck* (1964)	Double grip	$1.44
Shirt	*Time* (1960)	*Manhattan Mansmooth* shirt; the no-iron 100 percent cotton shirt that stays neat and wrinkle-free all day, Each	$5.00
Shirt	*Time* (1960)	*Sir Pendleton;* when leisure and dignity mix; 100 percent virgin wool shirt with impeccable tailoring	$17.50

Item	Source	Description	Price
Shirt	*New York Times* (1964)	Silk and knit sportshirt; tailored for comfort	$7.95
Shirt	*Chicago Tribune* (1962)	*Hathaway;* the world's coolest sportshirt	$8.95
Shirt	*Life* (1963)	*Manhattan Golf;* because it's 65% dacron, 35% combed cotton, it's light; solids, iridescents, white	$5.00
Shoes	*Chicago Tribune* (1962)	*Johnston & Murphy;* regularly $29.95 and $34.95	$21.90
Shoes	*Chicago Tribune* (1962)	*Johnston & Murphy;* hand-sewn moccasins; regularly $16.95 and $17.95	$10.90
Shoes	*Saturday Evening Post* (1964)	*Nunn-Bush;* ankle-fashioning provides superior, tensile, coddling fit	$19.95–$39.95
Shoes	*Sears, Roebuck* (1964)	The priceless-looking wing-tip	$21.70
Slacks	*Sears, Roebuck* (1964)	Finely tailored all-wool worsted slacks	$11.90
Socks	*Life* (1960)	*Supp-hose;* how to be supported in style	$4.95
Suit	*Time* (1960)	*Michaels, Stern & Company;* gray worsted plaid suit	$80.00
Suit	*Time* (1961)	*Worsted-Tex;* the 10-monther suit; all-climate suit	$69.50
Suit	*Time* (1962)	Wrinkles are now obsolete for fall; and dacron did it	$90.00
Apparel, Women's			
Blazer	*Life* (1961)	*McGregor Meteor;* lined with batik-printed cotton	$25.95
Brassiere	*Life* (1961)	*Formfit;* lifts me lovely, and ends under-cup curl-up forever	$3.00
Dress	*Seventeen* (1960)	*DuPont 100% Dacon polyester fiber dress;* upkeep is almost non-existent	$20.00
Dress	*Seventeen* (1960)	*Lord & Taylor* dress; the dating costume in pure silk print; junior sizes 5 to 15	$24.95
Dress	*Chicago Tribune* (1962)	*Miller's Fashion Plate;* a divine shirtdress of exquisite dacron and cotton; newest Italian collar; price includes 3-letter monogram	$14.95
Dress	*Chicago Tribune* (1962)	*Norman;* cool-as-a-garden patio casual	$6.00
Dress	*Sears, Roebuck* (1964)	The positive flair for after five	$22.00
Dress	*Life* (1964)	*Macy's;* navy; flare-skirted, trimmed with gold braid	$120
Hair Bow	*Sears, Roebuck* (1964)	Double-fabric cotton and rayon grosgrain	$1.00
Hat	*Sears, Roebuck* (1964)	Pleated pillbox; veil	$3.97
Purse	*Seventeen* (1960)	*Princess Gardner French Purse;* made of lustrous leather	$5.00
Shoes	*Minneapolis Morning Tribune* (1964)	*QualiCraft Dress Shoes;* lots of styles	$2.99
Socks	*Seventeen* (1960)	Adler worsted wool knee high socks	$2.00
Shoe Cover	*Life* (1960)	*Rain Dears;* for all but spike heels	$2.00
Slacks	*Life* (1961)	*McGregor Meteor;* a terrific blend of 50% dacron polyester and 50% cotton	$10.00

Item	Source	Description	Price
Stockings	*Chicago Tribune* (1964)	Ultra-sheer seamless; box of 6 prs	$5.28
Stole	*Sears, Roebuck* (1964)	Natural brown mink; 5 skins	$149
Sweater	*Greenville News* (Greenville, SC) (1963)	*Belk's;* ribbon-front cardigan; in six fashion colors	$7.99
Swimsuit	*Life* (1964)	*Rose Marie Reid Vanessa;* the look based on bold nylon print; boldly designed	$24.00
Veil	*New York Times* (1964)	Imported French silk lace veiling; for keeping coiffures from the wind	$5.00

Appliances

Item	Source	Description	Price
Air Conditioner	*Chicago Tribune* (1962)	*Admiral;* 5800 btu	$158
Air Conditioner	*Chicago Tribune* (1962)	*Kelvinator* 6700 btu; 7 ½ amp	$169
Appliances	*New York Times* (1964)	*RCA Whirlpool Air Conditioners;* 1 HP, 7 ½ AMP	$179
Dryer	*Minneapolis Morning Tribune* (1964)	*Hamilton Gas Dryer;* ideal for all fabrics	$188
Hot Water Heater	*Sears, Roebuck* (1964)	Gas-type burner, oil fired; 30-gal glass lined tank	$229.95
Humidifier	*Minneapolis Morning Tribune* (1964)	*Air King* humidifier; sends out fresh air to many rooms; includes extra-large 346 cubic inch filter	$49.00
Mixer	*The Saturday Evening Post* (1961)	*Sunbeam's Deluxe Mixmaster Mixer;* the quality mixer that does everything	$49.95
Portable Radio	*Seventeen* (1960)	*Zenith's Royal 50;* the smallest pocket radio plays up to 75 hours on 40 cents worth of batteries	$29.95
Refrigerator	*Chicago Tribune* (1964)	*Admiral;* 11.1 cu ft; no money down—only $1.50 a week	$158.88
Refrigerator	*San Bernardino (California) Evening Telegram* (1963)	*Frigidaire Frostproof Refrigerator;* absolutely no frost, no defrosting, 162 lb. Freezer Easy Terms	$478.88
Stove	*San Bernardino (California) Evening Telegram* (1963)	*Modern Maid Gas Cook-Top;* drop-in type with thermal eye top 28" x 21"	$72.20
Stove	*Sears, Roebuck* (1964)	Automatic from top to bottom	$249.95

Baby Products

Item	Source	Description	Price
Bath Set	*Sears, Roebuck* (1964)	Attaches firmly to tub with 4 suction cups for bath-time safety	$2.57
Car Seat	*Sears, Roebuck* (1964)	Extra-safe style made of strong flexible, high impact styrene	$6.95
Doll	*San Bernardino (California) Evening Telegram* (1963)	Baby Doll in Cradle; 15" fully jointed doll with rooted hair and moving eyes; regular $5.98	$3.99
Feeding Set	*Sears, Roebuck* (1964)	3-piece; features the Flintstones; will delight any child	$1.99

Item	Source	Description	Price
Business Equipment and Services			
Briefcase	*Ivey's of Charlotte, NC* (1963)	*Digby;* sturdy vinyl and split-cowhide brief bag is roomy 16"	$8.00
Dictating System	*Time* (1960)	*Sound Scriber;* dictating system for the office of the space age; complete satellite system	$161.00
Fountain Pen	*Time* (1960)	*Sheaffer's PFM;* pen for men; with unique inlaid point and snorkel pen cleaning action	$14.95
Microfilm	*Time* (1961)	*Recordak;* 100-foot roll of 16mm microfilm, including processing cost	$4.90
Name Purchase	*The Scribner Encyclopedia of American Lives, 1987*	Price paid by Ray Kroc to obtain unrestricted use of the name McDonalds in 1961	$2.7 million
Store Rental	*San Bernardino (California) Evening Telegram* (1963)	*Northland Center;* attractive 16' X 50' store building at Highland's newest commercial center on Base Line just west of Palm Per month	$125
Typewriter	*Ivey's of Charlotte, NC* (1963)	*Royalite;* with latest feature, carry case, standard keyboard, pica or elite	$49.95
Education			
Dance Lessons	*Chicago Tribune* (1962)	*Fred Astaire;* you'll be dancing tonight; introductory offer, reg $56	$19.50
Driving Lessons	*Chicago Tribune* (1962)	*Goldblatt's Learn to Drive;* Illinois Easy Method; beginner's course	$46.88
Public School Education	*Time* (1961)	Per pupil expenditure in Delaware Mississippi	$460 $225
Tuition	*Boy's Life* (1962)	*Augusta Military Academy;* distinguished ROTC school in Shenandoah Valley; boys 8–20	$1,300/yr
Entertainment			
Broadway Play	*New York Times* (1964)	*Luv;* a new comedy; Booth Theatre Monday to Thursday evenings, Orchestra Friday and Saturday evenings, Orchestra	 $6.90 $7.50
Dance Concert	*San Bernardino (California) Evening Telegram* (1963)	*Beach Boys, The Astronauts, and The Torquays;* you might even be on TV. Channel 18 will telecast the dance from 9:30 pm to 10:30 pm, so no jeans, capris or toredors; couples only Per couple, in advance Per couple, at door	 $4.00 $4.50
Drive-In Movie	*San Bernardino (California) Evening Telegram* (1963)	*Mt. Vernon Motor-In Theatre;* Rock Hudson in *A Gathering of Eagles* Per Car	 $1.50
Hockey Game	*Minneapolis Morning Tribute* (1964)	Professional Hockey; Minneapolis vs. Cincinnati; per seat	$2.50 $2.00 $1.50
Ice Skate Show	*Minneapolis Morning Tribute* (1964)	*Ice Capades;* six nights Tickets	 $2.00 $2.50 $3.00 $3.50
Movie	*Minneapolis Morning Tribute* (1964)	Walt Disney's *The Sword and the Stone,* children	$0.50

Item	Source	Description	Price
Movie	*Minneapolis Morning Tribune* (1964)	Metro-Goldwyn-Mayer's *How the West Was Won*	$2.25
Movie Ticket	*Greenville Times* (Greenville, SC) (1963)	*Promises, Promises!;* Jayne Mansfield; uncut and uncensored European version	$0.75
Symphony	*Minneapolis Morning Tribune* (1964)	*Minneapolis Symphony Orchestra;* Andre Watts, pianist	$2.75 to $5.00
Theater Ticket	*Chicago Tribune* (1962)	*The Sound of Music;* Schubert Theater; evenings Friday and Saturday	$2.50–$6.60

Entertainment, Home

Item	Source	Description	Price
Board Game	*San Bernardino (California) Evening Telegram* (1963)	*Parker Brothers Monopoly;* fun for all	$3.33
Camera	*Boy's Life* (1963)	*Kodak Brownie Super 27;* includes camera, neck strap, flash bulbs, batteries, film, instruction book	$22.00
Camera	*Chicago Tribune* (1964)	*Bell and Howell Canon 7;* F/1.8 lens	$149.50
Camera	*Chicago Tribune* (1964)	*Polaroid 100*	$99.95
Camera	*The Saturday Evening Post* (1961)	*Kodak;* The Brownie Starmite Camera; most compact camera with built-in flash ever offered	$12.00
Hi-Fi	*Seventeen* (1960)	*Webcor Hi-Fi Fonografs;* with the record changer that keeps things going	$29.95
High-Fi	*Time* (1961)	*Stereophonic Console Phonograph;* The Voice of Music; preserve the natural musical beauty of the live performance	$350
Movie Camera	*Popular Mechanics* (1962)	*Kodak Electric 8;* automatic; no lens setting, an electric eye automatically adjusts the super-fast F/1.6 lens to the light	$1,000
Projector	*Time* (1960)	*Keystone;* 8mm movie projector with motorized action-editor; with case	$220
Radio	*New York Times* (1964)	*Emerson Clock Radio;* wakes you to music; 5 tube chassis for crisp, clear highs, resonant lows	$19.88
Record	*Chicago Tribune* (1964)	*Peter, Paul & Mary*	$1.77
Record	*Chicago Tribune* (1964)	*Ella Fitzgerald*	$2.77
Record	*Chicago Tribune* (1964)	*Leontyne Price*	$2.77
Record Club	*Life* (1960)	*Columbia Record Club;* any 5 records, regular or stereo	$1.97
Stereo	*Saturday Evening Post* (1964)	*Admiral Playmate;* full-automatic phonograph with a long-distance radio	$59.95
Stereo	*Sears, Roebuck* (1964)	Four great speakers create a living wall of sound	$124.95
Stereo Phonograph	*Time* (1960)	*Magnavox Imperial Classic;* stereophonic high fidelity phonograph with superb FM/AM radio	$650
Stereo Theater	*Life* (1961)	*Magnavox Broadway;* superb stereophonic high fidelity; big optically filtered 23" television, FM/AM radio; automatic record player	$495

Item	Source	Description	Price
Tape Recorder	*Time* (1962)	*RCA Victor;* tape cartridge recorder; ends forever the loose tape worries of conventional reel to reel recorders	$99.95
Tape Recorder	*Time* (1960)	*Webcor Regent Cornet;* professionally engineered for three-speed, 4-track stereo (and monaural) record and playback	$139.95
Television	*Sears, Roebuck* (1964)	All channel; 19" with VHF remote control	$179.95
Television	*Life* (1964)	*General Electric;* portable; black and white; 12-lb personal portable with 11" screen	$99.95
Television	*Chicago Tribune* (1964)	*General Electric;* 23" console; with lifetime circuit board guarantee	$179.88
Television	*Chicago Tribune* (1964)	*General Electric;* 19" portable	$139.95

Food Products

Item	Source	Description	Price
Apples	*Greenville News* (Greenville, SC) (1963)	Red Delicious	$0.10/lb
Baby Food	*Chicago Tribune* (1962)	*Clapp's;* what a variety to choose from; you can keep baby healthy 'n happy with all kinds of meal variety; 4-oz jar	$0.25/3
Baby Food	*San Bernardino (California) Evening Telegram* (1963)	*Beech-Nut Strained Baby Food* 3 jars for	$0.29
Bacon	*Chicago Tribune* (1962)	*Corn King;* fresh corn-country flavor	$0.49/lb
Baked Beans	*Chicago Tribune* (1962)	*Heinz Pork and Beans;* for outdoor suppers	$0.12
Bananas	*Minneapolis Morning Tribune* (1964)	Golden Ripe Bananas, per pound	$0.10
Bologna	*Minneapolis Morning Tribune* (1964)	*Swift's Premium Large Bologna* by the piece; per pound	$0.39
Bread	*Greenville News* (Greenville, SC) (1963)	*Big Star;* 14 oz; sandwich bread; per loaf	$0.19
Butter	*Minneapolis Morning Tribune* (1964)	*Land O' Lakes Sweet Cream Butter;* 1 pound carton	$0.69
Cake Mix	*Minneapolis Morning Tribune* (1964)	*Pillsbury Cake Mixes;* 4 packages	$1.00
Catsup	*Chicago Tribune* (1962)	*Hunt's;* a tangy sauce for picnic foods; 14-oz bottle	$0.39/2
Cheese	*Minneapolis Morning Tribune* (1964)	*Bongards' Natural Cheddar Cheese;* 2 pound package	$0.89
Coffee	*Greenville News* (Greenville, SC) (1963)	*Maxwell House*	$0.38/lb
Crackers	*Chicago Tribune* (1964)	*Nabisco;* 16-oz package	$0.25
Dates	*San Bernardino (California) Evening Telegram* (1963)	*Mac's Date Shop;* new crop 3 pounds	$0.98

Item	Source	Description	Price
Diet Drink	*Time* (1960)	*Metrecal by Mead Johnson and Company;* weight-reducing liquid drink; 8 oz. Can	$1.29
Drink Powder	*San Bernardino (California) Evening Telegram* (1963)	*Nestle's Quik;* nutritious chocolate drink; two pound tin	$0.66
Fish	*Minneapolis Morning Tribune* (1964)	*Booth's Frozen Walleye Fillets;* 12 ounce package	$0.59
Fish	*Minneapolis Morning Tribune* (1964)	*Del Monte Chunk Style Tuna Fish;* 6 ½ ounce can	$0.22
Flour	*Greenville News* (Greenville, SC) (1963)	*Golden Rose;* 5-lb bag	$0.28
Green Beans	*Chicago Tribune* (1962)	Fresh; just can't find fresher finer produce; 2 lbs	$0.29
Ham	*Greenville News* (Greenville, SC) (1963)	*K-Mart;* cooked	$0.46/lb
Margarine	*Chicago Tribune* (1962)	*Bluebrook;* Bluebrook margarine melts quickly and deliciously on steaming fresh buns, adding just the right moistness and flavor	$0.15/lb
Meat	*Minneapolis Morning Tribune* (1964)	*Peters Braunschweiger;* 1 ½ pound chub	$0.59
Meat	*Chicago Tribune* (1962)	*National Food Stores;* Boston Butt steak or roast	$0.35/lb
Milk	*Greenville News* (Greenville, SC) (1963)	*Big Star;* tall can	$0.10
Peanut Butter	*Chicago Tribune* (1964)	*Jif;* plain or crunchy; 18-oz jar	$0.51
Peas	*Greenville News* (Greenville, SC) (1963)	*Argo;* June peas	$0.05
Pie	*Greenville News* (Greenville, SC) (1963)	*Morton's;* pumpkin pie; 20-oz package	$0.25
Potato Chips	*Chicago Tribune* (1962)	*So Fresh;* crisp . . . fresh; twin pack; 1-lb box	$0.49
Potatoes	*Greenville News* (Greenville, SC) (1963)		$0.05/lb
Potatoes	*Minneapolis Morning Tribune* (1964)	*Burbank Russet Potatoes;* U.S. No. 1, B size, 20 pound bag	$0.49
Salad Dressing	*Chicago Tribune* (1964)	*Kraft Miracle Whip;* quart jar	$0.43
Shortening	*Greenville News* (Greenville, SC) (1963)	*Snowdrift;* 3-lb can	$0.48
Shrimp	*San Bernardino (California) Evening Telegram* (1963)	*Crystal Seafood;* shrimp, per pound	$1.00
Soup	*Chicago Tribune* (1962)	*Campbell Chicken Noodle;* quick to fix—nourishing too	$0.16

Item	Source	Description	Price
Sweet Peas	*Chicago Tribune* (1964)	*Del Monte;* 16-oz cans	$0.33/2
Veal	*Minneapolis Morning Tribune* (1964)	*Swift's Premium Boneless Rolled Veal Roast;* per pound	$0.59

Furniture

Item	Source	Description	Price
Bed	*Greenville News* (Greenville, SC) (1963)	Cherry poster; spool bed; double size	$89.99
Bed	*Sears, Roebuck* (1964)	Triple decker bunk	$149.95
Bed	*Sears, Roebuck* (1964)	Colonial divan; cloud soft comfort; becomes 72" x 53" bed	$194.95
Cigarette Table	*Sears, Roebuck* (1964)	Cut from the central core of the walnut tree	$28.95
Desk	*Greenville News* (Greenville, SC) (1963)	*Ethan Allen;* dresser desk; 4' 8"; 4 drawer	$85.60
Lounge	*Chicago Tribune* (1964)	*Estee Sleep Shops;* our popular Empress foam lounge; not the skinny lounges you've seen at this price but a full 30" x 74" foam cushion; 4" thick	$49.88
Patio Umbrella	*New York Times* (1964)	Giant 8-foot lawn umbrella with automatic lift	$29.95
Sofa	*Greenville News* (Greenville, SC) (1963)	*Custom Built Furniture;* demand to be shown the U.S. Naugahyde trademark seal on the back of the fabric you are buying	$19.97
Sofa	*Greenville News* (Greenville, SC) (1963)	*Kirby Quinn;* walnut; modern; purple; list $182	$139.99

Garden Equipment and Supplies

Item	Source	Description	Price
Chain Saw	*San Bernardino (California) Evening Telegram* (1963)	*HomeLite Chain Saw*	$149.95
Fence	*San Bernardino (California) Evening Telegram* (1963)	Chain Link fence installed, per foot	$0.85
Ladder	*New York Times* (1964)	Heavy Duty Aluminum Extension Ladder; automatic steel locks	$19.99

Hotel Rates

Item	Source	Description	Price
Room Rate	*San Bernardino (California) Evening Telegram* (1963)	*Clark Hotel,* Los Angeles; central location Per day	$5.00
Room Rate	*Time* (1960)	*Essex House on the Park;* make this executive suite your office in New York; per night Single from / Double from / Executive Suites from	$16.00 / $20.00 / $30.00

Household Products

Item	Source	Description	Price
Baby Walker	*New York Times* (1964)	*Dennis Mitchell Baby Walker;* extra-wide wheel base	$5.99

Item	Source	Description	Price
Can Opener	Chicago Tribune (1964)	Westinghouse; automatic electric; truly automatic—just slide the switch on and can opens; no fuss, no holding, just a clean rolled edge	$8.44
Carpet	Greenville News (Greenville, SC) (1963)	Wunda Weve; surplus stock	$9.88/sq yd
Cleaner	San Bernardino (California) Evening Telegram (1963)	Mr. Clean household cleaner; giant 20 oz. size	$0.59
Cooker	Chicago Tribune (1962)	Sunburst Broil-Mate; play it cool this summer—don't cope with stifling oven temperatures in the kitchen	$5.99
Cookware	San Bernardino (California) Evening Telegram (1963)	Ekco Stainless Steel flint cookware; sauce pan with cover; magic radiant heat; 4 quart size	$5.98
Detergent	San Bernardino (California) Evening Telegram (1963)	Tide Detergent powder; giant size	$0.69
Doorknob	Sears, Roebuck (1964)	Provincial knob; antique English finish	$0.46
Drill	Life (1964)	Black & Decker U-100; 1/4" power drill	$9.88
Humidifier	Sears, Roebuck (1964)	Put a fresh breath of spring into dry parched air	$64.95
Kitchen Gloves	Life (1961)	Pioneer Ebonetts; neoprene to outlast rubber in fast acting cleaning aids	$0.98
Level	Sears, Roebuck (1964)	68" magnesium level	$18.50
Light	Popular Mechanics (1962)	Magna-Lite shop light; put the light where it's needed; with magnet base	$6.95
Light Bulbs	Boy's Life (1962)	El-Tronics, Inc. Solar; handy six-pack	$1.50
Mailbox	Sears, Roebuck (1964)	What an elegant way to get mail	$8.25
Midget Pliers	Sears, Roebuck (1964)	Cutting pliers for fast accurate bench work	$2.64
Percolator	Chicago Tribune (1964)	Universal Coffiesta	$9.88
Sander	Popular Mechanics (1962)	Millers Falls; 12 times faster than hand sanding	$34.95
Sander-Polisher	Sears, Roebuck (1964)	It's almost like having three sanders and polishers in one	$48.99
Saw	Popular Mechanics (1962)	Dremel Model 572; in one compact, portable unit you have a jig saw, disc sander, buffing wheel, bench grinder and a flexible shaft machine	$49.95
Silverware	Seventeen (1960)	Reed & Barton solid silver patterns; six-piece place setting	$35 to $45
Soap	San Bernardino (California) Evening Telegram (1963)	Cascade for automatic dishwashers; 20 oz. size	$0.33
Soldering Gun	The Saturday Evening Post (1961)	Weller Soldering Gun Kit; a tool for repairs, electrical work and hobbies	$7.95
Switch Plate	Sears, Roebuck (1964)	Gleaming white ceramic accented with gold trim; double	$1.99
Tools and Tool Chest	Popular Mechanics (1962)	Craftsman; 59-piece set; regular separate prices total $69.95; all tools fit in 18" x 8" x 9" steel tool box	$39.99

Item	Source	Description	Price
Jewelry			
Bracelet	*Sears, Roebuck* (1964)	From West Germany	$3.30
Jewelry Box	*Seventeen* (1960)	*Mele Jewel Case;* the Pandora, the ultimate in luxury	$19.98
Necklace	*Chicago Tribune* (1962)	*Pakula;* new year-round tones; browns, blues, greens, orange; in a three-strand Cleopatra choker	$3.00
Necklace	*Sears, Roebuck* (1964)	Gold-color metal, intriguing textured balls strung on supple chain	$5.50
Ring	*New York Times* (1964)	*Lambert Brothers* oval diamond engagement ring	$350
Watch	*San Bernardino (California) Evening Telegram* (1963)	*Timex Wrist Watch;* ladies' and men's	$6.95 to $39.95
Watch	*Time* (1960)	*Omega Ladymatic* watch with stainless steel case, water and shock resistant	$115
Watch	*Seventeen* (1960)	*Bulova Senator Watch;* 17 jewels; shock-resistant	$35.75
Watch	*Boy's Life* (1962)	*Timex;* Boy Scout wrist watch; takes a licking and keeps on ticking	$9.95
Watch	*Saturday Evening Post* (1964)	*Longines Admiral Jubilee;* 5-star Admiral automatic watch	$125
Watch	*Saturday Evening Post* (1964)	*Longines-Wittnauer;* with the world's most advanced, self-powered wrist watch movement	$125
Watch	*Sears, Roebuck* (1964)	Barbie's picture is on the dial, a reminder of her favorite doll	$8.95
Meals			
Breakfast	*Chicago Tribune* (1962)	*Walgreens Cafeterias;* this week's breakfast buy; 2 hot cakes, 2 strips bacon, and maple syrup	$0.33
Dinner	*San Bernardino (California) Evening Telegram* (1963)	*San Franciscan Steak House;* family buffet Thanksgiving dinner; roast young Tom turkey and ham Adults Children	 $2.50 $1.50
Dinner	*San Bernardino (California) Evening Telegram* (1963)	*B&B Rancho;* broiled steak and lobster combination	$3.25
Dinner Theatre	*New York Times* (1964)	*Restaurant Voisin;* dinner menu and courtesy limousine service to theatre Prix-Fixe Price	 $9.50
Lunch	*Chicago Tribune* (1962)	*Walgreens Cafeterias;* delicious home-cooked flavor; chicken pot pie with garden vegetables under a flaky crust	 $0.49
Lunch	*San Bernardino (California) Evening Telegram* (1963)	*Taco Aqui;* taco, tostada and beans Tacos, 5 for	$0.50 $0.95
Medical Products and Services			
Acne Medicine	*Boy's Life* (1962)	*Clearasil;* the man's way to clear pimples fast	$0.98

Item	Source	Description	Price
Analgesic Powder	*Life* (1961)	*Stanback;* quick relief of pain due to headache, neuralgia, cold	$0.98
Antacid	*San Bernardino (California) Evening Telegram* (1963)	*Maalox Antacid;* non-constipating, 12 oz. Size	$0.96
Antacid	*Life* (1961)	*Tums;* for acid indigestion; per roll	$0.12
Cold Medicine	*Saturday Evening Post* (1964)	*Contac;* over 600 tiny time pills in each Contac capsule keeps working all day or night; 10 continuous-action capsules	$1.49
Lip Balm	*Life* (1961)	*Chap-et;* relieves chapped dry lips	$0.35
Make-Up Cream	*Seventeen* (1960)	*Dermacare,* a new plan for blemish control; per tube	$1.25

Motorized Vehicles, Supplies, and Services

Item	Source	Description	Price
Air Conditioner	*Chicago Tribune* (1962)	*Mark IV;* air condition your present car with Mark IV	$279
Air Conditioner	*American Motorist* (1963)	Be cool this summer, completely installed	$299.95
Air Conditioner	*American Motorist* (1963)	*Mark IV;* commuter, air conditioner; fits many American cars; starts cooling in seconds; completely installed	$289.50
Airplane	*Time* (1961)	*Cessna 310F;* leave your competitors behind	$62,500
Alignment	*American Motorist* (1963)	All American cars; foreign cars and parts additional	$3.95
Auto Leasing	*San Bernardino (California) Evening Telegram* (1963)	*Travel Leasing Company* Per Day Per Mile	$7.00 $0.07
Automobile	*Minneapolis Morning Tribune* (1964)	*Plymouth 2-Door Hardtop;* V-8 engine; 5-year, 50,000 mile warranty	$2,706
Automobile	*Life* (1961)	*Renault Dauphine;* have you ever jealously watched a Dauphine scoot in and out of heavy city traffic? You also get just a little bit more mileage than most other imports give, a lot more mileage than any bigger car	$1,385
Automobile	*Life* (1961)	*Chrysler Newport;* 60's price surprise; this is no junior edition; this is the full size Chrysler Newport with a small-size price tag	$2,964
Automobile	*Life* (1961)	*Rambler America;* look into Rambler excellence, classic 6	$1,845
Automobile	*Esquire* (1961)	*Chevrolet Corvair Monza;* suggested price $200 more than the '61 Corvair Monza with all sports options	$2,850
Automobile	*Esquire* (1961)	*Maserati*	$3,200
Automobile	*Popular Mechanics* (1962)	*Saab '96;* this car was built to be better and safer, not different	$1,895
Automobile	*Time* (1962)	*Peugeot;* the steel in a Peugeot is .9mm thick; you could overturn the car and remain unscathed; not that we recommend it, but Peugeots at the factory are tested this way	$2,250
Automobile	*Greenville News* (Greenville, SC) (1963)	*Ford Fastback Coupe;* radio, heater, whitewall tires	$3,095

Item	Source	Description	Price
Automobile	*Chicago Tribune* (1964)	*Pontiac Grand Prix*	$2,895
Automobile Painting Service	*American Motorist* (1963)	*Rainbow Auto Painters;* Washington's largest and busiest auto paint shop	$49.95
Automobile, Used	*Greenville News* (Greenville, SC) (1963)	*1957 Plymouth Belvedere;* hardtop coupe; v-8 powerflyte, radio, heater, whitewall tires, clean	$595
Automobile, Used	*Chicago Tribune* (1964)	*1963 Tempest;* here's a fine sedan 4 dr with low mileage	$1,593
Automobile, Used	*San Bernardino (California) Evening Telegram* (1963)	*1959 Cadillac Fleetwood Sedan;* 4-door hardtop	$2,895
Automobile, Used	*San Bernardino (California) Evening Telegram* (1963)	*1957 Dodge V-8 Lancer;* radio, heater, overhauled transmission, power steering and brakes	$595
Battery	*Chicago Tribune* (1964)	Installed free; guaranteed 24 months	$7.88
Brake Service	*Chicago Tribune* (1964)	*Korvette Tire Center;* all four wheels relined; free installation	$12.88
Car Bed	*New York Times* (1964)	*Teddy Tot's "Zip apart";* goes from car bed to car seat in a zip	$12.95
Convertible Tops	*Sears, Roebuck* (1964)	Appearance and pinpoint grain same as original equipment on most 1964 cars	$31.70
Floor Mats	*New York Times* (1964)	*Rubbermaid Heavy Duty Floor Mat* to protect your car Rear Front	 $6.99 $9.50
Garage Door Opener	*Minneapolis Morning Tribune* (1964)	*Auto-Mate Overhead Garage Door Operator;* completely installed	$159.95
Radio	*American Motorist* (1963)	*Motorola;* all transistor; installed free; with free antenna	$29.95
Repair	*San Bernardino (California) Evening Telegram* (1963)	Ring and valve grind special; includes labor and parts, new rings, wrist pins, grind valves and seats 6 cylinder 8 cylinder	 $48.50 $58.50
Seat Belts	*New York Times* (1964)	*Hickok Seat Belt;* Royal Traveler; Insist on Hickok, the largest manufacturer of seat belts	$12.95
Seat Belts	*American Motorist* (1963)	All-nylon caprolan, metal to metal installed	$5.95
Seat Covers	*Sears, Roebuck* (1964)	Channel quilted, all-vinyl seat covers	$23.49
Tires	*San Bernardino (California) Evening Telegram* (1963)	*Dary's Deluxe Retreads;* black wall Plus tax and tire exchange	 $7.88
Tires	*American Motorist* (1963)	*Fisk's;* 4-ply; custom tubeless nylon tires; rugged nylon carcass for added strength	$12.77
Tires	*Minneapolis Morning Tribune* (1964)	*B. F. Goodrich Black Tubeless Tires;* 6.50–13; per tire	$14.95
Washcloth	*American Motorist* (1963)	*Kozaks;* made by people you can depend on to do the right thing	$3.00

Musical Instruments

Item	Source	Description	Price
Clarinet	*Sears, Roebuck* (1964)	With standard B-flat Boehm style	$79.95

Item	Source	Description	Price
Keyboard Harmonica	*Sears, Roebuck* (1964)	25 keys, 2 octaves	$11.95
Organ	*San Bernardino (California) Evening Telegram* (1963)	*Estey Electric Organ,* used	$149.50

Other

Item	Source	Description	Price
Autograph Hound	*Ivey's of Charlotte, NC* (1963)	*Sutton;* the whole crowd will sign on Snippy, the long, long 25" autograph hound	$2.00
Bird Food	*San Bernardino (California) Evening Telegram* (1963)	*HAP Parakeet Seed;* contains millet, canary seed and oats; 2 pound bag	$0.29
Charcoal	*Chicago Tribune* (1962)	*Easy Life;* 20-lb bag	$0.85
Dog	*San Bernardino (California) Evening Telegram* (1963)	Registered Dachshund puppies; small deposit holds until Christmas Each	$35.00
Dog	*New York Times* (1964)	Poodle; all mamas had pups at once; special this week; each	$85.00
Flag	*Boy's Life* (1962)	American flag set; includes 3' x 5' printed cotton flat, 1-piece 6' pole of sturdy aluminum, metal wall bracket, halyard, flag courtesy holder	$3.95
Flower Delivery	*Life* (1963)	*FTD:* Mother's Day flower arrangement; glads, carnations, pompons and greens, delivered any place in the U.S. and Canada	$7.50
Glasses	*Chicago Tribune* (1964)	*Wieboldt's;* single vision; white lenses and frame	$9.95
Marker	*Life* (1960)	*Carter Marks-a-Lot;* with felt tip	$0.59
Model Paint	*Boy's Life* (1963)	*Testor's;* look at the models that win competitions and you'll see the difference PLA enamels make, matching colors	$0.15
Paneling	*San Bernardino (California) Evening Telegram* (1963)	*Wickes;* plywood paneling, ¼" width; 4' x 8' prefinished V groove sheets; per sheet Rustic Birch Philippine Mahogany Knotty Cedar Walnut	 $5.60 $4.00 $6.40 $10.08
Pen	*Ivey's of Charlotte, NC* (1963)	*Parker-T-Ball Jotter;* in black, light grey, green, bright red, dark blue	$1.98
Pen	*Saturday Evening Post* (1964)	*Scripto Tilt-Tip;* with skip-proof tungsten ball for smooth writing	$1.98
Pen/Pencil	*Boy's Life* (1962)	*Scripto;* official, dependable, rugged, slim, lightweight, vest-locking, smooth-writing	$1.95
Portrait	*New York Times* (1964)	*Stern's Father Day Special;* three photographs of you or your child; 5 x 7 portrait	$4.95
Schoolbag	*Ivey's of Charlotte, NC* (1963)	*Digby's;* in ginger, tan, olive; serv-a-lon	$3.00
Sea Horses	*Boy's Life* (1962)	*Florida Sea Horse Co.;* live; pair of dwarf species of living sea horses from Florida	$3.50
Slide Rule	*Popular Mechanics* (1962)	4"; non-warp with 2-color scales on white nitiate face	$2.95

Item	Source	Description	Price
Umbrella	*Ivey's of Charlotte, NC* (1963)	Your little girl's name personalized on the handle	$3.00
Wood	*Minneapolis Morning Tribune* (1964)	Dry firewood; per stove cord	$11.00

Personal Care Products

Item	Source	Description	Price
Bathroom Tissue	*San Bernardino (California) Evening Telegram* (1963)	*Chiffon Tissue;* assorted colors, first quality Per roll	$0.10
Cologne	*San Bernardino (California) Evening Telegram* (1963)	*Shuffton Old Spice for Men* Set	$1.25 and up
Face Lotion	*Esquire* (1961)	*English Leather After Shave;* after shower, after hours	$2–$10
Hair Cream	*San Bernardino (California) Evening Telegram* (1963)	*Brylcreem Hair Dressing;* king size tube	$0.59
Haircut	*Life* (1964)	Rothschild Barber Shop in Beverly Hills, California	$2.50
Lip Cream	*The Saturday Evening Post* (1961)	*Blistex;* cure; sore lips, cold sores, chapped lips, fever blisters	$0.39
Make-Up	*Seventeen* (1960)	*Pond's Angel Touch Liquid Make-Up;* nine soft-and-subtle shades; per bottle	$1.00
Makeup Kit	*Life* (1961)	*Merle Norman 3 Steps to Beauty;* includes all-purpose cold cream, miracle powder base	$6.50
Mouthwash	*Life* (1960)	*Vi-Jon;* for bad breath, colds, sore throat; 6-oz size bottle free with purchase of family size	$0.49
Perfume	*Seventeen* (1960)	*Lentheric Miracle* perfume; 1/2 ounce	$10.00
Perfume	*Seventeen* (1960)	*Chanel No. 5* spray perfume; good things come in small packages	$5.00
Perfume	*New York Times* (1964)	*Elizabeth Arden Blue Grass Flower Mist,* 4 ounces	$2.00
Permanent	*San Bernardino (California) Evening Telegram* (1963)	*Belladona Beauty Salon;* Brush Back Permanent special	$4.50
Permanent Wave	*Chicago Tribune* (1962)	*Helene Curtis Baroness Rhapsody;* permanent wave	$7.50
Shaver	*Seventeen* (1960)	*Lady Ronson Superbe Electric Shaver;* two different cutting actions	$16.50
Soap	*Minneapolis Morning Tribune* (1964)	*Dial Soap;* 4 regular bars	$0.49
Tissues	*Chicago Tribune* (1964)	*Scott;* 2 packages of 400	$0.39
Toothbrush	*Chicago Tribune* (1964)	*Sunbeam;* electric; cordless	$11.44
Washcloth	*New York Times* (1964)	*Wash-Away,* disposable washcloth with instant suds	$1.00

Item	Source	Description	Price
Publications			
Book	*Hobbies* (1963)	*New Manual of Model Ship-Building* by P. M. Wright	$6.95
Book	*Time* (1960)	*Victory in the Pacific* by Samuel Eliot Morison; Atlantic-Little-Brown, publisher	$6.50
Dictionary	*Time* (1961)	*Webster's New World Dictionary;* 142,000 entries, 1,760 pages	$5.57
Magazine	*Life* (1961)	*Life Magazine;* weekly	$0.20
Magazine	*Boy's Life* (1962)	*Boy's Life;* monthly	$0.25
Time Magazine	*Time* (1960)	*The Weekly News Magazine* Per issue Per Year	 $0.25 $7.00
Real Estate			
Apartment	*San Bernardino (California) Evening Telegram* (1963)	Clean bachelor apartment completely furnished; Civic Center location Per month	 $57.50
Apartment	*San Bernardino (California) Evening Telegram* (1963)	*Starlite Apartments;* new two-bedroom units; colored fixtures in kitchen, snack bar, carpet and drapes	$127.50
Apartment	*Chicago Tribune* (1964)	For rent; 3 ½ rooms; gas included; newly decorated; near Lincoln Park golf course	$110/mo
Apartment	*Chicago Tribune* (1964)	For rent; 5 rooms, 2 bedrooms	$135/mo
Apartment Building	*New York Times* (1964)	East Bronx five-story walk-up; 16 apartments, 83 rooms; rent $12,725	$49,000
Apartment Building	*Chicago Tribune* (1964)	For sale; deluxe 3 flats; excellent income property at this preopening price for a limited time only	$47,500
Cooperative Apartment	*New York Times* (1964)	Apartments of 3 1/2, 4, 5, 6 rooms; some terraces; centrally air conditioned; gas and electric Priced from	 $16,250
Cottage	*Chicago Tribune* (1962)	For sale; Valparaiso, Indiana; on choice, spectacular lakefront; nice summer cottage; 72' x 30'; full basement, private parking lot and boat; completely furnished; cash or contract	 $7,850
Home	*New York Times* (1964)	Bucks County, Pennsylvania summer home; knotty pine; 3 bedrooms; modern conveniences; good fishing	$3,600
House	*Chicago Tribune* (1962)	For rent; 3 bedrooms, 1 bath, attached garage	$125/mo
House	*San Bernardino (California) Evening Telegram* (1963)	Raintree Valley View Homes; near College site in North San Bernardino; 4 bedrooms	$17,100
Land	*Greenville News* (Greenville, SC) (1963)	For sale; 55 acres, highway 296, near Five Forks, 1,700 ft river frontage; lovely open land, passenger and wooded area; Greenville, South Carolina area	 $9,950
Lot	*Chicago Tribune* (1962)	For sale; 1/2 acre corner; paved streets; close in; nice homes in area; terms	$1,900
Mobile Home	*San Bernardino (California) Evening Telegram* (1963)	Great Lakes home; Belmont; two-bedroom, 10' x 50	$3,895
Townhome	*Chicago Tribune* (1962)	For rent; 2 bedrooms	$106/mo

Item	Source	Description	Price
Sewing Equipment and Supplies			
Cloth	*San Bernardino (California) Evening Telegram* (1963)	Heavy sport cottons; plain or print; per yard	$0.79
Sports Equipment			
BB Gas Rifle	*Boy's Life* (1962)	*Benjamin Super 100;* no pumping, uniform high power	$19.95
BB Gun	*Dell Comic Book 6 Black Horses* (1962)	*Daisy 1894;* a spitting image of the model 94 Winchester; easy 2-way cocking action	$12.98
BB Gun	*Dell Comic Book 6 Black Horses* (1962)	*Daisy;* easy 2-way cocking action; realistic side-loading slim-line barrel	$12.98
BBs	*Dell Comic Book 6 Black Horses* (1962)	*Daisy;* copper coated from the world's largest manufacturer of B-Bs; per tube	$0.05/$0.10/$0.25
Fishing Lure	*Boy's Life* (1962)	*Fred Arbogast Hawaiian Wiggler;* for heavy brush and cover	$1.25
Fishing Reel	*Boy's Life* (1963)	*Zebco 20Z;* the lowest-priced foolproof spinning reel made in America	$5.95
Knife	*Boy's Life* (1962)	*Boy Scout;* brass-lined knife has four tempered carbon-steel blades	$1.75
Sailboat	*New York Times* (1964)	*The Sea Shark;* lightweight, unsinkable; 11 feet long; sail area 45 square feet	$99.75
Shotgun	*Boy's Life* (1962)	*O. F. Mossberg & Son;* boy's; single-shot .410 gauge; with youth-size stock and short barrel so you can shoulder accurately	$27.95
Sunraft	*Chicago Tribune* (1962)	*Abercrombie & Fitch;* inflatable; almost 20 sq ft of sunning surface	$29.95
Waders	*Sears, Roebuck* (1964)	Chest high	$16.50
Weights	*Sears, Roebuck* (1964)	Vinyl jacketed; 110-lb set with 2 dumbbells	$20.00
Telephone Equipment and Services			
Telephone	*Popular Mechanics* (1962)	*Western Electric;* late-model dial phone same as used by all the telephone companies; cost $40 new	$6.95
Tobacco Products			
Lighter	*Saturday Evening Post* (1964)	*Scripto Goldenglo;* compact Vu-Lighter	$5
Pipe	*Time* (1960)	*Kaywoodie;* for flavor, mildness, relaxation without inhaling Standard Relief Grain Connoisseur	$5.95 $7.95 $15.00
Pipe	*Popular Mechanics* (1962)	*Kirsten;* patented radiator stem means cool smoking	$3.95
Toys			
Art Board	*San Bernardino (California) Evening Telegram* (1963)	*Enlarg-A-Graph;* complete with many figures and scenes to enlarge; operates on D cell batteries, not included	$5.98
Board Game	*Boy's Life* (1963)	*Cadaco All-Star Baseball;* select your lineup from 40 present-day stars and 20 all-time greats	$3.00
Boat	*San Bernardino (California) Evening Telegram* (1963)	*Mighty Matilda Nuclear Aircraft Carrier;* with 100 man crew; 3 feet long	$8.88

Item	Source	Description	Price
Cannon	*San Bernardino (California) Evening Telegram* (1963)	*Remco Mighty Mo Cannon;* breech loading, remote control firing	$9.88
Cars	*Boy's Life* (1962)	*Matchbox;* made in England of die-cast metal	$0.50
Chemistry Set	*San Bernardino (California) Evening Telegram* (1963)	*Gilbert Chemistry Set* of plastic and glass; make dozens of exciting glass objects	$7.98
Doll	*San Bernardino (California) Evening Telegram* (1963)	*Ideal Doll; Bidsy;* she eats then bubbles like a real baby	$12.88
Doll Clothes	*Barbie and Ken Catalogue* (1963)	*Barbie Nighty-Negligee;* luxurious full-length gown; Grecian bodice with embroidered flowers	$3.00
Doll Clothes	*Barbie and Ken Catalogue* (1963)	*Barbie Icebreaker;* red velveteen skating skirt top with furry white jacket; red knit leotard with turtleneck and long sleeves, long stockings and skates complete the set	$3.00
Doll Clothes	*Barbie and Ken Catalogue* (1963)	*Barbie American Airline Stewardess;* Barbie takes off for sky adventures in her flight blue uniform with flight insignia on cap and jacket	$3.50
Model Kit	*Boy's Life* (1962)	*Hubley;* scale model metal kit; 1930 Packard Sport Phaeton, die cast in durable metal	$2.98
Model Kit	*Boy's Life* (1962)	*Hawk;* starfighter airplane; each model is actually metal plated with a coat of real aluminum and then covered with a high glass lacquer	$2.00
Model Kit	*Popular Mechanics* (1962)	*Aurora;* who would prefer a pokey loco going around in circles to the pulse-pounding action of a road race; includes land-changing criss-cross layout	$21.98

Travel and Transportation

Item	Source	Description	Price
Airline Fare	*Time* (1964)	*American Airlines;* starting January 15; we reduced our first class fares and our coach fare for families; New York to Los Angeles; first class	$160.90
Cruise	*American Motorist* (1963)	*Canada Steamship Lines;* through French Canada; Richelieu cruises, six days; steamer your hotel throughout	$149.50
Cruise	*American Motorist* (1963)	*Canada Steamship Lines Aristo;* 8 days includes Ritz-Carlton, Manoir Richelieu; Chateau Frontenac hotels	$204.50
Cruise	*New York Times* (1964)	Cruise on Queen Elizabeth; the World's largest liner; New York to Europe, roundtrip	
		Tourist	$316
		Cabin	$406
		First Class	$660
Land Sales Trip	*Chicago Tribune* (1964)	*Mackie Brothers;* special; all expense trip to Deltona, Florida; including meals, lodging and transportation for only	$50.00
Subway Token	*Life* (1963)	New York City	$0.15
Tour	*Time* (1962)	*Lufthansa;* visit Europe on a Budget tour	$485
Travel Kit	*New York Times* (1964)	Celebrity's travel kit with two zipper compartments, removable vinyl case with plastic fitting	$5.00
Trip	*American Motorist* (1963)	*AAA Travel Service;* Washington to Waikiki by jet; 14-day tour including hotel accommodations	$640

MISCELLANY 1960-1964

People

To help raise money for taxes, friends of the London Library put several prized manuscripts on the block of a local auctioneer. The final hand-written draft of *A Passage to India,* the great West-confronts-East novel by E. M. Forster, was knocked down for $18,200—said to be the highest price ever paid for a living author's manuscript. The buyer, a Manhattan rare books dealer, also picked up (for another client) a hand copy of T. S. Eliot's *The Wasteland,* faithfully duplicated by the poet in his own script because the original—last seen many years ago in Manhattan—is missing and presumed lost. Price: $7,840.

Time, July 4, 1960

Plenty of Sugar

When President Eisenhower last week decided to give Fidel Castro his lumps, he set off a flurry of excitement on the New York Coffee and Sugar Exchange, clearinghouse for much of the world's sugar. Just before Ike announced a slash of 700,000 tons in the amount of sugar that the U.S. would buy from Cuba during the rest of 1960, world sugar prices dropped 3 to 8 points, i.e., hundredths of a cent a pound, in expectation of the cut—and in fear that Cuba would dump its surplus sugar on the world market. Instead, Cuba raised its minimum export price from $3 to $3.25 a hundred pounds in an effort to recover part of its losses on sugar sales. Thereupon, in heavy trading world sugar futures shot up again, only to level off at week's end.

Time, July 18, 1960

The Yankee Tinkerers

The most fascinating phenomenon on Wall Street these days is the spectacular rise of the growth and glamour stocks. For investors who know how to choose well, they have made some tidy profits. They have also created a new class of management millionaires who rank with the Rockefellers and the big rich of Texas, and who prove that—despite high taxes—it is still quite possible in the U.S. to get impressively rich in a short time.

Among listed growth stocks, none has risen faster than one that appears on the ticker tape as FAV—the Fairchild Camera & Instrument Corp. An investor who bought $1,000 worth of Fairchild stock when it was selling at its 1958 low of 19 1/2, and held onto it, last week would have had nearly $18,000 worth of stock. Fairchild makes a long list of imaginative products, ranging from a new silicon superconductor to the first 8-mm. home sound motion-picture camera. It is one of the Street's most cherished buys, ranking with such rapid risers as Texas Instruments (72 1/8 to 214 1/4 in 18 months), Polaroid (97 1/4 to 245 1/2) and Universal Match (46 1/4 to 271 1/8 on a presplit basis).

Time, July 25, 1960

N.Y.U. Operating Giant Computer; $3,000,000 Device Digests 750,000 Facts a Second

The Courant Institute of Mathematical Sciences at New York University has begun operating an IBM 7090—the most powerful computer in use at any Eastern university.

The computer, which cost $3,000,000, will be used by the Atomic Energy Commission's Computing and Applied Mathematics Center at N.Y.U., as well as by scientists and institutions engaged in basic and applied mathematical research.

New York Times, November 2, 1961

Liquor Revenues Rose 4.6% In Year

Governmental revenues from alcoholic beverages in 1961 came to $4,687,872,807, or 4.6 per cent above the level of 1960, and brought the total collected since Repeal twenty-eight years before, to 76,747,276,116. The report noted that the Federal excise tax on distilled spirits is $10.50 a gallon and on beer, $9 a barrel of thirty-one gallons. The tax on a still wine gallon is as follows: Wine not over 14 per cent alcohol by volume, 17 cents; more than 14 and not exceeding 21 per cent, 67 cents; over 21 and not exceeding 24 per cent, $2.25.

New York Times, September 2, 1962

MISCELLANY 1960-1964

Greenwich Homes' Cost Highest In Connecticut

The median value of one-family homes in this town was the highest in the state in 1960, according to a survey by the Connecticut Department of Public Works.

The survey was based on owner estimates in the 1960 census. It showed that the median value—midpoint between the upper and lower halves—of Greenwich homes was $32,800. The town of Woodridge in New Haven County was second with a median value of $30,600.

Other Fairfield County figures were:

New Canaan	$26,862;
Darien	$26,298;
Westport	$26,082;
Weston and Wilton	$25,000;
Stamford	$23,800;
Norwalk	$20,600;
Bridgeport	$16,000;
Bethel	$15,376.

New York Times, September 2, 1962

HISTORICAL SNAPSHOT
1965-1969

1965

- Vietnam War intensifies
- President Lyndon Johnson's "Great Society" plan unveiled
- Americans buy $60 million worth of prescription weight-loss drugs
- Production of soft-top convertibles peaks at 507,000
- Avis Rent-A-Car acquired by International Telephone and Telegraph
- Saint Louis's Gateway Arch completed
- 1,250-room Washington Hilton opens in Washington, D.C.
- U.S. immigration bill abolishes national origin quotas

1966

- Student Protest against Vietnam War begins
- National Organization for Women (NOW) is founded
- Largest year-to-year rise in cost of living since 1958 announced—2.8 percent
- 2,377 corporate mergers take place
- New York subway fares rise to 20 cents
- Per capita consumption of processed potatoes reaches 44.2 pounds per year

- Taster's Choice freeze-dried instant coffee introduced

1967

- 2,975 corporate mergers occur
- 41 percent of nonwhite families make less than $3,000 annually
- *New York World Journal & Tribune* closes; *Rolling Stone* magazine founded
- 2.7 million Americans receive food stamp assistance
- Nearly 10,000 farmers receive more than $20,000 each in subsidies
- Annual beef consumption reaches 105.6 pounds
- Burger King Corporation acquired by Pillsbury Corporation
- U.S. population passes 200 million

1968

- Vietnam War and protests intensify
- Richard Nixon elected president
- 4,462 corporate mergers take place
- BankAmericard holders number 14 million, up 12 million in two years
- Automobile production reaches 8.8 million

- Volkswagen captures 57 percent of U.S. import market
- Oil discovered on Alaska's North Slope
- Television advertising revenues hit $2 billion, twice that of radio
- First-class postage rates climb to 6 cents
- Uniform Monday Holiday Law enacted by Congress, creating 3-day holiday weekend
- Average farm subsidy is nearly $1,000

1969

- Neil Armstrong walks on moon
- Average U.S. automobile wholesales at $2,280
- Panty hose production reaches 624 million pairs, up from 200 million in 1968
- Average U.S. farm produces enough food for 47 people
- Blue Cross health insurance covers 68 million Americans
- *Penthouse* magazine begins publication; *Saturday Evening Post* folds
- National Association of Broadcasters begins cigarette advertising phaseout

SELECTED INCOME 1965-1969

Job	Source	Description	Pay
Accounting	*Chicago Tribune* (1966)	Accounting Clerks	$500/mo
Actress	Legrand and Karney, *Chronicle of the Cinema* (1995)	Elizabeth Taylor's salary for her role in *Cleopatra* in 1963	$1 million
Actress	Legrand and Karney *Chronicle of the Cinema* (1995)	Audrey Hepburn's salary for *My Fair Lady* in 1964	$1 million
Advertising Copywriter	*New York Times* (1965)	Fine NYC agency wants package-goods TV writer; 2–5 years 4A experience; no job hoppers	$15,000–$40,000/yr
Airline Trainees	*New York Times* (1965)	No experience; train as reservationist	$75–$100/wk
Baseball Player	Jim Hunter, *Catfish My Life is Baseball* (1988)	Salary of Oakland Athletics pitcher Jim "Catfish" Hunter in 1967	$13,000
Basketball Star	*Time* (1968)	Annual salary of professional basketball center Wilt Chamberlain	$250,000
Chauffeur	*New York Times* (1967)	With or without experience	$65–$160/wk
Clerk	*New York Times* (1967)	Shipping Stock	$70–$100/wk
Comparative Analyst	*New York Times* (1965)	Know major medical coverage; college degree	$8500/yr
Comptroller	*Chicago Tribune* (1966)	Any age to 42. Degree not required, varied duties, good future	$12,000/yr
Counterman	*Chicago Tribune* (1966)	For retail building supply; capable of selling plywood, paneling, tile, etc; 5 days	$2.75/hr to start
Dishwasher	*Chicago Tribune* (1968)	Nights or days; experienced; car needed for transportation	$100/wk
Doctors	*Time* (1968)	Average annual pay of U. S. doctors	$31,160
Editor/Assistant	*New York Times* (1967)	BA Engineering, rewriting, editing	$100/wk
Executive Director	*New York Times* (1965)	Washington, D.C., youth agency	$11,000/yr
Football Player (1968)	*Time*	Minimum annual salary for a second-year professional football player in the National Football League	$12,000
Girl Friday	*Chicago Tribune* (1966)	To baby doctor; no medical experience needed to welcome tiny patients and their parents, announce their arrival, escort them to examination rooms where you help by weighing babies	$90/wk
Girl/Man Friday	*New York Times* (1967)	Park Avenue management consultant needs takeover right hand for top-level work	$150/wk
Greeter	*Chicago Tribune* (1968)	100% public contact; chance of lifetime for girl with light office skills, a nice smile and friendly personality	$125/wk

Job	Source	Description	Pay
Highway Designers	*Chicago Tribune* (1966)	From trainees to actual experience	$150–$175/wk
Hospital Receptionist	*Chicago Tribune* (1966)	Age to 40; will be front-desk receptionist for famous Chicago hospital; will answer phones, screen calls, do customer service, greet new patients, process new patients through hospital	$382/mo
Industrial Relations	*Chicago Tribune* (1966)	College graduate; train under the industrial relations manager of a world famous Chicago-based company	$600/mo
Inventor's Apprentice	*Chicago Tribune* (1966)	He'll train jack-of-all-trades	$475–$600/mo
Judges	*Time* (1968)	Average annual pay of General Court judges across America	$20,620
Keypunch Operator	*New York Times* (1965)	A/N; good at punctuation; paid overtime	$85/wk
Manager	*New York Times* (1965)	College degree; 1 year supervisory experience; head up correspondence department; top company	$6,500/yr
Model	*Playboy* (1996)	Modeling fee of Victoria Valentino, the *Playboy* Playmate for September, 1963	$1,000
Painter	James E. B. Breslin, *Mark Rothko: A Biography* (1993)	Annual earnings of Mark Rothko in 1967	$129,451
Performer (1968)	*Guinness Book of World Records* (1981)	Size of three-year television contract between Dean Martin and NBC	$34 million
Personnel Interviewer	*New York Times* (1965)	Diversified spot at leading temporary personnel company Midtown; fee paid	$100/wk
Personnel Interviewer	*Chicago Tribune* (1966)	We will thoroughly train you to interview, test, evaluate white-collar workers in our offices; age no barrier; 18–45 years	$75–$125/wk
Porter	*Chicago Tribune* (1968)	For AM shift in north suburban nursing home; must have transportation	$2.50/hr
Programmer Trainee	*New York Times* (1967)	College graduates, any degree; immediate hire	$7,000+/yr
Programmer Trainee	*Chicago Tribune* (1968)	HS Graduate with good figure aptitude; top firm offers complete training in the fascinating field of automated equipment; full training is at company expense; new class is forming now	$725/mo
Purchaser	*New York Times* (1967)	Relocation paid to Manila, including housing and car	$12,000/yr
Sales Promotion	*Chicago Tribune* (1968)	National firm with home office in Chicago needs men who can meet and talk with management-level executives of their clients	$8,400/yr
Sales Trainee	*New York Times* (1965)	MBA preferable for wholesaling	$9,000/yr
Sales Trainee	*Chicago Tribune* (1966)	Pharmaceuticals	$550/mo
Security Management	*Chicago Tribune* (1968)	Ex-GIs: this is a terrific opportunity for you to put your service experience to work; very little training is necessary; this multi-million-dollar firm has had great success in the past with young vets	$150/wk
Singer (1965)	*Guinness Book of World Records* (1981)	Single year earnings of singer/actor Elvis Pressley	$4.7 million
Technical Writers	*New York Times* (1967)	Top metro electronic career	$8,000– $10,000/yr

Job	Source	Description	Pay
Teletype	*New York Times* (1965)	Days or nights; light experience and ability to read tape	$450/mo
Tour Clerk	*Chicago Tribune* (1966)		$85/wk
Trainee	*Chicago Tribune* (1966)	Learn new products tests; high school enough	$435/wk
Troubleshooter	*Chicago Tribune* (1968)	All around the plant into everybody's hair, training everywhere!	$110–$160/wk
TV Station Receptionist	*Chicago Tribune* (1966)	HURRY this choice position will not last long; meet and greet TV stars, help answer fan mail and be on the inside of the television world	$400/mo
TV Trainee	*New York Times* (1965)	Job future; join #1 TV company; reach management fast	$5,200/yr
Typist	*Chicago Tribune* (1966)	Any typing; hunt and peck, slow or fast; if you type at all we have the jobs right now	$90/wk
Typist	*Chicago Tribune* (1968)	TV-Radio Studio; long-term assignment to start immediately	$3/hour
Wall Street Sales Trainee	*New York Times* (1965)	MBA preferable for wholesaling	$9,000/yr
Writers	*Time* (1968)	Daily rate of Presidential historians assigned the task of recording President Lyndon Johnson's accomplishments	$50

CONSUMER EXPENDITURES 1965-1969

(Per Capita)

Expenditure Type	1965	1966	1967	1968	1969
Clothing	$147.19	$158.73	$164.06	$178.87	$189.96
Food	$519.81	$555.05	$565.14	$605.86	$643.88
Auto Usage	$283.58	$294.06	$299.43	$338.80	$361.66
New Auto Purchase	$110.14	$106.84	$100.65	$122.07	$123.84
Auto Parts	$18.01	$19.33	$20.13	$22.92	$26.64
Gas & Oil	$76.17	$81.40	$86.05	$92.67	$101.15
Housing	$336.59	$353.58	$372.90	$397.09	$428.27
Furniture	$33.45	$35.61	$38.71	$39.36	$41.45
Utilities	$89.55	$93.10	$97.13	$100.15	$105.09
Telephone & Telegraph	$33.45	$35.61	$38.75	$41.35	$45.89
Physicians	$43.75	$46.29	$50.23	$54.31	$61.18
Dentists	$14.41	$15.26	$15.60	$19.93	$21.22
Health Insurance	$13.89	$15.26	$15.60	$19.93	$20.72
Personal Business	$107.56	$117.52	$128.83	$141.00	$144.07
Personal Care	$41.69	$45.79	$49.32	$52.81	$54.77
Tobacco	$41.69	$43.24	$44.79	$46.83	$48.35
Local Transport	$10.81	$10.68	$11.70	$11.96	$13.32
Intercity Transport	$10.29	$11.70	$13.59	$15.45	$18.26
Recreation	$137.93	$156.69	$166.57	$182.85	$196.86
Religion/Welfare Activities	$39.63	$43.24	$47.30	$51.32	$54.27
Private Education & Research	$41.99	$39.68	$43.78	$49.33	$54.77
Per Capita Consumption	$2288.18	$2450.14	$2563.01	$2785.67	$2978.63

"Come back to Hawaii"   "Best way to learn the hula is from island girl."

"You who know Hawaii
only in your dreams...
you who know Hawaii well
...come back to Hawaii."

There's an island for you in Hawaii, only $300 and a few
relaxing jet hours away from Los Angeles and San Francisco.
Only United can fly you to Hawaii from so many U.S.
cities and show you wide-screen color movies on the way. Just
call your Travel Agent or United. And don't forget to return the
postcard for your exciting Hawaii Planning Kit, only $1.
Come back to Hawaii with United.

UNITED AIR LINES

Welcome aboard the extra care airline

INVESTMENTS 1965-1969

Investment	1965	1966	1967	1968	1969
Basic Yield, One-year Corporate Bonds	4.14	5.00	5.29	6.29	7.05
Short-term Interest Rates, 4–6 Months, Prime Commercial Paper	4.38	5.55	5.10	5.90	7.83
Basic Yield, Common Stocks, Total	3.06	3.57	3.35	3.22	3.42
Index of Common Stocks (Moody's)	21.03	13.66	6.93	8.96	9.84

COMMON STOCKS, CLOSING PRICE AND YIELD, FIRST BUSINESS DAY OF YEAR

(Parenthetical number is annual dividend in dollars)

	1965	1966	1967	1968	1969
Allis Chalmers	19 5/8	33 1/8	21 7/8	35 3/4	30 1/2
	(.50)	(.75)	(1)	(1)	(1)
AT&T	69 1/2	61 1/2	54 3/8	51 5/8	53 1/2
(2 for 1 split 5/28/64)	(2)	(2.20)	(2.20)	(2.40)	(2.40)
American Tobacco	33 7/8	36 1/2	31 3/4	32 1/4	39
	(1.60)	(1.70)	(1.80)	(1.80)	(1.90)
Anaconda	52 3/4	84 1/8	81 1/2	47 3/8	64
(split 2 shares for 1, 6/9/67)	(2.50)	(3.75)	(5)	(1.25)	(2.50)
Bethlehem Steel	35	39 7/8	30 3/8	33 1/2	31 1/4
	(1.50)	(1.50)	(1.50)	(1.50)	(1.60)
Corn Products	54 3/4	53	46 3/8	40 1/2	42 5/8
	(1.50)	(1.60)	(1.70)	(1.70)	(1.70)
Delta Air Lines	61 1/4	70 1/2	116 1/8	33 7/8	36 1/2
(2 for 1 split 12/13/65) (3 for 1 split 11/16/67)	(1.60)	(1)	(1)	(.40)	(.40)
General Electric	91 1/8	116 7/8	89	95 5/8	94 7/8
	(2.20)	(2.60)	(2.60)	(2.60)	(2.60)
General Motors	95 3/8	102 5/8	68 7/8	82 3/4	80 1/8
	(4.45)	(5.20)	(4.55)	(3.80)	(4.30)
International Business Machines	405 1/8	493 1/2	369	613 1/2	313 3/4
(3 shares for 2 split, 5/17/66) (2 1/2% stock dividend, 6/10/67) (2 shares for 1 split, 5/23)	(5)	(6)	(4.40)	(4.40)	(2.60)
Intl Harvester	74 1/8	45 3/4	34 7/8	35 5/8	37 1/8
(2 shares for 1 split, 4/9/65)	(2.80)	(1.50)	(1.80)	(1.80)	(1.80)
National Biscuit	58 3/8	54 3/8	47	43 1/2	50 1/8
	(1.70)	(1.80)	(1.90)	(2)	(2.10)
U.S. Steel	50 3/4	51 7/8	38 1/2	42 1/8	43 1/2
	(2)	(2)	(2.40)	(2.40)	(2.40)
Western Union	30 3/8	49 1/2	37	36 3/4	42 7/8
	(1.40)	(1.40)	(1.40)	(1.40)	(1.40)

STANDARD JOBS 1965-1969

Job Type	1965	1966	1967	1968	1969
Bituminous Coal Mining	$6543/yr	$7398/yr	$7663/yr	$8169/yr	$8582/yr
Building Trades	$6921/yr	$7363/yr	$7738/yr	$8332/yr	$9049/yr
Domestic Industries	$5812/yr	$6062/yr	$6312/yr	$6759/yr	$7230/yr
Domestics	$2657/yr	$2780/yr	$2961/yr	$3254/yr	$3543/yr
Farm Labor	$2661/yr	$2923/yr	$3136/yr	$3327/yr	$3646/yr
Federal Civilian	$7859/yr	$8170/yr	$8257/yr	$9002/yr	$9690/yr
Federal Employees, Executive Depts.	$5763/yr	$5921/yr	$5993/yr	$6520/yr	$7010/yr
Federal Military	$4477/yr	$4650/yr	$4732/yr	$5148/yr	$5526/yr
Finance, Insurance, & Real Estate	$5962/yr	$6239/yr	$6516/yr	$6994/yr	$7400/yr
Gas, Electricity, & Sanitation Workers	$7480/yr	$7801/yr	$8191/yr	$8666/yr	$9316/yr
Manufacturing, Durable Goods	$7001/yr	$7228/yr	$7475/yr	$8002/yr	$8454/yr
Manufacturing, Nondurable Goods	$5950/yr	$6172/yr	$6413/yr	$6849/yr	$7257/yr
Medical/Health Services Workers	$4410/yr	$4565/yr	$4861/yr	$5292/yr	$5845/yr
Miscellaneous Manufacturing	$5365/yr	$5548/yr	$5849/yr	$6252/yr	$6620/yr
Motion Picture Services	$7125/yr	$7397/yr	$7503/yr	$7946/yr	$8318/yr
Nonprofit Org. Workers	$4138/yr	$4280/yr	$4402/yr	$4655/yr	$5138/yr
Passenger Transportation Workers, Local and Highway	$5553/yr	$5737/yr	$5926/yr	$6279/yr	$6623/yr
Personal Services	$4375/yr	$4551/yr	$4705/yr	$4960/yr	$5254/yr
Private Industries, incl farm labor	$5810/yr	$6098/yr	$6342/yr	$6772/yr	$7237/yr
Public School Teachers	$5848/yr	$6142/yr	$6605/yr	$7129/yr	$7623/yr
Radio Broadcasting & Television Workers	$8515/yr	$8833/yr	$9000/yr	$9563/yr	$10,085/yr
Railroads	$7460/yr	$7708/yr	$8116/yr	$8663/yr	$9317/yr
State and Local Govt. Workers	$5558/yr	$5834/yr	$6284/yr	$7255/yr	$7894/yr
Telephone & Telegraph Workers	$6604/yr	$6858/yr	$7063/yr	$7506/yr	$8044/yr
Wholesale and Retail Trade Workers	$6981/yr	$7345/yr	$7690/yr	$8142/yr	$8685/yr

FOOD BASKET 1965-1969

(NR = Not Reported)

Commodity	Year	New York	Atlanta	Chicago	Denver	Los Angeles
Apples, Fresh, per pound	1965	20.10¢	NR	16.30¢	NR	20.50¢
	1966	21.20¢	NR	19¢	NR	21.20¢
	1967	23.30	NR	20.50¢	NR	23¢
	1968	26¢	23.90¢	24¢	NR	27.60¢
	1969	26¢	23.50¢	24.20¢	NR	26.90¢
Beans, Dried, per pound	1965	16.80¢	NR	17.70¢	NR	21¢
	1966	19.80¢	NR	20¢	NR	22.30¢
	1967	18.60¢	NR	18.50¢	NR	20¢
	1968	20.30¢	16.30¢	19.70¢	NR	23.20¢
	1969	17.40¢	17.40¢	18.80¢	NR	23.10¢
Beef, Rib Roasts, per pound	1965	84.70¢	NR	91¢	NR	$1.01
	1966	88.30¢	NR	95.70¢	NR	$1.01
	1967	88.70¢	NR	97.60¢	NR	99.30¢
	1968	91.50¢	99.40¢	99.60¢	NR	$1.08
	1969	$1.00	$1.19	$1.11	NR	$1.20
Beef, Steaks (Round), per pound	1965	$1.23	NR	91.90¢	NR	96.70¢
	1966	$1.27	NR	93.70¢	NR	99.80¢
	1967	$1.26	NR	93.10¢	NR	$1.01
	1968	$1.31	$1.09	96.30	NR	$1.05
	1969	$1.45	$1.26	$1.09	NR	$1.15
Bread, White, per pound	1965	24.20¢	NR	19.20¢	NR	29.40¢
	1966	25.20¢	NR	21.30¢	NR	27.80¢
	1967	25.40¢	NR	21¢	NR	26.50¢
	1968	26.30¢	22¢	21.50¢	NR	26.20¢
	1969	27¢	22.10¢	22.80¢	NR	26.10¢
Butter, per pound	1965	75¢	NR	77.70¢	NR	76.80¢
	1966	81.90¢	NR	86.30¢	NR	84.70¢
	1967	82.90¢	NR	87.10¢	NR	85.60¢
	1968	84¢	90.50¢	87.70¢	NR	84.70¢
	1969	85.10¢	91.80¢	87.50¢	NR	85.50¢
Cheese, per 8 ounces	1965	36.20¢	NR	36.90¢	NR	39.30¢
	1966	40.30¢	NR	41.50¢	NR	44.70¢
	1967	41.10¢	NR	42.40¢	NR	47¢
	1968	42.70¢	42.70¢	44.10¢	NR	46.80¢
	1969	45.30¢	45.70¢	48.40¢	NR	49.90¢
Chickens, per pound	1965	41.60¢	NR	37.10¢	NR	40.10¢
	1966	44.20¢	NR	39.60¢	NR	40¢
	1967	41.40¢	NR	36.10¢	NR	37.20¢
	1968	44.30¢	39.30¢	37.80¢	NR	38¢
	1969	47.20¢	40.20¢	41.10¢	NR	42.10¢
Coffee, per pound	1965	83.70¢	NR	85.30¢	NR	79.40¢
	1966	83.50¢	NR	84.60¢	NR	74.10¢
	1967	77.30¢	NR	77.80¢	NR	69.80¢
	1968	75.80¢	79.50¢	78¢	NR	70.50¢
	1969	74.50¢	76.50¢	79.10¢	NR	94.20¢
Cornmeal, per pound	1965	19.08¢	NR	21.80¢	NR	21.20¢
	1966	21¢	NR	23¢	NR	22¢
	1967	25.10¢	NR	27.90¢	NR	26.90¢
	1968	25.20¢	25.20¢	28.40¢	NR	26.80¢
	1969	NR	NR	NR	NR	NR
Eggs, per dozen	1965	56.70¢	NR	51.40¢	NR	48.90¢
	1966	64.70¢	NR	58.60¢	NR	55.60¢
	1967	51.30¢	NR	48.60¢	NR	47.90¢
	1968	56.20¢	51.70¢	54.40¢	NR	48¢
	1969	66.90¢	61.50¢	62.30¢	NR	56.20¢

Commodity	Year	New York	Atlanta	Chicago	Denver	Los Angeles
Flour, White, per pound	1965	11.44¢	NR	11.26¢	NR	12.02¢
	1966	11.64¢	NR	11.76¢	NR	11.62¢
	1967	12.06¢	NR	11.58¢	NR	11.80¢
	1968	11.70¢	12.84¢	11.56¢	NR	11.90¢
	1969	11.58¢	12.52¢	11.46¢	NR	12.14¢
Lamb Chops, Loin, per pound	1965	$1.45	NR	$1.46	NR	$1.59
	1966	$1.52	NR	$1.54	NR	$1.70
	1967	$1.57	NR	$1.57	81¢	$1.66
	1968	$1.66	$1.38	$1.71	NR	$1.73
	1969	$1.77	$1.48	$1.83	NR	$1.86
Margarine, per pound	1965	29.70¢	NR	30.20¢	NR	28¢
	1966	30.70¢	NR	31.40¢	NR	27.70¢
	1967	29.90¢	NR	30.50¢	NR	27.60¢
	1968	29.70¢	29.10¢	30.10¢	NR	27.20¢
	1969	30.10¢	29.50¢	29.80¢	NR	27.60¢
Milk, Fresh, per quart	1965	29.75¢	NR	27.10¢	NR	27.55¢
	1966	31.40¢	NR	28.45¢	NR	28.25¢
	1967	31¢	NR	30.30¢	NR	29¢
	1968	32.30¢	30.55¢	33.35¢	NR	30.75¢
	1969	33.10¢	31.60¢	33.80¢	NR	31.45¢
Pork, Bacon, Sliced, per pound	1965	85.50¢	NR	81.10¢	NR	78.40¢
	1966	$1.02	NR	94.90¢	NR	91.30¢
	1967	90.40¢	NR	84.10¢	NR	76.10¢
	1968	87.30¢	83.50¢	82¢	NR	75¢
	1969	91.60¢	90.10¢	90.10¢	NR	82¢
Pork Chops, per pound	1965	$1.03	NR	91.50¢	NR	$1.06
	1966	$1.14	NR	$1.02	NR	$1.14
	1967	$1.08	NR	92.60¢	NR	$1.09
	1968	$1.11	$1.01	90.20¢	NR	$1.08
	1969	$1.22	$1.09	98.10¢	NR	$1.19
Pork, Ham, Whole, per pound	1965	68¢	NR	64.10¢	NR	62.50¢
	1966	76.20¢	NR	69.90¢	NR	69.40¢
	1967	71.10¢	NR	62.70¢	NR	65.70¢
	1968	70.40¢	64.60¢	62.50¢	NR	65.20¢
	1969	75.60¢	65.40¢	69.70¢	NR	70¢
Potatoes, Irish, per 10 pounds	1965	90.70¢	NR	$1.10	NR	$1.18
	1966	79.20¢	NR	79.50¢	NR	85.20¢
	1967	75.30¢	NR	90¢	NR	88.90¢
	1968	76.80¢	75.10¢	93.60¢	NR	95.10¢
	1969	82.80¢	81.80¢	$1.07	NR	$1.00
Rice, per pound	1965	20.10¢	NR	19¢	NR	22.60¢
	1966	20.30¢	NR	19.60¢	NR	23.30¢
	1967	20.70¢	NR	19.30¢	NR	23.30¢
	1968	20.70¢	21.50¢	19.40¢	NR	23.20¢
	1969	20.90¢	19.30¢	19.90¢	NR	23.50¢
Sugar, per pound	1965	11.90¢	NR	12¢	NR	10.78¢
	1966	12.40¢	NR	12.22¢	NR	11.18¢
	1967	12.40¢	NR	11.70¢	NR	11.80¢
	1968	12.48¢	12.20¢	11.90¢	NR	11.76¢
	1969	12.76¢	12.30¢	12.16¢	NR	11.74¢
Tea, Bags, package of 48	1965	58.10¢	NR	66.40¢	NR	65.60¢
	1966	55.90¢	NR	66.40¢	NR	66.70¢
	1967	56.70¢	NR	60.70¢	NR	66¢
	1968	57.70¢	61.90¢	61.20¢	NR	64.40¢
	1969	57.90¢	64.20¢	61.80¢	NR	64.80¢
Veal, per pound	1965	$1.74	NR	$1.35	NR	$1.58
	1966	$1.85	NR	$1.46	NR	$1.68
	1967	$1.95	NR	$1.52	NR	$1.76
	1968	$2.09	$1.56	$1.68	NR	$1.78
	1969	$2.32	$1.89	$1.85	NR	$2.04

SELECTED PRICES 1965-1969

Item	Source	Description	Price
Alcohol			
Beer	*Chicago Tribune* (1968)	*Schlitz;* 12-oz quick chill cans; 6 pack	$0.99
Rum	*Chicago Tribune* (1968)	*Virgin Island Brugal;* choice of dark or light	$2.98/fth
Scotch	*New York Times* (1965)	*Clan MacGregor Rare Scotch;* light and smooth Full quart	$6.19
Scotch	*New York Times* (1965)	*King George IV Blended Scotch Whiskey;* per fifth	$4.99
Whiskey	*New York Times* (1965)	*Four Roses Blended Whiskey;* per fifth sized bottle	$4.99
Whiskey	*Chicago Tribune* (1968)	*Seagram's VO;* 6 years old; 86.8 proof	$5.79/fth
Apparel, Children's			
Briefs	*Life* (1969)	*Fruit of the Loom;* dacron and cotton is what makes our golden line of underwear the buy it is; package of 3	$2.65
Clothing	*Sears, Roebuck* (1967)	Sports set; yellow broadcloth blouse with shoulder epaulet; navy-and-white-striped denim culottes	$5.97
Dancing Shoes	*Sears, Roebuck* (1967)	*Sparking;* tap shoe	$5.77
Dress	*New York Times* (1965)	High-waisted sundress with bright carrot appliqués across the front	$12
Shorts	*Sears, Roebuck* (1967)	One low price for three pairs of smart snappy play shorts	$2.97
Slip	*Sears, Roebuck* (1967)	*Magic Grow;* packages of three; white cotton percale; one with nylon lace and schiffli embroidery; two with schiffli embroidery	$2.97
Apparel, Men's			
Boots	*Sears, Roebuck* (1967)	Cowboy; olive-brown 12" boot has fine water-buffalo calf uppers	$26.80
Hat	*Chicago Tribune* (1968)	*Bonds;* famous Executive Group hats with the hand-detailed extras that add to your wearing pleasure	$7.99
Jacket	*The Sporting News* (1966)	Major league warm-up jacket; satin jacket with team name in script	$12.95
Jacket	*Sears, Roebuck* (1967)	Authentic western wear	$5.27
Shirt	*Life* (1968)	*Arrow;* available in 19 solid colors; sanforized-plus-2 in a blend of dacron polyester and cotton	$7.50
Shoes	*Life* (1968)	*Jarman;* Jarman toes the mark of fashion	$22.00
Shoes	*Chicago Tribune* (1968)	Scotch-grain supple; long-wearing leathers with the added comfort of heel-to-toe-full leather lining	$13.80
Slacks	*Sears, Roebuck* (1967)	Fashion-right plaid slacks in smooth-weave fabric of Fortrel and combed cotton	$6.97
Apparel, Women's			
Brassier	*New York Times* (1965)	Longline with flatter band, B cup, 32 to 40	$11.00
Clothing	*Sears, Roebuck* (1967)	The weekend set; jacket, skirt and pants; crisp white with floral print	$9.90

Item	Source	Description	Price
Coat	Sears, Roebuck (1967)	Imported leather suede or cabretta; snappily seamed and shaped	$38.90
Dress	New York Times (1965)	Chiffon for Evening at Bonwit Teller; in blue and white or pink and white	$90.00
Dress	New York Times (1965)	B. Altman & Company; cotton and acetate dress and matching jacket	$70.00
Girdle	New York Times (1965)	Youthcraft's Long Leg "Shift" Girdle	$11.00
Hat	Sears, Roebuck (1967)	Garden party pillbox; high rounded dome covered with flowers	$4.97
Pullover	Life (1968)	James Douglas Goodson; challis; makes a splashy beach cover-up	$28.00
Shirt	Life (1968)	Gregory Sheer; printed with challis-like flowers	$20.00
Shoes	Sears, Roebuck (1967)	It's time for flats; young and impish	$6.97

Appliances

Item	Source	Description	Price
Air Conditioner	Western Auto Catalog (1965)	Pre-charged central unit; 2 1/2 hp, single phase, 28,000 btu; shipping weight 188 lbs	$319.95
Air Conditioner	Western Auto Catalog (1965)	Wizard Ex-pand-O; 8,000 btu, featuring the panelmatic cover that snaps off for instant cooling	$189.95
Air Conditioner	Chicago Tribune (1966)	Goldblatt's; whole house; completely installed at a new low price; includes unit and installation	$498.88
Air Conditioner	Sears, Roebuck (1967)	The only window air conditioners with separate controls for humidity and temperature; 11,000 btus	$254.95
Dishwasher	Western Auto Catalog (1965)	Fully automatic built-in dishwasher; two separate spray arms to clean every dish without pre-rinsing; special loading	$207.95
Dishwasher	Life (1968)	General Electric; now you can take your dishes from the table to the dishwasher to the cupboard	$119.25
Dryer	Western Auto Catalog (1965)	Wizard; electric; 8-cycle sunshine ozone lamp in drum freshens, sanitizes, and prevents mildew	$169.95
Dryer	Chicago Tribune (1968)	Speed Queen; 3-temperature automatic gas dryer; has normal, delicate, air-only fabric selection to leave everything from dura-press to denims fluffy and soft	$178
Freezer	Western Auto Catalog (1965)	Wizard; 21" chest; economical to operate, saves on electricity bills; coiling system is welded to sides of heavy-duty steel liner	$232.95
Oven	Western Auto Catalog (1965)	Wizard; built-in; new eye-level check-it oven pre-heats, thaws frozen food fast, warms finest china safely	$154.95
Oven	Western Auto Catalog (1965)	Automatic electric; lets you cook meals while away from home; includes roll-out broiler with 2-pc porcelain pilots	$164.95
Range	Western Auto Catalog (1965)	Wizard Citation; the convenience of a full-size 30" range, plus, a separate eye-level rotary broiler	$299.95
Refrigerator	Chicago Tribune (1968)	Frigidaire; 12.3 cu ft; keeps food really cool	$208
Refrigerator-Freezer	Western Auto Catalog (1965)	Wondermart 15; no-frost; 4.8-cu-ft-bottom freezer holds 171 lbs; never any frost in 9.69-cu-ft refrigerator	$299.95

Item	Source	Description	Price
Vacuum	*Sears, Roebuck* (1967)	Built-in; you can install system in existing or new home for floor-to-ceiling vacuuming and cleaning	$195
Washer	*Western Auto Catalog* (1965)	*Wizard Citation;* 7-cycle; does everything but put the laundry in and take it out	$247.95
Washer	*Western Auto Catalog* (1965)	*Wizard;* economical 10-lb capacity washer, wringer adjusts for all fabrics	$99.88

Baby Products

Item	Source	Description	Price
Auto Harness	*Sears, Roebuck* (1967)	Helps guard baby while you drive	$2.99
Bottles	*Sears, Roebuck* (1967)	34-piece feeding kit	$7.99
Crib	*Western Auto Catalog* (1965)	Portable crib and play yard; fits easily into car seats; masonite floor raises to make dressing table	$22.95
Gate	*Western Auto Catalog* (1965)	Portable; easiest way of letting baby have lots of room to play; yet keeps him out of places he shouldn't be	$3.95
Play Yard	*Western Auto Catalog* (1965)	Nylon mesh; A-frame construction is far more rigid, durable, and easier to fold than models with corner legs	$19.25
Sterilizer	*Western Auto Catalog* (1965)	Baby bottle; aluminum; has a lift-out storage rack; quick heating allows you to prepare day's formula in one sterilization	$3.99
Stroller	*Sears, Roebuck* (1967)	Two-seater stroller sleeper	$29.95
Walker-Stroller	*Western Auto Catalog* (1965)	Deluxe 3-in-1; easy-to-clean plastic coated snap-on fabric in ice-sparkler pattern	$18.95

Business Equipment and Services

Item	Source	Description	Price
Calculator	*Time* (1968)	*Friden Electric Printing Calculator*	$1,495
Calculator	*New York Times* (1965)	*Remington Electric Calculator*	$189.50
Calculator	*Time* (1966)	*Friden Model 132;* a division of Singer; how much faster is an electronic calculator? On accounts payable, Gimbels' found it 43% faster; with automatic square root	$1,950
Stapler	*Sears, Roebuck* (1967)	Variable-compression stapler	$10.79
Tape Recorder	*New York Times* (1965)	*Roberts 1640* 4-track stereo tape recorder with two speakers	$198.95
Typewriter	*Western Auto Catalog* (1965)	*Wizard Imperial;* manual; finger-tip control panel, push-button tabulator; stamped-steel frame	$89.95

Collectibles

Item	Source	Description	Price
Candelabra	*Antiques* (1966)	*Sheffield;* circa 1820, 22" high	$425
Clock	*Antiques* (1969)	*Seth Thomas;* pillar and scroll; running order circa 1809–1813	$600
Creamer	*Antiques* (1969)	Silver; creamer 7 1/2"; John Curry; Philadelphia circa 1830	$250
Desk	*Antiques* (1969)	*Lloyds of New York;* reproduction directoire; length 48", depth 24", height 30"	$545
Figurines	*Antiques* (1966)	Chelsea boy and girl; 10" high, 9" wide	$450

Item	Source	Description	Price
Harp	*Antiques* (1966)	Gilt; early-nineteenth-century harp by Sebastian Erard	$790
Print	*Antiques* (1969)	Rare folio; Mark Catesby, 1754; birds, animals, fish, snakes	$35.00
Printed Broadsheet	*Guinness Book of World Records* (1981)	Price paid in 1969 for one of the 16 known copies of The Declaration of Independence, printed in 1776 by Samuel T. Freeman & Co.	$404,000
Rug	*Antiques* (1966)	*Keshan;* 12' x 9'	$1,250
Rug	*Antiques* (1966)	*Herez;* 15.4' x 11.2'	$925
Sideboard	*Antiques* (1966)	*Hepplewhite;* circa 1790–1800; shaped front; hepplewhite legs ending in spade feet	$2,200
Statue	*Antiques* (1966)	Bronze; Ming horse and noble rider, height 20", width 17 1/2"; weight 13 lbs	$750
Sugar and Creamer	*Antiques* (1969)	Silver; 6" to 7"; circa 1830–1840	$450

Education

Item	Source	Description	Price
Dance Lessons	*Chicago Tribune* (1966)	*Fred Astaire;* take a tranquilizer; learn to dance; 8 private 1/2-hour lessons	$13.95

Entertainment

Item	Source	Description	Price
Ballet	*New York Times* (1965)	*New York City Ballet;* Apollo Orchestra	$4.95
Concert Ticket	*Life* (1969)	*Newport Jazz Festival;* featuring Buddy Rich, B.B. King, and Johnny Winter	$3.50-$6.50/day
Movie	*New York Times* (1965)	*The Yellow Rolls-Royce* at Radio City Music Hall Per Seat Noon Afternoon Evenings	 $0.99 $1.35 $1.85
Opera Ticket	*Chicago Tribune* (1968)	*Dyly Carte Opera Company;* Gilbert & Sullivan's *HMS Pinafore; The Mikado*	$3.50-$6.50
Play	*New York Times* (1965)	*Kiss Me, Kate* at New York City Center; Special Cole Porter Memorial Production Orchestra 2nd Balcony	 $4.95 $1.95
Play Ticket	*Chicago Tribune* (1968)	*Neil Simon's Plaza Suite;* Forrest Tucker and Betty Garrett; evening, Monday through Thursday, orchestra	$5.95

Entertainment, Home

Item	Source	Description	Price
Camera	*Time* (1968)	*Kodak Instamatic 814 Camera;* drop-in film cartridge	$240
Camera	*Western Auto Catalog* (1965)	*Argus;* 35mm cartridge; instant loading; with flash and slide reviewer	$69.95
Camera	*Life* (1968)	*Polaroid Color Pack;* the 60-second excitement	$50.00
Camera	*Life* (1969)	*Kodak Instamatic S-10;* it fits your pocket; palm or purse	$35.00
Camera and Projector	*Western Auto Catalog* (1965)	*Mansfield;* 8mm holiday electromatic; retain those once-in-a-lifetime occasions on film; includes a projector, camera combination and shadow box and wall screen; camera carrying case and accessories	$99.99
8mm Camera	*New York Times* (1965)	*Fujica 8mm Electric Power Zoom Reflex Camera;* normal, slow motion and sound speeds	$129.95

Item	Source	Description	Price
Film	*Western Auto Catalog* (1965)	*Technicolor;* 35mm indoor/outdoor color slide film; high-quality color film with the Hollywood difference	$2.49
Film Editor	*Western Auto Catalog* (1965)	*Mansfield Action Editor;* see your processed movie film in clear, sharp detail; in forward and reverse action or single-frame stills	$19.95
Slide Viewer	*Time* (1968)	*6AF Ansochrome Color Slide Film Viewer*	$2.45
Movie Outfit	*Chicago Tribune* (1968)	*Kodak Super 8;* movie outfit; it's the instant-loading camera that uses drop-in 50 ft film	$24.66
Radio	*Western Auto Catalog* (1965)	*Custom 7;* transistor; PM speaker for clear reception; includes handsome carrying case	$12.95
Radio	*National Geographic* (1966)	*Admiral All World Transistor;* portable radio; tune in the world; 10 bands for world-wide reception	$200
Slide Projector	*National Geographic* (1966)	*Kodak Carousel 600;* dependable as gravity because it works by gravity	$80.00
Slide Projector	*Time* (1966)	*Honeywell;* there are a lot of other built-in conveniences, too, including the handiest edit/preview gate on the market	$149.50
Slide Projector	*Life* (1968)	*Sawyer;* automatic focusing; you focus the first slide, the machine does the rest	$60.00
Stereo	*Western Auto Catalog* (1965)	*Truetone Skylark 200;* portable stereo; with console-like features	$64.95
Stereo	*Western Auto Catalog* (1965)	*Provincial 3000;* cabinet; enjoy the exciting depth of living stereophonic sound	$499.95
Tape Player	*Sears, Roebuck* (1967)	*Stereo;* play the new 8-track stereo tape cartridges on your present music system	$67.95
Television	*Western Auto Catalog* (1965)	*Truetone;* color; cabinet model; 21" long-*life* laminated etched picture tube	$629.95
Television	*Western Auto Catalog* (1965)	*Truetone Riviera;* 16" black & white portable; 16,000 volts of power for a bright, clear picture; weighs less than 24 pounds	$149.95
Television	*National Geographic* (1966)	*Magnavox;* contemporary S24 color; walnut with remote control	$650

Farm Equipment and Supplies

Item	Source	Description	Price
Arc Welder	*The Progressive Farmer* (1968)	*Wel-Dex Arc Welder;* does the work of an $85 welder; fits ordinary 110 outlet	$18.95
Bearing Lubricator	*The Progressive Farmer* (1968)	*T&M Sealed Bearing Lubricator;* made for farmers by farmers	$2.95
Cattle	*The Progressive Farmer* (1968)	Holstein heifers, two to four weeks old, each	$45.00
Chickens	*The Progressive Farmer* (1968)	Red Cross chicks, per 100	$6.75
Ducks	*The Progressive Farmer* (1968)	Muscovy Ducks, pair	$5.00

Food Products

Item	Source	Description	Price
Bread	*New York Times* (1965)	*la Vie's* sour dough bread; available at Bloomingdale's; per pound	$0.49

Item	Source	Description	Price
Catsup	*Chicago Tribune* (1968)	*Hunts;* 14-oz bottle	$0.22
Chocolate Covered Cherries	*Chicago Tribune* (1968)	*Brach's;* 12 oz; light or dark chocolate	$0.47
Coffee	*Chicago Tribune* (1968)	*Folgers;* 2-lb can	$1.27
Cola	*Chicago Tribune* (1968)	*Pepsi;* no deposit, 10-oz bottles; 6 pack	$0.59
Juice Drink	*Chicago Tribune* (1968)	*Del Monte;* pineapple-grapefruit; 46-oz can	$0.25
Liquid Diet	*Chicago Tribune* (1968)	*Sego;* 4 cans	$0.99

Furniture

Item	Source	Description	Price
Bunk Bed	*Western Auto Catalog* (1965)	Wagon-wheel; early American bunk bed; solid oak; bunkie mattress	$69.95
Cabinet	*Western Auto Catalog* (1965)	Multi-purpose; rich walnut finish, adds style; storage is an excellent room divider	$22.95
Chair	*American Home* (1966)	*Viking;* made of solid, clear birch	$11.95
Desk	*Western Auto Catalog* (1965)	Three-drawer; spacious dovetailed drawers with authentic antique-brass-finished hardware	$47.88
Dinette Set	*Western Auto Catalog* (1965)	High-pressure laminated plastic top; tapered legs; tubular braching; seats 8	$99.95
Dinette Set	*Western Auto Catalog* (1965)	Early American; 5 piece; 42 in table with leaf; laminated plastic table top, plus four chairs	$119.88
Living Room Suite	*Western Auto Catalog* (1965)	7-piece living room group; nylon frieze sofa and chair; 3 marproof occasional tables; 2 table lamps	$169.77
Mattress	*Western Auto Catalog* (1965)	*Englander;* innerspring or foam; quilted damask covers; twin or full	$59.95
Nightstand	*Western Auto Catalog* (1965)	Solid-oak construction with full-depth drawer and magazine shelf	$25.95
Recliner	*Western Auto Catalog* (1965)	King-size; pillow back; reinforced super glove-soft plastic; wears like iron; is easy to care for	$59.95

Garden Equipment and Supplies

Item	Source	Description	Price
Arbor	*Sears, Roebuck* (1967)	Aluminum; has baked-on white enamel finish so it never needs painting	$19.50
Bird Bath	*Sears, Roebuck* (1967)	Plastic bird bath; designed with the look of alabaster; fill the base with sand for stability	$2.89
Chaise	*Western Auto Catalog* (1965)	Redwood; three position; ideal for relaxing on lawn or patio	$25.95
Duster	*The Progressive Farmer* (1968)	*Whatley's Roller Duster;* dust 100 ft. per minute; use on Mason jar	$1.00
Edger-Trimmer	*Western Auto Catalog* (1965)	*Wizard;* 3 wheel, 2 hp, gas power; gives your lawn a manicured look	$69.96

Item	Source	Description	Price
Fertilizer	*Western Auto Catalog* (1965)	*Weed and Feed;* 20-10-5 fertilizer and 2-40 kills weeds; 18 lbs	$3.89
Grass	*The Progressive Farmer* (1968)	*Certified Meyer Z-52 Zoysia* grass; 1000 sprigs	$10.00
Hose	*Western Auto Catalog* (1965)	Red rubber; 50'; inner tubes reinforced with strong rayon-cord body and vulcanized	$7.95
Lawn Chair	*Western Auto Catalog* (1965)	Aluminum-web folding; 6 vertical, 5 horizontal webs in seat and back	$5.99
Lawn Flamingo	*Sears, Roebuck* (1967)	Our loveliest flamingos in natural pink	$3.69
Lawn Mower	*Western Auto Catalog* (1965)	*Wizard Holiday Alum-Lite;* 21"; has 3 hp Briggs and Stratton engine; 5 select-a-height trim size adjustments	$79.95
Outdoor Vacuum	*Sears, Roebuck* (1967)	Vacuum clean your lawn, hedges, patios, walks, and driveway	$194
Rider-Tractor	*Western Auto Catalog* (1965)	*Wizard Holiday;* has everything for easiest mowing; 5 hp Tecumseh engine, 25", 3 speeds	$352.95
Seeds	*The Progressive Farmer* (1968)	*Morris Heading* collard seeds, per pound	$2.00
Sprinkler	*Western Auto Catalog* (1965)	*Wizard Set 'N Spray;* oscillating; covers up to 2600 sq ft with just a twist of a dial	$9.19
Tiller	*Western Auto Catalog* (1965)	*Wizard Imperial;* deep-digging; 4 hp, with power reverse	$140.95
Wagon	*Western Auto Catalog* (1965)	*Western Auto Town & Country;* rugged wagons feature 10 in double-disc fit grip handles and self-lubricating bearings	$18.50

Household Products

Item	Source	Description	Price
Blender	*Chicago Tribune* (1968)	*Proctor;* 4 speeds, 6 pushbuttons, a perfect gift for the home	$13.49
Carpet	*The Progressive Farmer* (1968)	*DuPont 501 Nylon Carpet;* resists crushing and withstands the stiffest wear Per square yard	$5.95
Carpet	*Western Auto Catalog* (1965)	9 x 12 carpet; get extra service; extra-heavy-duty loop pile of 100% nylon at low cost	$38.95
Carpet	*American Home* (1966)	*Cabin Crafts Briarwood;* makes a great show of elegance, but it's really a toughie at heart	$10.95/yard
China	*Western Auto Catalog* (1965)	*Western Auto Estate;* the classic swirl design of estate dinnerware, accented by a fine platinum band; 57-piece service	$49.95
Clock	*Western Auto Catalog* (1965)	*Western Auto Sunburst;* wall clock; brilliant 23" brass spokes radiate from 7" diameter; battery operated	$16.25
Clock	*Western Auto Catalog* (1965)	*General Electric;* sparkle alarm clock; a shadow-box crystal enhances the white dial and black numerals and hands	$5.98
Clock Radio	*Western Auto Catalog* (1965)	*Truetone Imperial;* AM/FM; all the beauty and style of a console; 4" x 6" heavy magnet speaker	$62.95

Item	Source	Description	Price
Coffee Maker	*Chicago Tribune* (1966)	*West Bend;* perks and serves 12 to 230 cups of full flavored coffee automatically	$9.95
Coffee Maker	*Western Auto Catalog* (1965)	*General Electric Peek-a-Brew;* with a transparent indicator that actually lets you see the coffee level	$19.95
Disinfectant Spray	*American Home* (1966)	*Florient;* why pay $0.98 for the high-priced spray	$0.59
Drill	*Western Auto Catalog* (1965)	*Wizard;* 2-speed electric drill; 1/4" drill develops 1/4 hp, drills through 1/4 steel, 1/2" hardwood	$19.95
Drill	*Chicago Tribune* (1968)	*Black & Decker;* 1/4" electric; your very best value in a general-purpose powerful drill	$10.99
Electric Blanket	*Western Auto Catalog* (1965)	*Wizard;* electric; non-allergenic, machine wash, dry; snap fit corners; double size	$19.35
Fan	*Western Auto Catalog* (1965)	*Imperial;* 3-speed; reversible window fan; 20"; has a push-button switch control panel and automatic thermostat that shuts fan off at pre-set temperature	$44.95
Fan	*Western Auto Catalog* (1965)	*Wizard;* box fan; 20", 2-speed suitable-type handle on top for easy portability	$21.45
Fan	*Western Auto Catalog* (1965)	*Wizard Imperial;* oscillating fan; 12", 3-speed; highly polished; deep-pitched aluminum blades	$19.95
Fireplace Tools	*Western Auto Catalog* (1965)	Hanging; wrought iron; solid-polish brass pull chains; black fire-screen mesh	$5.95
Food Processor	*Western Auto Catalog* (1965)	*Wizard Meal Maker;* use as a juicer, mixer or grinder; seven speeds—from slow for easy blending to fast for grinding meats, vegetables	$39.95
Freezer Bags	*Western Auto Catalog* (1965)	Tear off roll—fill and tie—presto; seals in freshness; 80 pt size	
Glasses	*Western Auto Catalog* (1965)	*Western Auto;* cut-glass water set; clear crystal; beauty and economy; includes six 9-oz tumblers and one 72-oz pitcher	$2.49
Ice Cream Maker	*Chicago Tribune* (1966)	*Proctor;* makes delicious homemade ice cream	$16.95
Ice Cream Maker	*Western Auto Catalog* (1965)	Electric; turns smoothly easily; 4-qt capacity	$27.95
Iron	*Western Auto Catalog* (1965)	*Wizard Imperial;* economically priced iron with unusually fine performance	$6.95
Ironing Table	*Western Auto Catalog* (1965)	12-way all-metal queen-of-the-ironing table; weighs only 15 lbs	$7.99
Lamp	*American Home* (1966)	*Stiffel;* with base; early Renaissance in character with Mediterranean overtones; height 22"	$72.50
Light Bulbs	*Western Auto Catalog* (1965)	*Wizard Long Life;* each bulb in handy 4-pack lasts 3 *times* longer; pack contains two 100 watt; one 75 watt	$1.29
Mirror	*American Home* (1966)	*Pittsburgh Plate Glass Mirror;* Spanish provincial style 32" x 46"	$7.00
Ovenware	*Western Auto Catalog* (1965)	*Western Auto;* 12-pc, withstands oven temperature includes 6 5-oz custard cups, gelatin molds, round 1-qt pudding pan; 1 deep loaf pan for bread, meat loaf, 9" pie plate; baking utility dish; 1 1/2-qt casserole dish and cover	$3.95

395

Item	Source	Description	Price
Paint	Western Auto Catalog (1965)	*Wizard;* latex; interior flat; one application is all you need; balanced formula for high hiding power	$5.55/gallon
Pillow	Western Auto Catalog (1965)	Machine washable; foam; made from 100% virgin urethane flaked foam; non-allergic	$4.98/pair
Plate	American Home (1966)	Pottery; creamy white, 10" pottery plate has bamboo pattern and border	$6.00
Pliers	Western Auto Catalog (1965)	Needle nose; slender jaws give long reach; hardened wire-cutter edges	$2.95
Polish	Antiques (1966)	*Old Patina;* furniture polish and feeder with beeswax; an eighteenth-century formula	$2.25/pt
Rods	Sears, Roebuck (1967)	Gleaming rods for café curtains; solid brass 30" to 52"	$4.89
Roller Pan Set	Chicago Tribune (1968)	Lightweight and easy to use...makes your painting job a breeze	$0.49
Router	American Home (1966)	*Stanley Works Rout-About;* compact 1/4 hp unit that spins at 25,000 rpm	$34.95
Rug	Antiques (1966)	Semi-antique Persian Sehna-Kurd oriental rug; 7 x 4 gold medallion on blue field, orange-red design	$345
Saw	Chicago Tribune (1968)	*Black & Decker;* 7 1/4" circular saw; cuts 2" x 4"'s at 45 degree angle	$27.77
Scale	Sears, Roebuck (1967)	Get the type of scale the professionals use	$42.37
Slip Covers	Sears, Roebuck (1967)	Crystal clear; show off the beauty of your furniture; chair cover	$3.99
Socket Set	Western Auto Catalog (1965)	*Wizard;* 57-piece; includes 1/2", 3/8", and 1/4" drive parts	$56.95
Tableware	Western Auto Catalog (1965)	*Western Auto Paris Night;* stainless steel; is exactly as its name; 69-piece service for 8	$19.95
Tile	Western Auto Catalog (1965)	Vinyl asbestos tile for kitchen floors; 9" square; made for long lasting *life* even in areas of critical wear	$12.50
Toaster	Western Auto Catalog (1965)	*Wizard Imperial;* this toaster gives you fingertip control	$11.39
Toaster-Broiler-Baker	Western Auto Catalog (1965)	*Wizard;* use as a baker one way, flip over for a broiler-toaster	$15.25
Tool Set	Sears, Roebuck (1967)	*Craftsman;* 155-piece set	$128.60
Vacuum Cleaner	Western Auto Catalog (1965)	*Wizard;* canister; power to spare, return original carpet beauty, get floors, walls really clean; includes 13-piece set	$69.95
Varnish	Western Auto Catalog (1965)	*Wizard Spar Varnish;* with china-wood oil; can be used inside on trim, woodwork, or outside to protect wood surfaces	$5.79

Hotel Rates

Item	Source	Description	Price
Room Rate	Time (1968)	*Hotel Thomas Jefferson* in Birmingham, Alabama; completely new throughout Commercial Single Rate	$8.50
Room Rate	New York Times (1965)	*Hotel Shelburne;* Boardwalk, Atlantic City; 100% central system air conditioned; per room; two in a room	$7.00

Item	Source	Description	Price
Room Rate	*New York Times* (1965)	*Griswold Hotel and Country Club;* 4 days and 3 nights Per person	$59

Jewelry

Item	Source	Description	Price
Necklace	*Western Auto Catalog* (1965)	*Hallmark;* cultured pearl; perfectly matched set of cultured pearls; handknotted graduated pearl necklace	$29.95
Pin	*Sears, Roebuck* (1967)	Abstract-shaped dramatic accent to current fashion	$5.00
Pocket Watch	*Sears, Roebuck* (1967)	Fob watch; railroad type; minute-marked dial	$5.49
Ring	*Western Auto Catalog* (1965)	Diamond; 4-prong Tiffany or Illusion setting; 1 ct; 14k yellow or white gold	$795
Watch	*New York Times* (1965)	*Longines Watch;* self-winding automatic; two years to pay with small down payment	$135
Watch	*New York Times* (1965)	*Belforte Electronic* watch for men	$49.95
Watch	*Western Auto Catalog* (1965)	*Timex Marlin;* radiolite dial for telling time in the darkest room; chrome-plated bezel	$11.95
Watch	*Western Auto Catalog* (1965)	*Waltham Ultra-thin Guardsman;* man's; white-gold finished case; 17 jewels	$28.95
Watch	*Western Auto Catalog* (1965)	*Timex Cavatina;* lady's; beautifully styled, keeps perfect time; lasting chrome-plated bezel, comfortable nylon-cord band	$9.95

Meals

Item	Source	Description	Price
Dinner	*New York Times* (1965)	*Astrojet Room;* interesting people are just part of the fascination of airport dining; complete Dinners Supreme from	$2.95
Lunch	*New York Times* (1965)	*Paddy's Clam House;* Maine Lobsters a Specialty; lunch, 4-course fish meal	$1.48

Medical Products and Services

Item	Source	Description	Price
Acne Solution	*Hit Parade* (1968)	Wipe away pimples, blackheads, and other embarrassing surface symptoms; an 8-wk solution	$2.98

Motorized Vehicles, Supplies, and Services

Item	Source	Description	Price
Air Conditioner	*Western Auto Catalog* (1965)	1800 btu model; 2 big rotary blowers cool you with 315 cu ft minimum of refrigerated air	$269.95
Automobile	*Time* (1968)	*Datsun;* value wagon of the year; all synchromesh 4-speed	$2,196
Automobile	*Life* (1968)	*Volkswagen;* station wagon; half a Volkswagen station wagon holds as much as most whole wagons hold	$2,602
Battery	*Western Auto Catalog* (1965)	*Wizard Deluxe;* for cars; new inter-cell construction to give your car 25% more starting power	$12.88
Car Wax	*Western Auto Catalog* (1965)	*Simonize;* durable paste wax puts a gleaming shine on your car's finish that lasts for months	$0.99
Dimmer	*Western Auto Catalog* (1965)	Automatic headlight dimmer; less than half the cost of previous models, automatic or manual	$26.95
Exhaust Kit	*Sears, Roebuck* (1967)	Dual-exhaust kit for Corvair	$18.45
Header Set	*Sears, Roebuck* (1967)	Dual-header set for Falcon and Comet	$64.95

Item	Source	Description	Price
Radio	Western Auto Catalog (1965)	Truetone; 11-transistor AM/FM auto radio; have the pleasure and relaxation of FM listening while you drive; plus the added enjoyment of an AM radio— both in one radio	$84.95
Resonator Pipes	Sears, Roebuck (1967)	Heavy 18-gauge steel tubing; Ford 1957–1960	$1.29
Seat Belt	Western Auto Catalog (1965)	Borg-Warner Maji-Buckle; automatically adjusts to fit everyone in your family	$12.45
Seat Covers	Western Auto Catalog (1965)	Wizard Suburban Jetspun; polypropylene-coated Jetspun fibers are durable, resist stains, fading, burns, scuffs; jewel tone pattern	$24.45
Spray Paint	Western Auto Catalog (1965)	Dupli-Color; quick, easy way to touch up your car; 6-oz can	$1.49
Tire	Western Auto Catalog (1965)	Davis Safety Sentry; new wrap-around tread design adds style, handling ease; black-tube type	$16.48
Tire	Western Auto Catalog (1965)	Davis Super Highway; 7.50 x 16; 6-ply rating, tube type	$26.95
Tires	The Progressive Farmer (1968)	Western Auto Premium Each, with trade	$19.98

Musical Instruments

Item	Source	Description	Price
Guitar	Western Auto Catalog (1965)	Truetone Jazz King; masterful guitar construction; 4-way selector switch	$97.95
Guitar	Sears, Roebuck (1967)	Electric; hollow body; triple pickup, each with tone and volume controls	$199.95
Organ	Western Auto Catalog (1965)	Truetone Regency; electric cord; voice selector switch, 8 pedal buttons for bass tones	$379.95
Trumpet	Western Auto Catalog (1965)	Barclay; student; perfect for the beginner; durable nickel-plated valves and mouthpiece	$79.50

Other

Item	Source	Description	Price
Baseball Cards	The Sporting News (1966)	Topps; 1966 complete set	$11.95
Bookkeeping Record	Life (1968)	Dome; simplified weekly bookkeeping record; America's most widely used single entry system	$3.75
Cosmetic Case	Sears, Roebuck (1967)	14" x 9" x 8"	$15.67
Film Developing	Life (1968)	United Film Club; CX 35mm-20, Kodapak cartridge; with new film	$5.99
Flag Set	Western Auto Catalog (1965)	United States; includes 3' x 5' printed flag; 6' jointed metal pole, plus rope halyard	$44.88
Flight Bag	Sears, Roebuck (1967)	Unzips to hang for easy packing	$39.47
Gasoline Container	Western Auto Catalog (1965)	Wizard; 5 gal; made of rugged dependable 28-gauge steel	$3.05
Knife	Western Auto Catalog (1965)	Kutmaster; two-bladed pocket knife; stag-type handle	$1.00

Item	Source	Description	Price
Parking Fee	*Life* (1969)	Watergate, Washington, D.C.	$3,500/yr
Photograph	*Hit Parade* (1968)	*Friendship Photos;* plastic laminate of favorite photo with deep-sunk embossing; 30 pictures	$1.00
Portable Kitchen	*Western Auto Catalog* (1965)	Deluxe oblong; all-aluminum; chrome-plated hinged grid; 30" high for no-stoop cooking	$37.95
Reupholstery Service	*Chicago Tribune* (1966)	*Goldblatt's;* new fabrics, new colors; flawless workmanship; sofa	$94.00
Weapons	*Time* (1968)	Booty money paid in Vietnam for captured Communist weapons AK-47 Assault Rifle 120-mm Mortar	 $25 $200

Personal Care Products

Item	Source	Description	Price
Artificial Fingernails	*Hit Parade* (1968)	*Nu-Nails;* artificial fingernails, pink, rose, platinum	$0.49/10
Barber Set	*Sears, Roebuck* (1967)	17 piece	$10.88
Electric Shaver	*Sears, Roebuck* (1967)	*Lady Kenmore;* distinctive cameo styling plus convenient built-in light	$13.97
Electric Toothbrush	*Western Auto Catalog* (1965)	*Tru-dent;* re-chargeable battery-powered motor in handle; four individual snap-in brushes	$12.50
Hair Dryer	*Western Auto Catalog* (1965)	*Wizard Holiday;* dries like a console, yet it carries like a portable	$29.95
Hair Spray	*Chicago Tribune* (1968)	*Just Wonderful;* 12-oz can	$0.47
Razor Blades	*Chicago Tribune* (1968)	*Gillette;* $1.59 size, cartridges of 10	$0.99
Shaver	*Western Auto Catalog* (1965)	*Remington 25;* for men; contour head has six rows of diamond-honed cutters	$25.95
Shaving Cream	*Chicago Tribune* (1968)	*Gillette Foamy;* regular, menthol, or lemon-lime; 11-oz can	$0.59
Strop	*Sears, Roebuck* (1967)	*Craftsman;* leather strop	$5.77
Toothpaste	*Chicago Tribune* (1968)	*Colgate;* 6.75-oz tube	$0.55
Vitamins	*Western Auto Catalog* (1965)	*Western Auto;* contains more than the known minimum daily requirement; 100 tablets	$1.49

Publications

Item	Source	Description	Price
Book	*Time* (1968)	*This Timeless Moment: A Personal View of Aldous Huxley* by Laura Archera Huxley	$6.95
Book	*New York Times* (1968)	*Always Ask a Man,* Arlene Dahl's Key to Femininity	$5.95
Book	*New York Times* (1965)	*Portrait of A People* by Charles Raddock; *The Story of the Jews from Ancient to Modern Times;* three volume set	$18.75
Book	*New York Times* (1965)	*Note X For Treason* by Brian Cleeve; a Random House Mystery	$3.95
Encyclopedia	*Western Auto Catalog* (1965)	*World University;* 12-volume set, a treasury of information	$59.00

Item	Source	Description	Price
Magazine	*Antiques* (1966)	*Antiques Magazine;* monthly	$12/yr
Magazine	*Life* (1968)	*Life;* weekly	$0.40

Real Estate

Item	Source	Description	Price
Apartment	*Life* (1969)	*Watergate,* Washington, D.C.; cost of Attorney General John Mitchell's apartment	$140,000
Farm Land	*The Progressive Farmer* (1968)	740 acre farm bordering river in Culpepper, Virginia; 3 houses, 5 barns, 4 silos Per acre	$395
House	*New York Times* (1965)	Bayside Hills Home in Queens; 3 bedrooms, 1 1/2 baths	$35,000
House	*New York Times* (1965)	Sea Cliff home in Nassau—Suffolk area; 3 bedrooms	$34,000
House	*Chicago Tribune* (1968)	3 bedroom, 1 1/2 bath, large closets, family room, many extras; fenced yard	$25,500
House	*Chicago Tribune* (1968)	Outstanding 3-bedroom ranch; garage, screened-in porch; drive out today	$23,500
Loft	*New York Times* (1965)	Manhattan lofts; 2nd Ave.; 16,000 to 27,000 square feet Per Square Foot	$1.50
Lot	*New York Times* (1965)	Brooklyn lot; 16 St. W; 40 x 120 lot in unrestricted area	$10,500

Sewing Equipment and Supplies

Item	Source	Description	Price
Cloth	*American Home* (1966)	*Bloomcraft Art Nouveau;* printed cotton; has a protective finish, is about 54" wide, and has sufficient body to be used for draperies, slip covers or upholstery	$3.50/yard
Cloth	*Sears, Roebuck* (1967)	Man-made fabrics and blends, three 4' pieces; enough for three smart dresses	$5.97
Electric Scissors	*Western Auto Catalog* (1965)	*Dritz;* electric; cut pattern in a fraction of *time*	$7.45
Electric Scissors	*Sears, Roebuck* (1967)	Reduces cutting time and makes cutting so much easier	$7.65
Sewing Machine	*Western Auto Catalog* (1965)	*Wizard Imperial Zig-zag;* sews 101 fancy stitches, monograms, embroiders, buttonholes with ease	$119.95
Sewing Machine	*Sears, Roebuck* (1967)	*Kenmore 95;* with new stretch stitch for elasticized fabrics	$149.95
Sewing Machine	*Life* (1968)	*Singer Touch & Sew;* solid-state speed control, exclusive push-button bobbin	$149.95
Yarn	*Sears, Roebuck* (1967)	3-ply cotton	$2.37

Sports Equipment

Item	Source	Description	Price
Baseball Bat	*Western Auto Catalog* (1965)	*Revelation Little League;* 32 in; sturdy white ash, natural color	$2.25
Baseball Catcher's Mask	*Western Auto Catalog* (1965)	*Wilson;* full-size professional quality; made of lightweight magnesium	$11.50
Baseball Glove	*Western Auto Catalog* (1965)	*Revelation;* fielders; has wide, deep, and rugged professional styling	$8.95
Baseball Glove	*Western Auto Catalog* (1965)	*Wilson Harvey Kuenn;* fielders; a glove good enough for the majors	$15.95

Item	Source	Description	Price
Bicycle	*Chicago Tribune* (1968)	*Power King;* adjustable polo saddle and hi-rise handlebar	$29.99
Bow	*Western Auto Catalog* (1965)	*Ben Pearson Cougar;* durable, laminated construction; the ideal bow for adult beginners or the accomplished archer	$22.95
Fishing Bait	*Western Auto Catalog* (1965)	*Doc's Prepared Catfish Bait;* choice of 4 scents; 12-oz jar	69
Fishing Lure	*Western Auto Catalog* (1965)	*DeLong Red Worm;* best for bluegill, perch; package of 3	$0.49
Fishing Lure	*Western Auto Catalog* (1965)	*Heddon Toni;* yellow body; jewelry blade finish; 1/4 oz	$0.89
Fishing Lure	*Sears, Roebuck* (1967)	*Lucky Dozen;* actual replicas of 12 of the fish-takingest lures ever designed	$5.22
Fishing Reel	*Western Auto Catalog* (1965)	*Shakespeare Wonder-Cast;* push button; aluminum frame; full-circle micro-drag	$12.95
Golf Shoes	*New York Times* (1965)	Woman's spiked oxford golf shoes; exceptionally lightweight	$22.00
Gun Scope	*The Sporting News* (1966)	*Weaver K4 Scope;* see the magnified target in clear, sharp detail	$34.50
Pool Table	*Western Auto Catalog* (1965)	*Imperial;* 8'; our very best table; laminated slatite precision playing bed; 100% virgin-wool billiard cloth assures you a hard, smooth surface	$334.50
Rod and Reel	*Western Auto Catalog* (1965)	*Zebco 606;* spin-cast rod-reel fishing combination; 2-piece, solid glass rod, 4 guides; tip top; cork handle	$9.99
Rod and Reel	*Western Auto Catalog* (1965)	*Zebco 777;* fishing-spinning combination; Zebflex 6 1/2', 2-piece tubular glass rod and 777 open-face spinning reel	$15.49
Sailboat	*Sears, Roebuck* (1967)	*Puffer;* 10' sailing dinghy can be used with motor or oars	$385
Sleeping Bag	*Western Auto Catalog* (1965)	*Duraloft;* 3 lb washable; 100% polyester insulation; 36" x 80" cut size	$17.95
Softball	*Western Auto Catalog* (1965)	*Voit Collegiate;* official size and weight	$1.65
Table Tennis Set	*Western Auto Catalog* (1965)	*Revelation;* deluxe; complete set for 4 players includes 3-ply rubber-faced paddles with tapered walnut handles; extra-heavy posts; green cord netting; adjustable metal ends, 4 official table-tennis balls	$6.95
Table Tennis Set	*Sears, Roebuck* (1967)	Complete set	$10.00
Table Tennis Table	*Western Auto Catalog* (1965)	*Western Auto;* our very best table; 5' x 9' tournament size; formed by two 4 1/2' x 5' sections	$43.95
Tennis Ball	*Western Auto Catalog* (1965)	*Wilson Championship;* dacron-nylon-wool cover for best wear, approved U.S. International and Professional Lawn Tennis Association	$2.65/can
Tennis Racket	*Western Auto Catalog* (1965)	*Autograph;* a perfect racket for the economy-minded beginner; laminated frame	$1.95

Item	Source	Description	Price
Tennis Racket	*Western Auto Catalog* (1965)	*Spalding Pancho Gonzales;* our very best racket; laminated ash and beech shoulder overlays for extra strength	$10.85
Tent	*Western Auto Catalog* (1965)	*Eagle;* wall tent; excellent for rough Boy Scout use; cut size; 5' x 7'	$17.75
Water Skis	*Western Auto Catalog* (1965)	*Wizard;* combine regular and slalom skiing, graceful, fast, banana-shape style	$19.95

Tobacco Products

Cigarettes	*New York Times* (1965)	Pink cigarettes for weddings and other occasions; carton of 200	$9.50

Toys

Backyard Amusement Set	*Western Auto Catalog* (1965)	Includes lawn glider; 2 swings; 2 gym rings; trapeze, sky-shooter; pumper swing, 7 1/2' platform slide	$34.95
Bicycle	*Western Auto Catalog* (1965)	*Western Flyer Cosmic Flyer;* for boys; features a new double-strength frame with twin center bars	$49.95
Bicycle	*Western Auto Catalog* (1965)	*Western Flyer Standard Flyer;* for girls or boys; rugged and built to last; 26"	$31.95
Croquet Set	*Western Auto Catalog* (1965)	Regulation size; 4-player; knurled 3 3/8" rock maple balls	$6.95
Doll	*Western Auto Catalog* (1965)	*Mattel Teenage Barbie;* easy to dress; arms, legs and head move; 11 1/2" with stand	$2.29
Doll	*Western Auto Catalog* (1965)	*Mattel Midge Bride;* Barbie's best friend; wears Barbie's clothes	$3.49
Doll	*Western Auto Catalog* (1965)	*Mattel Ken;* Barbie's boyfriend; a living doll; neatest crew cut; big blue eyes; 12 1/2" with stand	$2.69
Doll	*Sears, Roebuck* (1967)	*Eeyore;* 10" high; 14" long; removable tail	$4.99
Lead Pellets	*Western Auto Catalog* (1965)	*Crossman;* .177 cal, 250 per can	$0.95
Locomotive	*Railroad Model Craftsman* (1966)	*Tyco Prairie Sante Fe;* locomotive and tender; 2-6-2 with operating headlight	$16.77
Motorcycle	*Western Auto Catalog* (1965)	*Western Flyer Thunder Rod;* roaring engine; hi-rise handlebar, pneumatic tires; banana seat	$34.95
Pistol	*Western Auto Catalog* (1965)	*Daisy;* CO2 pistol; shoot regular .177 calibre bb's; semi-automatic	$16.95
Racing Set	*Western Auto Catalog* (1965)	*Aurora HO;* two speed controls allow you and your opponent to brake the cars and control them on curves; set comes with track, powerpack, and two lightning fast cars—Corvette Sting Ray and Jaguar XKE	$19.77
Rifle	*Western Auto Catalog* (1965)	*Daisy 51 Scope Smoker Rifle;* shoots a captive cork with a pop and a shower of sparks and a puff of smoke; 21" long	$0.97

Item	Source	Description	Price
Rifle	*Western Auto Catalog* (1965)	*Daisy golden 750;* lever action air rifle; our most popular model Daisy; carbine styled, 750-shot lever-action repeater	$7.50
Rifle	*Western Auto Catalog* (1965)	*Hy-Score;* single-shot pellet; shoots .177 calibre pellets; single-breaking action cocks rifle	$19.95
Robots	*Chicago Tribune* (1968)	*Ideal Zeriods;* the workers of the future—robots that obey your every command; they grab, throw, push, haul, and much more	$3.97
Space Man	*Chicago Tribune* (1968)	*Eldon's Billy Blast-Off;* 9" high miniature space man in space suit; comes with his own 7-piece set of space equipment	$3.99
Sports Car	*Western Auto Catalog* (1965)	*Western Flyer;* pedals easy; steers easy; 33 1/2" long	$11.95
Station Wagon and Camper	*Western Auto Catalog* (1965)	*Buddy L;* an authentic replica of the Teepez Trailer; hi-impact plastic tent, tufted bed; tent flaps	$5.66
Tricycle	*Western Auto Catalog* (1965)	*Western Flyer;* 10"; sturdier, huskier frame for young Rough Riders	$7.95
Truck	*Western Auto Catalog* (1965)	*Tonka;* pick-up truck; features snap-open tailgate, glassed-in cab and rubber tires; 9 1/8" long	$1.69
Wading Pool	*Western Auto Catalog* (1965)	*Western Auto Playmate;* custom-styled steel wading pool; 147 gallon capacity	$8.45

Travel and Transportation

Item	Source	Description	Price
Air Fare	*New York Times* (1965)	New York to San Francisco by Jet	$217.65
Airline Fare	*Chicago Tribune* (1966)	*Delta;* Miami; Delta's got up to 11 jets daily; up to 4 non-stops on weekend; it's just 24 hours to Florida's most famous resort city; day jetourist	$74.70
Hawaii Tour	*Time* (1968)	Trans International Airlines offers two weeks in Hawaii; complete tour	$599 and up

MISCELLANY 1965-1969

Giving Is Growing

The annual survey of 50 U.S. colleges and universities by New York's John Price Jones Co., professional fund raisers, shows that gifts spurted 1 1/3% last year over 1963—from $335,456,000 to $373,446,000. Contributions from individuals still provide the biggest single source of such funds (39.3%), but foundation grants are growing (now 33.1%), while bequests (16.9%) and corporations (10.7%) provide the rest. The gifts of the past four years alone total more than a fourth of the $4.8 billion that the Jones surveys have tabulated in their 44 years of existence.

The top ten beneficiaries in 1964:

Harvard	$38,812,000
Stanford	$36,078,000
Cornell	$27,695,000
Yale	$22,538,000
M.I.T.	$21,233,000
Chicago	$20,555,000
California	$16,602,000
Princeton	$16,416,000
Columbia	$16,001,000
N.Y.U.	$15,741,000

Time, February 26, 1965

$8,000 a Year

By far the most controversial part of the President's program was a plan to provide direct subsidies, for rent or mortgage payments, for some 500,000 city families with incomes as high as $8,000 a year. Initially, the aid would be limited to families displaced by Government projects such as urban renewal and highway construction, to those presently in substandard housing, to the impoverished elderly, and to displaced or ill-housed families capable of increasing their income in the future. In general, the formula would call for such families to pay 20% of their income for housing—and the Government would make up any necessary difference. Critics might wonder if an $8,000-a-year family really ought to be on a dole, but the President insisted that this section might "prove the most effective instrument of our new housing policy."

Time, March 12, 1965

Divorced

By Mary Costa, 36, blonde and beautiful lyric soprano, who left a $150,000-a-year job as TV's Chrysler girl for an opera career, making her widely acclaimed 1964 Metropolitan debut as Violetta in *La Traviata;* Frank Tashlin, 53, Hollywood writer director of slapstick comedies (*The Man from the Diners' Club*); on grounds of cruelty; after twelve years of marriage, no children; in Santa Monica, Calif.

Time, April 22, 1966

Shape of Events from One Year to Next

And capital is in shorter supply. The American economy, the powerhouse of world progress these last few years, went under severe monetary restraint in 1966. The transition was not too skillfully handled—1966 should have seen, but did not see, a tax increase—and the economy entered 1967 with every prospect of a lower growth rate, if not an end to its unprecedented six-year boom. Yet the demands on that economy will not grow less. The rising costs of Vietnam were matched by a growing list of domestic problems ranging from smog to transportation, from ghettos to inadequate schools.

Life, January, 1967

Killebrew to Get $65,000 for 1967; Slugger and Twins Agree to Terms for This Season

Harmon Killebrew, one of the leading sluggers in baseball, has agreed to a 1967 contract for a salary estimated at $65,000, the Minnesota Twins said today.

Killebrew hit 281 last season, smashing 39 home runs and driving in 110 while playing first base, third base and the outfield for the American League club. He was second to Frank Robinson of the Baltimore Orioles in both homers and runs batted in.

New York Times, February 23, 1967

MISCELLANY 1965-1969

Watergate West

The interior of Watergate West's free-form super-structure includes a number of "luxury features." The lobby is resplendent with fake Chou Dynasty lamps and curtains handwoven in Swaziland. The elevators are flooded with Musak, and the bathrooms are paved with marble and equipped with bidets and golden faucets. The 143 apartments vary as much in design as they do in price (from $28,000 for a one-bedroom to $186,000 for a penthouse). Many living and dining rooms are trapezoids or obtuse-angled triangles, while a few entranceways are circles.

Life, August, 1969

Advertisement: Getting Rid of $176,000,999 Isn't as Easy as You Think

The next time you sit down to balance your checkbook, think about what it would be like if you had the job of balancing a *bank's* bank account.

Especially when the bank is the biggest in Michigan. And when the job has to be done not just once a month, but every day, all day long.

Time, August 8, 1969

HISTORICAL SNAPSHOT
1970-1974

1970

♦ Man-made fibers control 56 percent of U.S. textile market

♦ Gross National Product reaches $977 billion

♦ New York subway rates reach 30¢

♦ Daily volume on New York Stock Exchange nearly three times that of 1960 at 11.6 million shares

♦ 25.5 million Americans live below the $3,908 per year poverty level

♦ President Nixon calls for voluntary wage and price controls

1971

♦ President Nixon orders 90-day freeze on wages and prices

♦ The average taxpayer gives the government $400 for defense, $125 to fight the war in Indochina, $40 to build roads, $30 to explore space, and $315 for health activities

♦ First-class postal rates rise to 8 cents per ounce

♦ Chicago's 1,107-foot Standard Oil of Indiana building opens

♦ Annual per capita beef consumption reaches 11 pounds

♦ *Look* magazine ceases publication

1972

♦ Richard Nixon reelected; Watergate burglary occurs

♦ Nearly 30 percent of U.S. petroleum is imported

♦ Wages, prices, and profits remain controlled by Phase II economic measures

♦ Dow Jones closes at 1003.15 on November 14, above 1,000 for first time

♦ San Francisco Bay Area Rapid Transit System opens

♦ *Ms.* magazine begins publication; *Life* magazine suspends publication

♦ Polaroid SX-70 system produces colored print

♦ New York's 110-story World Trade Center opens

♦ Birth rate falls to 15.8 per 1,000, lowest since 1917

1973

♦ McDonald's introduces Egg McMuffin, pioneering fast-food breakfast

♦ U.S. troops leave South Vietnam

♦ Median sales price of an existing single-family house reaches $28,900

♦ Average farmer produces enough food for 50 people

♦ Farm labor represents 5 percent of work force

♦ President Nixon orders freeze on all retail food prices

♦ Vodka outsells whiskey for first time

♦ Energy crisis and soaring grain prices produce economic recession

1974

♦ Pocket calculator marketed

♦ President Nixon lowers highway speed limit to 55 mph to save gasoline

♦ 110,000 clothing workers stage nationwide strike

♦ Unemployment reaches 6.5 percent, highest since 1961

♦ Universal product code designed for supermarket industry

♦ Year-long daylight savings time adopted to save fuel

♦ 3M develops Post-it to stick paper to paper

♦ ITT's Harold Geneen is highest paid executive at $791,000 per year

♦ Time, Inc., issues *People* magazine, devoted to celebrity journalism

♦ Walgreen's drug chain exceeds $1 billion in sales for first time

♦ President Nixon resigns

SELECTED INCOME 1970-1974

Job	Source	Description	Pay
Accountant	*New York Times* (1971)	Park Avenue Public Co.	$15,000/yr
Accounting Clerks	*New York Times* (1971)	Night Students	$160/wk
Actor	Legrand and Karney, *Chronicle of the Cinema* (1995)	Mae West's fee for 10 days' work in the movie *Myra Breckinridge,* her first screen appearance since 1943	$335,000
Art Designer	*New York Times* (1973)	Children's book designer	$11,000/yr
Art Gallery Clerk	*New York Times* (1973)	Good appearance; sales personality	$150-$125/wk
Baseball Umpire	John Feinstein, *Play Ball: The Life and Troubled Times of Major League Baseball* (1993)	Annual salary of Bruce Froemming in 1972	$10,000
Bookkeeper	*New York Times* (1973)	Midtown music company seeks several assistant bookkeepers	$125–$170/wk
Branch Manager	*New York Times* (1970)	Bank seeks branch manager for operations, credit and new business; per year	To $16,000
Caretaker	*Chicago Tribune* (1970)	Free apartment, plus food; retired or nonretired couple; care for home on lake	$150/mo
Chess Player	*Life* (1972)	Prize money offered to Boris Spassley and Bobby Fisher to play chess in Iceland	$125,000
Clerk	*Chicago Tribune* (1970)	Maintain technical society membership records	$100/wk
Cocktail Waitress	*Chicago Tribune* (1970)	Nights	$120/wk
Dancer	*Chicago Tribune* (1972)	No experience necessary; daily pay	$350/wk
File Clerk	*New York Times* (1970)	Law firm seeks persons with light experience; legal experience helpful; per week	$100 to $110
Girl/Man Friday	*New York Times* (1971)	No stenography necessary; lovely office; 9–5	$110–$135/wk
Hostess	*Chicago Tribune* (1972)	Days-nights; full charge of 25 girls; seating capacity 150	$125/wk to start
Hotel Desk Clerk	*New York Times* (1971)	5 days, relief shift; must know NCR 4200	$125/wk
Hotel Room Clerk	*New York Times* (1973)	4–12 or nights	$541/mo
Housekeeper	*Chicago Tribune* (1970)	Experienced pleasant woman to live in	$80/wk
IBM Typist	*Chicago Tribune* (1970)	Must type 65 words per minute accurate and neat for small print shop	$2.90+/hr
Ice Skater	Guinness Book of World Records (1981)	Annual earnings of professional ice skater Janet Lynn [1974]	$750,000
Inventory Clerk	*Chicago Tribune* (1972)	Mail-order book concern in Niles needs intelligent young adult for inventory records	$520/mo

Job	Source	Description	Pay
Keypuncher	*Chicago Tribune* (1970)	For a world-famous airline; junior	$450/mo
Keypuncher	*New York Times* (1971)	3 mos + experience	$130/wk
Manager	*New York Times* (1971)	IBM System 3	$15,000/yr
Marketing Manager	*New York Times* (1973)	Paper	$20,000–$22,000/yr
Metallurgist	*Chicago Tribune* (1974)	Heat treat supervisor	$14,000/yr
Navy Recruit	*Life* (1972)	Monthly pay of Navy recruit, plus free food, free clothing and free housing	$288
Nurse	*Chicago Tribune* (1970)	Situation wanted: practical nurse; will care for elderly or invalid person; will live-in and give 24 hr care 6 days	$150/wk
Part-Time Typist	*Chicago Tribune* (1974)	Large publishing firm located in Loop area needs permanent part-time typist	$3.63–$4/hour
Psychiatric Social Worker	*Chicago Tribune* (1974)	Immediate opening; ACSW with three years or more experience	$11,138/yr
Receptionist	*Chicago Tribune* (1974)	Law firm; a well-established law firm is looking for a receptionist; will train on pushbutton console	$625/mo
Sales-Buyer	*Chicago Tribune* (1974)	Must love to sell and work; must be talented in sales, office skills and want to grow with a large wholesale firm	$200/wk
Secretary	*New York Times* (1970)	Will work as right-hand to dynamic executives in high profit brokerage firm; per week	$135 to $175
Truck Driver	*Chicago Tribune* (1974)	Must have good work and driving record	$14,000/yr
Wall Street Analysts	*New York Times* (1970)	Institution seeks topnotch senior analyst in oil; per year	To $40,000
Writer	Patrick Sameway, *Walker Percy: A Life* (1997)	Payment to Walker Percy for paperback rights to his novel *Love in the Ruins* in 1971	$75,000

CONSUMER EXPENDITURES 1970-1974

(Per Capita)

Expenditure Type	1970	1971	1972	1973	1974
Clothing	$194.26	$208.99	$225.83	$248.22	$261.86
Food	$693.58	$710.26	$755.114	$831.02	$926.33
Auto Usage	$362.16	$419.43	$460.70	$500.69	$506.89
New Auto Purchase	$106.89	$135.79	$150.55	$159.97	$126.25
Auto Parts	$29.77	$34.19	$38.11	$41.99	$44.42
Gas & Oil	$106.89	$111.72	$116.25	$132.60	$168.81
Housing	$458.81	$494.56	$534.07	$579.02	$627.06
Furniture	$41.98	$44.30	$45.55	$55.68	$58.45
Utilities	$110.79	$119.43	$131.02	$144.87	$169.74
Telephone & Telegraph	$49.29	$52.97	$59.08	$66.54	$72.48
Physicians	$68.33	$73.68	$79.09	$86.83	$94.92
Dentist	$23.92	$24.56	$26.68	$31.15	$34.14
Health Insurance	$21.48	$23.59	$28.59	$30.20	$29.93
Personal Business	$156.19	$169.51	$183.42	$196.31	$216.04
Personal Care	$57.59	$58.27	$61.46	$66.54	$72.01
Tobacco	$52.71	$54.42	$58.75	$62.29	$65.93
Local Transport	$14.64	$15.89	$16.19	$16.52	$17.30
Intercity Transport	$19.52	$21.19	$24.77	$27.84	$32.27
Recreation	$210.37	$221.51	$244.88	$272.29	$297.39
Religion/Welfare Activities	$59.06	$65.01	$72.42	$76.92	$84.17
Private Education & Research	$61.01	$65.97	$71.94	$78.34	$85.57
Per Capita Consumption	$3155.52	$3372.32	$3658	$4002.19	$4338.01

INVESTMENTS 1970-1974

Investment	1970	1971	1972	1973	1974
Basic Yield, One-year Corporate Bonds	8.51	7.94	7.63	7.80	8.98
Short-term Interest Rates, 4-6 Months, Prime Commercial Paper	7.72	5.11	4.69	8.15	4.87
Basic Yield, Common Stocks, Total	3.83	3.14	2.84	3.06	4.47
Index of Common Stocks (1941–1943=10)	83.22	98.29	109.20	107.43	82.85

COMMON STOCKS, CLOSING PRICE AND YIELD, FIRST BUSINESS DAY OF YEAR

(Parenthetical number is annual dividend in dollars)

	1970	1971	1972	1973	1974
Allis Chalmers	21 7/8	15 3/4	13	12 1/2	8 7/8
	(/)	(.05)	(.05)	(.20)	(.26)
American Brands	35 5/8	45 1/8	42 1/8	43	33 1/2
	(2)	(2.10)	(2.20)	(2.29)	(2.38)
AT&T	49 3/8	48 3/4	44 3/4	53 1/4	50
	(2.60)	(2.60)	(2.60)	(2.80)	(3.08)
Anaconda	30 3/4	21 1/8	16	19 3/4	27 3/4
	(1.90)	(1.90)	(/)	(.12)	(.50)
Bethlehem Steel	27 1/8	22 1/2	29 1/4	29 3/8	32 1/2
	(1.80)	(1.80	(1.20)	(1.20)	(1.60)
CPC Intl (Name changed from Corn Products, 4/22/69)	32 3/8	33 5/8	32 5/8	32 1/2	26 3/4
	(1.70)	(1.70)	(1.70)	(1.77)	(1.86)
Delta Air Lines	30 3/4	33 1/2	48	66	39 7/8
	(.40)	(.50)	(.50)	(.50)	(.60)
General Electric (2 shares for 1, 4/29/71)	76 5/8	93 7/8	63	73 7/8	62 5/8
	(2.60)	(2.60)	(1.40)	(1.40)	(1.60)
General Motors	71 1/4	78 7/8	79 3/4	82 1/8	46
	(4.30)	(3.40)	(3.40)	(4.45)	(5.25)
International Business Machines	364 3/4	313	333	409	242 3/4
	(4)	(4.80)	(5.20)	(5.40)	(4.48)
Intl Harvester	26 1/8	27 1/2	29 3/4	38 3/4	26 3/4
	(1.80)	(1.80)	(1.40)	(1.40)	(1.50)
National Biscuit (Name changed to Nabisco 4/27/71)	49 3/4	52 1/4	57 7/8	60 7/8	37 1/2
	(2.20)	(2.20)	(2.20)	(2.30)	(2.30)
US Steel	34 3/4	32 1/4	30 1/2	31 1/8	37 1/4
	(2.40)	(2.40)	(1.60)	(1.60)	(1.60)
Western Union	44 1/4	40 1/2	44 5/8	48 5/8	14 3/8
	(1.40)	(1.40)	(1.40)	(1.40)	(1.40)

STANDARD JOBS 1970-1974

Job Type	1970	1971	1972	1973	1974
Domestic Industries	$7747/yr	$8255/yr	$8794/yr	$9326/yr	$10,017/yr
Private Industries, incl farm labor	$7679/yr	$8144/yr	$8634/yr	$9154/yr	$9867/yr
Bituminous Coal Mining	$9790/yr	$10,331/yr	$11,323/yr	$12,335/yr	$13,580/yr
Building Trades	$9810/yr	$10,473/yr	$10,747/yr	$11,251/yr	$12,192/yr
Domestics	$3847/yr	$4159/yr	$4478/yr	$4833/yr	$5260/yr
Farm Labor	$3787/yr	$3783/yr	$3900/yr	$4391/yr	$4776/yr
Federal Civilian	$10,921/yr	$11,767/yr	$12,596/yr	$13,464/yr	$14,080/yr
Federal Employees, Executive Depts.	$8040/yr	$8995/yr	$10,331/yr	$11,003/yr	$12,446/yr
Federal Military	$6319/yr	$7139/yr	$8603/yr	$9070/yr	$9594/yr
Finance, Insurance, & Real Estate	$7823/yr	$8347/yr	$8861/yr	$9270/yr	$9853/yr
Gas, Electricity, & Sanitary Workers	$10,028/yr	$10,696/yr	$11,420/yr	$12,156/yr	$13,031/yr
Manufacturing, Durable Goods	$9810/yr	$10,473/yr	$10,747/yr	$11,251/yr	$12,192/yr
Manufacturing Nondurable Goods	$7691/yr	$8167/yr	$8636/yr	$9099/yr	$9925/yr
Medical/Health Services Workers	$6593/yr	$7043/yr	$7499/yr	$7980/yr	$8727/yr
Miscellaneous Manufacturing	$7097/yr	$7355/yr	$7800/yr	$8080/yr	$8679/yr
Motion Picture Services	$8359/yr	$8441/yr	$8882/yr	$9172/yr	$10,108/yr
Nonprofit Org. Workers	$5449/yr	$5924/yr	$6088/yr	$6645/yr	$7130/yr
Passenger Transportation Workers, Local and Highway	$6996/yr	$7309/yr	$7496/yr	$7973/yr	$8645/yr
Personal Services	$5636/yr	$5892/yr	$6268/yr	$7079/yr	$7459/yr
Public School Teachers	$8299/yr	$8813/yr	$9284/yr	$9774/yr	$10,249/yr
Radio Broadcasting & Television Workers	$10,712/yr	$10,885/yr	$11,575/yr	$12,168/yr	$12,779/yr
Railroads	$10,110/yr	$11,360/yr	$11,991/yr	$13,775/yr	$14,240/yr
State and Local Govt. Workers	$7894/yr	$8443/yr	$8898/yr	$9466/yr	$10,020/yr
Telephone & Telegraph Workers	$8512/yr	$9350/yr	$10,518/yr	$11,397/yr	$12,503/yr

FOOD BASKET 1970-1974

(NR = -Not Reported)

Commodity	Year	New York	Atlanta	Chicago	Denver	Los Angeles
Apples, Fresh, per pound	1970	25¢	22.40¢	20.20¢	NR	24.20¢
	1971	26.60¢	25.10¢	19.90¢	NR	
	1972	26.50¢	25¢	25.30¢	NR	28.40¢
	1973	32.10¢	31.30¢	31.70¢	NR	32.10¢
	1974	37.70¢	51.70¢	36.70¢	NR	39.60¢
Beans, Dried, per pound	1970	20.10¢	17.50¢	18.30¢	NR	21.70¢
	1971	22.60¢	18.30¢	19.40¢	NR	24.70¢
	1972	25.30¢	20.30¢	20.80¢	NR	29.20¢
	1973	32¢	30.30¢	29.70¢	NR	34¢
	1974	94¢	$1.02	50.30¢	NR	73.30¢
Beef, Rib Roasts, per pound	1970	$1.02	$1.19	$1.09	NR	$1.25
	1971	$1.70	$1.27	$1.11	NR	$1.27
	1972	$1.17	$1.39	$1.25	NR	$1.40
	1973	$1.41	$1.65	$1.42	NR	$1.65
	1974	$1.51	$1.85	$1.41	NR	$1.63
Beef, Steaks (Round), per pound	1970	$1.54	$1.32	$1.09	NR	$1.16
	1971	$1.64	$1.37	$1.14	NR	$1.21
	1972	$1.77	$1.49	$1.22	NR	$1.30
	1973	$2.02	$1.83	$1.49	NR	$1.58
	1974	$2.12	$1.89	$1.90	NR	$1.64
Bread, White, per pound	1970	28.50¢	22.90¢	24¢	NR	26.40¢
	1971	30.10¢	24.30¢	24.30¢	NR	26.80¢
	1972	30.30¢	24.10¢	24.60¢	NR	41.20¢
	1973	33.20¢	26.70¢	28.20¢	NR	28¢
	1974	40.90¢	32.70¢	35¢	NR	33.70¢
Butter, per pound	1970	88.10¢	93¢	86.70¢	NR	87.20¢
	1971	90.10¢	93¢	87.30¢	NR	88¢
	1972	89.50¢	91.10¢	87.40¢	NR	87.90¢
	1973	93.30¢	98.20¢	93.90¢	NR	91.30¢
	1974	97¢	$1.02	93.50¢	NR	92.90¢
Cheese, per 8 ounces	1970	49.10¢	50.20¢	51.10¢	NR	53.20¢
	1971	58.40¢	52.50¢	55.10¢	NR	55.30¢
	1972	52.10¢	53.60¢	57.80¢	NR	57.90¢
	1973	58¢	61.30¢	63.70¢	NR	64.70¢
	1974	72.40¢	73.50¢	74.30¢	NR	77.10¢
Chickens, per pound	1970	46.40¢	38.90¢	39.90¢	NR	39.70¢
	1971	46.90¢	39.20¢	40.40¢	NR	39.20¢
	1972	46.40¢	41.10¢	40.60¢	68.30¢	40.50¢
	1973	63.40¢	58.70¢	59.50¢	NR	57.40¢
	1974	60.60¢	55.30¢	55.80¢	NR	52.70¢
Coffee, per pound	1970	91¢	93.80¢	94.10¢	NR	85.30¢
	1971	93¢	95.80¢	97.60¢	92.50¢	86.20¢
	1972	91.80¢	93.90¢	96.60¢	NR	86.10¢
	1973	$1.03	$1.01	$1.08	NR	98.3¢
	1974	$1.24	$1.22	$1.29	NR	$1.11
Eggs, per dozen	1970	66.80¢	61.40¢	60.70¢	NR	56.20¢
	1971	57.90¢	53.20¢	52.50¢	NR	46.80¢
	1972	57.10¢	52.80¢	51.50¢	NR	9.20¢
	1973	83.50¢	77¢	77.10¢	NR	77¢
	1974	85.60¢	78.30¢	81¢	NR	72.30¢
Flour, White, per pound	1970	11.78¢	12.76¢	11.10¢	NR	12.12¢
	1971	11.72¢	13.40¢	10.90¢	NR	12.46¢
	1972	11.26¢	13.42¢	10.94¢	NR	12.62¢
	1973	14.62¢	16.04¢	14.72¢	NR	15.24¢
	1974	20.06¢	21.64¢	20.74¢	NR	19.90¢

Commodity	Year	New York	Atlanta	Chicago	Denver	Los Angeles
Lamb Chops, per pound	1970	$1.84	$1.46	$1.89	NR	$1.90
	1971	$1.92	$1.51	$1.93	NR	$1.94
	1972	$2.03	$1.69	$2.09	NR	$2.08
	1973	$2.29	$2.34	$2.30	NR	$2.25
	1974	$2.49	$2.56	$2.36	NR	$2.75
Margarine, per pound	1970	32.70¢	31.80¢	31.40¢	NR	29.50¢
	1971	37.40¢	35.50¢	34.60¢	NR	32.30¢
	1972	37¢	37.50¢	35.10¢	NR	33.10¢
	1973	41.50¢	39.30¢	37.70¢	NR	36.50¢
	1974	63.50¢	58.70¢	58.20¢	NR	55.10¢
Milk, Fresh, per quart	1970	35.60¢	32.85¢	34.95¢	NR	33.85¢
	1971	36.85¢	33.65¢	36.25¢	NR	35.05¢
	1972	37.05¢	34.40¢	37.10¢	NR	35.25¢
	1973	40.55¢	38.70¢	41.70¢	NR	36.95¢
	1974	41.80¢	44.95¢	39.20¢	NR	34.75¢
Pork, Bacon, Sliced, per pound	1970	$1.02	92.70¢	98.90¢	NR	88.70¢
	1971	92.40¢	78.60¢	83.10¢	NR	72.70¢
	1972	$1.02	97.70¢	$1.03	NR	88.20¢
	1973	$1.38	$1.34	$1.39	NR	$1.21
	1974	$1.41	$1.365	$1.37	NR	$1.21
Pork, Chops, per pound	1970	$1.30	$1.17	$1.01	NR	$1.21
	1971	$1.25	$1.09	93.70¢	NR	$1.12
	1972	$1.40	$1.22	$1.11	NR	$1.32
	1973	$1.66	$1.56	$1.44	NR	$1.67
	1974	$1.67	$1.65	$1.59	NR	$1.69
Pork, Ham, Whole, per pound	1970	82.40¢	71.30¢	73¢	NR	78.20¢
	1971	79¢	67.40¢	65.10¢	NR	72.20¢
	1972	84.80¢	78.50¢	71.60¢	NR	78.40¢
	1973	$1.10	$1.02	94.20¢	NR	$1.08
	1974	$1.12	98.50¢	$1.16	NR	$1.08
Potatoes, Irish, per 10 pounds	1970	94.40¢	$1.09	$1.15	NR	$1.00
	1971	94.20¢	$1.14	$1.10	NR	91.60¢
	1972	99.90¢	$1.27	$1.20	NR	$1.04
	1973	$1.47	$1.65	$1.57	NR	$1.47
	1974	$1.76	$1.89	$2.05	NR	$1.72
Rice, per pound	1970	22.10¢	19.40¢	19.90¢	NR	24.40¢
	1971	23.70¢	20.40¢	19.80¢	NR	25.20¢
	1972	23.70¢	20.80¢	20.60¢	NR	24.70¢
	1973	30.40¢	27¢	29¢	NR	32.10¢
	1974	51.20¢	44.80¢	46.60¢	NR	55.90¢
Sugar, per pound	1970	13.48¢	12.84¢	13.02¢	NR	12.34¢
	1971	13.90¢	13.42¢	14.10¢	NR	13.10¢
	1972	14.08¢	13.92¢	14.40¢	NR	13.84¢
	1973	15.50¢	15.12¢	15.32¢	NR	14.74¢
	1974	33.60¢	33.18¢	32¢	NR	30.80¢
Tea, Bags, per package of 48	1970	60.80¢	66.50¢	62.30¢	NR	65.20¢
	1971	62¢	66.10¢	64.10¢	NR	64.60¢
	1972	60.80¢	66.70¢	64¢	NR	65.20¢
	1973	62.10¢	65.40¢	65.80¢	NR	64.80¢
	1974	66.80¢	71.40¢	73¢	NR	69.50¢
Veal, per pound	1970	$2.65	$2.00	$1.98	NR	$2.11
	1971	$2.88	$2.10	$2.19	NR	$2.26
	1972	$3.29	$2.28	$2.77	NR	$2.77
	1973	$3.90	NR	$2.94	NR	$3.1
	1974	$3.92	NR	$3.18	NR	$4.06

SELECTED PRICES 1970-1974

Item	Source	Description	Price
Alcohol			
Whiskey	*New York Times* (1970)	*Canadian Club whiskey;* C.C., Canada's best tasting initials; per fifth	$7.10
Apparel, Children's			
Dress	*New York Times* (1970)	*Pandora;* ruffly-edged coat dress with white collar	$13
Jacket and Knit Cap	*Sears, Roebuck* (1974)	NFL; authentic team emblem on the left front	$17.99
Pajamas	*Sears, Roebuck* (1974)	Perma-press knit; features irresistible characters screen printed on chest	
		Tigger, Snoopy and Woodstock	$5.49
		Scooby-Doo	$5.99
Robe	*Sears, Roebuck* (1974)	Plaid-flannel robe	$8.99
Shoes	*New York Times* (1970)	*Penaljo* footwear for girls; ultra-comfortable walker	$19.95
Sweater	*New York Times* (1970)	*Justin Charles;* easy care Orlon acrylic sweater; monogram with three initials or first name	$7
Apparel, Men's			
Belt	*Smithsonian* (1973)	*Austral Enterprisers;* braided calfskin; 1 1/2" wide, pliant, comfortable, hand-braided from sixteen strands of specially tanned calfskin	$12.50
Belt	*Sears, Roebuck* (1973)	*Buck suede;* lucite-plastic insert buckle mixes textures with buck suede	$7
Jacket	*Ebony* (1972)	*Smith House of Leather, leather;* colors include black, brown, red, and blue	$80
Jacket	*Sears, Roebuck* (1973)	Lightweight; stitch-trimmed western style in smooth-grain leather	$65
Pants	*Ebony* (1972)	*Jaymar,* hemmed slack is fashioned of 100% Trevina polyester in a rare range of colors	$22.50
Shirt	*Sears, Roebuck* (1973)	*Kingsroad;* lightweight double-knit polyester stretch sports shirt with collar and placket	$7
Shoes	*Ebony* (1972)	*Flagg Brothers Outta Sight;* tan and brown leather wingtip lace-up; flared maxi heel	$16.99
Shoes	*Ebony* (1972)	*Navarro Brothers;* baby sharkskin slip-ons; benchmade by Mexico's finest shoemaker	$39.50
Shoes	*Smithsonian* (1973)	*Norm Thompson;* handcrafted moccasins from golden-tan deerskin for unbelievable comfort indoors or out	$15
Underwear	*Ebony* (1972)	*Kayser-Roth;* Paris zig-zag-colored boxer shorts; lily-white underwear was your Mother's idea	$4
Underwear	*Penthouse* (1973)	Imported Norwegian see-thru fish-net weave bikini briefs keep you cool in the summer, warm in the winter; 3 to a pack	$8.95
Apparel, Women's			
Blouse	*Ebony* (1972)	*Frederick's of Hollywood;* a shirtmaker that goes from prim to pow; buttons to the chin; blue or pink nylon	$9
Body Suit	*Sears, Roebuck* (1973)	High band-neck with 6-button placket adds a great look to this figure-hugging rib-knit stretch nylon body suit; was $7.97	$4.77
Coat	*New York Times* (1970)	*Bergdorf Goodman;* fierce tiger fake with natural brown Australian opossum borders; a sash of real leather holds everything in place	$260

Item	Source	Description	Price
Coat	*The New York Times Magazine* (1971)	*John Meyer* velvet midi coat	$80
Dress	*New York Times* (1970)	*The Young Individualist;* black velvet overalls with satin work-shirt top; rhinestone buckles	$60
Dress	*The New York Times Magazine* (1971)	*Kay Windsor* dress; spirited knit, squared off with eye-catching accents; Dacron polyester doubleknit	$32
Jeans	*Sears, Roebuck* (1973)	Our lowest price in five years; corduroy	$4.88
Overcoat	*Ebony* (1972)	*Swank Shirt Shop;* jazz-age wrap, featuring 47" wool velour, cashmere hand wrap	$74.50
Pants	*Ms.* (1972)	*Lady Wrangler;* corduroy flares	$15
Pantsuit	*The New York Times Magazine* (1971)	*ENKA Pantsuit* made of Encron polyester by Adamo Knits; will never wrinkle or crush	$26
Shirt	*Sears, Roebuck* (1973)	For today's individualist; great ways to express yourself; be creative in versatile coordinates	$11
Shoes	*Sears, Roebuck* (1973)	Sandals; cross straps for comfort	$12.99
Shoes	*The New York Times Magazine* (1971)	*B. Altman & Company* offers suede shoes with an Oxford accent; made by Sandler of Boston	$17
Skirt	*The New York Times Magazine* (1971)	*Alberoy Tie-Back Boot-Topper;* birch, beet and brick	$28
Skirt	*Ebony* (1972)	*Smith House of Leather,* leather; colors include blue, black, red, and burgundy	$19.00
Underwear	*Sears, Roebuck* (1973)	Brassiere and panties; suit-your-size; Antron nylon knit in yellow, green, and pink print on orange	$7

Appliances

Air Cleaner	*The New York Times Magazine* (1971)	*General Electric Air Cleaner;* keeps dirt off your furniture and out of the air you breathe	$319.95
Chain Saw	*Southern Living* (1973)	*Remington Mighty Mite Bantam Chain Saw;* weighs just 6 1/2 pounds	$89.95
Microwave Oven	*New York Times* (1970)	*Radarange Microwave Oven;* cook cool with electronics; so quick that usual cooking time is reduced up to 75%	$450
Reading Light	*The New York Times Magazine* (1971)	*Love Lights* for your bed; each reader has his or her own light source	$45

Baby Products

Bed-wetting Alarm	*Sears, Roebuck* (1973)	*Wee-alert Buzzer,* buzzer alarm helps keep sleeper dry and more comfortable by conditioning him to stop bedwetting	$19.95
Quilt	*The New York Times Magazine* (1971)	*Triboro Quilt* cuddles babies with a pram suit and comforter; with Disney characters	$5

Business Equipment and Services

Welding Torch	*Southern Living* (1973)	*Pyro Welding Torch kit;* produces 5000 degrees heat for welding, soldering and brazing	$24.88

Collectibles

Bowl	*Gourmet* (1973)	*Haviland & Co.;* Louis XV carette porcelain bowl	$33.50
Calendar	*Ms.* (1972)	*Reid & Reid Books;* Marilyn Monroe photo calendar, 1954; extremely rare	$10

Item	Source	Description	Price
Egg Box	*Gourmet* (1973)	*Georg Jensen;* sterling	$145
Painting	*Guinness Book of World Records* (1981)	Price paid in 1971 for painter Mary Cassatt's *Summertime*	$150,000
Paintings	*New York Times* (1970)	*Gimbels* magnificent collection of framed reproductions; Sunflower by Borg; walnut frame	$29.99
Plate	*New York Times* (1970)	*Franklin Mint;* annual Christmas collector's plate by Norman Rockwell; a sound investment	$100
Print	*Gourmet* (1973)	Nineteenth-century Chinese, on rice paper	$50
Sculpture	*Gourmet* (1973)	Cybis porcelain birds, limited edition, sold as a pair	$1,800
Sculpture	*Smithsonian* (1973)	Porcelain original; by conservationist Lowell Davis, 17 1/2" long, limited edition of 950 pieces	$1,000
Shop Box	*Gourmet* (1973)	Decoupage and lacquer	$75

Entertainment

Item	Source	Description	Price
Antique Show	*Southern Living* (1973)	High Museum Antiques Show and Sale in Atlanta, Georgia; featuring furniture influenced by 17th and 18th century China	$2.50
Concert Ticket	*New York Times* (1973)	*Mostly Mozart;* Philharmonic Hall, Lincoln Center; all seats reserved	$4.50
Theater Ticket	*New York Times* (1971)	*Hair,* Monday—Thursday evenings	
		Rear Mezzanine	$5–$9
		Front Mezzanine	$11
		Orchestra	$12
Theater Ticket	*New York Times* (1971)	*Oh! Calcutta!;* evenings	$5-$15
Theater Ticket	*New York Times* (1973)	*American Shakespeare Theatre; Measure for Measure; The Country Wife; Macbeth*	
		Saturday Matinee; Saturday Evening; Sunday Matinee	$5.50
		All Other Shows	$8
Theater Ticket	*New York Times* (1973)	*Sportsmen's Show;* 2 Hollywood stars	
		Children	$0.75
		Adult General Admission	$1.50

Entertainment, Home

Item	Source	Description	Price
Camera	*Life* (1972)	*Kodak* introduces the pocket camera; Just drop in the new little film cartridge and shoot.	$28
Camera	*Life* (1972)	*Polaroid's Focused Flash 400;* You can forget burnouts, you can forget blackouts	$70
Camera	*Life* (1971)	*Cannon Canonet QL 17;* this carry-it-anyplace camera gives you quick and precise rangefinder focus	$165
Camera	*Life* (1971)	*Polaroid's Square Shooter,* brings 60-second color pictures down to about the cost of shots you have developed at the factory	$35
Camera	*Popular Mechanics* (1972)	*Kodak Electric 8 Automatic Movie Camera;* no lens setting, an electric eye automatically adjusts the super-fast f/1.6 lens to the light.	$1,000
Camera	*Smithsonian* (1973)	*Kodak Pocket Instamatic 40;* an electronic shutter and CIS electric eye give you automatic exposure control	$68
Camera Outfit	*Ebony* (1972)	*Kodak Hawkeye Instamatic X;* includes camera, film, magicube, wrist strap and instruction book	$22.95
Camera Outfit	*Smithsonian* (1973)	*Polaroid Minute Maker Kit;* contains everything you need to take instant pictures, including Square Shooter 2 camera, 2 Sylvania Blue Dot flashcubes, a pack of square color film and a coupon for 3 free copies of a favorite instant picture	$36

Item	Source	Description	Price
Cassette Tapes	*Sears, Roebuck* (1974)	60-minute; 3 in package	$1.99
Projector	*Southern Living* (1973)	*Kodak Carousel Custom H Projector;* The slide projector that lives in the living room	$180
Radio	*New York Times* (1970)	*Hitachi Solid State AM/FM Radio;* works with batteries or AC; reduced from $79.99, now	$49.99
Record Album	*New York Times* (1970)	Simon & Garfunkel's *Bridge Over Troubled Water*	$5.98
Record Album	*New York Times* (1970)	Neil Young's *After the Gold Rush*	$4.98
Stereo	*Life* (1972)	*The Voice of Music;* This graduation gift is brought to you in glorious color by the class of '72; includes four speed, automatic changer; orange peel color, Model 346	$79.95
Television	*Ebony* (1972)	*Sears, Roebuck;* portable 19" screen; color with one-button tuning	$220

Food Products

Item	Source	Description	Price
Eggs	*Chicago Tribune* (1972)	*Sunnybrook;* fresh grade A	$0.39/dz
Pecans	*New York Times* (1970)	*Sunnyland Farms;* paper-shell pecans 5 lb. Box	$6.45
Shrimp	*Chicago Tribune* (1972)	Peeled and de-veined; 1 1/2 lb bag	$3.69

Furniture

Item	Source	Description	Price
Buffet	*The New York Times Magazine* (1971)	*Bennington* solid pine antiqued Welch buffet	$429
Chair	*New York Times* (1970)	*Beach Hill Furniture;* Wendell open-arm chair, tufted seat in muslin	$425
Chair	*New York Times* (1970)	Bean bag chair; sold everywhere for $50 or more; full adult size	$29.99
Chest	*New York Times* (1970)	*Beacon Hill Furniture;* Harcourt chest; oriental design, lacquer finish	$525
Mattress	*The New York Times Magazine* (1971)	*Sealy Posturepedic Mattress;* your back has to last a long time Queen size, 2 piece set King size, 3 piece set	$399.95 $499.95
Table	*New York Times* (1970)	*Maurice Villency;* stainless steel tables; made any size with glass top; dining table 36" x 60" x 28" with 1/2" glass top	$418

Garden Equipment and Supplies

Item	Source	Description	Price
Flower	*Smithsonian* (1973)	African Amaryllis; pre-planted, exotic Amaryllis grows nearly an inch a day	$5.95
Hedge Trimmer	*Life* (1972)	*Disston* cordless electric lawn products; the lightweight way to save trimming time Heavy duty model	$59.99
Wheelbarrow	*The Updated Last Whole Earth Catalog* (1974)	For brick and tile; carries up to 120 bricks; made of rugged, seasoned hardwood	$34.95

Hotels

Item	Source	Description	Price
Room Rate	*New York Times* (1970)	*Barbizon-Plaza Hotel,* 106 Central Park South, New York City; 24 hour operator attended elevators; choice doubles	$26 to $34
Room Rate	*New York Times* (1970)	*Sheraton Inn at LaGuardia;* free bus to/from LaGuardia Airport, free parking; singles, per night from	$22
Room Rate	*The New York Times Magazine* (1971)	*Downingtown Inn,* Downingtown, Pennsylvania; tour Penna Dutch Amish land; 3 days and 2 nights with gourmet meals; each	$60

Item	Source	Description	Price
Room Rate	*Southern Living* (1973)	*Del Webb's Hotel Sahara;* three days, two nights, two dinner shows; per person, double occupancy required	$43

Household Products

Item	Source	Description	Price
Blanket	*New York Times* (1970)	Thickly woven 100% virgin wool reversible animal design blanket from Peru	$22.50
Bundt Pan	*Sears, Roebuck* (1973)	Perfect for use with the Bundt-pan cake mixes; 12-cup colored aluminum Bundt pan with Teflon lining	$2.99
Capita Set	*Penthouse* (1973)	*Jose Cuervo;* hand-made, hand-painted potter tray	$2.50
China	*Gourmet* (1973)	*Royal Worchester;* tea cup and saucer; Royal Garden porcelain set	$15
Cleanser	*Chicago Tribune* (1972)	*Janitor in a Drum;* industrial strength; 64 oz.	$0.99
Cocktail Shaker	*Gourmet* (1973)	*Reed & Barton;* sterling; milk-can design	$47
Coffee Set	*Gourmet* (1973)	*Gorham;* pewter; 3-piece set includes 40 oz coffee pot, creamer, and sugar bowl	$125
Cookware Set	*Sears, Roebuck* (1973)	*Corning Ware;* 9-piece; the newest pattern and shape in freezer-to-oven; save $9.31	$34.99
Detergent	*Chicago Tribune* (1972)	*Dove;* liquid; 22-oz bottle	$0.57
Dish	*Gourmet* (1973)	*Bonniers Dansk;* porcelain; statement style, ovenproof	$18.50
Fabric Softener	*Chicago Trubune* (1972)	*Downy;* 64-oz bottle; with coupon in this ad	$0.99
Flatware	*Gourmet* (1973)	*Bergdorf Goodman;* stainless-steel Spectro style; 5-piece place setting	$10
Grill	*Gourmet* (1973)	Wrought iron; fish shaped	$12
Mattress and Box Spring	*Life* (1971)	*Sealy Posturepedic Sleep System;* queen-size mattress and posturepedic foundation	$249.95
Pasta Machine	*Gourmet* (1973)	*Bazaar De La Cuisine;* Italian chrome-plated machine	$30
Pepper Grinder	*Gourmet* (1973)	*Cartier;* 11" tall and handsome is our silver and mahogany pepper grinder	$35
Preserve Dish	*Gourmet* (1973)	*Wedgwood Queensware;* melon design	$20
Pressure Cooker	*Sears, Roebuck* (1973)	Non-electric; lets you cook complete meals in minutes and still keep food moist and flavorful	$18.99
Shoe Bag	*Gourmet* (1973)	*Louis Vuitton;* cotton bag	$8.50
Staple Gun	*Southern Living* (1973)	*Tru-Test Staple Gun* set; heavy-duty	$4.95
Valise	*Gourmet* (1973)	*Mark Cross;* canvas and leather	$175
Water Softener	*Sears, Roebuck* (1973)	Even at this low price, a manual water softener with up to 36,000 hardness-grain capacity	$99.95
Wok	*The Updated Last Whole Earth Catalog* (1974)	16" spun steel; one with a handy steel-ring base to sit on gas burners	$17.50

Jewelry

Item	Source	Description	Price
Bracelet	*New York Times* (1970)	*Tiffany & Company;* wide link bracelet of 18 karat gold	$1400
Brooch	*Gourmet* (1973)	Yellow sapphire and diamond; one of a kind	$6,500
Jewel Case	*Gourmet* (1973)	*Gucci;* leather with yellow and red accents	$99

Item	Source	Description	Price
Pendant	*Life* (1971)	*Alva Museum;* dragon; gold electroplated facsimile	$6.50
Ring	*New York Times* (1970)	Beautifully styled dome ring; approximately 3 karats of matched diamonds; 18 karat gold setting	$975
Watch	*Life* (1972)	*Haverhill's;* Get a fine Swiss diver's watch	$9.95
Watch	*Penthouse* (1973)	*Rolling Stones;* wristwatch; Swiss made	$15.95

Meals

Item	Source	Description	Price
Breakfast	*Chicago Tribune* (1972)	*Elliott's,* served all day	$0.95
Dinner	*Chicago Tribune* (1972)	*Magical Lamp of Aladdin;* imported turbot, sautéed with dainty mushrooms	$5.95
Dinner	*Chicago Tribune* (1972)	All you can eat; dessert included	$2.45
Dinner	*Gourmet* (1972)	*Coventry Forge Inn;* Coventryville, Pennsylvania; prix fixe	$12.50
Dinner	*Gourmet* (1973)	*Antolotti's,* New York, New York; table d'hôte	$8.25
Dinner	*Gourmet* (1973)	*Constantine's,* Mobile, Alabama; table d'hôte	$2.85
Dinner	*Gourmet* (1973)	*L'Etoile;* San Francisco; table d'hôte	$12
Dinner	*Gourmet* (1973)	*Alfio's La Trattoria;* Washington, D.C.; table d'hôte	$3.75
Meal	*Chicago Tribune* (1972)	*Sir Whoopee;* where a sandwich is a meal; chicken at 1/2 price with this coupon; 8 piece; regular price $2.40	$1.20

Medical Products and Services

Item	Source	Description	Price
Bed Pan	*Sears, Roebuck* (1973)	Hospital quality; contoured design for more comfortable and easier use	$4.98
Biofeedback Monitor Kit	*Smithsonian* (1973)	*Edmund Scientific Co.;* for greater relaxation, concentration, listen to your Alpha and Theta brain waves	$125.50
Cold Remedy	*Chicago Tribune* (1972)	*Neo-synephrine;* 1 oz drops; $1.06 value	$0.66
Eye Drops	*Chicago Tribune* (1972)	*Visine;* regular $1.33; for irritated eyes	$0.99
Nonprescription Drug	*Chicago Tribune* (1972)	*Bayer;* aspirin; manufacturer's list price $1.17; everyday low price; 100 tablets	$0.79
Nonprescription Drug	*Chicago Tribune* (1972)	*Excedrin;* 100 count; 1.69 value	$0.89
Weight Loss Tablets	*Sears, Roebuck* (1973)	*Naturama;* protein; to help you lose weight	$2.19
Wheelchair	*Sears, Roebuck* (1973)	Even at this low price a wheelchair with chrome-plated rims and handrims	$70

Motorized Vehicles, Supplies and Services

Item	Source	Description	Price
Automobile	*Life* (1972)	*Renault 12 Sedan;* front wheel drive, front disc brakes, independent front suspension	$2,295
Automobile	*Life* (1971)	*Volkswagen;* 4-door sedan; a big car as good as a Volkswagen	$2,999
Automobile, Used	*Chicago Tribune* (1972)	*Cougar;* 1969 model	$2,998
Automobile, Used	*Chicago Tribune* (1972)	*Oldsmobile Sport Coupe;* 1970 model; Oldsmobile V-8; never buy before you try	$2,899
Automobile, Used	*New York Times* (1971)	*Oldsmobile Cutlass;* 1968 model; 4 dr; A/C, power steering, power brakes, alarm, excellent condition	$1,850
Automobile, Used	*New York Times* (1971)	*BMW 2002;* early 1970 production; white; 5,000 miles, showroom condition	$2,900

Item	Source	Description	Price
Automobile, Used	*New York Times* (1971)	*Datsun;* 1966 model; sedan; good condition	$475
Automobile, Used	*Chicago Tribune* (1972)	*Ford Wagon;* 1968 model; full-size ranch wagon with 6-cylinder automatic and power	$545
Tires	*The New York Times Magazine* (1971)	*General Safety-Jet Tires* for Volkswagen owners; radial; Each plus $1.74 Federal Excise Tax	$16.95

Other

Item	Source	Description	Price
Beekeeping Set	*The Updated Last Whole Earth Catalog* (1974)	*Walter T. Kelly's Complete;* the necessary items that you need in starting with one hive of bees, including bees, necessary tools, and a book of instructions	$30
Bowhunter's License	*Southern Living* (1973)	Arkansas license fee for non-resident for bow hunting deer	$10
Cane	*Sears, Roebuck* (1973)	Pistol-grip; 1" thick maple shaft; walnut finish; 35"	$4.98
Center Punch	*Sears, Roebuck* (1973)	*Craftsman;* automatic; adjusts for light, heavy impression; steel; 5" long	$5.04
Christmas Tree	*Sears, Roebuck* (1974)	This Canadian pine is our best-selling 6' Christmas tree of all time; now reduced $6 to our lowest price ever	$29.95
Combination Square	*Sears, Roebuck* (1973)	*Craftsman;* hardened, ground-steel blade	$25.99
Dog Tag	*New York Times* (1970)	Silver plated dog bone shaped tag with animal's name, area code, phone number, city and state engraved	$7.50
Folding Chair	*Sears, Roebuck* (1973)	Aluminum-frame yacht chair	$11.65
Light	*Popular Mechanics* (1972)	*Magna-Lite;* shop light; put the light where it's needed; with magnet base	$6.95
Metal Detector	*Ebony* (1972)	*Relco;* finds buried gold, silver and coins	$19.95
Potter's Wheel	*Smithsonian* (1973)	*Gilbert's Potterycraft;* create your own ceramics; seat and flywheel adjust for adults or teenagers	$55
Puppy	*New York Times* (1970)	*American Kennels;* The Dog Department Store: Yorkshire Terrier	$199
		Lhasa Apsos	$249
		Pekingese	$99
		Huskies	$150
Rule	*Sears, Roebuck* (1973)	*Craftsman;* stainless steel; chrome plated	$1.99
Rule	*Sears, Roebuck* (1973)	Stainless steel; not Craftsman; flexible, 6" long	$0.89
Sander	*Popular Mechanics* (1972)	*Millers Falls;* 12 times faster than hand sanding	$34.95
Saw	*Sears, Roebuck* (1973)	9" saw; manual brake for stopping blade quickly; performs the same operations as our 12" saw on a smaller scale	$164
Saw	*Popular Mechanics* (1972)	*Dremel Model 572;* in one compact, portable unit you have a jig saw, disc sander, buffing wheel, bench grinder, and a flexible shaft machine	$49.95
Slide Rule	*Popular Mechanics* (1972)	4"; non-warp with 2-color scales on white nitrate face	$2.95
Tool Set	*Popular Mechanics* (1972)	*Craftsman;* 59-piece set; regular separate prices total $69.95; all tools fit in 18" x 8" x 9" steel tool box	$39.99
Tropical Fish Motor Filter	*Life* (1971)	*Dynaflo;* never change aquarium water	$13.50
Weight Loss Pants	*Life* (1971)	*Sauna Belt;* the amazing space-age slenderizer that is so sensationally effective	$13.50

Personal Care Products

Item	Source	Description	Price
Bath Oil	*Chicago Tribune* (1972)	*Calgon Bath Oil Beads;* 16-oz package	$0.98

Item	Source	Description	Price
Condoms	*Penthouse* (1973)	*Trojan;* made so thin, they're ultra-sensitive; special sampler includes 9 condoms	$3
Deodorant	*Chicago Tribune* (1972)	*Ban Roll-On;* 1 1/2-oz size; save $0.50; limit 1	$0.49
Hair Spray	*Chicago Tribune* (1972)	*Adorn Hard to Hold;* regular or unscented; 13 oz; $2.35 value	$1.09
Hair Treatment	*Ebony* (1972)	*LaCade Hormone Hair Growth Treatment;* with vitamins A and D	$3
Hair Treatment	*Ebony* (1972)	*Murray's Natural Sheen*	$1
Hair Treatment	*Ebony* (1972)	*Drake Persulan Blow-Out Cream;* make Afro twice as big	$2.25
Skin Cream	*Ebony* (1972)	*Bleach and Glow;* does beautiful things for your skin	$1.50
Soap	*Penthouse* (1973)	*English Leather Shower Soap;* our soap on a rope is tied to a great tradition	$2
Soap	*Chicago Tribune* (1972)	*Lifebuoy;* $0.07 off label; bath size	$0.40/2
Wig	*Ebony* (1972)	*Valmor High Fashion;* soul wig, hand styled; 100% human hair	$29.99
Wig	*Ebony* (1972)	*Valmor High Fashion;* Afro-American natural wig	$9.99

Publications

Item	Source	Description	Price
Book	*New York Times* (1970)	*A White House Diary* by Lady Bird Johnson; published by Holt, Rinehart and Winston, 806 pages	$10.95
Book	*New York Times* (1970)	*The Supreme Commander: The War Years of General Dwight D. Eisenhower* by Stephen E. Ambrose; published by Doubleday; 732 pages	$10.00
Book	*New York Times* (1970)	*Lawn Beauty the Organic Way* by Glenn Johns; Rodale Press books	$6.95
Book	*New York Times* (1973)	*Breakfast of Champions,* by Kurt Vonnegut, Jr.	$7.95
Book	*New York Times* (1973)	*Once Is Not Enough,* Jacqueline Susann	$7.95
Book	*New York Times* (1973)	*The Joy of Sex*	$12.95
Book with Cassette	*Sears, Roebuck* (1974)	You'll be enchanted when you pop in a cassette and hear a fairy tale dramatized complete with music and voices; fourteen-page story book follows the action; has full-color illustrations	$1.79
Magazine	*Ebony* (1972)	*Ebony* magazine; Johnson Publishing Co.; monthly	$0.75
Magazine	*Gourmet* (1973)	*Gourmet;* monthly	$0.50
Magazine	*Penthouse* (1973)	*Penthouse;* monthly	$1
Magazine	*Smithsonian* (1973)	*Smithsonian;* monthly	$1

Real Estate

Item	Source	Description	Price
Apartment	*New York Times* (1971)	For rent; 80s and Madison; a skyline view East and South; 2 bedrooms, 2 baths; year-round pool, doorman, security system; 16 months sublet or possible new lease	$680/mo
Apartment	*New York Times* (1971)	For rent; renovated brownstone; 2 bedrooms; large living room; working fireplace; A/C; all electric heat	$475/mo
House	*New York Times* (1971)	For sale; 2-bedroom ranch; double garage; 1 1/2 baths screened patio with triple-Hollywood pool; 1/2 acre beautifully landscaped; immaculate	$38,000

Item	Source	Description	Price
House	*New York Times* (1971)	For sale; must sell magnificent 7-room, 2 1/2-bath colonial; professionally landscaped and decorated; heated concrete pool, cabana and many extras; sacrifice	$55,500
House	*Chicago Tribune* (1972)	For sale; ranch style triplex in Florida; good income from three 2-bedroom apartments	$25,500
Hunting and Fishing Lodge	*New York Times* (1973)	For sale; 440 acres with 50 acre private lake near Minoquoa, Wisconsin; year-round lodge with two guest houses plus garage and out-camp hunting table	$75,000

Sports Equipment

Item	Source	Description	Price
Archery Set	*Sears, Roebuck* (1974)	*Bear Target;* includes bow, arrows, quiver, and target	$28.95
Basketball	*Sears, Roebuck* (1974)	Our lowest price this season for any basketball	$4.98
Basketball Goal	*Sears, Roebuck* (1974)	Portable; so stable, rebound action matches most permanent goals	$99.90
Binoculars	*New York Times* (1970)	*Quazar 2000 Binocular;* made in West Germany; weighs a mere 18 1/2 ounces	$149.95
Life Vest	*Sears, Roebuck* (1973)	Meets USCG specifications; adult ski vests	$20.59
Striking Bag Set	*Sears, Roebuck* (1974)	Wallmount; help develop your body while you sharpen timing, reflexes and coordination	$34.95
Tent	*Sears, Roebuck* (1973)	Pitches anywhere; even on solid rock or sand because it needs no stakes, and its frame anchors to tent, not in ground; plus tent fly adds additional protection from rain	$89
Tent	*Sears, Roebuck* (1973)	Two-man nylon pack; 5' x 7' sleeping area; tent with nylon case	$29.99
Weight Bench	*Sears, Roebuck* (1973)	500-lb capacity; adjustable back and adjustable barbell arms	$3,5.87

Telephone Equipment and Services

Item	Source	Description	Price
Telephone	*Popular Mechanics* (1972)	*Western Electric;* late-model dial phone same as used by all the telephone companies; cost $40 new	$6.95

Tobacco Products

Item	Source	Description	Price
Cigarette Box	*Gourmet* (1973)	*Bergdorf Goodman;* ceramic	$12
Cigarette Lighter	*New York Times* (1970)	A great little lighter with a big difference; works on butane fuel, ignites electronically, never needs flints; gold tone metal case	$30
Pipe	*Popular Mechanics* (1972)	*Kirsten;* patented radiator stem means cool smoking	$3.95
Pipe	*Penthouse* (1973)	*Kaywoodie;* custom-crafted smoking pipe; new relief grain; custom cut	$3.95
Tobacco	*Life* (1971)	*Laredo;* menthol filter blend cigarette tobacco; smoke the freshest menthol filter cigarettes ever for less than $0.20 a pack	$1

Toys

Item	Source	Description	Price
Baby Doll	*Sears, Roebuck* (1974)	*Tenerella;* cut $2; this lovely 19" doll has long, dark, rooted hair, sparkling go-to-sleep-eyes and smooth vinyl skin	$12.99
Buggy Kit	*Sears, Roebuck* (1974)	Assemble your own collection of NFL buggies; an officially licensed NFL product	$5
Coloring Book	*Chicago Tribune* (1972)	Regularly $0.29	$0.10
Doll	*Sears, Roebuck* (1974)	*Rub-A-Dub Dolly;* 17"; wash her, dry her, then bundle her up after the bath	$8.94
Doll	*Sears, Roebuck* (1974)	*Smokey the Bear;* acrylic pile and blue denim	$4.94
Doll Clothes	*Sears, Roebuck* (1974)	2-piece hand-knit outfits for 12"–18" baby dolls	$3.49

Item	Source	Description	Price
Race Track	*Popular Mechanics* (1962)	*Aurora;* who would prefer a pokey loco going around in circles to the pulse-pounding action of a road race; includes land-changing criss-cross layout	$21.98
Stuffed Animal	*Sears, Roebuck* (1974)	*Fashionable Friends;* cotton felt animal with pert cotton-print dresses and bonnets	$3.47
Toy Set	*Sears, Roebuck* (1974)	Get an entire wagonload of 5 of our all-time favorite toys, and we'll include the red wagon for just $1 more; here's what you get: Bugs Bunny toothbrush; 40-piece medical kit; all-steel cash register; 10-piece nesting blocks; talking telephone	$21.78
Walkie-Talkie	*Sears, Roebuck* (1974)	Pocket-size; keeps you in voice contact with your fellow secret agents	$19.99

Travel and Transportation

Item	Source	Description	Price
Air Fare	*The New York Times Magazine* (1971)	New York to Aruba on KLM or American Airlines; one way	$89.50
Airfare	*New York Times* (1973)	*American Airlines;* California and the West round-trip; purchase only 7 days in advance; regular coach fare $336; you save $156.05	$179.95
Airfare	*Smithsonian* (1973)	*American Airlines;* roundtrip group airfare from California to Sydney, Australia; includes 10-day lodging and Hertz Ford Falcon rental car with 500 free miles	$683
Bus Ticket	*Ebony* (1972)	*Greyhound Ameripass;* good for 60 days of almost limitless travel; a new way to see more of America on $2.50 a day	$149.50
Cruise	*Smithsonian* (1973)	*Orient Overseas Services;* 4-month cruise to Acapulco, Panama Canal, Rio de Janeiro, Santos, Buenos Aires, Capetown, Durban, Lourenco Marques, Singapore, Hong Kong, Kaohsiung, Kobe, Vancouver, San Francisco; up to 40 days in port	$3,105
European Tour	*Southern Living* (1973)	Icelandic; one-week car tour, per person, from New York, features roundtrip jet to Luxembourg and self-drive car with unlimited mileage	$250
Hawaiian Tour	*Southern Living* (1973)	Braniff International makes it easy for you to spend seven days and six nights discovering Hawaii; includes accommodations at The Outrigger Surf or Outrigger West hotel in Waikiki; all transfers between airport and hotel; a city tour of Honolulu; from Kansas City, per person	$356.31
Sponge Diving Tour	*Southern Living* (1973)	25-minute trip on Anclote River, Tarpon Springs, Florida where a diver will demonstrate the technique of sponge diving and bring up live sponges Adults Children	 $1.50 $.75
Safari	*Smithsonian* (1973)	East Africa; in-depth viewing of abundant, various wildlife concentrations in famous national parks and reserves of Kenya and Tanzania	$1,519
Trip	*Chicago Tribune* (1972)	*Cartan Travel;* Hawaii; lovely enchanting islands; enjoy 4 islands, top hotels, great sightseeing entertainment, 9 days in outer islands; 5 days in Honolulu, Waikiki Beach	$575
Trip	*Chicago Tribune* (1972)	*VIP Travel Service;* Las Vegas; 3 nights, 4 days; strip hotel	$149
Trip	*Chicago Tribune* (1972)	*Mr. Travel;* San Francisco, Los Angeles, Las Vegas; two weeks; jet to all three	$289

MISCELLANY 1970-1974

The Mafia Sells

Mafia business is not precisely booming these days, but business about the Mafia has never been better. There are nearly 1,000,000 *Godfather* hard covers in print, and over 10 million paperbacks. Jimmy Breslin's best selling comic novel *That Gang Couldn't Shoot Straight*—said to be a take-off of the chaotic exploits of Brooklyn's Gallo gang—was recently reincarnated as a movie. Gay Talese's *Honor Thy Father,* a detailed and understanding portrait of the son of Mafia Boss Joseph Bonanno, has been on the bestseller lists for four months, and recently brought a beefy $451,000 for paperback rights.

Time, March 13, 1972

U.S. Compensating Kin of Raid Dead; Cambodians In Town Hit by Error Will Get $400 Each

The United States made formal restitution to Cambodia today for an accidental American air raid Aug. 6 against the Mekong River town of Neak Buong in which 137 civilians and Cambodian Government soldiers were killed and 282 wounded.

Under an agreement signed today by the Cambodian and American Governments, the United States will pay surviving relatives of each of the dead the equivalent of about $400.

New York Times, August 23, 1973

The Aging American Indian

The indicators of Indian suffering are appalling. Their life expectancy is 44 years, compared with 71 for white Americans. The average income for each Indian family living on a reservation—and more than half do—is only $1,500. The average years of schooling is 5.5, well behind that of both the black and Mexican American. Some officials rate 90% of reservation housing as substandard. Unemployment ranges from a low of 20% on the more affluent reservations to 80% on the poorest. The birth rate of Indians is 2 1/2 times that of whites—a majority of Indians are under 20 years old. The average family has to carry water for its daily needs at least a mile. It is usually done afoot.

Time, February 9, 1970

Price Panel Okays Bra Price Stretch The Price Commission granted Warmaco Inc. permission Monday to lift prices on brassieres and girdles.

The Price Commission granted Warmaco Inc. permission Monday to lift prices on brassieres and girdles.

As the Price Commission put it, the company will be permitted to raise prices on the following items by the stated maximum amount: Bras-fiber, filler, 12 percent; bras, soft cup, 10 percent; bras, Love Touch, 7.5 percent; bras, Love Lace, 7.5 percent; coresellettes, 4.8 percent; and girdles, controlled 9 percent.

In another case, the commission approved requested price increases by Diamond International on toothpicks, clothes pins and wooden ice cream sticks. The request ranged from 2.95 percent to 5.02 percent.

Atlanta Constitution, February 15, 1972

$5.50 Kit Tells If You're Pregnant

Mrs. Earl Callan's menstrual period was eight days overdue. The Toronto, Ontario, housewife decided to wait no longer to determine if she was pregnant. As she completed the family shopping for the day, she stopped in the neighborhood drugstore and picked up a three-inch square paper box bearing the brand name of Confidelle. She paid $5.50 for it and hurried home.

Atlanta Constitution, February 17, 1972

MISCELLANY 1970-1974

PBA Plans a Job Action to Gain Pay Raise

In his brief news conference yesterday, Mr. Kiernan said that patrolmen were not satisfied with the money among other things in the rejected contract. The proposed increases would have raised the salaries of patrolmen $2,150 between Jan. 1, 1971, and Jan. 1, 1973, when the final $750 increase would have gone into effect. Thus, their pay would have gone from the present $12,150 to $14,308.

Various other benefits, such as night differential, paid holidays, uniform allowance, annuity fund payments, medical plan costs and city contributions to the PBA health and welfare fund, according to the PBA's computations, would have raised the annual wage and benefits of a patrolman to $16,894 as of Jan. 1, 1973.

Mr. Kiernan said that the delegates, representing the city's 27,000 patrolmen, had decided also to start a public relations program to tell people of the city why policemen should be paid more than firefighters and sanitation men.

New York Times, June 7, 1972

Gold Price Rises to a Record of $62,375; A Commercial Shortage Brings Heavy Buying In Long Market

A new gold rush prompted by a commercial shortage of the metal shot its price to new peaks today in Europe's free markets.

The flow of buying orders swept the price to a record closing level of $62.375 an ounce in London. This was more than $24 above the official United States price for monetary gold. The previous closing high was yesterday at $59.55.

The picture was much the same in Zurich, Switzerland, the other major trading center. Gold rose to $62.25 an ounce in Zurich, before it closed at $62. The previous recording in Switzerland just topped the $60 mark on May 31.

In Frankfurt active buying pushed the price to a record of $59.22, compared with the previous high of $58.49 last Friday, dealers said. In France, where the market is controlled the price was a more modest $58.16, up from $57.19 yesterday.

New York Times, June 7, 1972

HISTORICAL SNAPSHOT
1975-1979

1975

- First desktop microcomputer available
- Pet rocks go on sale, featuring obedience, loyalty, and low maintenance costs
- Unemployment hits 9.2%
- Minnesota first state to require businesses, restaurants, and institutions to establish no-smoking areas
- New York City averts bankruptcy with $2.3 billion federal loan
- Beef consumption falls 9%; chicken consumption rises nearly 35%
- McDonald's opens its first drive-thru restaurants
- Time-sharing of vacation real estate introduced in U.S.
- Record 120,000 Americans declare personal bankruptcy

1976

- Jimmy Carter elected president
- Cuisinart home food processor introduced
- $68 million football stadium opens in East Rutherford, NJ
- Colossus Cave, first computer game, designed at Princeton
- 3,420 lobbyists registered in Washington, DC
- Congress passes law to admit women in military academies

- ABC offers industry's first $1 million per-year contract, to Barbara Walters of NBC
- Clothier Abercrombie & Fitch declares bankruptcy
- 100 companies sponsor 76% of network TV ads
- Mobil Petroleum buys Montgomery Ward for $1 billion

1977

- Balloon angioplasty developed for reopening diseased arteries of the heart
- U.S. and Canada sign pact to build gas pipeline from Alaska to Midwest
- 1.9 million women operate businesses
- 20,000 shopping malls generate 50% of total retail sales
- Pepsi tops Coca-Cola in sales for first time
- Three major networks control 91% of prime-time audience
- American Express becomes first service company to top $1 billion in sales

1978

- Airline Deregulation Act eliminates federal controls on fares and routes
- California voters adopt Proposition 13 to control property taxes
- Gold sells for $245 per ounce

- Tax code permits 401(k) savings plans for first time
- 8 airlines control 81% of domestic market
- 26 major-league baseball teams show average profit of $4,526
- Pepsico acquires Mexican fast-food chain Taco Bell
- President Carter signs legislation raising the mandatory retirement age to 70
- Unemployment rises to 6 percent
- First class postal rate goes to 15 cents per ounce

1979

- New York City's Citicorp Building completed
- Multiple-mirror telescope installed at Mount Hopkins in Arizona
- Sony Walkman, a portable tape player with headphones, is introduced
- Gold sells for more than $400 per ounce
- First Jiffy Lube fast oil-change automotive service center opens
- Avon products acquires Tiffany & Co.
- Ford Motor Co. acquires 25% of Japan's Mazda Motor Co.
- Controls on oil prices lifted
- Three-Mile Island near meltdown arouses antinuclear forces
- Inflation worst in 33 years; prices increase over 13.3%
- Prime lending rate at banks hits 14.5%

SELECTED INCOME 1975-1979

Job	Source	Description	Pay
Account Executive	Chicago Tribune (1978)	Prefer college degree and background in teaching, sales or management	$12,000 $15,000/yr to start
Accountant	Los Angeles Times (1978)	Min 2 yrs experience in general accounting; diversified corporation in sales and distribution	$18,000/yr
Accountant	Los Angeles Times (1978)	Semi-sr to strong srs, audit and heavy tax positions; permanent with small to "BIG 8" firms	$30,000/yr
Accounting Clerk	Los Angeles Times (1978)	Accounting personnel service	$900/mo
Actor	Guinness Book of World Records (1981)	Per single episode fee paid to Peter Falk for his role in the television show Columbo [1976]	$350,000
Administrator	New York Times (1977)	Children's theater association	$13,000/yr
Author	Guinness Book of World Records (1981)	Advance paid by Bantam Books to Judith Krantz for Princess Daisy	$3.2 million
Baseball Player	USA Today Sports Weekly (2004)	Salary of Minnesota Twins baseball player Rod Carew in 1978	$150,000
Baseball Player	New York Times (2004)	1975 annual salary of relief pitcher Tug McGraw, Philadelphia Phillies	$75,000
Bookkeeper	Los Angeles Times (1978)	Full charge; CPA office	$18,000/yr
Bowler	Guinness Book of World Records (1981)	Earnings of professional bowler Mark Roth [1978]	$134,500
Bowling-alley Trainees	Los Angeles Times (1978)	Desk sales	$184/wk
Business Executive	Guinness Book of World Records (1981)	Salary, bonus, stock and other benefits paid to David Tendler of Englehardt Minerals and Chemical Corp. and President of Philipps Brothers trading division [In 1979]	$2,202,938
Business Manager	Los Angeles Times (1978)	Multimember university medical practice; billing and organization experience necessary	$18,000/yr
Cashier (Restaurant)	New York Times (1977)	Nights, 5–6 days	$3.50/hr
Chef	Los Angeles Times (1978)	Seafood	$1,500/mo
Executive Secretary	Los Angeles Times (1978)	Fast notes or light shorthand; one person only in busy sales firm	$1,200/mo
Football Player	The State Newspaper Columbia, SC (2004)	Payment in 1978 to each member of the Dallas Football team for winning the Super Bowl	$18,000
Golfer	Guinness Book of World Records (1981)	Earnings of professional golfer Nancy Lopez [In 1979]	$197,488
Industrial Engineer	Chicago Tribune (1978)	National consulting firm, enjoying 20 years of continuing growth, has opening for qualified engineer for consulting assignments involving full range of industrial-engineering disciplines	$22,000–$25,000/yr to start
Keypunch Operator	New York Times (1978)	3742 or Key Disc; minimum one year's experience; 35 hours, 5 days a week; per week	$130 to $180

427

Job	Source	Description	Pay
Nobel Prize Award (1979)	Guinness Book of World Records (1981)	Amount paid to each of the 1979 Nobel Prize winners in Physics, Chemistry, Medicine and Physiology, Literature, Peace and Economics	$192,775
Programmer/Analyst	Chicago Tribune (1978)	Do you know or want to learn any of the following applications: IMS, MRP, CICS, MVS, IOMS, VSAM, DB/DC, A/R, or A/P?	$1,450–$2,100/mo
Race Car Driver	Guinness Book of World Records (1981)	Earnings of NASCAR driver Richard Petty [In 1979]	$531,292
Receptionist	New York Times (1977)	Exciting Sportswear designer anxious to hire outward individual	$170–$190/wk
Receptionist	Los Angeles Times (1978)	Greet clients, handle phones; a variety of public contact and general office duties for top law firm	$850/mo
Research Coordinator	New York Times (1977)	Well-known Fifth Avenue firm seeks sharp, personal individual to act as coordinator in research effort	$12,800/yr
Respiratory Therapist	Los Angeles Times (1978)	2-year graduate or CRTT	$944/mo
Rodeo Cowboy	Kristine Fredriksson, American Rodeo (1985)	Annual winnings of Tom Ferguson in 1976	$114,000
Rodeo Rider	Guinness Book of World Records (1981)	Prize money earnings of rodeo rider Tom Ferguson [In 1978]	$131,233
Sales	Chicago Tribune (1978)	Art sales; long term security; fast advancement; no experience necessary	$800/wk, plus commission
Sales	Chicago Tribune (1978)	Dialysis equipment	$22,000–$24,000/yr
Secretary	New York Times (1978)	Gal/Guy Friday; Executive Secretary for health management company; per year	$10,000 to $12,000
Secretary	Chicago Tribune (1978)	Fantastic world famous ad agent will train you to work with him on million-dollar account	$13,000/yr
Secretary/Clerk	New York Times (1977)	2 days wkly, Tuesday & Thursday	$5/hr
Social Secretary	Chicago Tribune (1978)	Secretary will receive telephone messages and correspondence for employer	$175/wk
Stunt Man	Guinness Book of World Records (1981)	Fee paid to Dar Robinson for a 1,100-foot-high leap off the CN Tower in Toronto for the movie High Point [In 1979]	$100,000
Tennis Player	Guinness Book of World Records (1981)	Earnings of professional tennis player Martina Navratilova [In 1979]	$747,548
Wine Consultant	Chicago Tribune (1978)	Immediate openings with PIEROTH, a 371-year old internationally known German winery. Ours is an exclusive guaranteed-high-quality product.	$25,000/yr

CONSUMER EXPENDITURES 1975-1979

(Per Capita)

Expenditure Type	1975	1976	1977	1978	1979
Clothing	$279.66	$300.41	$326.01	$359.86	$377.68
Food	$1011.70	$1082.39	$1161.92	$1259.09	$1390.33
Auto Usage	$550.53	$654.02	$748.73	$808.68	$885.12
New Auto Purchase	$135.67	$175.20	$201.59	$217.89	$219.06
Auto Parts	$47.69	$52.29	$58.57	$60.65	$63.98
Gas & Oil	$183.82	$197.22	$212.95	$225.08	$294.15
Housing	$680.64	$740.71	$815.02	$906.17	$1006.86
Furniture	$59.27	$64.67	$74.76	$80.87	$90.20
Utilities	$196.32	$222.89	$251.54	$274.95	$309.26
Telephone & Telegraph	$81.95	$90.81	$97.62	$107.37	$114.19
Physicians	$108.81	$118.33	$134.39	$146.01	$163.52
Dentists	$37.97	$42.65	$46.77	$50.77	$54.65
Health Insurance	$30.56	$32.10	$42.68	$53.46	$55.09
Personal Business	$245.40	$273.81	$300.13	$359.41	$397.68
Personal Care	$77.32	$83.47	$93.99	$103.33	$111.53
Tobacco	$69.92	$77.05	$77.19	$82.22	$85.31
Local Transport	$18.52	$20.18	$21.79	$21.56	$21.33
Intercity Transport	$33.80	$39.44	$44.95	$49.87	$58.21
Recreation	$331.53	$328.28	$392.30	$435.79	$487.44
Religion/Welfare Activities	$91.22	$102.28	$112.60	$132.53	$148.85
Private Education & Research	$94.92	$102.74	$108.97	$119.95	$132.41
Per-Capita Consumption	$4745.50	$5242.74	$5773.33	$6384.98	$7036.95

INVESTMENTS 1975-1979

Investments	1975	1976	1977	1978	1979
Basic Yield, One-Year Corporate Bonds	9.57	9.01	8.43	9.07	10.12
Short-Term Interest Rates, 4–6 Months, Prime Commercial Paper	6.33	5.35	5.60	7.99	10.91
Basic Yield, Common Stocks, Total	4.31	3.77	4.56	5.28	5.46
Index of Common Stocks (1941–1943=10)	85.17	102.01	98.18	96.11	107.94

COMMON STOCKS, CLOSING PRICE AND YIELD, FIRST BUSINESS DAY OF YEAR

(Parenthetical number is annual dividend in dollars)

	1975	1976	1977	1978	1979
Allis Chalmers	6 3/4	12 1/8	26 1/2	24 3/4	29 5/8
	(.26)	(.40)	(.90)	(.60)	(1.70)
American Brands	31 1/2	38 3/4	45 1/4	42 1/2	50 3/8
	(2.56)	(2.68)	(2.80)	(3.04)	(4)
Anaconda (Merged as wholly owned subsidiary of Atlantic Richfield, 1/12/77)	14 1/2	(1) (.60)	17 1/8 (.60)	30	
Bethlehem Steel	24 7/8	33 1/2	39 7/8	20 3/8	19 7/8
	(4)	(2)	(2)	(1)	(1)
CPC Intl	33	43	46 7/8	45 3/4	49 1/2
	(2)	(2.14)	(2.30)	(2.50)	(2.70)
Delta Airlines	29 1/8	37 5/8	39 1/4	39 1/8	42
	(.60)	(.60)	(.70)	(.70)	(1)
General Electric	33 3/4	46 5/8	55 3/8	48 3/4	47
	(1.60)	(1.60)	(1.80)	(2.20)	(2.60)
General Motors	31 7/8	58 3/8	78	61 1/2	55
	(3.40)	(2.40)	(5.55)	(6.80)	(6)
IBM (5 shares for 4 split, 5/10/73) (4 shares for 1 split, 5/31/79)	168 7/8 (6)	226 1/2 (7)	276 1/2 (9)	268 3/4 (11.52)	303 1/2 (13.76)
Intl Harvester	20 1/4	23 1/8	32 7/8	29 5/8	36 7/8
	(1.70)	(1.70)	(1.85)	(2.10)	(2.30)
Nabisco	22 3/4	38 5/8	50 1/2	46 1/2	25 3/8
	(2.30)	(2.30)	(2.40)	(2.52)	(1.50)
US Steel	38 1/2	65 3/8	49 3/8	31 3/8	22 1/8
	(4)	(2.80)	(2.20)	(2.20)	(1.60)
Western Union	9 1/4	16 1/4	20 1/4	16 7/8	15 1/2
	(1.40)	(1.40)	(1.40)	(1.40)	(1.40)

STANDARD JOBS 1975-1979

Job Type	1975	1976	1977	1978	1979
Wages per Full-Time Employee	$10,817/yr	$11,585/yr	$12,370/yr	$13,263/yr	$14,373/yr
Private Industries, inc. farm labor	$10,655/yr	$11,430/yr	$12,222/yr	$13,143/yr	$14,310/yr
Bituminous Coal Mining	$15,924/yr	$17,018/yr	$18,292/yr	$20,160/yr	$22,363/yr
Building Trades	$13,447/yr	$14,242/yr	$14,639/yr	$15,394/yr	$16,785/yr
Domestics	$5774/yr	$6479/yr	$6844/yr	$7206/yr	$7912/yr
Farm Labor	$5073/yr	$5416/yr	$6021/yr	$6438/yr	$7154/yr
Federal Civilian	$15,024/yr	$16,238/yr	$17,488/yr	$18,905/yr	$19,907/yr
Federal Employees, Executive Depts.	$12,446/yr	$13,153/yr	$13,980/yr	$15,068/yr	$15,961/yr
Federal Military	$10,064/yr	$10,420/yr	$10,854/yr	$11,570/yr	$12,316/yr
Finance, Insurance, & Real Estate	$10,609/yr	$11,386/yr	$12,184/yr	$13,207/yr	$14,326/yr
Gas, Electricity, & Sanitation Workers	$14,231/yr	$15,653/yr	$16,916/yr	$18,277/yr	$19,697/yr
Manufacturing, Durable Goods	$12,594/yr	$13,622/yr	$14,730/yr	$15,841/yr	$17,212/yr
Manufacturing, Nondurable Goods	$10,901/yr	$11,710/yr	$12,578/yr	$13,564/yr	$14,738/yr
Medical/HealthServices Workers	$9624/yr	$10,465/yr	$11,248/yr	$12,179/yr	$13,276/yr
Miscellaneous Manufacturing	$9407/yr	$10,148/yr	$10,678/yr	$11,494/yr	$12,563/yr
Motion-Picture Services	$10,614/yr	$11,987/yr	$13,209/yr	$14,910/yr	$16,821/yr
Nonprofit Org. Workers	$7407/yr	$7701/yr	$8297/yr	$8933/yr	$9564/yr
Passenger-Transportation Workers, Local and Highway	$9462/yr	$10,121/yr	$10,780/yr	$11,590/yr	$12,266/yr
Personal Services	$7459/yr	$7943/yr	$8322/yr	$9048/yr	$9723/yr
Public-School Teachers	$11,182/yr	$12,038/yr	$12,738/yr	$13,391/yr	$14,306/yr
Radio-Broadcasting & Television Workers	$13,475/yr	$14,705/yr	$15,708/yr	$16,879/yr	$18,329/yr
Railroads	$14,987/yr	$17,292/yr	$18,784/yr	$20,605/yr	$23,021/yr
State- and Local-Govt. Workers	$10,831/yr	$11,594/yr	$12,359/yr	$13,022/yr	$13,879/yr
Telephone & Telegraph Workers	$13,948/yr	$15,756/yr	$17,279/yr	$19,032/yr	$20,646/yr
Wholesale and Retail Trade Workers	$12,930/yr	$13,684/yr	$14,584/yr	$15,711/yr	$17,113/yr

FOOD BASKET 1975-1979

(NR = Not Reported)

Commodity	Year	New York	Atlanta	Chicago	Denver	Los Angeles
Apples, Fresh, per pound	1975	35.60¢	40.30¢	34.30¢	NR	40¢
	1976	35.90¢	39.30¢	32.40¢	NR	36¢
	1977	41.50¢	45.10¢	38.50¢	NR	43.80¢
	1978	NR	NR	NR	NR	NR
	1979	NR	NR	NR	NR	NR
Beans, Dried, per pound	1975	52¢	43.90¢	39.90¢	NR	42.50¢
	1976	57.90¢	43.70¢	41.20¢	NR	53¢
	1977	50.20¢	38.80¢	43.20¢	NR	44.10¢
	1978	NR	NR	NR	NR	NR
	1979	NR	NR	NR	NR	NR
Beef, Rib Roasts, per pound	1975	$1.77	$1.99	$1.64	NR	$1.86
	1976	$1.75	$1.96	$1.58	NR	$1.75
	1977	$1.80	$1.97	$1.40	NR	$1.88
	1978	NR	NR	NR	NR	NR
	1979	NR	NR	NR	NR	NR
Beef, Steaks (Round), per pound	1975	$2.25	$1.99	$1.64	NR	$1.71
	1976	$2.12	$1.91	$1.49	NR	$1.59
	1977	$2.09	$1.78	$1.37	NR	$1.59
	1978	NR	NR	NR	NR	NR
	1979	NR	NR	NR	NR	NR
Bread, White, per pound	1975	42.30¢	33.50¢	35.30¢	NR	36.30¢
	1976	42.40¢	34¢	35.70¢	NR	35¢
	1977	41.20¢	34.10¢	35.80¢	NR	34.90¢
	1978	35.5¢ (U. S. Average)				
	1979	NR	NR	NR	NR	NR
Butter, per pound	1975	$1.05	$1.06	98.80¢	NR	$1.03
	1976	$1.32	$1.26	$1.21	NR	$1.24
	1977	$1.41	$1.37	$1.34	NR	$1.31
	1978	$1.33 (U. S. Average)				
	1979	NR	NR	NR	NR	NR
Cheese, per pound	1975	77.90¢	79.10¢	75.10¢	NR	80.80¢
	1976	86.70¢	89.60¢	80.40¢	NR	89.30¢
	1977	89.80¢	91.60¢	85.50¢	NR	89.70¢
	1978	NR	NR	NR	NR	NR
	1979	NR	NR	NR	NR	NR
Chickens, per pound	1975	68.20¢	61.20¢	63.80¢	NR	61.90¢
	1976	66¢	58.60¢	59.40¢	NR	61.10¢
	1977	65.40¢	56.40¢	59.60¢	NR	63.30¢
	1978	NR	NR	NR	NR	NR
	1979	NR	NR	NR	NR	NR
Coffee, per pound	1975	$1.40	$1.33	$1.35	NR	$1.22
	1976	$1.99	$1.80	$1.91	NR	$1.74
	1977	$3.58	$3.46	$3.39	NR	$3.37
	1978	$3.42 (U. S. Average)				
	1979	NR	NR	NR	NR	NR
Eggs, per dozen	1975	84.60¢	77¢	73.90¢	NR	72¢
	1976	91.40¢	82.40¢	83.80¢	NR	78.70¢
	1977	88.50¢	79.70¢	81¢	NR	79¢
	1978	82.30¢ (U. S. Average)				
	1979	NR	NR	NR	NR	NR

Commodity	Year	New York	Atlanta	Chicago	Denver	Los Angeles
Flour, Wheat, per pound	1975	19.78¢	21.50¢	20.06¢	NR	19.28¢
	1976	19.04¢	19.34¢	19.02¢	NR	16.28¢
	1977	17.86¢	17.80¢	17.48¢	NR	14.54¢
	1978	NR	NR	NR	NR	NR
	1979	NR	NR	NR	NR	NR
Lamb, Chops, per pound	1975	$2.80	$2.65	$2.75	NR	$2.74
	1976	$3.10	$3.09	$2.93	NR	$3.00
	1977	$3.21	$3.58	$2.94	NR	$3.14
	1978	NR	NR	NR	NR	NR
	1979	NR	NR	NR	NR	NR
Margarine, per pound	1975	68.70¢	68.50¢	63.10¢	NR	61.80¢
	1976	59¢	56.90¢	53.60¢	NR	53¢
	1977	63.20¢	62.60¢	60.90¢	NR	58.60¢
	1978	57.20¢ (U. S. Average)				
	1979	NR	NR	NR	NR	NR
Milk, Fresh, per quart	1975	41.40¢	45.40¢	38.75¢	NR	34.80¢
	1976	42.80¢	49.30¢	41.20¢	NR	34.40¢
	1977	43.05¢	51.15¢	42.35¢	NR	34.10¢
	1978	83.90¢ (U. S. Average)				
	1979	NR	NR	NR	NR	NR
Pork, Bacon, Sliced, per pound	1975	$1.85	$1.81	$1.80	NR	$1.60
	1976	$1.85	$1.70	$1.69	NR	$1.54
	1977	$1.69	$1.50	$1.62	NR	$1.45
	1978	$1.56 (U. S. Average)				
	1979	NR	NR	NR	NR	NR
Pork, Chops, per pound	1975	$1.92	$1.92	$1.79	NR	$1.95
	1976	$1.92	$1.85	$1.72	NR	$1.91
	1977	$1.85	$1.83	$1.62	NR	$1.90
	1978	$1.81 (U. S. Average)				
	1979	NR	NR	NR	NR	NR
Pork, Ham, Whole, per pound	1975	$1.26	$1.03	$1.05	NR	$1.28
	1976	$1.47	$1.17	$1.22	NR	$1.35
	1977	$1.40	$1.11	$1.14	NR	$1.33
	1978	NR	NR	NR	NR	NR
	1979	NR	NR	NR	NR	NR
Potatoes, Irish, per 10 pounds	1975	$1.41	$1.75	$1.75	NR	$1.24
	1976	$1.61	$1.87	$1.90	NR	$1.17
	1977	$1.67	$2.16	$2.08	NR	$1.16
	1978	$1.49 (U.S. Average)				
	1979	NR	NR	NR	NR	NR
Rice, per pound	1975	49.80¢	33.50¢	40.50¢	NR	51.50¢
	1976	47.70¢	39.40¢	34.70¢	NR	45.20¢
	1977	44.80¢	35.70¢	34.60¢	NR	40.40¢
	1978	40¢ (U. S. Average)				
	1979	NR	NR	NR	NR	NR
Sugar, per pound	1975	39.72¢	40.94¢	35.82¢	NR	35.24¢
	1976	25.24¢	25.58¢	24.52¢	NR	22.46¢
	1977	22.36¢	20.54¢	22.94¢	NR	20.22¢
	1978	$1.08 (U. S. Average)				
	1979	NR	NR	NR	NR	NR
Tea, Bags, per package of 48	1975	86.80¢	87.60¢	82.90¢	NR	84¢
	1976	89.10¢	82.60¢	87.90¢	NR	86.40¢
	1977	$1.04	$1.03	$1.19	NR	$1.03
	1978	NR	NR	NR	NR	NR
	1979	NR	NR	NR	NR	NR
Veal, per pound	1975	$3.68	NR	$3.16	NR	$2.75
	1976	$3.54	$3.05	$2.97	NR	$2.51
	1977	$3.45	$3.71	$2.84	NR	$2.88
	1978	NR	NR	NR	NR	NR
	1979	NR	NR	NR	NR	NR

SELECTED PRICES 1975-1979

Item	Source	Description	Price
Alcohol			
Beer	*Chicago Tribune* (1978)	*Stroh's;* 6-pack	$1.49
Vodka	*Chicago Tribune* (1978)	*Smirnoff;* 80-proof; 1.75 liter	$8.59
Wine Butler	*New York Times* (1978)	Never spill another drop of wine when you pour with Wine Butler; made from space-age material that cuts off the last drop cleanly, returning it to the bottle; with sterling silver crown	$24.50
Apparel, Children's			
Belt	*Sears, Roebuck* (1976)	Leather strap with all around three-hole perforations and three-prong metal buckle	$3.99
Boots	*Sears, Roebuck* (1976)	*Winnie-the-Pooh;* over the foot pull-on boot	$10.99
Briefs	*Sears, Roebuck* (1976)	Rib knit with two-way stretch	$2.99
Coat	*Sears, Roebuck* (1976)	*Winnie-the-Pooh;* all-weather trench coat	$19
Coat	*Sears, Roebuck* (1976)	*Balmecaan;* single-breasted styling	$8.99
Coverall	*Sears, Roebuck* (1976)	Corduroy	$3.99
Dress	*Sears, Roebuck* (1976)	No-iron dresses at low prices; save $1 when you buy any 2 dresses in any style, in any size	$5.49
Dress	*Sears, Roebuck* (1976)	Picture-perfect no-iron dresses	$3.49
Dress	*Sears, Roebuck* (1976)	*Winnie-the-Pooh;* dresses never need ironing	$10
Gown	*Sears, Roebuck* (1978)	Screen-printed across yoke, "My Heart Belongs to Daddy"	$4.99
Jacket	*Sears, Roebuck* (1976)	Denim jackets with screen-print back; motorcycle, *Budweiser,* American eagle	$9.99
Jeans	*Sears, Roebuck* (1976)	Perma-prest; denim jeans; wise buys for thrifty shoppers	$3.88
Jeans	*Sears, Roebuck* (1976)	*Toughskins;* the toughest of Sears, Roebuck tough casual jeans; lab tests prove it	$5.99
Pajamas	*Sears, Roebuck* (1978)	*Winnie-the-Pooh;* has pants that are hem-stitched at ankle	$5.99
Play Suit	*Sears, Roebuck* (1976)	*Winnie-the-Pooh;* our finest sleep 'n' play suit; heavyweight stretch-knit terry	$4.99
Raincoat	*Sears, Roebuck* (1976)	Water-repellent vinyl raincoat; boys' sizes 6 to 16	$3.79
Shirt	*Sears, Roebuck* (1976)	Cat appliqué	$6.99
Shirt	*Sears, Roebuck* (1976)	Perma-prest knit shirt	$2.99
Shirt	*Sears, Roebuck* (1976)	Tie-dyed shirt	$5.99
Shirt	*Sears, Roebuck* (1976)	Wet-look shirt	$5
Shoes	*Sears, Roebuck* (1976)	T-strap	$10.99

Item	Source	Description	Price
Slippers	*Sears, Roebuck* (1976)	Mom will love these slippers as much as the kids because they're so easy to keep clean; just machine wash, warm	$4.99
Socks	*Sears, Roebuck* (1976)	Novelty knee-high socks; multicolor florals	$1.59
Socks	*Sears, Roebuck* (1976)	Tube socks; three pairs	$2.97
Sweatshirt	*Sears, Roebuck* (1976)	Hooded sweatshirt	$5.99
Tank Top	*Sears, Roebuck* (1976)	Pullover contrast rib-knit trim at U-neck and sleeve openings	$4.99
Tights	*Sears, Roebuck* (1976)	Stretch nylon in opaque knit	$1.67
Underwear	*Sears, Roebuck* (1976)	Perma-prest underwear for girls and boys; three in package	$2.99
Vest	*Sears, Roebuck* (1976)	Girl's rosebud print vest	$2.99

Clothing, Man's

Item	Source	Description	Price
Briefs	*New York Times Magazine* (1975)	*Bravos;* bikinis and fly front briefs	$1.99
Coat	*New York Times Magazine* (1975)	*Antartex Main Shop;* from Scotland; 9 skin colours, 8 sheepskin types	$175
Jeans	*Sears, Roebuck* (1977)	100% cotton denim jeans; 3 proportioned cuts mean your jeans will fit and feel better; prewashed blue	$13
Jeans	*Sears, Roebuck* (1977)	*Toughskin;* casual jeans	$6.39
Moccasin	*Smithsonian* (1976)	*J&M After Hours Swanee I;* moccasin toe, clip-on styling for good looks and comfort	$37.50
Pants	*New York Magazine* (1975)	*Cable Car;* cotton corduroy hobby pants; fuller cut, pleated for leisure, travel, golf, or puttering	$19
Robe	*Smithsonian* (1976)	*L. L. Bean;* chamois cloth; a high grade 100% cotton flannel, thickly napped on both sides	$33
Shirt	*Popular Mechanics* (1977)	*Canadian Mist Chamois* cloth shirt; long sleeves and long tuck-in tails	$12.50
Shirt	*New York Times Magazine* (1975)	*Bravos;* tank shirt; bold, individually expressed in DuPont's 100% 2-ply stretch nylon	$2.99
Shirt	*Sears, Roebuck* (1977)	*Perma-Prest;* long-point banded collar; permanent stays; 65% polyester, 35% chambray	$7.99
Shirt	*Sears, Roebuck* (1977)	Rugby-style long-sleeve knit shirts	$4.49
Socks	*New York Times Magazine* (1975)	Interwoven satin stripe; the handsome alternating stripes of Antron nylon add just right lustre	$2
Socks	*Smithsonian* (1976)	*Eddie Bauer;* goose down; fully insulated and quilted in tough nylon taffeta	$9.95
Ties	*Smithsonian* (1976)	*Wm. Chelsea, Ltd.;* Tin Lizzie design, select blue or brown	$10
Touring Cap	*New York Times Magazine* (1975)	*L. L. Bean;* attractive and sturdy sports cap of brushed-pigskin leather	$7.50
Vest	*Smithsonian* (1976)	*Autstral Enterprises;* Welsh sheepworker's; a casual top for work or leisure; made of the best 12-oz Welsh flannel; 100% wool	$27.50

Item	Source	Description	Price
Apparel, Women's			
Blazer	*New York Times Magazine* (1975)	*Lord & Taylor;* smoothly knit; personal and Dacron, America's finest polyester	$50
Blouse	*New York Times Magazine* (1975)	*Lydia;* Edwardian; of white lawn with embroidery Anglaise and Irish-lace trimming	$200
Body Briefer	*Sears, Roebuck* (1977)	Featherweight all-in-one of sheer, glistening Antron nylon and spandex lets your clothes fall in sensuous unbroken lines; especially desirable under close-fitting outerwear	$16
Coatdress	*Sears, Roebuck* (1977)	Double-knit polyester; multicolor pali-print bodice with pique texture	$21
Coverup	*Sears, Roebuck* (1977)	Front-tie closing at rounded neckline, shirring at front and back yoke	$13
Gown	*New York Times* (1977)	*Elizabeth Arden Salon;* innocence is Blass; and very in	$125
Jacket Dress	*Atlanta Journal and Constitution* (1978)	*Lady Carol;* sleeveless striped dress and matching short-sleeve jacket, 100% encron polyester	$32
Jumpsuit	*Sears, Roebuck* (1977)	Easy-fitting step-in-style with a front-button opening	$21
Jumpsuit	*Sears, Roebuck* (1977)	Pre-washed denim; sized to be worn over underwear	$31.99
Kimono	*New York Times Magazine* (1975)	*Saks Happy Coat;* in woven textured polyester; traditional length 36"	$35
Maternity Top	*Sears, Roebuck* (1977)	Pull-over style with sweetheart neckline; front yoke of broadcloth with an inset of denim	$9
Maternity Top	*Sears, Roebuck* (1977)	With Mom motif	$8
Pants	*New York Times Magazine* (1975)	*Koret of California;* seersucker; creating resort wardrobes that set the pace for summer fashion; 65% Dacron polyester, 35% cotton	$20
Pants	*Sears, Roebuck* (1977)	Tailored; extra-smooth heavyweight single-knit polyester that looks woven	$12
Panty	*Sears, Roebuck* (1977)	Knee length; smoothes from waist through thighs	$10.38
Shirt	*New York Times Magazine* (1975)	*Koret of California;* printed polo; creating resort wardrobes that set the pace for summer fashion; 65% Dacron polyester, 35% cotton	$15
Shoes	*Atlanta Journal and Constitution* (1978)	*Bakers;* glazed cork; sure allure on 4" heels; from our collection of urethane beauties, timed for day or disco	$19.99
Shoes	*Atlanta Journal and Constitution* (1978)	*K-Mart Lighthearted Sandals;* cut out for fun, 3-tier upper bands in white vinyl, bone, or teak urethane	$4.91
Shoes	*Rolling Stone* (1975)	*Kalso Earth Shoe;* the theory of pure walking	$23.50
Shoes	*Sears, Roebuck* (1977)	Oxford with two-eyelet tie	$7.99
Shoes	*Sears, Roebuck* (1977)	Wedge pump; pillow-soft shoe insole of cushioned vinyl	$12.99
Slack-Companion	*Sears, Roebuck* (1977)	Calf-length panty gives a smooth line; stretch lace leg bands	$12.38

Item	Source	Description	Price
Suit	*Atlanta Journal and Constitution* (1978)	*Walden Classics;* 3-piece set; includes sleeveless dress, tailored blazer, and bias skirt; spring weight polyester in pink or blue plaid	$40
Sweater	*New York Times Magazine* (1975)	*Beldoch Popper;* a carefree rib-turtle by Sandy Starkman of luxurious Qiana nylon	$20
Sweater	*Sears, Roebuck* (1977)	Pullover; has a pointed collar, open-front placket, short sleeves and turn-back cuffs, a square bottom	$11
Sweatercoat	*New York Times* (1977)	*Rodier's Ravissant;* boot-brushing belted, beautifully ribbed	$140
Swimsuit	*Sears, Roebuck* (1977)	Bikini; bra-halter style with V-neckline, tie-bow trim, and princess seams; pants; pull-on style elasticized waist and leg opening	$13
Swimsuit	*Sears, Roebuck* (1977)	One-piece stretch; smooth knit of Antron nylon and Lycra	$20

Appliances

Item	Source	Description	Price
Circular Saw	*Popular Mechanics* (1977)	*Rockwell* 7 1/4" circular saw, cuts at 5800 RPMs	$22.88
Coffee Maker	*Chicago Tribune* (1978)	*Norelco;* 12-cup automatic drip filter coffeemaker; coffee never boils so it's never bitter	$23.88
Computer	*Cox News Service* (2004)	*Apple I;* [In 1976]	$666.66
Computer	*Cox News Service* (2004)	*Apple II;* [In 1977]	$1300
Dryer	*Sears, Roebuck* (1977)	*Kenmore;* this model has cycles for cotton, sturdy, and permanent press as well as an air-only cycle too	$149
Espresso Maker	*New York Times Magazine* (1975)	Brews four to six demitasses the Italian way by steam pressure	$40
Food Processor	*Sears, Roebuck* (1977)	Helps you prepare meals from everyday to gourmet, slices thick or thin, shreds most fruits and vegetables, nuts, cheese	$39.99
Food Sealer	*Sears, Roebuck* (1977)	*Seal-N-Save;* seals 8" individual pouches or holds 8" or 10" wide continuous rolls of pouch material for sealing long items	$16.49
Freezer	*Chicago Tribune* (1978)	8.3 cu. ft. compact freezer	$199.88
Freezer	*Sears, Roebuck* (1977)	Upright 16 cu. ft. conventional defrost model with painted steel interior	$219
Kitchen Machine	*Sears, Roebuck* (1977)	Basic outfit includes power unit plus attachments for grinding, blending, mixing, juicing	$99.99
Microwave Oven	*Chicago Tribune* (1978)	Big microwave oven cooks fast and cool	$168
Slow Cooker	*Sears, Roebuck* (1977)	Yellow metal exterior; glass lid; recipes and instructions	$13.79

Baby Products

Item	Source	Description	Price
Baby-Basket Set	*Sears, Roebuck* (1976)	3-piece set; save $1; includes print liner, hoodless basket, basket pad	$24.97
Baby Carrier	*Sears, Roebuck* (1976)	*Pak-A-Poose;* patented frame distributes baby's weight evenly; for babies from 4 months old to 35 pounds	$14
Baby Holder	*Sears, Roebuck* (1976)	*Johnny Jump-Up;* for babies 4 months old to 24 pounds	$6.99
Child Carrier	*Sears, Roebuck* (1976)	Sports denim-look rear-mount carrier	$11.88
Cradle	*Sears, Roebuck* (1976)	Automatic; converts cradle	$34.99

Item	Source	Description	Price
Food Grinder	*Sears, Roebuck* (1976)	Handy-size food grinder; convenient size for travel; only 5" high; serve fresh natural foods right at the table	$4.50
Mattress Pad	*Sears, Roebuck* (1976)	Our finest crib-size mattress pad; it's quilted, waterproof	$5.99
Nurser	*Sears, Roebuck* (1976)	26-piece disposable nurser kit; presterilized bag collapses as baby drinks, so baby takes in less air	$5.99
Pajamas	*Sears, Roebuck* (1976)	One-piece style; gripper snaps down front, crotch, both legs; short sleeves	$2.79
Pants	*Sears, Roebuck* (1976)	Corduroy boxer pant; 2 in package	$3.99
Seat Carrier	*Sears, Roebuck* (1976)	Lightweight, portable; cradles baby for feeding, rocking, toting from place to place	$9.99
Sleeper	*Sears, Roebuck* (1976)	*Winnie-the-Pooh;* our finest stretch terry sleep 'n' play suit	$4.99
Slippers	*Sears, Roebuck* (1976)	Infant's slippers and bag set; a cuddly combination that's sure to please; set includes Pooh slippers plus matching and handy hanging hook	$5.99
Stroller	*Sears, Roebuck* (1976)	Swivel-wheel stroll 'n' fold; handy ideas for outgoing mother; handle totes easily on mother's arm, leaves both swivel front wheels take corners easily, umbrella-type handles free	$24.99
Walker	*Sears, Roebuck* (1976)	Circular; easy to disassemble for compact storage	$10.88
Waterproof Sheets	*Sears, Roebuck* (1976)	Reversible waterproof sheets; two layers of warm fleeced cotton flannelette laminated to a pure gum rubber core; package of 2; 27" x 26"	$3.99

Business Equipment and Supplies

Item	Source	Description	Price
Briefcase	*Smithsonian* (1976)	*Paul McAfee & Friends;* natural leather; legal size, 11" by 16 3/4" case	$35.95
Calculator	*Chicago Tribune* (1978)	*Texas Instruments;* pocket calculator	$74.95
Calculator	*Chicago Tribune* (1978)	*Texas Instruments Exactra;* electronic calculators; adds, subtracts, multiplies, and divides; battery operated and easy to use	$29
Copier	*New York Times* (1977)	*Saxon;* plain paper; we'd like to demonstrate the reasons for our success	$2,995
Drill Press	*New York Times* (1978)	*Chicago Power Tools;* cast iron head, 1/2 horse power 1725 motor; 5 speed	$199
Phone Rates	*New York Times* (1978)	*Bell System;* three minute call from United States to Paris, Berlin or Amsterdam; station-to-station	$6.75

Collectibles

Item	Source	Description	Price
Automobile	*Guinness Book of World Records* (1981)	Price paid in 1979 for a 1936 Mercedes-Benz Roadster	$421,040
Bedside Cupboard	*Antiques* (1977)	With tambour door; circa 1790	$690
Book	*Art & Antiques* (1993)	William Falkner's one-act play entitled *"Marionettes,"* hand-lettered by author, sold in auction in 1975	$34,000
Bookcase	*Antiques* (1977)	Antique Chippendale cherry; especially noteworthy for its ventilated cornice, double-raised panel doors; circa 1790	$6,600
Camera	*Guinness Book of World Records* (1981)	1856 J. B. Dancer stereo camera sold in 1977	$42,000
Card Table	*Antiques* (1977)	Chippendale fold-over table; circa 1760; mahogany with cariole legs and claw-and-ball feet	$1,950
Clock	*Antiques* (1977)	Nineteenth-century country French Horloge cherry clock; height 7' 9 1/2", width 19 1/2", depth 11 1/2"	$2,800

Item	Source	Description	Price
Dough Table	*Antiques* (1977)	Rare watervleit, New York community dough-table, signed "E. L."; height 30 1/2', depth 21", length 47"; circa 1830	$1,650
Drum Table	*Antiques* (1977)	Georgia Coromandel wood; a charming, small antique table; circa 1780	$2,390
Figurine	*New York Times Magazine* (1975)	*Steuben;* glass penguin; height 6 1/2"; send $3 for 1975 catalogue of Christmas gifts	$130
Figurine	*Smithsonian* (1976)	*Burgues;* nature in porcelain; young walrus; 9" wide by 5 1/2" high; issue of 950	$225
Figurine	*Smithsonian* (1976)	*Steuben;* glass Stars and Stripes; crystal prism, cut and engraved	$160
Print	*Antiques* (1977)	Antique Audubon quadrupeds; 21" x 27"	$150
Print	*Antiques* (1977)	Antique Wilson birds; 1810; 13" x 6"	$17.50
Print	*Antiques* (1977)	*Catesbury;* bird; 1771 edition; 14" x 20"	$150
Print	*Antiques* (1977)	*Gould's Birds of Great Britain;* hand colored, 1862; 15" x 20"	$50
Rug	*Antiques* (1977)	Oriental; Tabriz; 9' 10" x 11' 2", from Iran	$1,950
Rug	*Antiques* (1977)	Persian Baktiari rug; 6' 4" x 4"; a fascinating combination of large-scale stylized floral design in a scatter rug size	$1,850
Sculpture	*Guinness Book of World Records* (1981)	Price paid in 1977 of a 4th-century BC bronze statue of a youth attributed to the school of Lysippus	$3.9 million
Seats	*New York Times* (1978)	Original reserved seats from Yankee Stadium; removed for the recent renovation Pair, connected	$45
Teddy Bear	*New York Times Magazine* (1975)	Antique; American Hurrah; circa 1910	$100
Tilt-Top Table	*Antiques* (1977)	Mahogany table; circa 1780; 31" diameter	$750

Education

Golf School	*New York Times* (1978)	*Concord Golf School;* six days and five nights based on double occupancy, per person; intense instruction	$650
TV/Audio Home Study	*Popular Mechanics* (1977)	*NRI School;* A complete course in black and white and color TV servicing, including 48 lessons, 10 special reference texts and 11 training kits	$550

Entertainment

Hockey Ticket	*Chicago Tribune* (1978)	Stanley Cup playoffs; Black Hawks vs. Boston	$6.50–$18.75
Movie Ticket	*Chicago Tribune* (1978)	*Dirty Mary Crazy Larry;* carload	$4
Movie Ticket	*Chicago Tribune* (1978)	*Golden Voyage of Sinbad*	$1
Movie Ticket	*Chicago Tribune* (1978)	*Serpico;* Al Pacino	$0.75
Resort Package	*New York Times* (1978)	*Granit Hotel and Country Club;* the only resort catering exclusively to adults; weekly package, 8 days, 7 nights, per person, double occupancy	$196–$229
Theater Ticket	*New York Times* (1977)	*Beatlemania;* phenomenal; a case example of the theater's miracle; Saturday evening	$11/$13/$15

Item	Source	Description	Price
Theater Ticket	*New York Times* (1977)	*A Chorus Line;* Pulitzer prize for drama, winner of 9 Tony awards; orchestra and boxes	$17.50
Theater Ticket	*Chicago Tribune* (1978)	*Rustic Barn Confidence Game;* 3-act comedy; dinner theater; play; gratuity; choice of 5 dinner entrees	$8.95

Entertainment, Home

Item	Source	Description	Price
Camera	*Smithsonian* (1976)	*Kodak EK$ Instant;* pictures that develop in minutes, the image protected by an elegant, textured, satinlux finish; automatic exposure control and electronic shutter	$54
Camera	*Smithsonian* (1976)	*Kodak TrimLite Instamatic 48;* has a superb f/2.7 Ektar lens and a coupled range finder	$129
CB Base Station and Walkie Talkie	*Atlanta Journal and Constitution* (1978)	*K-Mart;* AM/CB receiver with morse code function; transmits on channel 14	$16.97
CB Radio	*Chicago Tribune* (1978)	Basic 40-channel mobile CB radio	$39.88
Game	*New York Times* (1978)	*Pachinko Pinball Game;* A fast, challenging game of action	$22.50
Projector	*Smithsonian* (1976)	*Kodak Carousel Custom 850H;* auto-focus; quiet dependability	$275
Radio	*Sears, Roebuck* (1978)	Stereo headphone radio; plays anytime and anyplace	$39.50
Stereo Cassette System	*Smithsonian* (1976)	*Sony CF-580;* the first complete stereo cassette system that's portable	$400
Stereo Receiver	*Rolling Stone* (1975)	*Pioneer SX-737;* offers a level of performance that can only be described as awesome	$400
Turntable	*Rolling Stone* (1975)	*Dual 1225;* fully automatic, single-play/multi-play; viscous damped cue-control; pitch control	$199.95

Farm Equipment

Item	Source	Description	Price
Tractor (1978)	*Guinness Book of World Records* (1981)	65-ton *Northern Manufacturing Company* 8-wheeled, 16V-747 tractor	$325,000

Food Products

Item	Source	Description	Price
Alaskan King Crab	*Chicago Tribune* (1978)	*Al's Fishery;* split; precooked; 3 lb bag; reg. $3.99; while supply lasts	$2.50/lb
Fruit Cake	*New York Times Magazine* (1975)	*Marty's Ol Fashion;* fresh to you in time for the holidays; three one-pound loaf cakes	$6
Crackers	*New York Times* (1978)	*Carr's Table Wafers;* 12 ounce can	$3.99
Food	*New York Times* (1978)	*The Country Grocer;* the first all natural supermarket in New Jersey	
		Organic Roast Beef, per 1/2 pound	$1.99
		Turkey Breast, cooked on premises, per 1/2 pound	$1.89
		Alta Dena flavored Yoghurt, sweetened with honey, 8 ounces	$.49
Soup	*New York Times* (1978)	*Pepperidge Farm* cold fruit soups; fresh off-the-vine taste; strawberry, prune, peach, cherry, apricot and orange	
		Per 10 3/4 ounce can	$1.19

Furniture

Item	Source	Description	Price
Bean Bag	*Sears, Roebuck* (1977)	Wet-look vinyl; graphic prints	$37.95
Bunk Beds	*Sears, Roebuck* (1977)	Bunk outfit with 6 storage drawers and two bookcases	$439.95
Chair	*Atlanta Journal and Constitution* (1978)	*James David;* contemporary; designs in thick gleaming chrome with deep foam cushions covered in beautiful, durable rust corduroy	$109

Item	Source	Description	Price
Chair	*New York Times* (1978)	*Breuer Chairs;* black with hand-caned seat and back; the authentic Italian import	$32.50
Chaise Group	*Atlanta Journal and Constitution* (1978)	3-piece; includes chaise, armless love seat, cocktail table	$699
Cocktail Table	*Atlanta Journal and Constitution* (1978)	*Woodmere;* 32" square table, wormy chestnut finish	$139
Mate's Bed	*Sears, Roebuck* (1977)	With two storage drawers, mattress, and foundation	$169.95
Stereo Wall System	*Atlanta Journal and Constitution* (1978)	*Brazil Contempo;* units finished in exotic mercuro laminate; feature tempered-glass door, lighted cabinets and chrome trim; all units are a full 15" deep x 72" high 30" wide	$199
Trestle Table	*New York Times Magazine* (1975)	*Great North Woods;* butcher block; made from natural 2"-thick hard-rock maple and finished by hand; 24" x 60"	$62.40
Trestle Table and Benches	*Sears, Roebuck* (1977)	3-piece set includes table and 2 side benches	$289.95

Garden Equipment and Supplies

Item	Source	Description	Price
Fence	*New York Times* (1978)	Chain link and stockade fences; standard 2 inch mesh Per running foot	$.80
Flower	*Smithsonian* (1976)	Christmas crocus; twelve Holland bulbs, preplanted and ready to grow	$11.95
Hummingbird Feeder	*Smithsonian* (1976)	*Droll Yankee;* has three feeding stations, a three-year guarantee	$13.50
Lawn Sweeper	*Sears, Roebuck* (1977)	Self-propelled; brush adjusts to 9 different heights to whisk up grass, leaves; 3 1/2 hp	$229.99
Lawn Sweeper and Bagger	*Sears, Roebuck* (1977)	*Lawn Valet;* vacuum, compactor, and bagger; clears a 25" path; converts to blower to clear an 8' path; reduces 4 bushels of leaves to 1; no lower price since 1975	$186
Seeds	*Chicago Tribune* (1978)	*Excel;* flower and vegetable seeds; limit 6 packs; six packs	$0.59

Hotel Rates

Item	Source	Description	Price
Hotel Room	*New York Times Magazine* (1975)	*St. Moritz on the Park;* handsome views of New York's Central Park	$31/day
Hotel Room	*Chicago Tribune* (1978)	*Schwartz Resort Hotel;* 6 days, 5 nights	$110
Room Rate	*Guinness Book of World Records* (1981)	Cost of staying at the Celestial Suite on the 9th floor of the *Astro Village Hotel,* Houston, Texas Per day	$2,500
Room Rate	*New York Times* (1978)	*Stouffer's Inn* of Westchester; Get out of the jungle this weekend; swim, jog and exercise; enjoy in-room movies; per person based on double occupancy	$72
Room Rate	*New York Times* (1978)	*Barbizon Plaza Hotel;* Enjoy Central Park in bloom across the street; single anytime, per night	$35.90
Room Rate	*New York Times* (1978)	*Jeronimo's Place in the Country;* No big name stars; no planned activities; no yoga, reducing or any other courses; no rap sessions; no hassles; per person, per day	$30

Household Products

Item	Source	Description	Price
Apron	*Gourmet* (1976)	Cotton and polyester; adjustable	$12
Bath Scale	*Sears, Roebuck* (1977)	Extra-large bath scale has handle for easy portability	$17.99
Bedspread	*Sears, Roebuck* (1977)	Woven; an early American touch; no-iron coordinates	$34.96

Item	Source	Description	Price
Bedspread	*Atlanta Journal and Constitution* (1978)	*Singapore by Croscill;* twin; fully quilted spread is covered in polyester/cotton with Kodel polyester fiberfill	$39
Blanket	*Popular Mechanics* (1977)	*Canadian Mist American Trapper blanket;* 85% wool, 15% nylon; 71" x 90"	$26.75
Brief Bag	*New York Times Magazine* (1975)	*Chisholm Classics;* leather; hand-rubbed chestnut brown leather, brass hardware, legal size	$52
Casserole	*Gourmet* (1976)	Metal; two-quart flameproof casserole	$58
Cookware	*Sears, Roebuck* (1977)	Stainless-steel cookware, aluminum-clad bottom; save $10	$69.96
Drapes	*Sears, Roebuck* (1977)	Rod pocket draperies; tufted medallion design; 63" x 72"	$9.96
Drill Stand	*Sears, Roebuck* (1977)	*Portalign;* holds drill for perpendicular exact-angle holes	$19.99
Extension Cord	*Popular Mechanics* (1977)	*Carol* heavy-duty 25-foot extension cord; all purpose for indoor and outdoor use	$3.89
Fabric	*New York Times* (1978)	Upholstery Fabric; save on the best in designer seconds for your home Per yard	$4.95
Faucet	*Sears, Roebuck* (1977)	Our best single-control washerless faucet; chrome-plated, brass handle	$36.99
Floor Lamp	*Smithsonian* (1976)	*Light Crafters Wonderful Sight Light;* up to 5 times the light of conventional lamps; traditional style	$78.50
Garbage Can	*New York Times* (1978)	Dapol Blow Mold 30 gallon garbage can	$5.99
Ice Bucket	*New York Times Magazine* (1975)	Modern classic in stainless steel from Finland	$80
Ice Cream Machine	*Smithsonian* (1976)	*Salton's;* nothing tastes better than homemade ice cream	$24.95
Lamp	*Gourmet* (1976)	*Jean-Paul Beaujard;* French brass with glass shade	$95
Luggage	*Chicago Tribune* (1978)	*Amelia Earhart*	$12.90
Massage Shower Head	*Sears, Roebuck* (1977)	This massage shower is two showers in one; just turn for massage action or regular spray	$26.95
Nail Spinner	*Sears, Roebuck* (1977)	Sets in finishing nails without predrilling	$4.99
Platter	*Gourmet* (1976)	*Diane Love;* handmade; earthenware	$25
Plywood Sheet	*New York Times* (1978)	Interior plywood sheet; 4' x 8' x 1/4"	$6.99
Pressure Cooker	*Chicago Tribune* (1978)	*Presto;* 6-qt pressure cooker; speed, convenience and economy; cooks food 3 to 10 times faster	$10.88
Punch Bowl	*New York Times Magazine* (1975)	*Le Grenier;* hand-blown glass, a French import that holds over a gallon	$35
Quilt	*New York Times Magazine* (1975)	*Continental Quilt Shoppe;* dreamy white European Goose down, light as a cloud; you'll never make your bed again because the continental quilt eliminates a top sheet	$109.95
Replacement Chucks	*Sears, Roebuck* (1977)	Three-jaw keyed chuck for Sears, Roebuck, other electric drills; key included; 1/4" and 3/8" drills	$5.99

Item	Source	Description	Price
Restroom Radio	*Sears, Roebuck* (1978)	AM radio was $6.99 in our 1974 Christmas book	$5.95
Sheets	*New York Times Magazine* (1975)	Satin twin; flat and fitted; slip into the luxury of these acetate satin sheets	$12
Sheets	*Sears, Roebuck* (1977)	Perma-prest muslin sheets in fun prints; Peanuts, Dumbo, Tiger-Tiger, Budweiser; twin	$4.99
Sheets	*Atlanta Journal and Constitution* (1978)	*Country Lace by Suzanne Pleshette;* twin; a stylized gingham check, made of no-iron cotton/polyester percale from Utica	$7
Storm Windows	*Sears, Roebuck* (1977)	Triple-track insulating aluminum frame storm-screen windows; requires minimal maintenance	$32.95
Towel	*Atlanta Journal and Constitution* (1978)	In thick all-cotton terry, and measuring a generous 32" x 65"; imported from Brazil	$9.99
Trash Bags	*New York Times* (1978)	*Plastic City* trash bags; Our bags are double strength because they're virgin poly not repro; box of 500, 10-gallon size	$19.95
Vacuum Cleaner	*Chicago Tribune* (1978)	*Eureka;* bigger bag capacity to work harder, longer; fewer changes	$49.88

Jewelry

Item	Source	Description	Price
Cigarette Case	*New York Times Magazine* (1975)	*Colibri;* French enamel; precision-crafted with old world pride of craftsmanship, in Colibris hand-surfaced Cloisenamel finish	$34.95
Earrings	*New York Times Magazine* (1975)	*S. Marsh & Sons;* exquisite pave diamond earrings, with 96 full-cut diamonds weighing 4.53 karats, 18K gold and platinum	$2,290
Necklace	*New York Times Magazine* (1975)	*International Museum Talisman of Love;* the apple of Solomon—a love charm and talisman; 2" in diameter, struck in solid bronze	$22
Necklace	*Sears, Roebuck* (1977)	His or hers; elegant fine-link construction	$9
Watch	*New York Times Magazine* (1975)	*Baume & Mercier;* woman's; excitement in 14 karat gold	$650
Watch	*New York Times Magazine* (1975)	*Concord;* man's wrist watch; 18K gold electroplated; the second generation in digital watches by Concord	$395
Watch	*New York Times Magazine* (1975)	*Gruen Telestar;* clip bracelet for women; at the press of a button, brings you the hours, minutes, seconds, month and day; bracelet is in sterling silver with gold-filled highlighting	$300
Watch	*New York Times Magazine* (1975)	*Movado;* ladies wrist watch; sophisticated interwoven bracelet of 14K yellow gold	$925

Meals

Item	Source	Description	Price
Meal	*Chicago Tribune* (1978)	*Lobster Tail;* home of famous San Francisco sourdough bread	$7.95
Meal	*Chicago Tribune* (1978)	*Medium Rare;* featuring complete all inclusive dinners of prime rib of beef, fresh filet of red snapper, flaming shishkebob; or fixed price includes 2 cocktails before dinner, glass of wine with dinner, and one after dinner drink	$6.95

Item	Source	Description	Price
Meal	*Chicago Tribune* (1978)	*Nordic Steak 'n Pub;* broiled African lobster tail; huge salad bar	$6.95
Meal	*Chicago Tribune* (1978)	*Port of Entry;* featuring complete all inclusive dinners of prime filet mignon; African lobster tails; prime rib or beef succulent barbeque ribs; with your choice of 2 cocktails before dinner, a glass of vintage wine with dinner, and 1 after dinner drink; Sunday—Tuesday	$6.95

Motorized Vehicles, Supplies and Services

Item	Source	Description	Price
Automobile	*Popular Mechanics* (1977)	*1977 Toyota Corolla;* two door sedan; EPA 49 miles highway, 36 in the city	$2,788
Automobile	*Popular Mechanics* (1977)	*Oldsmobile Cutlass;* Cutlass style and Cutlass comfort	$4,811
Automobile	*Time* (1976)	*Volkswagen Rabbit*	$3,500
Battery	*Los Angeles Times* (1978)	*Firestone Forever;* maintenance-free battery; any size; 12-volt exchange	$59
Car Stereo	*Sears, Roebuck* (1977)	*Citizens Band Transceiver;* 40-channel with built in AM/FM stereo radio	$269.99
Electronic Engine Tune-Up	*Los Angeles Times* (1978)	Most 4-cylinder cars; foreign or American	$29
Motorcycle	*Popular Mechanics* (1977)	*Kawasaki 250cc F-11, Enduro;* two-stroke engine mated to five-speed transmission	$699
Motor Oil	*Chicago Tribune* (1978)	10W30 all-weather oil; one-quart can	$0.39
Tire	*Sears, Roebuck* (1977)	Steel-belted radials; warrantied 40,000 miles	$42
Tires	*Popular Mechanics* (1977)	*Sears Guardsman* 4-ply tires for mid-sized cars, 6-78-14 black wall prices, plus $2.23 for Federal excise tax	$21

Other

Item	Source	Description	Price
Batteries	*New York Times* (1977)	For all electronic watches, installed by experts	$2.95
Charcoal Starter	*Chicago Tribune* (1978)	*Gulf Lite;* for quick starts; one-quart can	$0.57
Charitable Donation	*New York Times Magazine* (1975)	*Save the Children Federation;* for sponsorship of a child in one of 27 countries	$16/mo
Stationery	*Atlanta Journal and Constitution* (1978)	*Sheridan;* 100 sheets and envelopes, antique vellum	$6.95
Sunglasses	*Sears, Roebuck* (1977)	Large sunglasses have radiant, smoke-color scratch-resistant plastic lenses	$7.99
Trophies (1978)	*The State Newspaper* Columbia, SC (2004)	Value of Vince Lombardi Trophy, given to the winner of the football Super Bowl game	$2000

Personal Care Products

Item	Source	Description	Price
Bandages	*Chicago Tribune* (1978)	*Curad;* box of 30 assorted sizes	$0.69
Bath Powder	*New York Times Magazine* (1975)	*Chanel No. 19*	$7
Compact	*New York Times Magazine* (1975)	*Miss Dior;* solid perfume designer miniature; brushed-silver toned oval has the famous Dior signature in gold-plated letters with long-lasting Miss Dior solid perfume inside	$4.50
Hair Dryer	*Chicago Tribune* (1978)	*Presto;* here's the quickest, easiest, most convenient hair dryer	$3.88

Item	Source	Description	Price
Makeup	*New York Times Magazine* (1975)	*Revlon Ultima II;* creme; 1.5 oz in Aurora, Beige, Bronze, Umber, Honey Tan, Tuscan Beige	$8.50
Mouthwash	*Chicago Tribune* (1978)	*Listerine;* 48-oz. mouthwash; price includes $0.50 off label	$1.99
Perfume	*New York Times Magazine* (1975)	*Chanel No. 19;* spray; it's another feeling; it's Chanel	$9.50
Razor Blades	*Chicago Tribune* (1978)	*Comfort II;* reg $1.79 packs	$1.29
Toothpaste	*Chicago Tribune* (1978)	*Ipana;* 7-oz tube of toothpaste	$0.59
Wrinkle Cream	*New York Times Magazine* (1975)	*Revlon Ultima II;* translucent	$15

Publications
Item	Source	Description	Price
Book	*New York Times* (1978)	*Isaac Bashevis Singer's Shosha,* a love story set between the two World Wars	$8.95

Real Estate
Item	Source	Description	Price
Apartment	*New York Times* (1977)	For rent; Ocean Avenue and Avenue Y; modern-elevator building; 3 1/2 rooms	$240/mo
Condominium	*New York Times* (1977)	For rent; 8 rooms, 4 baths	$1,025/mo
Country House	*Antiques* (1977)	For sale; 12 rooms built in 1929 in the English tradition; more than 207 acres	$300,000
Home	*New York Times* (1978)	Flushing, New York; six rooms, solid brick, 3 bedrooms, garage, gas heat	$48,500
Home	*New York Times* (1978)	Woodside/Queens Boulevard, New York; ranch type family home, garage, mint condition, modern kitchen, basement	$44,990
Rental	*New York Times* (1978)	Boca Raton, Florida; magnificent view of the ocean; furnished, 2 bedrooms, 2 baths, pool and recreation room; season rental (four month minimum)	$6,400
Summer Home	*New York Times* (1978)	Stratford, Connecticut; six room summer home; just completely remodeled and carpeted; on Long Island Sound	$49,900

Sewing Equipment and Supplies
Item	Source	Description	Price
Cloth	*Atlanta Journal and Constitution* (1978)	*K-Mart;* double knits; polyester yarn-dyed prints and double-blister crepes, 58–60	$1.33/yd
Sewing Machine	*Chicago Tribune* (1978)	Heavy-duty zigzag sewing head	$69.88

Sports Equipment
Item	Source	Description	Price
Basketball	*Sears, Roebuck* (1976)	Even at this low price, a basketball with long-wearing pebble-grain vinyl/rubber cover	$4.89
Basketball Goal	*Sears, Roebuck* (1976)	Adjustable-height goal for players 6–12 years old; you can set height from 7' to regulation 10'	$49.99
Bicycle	*Sears, Roebuck* (1976)	24" youth lightweights; for the shorter youth or the petite miss	$99
Bicycle	*Sears, Roebuck* (1976)	26" midweight bike is built for comfort	$64.99
Boat Motor	*Sears, Roebuck* (1977)	*Gamefisher;* 30-speed twin prop motor; whisper quiet electric fishing motors	$119
Motorcycle Helmet	*Sears, Roebuck* (1977)	Meets DOT safety specs where applicable	$30.99
Pump	*Sears, Roebuck* (1976)	Inflating pump; steel with 8" barrel	$2.80

Item	Source	Description	Price
Telescope	*Smithsonian* (1976)	*Edmund Newtonian Field Reflector;* clearest, brightest, most spectacular wide-angle view of moon, stars, comets, galaxies ever	$129.95
Tennis Balls	*Chicago Tribune* (1978)	*Wilson Pro;* yellow; package of 3	$2.29
Tricycle	*Sears, Roebuck* (1976)	With flowered basket	$16.99
Unicycle	*Sears, Roebuck* (1976)	Beginners	$21.88

Telephone Equipment and Services

Item	Source	Description	Price
Telephone Charges	*New York Times* (1977)	*Bell System;* wherever in the world you do business, a station-to-station call is the cheapest way to get there; France, Italy, Germany	$6.75

Toys

Item	Source	Description	Price
Baby Doll	*Sears, Roebuck* (1978)	*Tenerella;* cut $2; this lovely 19" doll has long, dark, rooted hair, sparkling go-to-sleep eyes, and smooth vinyl skin	$12.99
Big Slider Gym	*Sears, Roebuck* (1977)	Has three activities including 9 1/2' long slide that goes over the top	$64.99
Bird Model Kits	*Smithsonian* (1976)	*Ariel;* little owl card sculptures of wild birds in flight; easy to make in a few hours	$5.95
Car Set	*Sears, Roebuck* (1978)	*Matchbox*	$4.47
Collector's Case	*Sears, Roebuck* (1978)	*Matchbox;* store and carry up to 72 mini-cars in this collector's case	$6.97
Crazy Buggy	*Sears, Roebuck* (1978)	The do-anything stunt car set	$9.95
Dome Climber	*Sears, Roebuck* (1977)	When your muscles tire, take climber into a clubhouse, just cover with old sheets or blankets	$44.99
Fun Tunnel	*Sears, Roebuck* (1978)	*Winnie-the-Pooh;* a crawl-through tunnel of fun that's 22" in diameter; 9' long; plenty of room for roaming	$10.95
Horse and Wagon	*Sears, Roebuck* (1978)	*Weebles West;* mosey on down to the corral and hitch the Weebles' roly-poly cowpony to the 8" covered wagon	$2.97
Merry-Go-Round	*Sears, Roebuck* (1977)	2-seat; 6' diameter, seat height 24"	$43.99
Remote-Control Racer	*Smithsonian* (1976)	*JS&A;* computer logic has added a new fun way to control remote control products	$49.95
Rocks and Minerals Set	*Sears, Roebuck* (1978)	*Learning by Doing;* start a lifetime hobby	$3.66
Sno-Cone Maker	*Sears, Roebuck* (1978)	Crank out sno-cones from ice cubes; add flavors	$5.66
Top	*Sears, Roebuck* (1978)	*Winnie-the-Pooh* spinning top	$4.49
Viewer	*Sears, Roebuck* (1978)	*Viewmaster 3-D;* touch and see your world; one reel of 7 scenes	$17.44
Wagon	*Sears, Roebuck* (1976)	Remove green hardwood side panels to convert to coaster wagon	$28.87

Tobacco Products

Item	Source	Description	Price
Pipe	*New York Times* (1978)	*Connoisseur Pipes;* Bent Dublin	$18.75

Travel and Transportation

Item	Source	Description	Price
Airfare	*New York Times* (1978)	*Aerolineas Argentinas;* APEX fares from New York to Rio; requires minimum 29-day stay in Argentina; round trip	$775

Item	Source	Description	Price
Airfare	*New York Times* (1978)	TWA round trip fares from New York to San Francisco Monday–Thursday:	
		Night Coach	$229
		Day Coach	$252
		Friday–Sunday:	
		Night Coach	$275
		Day Coach	$298
Airplane Fare	*New York Times* (1977)	*United;* save to Los Angeles/San Francisco; freedom fare round trip; your savings $86	$342
Airplane Fare	*Los Angeles Times* (1978)	*TWA;* new economy coach for our lowest price; you'll save up to 56%; Los Angeles to Boston	$230
Cruise	*Chicago Tribune* (1978)	*Chandis Lines;* 7 nights, 8 days	$6.99
Ferry	*Chicago Tribune* (1978)	*Chessie;* the good ferry rides again between Michigan and Wisconsin; one-way adult	$8
Trip	*Chicago Tribune* (1978)	TWA from Chicago to Las Vegas; round trip; open bar & meals; 4 days at the hotel Frontier	$179.95

MISCELLANY 1975-1979

Now, The No-Frills House

Thanks to inflation and the continuing energy shortage, the compact car seems here to stay. Now, with driveway ready, comes the compact house. In suburban areas around the country, builders are turning out no-frills houses that sell for prices ranging in most areas from about $20,000 to $36,000. Aimed at buyers who would not otherwise be able to afford a home of their own in today's market, the small houses in some areas are breaking sales records in a recession-dogged industry.

Time, February 23, 1976

Hemingway Should Have Had It So Good

Former Domestic Affairs Chief John Ehrlichman, who received a $50,000 advance from Simon & Schuster for his first novel, has now peddled film rights to the book to Paramount Pictures. His price: an estimated $75,000. Titled *The Company* and due in the stores by May, it is about a U.S. President who dabbles in domestic spying, then faces blackmail by the CIA. "If I stick to a routine and don't get too loose, I can write 15 to 25 pages a day," says Ehrlichman. Now appealing his 1975 conviction for Watergate-related crimes, he has already started work on a second book, which he describes as another "purely fictional novel about Washington, D.C." So far, no nibbles from Hollywood.

Time, March 1, 1976

College Graduates Found to Earn More

Finance Facs, a monthly statistical bulletin issued by the National Consumer Finance Association says that a college education continues to play "a major determining role" in household income.

Its most recent survey based on 1975 figures, indicates that households headed by a college graduate averaged $21,734 in annual income, compared with $13,779 for all households.

Where the head of the household had completed only one to three years of college, income averaged $15,500. It slipped to $13,905 where the household head was only a high school graduate. At lower levels of education, average income ran still less, the survey found.

A wide discrepancy persists between households headed by men and women, the organization says. In fact, households headed by males average $15,873—or a little more than double the $7,201 average where a female headed the family.

New York Times, February 2, 1977

Rubber

The breakthrough in the 16-week strike by 60,000 members of the United Rubber Workers came after a 70-hour bargaining marathon, when union negotiators and Firestone agreed to a new pay package giving workers a 36% increase in wages and benefits over three years. The Firestone agreement, which will set the pattern for the other struck members of rubber's Big Four (Goodyear, Goodrich and Uniroyal), will boost the industry's average hourly wage in the first year by 88¢ to $6.38. In addition, the rubber workers got an escalator that provides an extra 1¢ an hour for each .4% increase in the cost of living index.

Time, August 23, 1976

1980-2004

From Recession to the Era of Possibilities

PRESIDENTS

Ronald Reagan	1981-1989
George Bush	1989-1993
William J. Clinton	1993-2001
George W. Bush	2001-

The decade of the 1980s began with serious economic problems. Both interest rates and inflation rates reached a staggering 18 percent. The economy was at a standstill and unemployment was rising. By 1982, America was in its deepest depression since the Great Depression that spanned most of the 1930s. One in 10 Americans was out of work. Convinced that inflation was the primary enemy of long-term economic growth, the Federal Reserve Board brought the economy to a halt in the early days of the decade. It was a shock treatment that worked. By 1984 the tight money policies of the government, stabilization of world oil prices and labor's declining bargaining power brought inflation to four percent, the lowest level since 1967. Despite the pain, the plan to strangle inflation succeeded; Americans not only prospered, but many began to believe it was their right to be successful. The decade came to be symbolized by self-indulgence and a soaring stock market. The Dow Jones Industrial Average tripled from 1,000 in 1980 to nearly 3,000 a decade later. In the center of the recovery was Mr. Optimism, President Ronald Reagan. During his presidential campaign he promised a "Morning in America" and during his eight years, his good nature helped transform the national mood. The collapse of communism at the end of the 1980s brought an end to the old world order of Cold War and set the stage for a realignment in which America was still regarded as the strongest nation in the world. However, in the postcommunist world, it was a strength defined by both military might and economic reach. As democracy swept across Eastern Europe in the 1990s, the U.S. economy began to feel the impact of a peace dividend generated by many corporations' willingness to invest in the newly created economies of countries such as Russia, its former satellites and the awakening giant of Asia, China.

Even though the 1990s opened on a down note, heavily burdened by a ballooning national debt, the chaotic collapse of the savings and loan industry and a war in Iraq, economists marvel at the prosperity achieved during the prosperous decade. This economic wave was driven by dramatic improvements in technology-headlined by advances in computerization and communications-as well as a willingness by consumers to assume higher levels of personal debt and the race toward globalization. The innovative advances in technology produced higher levels of personal efficiency and self-sufficiency, but contributed to the job losses suffered nationwide, most of which were blamed on globalization, especially the off-shoring of American manufacturing jobs. At the end of World War II, the U.S. economy accounted for almost 50 percent of the global economic product; by 1993 the U.S. share was less than 23 percent and declining. This need for a global reach inspired a round of corporate mergers as companies searched for efficiency, market share, new products, or advanced technology to survive in the rapidly shifting business environment. The increase in consumer credit fueled the boom years and also led to an increase in personal bankruptcy and a reduction in the overall savings rate. At the same time, the two-career family became the norm. Forty-two percent of all American workers were female, more than half of all married women and 90 percent of female college graduates worked outside the home. The rise of women in the work force, which had been accelerating since the 1960s, brought great social change, affecting married life, child rearing, family income, office culture and the growth of the national economy.

As the 1990s drew to a close it was labeled the "Era of Possibilities" by Fortune magazine and had produced the longest economic expansion in the nation's history. Its primary characteristics were steady growth, low inflation and low unemployment. The stock market set a succession of records throughout the period, attracting thousands of middle-class investors to stocks, especially to the so-called glamour offerings of high technology companies. This market boom eventually spawned new wealth and brought early retirement to legions of aging baby boomers. At the turn of the twentieth century, 63 percent of all men over the age of 65 were in the work force; by 1948 it was 47 percent, and by the mid-1990s, less than 16 percent. The economic boom did not benefit everyone, however. By 1997 a greater share of Americans were living in poverty than in 1973. Many of the new jobs created during the period were within the low wage sector. At the same time, the workplace was changing. As companies expanded and contracted adjusting to the new global economy, the job security American workers at large corporations had enjoyed was threatened. The rising cost of health insurance placed this essential benefit beyond the reach of many. To stay employed, workers became more willing to learn new job skills, establish their own companies and move from project to project aided by dramatic improvements in technology that altered the once expensive and insurmountable impact of distance and geography. Profit sharing, which allowed workers to benefit from increased productivity, became more common. Retirement programs and pension plans became more flexible and transferable, serving the needs of a highly mobile work force.

History will record that the twenty-first century began in the United States on September 11, 2001, when four American commercial airliners were hijacked and used as weapons of terror. After the tragedies at the World Trade Center in New York; Shanksville, Pennsylvania; and the Pentagon, Americans felt vulnerable to a foreign invasion for the first time in decades. Citizens in every part of the nation, even those thousands of miles from the targets, immediately began to question what was important. As a result, the economy, already reeling from the stock market crash in technology stocks, slowed to a crawl. This recession then stretched for 36 months as cautious companies reduced expansions, slowed product development and looked for technology-driven productivity gains to drive down costs. The slowdown allowed an increasingly global economy desperate to catch its breath, while creating a rise in unemployment.

America's military response to the attacks was to dispatch U.S. force around the world in a War on Terror. United in grief and outrage, the military mobilized its intelligence, law enforcement, diplomatic and financial resources. The first stop was the mountains of Afghanistan, where a new breed of suicidal terrorists, known as al Qaeda, were collected into an army of self-styled Islamic warriors determined to destroy America. Under the protection of the country's ruling Taliban, al Qaeda had trained thousands of terrorists. America's military response was swift and uncompromising. The stated goal was to hunt down and kill the al Qaeda leadership and free Afghanistan from Taliban rule. The initial fighting force combined billion-dollar U.S. technology, which struck distant primitive cave targets from the air using space-age laser-guided missiles. The Taliban was quickly routed. The prime target of the assault, al Qaeda leader Osama bin Laden, escaped capture. Within months of the invasion, more than 2,400 suspected terrorists in 90 countries were detained and the messy process of rebuilding Afghanistan had begun.

The United States quickly shifted from Afghanistan to Iraq, home of leader Saddam Hussein. Despite vehement opposition from Germany, France, Spain and the United Nations, President Bush launched Operation Iraqi Freedom to eliminate Saddam Hussein and the possibility of his employing weapons of mass destruction. As in the invasion of Afghanistan, the U.S. achieved a rapid victory, quickly capturing the Iraq capital of Baghdad. Bringing peace and stability to the Arab nation and finding the fearsome weapons of mass destruction proved to be more daunting. At mid-year 2004, the coalition forces bestowed partial sovereignty on an interim government, while retaining more than 144,000 soldiers in the country.

HISTORICAL SNAPSHOT
1980-1984

1980

- Sixty-five million Americans read daily newspapers
- 4,225 cable-television channels, 750 commercial television stations, and over 7,500 radio stations now in operation
- Gold hits record high $875 per ounce
- EPA superfund created to clean up toxic-waste sites
- Japan surpasses U.S. as world's largest auto producer
- 30 percent of U.S. auto sales are imports
- Double-digit inflation continues; prices rise 12.4 percent

1981

- IBM Personal Computer marketed
- 12,000 striking air-traffic controllers fired by President Ronald Reagan
- Public debt hits $1 trillion
- U.S. prime interest rate reaches 21.5 percent, highest since Civil War
- New York and Miami increase transit fares from 60¢ to 75¢
- Kellogg's introduces Nutri-Grain wheat cereal

- U.S. first-class postal rates go to 18¢, then 20¢
- Sears, Roebuck buys real estate broker, Coldwell Banker & Co. and securities concern, Dean Witter Reynolds
- U.S. population hits 228 million

1982

- Court order breaks up AT&T, U.S. telephone monopoly, into AT&T long lines and regional telephone companies
- Japanese market wristwatch-sized television with 1.2-inch screen
- *USA Today,* first national general-interest daily newspaper, introduced
- 2.9 million women operate businesses
- Braniff International declares bankruptcy
- United Auto Workers agree to wage concessions with Ford Motor Co.
- U.S. Steel acquires Marathon Oil
- Unemployment reaches 10.8 percent
- Computer "mouse" introduced by Apple
- First successful embryo transfer is performed

- NutraSweet introduced as a synthetic sugar substitute
- Martin Luther King Day becomes a national holiday
- One-of-a-kind Cabbage Patch dolls become overnight sensation
- 26 major league baseball teams show total loss of $45 million
- Wall Street's Dow Jones Industrials Average closes at new high 1258.64
- 35.3 million live below poverty line
- Cellular telephones become available to motorists, cost $3,000, plus $150 per month service

1984

- President Reagan reelected
- Laser disc computer data storage system becomes available
- Book publishers sell 2.164 billion books; total receipts reach $9.12 billion
- Three major networks control 73% of prime-time viewership
- New York State imposes first mandatory automobile seat belt law
- Inflation drops to 1972 levels
- Trivial Pursuit board game has sales of $777 million
- Average price of single-family house tops $101,000

SELECTED INCOME 1980-1984

Job	Source	Description	Pay
Adjuster	New Orleans Times-Picayune (1983)	1 to 2 yrs. multi-line exp.; 20% comp, 50% gen. liability, 30% comm lines; this position offers good advancement potential	$20,000/yr
Administrative Assistant	New Orleans Times-Picayune (1983)	For fund-raising director of non-profit organization; responsibilities include special events, proposal and grant writing, record-keeping and some typing; experience required	$12,000–$15,000/yr
Baseball Player	Bob Rains, St. Louis Cardinals: The 100th Anniversary History (1992)	Annual income of Milwaukee Brewers pitcher Don Sutton in 1982	$700,000
Boxer	Guinness Book of World Records (1981)	Purse paid to boxer Sugar Ray Leonard for a welter weight title fight against Roberto Duran in 1980	$8.5 million
Dancers-Hostesses	Chicago Tribune (1981)	No experience necessary; full or part-time	$500-$700/wk
Housekeeper-Cook	Chicago Tribune (1983)	Live in; private room and bath; 3 adults; must speak English; RECENT reference; 5-day week	$200/wk to start
Keypunch Operator	San Francisco Examiner (1982)	Min. 2 yrs. exper. nec.; 15,000 strokes/hr; IBM 129 exper. helpful	$6.45/hr
Mechanic	San Francisco Examiner (1982)	Will train; exc. co. benefits; flexible hours	$8–$10/hr
Medical Secretary	Chicago Tribune (1981)	No medical experience necessary; you'll deal with patients, get information for charts, histories; talk with hospital personnel to set up surgeries, therapy; good typing skills desired; no Saturdays; exceptional benefits; employer pays fee	$1,250/mo
Nurse	New York Times (1981)	LPN; Candidates must have a license to practice as a Practical Nurse in New York State	$10,755/yr
Performer (1980)	Guinness Book of World Records (1981)	Annual payment to television's Tonight Show host Johnny Carson for 125 days a year	$2.5 million
Playwright	Life Magazine (1983)	Payment in 1983 to Tennessee Williams for rights to a television remake of his 1947 play A Streetcar Named Desire	$750,000
Produce Stand Vendor	San Francisco Examiner (1982)	Pleasant Hill area; must have truck	$2,000/mo
Rehabilitation Assistant	New York Times (1981)	Bachelor's degree and 1 year experience in the care or rehabilitation of mental patients or a Masters degree in an appropriate field of study essential	$14,245/yr
Salesman	Chicago Tribune (1983)	Outside sales person for health organization; possible inside management position available	$300–$600/mo, plus weekly commission
Teacher	New York Times (1981)	Special Ed; work on transdisciplinary team serving multihandicapped	$14,500–$17,000/yr
Tennis Instructor	Chicago Tribune (1981)	600 hrs of group lessons per year plus private lessons; U.S.P.T.A. sanction preferred	$13/hr

CONSUMER EXPENDITURES 1980-1984

(Per Capita)

Expenditure Type	1980	1981	1982	1983	1984
Clothing	$394.35	$424.88	$435.45	$470.77	$511.35
Food	$1592.31	$1597.77	$1662.57	$1733.28	$1820.24
Auto Usage	$943.71	$1028.07	$1034.58	$1144.28	$1270.61
New Auto Purchase	$203.76	$220.49	$229.57	$282.55	$328.34
Auto Parts	$65.43	$66.97	$64.88	$70.85	$73.19
Gas & Oil	$380.73	$425.75	$405.30	$398.21	$399.84
Housing	$1120.68	$1248.56	$1339.96	$1428.11	$1532.94
Furniture	$90.90	$94.37	$90.45	$100.72	$112.97
Utilities	$356.14	$390.09	$425.55	$458.82	$480.23
Telephone & Telegraph	$121.20	$134.38	$151.18	$155.79	$163.39
Physicians	$187.95	$219.18	$237.76	$263.77	$291.10
Dentists	$60.16	$70.02	$74.94	$79.81	$85.89
Health Insurance	$56.21	$63.49	$77.09	$79.39	$82.51
Personal Business	$446.16	$471.85	$525.91	$626.98	$670.64
Personal Care	$118.13	$124.81	$127.92	$144.69	$156.13
Tobacco	$91.78	$99.15	$104.66	$121.21	$127.36
Local Transport	$21.08	$21.74	$23.26	$25.61	$28.35
Intercity Transport	$70.70	$76.11	$77.09	$79.81	$89.28
Recreation	$516.43	$567.53	$603	$662.41	$731.14
Religion/Welfare Activities	$169.51	$189.61	$206.31	$224.08	$248.79
Private Education & Research	$147.55	$164.82	$179.61	$195.48	$210.71
Per Capita Consumption	$7676.57	$8376.79	$8869.32	$8788.88	$10409.87

INVESTMENTS 1980-1984

Investment	1980	1981	1982	1983	1984
Basic Yield, One-year Corporate Bonds	12.75	15.06	14.84	12.78	13.49
Short-term Interest Rates, 4–6 Months, Prime Commercial Paper	12.29	14.76	11.89	8.89	10.16
Basic Yield, Common Stocks, Total	5.25	5.41	5.81	4.40	4.64
Index of Common Stocks (1941–1943=10)	118.71	128.05	119.71	160.41	160.50

COMMON STOCKS, CLOSING PRICE AND YIELD, FIRST BUSINESS DAY OF YEAR

(Parenthetical number is annual dividends in dollars)

	1980	1981	1982	1983	1984
Allis Chalmers	33 1/2 (2)	36 (2)	15 7/8 (/)	9 5/8 (/)	16 1/8 (/)
American Brands (2 for 1 split, 5/8/81)	66 7/8 (5.50)	77 1/8 (6.20)	36 3/4 (3.25)	45 1/2 (3.50)	59 3/8 (3.60)
AT&T	51 3/4 (5)	48 7/8 (5)	58 1/2 (5.40)	59 7/8 (5.40)	62 1/2 (5.40)
Bethlehem Steel	20 7/8 (1.60)	26 1/4 (1.60)	23 1/2 (1.60)	19 3/4 (1)	27 7/8 (.60)
CPC Intl	58 1/2 (3)	62 1/2 (3.40)	35 (1.92)	40 1/4 (2.10)	38 7/8 (2.20)
Delta Airlines (2 for 1 split, 12/1/81)	37 1/4 (1.20)	59 (1.20)	24 5/8 (1)	41 1/2 (1)	40 3/8 (.60)
General Electric (2 for 1 split, 4/23/83)	49 3/8 (2.80)	61 7/8 (3)	58 3/8 (3.20)	91 3/4 (3.40)	57 5/8 (2)
General Motors	49 3/8 (5.30)	45 3/8 (2.95)	39 3/4 (2.40)	61 (2.40)	74 1/8 (2.80)
Intl Harvester	37 (2.50)	25 3/8 (1.20)	7 1/4 (/)	4 3/8 (/)	11 5/8 (/)
Nabisco (merged as wholly owned subsidiary of R. J. Reynolds Industries, Inc.)	21 5/8 (1.62)	26 3/4 (1.80)	30 5/8 (1.85)	36 (2.05)	40 7/8 (2.28)
U.S. Steel	18 (1.60)	25 5/8 (1.60)	30 (2)	20 3/4 (1)	31 (1)
Western Union	20 3/8 (1.40)	25 3/8 (1.40)	35 7/8 (1.40)	43 3/4 (1.40)	36 7/8 (1.40)

STANDARD JOBS 1980-1984

Job Type	1980	1981	1982	1983	1984
Wages Per Full-Time Employees	$15,757/yr	$17,197/yr	$18,430/yr	$17,524/yr	$18,356/yr
Private Industries, inc. Farm Labor	$15,721/yr	$17,144/yr	$18,331/yr	$17,420/yr	$18,200/yr
Bituminous Coal Mining	$24,555/yr	$27,283/yr	$29,110/yr	$29,796/yr	$32,292/yr
Building Trades	$18,571/yr	$20,355/yr	$21,868/yr	$20,488/yr	$20,748/yr
Domestics	$8576/yr	$9327/yr	$10,260/yr	$6,665/yr	$6,760/yr
Farm Labor	$7434/yr	$7989/yr	$8781/yr	$6552/yr	$6864/yr
Federal Civilian	$21,206/yr	$23,029/yr	$24,452/yr	$23,972/yr	$25,083/yr
Federal Employees, Executive Depts.	$17,217/yr	$19,079/yr	$20,689/yr	$21,666/yr	$25,655/yr
Federal Military	$13,498/yr	$15,537/yr	$17,384/yr	NR	NR
Finance, Insurance, & Real Estate	$15,871/yr	$17,343/yr	$18,966/yr	$19,552/yr	$20,695/yr
Gas, Electricity, & Sanitation Workers	$21,701/yr	$23,959/yr	$26,185/yr	$27,508/yr	$29,276/yr
Manufacturing, Durable Goods	$19,014/yr	$20,810/yr	$22,256/yr	$21,476/yr	$22,568/yr
Manufacturing, Nondurable Goods	$16,323/yr	$17,739/yr	$19,272/yr	$19,188/yr	$19,916/yr
Medical/Health Services Workers	$14,728/yr	$16,288/yr	$17,861/yr	$17,108/yr	$17,888/yr
Miscellaneous Manufacturing	$13,990/yr	$15,169/yr	$16,680/yr	$17,680/yr	$18,512/yr
Motion Picture Services	$17,868/yr	$19,856/yr	$21,452/yr	$23,712/yr	$25,428/yr
Nonprofit Org. Workers	$10,400/yr	$11,153/yr	$11,971/yr	$10,504/yr	$10,972/yr
Passenger Transportation Workers, Local and Highway	$13,447/yr	$14,446/yr	$15,224/yr	$13,780/yr	$14,508/yr
Personal Services	$10,615/yr	$11,195/yr	$11,752/yr	$9308/yr	$9776/yr
Postal Employees	$20,280/yr	$23,384/yr	NR	$25,262/yr	$26,417/yr
Public School Teachers	$15,438/yr	$16,606/yr	$18,061/yr	$19,040/yr	$20,031/yr
Radio Broadcasting & Television Workers	$19,538/yr	$20,813/yr	$22,550/yr	$21,944/yr	$23,504/yr
Railroads	$25,372/yr	$27,452/yr	$29,692/yr	$21,840/yr	$22,724/yr
State and Local Govt. Workers	$15,078/yr	$16,362/yr	$17,762/yr	$17,160/yr	$18,252/yr
Telephone & Telegraph Workers	$22,515/yr	$25,090/yr	$27,313/yr	$27,716/yr	$28,574/yr
Wholesale and Retail Trade Workers	$18,822/yr	$20,324/yr	$21,694/yr	$21,476/yr	$22,724/yr

FOOD BASKET 1980-1984

(NR = Not Reported)

Commodity	Year	U.S. Average	North East	North Central	South	West
Bananas, per pound	1980	33.39¢	34.80¢	34.30¢	33.30¢	33.10¢
	1981	37.70¢	37.10¢	37.80¢	39.60¢	36.10¢
	1982	37.20¢	36.60¢	36.60¢	38.80¢	36.70¢
	1983	43.80¢	45.30¢	41.70¢	46.60¢	41.80¢
	1984	38.60¢	38.40¢	37.60¢	38.90¢	39.10¢
Beef, Ground, Hamburger, per pound	1980	$1.85	$1.87	$1.78	$1.88	$1.87
	1981	$1.78	$1.80	$1.69	$1.83	$1.83
	1982	$1.78	$1.79	$1.73	$1.85	$1.74
	1983	$1.77	$1.79	$1.69	$1.83	$1.79
	1984	$1.69	$1.71	$1.58	$1.73	$1.74
Beef, Steak, T-bone, per pound	1980	$3.64	NR	$3.66	$3.80	$3.32
	1981	$3.57	NR	$3.55	$3.68	$3.24
	1982	$3.89	NR	$3.90	$3.99	$3.73
	1983	$3.88	NR	$3.86	$3.73	$3.82
	1984	$4.06	NR	$4.01	$4.16	$3.82
Bread, White, per pound	1980	51.90¢	60¢	48.40¢	47¢	48.70¢
	1981	51.90¢	58.30¢	50.70¢	47.60¢	51.50¢
	1982	52.90¢	61.40¢	52.50¢	49.20¢	49.10¢
	1983	54.20¢	62.70¢	51.80¢	51.70¢	52.80¢
	1984	54.10¢	67¢	50¢	50.90¢	53.30¢
Butter, per pound	1980	$1.99	$1.98	$1.95	$2.08	$1.93
	1981	$1.99	$1.94	$2.02	$2.06	$1.93
	1982	$2.05	$1.98	$2.10	$2.12	$2.00
	1983	$2.07	$2.01	$2.06	$2.17	$2.06
	1984	$2.11	$2.06	$2.07	$2.20	$2.14
Chickens, per pound	1980	76.60¢	79.70¢	74.20¢	74.30¢	79.70¢
	1981	73.40¢	76.90¢	71.70¢	70.60¢	75.40¢
	1982	72¢	75¢	71.50¢	68.70¢	73.50¢
	1983	68.70¢	72.20¢	70.20¢	65.60¢	72.10¢
	1984	82.90¢	91.40¢	77.70¢	79.30¢	85.50¢
Coffee, per pound	1980	$2.19	$2.96	$2.90	$2.90	$2.80
	1981	$2.56	$2.48	$2.65	$2.53	$2.45
	1982	$2.56	$2.54	$2.56	$2.60	$2.57
	1983	$2.45	$2.51	$2.40	$2.49	$2.43
	1984	$2.60	$2.59	$2.60	$2.63	$2.59
Corn on the Cob, per pound	1980	40.90¢	NR	39.30¢	43.80¢	45.80¢
	1981	45.50¢	NR	42.90¢	64.70¢	53.90¢
	1982	46.80¢	43.10¢	50.10¢	42.90¢	56.90¢
	1983	56.70¢	NR	60.70¢	56.70¢	NR
	1984	45.80¢	60¢	46.70¢	41.30¢	34.90¢
Eggs, per dozen	1980	91.17¢	99.40¢	88.10¢	88.50¢	90.50¢
	1981	90.04¢	99.80¢	83.70¢	87.50¢	92.60¢
	1982	84.20¢	93.70¢	80¢	80.40¢	87.30¢
	1983	86.50¢	94¢	81.90¢	83.50¢	93.80¢
	1984	87.60¢	96.80¢	78¢	87.20¢	96.10¢
Crackers, Salted, per pound	1980	82¢	86.50¢	79.60¢	81.20¢	76.40¢
	1981	87.20¢	89.50¢	86.40¢	85.10¢	89.30¢
	1982	88.20¢	NR	87.30¢	85.10¢	NR
	1983	94.70¢	NR	94.70¢	89.60¢	NR
	1984	$1.00	NR	95.70¢	97.30¢	NR

Commodity	Year	U.S. Average	North East	North Central	South	West
Margarine, per pound	1980	73.10¢	NR	70¢	NR	69.40¢
	1981	73¢	NR	68.80¢	NR	75.80¢
	1982	NR	NR	NR	NR	NR
	1983	NR	NR	NR	NR	NR
	1984	80¢	81¢	78.20¢	76.20¢	91.30¢
Milk, Fresh, per half-gallon	1980	$1.08	$1.03	$1.08	$1.22	$1.03
	1981	$1.11	$1.06	$1.10	$1.24	$1.06
	1982	$1.12	$1.10	$1.11	$1.24	$1.05
	1983	$1.12	$1.11	$1.11	$1.23	$1.05
	1984	$1.12	$1.09	$1.09	$1.27	$1.06
Lettuce, Iceberg, per pound	1980	52.20¢	59.60¢	51.90¢	55.40¢	42.60¢
	1981	44.10¢	47¢	46.30¢	46.90¢	37.30¢
	1982	51.80¢	57.80¢	51.50¢	53.50¢	44.70¢
	1983	58¢	58.40¢	58.60¢	57.10¢	58.30¢
	1984	43.60¢	48.20¢	43.50¢	49¢	31.40¢
Orange Juice, Frozen, per 16 ounces	1980	$1.14	$1.31	$1.08	$1.04	$1.20
	1981	$1.41	$1.55	$1.37	$1.35	$1.42
	1983	$1.36	$1.45	$1.27	$1.36	$1.44
	1984	$1.66	$1.66	$1.63	$1.68	$1.69
Pork, Chops, per pound	1980	$2.05	$2.07	$1.91	$2.13	$2.20
	1981	$2.05	$2.07	$1.94	$2.10	$2.20
	1982	$2.32	$2.33	$2.16	$2.37	$2.52
	1983	$2.41	$2.39	$2.22	$2.51	$2.62
	1984	$2.43	$2.42	$2.26	$2.48	$2.63
Pork, Bacon, Sliced, per pound	1980	$1.68	$1.80	$1.64	$1.64	$1.65
	1981	$1.53	$1.61	$1.49	$1.49	$1.52
	1982	$1.98	$1.97	$2.00	$1.94	$2.00
	1983	$1.95	$1.98	$1.93	$1.92	$1.97
	1984	$1.90	$2.02	$1.80	$1.91	$1.87
Pork, Ham, Rump or Shank Half, per pound	1980	$1.39	$1.57	$1.32	$1.33	$1.53
	1981	$1.19	$1.31	$1.11	$1.13	$1.45
	1982	$1.38	$1.44	NR	$1.35	NR
	1983	$1.3230	$1.2810	NR	$1.30	NR
	1984	$1.2710	$1.2870	NR	$1.19	NR
Potato Chips, 16 ounces	1980	$2.13	$2.10	$2.03	$2.32	$2.13
	1981	$2.27	$2.30	$2.14	$2.35	$2.32
	1982	$2.40	$2.46	$2.25	$2.41	$2.51
	1983	$2.53	$2.53	$2.41	$2.52	$2.76
	1984	$2.57	$2.62	$2.50	$2.56	$2.67
Potatoes, per 10 pounds	1980	$2.20	$2.11	$2.32	$2.23	$2.15
	1981	$2.75	$2.59	$2.85	$2.93	$2.59
	1982	$2.29	$2.05	$2.29	$2.21	$2.67
	1983	$2.09	$2.12	$2.03	$2.34	$1.89
	1984	$2.99	$3.15	$3.12	$3.04	$3.17
Rice, per pound	1980	52¢	60.30¢	NR	43.20¢	55.50¢
	1981	57.20¢	64.40¢	NR	47.30¢	59.50¢
	1982	50.80¢	66.60¢	NR	42.60¢	49.20¢
	1983	46.80¢	NR	NR	38.50¢	49.10¢
	1984	48.40¢	59.40¢	NR	39.80¢	51.50¢
Sugar, per pound	1980	55¢	61.20¢	53.40¢	55.10¢	48.90¢
	1981	44.60¢	49.70¢	42.90¢	42.70¢	43.60¢
	1982	33.50¢	37.70¢	30.90¢	32.50¢	35.35¢
	1983	35.50¢	40.30¢	33.40¢	34.50¢	35.90¢
	1984	35.80¢	38.60¢	35.60¢	33¢	39.70¢

Commodity	Year	U.S. Average	North East	North Central	South	West
Soft Drink, Cola, per 16 ounces	1980	44.60¢	42.80¢	45.70¢	NR	45.50¢
	1981	46.40¢	45.50¢	47.60¢	45.50¢	46.60¢
	1982	47.30¢	47.50¢	48.40¢	46.30¢	47.40¢
	1983	46.90¢	45.40¢	48.70¢	46¢	47.50¢
	1984	47.50¢	49.80¢	49.20¢	46.50¢	46¢
Tuna, Light, Chunk, per pound	1980	$2.55	$2.46	$2.54	$2.64	$2.54
	1981	$2.58	$2.48	$2.59	$2.63	$2.62
	1982	$2.58	$2.54	$2.51	NR	$2.42
	1983	$2.38	$2.47	$2.34	$2.34	$2.46
	1984	$2.16	$2.05	$2.12	$2.16	$2.18

SELECTED PRICES 1980-1984

Item	Source	Description	Price
Advertising			
Advertising Rate	*Guinness Book of World Records* (1981)	Price of a single minute of television advertising on Super Bowl XIV in 1980	$468,000
Business Advertising Rate	*Guinness Book of World Records* (1981)	Price of a four-color back cover of *Parade* Magazine; circulation 21 million in 1980	$152,475
Alcohol			
Beer	*Los Angeles Times* (1981)	*Pabst;* 12 pack, 12-oz cans	$3.19
Bourbon	*Los Angeles Times* (1981)	*Old Crow;* 1.75 liter	$9.49
Vodka	*Los Angeles Times* (1981)	*Count Vasya;* 80 proof; 1.75 lt	$6.99
Wine	*Los Angeles Times* (1981)	*Bolla Soave;* dry white; 750 ml; save $1.40	$2.99
Wine	*Guinness Book of World Records* (1981)	1822 bottle of rare Chateau Lafite wine bought in 1980	$31,000
Apparel, Children's			
Shoes	*Yankee* (1981)	*Kangaroos;* Sebago's most noted quality casual shoes	$38.95
Apparel, Men's			
Boots	*Field & Stream* (1982)	*Browning Featherweight;* soft leather boot	$102.95
Cap	*Sears, Roebuck* (1983)	Genuine leather with acetate lining	$22
Gloves	*Sears, Roebuck* (1983)	Leather driving-style; soft, rich cowhide shell	$17
Gloves	*Sears, Roebuck* (1983)	Canvas-cloth work gloves	$6.49
Hat	*Field & Stream* (1982)	Gunslinger western style; flat crown, 4 1/4 high with oval indentations; made of 100% wool felt	$15.50
Hunting Suit	*Field & Stream* (1982)	*Cabela;* camouflage; reversible orange and camouflage; 2-piece suit	$74.95
Jacket	*The Scottish Lion Catalog* (1984)	Irish tweed; a washing in the River Eske in Ireland to soften the yarn is part of the special handling these jackets have been receiving since 1866	$185
Pants	*New York Times* (1981)	Genuine U.S. Marine; camouflage	$39
Pants	*Bon Appetit* (1984)	*REI Woolrich;* comfort in action; have fun and good fit in these Rugby-style pants	$18.95
Shirt	*Field & Stream* (1982)	*L. L. Bean;* chamois cloth shirt; in green, red, navy, ivory, tan, and slate blue	$18.25
Shoes	*Yankee* (1981)	*Deerskin Trading Post;* pile-lined suede mocs; sturdy cowhide suede lined with fleecy acrylic	$12.99
Shoes	*Sears, Roebuck* (1983)	Wing-tip oxford	$39.99
Socks	*Sears, Roebuck* (1983)	Even our very low-priced work socks are cotton-terry lined; 6 pairs in package	$5.99/pkg

Item	Source	Description	Price
Socks	*Sears, Roebuck* (1983)	Wool blend for boots	$5.99
Sportcoat	*Sears, Roebuck* (1983)	In a rich array of colors, patterns, and sizes	$59.99
Work Gloves	*Sears, Roebuck* (1983)	Long-wearing; split-cowhide leather palm	$4.99

Apparel, Women's

Item	Source	Description	Price
Bag	*The Scottish Lion* Catalog (1984)	Two thistle; 100% cotton canvas tote bag; zippered top opens to a roomy 12" x 10" x 4 1/2" interior	$25
Blouse	*Sears, Roebuck* (1983)	Coordinating Dacron polyester blouses with ties; solid colors; misses sizes	$12
Blouse	*The Scottish Lion Catalog* (1984)	In 100% Irish silk, tie front, dry clean	$85
Caftan	*Yankee* (1981)	Chain stitched embroidered caftan; 100% cambric cotton	$22
Dress	*The Scottish Lion Catalog* (1984)	*Liberty of London;* 100% cotton; top stitching around the collar, waist band, and placket front	$125
Jacket	*The Scottish Lion Catalog* (1984)	Belted; made in Scotland of 70% mohair, 23% wool, 7% nylon	$110
Kimono	*Bon Appetit* (1984)	*Horchow Collection;* Japanese cotton kimono robe	$29.50
Nightshirt	*The Scottish Lion Catalog* (1984)	Seersucker shortie; 100% cotton, button on the front placket and cuffs; made in Scotland	$19
Pocketbook	*The Scottish Lion Catalog* (1984)	Lovely leather bag from Wales; can be carried on the shoulder or the arm; wine, black, or navy	$49
Shoes	*Los Angeles Times* (1981)	*Lady Wellco The Mesh;* walking shoe; plenty of soft comfort in this mesh shoe	$19.99
Skirt	*The Scottish Lion Catalog* (1984)	Striped skirt; from Scotland; 100% linen in bold natural, black and red design	$59
Sweater	*The Scottish Lion Catalog* (1984)	Cardigan; 100% pure new wool with high crewneck for warmth	$95

Appliances

Item	Source	Description	Price
Air Conditioner	*Chicago Tribune* (1983)	*Hotpoint;* 5,950 BTU	$299
Computer (1984)	*Cox News Service* (2004)	*Apple Macintosh;* easy graphic user interface, includes mouse	$2500
Fan	*Sears, Roebuck* (1983)	Manually reversible 2-speed window fan	$34.99
Fan	*Sears, Roebuck* (1983)	Whole-house window fans can pull at least twice as much air through your home as any other fan sold on this page; 24"; 3-speed; with temperature control	$179.99
Gas Grill	*Los Angeles Times* (1981)	*Turco Saratoga;* deluxe twin-burner gas grill	$179.99
Microwave Oven	*Sears, Roebuck* (1981)	*GE Spacemaster;* 1.3 cu ft; mounts like range hoods to cook, vent, illuminate; all without using an inch of valuable counterspace	$689.99
Vacuum Cleaner	*Los Angeles Times* (1981)	*Eureka;* high-performance upright; originally $150	$119.95
Vacuum Cleaner	*Food & Wine* (1984)	*Eureka MiniMite;* the cordless rechargeable hand vacuum, the eighties answer to a dust pan and broom	$39.95

Item	Source	Description	Price
Washer	*Sears, Roebuck* (1983)	*Kenmore;* 2 speed; 5 fabric care cycles	$529.95
Washer	*Chicago Tribune* (1983)	*Westinghouse;* single speed	$318
Washer and Dryer	*Sears, Roebuck* (1983)	*Kenmore;* all-in-one; installs permanently	$719.95

Baby Products

Item	Source	Description	Price
Baby Bag	*Yankee* (1981)	*The Baby Bag;* warmer and easier to use than a snowsuit; fits children 3 months to two years	$32.50
Cradle	*Sears, Roebuck* (1983)	Suspends from hooks mounted on stand posts, swings or can be locked in stationary position	$79.99
Crib	*Sears, Roebuck* (1983)	*Homestead;* features a pine-frame crib with carved detail on the footboard	$129.99
Crib	*Sears, Roebuck* (1983)	*Laura Lynn;* has a pine frame and turned spindles; choose pine or maple finish	$119.99
Crib Set	*Sears, Roebuck* (1983)	Mattress and bumper pad; save $6; separate prices total $165.97; includes crib, 80-coil mattress, and polyurethane foam bumper pad	$159.97
Dressing Table	*Sears, Roebuck* (1983)	1" thick polyurethane foam pad covered in vinyl Sunny Days print that reverses to white	$79.99

Business Equipment and Supplies

Item	Source	Description	Price
Attaché Case	*Sears, Roebuck* (1983)	Our finest cowhide attaché won't open when upside down	$44.99
Attaché Case	*Sears, Roebuck* (1983)	Dark brown pigskin leather; molded handle; leather-look vinyl interior wipes clean; brass-plated double combination lock	$89.99
Chair	*Los Angeles Times* (1981)	*Ford Office Furniture;* secretary posture chair; list $70	$39.95
Computer	*New York Times* (1984)	*Panasonic Sr. Partner;* more powerful than IBM or Compaq portables plus a built-in printer	$2,195
Computer	*New York Times* (1984)	*IBM;* 256K RAM that's expandable to 512K	$1,795
Computer	*New York Times* (1984)	*Macintosh; 128K;* includes MacWrite and MacPaint	$1,788
Copier	*Los Angeles Times* (1981)	*Xerox 2300*	$2,995
Desk	*Los Angeles Times* (1981)	*Ford Office Furniture;* full executive desk, 36" x 72"	$139.95
Paper Shredder	*New York Times* (1984)	*Destroyit;* styled to fit into executive office	$474.95
Portfolio	*Sears, Roebuck* (1983)	Our business case collection; genuine pigskin leather	$49.99
Printer	*New York Times* (1984)	*Epson RX-80;* frills on a no-frills budget	$239

Collectibles

Item	Source	Description	Price
Furniture	*Atlanta Constitution* (1983)	Antique pub table	$150
Painting	*Guinness Book of World Records* (1981)	Price paid in 1980 for J. M. W. Turner's *Juliet and Her Nurse,* 1836	$6.4 million
Painting	*Guinness Book of World Records* (1981)	Auction price in 1980 of Picasso's 1923 portrait of an acrobat Saltimbanque	$3 million
Poster	*Bon Appetit* (1984)	By Robert Rauschenberg; 1984 Olympic; fine-art poster; 24" x 36"	$30

Item	Source	Description	Price
Entertainment, Home			
Camera	*New York Times* (1984)	*Canon Super Sure-Shot;* autofocus	$128.50
Movie Camera	*Sears, Roebuck* (1983)	Low-light silent movie camera; 2-to-1 manual zoom	$109.99
Movie Projector	*Sears, Roebuck* (1983)	*Dual 8;* silent movie projector	$99.99
Turntable	*Los Angeles Times* (1981)	*Sony;* direct-drive turntable; fully automatic straight-line tonearm tracks any record more accurately	$200
Video Camera	*Village Voice* (1981)	*Panasonic PK 750*	$645
Video Camera	*New York Times* (1984)	*Sharp;* save on world's smallest portable video cameras	$359.50
Video Disc Player	*Village Voice* (1981)	*Pioneer VP 1000*	$539
Video Games	*New York Times* (1981)	*Bally Professional Arcade Plus;* includes three built-in games, two hand controls; color calculator; Bally Basic cartridge worth $54.95	$299.95
Video Tapes	*Village Voice* (1981)	*Maxwell T-120*	$13.49
Entertainment			
Circus Ticket	*Los Angeles Times* (1981)	*Ringling Bros. and Barnum & Bailey Circus;* all seats reserved	$5–$8.50
Concert	*Village Voice* (1981)	*Musical Medicine Show;* General Mineral's musical comedy, Floating Hospital Children's Theater Adults Children	 $2 Free
Concert Ticket	*New York Times* (1984)	Pete Seeger at Carnegie Hall	$8.50–$10.50
Movie	*Village Voice* (1981)	*Mickey Mouse and Silly Symphonies;* Whitney Museum	$2
Music Concert	*Village Voice* (1981)	*Jazz in the Park;* Danny Holgate Ensemble and tap dancer Sandman Sims Each	 $2.50
Museum Ticket	*Mini-Vacation in the Mid-Atlantic* (1980)	*The Hagley Museum;* a complex of 19th-century industrial buildings on the site of the original DuPont black powder works	$2.50
Museum Ticket	*Mini-Vacation in the Mid-Atlantic* (1980)	*Old Dutch House Museum;* reputedly the oldest brick dwelling in the state	$0.50
Theater Ticket	*New York Times* (1984)	Dance; Ailey at City Center; evenings and Sunday matinee; orchestra and mezzanine	$30
Food Products			
Beef Jerky	*Los Angeles Times* (1981)	*Lowry's;* in plastic jar with screw top lid; 4 oz. size	$1.99
Beef Roast	*New York Times* (1981)	USDA Choice grade; top round, sirloin, tip round, bottom round	$1.89/lb
Candy	*The Scottish Lion Catalog* (1984)	Scottish Butterscotch; 1 lb; individually gold-foil wrapped, packed in assorted reusable tin of English shops; 4 1/2" x 3" x 3"	$7
Carrots	*New York Times* (1981)	3 1-lb bags	$1
Crabmeat	*Food & Wine* (1984)	*Stone Harbor;* whole; backfin lump crabmeat; now you can enjoy delicious Crab Louis or Crab Imperial; 12 6 1/2 oz tins; regular $70.95; introductory price	$62.95
Cranapple Juice	*Los Angeles Times* (1981)	*Oceanspray;* 32-oz jar	$0.93

Item	Source	Description	Price
Elephant Garlic	*Food & Wine* (1984)	*Willacrick Farm;* great gift item, contains over 2 pounds	$15
Lobster	*Bon Appetit* (1983)	*Barker's;* four 1 1/4-pound Maine lobsters with four pounds of live, clean Ipswich steamers	$79.50
Marmalade	*The Scottish Lion Catalog* (1984)	*Dundee;* four 1-lb jars of orange, lemon, grapefruit and 3-in-1 blend	$16
Milk	*Los Angeles Times* (1981)	*Sunnydell;* 1/2 gallon homogenized	$1.01
Pork Loin	*New York Times* (1981)	*Wilson;* rib end	$0.99/lb
Tomatoes	*New York Times* (1981)	Hard, ripe; selected for slicing; 18 oz package	$0.79
Yogurt	*New York Times* (1981)	*Breyers;* assorted flavors; 8-oz containers; 2 containers	$0.89

Furniture

Item	Source	Description	Price
Chair	*New York Times* (1981)	*Wild Boar;* taupe; regularly $1,795; sale	$895
Dresser	*New York Times* (1981)	*Welch;* dresser; regularly $2,405	$1,599
Sofa	*New York Times* (1981)	Green and pink floral contemporary; 80"; parsons style; upholstered; regularly $1,995	$1,495

Garden Equipment and Supplies

Item	Source	Description	Price
Lawn Mower	*Sears, Roebuck* (1983)	*Craftsman;* standard Eager-1 engine; 3.5 reserve power	$299.99
Plants	*Atlanta Constitution* (1983)	Ground covers; English Ivy, Pachysandra, or Vinca Minor; bundle of 25, per bundle	$7.25
Plants	*Atlanta Constitution* (1983)	Azaleas, full 6" pots; dwarf and tall, each	$.99
Shears	*The Scottish Lion Catalog* (1984)	Japanese gardeners' hedge shears; the stainless-steel model has a 6 1/2" blade, is 25" overall and weighs 30 oz	$19.95
Soil	*Atlanta Constitution* (1983)	*Hyponex Professional Mix Potting Soil;* spagnum peat moss, vermiculite, perlite, humus, charcoal, 16 quart	$3.88

Hotel Rates

Item	Source	Description	Price
Hotel	*Great Outdoors Vacation & Lodging Guide* (1980)	*Baranof Hotel;* Juneau, Alaska; 218 rooms and suites, the Latchstring restaurant, sauna and exercise room; double	$48.50/ngt
Hotel	*Great Outdoors Vacation & Lodging Guide* (1980)	*Holiday Inn;* Flagstaff, Arizona; 157 excellent rooms, restaurant, coffee shop, cocktail lounge, heated pool; double	$35/ngt
Hotel	*Great Outdoors Vacation & Lodging Guide* (1980)	*Ramada Inn;* Lake Havasu City, Arizona; 100 excellent rooms, restaurant, cocktail lounge, heated pool; double	$27/ngt
Hotel	*Great Outdoors Vacation & Lodging Guide* (1980)	*Holiday Inn;* Fayetteville, Arkansas; 165 excellent rooms, a famous resort area of the Ozarks; double	$28/ngt
Lodge	*Great Outdoors Vacation & Lodging Guide* (1980)	*Prince of Wales Lodge;* southeast Alaska; overlooks Klawock Bay and offers handsome accommodations in carpeted rooms with private bath; package trip includes airfare from Ketchikan, Seattle, or Anchorage; 4 days and 3 nights	$453

Item	Source	Description	Price
Lodge	*Great Outdoors Vacation & Lodging Guide* (1980)	*Afognak Wilderness Lodge;* Kodiak Island, Alaska; accommodations for 10 guests at a time; rates cover lodging, all meals, and boat travel	$100
Lodge	*Great Outdoors Vacation & Lodging Guide* (1980)	*Alexander Lake Lodge;* rustic fly-in resort in lowland lake country 50 miles northeast of Anchorage, offers unspoiled fishing; rates include all meals, lodging and boat service; per person	$75
Lodge	*Great Outdoors Vacation & Lodging Guide* (1980)	*Garland's Oak Creek Lodge;* Arizona; located in the heart of Oak Creek Canyon, surrounded by stunning red-rock mountains; rates include breakfast, dinner, and lodging; per couple, per night	$58
Resort	*Great Outdoors Vacation & Lodging Guide* (1980)	*Indian Rock Resort;* Fairfield Bay, Arkansas; guest-house for 4, located on 40,000 acre Greers Ferry Lake	$60

Household Products

Item	Source	Description	Price
China	*The Scottish Lion Catalog* (1984)	English, fine bone; 10-piece tea-for-two set includes 2-cup teapot with cover, sugar and creamer, 2 teacups and saucers, 2 6 1/2" plates	$69
Chisel Set	*The Scottish Lion Catalog* (1984)	*Marples;* beveled-edge chisel set; made of Sheffield steel; set of six: 1/4", 3/8", 1/2", 5/8", 3/4", 1"	$51.95
Clock	*The Scottish Lion Catalog* (1984)	Chiming, carriage; beautiful brass clock with silver face is made in Norfolk County in England; quartz movement	$115
Curtains	*Yankee* (1981)	*Country Curtains;* classic tightly woven pinwale corduroy curtains in colonial blue, bright red, natural or deep brown; 63 inches or 72 inches long; per pair	$37
Flatware	*Bon Appetit* (1984)	*International Lyon;* 60-piece service for 12, queen's fancy style	$219.95
Folding Rule	*The Scottish Lion Catalog* (1984)	Hardwood; 3', 4-fold rule, subdivided in 8ths, 16ths	$6.95
Footlocker	*Sears, Roebuck* (1983)	Antique-look burled-design vinyl exterior with nickel-plated steel hardware	$49.99
Furniture Finish	*Yankee* (1981)	Lemon oil with beeswax furniture polish; leaves no film; two 8 oz. Bottles	$4.98
Gadget Bag	*Sears, Roebuck* (1983)	Rugged, yet lightweight; great for carrying all your photographic equipment	$19.99
Hammer	*The Scottish Lion Catalog* (1984)	*Stanley;* 13 oz; hickory; rim-tempered face, curved claw, hickory handle; Stanley list price $12.25	$8.95
Handsaw	*The Scottish Lion Catalog* (1984)	*Model D-95;* precision set and beveled to provide smooth, accurate cuts, 26" x 8 points	$19.95
Knife	*Bon Appetit* (1984)	*Sabatier Gingko International;* 6" chef's knife, crafted of high-carbon stainless steel in La Monnerie, France	$10
Mattress Set	*Atlanta Constitution* (1983)	Queen Size, regular $399.95 to $649.95 Sale on sets	$165 to $292
Pillow	*Bon Appetit* (1984)	Queen size, 20" x 36"; for complete bedtime comfort; down	$40
Screwdriver	*The Scottish Lion Catalog* (1984)	*Stanley Blackhawk;* professional quality, forged-steel blades; set of 4; Stanley's list price $26.95	$14.95
Tray	*Bon Appetit* (1983)	*Bombay Raffles;* serving tray; adapted from our popular Raffles table; mahogany finished	$9

Item	Source	Description	Price
Workbench	The Scottish Lion Catalog (1984)	Swedish; woodworking; top is arctic birch; the body is three-layer laminated hardwood; 50 1/2" long, includes five drawers	$259.95
Jewelry			
Brooch	The Scottish Lion Catalog (1984)	Irish harp; a lyrical, lovely and treasured gift; British gold	$115
Pendant	The Scottish Lion Catalog (1984)	Thistle amethyst; a symbol of unity and pride in Scottish history; gold	$250
Pendant	Food & Wine (1984)	Diamond Desires; heart; it's scandalous what diamonds do to me	$1,650
Wristwatch	New York Times (1984)	Rolex Oysterquartz Date; just peerless performance, timeless style	$2,725
Wristwatch	New York Times (1984)	Seiko 12-L; ladies ultra thin	$84.95
Motorized Vehicles, Supplies and Services			
Automobile	Atlanta Constitution (1983)	1983 Honda Civic wagon; five speed transmission, air conditioning, stereo cassette, pin stripes; list price $8,317.85, now	$7,517.85
Automobile	Sports Illustrated (1980)	Pontiac Firebird; Pontiac takes on the imports	$6,132
Automobile	Los Angeles Times (1981)	Cadillac Eldorado; 1981	$19,700
Car Stereo	Sears, Roebuck (1983)	Sanyo Automatic; music-select system; auto reverse with locking fast forward and reverse	$179.99
Rental	Food & Wine (1984)	Budget; Budget has more Lincolns than Hertz, Avis, and National combined; so when you want a Lincoln call Budget	$44.95/day
Truck	Field & Stream (1982)	Dodge Ram 50; pick-up; now the world has turbo-diesel pickups	$5,999
Other			
Carving Kit	Yankee (1981)	Learn to carve a Cardinal; a complete kit, including ready to carve pine bird, material for eyes, legs and feet	$11.95
Figurine	The Scottish Lion Catalog (1984)	Blue Tit bird; a very lifelike pose; ceramic is signed by the sculptor; 3 1/2" height	$65
Photo Album	Sears, Roebuck (1983)	100-page loose-leaf album	$12.99
Photo Finishing	New York Times (1981)	First Class Photo; any size film, 110–126 and 35mm too; per picture from roll	$0.14
Tree Lease	Food & Wine (1984)	North County Corp.; rent Mother Nature; lease a sugar-maple tree or a sap bucket for one year	$25
Personal Care Products			
Cuticle Nipper	Yankee (1981)	German Cutlery; cuticle nipper, precision ground	$10.95
Publications			
Book	Food & Wine (1984)	The Gold and Fizdale Cookbook, by Arthur Gold and Robert Fizdale; asparagus, ampergios, and anecdotes	$19.95
Magazine	Village Voice (1981)	52 weeks	$26
Newspaper	Atlanta Constitution (1983)	The Atlanta Constitution (mornings) and Atlanta Journal (afternoons); 13 weeks	$25

Item	Source	Description	Price
Videotape	*Food & Wine* (1984)	*Video Manufacturing Concepts; The Videotape Italian Cookbook;* the perfect holiday gift for those with VHS/Beta recorders	$42.50

Real Estate

Item	Source	Description	Price
Apartment	*Chicago Tribune* (1983)	For rent; top of the line; deluxe 2 bedroom	$489/mo
Apartment	*Chicago Tribune* (1983)	For rent; 1 bedroom with underground parking	$400/mo
Apartment	*Chicago Tribune* (1983)	Furnished; elegant 3 1/2 rooms, 2 bedroom; carpeted, with appliances and furniture; all utilities paid	$350/mo
House	*Chicago Tribune* (1983)	The 5-bedroom fully furnished main residence, 4-room coach house, and enclosed horse arena/barn are situated on 7 wooded acres; originally priced at $475,000	$185,000
House	*New York Times* (1984)	Doctor's home; custom details throughout; huge living room, fireplace, formal dining room, 4 bedrooms, 3 baths	$156,000
House	*New York Times* (1984)	Very special; stunning colonial inside and out; living room with fireplace, dining room, new kitchen, screened terrace, playroom and office	$225,000
House	*New York Times* (1984)	Exciting; sprawling California contemporary ranch	$659,000

Sports Equipment

Item	Source	Description	Price
Bicycle	*Sears, Roebuck* (1983)	*FS300;* 20" has mag-style wheels, gumwall knobby tires, and 3 BMX pads	$139.99
Bicycle	*Sears, Roebuck* (1983)	*FS500;* 24" track-certified bike for competitive use	$179.99
Boat	*Field & Stream* (1982)	*Bass Tracker 1;* boats that can do the same job as the expensive $12,000–$15,000 fiberglass boats but not carry the additional weight, cost, and inefficiency	$3,795
Boat	*Field & Stream* (1982)	*Harrison-Hodge Sea Eagle;* inflatable; lightweight, 81-pound boat has 1200 pound capacity	$540
Fishing Spool	*Field & Stream* (1982)	*Lew Childre & Sons;* fresh water light bait casting reel; 9.7 ounces	$95
Fly Reel	*Field & Stream* (1982)	*Shakespeare;* 6 ounces; takes up to no. 8 fly line	$29.95
Golf Balls	*New York Times* (1981)	*Spalding Top-Flite;* 15-ball bonus packs	$13.99
Golf Clubs	*New York Times* (1981)	*Wilson;* 11-piece pro-style	$219.99
Heater	*Field & Stream* (1982)	*Kero-Sun Omni;* portable; ideal to heat extra-large areas; operates up to 18 hours on a 2-gallon tankful of kerosene	$289.95
Knee Pads	*Sears, Roebuck* (1983)	Red and white elastic	$5.99/pr
Rifle	*Field & Stream* (1982)	*Beeman Feinwerkbau 124 Air Rifle;* .177 caliber, 18.3", 12-groove rifled barrel, single shot	$299.50
Rod and Reel	*Field & Stream* (1982)	*Daiwa 4-Minimite;* ultra/light skirted spool spinning system	$59.95
Shotgun	*Field & Stream* (1982)	*Olin/Winchester;* pigeon grade lightweight, 12-gauge; 25 1/2" barrel	$1,200
Skate Helmet	*Sears, Roebuck* (1983)		$15.99
Skateboard	*Sears, Roebuck* (1983)	Our longest, widest board for stability; kicktail on board aids in trick riding; king bolts adjust for ease of turning	$59.99
Skates	*Sears, Roebuck* (1983)	*Young Star;* with sealed-greased bearings and durable nickel-plated steel chassis that resists corrosion	$24.99
Sleeping Bag	*Field & Stream* (1982)	*Coleman;* 31 lbs, spring to late fall comfort range	$32

Item	Source	Description	Price
Tackle Box	*Field & Stream* (1982)	*Plano Molding;* measures 19" x 19 1/2" x 13 5/8"; front panel opens and slides under bottom drawer	$89.95

Telephone Equipment and Services

Item	Source	Description	Price
Long Distance Rates	*Chicago Tribune* (1983)	Chicago to Detroit; 10 minutes	$3.08
Long Distance Rates	*Chicago Tribune* (1983)	Indianapolis to New York; 5 minutes	$1.78
Telephone	*New York Times* (1984)	*Cobra;* national best-seller; cordless	$139.95

Tobacco Products

Item	Source	Description	Price
Cigars	*Food & Wine* (1984)	*Thompson Cigar;* you don't need Castro's permission to smoke Cuban-seed handmade cigars; sampler	$10.90

Toys

Item	Source	Description	Price
Blocks	*Yankee* (1981)	We call this one Triple Up because the object of the game is to be the first to get three blocks of your color in a row; per set	$4.95
Doll	*Yankee* (1981)	*Yankee Doodle Dancer,* Dancer Folk Toy; an educational rhythm toy	$8.50

Travel and Transportation

Item	Source	Description	Price
Airfare	*Village Voice* (1981)	Ventura seaplane to Fire Island from 23rd Street, New York City	$40
Airfare	*Great Outdoors Vacation & Lodging Guide* (1980)	*Air Alaska;* from Anchorage to Brooks Lodge on Brooks River, Alaska; round trip	$135
Boat Tour	*Mini-Vacation in the Mid-Atlantic* (1980)	*Potomac Boat Tours;* cruises daily 10–9	$3
Cruise	*Yankee* (1981)	*Emerald Seas;* sailing from Miami to the Bahamas; three night cruise to Nassau, per person On season Off season	$230–$475 $215–$460
Expedition	*Great Outdoors Vacation & Lodging Guide* (1980)	*Alaska Discovery;* Yukon River 10-day canoeing and camping excursion; per person	$600
Festival	*Village Voice* (1981)	*Reggae Sunsplash, Jamaica's Music Festival;* one week includes roundtrip airfare from New York to Chicago Montego Bay; double occupancy hotel, admission to music events	$499
Houseboat Trip	*Great Outdoors Vacation & Lodging Guide* (1980)	*Colorado River Houseboat;* a unique means of vacation transport on 500 miles of the Colorado River and the entire expanse of Lake Havasu; rate includes 6 days on a 43-ft craft	$755
River Trip	*Great Outdoors Vacation & Lodging Guide* (1980)	*Miller's Float Services;* Cotter, Arkansas; one-day float trip for two on White River	$90

MISCELLANY 1980-1984

Sony Unit Links Camera to Recorder

In twin presentations in Tokyo and New York yesterday, the Sony Corporation introduced a single-unit combination video camera and video cassette recorder weighing 4.4 pounds, substantially more compact than existing equipment with the same functions.

The new Video Movie, as the product is called, is a prototype, however, and will not be commercially available until 1985.

The new single-unit prototype, which will sell for under $1,000, apparently offers an entirely new product to further stir the percolating video-recording field.

New York Times, July 2, 1980

Prices Farmers Get Fell 0.7% from May

Prices that farmers get for their raw products fell seventh-tenths of one percent in June from the May level but still averaged 11 percent more than in June of last year, the Agriculture Department said today.

The department's Crop Reporting Board, in releasing its preliminary estimates for June, said lower prices for wheat, soybeans, corn, hay and lettuce led the month's drop. These declines were partly offset, however, by higher prices for hogs, tomatoes, potatoes, broilers and turkeys.

New York Times, July 1, 1981

Video Games Go to Hollywood

Hollywood is cashing in on the video game craze. In 1981, game cartridges that can be plugged into home television sets and coin-operated arcades were an $8 billion business, while audiences paid less than $3 billion at United States movie theater box offices. In the past few weeks, nearly every movie studio has announced a joint venture or new division meant to siphon off some of those impressive video game revenues.

Each studio is aiming its laser guns and space ships down a different path, but all share at least one goal—replacing games titled "Pac-Man," "Berzerk," and "Frogger" with games called, "Jaws," "9 to 5," "Star Wars," and "Star Trek."

New York Times, July 1, 1982

Tobacco Market Opens Sluggishly

"We had anticipated a strong market opening. The quality was good, but the overall interest of the (buying) companies was something less than we expected," said [U.S. Senator Sam] Irvin. Georgia tobacco farmers are expected to produce a 117-million-pound crop this year.

The average opening day buying price ranged from $145 to $170 per hundred pounds, depending on the quality and grade, the commission said. Last year's average price was $162.50.

Atlanta Constitution, July 22, 1982

HISTORICAL SNAPSHOT
1985-1989

1985

♦ Single optical fiber carries 300,000 simultaneous phone calls in Bell Laboratory tests

♦ Coca-Cola introduces new-formula Coke; public outcry brings back old formula as Classic Coke one year later

♦ Capital Cities Communications buys television network ABC for $3.5 billion

♦ U.S. becomes net debtor nation for first time since 1914

♦ Philip Morris acquires General Foods for $5.7 billion

♦ First genetically engineered microorganisms are licensed for commercial purposes

♦ $39 billion in merger deals put together, largely through leveraged buyouts

♦ Supreme Court upholds affirmative-action hiring quotas

♦ World oil prices collapse, bottoming out at $7.20 per barrel

♦ Dow Jones Industrials average tops 1900

♦ U.S. national debt tops $2 billion

♦ New York transit fares rise from 75¢ to $1

1986

♦ Unisys incorporates as successor to Burroughs Corp.

♦ Sears celebrates its 100th anniversary

♦ Office Depot, one of the first office supply warehouse-type stores, opens in Lauderdale Lakes, FL

1987

♦ Supercomputer capable of 1,720 billion computations per second goes on-line

♦ First bioinsecticides, to eliminate insects without harming environment, announced

♦ Elementary and secondary school teachers earn average salary of $26,700

♦ 8 airlines control 90 percent of domestic market

♦ Clean water bill passed to address pollution of estuaries and rainwater

♦ Stock market plunges 508 points in one day (October 19), largest drop in history

♦ New York Stock Exchange seat sells for $1.5 million

♦ Trade deficit hits record $16.5 billion

1988

♦ Robots are used for fruit picking

♦ 1 million fax machines purchased

♦ U.S. automakers produce 13 million cars and trucks

♦ Unemployment falls to 5.4 percent

♦ Lawyers earn average $914 weekly; nurses, $516; secretaries, $299

♦ Philip Morris buys Kraft for $12.9 billion

♦ U.S. savings and loans lose $13.44 billion

1989

♦ Media conglomerates Warner Communications and Time, Inc. merge

♦ Exxon oil tanker runs aground off Alaska coastline, causing worst U.S. oil spill; costs Exxon $1.7 billion in lawsuits

♦ Eastern Airlines files for bankruptcy

♦ Stock market plunges 190.58 points in single day (October 17), 2nd largest drop in history

♦ Federal government spends $159 billion to bail out savings and loan industry

♦ General Motors acquires half of Sweden's Saab

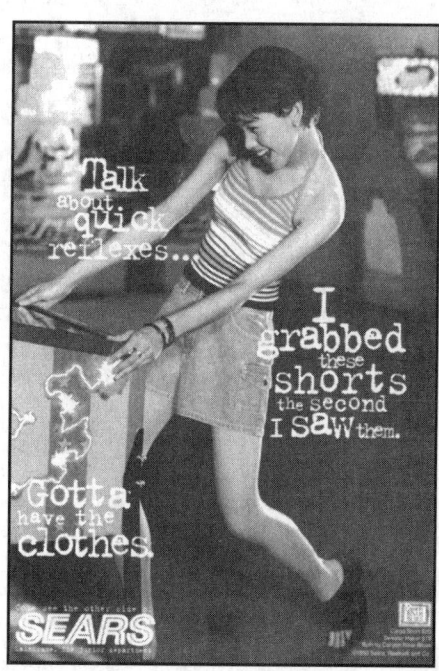

SELECTED INCOME 1985-1989

Job	Source	Description	Pay
Accountants	*New York Times* (1988)	Temporary	$12/hr
Administrative Assistant	*New York Times* (1988)	French/English; Gourmet Foods; work for top exec	$22,000/yr
Advertising	*New York Times* (1988)	Direct response account executives	$30,000–$40,000/yr
Assistant Service Manager	*New York Times* (1988)	Ford experience preferred; modern shop; excellent benefits	$30,000/yr
Attorney	*New York Times* (1988)	Major law firm seeks corporate SEC attorney; early responsibility and extensive client contact; 2–4 years experience	$50,000–$60,000/yr
Bookkeeper A/R	*New York Times* (1988)	You will know this leading sportswear importer; phenomenal growth has created this position for an experienced A/R adjuster	$15,000–$17,000/yr
Bookkeeper Billing Coordinator	*New York Times* (1988)	Brooklyn-based manufacturer; prerequisites include capacity to supervise small staff in all phases of computerized billing	$16,000–$21,000/yr
Carpenter	*New York Times* (1988)	Experienced kitchen/bathroom installer; fine carpentry; driver's license necessary	$11/hr
Chauffeur	*New York Times* (1988)	Early retiree ok; no violations; heavy OT; mature	to $19,000/yr
Chef	*New York Times* (1988)	Candidate must have at least 5 years experience in the industry and have formal culinary training in U.S. or abroad	$37,000/yr
Conference Planner	*Chicago Tribune* (1986)	Nat'l Association located near O'Hare offers excellent career opportunity for experienced conference planner who is skilled in working with volunteer program committees and hotel facilities	$20,000 (mid)/yr
Customer Service	*Chicago Tribune* (1986)	Entry level; will train; front-office appearance base salary	$14,400/yr
Delivery Driver	*Chicago Tribune* (1986)	Use your own vehicle; excellent part-time earnings; weekdays and weekends	to $20/delivery
Drafters	*New York Times* (1988)	Experienced inter or exter/detailing	$20,000/yr
Driver	*Chicago Tribune* (1986)	Pizza; Top pay! Part & full time plus tips	$1.75/delivery,
Driver	*Chicago Tribune* (1986)	Pizza; work for Chicago's top pizzeria; full or part time	$6/hr
EDP Auditor	*New York Times* (1988)	Prominent financial service organization is expanding its EDP audit division; candidate should possess 1+ years experience in audit reviews and programming	$28,000/yr
Golfer	Victor Bondi, ed., *American Decades: 1980–1989* (1996)	Average total purse in an official Professional Golf Association Event in 1985	$538,000
Industrial Engineer	*New York Times* (1988)	Major international bank seeks IE for operations analyst position; individual will perform work measurement studies; analyze manual and auto systems and review clerical procedures	$26,000–$30,000/yr
Insurance Claims	*Chicago Tribune* (1986)	Accident, health; two raises 1st year; looking for experienced major medical claims adjuster with willingness to grow with us	$19,000/yr

Job	Source	Description	Pay
Mechanical Artist	*New York Times* (1988)	Excellent entry-level career opportunity for art school graduate with at least one year experience to work in lively magazine art department of major publishing house	$230-$250/wk
Media Manager	*New York Times* (1988)	Media planning pro with strength in broadcasting to oversee agencies, assist managers; develop manufacturing and media strategies	to $42,000/yr
Model	*Playboy* (1986)	Modeling fee of Christine Richters, the Playboy Playmate for May, 1986	$15,000
Print Estimator	*New York Times* (1988)	2+ years agency media department	$16,000/yr
Production Manager	*New York Times* (1988)	Experienced residential interior retails	$45,000/yr
Salesman	*Chicago Tribune* (1986)	Manager trainees, students welcome	$7/hr part time $360/wk full time
Secretary	*New York Times* (1988)	German/English; diverse position for secretary to assist in lively office of European co.; skills in English a plus	$18,000-$20,000/yr
Transfer Supervisor	*New York Times* (1988)	Supervise 10 clerks; legal, transfer area	$20,000-$24,000/yr

CONSUMER EXPENDITURES 1985-1989

(Per Capita)

Expenditure Type	1985	1986	1987	1988	1989
Clothing	$542.22	$576.75	$611.98	$648.44	$706.29
Food	$1891.67	$1981.67	$2062.43	$2177.51	$2406.31
Auto Usage	$1398.52	$1411.96	$1447.16	$1538.05	$1567.01
New Auto Purchase	$366.51	$416.77	$385.06	$412.16	$403.07
Auto Parts	$75.90	$76.46	$77.42	$84.47	$131.39
Gas & Oil	$406.35	$331.18	$348.82	$354.62	$338.79
Housing	$1645.94	$1752.69	$1863.52	$1975.92	$2158.48
Furniture	$119.93	$130.06	$135.90	$138.75	$135.84
Utilities	$500.28	$487.41	$495.43	$519.48	$563.17
Telephone & Telegraph	$179.48	$187.40	$195.21	$204.86	$196.89
Physicians	$319.96	$349.46	$401.53	$451.33	$456.84
Dentists	$92.68	$97.65	$106.25	$113.85	$117.24
Health Insurance	$95.19	$91.83	$98.84	$107.73	$119.67
Personal Business	$775.37	$891.31	$963.68	$1040.59	$982.82
Personal Care	$167.32	$180.22	$195.21	$209.75	$211.44
Tobacco	$132.93	$137.54	$144.14	$147.72	$168.59
Local Transport	$31.03	$32.83	$32.95	$33.87	$35.98
Intercity Transport	$93.93	$94.32	$104.19	$114.26	$118.05
Recreation	$787.95	$846.84	$921.26	$1007.14	$1068.93
Religion/Welfare Activities	$265.45	$292.12	$312.99	$350.95	$335.15
Private Education & Research	$228.54	$245.16	$263.98	$292.18	$259.96
Per Capita Consumption	$11,185	$11,845	$12,569	$13,450	$13,948

INVESTMENTS 1985-1989

Investment	1985	1986	1987	1988	1989
Basic Yield, One-year Corporate Bonds	12.05	9.71	9.91	10.18	9.66
Short-term Interest Rates, 4–6 Months, Prime Commercial Paper	8.01	6.39	6.85	7.68	8.80
Basic Yield, Common Stocks, Total	4.25	3.48	3.08	3.64	3.45
Index of Common Stocks (1941–1943=10)	186.84	236.34	287.00	265.88	323.05

COMMON STOCKS, CLOSING PRICE AND YIELD, FIRST BUSINESS DAY OF YEAR

(Parenthetical number is annual dividends in dollars)

	1985	1986	1987	1988	1989
Allis Chalmers (Ch 11 Bankruptcy 12/2/88; 1 share common exchanged for .122039 new common)	6 1/8 (-)	4 1/4 (-)	2 3/4 (-)	1 3/8 (-)	
American Brands (2 for 1 split, 9/10/86)	63 3/4 (3.75)	65 1/2 (3.90)	43 3/8 (2.08)	48 1/2 (2.20)	62 1/4 (2.44)
AT&T	19 1/4 (1.20)	24 5/8 (1.20)	25 1/4 (1.20)	28 1/4 (1.20)	28 5/8 (1.20)
Bethlehem Steel	17 1/4 (.60)	15 3/8 (-)	7 (-)	17 3/4	22 5/8
CPC Intl	40 (2.20)	51 (2.20)	81 1/4 (2.48)	41 3/4 (1.44)	51 (1.60)
Delta Airlines	43 7/8 (.60)	39 1/4 (1)	48 (1.00)	37 3/4 (1.20)	49 3/8 (1.20)
General Electric (2 shares for 1 split, 4/23/87)	56 (2.20)	71 7/8 (2.32)	87 3/8 (2.52)	46 1/2 (1.40)	44 (1.64)
General Motors (distribution of 1 share of class E common stock @39 for each 20 shares of common held, 12/10/84) (distribution of 1 share of class H common stock 2 shares for 1 split, 2/17/89)	77 5/8 (4.75)	70 7/8 (5)	66 7/8 (5)	63 1/4 (5)	82 1/4 (5)
Intl Harvester	8 1/8 (-)	8 3/8 (-)			
Nabisco (Merged as wholly owned subsidiary of R. J. Reynolds Industries, 9/10/85)	51 (2.48)				
U.S. Steel (Name changed to U.S.X. 7/9/86)	25 3/4 (1)	26 1/2 (1.20)	21 7/8 (1.20)	31 1/2 (1.20)	29 1/4 (1.40)
Western Union	8 1/2 (/)	12 3/8 (/)	4 1/4 (/)	2 3/4 (/)	1 3/8 (/)

STANDARD JOBS 1985-1989

Job Type	1985	1986	1987	1988	1989
Wages Per Full-Time Employee	$19,188/yr	$21,915/yr	$22,872/yr	$24,032/yr	$22,568/yr
Private Industries, inc. farm labor	$18,980/yr	$21,699/yr	$22,629/yr	$23,794/yr	$22,256/yr
Bituminous Coal Mining	$32,968/yr	$34,837/yr	$35,924/yr	$36,660/yr	$37,908/yr
Building Trades	$21,372/yr	$23,590/yr	$24,537/yr	$25,872/yr	$25,220/yr
Domestics	$7072/yr	$10,061/yr	$10,289/yr	$11,353/yr	$8736/yr
Farm Labor	$7228/yr	$10,216/yr	$10,156/yr	$10,472/yr	$7904/yr
Federal Civilian	$25,591/yr	$27,833/yr	$28,828/yr	$29,957/yr	$28,775/yr
Federal Employees, Executive Depts.	$26,598/yr	$24,273/yr	$25,239/yr	$28,725/yr	$29,951/yr
Finance, Insurance, & Real Estate	$22,308/yr	$25,778/yr	$27,750/yr	$27,716/yr	$28,288/yr
Gas, Electricity, & Sanitary Workers	$31,096/yr	$33,222/yr	$34,730/yr	$35,308/yr	$36,972/yr
Manufacturing, Durable Goods	$23,868/yr	$27,147/yr	$27,899/yr	$129,170/yr	$27,768/yr
Manufacturing, Nondurable Goods	$20,800/yr	$23,313/yr	$24,141/yr	$25,407/yr	$23,764/yr
Medical/Health Services Workers	$18,668/yr	$21,652/yr	$23,724/yr	$25,665/yr	$23,608/yr
Miscellaneous Manufacturing	$18,200/yr	$20,145/yr	$20,918/yr	$20,904/yr	$21,528/yr
Motion Picture Services	$27,040/yr	$28,363/yr	$32,308/yr	$27,716/yr	$34,060/yr
Nonprofit Org. Workers	$11,440/yr	$14,350/yr	$15,017/yr	$15,635/yr	$13,832/yr
Passenger Transportation Workers, Local and Highway	$12,589/yr	$16,239/yr	$16,710/yr	$17,356/yr	$14,092/yr
Personal Services	$10,088/yr	$13,403/yr	$13,889/yr	$14,758/yr	$12,012/yr
Postal Employees	$26,995/yr	$26,362/yr	$27,262/yr	$28,364/yr	$28,479/yr
Public School Teachers	$20,973/yr	$21,920/yr	$22,940/yr	$23,992/yr	$22,413/yr
Radio Broadcasting & Television Workers	$25,064/yr	$28,721/yr	$31,125/yr	$30,857/yr	$28,860/yr
Railroads	$23,036/yr	$37,673/yr	$39,456/yr	$40,862/yr	$36,039/yr
State and Local Govt. Workers	$18,363/yr	$21,949/yr	$23,075/yr	$24,284/yr	$22,440/yr
Telephone & Telegraph Workers	$29,276/yr	$33,705/yr	$35,623/yr	$37,210/yr	$35,906/yr
Wholesale and Retail Trade Workers	$23,764/yr	$26,119/yr	$27,269/yr	$27,820/yr	$28,652/yr

FOOD BASKET 1985-1989

(NR = Not Reported)

Commodity	Year	New York	Atlanta	Chicago	Denver	Los Angeles
Bananas, per pound	1985	35.60¢	40.30¢	34.30¢	NR	40¢
	1986	41¢	35¢	NR	41¢	49¢
	1987	35¢	33¢	38.50¢	43¢	30¢
	1988	41¢	34¢	NR	31¢	32¢
	1989	NR	39¢	NR	48¢	48¢
Beef, Ground, Hamburger, per pound	1985	NR	NR	NR	NR	NR
	1986	$1.37	$1.13	NR	$1.26	$1.29
	1987	$1.59	$1.22	NR	91¢	$1.28
	1988	$1.59	$1.56	NR	$1.15	$1.09
	1989	NR	$1.71	NR	$1.13	$1.49
Beef, Steak, T-bone, per pound	1985	NR	NR	NR	NR	NR
	1986	$4.17	$4.49	NR	$3.54	$2.52
	1987	$4.25	$3.99	NR	$3.85	$3.22
	1988	$4.07	$3.98	NR	$3.95	$2.89
	1989	NR	$5.99	NR	$4.18	$4.02
Bread, White, per 24 ounces	1985	NR	NR	NR	NR	NR
	1986	71¢	50¢	NR	54¢	75¢
	1987	72¢	54¢	NR	45¢	59¢
	1988	69¢	57¢	NR	48¢	52¢
	1989	NR	65¢	NR	66¢	92¢
Chickens, per pound	1985	NR	NR	NR	NR	NR
	1986	88¢	79¢	NR	78¢	$1.25
	1987	77¢	84¢	NR	57¢	80¢
	1988	75¢	60¢	NR	50¢	51¢
	1989	NR	63¢	NR	67¢	99¢
Cheese, Parmesan, Grated, per 8 ounces	1985	NR	NR	NR	NR	NR
	1986	$2.75	$2.35	NR	$2.77	$2.09
	1987	$2.99	$2.29	NR	$2.76	$2.68
	1988	$2.93	$2.38	NR	$2.37	$2.74
	1989	NR	$2.52	NR	$2.39	$2.82
Coffee, per pound	1985	NR	NR	NR	NR	NR
	1986	$3.41	$3.97	NR	$2.96	$3.53
	1987	$2.97	$3.55	NR	$3.20	$2.86
	1988	$2.71	$2.34	NR	$2.52	$2.23
	1989	NR	$2.92	NR	$2.82	$3.05
Corn, Whole Kernel, Frozen, per 10 ounces	1985	NR	NR	NR	NR	NR
	1986	53¢	70¢	NR	53¢	46¢
	1987	55¢	65¢	NR	55¢	46¢
	1988	57¢	62¢	NR	55¢	50¢
	1989	NR	78¢	NR	52¢	64¢
Eggs, per dozen	1985	NR	NR	NR	NR	NR
	1986	92¢	68¢	NR	88¢	94¢
	1987	99¢	84¢	NR	83¢	$1.25
	1988	89¢	65¢	NR	72¢	$1.25
	1989	NR	78¢	NR	93¢	$1.56
Cereal, per 18 ounces	1985	NR	NR	NR	NR	NR
	1986	$1.54	$1.30	NR	$1.57	$1.44
	1987	$1.57	$1.40	NR	$1.73	$1.46
	1988	$1.73	$1.42	NR	$1.74	$1.41
	1989	NR	$1.55	NR	$1.66	$1.71

Commodity	Year	New York	Atlanta	Chicago	Denver	Los Angeles
Margarine, per pound	1985	NR	NR	NR	NR	NR
	1986	85¢	59¢	NR	62¢	68¢
	1987	91¢	58¢	NR	61¢	68¢
	1988	65¢	52¢	NR	45¢	64¢
	1989	NR	61¢	NR	64¢	78¢
Milk, Fresh, per half gallon	1985	NR	NR	NR	NR	NR
	1986	$1.27	$1.46	NR	$1.22	$1.02
	1987	$1.29	$1.40	NR	$1.22	$1.02
	1988	$1.15	$1.22	NR	$1.16	$1.02
	1989	NR	$1.33	NR	$1.12	$1.13
Lettuce, per 1 1/4 pound	1985	NR	NR	NR	NR	NR
	1986	71¢	56¢	NR	80¢	43¢
	1987	75¢	62¢	NR	71¢	34¢
	1988	$1.23	92¢	NR	82¢	$1.16
	1989	NR	83¢	NR	99¢	64¢
Pork, Bacon, Sliced, per pound	1985	NR	NR	NR	NR	NR
	1986	$2.61	$2.72	NR	$2.30	$2.14
	1987	$2.99	$2.82	NR	$3.10	$2.22
	1988	$2.59	$2.39	NR	$2.72	$2.22
	1989	NR	$1.42	NR	$1.95	$1.42
Potatoes, per 10 pounds	1985	NR	NR	NR	NR	NR
	1986	$2.28	$1.86	NR	$1.65	$1.46
	1987	$2.27	$1.74	NR	$1.25	$1.36
	1988	$1.97	$2.39	NR	$1.76	$1.34
	1989	NR	$2.90	NR	$3.14	$2.15
Sugar, per 5 pounds	1985	NR	NR	NR	NR	NR
	1986	$1.83	$1.44	NR	$1.36	$1.55
	1987	$1.69	$1.33	NR	$1.19	$1.62
	1988	$1.73	$1.32	NR	96¢	$1.46
	1989	NR	$1.55	NR	$1.17	$1.80
Soft Drink, Cola, per 2 liters	1985	NR	NR	NR	NR	NR
	1986	$1.23	$1.11	NR	$1.12	$1.44
	1987	$1.09	$1.19	NR	$1.26	$1.69
	1988	$1.03	$1.49	NR	$1.04	$1.24
	1989	NR	$1.03	NR	$1.51	97¢
Tuna, Canned, per 6 1/2 ounces	1985	NR	NR	NR	NR	NR
	1986	76¢	74¢	NR	59¢	95¢
	1987	85¢	74¢	NR	59¢	64¢
	1988	99¢	66¢	NR	64¢	72¢
	1989	NR	64¢	NR	65¢	68¢

SELECTED PRICES 1985-1989

Item	Source	Description	Price
Alcohol			
Beer	*New York Times* (1988)	*Michelob;* 12-oz n/r bottles	$9.95/case
Cocktails	*New York Times* (1988)	Martini for two	$1.08
Liqueur	*New York Times* (1987)	*Kahlua;* coffee liqueur	$9.97/btl
Wine	*New York Times* (1987)	Liebfraumilch	$3.99/btl
Wine	*New York Times* (1988)	*Bolla Soave*	$3.13/btl
Apparel, Children's			
Disposable Diaper	*Consumer Reports* (1987)	"In light of the unmitigated rave reviews for Pampers Super, it might be difficult to choose another model of disposable diaper."	
		Medium	$.21 ea
		Large	$.31 ea
Jackets	*Los Angeles Times* (1988)	Boys; express twill classics in fall colors	$12.70–$21.20
Socks	*Sears, Roebuck* (1988)	More of our crew-length tube socks; package of six pairs	$4.99
Underwear	*Sears, Roebuck* (1988)	A fun new underwear idea for the little guy; no problem; just choose GI Joe or our Fruit of the Loom Funpals Alf	$5.49
Apparel, Men's			
Shirt	*Sears, Roebuck* (1988)	100% cotton-knit shirts never had it so good and neither will you	$15.88
Shirt	*New York Times* (1988)	Velour	$14.92
Shoes	*New York Times* (1987)	*Asics Riger GT IIGEL;* this is the most advanced running shoe for serious runners	$89.95
Suit	*New York Times* (1988)	*Dunhill Tailors;* ready-to-wear suit for fall; the dollar remains strong	$525–$650
Sweater	*New York Times* (1988)	Long sleeve, bulk knit	$29.25
Sweatshirt	*European Travel & Life* (1987)	European trade sweatshirts	$17.95–$19.95
Apparel, Women's			
Blouse	*Sears, Roebuck* (1988)	Take a closer look at this soft laundered fabric that's so versatile it goes from beach to business with a quick change of accessories	$26
Clogs	*Better Homes and Gardens* (1986)	Genuine leather clog; lightweight, perforated to let your feet breathe	$19.95
Dress	*Charlotte Observer* (1986)	Strapless dress with sequin bodice and white ruffled organza skirt	$215
Fur	*Chicago Tribune* (1986)	Tibetan lamb jackets in white or pink; regularly $750	$399
Hose	*Sears, Roebuck* (1988)	Our sheerest nylon hosiery for your fanciest occasions; three pairs per package	$8.07
Jumpsuit	*Los Angeles Times* (1988)	Cotton sheeting with front snaps	$34.99

477

Item	Source	Description	Price
Shoes	*New York Times* (1987)	*Naturalizer;* cool comfort for spring; genuine leather uppers with cutout detail on a medium heel	$45
Skirt	*Sears, Roebuck* (1988)	Swirl potential; soft, full skirt with an easy wearing elastic waist	$26
Appliances			
Camcorder	*Charlotte Observer* (1986)	*RCA Small Wonder Camcorder;* 3-way AC/DC versatility	$994
Can Opener	*Los Angeles Times* (1988)	*Sunbeam;* electric; originally $25; sharpens knives; opens cans and plastic bags	$19.99
Coffee Maker	*Consumer Reports* (1987)	*Mr. Coffee,* the brand that fomented the drip-coffee revolution, still rules the market in terms of numbers	$36.00
Coffee Maker	*European Travel & Life* (1987)	Two-cup coffee brewer; coffee in your room in 3 minutes	$25
Heater	*Popular Mechanics* (1985)	*Arvin;* radiant; instant fan-forced heat	$23.88
Microwave	*Sears, Roebuck* (1988)	*Kenmore;* solid-state electronics; digital readout that doubles as time-of-day clock and 100-minute countdown timer; variable power settings from 100 to 700 watts	$199.99
Range	*Sears, Roebuck* (1988)	*Lady Kenmore;* 30" range; gives you cooking and cleaning convenience	$559.99
Refrigerator	*Sears, Roebuck* (1988)	America's smartest refrigerator; no one has an electronic system this innovative	$1,769.99
Television	*Charlotte Observer* (1986)	*NEC* 41 inch widescreen stereo TV	$1,995
Vacuum Cleaner	*Popular Mechanics* (1985)	*Shop-Vac Mighty Mini-Vac;* hardware can be the perfect gift	$44.88
Water Heater	*Sears, Roebuck* (1988)	*Kenmore;* compact style; tank has limited 5-year warranty against leaks; polyurethane or fiberglass insulation; adjustable thermostat with energy-saving setting	$89.99
Baby Products			
Bicycle Child Carrier	*Sears, Roebuck* (1988)	Hi-impact molded plastic carrier has contoured seat	$14.99
Bronze Shoes	*Better Homes and Gardens* (1986)	Baby's first shoes bronze-plated in solid metal	$5.99
Canisters	*Sears, Roebuck* (1988)	Clear-acrylic nursery canisters with My Bears decoration; come with vinyl-covered wire tray; safer than glass	$12.99
Car Seat	*Charlotte Observer* (1986)	*Century Car Seat;* meets Federal safety standards	$54.99
Diapers	*Charlotte Observer* (1986)	*Pampers Ultra Plus 64 Larger Diapers;* after $3 refund offer	$13.99
Dressing Table	*Sears, Roebuck* (1988)	*Cosco Quick Change;* dressing table has four interlocking plastic cubes that are used in a variety of ways; includes dressing table pad with wipe clean bin cover and safety strap	$77.99
Stroller	*Charlotte Observer* (1986)	*Graco Stroll-a-Bed;* features one hand opening and closing	$56.97
Business Equipment and Supplies			
Briefcase	*Gourmet* (1988)	*Lladro;* Spanish leather	$565
Calculator	*New York Times* (1987)	*Casio;* printing; 12 digit, 2 color	$54.95
Computer	*New York Times* (1987)	*Leading Edge Model D;* one-drive system	$895
Computer	*New York Times* (1987)	*Apple IIGS*	$795

Item	Source	Description	Price
Desk Set	*European Travel & Life* (1987)	Italian pearlwood desk set lined with calfskin	$250
Floppy Disks	*New York Times* (1987)	*Fuji;* 5 1/4" DS/DD; per box	$9.95
Modem	*New York Times* (1987)	*Maxum;* internal, 1,200 baud; 1/2 card	$119.95
Overhead Projector	*New York Times* (1987)	*Bell & Howell;* 14" triple lens	$262.99
Printer	*New York Times* (1987)	*Epson;* 48 cps nlq mode	$429
Software	*New York Times* (1987)	*Lotus;* spreadsheet	$339
Tape Backup	*New York Times* (1987)	*Mountain Filesafe 7000;* external 60 mb	$1,295

Collectibles

Item	Source	Description	Price
Antique Automobile	*Guinness Book of World Records* (1986)	*1931 Berline de Voyage Royale;* greatest price paid for used car; one of six Bugatti Royales	$8,100,000
Cel Animation	*Art & Antiques* (1993)	Cel and background for movie *Who Framed Roger Rabbit* sold in auction in 1989	$7,150
Coin	*Guinness Book of World Records* (1989)	The highest price paid at auction for a single coin; for a U.S. 1804 silver dollar in proof condition at Rarcoa's, Chicago, Illinois	$990,000
Quilt	*Village Voice* (1989)	*Kentucky Quilt Company;* individually hand-made at home in the foothills of the Appalachian Mountains	$299 to $499
Table	*Art & Antiques* (1993)	Console table once owned by Marie Antoinette; sold in auction in 1988	$2.97 million

Entertainment

Item	Source	Description	Price
Ballet Ticket	*Chicago Tribune* (1986)	*The Nutcracker;* Arie Crown Theatre, McCormick Place; main floor; Saturday and Sunday	$18
Concert Ticket	*New York Times* (1987)	*Indiana University Baroque Orchestra* Student General Admission	$5 $10
Concert Ticket	*New York Times* (1988)	*Victor Borge;* Carnegie Hall	$10–$30
Membership	*Village Voice* (1989)	YMCA summer membership; There's swimming, jogging, weights, fitness classes; the whole summer, one price	$125
Movie Ticket	*Chicago Tribune* (1986)	*Lady and the Tramp;* General Cinema; all showings before 6 pm	$2
Play Ticket	*Chicago Tribune* (1986)	*Pump Boys and Dinettes;* Tuesday–Thursday; 8 pm	$19.50

Entertainment, Home

Item	Source	Description	Price
Audio Tape	*New York Times* (1987)	*Sony;* high power; uniaxial; blank; three pack	$7.99
Camcorder	*Chicago Tribune* (1986)	*Kodak 3440;* modular; weighs slightly over 4 lbs; save $102	$893
Camcorder	*Audubon* (1989)	*Sharp 8x;* VHS; record your memories for years to come	$1,799.99
Camera	*New York Times* (1987)	*Nikon FP-Program*	$189.99
Cassette Player	*Chicago Tribune* (1986)	*Sony Walkman;* make great gifts	$19.95
Cassette Player and Recorder	*Chicago Tribune* (1986)	*Panasonic;* two 5" dynamic speakers, continuous-tone control, one-touch recording; regular $59.95	$37
Compact Disc	*Los Angeles Times* (1988)	Top hits	$11.99

Item	Source	Description	Price
Compact Disc Player	*New York Times* (1987)	*Technics;* programmable; fine-focus single-beam system	$229.95
Computer Game	*Sears, Roebuck* (1987)	*New York Times Fidelity;* par excellence; 5.0 computer chess	$149
Scanner	*Sears, Roebuck* (1988)	*Regency Informant;* instantly monitors 9 bands with the push of a button	$299.99
Telescope	*Popular Mechanics* (1985)	*Bausch & Lomb Criterion 400;* high-quality amateur telescope	$695
Television	*Chicago Tribune* (1986)	*Sony Watchman;* pocket-size black-and-white television; 2" screen with crisp, bright high-contrast picture; reference price $129.95	$95
Television	*New York Times* (1987)	*Sharp;* 19" color	$209.99
Television Satellite Dish	*Popular Mechanics* (1985)	*Radio Shack;* brings you over 100 channels of quality entertainment	$1,995

Food Products

Item	Source	Description	Price
Cereal	*Los Angeles Times* (1988)	*Kellogg's Corn Flakes;* 18-oz package	$1.59
Cheese	*Los Angeles Times* (1988)	*Kraft American;* cheese food; 1-lb singles	$2.79
Corn	*Los Angeles Times* (1988)	Fresh barbecue sweet corn; 5 ears	$1
Fruit	*Charlotte Observer* (1986)	Washington Fancy Red Apples; per pound	$.29
Fruit	*Charlotte Observer* (1986)	California Sweet Cantaloupe; large size; each	$.79
Fruit	*Charlotte Observer* (1986)	Oranges; Florida new crop; 5 pound bag	$1.59
Ice Cream	*Time* (1985)	*Dove Bar;* they're expensive, but they're worth it	$1.45
Meat	*Charlotte Observer* (1986)	Ground Beef, fresh family pack; per pound	$.99
Milk	*Chicago Tribune* (1986)	2 percent; plastic carton	$1.59
Olive Oil	*European Travel & Life* (1987)	*Green Gold;* the Christmas gift for the host who has everything	$8.28
Potato Chips	*Chicago Tribune* (1986)	*Ruffles;* 6 1/2-oz bag	$1.19
Potatoes	*Charlotte Observer* (1986)	U.S. No. 1 spuds; 10 pound bag	$.99
Pot Pie	*Charlotte Observer* (1986)	*Morton Chicken Pot Pies;* three for	$.99
Soft Drink	*New York Times* (1988)	*Coke;* 2 liter	$1

Furniture

Item	Source	Description	Price
Couch	*Village Voice* (1989)	*The Original Sii;* full-size reclining sofa bed with bentwood arms	$245
Chair	*Better Homes and Gardens* (1986)	*Adirondack;* remember lawn chairs; they're back	$129
Chair	*New York Times* (1987)	*Bon Marche;* all steel; black or white	$57.50
Chair	*New York Times* (1987)	*Scandinavian Gallery;* leather tub chair	$399.95

Item	Source	Description	Price
Chair	*Audubon* (1989)	*Adirondack;* outdoor chair and ottoman; made of kiln-dried western pine	$119.95
Coffee Table	*Better Homes and Gardens* (1986)	Quaint Victorian with imported marble top	$89.95
Couch	*New York Times* (1988)	*Eclectic Furniture of Manhasset;* sectional; two pieces with queen sleeper	$799
Entertainment Center	*Village Voice* (1989)	Complete wall unit and entertainment center	$699
Grandfather Clock	*Better Homes and Gardens* (1986)	*European Clock Company;* do-it-yourself kits; build your own grandfather clock	$280
Modular System	*New York Times* (1987)	*Bon Marche;* black or white hard melamine laminate; per unit	$85
Sofa	*Los Angeles Times* (1988)	*Eastman West;* full size 82"; imported leather; smooth, supple, sumptuous	$599
Table	*New York Times* (1988)	Handcrafted Italian marble table; 71" x 37"	$998
Table Pad	*Better Homes and Gardens* (1986)	Save 50% by buying direct	$49.95

Garden Equipment and Supplies

Item	Source	Description	Price
Azalea	*New York Times* (1987)	6" pot	$3.99
Easter Lily	*New York Times* (1987)	*Plant Shed;* special	$4.99
Lawn Mower	*Consumer Reports* (1987)	The *Homelite-Jacobsen HSD20* was judged a Best Buy	$300

Household Products

Item	Source	Description	Price
Bedspread	*Sears, Roebuck* (1988)	The look your star athlete will love; let the game begin; whether it's a kick-off or the first ball thrown your special athlete can be part of the action with these coordinates; bunk size	$16.99
Carving Set	*Gourmet* (1988)	*James Robinson;* ebony-handled, stainless steel, set of four	$675
Compote	*Gourmet* (1988)	*By Design;* frosted glass, large size, designed by Sugahara	$21.95
Dinner Plate	*Gourmet* (1988)	*Majolica;* Italian hand-painted plates, designed by Jacie Rice	$80
Flatware	*House & Garden Gardens* (1986)	*Oneida Heirloom;* 48-piece stainless set	$229.95
Glass	*House & Garden* (1987)	*Block;* full-lead crystal; Atlantis Chartres pattern designed by Gerald Gulotta	$37.50
Glue Gun	*Sears, Roebuck* (1988)	*Craftsman;* the best of both worlds is yours with this	$24.99
Light Bulb	*Popular Mechanics* (1985)	*DieHard;* has an average life of 6,000 hours—about six times longer than conventional bulbs; 2 bulb pack	$4
Pillow	*House & Garden* (1987)	*Hermes;* lotus design; 13" x 17"	$75
Pillow	*European Travel & Life* (1987)	*HedBed;* end stiff necks	$11
Plate	*Gourmet* (1988)	*Umbra;* on rubber feet; large frost-glass plate	$24
Plate and Knife	*Gourmet* (1988)	Cheese; earthenware	$45
Rug	*Chicago Tribune* (1986)	Handmade wool rugs from India; oriental King and Spring Garden pattern in blue; pure wool; 6' x 9'; regularly $1,199	$499

Item	Source	Description	Price
Shade	*Better Homes and Gardens* (1986)	*Burlington Voile Pouf Shade;* when delicate almost lacy romance is your style	$50
Sham	*Gourmet* (1988)	Cotton with lace trim; European-square, circa 1920	$95
Silk Azalea	*Sears, Roebuck* (1988)	Lovely azalea bush has 132 leaves, 48 rosy blooms in an 8" diameter whitewash rattan basket	$24.99
Silk Geranium	*Sears, Roebuck* (1988)	Double jumbo geranium has 294 leaves, 54 buds and an incredible 234 gorgeous blooms	$54.99
Silk Spider Plant	*Sears, Roebuck* (1988)	Double jumbo spider plant has 240 leaves and an unbelievable 80 bouncing babies	$54.99
Soufflé Dish	*Gourmet* (1988)	Frosted glass	$22
Tape/Rule	*Popular Mechanics* (1985)	*Master Mechanic;* 6' pocket tape rule free when you buy the 25" power tape in rugged cycolac case	$8.99

Jewelry

Item	Source	Description	Price
Bracelet	*New York Times* (1987)	Sapphire and diamond	$129
Earrings	*New York Times* (1987)	Sapphire earrings surrounded by diamonds; regularly $690	$190
Necklace	*New York Times* (1987)	Italian 14 kt gold herringbone chains; 16"; regularly $225	$79

Meals

Item	Source	Description	Price
Dinner	*Village Voice* (1989)	*Meson Toledo;* complete daily dinner with wine or Sangria; 318 W. 23rd Street, New York	$16.95
Dinner	*Village Voice* (1989)	*Kinoko;* Sushi, all you can eat	$15
Meal	*Gourmet* (1988)	*Shun Lee Restaurant;* New York City; Szechuan seafood salad	$13.50

Motorized Vehicles, Supplies and Services

Item	Source	Description	Price
Alignment	*Charlotte Observer* (1986)	Front Wheel Alignment; set front wheel castor, camber and toe on cars with adjustable suspension	$29
Automobile	*House & Garden* (1987)	*Mazda RX-7 Roadster;* the sensible sports car to buy	$22,000
Automobile	*New York Times* (1987)	*1988 Dodge Medallion;* 4-door sedan	$8,995
Automobile	*New York Times* (1987)	*1987 Wrangler;* 4-wheel drive; soft-top	$8,395
Car Phone	*Chicago Tribune* (1986)	*Metrocom;* the superior car phone; plus free hands-free speaker phone	$995
Luggage Carrier	*Sears, Roebuck* (1988)	X-cargo roof-top carrier provides 21 cu ft of storage; for mobile homes, RVs, and vans	$169.99
Radio	*New York Times* (1987)	*Alpine;* removable car radio	$199
Stereo	*New York Times* (1987)	*Audiovox;* car stereo; cassette player and quartz clock	$89
Tires	*Charlotte Observer* (1986)	*Eagle GT Radial Tire;* no trade needed; outline white letters	$78.70

Musical Instruments

Item	Source	Description	Price
Guitar	*Sears, Roebuck* (1988)	Beginner's guitar; comes with everything needed to get on the road to stardom	$89.99
Synthesizer	*Sears, Roebuck* (1988)	*Yamaha PSS-470;* our lowest price ever; custom drummer	$188.88

Other

Item	Source	Description	Price
Book Club Membership	*New York Times* (1987)	*Literary Guild;* you can't beat our benefits; unlimited time to buy; easy at-home shopping; 5 books	$1

Item	Source	Description	Price
Currency Calculator	*European Travel & Life* (1987)	Currency; calculator; clock; one-touch currency conversion to and from dollars	$32
Decals	*European Travel & Life* (1987)	Authentic international auto decals from Europe	$5
Pen Set	*House & Garden* (1987)	*Cross* for women; gray; pen and pencil set	$30
Radar Detector	*Chicago Tribune* (1986)	*FuzzBuster;* detects all types of police radar at 10 times their effective range; advanced filter system; reference price $89.95	$69
Sneaker Nameplates	*Better Homes and Gardens* (1986)	Stylish way to tag and identify your sports and jogging shoes	$2.50
Yacht	*Popular Mechanics* (1985)	*Hatteras 77;* lets you cruise the world	$1,700,000

Personal Care Products

Item	Source	Description	Price
Hand Lotion	*Los Angeles Times* (1988)	*Corn Huskers;* heavy-duty hand lotion	$1.59
Insect Repellent	*Consumer Reports* (1987)	*Off!* 6 oz. aerosol style; 15% active ingredient of deet	$2.99
Perfume	*Guiness Book of World Records* (1984)	Most expensive perfume; the Chicago based firm Jovan marketed from March 1984 a cologne called Andron that contains a trace of the attractant pheromone androstenol	$2,750/oz
Skin Moisturizer	*Consumer Reports* (1986)	*Sea Breeze Moisture Lotion* "felt less greasy than most" and "has a more pleasant consistency than most." 4 oz.	$3.31
Toothpaste	*Consumer Reports* (1986)	*Ultra Brite*—moderately abrasive 7 oz.	$.71

Publications

Item	Source	Description	Price
Catalogue	*House & Garden* (1987)	*P. E. Guerin;* everything from bathroom faucet sets to door knobs to decorative hardware	$7.50

Real Estate

Item	Source	Description	Price
Apartment	*Chicago Tribune* (1986)	For rent; Willow West; 2 bedroom, all carpeted; heat; air conditioning; all appliances; pool	$520/mo
Apartment	*Chicago Tribune* (1986)	For rent; furnished; newly decorated 3 rooms in quiet neighborhood; includes heat	$275/mo
Co-Op Condo	*Village Voice* (1989)	Sunny one bedroom in luxurious building; 1000 square feet; 4th Street, East, New York	$225,000
House	*Chicago Tribune* (1986)	Quick sale price; interesting price-wise buy for alert buyer; cute and cozy secluded cottage nestled in convenient Rogers Park	$50,000
Hotel	*Guiness Book of World Records* (1989)	Sale of hotel Bel-Air in Los Angeles; sold to Sekitei Kaihatsu Company of Tokyo, Japan; per room	$1,200,000
House	*Village Voice* (1989)	Crown Heights; one family, four story, 15 rooms, four baths	$240,000
House	*Charlotte Observer* (1987)	Ashebrook Villas Townhouses, York, South Carolina; 3 bedrooms, 2 baths; lots of room for living	$67,900

Sewing Equipment and Supplies

Item	Source	Description	Price
Labels	*Better Homes and Gardens* (1986)	Personalized sewing labels; your originals deserve these washable woven rayon taffeta labels	$4.95/20

Sports Equipment

Item	Source	Description	Price
Bicycle	*European Travel & Life* (1987)	*Aero Urban Cowboy;* perfect for city biking; it takes potholes like a Cadillac	$600

Item	Source	Description	Price
Gun Kit	*Popular Mechanics* (1985)	*Weller Soldering;* give a gift that will come in handy	$19.99
Helmet	*Sears, Roebuck* (1988)	Use of a helmet while biking is an investment in protection for you and for your child	$19.99

Telephone Equipment and Services

Long Distance Rates	*Newsweek* (1985)	*AT&T Reachout America;* you get an hour of AT & T long distance calls	$9.45
Long Distance Rates	*House & Garden* (1987)	*AT&T;* United States to Holland, standard rate from 7 am to 1 pm	$1.18/min
Long Distance Rates	*Gourmet* (1988)	*AT&T;* 6 pm to midnight, 10-minute call, United States to Brazil	$0.96/min

Tobacco Products

Cigars	*Los Angeles Times* (1988)	*Wm. Penn Invincible;* corona cigars; $5 value	$1.99

Toys

Doll	*Charlotte Observer* (1986)	*Playskool Doll;* My Buddy Wink or Kid Sister Wink; each	$24.97
Toy	*Charlotte Observer* (1986)	*Playskool;* Sesame Street Poppin Pals; 5 different activities	$11.97
Game	*Charlotte Observer* (1986)	*Fisher Price Bowling* game; easy set-up pins	$9.97

Travel and Transportation

Airfare	*Village Voice* (1989)	New York to Osaka; Seil Travel America	$715
New Orleans Weekend	*Village Voice* (1989)	New Orleans Labor Day Weekend Getaway; includes airfare, 3 nights with breakfast, transfers, each	$520
Tour	*Audubon* (1989)	*Wood Star;* birding tour of Argentina; 21 day trip	$3,595
Trip	*New York Times* (1988)	St. Kitts; the Royal St. Kitts Hotel & casino; includes round-trip air via BWIA; manager cocktail party; $25 casino chips, tennis, and admission to disco; 7 nights	$403
Trip	*New York Times* (1988)	Cupecoy Beach Resort; roundtrip American; Tuesday, Wednesday, Thursday departures; 8 days/7 nights; 1-bedroom suite	$545
Trip	*New York Times* (1988)	Deer Valley this year, don't just ski Deer Valley; live it; 7 nights/6 days; December 8–16; January 3–February 9	$499
Trip	*New York Times* (1988)	Paradise Island; 8 days/7 nights; including airfare	$249

MISCELLANY 1985-1989

Metromedia to Sell Mobile Phone Operations

The Southwestern Bell Corporation has agreed to buy the paging and mobile telephone businesses of Metromedia Inc. for $1.65 billion in cash.

The sale will vastly enrich John W. Kluge, already one of the nation's wealthiest men, who owns 93 percent of the voting stock of Metromedia.

Southwestern Bell, for its part, will become the largest investor in cellular telephones in the country. Its existing cellular operations, joined with Metromedia's interests in such major cities as New York, Chicago and Washington, would service markets with a total population of 45 million.

New York Times, July 1, 1985

Texas Instruments vs. Japan

To survive in a world market increasingly dominated by the Japanese, such American semiconductor manufacturers as the Intel Corporation and Advanced Micro Devices, Inc. have withdrawn to segments they think they can still defend. Others, including Motorola Inc. and Fairchild Semiconductor Corporation, are teaming up with their Japanese rivals.

But even though its semiconductor operations lost $89 million in 1985 and barely broke even in 1986, the battle cry at Texas Instruments Inc. is never give an inch to the Japanese.

New York Times, July 1, 1987

Mutual Fund Sales Decline

Monthly mutual fund sales fell to $7.1 billion in May, compared with $9 billion in April and $13.5 billion in May 1987, the Investment Company Institute said today.

Year-to-date mutual fund sales through May were $42.1 billion, compared with $111.2 billion for the comparable 1987 period, the institute said.

New York Times, July 1, 1988

Investor Group Buying South Carolina Resort Island

Charles S. Way Jr. and his associates have bought themselves some choice real estate: a sparkling South Carolina sea island that had been in the hands of Kuwaiti investors.

Mr. Way said yesterday that his group had paid $105 million for the 10,000 acre Kiawah Island near Charleston, making it one of the biggest real estate transactions in South Carolina history.

The Kuwaitis bought the island in 1974 for $17.4 million, and Mr. Way said they had sunk $200 million into its development as a resort.

New York Times, July 1, 1988

HISTORICAL SNAPSHOT
1990-1994

1990

- U.S. deploys combat aircraft to Persian Gulf to defend Saudi Arabia
- Banks are allowed to trade stocks
- Atlanta awarded 1996 Olympic Summer Games
- General Electric Foundation allots $2.1 million to 30 universities to attract women, African Americans, American Indians, and Hispanics to careers in science and business
- East and West Germany united after 45 years of separation

1991

- U.S. and allies wage war with Iraq
- U.S. Postal Service increases first-class postage stamp rate from 25 to 29 cents
- U.S. Supreme Court ends forced busing, originally designed to end racial segregation
- Federal Reserve slashes interest rates by 1/2 percent to spur economy
- Walter H. Annenberg bequeaths $1 billion art collection to Metropolitan Museum of Art
- Congress halts nationwide rail strike after one day
- U.S. Trade Deficit hits eight-year low
- National Commission on AIDS approves needle exchange program to reduce spread of the disease
- Congress approves family leave allowing up to 12 weeks for family emergencies

- General Motors announces plans to close more than 20 plants over several years, eliminating more than 70,000 jobs

1992

- TWA Airlines files bankruptcy
- President of United Way of America forced out by excessive spending allegations
- United Auto Workers end five-month-old strike against Caterpillar, maker of heavy equipment
- *Endeavor* astronauts repair $150 million communications satellite in space
- Third party presidential candidate Ross Perot withdraws from race, then reenters
- British Airways invests $750 million in US Air
- U.S. launches spacecraft to study Mars
- Bill Clinton elected president of the United States

1993

- Blast injures hundreds in World Trade Center bombing in New York City
- Major League baseball owners announce new initiatives on minority hiring
- Law agents raid religious cult in Waco, Texas
- U.S. pledges $1.6 billion aid package to assist Russian reforms
- Women receive combat roles in aerial and naval warfare
- Civil rights advocate Ruth Bader Ginsburg named to U.S. Supreme Court

- IBM announces $8.9 billion restructuring of world's largest computer maker; eliminates 60,000 jobs
- President Bill Clinton supports easing ban on homosexuals in military
- Chicago Bulls basketball star Michael Jordan retires to play professional baseball
- American novelist Toni Morrison wins Nobel Prize for literature
- Inflation rate remains at 2.7%, lowest in seven years

1994

- Supreme Court rules abortion clinics may sue violent antiabortion protesting groups for damages
- Viacom buys Paramount for $10 billion in cash and securities
- Astronauts grow crystals, melt metals, and test magnets and new drugs in low-gravity conditions aboard shuttle *Columbia*
- U.S. renews China's trade status despite human rights policy
- Tobacco companies accused of nicotine manipulation
- Major League baseball players go on strike, World Series canceled
- U.S. ends policy of accepting Cubans fleeing by sea
- U.S., French, and British troops leave Berlin without foreign presence for first time since World War II
- Hartford, CT, public schools hire private firm, Education Alternatives, to manage city schools
- Steven Spielberg, David Geffen, and Jeffrey Katzenberg form Dreamworks, a new Hollywood studio

SELECTED INCOME 1990-1994

Job	Source	Description	Pay
Administrative Assistant	*Atlanta Journal Constitution* (1994)	Must know Microsoft Word and Harvard Graphics	$20,000–$23,000/yr
Banker	*New Orleans Times-Picayune* (1993)	Demand Deposit Manager	$70,000/yr
Bookkeeper	*Atlanta Journal Constitution* (1994)	Office administrator and bookkeeper to calculate payroll of 120 employees and handle receivables	$25,000/yr
Budget Analyst	*Atlanta Journal Constitution* (1994)	City of Marietta; must have knowledge of state and city budgeting regulations	$22,693/yr
Business Executive	*Fortune* (1994)	Salary of CEO Billy Payne, Atlanta Committee for Olympic games in 1994	$600,000/yr
Business Executive	*San Francisco Examiner* (1994)	Eight months' salary and bonus for Apple Computer Chairman Gilbert Amelio in 1994	$3 million
Chemist	*New Orleans Times-Picayune* (1993)	Research and development; PhD; 10 years specialty in chemistry	$70,000/yr
Chief Financial Officer	*Wall Street Journal* (1993)	Major U.S. university	$175,000/yr
Chief Information Officer	*Wall Street Journal* (1993)	Medical college seeking candidates for planning, managing and orchestrating the use of Information Systems	$75,000–$80,000/yr
Collections	*Atlanta Journal Constitution* (1994)	Commercial collections representative; for calling on past-due accounts	$7.25/hr
Computer Support	*Chicago Tribune* (1990)	Wang Programmer	$35,000/yr
Computer Support	*Chicago Tribune* (1990)	Tape Librarian	$18,000/yr
Crafts	*Chicago Tribune* (1990)	Assemble craft items at home	To $525/wk
Dancer	*New Orleans Times-Picayune* (1993)	Go-Go dancer, guaranteed pay, good tips	$300/wk
Driver	*Chicago Tribune* (1990)	Pizza delivery	$6.50/hr
Finance and Administrative Director	*Wall Street Journal* (1993)	Global Environmental Fund; Responsible for all internal functions relating to accounting, financial management, information systems	$50,000–$65,000/yr
Football Player	*New Orleans Times-Picayune* (1993)	Three-year contract signed by Pittsburgh Steeler Kevin Greene in 1993	$5.3 million
Golfer	*Milwaukee Journal* (1991)	Earnings of John Daly for winning the Professional Golfers' Association Championship in 1991	$230,000
Investment Analyst	*Wall Street Journal* (1993)	Entails developing sophisticated strategies for the financing of goods sold by U.S. exporters premised on innovative structuring of credit facilities and discounting trade debt	$87,000/yr

Job	Source	Description	Pay
Investment Director	*Wall Street Journal* (1993)	Emerging Market Investments Director	$80,000–$100,000/yr
Legal Secretary	*San Francisco Chronicle* (1996)	Don't be on the wrong side of the door when opportunity knocks	to $42,000/yr
Marketing Trainee	*Chicago Tribune* (1990)	National Wholesale Management Trainee; no experience	$25,000–$35,000/yr
Mason	*Milwaukee Journal* (1991)	Employment for brick layers; quality a must	$23/hr
Model	*Playboy* (1993)	Modeling fee of 1993 Playmate of the Year, Anna Nicole Smith	$100,000 plus automobile
NFL Coach	*USA Today* (2004)	Annual salary, Washington Redskin Football Coach Joe Gibbs	$1.6 million
Phone Operator	*Chicago Tribune* (1990)	Switchboard operator	$7/hr
Postal Clerk	*Chicago Tribune* (1990)	No experience	$11.57/hr
Sales	*Chicago Tribune* (1990)	Engineering sales, two years experience in machine tools or robotics	$40,000/yr
Sales Manager	*Wall Street Journal* (1993)	U.S. West Communications needs manager to direct all sales activities targeting home-based business customers within a 14-state region	$75,000/yr
Sales Manager	*Wall Street Journal* (1993)	Sell franchises, distributorships, joint ventures	$100,000/yr
Stockers	*Chicago Tribune* (1990)	Major department store now hiring	$4.00–$4.75/hr

CONSUMER EXPENDITURES 1990-1994

(Per Capita)

Expenditure Type	1990	1991	1992	1993	1994
Clothing	$622	$667	$694	$670	$657
Food	$2,485	$2,651	$2,643	$2,735	$2,712
Auto Usage	$1,642	$1,741	$1,776	$1,843	$1,953
New Auto Purchase	$445	$414	$452	$486	$556
Auto Maintenance	$235	$245	$244	$248	$272
Gas & Oil	$402	$382	$389	$390	$394
Housing	$1,860	$1,996	$2,164	$2,166	$2,274
Furniture	$119	$113	$126	$126	$127
Utilities	$499	$527	$544	$581	$599
Telephone	$227	$237	$249	$263	$276
Health Care	$569	$597	$653	$710	$702
Health Insurance	$223	$252	$290	$320	$326
Personal Business	$996	$1,071	$1,100	$1,163	$1,175
Personal Care	$140	$153	$154	$154	$158
Tobacco	$105	$105	$110	$107	$103
Public Transportation	$116	$116	$116	$125	$152
Entertainment	$546	$566	$600	$650	$626
Per Capita Consumption	$10,915	$11,390	$11,938	$12,276	$12,692

INVESTMENTS 1990-1994

Investment	1990	1991	1992	1993	1994
Basic Yield, One-Year Corporate Bonds	9.69	9.46	8.56	7.55	8.41
Short-Term Interest Rates, 4–6 Months, Prime Commercial Paper	8.06	6.21	3.95	3.40	5.02
Basic Yield, Common Stocks, Total	3.39	3.28	3.05	2.80	2.90
Index of Common Stocks S&P 500	358.02	371.16	408.14	450.53	444.27

COMMON STOCKS, CLOSING PRICE AND YIELD, FIRST BUSINESS DAY OF YEAR

(Parenthetical number is annual dividends in dollars)

Investment	1990	1991	1992	1993	1994
AT&T (Name changed from American Telephone & Telegraph Company, 4/21/94) (1 per 16 spin-off, 12/13/96)	30 61/64 (1.29)	20 1/2 (1.32)	26 5/8 (1.32)	34 45/64 (1.32)	35 23/32 (1.32)
NationsBank N/C Bank of America (NCNB & C&S Sovran combine to form NationsBank, 1/2/92) (2 for 1 split, 2/7/97) (NationsBank combines with Bank of America, 10/1/98)			40 3/8 (0.76)	51 1/8 (0.82)	48 3/8 (0.94)
CPC Ind. N/C Best Foods (Pfd rights redepmt., 4/1/91) (2 for 1 split, 4/2/92) (1 per 4 spin-off, 12/15/97) (Name changed to Best Foods, 1/2/98) (2 for 1 stock split, 3/31/98)	17 5/32 (0.50)	19 3/8 (0.54)	21 3/64 (0.59)	23 9/16 (0.63)	22 5/32 (0.67)
Bethlehem Steel (1 per 1 poison pill rights, 10/18/98)	18 1/2 (0.40)	14 7/8 (0.40)	14 (0.00)	16 (0.00)	20 3/8 (0.00)
Delta Airlines (2 for 1 split, 11/2/98)	34 1/8 (0.60)	27 7/8 (0.60)	33 1/16 (0.60)	25 7/16 (0.10)	27 5/16 (0.10)
American Brands N/C Fortune Brands (2 for 1 split, 10/9/90) (1 per 1 spin-off, 5/29/97) (Name changed to Fortune Brands, Inc., 5/30/97)	29 3/8 (1.41)	26 15/32 (1.59)	28 45/64 (1.81)	25 53/64 (1.97)	21 13/64 (1.99)
General Electric (2 for 1 split, 4/28/94) (2 for 1 split, 4/28/97)	16 1/8 (0.47)	14 11/32 (0.51)	19 1/8 (0.56)	21 3/8 (0.63)	26 7/32 (0.72)
GM/E Electronic Data Sys. (2 for 1 split, 2/16/90) (2 for 1 split, 2/14/92) (Each share of CL "E" converted into 1 share of Electronic Data Systems, 6/10/96)	13 21/32 (0.28)	19 5/16 (0.32)	31 1/2 (0.36)	32 7/8 (0.40)	29 (0.48)
General Motors (1 spin-off, 12/17/97)	39 59/64 (3.00)	32 31/64 (1.60)	27 9/32 (1.40)	30 15/32 (0.80)	51 55/64 (0.80)
Microsoft (2 for 1 split, 3/26/90) (3 for 2 split, 6/18/91) (3 for 2 split, 6/3/92) (2 for 1 split, 5/6/94) (2 for 1 split, 11/22/96) (2 for 1 split, 2/6/98)	2 27/64 (0.00)	4 3/16 (0.00)	9 17/64 (0.00)	10 43/64 (0.00)	10 5/64 (0.00)
Ind Harvester N/C Navistar Int'l (Name change to Navista International Corp., 2/20/86) (1 for 10 split, 6/30/93)	38 3/4 (0.00)	22 1/2 (0.00)	26 1/4 (0.00)	22 1/2 (0.00)	23 5/8 (0.00)

Investment	1990	1991	1992	1993	1994
Nabisco/RJ Reynolds Inc.	-	-	53 3/4	43 1/8	31 7/8
(1 for 5 split, 4/12/95)	(0.00)	(0.00)	(0.00)	(0.00)	(0.00)
USX-U.S. Steel Group	36	29 3/4	27 5/8	33 1/8	42 1/8
(Formerly USX Corp.;	(1.00)	(1.00)	(1.00)	(1.00)	(1.00)
each share of USX Corp.					
was divided into 1 share of					
USX-Marathon Group and					
2 shares of USX-U.S. Steel					
Group eff. 5/6/91)					
Wal-Mart	47 1/8	30	59 1/8	62 7/8	25 1/2
(2 for 1 split, 6/15/90)	(0.07)	(0.08)	(0.10)	(0.12)	(0.16)
(2 for 1 split, 2/2/93)					
Warner Lambert	118 1/2	67 1/4	77 3/4	68 1/2	66 7/8
(2 for 1 split, 5/2/90)	(0.25)	(0.29)	(0.34)	(0.38)	(0.41)
(2 for 1 split, 5/3/96)					
(3 for 1 split, 5/8/98)					

STANDARD JOBS 1990-1994

Job Type	1990	1991	1992	1993	1994
Wages Per Full-Time Employee	$23,602	$24,578	$25,897	$26,361	$26,939
Private Industries, Incl. Farm Labor	$23,258	$24,178	$25,547	$25,934	$26,494
Bituminous Coal Mining	$38,552	$39,988	$39,649	$40,493	$42,236
Building Trades	$25,504	$25,945	$26,227	$26,739	$27,677
Domestics	$9,284	$9,527	$9,926	$10,275	$10,466
Farm Labor	$14,203	$14,493	$14,735	$15,019	$15,294
Finance, Insurance & Real Estate	$29,683	$31,008	$34,824	$36,013	$36,061
Gas, Electricity, & Sanitary Workers	$32,945	$33,940	$35,035	$36,755	$38,010
Manufacturing Durable Goods	$24,375	$25,112	$25,939	$26,992	$28,286
Manufacturing Non-Durable Goods	$21,049	$21,823	$22,541	$23,181	$23,905
Medical/Health Services Workers	$17,593	$18,522	$19,367	$20,091	$20,637
Miscellaneous Manufacturing	$18,678	$19,107	$20,042	$20,508	$21,154
Motion Picture Services	$31,833	$35,152	$35,417	$37,541	$40,811
Non Profit Org. Workers	$12,999	$13,368	$13,853	$14,094	$14,513
Passenger Transportation Workers, Local & Highway	$16,126	$16,770	$17,379	$17,802	$18,424
Postal Employees	$31,877	$33,210	$36,877	$37,609	$37,050
Public School Teachers	$23,653	$24,561	$25,270	$25,816	$26,372
Radio Broadcast and Television Workers	$27,679	$28,455	$29,543	$30,702	$31,382
Railroads	$37,794	$36,772	$38,291	$40,672	$40,874
State & Local Government Workers	$24,818	$25,863	$26,611	$27,369	$28,121
Telephone & Telegraph Workers	$30,253	$31,034	$32,454	$33,871	$34,941
Total Federal Government	$30,286	$32,609	$35,066	$36,940	$38,038
Wholesale & Retail Trade Workers	$12,588	$12,930	$13,277	$13,597	$14,056

FOOD BASKET 1990-1994

(NR = Not Reported)

Commodity	Year	U.S. Average	North East	North Central	South	West
Bacon, sliced, per pound	1990	$1.971	$2.094	$1.952	$1.942	$1.895
	1991	$2.261	$2.409	$2.266	$2.265	$2.102
	1992	$1.948	$2.232	$1.979	$1.757	$1.822
	1993	$1.861	$2.115	$1.793	$1.707	$1.830
	1994	$2.028	$2.209	$2.077	$1.894	$1.930
Bananas, per pound	1990	43.2¢	47.4¢	42.2¢	41.3¢	41.8¢
	1991	44.1¢	48.9¢	42.5¢	40.9¢	44.1¢
	1992	42.9¢	45.1¢	42.9¢	38.9¢	44.6¢
	1993	43.0¢	46.1¢	40.4¢	37.8¢	47.8¢
	1994	44.3¢	48.0¢	42.2¢	41.3¢	45.5¢
Bread, white pan, per pound	1990	72.0¢	87.1¢	66.3¢	59.7¢	74.8¢
	1991	72.9¢	87.6¢	69.6¢	59.6¢	74.6¢
	1992	74.2¢	90.5¢	72.6¢	60.0¢	73.8¢
	1993	76.5¢	86.7¢	76.6¢	64.6¢	78.2¢
	1994	79.2¢	87.6¢	80.6¢	63.9¢	84.8¢
Butter, salted, grade AA, stick, per pound	1990	$2.103	$2.195	$2.036	$2.074	$2.108
	1991	$1.941	$2.070	NR	$1.812	NR
	1992	$2.010	$2.010	NR	NR	NR
	1993	$1.927	$1.927	NR	NR	NR
	1994	$1.696	$1.835	$1.557	NR	NR
Chicken, fresh, whole, per pound	1990	89.9¢	$1.087	85.0¢	77.6¢	88.3¢
	1991	90.7¢	$1.050	84.3¢	80.7¢	92.8¢
	1992	89.3¢	$1.057	83.9¢	78.7¢	89.0¢
	1993	89.8¢	$1.059	83.3¢	78.4¢	91.4¢
	1994	91.8¢	$1.027	88.3¢	79.1¢	97.1¢
Coffee, 100%, ground roast, all sizes, per pound	1990	$2.912	$3.041	$2.765	$3.077	$2.764
	1991	$2.932	$3.028	$2.744	$3.060	$2.897
	1992	$2.656	$2.870	$2.562	$2.602	$2.589
	1993	$2.348	$2.615	$2.241	$2.413	$2.122
	1994	$2.533	$2.777	$2.478	$2.470	$2.408
Cola, nondiet, cans, 6 pack, 12-oz cans per 16 ounces	1990	41.7¢	NR	NR	NR	41.7¢
	1991	NR	NR	NR	NR	NR
	1992	NR	NR	NR	NR	NR
	1993	NR	NR	NR	NR	NR
	1994	NR	NR	NR	NR	NR
Corn on the cob, per pound	1990	NR	NR	NR	NR	NR
	1991	NR	NR	NR	NR	NR
	1992	NR	NR	NR	NR	NR
	1993	NR	NR	NR	NR	NR
	1994	NR	NR	NR	NR	NR
Crackers, soda, salted, per pound	1990	$1.249	NR	NR	$1.249	NR
	1991	$1.334	NR	NR	$1.334	NR
	1992	NR	NR	NR	NR	NR
	1993	$1.138	NR	NR	$1.138	NR
	1994	$1.023	NR	NR	$1.023	NR
Eggs, Grade A, large, per dozen	1990	$1.232	$1.356	$1.148	$1.193	NR
	1991	$1.135	$1.300	$1.093	$1.013	NR
	1992	94.5¢	$1.138	81.0¢	88.6¢	NR
	1993	92.3¢	$1.083	82.2¢	86.3¢	NR
	1994	94.6¢	$1.128	83.3¢	87.8¢	NR

Commodity	Year	U.S. Average	North East	North Central	South	West
Ground beef, 100% beef, per pound	1990	$1.545	NR	$1.566	$1.569	$1.501
	1991	$1.632	NR	$1.623	$1.657	$1.615
	1992	$1.597	NR	$1.615	$1.576	$1.600
	1993	$1.054	NR	$1.601	$1.561	NR
	1994	$1.533	NR	$1.588	$1.531	$1.480
Lettuce, iceberg, per pound	1990	61¢	68.6¢	54.9¢	61.4¢	59.0¢
	1991	69.2¢	77.8¢	67.3¢	69.6¢	62.0¢
	1992	58.2¢	63.5¢	59.2¢	58.8¢	51.4¢
	1993	62.8¢	70.0¢	62.9¢	63.8¢	54.5¢
	1994	50.7¢	57.1¢	49.1¢	52.0¢	44.6¢
Margarine, soft, tubs, per pound	1990	$1.138	NR	$1.090	NR	$1.186
	1991	NR	NR	NR	NR	NR
	1992	$1.097	NR	$1.097	NR	NR
	1993	NR	NR	NR	NR	NR
	1994	$1.076	NR	$1.076	NR	NR
Margarine, stick, per pound	1990	86.8¢	90.8¢	84.3¢	76.1¢	95.9¢
	1991	87.1¢	NR	86.0¢	80.3¢	94.9¢
	1992	87.2¢	80.2¢	78.5¢	98.1¢	91.9¢
	1993	86.5¢	NR	75.5¢	88.6¢	95.3¢
	1994	81.6¢	NR	82.8¢	80.3¢	NR
Milk, fresh, whole, fortified, per 1/2 gallon	1990	$1.444	$1.400	$1.457	$1.664	$1.255
	1991	$1.390	$1.379	$1.274	$1.593	$1.313
	1992	$1.364	$1.365	$1.393	NR	$1.335
	1993	$1.348	$1.325	NR	NR	$1.370
	1994	$1.461	$1.364	NR	NR	$1.558
Potatoes, frozen, French fried, per pound	1990	85¢	94.2¢	82.8¢	78.1¢	NR
	1991	85.7¢	98.5¢	87.6¢	71.1¢	NR
	1992	96.3¢	$1.019	95.3¢	91.6¢	NR
	1993	90.9¢	$1.014	89.6¢	81.8¢	NR
	1994	59.7¢	NR	88.0¢	91.2¢	NR
Steak, T-Bone, U.S. Choice, bone-in, per pound	1990	$5.199	NR	$5.134	$5.263	NR
	1991	$5.232	NR	$4.974	$5.489	NR
	1992	$5.159	NR	$5.145	$5.173	NR
	1993	$5.334	NR	$5.473	$5.194	NR
	1994	$5.716	NR	$5.731	$5.701	NR
Sugar, white, all sizes, per pound	1990	42.3¢	45.6¢	40.9¢	40.9¢	41.7¢
	1991	44¢	49.0¢	43.3¢	40.8¢	42.8¢
	1992	43¢	49.2¢	38.9¢	40.7¢	43.3¢
	1993	42¢	51.0¢	36.3¢	38.8¢	41.8¢
	1994	41.2¢	48.5¢	36.3¢	39.5¢	40.4¢
Tuna, light, chunk, per pound	1990	$1.986	NR	$2.057	$1.915	NR
	1991	$2.042	NR	$1.995	$2.088	NR
	1992	$2.064	$2.228	$1.979	$1.986	NR
	1993	$1.973	$2.240	$1.912	$1.768	NR
	1994	$2.074	$2.261	$2.016	$1.901	$2.116

SELECTED PRICES 1990-1994

Item	Source	Description	Price
Alcohol			
Gin	*New Orleans Times-Picayune* (1992)	*Seagram's Extra Dry Gin;* 1.75 liter	$14.39
Liquor	*Chicago Tribune* (1990)	*Grand Marnier Creme;* 750 ml	$6.99
Rum	*New Orleans Times-Picayune* (1992)	*Bacardi Rum;* 1.75 liter	$15.99
Vodka	*New Orleans Times-Picayune* (1992)	*Absolut Vodka;* 750 ml	$12.29
Whiskey	*New Orleans Times-Picayune* (1992)	*Seagram's 7 Crown;* blended whiskey; 750 ml	$6.79
Whiskey	*New Orleans Times-Picayune* (1992)	*Jack Daniel's Black Label;* 750 ml	$11.39
Whiskey	*New Orleans Times-Picayune* (1992)	*Canadian Mist;* 1.75 liter	$14.49
Wine	*New Orleans Times-Picayune* (1992)	*Glen Ellen White Zinfandel;* 750 ml	$3.99
Apparel, Children's			
Coat	*Chicago Tribune* (1990)	*Pacific Trail;* boy's ski jacket; waterproof nylon	$49.96
Jacket	*Sears Flyer* (1993)	Crinkle nylon jacket	$18
Leggings	*Sears Flyer* (1993)	Bends more the way you do	$15
Overalls	*Sears Flyer* (1993)	Osh Kosh overalls	$22
Pants	*Milwaukee Journal* (1991)	*Wild Thunder;* cotton canvas and twill with drawstrings	$19.99
Shirt	*New Orleans Times-Picayune* (1992)	*Blitzz;* knit shirt; 100% cotton; crew-neck styling	$5.50
Shoes	*New Orleans Times-Picayune* (1992)	*McGregor Boat Oxfords*	$9.96
Socks	*New Orleans Times-Picayune* (1992)	*Keds;* 4-pack cuff anklets, cotton-nylon blend	$4
Sweater	*Natural History Magazine* (1993)	Charming, handmade sweater with dinosaur design	$68
Tee Shirt	*Sears Flyer* (1993)	Skateboard tee shirt, rainbow hued, hand sprayed and sponged front and back	$9
Apparel, Men's			
Baseball Cap	*New Orleans Times-Picayune* (1992)	Choice of color	$2.99

Item	Source	Description	Price
Blazer	*Sears Flyer* (1993)	Wool blend	$95
Coat	*Chicago Tribune* (1990)	*Edelweiss Glenn;* nylon-fiber shell	$99.96
Jacket	*Sears Flyer* (1993)	Cotton polyester with poplin shell	$45
Jacket	*Natural History* (1993)	Genuine leather U. S. Army field jacket; available in brown or black	$199
Pants	*Milwaukee Journal* (1990)	*Maxx;* cargo pockets, tapered legs, matching belt	$14.99
Shirt	*Atlanta Journal Constitution* (1993)	*Spalding;* golf shirt; cotton blend	$14.98
Shirt	*Atlanta Journal Constitution* (1993)	*Kensington;* cotton pinpoint dress shirt	$29.99
Shoes	*New Orleans Times-Picayune* (1992)	*Brittania;* leather boat oxfords	$16
Shoes	*Milwaukee Journal* (1990)	*Nike Air;* cross-trainer	$58.99
Shoes	*Milwaukee Journal* (1990)	*Reebok Sir Jam;* basketball high top	$58.99
Shoes	*Atlanta Journal Constitution* (1993)	*Etonic Stableair Base 11;* running shoe	$49.96
Tennis Shoes	*Sears Flyer* (1993)	*Converse All Stars*	$24
Tie	*Natural History* (1993)	Dashing Dinosaur tie made exclusively for the American Museum of Natural History	$35
Underwear	*Milwaukee Journal* (1990)	*Hanes;* red-label briefs; 3 per pack	$4.49

Apparel, Women's

Item	Source	Description	Price
Blazer	*Sears Flyer* (1993)	Lined rollback cuffs, notched lapels, patch pockets	$38
Bodysuit	*Sears Flyer* (1993)	Figurehugging stretch cotton, lace trims neck and sleeves	$26
Cardigan	*Sears Flyer* (1993)	Bold graphics with shoulder pads	$40
Coat	*Chicago Tribune* (1990)	*Columbia Bugaloo;* parka; zip-out fleece liners	$119
Formal Wear	*Milwaukee Journal* (1990)	Mother-of-the-bride polyester georgette dress, in mauve or silver blue	$44.99
Girdle	*Sears Flyer* (1993)	Hi waist style	$25
Handbag	*New Orleans Times-Picayune* (1992)	Ladies' vinyl handbags, assortment of dressy or casual styles	$9.44
Jumpsuit	*Milwaukee Journal* (1990)	*Bonjour;* chambray jumpsuit	$29.99
Polo Shirt	*Sears Flyer* (1993)	Oversized	$18
Shirt	*Milwaukee Journal* (1990)	*Willow Bay;* ladies' rugby-stripe mock neck blouse	$7.99
Shoes	*New Orleans Times-Picayune* (1992)	*Gitano;* comfort walkers	$10.87

Item	Source	Description	Price
Shoes	*Atlanta Journal Constitution* (1993)	*Shelby Shoe;* cream, taupe, or navy leather	$68
Sweater	*Sears Flyer* (1993)	Cotton tunic sweater, wide scoop neck	$32

Appliances

Item	Source	Description	Price
Air Conditioner	*Sears Flyer* (1993)	Window air conditioning unit	$474.99
Air Purifier	*Sears Flyer* (1993)	Cleans up to 2250 sq. ft. per hour; 4 speed fan control	$234.50
Dishwasher	*Sears Flyer* (1993)	5 cycle, 5 option with Quiet Pack; plus installation	$629.99
Dishwasher	*New Orleans Times-Picayune* (1992)	*Whirlpool;* 5-cycle built-in dishwasher	$299
Microwave Oven	*Milwaukee Journal* (1990)	Ten-power microwave; touch control	$99
Refrigerator	*Milwaukee Journal* (1990)	*Frigidaire;* 18 cubic feet	$396
Refrigerator	*Sears Catalog* (1990)	*Kenmore Space Saver;* two-door, frostless model	$425.97
Vacuum Cleaner	*New Orleans Times-Picayune* (1992)	*Hoover Elite II;* vacuum with 5 amp motor	$89.96
Vacuum Cleaner	*New Orleans Times-Picayune* (1992)	*Dustbuster;* cordless vacuum; lightweight and compact	$17.99
Water Heater	*Sears Flyer* (1993)	40 gallon unit	$549.99

Baby Products

Item	Source	Description	Price
Car Seat	*Sears Flyer* (1993)	Converts to carrier or rocker	$65
Car Seat	*Sears Catalog* (1992)	*Travel 700 Car Seat;* padded shield and push-button release	$80
Chest	*Sears Flyer* (1993)	4 drawer chest, some assembly required	$200
Crib	*Sears Flyer* (1993)	Honey oak finish, double drop sides with stabilizer bar	$190
Crib Sheets	*Sears Flyer* (1993)	3 piece, Mickey Mouse design	$40
Diapers	*New Orleans Times-Picayun* (1992)	*Walgreen;* disposable diapers for boys or girls	$6.99
Dressing Table	*Sears Flyer* (1993)	Honey oak finish	$100

Business Equipment and Supplies

Item	Source	Description	Price
Calculator	*New Orleans Times-Picayune* (1992)	*Tozal;* compact desktop dual power with 8-digit display	$3.99
Computer	*Atlanta Journal Constitution* (1993)	*Apple MacIntosh Powerbook;* 180 4/80	$3,799
Office Machine	*Atlanta Journal Constitution* (1993)	*Brother Intellifax-600;* Home Office Fax Machine with cutter	$353.43
Pager	*New Orleans Times-Picayune* (1992)	*Motorola Lifestyle;* digital pager	$7.95/mo
Photocopier	*Sears Catalog* (1990)	*Xerox;* personal copier	$899.99

Item	Source	Description	Price
Telephone	Atlanta Journal Constitution (1993)	Oki-810; car phone, includes installation and antenna	$149

Collectibles

Item	Source	Description	Price
Bottle	*Glass-Works Auctions East Greenville, PA* (1992)	*Wahoo & Calisaya Bitters Bottle—Jacob Pinkerton;* medium amber semi-cabin 9 7/8" high, smooth base, applied mouth	$400
Boxing Trunks	*Art & Antiques* (1993)	Boxer *Muhammad Ali's* satin boxing trunks, sold in auction in 1992	$13,200
Calendar	*Natural History Magazine* (1993)	*Insects of the New World;* wall calendar	$12.85
Coin	*Boy's Life* (1992)	1652 Colonial Massachusetts silver sixpence	$35,200
Comic Book	*Art & Antiques* (1993)	Superman Comic Book, No. 1, from June 1938; good condition, sold in auction in 1992	$82,500
Furniture	*Art & Antiques* (1993)	Porcelain and tupliwood jewel casket and stand, once owned by Marie Antoinette; sold in auction in 1991	$4.93 million
Photograph	*Art & Antiques* (1993)	Photographer Nic Nicosia's scenes from daily life, each	$3,500
Photograph	*Boy's Life* (1992)	Simulated Special Edition of *Boy's Life* cover with your favorite picture plus $3.50 for postage and handling	$19.95
Political Button	*David J. Frent Political Auction* (1994)	George Washington, 1789 Inaugural Shank Button; GW raised in center with "Long Live the President" above in semicircular channel	$1,408
Snuff Box	*Art & Antiques* (1993)	18th century snuff box reading "On Thy Sweet Lips, To Print A Kiss, Is My Deal Girl The Price Of This"	$700
Sports Card	*Art & Antiques* (1993)	Baseball card for Honus Wagner, from 1910; sold in auction in1991	$451,000
Stamp Collection	*Natural History Magazine* (1993)	Endangered species stamp collection; U.N. postal administration	$8.50
Stamps	*Boy's Life* (1992)	109 stamps from around the world	$0.50

Education

Item	Source	Description	Price
Annual Tuition	*Boy's Life* (1994)	Military academy, Gainesville, Georgia, grades 8–12	$9,400
Camp	*Boy's Life* (1994)	Lake Toxaway, NC	$3,100
Tuition	*Boy's Life* (1992)	Carson Long Military Institute; New Bloomfield, Pennsylvania	$7,500/yr

Entertainment

Item	Source	Description	Price
Antique Show	*Art & Antiques* (1993)	*The Original Miami Beach Antiques Show;* 33 years in the same location; Miami Beach Convention Center Admission	$7
Antique Show	*Art & Antiques* (1993)	*Sacred Heart Antiques Show,* Chicago, Illinois; 45 dealers showing American, English, Continental and Oriental furniture Admission	$8
Camp	*Boy's Life* (1992)	*Northern Michigan Wilderness Camp;* backpacking, canoeing and bicycling, two weeks	$515
Festival Ticket	*New Orleans Times-Picayune* (1993)	*New Orleans Jazz and Heritage Festival;* Friday night	$25 reserved seat
Lecture	*Natural History* (1993)	Natural History Museum presents the latest scientific findings from the Hubble Space Telescope; slide-show illustrated lecture, each	$8

Item	Source	Description	Price
Tour	Natural History Magazine (1993)	American Museum of Natural History; Predators, Prey, and their Habitats	$10
Entertainment, Home			
Camcorder	New Orleans Times-Picayune (1992)	RCA compact 8mm 8:1 zoom camcorder with remote control	$699
Camera	New Orleans Times-Picayune (1992)	Kodak Star 435; 35mm camera, focus-free, built-in flash	$29.96
CD/Cassette Player	New Orleans Times-Picayune (1992)	Sony; three-piece portable CD and cassette player; 34-track programming	$166
Television	Chicago Tribune (1990)	Mitsubishi; Big-screen TV; 35"; stereo digital monitor	$2,599
Television	New Orleans Times-Picayune (1992)	Zenith; 25"; remote monitor receiver	$388
VCR	Chicago Tribune (1990)	JVC; VHS Hi-Fi stereo sound	$399
VCR	Milwaukee Journal (1990)	Toshiba; programmable VHS with remote	$227
VCR	Sears Catalog (1990)	RCA; 2 heads and up to 110 cable-compatible channels	$294.97
Videotape, Blank	Milwaukee Journal (1990)	3 T120 JVC videotapes	$8.49
Videotape, Prerecorded	New Orleans Times-Picayune (1992)	Walt Disney's Jungle Book	$19.76
Videotape, Prerecorded	Fine Woodworking Magazine (1994)	School of Classical Woodcarving; Acanthus Leaf Training; 72 minutes	$52.50
Food Products			
Apples	New Orleans Times-Picayune (1993)	Washington State Delicious apples	$0.59/lb
Chocolate	New Orleans Times-Picayune (1992)	Hershey's Chocolate Kisses; 14 oz	$1.97
Crackers	Milwaukee Journal (1990)	Nabisco Ritz Bits; box	$1.69
Eggs	New Orleans Times-Picayune (1993)	Large	$0.89/dz
Fish	Chicago Tribune (1990)	Farm-raised catfish	$2.29/lb
Flour	New Orleans Times-Picayune (1993)	Gold Medal Flour; 5-lb bag	$0.79
Shrimp	Chicago Tribune (1990)	Cooked tail-on shrimp; 12 oz	$8.99
Squid	Chicago Tribune (1990)	Federally inspected whole squid	$0.79/lb
Turkey	New Orleans Times-Picayune (1993)	10–22 lb average	$0.59/lb
Furniture			
Bed	New Orleans Times-Picayune (1992)	Cherrywood full-size bed	$399.88

Item	Source	Description	Price
Bed	*Atlanta Journal Constitution* (1993)	Solid pine bunk bed	$69
Dining Set	*Milwaukee Journal* (1990)	5-piece oak dining set, 42" round table, 4 high back chairs	$499
Easy Chair	*Milwaukee Journal* (1990)	*La-Z-Boy;* wall recliner; matching pair	$599
Lamp	*Atlanta Journal Constitution* (1993)	Brass lamps, 26" high	$36
Sofa	*Sears Catalog* (1990)	Sofa sleeper; has recessed handle sleeper mechanism with one-piece design	$499
Table	*Atlanta Journal Constitution* (1993)	Pine dinette with 2 benches	$99
Wall Shelves	*New Orleans Times-Picayune* (1992)	*Thomasville;* hand-crafted wall system; 3-piece wall system of cherry solids and veneers	$1,599
Wicker Furniture	*Sears Catalog* (1990)	Chaise lounge; frame and cushion	$493.99

Garden Equipment and Supplies

Item	Source	Description	Price
Ant Poison	*New Orleans Times-Picayune* (1992)	*Hyponex;* fire ant killer; 4 lb	$2.94
Fertilizer	*New Orleans Times-Picayune* (1992)	*Scott's Turf Builder;* lawn fertilizer; 5,000 square ft coverage	$7.88
Flowers	*New Orleans Times-Picayune* (1992)	4" flowering annuals, begonias, coleus, or salvia	$0.72
Hose	*Milwaukee Journal* (1991)	3 gauge sprinkler hose; 50'	$7.99
Lawn Mower	*New Orleans Times-Picayune* (1992)	*Lawn-Boy;* 4 HP 21" power mulch push mower; two cycle commercial grade engine	$289
Seed	*Chicago Tribune* (1990)	Wild bird food; 20 lbs	$2.99
Shrubbery	*New Orleans Times-Picayune* (1992)	1 gallon azalea, brilliant colors	$0.99
Spreader	*New Orleans Times-Picayune* (1992)	*Precision Green Drop;* 12" rubber tires	$54.75
Weed Killer	*Milwaukee Journal* (1991)	*Monsanto Round-Up;* 24-ounce; gallon	$16.99

Hotel Rates

Item	Source	Description	Price
Hotel Room	*Atlanta Journal Constitution* (1993)	*Sheraton New York;* New York City; Sure Saver Rate	$169/night
Hotel Room	*Atlanta Journal Constitution* (1993)	*Sheraton Boston;* Boston, Massachusetts; Sure Saver Weekend Rates	$104/night

Household Products

Item	Source	Description	Price
Alarm Clock	*Milwaukee Journal* (1990)	*Ingraham;* wood clock; round, square or octagonal shape	$9.99
Alarm Clock	*New Orleans Times-Picayune* (1992)	*Spartus;* electronic eurostyle	$9.99

Item	Source	Description	Price
All Purpose Cleaner	*New Orleans Times-Picayune* (1992)	*Formula 409;* 32-oz	$1.79
Bath Set	*Milwaukee Journal* (1990)	5-piece bath rug set and 2-piece tank cover	$12.99
Blinds	*Sears Catalog* (1990)	Kenney contoured mini blinds; ready-made; 35 x 42	$15.99
Caulk	*New Orleans Times-Picayune* (1992)	*Red Devil Speed Demon;* latex caulk; 10.3 oz tube	$0.89
Cleanser	*New Orleans Times-Picayune* (1992)	*Comet;* 14-oz	$0.49
Coffee Filters	*New Orleans Times-Picayune* (1992)	*Mr. Coffee;* basket type	$0.29/50
Coffee Maker	*Milwaukee Journal* (1990)	*Regal Drip Coffeemaker;* 1–10 cup capacity	$7.99
Comforter	*Sears Catalog* (1990)	Quilted comforter has polyester fill; twin 68 x 86	$26.88
Cookware	*New Orleans Times-Picayune* (1992)	*Anchor Hocking;* Microwave 20-piece pop top set; 9 containers and 4 cup pitcher with lids	$7.96
Cookware	*New Orleans Times-Picayune* (1992)	7-piece cookware set, non-stick interior	$10
Dishes	*New Orleans Times-Picayune* (1992)	*Corelle Livingware;* 16-piece dinnerware	$17.97
Flashlight	*New Orleans Times-Picayune* (1992)	*First Alert;* rechargeable	$7.99
Grill	*New Orleans Times-Picayune* (1992)	*Hibachi;* 2 adjustable grids	$6.99
Knife	*New Orleans Times-Picayune* (1992)	*Washington Forge;* 4-piece steak knife set	$3.50
Laundry Basket	*Milwaukee Journal* (1990)	*Rubbermaid*	$2.99
Laundry Cleaner	*New Orleans Times-Picayune* (1992)	*Ultra Tide;* 128 oz	$5.94
Light Bulb	*Atlanta Journal Constitution* (1993)	Halogen Accent Bulb	$8.96
Light Bulb	*Atlanta Journal Constitution* (1993)	*Philips Bag-A-Way;* 2 bulbs	$1.61
Light Bulb	*Atlanta Journal Constitution* (1993)	*Philips Director;* 150 watt	$2.09
Luggage	*New Orleans Times-Picayune* (1992)	*American Tourister;* garment bag	$39.96
Mattress	*Atlanta Journal Constitution* (1993)	*Loving Care Supreme Mattress;* queen size	$189.95
Mattress	*Milwaukee Journal* (1990)	*Sealy;* queen size; extra firm; 10 year warranty	$324

Item	Source	Description	Price
Paint	New Orleans Times-Picayune (1992)	Woolsey; gloss-white paint	$14.95/gal
Paint Additive	Country Living Magazine (1996)	Zinsser's Blend and Glaze Decorative Painting Liquid	$25/gal
Paint Roller	New Orleans Times-Picayune (1992)	EZ Painter; free frame with three covers	$6.88
Paper Towels	New Orleans Times-Picayune (1993)	Mardi Gras	$0.50
Plastic Wrap	New Orleans Times-Picayune (1992)	Reynolds Wrap; 100 sq ft	$1.99
Resin	New Orleans Times-Picayune (1992)	Fiberglass resin with hardener	$16.95/gal
Saw	Chicago Tribune (1990)	7 1/4" circular saw; 2 1/3 H.P. motor	$59.99
Sheets	New Orleans Times-Picayune (1992)	Smooth-touch twin sheet, fitted	$8.99
Sheets	New Orleans Times-Picayune (1992)	Percale sheet set; permanent press; cotton and polyester; 4-piece set	$17.96
Sheets	New Orleans Times-Picayune (1992)	Waterbed sheet set; cotton; queen size	$19.96
Shower Curtain	Sears Catalog (1990)	Priscilla-style shower curtain has mock valance	$19.77
Smoke Detector	New Orleans Times-Picayune (1992)	Family guard detector with test button and battery	$5.99
Tape	New Orleans Times-Picayune (1992)	Duct tape; 45 yds, 2" wide	$2.99
Teapot	New Orleans Times-Picayune (1992)	6-cup porcelain teapot, designs licensed by Corning	$5.50
Towel	New Orleans Times-Picayune (1992)	JC Penney; bath towel	$4.90
Trash Bag	New Orleans Times-Picayune (1992)	Hefty; 33 bonus size bags	$2.88
Trash Bag	Milwaukee Journal (1990)	Hefty; 20-count; 30-gallon size	$2.22
VCR	Sears Catalog (1990)	RCA; 2 heads and up to 110 cable-compatible channels	$294.97
Waterbed Conditioner	Milwaukee Journal (1990)	Add conditioner every 4 to 6 months to protect your waterbed mattress	

Item	Source	Description	Price
Jewelry			
Gold Chain	*New Orleans Times-Picayune* (1992)	Ladies 18" 14k gold diamond cut rope	$79.99
Ring	*Sears Catalog* (1992)	Round pearl ring	$79.99
Ring	*Sears Catalog* (1992)	Emerald cluster ring	$99.99
Ring	*Atlanta Journal Constitution* (1993)	*Artcarved* high-school class ring	$69.95
Watch	*New Orleans Times-Picayune* (1992)	*Citizen;* men's	$149.90
Watch	*Chicago Tribune* (1990)	*Raymond Weil;* white dial with 18k gold bezel and black sharkskin strap; men's	$750
Watch	*New Orleans Times-Picayune* (1992)	*Timex Analog Quartz*	$14.99
Watch	*Natural History* (1993)	Your dog on a wrist watch; see your favorite dog walk around the dial	$29.95
Meals			
Dinner	*Milwaukee Journal* (1990)	*Hales Corner Restaurant;* 8 oz filet mignon, relish tray, salad, soup and potato, cherries jubilee	$7.95
Easter Sunday	*New Orleans Times-Picayune* (1993)	*Salvatore Ristorante;* Easter Sunday menu	$15.95
Medical Products and Services			
Hydrogen Peroxide	*New Orleans Times-Picayune* (1992)	16-oz bottle	$0.39
Nonprescription Medicine	*Atlanta Journal Constitution* (1993)	*Nyquil;* 10-oz bottle	$4.93
Nonprescription Medicine	*Milwaukee Journal* (1990)	*Advil;* caplets, 100-count package	$6.68
Nonprescription Medicine	*New Orleans Times-Picayune* (1992)	*Dramamine;* for nausea, dizziness and vomiting; 12 tablets	$2.39
Ointment	*Milwaukee Journal* (1990)	*Preparation H;* 1-oz tube	$2.88
Motorized Vehicles, Supplies, and Services			
Anti-Freeze	*Milwaukee Journal* (1990)	*Prestone;* antifreeze/coolant	$5.45
Automobile	*Milwaukee Journal* (1990)	1990 *Ford Escort*	$5,999
Automobile	*Milwaukee Journal* (1990)	1990 *Ford Taurus;* 4 doors; fully equipped	$9,999
Automobile	*Chicago Tribune* (1990)	1991 *Oldsmobile Ninety-Eight Regency Elite*	$20,999
Automobile	*Atlanta Journal Constitution* (1993)	1992 *Miata*	$14,978
Automobile	*Atlanta Journal Constitution* (1993)	1993 *Nissan Altima GXE*	$14,484
Automobile	*Atlanta Journal Constitution* (1993)	1993 *Toyota Previa*	$20,893

Item	Source	Description	Price
Automobile, Used	*Atlanta Journal Constitution* (1993)	1990 *Cadillac Seville*	$11,900
Automobile, Used	*Atlanta Journal Constitution* (1993)	1990 *Eldorado*	$15,900
Automobile, Used	*Chicago Tribune* (1990)	1987 *Toyota Supra*	$11,995
Automobile, Used	*Chicago Tribune* (1990)	1988 *Chrysler LeBaron*	$8,495
Battery	*Atlanta Journal Constitution* (1993)	*Marine Deep Cycle;* 500 CCA	$39.99
Motor Oil	*New Orleans Times-Picayune* (1992)	*Quaker State;* 10W-30	$0.99/qt
Oil Filter	*Atlanta Journal Constitution* (1993)	*Fram*	$2.99
Tire	*Milwaukee Journal* (1990)	*Goodyear 54S;* radial, two steel belts	$41.95
Tire	*Atlanta Journal Constitution* (1993)	*Dunlop;* steel radial P195/70SR14	$65.77
Tire Cleaner	*Atlanta Journal Constitution* (1993)	*No Touch Tire Care*	$2.79

Other

Item	Source	Description	Price
Christmas Tree	*Chicago Tribune* (1990)	Artificial 7' Blue Alpine Fir	$124.99

Personal Care Products

Item	Source	Description	Price
Contact Lens Solution	*New Orleans Times-Picayune* (1992)	*Boston Advance conditioner;* 4-oz bottle for gas permeable lenses	$4.99
Mouthwash	*New Orleans Times-Picayune* (1992)	*Listerine;* 6-oz bottle	$1.79
Razor	*New Orleans Times-Picayune* (1992)	*Gillette;* disposable razors, with $2 rebate	$2.99
Scale	*Sears Flyer* (1993)	Bathroom scales, weighs up to 300 pounds	$27.99

Real Estate

Item	Source	Description	Price
Home	*Art & Antiques* (1993)	10,000 square foot house in Dallas, Texas suburb designed by architect Frank Lloyd Wright in 1958	$5.5 million

Sewing Equipment and Supplies

Item	Source	Description	Price
Sewing Machine	*New Orleans Times-Picayune* (1992)	*Brother;* lightweight free arm; sews 16 different stitches	$150

Sports Equipment

Item	Source	Description	Price
Backpack	*Natural History* (1993)q	Leather backpack; plus $3.95 shipping	$29.95
Baseball Bat	*Atlanta Journal Constitution* (1993)	*Louisville Slugger TPXBBL*	$79.96
Baseball Glove	*Atlanta Journal Constitution* (1993)	*Wilson Roger Clemens;* all leather	$34.98

Item	Source	Description	Price
Basketball Backboard	*Chicago Tribune* (1990)	Fiberglass backboard with rim and pole	$99.98
Binoculars	*Sears Catalog* (1992)	*Tasco;* 8–20 power x 50mm	$139.99
Exercise Bicycle	*Chicago Tribune* (1990)	*Air-gometer;* exercise cycle	$249.99
Exercise Equipment	*Natural History Magazine* (1993)	*Lifestep;* Model 550; proven effective in the nation's finest health clubs	$1,589
Exercise Equipment	*Natural History Magazine* (1993)	*Nordic Track;* takes weight off and keeps it off	$399.95
Exercise Machine	*Natural History* (1993)	*Lifestep 5500 Aerobic Trainer;* 20 minutes to a healthier body	$1,598
Golf Clubs	*Atlanta Journal Constitution* (1993)	*Dunlop Solution Golf Set;* stainless-steel woods and irons	$249
Knife	*Milwaukee Journal* (1990)	*Wormark Fish 'n Filet*	$9.99
Pistol	*New Orleans Times-Picayune* (1993)	*Smith & Wesson;* 38 caliber; SST, S-shot	$309
Pool Table	*Chicago Tribune* (1990)	*Canterbury;* 6'	$699
Rod and Reel	*Milwaukee Journal* (1990)	*Garcia Lite Plus Casting Combo*	$59.99
Scuba Equipment	*New Orleans Times-Picayune* (1993)	Pro scuba mask; list $79.95	$24.95
Scuba Equipment	*New Orleans Times-Picayune* (1993)	Scuba tank; 80 cu ft; 3000 PSI	$119.95
Tennis Racket	*Atlanta Journal Constitution* (1993)	*Wilson;* 3.0 tennis frame; wide-body graphite/kevlar construction	$129.97
Tent	*Atlanta Journal Constitution* (1993)	*Camel Genesis Sixty Second Tent;* 7' x 8' dome	$89.98

Toys

Item	Source	Description	Price
Tilt Walker	*Boy's Life* (1994)	Develops coordination	$21.95
Water Balloon Launcher	*Boy's Life* (1994)	200 yard model	$13.50

Travel and Transportation

Item	Source	Description	Price
Airline Ticket	*New Orleans Times-Picayune* (1993)	*American Airlines;* New Orleans to Miami	$290
Airline Ticket	*Chicago Tribune* (1990)	*Midway Airlines;* Chicago to Boston one way	$99
Airline Ticket	*Chicago Tribune* (1990)	*Midway Airlines;* Chicago to Saint Thomas; one way	$179
Airline Ticket	*New Orleans Times-Picayune* (1993)	*TransWorld Airlines;* New Orleans to Honolulu	$612
Cruise Ticket	*Natural History Magazine* (1993)	Alaska cruise; If you want authentic Alaska, don't gamble on another cruise	$2,395/person

MISCELLANY 1990-1994

Bordeaux Wines

At $40 or more for a bottle from a well-known chateau, a good Bordeaux wine comes at a price that can cramp the style of all but the most well-heeled wine lovers. Some Bordeaux producers have done something about this. Look for the 1990 Maitre d'Estournel ($8), 1989 Michel Lynch ($8.50), 1989 Christian Moueix Merlot ($10) and 1989 Mouton-Cadet ($8). They're all very good wines and real values.

Bon Appetit, February, 1993

Cheap Gas—For Now

Happy anniversary, drivers! Just a year after Iraqi troops conquered Kuwait and gasoline prices began spiking, a new study by oil historian Daniel Yergin says pretax, inflation adjusted gasoline prices are at their lowest point since 1947. Even with recent increases in federal and state fuel taxes, gasoline costs Americans 44% less in real terms than it did in 1980, and surprisingly, 24% less than it did in the halcyon days of 1960, before anyone had heard of Saddam Hussein or OPEC.

Time, August 5, 1991

Remember Cost Control

Eighteen months ago, everyone agreed that the bottom line to healthcare reform had to be controlling the skyrocketing costs that are busting the federal budget—and devastating families, businesses and the economy as a whole. Today you'd have to scour the *Congressional Record* for a mention of that goal. Instead, national leaders compete over who can give the most generous benefits to the most constituents . . . Consider the stark numbers. In 1993 the United States spent an estimated 14.3 percent of its gross domestic product on health care. That translates into $3,400 per person, more than three and a half times as much as the amount 30 years ago, even taking inflation into account.

Newsweek, July 25, 1994

PGA Championship Prize

Golfer John Daly has plans for at least part of the $230,000 first-place check (he earned as winner of the Professional Golfers' Association Championship).

"Pay off my house, van and BMW," said Daly, who bought the car for his fiancée. "I'm going to donate $30,000 to charity, whatever the PGA wants to donate it to."

Milwaukee Journal, August 21, 1991

Proof at last that money can buy happiness.

HISTORICAL SNAPSHOT 1995-1999

1995

- Chevron settles harassment charges concerning offensive jokes and comments for $2.2 million
- Michael Jordan leaves baseball, returns to professional basketball's Chicago Bulls
- U.S. opposes Microsoft's planned $2 billion merger with Intuit
- Longest Major League Baseball strike in history, 234 days, ends
- Courts force the Citadel Military College to admit first female cadet
- Oklahoma City Federal Courthouse bombed, the worst act of terrorism in U.S. history
- Twenty-fifth anniversary of Earth Day celebrated
- Supreme Court rules that only a constitutional amendment can enforce term limits on Congress
- Dow Corning declares bankruptcy after failure of its silicone breast device
- U.S. renews trade privileges with China despite human rights record
- U.S. space shuttle docks with Russian Space Station
- Federal Drug Administration rules nicotine an addictive drug, moves to regulate
- Walt Disney Company acquires Capital Cities/ABC for $19 billion
- Chemical Bank and Chase Manhattan merge to create nation's biggest bank
- Forty thousand African American men meet in Washington, D.C., pledge to take responsibility for their lives and communities
- 25 percent of Americans continue to smoke cigarettes despite health warnings

1996

- U.S. approves fat substitute olestra for snacks
- Budget crisis shuts down Federal Government temporarily
- Networks introduce Television Rating System
- General Motors strike settled after 16 days
- Liggett Group breaks with other tobacco companies, settles law suits
- Bell Atlantic and NYNEX merge to form nation's second largest telephone company
- Federal Drug Administration approves U.S. marketing of abortion pill RU-486
- Centennial Summer Olympics in Atlanta, GA, disrupted by bombing
- Safer whooping cough vaccine approved
- Jobless rate lowest in six years
- Incumbent U.S. president Bill Clinton defeats Bob Dole
- Minimum wage increased 90 cents to $5.15 per hour
- Wall Street's Dow Jones Industrial average surpasses 6,000 barrier
- Department of Agriculture says the cost of raising a child to age 17 is $149,820
- Dow ends year at 6,448

1997

- Thirty-year mortgage falls to 7 percent
- Leading tobacco companies make $368 billion settlement with states to settle smoking death claims
- Scottish researchers announce the first cloning of an adult mammal, a sheep named Dolly
- Despite a one-day plunge of 554 points, stock market soars; Dow up 20 percent for third straight year
- President Clinton gains line-item veto power for first time
- Affirmative Action programs, designed to aid minorities, come under attack

1998

- Tobacco companies make a $260 billion settlement with states for smoke-related illnesses
- Dow Jones industrial average closes year at 9,181, up 16%
- Seagrams acquires music giant Polygram for $10.4 billion to give the new company one quarter of the $11.4 billion market
- Inflation rate falls to 1.6%
- Professional basketball players are locked out by owners
- Biotechnological stocks show long anticipated potential, increase 44% for the year
- The Unabomber pleads guilty to all charges and accepts a sentence of life without parole
- President Bill Clinton impeached; admits to an affair with White House intern Monica Lewinsky
- In professional baseball Mark McGuire and Sammy Sosa compete to break Roger Maris's 1961 home run record; both succeed; Sosa hits 66 and McGuire hits 70
- Melissa Ward becomes the first black female captain in commercial aviation
- The television game show *The Price is Right* airs its 5,000th episode
- India resumes nuclear testing after Pakistan successfully tests its first nuclear weapon

1999

- Over 10,000 people protest the World Trade Summit in Seattle, Washington
- The United States officially hands over control of the Panama Canal to Panama
- Pokeman, a card game, is the largest toy craze of the year
- The cartoon movie *South Park* is released and found to have the most curse words per minute, of any movie ever distributed
- NATO bombs Serbia to stop Serbian aggression against the Croats
- The USA Women's soccer team wins the World Cup
- George W. Bush, son of former president George Bush, announces that he will run for president of the United States

SELECTED INCOME 1995-1999

Job	Source	Description	Pay
Administrative Assistant	*San Francisco* (1996)	Collections, pull credit reports, create spreadsheets	$20,000-$26,000/yr
Administrative Assistant	*San Francisco Chronicle* (1996)	International bank seeks French speaking candidate	to $30,000/yr
Administrative Assistant	*New York Times* (1998)	Chairman looking for an articulate assistant to coordinate all meetings and presentations	$52,000/yr plus bonus
Animal Control Officer	*San Francisco Chronicle* (1996)	Good people and animal handling skills required; law enforcement background preferred	$10.75/hr
Attorney	*San Francisco Chronicle* (1996)	City of Oakland, California; Deputy City Attorney	$7,094-$8,709/mo
Baseball Player	*People Weekly* (1998)	Annual salary of St. Louis Cardinal baseball player Mark McGwire	$9 million
Book Advance	*People Weekly* (1998)	Amount paid to Monica Lewinsky to write a tell-all book about her affair with President Bill Clinton	$600,000
Bus Driver	*Washington Post* (1999)	Require clean driving and criminal record. Must pass physical with drug test	$9/hr
Comedian	*San Francisco Examiner* (1997)	Per episode salary of television comic star Jerry Seinfeld in 1997	$1 million
Computer Engineer	*New York Times* (1998)	LAN/WAN engineer, routers, frame, SNA, ATM, NT	to $100,000
Dentist	*New York Times* (1998)	Endo, ortho, implants	$2,000/day
Football Player	*San Francisco Examiner* (1997)	Salary and bonus of San Diego Chargers player Junior Seau in 1997	$6.88 million
Hockey Player	*San Francisco Examiner* (1997)	Annual salary of Philadelphia hockey player Eric Lindros in 1997	$8 million
Housekeeper	*San Francisco Chronicle* (1996)	9 A.M. to 4 P.M. M-F	$15/hr
Housekeeper	*San Francisco Chronicle* (1996)	Must have car; English speaking	$1,000/mo
Housekeeper	*Washington Post* (1999)	Live-in, Monday through Friday, experience and references required	$225/wk
Informant	*People Weekly* (1998)	Reward paid to David Kaczynski for identifying his brother, Ted, as the Unabomber	$1 million
Legal Secretary	*San Francisco Chronicle* (1996)	Don't be on the wrong side of the door when opportunity knocks	to $42,000/yr
Medical Faculty	*Look Smart Website* (2000)	Annual salary of Dermatology faculty in 1999	$153,498
Medical Faculty	*Look Smart Website* (2000)	Annual salary of Internal Medicine faculty in 1999	$120,000
Packers	*Atlanta Constitution* (1999)	Warehouse has openings from 7:00 A.M. to 4:00 P.M.	$8/hr

Job	Source	Description	Pay
Secretary	*San Francisco Chronicle* (1996)	Human Resources Department; part-time; MS Word/Excel required	$12-$13/hr
Store Manager	*Atlanta Constitution* (1999)	If you have clean motor vehicle record, with 2 years college or management experience, are able to lift 75 lbs., we want you	$33,000/yr
Systems Administrator	*Washington Post* (1999)	Must have ability to maintain small Windows NT 4.0 network	$45,000/yr
Television Anchor	*People Weekly* (1998)	Annual salary of television's Today host Katie Couric	$7 million
U.S. President	*The Christian Science Monitor* (1996)	Annual salary of President Bill Clinton in 1996	$200,000
Wrestler	*People Weekly* (1998)	Estimated annual income of wrestler Stone Cold Steve Austin, not including merchandising royalties	$2 million

CONSUMER EXPENDITURES 1995-1999

(One Person)

Expenditure Type	1995	1996	1997	1998	1999
Clothing	991	886	866	961	933
Food at Home	1,401	1,461	1,354	1,408	1,449
Food Away from Home	1,098	1,138	1,225	1,232	1,236
Auto Usage	2,921	3,197	3,239	3,331	3,536
Auto Purchase (new)	1,042	1,189	1,244	1,362	1,507
Auto Maintenance	393	381	391	392	382
Gas and Oil	530	582	567	529	565
Housing	7,030	7,095	7,586	7,843	8,206
Utilities	1,421	1,488	1,563	1,536	1,551
Telephone	506	544	583	581	592
Health Care	1,110	1,155	1,249	1,220	1,336
Personal Taxes	2,013	1,828	2,011	2,040	2,218
Tobacco	172	166	169	175	189
Public Transportation	239	305	280	297	250
Entertainment	992	1,002	1,011	999	1,040
Total Average Expenditures	21,859	22,417	23,338	23,906	24,990

INVESTMENTS 1995-1999

Investment	1995	1996	1997	1998	1999
Basic Yield, One-Year Corporate Bonds	7.54	7.96	7.63	6.23	7.64
Short-Term Interest Rates, 4–6 Months, Prime Commercial Paper	5.79	5.61	5.65	4.80	5.71
Basic Yield, Common Stocks, Total	2.53	2.21	1.77	NR	NR
Index of Common Stocks (S&P-500)	544.75	670.63	885.14	1229.23	1469.25

COMMON STOCKS, CLOSING PRICE AND YIELD, FIRST BUSINESS DAY OF YEAR

(Parenthetical number is annual dividends in dollars)

	1995	1996	1997	1998	1999
Allis Chalmers	1	3/8	1	3 5/8	3.50
AT&T (Name changed from American Telephone & Telegraph Company, 4/21/94) (1 per 16 spin-off, 12/13/96) (3 for 1 split, 4/99; 1 for 5 split, 11/02)	34 3/16 (4.40)	44 3/64 (4.40)	41 1/4 (4.40)	58.82 (4.40)	77.88 (4.40)
NationsBank N/C Bank of America (NCNB & C&S Sovran combine to form NationsBank, 1/2/92) (2 for 1 split, 2/7/97) (NationsBank combines with Bank of America, 10/1/98)	45 3/4 (1.04)	69 3/8 (1.20)	97 3/8 (1.37)	60 3/4 (1.80)	60.50 (1.85)
Delta Airlines (2 for 1 split, 11/98)	25 1/4 (.10)	36 13/16 (.10)	35 7/16 (.10)	59 1/2 (.10)	51.94 (0.10)
American Brands N/C Fortune Brands (2 for 1 split, 10/9/90) (1 per 1 spinoff, 5/29/97) (Name changed to Fortune Brands, Inc., 5/30/97)	23 59/64 (2.00)	28 3/8 (2.00)	31 21/32 (1.41)	37.06 (1.67)	31.25 (1.99)
General Electric (2 for 1 split, 4/28/94) (2 for 1 split, 4/28/97) (3 for 1 split, 5/00)	25 1/2 (.82)	36 (.92)	49 7/16 (1.04)	73.31 (1.20)	100.56 (1.29)
GM/E Electronic Data Sys. (2 for 1 split, 2/16/90) (2 for 1 split, 2/14/92) (Each share of CL "E" converted into 1 share of Electronic Data Systems, 6/10/96)	38 3/8 (.52)	52 (.60)	43 1/4 (.60)	43 15/16 (.60)	
General Motors (1 spinoff, 12/17/97)	39 13/16 (1.10)	49 31/32 (1.60)	52 11/16 (2.00)	60 3/4 (2.00)	70.87 (2.00)
Microsoft (2 for 1 split, 3/26/90) (3 for 2 split, 6/18/91) (3 for 2 split, 6/3/92) (2 for 1 split, 5/6/94) (2 for 1 split, 11/22/96) (2 for 1 split, 2/6/98) (2 for 1 split, 3/99; 2 for 1 split, 2/03)	5 9/32	21 15/16	41 5/16	64 5/8	141.00
Ind Harvester N/C Navistar Int'l (Name change to Navistar (no dividends) International Corp., 2/20/86) (1 for 10 split, 6/30/93)	15 1/8	10 5/8	9 1/8	24 13/16	27.75

Investment	1995	1996	1997	1998	1999
Nabisco/RJ Reynolds Inc. (1 for 5 split, 4/12/95)	27 1/2 (1.50)	30 3/4 (1.76)	34 (2.00)	37 1/2 (2.05)	n/a (1.55)
USX-U.S. Steel Group (Formerly USX Corp; each share of USX Corp was divided into 1 share of USX-Marathon Group and .2 shares of USX-US Steel Group eff. 5/6/91)	35 5/8 (1.00)	31 7/8 (1.00)	32 1/8 (1.00)	34 7/8 (1.00)	n/a
Wal-Mart (2 for 1 split, 6/15/90) (2 for 1 split, 2/2/93) (2 for 1 split, 4/99)	20 7/8 (.10)	23 1/4 (.11)	23 (.14)	39 3/8 (.16)	80.63 (.19)
Warner Lambert (2 for 1 split, 5/2/90) (2 for 1 split, 5/3/96) (3 for 1 split, 5/8/98)	76 1/2 (.43)	98 1/2 (.46)	74 (.51)	125 7/8 (.64)	n/a

STANDARD JOBS 1995-1999

Job Type	1995	1996	1997	1998	1999
Wages Per Full-Time Employee	$27,845/yr	$28,946/yr	$25,272	$26,260	$27,092
Private Industries, Incl. Farm Labor	$27,440/yr	$28,581/yr	$28,170	$28,990	$28,640
Bituminous Coal Mining	$42,711/yr	$44,769/yr	$44,535	$44,811	$44,582
Building Trades	$28,465/yr	$28,846/yr	$33,649	$35,068	$36,379
Domestics	$10,854/yr	$11,173/yr	$11,180	$11,596	$12,636
Farm Labor	$15,863/yr	$15,316/yr	$14,196	$14,612	$15,808
Finance, Insurance, & Real Estate	$38,577/yr	$41,728/yr	$41,808	$42,380	$42,990
Gas, Electricity, & Sanitation Workers	$38,936/yr	$39,398/yr	$42,549	$44,592	$45,274
Manufacturing, Durable Goods	$28,507/yr	$28,366/yr	$30,122	$31,006	$32,051
Manufacturing, Nondurable Goods	$24,387/yr	$24,203/yr	$29,403	$29,767	$31,190
Medical / Health Services Workers	$21,234/yr	$21,555/yr	$21,667	$22,431	$23,290
Miscellaneous Manufacturing	$21,798/yr	$21,688/yr			
Motion Picture Services	$39,585/yr	$39,842/yr	$39,906	$40,606	$40,777
Nonprofit Org. Workers	$15,016/yr	$15,538/yr	$15,540	$16,030	$16,106
Passenger Transportation Workers, Local & Highway	$18,525/yr	$18,167/yr	$19,662	$21,149	$20,320
Postal Employees	$35,797/yr	$37,776/yr	$35,204	$35,412	$36,244
Public School Teachers	$27,130/yr	$27,875/yr	$34,060	$34,892	$35,776
Radio Broadcast and Television Workers	$32,223/yr	$32,822/yr	$32,811	$33,117	$33,222
Railroads	$42,175/yr	$42,983/yr	$42,328	$44,148	$42,432
State & Local Government Workers	$29,023/yr	$30,160/yr	$30,784	$31,824	$31,824
Telephone & Telegraph Workers	$35,844/yr	$36,571/yr	$33,696	$35,412	$36,140
Total Federal Government	$38,520/yr	$34,944/yr	$35,568	$36,088	$37,908
Wholesale & Retail Trade Workers	$14,412/yr	$14,415/yr	$20,332	$21,320	$21,892

FOOD BASKET 1995-1999

(NR = Not Reported)

Commodity	Year	U.S. Average	North East	North Central	South	West
Bacon, Sliced, per pound	1995	$1.921	$2.252	$1.969	$1.661	$1.801
	1996	$2.177	$2.353	$2.093	$2.207	$2.054
	1997	$2.658	$2.854	$2.595	$2.599	$2.585
	1998	$2.64	$2.78	$2.67	$2.51	$2.73
	1999	$2.52	$2.77	$2.61	$2.27	$2.64
Bananas, per pound	1995	50.6¢	56.2¢	47.3¢	47.5¢	51.3¢
	1996	46.7¢	50.0¢	43.2¢	43.1¢	50.3¢
	1997	50.3¢	54.3¢	46.9¢	46.6¢	53.2¢
	1998	$0.47	$0.52	$0.44	$0.43	$0.51
	1999	$0.48	$0.49	$0.48	$0.44	$0.55
Bread, White Pan, per pound	1995	78.2¢	85.2¢	76.1¢	69.2¢	82.2¢
	1996	86.8¢	90.3¢	84.6¢	81.7¢	90.5¢
	1997	87.1¢	89.0¢	87.4¢	81.4¢	90.6¢
	1998	$0.85	$0.96	$0.84	$0.75	$0.94
	1999	$0.87	$1.01	$0.87	$0.77	$0.89
Butter, Salted, Grade AA, Stick, per pound	1995	$1.610	$1.610	NR	NR	NR
	1996	$1.784	$1.771	$1.908	$1.673	NR
	1997	$1.959	NR	NR	$1.959	NR
	1998	$2.35	NR	NR	NR	NR
	1999	$3.00	NR	NR	$2.79	NR
Chicken, Fresh, Whole, per pound	1995	91.7¢	$1.058	86.4¢	79.5¢	95.0¢
	1996	96.2¢	$1.100	93.8¢	82.9¢	98.2¢
	1997	$1.029	$1.074	$1.000	93.6¢	$1.104
	1998	$1.02	$1.10	$0.97	$0.91	$1.15
	1999	$1.07	$1.21	$1.13	$0.98	$1.11
Coffee, 100%, Ground Roast, all sizes, per pound	1995	$4.478	$4.739	$4.236	NR	$4.459
	1996	$3.336	$3.097	$3.451	$3.254	$3.543
	1997	$3.333	$3.661	$3.135	NR	$3.204
	1998	$4.02	$4.40	$3.77	$3.89	$4.01
	1999	$3.43	$3.69	$3.17	$3.37	$3.48
Crackers, Soda, Salted, per pound	1995	NR	NR	NR	NR	NR
	1996	$1.306	NR	NR	$1.306	NR
	1997	$1.441	NR	NR	$1.441	NR
	1998	$1.66	NR	NR	$1.49	
	1999	$1.59	NR	NR	$1.41	
Eggs, Grade A, Large, per dozen	1995	92.4¢	$1.115	78.6¢	87.0¢	NR
	1996	$1.193	$1.330	$1.046	$1.202	NR
	1997	$1.167	$1.312	$1.052	$1.138	NR
	1998	$1.12	$1.20	$1.04	$1.11	NR
	1999	$1.05	$1.17	$1.00	$1.00	NR
Ground Beef, 100% beef, per pound	1995	$1.364	NR	$1.384	$1.343	$1.365
	1996	$1.305	NR	$1.297	$1.402	$1.215
	1997	$1.404	NR	$1.315	$1.492	NR
	1998	$1.45	NR	$1.42	$1.49	NR
	1999	$1.38	NR	$1.32	$1.42	NR
Lettuce, Iceberg, per pound	1995	82.1¢	98.6¢	75.3¢	82.0¢	72.5¢
	1996	76.3¢	83.1¢	73.2¢	81.0¢	67.7¢
	1997	64.7¢	67.2¢	57.4¢	70.6¢	63.7¢
	1998	$1.07	$1.16	$0.82	$1.15	$1.13
	1999	$0.64	$0.70	$0.59	$0.66	$0.62

Commodity	Year	U.S. Average	North East	North Central	South	West
Margarine, Soft, Tubs, per pound	1995	NR	NR	NR	NR	NR
	1996	NR	NR	NR	NR	NR
	1997	NR	NR	NR	NR	NR
	1998	NR	NR	NR	NR	NR
	1999	NR	NR	NR	NR	NR
Margarine, Stick, per pound	1995	80.9¢	NR	81.8¢	80.0¢	NR
	1996	NR	NR	NR	NR	NR
	1997	NR	NR	NR	NR	NR
	1998	NR	NR	NR	NR	NR
	1999	NR	NR	NR	NR	NR
Milk, Fresh, Whole, Fortified, per 1/2 gallon	1995	$1.446	$1.319	NR	NR	$1.572
	1996	$1.481	$1.327	NR	NR	$1.635
	1997	$1.616	$1.441	NR	NR	$1.790
	1998	NR	NR	NR	NR	NR
	1999	NR	NR	NR	NR	NR
Potatoes, Frozen, French Fried, per pound	1995	81¢	NR	78.0¢	83.2¢	81.9¢
	1996	83.5¢	NR	80.3¢	86.7¢	NR
	1997	90.8¢	NR	88.3¢	93.3¢	NR
	1998	$0.98	$1.13	NR	$0.87	NR
	1999	$1.00	$1.19	NR	$0.95	NR
Steak, T-Bone, U.S. Choice, Bone-in, per pound	1995	$5.660	NR	$5.577	$5.743	NR
	1996	$5.667	NR	$5.691	$5.643	NR
	1997	$5.799	NR	$5.776	$5.822	NR
	1998	$5.82	NR	NR	NR	NR
	1999	$6.36	NR	$6.04	NR	NR
Sugar, White, All Sizes, per pound	1995	40.1¢	45.3¢	36.1¢	39.4¢	39.6¢
	1996	40.9¢	43.4¢	37.7¢	41.0¢	41.5¢
	1997	43.5¢	45.2¢	43.7¢	42.9¢	42.2¢
	1998	$0.43	$0.45	$0.42	$0.41	$0.43
	1999	$0.43	$0.46	$0.42	$0.42	$0.44
Tuna, Light, Chunk, per pound	1995	$2.022	$2.122	$1.950	$1.922	$2.093
	1996	$2.016	$2.067	$2.007	$1.858	$2.132
	1997	$2.063	$2.087	$2.090	$1.911	$2.165
	1998	$2.10	NR	$2.15	$2.03	NR
	1999	$2.09	NR	$2.30	$1.93	NR

SELECTED PRICES 1995-1999

Item	Source	Description	Price
Alcohol			
Wine Bottle Holder	Playboy (1997)	Hand-crafted by artist Eric Kaposta; limited edition; bust of Bacchus	$150
Wine	*Playboy* (1997)	*1994 Cakebread Cellar's Chardonnay Reserve*	$36
Wine	*Viansa Catalog* (1998)	*Viansa;* 1997 Sauvignon Blanc, made from Napa Valley grapes	$12
Apparel, Men's			
Belt	*Coldwater Creek Catalog* (1998)	Fine-grained Italian leather, 1" wide	$42
Field Jacket	*Lands' End Catalog* (1998)	Gently stonewashed 7-oz cotton canvas, with corduroy collar	$69.50
Jacket	*Soccer Madness Catalog* (1997)	*Adidas Santiago Polar Fleece;* two-tone sleeves and body	$69.95
Jeans	*Los Angeles Times* (1997)	Todd Oldham style	$50
Shoes	*Los Angeles Times* (1997)	Bass Brompton style	$59.99
Shoes	*Coldwater Creek Catalog* (1998)	Loafers of flexible nappa leather	$68
Soccer Cleats	*Soccer Madness Catalog* (1997)	*Predator Touch liga;* features jets, fins, and ridges which offer better ball control and spin	$129.95
Suit	*Los Angeles Times* (1997)	*Savane;* double-gabardine suit	$149.99
Suit	*Boston Globe* (1997)	*Hickey-Freeman*	$760
Suit	*Boston Globe* (1997)	Oxford suit	$1,320
Apparel, Women's			
Brassiere	*Boston Globe* (1997)	*Maidenform*	$12.99
Brassiere	*Boston Globe* (1997)	*Best Form*	$5.99
Brassiere	*Los Angeles Times* (1997)	*Olga;* push-up sensuous solution style	$20.63
Brassiere	*Los Angeles Times* (1997)	*Vanity Fair;* underwire skin-to-skin style	$18
Dress	*Los Angeles Times* (1997)	*Versace;* stretch scuba dress	$295
Fur Coat	*Boston Globe* (1997)	Beaver jacket	$495
Fur Coat	*Boston Globe* (1997)	Blush fox coat	$2,595
Fur Coat	*Boston Globe* (1997)	Russian sable coat	$7,995
Handbag	*Los Angeles Times* (1997)	*Tignanello;* one-touch leather bag	$69.99

Item	Source	Description	Price
Hat	*Smith & Hawken* (1998)	Double-chemille stuffs into backpack or purse	$39
Jacket	*Boston Globe* (1997)	Cashmere-blend jacket	$69.99
Pants	*The State* (Columbia, SC) (1998)	*Diane Richard* washable flannel pants, styled in poly/rayon	$28
Purse	*Los Angeles Times* (1997)	*Kenneth Cole;* leather reaction bag	$148.50
Shoes	*Boston Globe* (1997)	*Salmon Evolution* 7.1 boots	$189.95
Shoes	*Los Angeles Times* (1997)	*Hush Puppies*	$29.99
Shoes	*Atlanta Constitution* (1999)	*Brooks Paragon;* cross-training tennis shoe	$55
Turtleneck Underwear	*Lands' End Catalog* (1998)	Pure silk; just as lightweight yet warm as our long, full bodied underwear	$32.50

Appliances

Item	Source	Description	Price
Breadmaker	*Consumer Reports* (1997)	The *Breadman TR800* made the best bread	$100
Vacuum Cleaner	*Consumer Reports* (1998)	*Hoover Windtunnel Deluxe* weighs 18 lb.; better than most on carpeting and at edge-cleaning	$280
VCR	*Consumer Reports* (1998)	The *Panasonic PV-8662* is a fine all-around performer that offers features for a range of family uses	$240
Whirlpool Tubs	*Consumer Reports* (1998)	*American Standard Luxury System II* is spacious and comfortable; holds 25 to 63 gallons	$1,660

Business Equipment and Supplies

Item	Source	Description	Price
Computer	*Boston Globe* (1997)	*Apple MacIntosh Performa;* 6115CD	$2,699
Computer	*Boston Globe* (1997)	*Apple MacIntosh Performa;* 475	$1,099
Computer	*New York Times*	*Compaq Presario 1235;* all-in-one color notebook (1999)	$1,199
Electronic Organizer	*Newsweek* (1998)	*The Palm III;* connected organizer keeps names, phone numbers, schedules, memos, and e-mail at your fingertips	$369
Envelope	*Los Angeles Times* (1997)	9 x 12 Brown Kraft Clasp Envelope	$4.65/100
Fax Machine	*Boston Globe* (1997)	*Brother Plain Paper Fax Machine;* features quickscan, 30-page document feeder	$799.99
Printer	*Newsweek* (1998)	*Epson Stylus;* color printers have the exclusive perfect-picture imaging system; Model 740	$279
Software	*Boston Globe* (1997)	*Microsoft Office 4.2*	$248.99
Software	*Boston Globe* (1997)	*Meca Managing Your Money 2.0*	$39.99
Telephone	*Boston Globe* (1997)	Handheld cellular with alpha memory	$49.99

Entertainment

Item	Source	Description	Price
Art Exhibit	*New York Times* (1999)	*Baule: African Art/Western Eyes;* Museum for African Art	$8

Item	Source	Description	Price
Museum	*Southern Living* (1999)	*Reedville Fisherman's Museum*, Reedville, Va.	$2

Entertainment, Home

Item	Source	Description	Price
Audio Tape	*Boston Globe* (1997)	*TDK audio tape;* 7-pack D90	$5
Camcorder	*Consumer Reports* (1999)	"The digital *Sony DCR-PC10* delivered the best image, but it's still extremely expensive."	$2,700
Camera	*Consumer Reports* (1999)	The *Nikon Coolpix 900* has 1.280 x 960-pixel resolution, compact flash memory card and Adobe Photo Deluxe 2.0 for Windows 95, Mac 05 7.2	$800
Camera	*American Photo* (1998)	*Canon;* EOS-3 35mm with eye control	$1,900.00
Film	*Boston Globe* (1997)	*Kodak Gold;* 110 film; 24 exposures; 3-pack; 200 speed	$6
Piano	*Atlanta Constitution* (1999)	*Yamaha;* digital piano	$997
Television	*Boston Globe* (1997)	*Zenith;* 19"; Digital; Color	$139
Television	*Playboy* (1997)	*Projectavision;* Digital Home Theater TV; combines 60" rear-projection TV with computer display	$10,000
Videotape, Prerecorded	*Playboy* (1997)	Farrah Fawcett, *All of Me*	$19.98
Videotape, Prerecorded	*Boston Globe* (1997)	Disney's *Lion King*	$29.97
Videotape, Prerecorded	*Atlanta Constitution* (1999)	*Lethal Weapon*	$15.99

Food Products

Item	Source	Description	Price
Cookies	*Viansa Catalog* (1998)	*Amaretti;* soft almond cookies in assorted fruit and nut flavors in spaghetti tin	$18
Jam	*Williams-Sonoma Catalog* (1997)	*La Trinquelinette;* organically grown fruits; 13-oz jar	$9
Olive Oil	*Viansa Catalog* (1998)	Extra-virgin oil from three olive varieties; comes in a handetched glass decanter, 23 oz	$32
Salt	*Williams-Sonoma Catalog* (1997)	*Brittany Grey Sea Salt;* 2 lb 2 oz box	$10.50
Tea	*Los Angeles Times* (1997)	*Tetley Iced Tea Mix;* 42 Servings	$0.99
Water	*Los Angeles Times* (1997)	*Niagara Pure Drinking Water;* 1.5 liter	$0.49

Furniture

Item	Source	Description	Price
Armoire	*Atlanta Constitution* (1999)	Port Royal entertainment armoire, holds 32" TV	$899
Bed	*Atlanta Constitution* (1999)	Campaign bed, made from steel with a protective coating; queen size	$699
Cabinet	*Boston Globe* (1997)	54" Utility cabinet, ready to finish	$44
Chair	*Boston Globe* (1997)	*La-Z-Boy;* 18 different elevations; 3-position foot rest	$332.99
Chair	*Los Angeles Times* (1997)	*Global Leather Task Tilter*	$99.99
Desk	*Los Angeles Times* (1997)	Recycled office furniture; 60" x 18"	$128

Item	Source	Description	Price
Ladderback Chair	*New York Times* (1998)	Walnut construction with rush seat	$195

Garden Equipment and Supplies

Item	Source	Description	Price
Arbor	*Southern Living* (1999)	Vinyl arbor	$495
Bulbs	*Fine Gardening Magazine* (1996)	100 pink/white lily-flowering tulips; delivered	$43
Garden Label	*Fine Gardening Magazine* (1996)	Flag-style markers	$20.95/100

Hotel Rates

Item	Source	Description	Price
Hotel Room	*Chicago Tribune* (1996)	*The Talbott Hotel;* includes deluxe accommodations, $20 Marshall Fields gift certificate, and holiday keepsake; available weekends	$160
Room Rate	*Southern Living* (1999)	Kiawah Island, SC	$260

Household Products

Item	Source	Description	Price
Answering Machine	*Playboy* (1998)	*Bank & Olufsen Beotalk 1100;* uses digital chip recorder to forward messages to three mailboxes	$250
Bath Towel	*The Company Store Catalog* (1998)	*Silhouette;* 100% cotton long terry loop, 27" X 54"	$24
Bath Tub Reglaze	*The State* (Columbia, SC) (1998)	Don't replace your old tub, reglaze it	$170
Battery	*Boston Globe* (1997)	*Eveready;* D-size; 2-pack	$6
Blender	*Los Angeles Times* (1997)	*Krups Power X;* 330-watt; 14 speeds	$49.99
Bowl Set	*Williams-Sonoma Catalog* (1997)	11-piece glass bowl set; tempered glass from France	$32
Breadmaker	*Los Angeles Times* (1997)	*Welbilt;* 2-lb convection bread machine	$129.99
Ceiling Fans	*Consumer Reports* (1998)	*Hunter Sojourn* is a very efficient fan with excellent air-moving ability	$190
Cell Phone	*Consumer Reports* (1998)	*Motorola StarTac* has excellent overall reception purity With contract Without contract	$199–$550 $349–$799
China	*Los Angeles Times* (1997)	5-piece place setting; festive pattern	$28.75
Cleanser	*Los Angeles Times* (1997)	*Purex All Purpose Cleaner;* 32 oz	$0.99
Cleanser	*Boston Globe* (1997)	*Ultra Downy;* 20 oz	$2
Cleanser	*Boston Globe* (1997)	*Ultra Mr. Clean;* 14 oz; Lemon Fresh	$2
Comforter	*Los Angeles Times* (1997)	*Quallowarm II;* hypoallergenic polyester fiberfill; king size	$160
Cookware	*Williams-Sonoma Catalog* (1997)	All-clad master soup pot; stainless steel; 12 qt	$230
Cookware	*Williams-Sonoma Catalog* (1997)	International clay pot; ideal for the health conscious	$14.95
Deodorizer	*Los Angeles Times* (1997)	*Arm & Hammer Pet Fresh Carpet and Room Refresher*	$0.99

Item	Source	Description	Price
Faucet	*Boston Globe* (1997)	Acrylic-handle lavatory faucet	$43
Flatware	*Williams-Sonoma Catalog* (1997)	Sierra four-piece setting; bakelite handles	$40
Food Processor	*Williams-Sonoma Catalog* (1997)	*Cuisinart;* perfect size to meet most families' day-to-day needs	$139
Glasses	*Williams-Sonoma Catalog* (1997)	Monogrammed beer mugs; 20-oz; 4 3/4" high	$40
Glue	*Boston Globe* (1997)	*Krazy Glue;* .07-oz tube	$1
Knife	*Los Angeles Times* (1997)	*J. A. Henckels;* 4-piece steak knife set	$39.99
Knife	*Williams-Sonoma Catalog* (1997)	*Schaaf;* forged 5" tomato knife	$44.95
Lamp	*Atlanta Constitution* (1999)	*Cresswell;* iron floor lamp; 60"	$69.99
Low Flush Toilets	*Consumer Reports* (1998)	*Gerber Ultra Flush* did an outstanding job of clearing waste and cleaning the bowl with each flush	$270
Luggage	*Playboy* (1998)	*Willis & Geiger;* leather chart case with multiple compartments and pockets	$470
Luggage	*Los Angeles Times* (1997)	*Samsonite 750;* jumbo hardside cart	$399.99
Mold	*Williams-Sonoma Catalog* (1997)	Butter molds; create rose- and leaf-shape pats with ease; one of each	$10
Mortar and Pestle	*Williams-Sonoma Catalog* (1997)	Process a small amount of peppercorns or spices with this porcelain tool	$9
Oriental-Style Rugs	*New York Times* (1998)	Geometrics from Pakistan, 9'1" X 12'1"	$2,458
Paint Additive	*Country Living Magazine* (1996)	*Zinsser's Blend and Glaze Decorative Painting Liquid*	$25/gal
Pillow	*Los Angeles Times* (1997)	European square 26" pillow with cotton cover	$15
Plates	*Williams-Sonoma Catalog* (1997)	Grape-leaf salad plates, green-grape-leaf design; 8" diameter, set of 4	$49
Roaster	*Los Angeles Times* (1997)	*Calphalon;* double roaster	$99.99
Silverware	*Southern Living* (1999)	Sterling, 46 piece setting	$2,999
Slumber Bag	*The Company Store Catalog* (1998)	Soft, bright and totally fun; 30 X 66	$89.99
Stairs	*Southern Living* (1999)	Victorian spiral stairs	$3,300
Tissue	*Los Angeles Times* (1997)	*Kleenex;* 150 count	$0.99
Toilet	*Boston Globe* (1997)	White, water-saver 1.6 gallon flush	$49
Towel	*Los Angeles Times* (1997)	*Fieldcrest Softique;* bath towel; 8 colors	$12
Trash Bag	*Boston Globe* (1997)	*Sure-Tuff Trash Bag;* 26-gallon size	$0.50/10

Item	Source	Description	Price
Vegetable Slicer	*Williams-Sonoma Catalog* (1997)	*Benriner;* shreds and juliennes fruits and vegetables	$45
Jewelry			
Bracelet	*Atlanta Constitution* (1999)	Garnet and diamond hugs and kisses bracelet in 18k gold over sterling	$160
Necklace	*Atlanta Constitution* (1999)	Cultured pearl necklace, 18" strand	$425
Ring	*New York Times* (1998)	*Givenchy;* sterling sliver cross band ring with cubic zirconia; woman's	$40
Watch	*Newsweek* (1998)	*Pulsar Solar;* charges with any light source, man's	$215
Watch	*Los Angeles Times* (1997)	*Kirium Chronometer;* men's	$1,695
Watch	*Playboy* (1997)	*Picasso Watch Collection;* featuring Pablo Picasso's "The Face"	$165
Meals			
Buffet	*The State* (Columbia, SC) (1998)	Daily seafood buffet, 60 items include crab legs, mussels, scallops, shrimp, fish, beef, and chicken dinner	$6.50
Dinner	*San Francisco Examiner* (1996)	*North India Restaurant;* featuring Baingan Bharta, mesquite-smoked eggplant	$7.95
Medical Products and Services			
Dental Services	*The State* (Columbia, SC) (1998)	Extractions, per tooth	$25
Nonprescription Drug	*Boston Globe* (1997)	*Pepto Bismol;* 8 oz	$4
Nonprescription Drug	*Boston Globe* (1997)	*Robitussin DM;* cough suppressant; 4 oz	$3
Motorized Vehicles, Supplies, and Services			
Automobile	*Southern Living* (1999)	1999 *Chevy Malibu*	$16,535
Automobile, New	*The State* (Columbia, SC) (1998)	1998 *Volvo S70* sedan	$26,895
Automobile, Used	*The State* (Columbia, SC) (1998)	1996 *Lincoln Mark VIII*	$20,292
Garage Door Opener	*Los Angeles Times* (1997)	*Lift Master 2000;* installed	$275
Radar Detector	*Playboy* (1997)	*SOLO Radar and Laser Detector;* cordless	$199
Tire	*Boston Globe* (1997)	*Bridgestone High Performance 65 HR 15*	$85
Other			
Bird Bath	*Smith & Hawken* (1998)	Cast-stone sundial design, 15" square with pedestal and base, including shipping	$236
Cat Food	*Boston Globe* (1997)	*Purina Cat Chow;* 20-lb bag	$7.99
Telescope	*Coldwater Creek Catalog* (1998)	*Bushnell;* compact spotting scope that weighs just over a pound; magnifies 20 to 50 times.	$225

Item	Source	Description	Price
Wreath	Smith & Hawken (1998)	Victorian Rose wreath combines rose buds, cedar tips, winter wheat and pink larkspur on a 12" grapevine base	$59

Personal Care Products

Item	Source	Description	Price
Denture Adhesive	*Boston Globe* (1997)	*Fixodent;* 1.4-oz cream	$2.50
Deodorant	*Boston Globe* (1997)	*Secret;* 1.7 oz	$1.50
Deodorant	*Boston Globe* (1997)	*Old Spice;* 2 oz	$1.79
Hand Lotion	*Boston Globe* (1997)	*Lubriderm Lotion;* relieves dry, chapped skin; 16-oz	$7
Shampoo	*Boston Globe* (1997)	*Vidal Sassoon Hair Care;* 13 oz	$2.50
Shaving Cream	*Los Angeles Times* (1997)	*Wilkinson Cream;* 11 oz	$0.99
Toothpaste	*Boston Globe* (1997)	*Crest;* gel, 6.4-oz Tartar Control	$2

Publications

Item	Source	Description	Price
Book	*Williams-Sonoma Catalog* (1997)	*Mediterranean Cooking Kitchen Library;* 108 pages; hardback	$14.95
Book	*Fortune Magazine* (1996)	*Success and the Fear of Success in Women,* by David Krueger, M.D.; paperback	$25
Book	*Times Past Catalog* (1998)	*VW Beetle: A Comprehensive Illustrated History of the World's Most Popular Car*	$24.98
Book	*Times Past Catalog* (1998)	*Roadside Memories: A Collection of Vintage Gas Station Photographs*	$29.95
Catalog	*Country Living Magazine* (1996)	*Waterworks Sink and Plumbing Fixtures Catalogue*	$8
Catalog	*Fine Gardening Magazine* (1996)	*Heirloom Old Garden Roses Catalog and Reference Guide*	$5
Magazine	*People Weekly* (1998)	Annual subscription to *People Weekly* magazine; published weekly	$103.98

Sports Equipment

Item	Source	Description	Price
Bicycle	*Playboy* (1997)	*Hotta TT;* racing bike; carbon-fiber monocoque frame	$4,000
Bicycle	*Boston Globe* (1997)	*Rand Barbie;* 12" girl's bike	$49.97
Exercise Equipment	*Boston Globe* (1997)	*Weider Jane Fonda Manual Treadmill*	$299.96
Exercise Equipment	*New York Times* (1999)	*Pro-Form* cage machine; multi work-out positions, weights not included	$299.99
Rollerblade Skates	*Boston Globe* (1997)	*Variflex*	$34.97
Soccer Ball	*Soccer Madness Catalog* (1997)	*Diadora;* signature ball; hand sewn	$69.95

Item	Source	Description	Price
Toys			
Bank	*Times Past Catalog* (1998)	*Mr. Potato Head* coin bank	$19.95
Travel and Transportation			
Airline Ticket	*Los Angeles Times* (1997)	*Southwest Airlines;* Los Angeles to Chicago	$198
Airline Ticket	*Los Angeles Times* (1997)	*Southwest Airlines;* Ontario to Salt Lake City	$69
Trip	*Boston Globe* (1997)	*Cancun Clipper Club;* includes round-trip airfare; seven nights in January	$399
Trip	*Boston Globe* (1997)	Lake Tahoe; includes round-trip airlines; 3 nights' hotel accommodations; ski lift discounts	$594
Trip	*Boston Globe* (1997)	*Radisson Inn;* Sanibel Island, Florida; package includes round-trip from Boston; 3 hotel nights; 3-day economy Alamo Rent-A-Car	$389
Trip	*Boston Globe* (1997)	Rex Saint Lucian; includes round-trip airfare, seven nights	$749

MISCELLANY 1995-1999

Expect to spend $60,000 or more for Net commerce

Online commerce "used to be an 'If you build it, they wouldn't have come,' situation because the audience was fearful of it," said Anita Bloch, president of Red Dot Interactive, San Francisco. "I don't think the technology has changed much, but the perception has changed that [the Web] is no less secure than any other credit card transactions." Medium-size sites wishing to include more secure transactions will face higher start-up costs, partially due to the need for "secure" servers such as those distributed by Netscape. Transactions like this could cost a company a median price of $21,250, according to our developers. Many sites have incorporated "shopping carts" on their transaction-based sites. This technology allows users to browse through a site and add items to their "cart" as they go. A site with a huge catalog of varied products would find this ideal, but could expect to pay a median price of $62,500 to set it up.

Advertising Age, January/February, 1997

The Cost of Bringing Up Baby

Rene Bellerive knew that bringing up a baby would cost a bundle. But $149,820? That's how much the Department of Agriculture says Bellerive and average new parents like her will spend to raise their newborns to age 17. The 1996 survey of 12,850 two-parent households and 3,395 single-parent households found that housing took the biggest chunk—33 percent, or $49,710. Food was No. 2, at $26,130; followed closely by transportation, clothing and child care. It costs about $8,300 a year, or $694 a month, to raise one child in a two-child, two-parent, middle-class family, the survey found. A generation earlier, raising a child cost one-sixth as much. Several expenses, such as child care, weren't a factor in earlier times. In 1960, the first year the department conducted the survey, raising a child cost $25,229.

San Francisco Examiner, November 25, 1997

Football Business

If the NFL ever changes some of the fundamental ways it does business, especially revenue sharing, it will impact old football stadiums. No less than 86% of the Green Bay Packers' revenue comes from shared sources—63% from the league's television contract and another 23% from ticket receipts, licensing agreements and other income that the NFL divides among its teams. Right now, business is booming. The Packers have a rainy-day fund of $21 million. Beginning last year they picked up an additional $2.5 million in annual skybox revenue by dropping an arrangement under which they placed three games a season at Milwaukee County Stadium.

Sports Illustrated, January 13, 1997

MISCELLANY 1995-1999

Same Price, More PC

Here's what you get in a $4,000 Gateway 2000 PC today compared with one in 1988:

$4,000 in 1988
—Intel 386 running at 20 megahertz
—DOS 3.3
—80-megabyte hard drive
—1 meg of RAM, expandable to 8
—3.5-inch disc drive
—5.25-inch disc drive

$4,000 in 1995
—Intel Pentium running at 133 megahertz
—Windows 95
—1.62-gigabyte hard drive
—16 megs of RAM
—3.5-inch disc drive
—6X CD-ROM drive
—28.8-kilobaud fax modem
—Surround Sound speakers with subwoofer
—Microsoft Office software

Newsweek: Computers and The Family, Fall/Winter 1995

Record-Breaking Folk Art

Robert S. Lee, Sr., bought the painting, Edward Hick's "Peaceable Kingdom" (circa 1837), at a Philadelphia auction in 1980 for $210,000, a record-breaking price for both the artist and folk art painting. While that may seem exorbitant 19 years ago, today Christie's estimates it will sell for $1.5 million to $2 million.

New York Times, January 1, 1999

Danger, Will Robinson

Can't find the perfect Christmas gift for the kid who has everything? How about the coolest little robot on the planet. R.A.D. from Toymax ($100; 800-222-9060)? It's 18 inches tall, speedy and can turn on a dime. But what makes the remote-controlled R.A.D. unique is its ability to bend over and pick things up. With articulated arms that open and close and the ability to bend over, R.A.D. can pick up a variety of objects and take them to you—it's even strong enough to carry a bulky basketball with ease.

Newsweek, November 30, 1998

HISTORICAL SNAPSHOT
2000-2004

2000

- The human genome is decoded after furious work including competition between private and government scientists
- George W. Bush wins the presidency in a disputed election after the U.S. Supreme Court rules that the Florida presidential vote will stand without a recount
- Los Alamos Scientist Dr. Wen Ho Lee is accused of spying and later found to be innocent
- The Whitewater investigation finally ends after six years; neither Bill nor Hillary Clinton is indicted
- Google, a popular search portal, indexes one billion Web sites
- *How the Grinch Stole Christmas* becomes the highest grossing film of the year, taking in over $260 million
- The Infatada starts in Israel over the breakdown of the peace talks
- Vermont approves same sex marriages
- Britain ends self rule in Northern Ireland after the IRA misses a deadline to disarm

2001

- American businessman Dennis Tito becomes the first space tourist after paying the Russian space program millions of dollars for the experience of space travel
- Oklahoma City bomber Timothy McVeigh is executed
- Terrorists hijack four airliners on September 11th; two are flown into the Twin Towers in New York City, a third into the Pentagon, while the fourth goes down 80 miles outside of Pittsburgh
- The United States invades Afghanistan in retaliation for its unwillingness to hand over Osama bin Laden, the head of al Qaeda, the group responsible for the September 11 attacks. The Taliban is deposed
- Enron, one of the world's largest energy trading firms, collapses because of massive fraud and accounting problems

- A U.S. spy plane collides with a Chinese fighter jet, igniting an international incident
- *Harry Potter and the Sorcerer's Stone* is the highest grossing movie of 2001

2002

- The euro debuts in 12 European countries, officially beginning the process of creating a common economy
- Arthur Andersen, one of the four largest accounting firms in the United States, collapses for its part in the Enron scandal
- Roadside snipers terrorize the Washington, DC area, killing 10 people before being apprehended
- The United Nations passes a unanimous motion calling on Iraq to disarm or face serious consequences
- *Spiderman* is the highest grossing movie of 2002, with over $400 million in ticket sales
- Reacting to the spate of high-profile fraud and bankruptcies at U.S. companies, Congress passes sweeping new anti-corruption laws
- Record companies continue to blame Internet music downloading for flat music sales; the industry responds by suing consumers
- North Korea admits to making nuclear bombs in defiance of signed treaties

2003

- Space shuttle Columbia explodes on reentry; seven astronauts are killed
- After Britain and the United States lose their attempt for UN resolution authorizing war against Iraq, they attack on March 19; coalition forces capture the Iraqi capital of Baghdad on April 9
- The Supreme Court upholds Affirmative Action
- Apple Music begins to sell songs for $0.99 over the Internet
- The Massachusetts Supreme Court rules that the legislature must craft a bill that gives gay couples the right to marry

- President George Bush signs a 10-year, $350 billion tax cut, the third-largest tax cut in U.S. history
- The Congressional Budget Office reveals that the deficit will be $480 billion in 2004 and projects a deficit of up to $5.8 trillion by 2013
- The European Union expands by 10 members

2004

- The Detroit Pistons beat the heavily favored Los Angeles Lakers in five games to win the National Basketball Association Championship
- American armed forces hand over partial sovereignty to Iraq; widespread violence persists throughout the country
- Kenneth Lay, the CEO of Enron, is indicted in connection with the giant energy company's collapse in 2001
- Massachusetts Senator John Kerry wins the democratic nomination and picks North Carolina Senator John Edwards as his running mate
- Abu Ghraib prison in Iraq becomes an international anti-American symbol after prisoner abuse by United States soldiers is uncovered
- Former President Ronald Reagan dies at age 93 after years of suffering from Alzheimer's disease
- Michael Moore releases the movie *Fahrenheit 9/11,* an attack on President George W. Bush, causing a political firestorm; the film becomes the highest grossing documentary of all time
- The U.S. Supreme Court rules that all prisoners of war and enemy combatants held at Guantanamo Bay, Cuba, are to be allowed access to a lawyer and the courts
- Jeopardy contestant Ken Jennings wins over a million dollars competing on the popular television game show

SELECTED INCOME 2000-2004

Job	Source	Description	Pay
Advertising Director	*New York Times* (2000)	Per day fee of Charles Stone III, Ad Director, *Budweiser's* "wassup" campaign	$18,000/day
Attorney	*The State Newspaper* Columbia, SC (2004)	Average annual income of lawyers in Myrtle Beach, South Carolina in 2002	$95,610
Bartender	*New York Times* (2000)	Bartender in fashionable restaurant in New York City	$600/night
Baseball Player	*USA Today Sports Weekly* (2004)	Salary of *Minnesota Twins* pitcher J. C. Romero	$820,000
Book Advance	*New York Times* (2004)	Fee paid in advance to John Welch, Jr., former Chairman of *General Electric,* to write a book on winning in the business world	$4 million
Carpet Cleaner	*San Francisco Chronicle* (2004)	*Stanley Steemer;* will train; weekly pay	$300 to $500
Chemist	*American Chemical Society Annual Survey* (2002)	Starting salary of a chemistry graduate with a Masters degree	$45,000
Clerical	*San Francisco Chronicle* (2004)	General office work with benefits; per hour	$20.70
Disc Jockey	*New York Times* (2000)	Nightly pay for DJ Mark Ronson	$7,500
Dog Walker	*New York Times* (2000)	Letting the dogs out for half hour walk	$20/half hr.
Endorsement Fee	*Charlotte (NC) Observer* (2004)	Amount paid to horse *Smarty Jones'* jockey Stewart Elliott to wear the logo for Infone, a telephone concierge service, on his pants and turtleneck during *Belmont Stakes* horse race	$200,000
Engineer	*Society of Fire Protection Engineers Website* (2001)	Fire protection engineers annual salary	$78,000
Firefighter	*The State Newspaper* Columbia, SC (2004)	Annual tax-free salary of firefighters in Iraq	$100,000
Focus Panelist Fee	*New York Times Magazine* (2003)	Amount paid by a pollster for less than two hours of participation in a focus panel concerning the upcoming Iowa Democratic presidential caucus	$60
Football Player	*USA Today Sports Weekly* (2004)	Annual salary of back-up quarterback Kurt Warner, *St. Louis Rams*	$9.5 million
Football Player	*The State Newspaper* Columbia, SC (2004)	Payment in 2004 to each member of the winning team in the *Super Bowl*	$68,000
Foundation Director	*New York Times* (2000)	Annual average salary for director of a nonprofit foundation in New York City	$224,000

Job	Source	Description	Pay
Garbageman	*New York Times* (2000)	City of New York, high school diploma or G.E.D. required, starting pay	$27,842
Information Manager	*Tech Target Survey* (2003)	Annual salary of storage architect	$80,836
Massage Therapist	*New York Times* (2000)	Average hourly wage of a massage therapist in a New York health club	$35
		Average hourly wage of a massage therapist working privately	$55
Medicine	*Ivy Tech State College Survey* (2000)	Annual salary of medical laboratory technician	$25,771
Medicine	*Ivy Tech State College Survey* (2000)	Top salary paid to radiology technician	$33,384
Model	*New York Times* (2000)	Hourly fee of super model Gisele Bundchen	$8,000/hr.
Movie Star	*Wall Street Journal* (2004)	Nicole Kidman's salary as lead in Sydney Pollack movie *The Interpreter*	$15 million
Movie Star	*Wall Street Journal* (2004)	Ben Affleck's salary as star of movie *Gigli*	$12.5 million
Musicians	*New York Times* (2000)	New York Philharmonic Cellist	$91,260
NFL Coach	*USA Today* (2004)	Annual salary of *Washington Redskin Football* Coach Joe Gibbs	$5 million
Nurse	*New York Times* (2001)	Dialysis RNs needed	$45/hr.
Physical Therapist	*New York Times* (2004)	Home health care; full time opening in all boroughs of New York City	
		Annual Salary of	$80,000
Physician	*New York Times* (2000)	Starting OB/GYN salary	$160,000
Physician	*American College of Physicians* (2002)	Median compensation of a doctor of internal medicine with ten years' experience	$162,872
Plumber	*Ivy Tech State College Survey* (2000)	Average hourly wage of plumber/pipefitter	$25
Policeman	*New York Times* (2000)	Average salary of first year police officer in New York City	$31,305
Police Sergeant	*New York Times* (2000)	Average salary of a New York City police sergeant	$59,299
Professor	*Association of Collegiate Schools of Planning* (2004)	Average salary of full professor at *Oklahoma State University* in 2001	$86,591
School Principal	*New York Times* (2004)	Rye City School District in Westchester County, New York, seeks talented, thoughtful and creative educator for Osborn Elementary School	
		Annual Salary	$117,000–$141,000
Software Developer	*SearchNetworking. com* (2004)	Annual salary of software developer in northwest	$87,000

Job	Source	Description	Pay
Teacher	*U. S. Department of Labor* (2004)	Median annual earnings of preschool teachers in 2002	$19,270
Teacher	*U. S. Department of Labor* (2004)	Annual salary of beginning teachers with a Bachelor's Degree in 2000	$30,719
Teacher	*New York Times* (2000)	Average wage of a New York City teacher with a Masters degree	$42,625
Tri-Athlete	*San Francisco Chronicle* (2004)	Winning prize for *The Escape from Alcatraz Triathlon;* includes 1.5 mile swim; 18 mile bike ride and 8 mile run	$5000
TV Anchor	*New York Times* (2000)	Co-Anchor, *Today Show*	$7 million
Writer	*Salary.com* (2004)	Median salary of a copywriter with an advertising agency	$34,603

CONSUMER EXPENDITURES 2000-2002

(One Person)

Expenditure Type	2000	2001	2002
Clothing	1,028	862	921
Food at Home	1,477	1,533	1,558
Food Away from Home	1,349	1,302	1,356
Auto Usage	3,732	4,012	3,890
New Auto Purchase	1,456	185	1,662
Auto Maintenance	396	419	437
Gas & Oil	682	659	646
Housing	8,189	8,371	8,619
Utilities	1,628	1,799	1,712
Telephone	607	620	624
Health Care	1,488	1,441	1,522
Personal Taxes	2,090	1,829	1,815
Tobacco	203	203	210
Public Transportation	322	273	276
Entertainment	1,026	1,097	1,193
Total Average Expenditures	25,673	24,605	26,441

INVESTMENTS 2000-2004

Investment	2000	2001	2002	2003	2004
Basic Yield, One-Year Corporate Bonds	7.16	6.61	6.09	5.64	
Short-Term Interest Rates, 4–6 Months, Prime Commercial Paper	6.19	1.78	1.28	1.05	
Basic Yield, Common Stocks, Total		1.36	1.81	1.92	
Index of Common Stocks (S&P-500)	1320.28	1148.08	879.82	1111.92	

COMMON STOCKS, CLOSING PRICE AND YIELD, FIRST BUSINESS DAY OF YEAR

(Parenthetical number is annual dividends in dollars)

	2000	2001	2002	2003	2004
Allis Chalmers	3.00	1.44	0.95	0.51	2.60
AT&T (3 for 1 split, 4/99; 1 for 5 split, 11/02)	53.38 (3.50)	18.25 (0.75)	18.70 (0.75)	27.00 (0.80)	20.87
Bank of America	48.43 (2.06)	46.75 (2.28)	62.96 (2.44)	70.68 (2.88)	79.09
Delta Airlines (2 for 1 split, 11/98)	50.00 (.10)	29.26 (.10)	29.21 (.10)	12.49 (.10)	11.99
Fortune Brands	32.25 (2.29)	30.50 (2.41)	39.64 (3.19)	47.57 (3.86)	70.80
General Electric (3 for 1 split, 5/00)	150.00 (1.29)	43.75 (1.41)	40.95 (1.51)	25.48 (1.55)	31.12
General Motors	74.62 (2.00)	52.18 (2.00)	48.64 (2.00)	38.95 (2.00)	53.64
Microsoft (2 for 1 split, 3/99; 2 for 1 split, 2/03)	116.56	43.37	67.04	53.72 (.08)	27.45
Navistar International Corp. (no dividends)	46.12	26.31	39.12	25.22	47.33
R.J. Reynolds Tobacco	18.00 (3.10)	51.00 (3.30)	57.64 (3.73)	42.37 (3.80)	57.61
United States Steel Corp. (formerly USX - U.S. Steel Group) 12/31/01	n/a	n/a	21.59	25.84	35.52
Wal-Mart (2 for 1 split, 4/99)	66.87 (.23)	53.87 (.27)	58.05 (.30)	51.60 (.36)	52.30
Warner Lambert (2/00 Warner-Lambert acquired)	30.68 (.36)	46.12 (.44)	39.90 (.52)	31.53 (.60)	35.55

STANDARD JOBS 2000-2003

Job Type	2000	2001	2002	2003
Wages Per Full-Time Employee	$28,548	$30,160	$31,001	$32,608
Private Industries, Incl. Farm Labor	$29,206	$29,606	$29,320	$30,171
Bituminous Coal Mining	$45,740	$47,839	$49,364	$49,681
Building Trades	$37,971	$38,101	$36,756	$38,655
Domestics	$13,728	$13,260	$14,404	$14,060
Farm Labor	$15,912	$16,276	$16,588	$16,702
Finance, Insurance & Real Estate	$43,001	$43,800	$43,080	$44,391
Gas, Electricity & Sanitation Workers	$47,998	$49,110	$51,792	$53,976
Manufacturing, Durable Goods	$33,043	$32,859	$32,744	$33,460
Manufacturing, Nondurable Goods	$28,917	$29,613	$29,999	$30,610
Medical/Health Services Workers	$23,972	$24,596	$26,052	$26,119
Motion Picture Services	$41,071	$42,308	$42,309	$44,001
Nonprofit Org. Workers	$16,312	$16,012	$17,091	$17,117
Passenger Transportation Workers, Local & Highway	$20,761	$22,131	$21,734	$22,297
Postal Employees	$37,596	$37,492	$38,792	$40,404
Public School Teachers	$36,972	$37,960	$38,110	$39,884
Radio Broadcast & Television Workers	$34,171	$34,206	$34,606	$34,671
Railroads	$44,876	$49,244	$44,668	$45,016
State & Local Government Workers	$33,800	$34,684	n/a	n/a
Telephone & Telegraph	$37,106	$38,195	$40,196	$41,606
Total Federal Government	$38,740	$35,568	$36,207	$37,551
Wholesale & Retail Trade Workers	$23,088	$24,336	$24,319	$25,406

FOOD BASKET 2000-2004

(NR = Not Reported)

Commodity	Year	U.S. Average	North East	North Central	South	West
Bacon, Sliced, per pound	2000	$2.75	$2.83	$2.79	$2.60	$2.93
	2001	$2.99	$3.05	$3.11	$2.75	$3.35
	2002	$3.27	$3.30	$2.97	$3.29	$3.69
	2003	$3.19	$3.13	$2.78	$3.32	$3.53
	2004	$3.15	$3.46	$2.93	$3.60	$2.81
Bananas, per pound	2000	$0.49	$0.53	$0.46	$0.44	$0.53
	2001	$0.50	$0.55	$0.47	$0.45	$0.53
	2002	$0.50	$0.54	$0.48	$0.47	$0.55
	2003	$0.52	$0.58	$0.50	$0.46	$0.59
	2004	$0.51	$0.54	$0.47	$0.45	$0.58
Bread, White Pan, per pound	2000	$0.90	$1.08	$0.90	$0.82	$0.89
	2001	$0.98	$1.03	$1.07	$0.86	$1.01
	2002	$1.00	$1.10	$1.06	$0.90	$0.98
	2003	$1.04	$1.15	$1.12	$0.95	$0.98
	2004	$0.94	$1.34	$0.72	$0.98	$0.99
Butter, Salted, Grade AA, Stick, per pound	2000	$2.42	NR	NR	$2.37	NR
	2001	$2.97	NR	$2.89	NR	NR
	2002	$3.41	NR	$2.90	$2.93	NR
	2003	$2.94	NR	$2.67	$2.35	NR
	2004	$2.84	$2.87	$2.63	$2.39	NR
Chicken, Fresh, Whole, per pound	2000	$1.05	$1.14	$1.01	$0.99	$1.13
	2001	$1.09	$1.10	$1.06	$1.03	$1.17
	2002	$1.09	$1.15	$1.09	$1.00	$1.17
	2003	$1.00	$0.98	$0.96	$0.91	$1.20
	2004	$1.06	$1.23	$1.02	$0.90	$1.23
Coffee, 100% Ground Roast, all sizes, per Pound	2000	$3.54	$3.86	$3.18	$3.51	$3.65
	2001	$3.22	$3.50	$2.75	$3.02	$3.77
	2002	$2.93	$3.19	$2.45	$2.75	$3.53
	2003	$2.99	$3.36	$2.62	$2.78	$3.35
	2004	$2.89	$3.21	$2.78	$2.75	$2.83
Crackers, Soda, Salted, per Pound	2000	$1.58	NR	NR	$1.52	
	2001	NR	NR	NR	NR	
	2002	NR	NR	NR	NR	
	2003	NR	NR	NR	NR	
	2004	NR	NR	NR	NR	
Eggs, Grade A, Large, per Dozen	2000	$0.97	$1.10	$0.88	$0.94	NR
	2001	$1.01	$0.65	$1.06	$1.17	NR
	2002	$0.97	$0.91	$1.01	$0.97	NR
	2003	$1.17	$1.41	$1.13	$1.05	NR
	2004	$1.57	$1.95	$1.45	$1.46	NR
Ground Beef, 100% beef, per Pound	2000	$1.48	NR	$1.33	$1.55	NR
	2001	$1.69	NR	$1.57	$1.76	NR
	2002	$1.73	NR	$1.63	$1.77	NR
	2003	$1.72	NR	$1.72	$1.72	NR
	2004	$2.26	NR	$2.30	$2.17	NR
Lettuce, Iceberg, per Pound	2000	$0.74	$0.85	$0.71	$0.73	$0.71
	2001	$0.73	$0.77	$0.69	$0.76	$0.69
	2002	$1.00	$1.00	$0.93	$1.03	$1.02
	2003	$0.73	$0.78	$0.76	$0.75	$0.62
	2004	$0.87	$0.90	$0.77	$0.91	$0.89

Commodity	Year	U.S. Average	North East	North Central	South	West
Margarine, Soft, Tubs, per Pound	2000	$0.82	NR	$0.86	NR	NR
	2001	$0.83	NR	$0.88	NR	NR
	2002	$0.89	NR	$0.93	$0.83	NR
	2003	$0.99	NR	$1.08	NR	NR
	2004	$0.99	NR	NR	NR	NR
Margarine, Stick, per Pound	2000	NR	NR	NR	NR	NR
	2001	NR	NR	NR	NR	NR
	2002	NR	NR	NR	NR	NR
	2003	$0.97	NR	NR	$1.00	NR
	2004	$1.03	NR	$1.05	NR	NR
Milk, Fresh, Whole, Fortified, per 1/2 Gallon	2000	NR	NR	NR	NR	NR
	2001	NR	NR	NR	NR	NR
	2002	NR	NR	NR	NR	NR
	2003	NR	NR	NR	NR	NR
	2004	NR	NR	NR	NR	NR
Potatoes, Frozen, French Fried, per Pound	2000	$1.06	NR	$1.03	$0.95	NR
	2001	$1.05	NR	$1.06	$1.01	NR
	2002	$1.13	NR	$1.18	$1.09	NR
	2003	$1.04	NR	NR	$1.03	NR
	2004	$0.98	NR	NR	$0.77	NR
Steak, T-Bone, US Choice, Bone-in, per Pound	2000	$6.59	NR	$6.66	NR	NR
	2001	$7.12	NR	NR	NR	NR
	2002	$7.55	NR	NR	NR	NR
	2003	NR	NR	NR	NR	NR
	2004	NR	NR	NR	NR	NR
Sugar, White, All Sizes, per Pound	2000	$0.43	$0.46	$0.42	$0.43	$0.44
	2001	$0.42	$0.46	$0.42	$0.40	$0.44
	2002	$0.44	$0.47	$0.43	$0.42	$0.46
	2003	$0.43	NR	$0.43	$0.41	$0.43
	2004	$0.42	NR	$0.43	$0.41	$0.44
Tuna, Light, Chunk, per Pound	2000	$1.98	NR	$2.17	$1.88	$2.02
	2001	$1.88	NR	$1.86	$1.77	$1.96
	2002	$1.97	NR	NR	$1.86	$2.04
	2003	$1.96	NR	NR	$1.69	NR
	2004	$1.82	NR	NR	$1.63	NR

SELECTED PRICES 2000-2004

Item	Source	Description	Price
Alcohol			
Beer	*Charlotte (NC) Observer* (2003)	*Budweiser,* 12-pack, bottles	$8.99
Beer	*The State Newspaper* Columbia, SC (2002)	*Coors Light;* 18 pack, 12 ounce cans	$8.99
Champagne	*San Francisco Chronicle* (2004)	*Roederer Estate Brut;* per bottle	$15.99
Wine	*Charlotte (NC) Observer* (2003)	*Gallo of Sonoma Chardonnay* 750 ml. Bottle	$9.99
Wine	*San Francisco Chronicle* (2004)	*La Crema Chardonnay;* per bottle	$11.99
Wine	*The State Newspaper* Columbia, SC (2002)	*Robert Mondavi wine;* 1.5 liter bottle	$11.49
Apparel, Children's			
Pants	*Campmor Catalog* (2004)	*Campmor Teckmor Girls Capri pants;* 100% quick dry nylon; back zippered security pocket; value $32	$14.99
Shoes	*Orlando (Fl.) Sentinel* (2004)	Boy's Michael James shoes	$17.99
Shorts	*Orlando (Fl.) Sentinel* (2004)	*Russell Athletic* reversible shorts Regular On sale	$16.00 $10.99
Shorts	*Goody's Flyer* (2004)	*Levi's* side-vent denim shorts for juniors 1–13, regular $30	$14.99
Shorts	*J C Penney Catalog* (2004)	*Big Flirt* active skorts; junior sizes; original $19.99	$9.99
Shorts	*J C Penney Catalog* (2004)	*Arizona* camper shorts; girls sizes 7–17; original $16.99	$8.49
Shorts	*J C Penney Catalog* (2004)	*Arizona* beach shorts; boys sizes 8–20; original $21.99	$9.99
Tank Tops	*J C Penney Catalog* (2004)	*Energie and One Step Up* tanks and halters; junior sizes; original $14.99	$7.49
Tee shirts	*Goody's Flyer* (2004)	*Choppers* screen tees for young men, regular $19.99	$12.99
Apparel, Men's			
Boots	*Campmor Catalog* (2004)	*Dunham* Men's Waffle Stomper Mid Leather Boots; list $110	$49.97
Boxers	*Kohl's Flyer* (2004)	Patriotic boxers and lounge pants for men; original $12–$20; sale	$6–$10
Fleece Top	*Campmor Catalog* (2004)	*Campmor Microfleece Zip-T Neck;* 100 weight micro-denier fleece with anti-piling technology; 12.5 inch zipper front opening; value $45	$19.99
Hat	*Seventeen* (2000)	Stetson style hat; black	$600

Item	Source	Description	Price
Pants	Goody's Flyer (2004)	Duck Head classic twill pants; in pleated and flat-front styles, regular $40	$20
Sandals	J C Penney Catalog (2004)	St. John's Bay men's Cayman leather sandals; regular $49.95	$24.96
Shirts	Goody's Flyer (2004)	Ivy Crew short sleeve rayon shirts, regular $29.99	$14.99
Shirts	J C Penney Catalog (2004)	Pierre Cardin boxed dress shirt and tie sets, regular $55	$27.50
Shoes	San Francisco Chronicle (2004)	Adidas Men's Pordoi II Trail Running Shoes; originally $74.99, on sale	$39.99
Shorts	Campmor Catalog (2004)	Columbia Shoshoni Falls water trunks; list $30	$19.95
Shorts	Kohl's Flyer (2004)	Dockers shorts for men; original $38, sale	$18.99
Shorts	Kohl's Flyer (2004)	Lee Dungaree shorts; twill or denim style; original $34, sale	$16.99
Tee Shirts	Kohl's Flyer (2004)	Novelty screen printed muscle and short-sleeved tees for young men; original $18, sale	$9

Apparel, Women's

Item	Source	Description	Price
Bra	Seventeen (2000)	Playtex bras; regularly $22.00 to $29.50, now	$10.97 to $13.97
Dress	Coldwater Creek Catalog (2004)	A darted, side-wrapped dress that buttons thrice at the sides and flares; USA made of imported polyester; back zip closure	$69
Dress	Seventeen (2000)	Ann Linn slip dress; bright designs	$86
Dress	Seventeen (2000)	All That Jazz floral pink dress	$54
Dress	Charlotte (NC) Observer (2004)	Donna Morgan silk leopard print halter dress	$79
Formal Dress	Seventeen (2000)	Zum Zum; sequin-embroidered organza ballgown with three frog enclosures in back; polyester	$185
Handbag	Seventeen (2000)	Jill Stuart sequined handbag	$175
Hand Bag	Seventeen (2000)	Rampage Blue Bag; available at specialty stores	$28
Handbag	Orlando (Fl.) Sentinel (2004)	St. John's Bay EZ organizers	$19.99
Hat	Coldwater Creek Catalog (2004)	Handwoven hat of red-hot rice paper; straw always springs back fresh; one size fits most	$25
Jacket	Charlotte (NC) Observer	Le Suit; short notched collar jacket with belt and pants	$99
Linen Shirt	jjill Catalog (2004)	Light weight and softly shaped. Scoop neckline. In pure linen washed for softness. Machine wash. Petite Size	$69
		Women's Size	$79
Pants	Goody's Flyer (2004)	Dockers twill capris for misses 4–18, regular $38	$21.99
Poncho	Seventeen (2000)	Tibi crocheted poncho	$165
Purse	Coldwater Creek Catalog (2004)	Straw, twisted and woven in three shades of blue; 23 inch leather-like straps; full-fabric lining and zip top	$25
Sandals	Coldwater Creek Catalog (2004)	Sling of soft, glossy leather; stretchy sides and flexible soles; 7/8 inch heel; red, blue or black	$49

Item	Source	Description	Price
Shirt	J C Penney Catalog (2004)	DCC shirts; misses sizes; original $30	$14.99
Shoes	San Francisco Chronicle (2004)	New Balance Women's 426 Running Shoes; originally $49.99, now	$39.99
Sleepwear	Kohl's Flyer (2004)	Nine and Company sleepwear separates for her; original $18, sale	$8.99
Socks	Kohl's Flyer (2004)	Novelty socks for her; original $5; sale	$2.50
Tank Tops	J C Penney Catalog (2004)	Worthington tank tops; misses sizes; original $20	$9.99
Tote Bag	Seventeen (2000)	Old Navy totes featuring the skyline of Seattle, San Francisco, New York and Chicago; each	$12.50
Underwear	Orlando (Fl.) Sentinel (2004)	Delicate lace boyshorts Regular Two for	 $12 $18

Appliances

Item	Source	Description	Price
Air Conditioner	Chicago Tribune (2004)	Sears window air conditioner	$99.99
Blender	New York Times Sunday Magazine (2003)	Oster's beehive blender	$80.00
Cordless Drill	Washington Post (2004)	DeWalt 12-volt Cordless Drill and Driver Kit	$129
Dishwasher	Asheville (NC) Times Citizen (2003)	Maytag JetClean II fits more dishes in a single load	$429.00
Electrical Cord	Washington Post (2004)	100' Doit Heavy-Duty Outdoor Extension Cord	$19.99
Fireplace Gas Logs	The Roanoke (Va.) Times (2004)	Appalachian Stove; 30" log set, manual control, 16,000 to 31,500 BTU	$399
Gas Grill	The State Newspaper Columbia, SC (2004)	The Big Easy, 36,000 BTU gas grill and smoker with side burner	$259
Gas Grill	Sears Flyer (2004)	Kenmore Gas Grill; wide body Delta Flame II cooking system; 580 sq. inches total cooking area	$134.99
Grill	Chicago Tribune (2003)	George Foreman 14-in. round grill; nonstick grilling surface, adjustable temperature	$29.99
Heater	New York Times (2004)	Toastmaster; fully automatic compact heater; thermostatically controlled	$19.95
Iron	Kohl's Flyer (2004)	Black & Decker Steam Xpress Iron; regular $34.99, sale	$17.49
Lantern	Asheville (NC) Times Citizen (2003)	8-In-1 Multi-function lantern; includes 5.5" black and white TV, AM/FM and weather band radio, fluorescent lantern, thermometer, flashlight, audible siren, compass and auto AC/DC adapter. Regularly $60	$39.99
Microwave	Chicago Tribune (2003)	Kenmore microwave; 1.4 cu. ft., 1100-watt. 6 Quick Touch sensor cooking keys	$64.99
Refrigerator	Charlotte (NC) Observer (2004)	Whirlpool No Frost Refrigerator; 17.6 cubic feet; upfront temperature control knobs	$397
Stereo System	Belk Flyer (2004)	Dolby Executive Stereo System; top loading CD player; black lit LCD readout; built-in AM/FM tuner; full function remote; desk or wall mount; regular $70	$49.99

Item	Source	Description	Price
Television	*Sears Flyer* (2004)	*Samsung* 42 inch wide-screen tabletop projection HDTV monitor; 30 watt audio system	$999.99
Walkman	*Men's Fitness* (2004)	*Sony Hi-MD Walkman;* downloads tunes 10 *times* faster than previous model	$200
Wine Cooler	*San Francisco Chronicle* (2004)	*Urbina* design wine storage cooler; electronic peltier cooling technology; 18 bottle size	$269.95

Baby Products

Diapers	*Charlotte Observer* (2004)	*Pampers Easy Ups* training pants; 40 per package	$14.99
Play Suits	*J C Penney Catalog* (2004)	*Baby Okie-Dokie* summer sets; original $12.99	$6.99
Sleep Outfit	*The Roanoke (Va.) Times* (2004)	*Little Me Stretchies;* each	$7.97

Business Equipment and Services

Computer Line	*Chicago Tribune* (2004)	*SBC Yahoo! DSL line;* up to two computers; price reduced when ordered on line; per month	$26.95
Computer	*Office Depot Flyer* (2004)	*Presario Desktop Computer Bundle with Intel Celeron Processor;* 2.7GHz	$417.49
Handheld Computer	*New York Times* (2003)	*Palm One Handheld;* 8M8 memory	$99.99
Phone	*Martinsville (Va.) Bulletin* (2004)	*Telos* new camera flip phone; Audiovox 8900	$99
Printer	*Office Depot Flyer* (2004)	*HP Flatbed All-In-One Printer*	$178.22
Rotary Tool Kit	*Home Depot Flyer* (2004)	*Dremel Multipro Rotary Toolkit*	$59.97
Scanner	*Office Depot Flyer* (2004)	*Canon CanoScan Flatbed Scanner*	$49.00
Software	*New York Times* (2003)	*Microsoft Office* standard edition *2003;* full version	$349.99
Telephone	*Martinsville (Va.) Bulletin* (2004)	*Motorola T731 color screen phone*	$79.95
Tool Set	*Sears Flyer* (2004)	*Craftsman* 137-piece mechanic's tool set; 82 sockets, 8 wrenches; includes case	$99.99
Want Ad	*San Francisco Chronicle* (2004)	Chronicle of available jobs; five days	$12
Wireless Telephone	*The Roanoke (Va.) Times* (2004)	*Verizon Wireless* color flip-phone *Audiovox CDM-8600;* retail $109.99, less $30 mail-in rebate and $40 instant savings	$39.99

Collectibles

Movie Memorabilia	*Associated Press* (2004)	Ray gun from *"Super Mario Brothers"* film	$75
Painting	*Art & Antiques Magazine* (2002)	Karl Schmidt-Rottluff's 1912 painting *"Die Lesende"* of a woman reading a book	$3.9 million
Painting	*Art & Antiques Magazine* (2002)	Norman Rockwell painting of *"Rosie the Riveter,"* which appeared on the May 29, 1943 cover of *The Saturday Evening Post*	$4.9 million
Sculpture	*Art & Antiques Magazine* (2002)	Carved Mezcala stone figure from Mexico dating from Preclassic period (circa 300–100 B.C.)	$71,700

Item	Source	Description	Price
Television Memorabilia (2004)	*Associated Press* (2004)	Set of yellow school lockers from the television series *"Dawson's Creek"*	$100
Used Automobile	*USA Today* (2004)	1970 *Pontiac GTO Convertible,* sold in auction	$27,000
Wine	*San Francisco Chronicle* (2004)	Case of 1999 *Pillar Rock;* sold in auction in 2001	$11,500
Education			
College Tuition	*Website* (2004)	*St. John's College* annual tuition	$30,570
Private High School	*Wall Street Journal* (2004)	*Hotchkiss School,* Lakeville, Conn.; school is building a new music and arts center Annual Tuition	$24,500
Private High School	*Wall Street Journal* (2004)	*St. Paul's School,* Concord, New Hampshire Annual Tuition	$31,125
Summer Camp	*New York Times* (2004)	*Camp Caribou* in Winslow, Maine; full seven-week program; per child	$7,150
Entertainment			
Boxing	*San Francisco Chronicle* (2004)	Professional live boxing, featuring Marco Angel Perez vs. Sergio Macias; Longshoreman's Hall, San Francisco Ringside Main Floor Balcony	 $75 $50 $25
Concert	*Chicago Tribune* (2004)	An evening with *Lyle Lovett;* Chicago Pavilion per ticket	$60
Concert	*Chicago Tribune* (2004)	*The Marriage of Figaro;* Chicago Symphony Orchestra	$20 to $40
Concert	*Chicago Tribune* (2004)	Piano legends: *Dave Brubeck Quartet; Marian McPartland Trio; Ramsey Lewis Trio;* Chicago Pavilion	$40
Concert Ticket	*Direct Mail Solicitation* (2003)	*Handel's Messiah,* David Tang, conducting Oratorio Singers of Charlotte, First United Methodist Church	$20.00
Concert Tickets	*Rolling Stone* (2004)	*Eric Clapton* in concert; Madison Square Garden, per person	$45 to $12
Concert Tickets	*Rolling Stone* (2004)	*Madonna* in concert; the Forum, Los Angeles, California, per person	$58.50 to $354.50
Dance Lessons	*Times-News* (Hendersonville, NC) (2004)	*Dance Lovers USA,* teaching basic dance; Foxtrot, Swing, Waltz, Rumba and Cha-Cha; 12-week course, per person	$91.25
Expo	*San Francisco Chronicle* (2004)	*Adult Entertainment Expo* in Las Vegas, Nevada; per person	$40
Movie	*Chicago Tribune* (2004)	*Harry Potter and the Prisoner of Azkaban;* Davis Theatre	$7.50
Music Concert Ticket	*Times-News* (Hendersonville, NC) (2004)	*Flatrock Music Festival* starring Ralph Stanley and the Clinch Mountain Boys, Snake Oil Medicine Show and Ras Alan and The Lions Advance adult weekend pass	 $60
Pool	*Charlotte (NC) Observer* (2004)	*Intex* Easy Set Pool; 10 feet by 30 feet; includes pool, filter pump and set-up video	$49.99
Theater	*San Francisco Chronicle* (2004)	*Buddy, the Buddy Holly Story;* the hit rock 'n roll musical; all seats	$35

Item	Source	Description	Price
Entertainment, Home			
Cable Television	Martinsville (Va.) Bulletin (2004)	Adelphia Cable Service; Get up to 140 channels; per month	$24.95
Camcorder	Chicago Tribune (2003)	Samsung mini-DV digital camcorder, Sears low price 2.5-in. color LCD, built-in digital still camera	$399.99
Camera	Sears Flyer (2003)	Canon Rebel SLR digital camera; 6.3 mega-pixels	$999.99
Camera	Men's Fitness (2004)	Olympus Stylus 410; 4 mega-pixel digital camera can shoot short videos with sound	$800
Disposable Camera	Publix Flyer (2004)	Kodak Max HQ Camera; 27 exposure film	$7.99
DVD	New York Times (2004)	The Lord of the Rings; DVD	$21.85
DVD Deck	Sears Flyer (2003)	Sony DVD/VCR dual desk	$179.99
Electronic Game System	Charlotte (NC) Observer (2004)	Game Boy Advance SP System; features backlit screen	$99.99
Electronic Game Software	Charlotte (NC) Observer (2004)	Harry Potter and the Prisoner of Azkaban on Gameboy Advance	$29.99
Exercise Equipment	Chicago Tribune (2003)	ProForm 545S treadmill, 2.50 HP treadmill-duty, 19x50-in. walking belt.	$599.99
Exercise Equipment	Wall Street Journal (2004)	Nautilus TreadClimber TC5000; Combines treadmill, stair-stepper or elliptical machine	$2,199
Exercise Equipment	Wall Street Journal (2004)	Precor EFX 5.23 elliptical trainer; keeps track of customized exercise routines for two different users	$3,999
i Tunes Album	USA Today (2004)	Dark Side of the Moon by Pink Floyd	$16.99
Music	Charlotte (NC) Observer (2004)	Music DVDs; Bob Dylan MTV Unplugged	$10.99
Radio/CD Player	Direct Mail Letter (2003)	Bose Wave Radio/CD; remarkably clear, natural sound	$499
Television Combination Set	Sears Flyer (2003)	Toshiba 24-inch TV/DVD/VCR combination	$499.99
Television	Sears Flyer (2003)	Pioneer 50-inch PureVision plasma HDTV monitor	$7,999
Video Camera	Sears Flyer (2003)	Fisher Digital CameraCorder; combines 3.0 mega-pixel digital camera with digital camcorder	$899.99
Water Filtration System	Kohl's Flyer (2004)	Pur Ultimate, faucet mount; regular $39.99, sale	$19.99
Food Products			
Apples	Charlotte (NC) Observer (2003)	Granny Smith Apples per pound	$.99
Bananas	Charlotte (NC) Observer (2003)	Chiquita Bananas; Healthy Favorite per pound	$.39
Beer	Publix Flyer (2004)	Heineken beer, 12-pack	$11.49
Bottled Water	Publix Flyer (2004)	Deer Park Spring Water; 25-pack, 26.9 oz. bottles	$4.99
Bread	Publix Flyer (2004)	Publix Bakery sourdough French bread; baked fresh throughout the day; 16 oz. Loaf	$1.99

Item	Source	Description	Price
Bread	*The State Newspaper* Columbia, SC (2002)	French Bread; each	$.99
Broth	*Charlotte (NC) Observer* (2003)	*Swanson Beef Broth* 14.5 oz. Can	$.59
Carrots	*The State Newspaper* Columbia, SC (2004)	Organic carrots; 5 pound bag	$2.99
Cereal	*The State Newspaper* Columbia, SC (2004)	*Nature's Patch organic Heritage O's cereal*	2 for $5
Chicken	*The State Newspaper* Columbia, SC (2002)	Split chicken breasts; bonus pack, per pound	$1.29
Coffee	*San Francisco Chronicle* (2004)	*Folgers Classic Roast;* 39 ounce can	$4.99
Coffee	*Bi-Lo Flyer* (2003)	*Maxwell House coffee;* 39 ounce can	$2.99
Coffee Cake	*Publix Flyer* (2004)	*Publix Bakery cinnamon nut coffee cake,* 11 oz. Size	$3.39
Cooking Oil	*Publix Flyer* (2004)	*Mazola Oil;* assorted varieties; 48 oz. bottle	$2.49
Deli Meat	*The State Newspaper* Columbia, SC (2002)	*Sahlen's Deli Ham;* per pound	$4.99
Fish	*The State Newspaper* Columbia, SC (2004)	*Wild Alaskan Sockeye Salmon Fillets;* per pound	$7.99
Frozen Food	*San Francisco Chronicle* (2004)	*Banquet Crock-Pot Classics;* 41.5 ounce package	$4.99
Fruit	*The State Newspaper* Columbia, SC (2002)	*Athena Cantaloupes,* each	$1.79
Ham	*Charlotte (NC) Observer* (2003)	*Armour Hostess Canned Ham* 4 pounds	$7.99
Juice	*Charlotte (NC) Observer* (2003)	*Ocean Spray Cranberry Juice* 64 oz. Bottle	$2.69
Pecan	*Charlotte (NC) Observer* (2003)	Shelled pecans in 1 lb. ziplock bag	$4.99
Shrimp	*Charlotte (NC) Observer* (2003)	*Kroger* 100 count shrimp ring, sold frozen	$19.99
Soft Drink	*Charlotte (NC) Observer* (2004)	*Pepsi 12-pack;* 12 oz. cans; two for	$5
Sour Cream	*Charlotte (NC) Observer* (2003)	*Kroger Sour Cream* 16 oz. container	$1.19

Item	Source	Description	Price
Sour Cream	*San Francisco Chronicle* (2004)	*Daisy Sour Cream;* 16 ounce cup	$1.39
Sour Cream	*Publix Flyer* (2004)	*Publix Sour Cream;* 16 oz. cup; comes in regular, fat free and light	$1.09
Steak	*Publix Flyer* (2004)	Beef ribeye steak; bone in, per pound	$7.99
Steak	*Bi-Lo Flyer* (2003)	T-bone bonus pack, per pound	$4.99
Vegetables	*The State Newspaper* Columbia, SC (2002)	Zucchini squash; per pound	$.69
Yogurt	*The State Newspaper* Columbia, SC (2004)	*Storyfield Farm* organic yogurt; low fat blueberry	4 for $3

Furniture

Item	Source	Description	Price
Bed	*New York Times* (2004)	*Campaign* bed; queen-sized hand forged iron	$999
Bookcase	*San Francisco Chronicle* (2004)	*Akio* two-shelf bookcase	$119
Chair	*San Francisco Chronicle* (2004)	*La-Z-Boy Pinnacle Recliner;* leather finesse; two chairs	$999
Chair	*Charlotte (NC) Observer* (2004)	*Revista Magazine Chair;* suggested retail price $1,067, now	$640
Chandelier	*Home Depot Flyer* (2004)	*Easy Street* 6-light chandelier; champagne marbled glass shades	$199
Computer Desk	*Havertys Flyer* (2004)	*Oak Canyon* computer desk with return; oak solids and veneers	$999
Queen Bed	*Havertys Flyer* (2004)	*Broyhill's Generation X;* built of hardwood solids and walnut veneers; was $499, now	$399
Recliner	*Havertys Flyer* (2004)	*Lane Home Furnishings* Montana mission-style high-leg recliner	$799
Reclining Sofa	*Havertys Flyer* (2004)	*Lane Home Furnishings* Markham collection; sofa covered with burgundy leather upholstery; pillow top arms and seating; padded back and outside arms; was $1199, now	$1099
Rug	*J C Penney Catalog* (2004)	The Bigger Accent Rug; *J C Penney Home Collection;* 22 x 36 inches; regular $25	$12.50
Sofa	*San Francisco Chronicle* (2004)	*Gatsby* Italian leather sofa	$899
Table & 2 Sidechairs	*Havertys Flyer* (2004)	*Havertys' British Inn* collection; 42 in. round drop-leaf table with two side chairs; was $349, now	$299

Garden Equipment and Supplies

Item	Source	Description	Price
Birdhouses	*Michaels Arts & Crafts Store Flyer* (2003)	Ready to finish wood birdhouses; each	$3.99
Fencing	*The State Newspaper* Columbia, SC (2002)	Chain-link fencing; 48" x 50' roll	$39.90
Flowers	*Jackson & Perkins 2004 Catalog*	10 giant begonias, tubers a full 1/2" larger than store-bought begonias produce huge 6" - 9" blooms on 24" stalks	$29.95

Item	Source	Description	Price
Lawnmower	*Home Depot Flyer* (2004)	*Murray* 6.5 hp, 22 inch high wheel mower; *Briggs & Stratton* engine	$219
Mulch	*Martinsville (Va.) Bulletin* (2004)	*Rubberific* mulch; buy 10 bags and get one free; covers 250 square feet	$273
Patio Furniture	*San Francisco Chronicle* (2004)	Teak grade A bow bench	$375
Plants	*Martinsville (Va.) Bulletin* (2004)	Geraniums; 6 1/2 inch pot	$5.99
Plants	*Martinsville (Va.) Bulletin* (2004)	Hosta; excellent in all landscaping	$3.59
Roses	*Jackson & Perkins 2004 Catalog*	Hybrid tea rose plant, powerful fragrance, light-filled color, petal-laden flowers	$17.95 ea.
Storage Building	*The State Newspaper* Columbia, SC (2002)	Gable style lap building; 10 x 16 x 10	$1,249
Torch	*Charlotte (NC) Observer* (2004)	Copper torch for outdoor living; regular $59, now	$19.99
Weedwacker	*Sears Flyer* (2004)	*Craftsman* 13-inch electric Weedwacker line trimmer with extra line	$29.99
Hotel Rates			
Room Rate	*New York Times* (2004)	*Henryetta Inn and Dome* near Okemah, Oklahoma, birthplace of *Woody Guthrie,* per night	$81
Room Rate	*Chicago Tribune* (2004)	*Cincinnati Hotel;* weekend getaway package at the most celebrated four-star luxury hotel in Ohio; one night, luxury queen	$175
Room Rate	*New York Times* (2004)	*Delta Bow Valley Hotel,* Calgary, Alberta, Canada; per night	$137
Household Products			
Bathroom Tissue	*The State Newspaper* Columbia, SC (2002)	*Charmin Bath Tissue,* 24 double rolls	$9.99
Batteries	*Charlotte (NC) Observer* (2003)	*Duracell* 8-pack "AA" batteries	$3.99
Beach Towel	*Belk Flyer* (2004)	*Home Accents* beach towels; 34 x 64 inches, regular $20	$10
Brushes	*A. C. Moore Flyer* (2002)	*Surprize Ink Game Books;* regular $4.99, now	$3.99
Charcoal	*Publix Flyer* (2004)	*Kingsford Original Charcoal Briquets;* 20 pound bag	$5.99
Charcoal	*Bi-Lo Flyer* (2003)	*Southern Home Instant Light Charcoal;* 8 pound bag	$3.29
Crystal Figurines	*Belk Flyer* (2004)	*Godinger* crystal animal figurines; regular $40	$19.99
Cutlery Set	*Kohl's Flyer* (2004)	Basic essentials 22-piece cutlery and tool set; regular $19.99, sale	$9.99
Dish Detergent	*Publix Flyer* (2004)	*Dawn Dish Liquid;* assorted varieties; 20.2 to 25-oz. bottle or pretreater power grease dissolver, 12.8 oz. bottle	$2.19
Drill	*New York Times* (2004)	*Stanley* model H131 drill; designed for comfort and balance	$19.95

Item	Source	Description	Price
Glasses	*New York Times Sunday Magazine* (2003)	Essential stemware; *Deborah Ehrlich's* glasses	$200.00 a pair
Glue	*A. C. Moore Flyer* (2002)	Super tacky glue; four ounce size	$.79
Glue Sticks	*A. C. Moore Flyer* (2002)	Hot metal glue sticks; four inch, each	$.04
Luggage	*Belk Flyer* (2004)	*Ciao Roll-A-Ton* rolling duffel; black/blue or black/red; regular $50	$19.99
Pepper Grinder	*Chicago Tribune* (2004)	*Michael Graves* design pepper mill	$12.99
Pillow	*Belk Flyer* (2004)	*Carpenter* comfort pillows; sensafoam pillow with 100% Visco elastic "memory" foam; regular $80	$39.99
Punch	*A. C. Moore Flyer* (2002)	*Fiskars* border punch	$10
Sheets	*Seventeen* (2000)	*Springs Registry* cotton sheet set; reduced	$29.99
Tape Measure	*Home Depot Flyer* (2004)	*MaxSteel* 25' and 12' tape measure combination	$19.99
Trees	*Michaels Arts & Crafts Store Flyer* (2003)	Six foot silk Ficas trees; each	$19.99

Jewelry

Item	Source	Description	Price
Bracelet	*Seventeen* (2000)	*Tarina Tarantino* coil bracelet	$80
Cross	*Parisian Gift Guide* (2003)	*Faith Collection;* bronze cross	$28
Earrings	*Coldwater Creek Catalog* (2004)	Two-tone matching teardrops in sterling silver and stabilized turquoise; 1 1/8 inches long; in posts or clips	$34
Necklace	*Seventeen* (2000)	Freshwater cultured pearl necklace	$105
Necklace	*J C Penney Catalog* (2004)	Reversible *Omega and Slide;* one necklace, four great looks; 10k gold; regular $249.99	$99.99
Necklace	*Kohl's Flyer* (2004)	10k gold diamond accent initial pendant; regular $100, sale	$34.99
Necklace	*Chicago Tribune* (2004)	*Ono* pendant in 18k gold with diamonds	$2,495
Pin	*Coldwater Creek Catalog* (2004)	Matte goldtone pin measures 2 3/8 inches across cast metal; USA-made	$24
Sports Watch	*Campmor Catalog* (2004)	*Timex Kids Tattoo You* analog watch; water resistant to 30 meters; center of face features a rotating disc design; elastic fabric straps; list $19.95	$5.97
Watch	*Parisian Gift Guide* (2003)	*Fossil* watch; ladies' stainless steel with adjustable bangle band; silver dial	$55
Watch	*Men's Fitness* (2004)	*Tommy Hilfiger;* multi-dial	$125

Meals

Item	Source	Description	Price
Buffet	*Martinsville (Va.) Bulletin* (2004)	*Aloha Wok;* Mother's Day buffet, Collinsville, Virginia Adult Child	 $6.95 $3.95
Oyster Roast	*The State Newspaper* Columbia, SC (2004)	*Ducks Unlimited Annual Oyster Roast and Program;* per person	$25
Pizza	*Atlanta Constitution* (2002)	*Little Caesars;* one large pizza; one topping	$12.95

Item	Source	Description	Price
Steak	*Menu* (2003)	Prime Rib at *Morton's Steak House,* San Francisco	$48

Medical Products and Services

Item	Source	Description	Price
Eye Surgery	*Direct Mail* (2004)	*Lasik* laser vision Correction–Imagine life without glasses, per eye	$599
Eye Surgery	*Charlotte (NC) Observer* (2004)	Custom *Lasik* New Wave Front Zyoptix Technology; per eye, starting at	$299.00
Fertilization	*New York Times* (2003)	In vitro fertilization with donor eggs	$35,000
Medical Care	*Martinsville (Va.) Bulletin* (2004)	Professional Eye Exam	$43
Pain Relief Tables	*Charlotte (NC) Observer* (2003)	*Tylenol Extra Strength Caplets* Bottle of 50	$4.87
Pain Reliever	*CVS Pharmacy Flyer* (2004)	*Aleve;* all day relief; 100 count	$5.99
Pain Reliever	*Bi-Lo Flyer* (2003)	*Advil;* 50 count bottle	$3.99
Pain Reliever	*CVS Pharmacy Flyer* (2004)	*Afrin No Drip Nasal Spray;* per bottle	$4.99
Plastic Surgery	*New York Times* (2004)	Female breast reduction, 2003 average	$5,351
Plastic Surgery	*New York Times* (2004)	Liposuction, 2003 average	$2,578
Plastic Surgery	*New York Times* (2004)	Hair transplant, 2003 average	$3.084
Skin Care	*CVS Pharmacy Flyer* (2004)	*Scarguard;* Improves the appearance of old and new scars	$29.99
Vitamins	*Bi-Lo Flyer* (2003)	*Centrum Vitamins;* 130 count bottle	$7.99
Vitamins	*CVS Pharmacy Flyer* (2004)	*One A Day Vitamins;* 100 count	$5.99

Motorized Vehicles, Supplies, and Services

Item	Source	Description	Price
Airplane	*Wall Street Journal* (2003)	2004 *Hawker 400XP,* cruising speed 529 mph, passenger capacity 7, 1/16th share (50 hrs)	$387,500
Automobile	*Wall Street Journal* (2003)	2003 *Jaguar X-Type 2.5;* manual with single-disc CD player; permanent all-wheel drive; $1,999 due at signing. Security deposit waived.	$279/mo 36-mo. Lease
Automobile	*Orlando (Fl.) Sentinel* (2004)	2004 *Honda Element EX,* 4 x 4 Total cost 48-month lease	$19,990 $249 per month
Automobile	*Orlando (Fl.) Sentinel* (2004)	2005 *Chevy Equinox;* automatic transition, towing package, power driver's seat Regular Sale price	$24,175 $18,995
Automobile	*Orlando (Fl.) Sentinel* (2004)	2004 *Ford F-250* super duty *Harley-Davidson* edition; V-10 engine Base price Fully equipped	$35,930 $48,805
Automobile	*San Francisco Chronicle* (2004)	2004 *Jaguar XK;* 294-horsepower engine; $3,999 due at signing; lease for 24 months	$899 per month

Item	Source	Description	Price
Automobile	Asheville (NC) Citizen–Times (2004)	Isuzu 2004 Ascender; 4 wheel drive; seven passenger	$26,990
Automobile	The State Newspaper Columbia, SC (2004)	Isuzu Rodeo 2004 Model	$16,995
Automobile	Men's Fitness (2004)	Nissan 350Z Roadster	$33,850
Automobile	The State Newspaper Columbia, SC (2004)	Toyota Prius hybrid automobile; advertised to get 50 to 66 miles per gallon	$20,810
Gasoline	Times-News (Hendersonville, NC) (2004)	Price of one gallon of regular gasoline	$1.78
Navigation	USA Today (2003)	Delphi; always know where you are headed with the portable in-car GPS navigation system	$999.99
Parking Cost	Times-News (Hendersonville, NC) (2004)	Cost to park in a metered space in downtown Hendersonville, N.C. per hour	$.25
Radio	The Roanoke (Va.) Times (2004)	Sirius Satellite Radio equipment and service unit Installation in car per month	$100 $30 $30 $12.95
Tires	Charlotte (NC) Observer (2004)	Tires and wheels; four 225/60R 16; 16x7 MBM 747	$449
Used Automobile	San Francisco Chronicle (2004)	1997 Chevrolet Suburban; fully loaded 4x4	$15,500
Used Automobile	San Francisco Chronicle (2004)	2000 Jeep Wrangler, 70,000 miles; air conditioning; tow package	$12,500
Used Motorcycle	San Francisco Chronicle (2004)	1997 Harley Davidson Custom Softtail; 12,000 miles	$17,500

Other

Item	Source	Description	Price
Carpet Cleaning	Direct Mail (2003)	Stanley Steemer Carpet Cleaner; 6 areas cleaned and protected	$224
Dog Food	The State Newspaper Columbia, SC (2004)	One Earth natural adult dry dog food; 17.6 pounds	$18.99
Figurines	Parisian Gift Guide (2003)	A Breed Apart; dog and cat figurines, each	$34
Kitchen Counters	San Francisco Chronicle (2004)	Granite kitchen counters; custom made to your specs; 100 colors to choose from; as low as	$1,849
Puppies	San Francisco Chronicle (2004)	Chihuahua pups; 11 weeks; first shots Each	$350
Puppies	San Francisco Chronicle (2004)	English Bulldog puppies; male or female Each	$1,200
Trophies (2004)	The State Newspaper Columbia, SC (2004)	Value of Vince Lombardi Trophy, given to the winner of the football Super Bowl game	$2000

Item	Source	Description	Price
Water and Sewer Rates	*Times-News* (Hendersonville, NC) (2004)	Cost of monthly use of water and sewer service in Hendersonville County, N.C.; based on a 5,000 gallon a month usage rate	
		Inside city of Hendersonville	$29.80
		Outside city	$47.10

Personal Care Products

Item	Source	Description	Price
Bathroom Tissue	*CVS Pharmacy Flyer* (2004)	*Scott Tissue;* 12 pack	$5.49
Body Gems	*Seventeen* (2000)	*Natural Desire's Girlstuff Birthstone Body Gems in Topaz;* put star and moon-shaped glitter bits on shoulders, cheeks or hair	$9.99
Deodorant	*San Francisco Chronicle* (2004)	*Right Guard Extreme Deodorant;* 2 ounce package	$3.49
Feminine Pads	*San Francisco Chronicle* (2004)	*Kotex Maxi Pads;* 14 count	$2.50
Lipstick	*Seventeen* (2000)	*Maybelline's East Mystique Brush Blush in Pink Tangerine;* each	$4.70
Shampoo	*CVS Pharmacy Flyer* (2004)	*Pantene Hair Care;* 5.1 ounce size	$2.99
Shampoo	*Bi-Lo Flyer* (2003)	*Pantene Shampoo;* 13.5 ounce size, two for	$7
Sunglasses	*Campmor Catalog* (2004)	*Julbo Sherpa;* blocks 100% UVA, Band C light; leather side shields; black nylon frame with amber polycarbonate lens; includes hard case	$29.99
Toothpaste	*Charlotte (NC) Observer* (2003)	*Colgate Simply White Toothpaste,* mint, 4 oz. tube	$3.49
Whitestrips	*CVS Pharmacy Flyer* (2004)	*Crest Whitestrips;* dental whitening system, 56 count	$24.99

Publications

Item	Source	Description	Price
Book	*Rock & Ice* (2001)	*Fearless on Everest, the Quest of Sandy Irvine;* 320 pages; paperback	$18.95
Book	*Charlotte (NC) Observer* (2004)	Lisa Scottoline's mystery novel *Killer Smile*	$18.00
Book	*Seventeen* (2000)	*Playing Botticelli* by Liza Nelson; G. P. Putnam & Sons	$23.95
DVD	*San Francisco Chronicle* (2004)	*Speaking to the Big Dogs: A Boardroom Survival Kit;* features comments of 17 top corporate executives	$239
Magazine	*USA Today* (2003)	*USA Today Sports Weekly.* Puts you inside the game with total baseball and pro football coverage for 52 weeks	$39.95
Magazine	*Men's Fitness* (2004)	12 issues of *Men's Fitness* magazine	$12

Real Estate

Item	Source	Description	Price
Co-Op	*New York Times* (2004)	Washington Heights, New York City, 2-bedroom, 1-bath 1,050 square foot co-op in a pre-war tutor-style building	$435,000
House	*Asheville (NC) Citizen-Times* (2004)	Newly constructed home in Weaverville, N.C.; three bedrooms, two baths, open floor plan	$179,900
House	*Chicago Tribune* (2004)	Five bedroom, 5.5 bath custom home in all brick and limestone; 6,200 square feet; 1844 North Burling, Chicago	$3,725,000

Item	Source	Description	Price
House	*Chicago Tribune* (2004)	Four bedroom, 3 bath home with open floor plan; 1917 West Grale, Chicago	$799,000
House	*New York Times* (2004)	Stonington, Connecticut house perched above the water on Mason's Island; Georgian-style home	$1.8 million
Loft	*Chicago Tribune* (2004)	South Loop location, granite in bathrooms, open layout	$294,999
Lot	*Wall Street Journal* (2004)	Homesite #8 at Sunwest Ranch on The Madison River, Ennis, Montana; private community of 55 homesites on 2000 acres	$335,000
Residential Water Use Rates	*The Roanoke (Va.) Times* (2004)	Henry County, Virginia, based on a monthly minimum of 6,000 gallons; per month	$24
Studio Apartment	*New York Times* (2001)	46th St. & 9th Ave. studio, furnished, with separate kitchen, 3rd floor walk-up	$1300/ month
Townhouse	*Chicago Tribune* (2004)	RP Fox development; 3 bedroom, 2 bath, chef's kitchen, granite countertops; designer appliances; 5115 North Damen Ave., Chicago	$419,000

Sewing Equipment and Supplies

Item	Source	Description	Price
Beads	*Michaels Arts & Crafts Store Flyer* (2003)	*Halcraft Bead Boxes;* each	$4.88
Ribbon	*Michaels Arts & Crafts Store Flyer* (2003)	*Tulle Circles Ribbon;* 100 yard roll	$6.88
Scissors	*Michaels Arts & Crafts Store Flyer* (2003)	*Provo Craft Decorative Edge Scissors;* three pair	$2

Sports Equipment

Item	Source	Description	Price
Basketball Goal	*San Francisco Chronicle* (2004)	*Lifetime World Class Acrylic Portable Basketball System;* on sale	$124.50
Binocular Set	*Belk Flyer* (2004)	*Meade;* binocular gift set; regular $50	$29.99
Boot	*Rock & Ice* (2001)	*Salomon Super Mountain 9;* features memofit lacing system; contragrip soles for traction; regularly $375, sale	$219
Compass	*Campmor Catalog* (2004)	*Lensatic Compass;* has sighting mechanics and cover; weighs 2 1/2 ounces	$7.99
Daypack	*Campmor Catalog* (2004)	*Eddie Bauer Ocean Daypack;* zippered bottom hideaway pocket; organizer compartment with key clip; detachable cell phone pocket; weighs 2 pounds; list $34.99	$14.97
Fishing Reel	*San Francisco Chronicle* (2004)	*Shimano Spheros Spinning Reel*	$99.99
Glove	*Men's Fitness* (2004)	*Wilson A900 3X glove;* triple welted constructed	$99
Shotgun	*San Francisco Chronicle* (2004)	*Legacy Escort;* 12-gauge fast pump action	$189.50
Sleeping Bag	*Campmor Catalog* (2004)	*Cocoon Ripstop Nylon/Fleece Kidbag;* 71" x 30"; temperature rating 58 degrees F; navy blue; stuff sack included; list $65	$29.96
Tent	*San Francisco Chronicle* (2004)	*Coleman 13' x 11' Hex Dome Tent*	$74.99

Item	Source	Description	Price
Tent	*Rock & Ice* (2001)	*TNF Perigrine two-person tent;* two doors; ample ventilation; seven pounds	$239
Tennis Racquet	*San Francisco Chronicle* (2004)	*Prince,* More Technology tennis racquets; on sale	$79.99
Travel Chair	*Campmor Catalog* (2004)	*Travel Chair Company* deluxe hi-back chair; armrests with drink holder; matching storage/carrying bag with shoulder strap and drawstring closure; regular $39.99	$29.97
Treadmill	*Sears Flyer* (2004)	*Proform 350S* treadmill with hand weights; 2 hp; 16" x 45" treadbelt; was $499.99, now	$399.88

Tobacco Products

Item	Source	Description	Price
Cigarettes	*Charlotte (NC) Observer* (2003)	*Marlboro Cigarettes;* Flip Top Box Carton	$21.99

Toys

Item	Source	Description	Price
Car	*Parisian Gift Guide* (2003)	*Tyco's Canned Heat Cars;* runs on batteries	$24.95
Chalk	*A. C. Moore Flyer* (2002)	*Crayola* 20 piece sidewalk chalk	$.99
Game	*New York Times* (2004)	*Radica 20Q;* can name the object you are thinking about	$9.99
Kit	*Parisian Gift Guide* (2003)	*Supermag Genius* 50-piece construction kit; Building is a breeze with the magnetic spheres	$21.95
Scooter	*Seventeen* (2000)	*Razor Scooter;* up to 40 minutes of continuous use; speeds up to 10 mph	$79.97
Slide	*Charlotte (NC) Observer* (2004)	*Wham-O Heat Wave Slip 'N Slide;* 22 feet long with *Drench-O-Matic* overhead hydrant system; as seen on TV	$19.99
Wiffle Ball	*Men's Fitness* (2004)	Wiffle ball and bat; much fun for little cash	$3.69

Travel and Transportation

Item	Source	Description	Price
Airline Fare	*Wall Street Journal* (2004)	New York to Miami flight; U. S. Airways Business Class Leisure Class	$667 $257
Airline Fare	*The State Newspaper* Columbia, SC (2004)	Cost of a roundtrip airline ticket on Independence Air from Columbia, SC to Newark, NJ	$178.30
Airline Fare	*New York Times* (2004)	Continental; cost of an airline ticket from New York City to Tulsa, Oklahoma	$450
Cruise	*San Francisco Chronicle* (2004)	*Norwegian Spirit Cruise* to Alaska; six nights	$658
Getaway	*San Francisco Chronicle* (2004)	Costa Rica Eight-Day Package; *Villa Sol Hotel;* package includes airfare, hotel and transfers; from San Francisco	$749
Mountain Climb	*San Francisco Chronicle* (2004)	Mount Kilimanjaro in Tanzania; 15-day tour of Mount Kilimanjaro, visits to wildlife sanctuaries and game drive Per person, land-only	$2,799
Tour	*San Francisco Chronicle* (2004)	Four-day trip to Santa Fe, New Mexico sponsored by *Oakland Museum* of California; includes private tours; per person, double occupancy and meals	$1,725

MISCELLANY 2000-2004

Permissions on Digital Media Drive Scholars to Lawbooks

When some 20,000 first-year American medical students reported to their schools last summer, they received a free 20-minute multimedia collage of music, text and short video clips from television doctor dramas, past and present, burned onto a CD-ROM.

"The patients you meet in the coming years may have doubts about you because of the doctors they see on prime-time television," the introduction reads. "The aim of this presentation is to explore why that is, and suggest what you can do about it."

But the CD was perhaps more of an education for its developer, Joseph Turow, a professor at the University of Pennsylvania's Annenberg School for Communication.

"It's crazy," Professor Turow said of the labyrinth of permissions, waivers and fees he navigated to get the roughly three minutes of video clips included on the CD, which was paid for by a grant from the Robert Wood Foundation. The process took months, Professor Turow said, and cost about $17,000 in fees and royalties paid to the various studios and guilds for the use of the clips. The film used ranged from, for example, a 1961 episode of "Ben Casey" to a more recent scene from "ER."

This Friday, Professor Turow and other experts will meet at a conference sponsored by the Annenberg School to debate how digital media fits into the concept of "fair use"—a murky safe harbor in copyright law that allows scholars and researchers limited use of protected materials for educational or commentary purposes.

The New York Times, June 14, 2004

Fed Expected to Raise Rate

The price of borrowing money is going up.

The Federal Reserve Board today begins a two-day meeting that will lead to the first increase in its key interest rate since May 2000.

The Fed has cut its key interest rate 13 times since then, propping up an economy choked by recession, terrorism, corporate scandals and war.

On Wednesday, it is expected to raise the target for its federal funds rate to 1.25 percent, up a quarter of a percentage point.

The move is a shot across the bow at inflation. The nation's inflation rate jumped 3.2 percent in the first three months of this year, significantly more than the 1 percent increase in the first quarter of 2003.

The federal funds interest rate is what banks pay when they make short-term loans to each other. It is a benchmark used directly or indirectly to set other interest rates.

The State, June 29, 2004 (Columbia, SC)

The Ultimate Luxury Item Is Now Made in China

Zhongshan, China—Among the carp ponds, duck farms and moldering plywood huts that have long lined the bank of a Pearl River estuary here, a most incongruous newcomer has appeared: a long, towering shed for building very large luxury yachts, a product that has no market in mainland China.

Lion dancers bobbed and weaved as strings of firecrackers sizzled and boomed on July 3 at the official opening of the yacht factory—an emblem of how China is shifting its sights upmarket. Having mastered the manufacture of many inexpensive goods for mass consumption here and abroad, the country is getting into luxury goods, the kinds coveted by the world's most demanding buyers. China's competitive advantage is that it is doing this at lower cost.

Increasingly expensive brands of shoes, clothing and furniture are being made in this country, mostly for domestic consumption but sometimes for export. BMW has begun assembling some of its latest models in China for sale here, and Mercedes and Cadillac are preparing to do the same.

With yachts, though, China is braving a market where it has little recent experience or demand at home.

The New York Times, July 13, 2004

MISCELLANY 2000-2004

Meet Me Online

When running a small business, you don't always have the space to hold meetings with staff and clients. And renting a hotel conference room or meeting site for a day or two can cost a small fortune. So, how do you get your team together to work on projects? Consider Web collaboration.

What is Web collaboration? It's a way for teams to work on a project together—online and off—while eliminating travel costs and paper. Online collaboration works pretty much like this:

One person signs up and sets up a virtual meeting room. That person then informs the rest of the group where to meet online. It's a bit like a personal chat room, where members can communicate and work securely.

In addition to Microsoft's NetMeeting (www.microsoft.com), which is free, there are several services that let you collaborate with far-flung clients and employees. Punch Networks' WebGroups (www.punchnetworks.com), for example, lets you automatically and securely work on important projects. WebGroups also features document management tools such as version tracking, audit trails, and automatic change notification.

Black Enterprise, July 2001

The Pajama Game: Not Just for Bedtime

What do you do when pulling on a sweat suit for a trip to the corner Starbucks is too much effort? How about just keeping on your pj's? Everyone from carpooling moms to yoga-bodied Hollywood celebs is taking the concept of dressing down a few notches lower by turning their pajamas into outerwear. Classic men's cuts in fun colors and prints, often more than $100 a pair, are being worn in pieces: bottoms only with a T-shirt, a camisole or a swimsuit; or just the long-sleeved top over a sexy T-shirt as a jacket for the evening. "My daughter at college in Santa Barbara wants to sell pj bottoms out of her dorm," says Dory Forge, designer of the spirited pj line Lounge Act. "Kids there are living in them."

Time, March 3, 2003

Closing The Pay Gap

In 1999, the weekly pay of American women with full-time jobs was 76.5% of what men got, up from 61% in 1974. That's a big gain. But progress has stalled since the mid-1990s. A study by Cornell University economists Francine D. Blau and Lawrence M. Kahn, to be published in the fall 2000 issue of the Journal of Economic Perspectives, argues that the stall is only temporary, and that the gap should narrow in the years ahead.

The primary reason for the shrinking pay gap in the 1980s and early 1990s was a rise in the full-time work experience of women, Blau and Kahn say. At the outset of the 1980s, men had an average of 7.5 more years of work experience than women. That's important, because work experience increases both productivity and pay. By the end of the 1980s, the experience disparity had fallen to 4.6 years.

Women also caught up because more of them went into professional and managerial jobs, and because of a decline in union membership, which hurt the wages of men more than those of women. Although the government scaled back anti-discrimination enforcement in this period, Blau and Kahn believe it's likely that discrimination still decreased in those years. Employers, they argue, began to realize that women were more committed to staying on the job than they had been in the past. Also, they say, changes in social attitudes made gender bias "increasingly unpalatable."

BusinessWeek, August 21-28, 2000

MISCELLANY 2000-2004

For Many Low-Income Workers, High Gasoline Prices Take a Toll

Tampa, Fla.—Denise Quenneville drives 30 miles each way to her $7-an-hour job as a cashier at a Krispy Kreme doughnut shop here. With this year's surge in gas prices, she's paying $23 every couple of days to fill up her car, up from about $19 a year ago.

"A $4 difference is a lot," says Ms. Quenneville, who now is pouring about a quarter of her take-home pay into the tank of her blue 2000 Oldsmobile Alero. To keep her car on the road, the 19-year-old has run up a balance of about $500 on her gas-company credit card.

The cost of gas, currently averaging $1.89 a gallon nationwide, is creating a new burden for everyone who drives a car. But the toll is particularly heavy among low-income workers, for whom higher gas prices amount to a palpable pay cut.

The average U.S. price of a gallon of regular unleaded gasoline topped $2 this spring for the first time. That's cheaper in inflation-adjusted terms than during the price peaks of the early 1980s, and prices have begun to fall over the past month. But at $1.89, the average price still is up 40 cents, or 27%, from a year ago.

At that level, assuming a car travels 15,000 miles a year, which is typical, and gets 21 miles per gallon, approximately the national average, its driver will spend $1,350 annually on gas, or $286 more than last year. Families that need two or three cars to get around, as many do, could be spending $3,000 or $4,000 a year on gas.

The Wall Street Journal, July 12, 2004

Pricing Trends
1900-2000*

This new *Pricing Trends* section, has been created because of suggestions from the readership of the previous edition. To fully understand the practical economy in which we live, it is often necessary to study the cost of buying common objects, such as an automobile or a vacuum cleaner, over long periods of time. While it is helpful to know the cost of a man's dress shirt in any given year, which is the essence of *The Value of a Dollar,* it is truly insightful to view that same knowledge over a 100-year panorama. New products, innovations, competition, new materials and fads can all impact what we are willing to pay for something we desire. *Trends* help unravel the mystery of price over time.

With this knowledge we can understand the relative value—and financial strain—placed on owning a baseball glove in 1910 versus 1990. *Trends* provide insight into what percentage of the family's income is required to buy a candy bar, or a dozen eggs, or a lovely summer dress throughout the last 100-plus years. During the last several years students, librarians, social studies teachers, historians, journalists and friends have asked for the relative meaning of an individual price as it changes over time. In hundreds of conversations, the suggestion has been made that this edition of *The Value of a Dollar* include a way to look at pricing from a historical perspective. Thus, *Trends* was created, thanks to you.

Each section has been arranged within topics such as *Travel & Entertainment,* where theater tickets can be found; *Outdoors,* which includes the cost of a Harley-Davidson motorcycle or a shotgun; and even *Want Ads,* which features a variety of jobs from coal miner to professional baseball player. Hopefully, each of these miniature pricing profiles can breathe new fascination into ordinary data.

At the same time, each pricing chart includes an index to current pricing. The indexing of these long pricing trends provides us another way of seeing how much each item would cost in today's terms. While it is essential to know what people were willing to pay for a certain item in a given year, it is also important to understand how those prices change over a long period of time. In this way, we are provided a window into the minds of consumers we have never met. Is it more or less expensive to attend professional football's premier event, The Super Bowl, today versus 10 years ago? How does the actual cost and relative cost of a Broadway play in 1920 compare to 1980? When were price changes over time the most dramatic and what influenced those costs? Historians and economists use this type of information to study the value of money and how it relates to human events. Their purpose often is to comprehend how values influence economic and cultural events—not just on the national level, but also the individual level. For all of us, this data allows us to anticipate events that may occur in the future, especially as it relates to how we spend our money.

By employing indexes based upon consumer expenditures, economists and historians can look back and compare monetary trends over periods of time. If we know that a comic book was worth $0.10 in 1939, we can compare the price to the Consumer Price Index and determine what it was worth in the dollar value of the year being compared. If one compares the value of the comic book in 2002 dollars, the 1939 comic book would cost approximately $1.29. The United States government did not focus on actual inflation rates and indexing consumer pricing until the twentieth century. During World War I, prices were rising rapidly, especially in shipbuilding centers

---

* The range of years will vary slightly from item to item, based on available data.

in the United States. It was during this period that the federal government started compiling an index essential for calculating cost-of-living adjustments in wages. Most of this work began around 1917, but the government developed indexes with estimates back to 1913. This information is compiled today by the U.S. Department of Labor under the Bureau of Labor Statistics.

When developing the charts for *The Value of a Dollar,* information was not available prior to 1913. To include the material prior to 1913, an alternative index was utilized based upon John J. McCusker's principle of determining the value of money prior to 1913. Charts in this book expressing values prior to 1913 should be viewed as approximations when compared to the year 2000 dollars. Charts that begin at or after 1913 used the Consumer Price Index and provide a closer comparison of actual dollars in 2002. During the development of this book, government indexes for the year 2003 were unavailable.

The use of indexing in this way gives each of us a deeper knowledge of economics. For example, the often discussed inflation index is a product of thousands of issues and items. Using individual trend data, we no longer look only at an average cost of change over time, but a specific change. This additional information then tells us that while most items experience price increases decade to decade, the relative price of many is less than it was 100 years ago. Thanks to improved agricultural techniques, many products—such as a dozen eggs—have a lower relative cost today and thus have a lower impact on the family budget.

As noted before, pricing is an inexact science. In any given year the same item—a woman's dress, for example—might be sold at widely varying prices in the same store, based on the season, the availability, the retailer's need for cash, or the consumer's demand. View this same item over 100 years and the variables—from workmanship to material quality, innovations in manufacture, changing fashion or the type of store selling the item—all have an impact. For that reason every effort has been made to appropriately price items. For example, the Broadway ticket price shows the best seat available, and indicates such in the description. The automobile pricing is the lowest list price over time, before dozens of extras are added in. Most of the prices came from catalogs and advertisements, meticulously traced back for 100 years. Some were provided by the companies themselves, recognizing that products, like a lawn mower, bear little resemblance to the whirling push device first employed decades ago. No mention is made of whether yesterday's sun was really hotter or the weeds more stubborn.

AROUND THE HOUSE

Atlantic Monthly

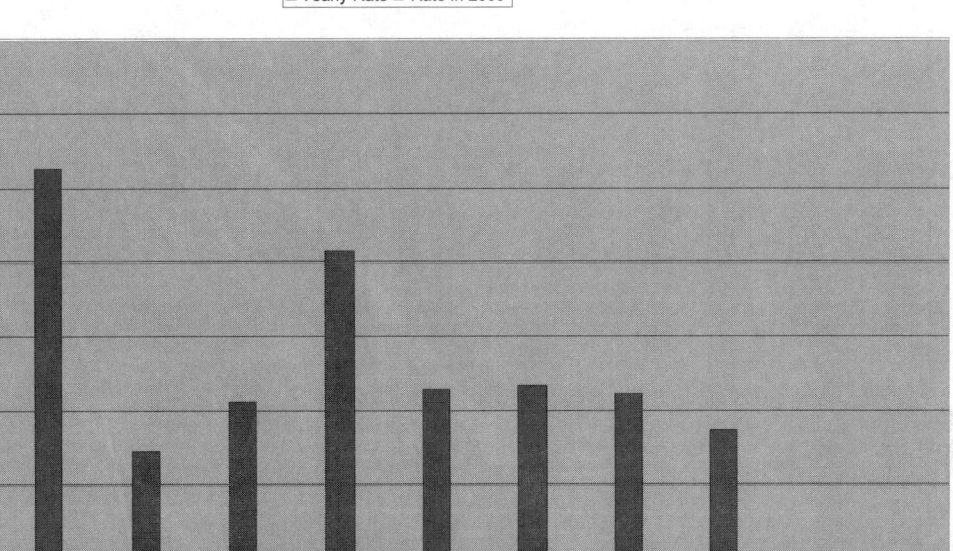

	1900	1910	1920	1930	1940	1950	1960	1970	1980	1990	2000
Yearly Rate	$4.00	$4.00	$4.00	$4.00	$5.00	$6.00	$7.50	$9.50	$18.00	$14.95	$17.94
Dollar Value in 2000	$81.63	$72.73	$34.48	$41.24	$61.73	$42.86	$43.60	$42.22	$37.58	$19.70	$17.94

AROUND THE HOUSE

Bath Towel

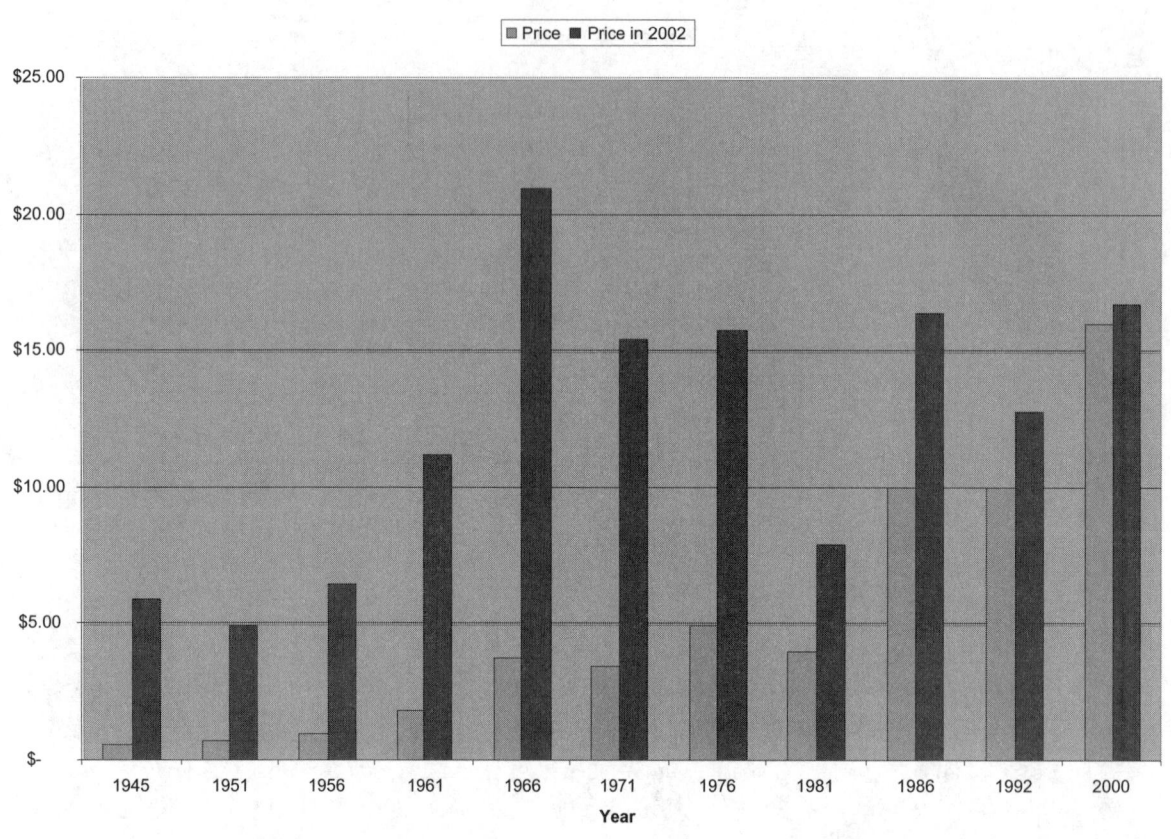

	1945	1951	1956	1961	1966	1971	1976	1981	1986	1992	2000
Price	$0.59	$0.72	$0.98	$1.86	$3.77	$3.48	$4.99	$3.99	$9.99	$10.00	$15.99
Dollar Value in 2002	$5.90	$4.98	$6.48	$11.19	$20.93	$15.46	$15.78	$7.90	$16.40	$12.82	$16.71

AROUND THE HOUSE

Chicago Daily Tribune

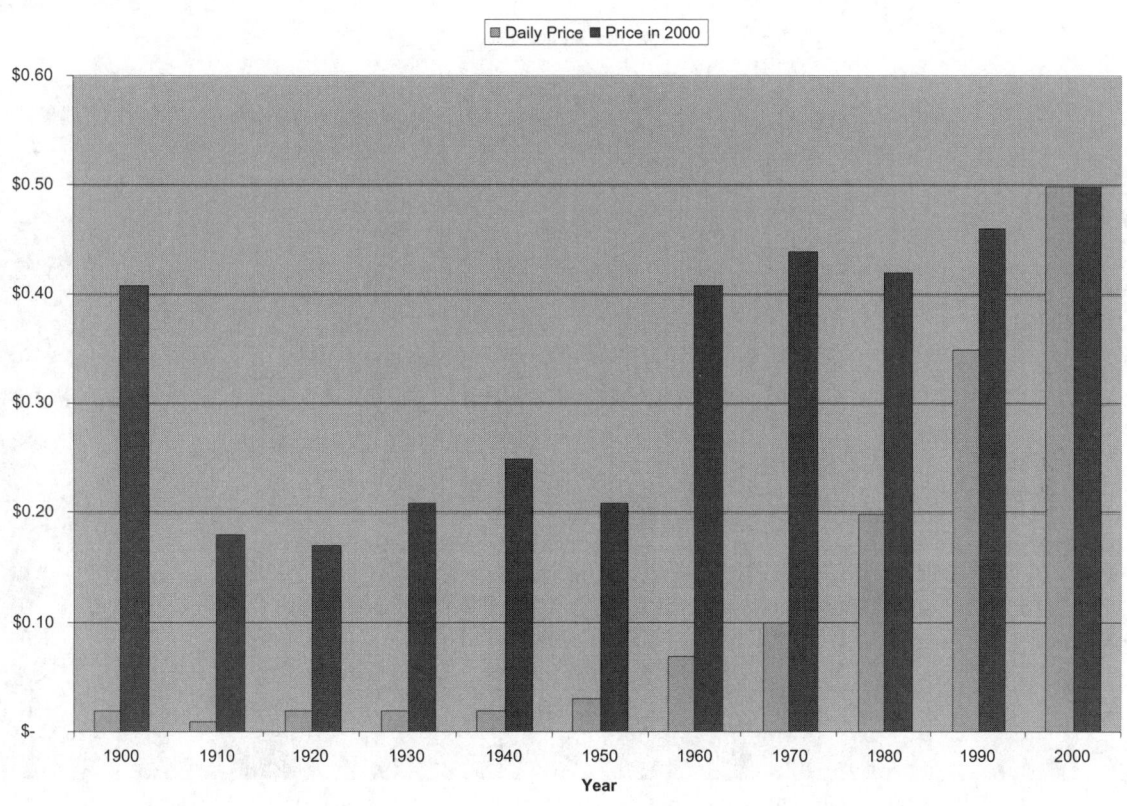

	1900	1910	1920	1930	1940	1950	1960	1970	1980	1990	2000
Daily Price	$0.02	$0.01	$0.02	$0.02	$0.02	$0.03	$0.07	$0.10	$0.20	$0.35	$0.50
Dollar Value in 2000	$0.41	$0.18	$0.17	$0.21	$0.25	$0.21	$0.41	$0.44	$0.42	$0.46	$0.50

AROUND THE HOUSE

Electric Clothes Iron

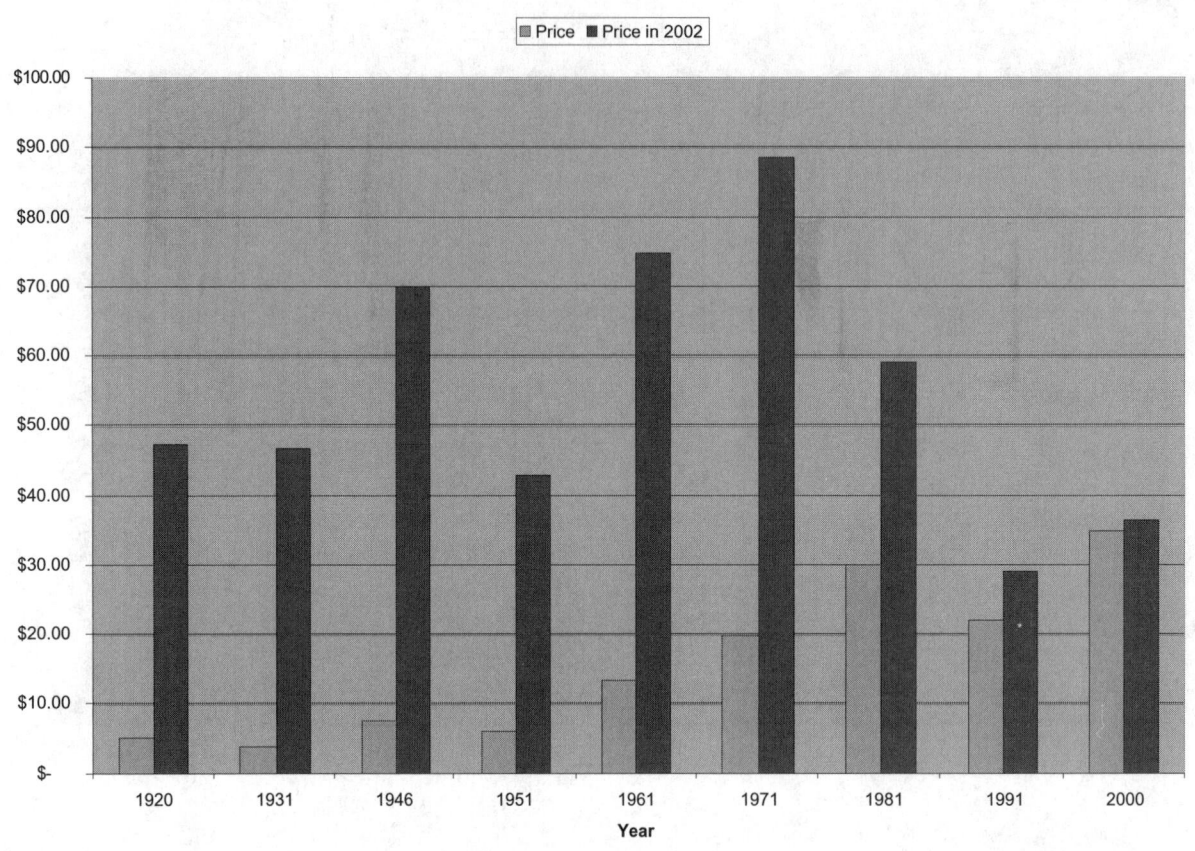

	1920	**1931**	**1946**	**1951**	**1961**	**1971**	**1981**	**1991**	**2000**
Price	$5.25	$3.95	$7.60	$6.19	$13.50	$19.95	$29.99	$21.95	$35.00
Dollar Value in 2002	$47.22	$46.75	$70.00	$42.83	$74.56	$88.62	$59.35	$28.99	$36.56

AROUND THE HOUSE

Electric Washing Machine

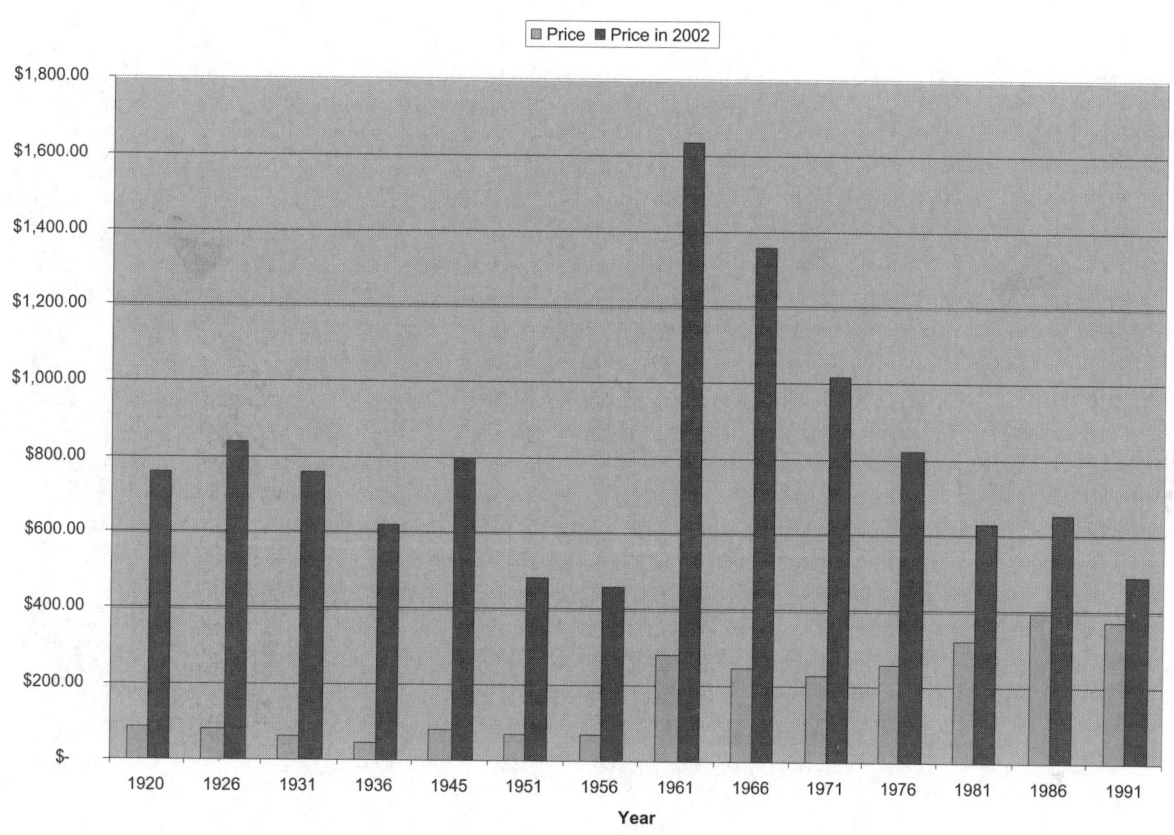

	1920	1926	1931	1936	1945	1951	1956	1961	1966	1971	1976	1981	1986	1991
Price	$84.75	$82.50	$64.50	$47.95	$79.95	$69.95	$69.95	$279.95	$244.95	$229.95	$259.95	$319.95	$399.99	$374.99
Dollar Value in 2002	$762	$839	$763	$621	$799	$484	$463	$1,634	$1,360	$1,021	$822	$633	$656	$495

AROUND THE HOUSE

Eureka Vacuum Cleaner

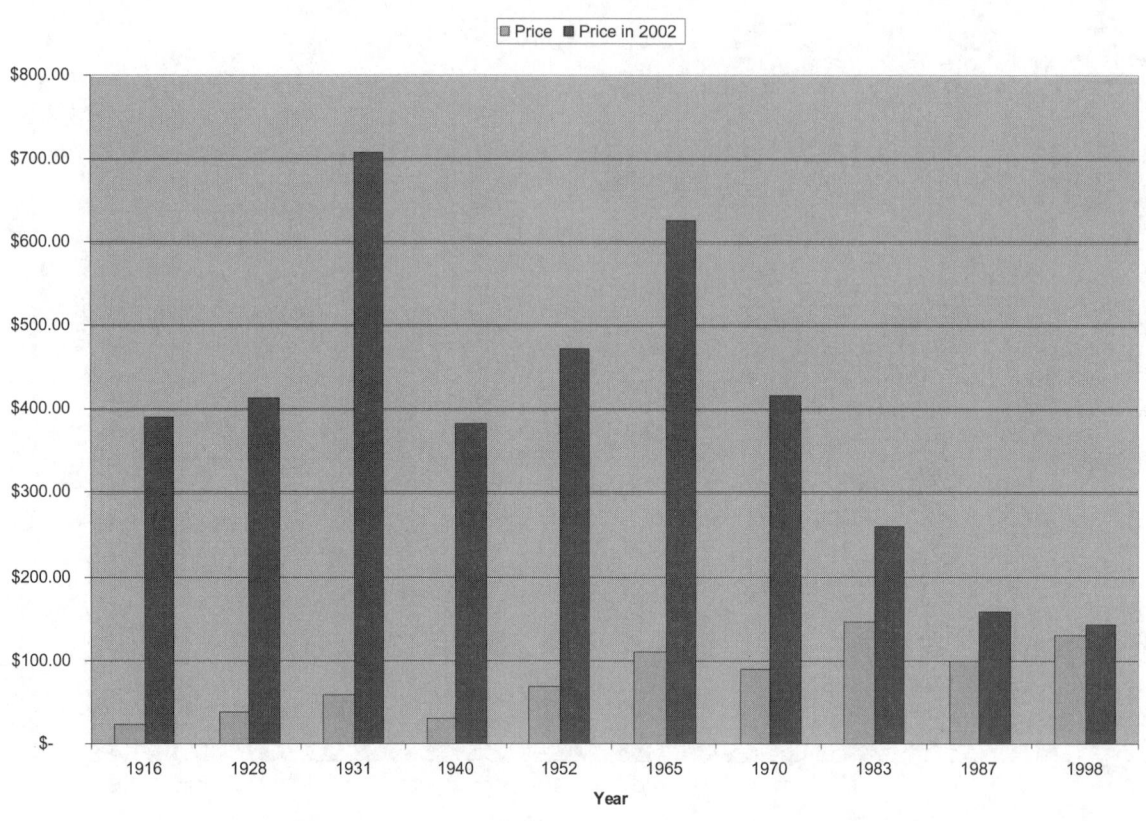

	1916	1928	1931	1940	1952	1965	1970	1983	1987	1998
Price	$23.75	$39.50	$59.95	$29.95	$69.95	$109.95	$89.95	$145.00	$99.97	$129.99
Dollar Value in 2002	$392	$416	$710	$385	$475	$628	$417	$262	$159	$143

AROUND THE HOUSE

Flashlight Battery

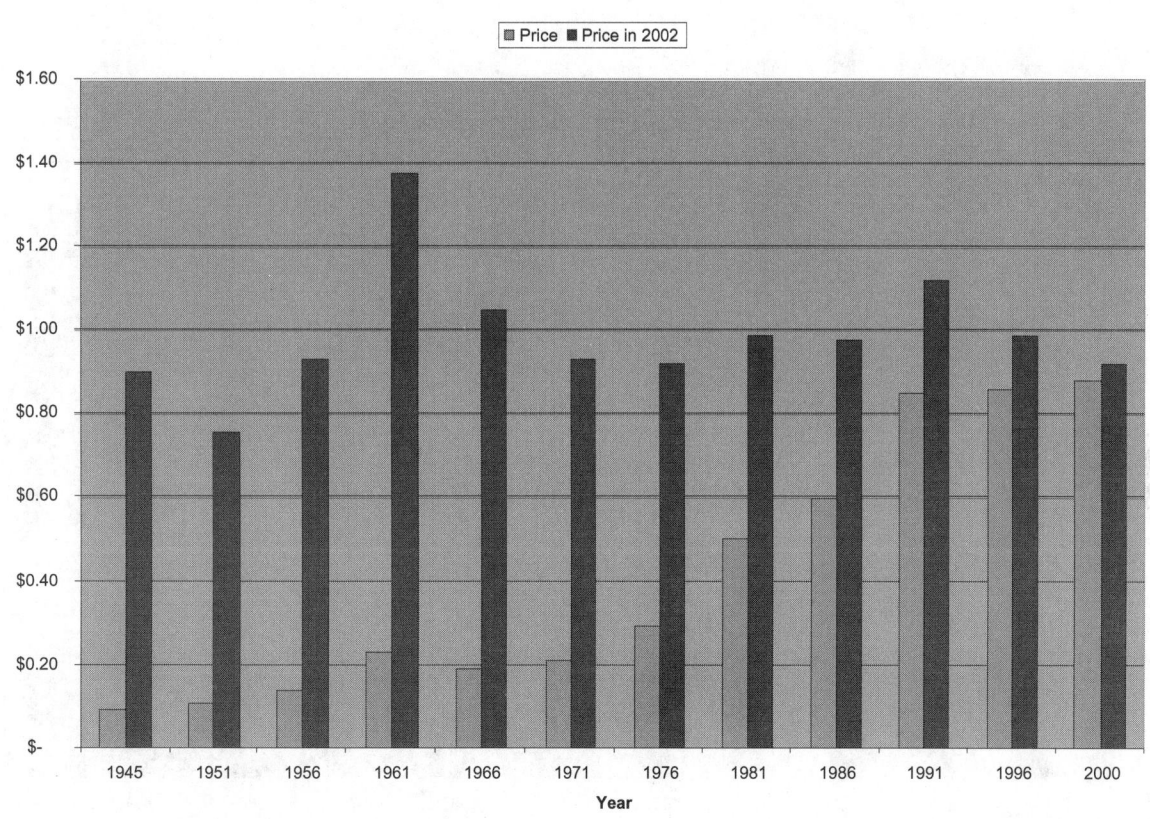

	1945	1951	1956	1961	1966	1971	1976	1981	1986	1991	1996	2000
Price	$0.09	$0.11	$0.14	$0.23	$0.19	$0.21	$0.29	$0.50	$0.60	$0.85	$0.86	$0.88
Dollar Value in 2002	$0.90	$0.76	$0.93	$1.38	$1.05	$0.93	$0.92	$0.99	$0.98	$1.12	$0.99	$0.92

AROUND THE HOUSE

Ladies Home Journal

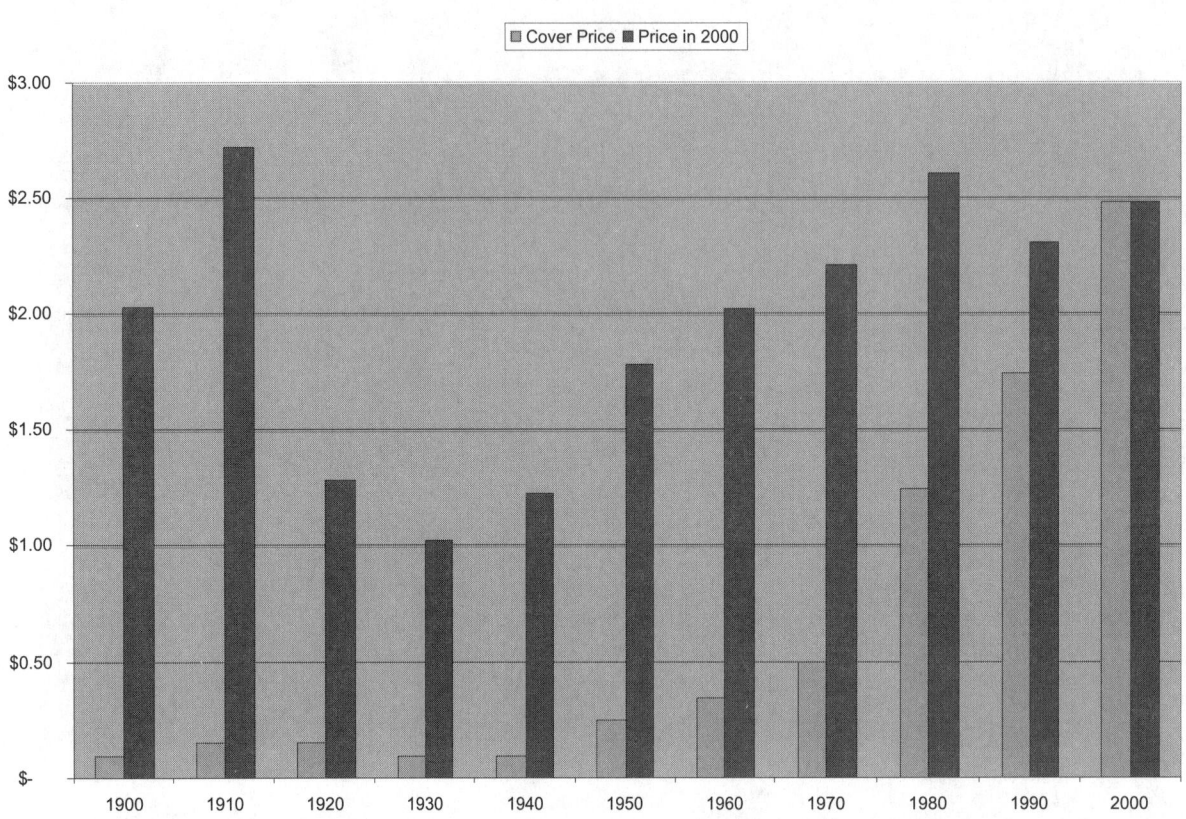

	1900	1910	1920	1930	1940	1950	1960	1970	1980	1990	2000
Cover Price	$0.10	$0.15	$0.15	$0.10	$0.10	$0.25	$0.35	$0.50	$1.25	$1.75	$2.49
Dollar Value in 2000	$2.04	$2.73	$1.29	$1.03	$1.23	$1.79	$2.03	$2.22	$2.61	$2.31	$2.49

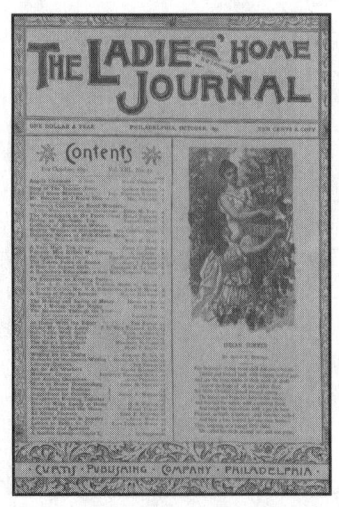

AROUND THE HOUSE

New Home*

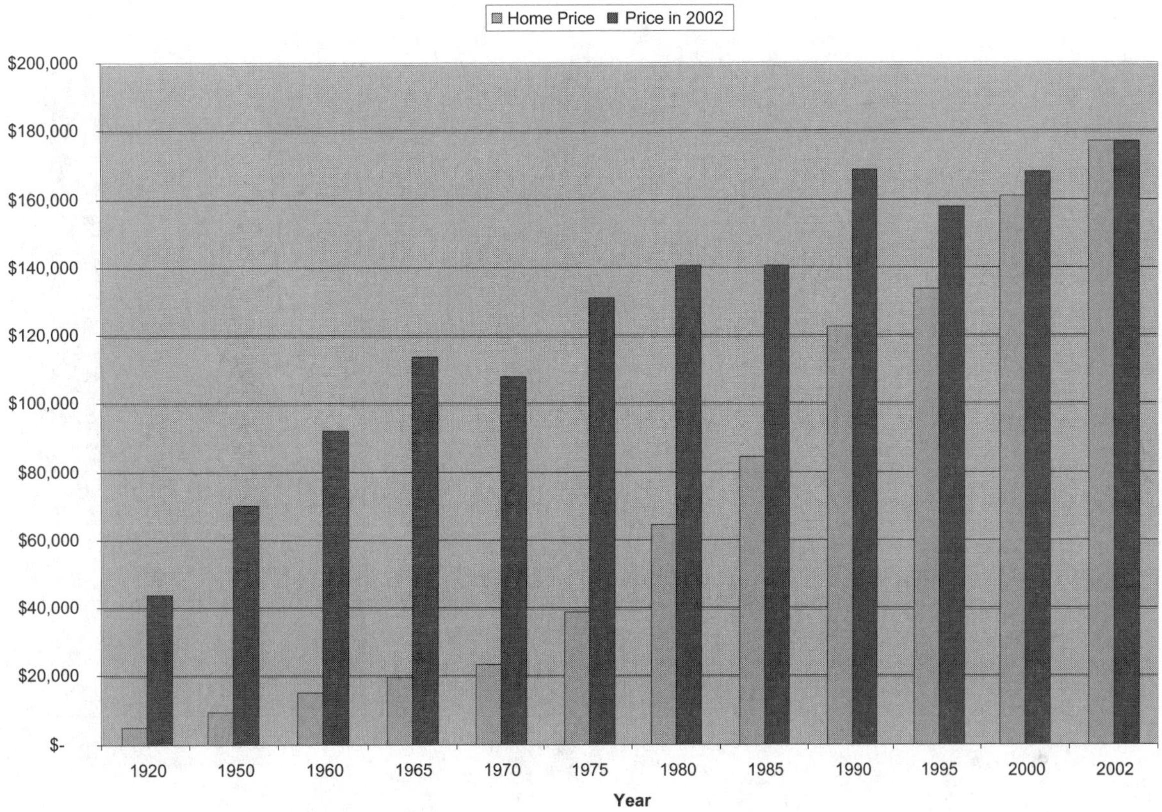

| Home Price | Price in 2002 |

	1920	1950	1960	1965	1970	1975	1980	1985	1990	1995	2000	2002
Home Price	$4,938	$9,422	$15,200	$20,000	$23,400	$39,300	$64,600	$84,300	$122,900	$133,900	$161,400	$177,300
Dollar Value in 2002	$44,417	$70,332	$92,381	$114,222	$108,496	$131,413	$141,038	$140,943	$169,163	$158,061	$168,617	$177,300

* Median Sales Price

AROUND THE HOUSE

New York Daily Times*

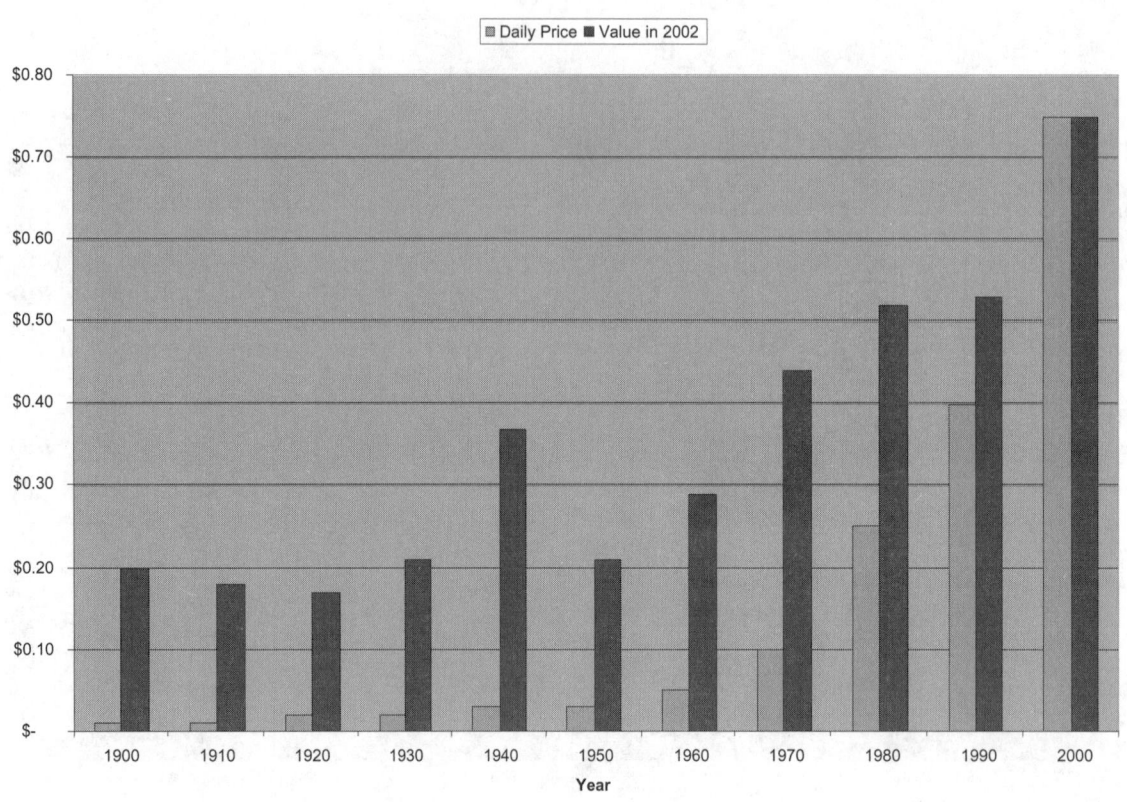

	1900	1910	1920	1930	1940	1950	1960	1970	1980	1990	2000
Daily Price	$0.01	$0.01	$0.02	$0.02	$0.03	$0.03	$0.05	$0.10	$0.25	$0.40	$0.75
Dollar Value in 2002	$0.20	$0.18	$0.17	$0.21	$0.37	$0.21	$0.29	$0.44	$0.52	$0.53	$0.75

* Cost is for papers purchased in the New York City area (within 200 mile radius of New York City).

AROUND THE HOUSE

New York Sunday Times

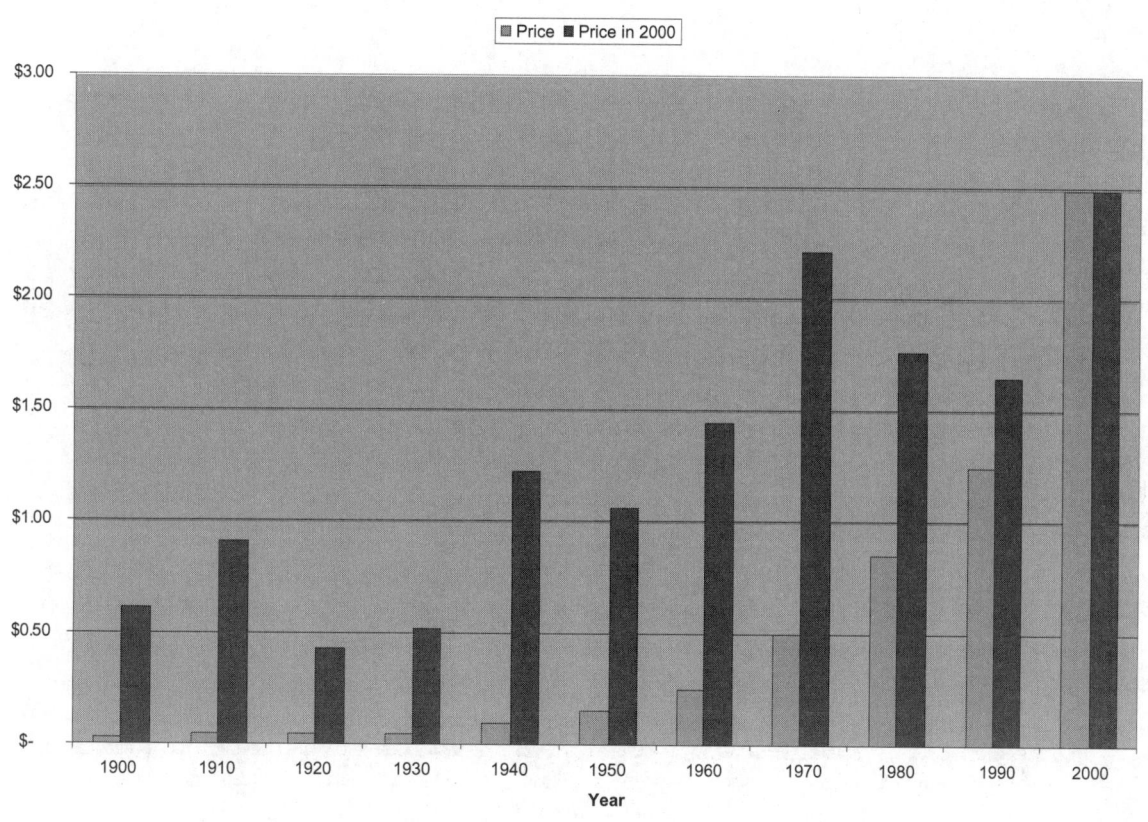

	1900	1910	1920	1930	1940	1950	1960	1970	1980	1990	2000
Price	$0.03	$0.05	$0.05	$0.05	$0.10	$0.15	$0.25	$0.50	$0.85	$1.25	$2.50
Dollar Value in 2000	$0.61	$0.91	$0.43	$0.52	$1.23	$1.07	$1.45	$2.22	$1.77	$1.65	$2.50

AROUND THE HOUSE

Postage Stamp for 1oz. First Class Mail

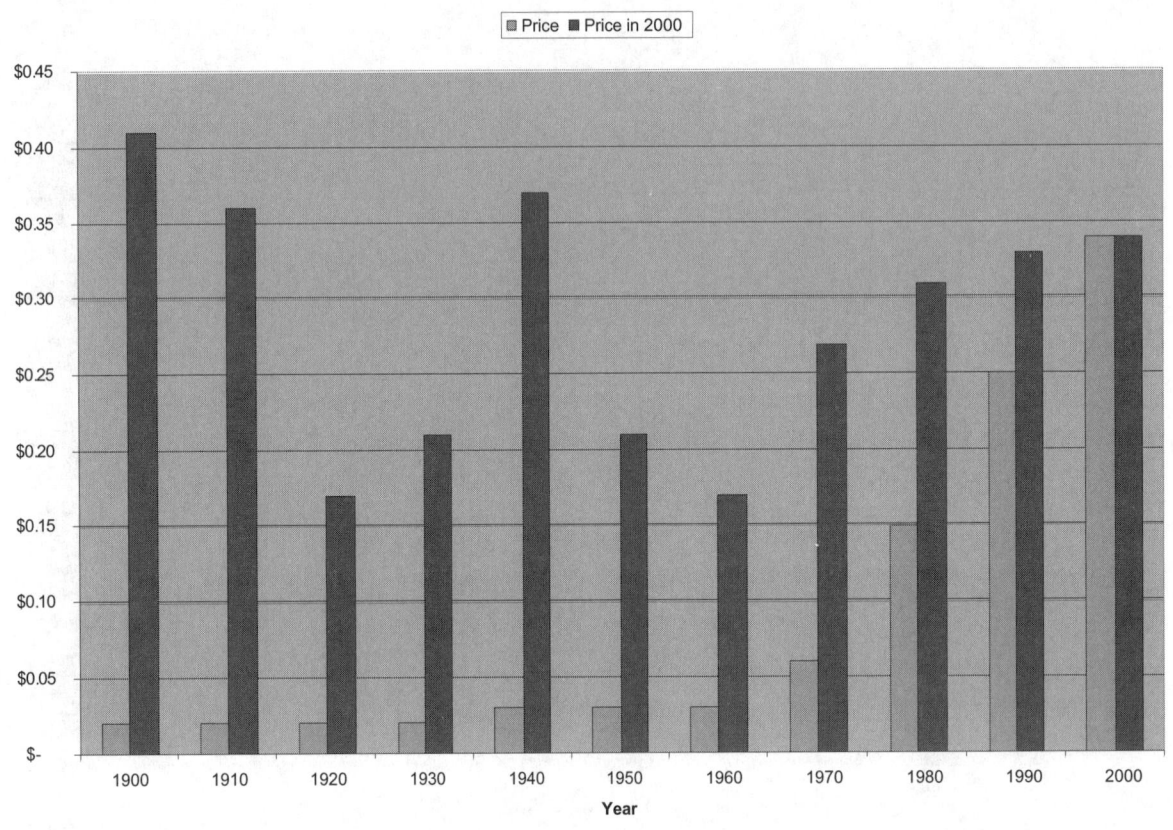

Price ■ Price in 2000

	1900	1910	1920	1930	1940	1950	1960	1970	1980	1990	2000
Price	$0.02	$0.02	$0.02	$0.02	$0.03	$0.03	$0.03	$0.06	$0.15	$0.25	$0.33
Dollar Value in 2000	$0.41	$0.36	$0.17	$0.21	$0.37	$0.21	$0.17	$0.27	$0.31	$0.33	$0.33

AROUND THE HOUSE

Sunbeam Toaster

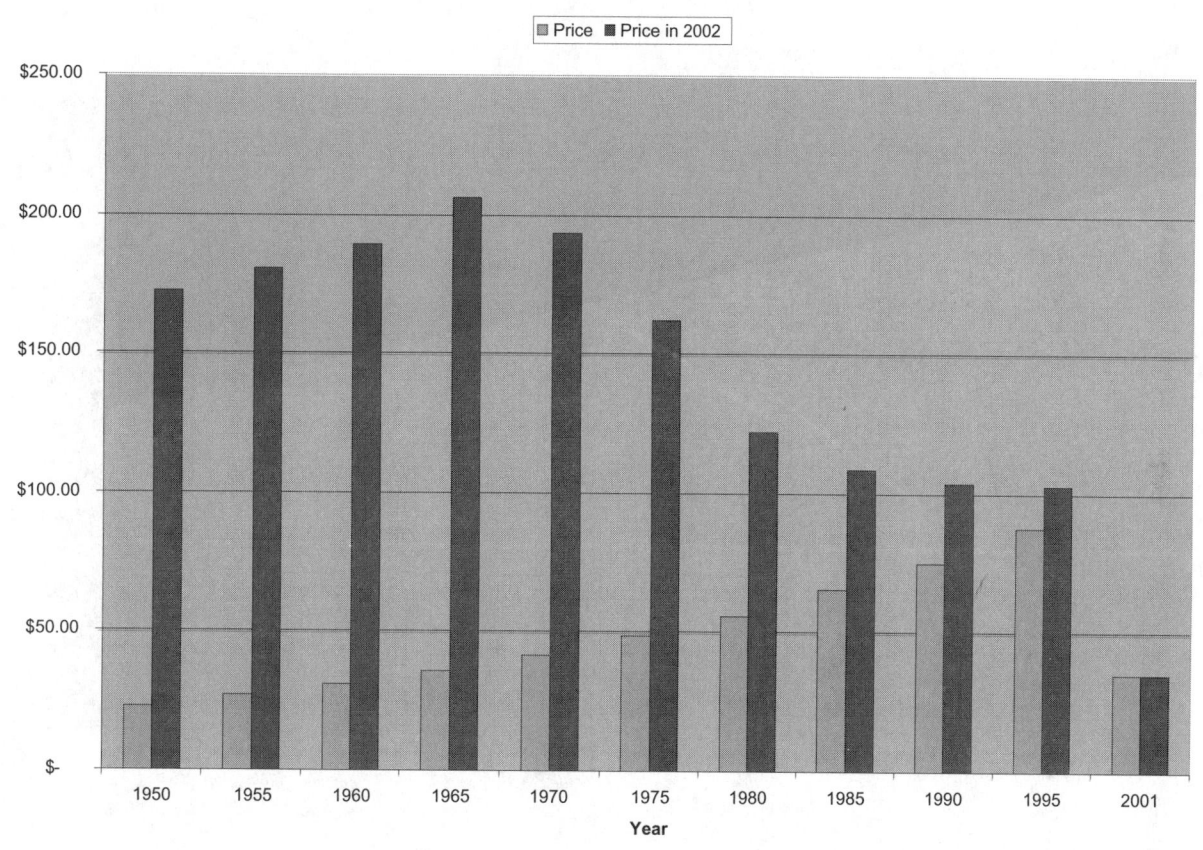

	1950	**1955**	**1960**	**1965**	**1970**	**1975**	**1980**	**1985**	**1990**	**1995**	**2001**
Price	$23.17	$26.90	$31.20	$36.10	$41.85	$48.50	$56.25	$65.25	$75.50	$87.65	$34.99
Dollar Value in 2002	$172.96	$180.57	$189.62	$206.17	$194.04	$162.18	$122.81	$109.09	$103.92	$103.47	$35.54

AROUND THE HOUSE

Superman Comic Book

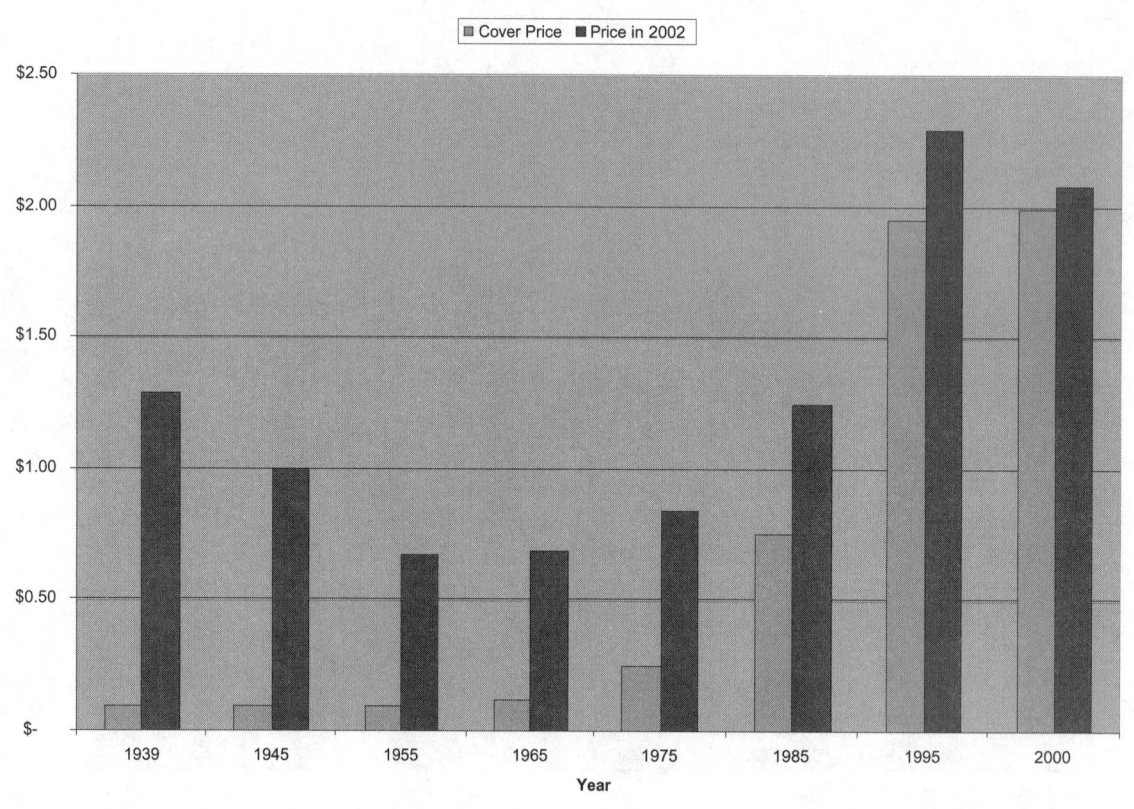

	1939	1945	1955	1965	1975	1985	1995	2000
Cover Price	$0.10	$0.10	$0.10	$0.12	$0.25	$0.75	$1.95	$1.99
Dollar Value in 2002	$1.29	$1.00	$0.67	$0.69	$0.84	$1.25	$2.30	$2.08

AROUND THE HOUSE

Time Magazine

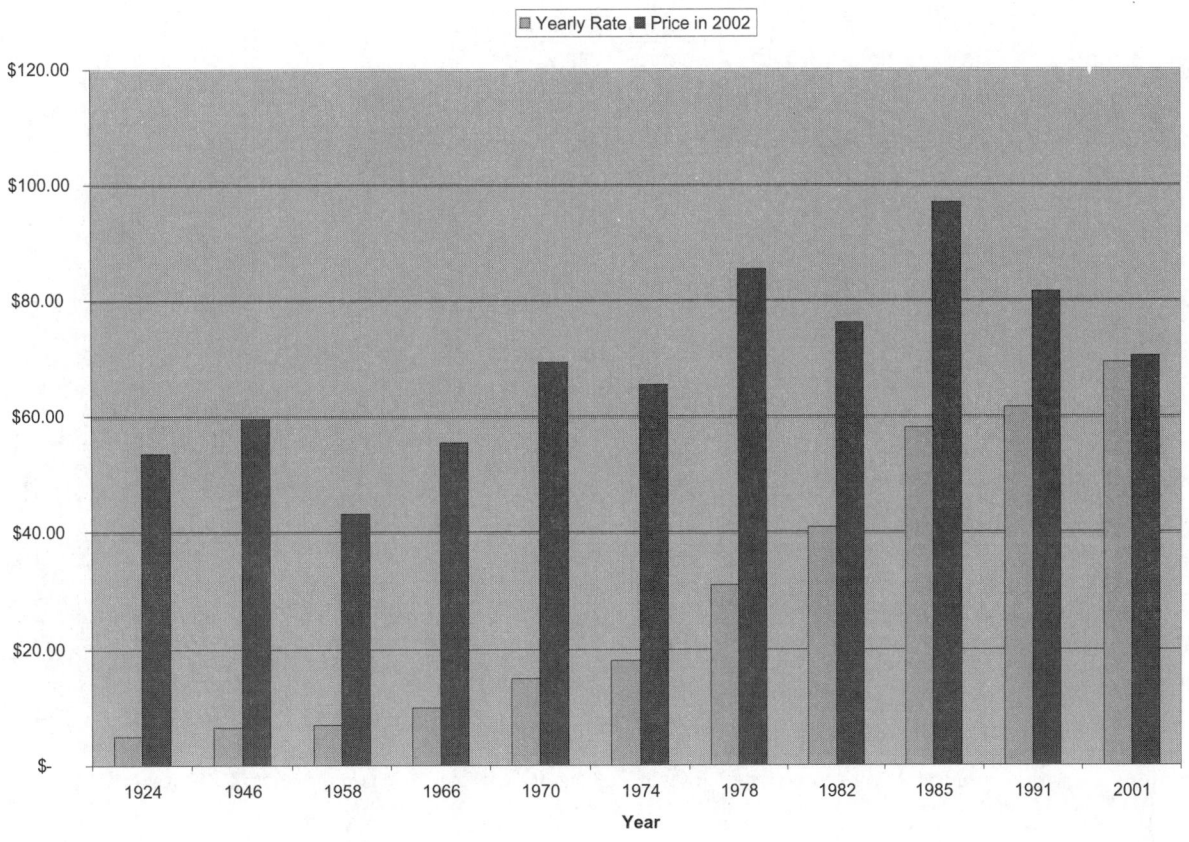

	1924	1946	1958	1966	1970	1974	1978	1982	1985	1991	2001
Yearly Rate	$5.00	$6.50	$7.00	$10.00	$15.00	$18.00	$31.00	$41.00	$58.24	$61.88	$69.66
Dollar Value in 2002	$53.60	$59.97	$43.57	$55.52	$69.55	$65.68	$85.54	$76.43	$97.37	$81.73	$70.76

AROUND THE HOUSE

Vogue Magazine

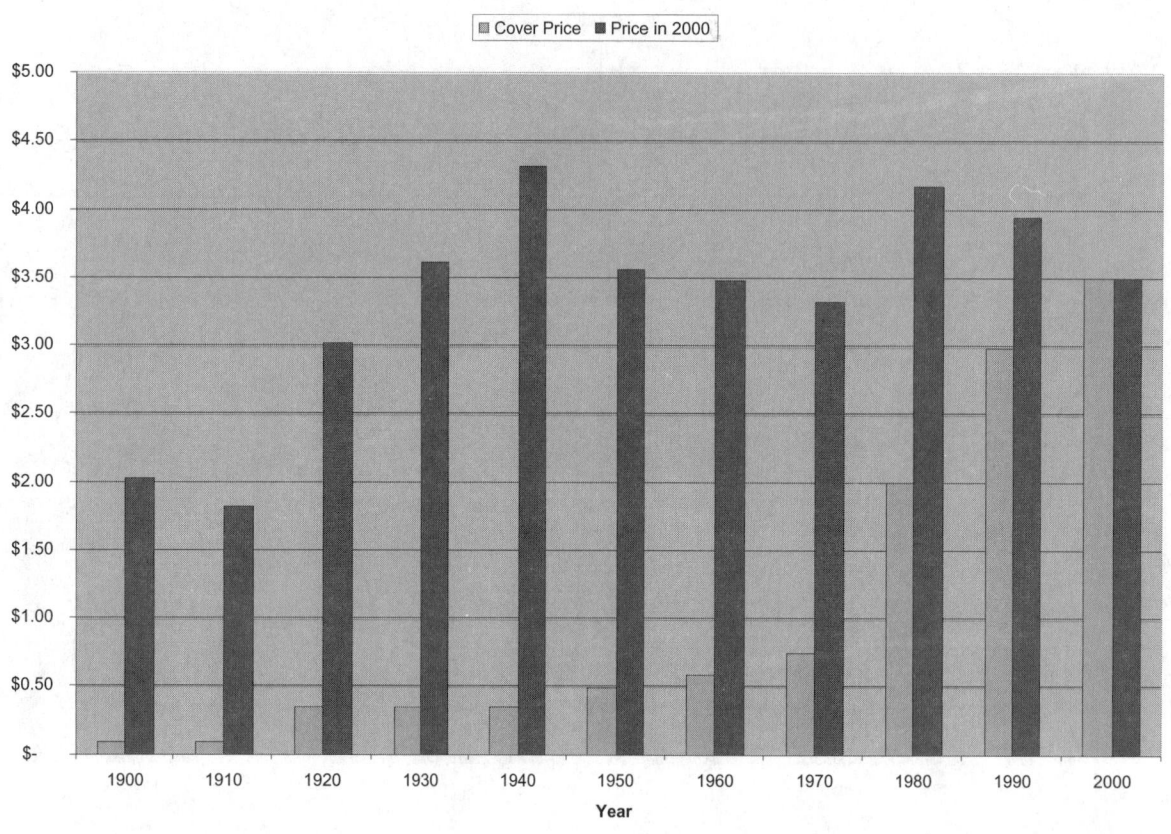

	1900	1910	1920	1930	1940	1950	1960	1970	1980	1990	2000
Cover Price	$0.10	$0.10	$0.35	$0.35	$0.35	$0.50	$0.60	$0.75	$2.00	$3.00	$3.50
Dollar Value in 2000	$2.04	$1.82	$3.02	$3.61	$4.32	$3.57	$3.49	$3.33	$4.18	$3.95	$3.50

AROUND THE HOUSE

Zippo Standard Brush Chrome Lighter

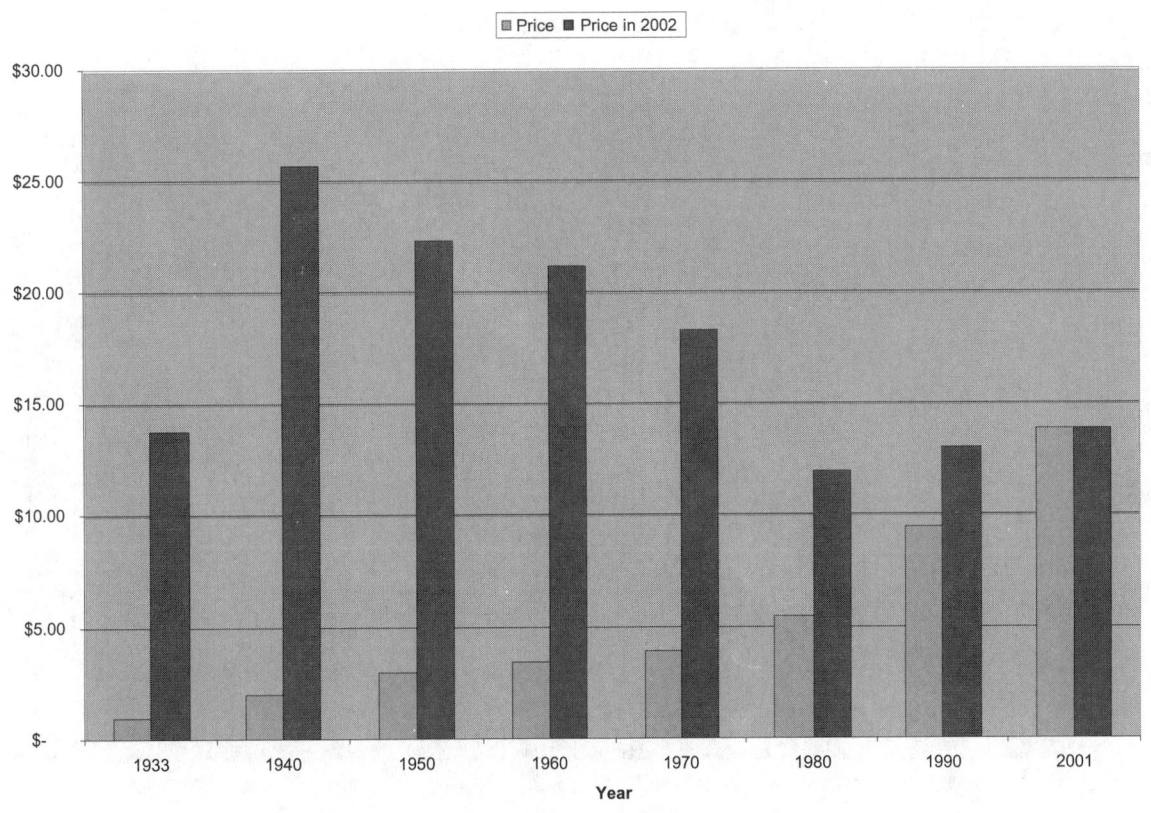

	1933	1940	1950	1960	1970	1980	1990	2001
Price	$1.00	$2.00	$3.00	$3.50	$3.95	$5.50	$9.50	$13.95
Dollar Value in 2002	$13.84	$25.70	$22.39	$21.27	$18.31	$12.01	$13.08	$13.95

FASHION

Brooks Brothers White Button Down Shirt

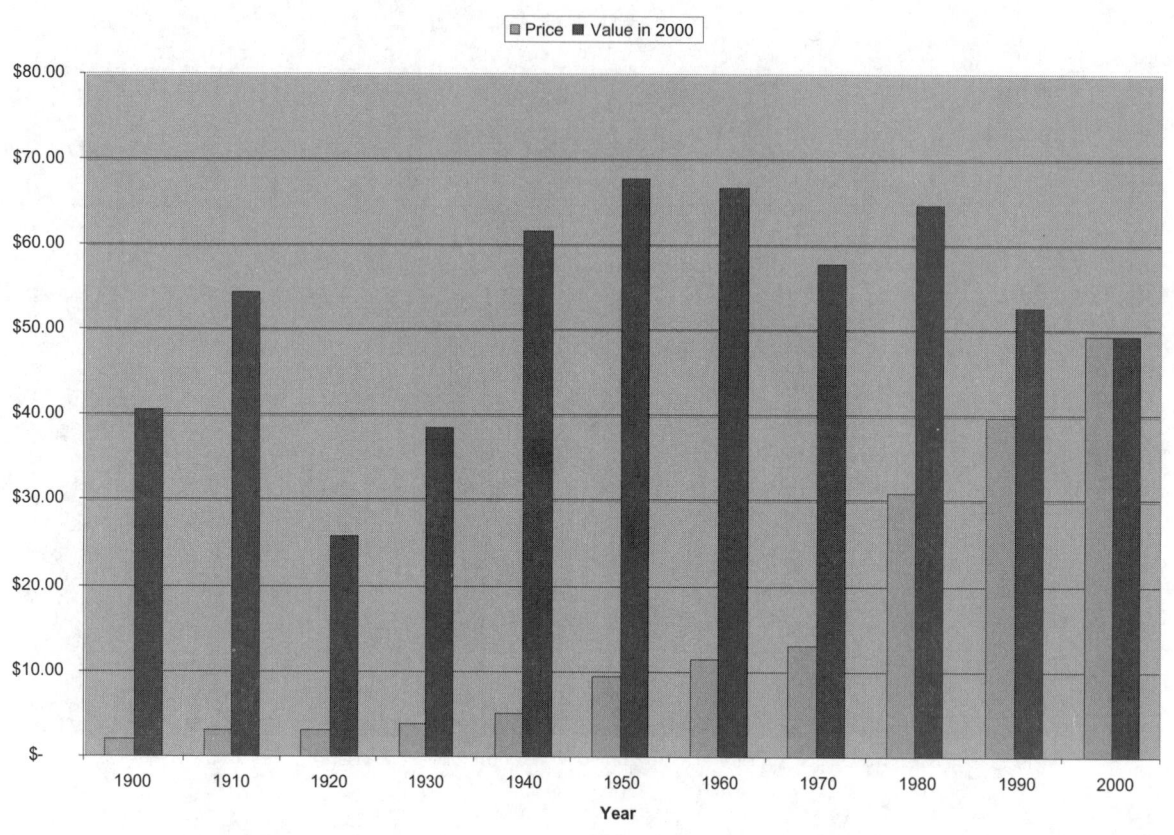

	1900	1910	1920	1930	1940	1950	1960	1970	1980	1990	2000
Price	$2.00	$3.00	$3.00	$3.75	$5.00	$9.50	$11.50	$13.00	$31.00	$40.00	$49.50
Dollar Value in 2000	$40.82	$54.55	$35.86	$38.66	$61.73	$67.86	$66.86	$57.78	$64.72	$52.70	$49.50

FASHION

Men's Dress (Overcoat/Trench) Coat

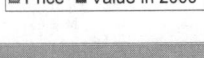

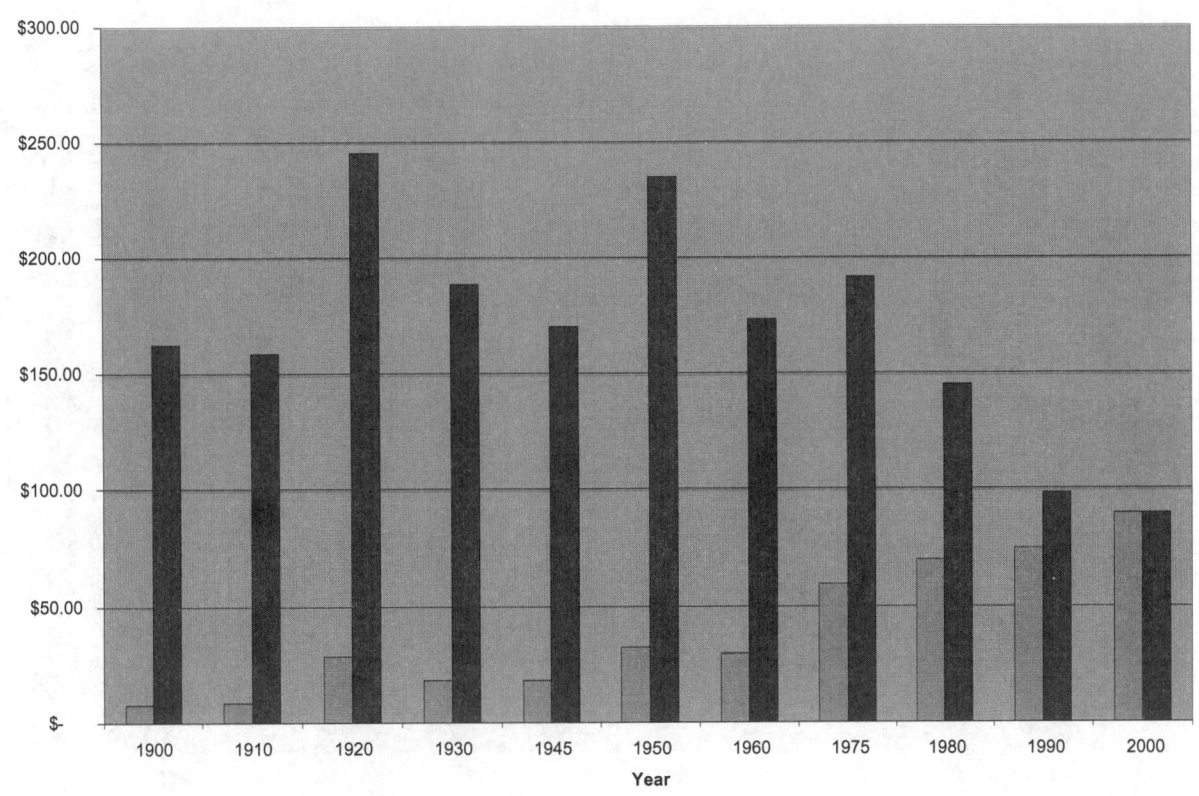

	1900	1910	1920	1930	1945	1950	1960	1975	1980	1990	2000
Price	$8.00	$8.75	$28.50	$18.35	$17.95	$32.95	$29.90	$59.80	$70.00	$74.75	$89.99
Dollar Value in 2000	$163.27	$159.09	$245.69	$189.18	$170.95	$235.36	$173.84	$191.67	$146.14	$98.48	$89.99

FASHION

Men's Black Leather Dress Shoes

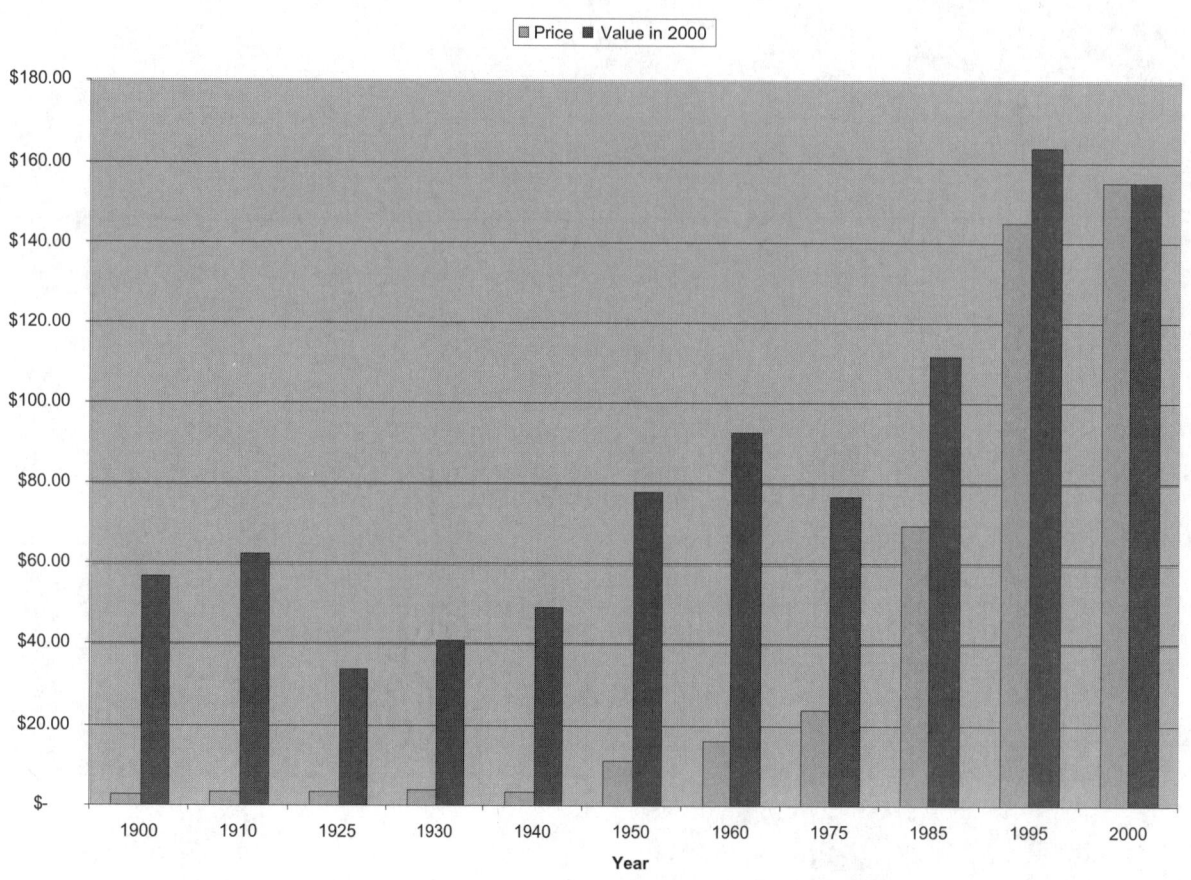

	1900	1910	1925	1930	1940	1950	1960	1975	1985	1995	2000
Price	$2.80	$3.45	$3.48	$4.00	$3.39	$10.95	$15.97	$23.99	$70.00	$145.00	$155.00
Dollar Value in 2000	$57.14	$62.73	$34.12	$41.24	$49.14	$78.21	$92.85	$76.89	$112.00	$163.84	$155.00

Excerpts from Ad Descriptions:

♦ **1900:** Velours Calf Goodyear Walt: Velours calf is a new tannage of calfskin finishing it in such a manner as to retain the strength and still give the appearance of a fine shoe.

♦ **1925:** The Brogue: We think these splendid looking black or brown GENUINE GOODYEAR WELT oxfords are the best bargains we now of. Rubber heels for comfort.

♦ **1940:** Peg Shanks: French toes –"must haves" for every shoe wardrobe. Pegged shanks, steel arch supports…rubber heels.

♦ **1960:** Cushion Insole GOLD BONDS. Wing tip with bold, distinctive rugged looks. Supple, premium leather uppers. Pacifate twill vamp lining. Pliant leather sole and rubber heel. Goodyear welt construction.

♦ **1985:** Luxurious, lightweight ghillie tie dress shoe. Designed of incredibly soft and supple leather uppers, unlined for comfort and flexibility. Stacked leather heel has leather and rubber toplift. Imported from Italy.

FASHION

Men's Two-Piece Dress Suit

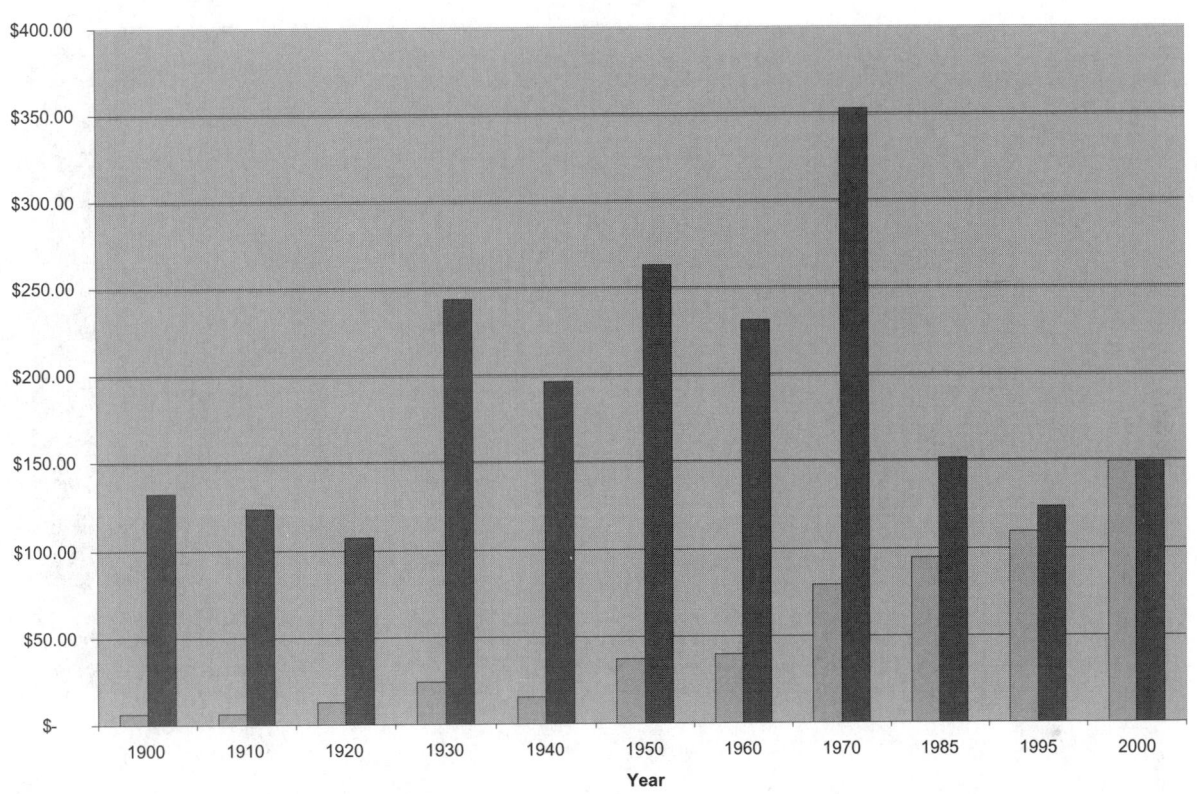

	1900	**1910**	**1920**	**1930**	**1940**	**1950**	**1960**	**1970**	**1980**	**1990**	**2000**
Price	$6.50	$6.83	$12.45	$23.75	$15.95	$36.95	$39.90	$79.50	$95.00	$110.00	$150.00
Dollar Value in 2000	$132.65	$124.18	$107.33	$244.85	$196.91	$263.93	$231.98	$353.33	$152.00	$124.29	$150.00

Excerpts from Ad Descriptions:

♦ **1900:** Men's Ready Made Suits. A very handsome ready made suit…dark background, covered with mixture of reddish brown and olive. Coat is satin piped throughout…pants made in first class style.

♦ **1920:** *Model S.* Gray stribed worsted material, about 55 percent wool, 45 percent cotton. Well made in our popular waistline Model S. Well fitted trousers have cuff bottoms.

♦ **1940:** *2-Button Single Breasted Model.* Trim in every line. When you put it on you feel *progressive*…you *look* it…your boss and friends *believe* it.

♦ **1960:** *a trend to quiet elegance.* A muted miniature check pattern in a year-around weigh suit of 55% Dacron polyester fiber, 45% rich virgin wool worsted.

♦ **1985:** *American Trend silk-blend.* Impeccably-tailored…woven of a luxurious blend of polyester, silk and linen.

FASHION

Men's Dress Shirt

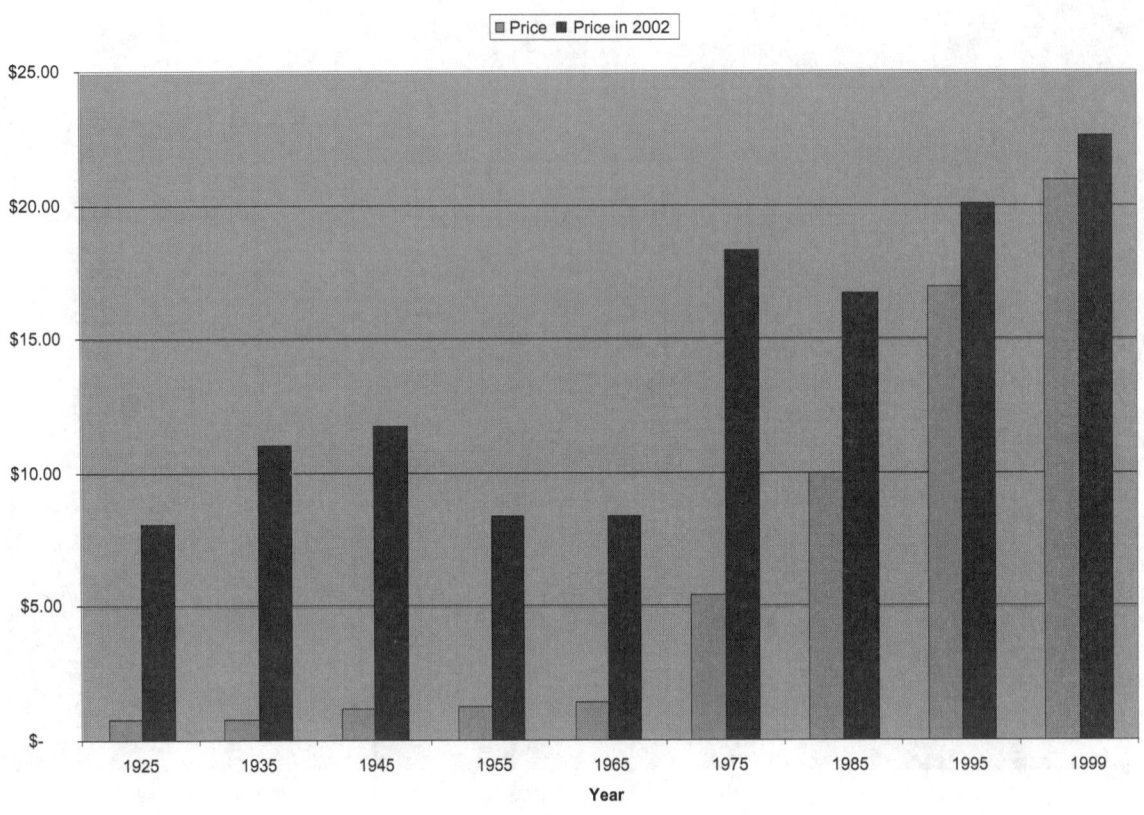

Price ▫ Price in 2002 ■

	1925	1935	1945	1955	1965	1975	1985	1995	1999
Price	$0.79	$0.84	$1.18	$1.25	$1.46	$5.47	$9.99	$16.99	$21.00
Dollar Value in 2002	$8.12	$11.03	$11.79	$8.39	$8.43	$18.29	$16.70	$20.06	$22.68

FASHION

Men's Dress Slacks

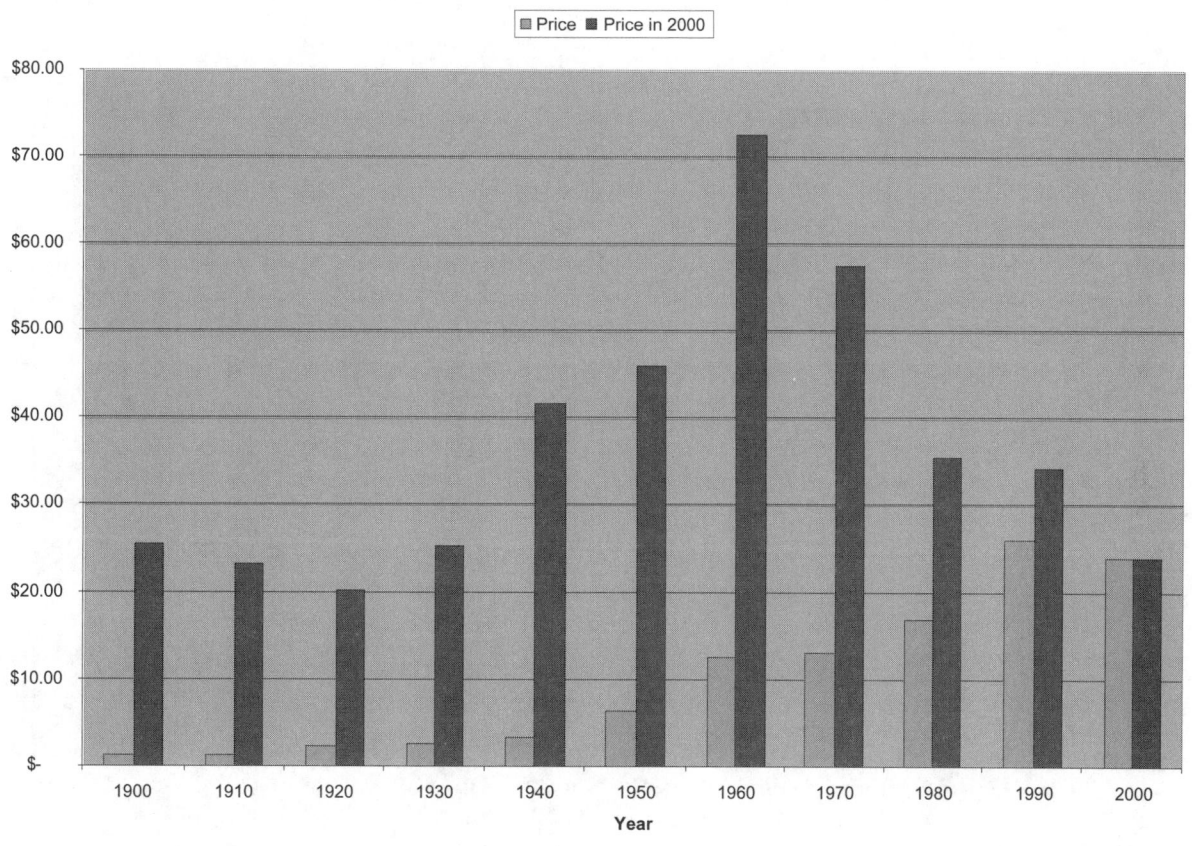

Price   Price in 2000

	1900	**1910**	**1920**	**1930**	**1940**	**1950**	**1960**	**1970**	**1980**	**1990**	**2000**
Price	$1.25	$1.28	$2.35	$2.45	$3.39	$6.45	$12.50	$12.95	$16.99	$26.00	$23.99
Dollar Value in 2000	$25.51	$23.27	$20.26	$25.26	$41.85	$46.07	$72.67	$57.56	$35.47	$34.26	$23.99

Excerpts from Ad Descriptions:

♦ **1900:** Men's Dark Neat Stripe Pants, pin check and plain effects
♦ **1920:** Striped Trousers Always Popular, Neat self stripe worsted trousers furnished in dark blue, brown or green colors.
♦ **1940:** 12_-ounce All Wool Navy Blue "Famo" Serge, Durable Serge – color-fast, smoothly finished.
♦ **1960:** Men's Slacks go casually continental.., Scotchgard Treated Sheen Gabardine of 100% virgin wool worsted.
♦ **1980:** The Coordinated Slacks, Dacron polyester double knit. Slanted front pockets' set in back pockets.
♦ **2000:** Barrington dress slacks, Comfortable polyester/rayon blend.

FASHION

Men's Sweater

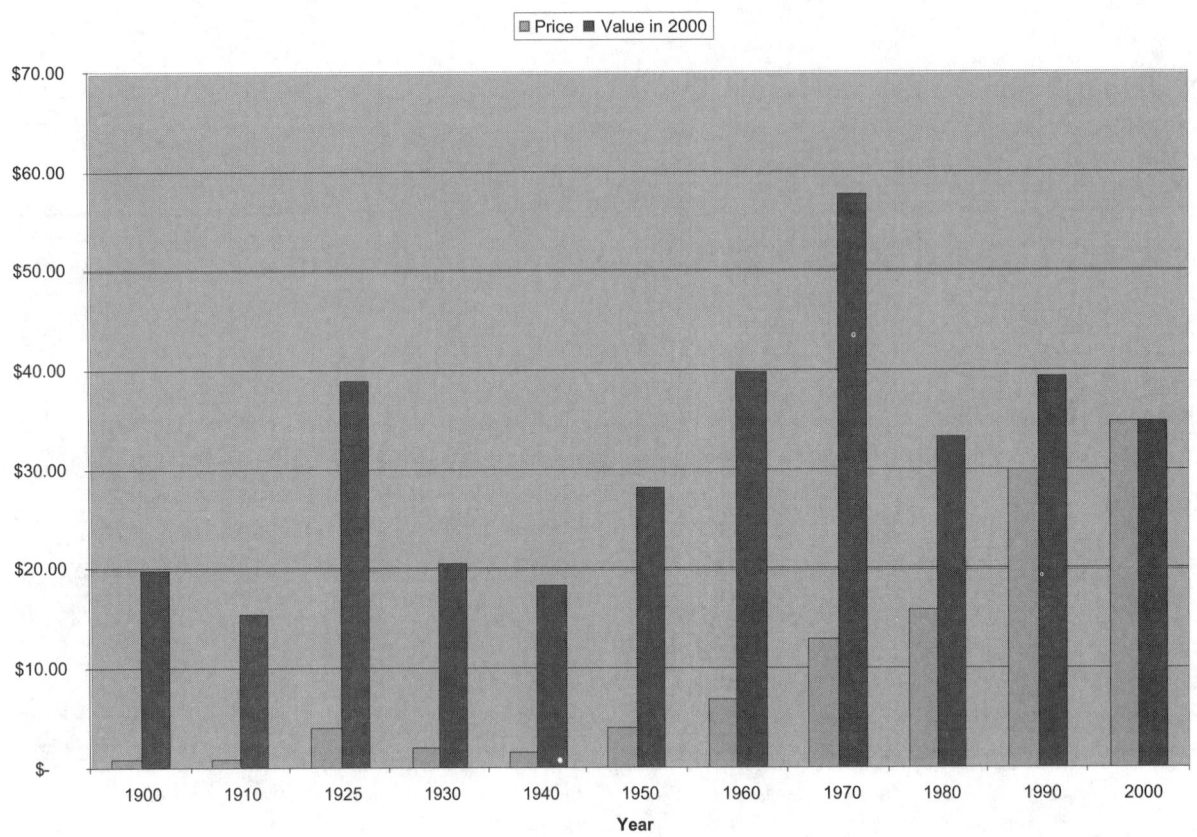

Price ■ Value in 2000

	1900	1910	1925	1930	1940	1950	1960	1970	1980	1990	2000
Price	$0.98	$0.85	$3.98	$2.00	$1.49	$3.95	$6.86	$13.00	$15.99	$29.99	$35.00
Dollar Value in 2000	$20.00	$15.45	$39.02	$20.62	$18.40	$28.21	$39.88	$57.78	$33.38	$39.41	$35.00

FASHION

Women's Black Purse

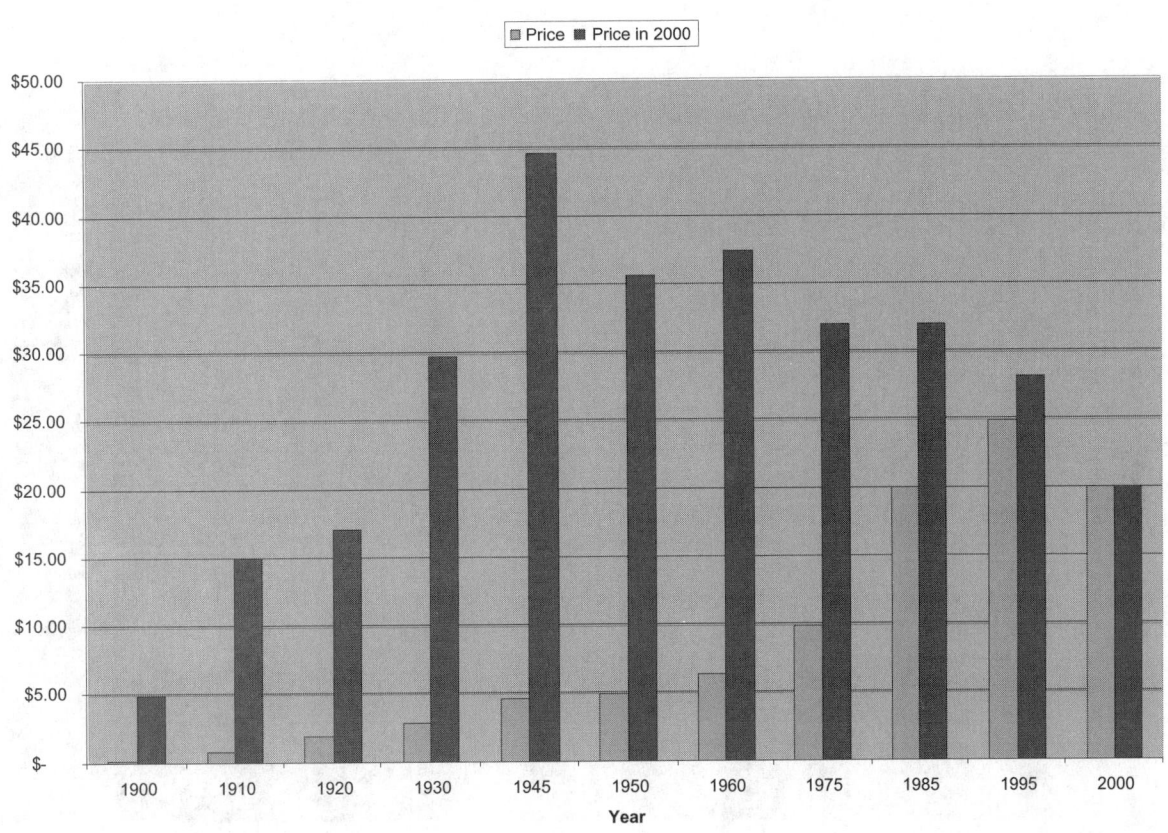

Legend: Price / Price in 2000

	1900	1910	1920	1930	1945	1950	1960	1975	1985	1995	2000
Price	$0.24	$0.83	$1.98	$2.89	$4.69	$5.00	$6.44	$10.00	$20.00	$24.95	$19.99
Dollar Value in 2000	$4.90	$15.09	$17.07	$29.79	$44.67	$35.71	$37.44	$32.05	$32.00	$28.19	$19.99

Excerpts from Ad Descriptions:

- ♦ **1900:** Black Seal Grain, Large outside pocket with embossed silvered clasp. Leather handles and drawstring top.
- ♦ **1920:** A beautifully embossed Leather Bag, wide opening conceled frame and large inner pocket and coin purse to match bag.
- ♦ **1945:** Dressmaker-Detail Pouches, Popular Capeskin in a tucked pouch with rayon faille gussets, Lucite clasp. Has a strong metal frame. Rayon lined, coin case, mirror.
- ♦ **1960:** Kerrybooke Classics, Roomy Swagger bag with 4-part frame has seven sections in all! 3 are inside compartments with separate openings at top, 2 are outside swagger pockets.
- ♦ **1980:** The Handbag, Polyester, rayon and flax bag. Beige plastic frame. Twist snap closure. Rope strap slips inside for use as a clutch.
- ♦ **2000:** Rosettti Bags, Microfiber handbags.

FASHION

Women's Dress Suit

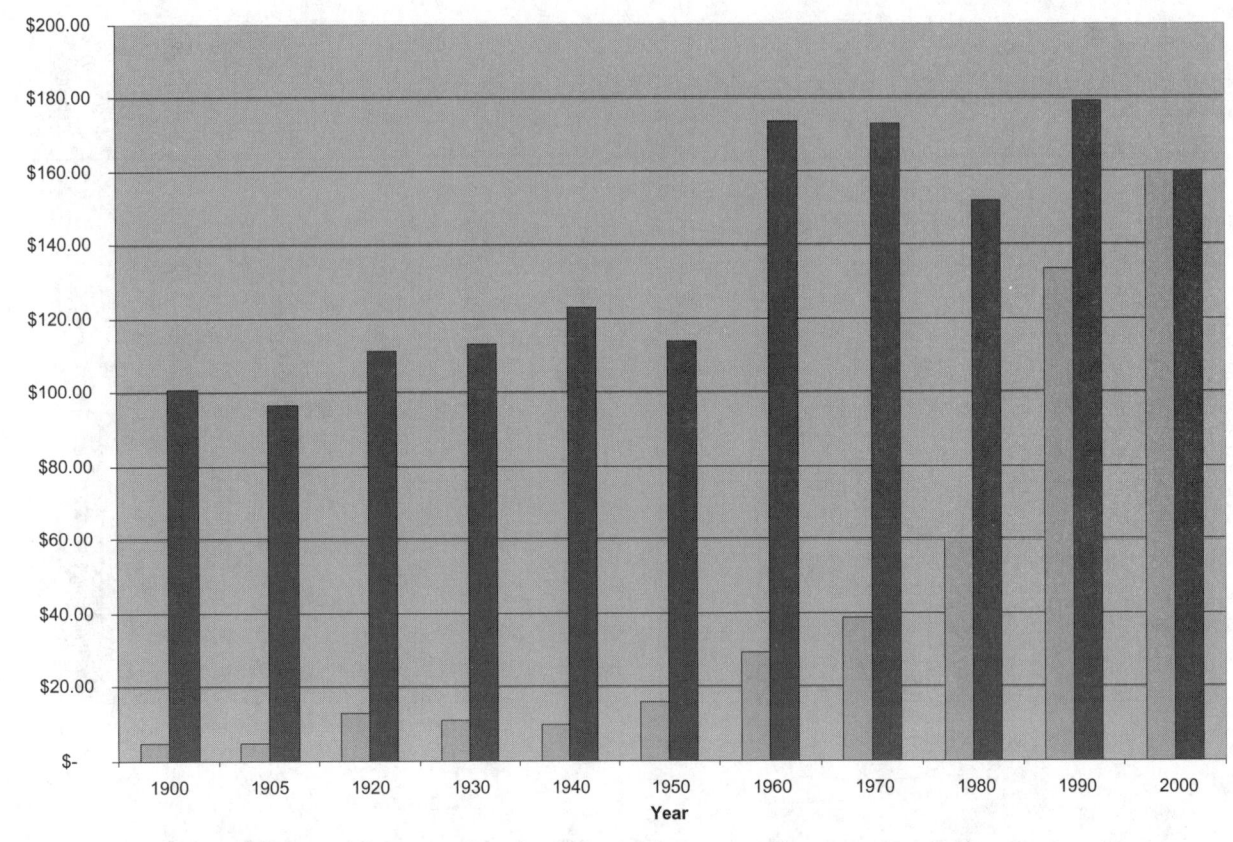

	1900	**1905**	**1920**	**1930**	**1940**	**1950**	**1960**	**1970**	**1980**	**1995**
Price	$4.95	$4.95	$12.95	$10.98	$9.98	$15.98	$29.90	$39.00	$60.54	$64.99
Dollar Value in 2000	$101.02	$97.06	$111.64	$113.20	$123.21	$114.14	$173.84	$173.33	$152.00	$73.44

FASHION

Women's High Heel Shoes

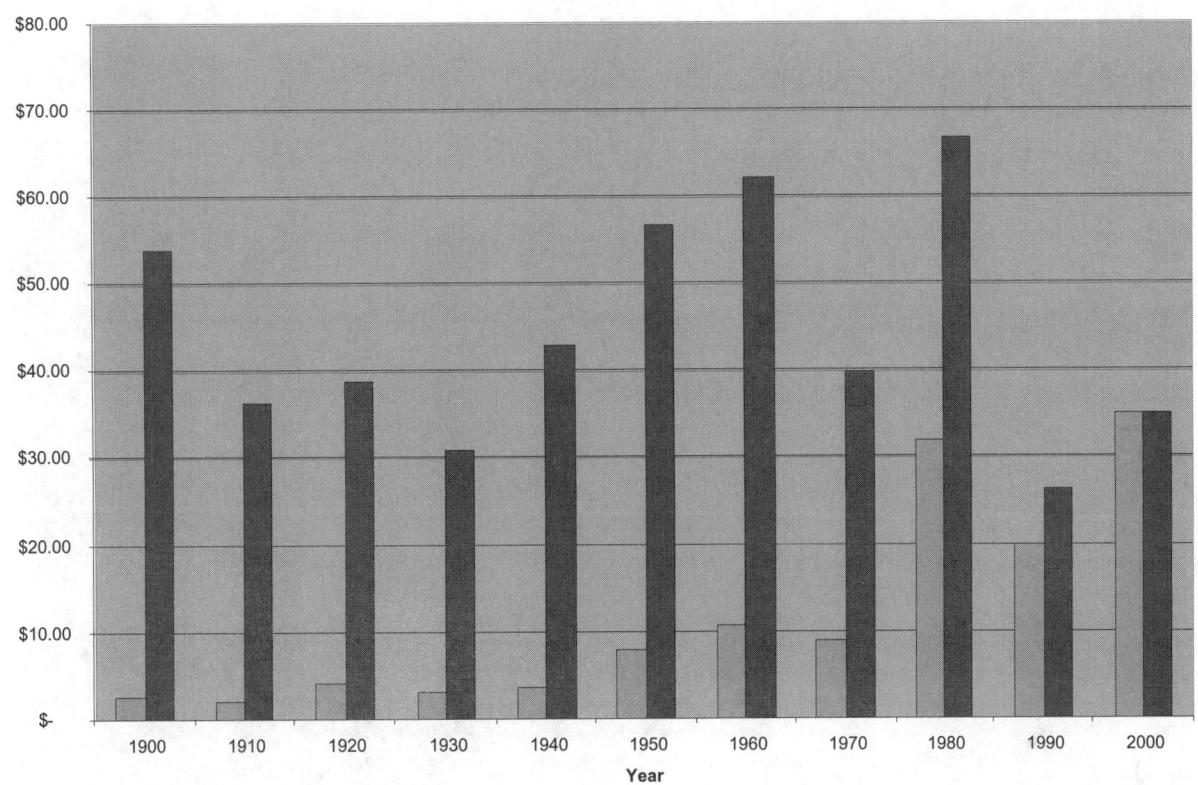

	1900	1910	1925	1930	1940	1950	1960	1970	1980	1990	2000
Price	$2.65	$2.00	$3.98	$3.00	$3.59	$7.95	$10.70	$8.99	$31.99	$19.94	$34.99
Dollar Value in 2000	$54.08	$36.36	$39.02	$30.93	$43.09	$56.79	$62.21	$39.96	$66.78	$26.27	$34.99

Excerpts from Ad Descriptions:

♦ **1900:** Lilian. This shoe is built from the best materials money can buy…put together by the very best workmen, combines more grace, style and good fitting qualities…suitable for dress wear.

♦ **1920:** The Pair. Brown Kid Lace..French Heel…Flexible Sewed Sole.

♦ **1940:** To Accent Foot Loveliness. Elasticized gabardine step-in slips on so easily – then fairly molds itself to your foot as you walk. Softly pleated vamp. Leather sole, 2-inch Cuban heel.

♦ **1950:** Costume Drama. High platforms, high heel..to star you as a leading lady…wherever you go. Superbly beautiful bracelet sandal for dining, dancing hours; soaring high on a _ -inch platform and slender 3-inch heels.

♦ **1960:** The classic Spectator. Flexible Featherlite pointed toe pump of supple textured leather. Leather sole and 2_-inch heel.

♦ **1970:** Step into the Classic Pump. Neatly-stitched topline and softly-shaped toe..here's the perfect underscore for your dressy as well as tailored clothes. Choose uppers of smooth leather or gleaming patent vinyl.

♦ **1980:** The Spectator Pump. A classic shoe to complement this year's suit styles.

FASHION

Women's One-Piece Dress

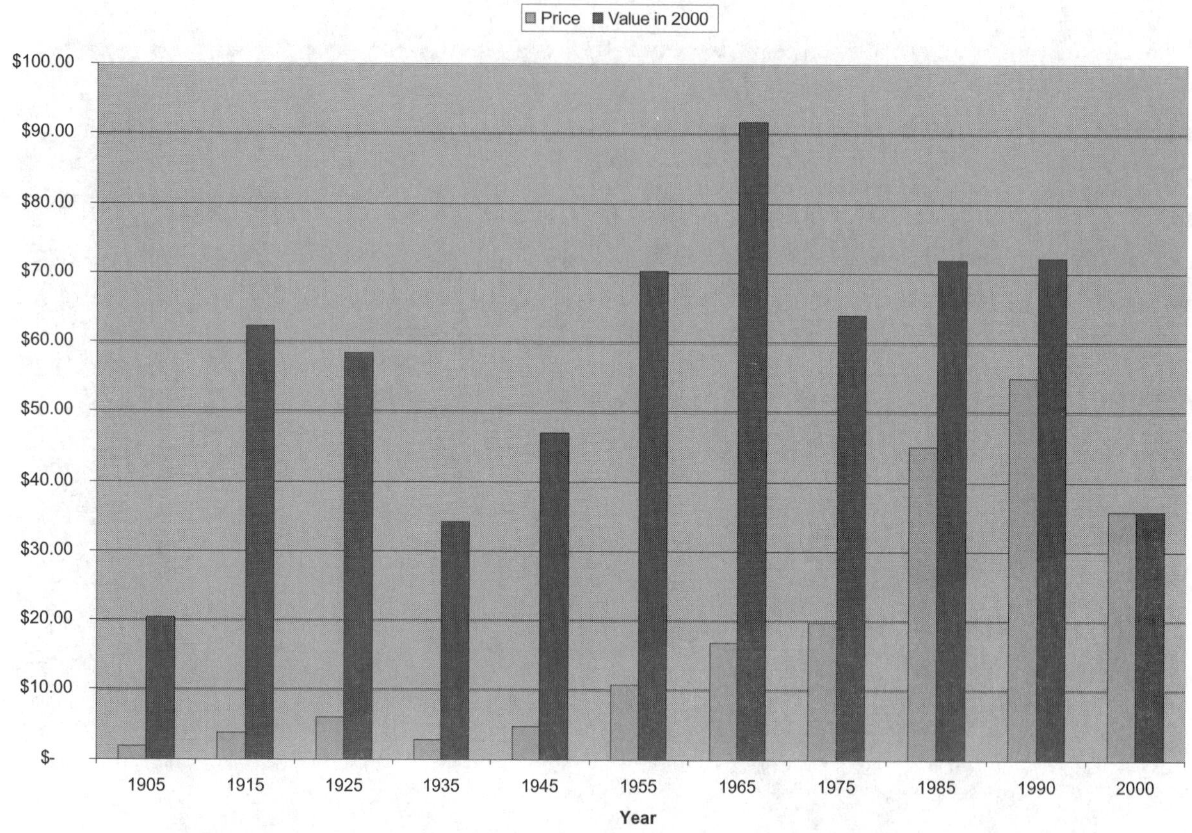

Legend: ▨ Price ■ Value in 2000

	1905	1915	1925	1935	1945	1955	1965	1975	1985	1990	2000
Price	$1.95	$3.69	$5.98	$2.74	$4.95	$10.98	$16.81	$20.00	$45.00	$55.00	$36.00
Dollar Value in 2000	$20.59	$62.54	$58.63	$34.25	$47.14	$70.38	$91.86	$64.10	$72.00	$72.46	$36.00

Excerpts from Ad Descriptions:

♦ **1905:** Ladies Shirt Waist Suit. Mode of good quality Sicilian cloth, consists of tailor made waist trimmed with side plaits...full sleeves, stylish cuffs...Silk buttons.

♦ **1915:** Rich Lace Trimmed Black Lawn One-Piece Dress. Popular semi-Princess style in a good weight...attached collar of same material edged with narrow black braided straps...Long sleeve.

♦ **1925:** Fine Quality Drawnwork Voile. Just to see this dainty, demure summer wash frock of fine, sheet voile will convey to you its delicate loveliness.

♦ **1945:** The Peplum Dress. ...Making fashion headlines everywhere with its jaunty newness. Gathered peplum covers skirt in front. Cinched in by set-in belt. Collar double looped. French-type rayon crepe.

♦ **1955:** This is the year for pleats...and these wash! 100% Nylon...Crisp, sheer ribbon puckered nylon in a dress as cool as a tall lemonade. Printed roses float here and there...pleated skirt whirls out to a full circle.

♦ **1975:** Softly Draped Dresses. They are of Dacron polyester double-knit in a smooth interlock-stitch...Step-in style dress has a front zipper opening; elasticized waistband.

FASHION

Women's Skirt

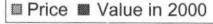
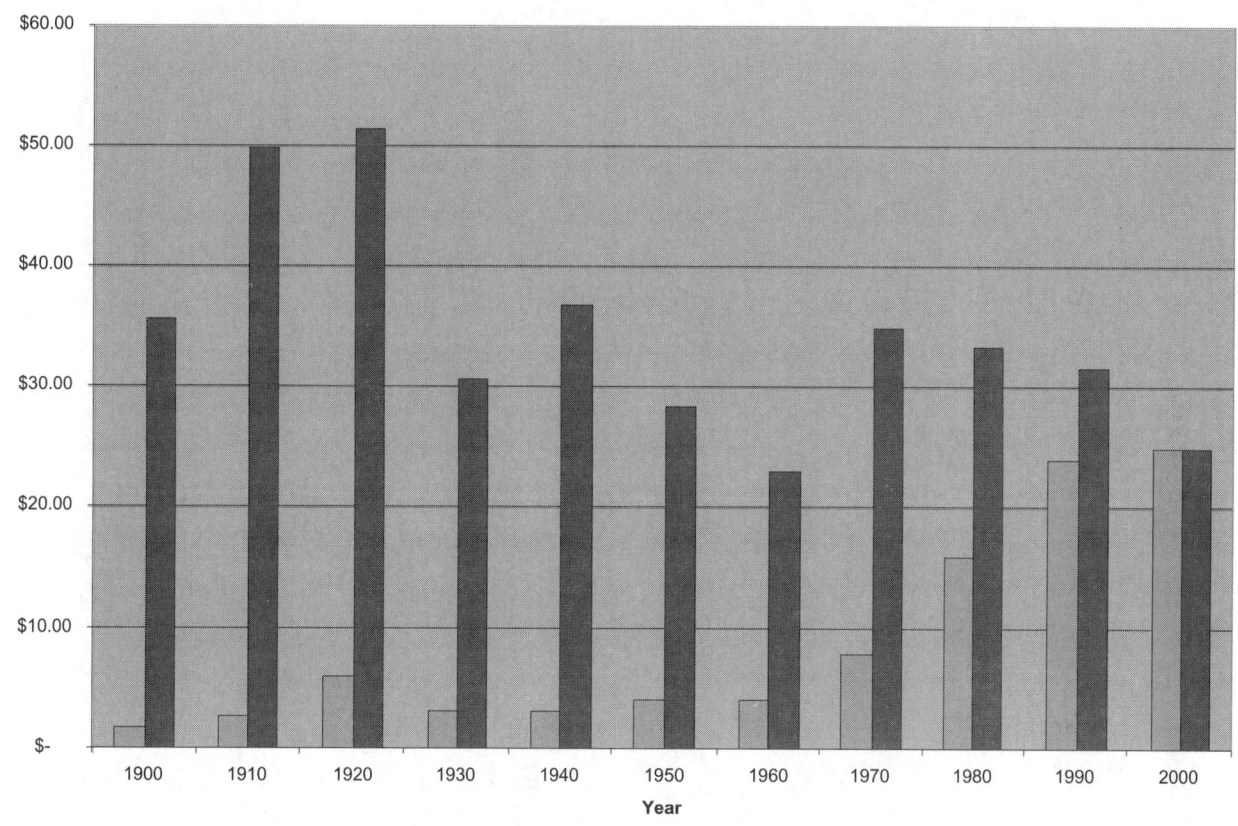

	1900	**1910**	**1920**	**1930**	**1940**	**1950**	**1960**	**1970**	**1980**	**1990**	**2000**
Price	$1.75	$2.75	$5.98	$2.98	$2.98	$3.98	$3.97	$7.97	$16.00	$24.00	$24.99
Dollar Value in 2000	$35.71	$50.00	$51.55	$30.72	$36.79	$28.43	$23.08	$35.02	$33.40	$31.62	$24.99

Excerpts from Ad Descriptions:

♦ **1900:** Ladies Skirt made of good quality Manchester cloth, measures 3_ yards around the bottom. Good value for the money.

♦ **1920:** Typical of youth in every line, this fashionable skirt is all the miss wants for all around service.

♦ **1940:** Fan Pleated; Handsomely tailored skirt in two fine fabrics that mate beautifully with blouses and jackets.

♦ **1960:** Woven Plaid.. Dan River wash-and-wear cotton. Simulated pockets; back zipper; kick pleats. Washable.

♦ **1980:** The Slim Skirt; Ours is a lightweight gabardine that's classically styled with self-piped, button-down pockets in front and back.

♦ **2000:** Apostrophe print ruffle skirt. A fun look.

FASHION

Women's Swim Suit

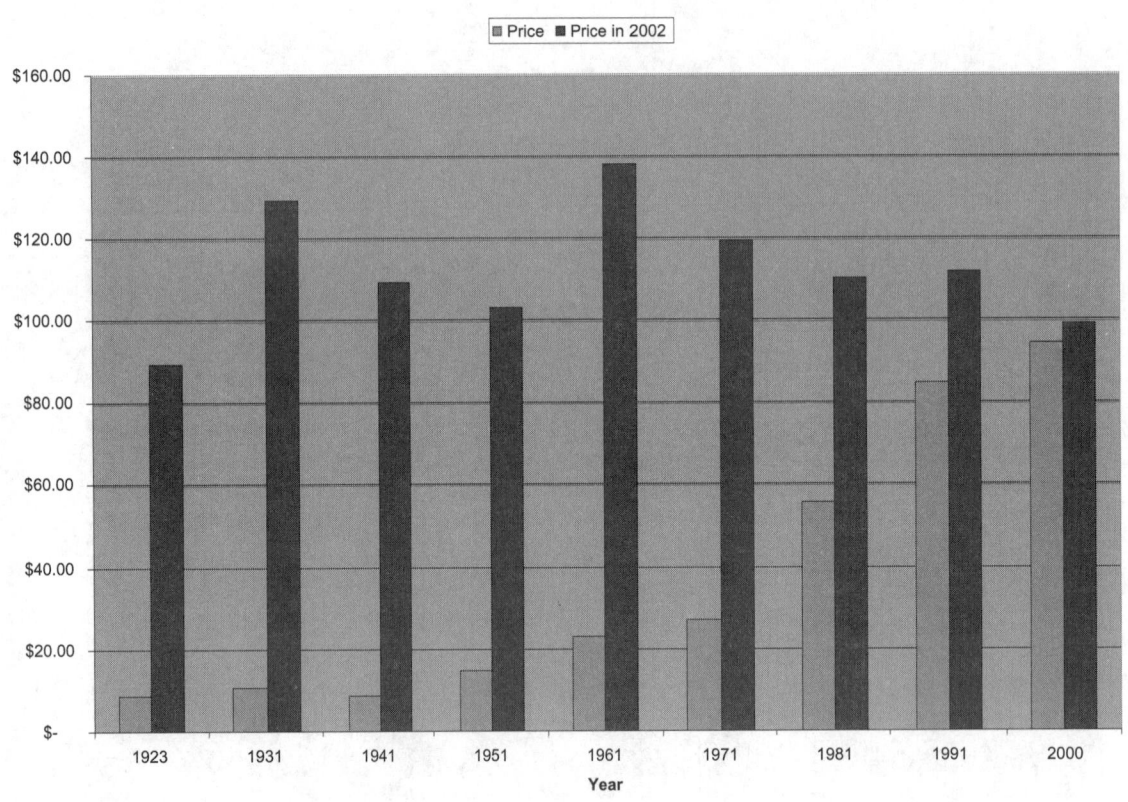

	1923	1931	1941	1951	1961	1971	1981	1991	1999
Price	$8.50	$10.95	$ 8.95	$14.95	$22.95	$26.99	$56.00	$85.00	$95.00
Dollar Value in 2002	$89.42	$129.60	$109.53	$103.44	$138.08	$119.89	$110.83	$112.27	$99.25

HELP WANTED

Average Major League Baseball Player's Salary

☐ Avg. Player Salary ■ Earnings in 2000

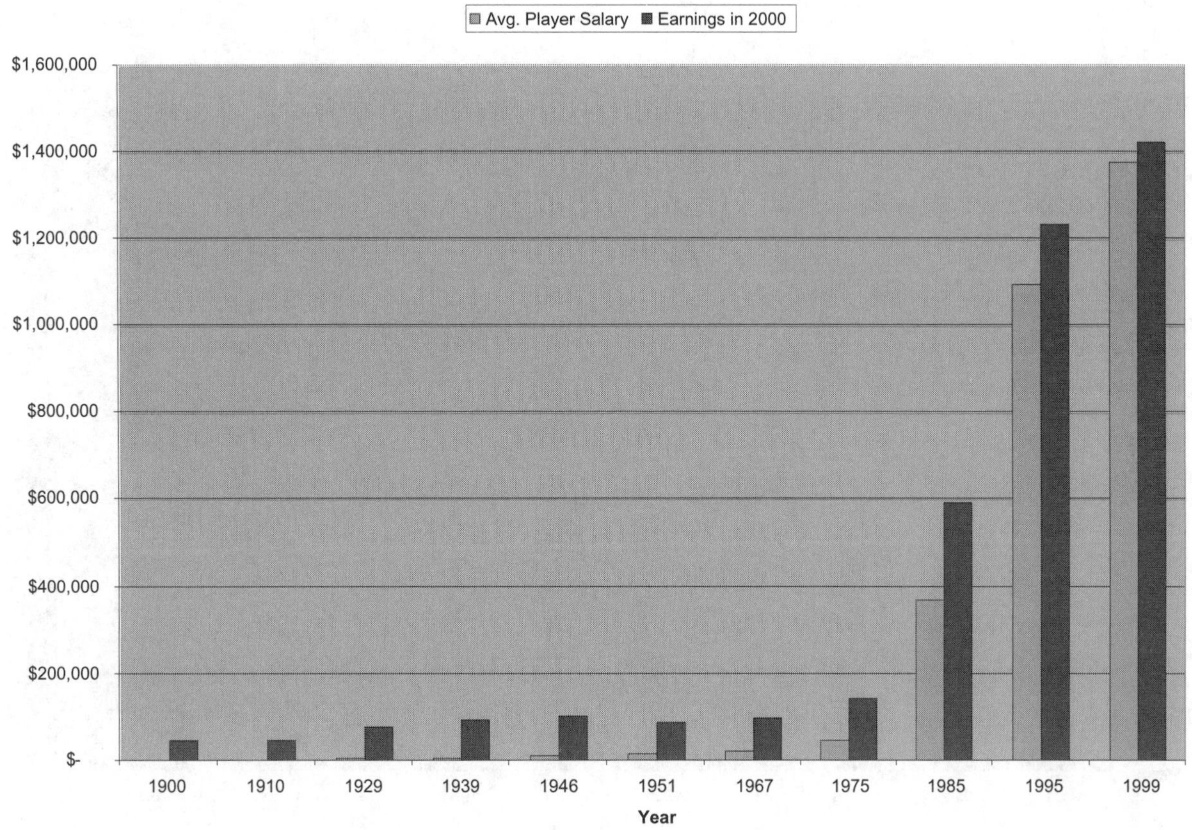

	1900	1910	1929	1939	1946	1951	1967	1975	1985	1995	1999
Avg. Player Salary	$2,200	$2,500	$7,531	$7,306	$11,294	$13,300	$19,000	$44,676	$371,157	$1,094,400	$1,377,196
Dollar Value in 2000	$44,898	$45,455	$76,071	$90,198	$99,947	$88,079	$97,938	$143,192	$593,851	$1,236,610	$1,424,194

Professional Baseball Salary Facts:

♦ Ty Cobb played with Detroit in 1908 for $4,500 ($83,333 in 2000 dollars).

♦ Babe Ruth earned $10,000 in 1921 with the New York Yankees ($100,502 in 2002 dollars). By 1923, he earned a $52,000 salary ($547,064 in 2002 dollars).

♦ Joe DiMaggio earned $37,000 in 1941 on the New York Yankee payroll ($458,928 in 2002 dollars). In 1949, his salary was $100,000 ($755,852 in 2002 dollars).

♦ Willie Mays started his rookie year earning $5,000 in 1951 ($34,596 in 2002 dollars). He earned $170,000 near the end of his career in 1971 ($755,135 in 2002 dollars).

♦ In 1999, the average baseball player's salary was $1,377,196 ($1,424,194 in 2000 dollars).

HELP WANTED

Average US National Annual Salary

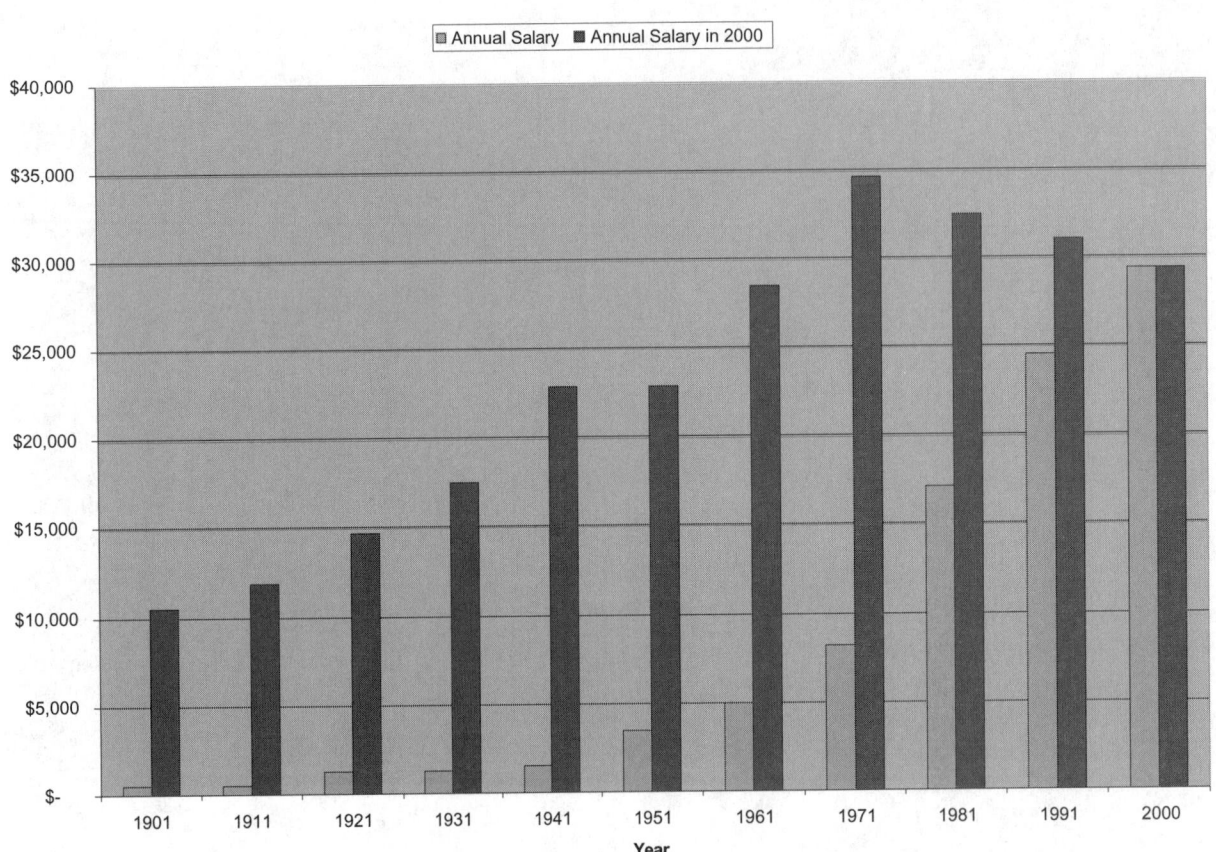

Legend: ▨ Annual Salary ■ Annual Salary in 2000

	1901	1911	1921	1931	1941	1951	1961	1971	1981	1991	2000
Annual Salary	$454	$575	$1,233	$1,289	$1,492	$3,452	$4,961	$8,144	$17,197	$24,578	$29,469
Dollar Value in 2000	$10,455	$11,855	$14,750	$17,553	$22,861	$22,860	$28,511	$34,655	$32,570	$31,072	$29,469

HELP WANTED

Bookkeeper Annual Salary

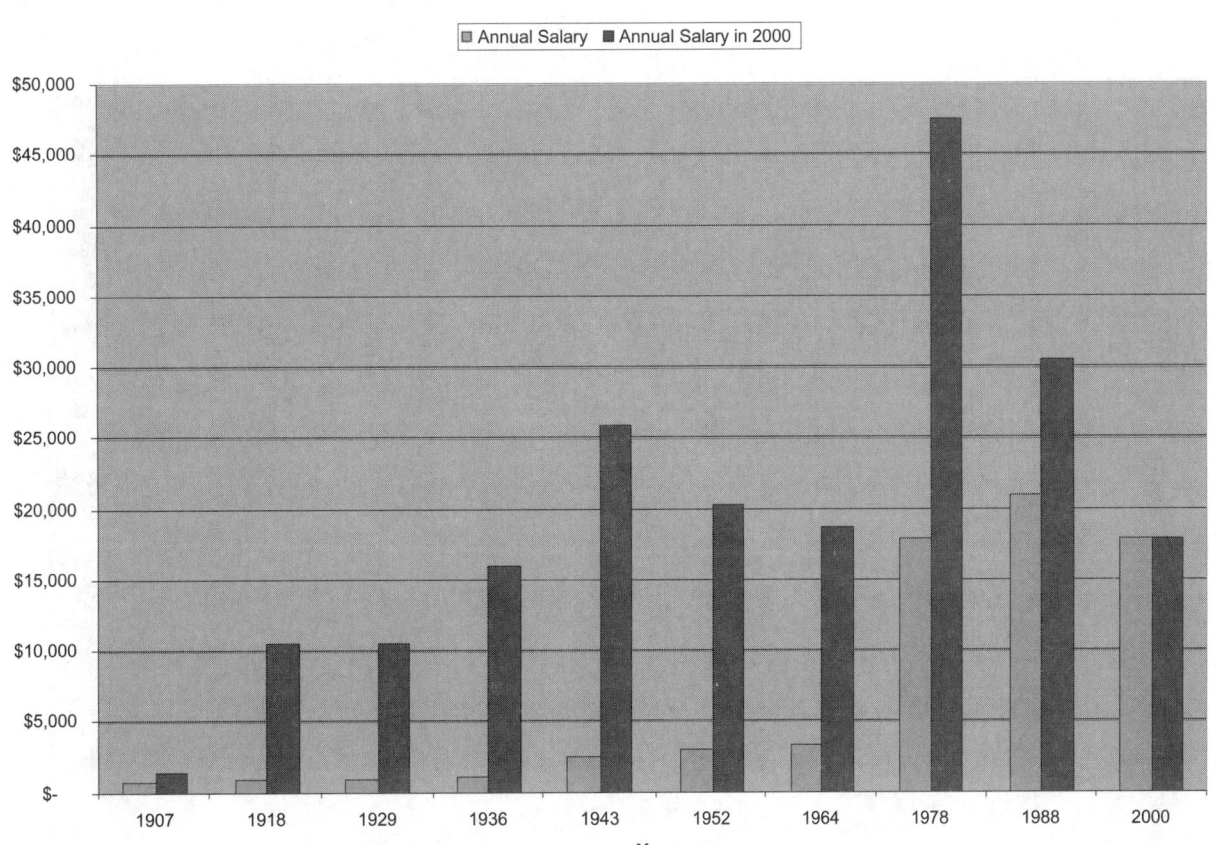

◻ Annual Salary ◼ Annual Salary in 2000

	1907	**1918**	**1929**	**1936**	**1943**	**1952**	**1964**	**1978**	**1988**	**1999**
Annual Salary	$780	$930	$1,040	$1,200	$2,600	$3,120	$3,360	$18,000	$21,000	$25,000
Dollar Value in 2000	$1,418	$10,568	$10,505	$16,049	$26,000	$20,260	$18,667	$47,493	$30,568	$25,583

Excerpts from Help Wanted Ads:

1907 Manufacturing Concern
1918 Assistant in office of large manufacturing concern
1929 Manufacturing concern; experience a must, some typing involved
1936 Complete charge of assistants
1952 Accounts payable, dress manufacturing experience
1964 Downtown company: good hours and benefits for keypunch experience
1978 Full charge: CPA office
1988 Manufacturer; supervise staff in all phases of computerized billing
1999 Bookkeeper: US National Average

HELP WANTED

Boston Red Sox Baseball Team Payroll

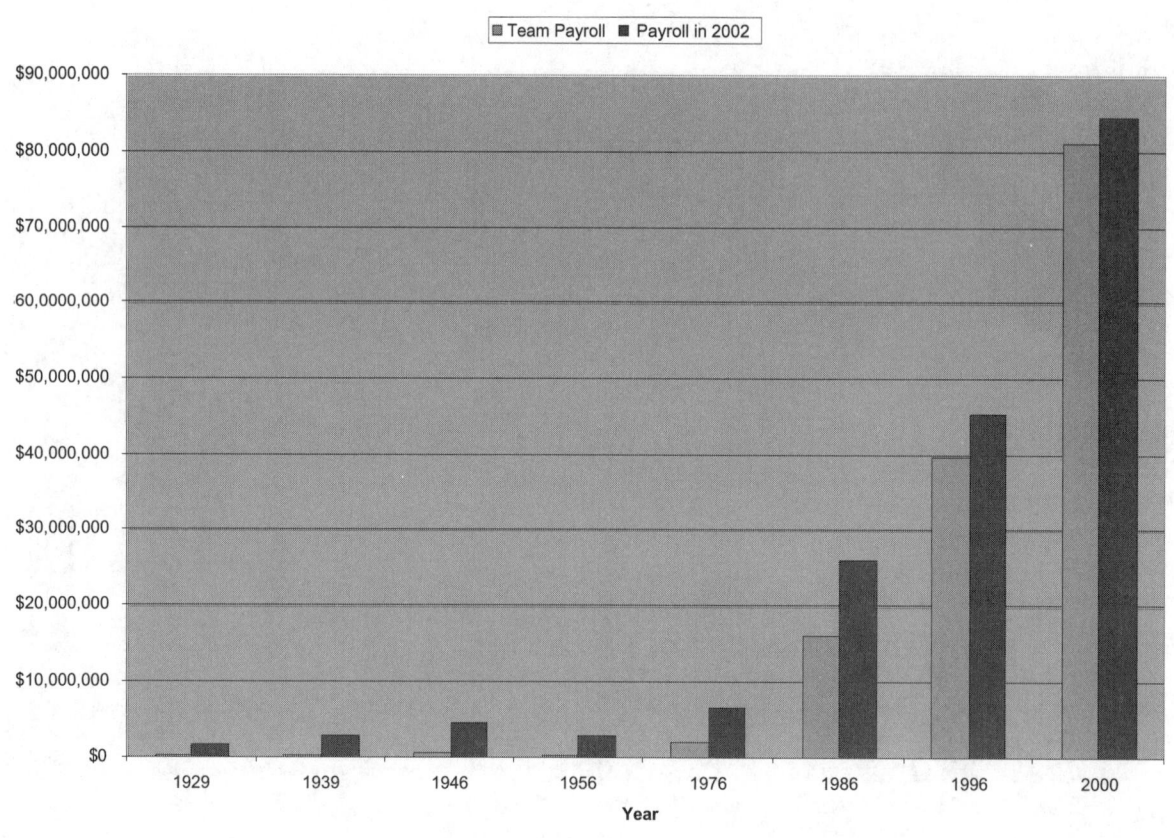

	1929	1939	1946	1956	1976	1986	1996	2000
Team Payroll	$171,260	$227,237	$511,025	$421,000	$2,052,460	$16,003,236	$39,676,000	$81,210,333
Dollar Value in 2002	$1,801,735	$2,941,003	$4,714,533	$2,784,482	$6,789,236	$26,268,085	$45,492,112	$84,841,689

HELP WANTED

Coal Miner Annual Salary*

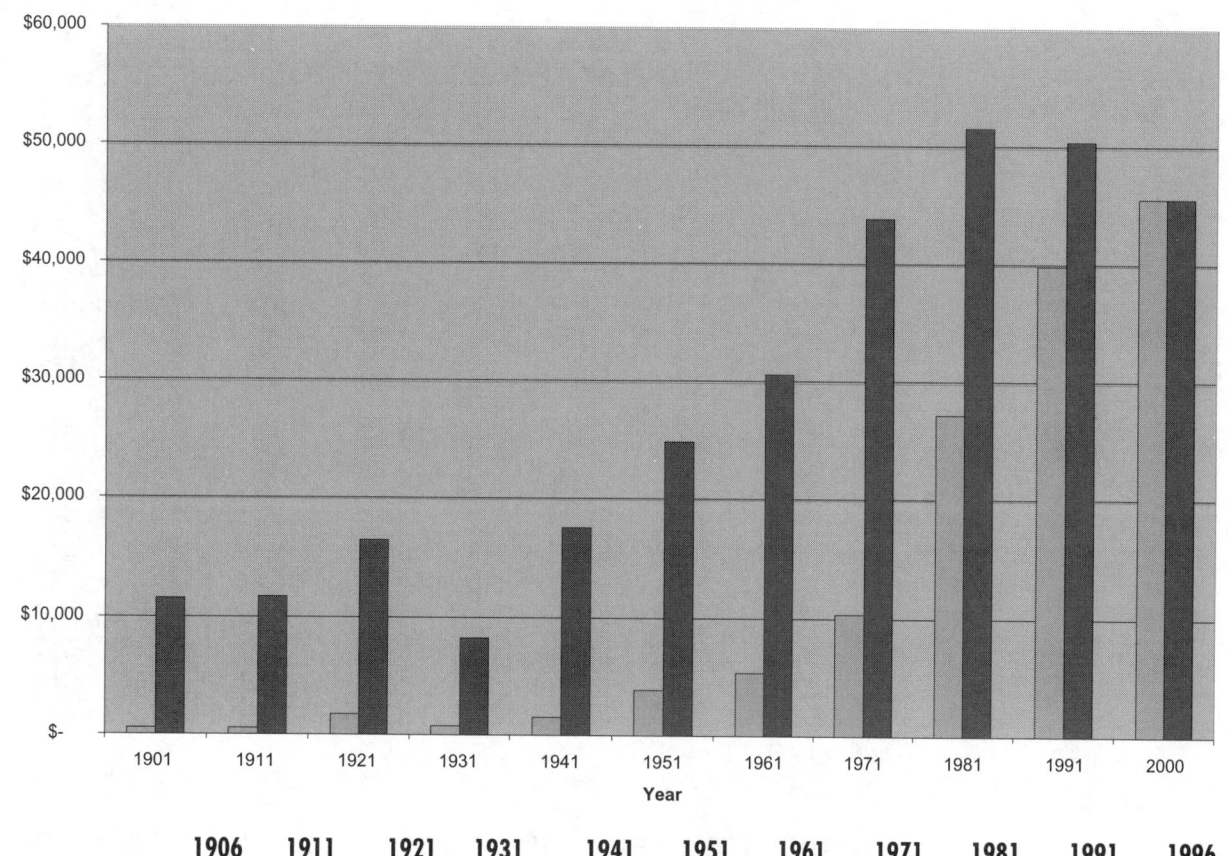

Annual Salary ■ Annual Salary in 2000

	1906	1911	1921	1931	1941	1951	1961	1971	1981	1991	1996
Annual Salary	$603	$644	$1,726	$723	$1,500	$3,762	$5,357	$10,331	$27,283	$39,988	$44,769
Dollar Value in 2000	$11,596	$11,709	$16,596	$8,215	$17,647	$24,914	$30,787	$43,961	$51,672	$50,554	$49,143

* Based on National Average

HELP WANTED

Domestic Annual Salary*

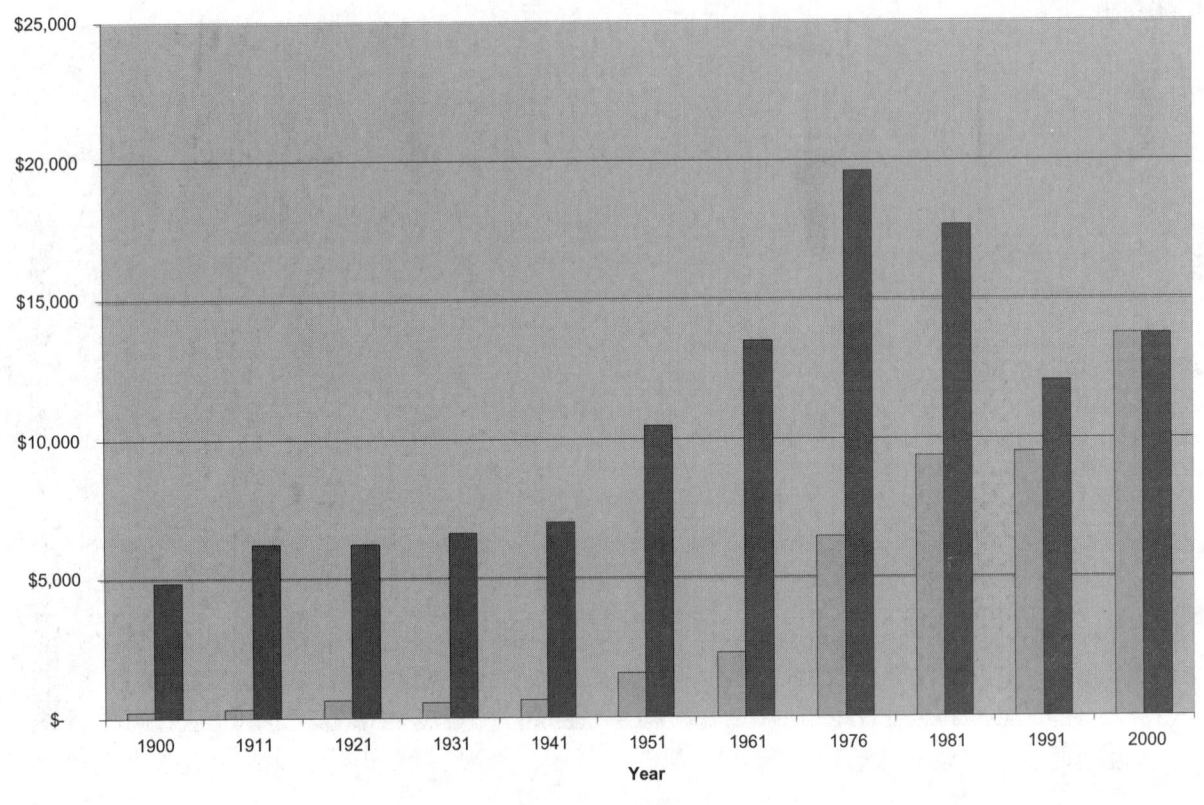

Legend: ▪ Annual Salary ▪ Annual Salary in 2000

	1900	1911	1921	1931	1941	1951	1961	1976	1981	1991	1999
Annual Salary	$240	$343	$649	$584	$601	$1,588	$2,356	$6,479	$9,327	$9,527	$15,000
Dollar Value in 2000	$4,897	$6,236	$6,240	$6,636	$7,071	$10,517	$13,540	$19,633	$17,665	$12,044	$15,512

* Based on National Average

HELP WANTED

Durable Goods Manufacturer Annual Salary*

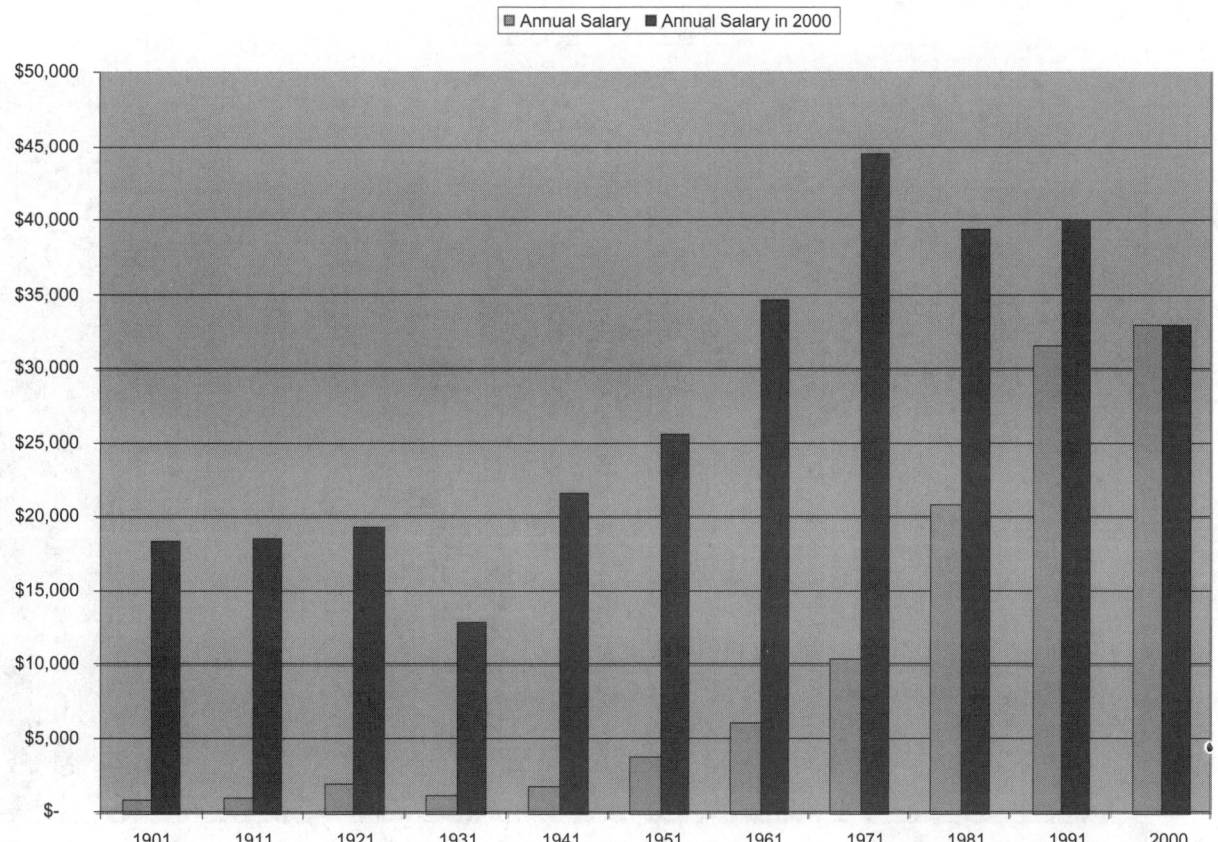

	1901	1911	1921	1931	1941	1951	1961	1971	1981	1991	2000
Annual Salary	$917	$1,020	$2,010	$1,127	$1,840	$3,862	$6,048	$10,473	$20,810	$31,658	$47,930
Dollar Value in 2000	$18,340	$18,545	$19,326	$12,806	$21,647	$25,576	$34,758	$44,566	$39,413	$40,023	$47,930

* Based on National Average

HELP WANTED

Federal Hourly Minimum Wage

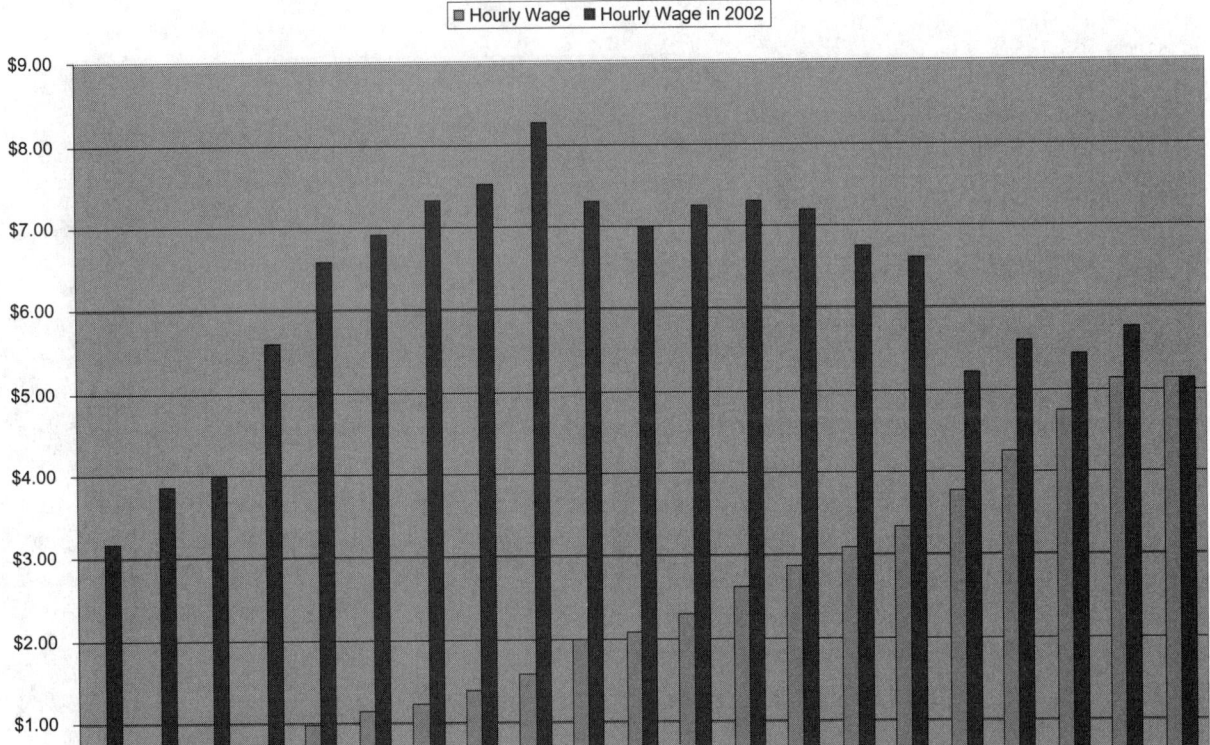

	1938	**1939**	**1945**	**1950**	**1956**	**1961**	**1963**	**1967**	**1968**	**1974**	**1975**
Hourly Wage	$0.25	$0.30	$0.40	$0.75	$1.00	$1.15	$1.25	$1.40	$1.60	$2.00	$2.10
Dollar Value in 2002	$3.19	$3.88	$4.00	$5.60	$6.61	$6.92	$7.35	$7.54	$8.27	$7.30	$7.02

	1976	**1978**	**1979**	**1980**	**1981**	**1990**	**1991**	**1996**	**1997**	**2001**
Hourly Wage	$2.30	$2.65	$2.90	$3.10	$3.35	$3.80	$4.25	$4.75	$5.15	$5.15
Dollar Value in 2002	$7.27	$7.31	$7.19	$6.77	$6.63	$5.23	$5.61	$5.45	$5.77	$5.15

HELP WANTED

Gas & Electric Worker Annual Salary*

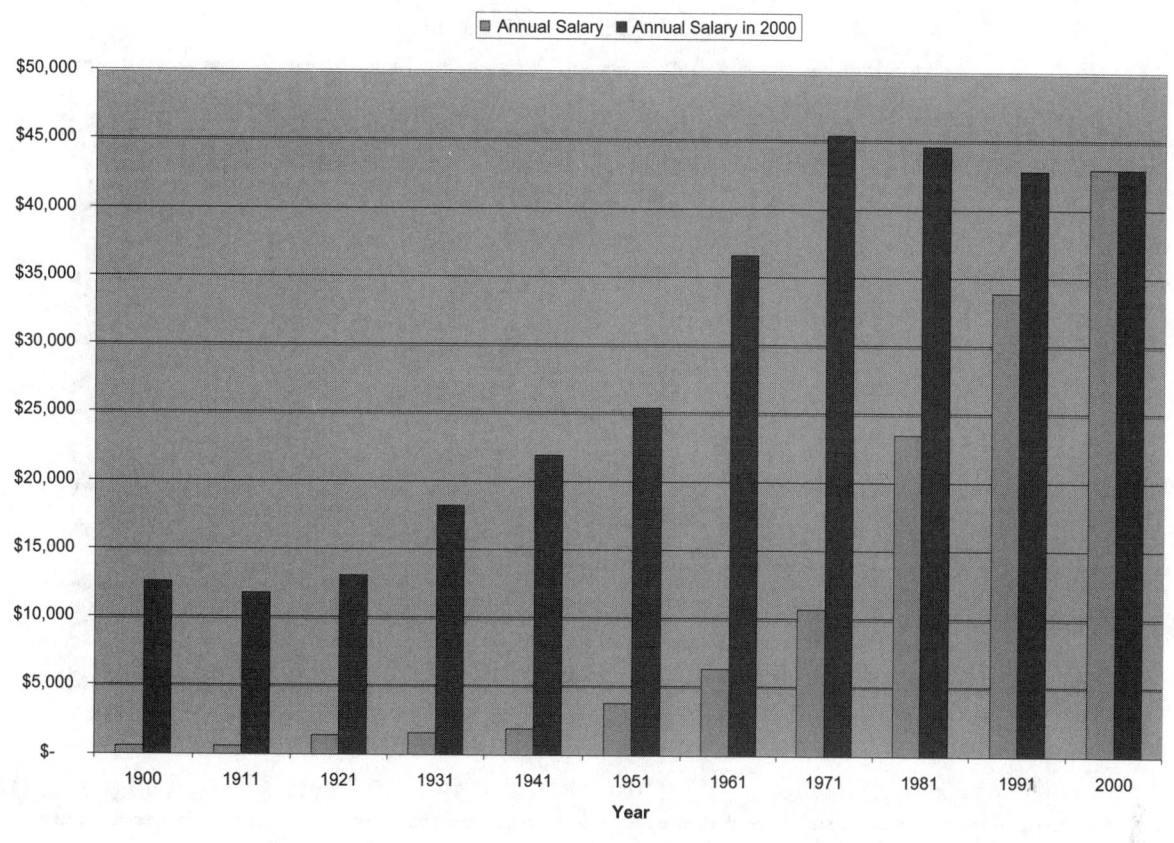

	1900	1911	1921	1931	1941	1951	1961	1971	1981	1991	1996
Annual Salary	$620	$648	$1,364	$1,600	$1,870	$3,851	$6,390	$10,696	$23,595	$33,940	$39,398
Dollar Value in 2000	$12,653	$11,782	$13,115	$18,181	$22,000	$25,503	$36,724	$45,514	$44,688	$42,908	$43,247

* Based on National Average

HELP WANTED

Golf Master Champions Earnings

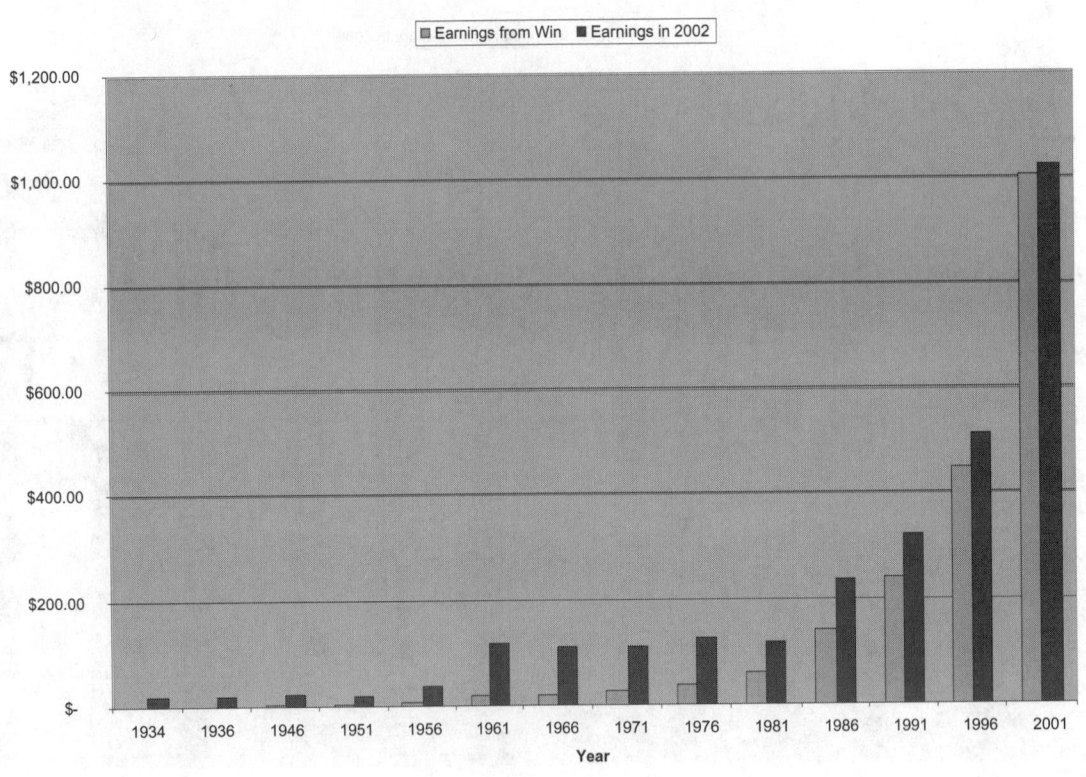

	1934	1936	1946	1951	1956	1961	1966
Winning Player	Horton Smith	Henry Picard	Herman Keiser	Ben Hogan	Jack Burke, Jr.	Gary Player	Jack Nicklaus
Total Score	−4	−3	−6	−8	1 over par	−8	Even
Earnings from Win	$1,500	$1,500	$2,500	$3,000	$6,000	$20,000	$20,000
Dollar Value in 2002	$20,138	$19,138	$23,064	$20,758	$39,684	$120,334	$25,000

	1971	1976	1981	1986	1991	1996	2001
Winning Player	Charles Coody	Raymond Floyd	Tom Watson	Jack Nicklaus	Ian Woosnam	Nick Faldo	Tiger Woods
Total Score	−9	−17	−8	−9	−11	−12	−16
Earnings from Win	$25,000	$40,000	$60,000	$144,000	$243,000	$450,000	$1,008,000
Dollar Value in 2002	$111,049	$126,467	$118,746	$236,365	$320,967	$515,966	$1,023,937

Master's Facts:

♦ Bobby Jones, a celebrated golfer in the 1920's, developed Augusta National's golf course from a 365 acre nursery.
♦ The first four years, the Masters Tournament was originally called the "Augusta National Invitational".
♦ The Masters is the only one of professional golf's four major golf tournaments with a permanent home.
♦ Each of the 18 holes designed by Bobby Jones is named after a plant or tree that adorns that hole.

HELP WANTED

Medical/Health Service Provider Annual Salary*

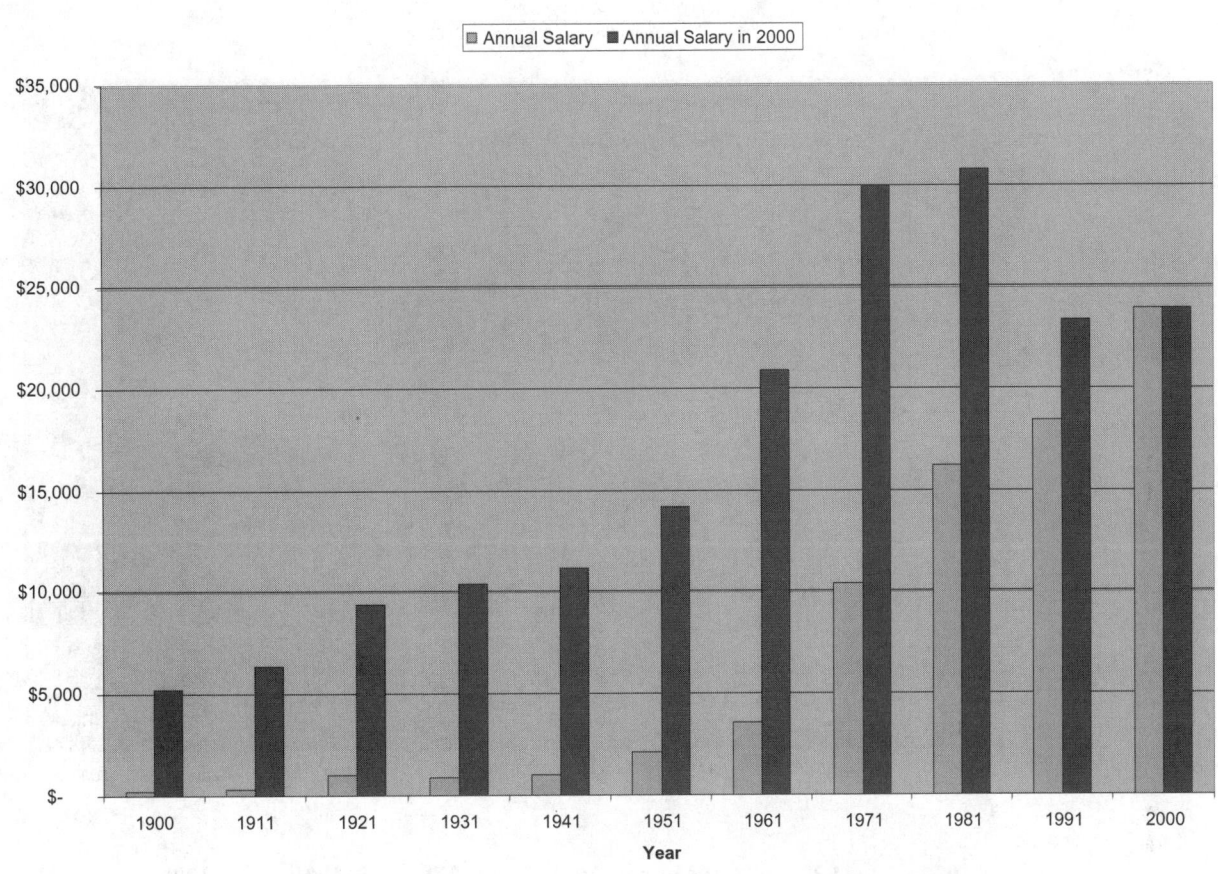

Legend: Annual Salary — Annual Salary in 2000

	1900	1911	1921	1931	1941	1951	1961	1971	1981	1991	1999
Annual Salary	$256	$352	$983	$919	$955	$2,143	$3,636	$10,465	$16,288	$18,522	$20,000
Dollar Value in 2000	$5,224	$6,400	$9,451	$10,443	$11,235	$14,192	$20,896	$29,970	$30,848	$23,416	$20,862

* Based on National Average

HELP WANTED

New York Yankees Baseball Team Payroll

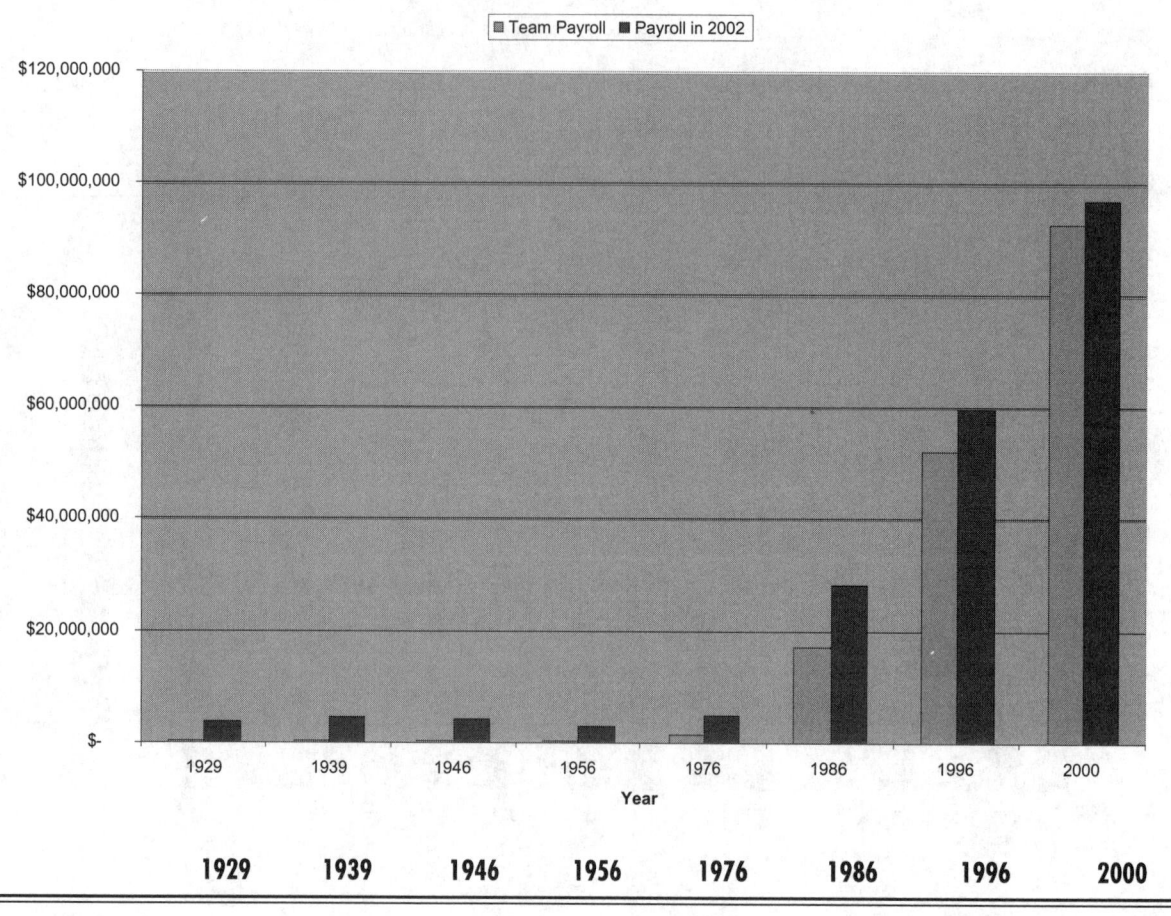

□ Team Payroll ■ Payroll in 2002

	1929	1939	1946	1956	1976	1986	1996	2000
Team Payroll	$365,741	$361,471	$442,854	$492,000	$1,630,900	$17,254,360	$52,189,370	$92,938,260
Dollar Value in 2002	$3,847,766	$4,678,319	$4,085,612	$3,254,074	$5,156,396	$28,311,861	$59,839,819	$97,094,036

HELP WANTED

Playboy Playmate Modeling Fee

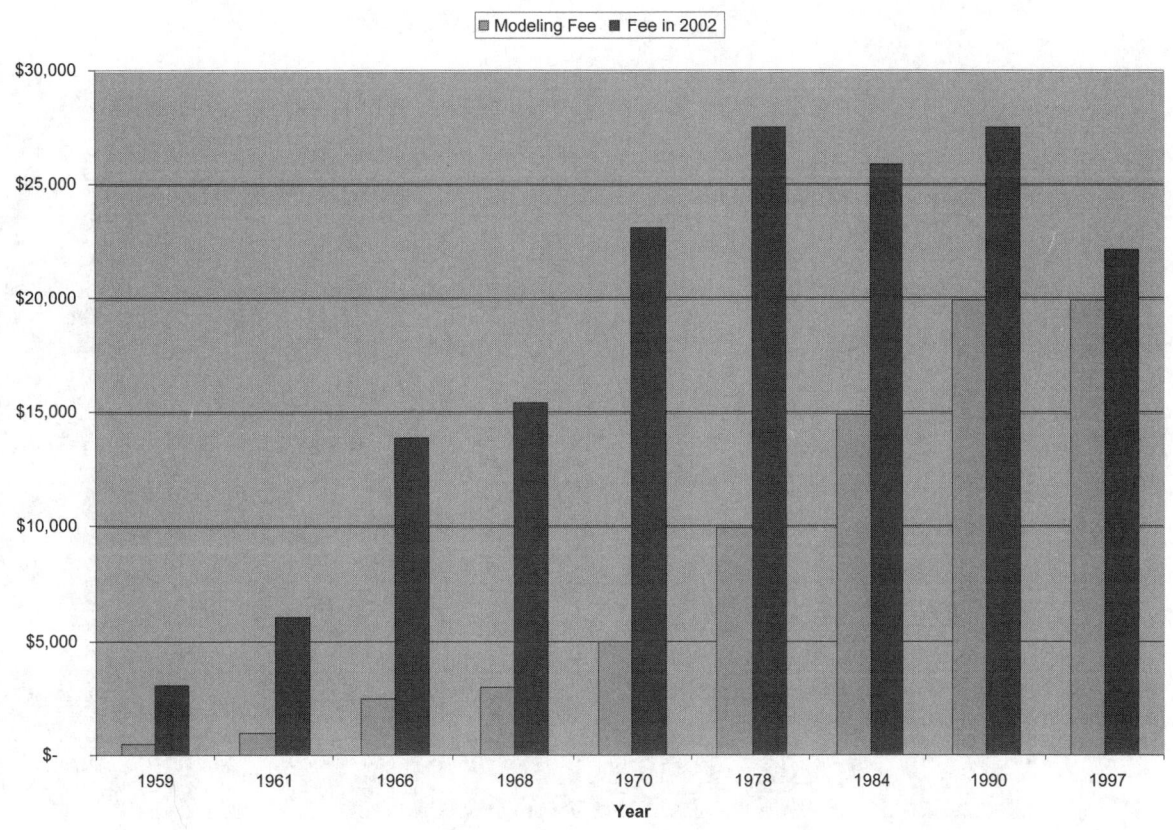

	1959	1961	1966	1968	1970	1978	1984	1990	1997
Modeling Fee	$500	$1,000	$2,500	$3,000	$5,000	$10,000	$15,000	$20,000	$20,000
Dollar Value in 2002	$3,091	$6,016	$13,881	$15,508	$23,182	$27,592	$25,972	$27,528	$22,214

HELP WANTED

President of the United States Annual Salary

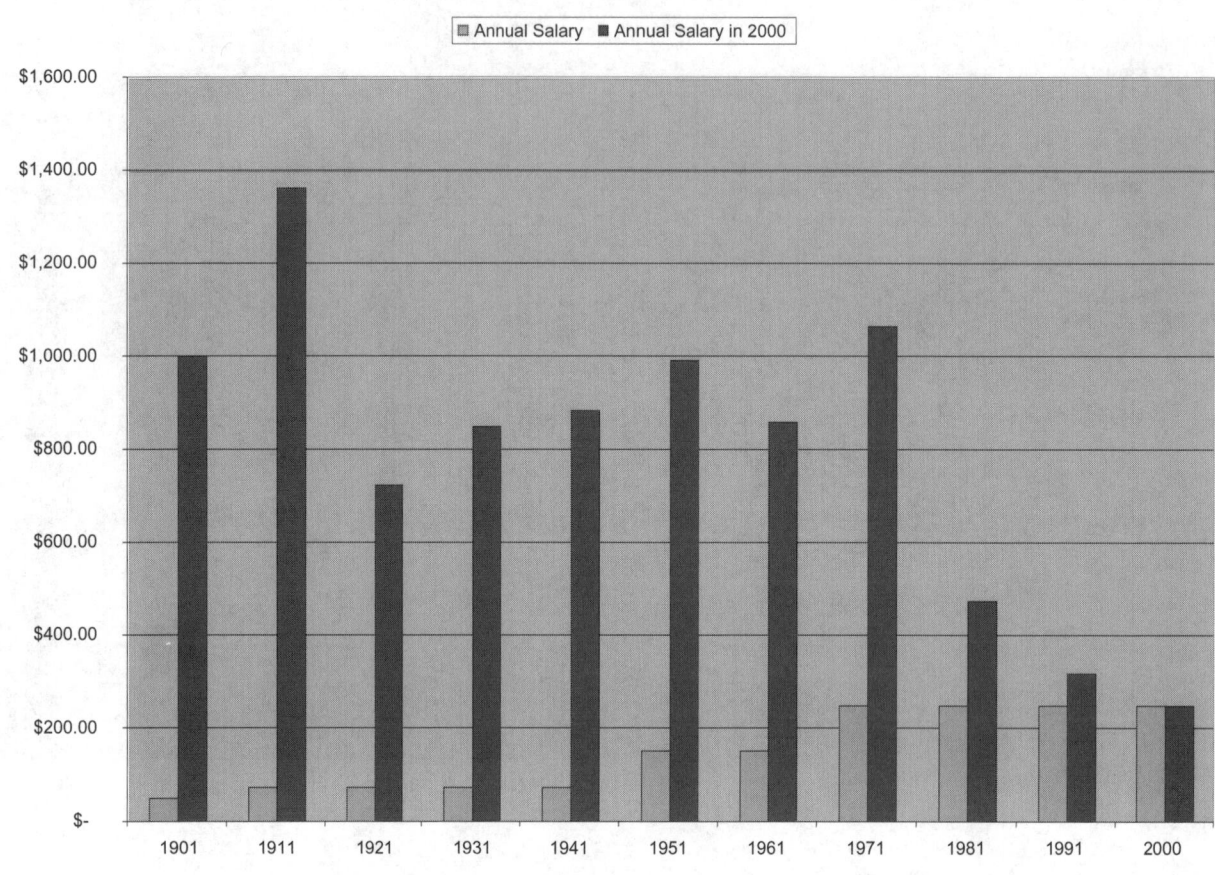

Legend: ▨ Annual Salary ■ Annual Salary in 2000

	1901	**1911**	**1921**	**1931**	**1941**	**1951**
President	William McKinley	William H. Taft	Warren Harding	Herbert Hoover	Franklin D. Roosevelt	Harry S. Truman
Salary	$50,000	$75,000	$75,000	$75,000	$75,000	$100,000 + $50,000 expense account
Dollar Value in 2000	$1,000,000	$1,363,636	$721,154	$852,273	$882,353	$993,377

	1961	**1971**	**1981**	**1991**	**2000**
President	John F. Kennedy	Richard M. Nixon	Ronald W. Reagan	George H. W. Bush	George W. Bush
Salary	$100,000 + $50,000 expense account (refused by Kennedy)	$200,000 + $50,000 expense account	$200,000 + $50,000 expense account	$200,000 + $50,000 expense account	$400,000 + $50,000 expense account
Dollar Value in 2000	$862,069	$1,063,830	$473,485	$316,056	$450,000

HELP WANTED

Public School Teacher Annual Salary*

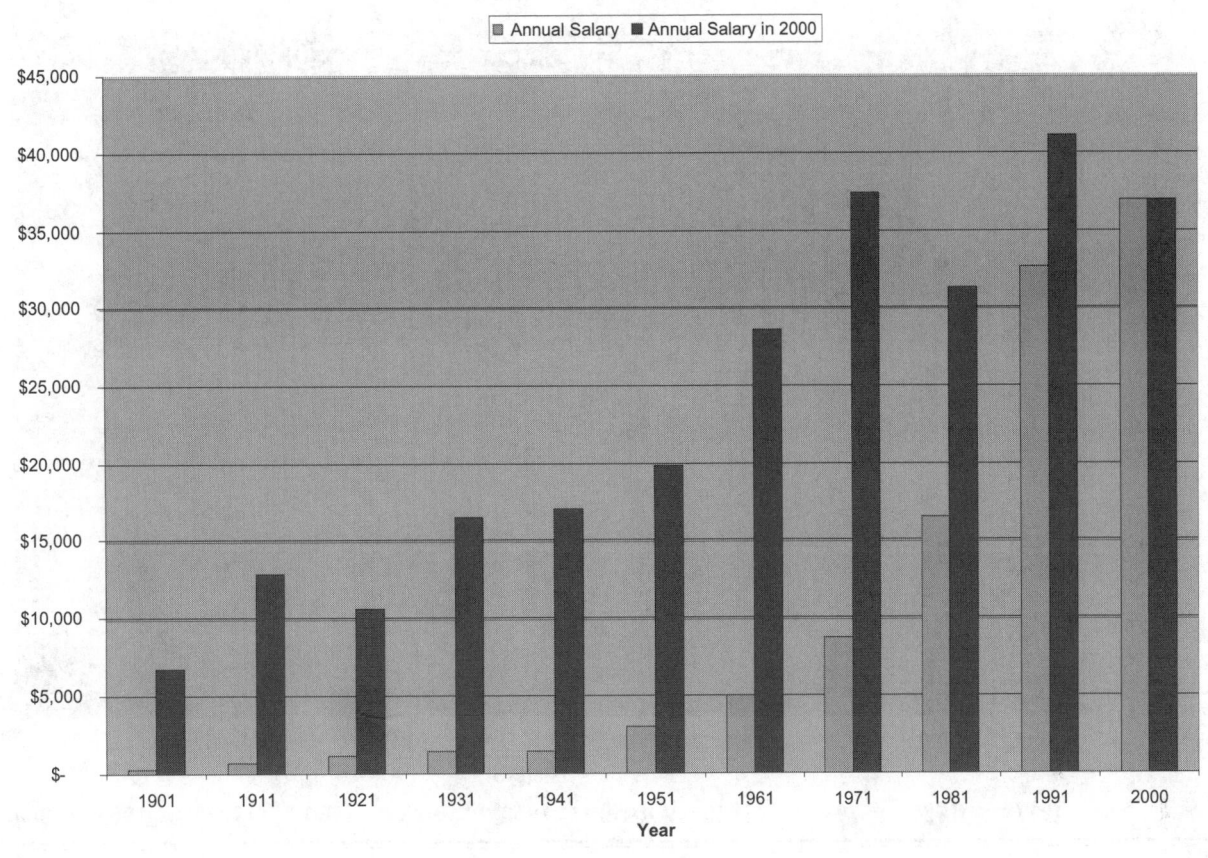

■ Annual Salary ■ Annual Salary in 2000

	1901	1911	1921	1931	1941	1951	1961	1971	1981	1991	2000
Annual Salary	$337	$712	$1,109	$1,463	$1,462	$2,998	$4,991	$8,813	$16,606	$32,638	$43,740
Dollar Value in 2000	$6,740	$12,945	$10,663	$16,625	$17,200	$19,854	$28,683	$37,502	$31,451	$41,262	$43,740

* Based on National Average

HELP WANTED

Pulitzer Prize Award Amount

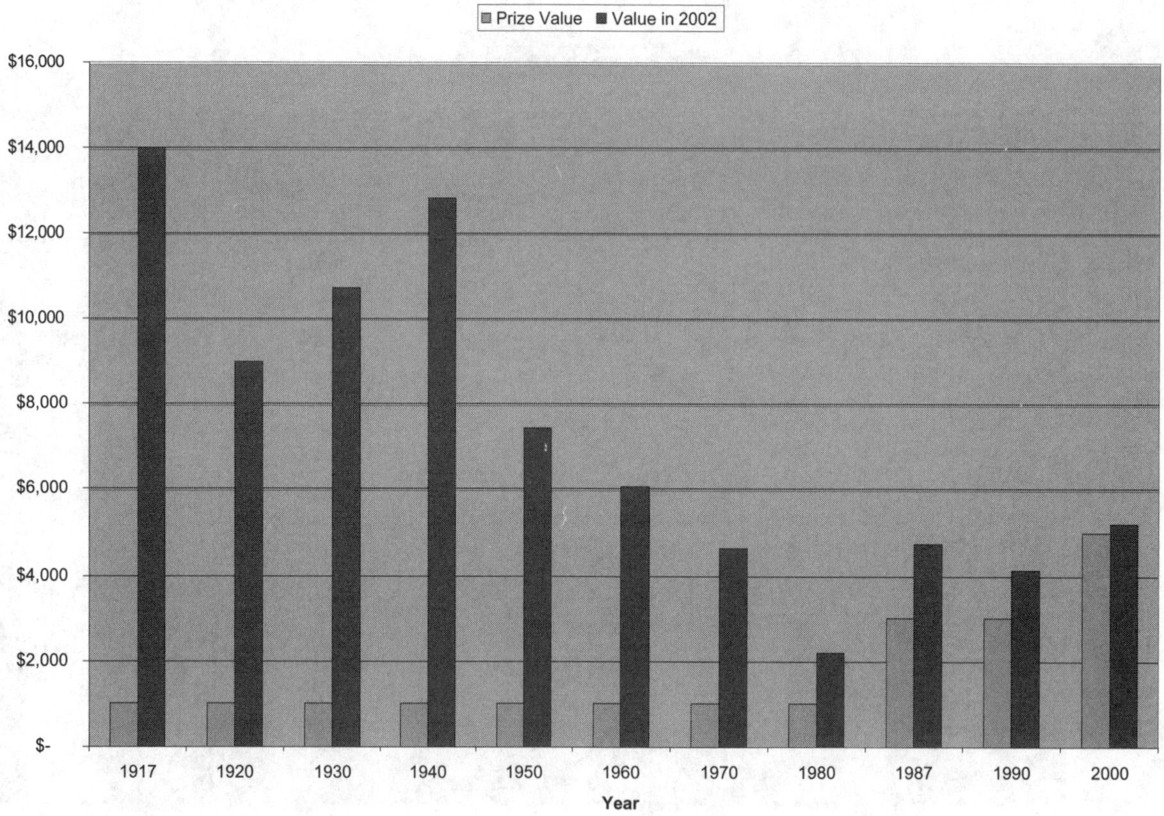

| | Prize Value | Value in 2002 |

	1917	**1920**	**1930**	**1940**	**1950**	**1960**	**1970**	**1980**	**1987**	**1990**	**2000**
Prize Value	$1,000	$1,000	$1,000	$1,000	$1,000	$1,000	$1,000	$1,000	$3,000	$3,000	$5,000
Dollar Value in 2002	$14,055	$8,995	$10,772	$12,850	$7,464	$6,077	$4,636	$2,183	$4,750	$4,129	$5,223

Awards in Journalism for National Reporting*

Year	Journalist(s)	Subject
1917	H. B. Swope	"Inside the German Empire."
1920	John J. Leary	National coal strike in the winter of 1919
1930	R. D. Owen	The Byrd Antarctic Expedition.
1940	S. Burton Heath	The frauds perpetrated by Federal Judge Martin T. Manton
1950	Edwin Guthman	The clearing of Communist charges of Professor Melvin Rader
1960	Vance Trimble	The extent of nepotism in the Congress of the United States
1970	William Eaton	Disclosures about the background of Judge Clement F. Haynesworth Jr
1980	Orsini & Stafford	Investigation of the Church of Scientology
1990	Anderson, Dietrich, Gwinn & Nalder	The Exxon Valdez oil spill and its aftermath
2000	Staff of Wall Street Journal	Stories that question U.S. defense spending and military deployment in the post-Cold War era

* Prior to 1948, the award was only for "Reporting"

HELP WANTED

Railroad Worker Annual Salary*

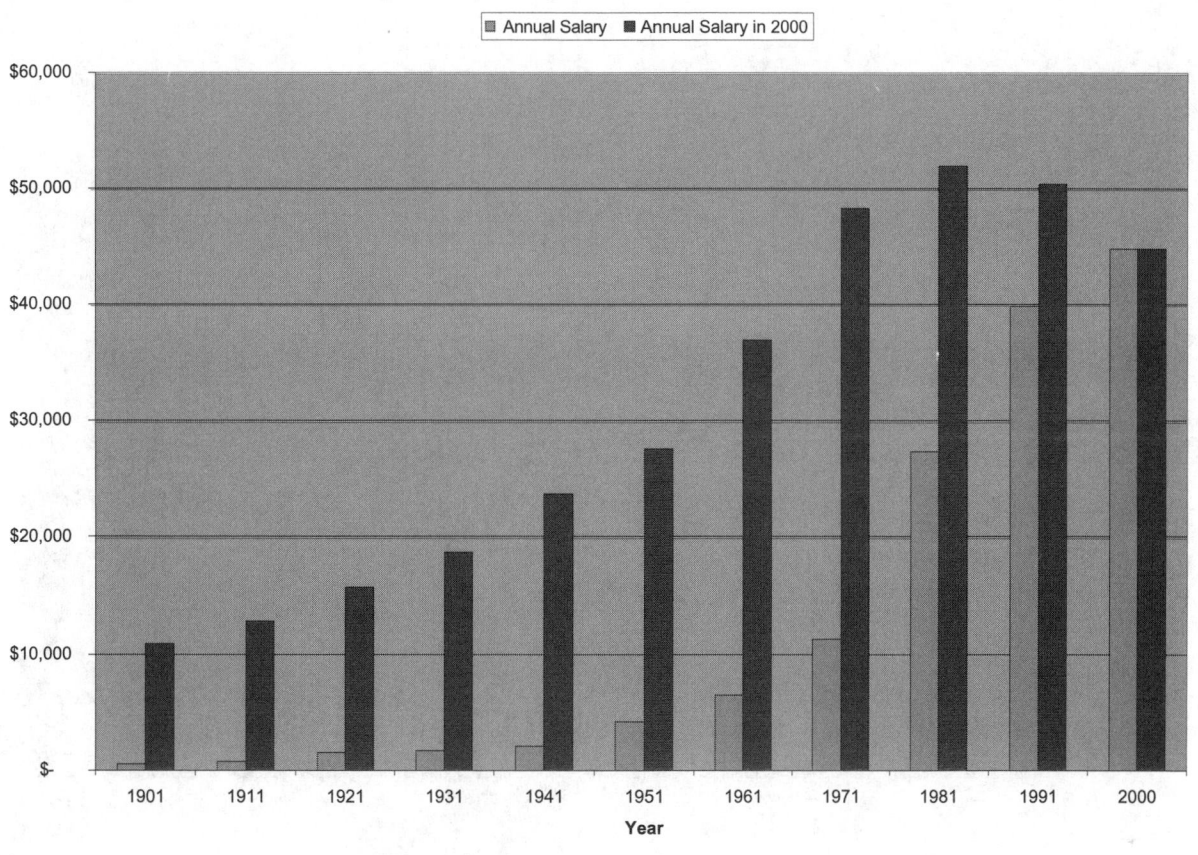

Legend: ☐ Annual Salary ■ Annual Salary in 2000

	1901	1911	1921	1931	1941	1951	1961	1971	1981	1991	2000
Annual Salary	$549	$705	$1,632	$1,661	$2,030	$4,163	$6,440	$11,360	$27,452	$39,987	$57,157
Dollar Value in 2000	$10,980	$12,818	$15,692	$18,875	$23,882	$27,569	$37,011	$48,340	$51,992	$50,552	$57,157

* Based on National Average

HELP WANTED

State & Local Government Worker Annual Salary*

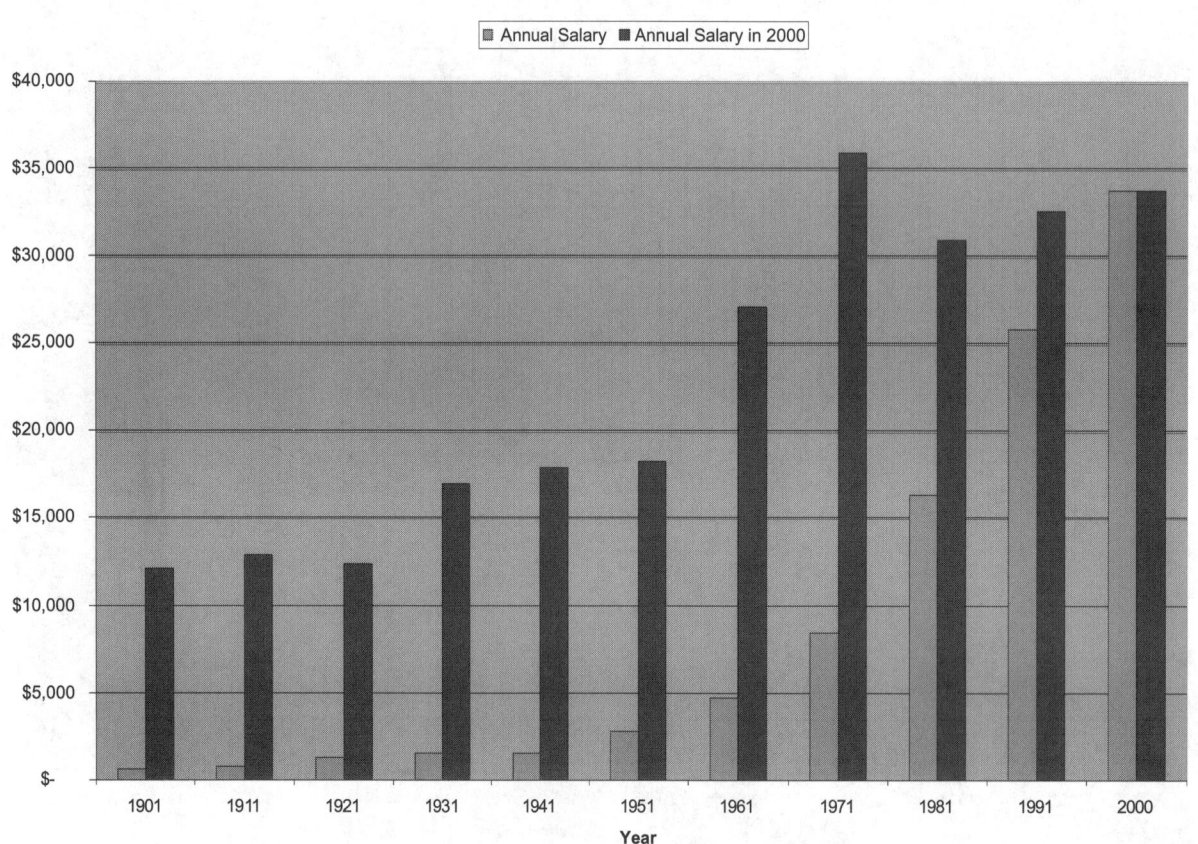

	1901	1911	1921	1931	1941	1951	1961	1971	1981	1991	2000
Annual Salary	$605	$712	$1,296	$1,497	$1,522	$2,758	$4,721	$8,443	$16,368	$25,863	$35,320
Dollar Value in 2000	$12,100	$12,945	$12,461	$17,011	$17,905	$18,264	$27,132	$35,927	$30,989	$32,697	$35,320

* Based on National Average

HELP WANTED

University of South Carolina Yearly Tuition*

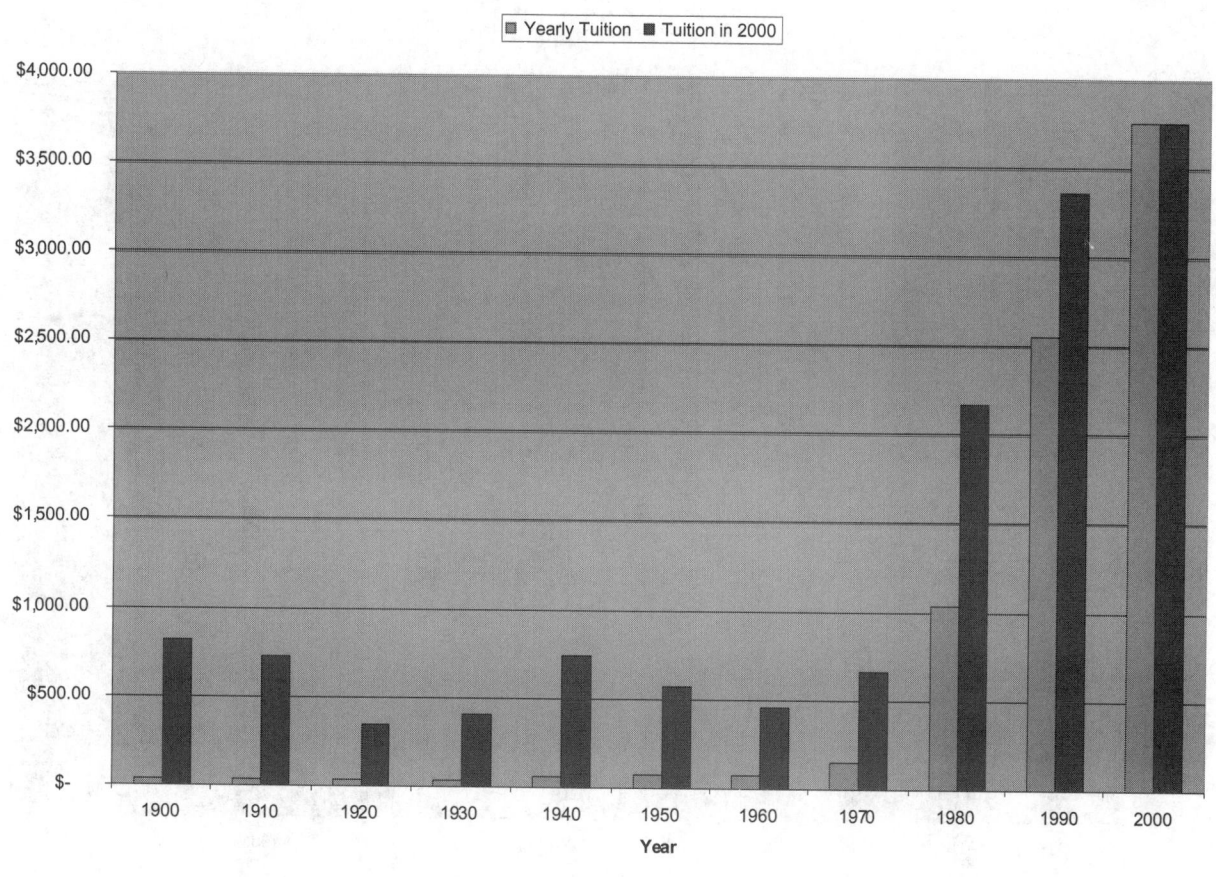

	1900	1910	19210	1930	1940	1950	1960	1970	1980	1990	2000
Yearly Tuition	$40.00	$40.00	$40.00	$40.00	$60.00	$80.00	$80.00	$150.00	$1,040.00	$2,560.00	$3,768.00
Dollar Value in 2000	$816.33	$727.27	$344.33	$412.37	$740.74	$571.43	$465.12	$666.67	$2,171.19	$3,372.86	$3,768.00

* Does not include other University expenses

HELP WANTED

United States Federal Civilian Annual Salary*

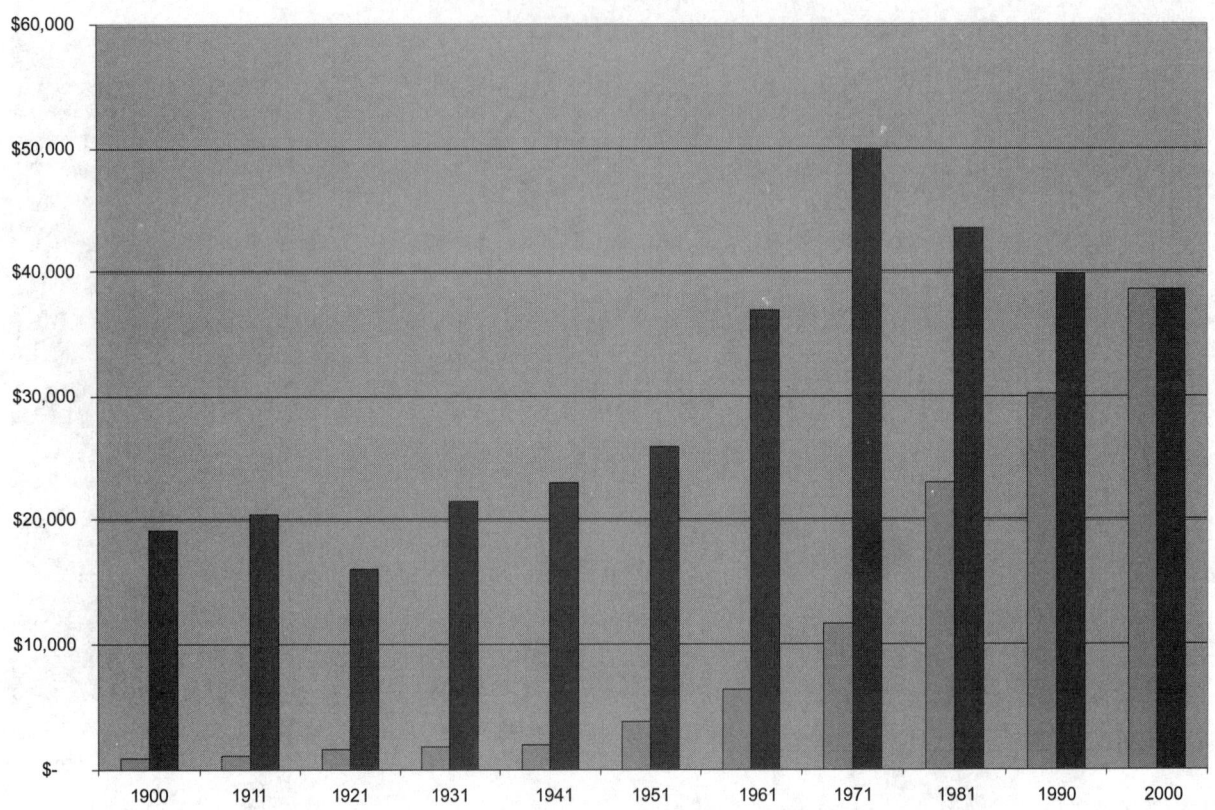

	1900	1911	1921	1931	1941	1951	1961	1971	1981	1990	2000
Annual Salary	$940	$1,133	$1,683	$1,895	$1,970	$3,924	$6,451	$11,767	$23,029	$31,174	$50,429
Dollar Value in 2000	$19,183	$20,600	$16,182	$21,534	$23,176	$25,986	$37,074	$50,072	$43,616	$41,072	$50,429

* Based on National Average

HELP WANTED

Winning Player's Share of Football Championship Game*

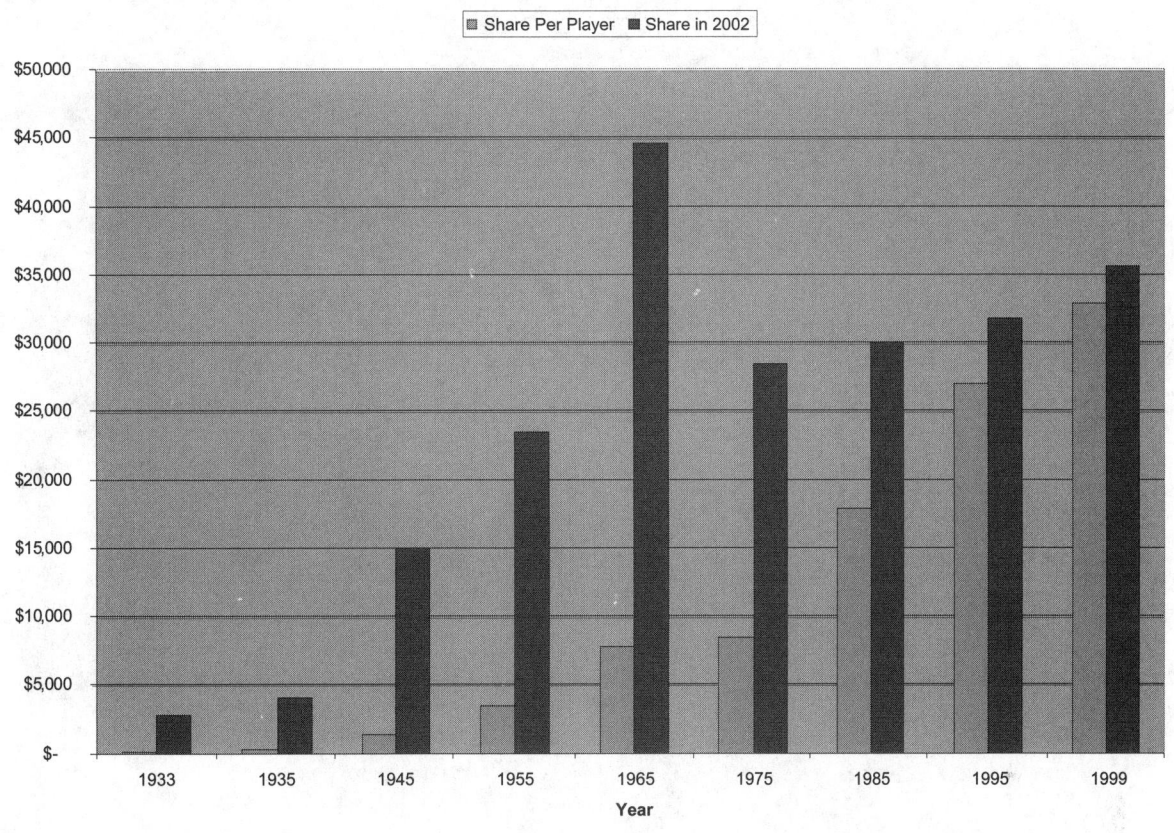

	1933	1935	1945	1955	1965	1975	1985	1995	1999
Team	Chicago	Detroit	Cleveland	Cleveland	Green Bay	Dallas	Chicago	Dallas	St. Louis
Share Per Player	$210	$313	$1,469	$3,508	$7,819	$8,500	$18,000	$27,000	$33,000
Dollar Value in 2002	$2,911	$4,115	$15,016	$23,548	$44,655	$28,423	$30,095	$31,872	$35,634

* (NFL/NFC); NFC Championship Games began in 1970

ITEMS IN THE REFRIGERATOR

Bread (1 loaf)

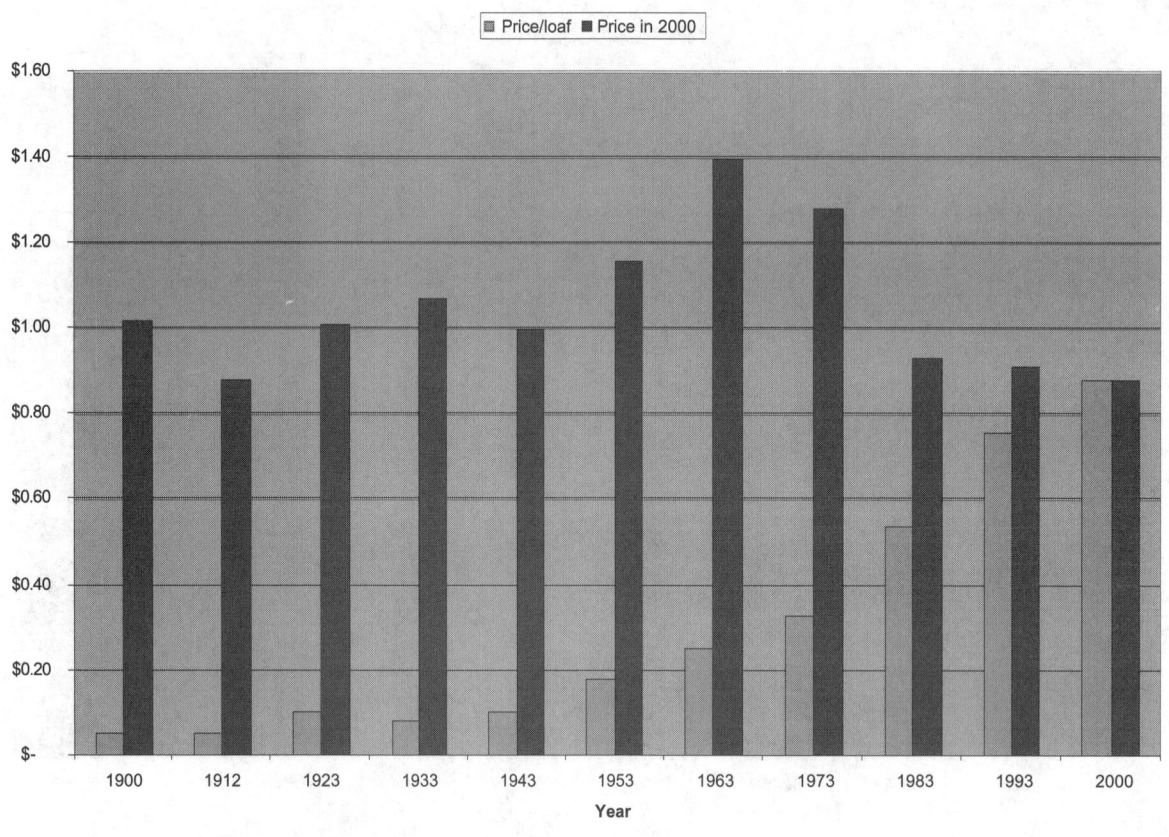

Legend: ▦ Price/loaf ■ Price in 2000

	1900	1912	1923	1933	1943	1953	1963	1973	1983	1993	2000
Price/loaf	$0.05	$0.05	$0.10	$0.08	$0.10	$0.18	$0.25	$0.33	$0.54	$0.76	$0.88
Dollar Value in 2000	$1.02	$0.88	$1.01	$1.07	$1.00	$1.16	$1.40	$1.28	$0.93	$0.91	$0.88

ITEMS IN THE REFRIGERATOR

Butter (1 pound)

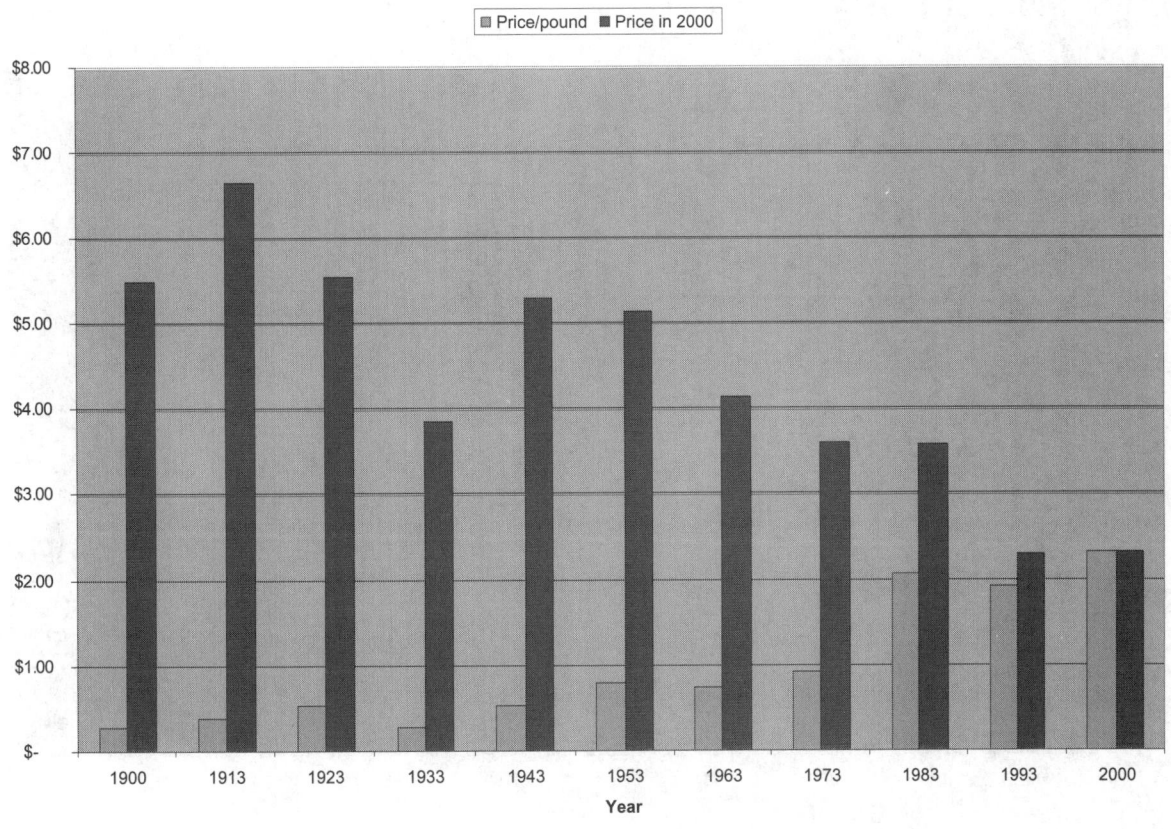

	1900	1913	1923	1933	1943	1953	1963	1973	1983	1993	1999
Price/pound	$0.27	$0.38	$0.55	$0.29	$0.53	$0.80	$0.74	$0.93	$2.07	$1.93	$2.27
Dollar Value in 2000	$5.51	$6.67	$5.56	$3.87	$5.30	$5.16	$4.16	$ 3.60	$3.58	$ 2.30	$2.35

ITEMS IN THE REFRIGERATOR

Cheese (1 pound)

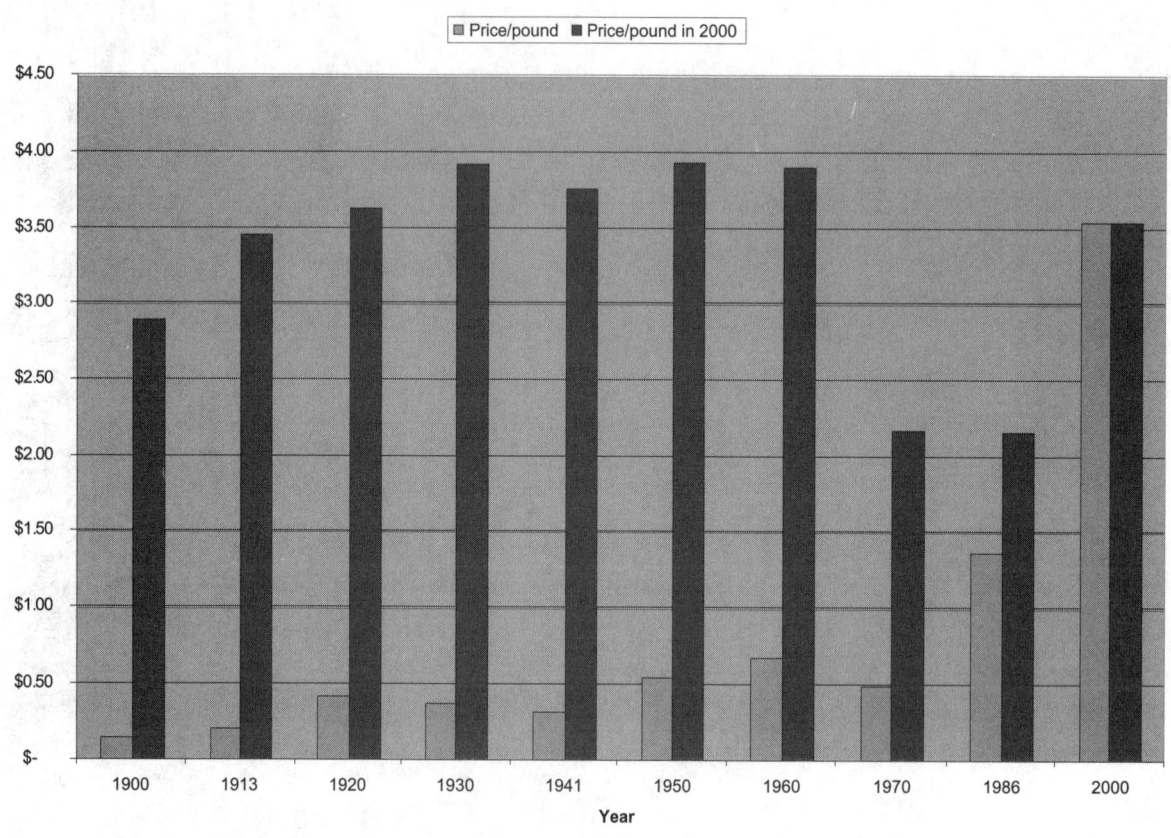

Legend: ■ Price/pound ■ Price/pound in 2000

	1900	1913	1923	1933	1943	1953	1963	1973	1983	2000
Price/pound	$0.14	$0.20	$0.42	$0.38	$0.32	$0.55	$0.67	$0.49	$1.38	$3.55
Dollar Value in 2000	$2.90	$3.46	$3.63	$3.92	$3.76	$3.93	$3.90	$2.18	$2.16	$3.55

ITEMS IN THE REFRIGERATOR

Chicken (1 pound)

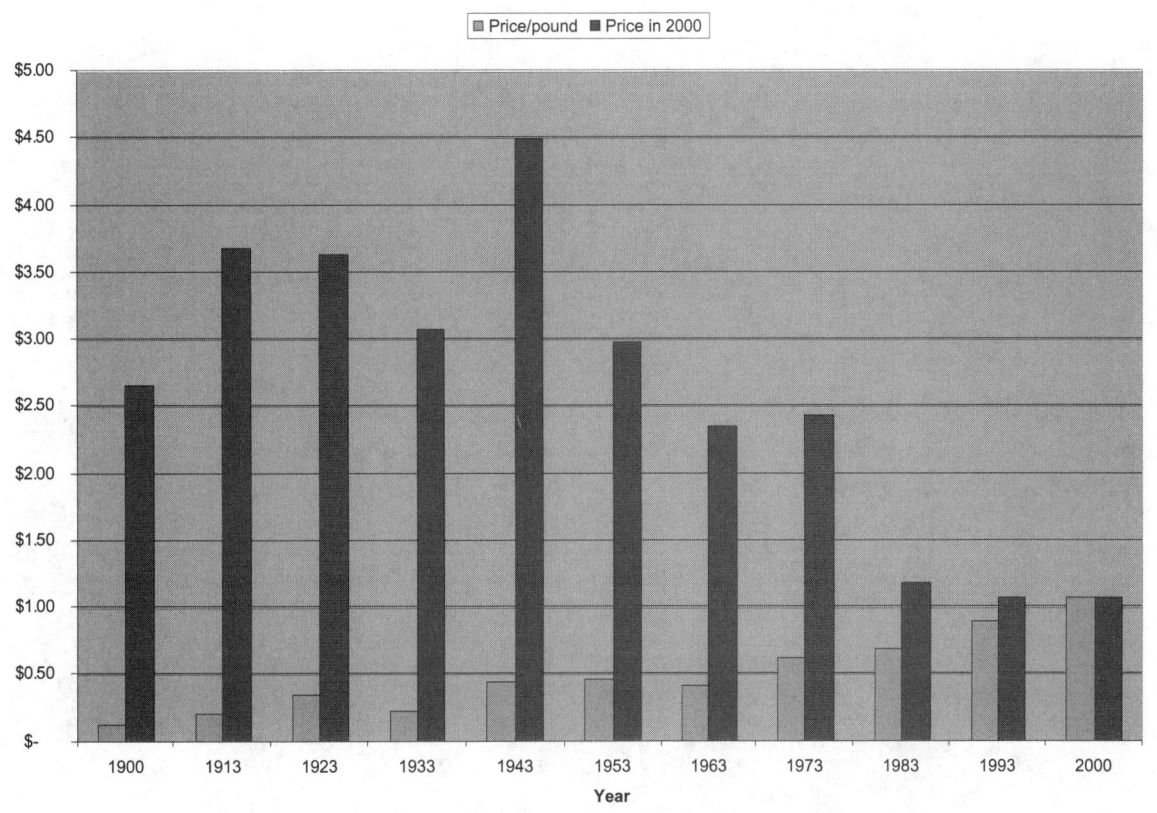

	1900	1913	1923	1933	1943	1953	1963	1973	1983	1993	1999
Price/pound	$0.13	$0.21	$0.36	$0.23	$0.45	$0.46	$0.42	$0.63	$0.69	$0.90	$1.07
Dollar Value in 2000	$2.65	$3.68	$3.64	$3.07	$4.50	$2.97	$2.36	$2.44	$1.19	$1.07	$1.07

ITEMS IN THE REFRIGERATOR

Coffee (1 pound)

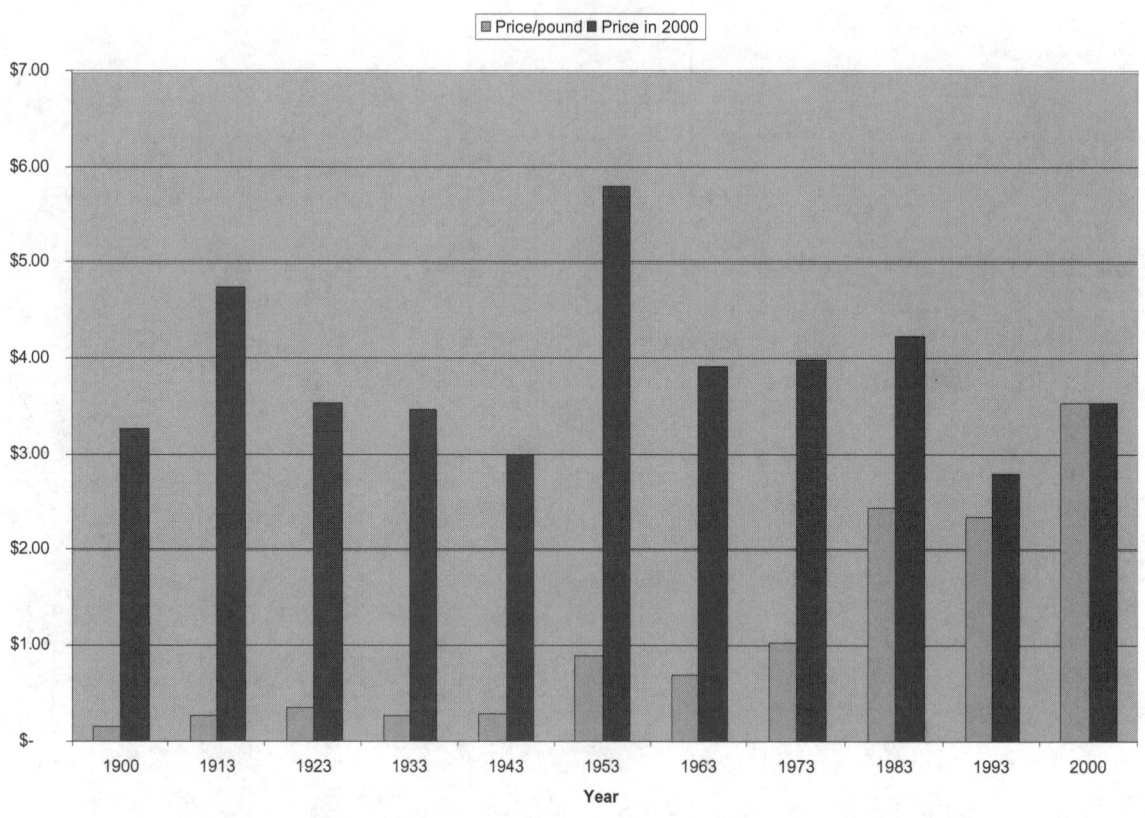

	1900	**1913**	**1923**	**1933**	**1943**	**1953**	**1963**	**1973**	**1983**	**1993**	**2000**
Price/pound	$0.16	$0.27	$0.35	$0.26	$0.30	$0.90	$0.70	$1.03	$2.45	$2.35	$3.54
Dollar Value in 2000	$3.27	$4.74	$3.54	$3.47	$3.00	$5.81	$3.93	$3.99	$4.24	$2.80	$3.54

ITEMS IN THE REFRIGERATOR

Dr. Pepper (8oz.)

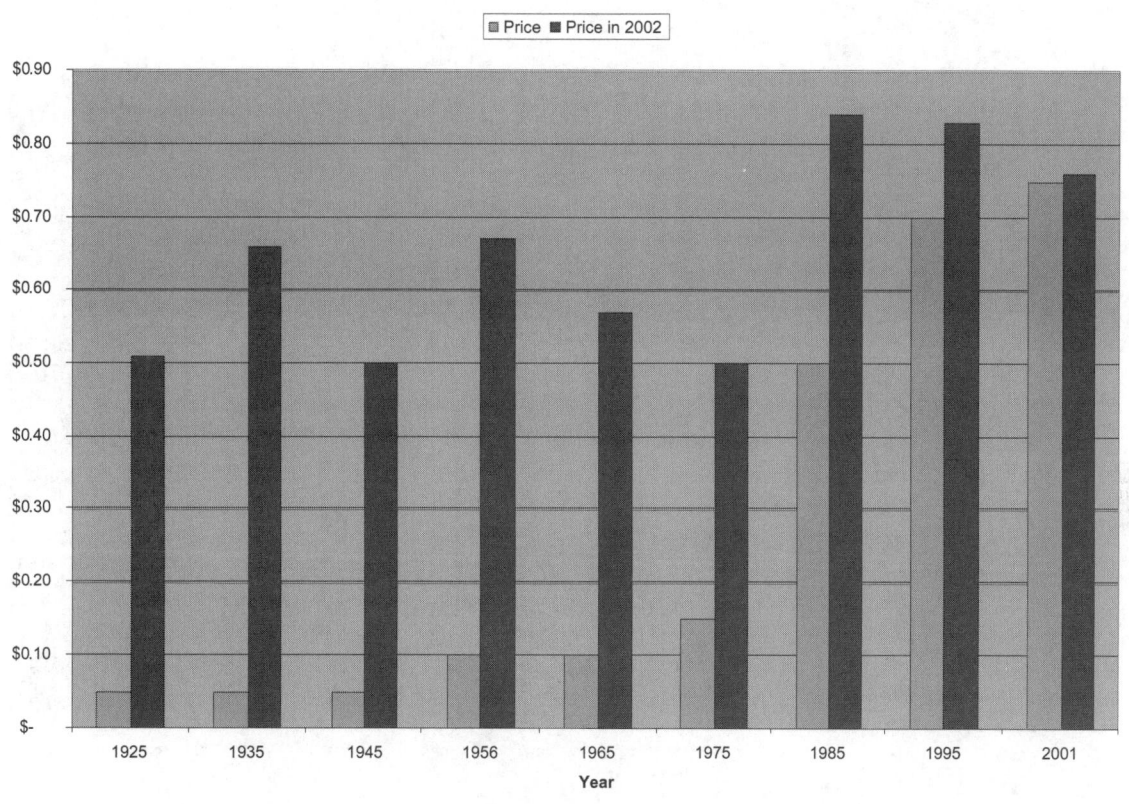

	1925	1935	1945	1955	1965	1975	1985	1995	2001
Price	$0.05	$0.05	$0.05	$0.10	$0.10	$0.15	$0.50	$0.70	$0.75
Dollar Value in 2002	$0.51	$0.66	$0.50	$0.67	$0.57	$0.50	$0.84	$0.83	$0.76

Comparison of Serving Price and Size

Year	Serving Size (oz.)	Serving Price	Price in 2000 Serving Price	Price/oz.
1925	6.5	$0.05	$0.51	$0.08
1935	6.5	$0.05	$0.66	$0.10
1945	6.5	$0.05	$0.50	$0.08
1955	6.5	$0.10	$0.67	$0.10
1965	10	$0.10	$0.57	$0.06
1975	10	$0.15	$0.50	$0.05
1985	12	$0.50	$0.84	$0.07
1995	12	$0.70	$0.83	$0.07
2001	12	$0.75	$0.76	$0.06

ITEMS IN THE REFRIGERATOR

Eggs (1 dozen)

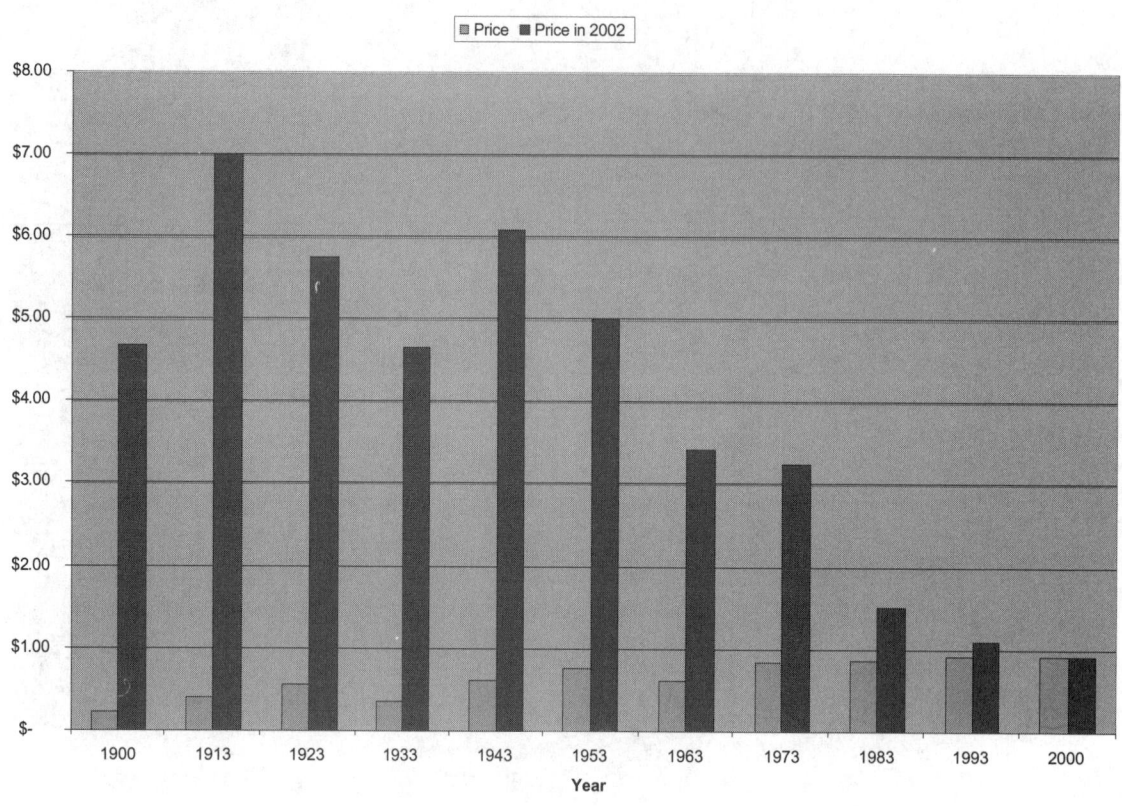

	1900	1913	1923	1933	1943	1953	1963	1973	1983	1993	2000
Price/dozen	$0.23	$0.40	$0.57	$0.35	$0.61	$0.78	$0.61	$0.84	$0.87	$0.92	$0.91
Dollar Value in 2000	$4.69	$7.02	$5.76	$4.67	$6.10	$5.03	$3.43	$3.26	$1.51	$1.10	$0.91

ITEMS IN THE REFRIGERATOR

Hershey's Milk Chocolate Bar

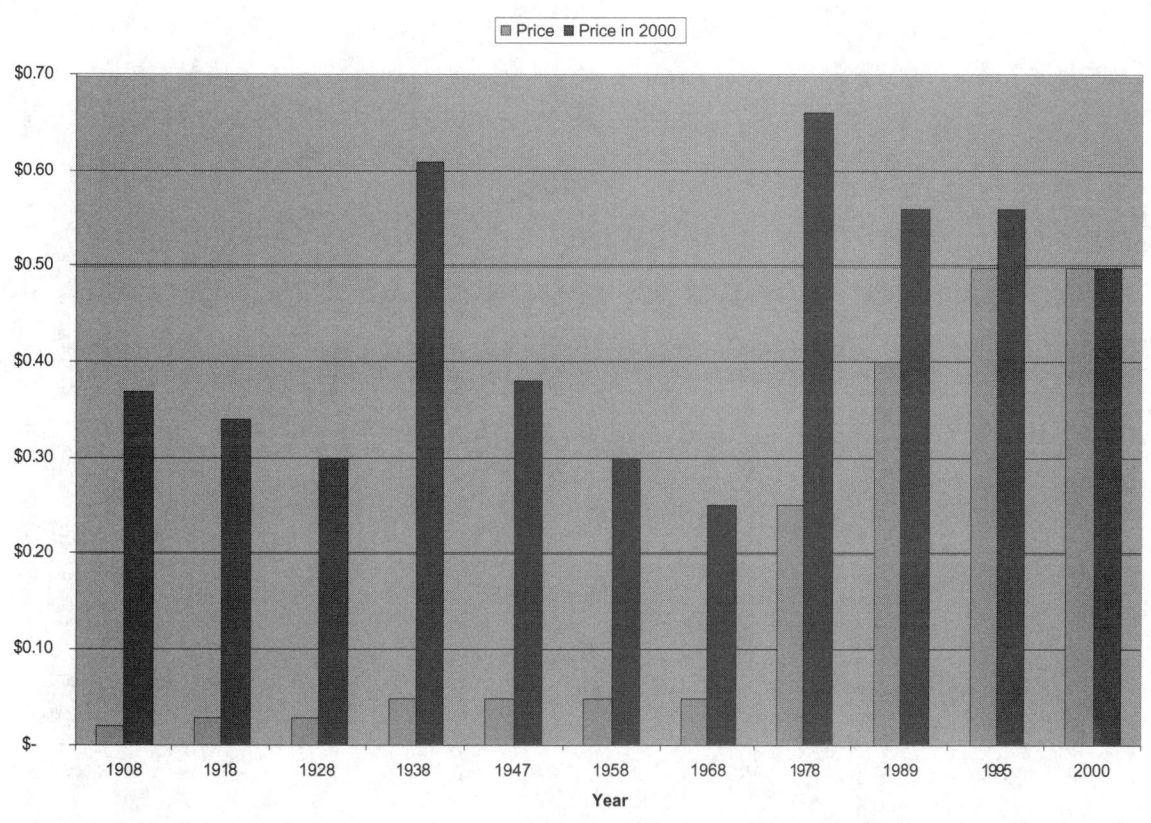

	1908	1918	1928	1938	1947	1958	1968	1978	1989	1995	2000
Price	$0.02	$0.03	$0.03	$0.05	$0.05	$0.05	$0.05	$0.25	$0.40	$0.50	$0.50
Dollar Value in 2000	$0.37	$0.34	$0.30	$0.61	$0.38	$0.30	$0.25	$0.66	$0.56	$0.56	$0.50

Comparison of Serving Price and Size

Year	Price	Bar Size	Value in 2000 Price/Bar	Price/oz.
1908	$0.02	9/16 oz	$0.37	$0.66
1918	$0.03	15/16 oz.	$0.34	$0.36
1928	$0.03	9/16 oz.	$0.30	$0.53
1938	$0.05	1 3/8 oz.	$0.61	$0.44
1947	$0.05	1.0 oz	$0.38	$0.38
1958	$0.05	7/8 oz.	$0.30	$0.34
1968	$0.05	3/4 oz.	$0.25	$0.33
1978	$0.25	1.2 oz.	$0.66	$0.55
1989	$0.40	1.55 oz.	$0.56	$0.36
1995	$0.50	1.55 oz.	$0.56	$0.36
2000	$0.50	1.55 oz.	$0.50	$0.32

ITEMS IN THE REFRIGERATOR

Margarine (1 pound)

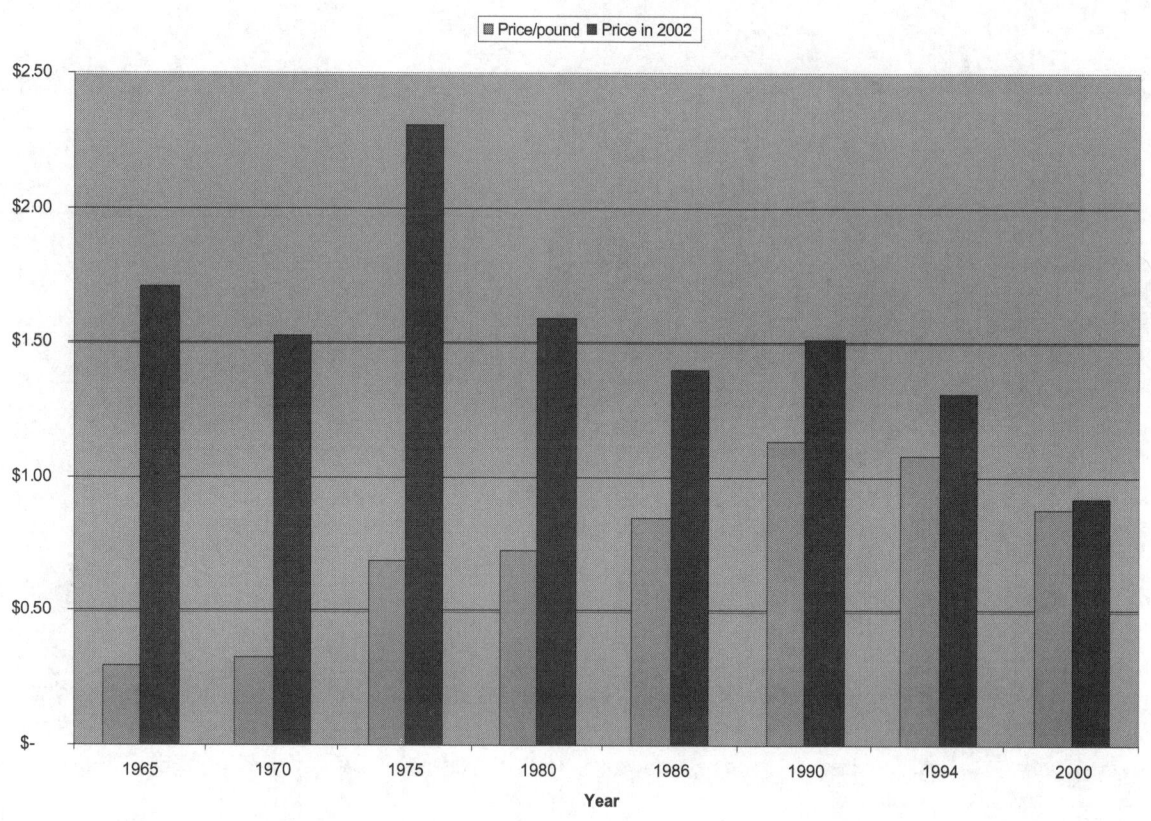

	1965	1970	1975	1980	1986	1990	1994	2000
Price/pound	$0.30	$0.33	$0.69	$0.73	$0.85	$1.14	$1.08	$0.88
Dollar Value in 2000	$1.71	$1.53	$2.31	$1.59	$1.40	$1.51	$1.31	$0.92

ITEMS IN THE REFRIGERATOR

McDonald's Hamburger

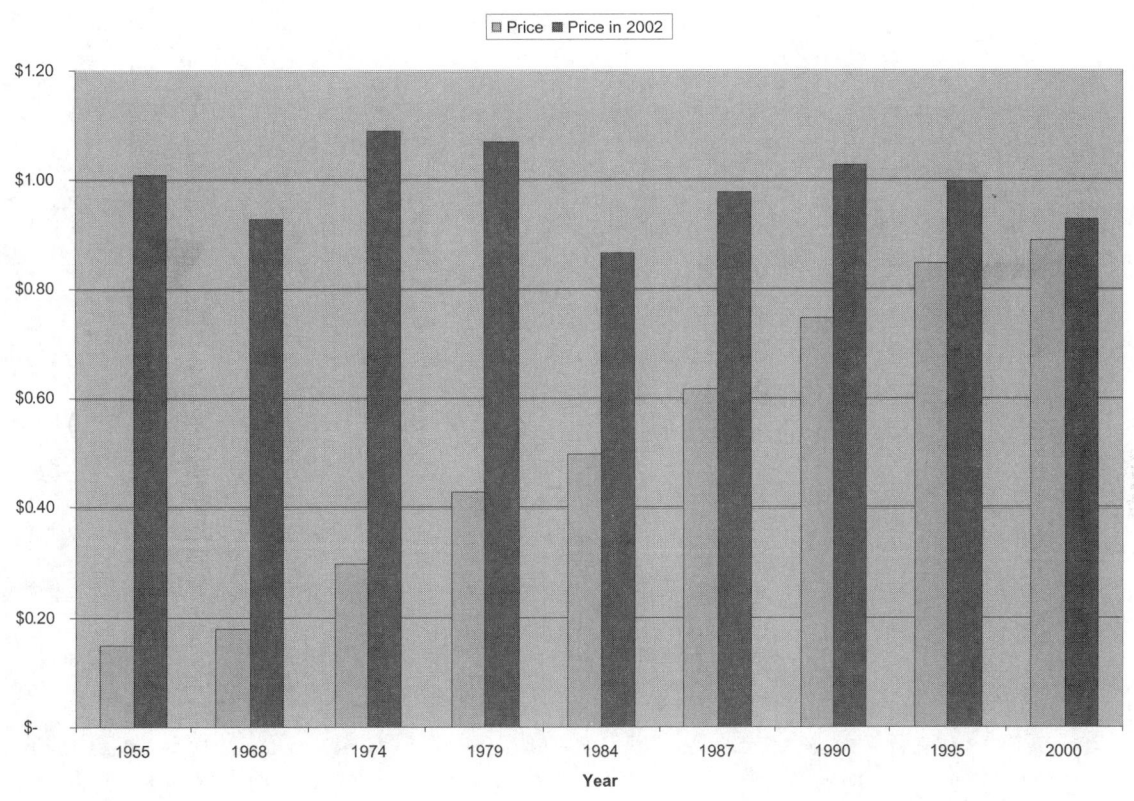

	1955	1968	1974	1979	1984	1987	1990	1995	2000
Price	$0.15	$0.18	$0.30	$0.43	$0.50	$0.62	$0.75	$0.85	$0.89
Dollar Value in 2002	$1.01	$0.93	$1.09	$1.07	$0.87	$0.98	$1.03	$1.00	$0.93

ITEMS IN THE REFRIGERATOR

Milk (1 quart)

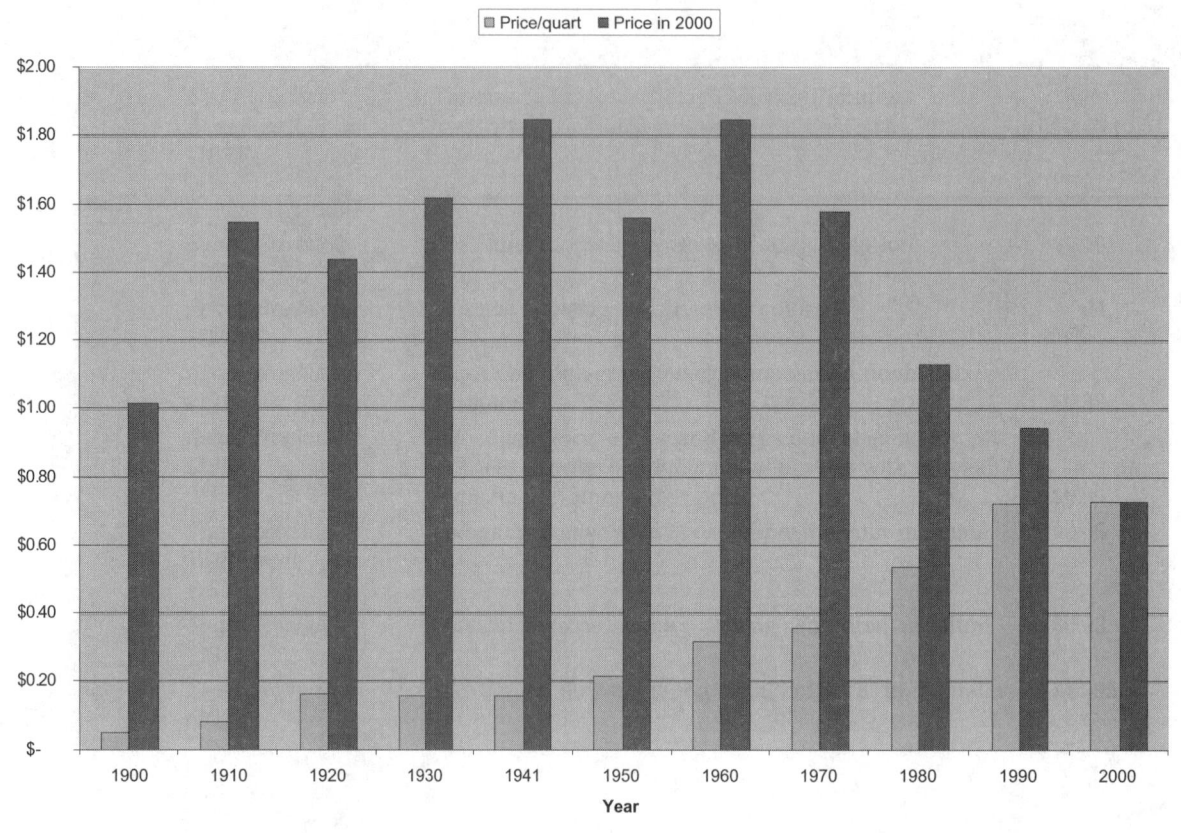

Legend: ☐ Price/quart ■ Price in 2000

	1900	**1910**	**1920**	**1930**	**1941**	**1950**	**1960**	**1970**	**1980**	**1990**	**2000**
Price/quart	$0.05	$0.09	$0.17	$0.16	$0.16	$0.22	$0.32	$0.36	$0.54	$0.72	$0.73
Dollar Value in 2000	$1.02	$1.55	$1.44	$1.62	$1.85	$1.56	$1.85	$1.58	$1.13	$0.95	$0.73

THE OUTDOORS

Basketball

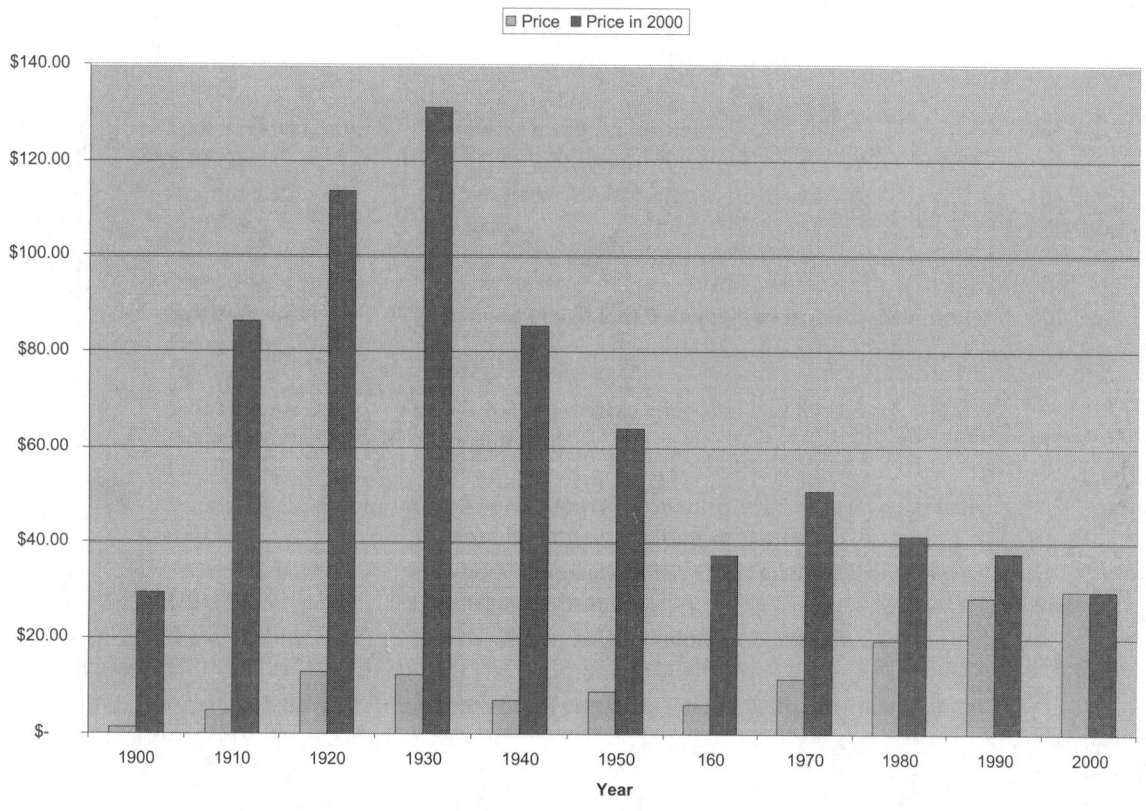

	1900	1910	1920	1930	1941	1950	1960	1970	1980	1990	2000
Price	$1.45	$4.75	$13.20	$12.75	$6.95	$8.95	$6.47	$11.50	$19.89	$28.88	$29.99
Dollar Value in 2000	$29.59	$86.36	$113.79	$131.44	$85.80	$63.93	$37.62	$51.11	$41.52	$38.05	$29.99

Excerpts from Ad Descriptions:

♦ **1900:** *Basket Ball*—Made of high grade pebbled leather, canvas lined and well made.

♦ **1910:** *The J.C. Higgins Official Basket Ball*—We guarantee this basket ball to be the best made, regardless of the brand or price.

♦ **1930:** *"J.C. Higgins" Regulation Basket Ball*—Laced and ready to inflate. Sold to schools and colleges under Nationally Advertised Brand for $14.00. Save Money!

♦ **1950:** *J.C. Higgins Official Laceless Basketball*—No laces. No dead spots. Official size, weight, handling ability. Select quality pebble-grained cowhide leather.

♦ **1960:** *No Stronger Basketballs Made!*—Extra yards of nylon cord assures more wear, more games. Tan cover is heat and pressured cured.

♦ **1980:** *5-Star Basketball with pebble-grained leather-look vinyl and nylon cover*—Ball is designed to minimize the effect temperature has on the bouncing....

THE OUTDOORS

Bicycle*

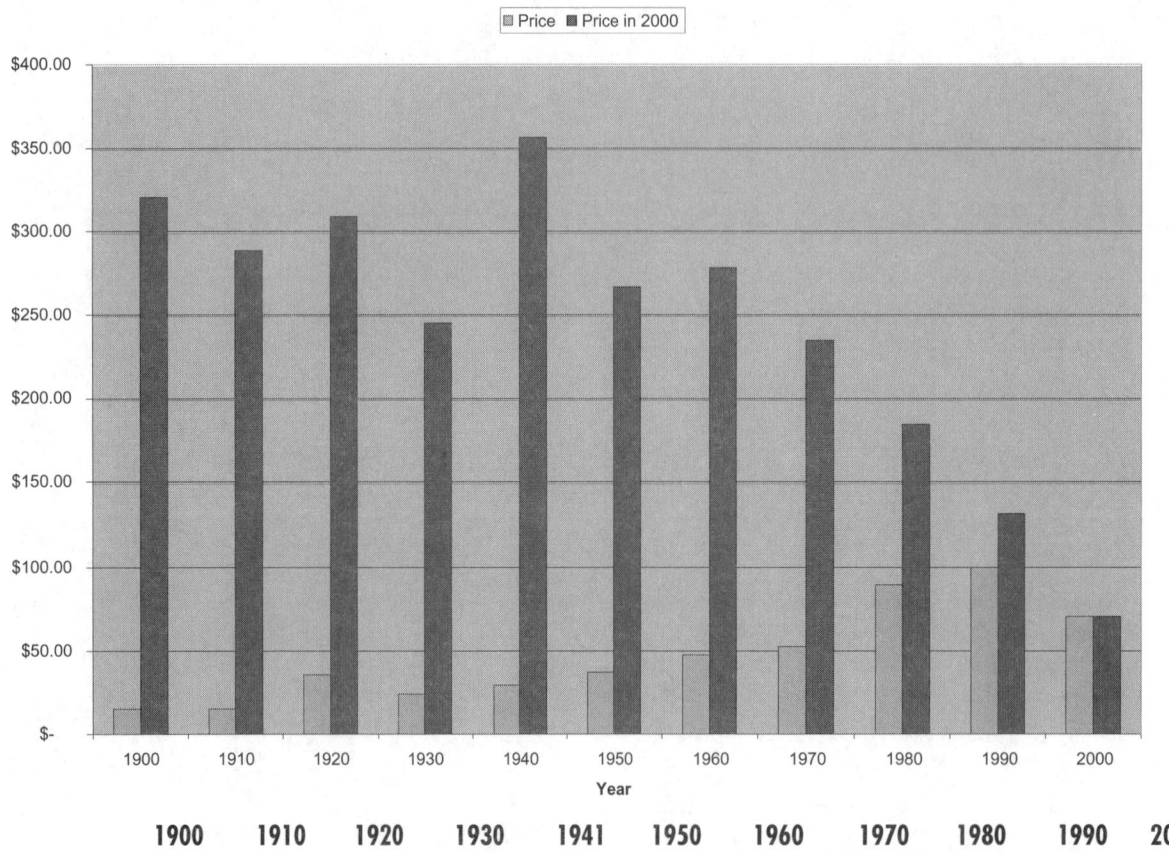

	1900	1910	1920	1930	1941	1950	1960	1970	1980	1990	2000
Price	$15.75	$15.95	$35.95	$23.85	$28.95	$37.50	$47.95	$52.95	$89.99	$99.99	$69.99
Dollar Value in 2000	$321.43	$290.00	$309.91	$245.88	$357.41	$267.86	$278.78	$235.33	$185.78	$131.74	$69.99

Excerpts from Ad Descriptions:

- ◆ **1900:** *The Celebrated Acme King*—We have sold the Acme King...in competition with the highest of the high grades.
- ◆ **1910:** *Our New Napoleon Bicycle*—For quality and value...One of the best know and most reliable bicycles on the market.
- ◆ **1930:** *The Elgin Redbird*—A sturdily build men's Elgin, single bar Motor Bike style. Red with white markings...Frame made of high carbon steel...
- ◆ **1940:** *Sears 4-Star DeLuxe Twin Bar Elgin*—Like a greyhound straining at the lead, this chambion Elgin fairly best to go places...and in a hurry!
- ◆ **1950:** *J.C. Higgins Semi-Equipped Bicycle*—Keen-looking...smooth riding...a bike that will give please to the "extra-special" youngster.
- ◆ **1960:** *Equipped Flightliner..Flo-bar frame*—New for 1960. Regular coaster break for sure stops, effortless coasting. Boys' are metallic red; girls' are metallic blue.

---

* Least Expensive Advertised

THE OUTDOORS

Fishing Reel

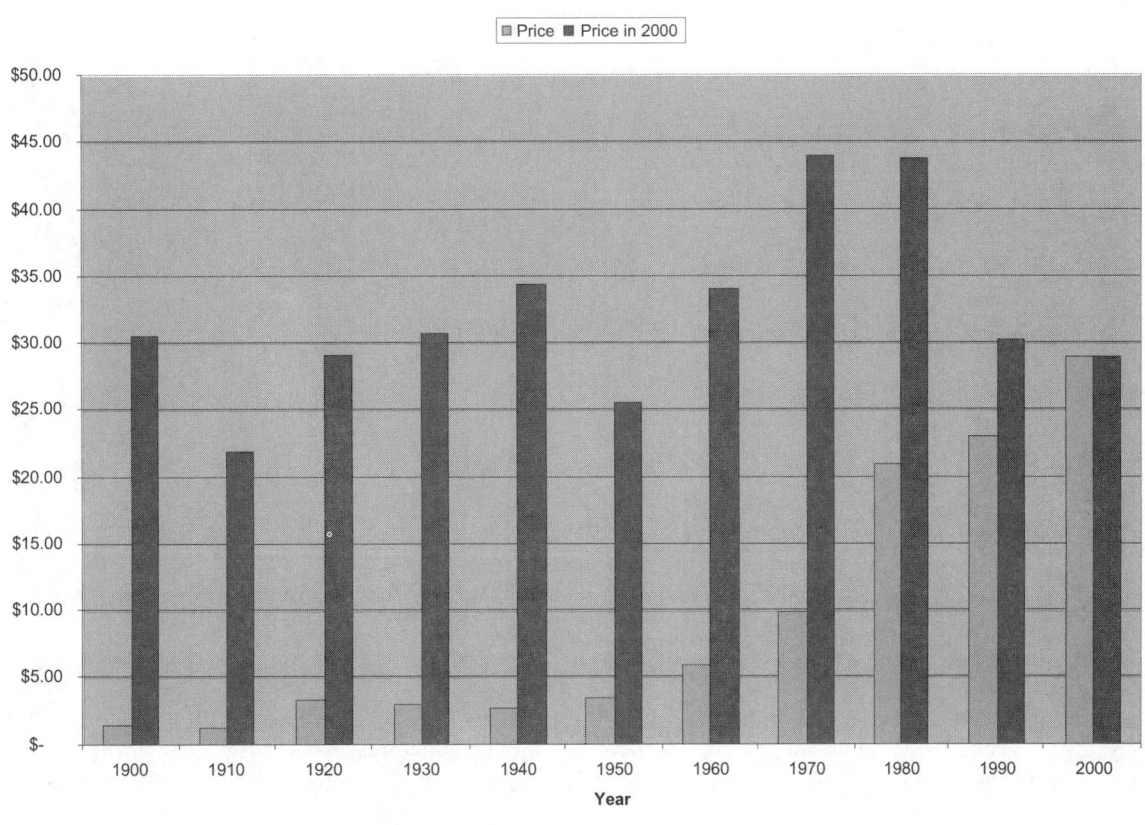

□ Price ■ Price in 2000

	1900	1910	1920	1930	1941	1950	1960	1970	1980	1990	2000
Price	$1.50	$1.21	$3.38	$2.98	$2.79	$3.59	$5.87	$9.89	$21.00	$22.99	$29.00
Dollar Value in 2000	$30.61	$22.00	$29.14	$30.72	$34.44	$25.64	$34.13	$43.98	$43.84	$30.29	$29.00

THE OUTDOORS

Fishing Rod

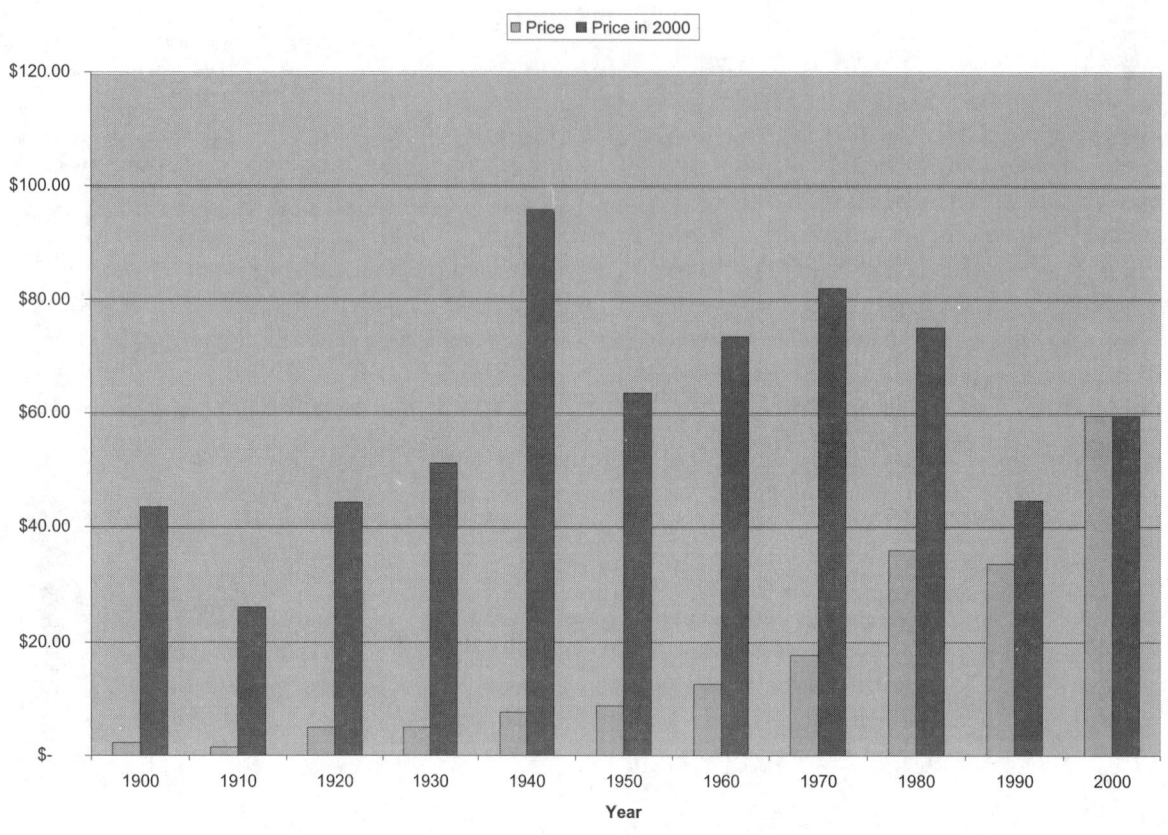

	1900	1910	1920	1930	1941	1950	1960	1970	1980	1990	2000
Price	$2.15	$1.43	$5.18	$4.98	$7.79	$8.95	$12.67	$17.50	$35.99	$33.99	$59.99
Dollar Value in 2000	$106.12	$54.18	$81.47	$70.00	$91.98	$124.64	$174.13	$177.73	$112.73	$97.50	$99.97

THE OUTDOORS

Golf Ball

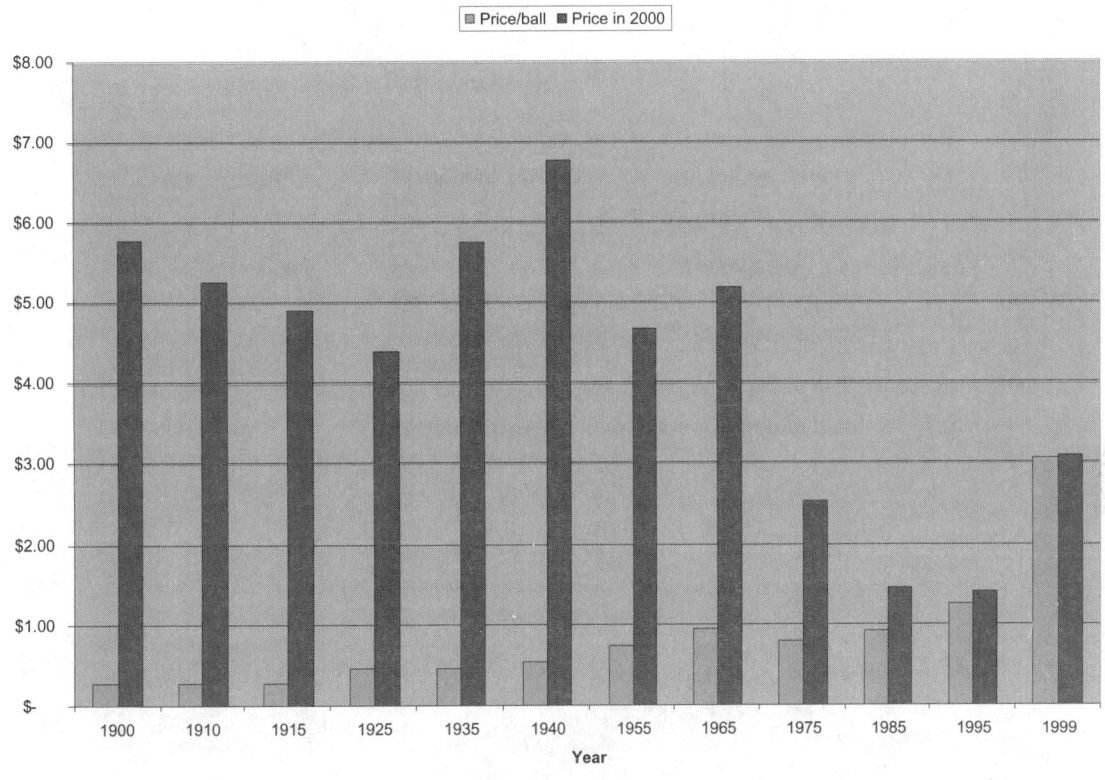

	1901	**1910**	**1915**	**1925**	**1935**	**1940**	**1955**	**1965**	**1975**	**1985**	**1995**	**1999**
Brand	Park Ball	Practice Ball	Goodrich Stag	Eclipse	Aristo Cover Ball	X-Pert High Grade	Johnny Bulla Tournament	Gene Sarazen	Advisory Staff	Power-Flite	MacGregor	Titleist Dt Spin
Price/Ball	$0.29	$0.08	$0.29	$0.45	$0.46	$0.55	$0.73	$0.95	$0.79	$0.92	$1.25	$3.08
Dollar Value in 2000	$5.80	$1.51	$4.92	$4.41	$5.75	$6.79	$4.68	$5.19	$2.53	$1.47	$1.41	$3.11

Golf Ball Facts:

♦ The first golf balls were sewn spheres stuffed with approximately a half a gallon of boiled feathers. A skilled worker could make 3 to 4 balls a day.

♦ By 1850, Malaysian gum (gutta percha) was discovered and used to create molded golf balls that were perfect spheres.

♦ It was discovered by golfers that dented gutta percha balls flew better. It was then when golfers hammered dents into their balls to create "dimples".

♦ At the beginning of the 20th Century, soft-cored elastic wound balls were developed and became popular because of there resiliency.

♦ By 1968, the PGA standardized the size of the golf ball to a sphere with 1.68 inch diameter for tournament play.

THE OUTDOORS

Golf Club (1 set)

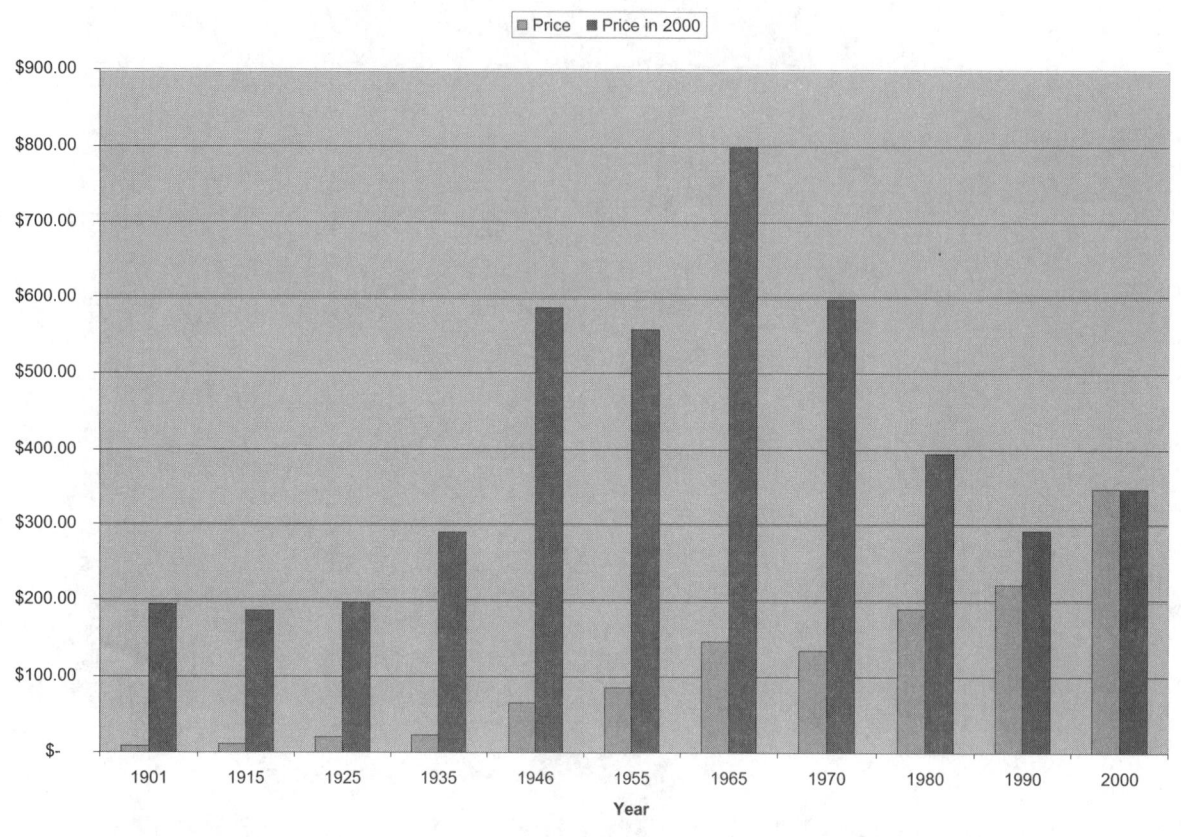

	1901	1915	1925	1935	1946	1955	1965	1970	1980	1990	2000
Price	$9.85	$11.10	$20.25	$23.31	$66.54	$87.00	$146.49	$135.00	$189.99	$222.00	$349.00
Dollar Value in 2000	$197.00	$188.14	$198.53	$291.38	$588.85	$557.69	$801.58	$600.00	$394.57	$292.49	$349.00

THE OUTDOORS

Hammock

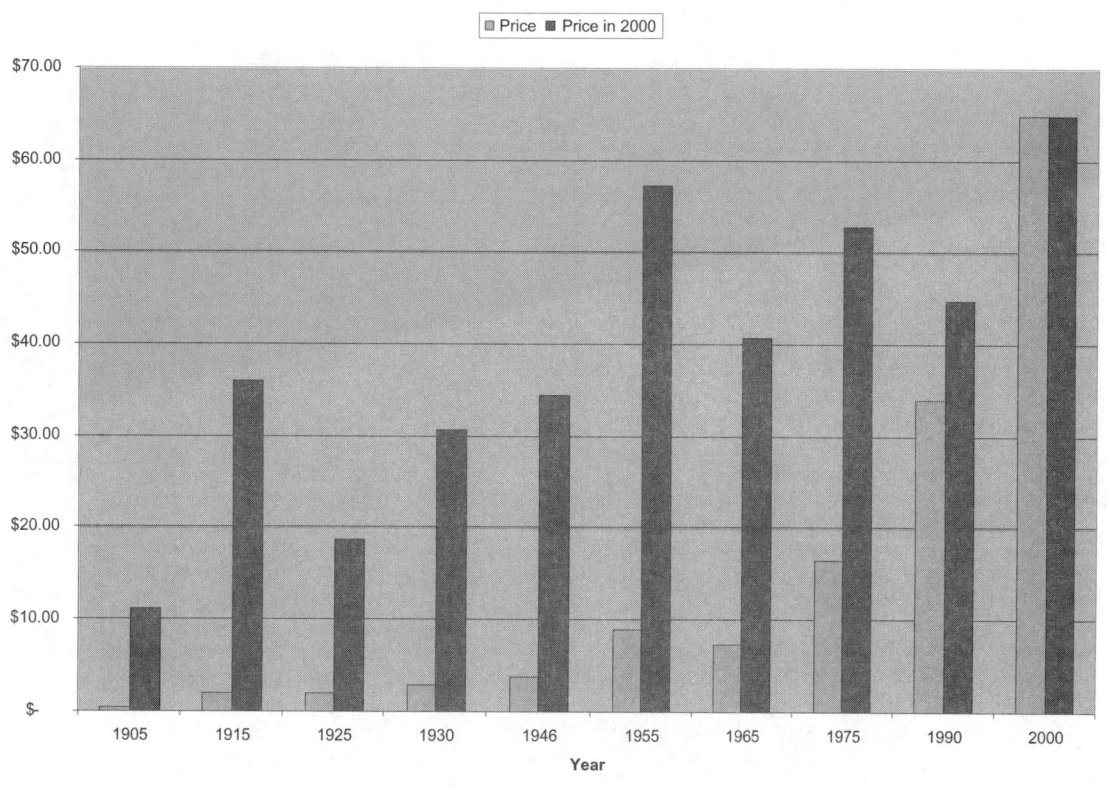

	1905	**1915**	**1925**	**1930**	**1946**	**1955**	**1965**	**1975**	**1990**	**2000**
Price	$0.55	$1.98	$1.95	$2.98	$3.89	$8.95	$7.47	$16.50	$34.00	$64.99
Dollar Value in 2000	$11.22	$36.00	$18.93	$30.72	$34.42	$57.37	$40.82	$52.88	$44.80	$64.99

Excerpts from Ad Descriptions:

♦ **1915:** *Our Great Standard Leader*—A hammock of great strength and wearing qualities offered specially at a low price.

♦ **1925:** *Fancy Weave Hammock*—Medium weight, fancy weave cotton hammock.

♦ **1930:** *For Summer Comfort*—A Jacquard weave hammock! Completely comfortable, thoroughly durable, made of strong tested warp year.

♦ **1955:** *Heavy Jacquard Woven Cotton Hammock*—3-point suspension style. Colorful white diamond design on red background.

♦ **1965:** *Sleeper Hammock won't rock or tilt*—Just swings gently to coax you to sleep. Green cotton plaid.

623

THE OUTDOORS

Harley-Davidson Motorcycle*

Legend: ■ Average Price ■ Price in 2000

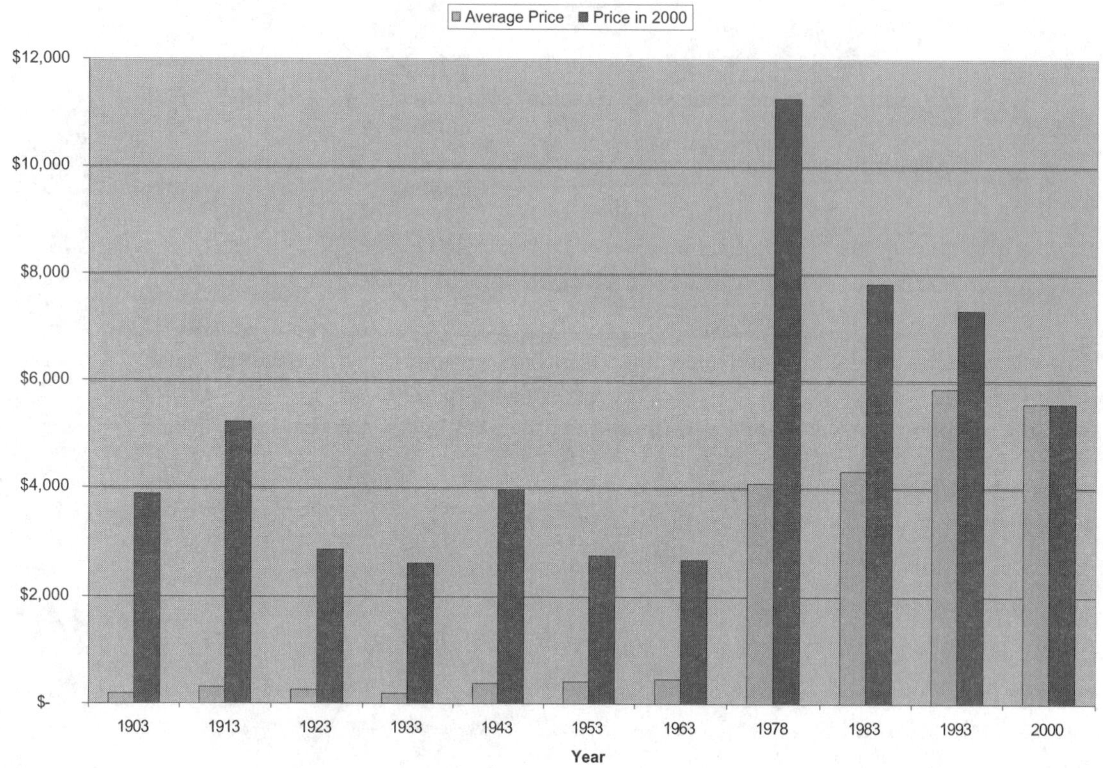

	1903	1913	1923	1933	1943	1953	1963	1978	1983	1993	2000
Price	$200	$290	$275	$188	$385	$405	$460	$4,100	$4,345	$5,895	$5,595
Dollar Value in 2000	$3,922	$5,269	$2,893	$2,601	$4,003	$2,782	$2,704	$11,312	$7,848	$7,339	$5,595

Harley-Davidson Facts:

♦ In 1909, the company developed and introduced a new engine that permitted riders to travel at 60 miles per hour.

♦ By the end of World War I, twenty thousand Harley-Davidson motorcycles were utilized by the United States.

♦ The "Teardrop" gas tank was introduced in 1926.

♦ During the 1930's, Harley-Davidson was one of only two motorcycle manufacturers to survive the Great Depression.

♦ During World War II, Harley-Davidson built over 90,000 motorcycles for the United States and its allies for military use.

♦ Black leather jackets developed as a "lifestyle" statement during the 1950s and 1960s.

♦ By the late 1960's and the1970's, the company had to compete against low-priced imports from Asia.

♦ By the early 1980's, the company's management developed a focus on quality and improved manufacturing processes. By 1986, the company went public with a stock offering.

*Prices listed are for least expensive Harley Davidson motorcycle available during that year.

THE OUTDOORS

Hiking Boots

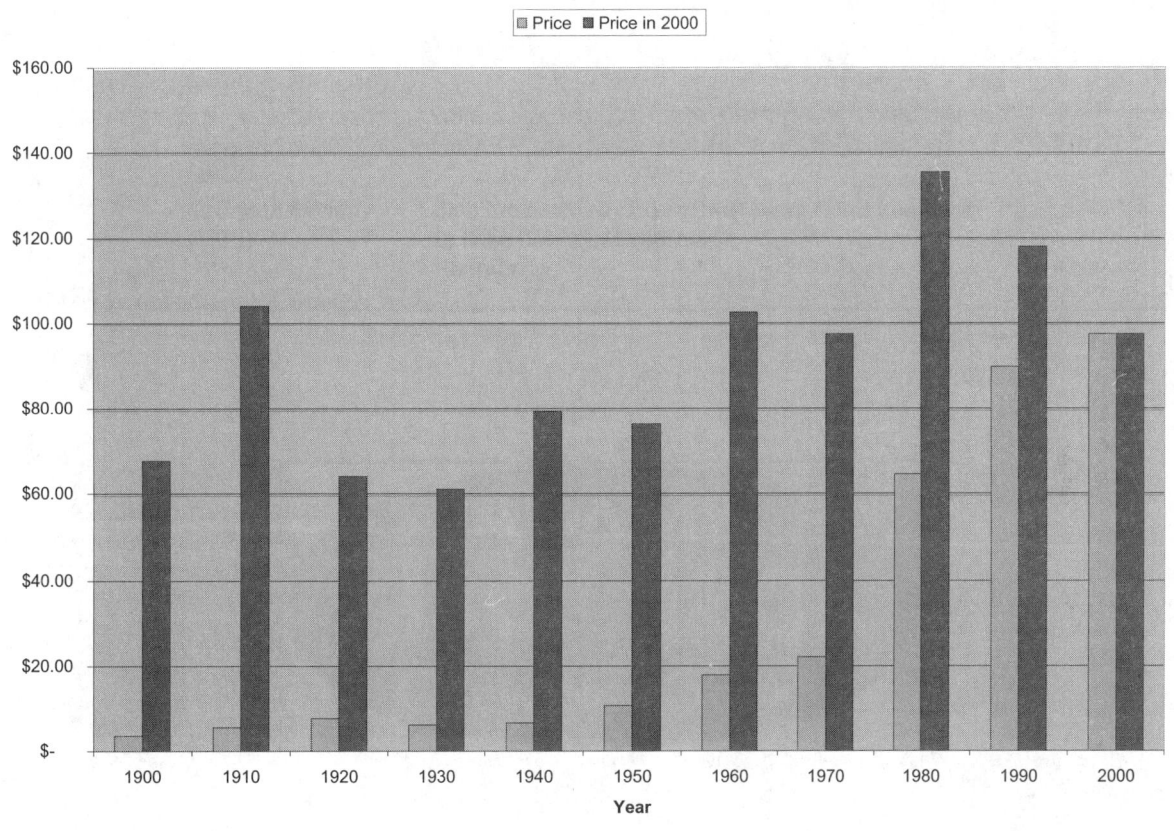

	1900	1910	1920	1930	1940	1950	1960	1970	1980	1990	2000
Price	$3.35	$5.75	$7.50	$5.95	$6.45	$10.75	$17.70	$21.97	$64.99	$89.97	$98.00
Dollar Value in 2000	$68.37	$104.55	$64.66	$61.34	$79.83	$76.79	$102.91	$97.64	$135.68	$118.54	$98.00

THE OUTDOORS

Lawn Mower*

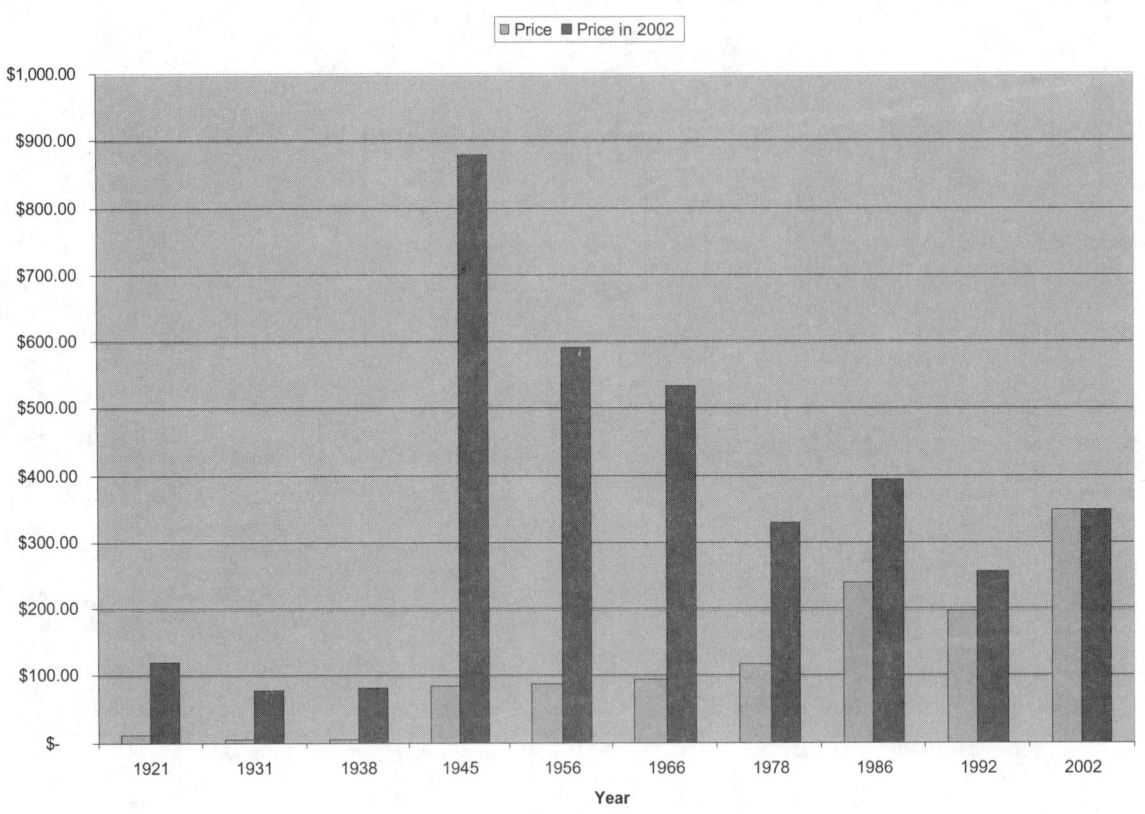

	1921	1931	1938	1945	1956	1966	1978	1986	1992	2002
Price	$12.00	$6.85	$6.42	$87.95	$89.50	$96.50	$119.00	$239.99	$199.99	$350.00
Dollar Value in 2002	$121.00	$81.07	$82.00	$879.01	$591.95	$535.31	$328.35	$393.93	$256.44	$354.38

---

* From 1920-1944 lawnmowers were push design. By 1945, power motors were available.

THE OUTDOORS

Shotgun*

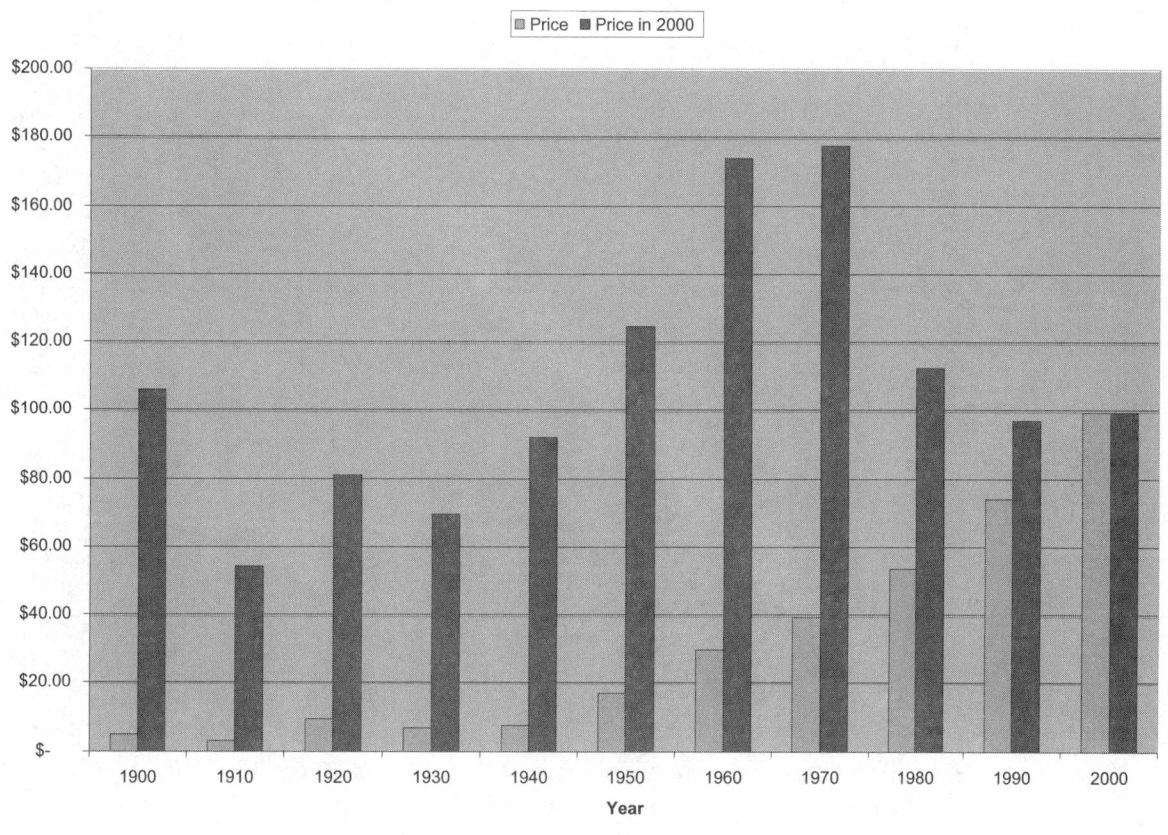

	1900	1910	1920	1930	1940	1950	1960	1970	1980	1990	2000
Price	$5.20	$2.98	$9.45	$6.79	$7.45	$17.45	$29.95	$39.99	$54.00	$74.00	$99.97
Dollar Value in 2000	$106.12	$54.18	$81.47	$70.00	$91.98	$124.64	$174.13	$177.73	$112.73	$97.50	$99.97

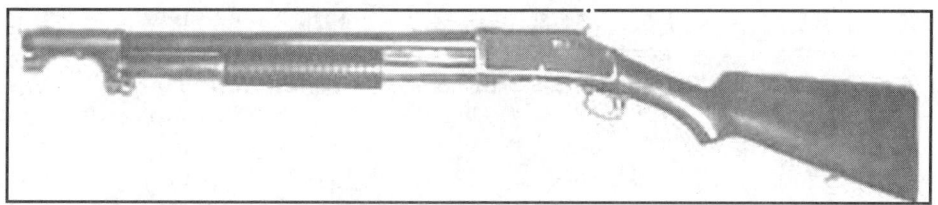

* Least Expensive Advertised

THE OUTDOORS

Tennis Racquet

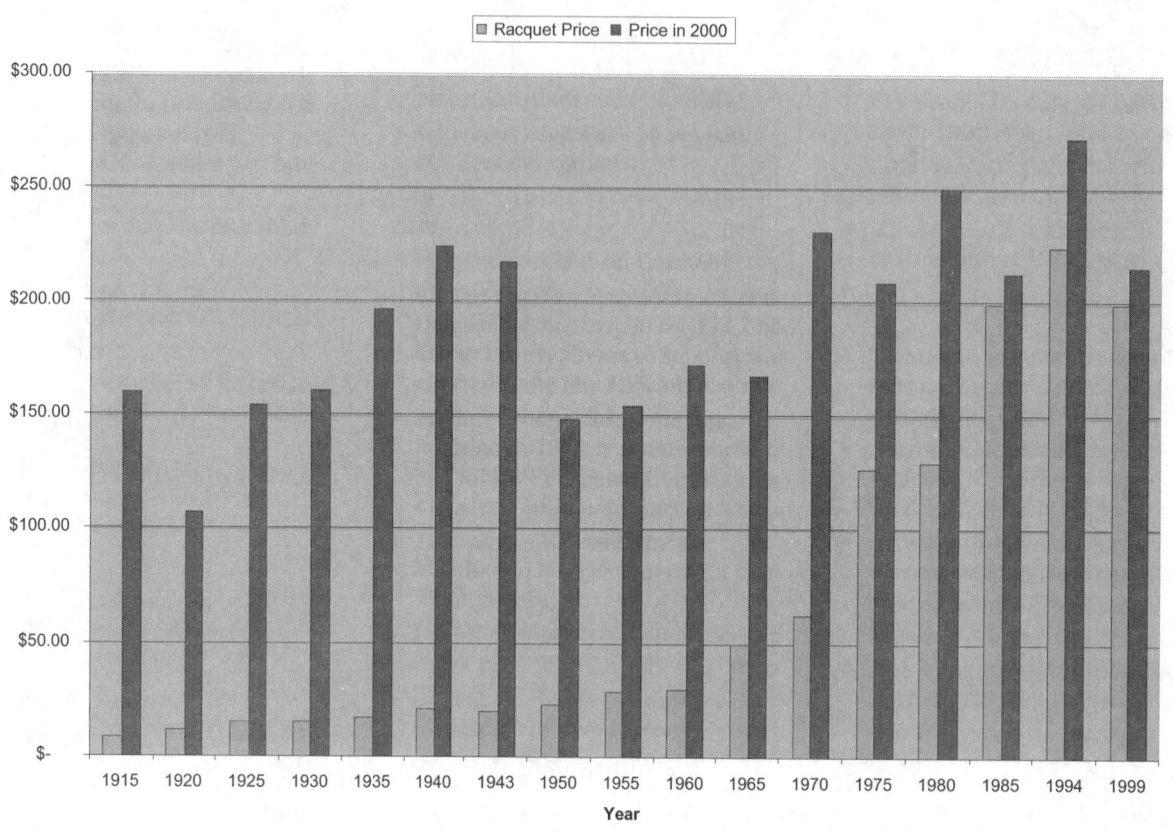

	1915	1920	1925	1930	1935	1940	1943	1950	1955
Brand	New Bancroft	Invincible Driver	Super Stroke	Laminated AAA	Ellsworth Vines	Squire	Squire	Jack Kramer Autograph	Sedgeman Squire
Price	$9.00	$12.00	$15.00	$15.00	$15.00	$17.50	$21.00	$20.00	$23.00
Dollar Value in 2000	$160.31	$107.94	$154.20	$161.59	$196.97	$224.88	$218.38	$149.29	$154.39

	1960	1965	1970	1975	1981	1986	1994	1999
Brand	Kramer Autograph	Kramer Autograph	T-2000	T-3000	Bancroft Limited Edition	Bancroft Boron	Wilson Sledgehammer	Wilson Hyper Hammer
Price	$28.50	$29.50	$50.00	$62.50	$126.50	$130.00	$224.94	$200.00
Dollar Value in 2000	$173.21	$168.48	$231.83	$208.99	$250.36	$213.39	$273.05	$215.97

THE SPORTS PAGE

Average Ticket Price for Baseball World Series Game*

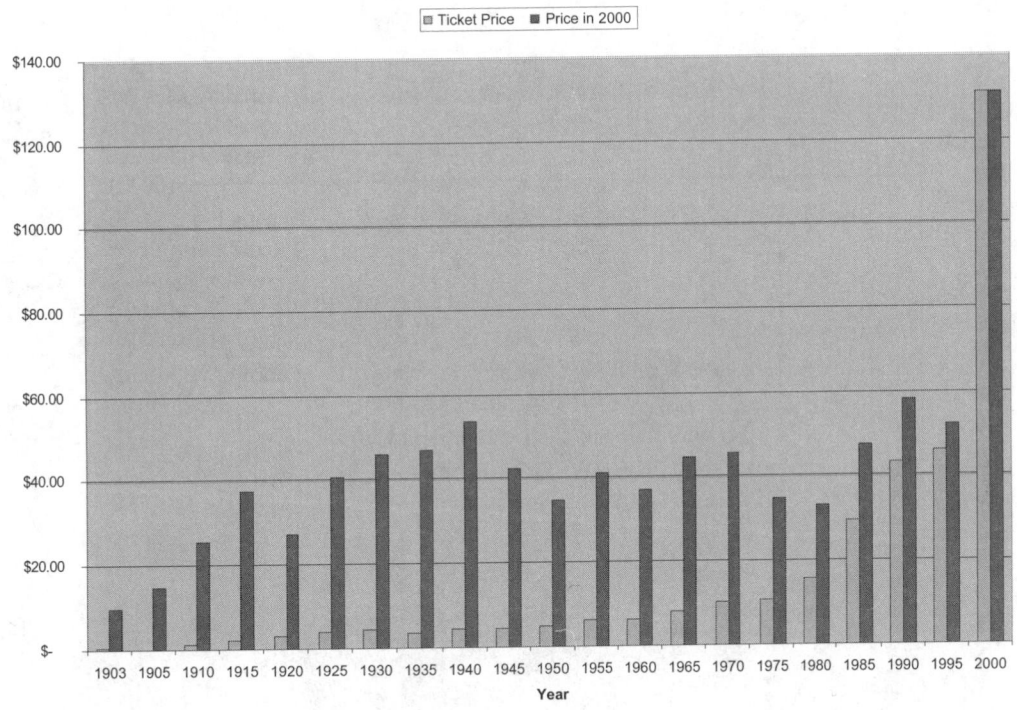

	1903	**1905**	**1910**	**1915**	**1920**	**1925**	**1930**	**1935**	**1940**	**1945**	**1950**
# Games Played	8	5	5	5	7	7	6	6	7	7	4
Avg. Ticket Price	$0.50	$0.75	$1.40	$2.23	$3.16	$4.18	$4.49	$3.75	$4.34	$4.48	$4.87
Dollar Value in 2000	$9.80	$14.71	$25.45	$37.80	$27.24	$40.98	$46.29	$46.88	$53.58	$42.67	$34.79

	1955	**1960**	**1965**	**1970**	**1975**	**1980**	**1985**	**1990**	**1995**	**2000**
# Games Played	7	7	7	5	7	6	7	4	6	5
Avg. Ticket Price	$6.45	$6.38	$8.17	$10.27	$10.97	$15.81	$29.56	$43.33	$46.31	$131.42
Dollar Value in 2000	$41.35	$37.09	$44.62	$45.64	$35.16	$33.01	$47.30	$58.41	$52.33	$131.42

* Based upon total attendance and total receipts collected.

THE SPORTS PAGE

Average Ticket Price for Chicago Cubs Baseball Game

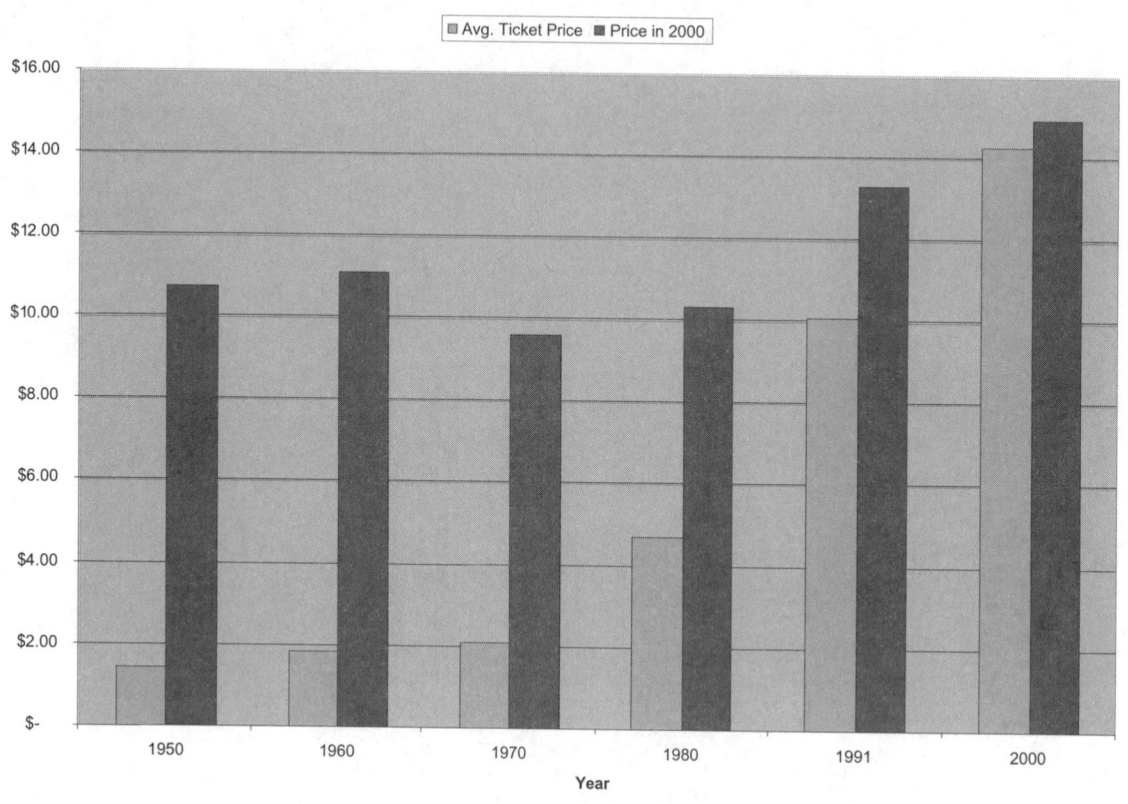

■ Avg. Ticket Price   ■ Price in 2000

	1950	1960	1970	1980	1991	2000
Avg. Ticket Price	$1.44	$1.83	$2.08	$4.73	$10.10	$14.30
Dollar Value in 2002	$10.75	$11.12	$9.64	$10.33	$13.34	$14.94

THE SPORTS PAGE

Average Ticket Price for Denver Broncos Football Game

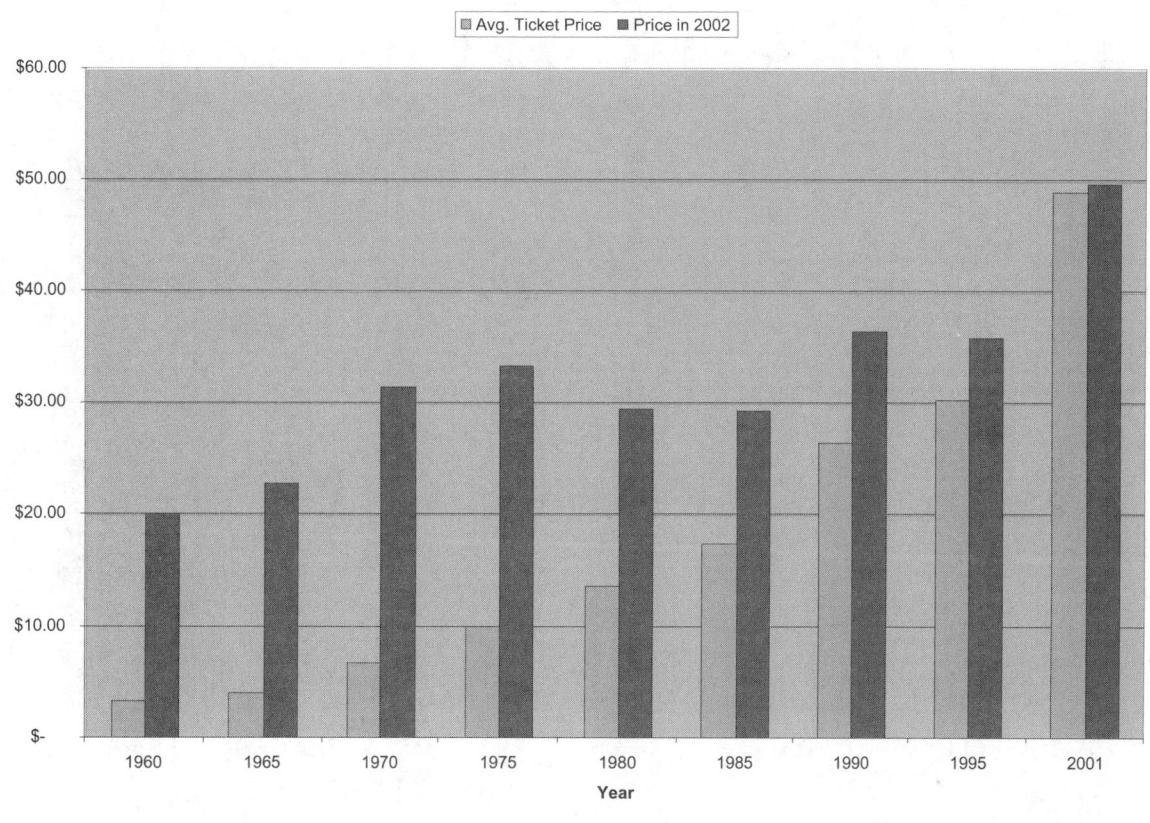

Avg. Ticket Price ■ Price in 2002

	1960	1965	1970	1975	1980	1985	1990	1995	2001
Avg. Ticket Price	$3.33	$4.00	$6.78	$10.00	$13.57	$17.54	$26.50	$30.40	$49.00
Dollar Value in 2002	$20.24	$22.84	$31.44	$33.44	$29.63	$29.33	$36.48	$35.89	$49.77

THE SPORTS PAGE

Average Ticket Price for Football Super Bowl Game

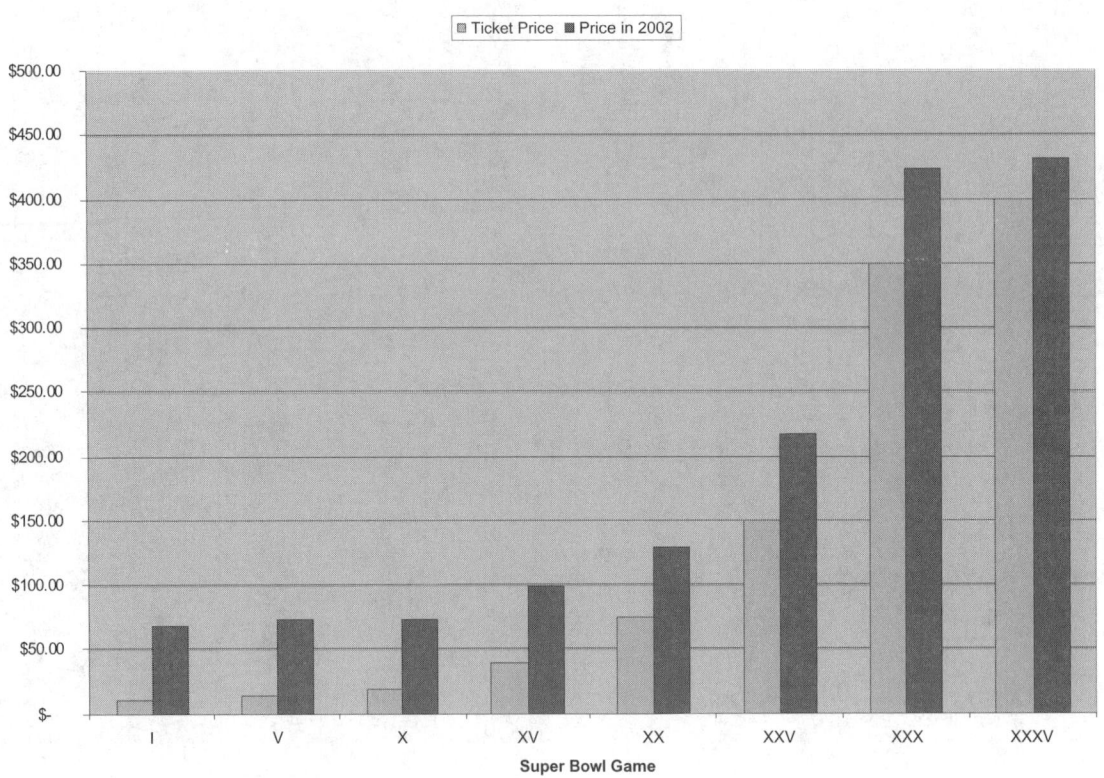

□ Ticket Price ■ Price in 2002

Super Bowl Game

Super Bowl Prices

	I	V	X	XV	XX	XXV	XXX	XXXV
Year	1967	1971	1976	1981	1986	1991	1996	2001
Ticket Price	$12.00	$15.00	$20.00	$40.00	$75.00	$150.00	$350.00	$400.00
Dollar Value in 2002	$64.63	$66.63	$63.23	$79.16	$123.11	$198.13	$401.31	$406.32

Super Bowl Facts:

♦ The Super Bowl was originally called the "AFC-NFC World Championship Game."

♦ Television audience for Super Bowl I was approximately 60,000 viewers.

♦ Super Bowl XIV had over 35 million television viewers and Super Bowl XX was over 127 million television viewers.

♦ A one-minute television commercial sold for $75,000 to $85,000 during Super Bowl I (approximately $400,000 to $460,000 in 2002 dollars).

♦ Super Bowl V was the first played on artificial turf.

THE SPORTS PAGE

Kentucky Derby Winners

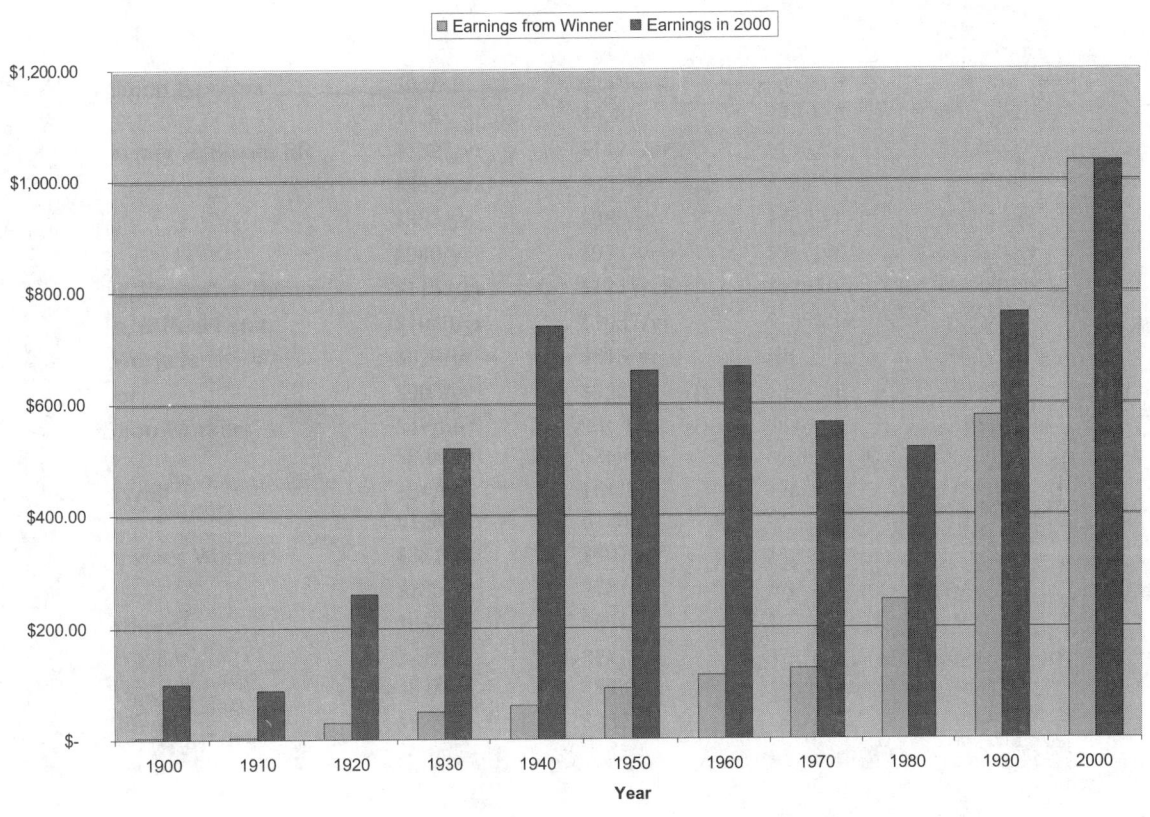

Legend: Earnings from Winner | Earnings in 2000

	1900	**1910**	**1920**	**1930**	**1940**	**1950**
Winning Horse	Lieut. Gibson	Donau	Paul Jones	Gallan Fox	Gallahadion	Middleground
Earnings from Winning Horse	$4,850	$4,850	$30,375	$50,725	$60,150	$92,650
Dollar Value in 2000	$98,980	$88,182	$261,853	$522,938	$742,593	$661,786

	1960	**1970**	**1980**	**1990**	**2000**
Winning Horse	Venetian Way	Dust Commander	Genuine Risk	Unbridled	Fusaichi Pegasus
Earnings from Winning Horse	$114,850	$127,800	$250,550	$581,000	$1,038,400
Dollar Value in 2000	$667,733	$568,000	$523,069	$765,481	$1,038,400

THE SPORTS PAGE

National Basketball Association's TV Contracts

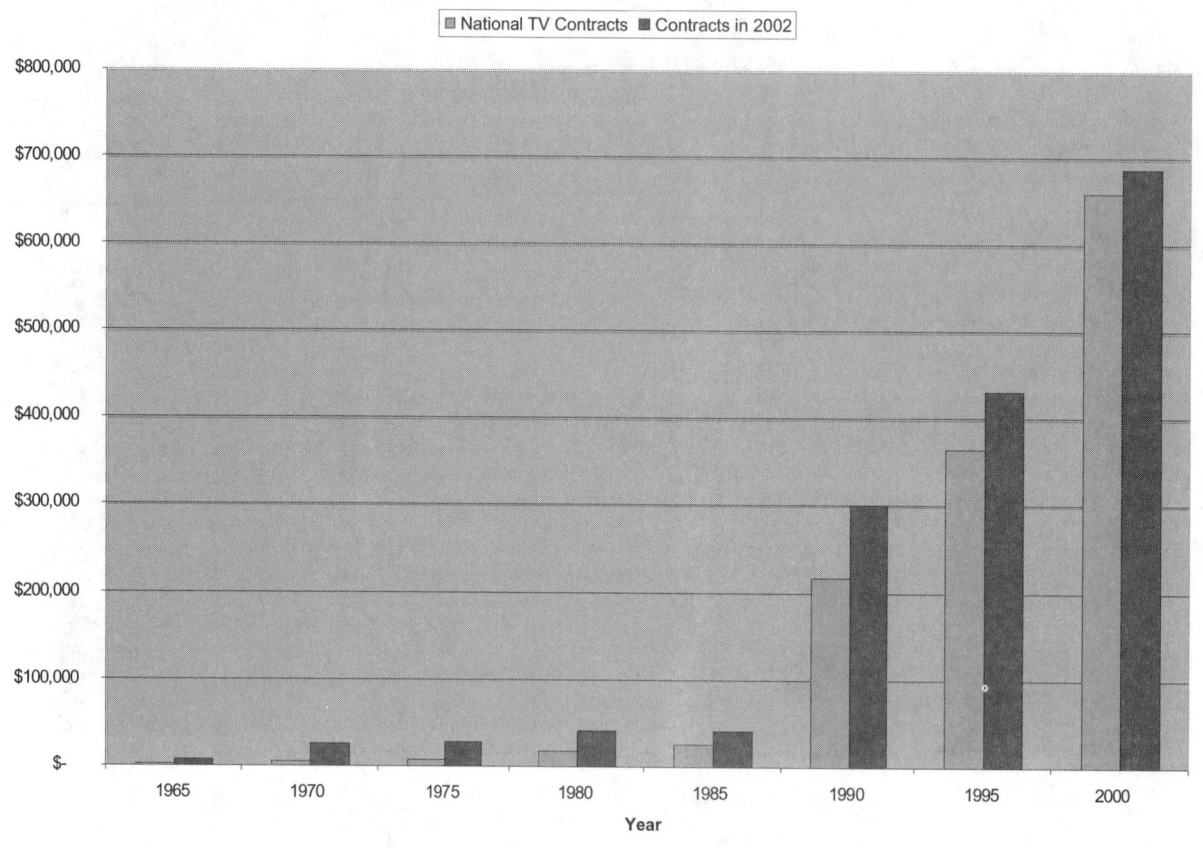

□ National TV Contracts ■ Contracts in 2002

	1965	1970	1975	1980	1985	1990	1995	2000
National TV Contracts	$1,500	$5,500	$8,800	$18,500	$25,000	$218,800	$366,670	$660,000
Dollar Value in 2002	$8,567	$25,501	$29,426	$40,390	$41,798	$301,164	$432,834	$689,512

TRAVEL & ENTERTAINMENT

Adult Ticket to Disneyland

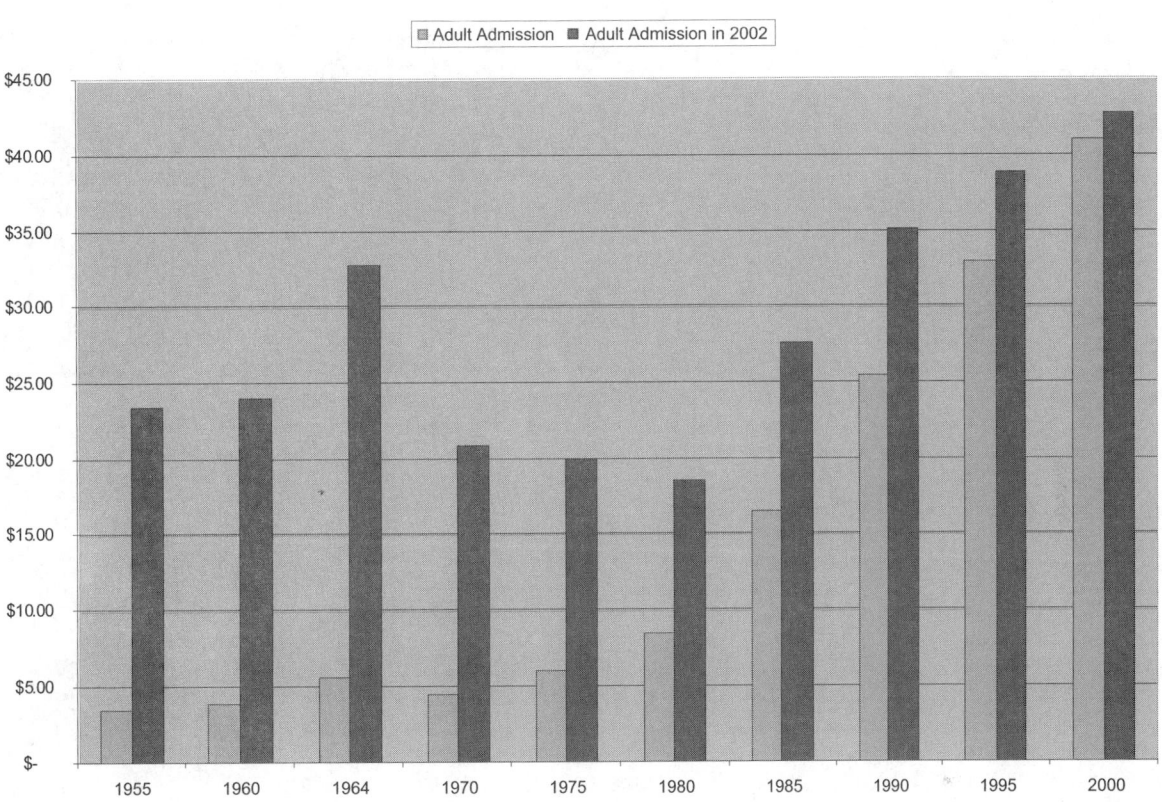

■ Adult Admission ■ Adult Admission in 2002

	1955	1960	1964	1970	1975	1980	1985	1990	1995	2000
Adult Admission	$3.50	$3.95	$5.65	$4.50	$6.00	$8.50	$16.50	$25.50	$33.00	$41.00
Dollar Value in 2002	$23.49	$24.01	$32.79	$20.86	$20.06	$18.56	$27.59	$35.10	$38.95	$42.83

Disneyland Ticket Facts:

♦ In 1955, the General Admission Ticket was only $1, but that did not include any of the eight attractions at the park.

♦ When the park first opened, Disneyland sold books with coupons that permitted guests to ride select attractions. Each coupon permitted the guest to ride a select number of attractions, depending on the coupons' classification level.

♦ Many guests typically returned home with unused coupons, but could have used them in future visits.

♦ Disney started phasing out the tickets in the late 1970's and early 1980's and began instituting the unlimited passports. This occurred when other theme parks started selling all-inclusive tickets in the 1970's.

♦ Disneyland established the all-inclusive passport by June of 1982.

TRAVEL & ENTERTAINMENT

Airline Ticket from New York City to Chicago

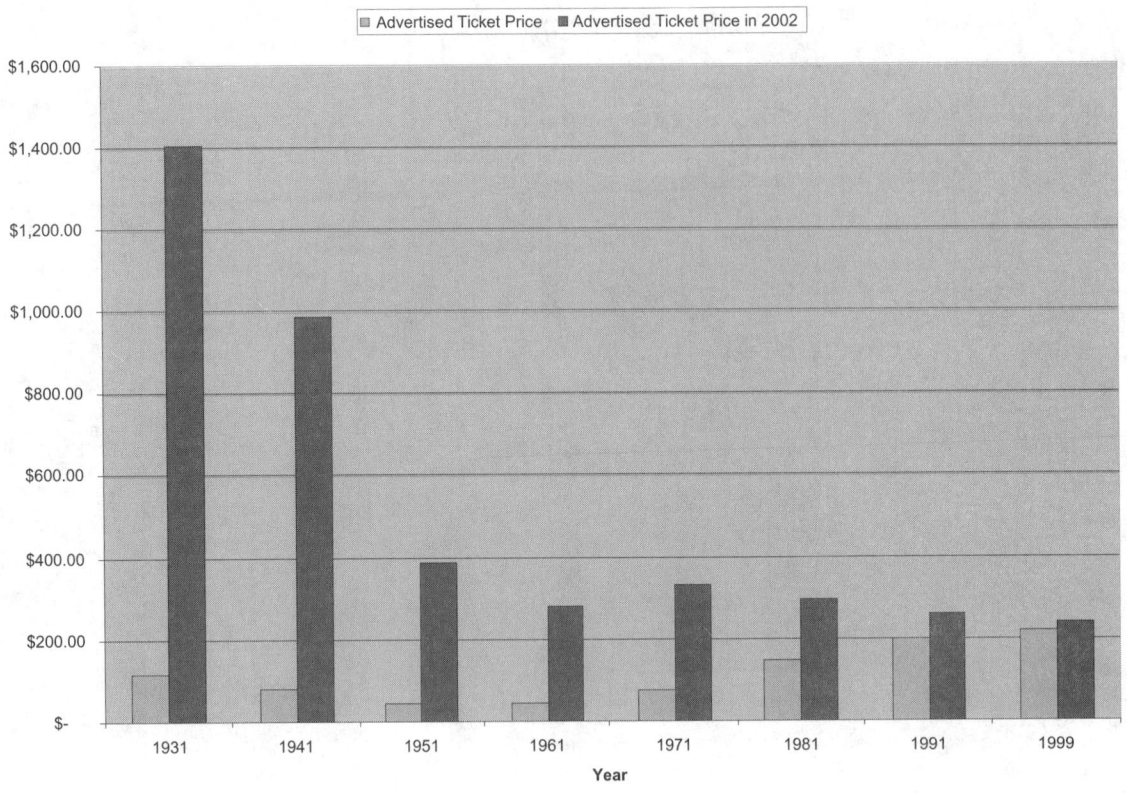

	1931	1941	1951	1961	1971	1981	1991	1999
Advertised Ticket Price	$119.00	$80.91	$48.00	$46.50	$75.00	$149.00	$198.00	$222.00
Dollar Value in 2002	$1,408.83	$990.18	$390.94	$282.61	$333.15	$294.89	$261.53	$239.72

Airline Ticket Facts:

♦ In 1931, Transcontinental & Western Air (TWA) advertised flights from New York City to Chicago.

♦ In 1941, TWA began flights from New York to Las Angeles for $149.94 one way ($1,835 in 2002 dollars). The flights were "only 15 hours, 8 minutes" on "TWA's transcontinental Stratoliner.

♦ "Fast and luxurious" and "pressurized comfort" were some of the advertising phrases during the 1930's and 1960's.

TRAVEL & ENTERTAINMENT

Average Cost of Ford Automobile*

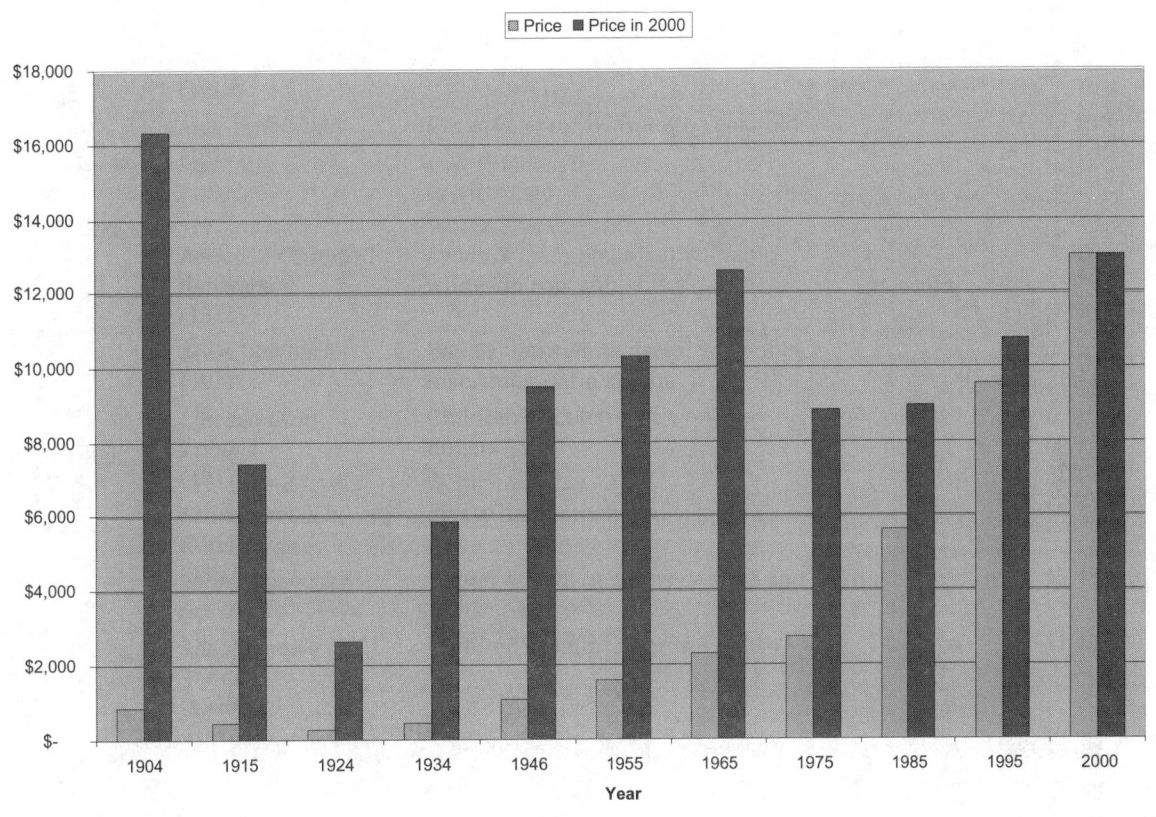

	1904	1915	1924	1934	1946	1955	1965	1975	1985	1995	1998
Price	$850	$440	$260	$460	$1,074	$1,606	$2,313	$2,769	$5,620	$9,560	$11,280
Dollar Value in 2000	$16,346	$7,458	$2,626	$5,897	$9,504	$10,294	$12,639	$8,875	$8,992	$10,802	$11,911

* Least Expensive Car

TRAVEL & ENTERTAINMENT

Average Movie Ticket Price

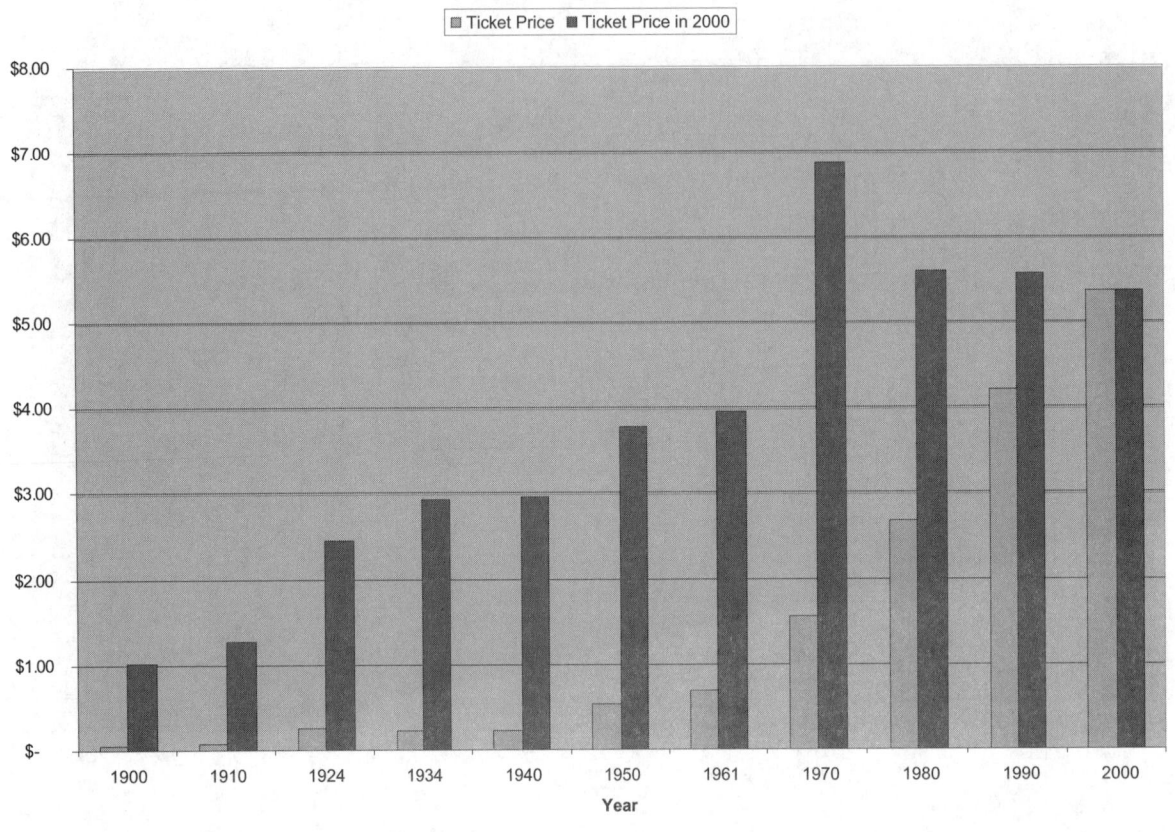

	1900	1910	1924	1934	1940	1950	1961	1970	1980	1990	2000
Ticket Price	$1.25	$1.28	$2.35	$2.45	$3.39	$6.45	$12.50	$12.95	$16.99	$26.00	$23.99
Dollar Value in 2000	$25.51	$23.27	$20.26	$25.26	$41.85	$46.07	$72.67	$57.56	$35.47	$34.26	$23.99

TRAVEL & ENTERTAINMENT

Bottle of Beaulieu Vineyard Wine

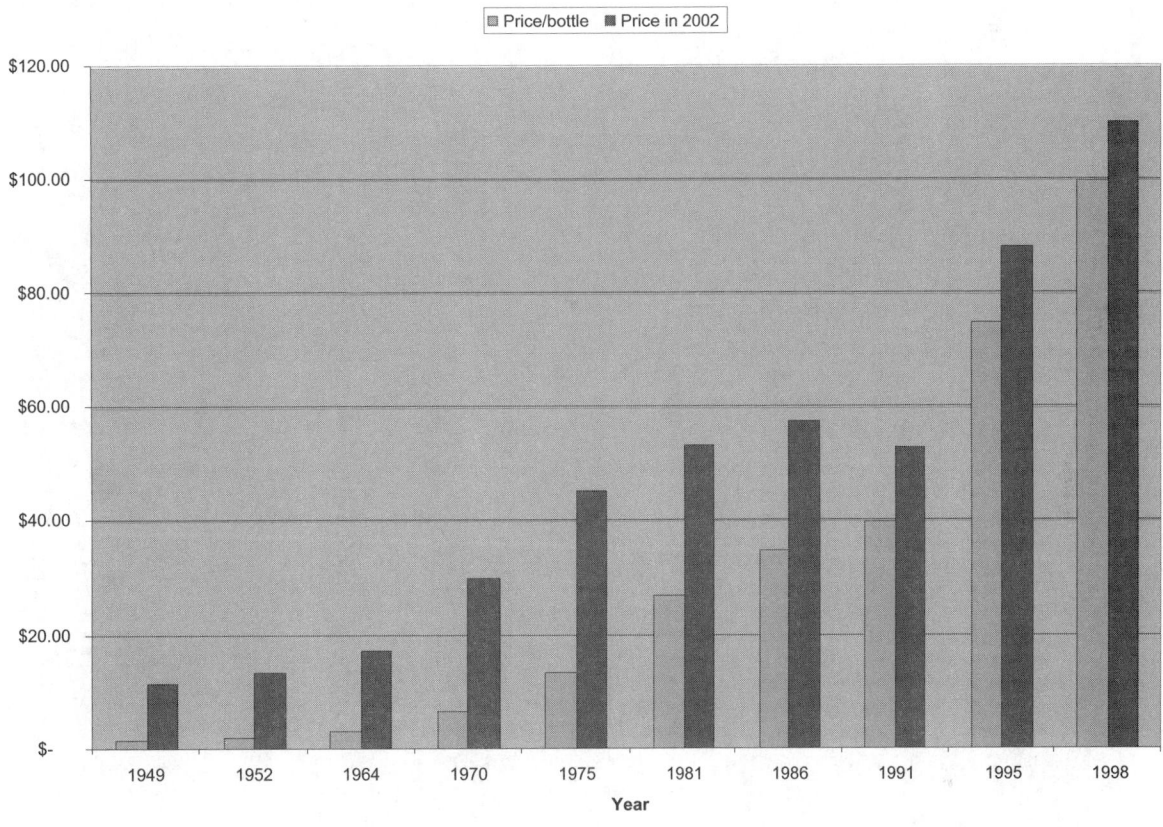

	1949	1952	1964	1970	1975	1981	1986	1991	1995	1998
Price/Bottle	$1.50	$2.00	$3.00	$6.50	$13.50	$27.00	$35.00	$40.00	$75.00	$100.00
Dollar Value in 2002	$11.34	$13.56	$17.41	$30.14	$45.14	$53.44	$57.45	$52.83	$88.53	$110.37

TRAVEL & ENTERTAINMENT

Hotel Nightly Rate

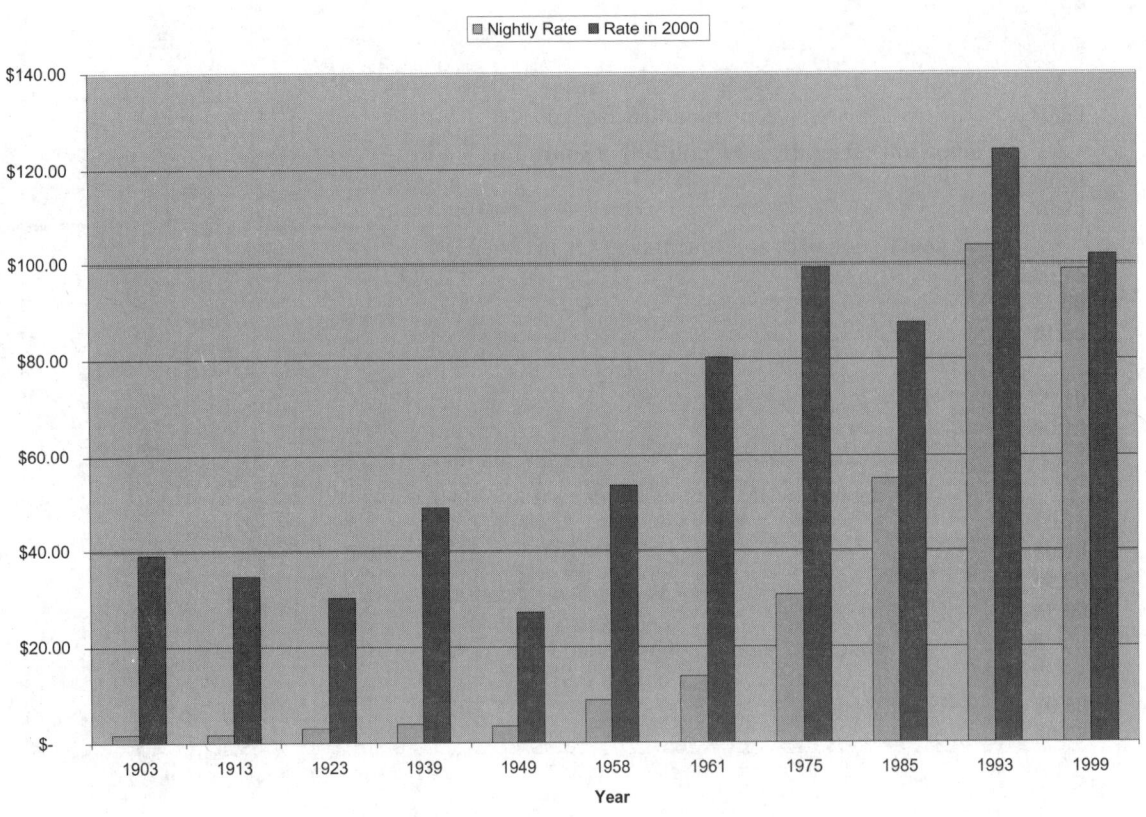

	1903	1913	1923	1939	1949	1958	1961	1975	1985	1993	1999
Nightly Rate	$2.00	$2.00	$3.00	$4.00	$3.75	$9.00	$14.00	$31.00	$55.00	$104.00	$99.00
Dollar Value in 2000	$39.22	$35.09	$30.30	$49.38	$27.17	$53.57	$80.46	$99.36	$88.00	$123.96	$102.38

TRAVEL & ENTERTAINMENT

Ocean Cruise from New York City to Bermuda

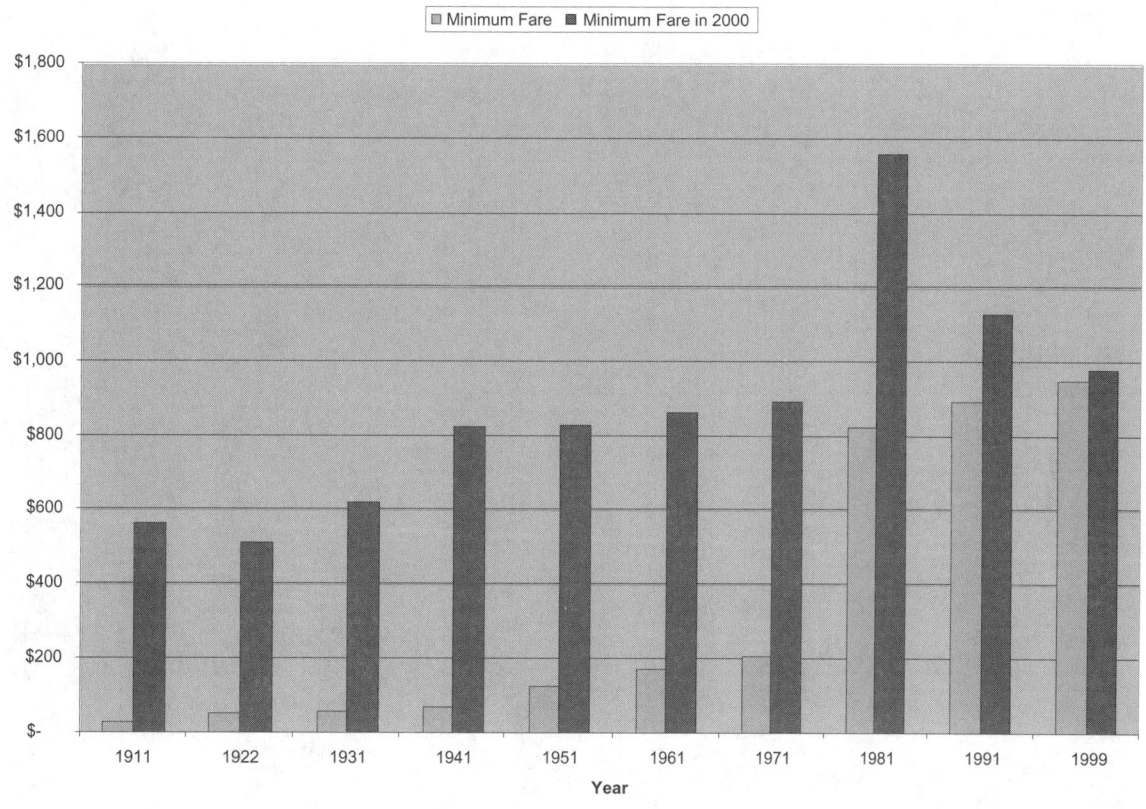

	1911	**1922**	**1931**	**1941**	**1951**	**1961**	**1971**	**1981**	**1991**	**1999**
Minimum Fare	$31	$50	$55	$70	$125	$175	$210	$825	$895	$950
Dollar Value in 2000	$564	$510	$625	$824	$828	$862	$894	$1,563	$1,131	$982

Excerpts from Ad Descriptions:

♦ **1911:** All expenses for 7 days; including 1,400 miles Superb Ocean trip. Stateroom and meals, Carriage Drives, Shore, Trips, Admission to Principal Attractions.

♦ **1922:** Go in May and June when Bermuda is ablaze with Flowers – perfect days for rest or play.

♦ **1941:** Sail with Alcoa to Bermuda…a wonderful vacation combination! Expert Cruise Director, deck sports, movies, dancing to Al Donahue orchestra…round-the-clock enjoyment all the way.

♦ **1951:** Sail into a world of Fun! Cruise on the "Queen of Bermuda" for the best vacation of your life! Take this gay cruise in one week or stay longer in Bermuda if you wish.

♦ **1971:** This sparkling new ship will appeal to everyone…The Bermuda Government has selected SEA VENTURE as its official contract ship, a highly prized endorsement.

♦ **1991:** Grant Resort to Bermuda. 7-night cruises from New York to Britain's beautiful crown jewel.

TRAVEL & ENTERTAINMENT

Rail Fare from New York City to San Francisco

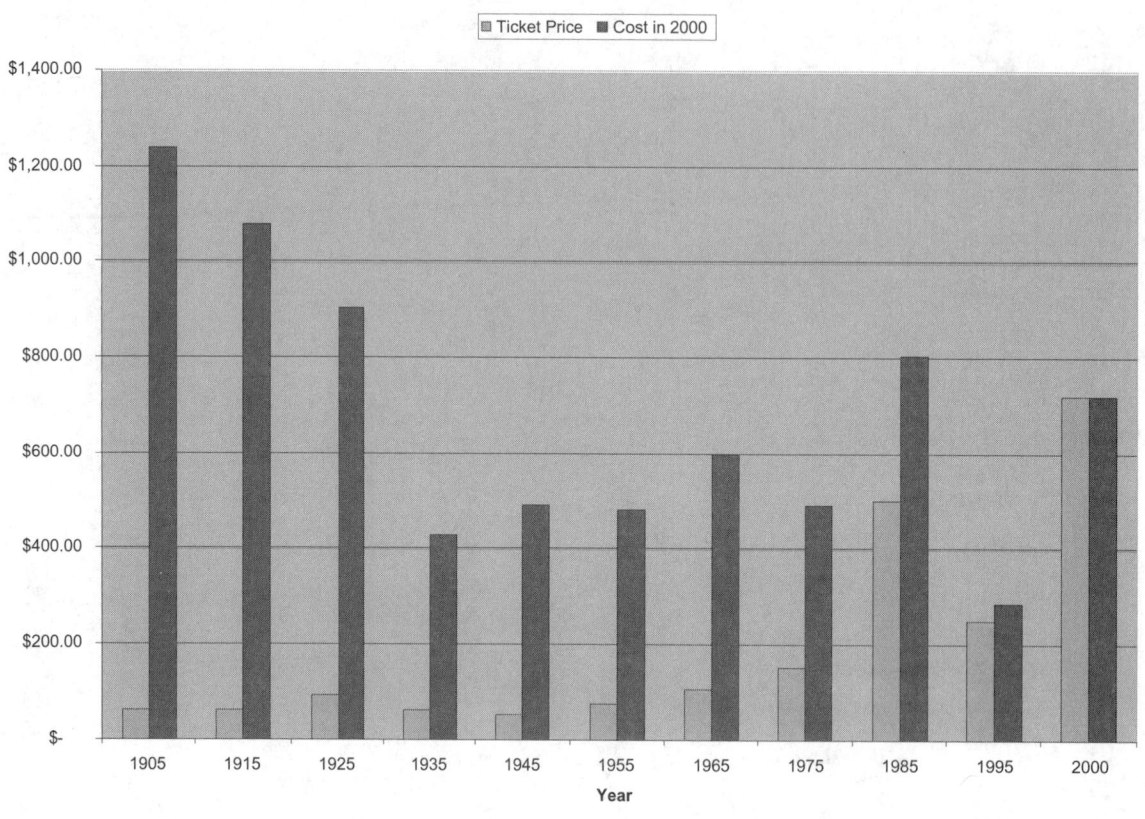

	1905	1915	1925	1935	1945	1955	1965	1975	1985	1995	2000
Ticket Price	$63.34	$ 63.66	$92.55	$64.49	$51.77	$75.77	$109.55	$153.50	$504.00	$253.00	$720.00
Dollar Value in 2000	$1,241.96	$1,078.98	$907.35	$429.88	$493.05	$485.71	$598.63	$491.99	$806.40	$285.88	$720.00

TRAVEL & ENTERTAINMENT

Roll of Film

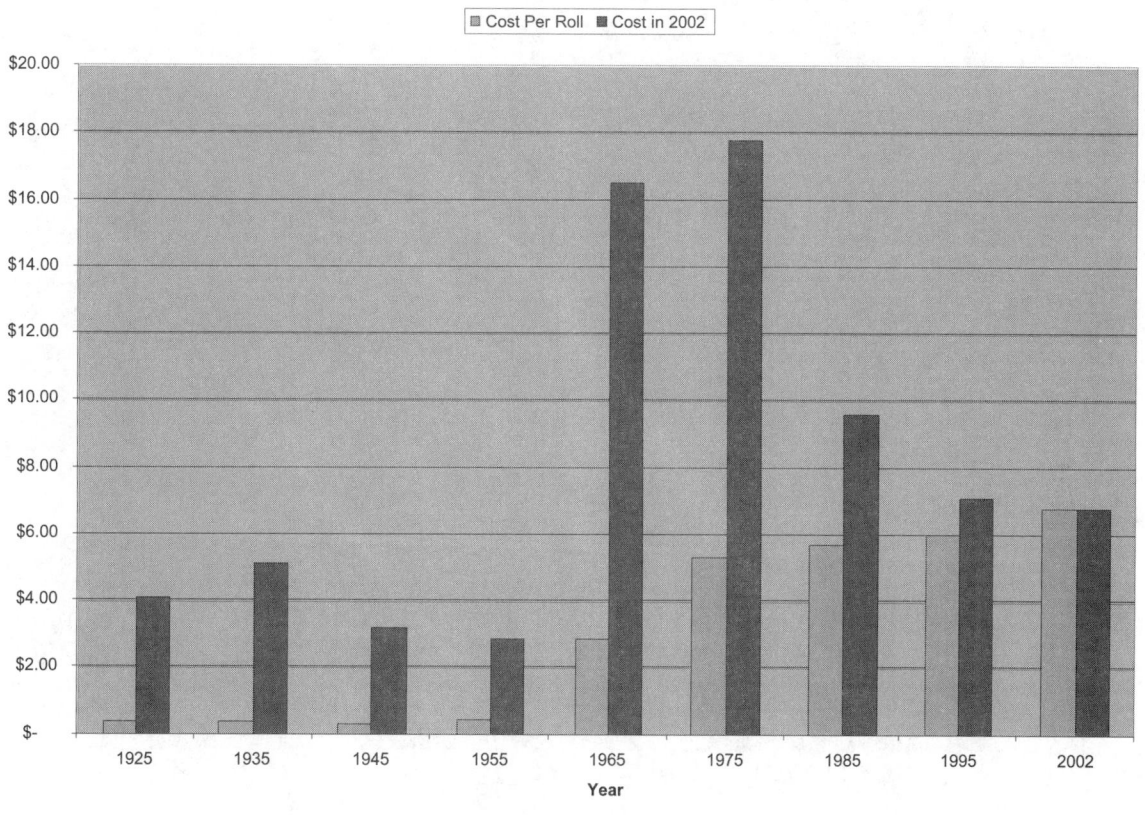

	1925	1935	1945	1955	1965	1975	1985	1995	1999
Cost Per Roll	$0.40	$0.39	$0.32	$0.43	$2.89	$5.33	$5.70	$6.00	$6.50
Dollar Value in 2002	$4.11	$5.12	$3.20	$2.89	$16.51	$17.82	$9.61	$7.08	$7.02

TRAVEL & ENTERTAINMENT

Suitcase

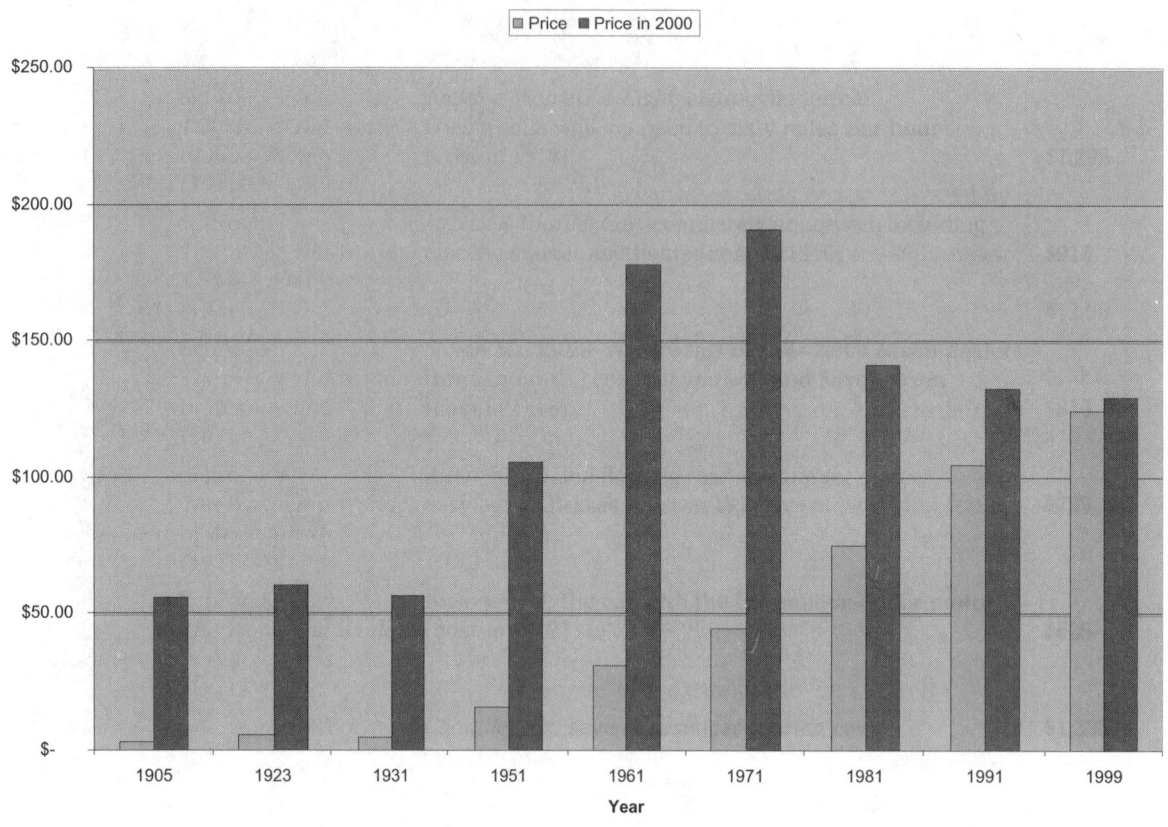

	1905	1923	1931	1951	1961	1971	1981	1991	1999
Price	$3.00	$6.00	$5.00	$15.95	$31.00	$44.50	$75.00	$105.00	$125.00
Dollar Value in 2000	$55.82	$60.61	$56.82	$105.63	$178.16	$191.49	$142.02	$132.74	$129.27

Excerpts from Ad Descriptions:

- **1923:** Black enameled; leather corners and handles; 24"x15"x9"
- **1931:** Top grain cowhide suitcase; 12"x16"x18"; Lowest price since 1910
- **1951:** Famous American Tourister Luggage; 24" Weekender
- **1971:** 24" Jr. Pullman; First Flite Aluminum Frame; Prestige Luggage
- **1991:** Samsonite Silhouette Valet

TRAVEL & ENTERTAINMENT

Ticket to Broadway Show*

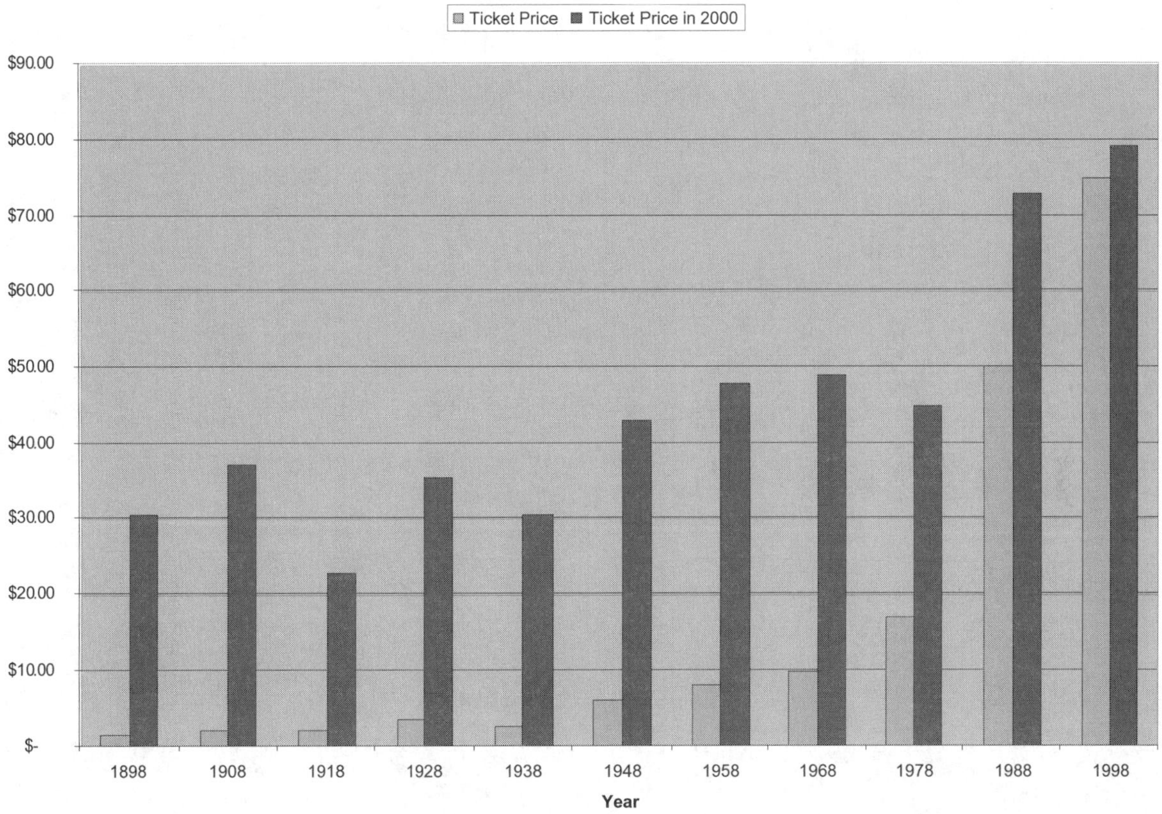

□ Ticket Price ■ Ticket Price in 2000

	1898	1908	1918	1928	1938	1948	1958	1968	1978	1988	1998
Ticket Price	$1.50	$2.00	$2.00	$3.50	$2.50	$6.00	$8.05	$9.90	$17.00	$50.00	$75.00
Dollar Value in 2000	$30.61	$37.04	$22.73	$35.35	$30.49	$42.86	$47.92	$49.01	$44.85	$72.78	$79.20

Shows Performing on Broadway:

- **1898:** Oh, Susannah!
- **1908:** The Soul Kill with Genee
- **1918:** Oh, Boy
- **1928:** 5 O'Clock Girl
- **1938:** Of Mice and Men
- **1948:** Macbeth
- **1958:** West Side Story
- **1968:** Fiddler on the Roof
- **1978:** A Chorus Line
- **1988:** The Phantom of the Opera
- **1998:** Chicago

* Best Seating

General Sources

Chapter Introductions: Primary sources are Charles Sellers, Henry May, Neil R. McMillen, *A Synopsis of American History,* 7th edition (Chicago: Dee, 1992); Richard B. Morris, ed., *Encyclopedia of American History* (New York, Evanston, San Francisco, & London: Harper & Row, 1975); and *Historical Statistics of the United States, Colonial Times to 1970* (Washington, D.C.: Government Printing Office, 1975).

Historical Snapshots: Primary sources are James Trager, ed., *The People's Chronology; A Year-by-Year Record of Human Events from Prehistory to the Present* (New York: Holt, 1992); and *Encyclopedia of American History.*

Consumer Expenditures: Sources for these figures are J. Frederick Dewhurst, *America's Needs and Resources: A New Survey* (New York: Twentieth-Century Fund, 1955); Department of Commerce, Bureau of Economic Analysis, *The National Income and Product Accounts, 1929–1988 Statistical Tables* (Washington, D.C.: Government Printing Office, 1989); Bureau of Foreign and Domestic Commerce, *Statistical Abstract of the United States, 1990 and 1991* (Washington, D.C.: Government Printing Office, 1990 and 1991); and U.S. Bureau of the Census, *Current Population Reports,* series P-25, nos. 311, 1045, and 1069.

Investments: For Basic Yields of Corporate Bonds, Short-term Interest Rates, Basic Yield Common Stocks, and Index of Common Stocks, the source is *Historical Statistics of the United States, Colonial Times to 1970,* and for the period from 1970 to 1989, Board of Governors of the Federal Reserve System, *Federal Reserve Bulletin,* May issue, 1971–1990; U.S. Department of Commerce, Bureau of Economic Analysis, *Survey of Current Business* (Washington, D.C.: Government Printing Office, 1971–1990). For price quotes and dividends, *The Wall Street Journal.* For information about stock splits, *Capital Changes Reports* (Chicago: Commerce Clearing House, 1993). Note that only splits and dividends are reported. Other factors affecting stock value, such as rights offered to debentures or other offerings, are omitted.

Selected Income: Sources are indicated in individual entries.

Standard Income: Paul H. Douglas, *Real Wages in the United States, 1890–1926* (New York: Augustus Kelley, 1966); Stanley Lebergott, *Manpower in Economic Growth: The American Record Since 1800* (New York: McGraw-Hill, 1964); Department of Commerce Bureau of Economic Analysis, *The National Income and Product Accounts of the United States, 1929–1988 Statistical Tables* (Washington, D.C.: Government Printing Office, 1989); and Department of Commerce, Bureau of Economic Analysis, *Business Statistics, 1963–1991* (Washington, D.C.: Government Printing Office, 1992).

Food Basket: Department of Commerce and Labor, *Bulletin of Bureau of Labor* (Washington, D.C.: Government Printing Office) no. 71 (1907), no. 105 (1912); Department of Labor, Bureau of Labor Statistics, *Retail Prices* (Washington, D.C.: Government Printing Office) Bulletin 140 (1914), 270 (1921), 300 (1922), 315 (1923), 334 (1923), 366 (1925), 418 (1926), 464 (1928), 495 (1929), 635 (1937), 707 (1942), 799 (1944), 899 (1947), 938 (1948), 965 (1949), 1032 (1950), 1055 (1951), 1141 (1953), 1183 (1955), 1217 (1957), 1254 (1959), 1301 (1961), 1446 (1964), 1632 (1969); *Estimated Retail Food Prices by Cities, 1969–1977* (Washington, D.C.: Government Printing Office, 1978); *Handbook of Labor Statistics, 1978, Bulletin 20* (Washington, D.C.: Government Printing Office, 1979); American Chamber of Commerce Researcher's Association, *Cost of Living Index, 1986–1987* (Alexandria, Va.: American Chamber of Commerce Researcher's Association, 1987); *Inter-City Cost of Living Index, 1988–1990* (Alexandria, Va.: American Chamber of Commerce Researcher's Association, 1990).

Selected Prices: Sources are indicated in individual entries; complete citations for books are provided in the bibliography.

Standard Prices: Sears, Roebuck Catalogues (ceased publication after 1992).

Miscellany: Sources are indicated in individual entries.

Pricing Trends Sources

Amtrak

Beaulieu Vineyard

Brooks Brothers

Cantigny First Division Foundation

Center of Disease Control

Chicago Historical Society

Chicago Tribune

Cleveland Public Library

CNN

Conde Nast

Consumer Digest

Dublin Dr. Pepper Bottling Company Museum

Eureka

Ford Motor Company

Golf Digest

Harley Davidson Data Book

Harley Davidson Sales Company

Herman's

Hershey

J.C.Penny

Lady's Home Journal

Major League Baseball

McDonald's

National Association of Home Builders

National Association of Theatre Owners and Box
  Office Managers

National Football League

National Railroad Historical Society

New York Times

Playboy Magazine

Richland County Library

Sears Roebuck

Statistical Abstract of the United States

Sunbeam Corporation

The Atlanta Constitution

The Atlantic Monthly Group

*The Sporting News Pro Football Guide 2002
  Edition*

*The Standard Catalog of Comic Books,
  2nd Edition*

The State

Time Warner

United States Census Bureau

United States Domestic Postage Rate: History

University of Oregon

University of South Carolina

US Treasury of the United States

USA Today

Yesterland Website

Zippo

Bibliography

Victor Bondi, ed. *American Decades: 1930–1939.* Detroit, Washington, D.C. & London: Gale Research/Manly, 1995.

Bondi, ed. *American Decades: 1940–1949.* Detroit, Washington, D.C. & London: Gale Research/Manly, 1995.

Bondi, ed. *American Decades: 1980–1989.* Detroit, Washington, D.C. & London: Gale Research/Manly, 1996.

James E. B. Breslin. *Mark Rothko: A Biography.* Chicago: University of Chicago Press, 1993.

John Brooks. *Telephone: The First Hundred Years.* New York: Harper & Row, 1976.

Mary A. Bufwack and Robert K. Oerman. *Finding Her Voice, The Saga of Women in Country Music.* New York: Crown Publisher, 1993.

Lyle W. Dorsett. *Billy Sunday and the Redemption of Urban America.* Grand Rapids, Mich.: Eerdmanns, 1991.

Susan J. Douglas. *Inventing American Broadcasting.* Baltimore, Md.: Johns Hopkins University Press, 1987.

Scott Eyman. *Mary Pickford: America's Sweetheart.* New York: Donald I. Fine, 1990.

John Feinstein. *Play Ball: The Life and Troubled Times of Major League Baseball.* New York: Villard, 1993.

Kristine Fredriksson. *American Rodeo: From Buffalo Bill to Big Business.* College Station: Texas A&M University Press, 1985.

Harvey Frommer. *Shoeless Joe and Ragtime Baseball.* Dallas, Tex.: Taylor, 1992.

James Grant. *Bernard Baruch: The Adventures of a Wall Street Legend.* New York: Simon & Schuster, 1983.

Warren G. Harris. *Lucy and Desi: The Legendary Love Story.* Simon & Schuster: New York, 1991.

Adelaide Hechtinger. *The Great Patent Medicine Era.* New York: Madison Square Press, 1970.

James D. Horan. *Mathew Brady: Historian with a Camera.* New York: Bonanza Books, 1965.

Harry Hunt III, *Texas Rich: The Hunt Dynasty From The Early Oil Days Through The Silver Crash.* New York: Norton, 1981.

Jim Hunter. *Catfish: My Life in Baseball.* New York: McGraw-Hill, 1988.

Justin Kaplan. *Lincoln Steffens.* New York: Simon & Schuster, 1974.

Philip B. Kunhardt, Philip B. Kunhardt III, and Peter W. Kunhardt. *P.T. Barnum, America's Greatest Showman.* New York: Knopf, 1995.

Richard M. Langworth and Graham Robson. *Complete Book of Collectible Cars, 1930–1980.* New York: Beekman House, 1985.

Richard Layman, ed. *American Decades: 1950–1959.* Detroit, Washington, D.C. & London: Gale Research/Manly, 1994.

Catherine Legrand and Robyn Karney. *Chronicle of the Cinema.* New York: Dorling Kindersley, 1995.

Robert A. Margo. *Race and Schooling in the South.* Chicago: University of Chicago Press, 1990.

Lee O. Miller. *The Great Cowboy Stars of Movies and Television.* New Rochelle, N.Y.: Arlington House, 1979.

Joyce Milton. *Loss of Eden: A Biography of Charles and Anne Morrow Lindbergh.* New York: Harper Collins, 1993.

Ward Morehouse. *George Cohan: Prince of the American Theater.* Philadelphia: Lippincott, 1943.

Cecil Munsey. *The Illustrated Guide to the Collectibles of Coca-Cola.* New York: Hawthorn, 1972.

Steven Naifeh and Gregory White Smith. *Jackson Pollock: An American Saga.* New York: C. N. Potter, 1989.

Bob Rains, *St. Louis Cardinals: The 100th Anniversary History.* New York: St. Martin's Press, 1992.

Arnold Rampersad. *Jackie Robinson: A Biography.* New York: Knopf, 1997.

Jeffrey Robinson. *Bardot: An Intimate Portrait.* New York: Donald I. Fine, 1994.

Patrick Sameway. *Walker Percy: A Life.* New York: Farrar, Strauss & Giroux, 1997.

Joseph J. Schroeder Jr. *The Wonderful World of Automobiles.* Chicago: Follett, 1971.

Edward L. Throm, ed. *Popular Mechanics Picture History of American Transportation.* New York: Simon & Schuster, 1952.

Vincent Tompkins, ed. *American Decades: 1900–1909.* Detroit, Washington, D.C. & London: Gale Research/Manly, 1996.

Tompkins, ed. *American Decades: 1910–1919.* Detroit, Washington, D.C. & London: Gale Research/Manly, 1996.

J. Chal Vinson. *Thomas Nast: Political Cartoonist.* Athens: University of Georgia Press, 1967.

Index

Universal Reference Publications
Statistical & Demographic Reference Books

Working Americans 1880-1999
Volume I: The Working Class, Volume II: The Middle Class, Volume III: The Upper Class

Each of the volumes in the *Working Americans 1880-1999* series focuses on a particular class of Americans, The Working Class, The Middle Class and The Upper Class over the last 120 years. Chapters in each volume focus on one decade and profile three to five families. Family Profiles include real data on Income & Job Descriptions, Selected Prices of the Times, Annual Income, Annual Budgets, Family Finances, Life at Work, Life at Home, Life in the Community, Working Conditions, Cost of Living, Amusements and much more. Each chapter also contains an Economic Profile with Average Wages of other Professions, a selection of Typical Pricing, Key Events & Inventions, News Profiles, Articles from Local Media and Illustrations. The *Working Americans* series captures the lifestyles of each of the classes from the last twelve decades, covers a vast array of occupations and ethnic backgrounds and travels the entire nation. These interesting and useful compilations of portraits of the American Working, Middle and Upper Classes during the last 120 years will be an important addition to any high school, public or academic library reference collection.

> *"These interesting, unique compilations of economic and social facts, figures and graphs will support multiple research needs. They will engage and enlighten patrons in high school, public and academic library collections." –Booklist*

Volume I: The Working Class ◆ 558 pages; Hardcover ISBN 1-891482-81-5, $145.00
Volume II: The Middle Class ◆ 591 pages; Hardcover ISBN 1-891482-72-6; $145.00
Volume III: The Upper Class ◆ 567 pages; Hardcover ISBN 1-930956-38-X, $145.00

Working Americans 1880-1999 Volume IV: Their Children

This Fourth Volume in the highly successful *Working Americans 1880-1999* series focuses on American children, decade by decade from 1880 to 1999. This interesting and useful volume introduces the reader to three children in each decade, one from each of the Working, Middle and Upper classes. Like the first three volumes in the series, the individual profiles are created from interviews, diaries, statistical studies, biographies and news reports. Profiles cover a broad range of ethnic backgrounds, geographic area and lifestyles – everything from an orphan in Memphis in 1882, following the Yellow Fever epidemic of 1878 to an eleven-year-old nephew of a beer baron and owner of the New York Yankees in New York City in 1921. Chapters also contain important supplementary materials including News Features as well as information on everything from Schools to Parks, Infectious Diseases to Childhood Fears along with Entertainment, Family Life and much more to provide an informative overview of the lifestyles of children from each decade. This interesting account of what life was like for Children in the Working, Middle and Upper Classes will be a welcome addition to the reference collection of any high school, public or academic library.

600 pages; Hardcover ISBN 1-930956-35-5, $145.00

Working Americans 1880-2003 Volume V: Americans At War

Working Americans 1880-2003 Volume V: Americans At War is divided into 11 chapters, each covering a decade from 1880-2003 and examines the lives of Americans during the time of war, including declared conflicts, one-time military actions, protests, and preparations for war. Each decade includes several personal profiles, whether on the battlefield or on the homefront, that tell the stories of civilians, soldiers, and officers during the decade. The profiles examine: Life at Home; Life at Work; and Life in the Community. Each decade also includes an Economic Profile with statistical comparisons, a Historical Snapshot, News Profiles, local News Articles, and Illustrations that provide a solid historical background to the decade being examined. Profiles range widely not only geographically, but also emotionally, from that of a girl whose leg was torn off in a blast during WWI, to the boredom of being stationed in the Dakotas as the Indian Wars were drawing to a close. As in previous volumes of the *Working Americans* series, information is presented in narrative form, but hard facts and real-life situations back up each story. The basis of the profiles come from diaries, private print books, personal interviews, family histories, estate documents and magazine articles. For easy reference, *Working Americans 1880-2003 Volume V: Americans At War* includes an in-depth Subject Index. The *Working Americans* series has become an important reference for public libraries, academic libraries and high school libraries. This fifth volume will be a welcome addition to all of these types of reference collections.

600 pages; Hardcover ISBN 1-59237-024-1; $145.00
Five Volume Set (Volumes I-V), Hardcover ISBN 1-59237-034-9, $675.00

To preview any of our Directories Risk-Free for 30 days, call (800) 562-2139 or fax to (518) 789-0556

The Environmental Resource Handbook, 2004

The Environmental Resource Handbook, now in its second edition, is the most up-to-date and comprehensive source for Environmental Resources and Statistics. Section I: Resources provides detailed contact information for thousands of information sources, including Associations & Organizations, Awards & Honors, Conferences, Foundations & Grants, Environmental Health, Government Agencies, National Parks & Wildlife Refuges, Publications, Research Centers, Educational Programs, Green Product Catalogs, Consultants and much more. Section II: Statistics, provides statistics and rankings on hundreds of important topics, including Children's Environmental Index, Municipal Finances, Toxic Chemicals, Recycling, Climate, Air & Water Quality and more. This kind of up-to-date environmental data, all in one place, is not available anywhere else on the market place today. This vast compilation of resources and statistics is a must-have for all public and academic libraries as well as any organization with a primary focus on the environment.

"…the intrinsic value of the information make it worth consideration by libraries with environmental collections and environmentally concerned users." –Booklist

1,000 pages; Softcover ISBN 1-59237-030-6, $155.00 ◆ Online Database $300.00

Weather America, A Thirty-Year Summary of Statistical Weather Data and Rankings

This valuable resource provides extensive climatological data for over 4,000 National and Cooperative Weather Stations throughout the United States. *Weather America* begins with a new Major Storms section that details major storm events of the nation and a National Rankings section that details rankings for several data elements, such as Maximum Temperature and Precipitation. The main body of *Weather America* is organized into 50 state sections. Each section provides a Data Table on each Weather Station, organized alphabetically, that provides statistics on Maximum and Minimum Temperatures, Precipitation, Snowfall, Extreme Temperatures, Foggy Days, Humidity and more. State sections contain two brand new features in this edition – a City Index and a narrative Description of the climatic conditions of the state. Each section also includes a revised Map of the State that includes not only weather stations, but cities and towns.

"Best Reference Book of the Year." –Library Journal

2,013 pages; Softcover ISBN 1-891482-29-7, $175.00

Profiles of America: Facts, Figures & Statistics for Every Populated Place in the United States

Profiles of America is the only source that pulls together, in one place, statistical, historical and descriptive information about every place in the United States in an easy-to-use format. This award winning reference set, now in its second edition, compiles statistics and data from over 20 different sources – the latest census information has been included along with more than nine brand new statistical topics. This Four-Volume Set details over 40,000 places, from the biggest metropolis to the smallest unincorporated hamlet, and provides statistical details and information on over 50 different topics including Geography, Climate, Population, Vital Statistics, Economy, Income, Taxes, Education, Housing, Health & Environment, Public Safety, Newspapers, Transportation, Presidential Election Results and Information Contacts or Chambers of Commerce. Profiles are arranged, for ease-of-use, by state and then by county. Each county begins with a County-Wide Overview and is followed by information for each Community in that particular county. The Community Profiles within the county are arranged alphabetically. *Profiles of America* is a virtual snapshot of America at your fingertips and a unique compilation of information that will be widely used in any reference collection.

A Library Journal Best Reference Book   "An outstanding compilation." –Library Journal

10,000 pages; Four Volume Set; Softcover ISBN 1-891482-80-7, $595.00

Ancestry in America: A Comparative Guide to Over 200 Ethnic Backgrounds

This brand new reference work pulls together thousands of comparative statistics on the Ethnic Backgrounds of all populated places in the United States with populations over 10,000. Section One, Statistics by Place, is made up of a list of over 200 ancestry and race categories arranged alphabetically by each of the 5,000 different places with populations over 10,000. This informative city-by-city section allows the user to quickly and easily explore the ethnic makeup of all major population bases in the United States. Section Two, Comparative Rankings, contains three tables for each ethnicity and race. In the first table, the top 150 populated places are ranked by population number for that particular ancestry group, regardless of population. In the second table, the top 150 populated places are ranked by the percent of the total population for that ancestry group. In the third table, those top 150 populated places with 10,000 population are ranked by population number for each ancestry group. These easy-to-navigate tables allow users to see ancestry population patterns and make city-by-city comparisons as well. Plus, as an added bonus with the purchase of *Ancestry in America*, a free companion CD-ROM is available that lists statistics and rankings for all of the 35,000 populated places in the United States. This brand new, information-packed resource will serve a wide-range or research requests for demographics, population characteristics, relocation information and much more. *Ancestry in America: A Comparative Guide to Over 200 Ethnic Backgrounds* will be an important acquisition to all reference collections.

"This compilation will serve a wide range of research requests … it offers much more detail than other sources." –Booklist

1,500 pages; Softcover ISBN 1-59237-029-2, $225.00

To preview any of our Directories Risk-Free for 30 days, call (800) 562-2139 or fax to (518) 789-0556

The Asian Databook: Statistics for all US Counties & Cities with Over 10,000 Population

This is the first-ever resource that compiles statistics and rankings on the US Asian population. *The Asian Databook* presents over 20 statistical data points for each city and county, arranged alphabetically by state, then alphabetically by place name. Data reported for each place includes Population, Languages Spoken at Home, Foreign-Born, Educational Attainment, Income Figures, Poverty Status, Homeownership, Home Values & Rent, and more. Next, in the Rankings Section, the top 75 places are listed for each data element. These easy-to-access ranking tables allow the user to quickly determine trends and population characteristics. This kind of comparative data can not be found elsewhere, in print or on the web, in a format that's as easy-to-use or more concise. A useful resource for those searching for demographics data, career search and relocation information and also for market research. With data ranging from Ancestry to Education, *The Asian Databook* presents a useful compilation of information that will be a much-needed resource in the reference collection of any public or academic library along with the marketing collection of any company whose primary focus in on the Asian population.

1,000 pages; Softcover ISBN 1-59237-044-6 $150.00

The Hispanic Databook: Statistics for all US Counties & Cities with Over 10,000 Population

Previously published by Toucan Valley Publications, this second edition has been completely updated with figures from the latest census and has been broadly expanded to include dozens of new data elements and a brand new Rankings section. The Hispanic population in the United States has increased over 42% in the last 10 years and accounts for 12.5% of the total US population. For ease-of-use, *The Hispanic Databook* presents over 20 statistical data points for each city and county, arranged alphabetically by state, then alphabetically by place name. Data reported for each place includes Population, Languages Spoken at Home, Foreign-Born, Educational Attainment, Income Figures, Poverty Status, Homeownership, Home Values & Rent, and more. Next, in the Rankings Section, the top 75 places are listed for each data element. These easy-to-access ranking tables allow the user to quickly determine trends and population characteristics. This kind of comparative data can not be found elsewhere, in print or on the web, in a format that's as easy-to-use or more concise. A useful resource for those searching for demographics data, career search and relocation information and also for market research. With data ranging from Ancestry to Education, *The Hispanic Databook* presents a useful compilation of information that will be a much-needed resource in the reference collection of any public or academic library along with the marketing collection of any company whose primary focus in on the Hispanic population.

"This accurate, clearly presented volume of selected Hispanic demographics is recommended for large public libraries and research collections."-Library Journal

1,000 pages; Softcover ISBN 1-59237-008-X, $150.00

America's Top-Rated Cities, 2004

America's Top-Rated Cities provides current, comprehensive statistical information and other essential data in one easy-to-use source on the 100 "top" cities that have been cited as the best for business and living in the U.S. This handbook allows readers to see, at a glance, a concise social, business, economic, demographic and environmental profile of each city, including brief evaluative comments. In addition to detailed data on Cost of Living, Finances, Real Estate, Education, Major Employers, Media, Crime and Climate, city reports now include Housing Vacancies, Tax Audits, Bankruptcy, Presidential Election Results and more. This outstanding source of information will be widely used in any reference collection.

"The only source of its kind that brings together all of this information into one easy-to-use source. It will be beneficial to many business and public libraries." –ARBA

2,500 pages, 4 Volume Set; Softcover ISBN 1-59237-038-1, $195.00

America's Top-Rated Smaller Cities, 2004

A perfect companion to *America's Top-Rated Cities*, *America's Top-Rated Smaller Cities* provides current, comprehensive business and living profiles of smaller cities (population 25,000-99,999) that have been cited as the best for business and living in the United States. Sixty cities make up this 2004 edition of *America's Top-Rated Smaller Cities*, all are top-ranked by Population Growth, Median Income, Unemployment Rate and Crime Rate. City reports reflect the most current data available on a wide-range of statistics, including Employment & Earnings, Household Income, Unemployment Rate, Population Characteristics, Taxes, Cost of Living, Education, Health Care, Public Safety, Recreation, Media, Air & Water Quality and much more. Plus, each city report contains a Background of the City, and an Overview of the State Finances. *America's Top-Rated Smaller Cities* offers a reliable, one-stop source for statistical data that, before now, could only be found scattered in hundreds of sources. This volume is designed for a wide range of readers: individuals considering relocating a residence or business; professionals considering expanding their business or changing careers; general and market researchers; real estate consultants; human resource personnel; urban planners and investors.

"Provides current, comprehensive statistical information in one easy-to-use source... Recommended for public and academic libraries and specialized collections." –Library Journal

1,100 pages; Softcover ISBN 1-59237-043-8, $160.00

To preview any of our Directories Risk-Free for 30 days, call (800) 562-2139 or fax to (518) 789-0556

The American Tally, 2003/04 Statistics & Comparative Rankings for U.S. Cities with Populations over 10,000

This important statistical handbook compiles, all in one place, comparative statistics on all U.S. cities and towns with a 10,000+ population. *The American Tally* provides statistical details on over 4,000 cities and towns and profiles how they compare with one another in Population Characteristics, Education, Language & Immigration, Income & Employment and Housing. Each section begins with an alphabetical listing of cities by state, allowing for quick access to both the statistics and relative rankings of any city. Next, the highest and lowest cities are listed in each statistic. These important, informative lists provide quick reference to which cities are at both extremes of the spectrum for each statistic. Unlike any other reference, *The American Tally* provides quick, easy access to comparative statistics – a must-have for any reference collection.

"A solid library reference." –Bookwatch

500 pages; Softcover ISBN 1-930956-29-0, $125.00

The Comparative Guide to American Suburbs, 2001

The Comparative Guide to American Suburbs is a one-stop source for Statistics on the 2,000+ suburban communities surrounding the 50 largest metropolitan areas – their population characteristics, income levels, economy, school system and important data on how they compare to one another. Organized into 50 Metropolitan Area chapters, each chapter contains an overview of the Metropolitan Area, a detailed Map followed by a comprehensive Statistical Profile of each Suburban Community, including Contact Information, Physical Characteristics, Population Characteristics, Income, Economy, Unemployment Rate, Cost of Living, Education, Chambers of Commerce and more. Next, statistical data is sorted into Ranking Tables that rank the suburbs by twenty different criteria, including Population, Per Capita Income, Unemployment Rate, Crime Rate, Cost of Living and more. *The Comparative Guide to American Suburbs* is the best source for locating data on suburbs. Those looking to relocate, as well as those doing preliminary market research, will find this an invaluable timesaving resource.

"Public and academic libraries will find this compilation useful...The work draws together figures from many sources and will be especially helpful for job relocation decisions." – Booklist

1,681 pages; Softcover ISBN 1-930956-42-8, $130.00

Sedgwick Press
Education Directories

Educators Resource Directory, 2003/04

Educators Resource Directory is a comprehensive resource that provides the educational professional with thousands of resources and statistical data for professional development. This directory saves hours of research time by providing immediate access to Associations & Organizations, Conferences & Trade Shows, Educational Research Centers, Employment Opportunities & Teaching Abroad, School Library Services, Scholarships, Financial Resources, Professional Consultants, Computer Software & Testing Resources and much more. Plus, this comprehensive directory also includes a section on Statistics and Rankings with over 100 tables, including statistics on Average Teacher Salaries, SAT/ACT scores, Revenues & Expenditures and more. These important statistics will allow the user to see how their school rates among others, make relocation decisions and so much more. In addition to the Entry & Publisher Index, Geographic Index and Web Sites Index, our editors have added a Subject & Grade Index to this 2003/04 edition. *Educators Resource Directory* will be a well-used addition to the reference collection of any school district, education department or public library.

"Recommended for all collections that serve elementary and secondary school professionals." –Choice

1,000 pages; Softcover ISBN 1-59237-002-0, $145.00 ◆ Online Database $195.00 ◆ Online Database & Directory Combo $280.00

The Comparative Guide to American Elementary & Secondary Schools, 2004/05

The only guide of its kind, this award winning compilation offers a snapshot profile of every public school district in the United States serving 1,500 or more students – more than 5,900 districts are covered. Organized alphabetically by district within state, each chapter begins with a Statistical Overview of the state. Each district listing includes contact information (name, address, phone number and web site) plus Grades Served, the Numbers of Students and Teachers and the Number of Regular, Special Education, Alternative and Vocational Schools in the district along with statistics on Student/Classroom Teacher Ratios, Drop Out Rates, Ethnicity, the Numbers of Librarians and Guidance Counselors and District Expenditures per student. As an added bonus, *The Comparative Guide to American Elementary and Secondary Schools* provides important ranking tables, both by state and nationally, for each data element. For easy navigation through this wealth of information, this handbook contains a useful City Index that lists all districts that operate schools within a city. These important comparative statistics are necessary for anyone considering relocation or doing comparative research on their own district and would be a perfect acquisition for any public library or school district library.

"This straightforward guide is an easy way to find general information. Valuable for academic and large public library collections." –ARBA

2,400 pages; Softcover ISBN 1-59237-047-0, $125.00

To preview any of our Directories Risk-Free for 30 days, call (800) 562-2139 or fax to (518) 789-0556

Sedgwick Press
Health Directories

The Complete Learning Disabilities Directory, 2004/05

The Complete Learning Disabilities Directory is the most comprehensive database of Programs, Services, Curriculum Materials, Professional Meetings & Resources, Camps, Newsletters and Support Groups for teachers, students and families concerned with learning disabilities. This information-packed directory includes information about Associations & Organizations, Schools, Colleges & Testing Materials, Government Agencies, Legal Resources and much more. For quick, easy access to information, this directory contains four indexes: Entry Name Index, Subject Index and Geographic Index. With every passing year, the field of learning disabilities attracts more attention and the network of caring, committed and knowledgeable professionals grows every day. This directory is an invaluable research tool for these parents, students and professionals.

"Due to its wealth and depth of coverage, parents, teachers and others… should find this an invaluable resource." -Booklist

900 pages; Softcover ISBN 1-59237-049-7, $145.00 ◆ Online Database $195.00 ◆ Online Database & Directory Combo $280.00

The Complete Directory for People with Disabilities, 2005

A wealth of information, now in one comprehensive sourcebook. Completely updated for 2005, this edition contains more information than ever before, including thousands of new entries and enhancements to existing entries and thousands of additional web sites and e-mail addresses. This up-to-date directory is the most comprehensive resource available for people with disabilities, detailing Independent Living Centers, Rehabilitation Facilities, State & Federal Agencies, Associations, Support Groups, Periodicals & Books, Assistive Devices, Employment & Education Programs, Camps and Travel Groups. Each year, more libraries, schools, colleges, hospitals, rehabilitation centers and individuals add *The Complete Directory for People with Disabilities* to their collections, making sure that this information is readily available to the families, individuals and professionals who can benefit most from the amazing wealth of resources cataloged here.

"No other reference tool exists to meet the special needs of the disabled in one convenient resource for information." –Library Journal

1,200 pages; Softcover ISBN 1-59237-054-3, $165.00 ◆ Online Database $215.00 ◆ Online Database & Directory Combo $300.00

The Complete Directory for People with Chronic Illness, 2003/04

Thousands of hours of research have gone into this completely updated 2003/04 edition – several new chapters have been added along with thousands of new entries and enhancements to existing entries. Plus, each chronic illness chapter has been reviewed by an medical expert in the field. This widely-hailed directory is structured around the 90 most prevalent chronic illnesses – from Asthma to Cancer to Wilson's Disease – and provides a comprehensive overview of the support services and information resources available for people diagnosed with a chronic illness. Each chronic illness has its own chapter and contains a brief description in layman's language, followed by important resources for National & Local Organizations, State Agencies, Newsletters, Books & Periodicals, Libraries & Research Centers, Support Groups & Hotlines, Web Sites and much more. This directory is an important resource for health care professionals, the collections of hospital and health care libraries, as well as an invaluable tool for people with a chronic illness and their support network.

"A must purchase for all hospital and health care libraries and is strongly recommended for all public library reference departments." –ARBA

1,200 pages; Softcover ISBN 1-930956-83-5, $165.00 ◆ Online Database $215.00 ◆ Online Database & Directory Combo $300.00

The Complete Mental Health Directory, 2004

This is the most comprehensive resource covering the field of behavioral health, with critical information for both the layman and the mental health professional. For the layman, this directory offers understandable descriptions of 25 Mental Health Disorders as well as detailed information on Associations, Media, Support Groups and Mental Health Facilities. For the professional, *The Complete Mental Health Directory* offers critical and comprehensive information on Managed Care Organizations, Information Systems, Government Agencies and Provider Organizations. This comprehensive volume of needed information will be widely used in any reference collection.

"… the strength of this directory is that it consolidates widely dispersed information into a single volume." –Booklist

800 pages; Softcover ISBN 1-59237-046-2, $165.00 ◆ Online Database $215.00 ◆ Online & Directory Combo $300.00

To preview any of our Directories Risk-Free for 30 days, call (800) 562-2139 or fax to (518) 789-0556

The Complete Directory for Pediatric Disorders, 2004/05

This important directory provides parents and caregivers with information about Pediatric Conditions, Disorders, Diseases and Disabilities, including Blood Disorders, Bone & Spinal Disorders, Brain Defects & Abnormalities, Chromosomal Disorders, Congenital Heart Defects, Movement Disorders, Neuromuscular Disorders and Pediatric Tumors & Cancers. This carefully written directory offers: understandable Descriptions of 15 major bodily systems; Descriptions of more than 200 Disorders and a Resources Section, detailing National Agencies & Associations, State Associations, Online Services, Libraries & Resource Centers, Research Centers, Support Groups & Hotlines, Camps, Books and Periodicals. This resource will provide immediate access to information crucial to families and caregivers when coping with children's illnesses.

"Recommended for public and consumer health libraries." –Library Journal

1,200 pages; Softcover ISBN 1-59237-045-4, $165.00 ♦ Online Database $215.00 ♦ Online Database & Directory Combo $300.00

Older Americans Information Directory, 2004/05

Completely updated for 2004/05, this Fifth Edition has been completely revised and now contains 1,000 new listings, over 8,000 updates to existing listings and over 3,000 brand new e-mail addresses and web sites. You'll find important resources for Older Americans including National, Regional, State & Local Organizations, Government Agencies, Research Centers, Libraries & Information Centers, Legal Resources, Discount Travel Information, Continuing Education Programs, Disability Aids & Assistive Devices, Health, Print Media and Electronic Media. Three indexes: Entry Index, Subject Index and Geographic Index make it easy to find just the right source of information. This comprehensive guide to resources for Older Americans will be a welcome addition to any reference collection.

"Highly recommended for academic, public, health science and consumer libraries…" –Choice

1,200 pages; Softcover ISBN 1-59237-037-3, $165.00 ♦ Online Database $215.00 ♦ Online Database & Directory Combo $300.00

The Complete Directory for People with Rare Disorders, 2002/03

This outstanding reference is produced in conjunction with the National Organization for Rare Disorders to provide comprehensive and needed access to important information on over 1,000 rare disorders, including Cancers and Muscular, Genetic and Blood Disorders. An informative Disorder Description is provided for each of the 1,100 disorders (rare Cancers and Muscular, Genetic and Blood Disorders) followed by information on National and State Organizations dealing with a particular disorder, Umbrella Organizations that cover a wide range of disorders, the Publications that can be useful when researching a disorder and the Government Agencies to contact. Detailed and up-to-date listings contain mailing address, phone and fax numbers, web sites and e-mail addresses along with a description. For quick, easy access to information, this directory contains two indexes: Entry Name Index and Acronym/Keyword Index along with an informative Guide for Rare Disorder Advocates. The Complete Directory for People with Rare Disorders will be an invaluable tool for the thousands of families that have been struck with a rare or "orphan" disease, who feel that they have no place to turn and will be a much-used addition to the reference collection of any public or academic library.

"Quick access to information… public libraries and hospital patient libraries will find this a useful resource in directing users to support groups or agencies dealing with a rare disorder." –Booklist

726 pages; Softcover ISBN 1-891482-18-1, $165.00

The Directory of Drug & Alcohol Residential Rehabilitation Facilities, 2004

This brand new directory is the first-ever resource to bring together, all in one place, data on the thousands of drug and alcohol residential rehabilitation facilities in the United States. *The Directory of Drug & Alcohol Residential Rehabilitation Facilities* covers over 1,000 facilities, with detailed contact information for each one, including mailing address, phone and fax numbers, email addresses and web sites, mission statement, type of treatment programs, cost, average length of stay, numbers of residents and counselors, accreditation, insurance plans accepted, type of environment, religious affiliation, education components and much more. It also contains a helpful chapter on General Resources that provides contact information for Associations, Print & Electronic Media, Support Groups and Conferences. Multiple indexes allow the user to pinpoint the facilities that meet very specific criteria. This time-saving tool is what so many counselors, parents and medical professionals have been asking for. *The Directory of Drug & Alcohol Residential Rehabilitation Facilities* will be a helpful tool in locating the right source for treatment for a wide range of individuals. This comprehensive directory will be an important acquisition for all reference collections: public and academic libraries, case managers, social workers, state agencies and many more.

"This is an excellent, much needed directory that fills an important gap…" –Booklist

300 pages; Softcover ISBN 1-59237-031-4, $135.00

To preview any of our Directories Risk-Free for 30 days, call (800) 562-2139 or fax to (518) 789-0556

Grey House Publishing
Business Directories

Nations of the World, 2005 A Political, Economic and Business Handbook

This completely revised edition covers all the nations of the world in an easy-to-use, single volume. Each nation is profiled in a single chapter that includes Key Facts, Political & Economic Issues, a Country Profile and Business Information. In this fast-changing world, it is extremely important to make sure that the most up-to-date information is included in your reference collection. This 2005 edition is just the answer. Each of the 200+ country chapters have been carefully reviewed by a political expert to make sure that the text reflects the most current information on Politics, Travel Advisories, Economics and more. You'll find such vital information as a Country Map, Population Characteristics, Inflation, Agricultural Production, Foreign Debt, Political History, Foreign Policy, Regional Insecurity, Economics, Trade & Tourism, Historical Profile, Political Systems, Ethnicity, Languages, Media, Climate, Hotels, Chambers of Commerce, Banking, Travel Information and more. Five Regional Chapters follow the main text and include a Regional Map, an Introductory Article, Key Indicators and Currencies for the Region. New for 2004, an all-inclusive CD-ROM is available as a companion to the printed text. Noted for its sophisticated, up-to-date and reliable compilation of political, economic and business information, this brand new edition will be an important acquisition to any public, academic or special library reference collection.

"A useful addition to both general reference collections and business collections." –RUSQ

1,700 pages; Print Version Only Softcover ISBN 1-59237-051-9, $145.00 ◆ Print Version and CD-ROM $180.00

Sports Market Place Directory, 2005

For over 20 years, this comprehensive, up-to-date directory has offered direct access to the Who, What, When & Where of the Sports Industry. With over 20,000 updates and enhancements, the *Sports Market Place Directory* is the most detailed, comprehensive and current sports business reference source available. In 1,800 information-packed pages, *Sports Market Place Directory* profiles contact information and key executives for: Single Sport Organizations, Professional Leagues, Multi-Sport Organizations, Disabled Sports, High School & Youth Sports, Military Sports, Olympic Organizations, Media, Sponsors, Sponsorship & Marketing Event Agencies, Event & Meeting Calendars, Professional Services, College Sports, Manufacturers & Retailers, Facilities and much more. *The Sports Market Place Directory* provides organization's contact information with detailed descriptions including: Key Contacts, physical, mailing, email and web addresses plus phone and fax numbers. For over twenty years, *The Sports Market Place Directory* has assisted thousands of individuals in their pursuit of a career in the sports industry. Why not use "THE SOURCE" that top recruiters, headhunters and career placement centers use to find information on or about sports organizations and key hiring contacts.

1,800 pages; Softcover ISBN 1-59237-077-2, $225.00 ◆ CD-ROM $479.00

The Directory of Business Information Resources, 2005

With 100% verification, over 1,000 new listings and more than 12,000 updates, this 2005 edition of *The Directory of Business Information Resources* is the most up-to-date source for contacts in over 98 business areas – from advertising and agriculture to utilities and wholesalers. This carefully researched volume details: the Associations representing each industry; the Newsletters that keep members current; the Magazines and Journals - with their "Special Issues" - that are important to the trade, the Conventions that are "must attends," Databases, Directories and Industry Web Sites that provide access to must-have marketing resources. Includes contact names, phone & fax numbers, web sites and e-mail addresses. This one-volume resource is a gold mine of information and would be a welcome addition to any reference collection.

"This is a most useful and easy-to-use addition to any researcher's library." –The Information Professionals Institute

2,500 pages; Softcover ISBN 1-59237-050-0, $195.00 ◆ Online Database $495.00

The Grey House Performing Arts Directory, 2005

The Grey House Performing Arts Directory is the most comprehensive resource covering the Performing Arts. This important directory provides current information on over 8,500 Dance Companies, Instrumental Music Programs, Opera Companies, Choral Groups, Theater Companies, Performing Arts Series and Performing Arts Facilities. Plus, this edition now contains a brand new section on Artist Management Groups. In addition to mailing address, phone & fax numbers, e-mail addresses and web sites, dozens of other fields of available information include mission statement, key contacts, facilities, seating capacity, season, attendance and more. This directory also provides an important Information *The Grey House Performing Arts Directory* pulls together thousands of Performing Arts Organizations, Facilities and Information Resources into an easy-to-use source – this kind of comprehensiveness and extensive detail is not available in any resource on the market place today.

"Immensely useful and user-friendly ... recommended for public, academic and certain special library reference collections." –Booklist

1,500 pages; Softcover ISBN 1-59237-023-3, $170.00 ◆ Online Database $335.00

To preview any of our Directories Risk-Free for 30 days, call (800) 562-2139 or fax to (518) 789-0556

The Directory of Venture Capital Firms, 2005

This edition has been extensively updated and broadly expanded to offer direct access to over 2,800 Domestic and International Venture Capital Firms, including address, phone & fax numbers, e-mail addresses and web sites for both primary and branch locations. Entries include details on the firm's Mission Statement, Industry Group Preferences, Geographic Preferences, Average and Minimum Investments and Investment Criteria. You'll also find details that are available nowhere else, including the Firm's Portfolio Companies and extensive information on each of the firm's Managing Partners, such as Education, Professional Background and Directorships held, along with the Partner's E-mail Address. *The Directory of Venture Capital Firms* offers five important indexes: Geographic Index, Executive Name Index, Portfolio Company Index, Industry Preference Index and College & University Index. With its comprehensive coverage and detailed, extensive information on each company, *The Directory of Venture Capital Firms* is an important addition to any finance collection.

"The sheer number of listings, the descriptive information provided and the outstanding indexing make this directory a better value than its principal competitor, Pratt's Guide to Venture Capital Sources. Recommended for business collections in large public, academic and business libraries." –Choice

1,300 pages; Softcover ISBN 1-59237-062-4, $450.00 ◆ Online Database (includes a free copy of the directory) $889.00

The Directory of Mail Order Catalogs, 2005

Published since 1981, this 2005 edition features 100% verification of data and is the premier source of information on the mail order catalog industry. Details over 12,000 consumer catalog companies with 44 different product chapters from Animals to Toys & Games. Contains detailed contact information including e-mail addresses and web sites along with important business details such as employee size, years in business, sales volume, catalog size, number of catalogs mailed and more. Four indexes provide quick access to information: Catalog & Company Name Index, Geographic Index, Product Index and Web Sites Index.

"This is a godsend for those looking for information." –Reference Book Review

1,700 pages; Softcover ISBN 1-59237-066-7 $250.00 ◆ Online Database (includes a free copy of the directory) $495.00

The Directory of Business to Business Catalogs, 2005

The completely updated 2005 *Directory of Business to Business Catalogs*, provides details on over 6,000 suppliers of everything from computers to laboratory supplies… office products to office design… marketing resources to safety equipment… landscaping to maintenance suppliers… building construction and much more. Detailed entries offer mailing address, phone & fax numbers, e-mail addresses, web sites, key contacts, sales volume, employee size, catalog printing information and more. Jut about every kind of product a business needs in its day-to-day operations is covered in this carefully-researched volume. Three indexes are provided for at-a-glance access to information: Catalog & Company Name Index, Geographic Index and Web Sites Index.

"An excellent choice for libraries… wishing to supplement their business supplier resources." –Booklist

800 pages; Softcover ISBN 1-59237-064-0, $165.00 ◆ Online Database (includes a free copy of the directory) $325.00

Thomas Food and Beverage Market Place, 2005

Thomas Food and Beverage Market Place is bigger and better than ever with thousands of new companies, thousands of updates to existing companies and two revised and enhanced product category indexes. This comprehensive directory profiles over 18,000 Food & Beverage Manufacturers, 12,000 Equipment & Supply Companies, 2,200 Transportation & Warehouse Companies, 2,000 Brokers & Wholesalers, 8,000 Importers & Exporters, 900 Industry Resources and hundreds of Mail Order Catalogs. Listings include detailed Contact Information, Sales Volumes, Key Contacts, Brand & Product Information, Packaging Details and much more. *Thomas Food and Beverage Market Place* is available as a three-volume printed set, a subscription-based Online Database via the Internet, on CD-ROM, as well as mailing lists and a licensable database.

"An essential purchase for those in the food industry but will also be useful in public libraries where needed. Much of the information will be difficult and time consuming to locate without this handy three-volume ready-reference source." –ARBA

8,500 pages, 3 Volume Set; Softcover ISBN 1-59237-058-6, $495.00 ◆ CD-ROM $695.00 ◆
CD-ROM & 3 Volume Set Combo $895.00 ◆ Online Database $695.00 ◆ Online Database & 3 Volume Set Combo, $895.00

To preview any of our Directories Risk-Free for 30 days, call (800) 562-2139 or fax to (518) 789-0556

The Grey House Safety & Security Directory, 2005

The Grey House Safety & Security Directory is the most comprehensive reference tool and buyer's guide for the safety and security industry. Arranged by safety topic, each chapter begins with OSHA regulations for the topic, followed by Training Articles written by top professionals in the field and Self-Inspection Checklists. Next, each topic contains Buyer's Guide sections that feature related products and services. Topics include Administration, Insurance, Loss Control & Consulting, Protective Equipment & Apparel, Noise & Vibration, Facilities Monitoring & Maintenance, Employee Health Maintenance & Ergonomics, Retail Food Services, Machine Guards, Process Guidelines & Tool Handling, Ordinary Materials Handling, Hazardous Materials Handling, Workplace Preparation & Maintenance, Electrical Lighting & Safety, Fire & Rescue and Security. The Buyer's Guide sections are carefully indexed within each topic area to ensure that you can find the supplies needed to meet OSHA's regulations. Six important indexes make finding information and product manufacturers quick and easy: Geographical Index of Manufacturers and Distributors, Company Profile Index, Brand Name Index, Product Index, Index of Web Sites and Index of Advertisers. This comprehensive, up-to-date reference will provide every tool necessary to make sure a business is in compliance with OSHA regulations and locate the products and services needed to meet those regulations.

"Presents industrial safety information for engineers, plant managers, risk managers, and construction site supervisors…" –Choice

1,500 pages, 2 Volume Set; Softcover ISBN 1-59237-067-5, $225.00

The Grey House Homeland Security Directory, 2005

This updated edition features the latest contact information for government and private organizations involved with Homeland Security along with the latest product information and provides detailed profiles of nearly 1,000 Federal & State Organizations & Agencies and over 3,000 Officials and Key Executives involved with Homeland Security. These listings are incredibly detailed and include Mailing Address, Phone & Fax Numbers, Email Addresses & Web Sites, a complete Description of the Agency and a complete list of the Officials and Key Executives associated with the Agency. Next, *The Grey House Homeland Security Directory* provides the go-to source for Homeland Security Products & Services. This section features over 2,000 Companies that provide Consulting, Products or Services. With this Buyer's Guide at their fingertips, users can locate suppliers of everything from Training Materials to Access Controls, from Perimeter Security to BioTerrorism Countermeasures and everything in between – complete with contact information and product descriptions. A handy Product Locator Index is provided to quickly and easily locate suppliers of a particular product. Lastly, an Information Resources Section provides immediate access to contact information for hundreds of Associations, Newsletters, Magazines, Trade Shows, Databases and Directories that focus on Homeland Security. This comprehensive, information-packed resource will be a welcome tool for any company or agency that is in need of Homeland Security information and will be a necessary acquisition for the reference collection of all public libraries and large school districts.

"Compiles this information in one place and is discerning in content. A useful purchase for public and academic libraries." –Booklist

800 pages; Softcover ISBN 1-59237-057-8, $195.00 ◆ Online Database (includes a free copy of the directory) $385.00

The Grey House Transportation Security Directory & Handbook, 2005

This brand new title is the only reference of its kind that brings together current data on Transportation Security. With information on everything from Regulatory Authorities to Security Equipment, this top-flight database brings together the relevant information necessary for creating and maintaining a security plan for a wide range of transportation facilities. With this current, comprehensive directory at the ready you'll have immediate access to: Regulatory Authorities & Legislation; Information Resources; Sample Security Plans & Checklists; Contact Data for Major Airports, Seaports, Railroads, Trucking Companies and Oil Pipelines; Security Service Providers; Recommended Equipment & Product Information and more. Using the *Grey House Transportation Security Directory & Handbook*, managers will be able to quickly and easily assess their current security plans; develop contacts to create and maintain new security procedures; and source the products and services necessary to adequately maintain a secure environment. This valuable resource is a must for all Security Managers at Airports, Seaports, Railroads, Trucking Companies and Oil Pipelines.

800 pages; Softcover ISBN 1-59237-075-6, $195

International Business and Trade Directories, 2003/04

Completely updated, the Third Edition of *International Business and Trade Directories* now contains more than 10,000 entries, over 2,000 more than the last edition, making this directory the most comprehensive resource of the worlds business and trade directories. Entries include content descriptions, price, publisher's name and address, web site and e-mail addresses, phone and fax numbers and editorial staff. Organized by industry group, and then by region, this resource puts over 10,000 industry-specific business and trade directories at the reader's fingertips. Three indexes are included for quick access to information: Geographic Index, Publisher Index and Title Index. Public, college and corporate libraries, as well as individuals and corporations seeking critical market information will want to add this directory to their marketing collection.

"Reasonably priced for a work of this type, this directory should appeal to larger academic, public and corporate libraries with an international focus." –Library Journal

1,800 pages; Softcover ISBN 1-930956-63-0, $225.00 ◆ Online Database (includes a free copy of the directory) $450.00

To preview any of our Directories Risk-Free for 30 days, call (800) 562-2139 or fax to (518) 789-0556

Sedgwick Press
Hospital & Health Plan Directories

The Directory of Hospital Personnel, 2005

The Directory of Hospital Personnel is the best resource you can have at your fingertips when researching or marketing a product or service to the hospital market. A "Who's Who" of the hospital universe, this directory puts you in touch with over 150,000 key decision-makers. With 100% verification of data you can rest assured that you will reach the right person with just one call. Every hospital in the U.S. is profiled, listed alphabetically by city within state. Plus, three easy-to-use, cross-referenced indexes put the facts at your fingertips faster and more easily than any other directory: Hospital Name Index, Bed Size Index and Personnel Index. *The Directory of Hospital Personnel* is the only complete source for key hospital decision-makers by name. Whether you want to define or restructure sales territories... locate hospitals with the purchasing power to accept your proposals... keep track of important contacts or colleagues... or find information on which insurance plans are accepted, *The Directory of Hospital Personnel* gives you the information you need – easily, efficiently, effectively and accurately.

"Recommended for college, university and medical libraries." -ARBA

2,500 pages; Softcover ISBN 1-59237-065-9 $275.00 ◆ Online Database $545.00 ◆ Online Database & Directory Combo, $650.00

The Directory of Health Care Group Purchasing Organizations, 2004

This comprehensive directory provides the important data you need to get in touch with over 800 Group Purchasing Organizations. By providing in-depth information on this growing market and its members, *The Directory of Health Care Group Purchasing Organizations* fills a major need for the most accurate and comprehensive information on over 800 GPOs – Mailing Address, Phone & Fax Numbers, E-mail Addresses, Key Contacts, Purchasing Agents, Group Descriptions, Membership Categorization, Standard Vendor Proposal Requirements, Membership Fees & Terms, Expanded Services, Total Member Beds & Outpatient Visits represented and more. With its comprehensive and detailed information on each purchasing organization, *The Directory of Health Care Group Purchasing Organizations* is the go-to source for anyone looking to target this market.

"The information is clearly arranged and easy to access...recommended for those needing this very specialized information." –ARBA

1,000 pages; Softcover ISBN 1-59237-036-5, $325.00 ◆ Online Database, $650.00 ◆ Online Database & Directory Combo, $750.00

The HMO/PPO Directory, 2005

The HMO/PPO Directory is a comprehensive source that provides detailed information about Health Maintenance Organizations and Preferred Provider Organizations nationwide. This comprehensive directory details more information about more managed health care organizations than ever before. Over 1,100 HMOs, PPOs and affiliated companies are listed, arranged alphabetically by state. Detailed listings include Key Contact Information, Prescription Drug Benefits, Enrollment, Geographical Areas served, Affiliated Physicians & Hospitals, Federal Qualifications, Status, Year Founded, Managed Care Partners, Employer References, Fees & Payment Information and more. Plus, five years of historical information is included related to Revenues, Net Income, Medical Loss Ratios, Membership Enrollment and Number of Patient Complaints. *The HMO/PPO Directory* provides the most comprehensive information on the most companies available on the market place today.

"Helpful to individuals requesting certain HMO/PPO issues such as co-payment costs, subscription costs and patient complaints. Individuals concerned (or those with questions) about their insurance may find this text to be of use to them." -ARBA

600 pages; Softcover ISBN 1-59237-057-8, $275.00 ◆ Online Database, $495.00 ◆ Online Database & Directory Combo, $600.00

The Directory of Independent Ambulatory Care Centers, 2002/03

This first edition of *The Directory of Independent Ambulatory Care Centers* provides access to detailed information that, before now, could only be found scattered in hundreds of different sources. This comprehensive and up-to-date directory pulls together a vast array of contact information for over 7,200 Ambulatory Surgery Centers, Ambulatory General and Urgent Care Clinics, and Diagnostic Imaging Centers that are not affiliated with a hospital or major medical center. Detailed listings include Mailing Address, Phone & Fax Numbers, E-mail and Web Site addresses, Contact Name and Phone Numbers of the Medical Director and other Key Executives and Purchasing Agents, Specialties & Services Offered, Year Founded, Numbers of Employees and Surgeons, Number of Operating Rooms, Number of Cases seen per year, Overnight Options, Contracted Services and much more. Listings are arranged by State, by Center Category and then alphabetically by Organization Name. *The Directory of Independent Ambulatory Care Centers* is a must-have resource for anyone marketing a product or service to this important industry and will be an invaluable tool for those searching for a local care center that will meet their specific needs.

"Among the numerous hospital directories, no other provides information on independent ambulatory centers. A handy, well-organized resource that would be useful in medical center libraries and public libraries." –Choice

986 pages; Softcover ISBN 1-930956-90-8, $185.00 ◆ Online Database, $365.00 ◆ Online Database & Directory Combo, $450.00

To preview any of our Directories Risk-Free for 30 days, call (800) 562-2139 or fax to (518) 789-0556

JAN 1 7 2005

Reference

Reference
317
Derks
2/05 $135